American Casebook Series
Hornbook Series and Basic Legal Texts
Black Letter Series and Nutshell Series

of

WEST PUBLISHING COMPANY
P.O. Box 64526
St. Paul, Minnesota 55164–0526

Accounting

FARIS' ACCOUNTING AND LAW IN A NUT-SHELL, 377 pages, 1984. Softcover. (Text)

FIFLIS, KRIPKE AND FOSTER'S TEACHING MATERIALS ON ACCOUNTING FOR BUSINESS LAWYERS, Third Edition, 838 pages, 1984. (Casebook)

SIEGEL AND SIEGEL'S ACCOUNTING AND FINANCIAL DISCLOSURE: A GUIDE TO BASIC CONCEPTS, 259 pages, 1983. Softcover. (Text)

Administrative Law

BONFIELD AND ASIMOW'S STATE AND FEDERAL ADMINISTRATIVE LAW, 826 pages, 1989. Teacher's Manual available. (Casebook)

GELLHORN AND LEVIN'S ADMINISTRATIVE LAW AND PROCESS IN A NUTSHELL, Third Edition, 479 pages, 1990. Softcover. (Text)

MASHAW AND MERRILL'S CASES AND MATERIALS ON ADMINISTRATIVE LAW—THE AMERICAN PUBLIC LAW SYSTEM, Second Edition, 976 pages, 1985. (Casebook) 1989 Supplement.

ROBINSON, GELLHORN AND BRUFF'S THE ADMINISTRATIVE PROCESS, Third Edition, 978 pages, 1986. (Casebook)

Admiralty

HEALY AND SHARPE'S CASES AND MATERIALS ON ADMIRALTY, Second Edition, 876 pages, 1986. (Casebook)

MARAIST'S ADMIRALTY IN A NUTSHELL, Second Edition, 379 pages, 1988. Softcover. (Text)

SCHOENBAUM'S HORNBOOK ON ADMIRALTY AND MARITIME LAW, Student Edition, 692 pages, 1987 with 1989 pocket part. (Text)

Agency—Partnership

DEMOTT'S FIDUCIARY OBLIGATION, AGENCY AND PARTNERSHIP: DUTIES IN ONGOING BUSINESS RELATIONSHIPS, Approximately 750 pages, April, 1991 Pub. (Casebook)

FESSLER'S ALTERNATIVES TO INCORPORATION FOR PERSONS IN QUEST OF PROFIT, Second Edition, 326 pages, 1986. Softcover. Teacher's Manual available. (Casebook)

HENN'S CASES AND MATERIALS ON AGENCY, PARTNERSHIP AND OTHER UNINCORPORATED BUSINESS ENTERPRISES, Second Edition, 733 pages, 1985. Teacher's Manual available. (Casebook)

REUSCHLEIN AND GREGORY'S HORNBOOK ON THE LAW OF AGENCY AND PARTNERSHIP, Second Edition, 683 pages, 1990. (Text)

SELECTED CORPORATION AND PARTNERSHIP STATUTES, RULES AND FORMS. Softcover. 727 pages, 1989.

STEFFEN AND KERR'S CASES ON AGENCY-PARTNERSHIP, Fourth Edition, 859 pages, 1980. (Casebook)

STEFFEN'S AGENCY-PARTNERSHIP IN A NUTSHELL, 364 pages, 1977. Softcover. (Text)

Agricultural Law

MEYER, PEDERSEN, THORSON AND DAVIDSON'S AGRICULTURAL LAW: CASES AND MATERIALS, 931 pages, 1985. Teacher's Manual avail-

Agricultural Law—Cont'd

able. (Casebook)

Alternative Dispute Resolution

KANOWITZ' CASES AND MATERIALS ON ALTERNATIVE DISPUTE RESOLUTION, 1024 pages, 1986. Teacher's Manual available. (Casebook) 1990 Supplement.

RISKIN AND WESTBROOK'S DISPUTE RESOLUTION AND LAWYERS, 468 pages, 1987. Teacher's Manual available. (Casebook)

RISKIN AND WESTBROOK'S DISPUTE RESOLUTION AND LAWYERS, Abridged Edition, 223 pages, 1987. Softcover. Teacher's Manual available. (Casebook)

American Indian Law

CANBY'S AMERICAN INDIAN LAW IN A NUTSHELL, Second Edition, 336 pages, 1988. Softcover. (Text)

GETCHES AND WILKINSON'S CASES AND MATERIALS ON FEDERAL INDIAN LAW, Second Edition, 880 pages, 1986. (Casebook)

Antitrust—see also Regulated Industries, Trade Regulation

FOX AND SULLIVAN'S CASES AND MATERIALS ON ANTITRUST, 935 pages, 1989. Teacher's Manual available. (Casebook)

GELLHORN'S ANTITRUST LAW AND ECONOMICS IN A NUTSHELL, Third Edition, 472 pages, 1986. Softcover. (Text)

HOVENKAMP'S BLACK LETTER ON ANTITRUST, 323 pages, 1986. Softcover. (Review)

HOVENKAMP'S HORNBOOK ON ECONOMICS AND FEDERAL ANTITRUST LAW, Student Edition, 414 pages, 1985. (Text)

OPPENHEIM, WESTON AND McCARTHY'S CASES AND COMMENTS ON FEDERAL ANTITRUST LAWS, Fourth Edition, 1168 pages, 1981. (Casebook) 1985 Supplement.

POSNER AND EASTERBROOK'S CASES AND ECONOMIC NOTES ON ANTITRUST, Second Edition, 1077 pages, 1981. (Casebook) 1984–85 Supplement.

SULLIVAN'S HORNBOOK OF THE LAW OF ANTITRUST, 886 pages, 1977. (Text)

Appellate Advocacy—see Trial and Appellate Advocacy

Architecture and Engineering Law

SWEET'S LEGAL ASPECTS OF ARCHITECTURE, ENGINEERING AND THE CONSTRUCTION PROCESS, Fourth Edition, 889 pages, 1989. Teacher's Manual available. (Casebook)

Art Law

DUBOFF'S ART LAW IN A NUTSHELL, 335 pages, 1984. Softcover. (Text)

Banking Law

BANKING LAW: SELECTED STATUTES AND REGULATIONS. Softcover. Approximately 265 pages, 1991.

LOVETT'S BANKING AND FINANCIAL INSTITUTIONS LAW IN A NUTSHELL, Second Edition, 464 pages, 1988. Softcover. (Text)

SYMONS AND WHITE'S BANKING LAW: TEACHING MATERIALS, Third Edition, approximately 775 pages, 1991. Teacher's Manual available. (Casebook)

Statutory Supplement. *See Banking Law: Selected Statutes*

Business Planning—see also Corporate Finance

PAINTER'S PROBLEMS AND MATERIALS IN BUSINESS PLANNING, Second Edition, 1008 pages, 1984. (Casebook) 1990 Supplement.

Statutory Supplement. *See Selected Corporation and Partnership*

SELECTED CORPORATION AND PARTNERSHIP STATUTES, RULES AND FORMS. 727 pages, 1989. Softcover.

Civil Procedure—see also Federal Jurisdiction and Procedure

AMERICAN BAR ASSOCIATION SECTION OF LITIGATION—READINGS ON ADVERSARIAL JUSTICE: THE AMERICAN APPROACH TO ADJUDICATION, 217 pages, 1988. Softcover. (Coursebook)

CLERMONT'S BLACK LETTER ON CIVIL PROCEDURE, Second Edition, 332 pages, 1988. Softcover. (Review)

COUND, FRIEDENTHAL, MILLER AND SEXTON'S CASES AND MATERIALS ON CIVIL PROCEDURE, Fifth Edition, 1284 pages, 1989. Teacher's Manual available. (Casebook)

COUND, FRIEDENTHAL, MILLER AND SEXTON'S CIVIL PROCEDURE SUPPLEMENT. 460 pages,

Civil Procedure—Cont'd

1990. Softcover. (Casebook Supplement)

FEDERAL RULES OF CIVIL PROCEDURE—EDUCATIONAL EDITION. Softcover. 632 pages, 1990.

FRIEDENTHAL, KANE AND MILLER'S HORNBOOK ON CIVIL PROCEDURE, 876 pages, 1985. (Text)

KANE AND LEVINE'S CIVIL PROCEDURE IN CALIFORNIA: STATE AND FEDERAL 498 pages, 1989. Softcover. (Casebook Supplement)

KANE'S CIVIL PROCEDURE IN A NUTSHELL, Second Edition, 306 pages, 1986. Softcover. (Text)

KOFFLER AND REPPY'S HORNBOOK ON COMMON LAW PLEADING, 663 pages, 1969. (Text)

MARCUS, REDISH AND SHERMAN'S CIVIL PROCEDURE: A MODERN APPROACH, 1027 pages, 1989. Teacher's Manual available. (Casebook)

MARCUS AND SHERMAN'S COMPLEX LITIGATION—CASES AND MATERIALS ON ADVANCED CIVIL PROCEDURE, 846 pages, 1985. Teacher's Manual available. (Casebook) 1989 Supplement.

PARK'S COMPUTER-AIDED EXERCISES ON CIVIL PROCEDURE, Second Edition, 167 pages, 1983. Softcover. (Coursebook)

SIEGEL'S HORNBOOK ON NEW YORK PRACTICE, Second Edition, Student Edition, approximately 900 pages, 1991. (Text)

Commercial Law

BAILEY AND HAGEDORN'S SECURED TRANSACTIONS IN A NUTSHELL, Third Edition, 390 pages, 1988. Softcover. (Text)

EPSTEIN, MARTIN, HENNING AND NICKLES' BASIC UNIFORM COMMERCIAL CODE TEACHING MATERIALS, Third Edition, 704 pages, 1988. Teacher's Manual available. (Casebook)

HENSON'S HORNBOOK ON SECURED TRANSACTIONS UNDER THE U.C.C., Second Edition, 504 pages, 1979, with 1979 pocket part. (Text)

MURRAY'S COMMERCIAL LAW, PROBLEMS AND MATERIALS, 366 pages, 1975. Teacher's Manual available. Softcover. (Coursebook)

NICKLES' BLACK LETTER ON COMMERCIAL PAPER, 450 pages, 1988. Softcover. (Review)

NICKLES, MATHESON AND DOLAN'S MATERIALS FOR UNDERSTANDING CREDIT AND PAYMENT SYSTEMS, 923 pages, 1987. Teacher's Manual available. (Casebook)

NORDSTROM, MURRAY AND CLOVIS' PROBLEMS AND MATERIALS ON SALES, 515 pages, 1982. (Casebook)

NORDSTROM, MURRAY AND CLOVIS' PROBLEMS AND MATERIALS ON SECURED TRANSACTIONS, 594 pages, 1987. (Casebook)

RUBIN AND COOTER'S THE PAYMENT SYSTEM: CASES, MATERIALS AND ISSUES, 885 pages, 1989. Teacher's Manual Available. (Casebook)

SELECTED COMMERCIAL STATUTES. Softcover. 1776 pages, 1990.

SPEIDEL'S BLACK LETTER ON SALES AND SALES FINANCING, 363 pages, 1984. Softcover. (Review)

SPEIDEL, SUMMERS AND WHITE'S COMMERCIAL LAW: TEACHING MATERIALS, Fourth Edition, 1448 pages, 1987. Teacher's Manual available. (Casebook)

SPEIDEL, SUMMERS AND WHITE'S COMMERCIAL PAPER: TEACHING MATERIALS, Fourth Edition, 578 pages, 1987. Reprint from Speidel et al., Commercial Law, Fourth Edition. Teacher's Manual available. (Casebook)

SPEIDEL, SUMMERS AND WHITE'S SALES: TEACHING MATERIALS, Fourth Edition, 804 pages, 1987. Reprint from Speidel et al., Commercial Law, Fourth Edition. Teacher's Manual available. (Casebook)

SPEIDEL, SUMMERS AND WHITE'S SECURED TRANSACTIONS: TEACHING MATERIALS, Fourth Edition, 485 pages, 1987. Reprint from Speidel et al., Commercial Law, Fourth Edition. Teacher's Manual available. (Casebook)

STOCKTON'S SALES IN A NUTSHELL, Second Edition, 370 pages, 1981. Softcover. (Text)

STONE'S UNIFORM COMMERCIAL CODE IN A NUTSHELL, Third Edition, 580 pages, 1989. Softcover. (Text)

WEBER AND SPEIDEL'S COMMERCIAL PAPER IN

Commercial Law—Cont'd

A NUTSHELL, Third Edition, 404 pages, 1982. Softcover. (Text)

WHITE AND SUMMERS' HORNBOOK ON THE UNIFORM COMMERCIAL CODE, Third Edition, Student Edition, 1386 pages, 1988. (Text)

Community Property

MENNELL AND BOYKOFF'S COMMUNITY PROPERTY IN A NUTSHELL, Second Edition, 432 pages, 1988. Softcover. (Text)

VERRALL AND BIRD'S CASES AND MATERIALS ON CALIFORNIA COMMUNITY PROPERTY, Fifth Edition, 604 pages, 1988. (Casebook)

Comparative Law

BARTON, GIBBS, LI AND MERRYMAN'S LAW IN RADICALLY DIFFERENT CULTURES, 960 pages, 1983. (Casebook)

GLENDON, GORDON AND OSAKWE'S COMPARATIVE LEGAL TRADITIONS: TEXT, MATERIALS AND CASES ON THE CIVIL LAW, COMMON LAW AND SOCIALIST LAW TRADITIONS, 1091 pages, 1985. (Casebook)

GLENDON, GORDON AND OSAKWE'S COMPARATIVE LEGAL TRADITIONS IN A NUTSHELL. 402 pages, 1982. Softcover. (Text)

LANGBEIN'S COMPARATIVE CRIMINAL PROCEDURE: GERMANY, 172 pages, 1977. Softcover. (Casebook)

Computers and Law

MAGGS AND SPROWL'S COMPUTER APPLICATIONS IN THE LAW, 316 pages, 1987. (Coursebook)

MASON'S USING COMPUTERS IN THE LAW: AN INTRODUCTION AND PRACTICAL GUIDE, Second Edition, 288 pages, 1988. Softcover. (Coursebook)

Conflict of Laws

CRAMTON, CURRIE AND KAY'S CASES–COMMENTS–QUESTIONS ON CONFLICT OF LAWS, Fourth Edition, 876 pages, 1987. (Casebook)

HAY'S BLACK LETTER ON CONFLICT OF LAWS, 330 pages, 1989. Softcover. (Review)

SCOLES AND HAY'S HORNBOOK ON CONFLICT OF LAWS, Student Edition, 1085 pages, 1982, with 1988–89 pocket part. (Text)

SIEGEL'S CONFLICTS IN A NUTSHELL, 470

pages, 1982. Softcover. (Text)

Constitutional Law—Civil Rights—see also Foreign Relations and National Security Law

ABERNATHY'S CASES AND MATERIALS ON CIVIL RIGHTS, 660 pages, 1980. (Casebook)

BARRON AND DIENES' BLACK LETTER ON CONSTITUTIONAL LAW, Third Edition, approximately 400 pages, 1991. Softcover. (Review)

BARRON AND DIENES' CONSTITUTIONAL LAW IN A NUTSHELL, Second Edition, approximately 475 pages, 1991. Softcover. (Text)

ENGDAHL'S CONSTITUTIONAL FEDERALISM IN A NUTSHELL, Second Edition, 411 pages, 1987. Softcover. (Text)

FARBER AND SHERRY'S HISTORY OF THE AMERICAN CONSTITUTION, 458 pages, 1990. Softcover. Teacher's Manual available. (Text)

GARVEY AND ALEINIKOFF'S MODERN CONSTITUTIONAL THEORY: A READER, 494 pages, 1989. Softcover. (Reader)

LOCKHART, KAMISAR, CHOPER AND SHIFFRIN'S CONSTITUTIONAL LAW: CASES–COMMENTS–QUESTIONS, Sixth Edition, 1601 pages, 1986. (Casebook) 1990 Supplement.

LOCKHART, KAMISAR, CHOPER AND SHIFFRIN'S THE AMERICAN CONSTITUTION: CASES AND MATERIALS, Sixth Edition, 1260 pages, 1986. Abridged version of Lockhart, et al., Constitutional Law: Cases–Comments–Questions, Sixth Edition. (Casebook) 1990 Supplement.

LOCKHART, KAMISAR, CHOPER AND SHIFFRIN'S CONSTITUTIONAL RIGHTS AND LIBERTIES: CASES AND MATERIALS, Sixth Edition, 1266 pages, 1986. Reprint from Lockhart, et al., Constitutional Law: Cases–Comments–Questions, Sixth Edition. (Casebook) 1990 Supplement.

MARKS AND COOPER'S STATE CONSTITUTIONAL LAW IN A NUTSHELL, 329 pages, 1988. Softcover. (Text)

NOWAK, ROTUNDA AND YOUNG'S HORNBOOK ON CONSTITUTIONAL LAW, Third Edition, 1191 pages, 1986 with 1988 pocket part. (Text)

ROTUNDA'S MODERN CONSTITUTIONAL LAW:

Constitutional Law—Civil Rights—Cont'd

CASES AND NOTES, Third Edition, 1085 pages, 1989. (Casebook) 1990 Supplement.

SHIFFRIN AND CHOPER'S FIRST AMENDMENT, CASES—COMMENTS—QUESTIONS, Approximately 700 pages, April, 1991 Pub. (Casebook)

VIEIRA'S CONSTITUTIONAL CIVIL RIGHTS IN A NUTSHELL, Second Edition, 322 pages, 1990. Softcover. (Text)

WILLIAMS' CONSTITUTIONAL ANALYSIS IN A NUTSHELL, 388 pages, 1979. Softcover. (Text)

Consumer Law—see also Commercial Law

EPSTEIN AND NICKLES' CONSUMER LAW IN A NUTSHELL, Second Edition, 418 pages, 1981. Softcover. (Text)

SELECTED COMMERCIAL STATUTES. Softcover. 1776 pages, 1990.

SPANOGLE, ROHNER, PRIDGEN AND RASOR'S CASES AND MATERIALS ON CONSUMER LAW, Second Edition, approximately 900 pages, 1991. (Casebook)

Contracts

CALAMARI AND PERILLO'S BLACK LETTER ON CONTRACTS, Second Edition, 462 pages, 1990. Softcover. (Review)

CALAMARI AND PERILLO'S HORNBOOK ON CONTRACTS, Third Edition, 1049 pages, 1987. (Text)

CALAMARI, PERILLO AND BENDER'S CASES AND PROBLEMS ON CONTRACTS, Second Edition, 905 pages, 1989. Teacher's Manual Available. (Casebook)

CORBIN'S TEXT ON CONTRACTS, One Volume Student Edition, 1224 pages, 1952. (Text)

FESSLER AND LOISEAUX'S CASES AND MATERIALS ON CONTRACTS—MORALITY, ECONOMICS AND THE MARKET PLACE, 837 pages, 1982. Teacher's Manual available. (Casebook)

FRIEDMAN'S CONTRACT REMEDIES IN A NUTSHELL, 323 pages, 1981. Softcover. (Text)

FULLER AND EISENBERG'S CASES ON BASIC CONTRACT LAW, Fifth Edition, 1037 pages, 1990. (Casebook)

HAMILTON, RAU AND WEINTRAUB'S CASES AND MATERIALS ON CONTRACTS, 830 pages, 1984. (Casebook)

JACKSON AND BOLLINGER'S CASES ON CONTRACT LAW IN MODERN SOCIETY, Second Edition, 1329 pages, 1980. Teacher's Manual available. (Casebook)

KEYES' GOVERNMENT CONTRACTS IN A NUTSHELL, Second Edition, 557 pages, 1990. Softcover. (Text)

SCHABER AND ROHWER'S CONTRACTS IN A NUTSHELL, Third Edition, 457 pages, 1990. Softcover. (Text)

SUMMERS AND HILLMAN'S CONTRACT AND RELATED OBLIGATION: THEORY, DOCTRINE AND PRACTICE, 1074 pages, 1987. Teacher's Manual available. (Casebook)

Copyright—see Patent and Copyright Law

Corporate Finance

HAMILTON'S CASES AND MATERIALS ON CORPORATION FINANCE, Second Edition, 1221 pages, 1989. (Casebook)

Corporations

HAMILTON'S BLACK LETTER ON CORPORATIONS, Second Edition, 513 pages, 1986. Softcover. (Review)

HAMILTON'S CASES AND MATERIALS ON CORPORATIONS—INCLUDING PARTNERSHIPS AND LIMITED PARTNERSHIPS, Fourth Edition, 1248 pages, 1990. Teacher's Manual available. (Casebook) 1990 Statutory Supplement.

HAMILTON'S THE LAW OF CORPORATIONS IN A NUTSHELL, Third Edition, approximately 500 pages, 1991. Softcover. (Text)

HENN'S TEACHING MATERIALS ON THE LAW OF CORPORATIONS, Second Edition, 1204 pages, 1986. Teacher's Manual available. (Casebook)

   Statutory Supplement. *See Selected Corporation and Partnership*

HENN AND ALEXANDER'S HORNBOOK ON LAWS OF CORPORATIONS, Third Edition, Student Edition, 1371 pages, 1983, with 1986 pocket part. (Text)

SELECTED CORPORATION AND PARTNERSHIP STATUTES, RULES AND FORMS. Softcover. 727 pages, 1989.

SOLOMON, SCHWARTZ AND BAUMAN'S MATERI-

Corporations—Cont'd

ALS AND PROBLEMS ON CORPORATIONS: LAW AND POLICY, Second Edition, 1391 pages, 1988. Teacher's Manual available. (Casebook) 1990 Supplement.

Statutory Supplement. *See Selected Corporation and Partnership*

Corrections

KRANTZ' THE LAW OF CORRECTIONS AND PRISONERS' RIGHTS IN A NUTSHELL, Third Edition, 407 pages, 1988. Softcover. (Text)

KRANTZ AND BRANHAM'S CASES AND MATERIALS ON THE LAW OF SENTENCING, CORRECTIONS AND PRISONERS' RIGHTS, Fourth Edition, approximately 625 pages, 1991. (Casebook)

ROBBINS' CASES AND MATERIALS ON POST-CONVICTION REMEDIES, 506 pages, 1982. (Casebook)

Creditors' Rights

BANKRUPTCY CODE, RULES AND OFFICIAL FORMS, LAW SCHOOL EDITION. 829 pages, 1990. Softcover.

EPSTEIN'S DEBTOR-CREDITOR LAW IN A NUTSHELL, Fourth Edition, approximately 400 pages, 1991. Softcover. (Text)

EPSTEIN, LANDERS AND NICKLES' CASES AND MATERIALS ON DEBTORS AND CREDITORS, Third Edition, 1059 pages, 1987. Teacher's Manual available. (Casebook)

LOPUCKI'S PLAYER'S MANUAL FOR THE DEBTOR-CREDITOR GAME, 123 pages, 1985. Softcover. (Coursebook)

NICKLES AND EPSTEIN'S BLACK LETTER ON CREDITORS' RIGHTS AND BANKRUPTCY, 576 pages, 1989. (Review)

RIESENFELD'S CASES AND MATERIALS ON CREDITORS' REMEDIES AND DEBTORS' PROTECTION, Fourth Edition, 914 pages, 1987. (Casebook) 1990 Supplement.

WHITE'S CASES AND MATERIALS ON BANKRUPTCY AND CREDITORS' RIGHTS, 812 pages, 1985. Teacher's Manual available. (Casebook) 1987 Supplement.

Criminal Law and Criminal Procedure—see also Corrections, Juvenile Justice

ABRAMS' FEDERAL CRIMINAL LAW AND ITS ENFORCEMENT, 866 pages, 1986. (Casebook)

1988 Supplement.

AMERICAN CRIMINAL JUSTICE PROCESS: SELECTED RULES, STATUTES AND GUIDELINES. 723 pages, 1989. Softcover.

CARLSON'S ADJUDICATION OF CRIMINAL JUSTICE: PROBLEMS AND REFERENCES, 130 pages, 1986. Softcover. (Casebook)

DIX AND SHARLOT'S CASES AND MATERIALS ON CRIMINAL LAW, Third Edition, 846 pages, 1987. (Casebook)

GRANO'S PROBLEMS IN CRIMINAL PROCEDURE, Second Edition, 176 pages, 1981. Teacher's Manual available. Softcover. (Coursebook)

HEYMANN AND KENETY'S THE MURDER TRIAL OF WILBUR JACKSON: A HOMICIDE IN THE FAMILY, Second Edition, 347 pages, 1985. (Coursebook)

ISRAEL, KAMISAR AND LAFAVE'S CRIMINAL PROCEDURE AND THE CONSTITUTION: LEADING SUPREME COURT CASES AND INTRODUCTORY TEXT. 747 pages, 1990 Edition. Softcover. (Casebook)

ISRAEL AND LAFAVE'S CRIMINAL PROCEDURE—CONSTITUTIONAL LIMITATIONS IN A NUTSHELL, Fourth Edition, 461 pages, 1988. Softcover. (Text)

JOHNSON'S CASES, MATERIALS AND TEXT ON CRIMINAL LAW, Fourth Edition, 759 pages, 1990. Teacher's Manual available. (Casebook)

JOHNSON'S CASES AND MATERIALS ON CRIMINAL PROCEDURE, 859 pages, 1988. (Casebook) 1990 Supplement.

KAMISAR, LAFAVE AND ISRAEL'S MODERN CRIMINAL PROCEDURE: CASES, COMMENTS AND QUESTIONS, Seventh Edition, 1593 pages, 1990. (Casebook) 1990 Supplement.

KAMISAR, LAFAVE AND ISRAEL'S BASIC CRIMINAL PROCEDURE: CASES, COMMENTS AND QUESTIONS, Seventh Edition, 792 pages, 1990. Softcover reprint from Kamisar, et al., Modern Criminal Procedure: Cases, Comments and Questions, Seventh Edition. (Casebook) 1990 Supplement.

LAFAVE'S MODERN CRIMINAL LAW: CASES, COMMENTS AND QUESTIONS, Second Edition, 903 pages, 1988. (Casebook)

Criminal Law and Criminal Procedure— Cont'd

LaFAVE AND ISRAEL'S HORNBOOK ON CRIMINAL PROCEDURE, Second Edition, Student Edition, approximately 1200 pages, June, 1991 Pub. (Text)

LaFAVE AND SCOTT'S HORNBOOK ON CRIMINAL LAW, Second Edition, 918 pages, 1986. (Text)

LANGBEIN'S COMPARATIVE CRIMINAL PROCEDURE: GERMANY, 172 pages, 1977. Softcover. (Casebook)

LOEWY'S CRIMINAL LAW IN A NUTSHELL, Second Edition, 321 pages, 1987. Softcover. (Text)

LOW'S BLACK LETTER ON CRIMINAL LAW, Revised First Edition, 443 pages, 1990. Softcover. (Review)

SALTZBURG'S CASES AND COMMENTARY ON AMERICAN CRIMINAL PROCEDURE, Third Edition, 1302 pages, 1988. Teacher's Manual available. (Casebook) 1990 Supplement.

UVILLER'S THE PROCESSES OF CRIMINAL JUSTICE: INVESTIGATION AND ADJUDICATION, Second Edition, 1384 pages, 1979. (Casebook) 1979 Statutory Supplement. 1986 Update.

VORENBERG'S CASES ON CRIMINAL LAW AND PROCEDURE, Second Edition, 1088 pages, 1981. Teacher's Manual available. (Casebook) 1990 Supplement.

Decedents' Estates—see Trusts and Estates

Domestic Relations

CLARK'S HORNBOOK ON DOMESTIC RELATIONS, Second Edition, Student Edition, 1050 pages, 1988. (Text)

CLARK AND GLOWINSKY'S CASES AND PROBLEMS ON DOMESTIC RELATIONS, Fourth Edition. 1150 pages, 1990. Teacher's Manual available. (Casebook)

KRAUSE'S BLACK LETTER ON FAMILY LAW, 314 pages, 1988. Softcover. (Review)

KRAUSE'S CASES, COMMENTS AND QUESTIONS ON FAMILY LAW, Third Edition, 1433 pages, 1990. (Casebook)

KRAUSE'S FAMILY LAW IN A NUTSHELL, Second Edition, 444 pages, 1986. Softcover. (Text)

KRAUSKOPF'S CASES ON PROPERTY DIVISION AT MARRIAGE DISSOLUTION, 250 pages, 1984. Softcover. (Casebook)

Economics, Law and—see also Antitrust, Regulated Industries

GOETZ' CASES AND MATERIALS ON LAW AND ECONOMICS, 547 pages, 1984. (Casebook)

MALLOY'S LAW AND ECONOMICS: A COMPARATIVE APPROACH TO THEORY AND PRACTICE, 166 pages, 1990. Softcover. (Text)

Education Law

ALEXANDER AND ALEXANDER'S THE LAW OF SCHOOLS, STUDENTS AND TEACHERS IN A NUTSHELL, 409 pages, 1984. Softcover. (Text)

YUDOF, KIRP AND LEVIN'S EDUCATIONAL POLICY AND THE LAW, Third Edition, approximately 975 pages, April, 1991 Pub. (Casebook)

Employment Discrimination—see also Women and the Law

ESTREICHER AND HARPER'S CASES AND MATERIALS ON THE LAW GOVERNING THE EMPLOYMENT RELATIONSHIP, 962 pages, 1990. Teacher's Manual available. (Casebook) Statutory Supplement.

JONES, MURPHY AND BELTON'S CASES AND MATERIALS ON DISCRIMINATION IN EMPLOYMENT, (The Labor Law Group). Fifth Edition, 1116 pages, 1987. (Casebook) 1990 Supplement.

PLAYER'S FEDERAL LAW OF EMPLOYMENT DISCRIMINATION IN A NUTSHELL, Second Edition, 402 pages, 1981. Softcover. (Text)

PLAYER'S HORNBOOK ON EMPLOYMENT DISCRIMINATION LAW, Student Edition, 708 pages, 1988. (Text)

PLAYER, SHOBEN AND LIEBERWITZ' CASES AND MATERIALS ON EMPLOYMENT DISCRIMINATION LAW, 827 pages, 1990. Teacher's Manual available. (Casebook)

Energy and Natural Resources Law—see also Oil and Gas

LAITOS' CASES AND MATERIALS ON NATURAL RESOURCES LAW, 938 pages, 1985. Teacher's Manual available. (Casebook)

SELECTED ENVIRONMENTAL LAW STATUTES— EDUCATIONAL EDITION. Softcover. 1020 pages, 1990.

Environmental Law—see also Energy and Natural Resources Law; Sea, Law of

BONINE AND MCGARITY'S THE LAW OF ENVIRONMENTAL PROTECTION: CASES—LEGISLATION—POLICIES, 1076 pages, 1984. Teacher's Manual available. (Casebook)

FINDLEY AND FARBER'S CASES AND MATERIALS ON ENVIRONMENTAL LAW, Second Edition, 813 pages, 1985. (Casebook) 1988 Supplement.

FINDLEY AND FARBER'S ENVIRONMENTAL LAW IN A NUTSHELL, Second Edition, 367 pages, 1988. Softcover. (Text)

RODGERS' HORNBOOK ON ENVIRONMENTAL LAW, 956 pages, 1977, with 1984 pocket part. (Text)

SELECTED ENVIRONMENTAL LAW STATUTES—EDUCATIONAL EDITION. Softcover. 1020 pages, 1990.

Equity—see Remedies

Estate Planning—see also Trusts and Estates; Taxation—Estate and Gift

LYNN'S AN INTRODUCTION TO ESTATE PLANNING IN A NUTSHELL, Third Edition, 370 pages, 1983. Softcover. (Text)

Evidence

BROUN AND BLAKEY'S BLACK LETTER ON EVIDENCE, 269 pages, 1984. Softcover. (Review)

BROUN, MEISENHOLDER, STRONG AND MOSTELLER'S PROBLEMS IN EVIDENCE, Third Edition, 238 pages, 1988. Teacher's Manual available. Softcover. (Coursebook)

CLEARY, STRONG, BROUN AND MOSTELLER'S CASES AND MATERIALS ON EVIDENCE, Fourth Edition, 1060 pages, 1988. (Casebook)

FEDERAL RULES OF EVIDENCE FOR UNITED STATES COURTS AND MAGISTRATES. Softcover. 381 pages, 1990.

FRIEDMAN'S PROBLEMS AND MATERIALS FOR AN INTRODUCTORY COURSE IN EVIDENCE, Approximately 290 pages, April, 1991 Pub. (Coursebook)

GRAHAM'S FEDERAL RULES OF EVIDENCE IN A NUTSHELL, Second Edition, 473 pages, 1987. Softcover. (Text)

LEMPERT AND SALTZBURG'S A MODERN APPROACH TO EVIDENCE: TEXT, PROBLEMS, TRANSCRIPTS AND CASES, Second Edition, 1232 pages, 1983. Teacher's Manual available. (Casebook)

LILLY'S AN INTRODUCTION TO THE LAW OF EVIDENCE, Second Edition, 585 pages, 1987. (Text)

MCCORMICK, SUTTON AND WELLBORN'S CASES AND MATERIALS ON EVIDENCE, Sixth Edition, 1067 pages, 1987. (Casebook)

MCCORMICK'S HORNBOOK ON EVIDENCE, Third Edition, Student Edition, 1156 pages, 1984, with 1987 pocket part. (Text)

ROTHSTEIN'S EVIDENCE IN A NUTSHELL: STATE AND FEDERAL RULES, Second Edition, 514 pages, 1981. Softcover. (Text)

Federal Jurisdiction and Procedure

CURRIE'S CASES AND MATERIALS ON FEDERAL COURTS, Fourth Edition, 783 pages, 1990. (Casebook)

CURRIE'S FEDERAL JURISDICTION IN A NUTSHELL, Third Edition, 242 pages, 1990. Softcover. (Text)

FEDERAL RULES OF CIVIL PROCEDURE—EDUCATIONAL EDITION. Softcover. 632 pages, 1990.

REDISH'S BLACK LETTER ON FEDERAL JURISDICTION, Second Edition, approximately 230 pages, 1991. Softcover. (Review)

REDISH'S CASES, COMMENTS AND QUESTIONS ON FEDERAL COURTS, Second Edition, 1122 pages, 1989. (Casebook) 1990 Supplement.

VETRI AND MERRILL'S FEDERAL COURTS PROBLEMS AND MATERIALS, Second Edition, 232 pages, 1984. Softcover. (Coursebook)

WRIGHT'S HORNBOOK ON FEDERAL COURTS, Fourth Edition, Student Edition, 870 pages, 1983. (Text)

Foreign Relations and National Security Law

FRANCK AND GLENNON'S FOREIGN RELATIONS AND NATIONAL SECURITY LAW, 941 pages, 1987. (Casebook)

Future Interests—see Trusts and Estates

Health Law—see Medicine, Law and

Human Rights—see International Law

Immigration Law

ALEINIKOFF AND MARTIN'S IMMIGRATION: PROCESS AND POLICY, Interim Second Edition, approximately 1075 pages, 1991. (Casebook)

   Statutory Supplement. *See Immigration and Nationality Laws*

IMMIGRATION AND NATIONALITY LAWS OF THE UNITED STATES: SELECTED STATUTES, REGULATIONS AND FORMS. Softcover. 400 pages, 1990.

WEISSBRODT'S IMMIGRATION LAW AND PROCEDURE IN A NUTSHELL, Second Edition, 438 pages, 1989, Softcover. (Text)

Indian Law—see American Indian Law

Insurance Law

DEVINE AND TERRY'S PROBLEMS IN INSURANCE LAW, 240 pages, 1989. Softcover. Teacher's Manual available. (Coursebook)

DOBBYN'S INSURANCE LAW IN A NUTSHELL, Second Edition, 316 pages, 1989. Softcover. (Text)

KEETON'S CASES ON BASIC INSURANCE LAW, Second Edition, 1086 pages, 1977. Teacher's Manual available. (Casebook)

KEETON'S COMPUTER-AIDED AND WORKBOOK EXERCISES ON INSURANCE LAW, 255 pages, 1990. Softcover. (Coursebook)

KEETON AND WIDISS' INSURANCE LAW, Student Edition, 1359 pages, 1988. (Text)

WIDISS AND KEETON'S COURSE SUPPLEMENT TO KEETON AND WIDISS' INSURANCE LAW, 502 pages, 1988. Softcover. Teacher's Manual available. (Casebook)

WIDISS' INSURANCE: MATERIALS ON FUNDAMENTAL PRINCIPLES, LEGAL DOCTRINES AND REGULATORY ACTS, 1186 pages, 1989. Teacher's Manual available. (Casebook)

YORK AND WHELAN'S CASES, MATERIALS AND PROBLEMS ON GENERAL PRACTICE INSURANCE LAW, Second Edition, 787 pages, 1988. Teacher's Manual available. (Casebook)

International Law—see also Sea, Law of

BUERGENTHAL'S INTERNATIONAL HUMAN RIGHTS IN A NUTSHELL, 283 pages, 1988. Softcover. (Text)

BUERGENTHAL AND MAIER'S PUBLIC INTERNA-

TIONAL LAW IN A NUTSHELL, Second Edition, 275 pages, 1990. Softcover. (Text)

FOLSOM, GORDON AND SPANOGLE'S INTERNATIONAL BUSINESS TRANSACTIONS—A PROBLEM-ORIENTED COURSEBOOK, 1160 pages, 1986. Teacher's Manual available. (Casebook) 1989 Documents Supplement.

FOLSOM, GORDON AND SPANOGLE'S INTERNATIONAL BUSINESS TRANSACTIONS IN A NUTSHELL, Third Edition, 509 pages, 1988. Softcover. (Text)

HENKIN, PUGH, SCHACHTER AND SMIT'S CASES AND MATERIALS ON INTERNATIONAL LAW, Second Edition, 1517 pages, 1987. (Casebook) Documents Supplement.

JACKSON AND DAVEY'S CASES, MATERIALS AND TEXT ON LEGAL PROBLEMS OF INTERNATIONAL ECONOMIC RELATIONS, Second Edition, 1269 pages, 1986. (Casebook) 1989 Documents Supplement.

KIRGIS' INTERNATIONAL ORGANIZATIONS IN THEIR LEGAL SETTING, 1016 pages, 1977. Teacher's Manual available. (Casebook) 1981 Supplement.

WESTON, FALK AND D'AMATO'S INTERNATIONAL LAW AND WORLD ORDER—A PROBLEM-ORIENTED COURSEBOOK, Second Edition, 1335 pages, 1990. Teacher's Manual available. (Casebook) Documents Supplement.

Interviewing and Counseling

BINDER AND PRICE'S LEGAL INTERVIEWING AND COUNSELING, 232 pages, 1977. Teacher's Manual available. Softcover. (Coursebook)

BINDER, BERGMAN AND PRICE'S LAWYERS AS COUNSELORS: A CLIENT–CENTERED APPROACH, Approximately 425 pages, 1991. Softcover. (Coursebook)

SHAFFER AND ELKINS' LEGAL INTERVIEWING AND COUNSELING IN A NUTSHELL, Second Edition, 487 pages, 1987. Softcover. (Text)

Introduction to Law—see Legal Method and Legal System

Introduction to Law Study

HEGLAND'S INTRODUCTION TO THE STUDY AND PRACTICE OF LAW IN A NUTSHELL, 418 pages,

Introduction to Law Study—Cont'd
1983. Softcover. (Text)

KINYON'S INTRODUCTION TO LAW STUDY AND LAW EXAMINATIONS IN A NUTSHELL, 389 pages, 1971. Softcover. (Text)

Judicial Process—see Legal Method and Legal System

Jurisprudence

CHRISTIE'S JURISPRUDENCE—TEXT AND READINGS ON THE PHILOSOPHY OF LAW, 1056 pages, 1973. (Casebook)

Juvenile Justice

FOX'S CASES AND MATERIALS ON MODERN JUVENILE JUSTICE, Second Edition, 960 pages, 1981. (Casebook)

FOX'S JUVENILE COURTS IN A NUTSHELL, Third Edition, 291 pages, 1984. Softcover. (Text)

Labor and Employment Law—see also Employment Discrimination, Social Legislation

FINKIN, GOLDMAN AND SUMMERS' LEGAL PROTECTION OF INDIVIDUAL EMPLOYEES, (The Labor Law Group). 1164 pages, 1989. (Casebook)

GORMAN'S BASIC TEXT ON LABOR LAW—UNIONIZATION AND COLLECTIVE BARGAINING, 914 pages, 1976. (Text)

LESLIE'S LABOR LAW IN A NUTSHELL, Second Edition, 397 pages, 1986. Softcover. (Text)

NOLAN'S LABOR ARBITRATION LAW AND PRACTICE IN A NUTSHELL, 358 pages, 1979. Softcover. (Text)

OBERER, HANSLOWE, ANDERSEN AND HEINSZ' CASES AND MATERIALS ON LABOR LAW—COLLECTIVE BARGAINING IN A FREE SOCIETY, Third Edition, 1163 pages, 1986. Teacher's Manual available. (Casebook) Statutory Supplement.

RABIN, SILVERSTEIN AND SCHATZKI'S LABOR AND EMPLOYMENT LAW: PROBLEMS, CASES AND MATERIALS IN THE LAW OF WORK, (The Labor Law Group). 1014 pages, 1988. Teacher's Manual available. (Casebook) 1988 Statutory Supplement.

Land Finance—Property Security—see Real Estate Transactions

Land Use

CALLIES AND FREILICH'S CASES AND MATERIALS ON LAND USE, 1233 pages, 1986. (Casebook) 1988 Supplement.

HAGMAN AND JUERGENSMEYER'S HORNBOOK ON URBAN PLANNING AND LAND DEVELOPMENT CONTROL LAW, Second Edition, Student Edition, 680 pages, 1986. (Text)

WRIGHT AND GITELMAN'S CASES AND MATERIALS ON LAND USE, Fourth Edition, approximately 1225 pages, 1991. Teacher's Manual available. (Casebook)

WRIGHT AND WRIGHT'S LAND USE IN A NUTSHELL, Second Edition, 356 pages, 1985. Softcover. (Text)

Legal History—see also Legal Method and Legal System

PRESSER AND ZAINALDIN'S CASES AND MATERIALS ON LAW AND JURISPRUDENCE IN AMERICAN HISTORY, Second Edition, 1092 pages, 1989. Teacher's Manual available. (Casebook)

Legal Method and Legal System—see also Legal Research, Legal Writing

ALDISERT'S READINGS, MATERIALS AND CASES IN THE JUDICIAL PROCESS, 948 pages, 1976. (Casebook)

BERCH AND BERCH'S INTRODUCTION TO LEGAL METHOD AND PROCESS, 550 pages, 1985. Teacher's Manual available. (Casebook)

BODENHEIMER, OAKLEY AND LOVE'S READINGS AND CASES ON AN INTRODUCTION TO THE ANGLO-AMERICAN LEGAL SYSTEM, Second Edition, 166 pages, 1988. Softcover. (Casebook)

DAVIES AND LAWRY'S INSTITUTIONS AND METHODS OF THE LAW—INTRODUCTORY TEACHING MATERIALS, 547 pages, 1982. Teacher's Manual available. (Casebook)

DVORKIN, HIMMELSTEIN AND LESNICK'S BECOMING A LAWYER: A HUMANISTIC PERSPECTIVE ON LEGAL EDUCATION AND PROFESSIONALISM, 211 pages, 1981. Softcover. (Text)

KEETON'S JUDGING, 842 pages, 1990. Softcover. (Coursebook)

KELSO AND KELSO'S STUDYING LAW: AN IN-

Legal Method and Legal System—Cont'd

TRODUCTION, 587 pages, 1984. (Coursebook)

KEMPIN'S HISTORICAL INTRODUCTION TO AN-GLO-AMERICAN LAW IN A NUTSHELL, Third Edition, 323 pages, 1990. Softcover. (Text)

REYNOLDS' JUDICIAL PROCESS IN A NUTSHELL, 292 pages, 1980. Softcover. (Text)

Legal Research

COHEN'S LEGAL RESEARCH IN A NUTSHELL, Fourth Edition, 452 pages, 1985. Soft-cover. (Text)

COHEN, BERRING AND OLSON'S HOW TO FIND THE LAW, Ninth Edition, 716 pages, 1989. (Text)

COHEN, BERRING AND OLSON'S FINDING THE LAW, 570 pages, 1989. Softcover reprint from Cohen, Berring and Olson's How to Find the Law, Ninth Edition. (Course-book)

Legal Research Exercises, 3rd Ed., for use with Cohen, Berring and Olson, 229 pages, 1989. Teacher's Manual availa-ble.

ROMBAUER'S LEGAL PROBLEM SOLVING—ANALYSIS, RESEARCH AND WRITING, Fourth Edition, 424 pages, 1983. Teacher's Man-ual with problems available. (Coursebook)

STATSKY'S LEGAL RESEARCH AND WRITING, Third Edition, 257 pages, 1986. Softcover. (Coursebook)

TEPLY'S LEGAL RESEARCH AND CITATION, Third Edition, 472 pages, 1989. Softcover. (Coursebook)

Student Library Exercises, 3rd ed., 391 pages, 1989. Answer Key available.

Legal Writing

CHILD'S DRAFTING LEGAL DOCUMENTS: MATERIALS AND PROBLEMS, 286 pages, 1988. Softcover. Teacher's Manual available. (Coursebook)

DICKERSON'S MATERIALS ON LEGAL DRAFT-ING, 425 pages, 1981. Teacher's Manual available. (Coursebook)

FELSENFELD AND SIEGEL'S WRITING CON-TRACTS IN PLAIN ENGLISH, 290 pages, 1981. Softcover. (Text)

GOPEN'S WRITING FROM A LEGAL PERSPEC-

TIVE, 225 pages, 1981. (Text)

MELLINKOFF'S LEGAL WRITING—SENSE AND NONSENSE, 242 pages, 1982. Softcover. Teacher's Manual available. (Text)

PRATT'S LEGAL WRITING: A SYSTEMATIC AP-PROACH, 468 pages, 1990. Teacher's Manu-al available. (Coursebook)

RAY AND RAMSFIELD'S LEGAL WRITING: GET-TING IT RIGHT AND GETTING IT WRITTEN, 250 pages, 1987. Softcover. (Text)

SQUIRES AND ROMBAUER'S LEGAL WRITING IN A NUTSHELL, 294 pages, 1982. Softcover. (Text)

STATSKY AND WERNET'S CASE ANALYSIS AND FUNDAMENTALS OF LEGAL WRITING, Third Edition, 424 pages, 1989. Teacher's Man-ual available. (Text)

TEPLY'S LEGAL WRITING, ANALYSIS AND ORAL ARGUMENT, 576 pages, 1990. Softcover. Teacher's Manual available. (Coursebook)

WEIHOFEN'S LEGAL WRITING STYLE, Second Edition, 332 pages, 1980. (Text)

Legislation

DAVIES' LEGISLATIVE LAW AND PROCESS IN A NUTSHELL, Second Edition, 346 pages, 1986. Softcover. (Text)

ESKRIDGE AND FRICKEY'S CASES AND MATERI-ALS ON LEGISLATION: STATUTES AND THE CRE-ATION OF PUBLIC POLICY, 937 pages, 1988. Teacher's Manual available. (Casebook) 1990 Supplement.

NUTTING AND DICKERSON'S CASES AND MATERIALS ON LEGISLATION, Fifth Edition, 744 pages, 1978. (Casebook)

STATSKY'S LEGISLATIVE ANALYSIS AND DRAFTING, Second Edition, 217 pages, 1984. Teacher's Manual available. (Text)

Local Government

FRUG'S CASES AND MATERIALS ON LOCAL GOVERNMENT LAW, 1005 pages, 1988. (Casebook)

MCCARTHY'S LOCAL GOVERNMENT LAW IN A NUTSHELL, Third Edition, 435 pages, 1990. Softcover. (Text)

REYNOLDS' HORNBOOK ON LOCAL GOVERN-MENT LAW, 860 pages, 1982, with 1990 pocket part. (Text)

Local Government—Cont'd

VALENTE'S CASES AND MATERIALS ON LOCAL GOVERNMENT LAW, Third Edition, 1010 pages, 1987. Teacher's Manual available. (Casebook) 1989 Supplement.

Mass Communication Law

GILLMOR, BARRON, SIMON AND TERRY'S CASES AND COMMENT ON MASS COMMUNICATION LAW, Fifth Edition, 947 pages, 1990. (Casebook)

GINSBURG, BOTEIN, DIRECTOR AND RICE'S REGULATION OF BROADCASTING: LAW AND POLICY TOWARDS RADIO, TELEVISION AND CABLE COMMUNICATIONS, Second Edition, approximately 750 pages, April, 1991 Pub. (Casebook)

ZUCKMAN, GAYNES, CARTER AND DEE'S MASS COMMUNICATIONS LAW IN A NUTSHELL, Third Edition, 538 pages, 1988. Softcover. (Text)

Medicine, Law and

FISCINA, BOUMIL, SHARPE AND HEAD'S MEDICAL LIABILITY, 487 pages, 1991. Teacher's Manual available. (Casebook)

FURROW, JOHNSON, JOST AND SCHWARTZ' HEALTH LAW: CASES, MATERIALS AND PROBLEMS, Second Edition, approximately 1200 pages, June, 1991 Pub. Teacher's Manual available. (Casebook)

HALL AND ELLMAN'S HEALTH CARE LAW AND ETHICS IN A NUTSHELL, 401 pages, 1990. Softcover (Text)

JARVIS, CLOSEN, HERMANN AND LEONARD'S AIDS LAW IN A NUTSHELL, Approximately 350 pages, 1991. Softcover. (Text)

KING'S THE LAW OF MEDICAL MALPRACTICE IN A NUTSHELL, Second Edition, 342 pages, 1986. Softcover. (Text)

SHAPIRO AND SPECE'S CASES, MATERIALS AND PROBLEMS ON BIOETHICS AND LAW, 892 pages, 1981. (Casebook)

Military Law

SHANOR AND TERRELL'S MILITARY LAW IN A NUTSHELL, 378 pages, 1980. Softcover. (Text)

Mortgages—see Real Estate Transactions

Natural Resources Law—see Energy and Natural Resources Law, Environmental Law

Negotiation

GIFFORD'S LEGAL NEGOTIATION: THEORY AND APPLICATIONS, 225 pages, 1989. Softcover. (Text)

WILLIAMS' LEGAL NEGOTIATION AND SETTLEMENT, 207 pages, 1983. Softcover. Teacher's Manual available. (Coursebook)

Office Practice—see also Computers and Law, Interviewing and Counseling, Negotiation

HEGLAND'S TRIAL AND PRACTICE SKILLS IN A NUTSHELL, 346 pages, 1978. Softcover (Text)

MUNNEKE'S LAW PRACTICE MANAGEMENT, MATERIALS AND CASES, May, 1991 Pub. (Casebook)

STRONG AND CLARK'S LAW OFFICE MANAGEMENT, 424 pages, 1974. (Casebook)

Oil and Gas—see also Energy and Natural Resources Law

HEMINGWAY'S HORNBOOK ON OIL AND GAS, Second Edition, Student Edition, 543 pages, 1983, with 1989 pocket part. (Text)

KUNTZ, LOWE, ANDERSON AND SMITH'S CASES AND MATERIALS ON OIL AND GAS LAW, 857 pages, 1986. Teacher's Manual available. (Casebook) Forms Manual. Revised.

LOWE'S OIL AND GAS LAW IN A NUTSHELL, Second Edition, 465 pages, 1988. Softcover. (Text)

Partnership—see Agency—Partnership

Patent and Copyright Law

CHOATE, FRANCIS AND COLLINS' CASES AND MATERIALS ON PATENT LAW, INCLUDING TRADE SECRETS, COPYRIGHTS, TRADEMARKS, Third Edition, 1009 pages, 1987. (Casebook)

MILLER AND DAVIS' INTELLECTUAL PROPERTY—PATENTS, TRADEMARKS AND COPYRIGHT IN A NUTSHELL, Second Edition, 437 pages, 1990. Softcover. (Text)

NIMMER, MARCUS, MYERS AND NIMMER'S CASES AND MATERIALS ON COPYRIGHT AND OTHER ASPECTS OF ENTERTAINMENT LITIGA-

Patent and Copyright Law—Cont'd

TION ILLUSTRATED—INCLUDING UNFAIR COMPETITION, DEFAMATION AND PRIVACY, Fourth Edition, Approximately 1,000 pages, April, 1991 Pub. (Casebook)

Products Liability

FISCHER AND POWERS' CASES AND MATERIALS ON PRODUCTS LIABILITY, 685 pages, 1988. Teacher's Manual available. (Casebook)

NOEL AND PHILLIPS' CASES ON PRODUCTS LIABILITY, Second Edition, 821 pages, 1982. (Casebook)

PHILLIPS' PRODUCTS LIABILITY IN A NUTSHELL, Third Edition, 307 pages, 1988. Softcover. (Text)

Professional Responsibility

ARONSON, DEVINE AND FISCH'S PROBLEMS, CASES AND MATERIALS IN PROFESSIONAL RESPONSIBILITY, 745 pages, 1985. Teacher's Manual available. (Casebook)

ARONSON AND WECKSTEIN'S PROFESSIONAL RESPONSIBILITY IN A NUTSHELL, Second Edition, approximately 500 pages, April, 1991 Pub. Softcover. (Text)

MELLINKOFF'S THE CONSCIENCE OF A LAWYER, 304 pages, 1973. (Text)

PIRSIG AND KIRWIN'S CASES AND MATERIALS ON PROFESSIONAL RESPONSIBILITY, Fourth Edition, 603 pages, 1984. Teacher's Manual available. (Casebook)

ROTUNDA'S BLACK LETTER ON PROFESSIONAL RESPONSIBILITY, Second Edition, 414 pages, 1988. Softcover. (Review)

SCHWARTZ AND WYDICK'S PROBLEMS IN LEGAL ETHICS, Second Edition, 341 pages, 1988. (Coursebook)

SELECTED STATUTES, RULES AND STANDARDS ON THE LEGAL PROFESSION. Softcover. 678 pages, 1990.

SMITH AND MALLEN'S PREVENTING LEGAL MALPRACTICE, 264 pages, 1989. Reprint from Mallen and Smith's Legal Malpractice, Third Edition. (Text)

SUTTON AND DZIENKOWSKI'S CASES AND MATERIALS ON PROFESSIONAL RESPONSIBILITY FOR LAWYERS, 839 pages, 1989. Teacher's Manual available. (Casebook)

WOLFRAM'S HORNBOOK ON MODERN LEGAL ETHICS, Student Edition, 1120 pages, 1986. (Text)

Property—see also Real Estate Transactions, Land Use, Trusts and Estates

BERNHARDT'S BLACK LETTER ON PROPERTY, 318 pages, 1983. Softcover. (Review)

BERNHARDT'S REAL PROPERTY IN A NUTSHELL, Second Edition, 448 pages, 1981. Softcover. (Text)

BOYER, HOVENKAMP AND KURTZ' THE LAW OF PROPERTY, AN INTRODUCTORY SURVEY, Fourth Edition, approximately 640 pages, April, 1991 Pub. (Text)

BROWDER, CUNNINGHAM, NELSON, STOEBUCK AND WHITMAN'S CASES ON BASIC PROPERTY LAW, Fifth Edition, 1386 pages, 1989. Teacher's Manual available. (Casebook)

BRUCE, ELY AND BOSTICK'S CASES AND MATERIALS ON MODERN PROPERTY LAW, Second Edition, 953 pages, 1989. Teacher's Manual available. (Casebook)

BURKE'S PERSONAL PROPERTY IN A NUTSHELL, 322 pages, 1983. Softcover. (Text)

CUNNINGHAM, STOEBUCK AND WHITMAN'S HORNBOOK ON THE LAW OF PROPERTY, Student Edition, 916 pages, 1984, with 1987 pocket part. (Text)

DONAHUE, KAUPER AND MARTIN'S CASES ON PROPERTY, Second Edition, 1362 pages, 1983. Teacher's Manual available. (Casebook)

HILL'S LANDLORD AND TENANT LAW IN A NUTSHELL, Second Edition, 311 pages, 1986. Softcover. (Text)

KURTZ AND HOVENKAMP'S CASES AND MATERIALS ON AMERICAN PROPERTY LAW, 1296 pages, 1987. Teacher's Manual available. (Casebook) 1988 Supplement.

MOYNIHAN'S INTRODUCTION TO REAL PROPERTY, Second Edition, 239 pages, 1988. (Text)

Psychiatry, Law and

REISNER AND SLOBOGIN'S LAW AND THE MENTAL HEALTH SYSTEM, CIVIL AND CRIMINAL ASPECTS, Second Edition, 1117 pages, 1990. (Casebook)

Real Estate Transactions

BRUCE'S REAL ESTATE FINANCE IN A NUT-SHELL, Second Edition, 262 pages, 1985. Softcover. (Text)

MAXWELL, RIESENFELD, HETLAND AND WARREN'S CASES ON CALIFORNIA SECURITY TRANSACTIONS IN LAND, Third Edition, 728 pages, 1984. (Casebook)

NELSON AND WHITMAN'S BLACK LETTER ON LAND TRANSACTIONS AND FINANCE, Second Edition, 466 pages, 1988. Softcover. (Review)

NELSON AND WHITMAN'S CASES ON REAL ESTATE TRANSFER, FINANCE AND DEVELOPMENT, Third Edition, 1184 pages, 1987. (Casebook)

NELSON AND WHITMAN'S HORNBOOK ON REAL ESTATE FINANCE LAW, Second Edition, 941 pages, 1985 with 1989 pocket part. (Text)

Regulated Industries—see also Mass Communication Law, Banking Law

GELLHORN AND PIERCE'S REGULATED INDUSTRIES IN A NUTSHELL, Second Edition, 389 pages, 1987. Softcover. (Text)

MORGAN, HARRISON AND VERKUIL'S CASES AND MATERIALS ON ECONOMIC REGULATION OF BUSINESS, Second Edition, 666 pages, 1985. (Casebook)

Remedies

DOBBS' HORNBOOK ON REMEDIES, 1067 pages, 1973. (Text)

DOBBS' PROBLEMS IN REMEDIES. 137 pages, 1974. Teacher's Manual available. Softcover. (Coursebook)

DOBBYN'S INJUNCTIONS IN A NUTSHELL, 264 pages, 1974. Softcover. (Text)

FRIEDMAN'S CONTRACT REMEDIES IN A NUTSHELL, 323 pages, 1981. Softcover. (Text)

LEAVELL, LOVE AND NELSON'S CASES AND MATERIALS ON EQUITABLE REMEDIES, RESTITUTION AND DAMAGES, Fourth Edition, 1111 pages, 1986. Teacher's Manual available. (Casebook)

MCCORMICK'S HORNBOOK ON DAMAGES, 811 pages, 1935. (Text)

O'CONNELL'S REMEDIES IN A NUTSHELL, Second Edition, 320 pages, 1985. Softcover. (Text)

SCHOENBROD, MACBETH, LEVINE AND JUNG'S CASES AND MATERIALS ON REMEDIES: PUBLIC AND PRIVATE, 848 pages, 1990. Teacher's Manual available. (Casebook)

YORK, BAUMAN AND RENDLEMAN'S CASES AND MATERIALS ON REMEDIES, Fourth Edition, 1029 pages, 1985. Teacher's Manual available. (Casebook)

Sea, Law of

SOHN AND GUSTAFSON'S THE LAW OF THE SEA IN A NUTSHELL, 264 pages, 1984. Softcover. (Text)

Securities Regulation

HAZEN'S HORNBOOK ON THE LAW OF SECURITIES REGULATION, Second Edition, Student Edition, 1082 pages, 1990. (Text)

RATNER'S SECURITIES REGULATION IN A NUTSHELL, Third Edition, 316 pages, 1988. Softcover. (Text)

RATNER AND HAZEN'S SECURITIES REGULATION: CASES AND MATERIALS, Fourth Edition, approximately 1,075 pages, 1991. (Casebook) Problems and Sample Documents Supplement.

    Statutory Supplement. *See Securities Regulation, Selected Statutes*

SECURITIES REGULATION, SELECTED STATUTES, RULES, AND FORMS. Softcover. Approximately 1,300 pages, 1991.

Social Legislation—see Workers' Compensation

Sports Law

SCHUBERT, SMITH AND TRENTADUE'S SPORTS LAW, 395 pages, 1986. (Text)

Tax Practice and Procedure

GARBIS, STRUNTZ AND RUBIN'S CASES AND MATERIALS ON TAX PROCEDURE AND TAX FRAUD, Second Edition, 687 pages, 1987. (Casebook)

MORGAN'S TAX PROCEDURE AND TAX FRAUD IN A NUTSHELL, 400 pages, 1990. Softcover. (Text)

Taxation—Corporate

KAHN AND GANN'S CORPORATE TAXATION, Third Edition, 980 pages, 1989. Teacher's Manual available. (Casebook)

Taxation—Corporate—Cont'd

WEIDENBRUCH AND BURKE'S FEDERAL INCOME TAXATION OF CORPORATIONS AND STOCKHOLDERS IN A NUTSHELL, Third Edition, 309 pages, 1989. Softcover. (Text)

Taxation—Estate & Gift—see also Estate Planning, Trusts and Estates

MCNULTY'S FEDERAL ESTATE AND GIFT TAXATION IN A NUTSHELL, Fourth Edition, 496 pages, 1989. Softcover. (Text)

PENNELL'S CASES AND MATERIALS ON INCOME TAXATION OF TRUSTS, ESTATES, GRANTORS AND BENEFICIARIES, 460 pages, 1987. Teacher's Manual available. (Casebook)

Taxation—Individual

DODGE'S THE LOGIC OF TAX, 343 pages, 1989. Softcover. (Text)

GUNN AND WARD'S CASES, TEXT AND PROBLEMS ON FEDERAL INCOME TAXATION, Second Edition, 835 pages, 1988. Teacher's Manual available. (Casebook) 1990 Supplement.

HUDSON AND LIND'S BLACK LETTER ON FEDERAL INCOME TAXATION, Third Edition, 406 pages, 1990. Softcover. (Review)

KRAGEN AND MCNULTY'S CASES AND MATERIALS ON FEDERAL INCOME TAXATION—INDIVIDUALS, CORPORATIONS, PARTNERSHIPS, Fourth Edition, 1287 pages, 1985. (Casebook)

MCNULTY'S FEDERAL INCOME TAXATION OF INDIVIDUALS IN A NUTSHELL, Fourth Edition, 503 pages, 1988. Softcover. (Text)

POSIN'S HORNBOOK ON FEDERAL INCOME TAXATION, Student Edition, 491 pages, 1983, with 1989 pocket part. (Text)

ROSE AND CHOMMIE'S HORNBOOK ON FEDERAL INCOME TAXATION, Third Edition, 923 pages, 1988, with 1989 pocket part. (Text)

SELECTED FEDERAL TAXATION STATUTES AND REGULATIONS. Softcover. 1558 pages, 1991.

SOLOMON AND HESCH'S PROBLEMS, CASES AND MATERIALS ON FEDERAL INCOME TAXATION OF INDIVIDUALS, 1068 pages, 1987. Teacher's Manual available. (Casebook)

Taxation—International

DOERNBERG'S INTERNATIONAL TAXATION IN A NUTSHELL, 325 pages, 1989. Softcover. (Text)

KAPLAN'S FEDERAL TAXATION OF INTERNATIONAL TRANSACTIONS: PRINCIPLES, PLANNING AND POLICY, 635 pages, 1988. (Casebook)

Taxation—Partnership

BERGER AND WIEDENBECK'S CASES AND MATERIALS ON PARTNERSHIP TAXATION, 788 pages, 1989. Teacher's Manual available. (Casebook)

BISHOP AND BROOKS' FEDERAL PARTNERSHIP TAXATION: A GUIDE TO THE LEADING CASES, STATUTES, AND REGULATIONS, 545 pages, 1990. Softcover. (Text)

Taxation—State & Local

GELFAND AND SALSICH'S STATE AND LOCAL TAXATION AND FINANCE IN A NUTSHELL, 309 pages, 1986. Softcover. (Text)

HELLERSTEIN AND HELLERSTEIN'S CASES AND MATERIALS ON STATE AND LOCAL TAXATION, Fifth Edition, 1071 pages, 1988. (Casebook)

Torts—see also Products Liability

CHRISTIE AND MEEKS' CASES AND MATERIALS ON THE LAW OF TORTS, Second Edition, 1264 pages, 1990. (Casebook)

DOBBS' TORTS AND COMPENSATION—PERSONAL ACCOUNTABILITY AND SOCIAL RESPONSIBILITY FOR INJURY, 955 pages, 1985. Teacher's Manual available. (Casebook) 1990 Supplement.

KEETON, KEETON, SARGENTICH AND STEINER'S CASES AND MATERIALS ON TORT AND ACCIDENT LAW, Second Edition, 1318 pages, 1989. (Casebook)

KIONKA'S BLACK LETTER ON TORTS, 339 pages, 1988. Softcover. (Review)

KIONKA'S TORTS IN A NUTSHELL: INJURIES TO PERSONS AND PROPERTY, 434 pages, 1977. Softcover. (Text)

MALONE'S TORTS IN A NUTSHELL: INJURIES TO FAMILY, SOCIAL AND TRADE RELATIONS, 358 pages, 1979. Softcover. (Text)

PROSSER AND KEETON'S HORNBOOK ON TORTS, Fifth Edition, Student Edition, 1286 pages, 1984 with 1988 pocket part. (Text)

ROBERTSON, POWERS AND ANDERSON'S CASES

Torts—Cont'd

AND MATERIALS ON TORTS, 932 pages, 1989. Teacher's Manual available. (Casebook)

Trade Regulation—see also Antitrust, Regulated Industries

MCMANIS' UNFAIR TRADE PRACTICES IN A NUTSHELL, Second Edition, 464 pages, 1988. Softcover. (Text)

OPPENHEIM, WESTON, MAGGS AND SCHECHTER'S CASES AND MATERIALS ON UNFAIR TRADE PRACTICES AND CONSUMER PROTECTION, Fourth Edition, 1038 pages, 1983. Teacher's Manual available. (Casebook) 1986 Supplement.

SCHECHTER'S BLACK LETTER ON UNFAIR TRADE PRACTICES, 272 pages, 1986. Softcover. (Review)

Trial and Appellate Advocacy—see also Civil Procedure

APPELLATE ADVOCACY, HANDBOOK OF, Second Edition, 182 pages, 1986. Softcover. (Text)

BERGMAN'S TRIAL ADVOCACY IN A NUTSHELL, Second Edition, 354 pages, 1989. Softcover. (Text)

BINDER AND BERGMAN'S FACT INVESTIGATION: FROM HYPOTHESIS TO PROOF, 354 pages, 1984. Teacher's Manual available. (Coursebook)

CARLSON AND IMWINKELRIED'S DYNAMICS OF TRIAL PRACTICE: PROBLEMS AND MATERIALS, 414 pages, 1989. Teacher's Manual available. (Coursebook) 1990 Supplement.

DESSEM'S PRETRIAL LITIGATION: LAW, POLICY AND PRACTICE, Approximately 615 pages, March, 1991 Pub. Softcover. (Coursebook)

GOLDBERG'S THE FIRST TRIAL (WHERE DO I SIT? WHAT DO I SAY?) IN A NUTSHELL, 396 pages, 1982. Softcover. (Text)

HAYDOCK, HERR, AND STEMPEL'S FUNDAMENTALS OF PRE-TRIAL LITIGATION, 768 pages, 1985. Softcover. Teacher's Manual available. (Coursebook)

HAYDOCK AND SONSTENG'S TRIAL: THEORIES, TACTICS, TECHNIQUES, 711 pages, 1991. Softcover. (Text)

HEGLAND'S TRIAL AND PRACTICE SKILLS IN A NUTSHELL, 346 pages, 1978. Softcover. (Text)

HORNSTEIN'S APPELLATE ADVOCACY IN A NUTSHELL, 325 pages, 1984. Softcover. (Text)

JEANS' HANDBOOK ON TRIAL ADVOCACY, Student Edition, 473 pages, 1975. Softcover. (Text)

LISNEK AND KAUFMAN'S DEPOSITIONS: PROCEDURE, STRATEGY AND TECHNIQUE, Law School and CLE Edition. 250 pages, 1990. Softcover. (Text)

MARTINEAU'S CASES AND MATERIALS ON APPELLATE PRACTICE AND PROCEDURE, 565 pages, 1987. (Casebook)

NOLAN'S CASES AND MATERIALS ON TRIAL PRACTICE, 518 pages, 1981. (Casebook)

SONSTENG, HAYDOCK AND BOYD'S THE TRIALBOOK: A TOTAL SYSTEM FOR PREPARATION AND PRESENTATION OF A CASE, 404 pages, 1984. Softcover. (Coursebook)

WHARTON, HAYDOCK AND SONSTENG'S CALIFORNIA CIVIL TRIALBOOK, Law School and CLE Edition. 148 pages, 1990. Softcover. (Text)

Trusts and Estates

ATKINSON'S HORNBOOK ON WILLS, Second Edition, 975 pages, 1953. (Text)

AVERILL'S UNIFORM PROBATE CODE IN A NUTSHELL, Second Edition, 454 pages, 1987. Softcover. (Text)

BOGERT'S HORNBOOK ON TRUSTS, Sixth Edition, Student Edition, 794 pages, 1987. (Text)

CLARK, LUSKY AND MURPHY'S CASES AND MATERIALS ON GRATUITOUS TRANSFERS, Third Edition, 970 pages, 1985. (Casebook)

DODGE'S WILLS, TRUSTS AND ESTATE PLANNING—LAW AND TAXATION, CASES AND MATERIALS, 665 pages, 1988. (Casebook)

KURTZ' PROBLEMS, CASES AND OTHER MATERIALS ON FAMILY ESTATE PLANNING, 853 pages, 1983. Teacher's Manual available. (Casebook)

MCGOVERN'S CASES AND MATERIALS ON WILLS, TRUSTS AND FUTURE INTERESTS: AN INTRODUCTION TO ESTATE PLANNING, 750 pages, 1983. (Casebook)

Trusts and Estates—Cont'd

MCGOVERN, KURTZ AND REIN'S HORNBOOK ON WILLS, TRUSTS AND ESTATES–INCLUDING TAXATION AND FUTURE INTERESTS, 996 pages, 1988. (Text)

MENNELL'S WILLS AND TRUSTS IN A NUTSHELL, 392 pages, 1979. Softcover. (Text)

SIMES' HORNBOOK ON FUTURE INTERESTS, Second Edition, 355 pages, 1966. (Text)

TURANO AND RADIGAN'S HORNBOOK ON NEW YORK ESTATE ADMINISTRATION, 676 pages, 1986. (Text)

UNIFORM PROBATE CODE, OFFICIAL TEXT WITH COMMENTS. 615 pages, 1989. Softcover.

WAGGONER'S FUTURE INTERESTS IN A NUTSHELL, 361 pages, 1981. Softcover. (Text)

WATERBURY'S MATERIALS ON TRUSTS AND ESTATES, 1039 pages, 1986. Teacher's Manual available. (Casebook)

Water Law—see also Energy and Natural Resources Law, Environmental Law

GETCHES' WATER LAW IN A NUTSHELL, Second Edition, 459 pages, 1990. Softcover.

(Text)

SAX AND ABRAMS' LEGAL CONTROL OF WATER RESOURCES: CASES AND MATERIALS, 941 pages, 1986. (Casebook)

TRELEASE AND GOULD'S CASES AND MATERIALS ON WATER LAW, Fourth Edition, 816 pages, 1986. (Casebook)

Wills—see Trusts and Estates

Women and the Law—see also Employment Discrimination

KAY'S TEXT, CASES AND MATERIALS ON SEX–BASED DISCRIMINATION, Third Edition, 1001 pages, 1988. (Casebook) 1990 Supplement.

THOMAS' SEX DISCRIMINATION IN A NUTSHELL, 399 pages, 1982. Softcover. (Text)

Workers' Compensation

HOOD, HARDY AND LEWIS' WORKERS' COMPENSATION AND EMPLOYEE PROTECTION LAWS IN A NUTSHELL, Second Edition, 361 pages, 1990. Softcover. (Text)

MALONE, PLANT AND LITTLE'S CASES ON WORKERS' COMPENSATION AND EMPLOYMENT RIGHTS, Second Edition, 951 pages, 1980. Teacher's Manual available. (Casebook)

CASES AND MATERIALS ON
CORPORATIONS
INCLUDING PARTNERSHIPS
AND
LIMITED PARTNERSHIPS

Fourth Edition

By

Robert W. Hamilton
Minerva House Drysdale
Regents Chair in Law
The University of Texas at Austin

AMERICAN CASEBOOK SERIES®

WEST PUBLISHING CO.
ST. PAUL, MINN., 1990

American Casebook Series, the key number appearing on the front cover and the WP symbol are registered trademarks of West Publishing Co. Registered in U.S. Patent and Trademark Office.

Library of Congress Cataloging-in-Publication Data

Hamilton, Robert W., 1931–
    Cases and materials on corporations, including partnerships and limited partnerships / by Robert W. Hamilton. — 4th ed.
      p. cm. — (American casebook series)
    ISBN 0–314–74327–8
    1. Corporation law—United States—Cases. 2. Partnership—United States—Cases. I. Series.
    KF1413.H35 1990
    346.73'066—dc20
    [347.30666]   90–36457
                                        CIP

ISBN 0–314–74327–8

Hamilton, Corp. 4th Ed. ACB
1st Reprint—1991

Preface

This book is designed for introductory courses in the law of business associations or corporations. With a minimum of adjustment it may be used in courses covering anywhere from three to six semester hours. Chapters are included on the law of partnerships, limited partnerships and selection of business form. These chapters, which may readily be omitted in courses dealing exclusively with the law of corporations, should occupy approximately three weeks of classes. This book is not designed for use in advanced courses such as securities regulation or corporation finance, nor for an introductory course devoted exclusively to agency and partnership.

I am strongly of the view that the modern law of corporations can be most effectively taught only in the context of a specific set of statutes. The statutory supplement contains the full text of the Uniform Partnership Act, the Revised Uniform Limited Partnership Act (1976) with the 1985 amendments, and the Revised Model Business Corporation Act (1984) (except for transition provisions). In earlier editions, the statutory supplement also included the original Uniform Limited Partnership Act approved in 1916. This older statute has been eliminated because in the last fifteen years more than forty-five states have adopted new limited partnership statutes based on or heavily influenced by RULPA. I have quoted from the original ULPA in the text of the casebook in the few instances where a comparison with that earlier statute may be useful. The statutory supplement also includes the financial provisions of the 1969 Model Business Corporation Act.

The publication "Selected Corporation and Partnership Statutes" contains most of the same statutes (and a lot of other materials as well), and may be used instead of the statutory supplement.

Students are encouraged to become familiar with these statutes in the statutory supplement by the simple practice of referring to, but not quoting, the relevant provisions of these statutes throughout this casebook. The statutes of most states today are sufficiently close to these Uniform or Model Acts that their choice should create little or no problem even where instruction is more or less explicitly directed to the laws of a specific state. Nevertheless it is feasible to use both the Uniform and Model Acts and the statutes of a specific state if one is willing to impose on his or her students the obligation first to examine the Uniform or Model Act provision and then search for the similar or correlative provision in the state statute. Such a procedure often has the distinct advantage of encouraging discussion of variations in language and substantive requirements between two sets of statutes dealing with a single subject.

In the preparation of this book, numerous citations and footnotes have been omitted without specification. All footnotes have been renumbered in each chapter. In a few instances the location of footnotes taken from original sources has been changed. In order to identify the source of footnotes, the bracketed phrases "[By the Court]" or "[By the Author]" appear at the beginning of footnotes that appear in the original source. Footnotes beginning "[By the Editor]" or footnotes without bracketed introduction were prepared by the undersigned.

Ellipsis ("∗ ∗ ∗") may indicate the omission of single words in a paragraph or entire paragraphs.

Permission to use copyrighted materials is gratefully acknowledged from Donna D. Adler, Albany Law Review, Barbara Bader Aldave, John R. Alexander, American Bar Association, American Business Law Journal, American Law Institute, American Enterprise Institute for Public Policy Research, Mark Andrews, William D. Andrews, Arizona State Law Journal, S. Samuel Arsht, Atlantic Richfield, Richard J. Barber, Joseph J. Basile, Dennis J. Block, Ward Bower, Douglas Branson, William W. Bratton, Jr., Alan Bromberg, Victor Brudney, The Business Lawyer, Henry N. Butler, Cardozo Law Review, William Carley, Dennis W. Carlton, William J. Carney, Case Western Reserve Law Review, Cincinnati Law Review, Robert Clark, Cleveland State Law Review, John C. Coffee, Jr., Directors of the Columbia Law Review, Alfred F. Conard, James D. Cox, Arthur B. Crozier, Lynne L. Dallas, Delaware Journal of Corporate Law, Deborah DeMott, Michael P. Dooley, David M. Doret, Duke Law Journal, Richard W. Dusenberg, E.P. Dutton New American Library, Frank H. Easterbrook, Melvin Eisenberg, Peter L. Faber, Ted J. Fiflis, Jesse A. Finkelstein, Daniel R. Fischel, Paul M. Foster, Milton V. Freeman, George Mason University Law Review, William A. Gregory, William P. Hackney, James J. Hanks, Jr., Charles Hansen, Harvard Business Review, Harvard Law Review Association, Harry J. Haynsworth, James E. Heard, Harry G. Henn, Leo Herzel, Joseph Hinsey, IV, Michael C. Jensen, Joseph F. Johnston, Dennis S. Karjala, Leo Katz, Stanley Keller, Richard H. Koppes, Reinier Kraakman, Homer Kripke, Donald C. Langevoort, Norman D. Lattin, J. B. Lippincott Co., Little Brown & Company, J. Livingston, Myles L. Mace, Manhattan Lawyer, Bayless Manning, The Michie Company, Alan M. Miller, Minnesota Law Review, New York Times, Stephen P. Norman, North Carolina Law Review, Northwestern Law Review, Ohio State Law Journal, Denis Orme, Andrew D. Orrick, Playboy Magazine, The Practical Accountant, Prentice Hall Law & Business, H. Adam Prussin, William J. Rands, Harold G. Reuschlein, Larry Ribstein, Richard Rodewald, Roberta Romano, Fred B. Rothman & Company, San Diego Law Review, Section of Corporation, Banking & Business Law of the American Bar Association, Joel Seligman, Robert J. Shaughnessy, G. Richard Shell, Stanford Law Review, Texas Law Review, Wall Street Journal, University of Florida Law Review, University of Chicago Law Review, University of Michigan Journal of Law Reform, University of

Pennsylvania Law Review, Vanderbilt Law Review, E. Norman Veasey, Virginia Law Review Association, Wachtell, Lipton, Rosen & Katz, Wake Forest Law Review, Alvin C. Warren, Jr., Washington University Law Quarterly, Ralph K. Winter, Jr., Wisconsin Law Review, and Yale Law Journal.

Finally, I express my gratitude to my colleague, David Sokolow, for his suggested reorganization of the introductory chapters dealing with partnership and selection of business forms.

ROBERT W. HAMILTON

AUSTIN, TEXAS
January 31, 1990

*

Summary of Contents

*

Table of Contents

Table of Cases

The principal cases are in bold type. Cases cited or discussed in the text are roman type. References are to pages. Cases cited in principal cases and within other quoted materials are not included.

*

CASES AND MATERIALS ON
CORPORATIONS
INCLUDING PARTNERSHIPS AND LIMITED PARTNERSHIPS

Fourth Edition

*

Chapter One

INTRODUCTION

A. THE SUBJECT IN GENERAL

The subject of corporations or business associations involves a study of the means and devices by which business is conducted either by a single individual or cooperatively by a few or many individuals. "Business" is a broad term describing all kinds of profit-making activity excluding the performance of services for another in an employment relationship. Of course, broad definitions such as the foregoing give little indication of the diversity and richness of the problems to be encountered.

Business associations has been broken down traditionally into *unincorporated* associations, e.g. agency, partnership, limited partnership, and *corporations*, and many law school curricula continue to reflect this approach. See the preceding *Preface: Primarily for the Teacher*. Viewed in this light, this book is primarily about corporations. It includes materials on partnerships and limited partnerships because those forms of business association are in fact functional alternatives to a corporation where the number of owners of the business is small, and may also be used to a limited extent where the number is large.

In the materials that follow, a basic distinction is drawn between *closely held* businesses, that is, ones with one or a few owners, and *publicly held* businesses, with hundreds or thousands of owners. At first glance there appears to be little in common between a very large corporation such as General Motors Corporation, with millions of shareholders, sales and revenues of over 110 billion dollars in 1988 and some 766,000 employees, and a small grocery store partnership with two owners, two employees, and annual sales of perhaps two hundred thousand dollars. Indeed, some law schools have departed radically from the traditional division and created two basic courses in business associations to consider separately the problems of the very large and the very small. There is some artificiality in this distinction, however, because in the real world there is a continuum of size and complexity of businesses, and to a surprising extent the closely-held and publicly-held business draw from a common reservoir of principles and tradition.

B. THE STATUTES

Unlike subjects such as property and torts, the subject of corporations or business associations is largely governed by statute. This is true not only in the large commercial states such as New York and California but in the smaller states as well. Answers to many but not all questions must be found in the statutes and cannot be answered solely on the basis of common sense. In this respect the law of corporations or business associations is similar to many other areas of the law in the modern commercial and government-oriented society.

An experienced attorney does not attempt to memorize the detailed provisions of the numerous complex statutes with which he or she must be familiar. Rather, the attorney becomes generally familiar with the provisions and keeps copies of them available for easy reference. Each student should follow approximately the same process. To encourage this process, the materials that follow refer to but do not quote the basic statutory materials.[1] Statutory references should be looked up in the statutes, since the materials cannot be fully understood without doing so.

The supplement to this book contains the verbatim text of the following statutes:

(1) The Uniform Partnership Act (UPA);

(2) The Revised Uniform Limited Partnership Act of 1976 with the 1985 Amendments (RULPA); and

(3) The Revised Model Business Corporation Act (1984) as amended (RMBCA).

The supplement describes the states that have incorporated these uniform or model statutes into their statutes. The following general comments give an indication of the extent of uniformity actually achieved by these statutes.

(1) *The Uniform Partnership Act (UPA).* Generally, the UPA, originally approved in 1913, has achieved virtual unanimous acceptance, though some states have departed from the Uniform Act language in minor respects. The longevity of this statute in the face of basic—indeed, revolutionary—changes in business practice, business ethics, the enactment of the Internal Revenue Code and the numerous recodifications and amendments to that law during the last seventy-five years can only be described as astonishing. Nevertheless, the 1980s saw the first tangible signs of dissatisfaction with this venerable statute. In 1984, Georgia enacted substantial amend-

---

1. [By the Editor] This statement refers to the basic statutory codification of the forms of business enterprise covered in the supplement or in the statutes of a specific state. Relevant federal statutes and individual statutes of specific states are quoted in the text or notes where appropriate.

ments to its version of the UPA. In January, 1986, an American Bar Association Subcommittee issued a detailed report that proposed a large number of changes to the UPA, many based on the Georgia revisions. Consult UPA Revision Subcommittee of the Committee on Partnerships and Unincorporated Business Organizations, Section of Business Law, American Bar Association, Should the Uniform Partnership Act Be Revised? 43 Bus.Law. 121 (1987). In 1987, the National Conference of Commissioners on Uniform State Laws created a Drafting Committee and named a Reporter (Professor Donald Weidner of Florida State University College of Law) to draft a revision of the UPA. A draft version of a new statute was presented for discussion by the Conference in the Summer of 1989; final action on this new statute, which undoubtedly will be known as the Revised Uniform Partnership Act (or "RUPA"), may occur in 1990, or more likely, in 1991. Because of the tentative nature of this revision, the original UPA remains the principal emphasis of the present edition, and the text of that statute is included in the statutory supplement. In a few instances the text of the casebook discusses some of the major policy changes proposed by this draft.

(2) *Revised Uniform Limited Partnership Act (RULPA)*. The original Uniform Limited Partnership Act (ULPA) was approved in 1917, the same year as the enactment of the first federal income tax of the modern era. This early statute also achieved virtually unanimous acceptance, but increasing dissatisfaction with its rather simplistic and often inadequate language occurred somewhat earlier than in connection with the UPA. The Conference of Commissioners on Uniform State Laws approved a substitute statute in 1976. Acceptance of this statute, however, was relatively slow, in large part because of uncertainty about the status for federal income tax purposes of organizations created under the new statute. When the tax status was clarified, a number of states promptly adopted new limited partnership statutes but a number of them also adopted deviating amendments because of dissatisfaction with some of the provisions of the RULPA itself. In 1983 and 1985 the Commissioners made significant amendments to the RULPA to increase its attractiveness; many of these amendments were suggested by the deviating amendments adopted by states. By 1989 more than 45 states have adopted the RULPA or some version of a modern limited partnership statute broadly based on that statute, and most of the remaining states have adopted amendments to the original ULPA.

Because of the numerous amendments to the RULPA and the deviating amendments adopted in many states, the degree of uniformity in state law relating to limited partnerships is much less than that relating to general partnerships.

(3) *The Revised Model Business Corporation Act (RMBCA)*. The RMBCA is a recent revision of the Model Business Corporation Act

(MBCA)[2], a statute that was extremely influential in the development of state corporation statutes since it was first widely published in 1950. The MBCA was used by more than 30 states in the period after 1950 as a model in the recodification of their business corporation statutes, and it had noticeable but lesser influence in a number of additional states. It appears likely that the RMBCA will have strong influence on state statutes in the future; it has been used as a model in the recodification of corporation statutes in about a dozen states between 1984 and 1989. Even with the wide popularity of the original MBCA, the variations in corporation statutes from state to state are greater than the variations in the partnership statutes—including variations in modern limited partnership statutes described above. For one thing, a number of important commercial states (as well as the ubiquitous state of Delaware long known for its success in attracting corporate business) have not followed the MBCA but have developed their own corporation statutes with their own resources. For another, there may be a subtle difference between a "uniform" statute and a "model" statute. A uniform statute is designed for enactment *in haec verba* so that the ultimate goal is nation-wide uniformity of provisions applicable to the subject matter in question. A "model" statute, on the other hand, contemplates that there may be amendments or changes to reflect local interests, needs, or problems: it is a "model" from which jurisdictions may draw but is not presented as a "uniform" statute. Thus, it should not be surprising that considerable diversity exists in state corporation statutes.

This book may be used either with the uniform and model statutes in the supplement or with the statutes of a particular state. If the latter are assigned, it will be necessary to master the numeration of the specific statutes and to locate the most analogous provisions to the model and uniform statutes cited in the following materials. This is "a good thing" since it doubtless will speed your mastery of the statutory materials.

To repeat: a lawyer does not need to memorize the detailed provisions of statutes. Rather, he or she keeps them close at hand, is generally familiar with what is in them, and, most importantly, knows about where in the statutes the specific provision is so that the precise language can be located quickly.

The statutes in most jurisdictions today are modern, up-to-date, and, as described above, draw from the common core of the model and uniform statutes. However, it should not be assumed that statutes always clarify and simplify. In specific circumstances, statutory language may appear to require an unjust or unreasonable result; where this occurs, the statute must be viewed as an obstacle to overcome rather than a rule to be followed. This is probably more likely to be

---

2. [By the Editor] The editor of this casebook served as the Reporter for the RMBCA.

true in jurisdictions that have not drawn from the common core of the model and uniform statutes, but it is also true in some circumstances under these statutes as well.

C. THE BASIC BUSINESS FORMS

Consider the following simple situation:

A and B are planning to go into the retail furniture business. A will invest $100,000 while B will make no cash contributions but will operate the store on a day-to-day basis. A desires first, assurance that he will not be called upon to increase his investment and second, a veto power over basic decisions made by B in order to protect his investment. Profits are to be divided equally after B is paid a "salary" of $1500 per month.

What is the legal relationship if, without legal advice, A and B shake hands on the deal, A gives B a check for $100,000 and B proceeds to rent a store, buy stock and commence business?

RESTATEMENT OF AGENCY, SECOND *

§ 1. Agency; Principal; Agent

(1) Agency is the fiduciary relation which results from the manifestation of consent by one person to another that the other shall act on his behalf and subject to his control, and consent by the other so to act.

(2) The one for whom action is to be taken is the principal.

(3) The one who is to act is the agent.

§ 2. Master; Servant; Independent Contractor

(1) A master is a principal who employs an agent to perform service in his affairs and who controls or has the right to control the physical conduct of the other in the performance of the service.

(2) A servant is an agent employed by a master to perform service in his affairs whose physical conduct in the performance of the service is controlled or is subject to the right to control by the master.

(3) An independent contractor is a person who contracts with another to do something for him but who is not controlled by the other nor subject to the other's right to control with respect to his physical conduct in the performance of the undertaking. He may or may not be an agent.

§ 220. Definition of Servant

* * * (2) In determining whether one acting for another is a servant or an independent contractor, the following matters of fact, among others, are considered:

(a) the extent of control which, by the agreement, the master may exercise over the details of the work;

(b) whether or not the one employed is engaged in a distinct occupation or business;

(c) the kind of occupation, with reference to whether, in the locality, the work is usually done under the direction of the employer or by a specialist without supervision;

(d) the skill required in the particular occupation;

(e) whether the employer or the workman supplies the instrumentalities, tools, and the place of work for the person doing the work;

(f) the length of time for which the person is employed;

(g) the method of payment, whether by the time or by the job;

(h) whether or not the work is a part of the regular business of the employer;

(i) whether or not the parties believe they are creating the relation of master and servant; and

(j) whether the principal is or is not in business.

---

(1) Was a traditional agency or master-servant relationship created?

A servant, in the foregoing definitions, is not limited to a menial position but includes all relationships usually described as involving "employment." Is B a "servant" or "employee" of A? What elements are present in the relationship between A and B which are missing in the usual employer-employee relationship? Is B an "independent contractor"? Is he working for another or for himself? Or for both?

(2) Is the relationship between A and B that of creditor and debtor? Is there, for example, a promise to repay and a repayment date?

(3) Are A and B partners? Consider UPA §§ 6(1), 7. Assuming so, can A be assured that he will not be called upon to increase his investment against his will despite the agreement? Consider the implications of UPA § 15.

(4) Can A be considered a limited partner and B a general partner in a limited partnership? Consider RULPA §§ 101(7), 201, 303(a). However, even assuming that the necessary certificate has been filed in the proper form [see RULPA §§ 201, 206], can the control arrangements desired by A be worked out in light of RULPA § 303? The problem of the limited partner who wished to keep a "hand" in the business (as did A) was even more uncertain under the 1916 Uniform Limited Partnership Act (ULPA). ULPA § 7 merely stated "A limited partner shall not become liable as a general partner unless, in addition to the exercise of his rights and powers as a limited partner, he takes part in the control of the business." The bare phrase "takes part in the

control of the business" without the enumeration and embroidery of section 303 of RULPA provided little guidance as to what controls a limited partner might safely retain and therefore greatly decreased the attractiveness of the limited partnership form of business, at least from the standpoint of the risk-adverse investor.

(5) Can A obtain what he desires through the device of a corporation? A corporation is formed by following the relatively simple procedures set forth in the corporation statute, see RMBCA §§ 2.01–2.03, 2.05. Section 2.03 states that "the corporate existence begins" upon the filing of articles of incorporation. This language accepts the customary theory that incorporation results in the creation of a new legal entity, a fictitious person, so to speak. In the above hypothetical, the "corporation" would be liable for business debts of the furniture store and neither A nor B would be liable. The "corporation" might enter into contracts, borrow money, sue and be sued, and otherwise conduct the furniture store business. It may also own real estate in its own name and may own property free and clear of claims of a spouse of a shareholder or other claims of creditors or shareholders. However, the shares of stock of the corporation owned by the shareholder might be subject to such claims.

A corporation offers advantages in internal management structure over the other forms of business enterprise discussed above. Unlike a limited partnership, management powers and limited liability may co-exist in a single individual in a corporation. Theoretically, a corporation consists of three layers or tiers—(1) the shareholders who are traditionally viewed as the ultimate owners of the enterprise, (2) the board of directors, who are the managers of the corporation's affairs [see RMBCA § 8.01(b)], and (3) the officers, who traditionally act for the corporation to implement the decisions of the directors [compare RMBCA § 8.41]. A single individual may simultaneously act as an officer, a director, and a shareholder. It is possible, for example, for A and B each to own 50 per cent of the shares and to be the directors of the corporation; A may be president of the corporation with power to approve or disapprove of all expenditures, while B may be vice president, secretary, "general manager," and whatever other office the parties desire to create. In this way, profits may be shared equally in the form of dividends without personal liability for corporate obligations, B is entitled to a salary, and A has the veto power he desires. The essentials of the desired control arrangement are therefore achieved.

Of course, in the above hypothetical, a corporation was not actually formed since A and B did not take the simple but essential steps to form a corporation. See RMBCA § 2.04.

Notes

(1) Both the RULPA and the RMBCA require a document to be filed with a public official as an essential step in the formation of a limited

partnership or a corporation. The contents of the articles of incorporation are described in RMBCA § 2.02, while the formal requirements of execution are set forth in RMBCA §§ 1.20 and 1.22. The contents of the limited partnership certificate are described in RULPA § 201(a). The original ULPA required much more complete disclosure than either of these modern statutes. The ULPA disclosure requirements were:

    I. The name of the partnership,

    II. The character of the business,

    III. The location of the principal place of business,

    IV. The name and place of residence of each member; general and limited partners being respectively designated,

    V. The term for which the partnership is to exist,

    VI. The amount of cash and a description of and the agreed value of the other property contributed by each limited partner,

    VII. The additional contributions, if any, agreed to be made by each limited partner and the times at which or events on the happening of which they shall be made,

    VIII. The time, if agreed upon, when the contribution of each limited partner is to be returned,

    IX. The share of the profits or the other compensation by way of income which each limited partner shall receive by reason of his contribution,

    X. The right, if given, of a limited partner to substitute an assignee as contributor in his place, and the terms and conditions of the substitution,

    XI. The right, if given, of the partners to admit additional limited partners,

    XII. The right, if given, of one or more of the limited partners to priority over other limited partners, as to contributions or as to compensation by way of income, and the nature of such priority,

    XIII. The right, if given, of the remaining general partner or partners to continue the business on the death, retirement or insanity of a general partner, and

    XIV. The right, if given, of a limited partner to demand and receive property other than cash in return for his contribution.

Prior to the 1985 amendments to the RULPA, its certificate requirements were similar to those in the ULPA, but these amendments adopted the "short form certificate" approach modeled in the RMBCA that now appears in the RULPA. Do you agree with the general trend of restricting mandatory public disclosure? What purposes might be served, for example, by the disclosure of residential addresses of partners and the amounts of contributions by limited partners? Might the public availability of such information be subject to abuse?

(2) The RMBCA contemplates that articles of incorporation will be filed with the secretary of state of the state of incorporation; the RULPA specifies the same office for filing the limited partnership certificate

(RULPA § 206). On the other hand, the original Uniform Limited Partnership Act left the place of filing open and under this older statute, a number of states, including the commercially important states of California, Illinois, Michigan, New York, Ohio, and Pennsylvania, originally provided for filing limited partnership certificates in an office of the county where the principal place of business of the limited partnership is located. Does this preference for local filing of limited partnership certificates in sophisticated states cast light on the traditional view of the role of limited partnerships in the economy? Prior to the RULPA, some states, including Texas, provided for central filing for limited partnership certificates, so that the RULPA does not represent a major change in this regard. Some states provided for both central and local filing of limited partnership certificates under ULPA, and some still require publication, e.g. in a local newspaper, in addition to a public filing.

(3) Do you see any practical problems with the corporate structure for the AB furniture store corporation proposed in the text? What would happen, for example, if A and B have a fundamental disagreement?

(4) Section 50 of the 1969 Model Business Corporation Act provided that "[t]he officers of a corporation shall consist of a president, one or more vice presidents as may be prescribed by the by-laws, a secretary, and a treasurer * * *. Any two or more offices may be held by the same person, except the offices of president and secretary." Contrast RMBCA § 8.40(a), (d). If the AB Furniture Store were being incorporated under the 1969 MBCA, A could not be named both president and secretary. Do you see any reason for this restriction? Do you see any reason why a corporation statute should require, like the 1969 MBCA, that every corporation have officers with designated titles? What possible problems might be created by such a requirement? (Rather peculiarly, corporation statutes that designate required officers usually do not attempt to specify what duties, responsibilities, or powers reside in the person holding an office with a designated title; rather, they contain a provision similar to RMBCA § 8.41.)

D. ROLE OF THE LAW OF AGENCY IN BUSINESS ASSOCIATIONS

Many problems that arise in connection with business associations involve simple and direct application of principles of agency. Assume, for example, that the AB Furniture Store employs C as a salesman, truck driver, office manager, or what have you. C is not a partner but purely a "servant" in the Restatement's nomenclature; a major question is whether C's "master," the AB Furniture Store, is liable for a variety of possible problems created by C's activities: contracts entered into by C in the name of the AB Furniture Store, injuries caused by C's negligence, liability for C's intentional torts committed in the course of his employment, and so forth. Such questions are usually thought of as involving primarily agency principles that are not dependent on whether the AB Furniture Store is doing business as a proprietorship, partnership, limited partnership or corporation. Other questions also addressed by the law of agency include whether C may be personally liable to persons with whom he or she dealt on behalf of the AB Furniture Store, whether the AB Furniture Store may enforce promises or commitments made by third persons to C, and whether AB Furniture Store may sue C if C is disloyal or disobeys instructions so that the store becomes liable to a third person as a result of C's unauthorized activities.

Many law students are not exposed to a systematic analysis of agency principles during the first year of law school. For the benefit of such students, Appendix One (pages 1192–1201, infra) sets forth the most significant sections of the Restatement of Agency, Second. It is important to recognize the limitations inherent in any such set of generalizations presented as "black letter" rules. For students desiring more comment or explanation the official comments to the Restatement of Agency, Second, are invaluable as are the hornbooks on agency prepared by various authors.

Agency principles are directly involved in a number of issues considered throughout this book. References to the "black letter" sections of the Restatement set forth in the appendix are usually included in the text where these issues arise.

Notes

Under the agency principles set forth in the appendix what is the responsibility of the AB Furniture Store if—

(a) C is the "office manager" who, contrary to specific instructions, buys 10 variety tables from a visiting "manufacturer's rep"? (See Restatement 2d Agency, § 160)

(b) C is the delivery truck operator who negligently runs into a pedestrian while delivering furniture? Does it make any difference whether C is normally a careful driver and whether the store owners investigated his driving record before hiring him or her? (See Restatement 2d Agency, § 219(1))

(c) C is the store's "security officer" who wrongly accuses X of being a shoplifter and holds X against his will for an hour until the police arrive? (See Restatement 2d Agency, § 231)

E. THEORIES OF CORPORATENESS

The theory that a corporation is a separate legal entity can be traced far back in legal history. In England, acceptance of the concept that a corporation is an entity separate from its shareholders or members long antedates the development of limited liability for shareholders, which occurred in the middle of the nineteenth century. Consult P. Blumberg, The Law of Corporate Groups: Procedural Law 1–2 (1983).

In the United States, the entity theory has received virtual universal legal acceptance. Indeed, the fictitious person so created has been given many of the constitutional protections available to individuals. As recently described by Justice O'Connor:

> In the words of Chief Justice Marshall, a corporation is "an artificial being, invisible, intangible, and existing only in contemplation of law." Dartmouth College v. Woodward, 4 Wheat. 518, 636, 4 L.Ed. 629 (1819). As such, it is not entitled to "'purely personal' guarantees" whose "'historic function' . . . has been limited to the protection of individuals." First National Bank of Boston v. Bellotti, 435 U.S. 765, 779, n. 14, 98 S.Ct. 1407, 1417, n. 14, 55 L.Ed.2d 707 (1978). Thus, a corporation has no Fifth Amendment privilege against self-incrimination, Wilson v. United States, 221 U.S. 361, 31 S.Ct. 538, 55 L.Ed. 771 (1911), or right to privacy, United States v. Morton Salt Co., 338 U.S. 632, 70 S.Ct. 357, 94 L.Ed. 401 (1950). On the other hand, a corporation has a First Amendment right to freedom of speech, Virginia Pharmacy Bd. v. Virginia Citizens Consumer Council, Inc., 425 U.S. 748, 96 S.Ct. 1817, 48 L.Ed.2d 346 (1976), and cannot have its property taken without just compensation, Penn Central Transportation Co. v. New York City, 438 U.S. 104, 98 S.Ct. 2646, 57 L.Ed.2d 631 (1978). A corporation is also protected from unreasonable searches and seizures, Marshall v. Barlow's, Inc., 436 U.S. 307, 98 S.Ct. 1816, 56 L.Ed.2d 305 (1978), and can plead former jeopardy as a bar to a prosecution, United States v. Martin Linen Supply Co., 430 U.S. 564, 97 S.Ct. 1349, 51 L.Ed.2d 642 (1977). Furthermore, a corporation is entitled to due process, Helicopteros Nacionales de Colombia v. Hall, 466 U.S. 408, 104 S.Ct. 1868, 80 L.Ed.2d 404 (1984), and equal protection, Metropolitan Life Ins. Co. v. Ward, 470 U.S. 869, 105 S.Ct. 1676, 84 L.Ed.2d 751 (1985), of law.
>
> Whether a particular constitutional guarantee applies to corporations "depends on the nature, history, and purpose" of the guarantee. First National Bank, 435 U.S., at 779, n. 14, 98 S.Ct., at 1417, n. 14.

* * *

Browning–Ferris Industries v. Kelco Disposal, Inc., ___ U.S. ___, ___, 109 S.Ct. 2909, 2925, 106 L.Ed.2d 219 (1989) (dissenting opinion).

The entity approach has been subject to criticism. Consider W. Hohfeld, Fundamental Legal Conceptions 197 (1923):

> Strangely enough, it has not always been perceived with perfect clearness that transacting business under the forms, methods and procedure pertaining to so-called corporations is simply another mode by which *individuals* or *natural persons* can enjoy their property and engage in business. Just as several individuals may transact business collectively as partners, so they may as members of a corporation—the corporation being nothing more than an association of such individuals
>   * * *.

Hohfeld represents the "realist" theory. Despite the general recognition and usefulness of the entity theory, the fictional nature of this theory should be recognized, as Hohfeld suggests.

Other theories of corporateness have also been put forward. "What is the nature of a corporation?" Professor Alfred Conard writes.

"Is it a fund of property, a band of investors, a crew of workers, a place, an entry in official records, or a mere figment of legislative and judicial imaginations? What principle of justice grants it the same capacities to sue and be sued, to convey and to receive conveyances, to promise and receive promises, to trespass and be trespassed against, as a free and mature human individual?" A. Conard, Corporations in Perspective 416 (1976).

The economist has evolved an unique theory of corporateness that permits analysis of the corporation within the confines of that discipline, and harks back to the realism of Hohfeld, but rejects the notion that the shareholders are the ultimate owners of the enterprise.

BUTLER, THE CONTRACTUAL THEORY OF THE CORPORATION
11 Geo. Mason U.L.Rev. 99 (1989)

The contractual theory of the corporation is in stark contrast to the legal concept of the corporation as an entity created by the state. The entity theory of the corporation supports state intervention—in the form of either direct regulation or the facilitation of shareholder litigation—in the corporation on the ground that the state created the corporation by granting it a charter. The contractual theory views the corporation as founded in private contract, where the role of the state is limited to enforcing contracts. In this regard, a state charter merely recognizes the existence of a "nexus of contracts" called a corporation. Each contract in the "nexus of contracts" warrants the same legal and constitutional protections as other legally enforceable contracts. Moreover, freedom of contract requires that parties to the "nexus of contracts" must be allowed to structure their relations as they desire.

The contractual theory of the corporation should be of practical as well as academic interest. * * * Recently, corporation law scholars antagonistic to the contractual theory have adopted the methodology and terminology of the contractual theory, but have misapplied it in a way that reaches contrary policy positions. * * * [T]hese mistakes might be due to something other than a mere misunderstanding of the contractual theory. * * *

The attractiveness of the corporation relative to other forms of business associations is due in large part to the economic benefits of issuing shares of stock that limit the shareholders liability to the initial investment in the firm. The issuing of stock facilitates the productive specialization of activities. The publicly traded corporation allows individuals with no managerial expertise to participate in corporations as owners by purchasing shares of stock. The corporate form also allows specialization, or centralization, of management functions through the hiring of professional managers. Specifically, the corporation allows individuals with little financial capital, but considerable managerial talents, to specialize as professional managers of corporations. The talents of such individuals would be much more difficult to tap in the absence of the corporate form of business association based on the separation of ownership and management functions.

* * * Common stockholders are the residual claimants in the publicly traded corporation because, in basic terms, the common shareholders get what is left after everyone else has been paid. As a consequence, common stock prices, which reflect the present discounted value of the residual claim, are extremely sensitive to changes in expectations about the future prospects of the business. Other types of financial instruments, backed by contractual claims, have a more stable rate of return.

The residual claimant status of common shareholders means that they are the primary risk bearers of the corporation. Common shareholders sell their risk bearing services to the corporation. In fact, it is often suggested in the economic literature on the theory of the firm that the productive role of common shareholders is that of risk bearers, rather than owners. * * *

The managers of firms select the mix of legal and market governance mechanisms that is optimal given the particular circumstances of the firm. The "nexus of contracts" specifies the extent of reliance upon differing mechanisms. Managers substitute among the various governance mechanisms until the marginal net productivity of each mechanism is equal. The corporate governance mechanisms, when combined in the manner most appropriate for the particular circumstances of each firm, resolve most of the conflicts between shareholders and managers * * *.

It is reasonable to assume that the parties to the nexus of contracts that form a firm anticipate the numerous problems associated with specialization, delegation, team production, and agency relationships. Freedom of contract allows the parties to structure their relations in a manner that ameliorates most of the agency problems inherent in the large corporation. * * *

[T]he contractual theory of the corporation offers a new perspective on the corporation and the role of corporation law. The corporation is in no sense a ward of the state; it is, rather, the product of contracts among the owners and others. Once this point is fully recognized by the state legislators and legal commentators, the corporate form may finally be free of unnecessary and intrusive legal chains.

Notes

(1) The notion that a corporation should be viewed essentially as contractual in nature is not original with the economic theorists of the late Twentieth Century. The corporate charter was viewed as a "contract" between the state and the corporation in the famous Dartmouth College case in 1819 [Trustees of Dartmouth College v. Woodward, 17 U.S. (4 Wheat.) 518, 4 L.Ed. 629 (1819)]. The conclusion reached in that case was that this contract could not be unilaterally amended by New Hampshire since that would constitute an unconstitutional impairment of contract in

violation of section 10 of article I of the United States Constitution. By the middle of the Twentieth Century this "contract" analysis had been modified into a tripartite analysis: The corporate charter was not only a contract between the corporation and the state but also a contract between the corporation and its shareholders and a contract among the shareholders themselves. These modifications of a "contract" theory arose because of the general recognition that many rights of shareholders may be modified by agreement, traditionally embodied in provisions in articles of incorporation.

(2) Attempting to put the "nexus of contracts" theory into historical perspective, Professor Bratton has written:

> The new theory's proponents made strong claims on its behalf. The economists who originated it proclaimed a major discovery: Professor Michael Jensen, for example, predicted that this infant "science of organizations" will produce a "revolution . . . in our knowledge about organizations" during "the next decade or two. . . ."[3] In the law schools, its enthusiasts moved aggressively for equal academic status (including representation among the drafters of the American Law Institute's Corporate Governance Project).[4] Even outside observers expressed enthusiasm about the new perspective's potential. Professor Bruce Ackerman saw "the stage . . . being set for a complex, yet broad-based analysis of the way in which activist law, by controlling the legal forms provided to the parties, can shape the way they use their legal freedom to plan their activities."[5]

> * * * [These claims are not supported by historical analysis.] History contains essential information about theories of the firm: Lawyers and economists have formulated principles to describe and regulate the relationship between individuals and producing institutions on repeated past occasions. * * *

> Once seen in historical context, the theory loses the revolutionary impact claimed by its proponents. It constitutes a significant innovation in neoclassical microeconomic theory. But, outside that limited methodological context, it is merely the latest in a long series of attempts to describe and justify the phenomenon of collective production in individualist terms. Such theories have followed from and responded to economic practice; they have not dominated and determined it.

3. [By the Author] Michael C. Jensen, *Organization Theory and Methodology,* 58 Acct.Rev. 319, 324 (1983). Professor Jensen is one of the originators and masters of the new theory.

4. [By the Author] Judge Ralph Winter attacks the American Law Institute Corporate Governance Project because the new economic theory, a "large body of reputable academic opinion in major law schools," is "astonishingly unrepresented" among its drafters. Ralph K. Winter, Jr., *The Development of the Law of Corporate*

Governance, 9 Del.J.Corp.L. 524, 528–29 (1984).

5. [By the Author] Bruce A. Ackerman, Reconstructing American Law 62 (1984). Ackerman's "activist" seeks to use the law "to design a better form of accommodation between competing activities than the one thrown up by the invisible hand." *Id.* at 31. Ackerman's statist perspective contrasts sharply with the anti-statism that prevails throughout the economic literature of the new theory of the firm. * * *

History also shows that contract always has held a constitutive place in corporate legal theory. This helps explain the new theory's success in the law. Its microeconomic innovations resonate well because they reconfirm and highlight antecedent concepts. However, history also suggests that the new theory goes too far in demanding that corporate law privilege contract. Historically, contract has had an equal, or more often subordinate, position in corporate legal theory—a position closely grounded in and responsive to economic practice. Changes in economic practice during the past two decades, while substantial, have not been so fundamental as to mandate that corporate law become absolutely contractual.

These recent changes in economic practice have played a role in the new theory's appearance. * * * [P]articular economic and legal practices of the 1960s and 1970s enabled the new theory's formulation. The theory, thus viewed, becomes an academic by-product of practical changes in the governance of the management corporation. It stems from and follows the events, repeating time-honored concepts about large-scale production in a form responsive to contemporary ways of doing business. Thus bound to history, it seems a vehicle unsuited to the control and reconstruction of legal practice.

Bratton, The New Economic Theory of the Firm: Critical Perspectives from History, 41 Stan.L.Rev. 1471, 1472–3 (1989).*

(3) As should be evident from the tenor of Professor Butler's analysis, proponents of the "nexus of contracts" analysis are strong believers in laissez faire, the absence of governmental regulation of or intervention in economic activity. Indeed, the "nexus of contracts" appears to be a proprietary invention of laissez faire economists. Suggestions that even if the corporation is viewed as a "nexus of contracts" there may be problems because some parties to these contracts may lack full cognition and volition about risks and benefits, or that the relationships within a large corporation may not successfully prevent self-aggrandizing behavior by managers, are sternly rejected: in the words of Professor Butler, "Recently, corporation-law scholars antagonistic to the contractual theory have adopted the methodology and terminology of the contractual theory, but have misapplied it in a way that reaches contrary policy positions."

(4) Whatever the merits of the "nexus of contracts" theory, it is clear today that "the law" is otherwise. Corporation statutes are studded with provisions that are mandatory and cannot be modified by contract among the participants. See, for example, RMBCA §§ 8.03(b), 16.02(d). Of course, the economic theorist may respond that such mandatory provisions are archaic and should be eliminated, or that some minimal mandatory regulation may be necessary even if the corporation is a "nexus of contracts." The latter appears to be the position taken in Easterbrook and Fischel, The Corporate Contract, 89 Colum.L.Rev. 1416 (1989), though it is unlikely that those authors would accept the types of mandatory regulation currently being imposed. See generally Symposium, Contractual Freedom in Corpo-

rate Law, 89 Colum.L.Rev. 1395 (1989); Bratton, The "Nexus of Contracts" Corporation: A Critical Appraisal, 74 Corn.L.Rev. 407 (1989).

(5) The holding in *Trustees of Dartmouth College* described in note (1) above appears at first blush to prohibit all amendments to state corporation statutes from affecting already-formed corporations. This result has been largely avoided by the practice of including reservations of the power to amend in virtually all general corporation statutes enacted after 1819. For a modern example of a reservation of power to amend see RMBCA § 1.02. Mr. Justice Story originally suggested in the *Dartmouth College* case that such a provision—or rather such a provision in a charter granted directly by the legislature—would avoid the application of section 10 of article I of the Constitution.

Chapter Two

THE PARTNERSHIP

A. THE NEED FOR A WRITTEN AGREEMENT

Returning to the furniture store partnership between A and B referred to in Chapter 1, let us assume that the business is to be conducted as a partnership. Is it necessary for A and B to enter into a written agreement? If not, is it desirable for them to do so?

One major advantage of having a written agreement is that it may avoid future disagreements over what the arrangement actually was. It avoids litigation similar to that involved in Fulbright v. Culbertson, 429 S.W.2d 179 (Tex.Civ.App.—Fort Worth 1968) where the Court commenced its opinion by stating:

> The case on appeal exhibits an example of a situation where two persons have entered into a "relationship" without any clearly defined understanding of either as to duties, if any of one to the other, or rights, if any, of one against the other.

Second, a written agreement is readily proved in court while proof of an oral agreement may involve substantial factual controversy. Third, a written agreement may focus attention on potential trouble spots in the relationship which may be unnoticed if the partners proceed on a "handshake" deal. Fourth, the Internal Revenue Code treatment of partnerships permits partners by agreement to allocate the tax burdens among themselves within limits, and a written agreement is clearly desirable where advantage of such provisions is taken. Fifth, the Uniform Partnership Act contemplates that upon the death or retirement of a partner, the business is terminated, wound up and disposed of. Usually, the surviving partners wish to continue the business and some provision should be made for the liquidation of the deceased or retiring partner's interest. Such provisions should be in writing since they may affect surviving spouses, executors, heirs and others who are strangers to the agreement and are unfamiliar with their rights. Sixth, as noted subsequently a partner may wish to lend rather than contribute specific property to a partnership. A written agreement clearly identifying which property is contributed and which is loaned is

17

necessary to protect the partner's interest in the loaned property. Seventh, where real estate is to be contributed as partnership property or the agreement includes a term of more than one year, a written agreement may be necessary to comply with the Statute of Frauds. In Gano v. Jamail, 678 S.W.2d 152 (Tex.App.1984), for example, Gano claimed that he was made a partner by oral agreement in Jamail's one-person law practice in 1969 on a fifty per cent participation basis; the firm was thereafter known as "Jamail and Gano." In 1978, Jamail terminated the arrangement, and Gano brought suit on the alleged partnership agreement; he lost because of the one-year provision of the statute of frauds, the court accepting the argument that the firm "was involved almost exclusively in a personal injury practice in which cases were based on contingent fee contracts, and almost always took more than a year to conclude," and the agreement contemplated that the partnership was to last until all of the cases signed up during the partnership were resolved. Finally, a written partnership agreement is advantageous to the attorney: not only may it justify a higher fee but also it places suggestions and advice in concrete form so that there is less possibility of misunderstanding.

Even though the advantages of a written agreement are undeniably substantial, it should be recognized that many successful partnerships have operated for years without a written agreement. Included within this group are many law partnerships.

A well drafted partnership agreement appears in Appendix Two. This agreement should be read carefully. It illustrates possible solutions to the principal problems encountered in the drafting of partnership agreements.

B. SHARING OF PROFITS AND LOSSES

One important non-tax issue is how the profits and losses of the business are to be shared. In the absence of agreement, how are profits and losses shared? See UPA § 18(a). Does it make any difference if the partners contributed unequal amounts of capital? See Dunn v. Summerville, 669 S.W.2d 319 (Tex.1984).

Profits of a business may be divided by agreement in numerous possible ways including:

(a) The partners may share on a flat percentage basis without regard to any other factor.

(b) One or more partners may be entitled to a fixed weekly or monthly "salary." This payment may be treated as a "cost" and subtracted before the "profit" is computed for division on some other basis, or it may be considered an advance to be credited against the amount the partner is otherwise entitled to after division of the profit. In the latter case, the agreement should consider the responsibility of the partner receiving the "salary" if the "salary" exceeds the actual profit allocable to him or her during any period.

(c) The partners may share on a percentage basis, with the percentages recomputed each year on the basis of the average amount invested in the business during the year by each partner. This type of arrangement is appropriate where the business is largely dependent on capital for generation of income.

(d) The partners may share on a percentage basis, with the percentages recomputed each year on the basis of total income, the sales or billings by each partner, time devoted to the business, or on the basis of some other factor.

(e) In large partnerships, each partner may be entitled to a fixed percentage applied against perhaps 80 per cent of the income. The remaining 20 per cent is allocated among the junior partners as a form of incentive compensation by a committee of senior partners on the basis of productivity, billings, or some other factor. Usually committee members are not themselves eligible to share in the "incentive pie."

(f) The agreement may remain silent on the division of profits, it being contemplated each year that the partners will work out the division of profits by agreement on a mutually acceptable basis.

The division of profits is, of course, basically a function of the relative bargaining power of each partner. An attorney may be helpful in suggesting techniques to divide the income on a reasonable basis which may not have occurred to the partners. Also, he or she may be able to formulate precisely the vague ideas that the partners may have expressed as to how profits should be shared.

In what types of business would the various ways of sharing profits described above be most appropriate?

Assume that in ABC law firm, A is responsible for bringing 70% of the year's business to the firm. As the principal business getter, A spends most of his time entertaining potential clients on the local golf course so that his office time billed to clients constitutes only ten per cent of the total. B brings 30% of the business and her time billings constitute 35% of the total. C brought no business to the firm, but handled the bulk (55%) of the actual legal work. What formula might be used to divide the year's profits? Or might it be better not to have a fixed formula, and negotiate the division of the pie each year. (As a matter of political power in a small law firm, A in such a situation is likely to have the predominant voice in any such negotiation, and C the smallest voice.)

ORME, PAYING PARTNERS FOR NEW BUSINESS: AN EQUITABLE LAW FIRM PARTNER COMPENSATION SCHEME

70 A.B.A.J. 60 (Dec.1984).*

In recent years, possibly because of economic pressure, law firms have begun to swing away from lock-step systems of partner compensation. Less emphasis is being placed on tenure and seniority, and more consideration is being given to merit performance and attraction of new business.

In a true partnership all income derived from the practice of law goes first to the firm and then is divided among the members on the basis of individual performance, which is a measure of the individual's contribution to the prosperity of the firm. A generally accepted principle is that not all partners are equal in income distribution.

An equitable partner compensation system should divide profits primarily according to a partner's percentage of equity ownership in the firm, but it also should set apart a portion of profits into a "bonus pool" to be distributed according to new business brought in.

COMPENSATION FACTORS

Among the various compensation schemes several factors govern the size of individual allocations. The following are perhaps the most common:

• **Productivity and billable hours.** Given that all partners achieve a threshold level of performance, special recognition should be given to those who regularly contribute the most billed and collected hours.

• **New business.** If a partner's activities produce new business for the firm, the compensation scheme should give that partner credit. This credit usually is a percentage of the total fees generated by the new business. The credit continues for a predetermined time period.

• **Client liaison.** Recognition should be given to efforts to retain the larger clients, although those efforts may not produce discernible, tangible results.

• **Practice economics.** Credit should be given to such efforts as client matter planning and control, prompt billing, accounts receivable follow-up and cash collection, fees received from clients, other fees directly resulting from partners' work, profitability by type of law, avoiding write-offs and overhead control.

• **Management, administration, training and supervision.** Recognition should be given for effective work delegation, supervision and good staff relations. Those contributions are hard to quantify, but they are essential to a true partnership.

* Reprinted with permission from the ABA Journal, The Lawyer's Magazine.

• **Marketing advancement.** This includes firm promotion, enhancement of the firm's public and professional image and the pursuit of specific marketing opportunities.

A starting point in choosing a compensation scheme is to decide which factors to use and their relative weight. Regardless of which method is chosen, the goal is to arrive at a plan that will enable the partners to deal fairly with each other and to let them work together without friction.

THE SMITH SYSTEM

One scheme that takes the various compensation factors into account is the Smith system devised by Reginald Heber Smith, a Boston lawyer who wrote widely on lawyer compensation schemes before he died in 1966. The Smith system and its variations consider "value produced" as follows:

Activity and Multiplier value		
Productivity and billable hours		
x6 or x7	or	x5
....		
New business		
x3 or x3	or	x3
....		
Client liaison, practice economics management, practice development or firm projects		
x1 or x0	or	x2
....		
Total		
10	10	10

These values are multiplied against the number of dollars in fees generated from a particular client to produce a lawyer's total number of credit points. Firm profits are paid according to a lawyer's number of points. "Net profit," as used here, is the firm's profit available for partner distribution.

The use of a system of point allocation rather than percentages eliminates the requirement that all allocations add to 100 percent. When a new partner is added or a partner retires, adjustments can be made by assigning additional points or reallocating existing points. A partner's share is determined by comparing his points (the numerator) to the total points of the firm (the denominator). * * *

Notes

Contemporaneously with the Orme article, the American Bar Association Journal published the results of a "Law Poll" of 521 regular ABA members as to the manner of dividing partners' income by size of firm and type of practice. The results may be summarized as follows:

Manner of Division	Size of Firm		
	1–2	3–10	more than 10
Equal sharing	43%	23%	2.5%
Lock step increases	2%	10%	11%
Various factors	50%	61%	72.5%
Not sure	5%	6%	14%

Manner of Division	Type of Firm		
	General	Business	Litigation
Equal sharing	27.5%	5%	10.5%
Lock step increases	7%	12.3%	12.5%
Various factors	59%	65.4%	67%
Not sure	6.5%	17.3%	10%

Factors that were listed as important among the "various factors" included number of hours billed or revenue generated, new business and clients brought into the firm, excellence of legal and analytical skills, being a founder of the firm, recommendation of influential partners, and seniority or longevity. Relatively little weight was given to recommendations of influential clients and the assumption of office management duties. 70 A.B.A.J. 48 (May 1984).*

BOWER, RETHINKING LAW FIRM ORGANIZATION—THE NEW PYRAMID

75 A.B.A.J. 90 (April 1989).

Conventional wisdom suggests that the successful law firm is structured as a pyramid, with the partners (profit sharers) at the top and the associates (profit contributors) at the bottom. Each associate produces sufficient income to pay himself, defray his overhead and generate profit to be distributed among the partners. This is the essential rationale behind group law practice: Lawyers can make more money in a law firm, provided they make partner, than they can in solo practice.

The leveraging of profits from associates is the structure upon which many successful law firms have built. The dynamics of the pyramid in the not-so-distant past provided for an expected 33 percent return on associates, as leveraged assets. Under a commonly accepted doctrine, the "Rule of Three," one-third of expected revenue was used to pay the associate, one-third to defray overhead, and the remaining one-third inured to partners as profit.

* Reprinted with permission from the ABA Journal, The Lawyer's Magazine, published by the American Bar Association.

Under the conventional model, law firm profitability became a "Ponzi scheme": Adding a partner lowered the line of demarcation on the pyramid between profit sharer and profit contributors. This reduced average partner income unless productive associates (profit contributors) were added in a ratio equal to that existing before the admission of the new partner.

In the embryonic legal services marketplace of the past, in which the demand for services exceeded the supply, this presented little problem. There was enough work to keep new associates productive while maintaining partner incomes, despite the fact that profits were divided among an increased number of partners.

The logical extension of the conventional wisdom of the past was a law firm that continually grew at practically geometrical proportions. Associates were recruited with the expectation of becoming partners. It was the exception, rather than the rule, not to admit an associate to partnership after a specified number of years.

Developments of the past decade, however, have introduced a new reality to the conventional law firm profitability model. The legal services profession has matured from an embryonic to a fully mature marketplace, in which there is an oversupply of services. * * *

Over the same period, the microeconomics of law practice have changed dramatically. Due to competition for top legal talent, starting salaries for highly qualified new law graduates have skyrocketed. At the same time, per-lawyer overhead has increased from 38 percent of gross-fee receipts in 1977 to 46 percent in 1988. * * *

Maturation has also induced an element of price competition, so that many firms cannot arbitrarily raise billing rates in response to increasing costs without losing market share. As a result, profit margins on associates have deteriorated to the point that net returns of 10 to 15 percent are considered acceptable. The "Rule of Three" no longer applies to most firms.

At the same time, many law firms, especially those founded shortly after World War II, find themselves supporting partners of retirement age without retirement policies, and dealing with problems of unproductive partners. * * *

Larger, more sophisticated law firms, such as major firms in New York, long ago realized the importance of the dynamics of the pyramid and began to take measures to deal with it. Typically, such firms have pursued a policy of a longer apprenticeship for associates, combined with a lower rate of admission (sometimes as low as one in 10), and an "up-or-out" policy. Outplacement from these firms is relatively easy, due to their prestige, reputations and the credentials of their associates.

Wasteful as these policies may seem, they have served to preserve and increase profitability. Combined with payment of top salary dollars to associates, these firms have attracted the best of legal talent, while constantly improving the quality of their client base by limiting their practice to serving only the most economically desirable clients.

For "second-tier" law firms, however, the results have been different. * * *

The solution for many law firms is to alter the traditional pyramid in pursuit of a new organizational structure, better suited to the realities of today's marketplace. This will require attention not only at the point at which associates are considered for partnership, but also at the top and the bottom of the pyramid.

The obvious first focus of a new organizational structure is at the middle of the pyramid. Here are three possible organizational strategies:

Partnership Criteria. Changing the criteria for partnership. This might involve a combination of (1) increasing the time for consideration as a partner and requiring any partner to display an ability to generate more clients than one can serve, or, (2) requiring contribution to the management of the practice or the training of young lawyers—the means by which the leveraged pyramid can be supported.

The Profit Sharer Concept. Separating the partnership decision from the decision regarding profit sharing. Those whose contributions are not greater than their consumption cannot be permitted to erode profits of those economically entitled to a profit share. Although adjusting the profit distribution plan might accomplish this, the compensation expectations of new partners, who frequently do not make a contribution justifying true profit sharing, often result in erosion of the compensation of those entitled to profit sharing.

Another approach which avoids the problem is to create a second tier of partners with different incidents of ownership, in terms not only of compensation, but also of management, voting rights, and entitlement upon death, disability, retirement or withdrawal. This second tier of owners might formally be identified as such, in order to avoid unrealistic expectations.

Senior Attorneys. Upgrading partnership criteria but retaining productive associates without making them partners. This approach involves abdication of the rigid "up-or-out" policy in favor of a non-partner class of senior, experienced lawyers, identified as senior attorneys or permanent associates.

These individuals can be well compensated and extended a degree of job security, but not held up to the outside world as partners. They may or may not be profit contributors, although they certainly would not be profit sharers. There may be justification for compensating them by paying them the difference between fees they produce and their allocated overhead.

Although it is infrequently addressed, reshaping the top of the pyramid can be just as effective, if not more so, in improving profitability of the leveraged pyramid. These significant, primary courses of action are available:

Peer Review. Peer review can be used in order to assess the contribution of each partner. Those not contributing adequately can be relegated to a new class of partners or given a compensation reduction.

Mandatory Retirement. Mandatory retirement policies can be implemented and enforced, reducing the number of profit sharers while encouraging effective retirement planning.

However, if any retiring partners will earn less than $44,000 a year, it may be illegal to require retirement. (The courts are split on the issue.) [1]

"Of Counsel" Status. Unproductive or underachieving partners might be employed in a different, "of counsel" status, taking them out of the profit-sharing group and, possibly, positioning them as profit contributors, or at least as profit neutral.

The third means to improve the dynamics of the leveraged pyramid focuses on the bottom tier. Here are four considerations:

Recruiting. Intensifying recruiting efforts, focusing on different sources of new law graduates, or recruiting laterally from other law firms. Many quality law graduates are available either from lower in their classes in first-tier, national law schools, or in regional or local schools. In addition, quality associates often can be recruited laterally from other law firms for compensation levels only slightly more than one would pay for a comparably credentialed new law graduate, but without the same need for training.

Staff Attorneys. Just as senior attorneys or permanent associates represent a "layer" of permanent leverage, the dynamics of the labor market for new law graduates also present opportunities. All national law firms, many regional firms, and most of those aspiring to become either of the two find themselves pursuing the top graduates of the national law schools. While this group of 2,000 to 4,000 of the 30,000 law graduates each year can pick and choose among high-paying jobs, the remaining 90 percent are often available for legal employment at compensation rates considerably below those paid to the top graduates.

As a result, not only can associates often be hired for less than going rates, but a separate, permanent tier of contract or staff attorneys can be created below the associate level to improve profitability. Individuals in such positions are normally hired for a one- or two-year contract period, after which consideration is given to renewal of their status. They are typically paid at one-half to two-thirds of the going

1. [By the Editor] The issue apparently raised by the unreported cases referred to is whether a partner may be retired involuntarily under the Age Discrimination in Employment Act, 29 U.S.C. § 631(c)(1), which permits compulsory retirement for an employee "who has attained 65 years of age and who, for the 2 year period immediately before retirement, is employed in a bona fide executive or a high policymaking position" if that person is entitled to pensions aggregating at least $44,000 per year following retirement.

rate for new associates, with no assurance—and little prospect—of ever becoming an associate, let alone a partner.

Provided they can be fully utilized, staff attorneys can be exceptionally profitable. Typically, their time can be billed to clients at rates approaching those of the top law graduates, whose compensation levels are 50 to 100 percent greater. Experience in large and small firms, and in large and small cities, has shown that this is true.

To the extent that the firm is able to fulfill its leverage requirements by adding staff attorneys rather than associates, recruiting pressures are decreased. That is, fewer of the top law graduates are needed in order to maintain leverage. It also becomes easier to compete for top graduates at *or above* the going rate, without adversely affecting profitability, since overall employment costs are reduced. Also, pressure on admission of new partners is decreased, as a lesser number of associates each year will be reaching a point for consideration for partnership status.

Paralegals. Another layer of permanent leverage, already available to many law firms, is that of paralegals. Properly used and managed, such individuals can provide profit to the firm, although typically less than that available from either staff attorneys or associates. Some problems with using paralegals: They bill fewer hours per year than that of the typical associate, and bill at rates that are 50 percent or less than those of associates. * * * And overhead may approach that of associates if secretaries are assigned to paralegals.

In addition, turnover is a problem with paralegals. Those good enough to perform effectively are also bright enough to discover that if one is to work in a law firm, it is much better to be a lawyer. Many law firms find that good paralegals often leave to go to law school.

Part-time Attorneys. The final consideration in optimizing the leveraged law firm is that, due to the number of women lawyers entering the profession, there are more two-lawyer families than ever before. And there are more lawyers facing the conflicting obligations of raising a family and continuing a career. As a result, many firms have found that part-time lawyers can be used much as staff attorneys, at compensation and overhead levels less than those of full-time attorneys, but with greater proportional productivity.

Part-time lawyers, if they previously have been full-time lawyers, require little or no training, and are almost totally utilized (billable) to the extent of their time commitment. Often they are appreciative enough to have such an opportunity that they actually produce more billable hours than expected, thus presenting a considerable opportunity to the leveraged law firm.

As a result of all the factors identified above, it is likely that the profitable law firm of the future will be organized quite differently from the simple pyramid of the past. It is likely to exhibit a number of layers of lawyers and leverage—the range of possible structures is myriad. * * *

Turning to the unfortunate situation where the venture does not prove to be profitable, who is responsible for losses? Compare UPA § 18(a) with UPA §§ 13–15. Why is § 18 modified by the phrase "subject to any agreement between them," while §§ 13–15 are not? Is it clear that an individual partner may be held personally liable on a partnership obligation even if the partnership is solvent and able to satisfy all its obligations? If so, why might a creditor elect to sue a partner and ignore a solvent partnership? How does the Act contemplate the working out of the financial relations between the partners when one is called upon to satisfy a partnership liability in excess of his or her liability therefor under the partnership agreement? Consider UPA §§ 18(b), 40(d).

The ABA Report on the Uniform Partnership Act suggests two important changes in section 15: (a) all liability should be made joint and several, and (b) a judgment creditor should first be required to exhaust partnership assets before proceeding directly against one or more partners individually. With respect to the latter suggestion, the Report suggests that this "rule would respect the concept of the partnership as an entity and would provide that the partners are more in the nature of guarantors than principal debtors on every partnership debt. We believe that this result would be most consistent with general business expectations today." 43 Bus.Law., at 143. The tentative draft of the Revised Uniform Partnership Act incorporates both of these suggestions. 1 A. Bromberg and L. Ribstein, Bromberg and Ribstein on Partnership, 1989 Supp. at 125.

In evaluating both of these ABA suggestions one must recognize the reality that many modern partnerships are not small local entities. Rather they may have partners resident in several states and may own partnership property located in different states. Joint liability, as contemplated by UPA § 15(b) requires joinder of all partners in litigation and may create serious practical enforcement problems where service cannot readily be obtained on some partners. As a result about a dozen states have amended section 15 to provide for "joint and several" liability for all partnership obligations. With respect to the exhaustion of partnership assets issue, what should be done about the partnership composed partially of California residents that owns real property in Kansas? Does a California creditor of the partnership who dealt with the California partners have to first file suit in Kansas before proceeding against the California partners? Are such problems arguments against the ABA suggestion, or may they be handled in some other way, e.g. by permitting courts to dispense with exhaustion of partnership assets in some situations?

In the AB furniture store, can A obtain protection against possible future liabilities by requiring B to execute a written agreement that provides: "It is understood and agreed that the parties hereto are not partners and that no partnership is formed by this agreement?" If this clause is given effect, what is the relationship between A and B? What about a clause that states that A will not be liable for any losses incurred in the business in excess of A's $100,000 investment? Would such an agreement have any legal effect at all? If so, what?

It is not uncommon in informal ventures for the parties to agree on a sharing of the profits but not discuss the sharing of losses. There is often some judicial sympathy for the unfortunate investor who is unexpectedly caught in a losing venture with the threat of personal liability for the venture's obligations that were incurred by others. In these cases, a court may be willing to accept the argument that the absence of an express agreement to share losses indicates that no partnership was ever created in the first place. See e.g. In re Tingle, 34 B.R. 676 (Bkrtcy.D.Fla.1983); Long v. Gonzales, 650 S.W.2d 173 (Tex. App.1983). Many cases, however, recognize that an express agreement to share losses is not essential for the existence of a partnership, a result that seems clear from the language of section 7 of the UPA. Parks v. Riverside Ins. Co., 308 F.2d 175 (10th Cir.1962).

Could A obtain the desired protection by being a "silent" partner? For example, the store might be known as B Furniture Store; A might advance the money but never appear in the store or participate in any public way in the management of the store. Assuming that creditors extend credit without knowing of A's interest in the business, can A escape liability? Should a negative inference be drawn from UPA § 35(2), a provision applicable only "after dissolution"? How might a creditor learn that A is a silent partner?

RICHERT v. HANDLY

Supreme Court of Washington, 1957.
50 Wn.2d 356, 311 P.2d 417.

ROSELLINI, JUSTICE.

This is an action for an accounting, wherein the plaintiff alleged that he entered into a partnership agreement with the defendant husband (hereafter referred to as the defendant), under the terms of which he, the plaintiff, was to purchase a stand of timber and the defendant was to log it, using his equipment, and the two were to share equally in the profits or losses resulting from the venture. He further alleged that the undertaking was unsuccessful; that after the payment of all operating expenses, the partnership suffered a loss of $9,825.12; that he had advanced $26,842 but had been repaid only $10,000 for his advances; and that he was entitled to $16,842 less $4,912.56 (one half of the net loss), or $11,929.44. In his amended answer, the defendant admitted that the parties had contracted with each other, but alleged that "there was no settled agreement between the partners as to recovery by the plaintiff for loss upon his capital contribution, nor as to the priority of any right to recover upon his capital contribution." In addition, he claimed certain offsets and asked that the complaint be dismissed.

The cause was tried to the court, which found in favor of the defendant in the amount of $1,494.51, plus costs. * * *

The facts found by the trial court are as follows:

"I   That defendants C.C. Handly and Mildred Handly are husband and wife constituting a marital community resident in Mason County, Washington.

"II   During the month of April 1953 plaintiff Richert advised defendant Handly that he had available for purchase according to his cruise 1,700,000 feet of timber in the State of Oregon, that he, Richert proposed to purchase said timber with his funds and requested Handly to log said timber on the basis that the two of them would share the profit or loss on the transaction.

"III   Prior to the purchase of the timber by the plaintiff the parties inspected the same and defendant Handly advised Richert that there was no more than approximately 1,000,000 feet of timber on the tract in question, and that the cruise was in error.

"IV   The plaintiff Richert purchased the timber for a price of $24,300.00 after the parties had inspected it as aforesaid, and Handly proceeded to log the same under an oral working agreement.   The essential elements of this agreement were as follows: Handly was to furnish a tractor for which he was to be paid rental at the rate of $13.00 per hour and was to haul the logs on his trucks at the rate of $8.00 per thousand.   He was also to manage the operation, keep the records and handle and account for the funds received and expended during the course of the same.   The profit or loss resulting from this single logging venture was to be borne equally.   There was no requirement that Handly contribute to Richert for the purchase price of the timber in the event of loss.

"V   The tract involved yielded between 800,000 and 900,000 feet of timber and the transaction resulted in a loss, the loss being caused by the deficiency in timber.

"VI   The defendant Handly employed a bookkeeper and accountant in the State of Oregon to keep the records of this venture.

"VII   The gross receipts of the venture amounted to $41,629.83. These funds were banked and accounted for by Handly.   There was no concealment nor unlawful withholding or conversion of any of the funds.

"VIII   Handly drew from the proceeds of the sale of the timber the sum of $7,016.88.   Richert received from the proceeds of the sale of the timber the sum of $10,000.00.

"IX   There was no agreement express or implied on the part of Handly to repay Richert for his investment in the timber.

"X   A partnership income tax was prepared for the year 1953 by Elliott B. Spring, accountant in Shelton, Washington.   This return was signed by Handly after he protested the accounting shown thereon.

The accounting appearing on said return was set up on the basis of Spring's understanding and opinion as to what the legal relationship of the parties was with reference to this single logging transaction.

"XI The $10,000.00 received by Richert and the $7,016.88 drawn by Handly are unexpended gross revenues of the undertaking."

Upon these facts, the court entered the following conclusions of law:

"I The arrangement of the parties hereto with reference to the single transaction involved constitutes a joint venture.

"II The defendant Handly is in no way responsible for plaintiff's loss on the purchase of the timber involved.

"III Of the total amount of $17,016.88 heretofore identified as unexpended gross revenue of the undertaking each party hereto is entitled to $8,508.44. Richert has been overpaid in the amount of $1491.56, and Handly is entitled to judgment against him in the amount of $1491.56.

"IV Plaintiff is entitled to take nothing by his complaint.
* * *"

Although the plaintiff maintains that the court erred in holding the undertaking to be a "joint venture" rather than a "partnership," we think the distinction is immaterial in this action. Deciding whether the relationship between the parties was that of partners or joint venturers does not determine their rights and duties under their contract or the status of their account. We will disregard, therefore, the conclusion of law that the arrangement constituted a joint venture.

On the other hand, it is manifest that the findings are inadequate to support the judgment entered, or any other judgment. There is a finding that the parties to the contract had agreed to share the profits or losses equally; but there is a further finding that the defendant had not agreed to contribute to the plaintiff for his investment in the timber in the event of loss; in other words, that they had not agreed to share the losses equally. Aside from the finding that the profit or loss was to be borne equally, which is inconsistent with the further finding that the defendant was not to contribute to the plaintiff for the purchase price of the timber in the event of loss, the findings are silent as to the basis on which the profit or loss was to be shared, whether proportionately to the contribution of each party, or otherwise. The mere fact that the defendant was not to be personally liable to the plaintiff for his losses does not mean that the plaintiff was not to be reimbursed out of the proceeds of the venture.

The findings also fail to reveal whether there was an understanding that the defendant was to be compensated for his services in managing the operation, apart from his share in the profits, and if so, in what amount. The only allegation contained in the amended answer pertaining to an agreement to reimburse the defendant for his services, was that he was owed $400 for maintaining fire watch and $25 for running property lines; and yet inherent in the court's disposition of the matter is a finding that these services were worth the full amount of the plaintiff's investment, or $26,842; for the court treated all of the "unexpended gross revenues" as profits and divided them equally between the parties, one of whom had lost nothing (unless his claimed offsets in the total amount of $4,800 were valid), while the other had lost an investment of $26,842.

The court appears to have lost sight of the fact that there could be no profits until the expenses of the operation were paid, including the cost of the timber. The conclusion that all of the "unexpended gross revenues" were to be divided equally between the parties could only be reached if it had been agreed that the plaintiff would not be reimbursed for his contribution. Such an intention cannot be inferred from any of the findings entered.

Since the findings are inadequate to support the conclusions and judgment, or any judgment on the matter in question, the cause must be remanded with directions to make findings regarding the basis on which the parties agreed that the losses were to be shared and whether the claims of one partner were to take priority over the claims of the other; the amount contributed by each (including cost of timber, and equipment rental, and also including services if there was an agreement that the defendant was to be compensated for his services, in addition to his share in the profits, if any); the total receipts and the authorized disbursements; the amount which each of the parties has received to date; and the amount due each on the basis of their agreement.

The judgment is reversed and the cause is remanded with directions to enter findings on the matters indicated above, conclusions, and judgment based thereon. * * *

RICHERT v. HANDLY

Supreme Court of Washington, 1958.
53 Wn.2d 121, 330 P.2d 1079.

HUNTER, JUSTICE. * * *

At the hearing on this matter pursuant to the remittitur, counsel for the respective parties agreed that no additional proof would be produced. Therefore, the trial court, after hearing argument of counsel, entered the following additional findings of fact in compliance with the remittitur:

"XII. The parties *did not agree upon or specify the basis* upon which losses were to be shared, nor whether the claims of *one partner* were to take priority over the claims of *the other*.

"XIII. Richert [appellant] contributed a total of $26,842 for cost of timber and incidental advancements. Handly [respondent husband] used his own equipment to haul logs, as agreed by the parties, and was paid $8,673.84 for this service. Handly used his own tractor, as agreed by the parties, and was paid $9,240 for this service. *There was no agreement that Handly was to be compensated for his services, in addition to his share in the profits, if any, (and except for the equipment and tractor services as last hereinbefore stated), and the accounting between the parties does not disclose any such compensation.*

"XIV. The gross receipts from the sale of logs were $41,629.83. The disbursements were hauling (as per Finding XIII), $8,673.84; falling and bucking, $3,474.21; tractor (as per Finding XIII), $9,240.00; payroll and taxes, $4,786.56; cruising, $35.00; right of way, $200.00; commission, $500.00; paid to Richert, $10,000.00; withdrawn by Handly, $7,016.88; Total $43,926.49.

"XV. *There was no agreement* of the parties as to how a loss of the capital contributed by Richert in the amount of $26,842.00 was to be borne, and *accordingly it cannot be determined the amount due each on the basis of their agreement."* (Italics ours.)

On the basis of such findings, the court concluded neither party was entitled to judgment against the other, that the complaint should be dismissed, and that the costs should abide the ultimate outcome of the case as provided by remittitur.

Mr. Richert has again appealed to this court from the judgment entered.

Since the trial court found that the parties had not agreed upon or specified the basis upon which losses were to be shared, or whether the claims of *one partner* were to take priority over the claims of the *other,* the provisions of the uniform partnership act are controlling. [The court quotes UPA §§ 18(a), 18(f).]

Therefore, applying the statute to the additional facts found by the trial court, to which no error was assigned, we find the following account established:

Capital Contribution:

Appellant Richert	$26,842.00
Respondent Handly	None
Gross Receipts From Sale of Timber	41,629.83

Expenses:

Tractor	9,240.00
Hauling	8,673.84
Falling & Bucking	3,474.21
Payroll & Taxes	4,786.56
Cruising	35.00
Right of Way	200.00
Commission	500.00
	$26,909.61
Gross Receipts	41,629.83
Less Expenses	26,909.61
Net Receipts	$14,720.22
Appellant's Capital Contribution	26,842.00
Less Net Receipts	14,720.22
Net Loss	$12,121.78

Appellant has received $10,000 from the venture leaving a
balance due on his Capital Contribution of $16,842.00

Less ½ of net loss ($12,121.78) 6,060.89

Amount respondent must reimburse appellant for loss resulting from logging venture $10,781.11

It follows that the judgment of the trial court is incorrect, as a
matter of law, under the facts found. Therefore, the judgment is
reversed, and the cause remanded with directions to enter judgment in
favor of the appellant in accordance with the views expressed herein.

Notes

(1) What was the theory adopted by the trial court in its first judgment?

(2) What was the theory adopted by the Supreme Court of Washington
in its second opinion? Is this conclusion logically and irresistibly compelled by the Uniform Partnership Act?

(3) The problem in *Richert* potentially arises whenever partners make
unequal contributions of capital and services and decide precisely how they
will split the profits but do not consider the possibility that the venture will
result in a loss. UPA § 18(a) provides a rule of thumb for such situations
that seems inconsistent with the parties' probable intention where one
person is providing only capital and the other only services. In the AB
furniture store, assume there is a fire shortly after B has invested A's
$100,000 in inventory and fixtures, and there is a total loss not covered by
insurance. Following the theory of *Richert*, would it not follow that B is
liable to A for $50,000? In a sense, A is risking his capital and B is risking
his services; it probably never occurred to B that he might have to restore
a portion of A's risk capital. Cannot the same argument be made in
Richert v. Handly? Or should the solution be to recognize that Handly
made a "capital contribution" by providing his services in the form of his
knowledge and skill in cutting and marketing the timber (other than the
costs of the tractor and trucks for which he was entitled to compensation
under the agreement)? But see UPA § 18(f).

(4) The proposed Revised Uniform Partnership Act does not attempt to
address the basic problem of *Richert*. The Reporter suggested a provision
that a court might award compensation "in other appropriate circumstances" to address this problem but the Committee rejected this language
on the ground that it was too much an invitation to litigation.

(5) If you were drafting a partnership agreement where one partner is
contributing capital and the other services, how would you phrase a
provision to effectuate the intent of the partners that the partner contributing services would not be called upon to replace part of the other
partner's risk capital?

C. MANAGEMENT

NATIONAL BISCUIT CO. v. STROUD
Supreme Court of North Carolina, 1959.
249 N.C. 467, 106 S.E.2d 692.

PARKER, JUSTICE.

C.N. Stroud and Earl Freeman entered into a general partnership to sell groceries under the firm name of Stroud's Food Center. There is nothing in the agreed statement of facts to indicate or suggest that Freeman's power and authority as a general partner were in any way restricted or limited by the articles of partnership in respect to the ordinary and legitimate business of the partnership. Certainly, the purchase and sale of bread were ordinary and legitimate business of Stroud's Food Center during its continuance as a going concern.

Several months prior to February 1956 Stroud advised plaintiff that he personally would not be responsible for any additional bread sold by plaintiff to Stroud's Food Center. After such notice to plaintiff, it from 6 February 1956 to 25 February 1956, at the request of Freeman, sold and delivered bread in the amount of $171.04 to Stroud's Food Center.

In Johnson v. Bernheim, 76 N.C. 139, this Court said: "A and B are general partners to do some given business; the partnership is, by operation of law, a power to each to bind the partnership in any manner legitimate to the business. If one partner go to a third person to buy an article on time for the partnership, the other partner cannot prevent it by writing to the third person not to sell to him on time; or, if one party attempt to buy for cash, the other has no right to require that it shall be on time. And what is true in regard to buying is true in regard to selling. What either partner does with a third person is binding on the partnership. It is otherwise where the partnership is not general, but is upon special terms, as that purchases and sales must be with and for cash. There the power to each is special, in regard to all dealings with third persons at least who have notice of the terms." There is contrary authority. 68 C.J.S. Partnership § 143, pp. 578–579. However, this text of C.J.S. does not mention the effect of the provisions of the Uniform Partnership Act.

The General Assembly of North Carolina in 1941 enacted a Uniform Partnership Act, which became effective 15 March 1941. G.S. Ch. 59, Partnership, Art. 2. * * *

[The court quotes UPA §§ 9(1), 9(4), 18(e), 18(h) and the North Carolina version of UPA § 15, which reads, "All partners are jointly and severally liable for the acts and obligations of the partnership."]

Freeman as a general partner with Stroud, with no restrictions on his authority to act within the scope of the partnership business so far as the agreed statement of facts shows, had under the Uniform Partnership Act "equal rights in the management and conduct of the partnership business." Under [UPA § 18(h)] Stroud, his co-partner, could not restrict the power and authority of Freeman to buy bread for the partnership as a going concern, for such a purchase was an "ordinary matter connected with the partnership business," for the purpose of its business and within its scope, because in the very nature of things Stroud was not, and could not be, a majority of the partners. Therefore, Freeman's purchases of bread from plaintiff for Stroud's Food Center as a going concern bound the partnership and his co-partner Stroud. * * *

In Crane on Partnership, 2d Ed., p. 277, it is said: "In cases of an even division of the partners as to whether or not an act within the scope of the business should be done, of which disagreement a third person has knowledge, it seems that logically no restriction can be placed upon the power to act. The partnership being a going concern, activities within the scope of the business should not be limited, save by the expressed will of the majority deciding a disputed question; half of the members are not a majority." * * *

At the close of business on 25 February 1956 Stroud and Freeman by agreement dissolved the partnership. By their dissolution agreement all of the partnership assets, including cash on hand, bank deposits and all accounts receivable, with a few exceptions, were assigned to Stroud, who bound himself by such written dissolution agreement to liquidate the firm's assets and discharge its liabilities. It would seem a fair inference from the agreed statement of facts that the partnership got the benefit of the bread sold and delivered by plaintiff to Stroud's Food Center, at Freeman's request, from 6 February 1956 to 25 February 1956. But whether it did or not, Freeman's acts, as stated above, bound the partnership and Stroud.

The judgment of the court below is affirmed.

RODMAN, J., dissents.

SMITH v. DIXON

Supreme Court of Arkansas, 1965.
238 Ark. 1018, 386 S.W.2d 244.

HOLT, JUSTICE.

The appellee, as purchaser, brought this action against appellants, as sellers, for the specific performance of a contract for the sale of realty and in the alternative sought damages for nonperformance of the contract.

The appellants are E.F. Smith, his wife, and their children and spouses. This entire family constitutes a business firm known as E.F. Smith & Sons, A Partnership. The "Contract For Sale of Realty With Lease" was signed by one of the appellants, W.R. Smith, on behalf of the family partnership.

By the terms of the contract, executed in March 1962, the partnership agreed to sell the 750 acre "Cracraft" plantation for $200,000.00 and convey title to the appellee on January 3, 1963. In the interim, by the lease provisions, the appellee took possession, farmed, and improved a portion of the property. Upon refusal of the appellants to convey the land as recited in the contract, the appellee instituted this action. The chancellor denied specific performance and awarded appellee special damages in the amount of $11,512.73. * * *

The partnership was created a short time after the lands in controversy were acquired by the family in 1951. The court found that:

"Soon after the purchase of 'Cracraft' [the lands in question] and the 'Sterling Place,' the Smiths, at the suggestion and on the recommendation of the financial institutions, who were to finance the farming operations for them on the farms, organized and formed a partnership known as E.F. Smith & Sons. They term the partnership an 'operating partnership'. The general purpose of the firm was to engage in farming operations on the farms, including direct cultivation and renting to others. The operation was later expanded to engage in the general farming business in the area. The partnership agreement was oral and has never been reduced to writing. Mr. W.R. Smith is the predominant member of both the partnership and the Smiths. He serves as the managing partner with general powers, with Mr. Charles Smith in charge of production. The other members of the partnership did not, nor at the present time, appear to have any direct participation or responsibility in the operation. * * *

"The firm, by and through its managing partner, Mr. W.R. Smith, has acted as agent for or under contract with, the Smiths, in the sale of the 'Sterling Place' to Mr. Rankin, in a similar capacity in another land conveyance and as trustee for another purchase."

It appears undisputed that appellant W.R. Smith was authorized by the members of the partnership to negotiate for the sale of the lands in question to the appellee. However, it is claimed that his authorization was based upon different terms of sale, mainly, a price of $225,000.00 instead of $200,000.00. Therefore, it is urged that the contract is unenforceable since it was not signed nor ratified by other members of the family.

In the case of May v. Ewan, 169 Ark. 512, 275 S.W. 754, we held that a partnership is bound by the acts of a partner when he acts within the scope or *apparent* scope of his authority. There we quoted with approval:

"* * * In order to determine the apparent scope of the authority of a partner, recourse may frequently be had to past transactions indicating a custom or course of dealing peculiar to the firm in question".

See, also [UPA §§ 8–10]. In the case at bar it was customary in past transactions, as in the present one, for the partnership to rely upon the co-partner, W.R. Smith, to transact the business affairs of the firm. We agree with the chancellor that appellant W.R. Smith was acting within the apparent scope of his authority as a partner when he signed the contract and that it is binding and enforceable upon the partnership.

* * *

Notes

(1) Consider Restatement of Agency, Second, §§ 7, 8. [Appendix One] Is National Biscuit Co. v. Stroud a case of actual authority or apparent authority? What about Smith v. Dixon?

(2) Many agency relationships may involve simultaneously actual and apparent authority. For example, if Freeman had been an employee or agent of Stroud rather than a partner, it is clear that Stroud could revoke any actual authority that Freeman might have to bind him to a purchase of bread simply by notifying Freeman. See Restatement of Agency, Second, § 118. [Appendix One] However, despite such notice, Freeman might still have the power under concepts of apparent authority to bind Stroud to a purchase of bread unless Nabisco is advised of the revocation of authority. See Restatement of Agency, Second, § 125. [Appendix One] In the actual case, of course, Stroud actually advised Nabisco that he did not intend to be bound by further purchases by Freeman yet he was held liable as a result of the court's decision. How can this be?

(3) Would the result in Smith v. Dixon be changed if W.R. Smith had been an agent or employee of E.F. Smith & Sons rather than the "predominant member" or "managing partner with general powers?" See Restatement of Agency, Second, § 160. [Appendix One]

(4) To what extent do the basic concepts of actual authority and apparent authority appear in UPA §§ 9(1), 9(2), and 9(4)?

(5) What should a person in Stroud's position do if he or she no longer trusts the co-partner and wishes to avoid liability for future bread purchases by the partnership?

(6) How does one ascertain the scope of the phrase "for apparently carrying on in the usual way the business of the partnership" in Section 9(1)?

(a) Many partnership agreements contain a recitation of the business to be carried on. [See e.g. art. 1.4, Appendix Two] Are such recitations relevant?

(b) Consider Burns v. Gonzalez, 439 S.W.2d 128, 131 (Tex.Civ.App.— San Antonio 1969, writ ref'd n.r.e.):

> As we interpret Sec. 9(1), the act of a partner binds the firm, absent an express limitation of authority known to the party dealing with such partner, if such act is for the purpose of "apparently carrying on" the business of the partnership in the way in which other firms engaged in the same business in the locality usually transact business, or in the way in which the particular partnership usually transacts its business. In this case, there is no evidence relating to the manner in which firms engaged in the sale of advertising time on radio stations usually transact business. Specifically, there is no evidence as to whether or not the borrowing of money, or the execution of negotia-

ble instruments, was incidental to the transaction of business, "in the usual way," by other advertising agencies or by this partnership, Inter–American Advertising Agency. It becomes important, therefore, to determine the location of the burden of proof concerning the "usual way" of transacting business by advertising agencies.

The court concluded that there was no reason to depart from the normal rule that the party who asserts that the particular act of an agent is within the scope of the agent's authority has the burden of proving the extent of that authority.

(7) To what extent may the management rights of partners be varied by agreement? The partnership agreement is often referred to as "the law of the partnership" for that particular partnership. This statement reflects the fact that a partnership is a consensual arrangement, and that the substantive rules governing the internal affairs of a partnership set forth in § 18 of the UPA may be altered by agreement. As we have seen, however, third parties may not be bound by provisions in the agreement and may enforce rights and liabilities created by the UPA without regard to the agreement. May the authority granted partners in UPA § 9 be eliminated by agreement if potential creditors are given notice?

(8) A common practice in some partnerships is to designate certain partners as "senior partners," "junior partners," "managing partners," and the like. There is statutory authority confirming this practice in a few states. Do such designations have any legal effect? Does designation of B as "managing partner" limit the scope of A's agency to bind the partnership under § 9(1)? Does a "senior partner" have greater actual or apparent authority to bind the partnership than a "junior partner?" May a "managing partner" confess a judgment despite UPA § 9(3)(d)?

In some partnerships, including some law firms, the partner in charge of office management—hiring of support staff, ordering of supplies, keeping the books, etc.—is designated the "managing partner."

(9) May a partnership agreement eliminate the power of one or more partners to participate in the management of the business? What about the introductory clause to section 18 of the UPA to the effect that the section governs the "rights and duties of the partners in relation to the partnership * * * *subject to any agreement between them*"? Can centralized management be provided in a partnership by agreement? Or to put the same question in a concrete way, what is the legal effect of a partnership agreement giving X "centralized management": e.g. "X shall have the sole power to manage the business and affairs of the partnership and Y shall have no power to manage the business or bind the partnership."? Compare UPA §§ 9(1), 13, 14, 15. If, despite such a provision, Y obtains a loan from a bank in the partnership name, is the partnership liable to the bank even though Y subsequently misappropriates the money? Does X thereafter have any claim over against Y? What would be the situation if X manages the business for her own sole benefit, e.g. by paying herself a "salary" equal to the profits each month? Is Y totally at the mercy of X as a result of the partnership agreement?

(10) The statutes of a handful of states authorize the public filing of a "Statement of Partnership" by general partnerships. Such a Statement

must be executed by all the partners and may affect the actual authority of partners. Most of these statutes limit the effect of Statements of Partnership to real estate transactions (in which event the Statement becomes one more public record to be examined by the title examiner), but Georgia's statute is broader. It authorizes a Statement of Partnership to contain any "limitations on the authority of one or more partners" as well as grants of "any authority beyond that defined" in the UPA "which the partnership desires to disclose." Ga.Code Ann. § 14–8–10.1. Do you think this broader statute is a good idea? Would it mean that Nabisco would have to check the public filings in Georgia before it can safely sell bread on credit to a business such as Stroud's Food Center?

ROUSE v. POLLARD

Court of Chancery of New Jersey, 1941.
129 N.J.Eq. 47, 18 A.2d 5, affirmed 130 N.J.Eq. 204, 21 A.2d 801 (1941).

BIGELOW, VICE CHANCELLOR.

The seven defendants were partners engaged in the general practice of law, their firm well-known and enjoying a high reputation for skill and integrity. Complainant was their client. The member of the firm who took care of her legal business was Thomas E. Fitzsimmons. At almost her first interview with him, she disclosed that she owned valuable securities, whereupon he immediately suggested that she sell them and turn the money over to the firm, saying that they would invest for her in good mortgages, and send her the interest every six months. Accordingly, on June 21, 1927, complainant endorsed to Fitzsimmons a check for the proceeds of her securities, $28,253, which he deposited in his personal bank account. Out of this sum, he gave the firm's bookkeeper $350 on account of complainant, for legal services unconnected with this transaction. He paid to her or on her order $403, retaining the balance. For several years he sent her a check every January and July for an amount equal to three per cent of the principal sum. In 1931, at her request, he paid complainant $7,000 and thereafter through 1937 continued to pay her interest on $20,500. Meanwhile, the law firm, of which defendants were members, was dissolved at the end of 1932.

In January, 1938, Fitzsimmons was arrested for embezzlement, was found to have defrauded a large number of persons and was sentenced to the State Prison. No mortgages or other securities representing complainant's $20,500 have been discovered and from the vagueness of Fitzsimmons' testimony, I am satisfied that immediately upon receipt of her money in 1927, he converted it to his own use. She may, of course, have a decree against Fitzsimmons but he is insolvent. The question is whether the other defendants as well are liable to her.

Until after Fitzsimmons' exposure, his co-defendants were entirely ignorant that complainant had entrusted him with any money, or had any dealings with him except for ordinary law work. Neither the payment to the firm of $350 by Fitzsimmons on complainant's account, nor any other circumstance which has been proved, was sufficient to put the partners on notice that he held other funds of complainant. They did not suspect or have reason to suspect him of improper conduct in this or other matters until long after the partnership was dissolved. Complainant can recover only if the partners are answerable for Fitzsimmons' malfeasance. They are responsible only if he was acting as their agent in accepting complainant's money. Certainly he had no express authority to act for his co-defendants in this regard. If there were authority, it existed only by implication from the fact that he and they were partners.

As a general rule, each partner is, by virtue of the partnership relation, authorized to act as the general agent for his co-partners in all matters coming within the scope of the business of the firm, in the same manner and to the same extent as if he had full power of attorney from his co-partners. All the partners are responsible for the act of one of their number as agent, even though he acts for some secret purpose of his own, and not really for the benefit of the firm. Restatement–Agency [2d], sec. 165. [Appendix One] Where one partner, by fraudulent promises made in a transaction within the scope of the partnership business, obtains money from a third person and misappropriates it, the other partners are liable. While the agency of a partner extends to all matters connected with the business in which the partnership is engaged, his authority extends no further. If the transaction is outside the partnership business, the other partners are not liable and they are not bound by a statement of the partner who conducts such transaction that he is acting on behalf of the firm.

So we come to the question whether the receipt of complainant's money by Fitzsimmons was a transaction within the scope of defendant's business. The scope of any line of business may be gauged by the usual and ordinary course in which such business is carried on by those engaged in it in the locality where the partnership has its seat. But the scope may be broadened by the actual though exceptional course and conduct of the business of the partnership itself, as carried on with the knowledge, actual or presumed, of the partner sought to be charged.

In their practice, defendants frequently had in their hands moneys belonging to clients, held for a particular purpose such as investment in a certain mortgage. But they were not in the habit of receiving, and indeed never received, money from a client to place on mortgage at their discretion. Fitzsimmons, doubtless in other cases besides the present one, received money for general investment and represented when doing so that he was acting for the firm. But the other members of the firm had no knowledge of such actions or representations on his part.

In England, although the receipt of money to be invested on a particular security may be considered an incident of an attorney's or solicitor's business, the receipt of money for the purpose of investment generally, or to invest it in mortgage as soon as a good mortgage can be found, is not so considered. No proof has been presented to show how the practice of law is usually carried on in New Jersey, and none is necessary, for that is a subject with which the court is familiar. Some few lawyers have made a habit of receiving money for general investment, and such practice has too often led to disastrous results. The prudent lawyer never retains funds or securities of his client in his hands longer than is necessary. He does not accept money until an investment has been found and approved by his client. The receipt of money for the purpose of investing it as soon as a good mortgage can be found, as was done by Fitzsimmons in the case at bar, is not part of the practice of law according to the usual and ordinary course pursued in New Jersey.

It follows that Fitzsimmons' partners are not answerable to complainant and as to them the bill will be dismissed.

Notes

(1) If Rouse v. Pollard arose under the UPA, which sections would be decisive? § 9? § 13? § 14? § 15?

(2) The opinion of the Court of Errors and Appeals of New Jersey affirming the principal case contains a somewhat fuller description of what happened (130 N.J.Eq., at 205–206, 21 A.2d, at 802–3).

In the course of the incidental conferences Fitzsimmons asked Mrs. Rouse what money she possessed and was informed by her of the amount thereof and the manner in which it was invested. According to Mrs. Rouse:

"He said that securities was a bad thing for a woman in my position to have and he suggested that I turn over my securities and sell them and turn the money over to the firm, that they dealt in gilt edge mortgage bonds, as he said. He said that they did that for their clients and it was perfectly secure. I asked if it was all right for me and he said that is the only way they would take care of it and I would get my check every six months. He said if I handed it at once they would place it the first of July and I did place it the 15th and the 15th of January was the first check."

Mrs. Rouse wrote to her brokers directing them to sell her securities and to "forward a check for the same payable to me to my attorney, Mr. Thomas E. Fitzsimmons, c/o Riker & Riker, 24 Commerce Street, Newark, N.J.". A check for $28,252.67 was sent as directed, was endorsed by Mrs. Rouse "Pay to the order of Thos. E. Fitzsimmons" and was deposited by Fitzsimmons in his personal bank account. No part ever came to the firm except $350, or thereabouts, which was paid by Fitzsimmons to the firm for the legal services rendered, and no member of the firm, other than Fitzsimmons, knew of the transaction. The bill of complaint specifically exonerates the remaining members from any fraud, deceit or misappropriation. On January 16, 1928, Fitzsimmons wrote Mrs. Rouse: "Enclosed herewith find my check for $825., being six months' interest at 6% on the

$27,500., which I have invested for you." On July 19, 1932, Fitzsimmons wrote: "I enclose herewith check for $615., representing six months' interest on the money which I have invested for you." For more than ten years interest payments went to Mrs. Rouse by Fitzsimmons' personal check. $7,000 of the principal was returned to her, likewise by Fitzsimmons' check, and the receipt was by Mrs. Rouse to Fitzsimmons, personally. The letter from Fitzsimmons to Mrs. Rouse accompanying the check reads:

"As requested, I enclose herewith check for $7,000., which sum is to be deducted from the amount which I have invested for you on bond and mortgage. I am also enclosing a receipt for such amount which I would request you to sign and return to me."

So, too, the receipt to Mrs. Rouse showing a balance retained to invest is by Fitzsimmons, personally. That was in October of 1931. On December 31, 1932, Fitzsimmons retired from the firm of Riker and Riker, and complainant had actual notice of this fact at that time or shortly thereafter. From then on Fitzsimmons' letters to Mrs. Rouse were written on his own stationery from his new office address, and Mrs. Rouse never thereafter went to, or communicated with, the Riker firm until after she had learned, in the early spring of 1938, of Fitzsimmons' defalcations and arrest.

Do these facts suggest an alternative ground for the decision in Rouse v. Pollard?

(2) The opinion of the Court of Errors and Appeals also gives additional information and detail about the nature of the firm practice of Riker and Riker (130 N.J.Eq., at 208–209, 21 A.2d, at 803–4):

The firm did engage extensively in what is known as a "real estate practice"; it represented banks, building and loan associations and estates; it examined titles, closed mortgages and drew necessary documents relating to mortgage investments by clients; it had clients' funds and trust funds on deposit awaiting the closing or other requirements of transactions for which such funds were held; it did not do a general investment business and it did not accept funds for future, unspecified investment, at the firm's discretion, in mortgages or otherwise.

It has long been a recognized incident to the general practice of law, more extensively developed in some offices than in others, to make note of such clients as have moneys to invest on bond and mortgage, to bring the attention of those clients to the applications of proposed borrowers and, after the principals come to an agreement, to search the title, draw the necessary documents, even hold the money against the event, place the recordable papers on record and in general superintend the closing of the transaction. But we do not understand that it is a characteristic function of the practice of law to accept clients' money for deposit and future investment in unspecified securities at the discretion of the attorney, and we find to the contrary. It is possible that attorneys in isolated instances have done this; just as it is possible that a person of any profession or occupation has done so. It has not, however, been done by lawyers, in this jurisdiction at least, with such frequency or appropriateness as to become a phase of the practice.

Assuming that a person knowledgeable about law firms would understand this, should Mrs. Rouse be held to this standard? If she goes to a well known law firm for assistance in a divorce settlement, is introduced to a partner, Mr. Fitzsimmons, and is told by him what the business of the firm is, can't she rely on the accuracy of this information?

(3) What would you suggest an attorney do if he or she learns that a partner has accepted money under the circumstances Fitzsimmons accepted Mrs. Rouse's funds in the principal case? Obviously the selection of a law partner is a serious matter since, even if the scope of the agency is limited to legal matters, there is unlimited liability for losses caused by negligence or incompetence as well as willful defalcation.

ROACH v. MEAD

Supreme Court of Oregon, 1986.
301 Or. 383, 722 P.2d 1229.

Before PETERSON, C.J., and LENT, LINDE, CAMPBELL, CARSON and JONES, JJ.

JONES, JUSTICE.

* * * At trial, defendant, David J. Berentson, moved for a directed verdict, contending that he was not vicariously liable for the negligent acts of his partner, Kenneth E. Mead, because the negligent acts were outside the scope of the partnership's business. The trial court denied the motion, and the jury found defendant liable for $20,000 damages * * *. The Court of Appeals held that defendant attorney was vicariously liable for his former partner's negligence. We affirm the Court of Appeals. * * *

Mead, defendant's former law partner, first represented plaintiff in December 1974 on a traffic charge and later represented plaintiff on several occasions. On November 1, 1979, Mead and defendant formed a law partnership. Mead continued to advise plaintiff on other traffic charges and on business dealings. Defendant prepared plaintiff's income tax returns.

In June 1980, plaintiff sold his meter repair business for $50,000. On November 25, 1980, plaintiff asked for Mead's advice on investing $20,000 in proceeds from the sale. Plaintiff testified that Mead told plaintiff that "he would take [the money] at 15 percent. So, I let him have it. * * * I trusted him and felt he would look out for me." Plaintiff considered Mead's advice to be legal advice; he testified that otherwise he would not have consulted an attorney.

After plaintiff agreed to the loan, Mead executed a promissory note for $20,000 payable on or before November 25, 1982, at 15 percent interest. Mead said that he would be receiving a large sum of money with which he would repay plaintiff. Mead offered to secure the loan with a second mortgage on his house, and plaintiff replied that he should do "whatever you think is best." Mead did not secure the loan.

On May 1, 1981, Mead went to plaintiff's home and requested a $1,500 loan, telling plaintiff he was in financial trouble but "had big money coming in." Plaintiff agreed to the loan and Mead added the $1,500 to the amount due on the promissory note.[2] Mead did not repay any money to plaintiff and later was declared bankrupt.[3]

Plaintiff sued defendant's partnership for negligence, alleging that the partnership failed to disclose the conflicting interests of plaintiff and Mead, to advise plaintiff to seek independent legal advice, to inform plaintiff of the risks involved in an unsecured loan, and to advise plaintiff that the loan would not be legally enforceable because the rate of interest was usurious. * * *

I. VICARIOUS LIABILITY

Plaintiff contends that Mead negligently advised him about the loan and that defendant should be vicariously liable for Mead's negligent legal advice. Defendant, while conceding that Mead was negligent, argues that the transaction between plaintiff and Mead was a personal loan outside the scope of the partnership, and that the evidence did not prove that soliciting personal loans was within Mead's express, implied or apparent authority as defendant's law partner. * * *

[The Court quotes UPA §§ 9(1), 9(2), 9(4), 13, and 15(a).]

Liability of partners for the acts of co-partners is based on a principal-agent relationship between the partners and the partnership. "Partners are jointly and severally liable for the tortious acts of other partners if they have authorized those acts or if the wrongful acts are committed 'in the ordinary course of the business of the partnership.' [UPA §§ 13, 15]" *Wheeler v. Green,* 286 Or. 99, 126, 593 P.2d 777 (1979). The issue in this case is whether Mead's failure to advise plaintiff on the legal consequences of the loan was "in the ordinary course of the business of the partnership."

In *Croisant v. Watrud,* 248 Or. 234, 432 P.2d 799 (1967), this court confronted a similar issue of the vicarious liability of a partnership for the wrongful acts of a partner. In *Croisant,* the client of an accountant sued the accounting partnership, claiming damages for the accountant's breach of trust. The accountant collected income from the client's property and then made unauthorized payments to the client's husband

2. [By the Court] The jury found defendant not liable for [this] additional $1,500 loan, presumably because it determined that the loan was personal and that giving legal advice concerning the loan was not within the scope of the partnership's business.

3. [By the Court] On January 18, 1983, this court accepted Mead's resignation from the bar. He stated that he had chosen not to contest disciplinary charges alleging that he had "borrowed $45,000 from a client, that he misrepresented the priority of the security given for the loan and that he subsequently forged a satisfaction of the mortgage given as security." 43 Or. St.B.Bull., June 1983, at 42. Mead was convicted of theft by deception because of the loan referred to in the disciplinary charges.

from the money. The defendant partnership contended that the collection services were personal dealings of the accountant with the client and not part of the partnership's business. This court held:

> "If a third person reasonably believes that the services he has requested of a member of an accounting partnership is undertaken as a part of the partnership business, the partnership should be bound for a breach of trust incident to that employment even though those engaged in the practice of accountancy would regard as unusual the performance of such services [collecting and disbursing funds] by an accounting firm." 248 Or. at 242, 432 P.2d 799.

The court stated that the reasonableness of the third person's belief that "the service he seeks is within the domain of the profession is a question which must be answered upon the basis of the facts in the particular case." *Id.* at 243, 432 P.2d 799.

Defendant contends that *Croisant* may be distinguished from the case at bar because in *Croisant* "the misconduct occurred in the course of * * * activities which the court held could reasonably be viewed as within the scope of the accounting firm's business," while in this case "[t]here was no evidence that the act of an attorney in taking a personal loan from a client could reasonably be viewed as part of the business of a law firm." However, defendant admits that "the evidence most favorable to Plaintiff was simply that Plaintiff thought Mead was giving him investment advice and that the giving of advice regarding legal aspects of loans and investments in general is a normal part of law practice." Defendant thus concedes the validity of plaintiff's argument that plaintiff reasonably believed that investment advice was within the scope of the partnership's business; plaintiff does not contend that soliciting loans from clients was partnership business.

In the case at bar, the jury determined that plaintiff reasonably believed that the partnership's legal services included investment advice. We agree with the Court of Appeals that:

> " * * * There is expert and other testimony from which the jury could have found that plaintiff relied on Mead for legal advice concerning the loan, that a lawyer seeking a loan from a client would be negligent if the lawyer did not tell the client to get independent legal advice and that a lawyer advising a client about this particular loan would seek to secure it and would warn the client of the risks involved in providing a usurious interest rate." 76 Or.App. at 85, 709 P.2d 246.

The Court of Appeals' rationale is buttressed by our decisions in bar disciplinary proceedings concerning loans from clients to lawyers.

* * *

When a lawyer borrows money from a client, this court requires that the lawyer advise the client about the legal aspects of the loan. Mead's failure to advise plaintiff to seek independent legal advice, that loans usually should be secured and the debtor's financial status checked, and that the rate of interest was usurious were all failures of Mead as a lawyer advising his client. Because these failures occurred within the scope of the legal partnership, responsibility for Mead's negligence was properly charged to defendant as Mead's law partner. The trial court did not err in submitting the negligence issue to the jury. * * *

The Court of Appeals is affirmed.

Notes

(1) Can this case be distinguished from *Rouse v. Pollard?* There were several cases during the 1980s in which liability was imposed on the partnership or copartners in situations similar to *Roach v. Mead.* See Kalish, When a Law Firm Member Borrows From a Client—The Law Firm's Responsibility: A Professional Model Replaces a Club Model, 37 U.Kans.L.Rev. 107 (1988). Professor Kalish views *Rouse v. Pollard* as illustrative of the "club model" of law partnerships and *Roach v. Mead* as illustrative of a "professional model."

(2) In the principal case, what differences are there, if any, between the $20,000 loan on which liability was found and the $1500 loan, on which it was not?

(3) Model Rules of Professional Conduct, Rule 1.8:

(a) A lawyer shall not enter into a business transaction with a client or knowingly acquire an ownership, possessory, security or other pecuniary interest adverse to a client unless:

(1) the transaction and terms on which the lawyer acquires the interest are fair and reasonable to the client and are fully disclosed and transmitted in writing to the client in a manner which can be reasonably understood by the client;

(2) the client is given a reasonable opportunity to seek the advice of independent counsel in the transaction; and

(3) the client consents in writing thereto.

Is a law firm liable for malpractice if a partner fails to obtain the written consent required by Rule 1.8(a)(3) for a personal loan from a client?

(4) R. Hamilton, Fundamentals of Modern Business (1989), 521:*

[I]f a lawyer is representing an unsophisticated client, the lawyer often gradually assumes the roles of both legal and business adviser. Where an unsophisticated client is involved, business risks should be pointed out clearly, forcefully, and without hesitation. To take an extreme example, a lawyer who is handling the estate of a corporate executive may learn that a securities broker has suggested to the widow that she attempt to augment the size of the estate by engaging in options trading (a highly speculative and sophisticated market * * * in which it is easy to lose one's entire capital investment in a very brief period). Probably every lawyer in this situation would feel compelled to speak up and warn the widow of the dangers of following the advice of the securities broker. This general type of situation is probably more common than many people realize: Most sophisticated

* Reprinted with permission of Little, Brown & Company.

business lawyers at one time or another represent relatively unsophisticated clients. In these situations, the client may end up relying on the lawyer for both financial and legal advice. Usually the lawyer should try to persuade the client that he or she should seek appropriate business advice, and that reliance on a lawyer for advice on such matters is not desirable. Often, however, the client is happy with the lawyer's advice or is unwilling to incur the cost of direct business advice or does not know who to ask.

It is perhaps unnecessary to point out that there is a difference between a lawyer warning a client that a proposed business transaction with third persons is risky or inappropriate, and the lawyer engaging in a direct business transaction with a client. However, what happens if the advice turns out badly? For example, the value of the recommended options may increase dramatically; can the client then sue the attorney for bad advice or for advice that is beyond the competence of a lawyer to give? If the lawyer fails to warn the client about the risk of options and significant losses are incurred, might the lawyer be liable on the theory that attorneys of ordinary competence would have warned the client under such circumstances?

(5) What principles determine the liability of a partner for the negligence or incompetence of an associate, i.e., an attorney employed by the partnership? Cf. Restatement of Agency, Second, §§ 165, 219, 228(1)(a). [Appendix One]

(6) In a well known novel of a few years ago, an incoming partner in a law partnership learns that a senior partner handling estate accounts has a substantial shortage of assets in his accounts which he is covering by commingling accounts and robbing Peter to pay Paul. What is the new partner's liability with regard to the original shortage? See UPA § 17. On the above facts is the new partner entirely safe? Might the last clause be inoperative if the new partner arguably assumes liability for existing or future obligations, e.g. by letting the practice continue?

D. DUTIES OF PARTNERS TO EACH OTHER

MEINHARD v. SALMON

Court of Appeals of New York, 1928.
249 N.Y. 458, 164 N.E. 545.

CARDOZO, C.J. On April 10, 1902, Louisa M. Gerry leased to the defendant Walter J. Salmon the premises known as the Hotel Bristol at the northwest corner of Forty–Second street and Fifth avenue in the city of New York. The lease was for a term of 20 years, commencing May 1, 1902, and ending April 30, 1922. The lessee undertook to change the hotel building for use as shops and offices at a cost of $200,000. Alterations and additions were to be accretions to the land.

Salmon, while in course of treaty with the lessor as to the execution of the lease, was in course of treaty with Meinhard, the plaintiff, for the necessary funds. The result was a joint venture with terms embodied in a writing. Meinhard was to pay to Salmon half of the moneys requisite to reconstruct, alter, manage, and operate the property. Salmon was to pay to Meinhard 40 per cent. of the net profits for the first five years of the lease and 50 per cent. for the years thereafter. If there were losses, each party was to bear them equally. Salmon, however, was to have sole power to "manage, lease, underlet and operate" the building. There were to be certain pre-emptive rights for each in the contingency of death.

The two were coadventurers, subject to fiduciary duties akin to those of partners. King v. Barnes, 109 N.Y. 267, 16 N.E. 332. As to this we are all agreed. The heavier weight of duty rested, however, upon Salmon. He was a coadventurer with Meinhard, but he was manager as well. During the early years of the enterprise, the building, reconstructed, was operated at a loss. If the relation had then ended, Meinhard as well as Salmon would have carried a heavy burden. Later the profits became large with the result that for each of the investors there came a rich return. For each the venture had its phases of fair weather and of foul. The two were in it jointly, for better or for worse.

When the lease was near its end, Elbridge T. Gerry had become the owner of the reversion. He owned much other property in the neighborhood, one lot adjoining the Bristol building on Fifth avenue and four lots on Forty–Second street. He had a plan to lease the entire tract for a long term to some one who would destroy the buildings then existing and put up another in their place. In the latter part of 1921, he submitted such a project to several capitalists and dealers. He was unable to carry it through with any of them. Then, in January, 1922, with less than four months of the lease to run, he approached the defendant Salmon. The result was a new lease to the Midpoint Realty Company, which is owned and controlled by Salmon, a lease covering the whole tract, and involving a huge outlay. The term is to be 20 years, but successive covenants for renewal will extend it to a maximum of 80 years at the will of either party. The existing buildings may remain unchanged for seven years. They are then to be torn down, and a new building to cost $3,000,000 is to be placed upon the site. The rental, which under the Bristol lease was only $55,000, is to be from $350,000 to $475,000 for the properties so combined. Salmon personally guaranteed the performance by the lessee of the covenants of the new lease until such time as the new building had been completed and fully paid for.

The lease between Gerry and the Midpoint Realty Company was signed and delivered on January 25, 1922. Salmon had not told Meinhard anything about it. Whatever his motive may have been he had kept the negotiations to himself. Meinhard was not informed even of the bare existence of a project. The first that he knew of it was in February, when the lease was an accomplished fact. He then made demand on the defendants that the lease be held in trust as an asset of

the venture, making offer upon the trial to share the personal obligations incidental to the guaranty. The demand was followed by refusal,
and later by this suit. A referee gave judgment for the plaintiff,
limiting the plaintiff's interest in the lease, however, to 25 per cent.
The limitation was on the theory that the plaintiff's equity was to be
restricted to one-half of so much of the value of the lease as was
contributed or represented by the occupation of the Bristol site. Upon
cross-appeals to the Appellate Division, the judgment was modified so
as to enlarge the equitable interest to one-half of the whole lease. With
this enlargement of plaintiff's interest, there went, of course, a corresponding enlargement of his attendant obligations. The case is now
here on an appeal by the defendants.

The owner of the reversion, Mr. Gerry, had vainly striven to find a
Joint adventurers, like copartners, owe to one another, while the
enterprise continues, the duty of the finest loyalty. Many forms of
conduct permissible in a workaday world for those acting at arm's
length, are forbidden to those bound by fiduciary ties. A trustee is held
to something stricter than the morals of the market place. Not honesty
alone, but the punctilio of an honor the most sensitive, is then the
standard of behavior. As to this there has developed a tradition that is
unbending and inveterate. Uncompromising rigidity has been the
attitude of courts of equity when petitioned to undermine the rule of
undivided loyalty by the "disintegrating erosion" of particular exceptions. Wendt v. Fischer, 243 N.Y. 439, 444, 154 N.E. 303. Only thus
has the level of conduct for fiduciaries been kept at a level higher than
that trodden by the crowd. It will not consciously be lowered by any
judgment of this court.

The owner of the reversion, Mr. Gerry, had vainly striven to find a
tenant who would favor his ambitious scheme of demolition and construction. Baffled in the search, he turned to the defendant Salmon in
possession of the Bristol, the keystone of the project. He figured to
himself beyond a doubt that the man in possession would prove a likely
customer. To the eye of an observer, Salmon held the lease as owner in
his own right, for himself and no one else. In fact he held it as a
fiduciary, for himself and another, sharers in a common venture. If
this fact had been proclaimed, if the lease by its terms had run in favor
of a partnership, Mr. Gerry, we may fairly assume, would have laid
before the partners, and not merely before one of them, his plan of
reconstruction. The pre-emptive privilege, or, better, the pre-emptive
opportunity, that was thus an incident of the enterprise, Salmon
appropriated to himself in secrecy and silence. He might have warned
Meinhard that the plan had been submitted, and that either would be
free to compete for the award. If he had done this, we do not need to
say whether he would have been under a duty, if successful in the
competition, to hold the lease so acquired for the benefit of a venture
then about to end, and thus prolong by indirection its responsibilities
and duties. The trouble about his conduct is that he excluded his
coadventurer from any chance to compete, from any chance to enjoy
the opportunity for benefit that had come to him alone by virtue of his

agency. This chance, if nothing more, he was under a duty to concede. The price of its denial is an extension of the trust at the option and for the benefit of the one whom he excluded.

No answer is it to say that the chance would have been of little value even if seasonably offered. Such a calculus of probabilities is beyond the science of the chancery. * * *

We have no thought to hold that Salmon was guilty of a conscious purpose to defraud. Very likely he assumed in all good faith that with the approaching end of the venture he might ignore his coadventurer and take the extension for himself. He had given to the enterprise time and labor as well as money. He had made it a success. Meinhard, who had given money, but neither time nor labor, had already been richly paid. There might seem to be something grasping in his insistence upon more. Such recriminations are not unusual when coadventurers fall out. They are not without their force if conduct is to be judged by the common standards of competitors. That is not to say that they have pertinency here. Salmon had put himself in a position in which thought of self was to be renounced, however hard the abnegation. He was much more than a coadventurer. He was a managing coadventurer. For him and for those like him the rule of undivided loyalty is relentless and supreme. Wendt v. Fischer, supra, Munson v. Syracuse, etc., R.R. Co., 103 N.Y. 58, 74, 8 N.E. 355. A different question would be here if there were lacking any nexus of relation between the business conducted by the manager and the opportunity brought to him as an incident of management. For this problem, as for most, there are distinctions of degree. If Salmon had received from Gerry a proposition to lease a building at a location far removed, he might have held for himself the privilege thus acquired, or so we shall assume. Here the subject-matter of the new lease was an extension and enlargement of the subject-matter of the old one. A managing coadventurer appropriating the benefit of such a lease without warning to his partner might fairly expect to be reproached with conduct that was underhand, or lacking, to say the least, in reasonable candor, if the partner were to surprise him in the act of signing the new instrument. Conduct subject to that reproach does not receive from equity a healing benediction.

A question remains as to the form and extent of the equitable interest to be allotted to the plaintiff. The trust as declared has been held to attach to the lease which was in the name of the defendant corporation. We think it ought to attach at the option of the defendant Salmon to the shares of stock which were owned by him or were under his control. The difference may be important if the lessee shall wish to execute an assignment of the lease, as it ought to be free to do with the consent of the lessor. On the other hand, an equal division of the shares might lead to other hardships. It might take away from Salmon the power of control and management which under the plan of the joint venture he was to have from first to last. The number of shares to be

allotted to the plaintiff should, therefore, be reduced to such an extent as may be necessary to preserve to the defendant Salmon the expected measure of dominion. To that end an extra share should be added to his half.

Subject to this adjustment, we agree with the Appellate Division that the plaintiff's equitable interest is to be measured by the value of half of the entire lease, and not merely by half of some undivided part. A single building covers the whole area. Physical division is impracticable along the lines of the Bristol site, the keystone of the whole. Division of interests and burdens is equally impracticable. Salmon, as tenant under the new lease, or as guarantor of the performance of the tenant's obligations, might well protest if Meinhard, claiming an equitable interest, had offered to assume a liability not equal to Salmon's, but only half as great. He might justly insist that the lease must be accepted by his coadventurer in such form as it had been given, and not constructively divided into imaginery fragments. What must be yielded to the one may be demanded by the other. The lease as it has been executed is single and entire. If confusion has resulted from the union of adjoining parcels, the trustee who consented to the union must bear the inconvenience. Hart v. Ten Eyck, 2 Johns. Ch. 62. * * *

The judgment should be modified by providing that at the option of the defendant Salmon there may be substituted for a trust attaching to the lease a trust attaching to the shares of stock, with the result that one-half of such shares together with one additional share will in that event be allotted to the defendant Salmon and the other shares to the plaintiff, and as so modified the judgment should be affirmed with costs.

ANDREWS, J. (dissenting). * * *

Were this a general partnership between Mr. Salmon and Mr. Meinhard, I should have little doubt as to the correctness of this result, assuming the new lease to be an offshoot of the old. Such a situation involves questions of trust and confidence to a high degree; it involves questions of good will; many other considerations. As has been said, rarely if ever may one partner without the knowledge of the other acquire for himself the renewal of a lease held by the firm, even if the new lease is to begin after the firm is dissolved. Warning of such an intent, if he is managing partner, may not be sufficient to prevent the application of this rule.

We have here a different situation governed by less drastic principles. I assume that where parties engage in a joint enterprise each owes to the other the duty of the utmost good faith in all that relates to their common venture. Within its scope they stand in a fiduciary relationship. I assume prima facie that even as between joint adventurers one may not secretly obtain a renewal of the lease of property actually used in the joint adventure where the possibility of renewal is expressly or impliedly involved in the enterprise. I assume also that Mr. Meinhard had an equitable interest in the Bristol Hotel lease.

Further, that an expectancy of renewal inhered in that lease. Two questions then arise. Under his contract did he share in that expectancy? And if so, did that expectancy mature into a graft of the original lease? To both questions my answer is "No." * * *

What then was the scope of the adventure into which the two men entered? It is to be remembered that before their contract was signed Mr. Salmon had obtained the lease of the Bristol property. Very likely the matter had been earlier discussed between them. The $5,000 advance by Mr. Meinhard indicates that fact. But it has been held that the written contract defines their rights and duties. Having the lease, Mr. Salmon assigns no interest in it to Mr. Meinhard. He is to manage the property. It is for him to decide what alterations shall be made and to fix the rents. But for 20 years from May 1, 1902, Salmon is to make all advances from his own funds and Meinhard is to pay him personally on demand one-half of all expenses incurred and all losses sustained "during the full term of said lease," and during the same period Salmon is to pay him a part of the net profits. There was no joint capital provided.

It seems to me that the venture so inaugurated had in view a limited object and was to end at a limited time. There was no intent to expand it into a far greater undertaking lasting for many years. The design was to exploit a particular lease. Doubtless in it Mr. Meinhard had an equitable interest, but in it alone. This interest terminated when the joint adventure terminated. There was no intent that for the benefit of both any advantage should be taken of the chance of renewal—that the adventure should be continued beyond that date. Mr. Salmon has done all he promised to do in return for Mr. Meinhard's undertaking when he distributed profits up to May 1, 1922. Suppose this lease, nonassignable without the consent of the lessor, had contained a renewal option. Could Mr. Meinhard have exercised it? Could he have insisted that Mr. Salmon do so? Had Mr. Salmon done so could he insist that the agreement to share losses still existed, or could Mr. Meinhard have claimed that the joint adventure was still to continue for 20 or 80 years? I do not think so. The adventure by its express terms ended on May 1, 1922. The contract by its language and by its whole import excluded the idea that the tenant's expectancy was to subsist for the benefit of the plaintiff. On that date whatever there was left of value in the lease reverted to Mr. Salmon, as it would had the lease been for thirty years instead of twenty. Any equity which Mr. Meinhard possessed was in the particular lease itself, not in any possibility of renewal. There was nothing unfair in Mr. Salmon's conduct. * * *

The judgment of the courts below should be reversed and a new trial ordered, with costs in all courts to abide the event.

POUND, CRANE, and LEHMAN, JJ., concur with CARDOZO, C.J., * * *

ANDREWS, J., dissents in opinion in which KELLOGG and O'BRIEN, JJ., concur.

Notes

(1) Consider UPA §§ 20–22. The broad fiduciary duty between partners is one of the more important aspects of the partnership relation. "The unique feature ＊ ＊ ＊ is their symmetry; each partner is, roughly speaking, both a principal and an agent, both a trustee and a beneficiary, for he has the property, authority and confidence of his co-partners, as they do of him. He shares their profits and losses, and is bound by their actions. Without the protection of fiduciary duties, each is at the others' mercy." J. Crane and A. Bromberg, Law of Partnership 389 (1968). Compare 2 Bromberg & Ribstein on Partnership, § 6.07 (1989):

> Judge Cardozo's eloquent statement makes it clear that partners cannot act vis-à-vis each other as they can with third parties. The main elements of the partners' fiduciary duties are well recognized: utmost good faith, fairness, and loyalty. The problem becomes one of precise delineation. ＊ ＊ ＊

> It is helpful to contrast partnership with other fiduciary relationships. Fiduciary duties in the partnership arguably should be less extensive than those in other agency or trust relationships because of the greater availability in the partnership of extrajudicial controls, including joint management by the partners, the relatively equal expertise of the partners, the terminability of the relationship, and the alignment of incentives of the partners through profit sharing and personal liability for partnership debts. The latter factor also distinguishes partners from corporate directors ＊ ＊ ＊.

> [S]ome of the considerations discussed immediately above that justify distinctions between fiduciary duties among partners and those in other fiduciary relationships justify distinctions between types of partnerships. Thus, the duties of a general partner in a limited partnership have been held to be somewhat more intense than those of a general partner in a general partnership, because the limited partners do not directly participate in management. The duties of joint venturers are also similar to those of partners, but here, too, it is necessary to avoid overgeneralization. The primary difference between joint venturers and partners is in connection with the scope of partnership opportunities and of permissible outside activities of partners.

(2) Is it significant whether or not the partners are dealing with each other at arms length? In Johnson v. Peckham, 132 Tex. 148, 120 S.W.2d 786 (1938) strained relations had developed between two partners and a suit for an accounting and dissolution was pending in a court. Peckham agreed to purchase Johnson's interest in two oil leases that constituted the partnership property for $1,500. Shortly after this transaction was completed Peckham resold the leases for $10,500. Upon a showing that negotiations for this resale had begun prior to the time Peckham purchased Johnson's interest, Peckham was required to share the profitable resale with Johnson. A judgment for $3,750 [one-half of $10,500 minus $1,500]

was entered, the Court quoting the ringing language of Mr. Justice Cardozo in Meinhard v. Salmon.

Same result under the UPA?

(3) From the facts of Meinhard v. Salmon it appears likely that the written joint venture agreement entered into by those individuals was drafted by a lawyer. Assume that this lawyer was Salmon's personal attorney, and that he continued to render legal assistance from time to time both to Salmon individually and to the Meinhard/Salmon joint venture without seriously considering whether there might be a potential conflict of interest between these two roles. Does that lawyer thereby become Meinhard's lawyer as well as Salmon's? Or does the lawyer become attorney for the venture (as well as lawyer for Salmon) but not Meinhard's personal lawyer? In either event, if the lawyer becomes involved with Salmon's negotiations with Gerry near the end of the joint venture, does he or she have an obligation to disclose that information to Meinhard? If the answer is "no," are you concerned that the lawyer may in fact be assisting one joint venturer to breach his fiduciary duties to the other? Can a lawyer avoid such nasty ethical questions by refusing to do work for the Meinhard/Salmon joint venture?

(4) A partner secretly takes $1,000 from the partnership and invests it in another venture. What rights do his copartners have if the other venture fails? If it is profitable?

(5) What is the "formal account" referred to in UPA § 22? H. Reuschlein and W. Gregory, Agency and Partnership, pp. 281–82 (1979):

> The significance of a partner's duty to account is that it may be enforced by an action for an accounting, traditionally an equitable remedy. * * * An accounting is intended to bring to the attention of the court all matters which might affect the obligations of the opartners inter se. Most accounting actions deal with attempts to ascertain the status of the partnership capital accounts.
>
> Courts most often decide how much cash or other assets each partner invested in the partnership, what share of profits each was to be entitled to, and what were the actual profits (or losses) of the partnership during its existence. These questions often involve a determination as to whether or not property was partnership property or individual property. Since the U.P.A. permits great flexibility in partnerships, questions often arise as to whether or not there was a contrary agreement, i.e., does the general rule of the U.P.A. apply, or has a partner successfully shouldered his burden of proof that a contrary agreement has been reached, e.g., to pay one partner a salary? The decisions reflect great skepticism toward claims of various forms of novel agreements, especially where they are asserted only on dissolution of the partnership.
>
> Accounting actions, in perhaps their most important aspect, deal with questions of fiduciary duty. Oftentimes, it is essential to resolve questions of partnership law so that the extent of the duty of loyalty may be defined by a court. Further, the abstract rules can take on

meaning only when applied in specific situations. The advantage of an accounting action in this context is inestimable.

If a partner has reason to believe that he has been defrauded by his partner, but lacks the documentation to prove by exactly what amount, an accounting action has great merit. The court will hear evidence and can determine what amount of profits have been siphoned off or exactly how much profit the disloyal partner made in a competing business.

Of course, it should be kept in mind that when a partner asks for a formal account, i.e., a review of all financial transactions of the partnership, which as a minimum would include the financial statements and books of account, he may well be satisfied with it, and after some questioning of his partners may decide that an accounting action is not necessary. Thus, in ordinary circumstances a partner's right to an account gives him formidable protection of his economic interests, especially when backed up by the ever present threat of an accounting action.

E. THE PARTNERSHIP AS AN ENTITY

Should a partnership be considered an entity separate and apart from the individual partners, or should it be considered as an extension of the partners themselves, without separate legal existence? The latter theory, usually referred to as the "aggregate" theory (as contrasted with the "entity" or mercantile theory) was the position usually taken by common law courts. Typical is the statement in Aboussie v. Aboussie, 270 S.W.2d 636, 639 (Tex.Civ.App.—Fort Worth 1954, writ ref'd), "A partnership is not a legal entity. The law recognizes no personality in a partnership other than that of the partners who compose it."

Which view of the partnership most nearly reflects the general business or lay approach? Consider for example, a large New York City law firm. Does the firm have a personality or existence independent of the identity of the partners themselves? What about our hypothetical AB Furniture Store partnership? The Meinhard/Salmon joint venture?

Legal discussion about the "true" nature of a partnership has generated a tremendous amount of heat and very little light. Which view is correct? The proper answer to this question is: both views.

Many provisions of the Uniform Partnership Act clearly reflect an entity approach. E.g. UPA § 18(b): "*The partnership* must indemnify *every partner* * * * " or UPA § 9(1): each partner is an "agent *of the partnership* * * *." Conceptually a person cannot be his or her own agent nor indemnify oneself. On the other hand, UPA § 6(1) defines a partnership as "an association of two or more persons." And certainly one of the basic provisions of the Act, joint and several liability for debts, is an aggregate concept.

JENSEN, IS A PARTNERSHIP UNDER THE UNIFORM PARTNERSHIP ACT AN AGGREGATE OR AN ENTITY?

16 Vand.L.Rev. 377, 377–379 (1963).

* * * The first committee appointed to draft the act in 1902 was chaired by Dean James Barr Ames of Harvard Law School. The original charge to the committee was to draft a uniform act based on the mercantile or entity theory, adopted by the civil law countries. The drafting committee was staffed in large part by practicing lawyers, psychologically imbued with stare decisis, who had practised partnership law under the common law aggregate doctrine that a partnership was not a legal person in addition to the natural persons who were the partners. Nevertheless the two first drafts contained a single definition that a partnership was a legal person. That definition was never adopted.

Dean Ames, who was loyally wedded to the entity theory of partnership, pursued his efforts to secure support for his views on each of the succeeding sections and subdivisions wherever he and his colleagues regarded the entity idea of the civil law as superior to the burdensome rules of common law partnerships. Illustrative are provisions designed to obviate the dangers of the concept of joint property subject to a partner's liens in favor of firm creditors which by successive transfers would be wiped out, and the disastrous rule that a partner's creditor had a right to interrupt or destroy the continuity of the firm by attaching and selling firm property to satisfy a partner's non-firm debt. After seven years as draftsman, chairman Dean Ames died in 1909 and Dean William Draper Lewis was appointed as chairman of the committee.

Partly as a result of the deep cleavage between members of the committee on the entity-aggregate controversy the Commissioners on Uniform Laws directed the reorganized committee to consider the subject at large and disregard the original directive to draft an act on the entity theory. * * *

This late, radical switch to a committee directive not to continue to draft the act on the entity view but to work on the project "at large" made it virtually inevitable that the final draft of the proposed act would reveal strong internal evidence of compromise, and so it did. The seven years of work by the committee with Dean Ames as draftsman accomplished so many committee agreements on specific provisions based on the entity concept that these provisions were bound to appear in the act. It is fair to say that the Ames committee was victorious in securing approval of the entity view in a score of specific, substantive provisions of the act wherein the law needed alteration, while the Lewis committee won approval of exclusion of the right of the firm to sue and be sued and inclusion of a definition of partnership as an aggregate association. This compromise produced ambiguities between the numerous specific provisions of the act espousing the entity principle and the act's general aggregate definition. These ambiguities became, and to a considerable degree still remain, a source of legal controversy as different problems arise.

That the act adopts both the entity and the aggregate theory of partnership, depending upon the particular problem involved was the position of Professor Crane, as his view is succinctly summarized in the reply of Dean Lewis: "That though the intention of the draftsmen was apparently to proceed on the aggregate theory, the Act does not explicitly adopt either the entity or the aggregate theory of the nature of a partnership." [4]

Notes

(1) The question whether a partnership should be considered an entity or an aggregate arises in a number of miscellaneous situations in which the question appears critical but the court has no clear guidelines. For example, what is your reaction to the following situations:

(a) A wife is injured in a store operated by a partnership composed of three persons, one of whom is the woman's husband. May the wife maintain a suit against the partnership in the face of a strong State policy against suits between spouses?

(b) A partnership, Hartigan and Dwyer, operates a department store in Troy, New York, while a partnership, Hartigan, Dwyer, and O'Brien, operates a department store in Albany, New York. An insurance company issues a policy in the name of "Hartigan and Dwyer, department store merchant, Troy, New York" insuring against liabilities arising from the operation of a delivery truck. The truck, while being used for deliveries from the Albany store operated by Hartigan, Dwyer, and O'Brien, strikes and kills a child. If Hartigan and Dwyer are called upon individually to pay a tort judgment, are they protected by the policy? See Hartigan v. Casualty Co., 227 N.Y. 175, 124 N.E. 789 (1919), holding the company not liable.

(c) A statute prohibits a bank from making loans to its directors. May a bank lawfully make a loan to a partnership one of whose partners is a director? Compare People v. Knapp, 206 N.Y. 373, 99 N.E. 841 (1912), holding that such a loan violates the statute, with State v. Pielsticker, 118 Neb. 419, 225 N.W. 51 (1929), holding that it does not. Should it make any difference that the statute prohibits such loans "directly or indirectly"?

(d) A partner is served with a subpoena to produce records of the partnership. May he decline on the grounds of self incrimination? See e.g. United States v. Silverstein, 314 F.2d 789 (2d Cir.1963); Bellis v. United States, 417 U.S. 85, 94 S.Ct. 2179, 40 L.Ed.2d 678 (1974).

4. [By the Editor] Lewis, The Uniform Partnership Act—A Reply to Mr. Crane's Criticism, 29 Harv.L.Rev. 158 (1915). The second installment of Dean Lewis' article appears at 29 Harv.L.Rev. 291. Dean Lewis was responding to Crane, The Uniform Partnership Act—A Criticism, 28 Harv.L.Rev. 762 (1915). See also Lewis, The Uniform Partnership Act, 24 Yale L.J. 617 (1915); Crane, Twenty Years Under the Uniform Partnership Act, 2 U.Pitt.L. Rev. 129 (1936); Drake, Partnership Entity and Tenancy in Partnership: The Struggle for Definition, 15 Mich.L.Rev. 609 (1917).

Can you see any underlying theory or approach which might permit courts to resolve questions such as the foregoing?

(2) The same question may be involved in the Internal Revenue Code's treatment of partnerships, and in Worker's Compensation Acts and other State statutes relating to business relationships. The Internal Revenue Code, for example, clearly takes a hybrid approach. See McKee, Partnership Allocations: The Need for an Entity Approach, 66 Va.L.Rev. 1039 (1980). The allocation of the partnership income automatically to the partners appears to be based on an aggregate notion; however, the requirement that the partnership prepare and file a separate information return, accounting for its own receipts and expenses, appears to be based on an entity notion. Other sections of the IRC also can be cited as reflecting an entity approach, e.g. § 707(a), which states that if a "partner engages in a transaction with a partnership other than in his capacity as a member of such partnership, the transaction shall ∗ ∗ ∗ be considered as occurring between the partnership and one who is not a partner."

Does the "rule" that a partner is not an "employee" of the partnership for purposes of employee retirement benefits reflect an entity or aggregate approach? What about the "rule" that a partner may qualify as an employee of the partnership for purposes of the "meals or lodging furnished for the convenience of the employer" rule under § 119? Armstrong v. Phinney, 394 F.2d 661 (5th Cir.1968).

(3) Probably all states have statutes that answer such questions as whether a partnership may sue in the firm name or whether it must sue in the name of all the partners, or whether service on one partner is effective service on the partnership or other partners? Do the following California statutes relating to such questions reflect an entity or aggregate approach?

§ 388. Associates Sued Under Common Name; Service; Judgment

(a) Any partnership or other unincorporated association, whether organized for profit or not, may sue and be sued in the name which it has assumed or by which it is known.

(b) Any member of the partnership or other unincorporated association may be joined as a party in an action against the unincorporated association. If service of process is made on such member as an individual, whether or not he is also served as a person upon whom service is made on behalf of the unincorporated association, a judgment against him based on his personal liability may be obtained in the action, whether such liability be joint, joint and several, or several.

§ 412.30   Action Against Corporation or Unincorporated Association; Notice; Contents; Default Judgment

In an action against a corporation or an unincorporated association (including a partnership), the copy of the summons that is served shall contain a notice stating in substance: "To the person served: You are hereby served in the within action (or special proceeding) on behalf of (here state the name of the corporation or the unincorporated association) as a person upon whom a copy of the summons and of the complaint may be delivered to effect service on said party under the provisions of (here state appropriate provisions of Chapter 4 (commencing with Section 413.10) of the Code of Civil Procedure)." If service is also made on such person as an individual, the notice shall also indicate that service is being made on such person as an individual as well as on behalf of the corporation or the unincorporated association.

If such notice does not appear on the copy of the summons served, no default may be taken against such corporation or unincorporated association or against such person individually, as the case may be.

§ 416.40 Unincorporated Association

A summons may be served on an unincorporated association (including a partnership) by delivering a copy of the summons and of the complaint:

(a) If the association is a general or limited partnership to the person designated as agent for service of process as provided in Section 24003 of the Corporations Code or to a general partner or the general manager of the partnership; * * *

[West's Ann.Calif.Code Civ.Proc. §§ 388, 412.30, 416.40]

Many statutes relating to such questions are of long standing and may have been enacted in order to achieve procedural simplicity without regard to a debate over the "true" nature of a partnership. Section 388 of the California Code of Civil Procedure, for example, may be traced back to 1872.

(4) In general terms, the proposed Revised Uniform Partnership Act, while not changing the language of Section 6(1) of the UPA "includes a number of steps that move partnership law more toward an entity approach. In general, an entity approach is adopted for its simplicity. The RUPA does not, however, take an extreme entity position. If it did Section 6(1) would provide that a partnership is 'a *legal person* formed by an association of' two or more people." Comment to Section 6, reprinted in 1 A. Bromberg and L. Ribstein, Bromberg and Ribstein on Partnerships, 1989 Supplement at 54–55.

UNITED STATES v. A & P TRUCKING CO.

Supreme Court of the United States, 1958.
358 U.S. 121, 79 S.Ct. 203, 3 L.Ed.2d 165.

MR. JUSTICE HARLAN delivered the opinion of the Court.

This case raises issues similar to those involved in United States v. American Freightways Co., 352 U.S. 1020, 77 S.Ct. 588, 1 L.Ed.2d 595, where a dismissal of an information charging a partnership entity with violations of 18 U.S.C.A. § 835 was affirmed by an equally divided Court.

Appellees, two partnerships, were charged, as entities, in separate informations with violations of 18 U.S.C.A. § 835, which makes it criminal knowingly to violate Interstate Commerce Commission regulations for the safe transportation in interstate commerce of "explosives and other dangerous articles." Appellee A & P Trucking Company was also charged with numerous violations of 49 U.S.C.A. § 322(a) (§ 222(a) of the Motor Carrier Act of 1935). [5] The District Court dismissed, on motion, the informations on the ground that a partnership entity cannot be guilty of violating the statutes involved. The Government appealed directly to this Court under the Criminal Appeals Act, 18 U.S. C.A. § 3731, and we noted probable jurisdiction. For reasons set forth below we hold that the informations were erroneously dismissed.

49 U.S.C.A. § 322(a), the comprehensive misdemeanor provision of the Motor Carrier Act, provides that "any person knowingly and willfully violating any provision of this chapter [Part II of the Interstate Commerce Act], or any rule, regulation, requirement, or order [of the Interstate Commerce Commission] thereunder, or any term or condition of any certificate, permit, or license, for which a penalty is not otherwise herein provided, shall, upon conviction thereof, be fined * * *." The Motor Carrier Act also contains its own definition of the word "person": "The term 'person' means any individual, firm, *copartnership,* corporation, company, association, or joint-stock association; * * *." (Italics supplied.) 49 U.S.C.A. § 303(a).

18 U.S.C.A. § 835 provides that "whoever knowingly violates any such regulation [ICC regulations pertaining to the safe transport of dangerous articles] shall be fined not more than $1,000 or imprisoned not more than one year, or both; * * *." The section makes such regulations binding on "all common carriers" engaged in interstate commerce. And 1 U.S.C.A. § 1, part of a chapter entitled "Rules of Construction" and in light of which § 835 must be read, provides that "in determining the meaning of any Act of Congress, unless the context indicates otherwise—* * * the words 'person' and 'whoever' include corporations, companies, associations, firms, *partnerships,* societies, and joint stock companies, as well as individuals; * * *." (Italics supplied.) The word "whoever" in 18 U.S.C.A. § 835 must, therefore, be construed to include partnerships "unless the context indicates otherwise." [6]

5. [By the Court] The information as to appellee A & P Trucking Company charged in one count an offense under 18 U.S.C.A. § 835 through the transportation by truck of chromic acid without the markings or placardings prescribed by 49 CFR § 77.823(a). It charged in 34 other counts offenses under 49 U.S.C.A. § 322(a), consisting of failure to comply with 49 CFR § 191.8, which prescribes physical examinations and certificates for drivers of trucks (one count), violation of 49 CFR, 1958 Cum. Pocket Supp., § 193.95(a), which requires that common-carrier trucks be equipped with fire extinguishers (one count), and violation of 49 U.S.C.A. § 306(a), which forbids the operation of a common-carrier truck in interstate commerce without a certificate of convenience and necessity (32 counts). The information as to appellee Hopla Trucking Company charged two violations of 18 U.S.C.A. § 835, in that Hopla shipped methanol, a flammable liquid, without properly marking or placarding the truck as required by 49 CFR § 77.823(a), and without its driver having in his possession a paper showing the prescribed labels required for the outside containers of the methanol as required by 49 CFR § 77.817.

6. [By the Court] It is significant that the definition of "whoever" in 1 U.S.C.A. § 1 was first enacted into law as part of the very same statute which enacted into positive law the revised Criminal Code. 62 Stat. 683, 859 (1948). The connection between 1 U.S.C.A. § 1 and the Criminal

We think that partnerships as entities may be proceeded against under both § 322(a) and § 835. The purpose of both statutes is clear: to ensure compliance by motor carriers, among others, with safety and other requirements laid down by the Interstate Commerce Commission in the exercise of its statutory duty to regulate the operations of interstate carriers for hire. In the effectuation of this policy it certainly makes no difference whether the carrier which commits the infraction is organized as a corporation, a joint stock company, a partnership, or an individual proprietorship. The mischief is the same, and we think that Congress intended to make the consequences of infraction the same.

True, the common law made a distinction between a corporation and a partnership, deeming the latter not a separate entity for purposes of suit. But the power of Congress to change the common-law rule is not to be doubted. See United States v. Adams Express Co., 229 U.S. 381, 33 S.Ct. 878, 57 L.Ed. 1237. We think it beyond dispute that it has done so in § 322(a) for, as we have seen, "person" in that section is expressly defined in the Motor Carrier Act to include partnerships. We think it likewise has done so in § 835, since we find nothing in that section which would justify our not applying to the word "whoever" the definition given it in 1 U.S.C.A. § 1, which includes partnerships. Section 835 makes regulations promulgated by the ICC for the transportation of dangerous articles binding on *all* common carriers. In view of the fact that many motor carriers are organized as partnerships rather than as corporations, the conclusion is not lightly to be reached that Congress intended that some carriers should not be subject to the full gamut of sanctions provided for infractions of ICC regulations merely because of the form under which they were organized to do business.[7] More particularly, we perceive no reason why Congress should have intended to make partnership motor carriers criminally liable for infractions of § 322(a), but not for violations of § 835.[8]

It is argued that the words "knowingly" (§ 835) and "knowingly and willfully" (§ 322(a)) by implication eliminate partnerships from the coverage of the statutes, because a partnership, as opposed to its individual partners, cannot so act. But the same inability so to act *in fact* is true, of course, with regard to corporations and other associations; yet it is elementary that such impersonal entities can be guilty of "knowing" or "willful" violations of regulatory statutes through the doctrine of *respondeat superior*. Thus in United States v. Adams Express Co., supra, in which the Adams Express Co., a joint stock association, was indicted for "wilfully" receiving sums for expressage in

Code, which includes § 835, is thus more than a token one, the very same statute which creates the crime admonishing that "whoever" is to be liberally interpreted.

7. [By the Court] Congress has specifically included partnerships within the definition of "person" in a large number of regulatory Acts, thus showing its intent to treat partnerships as entities.

8. [By the Court] The fact that § 835 provides for imprisonment, as well as fine, for its violation, whereas § 322(a) provides only for fines, does not lead to a different conclusion.

excess of its scheduled rates, Mr. Justice Holmes said, 229 U.S. at pages 389–390, 33 S.Ct. at page 879:

"It has been notorious for many years that some of the great express companies are organized as joint stock associations, and the reason for the amendment hardly could be seen unless it was intended to bring those associations under the act. As suggested in the argument for the government, no one, certainly not the defendant, seems to have doubted that the statute now imposes upon them the duty to file schedules of rates. * * * But if it imposes upon them the duties under the words 'common carrier,' as interpreted, it is reasonable to suppose that the same words are intended to impose upon them the penalty inflicted on common carriers in case those duties are not performed. * * *

"The power of Congress hardly is denied. The constitutionality of the statute as against corporations is established, (New York Central & Hudson River R.R. Co. v. United States, 212 U.S. 481, 492, 29 S.Ct. 304, [306], 53 L.Ed. 613, 621,) and no reason is suggested why Congress has not equal power to charge the partnership assets with a liability and to personify the company so far as to collect a fine by a proceeding against it by the company name. That is what we believe that Congress intended to do. * * *"

The policy to be served in this case is the same. The business entity cannot be left free to break the law merely because its owners, stockholders in the Adams case, partners in the present one, do not personally participate in the infraction. The treasury of the business may not with impunity obtain the fruits of violations which are committed knowingly by agents of the entity in the scope of their employment. Thus pressure is brought on those who own the entity to see to it that their agents abide by the law.

We hold, therefore, that a partnership can violate each of the statutes here in question quite apart from the participation and knowledge of the partners as individuals. The corollary is, of course, that the conviction of a partnership cannot be used to punish the individual partners, who might be completely free of personal guilt. As in the case of corporations, the conviction of the entity can lead only to a fine levied on the firm's assets.

Reversed.

MR. JUSTICE DOUGLAS, with whom MR. JUSTICE BLACK, MR. JUSTICE FRANKFURTER, and MR. JUSTICE WHITTAKER, concur, dissenting in part.

18 U.S.C.A. § 835, unlike the Motor Carrier Act, has not explicitly subjected partnerships to criminal liability, and I do not think that such liability should be implied, for we are dealing with a penal statute which should be narrowly construed.

As Chief Justice Marshall wrote in United States v. Wiltberger, 5 Wheat. 76, 95, 5 L.Ed. 37, "The rule that penal laws are to be construed strictly, is perhaps not much less old than construction itself. It is founded on the tenderness of the law for the rights of individuals; and on the plain principle that the power of punishment is vested in the legislative, not in the judicial department."

With that approach we would not allow this criminal sanction to attach under 18 U.S.C.A. § 835. A corporation is an artificial, legally created entity that can have no "knowledge" itself and is said to have "knowledge" only through its employees. On the other hand a partnership means A, B, and C—the individuals who compose it. In this country the entity theory has not in general been extended to the partnership. Judge Learned Hand summarized the history in Helvering v. Smith, 2 Cir., 90 F.2d 590, 591–592. If Dean Ames had had his way, the mercantile or entity theory of the partnership would have prevailed. But those who took up the drafting of the Uniform Partnership Act after his death adhered to the common-law attitude toward a partnership—that it is an aggregation of individuals. That is to say, the Act adopted the aggregate rather than the entity theory. And that Act is in force in about three-fourths of the States. One who combs the reports today can find cases espousing the entity theory. But they are in the minority and consciously reject the other theory. As Professor Williston has shown, the main stream of American partnership law follows the British course of treating the partnership in the pluralistic sense. The Uniform Partnership Act, 68 U. of Pa.L.Rev. 196, 208. We should therefore assume that this criminal statute, written against that background, reflects the conventional aggregate, not the exceptional entity, theory of the partnership.

We are dealing with a statute where liability depends on "culpable intent," as stated in Boyce Motor Lines, Inc. v. United States, 342 U.S. 337, 342, 72 S.Ct. 329, 331, 96 L.Ed. 367. The partners could not be held criminally responsible for the acts of their employees. Gordon v. United States, 347 U.S. 909, 74 S.Ct. 473, 98 L.Ed. 1067. The partnership, being no more than the aggregate of the partners, should stand on the same footing, unless Congress explicitly provides otherwise. Title 1 U.S.C.A. § 1 defines "person" in any Act of Congress to include a partnership, "unless the context indicates otherwise." The context of 18 U.S.C.A. § 835 does indicate otherwise for the Act punishes only those who knowingly violate it. The aggregate theory of partnership law teaches that there can be no vicarious criminal liability where no partner is culpable.

If the rule of strict construction of a criminal statute is to obtain, 18 U.S.C.A. § 835 must be read narrowly to reflect the prevailing view of partnership law. If the entity theory is to be applied for the purpose of imposing criminal penalties on partnership assets, where the partners are wholly innocent of any wrongful act, it should be done only on the unequivocal command of Congress, as is the case under the Motor Carrier Act.

Notes

(1) The position taken in the principal case is inconsistent with the holdings of, or at least language in, a large number of decisions by state courts. Many of these decisions predate the enactment of the Uniform Partnership Act. The Model Penal Code contains provisions imposing liability on unincorporated associations, including partnerships, and specific references to possible criminal liability of partnerships now appear in several State penal codes. Consult A.L.I. Model Penal Code, Proposed Official Draft, §§ 2.07(3), 6.04 (1962).

(2) Is the last paragraph of Mr. Justice Harlan's opinion consistent with UPA §§ 13, 15(a)?

(3) Can you see any policy justification for holding partnerships, as such, criminally liable? Would it not be better to hold the persons committing the criminal act liable? The same question, of course, is present where a corporation is held criminally liable. Consider G. Williams, Criminal Law: The General Part, ch. 22, particularly § 283 (1961).

(4) There is a burgeoning literature on the policies underlying the imposition of criminal liability on corporations, but little attention has been paid to the related but somewhat different problems associated with the imposition of criminal liability on partnerships. For general discussions of corporate criminal liability see K. Brickey, Corporate Criminal Law (1984); Brickey, Rethinking Corporate Liability Under the Model Penal Code, 19 Rutgers L.Rev. 593 (1983); Metzger, Corporate Criminal Liability for Defective Products: Policies, Problems, and Prospects, 73 Geo.L.J. 1 (1984).

(5) United States Sentencing Commission, Discussion Materials on Organizational Sanctions (July 1988), 8.1:

> In general, the Comprehensive Crime Control Act of 1984 sets the same broad objectives for sentencing organizations as for sentencing individuals. However, there are differences between individuals and organizations—in terms of available sentencing options, the standards of criminal liability, and the importance of collateral remedies outside the criminal justice system—that call for a distinct approach to sentencing organizations.

> First, organizations can not be imprisoned. Sentencing standards for organizations must be structured around the five available sentencing options for organizations: three types of monetary sanctions— restitution, fines, and forfeitures; and two types of non-monetary sanctions—notice to victims and probation. With few exceptions, organizational defendants in the federal courts are business corporations, which are motivated primarily by monetary profit and loss. Monetary sanctions have the most direct impact on a business firm's fundamental interest. Even where non-monetary sanctions are imposed, their ultimate impact will be largely monetary in any event, because financial results are the measure of a business organization's value and effectiveness.

Second, organizations can act only through agents. Under federal law, organizations generally are held to a strict standard of vicarious criminal liability for offenses committed by their agents. Therefore, principles for organizational sentencing should provide an appropriate incentive for the organization to control its agents. At the same time, the individual agent remains criminally responsible for his or her own offense. Most federal prosecutions of organizations involve individual co-defendants who are agents and, in many cases, owners of the organizational offender. Consequently, sentencing principles for organizations should encourage effective coordination between organizational and individual sentencing.

Third, for many if not most offenses committed by organizations, criminal prosecution is only one aspect of federal law enforcement. Generally, criminal offenses committed by organizations also are subject to punitive and compensatory remedies through administrative or civil enforcement proceedings brought by federal agencies, and to compensatory and punitive damages in private litigation. These civil sanctions can complement or partially substitute for criminal sentences. Compensatory damages, civil penalties, and civil forfeitures can substitute for criminal restitution, fines, and forfeitures; and civil injunctions or administrative orders can substitute for criminal probation or notice to victims. Enforcement agencies in fact do coordinate among the parallel enforcement systems, in order to achieve an appropriate overall sanction in the most effective manner. Criminal sentencing standards for organizations should recognize and promote that goal. * * *

The draft sentencing guidelines and policy statements embody three basic principles: (a) a total monetary sanction is determined by multiplying the loss caused by the offense times a "multiple" representing the difficulty of detecting and punishing the offender, and adding enforcement costs; (b) non-monetary sanctions are added as necessary to reinforce the monetary sanctions; and (c) criminal and civil sanctions are coordinated.

The principal non-monetary sanction proposed is "organization probation." The goals of such probation are to enforce monetary sanctions and to reduce the likelihood of future offenses by increasing their detectability or by requiring the implementation of internal compliance measures.

This effort to provide sentencing guidelines for associations was highly controversial. Complaints were voiced about the leniency of the sentencing standards by prosecutors, by academics, and by members of the sentencing commission's own staff. See Coffee, Let's Not Shield Corporations from Criminal Penalties, Legal Times, February 13, 1989, p. 19:

> * * * [T]he draft proposals (1) are unworkable on a practical level (chiefly because they impose excessive burdens on prosecutors), (2) undercount the social loss from many crimes (because they ignore the externalities that crimes impose on third parties other than the immediate victim), and (3) institutionalize underdeterrence by adopting artificially low offense multiples that lack any foundation in empirical research.

Beyond all this, however, the truly radical idea in these proposals is the view that overdeterring the offender is as great a danger (and serious a harm) as underprotecting the victim. Based on this ideological view that no distinction can be drawn between the victim's losses and the offender's, these guidelines seek to minimize not the victim's losses, but rather the sum of (1) the victim's losses, (2) the offender's losses and (3) public enforcement costs. The problem with this overly simple attempt to achieve allocational efficiency is that we ignore distributive justice. The victim and the offender possess different moral entitlements, and their losses should not be weighted equally. Moreover, the goal of total cost minimization assumes that which society has never taken as a given: namely, that it is wrong to impose $2 on criminals to prevent $1 in losses to innocent victims. Learned Hand's formula for tort law should not govern the criminal law.

For a general defense of the Commission's proposals, see Parker, Criminal Sentencing Policy for Organizations: The Unifying Approach of Optimal Remedies, 26 Am.Crim.L.Rev. 513 (1989); Cohen, Corporate Crime and Punishment: A Study of Social Harm and Sentencing Practice in the Federal Courts, 1984–1987, 26 Am.Crim.L.Rev. 605 (1989). In November, 1989, the Commission published for comment a revised set of guidelines containing an alternative approach by which sentencing would be governed only by the offense level together with mitigating or aggravating factors. 54 Fed.Reg. 47056–01 (Nov. 8, 1989). Do you believe that sentencing of associations should be governed only by the nature of the offense, or should the losses suffered by victims be taken into account?

F. PARTNERSHIP PROPERTY

OFFICIAL COMMENT TO SUBDIVISIONS (1) AND (2–b) OF SECTION 25 OF THE UNIFORM PARTNERSHIP ACT

6 Uniform Laws Annotated: Uniform Partnership Act 327 (1969).

Subdivision (1). One of the present principal difficulties in the Administration of the law of partnerships arises out of the difficulty of determining the exact nature of the rights of a partner in specific partnership property. That the partners are co-owners of partnership property is clear; but the legal incidents attached to the right of each partner as co-owner are not clear. When the English courts in the seventeenth century first began to discuss the legal incidents of this co-ownership, they were already familiar with two other kinds of co-ownership, joint tenancy and tenancy in common. In joint tenancy on the death of one owner his right in the property passes to the other co-owners. This is known as the right of survivorship. The incident of survivorship fits in with the necessities of partnership. On the death of a partner, the other partners and not the executors of the deceased partner should have a right to wind up partnership affairs. (See [UPA § 25(d).].) The early courts, therefore, declared that partners were joint tenants of partnership property, the consequence being that all the other legal incidents of joint tenancy were applied to partnership co-ownership. Many of these incidents, however, do not apply to the necessities of the partnership relation and produce most inequitable results. This is not to be wondered at because the legal incidents of joint tenancy grew out of a co-ownership of land not held for the purposes of business. The attempt of our courts to escape the inequitable results of applying the legal incidents of joint tenancy to partnership has produced very great confusion. Practically this confusion has had more unfortunate effect on substantive rights when the separate creditors of a partner attempt to attach and sell specific partnership property than when a partner attempts to assign specific partnership property not for a partnership purpose but for his own purposes.

The Commissioners, however, believe that the proper way to end the confusion which has arisen out of the attempt to treat partners as joint tenants, is to recognize the fact that the rights of a partner as co-owner with his partners of specific partnership property should depend on the necessities of the partnership relation. In short, that the legal incidents of the tenancy in partnership are not necessarily those of any other co-ownership.

In the clauses of this section these incidents of tenancy in partnership are stated with several practical results of value. In the first place the law is greatly simplified in expression. In the second place the danger of the courts reaching an inequitable conclusion by refusing to modify the results of applying the legal incidents of joint tenancy to the partnership relation is done away with. Finally, ground is laid for the simplification of a procedure in those cases where the separate creditor desires to secure satisfaction out of his debtor's interest in the partnership. (Compare [UPA § 25(2)(c)] with [UPA § 28(1).].)

Subdivision (2–b). Clause (b) asserts that the right of a partner as co-owner in specific partnership property is not separately assignable. This peculiarity of tenancy in partnership is a necessary consequence of the partnership relation. If A and B are partners and A attempts to assign all his right in partnership property, say a particular chattel, to C, and the law recognizes the possibility of such a transfer, C would pro tanto become a partner with B; for the rights of A in the chattel are to possess the chattel for a partnership purpose. But partnership is a voluntary relation. B cannot have a partner thrust upon him by A without his, B's, consent.

A cannot confer on C his, A's, right to possess and deal with the chattel for a partnership purpose. Neither can he confer any other rights which he has in the property. A partner has a beneficial interest in partnership property considered as a whole. As profits accrue, he has a right to be paid his proportion, and on the winding up of the business, after the obligations due third persons have been met, he has a right to be paid in cash his share of what remains of the partnership property. These rights considered as a whole are his interest in the partnership; and this beneficial interest he may assign in whole or fractional part, as is indicated in [UPA § 27]. In a sense, each partner, having thus a beneficial interest in the partnership property considered as a whole, has a beneficial interest in each part, and such beneficial interest might be regarded as assignable if it were not impossible, except by purely arbitrary and artificial rules, to measure a partner's beneficial interest in a specific chattel belonging to the partnership, or any other specific portion of partnership property.

Notes

(1) As indicated in the official comment, the problem of ownership of property, the rights of partners, and the rights of creditors of the partnership and of individual partners are covered in some detail in sections 24 through 28 of the Act. These sections should be read carefully since they provide firm (and sometimes startling) answers to questions. For example, a person dies leaving a will that provides that son A inherits all his personal property and daughter B inherits all his real estate. His only asset on his death is a one-half interest in a partnership whose sole asset is a valuable piece of real estate. Who is entitled to his interest in that real estate? See UPA § 26.

(2) The ability of a partnership creditor to proceed against the individual property of a partner is dependent only on naming and serving the partner as a defendant in the suit. If this is done, the partner's individual property may be subject to execution, attachment or other process. However, the ability of an individual creditor to proceed against partnership property is sharply circumscribed by UPA §§ 25(2)(c), 28 and RULPA § 703. Why are individual creditors seeking to recover from partnership assets treated differently from partnership creditors seeking to recover from individual assets?

(3) Precisely what rights does a judgment creditor of a partner get upon obtaining the charging order contemplated by § 28? Is it a "lien" on the partnership interest? Consult Kerry v. Schneider, 239 F.2d 896 (9th Cir.1956). What other rights does the creditor have or can thereafter obtain? Gose, The Charging Order Under the Uniform Partnership Act, 28 Wash.L.Rev. 1, 15–18 (1953), describes the relationship between creditor, debtor, and partnership as follows:

> In the somewhat doubtful state of the law,[9] the following propositions seem to accord best with the language and purpose of the statute and the philosophy of the American courts with respect thereto.
>
> First, the charging order may enjoin the members of the partnership from making further disbursements of any kind to the debtor partner, except such payments as may be permissible under a legal exemption right properly asserted by the debtor.
>
> Second, the charging order may formally require the members of the partnership to pay to the creditor any amounts which it would otherwise pay to the debtor partner, exclusive of any amounts payable to the latter under a properly asserted legal exemption right.

9. [By the Author] No substantial aid to specific interpretations of the statute is obtained from the texts or other non-judicial literature. * * *

Third, the appointment of a receiver is not indispensable to the collection of the claim out of the debtor partner's share. A receiver should be appointed only where he has some useful function to serve such as the maintenance of a lawsuit, the conduct of a sale or the representation of competing creditors of the debtor partner. It may be that even in such a case, no receiver is necessary since there is no insuperable reason why these services cannot be obtained by some other method. Certainly the court should not appoint a receiver where he would serve no useful purpose while adding to the expense of the proceeding.

Fourth, the debtor's interest should be sold if, and only if, the court is convinced that the creditor's claim will not be satisfied with reasonable expedition by the less drastic process of diverting the debtor's income from the partnership to the payment of the debt.[10] Even in the case of a wholly solvent partnership, the creditor's claim may be so large in relation to the current income of the debtor from the firm as to require sale as the only alternative to long delay in payment.

Fifth, the courts should liberally employ the general language of the act concerning "orders, directions, accounts and inquiries * * * which the circumstances of the case may require." By this means information as to the nature and extent of the debtor's interest in the partnership can be obtained and the whole range of unusual problems which are bound to arise may be dealt with as the occasion demands. Included in this general power should be the power to prescribe the manner in which a sale of the partnership interest is to be made.[11]

One other question prominently posed by both the English and American statutes and not touched upon by any decision in either country since the adoption of the respective acts goes to the rights of a non-debtor partner who redeems or purchases the interest of a debtor partner. Both statutes expressly recognize the right to redeem and, in the event of a sale being ordered, the right to purchase at the sale. The American statute is somewhat more detailed, specifying that the right to redeem exists "before foreclosure." [12] and that a purchase or redemption may be made with separate property of the redemptioner or, if all of the non-debtor partners consent, with partnership property.

10. [By the Author] There is actually no authority whatsoever as to when a sale should be ordered. Necessarily the order must fall in the area of those "which the circumstances of the case require." The apparent situations in which sale would be necessary are those in which, owing to the size of the claim or the absence of current liquid income, an order to pay over the debtor partner's share of current income and other moneys would not be effective.

11. [By the Author] The statute is utterly silent as to the procedure to be followed in making a sale. * * * Whether [a sheriff] can be called on to make judicial sales in the absence of a special statutory provision is questionble. Unless the re-

ceiver contemplated by Section 28 is to be regarded as limited to the express duties mentioned in the statute, the logical procedure would be for him to conduct the sale on such notice and terms as the court might fix. * * *

12. [By the Author] No definition of these words appears elsewhere in the Act or in the cases decided thereunder. Doubtless the language would mean before sale or before the expiration of a redemption period fixed by the court in its order of sale. There appears to be no unqualified right to a redemption period extending after sale, the matter being controlled by the court's discretion.

Both statutes present the question whether a non-debtor partner who redeems or purchases thereby acquires the interest of the debtor partner free and clear of the latter's claim or in trust for him.

Considering the statute only, a possible distinction between the redemption and purchase situations can be urged. The price realized on a competitive sale theoretically represents the full value of the thing sold, although in practice this ideal result is seldom achieved. Upon a redemption before sale, however, there is not even a theoretical logical connection between the redemption price and the value of the redeemed interest. Normally the redemption price would be the amount of the creditor's claim and any identity between the amount of the claim and the value of the interest would be merely a coincidence.

Under these circumstances it might be maintained with some force that the non-debtor partners who purchase at a sale held under the statute acquire the debtor partner's interest absolutely [13] whereas the non-debtor partner who redeems has merely advanced moneys for the benefit of the debtor and holds the interest in trust for him. The theory would be that, in the former situation, the debtor's interest is entirely represented by the purchase money while, in the latter case, the value of the interest and its relation to the redemption price can be determined only by an accounting.

More likely, however, the courts would in all cases invoke principles of fiduciary relationship which are so deeply rooted in the law of partnership and would in every instance require the non-debtor partners to account for the full value of the debtor partner's interest, less the amount paid by way of redemption or purchase. * * *

(4) Where the partnership or a partner is insolvent § 40(h) and (i) of the UPA establish the "jingle rule" for priority of payment: individual creditors have priority with regard to individual property and partnership creditors have priority with regard to partnership property. For may years the Federal Bankruptcy Act followed the same pattern, but in 1978 it was changed to provide, essentially, that partnership creditors have priority as to partnership property and equivalence with individual creditors as to individual property. 11 U.S.C.A. § 723(c). The most serious criticism of the old "jingle rule" was that partnership creditors consider the net worth of both the partnership and the individual partners in deciding to extend credit to the partnership and should not therefore be subordinated to individual creditors with respect to individual assets. The proposed Revised Uniform Partnership Act eliminates sections 40(h) and 40(i).

(5) Is it desirable to have one set of priorities applicable in state insolvency and receivership proceedings and a different set of priorities applicable in federal bankruptcy proceedings? This was the principal objection to the 1978 change when it was being considered. Since the federal set of priorities is always more favorable to partnership creditors, the likely result will be that such creditors will resort to the federal forum whenever their claims exceed partnership assets and the partnership fails

---

13. [By the Author] Upon this theory, it would be immaterial whether separate or partnership funds were used by the non-debtor partners. The debtor would have received the full value of his interest in either event.

to meet its obligations as they become due. In other words, the 1978 change may increase the number of federal bankruptcy cases involving partners and partnerships.

(6) What rights does an assignee of a partnership interest obtain if the other partners do not accept the assignee as a partner? See UPA §§ 18(g), 27. Does § 29 cause such an assignment to effect a dissolution of the partnership? What is the relationship between sections 27 and 29? Under § 27 of the UPA, an assignee has no right to interfere in the management or administration of the affairs of the continuing partnership, to require any information or account of partnership transactions, or to inspect its books. An assignee merely obtains the right to receive the profits to which the assignor would otherwise be entitled. Is the assignee liable for partnership debts? An assignee may compel a dissolution only pursuant to UPA § 32(2), which involves a judicial proceeding. Clearly, an assignee of a partnership interest is not favored by the Uniform Partnership Act.

G. PARTNERSHIP ACCOUNTING

From an accounting standpoint, the business of the partnership is almost universally recognized as being distinct from the financial affairs of the individual partners. The interests of the partners are usually reflected in capital accounts which are adjusted periodically for income, drawings, and contributions or withdrawals of capital. In some partnerships, the capital and income accounts are segregated, so that separate income accounts are maintained for the allocation of income or loss to each partner and for drawings.

Partnership accounting in other respects closely resembles corporate accounting for profits and losses, assets and liabilities. A simple illustration based on the first year's successful operation of the AB Furniture Company might be helpful.

(1) Income Statement

AB FURNITURE COMPANY
Statement of Profit and Loss for Year Ending December 31, 19__

Sales	$417,000	
Cost of Sales	270,000	
GROSS PROFIT		$147,000
Other Expenses:		
Advertising	8,000	
Rentals	24,000	
Depreciation	5,000	
Salaries	32,000	
Miscellaneous	18,000	87,000
NET PROFIT		$60,000

(2) Balance Sheet

AB FURNITURE COMPANY
Balance Sheet, December 31, 19__

Assets		Liabilities	
Cash	$ 19,000	Accounts Payable	$ 73,000
Accounts Receivable	93,000	Note Payable to A	25,000
Inventory	95,000		
Fixtures (Net of depreciation)	42,000		
Truck (Net of depreciation)	9,000	**Equity** Partner's Capital *	160,000
	$258,000		$258,000

* The details of the partners' capital accounts may be shown in separate accounts that might appear like this:

Capital Accounts for 19__

	Opening	Income for Year	Drawing for Year	Closing
A	$100,000	$30,000	–0–	$130,000
B	–0–	30,000	–0–	30,000
				$160,000

R. HAMILTON, FUNDAMENTALS OF MODERN BUSINESS
P. 152–157 (1989).

The starting point of the whole subject of accountancy is a very simple equation:

$$\text{Equity} = \text{Assets} - \text{Liabilities}$$

Equity in this equation has nothing to do with the historical courts of equity or with notions of fairness or simple justice: It means *ownership* or *net worth*. This equation simply states that the net worth of a business is equal to its assets minus its liabilities.

A *balance sheet* is in many ways the most fundamental financial statement: It is simply a restatement of this fundamental equation in the form:

$$\text{Assets} = \text{Liabilities} + \text{Equity}$$

A balance sheet simply is a presentation of this equation in a chart form:

Assets:	Liabilities + Equity
_____	_____

Every balance sheet, whether it is for General Motors or the smallest retail grocery store, is based on this format. * * *

The asset side of a balance sheet is always referred to as the *left hand side* [and] the liability/equity side is always the *right hand side* * * *.

There are four fundamental premises underlying financial accounting that can readily be grasped from this simple introduction. First, *financial accounting assumes that the business that is the subject of the financial statements is an entity.* A person may own several different businesses; if each maintains its own records, it will be on the assumption that it is independent from the person's other businesses. The equity referred to in that business's balance sheet will be limited to the person's investment in that single business. If a person owns two businesses that keep separate financial records, a debt owed by one business to the other will be reflected as an asset on one balance sheet and a liability on the other. Second, *all entries have to be in terms of dollars.* All property, tangible or intangible, shown on a balance sheet, must be expressed in dollars, either *historical cost* or *fair market value* or some other method of valuation. Many "assets" or "liabilities" of a business, however, are not reflected at all. A person's friendly smile may be an asset in a sense, but will not appear on a balance sheet since a dollar value is not normally given to a smile. Intangible assets, such as a debt owed to the company or rights to a patent, on the other hand, are assets that appear in balance sheets. * * * Similarly, a company may have a reputation for sharp practices or questionable dealing; while that reputation is doubtless a liability in a sense, it is not the type of liability that appears on a balance sheet. A liability in the balance sheet sense is a recognized debt or obligation to someone else, payable either in money or in something reducible to money. Not all liabilities that in the legal or lay sense meet this test are recognized as liabilities in the accounting sense. * * * Third, *a balance sheet has to balance.* The fundamental accounting equation itself states an equality: The two sides of the balance sheet restate that equality in somewhat reorganized form. A balance sheet therefore is itself an equality and the sum of the left hand side of the balance sheet must precisely equal the sum of the right hand side. Indeed, when accountants are involved in auditing a complex business, they take advantage of this characteristic by running *trial balances* on their work to make sure that they have not inadvertently transposed or omitted figures: The mathematical equality of the two sides of the balance sheet provides a check on the accuracy of the accountant's labors. In short, if a balance sheet doesn't balance, somewhere there is a mistake. Fourth, *every transaction entered into by a business must be recorded in at least two ways if the balance sheet is to continue to balance.* This last point underlies the concept of that mysterious subject, *double entry bookkeeping,* and is the cornerstone on which modern accounting is built.

Assume that we have a new business, just starting out, in which the owner has invested $10,000 in cash (for this purpose it makes no difference whether the business is going to be conducted in the form of a proprietorship, partnership, or corporation; all that is important is that it will be accounted for as an entity separate from the owner). The opening balance sheet will look like this:

Assets:		Liabilities	–0–
Cash	10,000	Owner's Equity	10,000

Now let us assume that the owner buys a used truck for $3,000 cash. The effect of this transaction is to reduce cash by $3,000 and create a new asset on the balance sheet:

Assets:		Liabilities	–0–
Cash	7,000	Owner's Equity	10,000
Used Truck	3,000		
	10,000		10,000

Voila! The balance sheet still balances. Let us assume next that the owner goes down to the bank and borrows an additional $1,000. This also has a dual effect: it increases cash by $1,000 (since the business is receiving the proceeds of the loan) and increases liabilities by $1,000 (since the business thereafter has to repay the loan). Yet another balance sheet can be created showing the additional effect of this second transaction:

Assets:		Liabilities	
Cash	8,000	Debt to Bank	1,000
Used Truck	3,000	Owner's Equity	10,000
	11,000		11,000

A couple of further insights should be evident from these two examples: First, *a balance sheet records a situation at one instant in time.* It is a static concept, an equilibrium that exists at one point in time rather than a record of change from an earlier period. Put another way, every transaction potentially creates a different or new balance sheet when the transaction is recorded. Second, *the bottom line of a balance sheet—$11,000 in this example—is not itself a meaningful figure,* since transactions such as the bank loan that do not affect the real worth of the business to the owners may increase or decrease it. * * *

The two transactions described above—the purchase of a used truck and a short-term bank loan—involve a reshuffling of assets and liabilities. From an accounting standpoint, the owner of the business is neither richer nor poorer as a result of them. However, most transactions that a business enters into are of a different type: They involve ordinary business operations leading to a profit or loss in the current accounting period. Let us take a simple example: The business involves hauling things in the truck for customers. The day that it opens for business, it hires a truck driver at a cost of $200 per day to drive the truck and pick up and deliver for it. During that first day the truck driver works very hard and for long hours making deliveries for which the business is paid $500. It is simple to create a *profit and loss statement* or *income statement* for the business for the one day of operation. "Profit and loss" and "income" are synonyms for this purpose. The basic formula is:

$$\text{Income} = \text{Revenues} - \text{Expenses}$$

Obviously, the business had income of $300 ($500 of revenue minus $200 of expense for the truck driver) for its first day of operation. There may have been other expenses as well that arguably should be charged to that first day of operation, but for simplicity we are ignoring that possibility.

At first glance the income statement appears to have nothing to do with the balance sheet described in the previous section. However, one should not jump too quickly to conclusions. It is possible to create a new balance sheet to reflect each of these transactions as well:

First, the payment of the $200 to the truck driver involves a cash payment of $200 by the business; it is easy to record that. But where should the offsetting entry be? The balance sheet cannot look like this:

Assets:		Liabilities	
Cash	7,800	Debt to bank	1,000
Used truck	3,000	Equity	10,000
	10,800		11,000

Something is obviously wrong since this balance sheet does not balance. There has to be an offsetting entry. It certainly should not be a reduction of liabilities (since the amount of the bank loan is unchanged) or an increase in value of the truck. Perhaps one could view the services as an asset something like the truck, but that does not make much sense since the services are transient and performed at the time the payment is made. One could perhaps argue that no balance sheet should be created until the payment to the truck driver is offset by whatever he earns during the rest of the day, but that cannot be correct either, because the balance sheet should balance after every transaction, not just at the end of a sequence of transactions. The only possible solution is to reduce "owner's equity" by the payment:

Assets:		Liabilities	
Cash	7,800	Debt to bank	1,000
Used truck	3,000	Equity	9,800
	10,800		10,800

Second, the $500 payment for the services rendered:

Assets:		Liabilities	
Cash	8,300	Debt to bank	1,000
Used truck	3,000	Equity	10,300
	11,300		11,300

Admittedly, these two balance sheets are not very helpful in showing the relationship between the balance sheet and the income statement. What is needed is a segregation of income items *within the equity account* so that the permanent investment and the transient changes are shown separately. If we take as the period of time the one-day period in which the truck driver was hired and his services were performed, the following balance sheet at the end of the period is much more illuminating:

Assets:		Liabilities	
Cash	8,300	Debt to bank	1,000
Used truck	3,000	Original capital	10,000
		Earnings	300
	11,300		11,300

The important point at present is that *the statement of income or profit and loss is itself a right-hand entry on the balance sheet.*

The balance sheet is a static concept showing the status of a business at a particular instant in time while the income statement describes the results of operations over some period of time: daily, monthly, quarterly, or annually. In a sense, the balance sheet is a photograph, the income statement a motion picture. However, the income statement for a period provides the bridge between the balance sheet at the beginning of the period and the balance sheet at the end of the period because positive income items (revenues) increase the owner's equity account while negative income items (expenses) reduce that account. Logically, the balance sheet is the basic document around which all financial statements are constructed while the income statement is a bridge between successive balance sheets.

Notes

(1) It is important for every law student to understand enough of the rudiments of accounting principles to be able to distinguish between the balance sheet and profit and loss statement set forth above.

(2) Turning to AB Furniture Store partnership financial statements, how would the partners' accounts (shown in the footnote) look if the store had spent $10,000 rather than $8,000 on advertising in the year in question without any increase in sales? How would they look if both A and B had drawn $5,000 each out of the business at the end of the year in question? If the partnership had lost $6,000 rather than showing a profit of $60,000?

(3) While AB Furniture Store has had a smashing first year incomewise, it is not blessed with an overabundance of cash. In this respect

it is like many new, struggling businesses. Do you look at the profit and loss statement or balance sheet to determine the cash position of the business? Why? The year-end balance sheet shows that the bulk of the current assets of the business are tied up in inventory and accounts receivable (amounts representing goods sold on credit). However, the AB Furniture Store, like most businesses, can safely work on the assumption that there will be continuous sales from inventories and payments by customers on account so that a cash crisis is unlikely even though the business's current liabilities significantly exceed its cash on hand.

(4) In addition to the profit and loss statement and balance sheet, it is customary to provide a third financial statement, usually called the "Statement of Changes in Financial Position," which analyzes changes in the various accounts from the end of last year to the end of the current year. Such a statement would have limited usefulness for the AB Furniture Store since, by hypothesis, it started out in business at the beginning of the current year with $100,000 in cash contributed by A, and no other assets or liabilities.

(5) You are advising A about his income tax liability. How much, if any, of the income of the AB Furniture Store does A have to include in his return? What about B? If A is in the 50 per cent bracket how much will this increase his tax bill?

(6) A, despite his desire to limit his financial investment to $100,000, agreed to lend the partnership an additional $25,000, presumably because the store was successful. He therefore has the status both of creditor and of partner. What are his rights as against other general creditors with respect to his loan if the partnership goes under? See UPA § 40.

(7) Also, neither A nor B withdrew any portion of the profit for the year, though, of course, B received his "salary." Why did they do this? Do you think A would object if B proposed to pay himself $10,000 as a distribution of his share of the profits? After all, it is his money, isn't it?

(8) Assets are usually recorded in a business's accounting records at their historical cost with no subsequent adjustment for variations in market value but with an annual charge (called "depreciation") to reflect the gradual "wearing out" or "using up" of the asset. See R. Hamilton, Fundamentals of Modern Business, § 8.6 (1989), for a fuller discussion. The AB Furniture Company has adopted this practice. Assume that AB Furniture Company decides to liquidate and wind up after one year—all the assets are sold, the proceeds used to discharge liabilities, and the balance distributed to the partners. Given the conventions described in this note, can one determine how much will be available for A and B from the balance sheet?

(9) Rather than winding up the AB Furniture Company, A and B decide they will sell the business as an operating entity to a third person, X. Presumably, X is buying the business in order to continue to operate it, not to close it down. Can one use the financial statements set forth above to determine how much X should offer for the business? See R. Hamilton, Fundamentals of Modern Business, Ch. 11. Does this depend in part on whether B is willing to remain as manager?

H. PARTNERSHIP DISSOLUTION

The provisions of the Uniform Partnership Act dealing with dissolution of a partnership are the most complicated sections of the Act. See generally Bromberg, Partnership Dissolution—Causes, Consequences, and Cures, 43 Tex.L.Rev. 631 (1965). Further, unexpected and unplanned dissolution or termination may force the liquidation of a profitable business and have devastating tax consequences. The provisions of the Internal Revenue Code dealing with the liquidation of partnership interests are themselves elaborate and formidable.

In partnership agreements prepared by attorneys it is customary to make careful provision for dissolution, expulsion, and termination. Since the provisions of the UPA dealing with termination and winding up are applicable only in the absence of agreement, their practical applicability is limited to oral partnerships, and others in which for some reason special attention was not focused on dissolution.

It is important to understand the different legal concepts involved in partnership "dissolution" as contrasted with "termination." These concepts are described in UPA §§ 29 and 30. The causes of dissolution are set forth in §§ 31 and 32. A sharp distinction should also be drawn between partnerships terminable at will and partnerships for a definite term or definite undertaking.

Notes

(1) It should be apparent from a careful reading of sections 29, 30, and 31 that the Uniform Partnership Act uses the word "dissolution" in a technical sense that differs from the lay understanding of that word. As a result there is a considerable risk of misunderstanding and confusion when the word "dissolution" is used in the partnership context. For example, in a partnership of three doctors, A, B, and C, assume that C withdraws and A and B continue the same practice at the same location under the same name. Under UPA § 29 has the partnership between A, B and C been dissolved when C withdraws and a "new" partnership between A and B been formed? For a court that refused to apply literally the language of section 29, see Adams v. Jarvis, page 88 infra.

(2) The issue described in note (1) is not entirely academic. For example, leases usually prohibit assignments by tenants without the landlord's consent and may also authorize landlords to cancel the lease if a prohibited assignment occurs. May a landlord use C's withdrawal from the partnership as a ground to evict A and B?

(3) The proposed Revised Uniform Partnership Act eliminates all reference to "dissolution" and uses "cessation of partner status" to describe events similar to those causing "dissolution" under UPA § 31. In a major conceptual simplification, the RUPA proposes to make clear that the "cessation of partner status" by one partner does not necessarily mean that the partnership has "ceased" with respect to the remaining partners. See

A. Bromberg and L. Ribstein, Bromberg and Ribstein on Partnership (1989 Supp.), 125–6.

(4) The UPA does not define what the process of "winding up" consists of, and only inferentially states when it must occur. See UPA § 38(1). The RUPA, on the other hand, proposes a new section that describes the specific events that cause winding up and provides that where such an event occurs "the assets of the partnership shall be applied to discharge its liabilities, and the surplus applied to pay in cash the net amount distributable to the partners." In a winding up, the business may be sold either piece-meal or as a single entity.

(5) Yet another new section of the RUPA provides that where a partner ceases to be a partner but the partnership is not to be wound up, the interest of the withdrawing partner is to be purchased at its "fair market value." The definition of "fair market value" is described below, infra page 88. As is the case with the UPA, the proposed sections of the RUPA are complicated and controversial, and will doubtless create unanticipated problems.

COLLINS v. LEWIS

Texas Court of Civil Appeals, 1955.
283 S.W.2d 258, writ ref'd n.r.e.

HAMBLEN, CHIEF JUSTICE.

This suit was instituted in the District Court of Harris County by the appellants, who, as the owners of a fifty per cent (50%) interest in a partnership known as the L–C Cafeteria, sought a receivership of the partnership business, a judicial dissolution of the partnership, and foreclosure of a mortgage upon appellees' interest in the partnership assets. Appellees denied appellants' right to the relief sought, and filed a cross-action for damages for breach of contract in the event dissolution should be decreed. Appellants' petition for receivership having been denied after a hearing before the court, trial of the issues of dissolution and foreclosure, and of appellees' cross-action, proceeded before the court and a jury. At the conclusion of such trial, the jury, in response to special issues submitted, returned a verdict upon which the trial court entered judgment denying all relief sought by appellants.

The facts are substantially as follows:

In the latter part of 1948 appellee John L. Lewis obtained a commitment conditioned upon adequate financial backing from the Brown–Bellows–Smith Corporation for a lease on the basement space under the then projected San Jacinto Building for the purpose of constructing and operating a large cafeteria therein. Lewis contacted appellant Carr P. Collins, a resident of Dallas, proposing that he (Lewis) would furnish the lease, the experience and management ability for the operation of the cafeteria, and Collins would furnish the money; that all revenue of the business, except for an agreed salary to Lewis, would be applied to the repayment of such money, and that thereafter all profits would be divided equally between Lewis and Collins. These

negotiations * * * culminated in the execution between the building owners, as lessors, and Lewis and Collins, as lessees, of a lease upon such basement space for a term of 30 years. Thereafter Lewis and Collins entered into a partnership agreement to endure throughout the term of the lease contract. This agreement is in part evidenced by a formal contract between the parties, but both litigants concede that the complete agreement is ascertainable only from the verbal understandings and exchanges of letters between the principals. It appears to be undisputed that originally a corporation had been contemplated, and that the change to a partnership was made to gain the advantages which such a relationship enjoys under the internal revenue laws. The substance of the agreement was that Collins was to furnish all of the funds necessary to build, equip, and open the cafeteria for business. Lewis was to plan and supervise such construction, and, after opening for business, to manage the operation of the cafeteria. As a part of this undertaking, he guaranteed that moneys advanced by Collins would be repaid at the rate of at least $30,000, plus interest, in the first year of operation, and $60,000 per year, plus interest, thereafter, upon default of which Lewis would surrender his interest to Collins. In addition Lewis guaranteed Collins against loss to the extent of $100,000.
* * *

Immediately after the lease agreement had been executed Lewis began the preparation of detailed plans and specifications for the cafeteria. Initially Lewis had estimated, and had represented to Collins, that the cost of completing the cafeteria ready for operation would be approximately $300,000. Due to delays on the part of the building owners in completing the building, and delays in procuring the equipment deemed necessary to opening the cafeteria for business, the actual opening did not occur until September 18, 1952, some 2½ years after the lease had been executed. The innumerable problems which arose during that period are in part reflected in the exchange of correspondence between the partners. Such evidence reflects that as to the solution of most of such problems the partners were in entire agreement. It further reflects that such disagreements as did arise were satisfactorily resolved. It likewise appears that the actual costs incurred during that period greatly exceeded the amount previously estimated by Lewis to be necessary. The cause of such increase is disputed by the litigants. Appellants contend that it was brought about largely by the extravagance and mismanagement of appellee Lewis. Appellees contend that it resulted from inflation, increased labor and material costs, caused by the Korean War, and unanticipated but necessary expenses. Whatever may have been the reason it clearly appears that Collins, while expressing concern over the increasing cost, and urging the employment of every possible economy, continued to advance funds and pay expenses, which, by the date of opening for business, had exceeded $600,000.

Collins' concern over the mounting costs of the cafeteria appears to have been considerably augmented by the fact that after opening for business the cafeteria showed expenses considerably in excess of receipts. Upon being informed, shortly after the cafeteria had opened for business, that there existed incurred but unpaid items of cost over and above those theretofore paid, Collins made demand upon Lewis that the cafeteria be placed immediately upon a profitable basis, failing which he (Collins) would advance no more funds for any purpose. There followed an exchange of recriminatory correspondence between the parties, Collins on the one hand charging Lewis with extravagant mismanagement, and Lewis on the other hand charging Collins with unauthorized interference with the management of the business. Futile attempts were made by Lewis to obtain financial backing to buy Collins' interest in the business. Numerous threats were made by Collins to cause Lewis to lose his interest in the business entirely. This suit was filed by Collins in January of 1953.

The involved factual background of this litigation was presented to the jury in a trial which extended over five weeks * * *. At the conclusion of the evidence 23 special issues of fact were submitted to the jury. The controlling issues of fact, as to which a dispute existed, were resolved by the jury in their answers to Issues 1 to 5, inclusive, in which they found that Lewis was competent to manage the business of the L–C Cafeteria; that there is not a reasonable expectation of profit under the continued management of Lewis; that but for the conduct of Collins there would be a reasonable expectation of profit under the continued management of Lewis; that such conduct on the part of Collins was not that of a reasonably prudent person acting under the same or similar circumstances; and that such conduct on the part of Collins materially decreased the earnings of the cafeteria during the first year of its operation. * * * [W]e conclude not only that there is ample support for the findings of the jury which we consider to be controlling, but further that upon the entire record, including such findings, the trial court entered the only proper judgment under the law, and that judgment must be in all things affirmed. * * *

As we understand appellants' position * * * they contend that there is no such thing as an indissoluble partnership; that it is not controlling or even important, in so far as the right to a dissolution is concerned, as to which of the partners is right or wrong in their disputes; and finally, that whenever it is made to appear that the partners are in hopeless disagreement concerning a partnership which has no reasonable expectation of profit, the legal right to dissolution exists. In support of these contentions appellants cite numerous authorities, all of which have been carefully examined. We do not undertake to individually distinguish the authorities cited for the reason that in no case cited by appellants does a situation analogous to that here present exist, namely, that the very facts upon which appellants predicate their right to a dissolution have been found by the jury to have been brought about by appellant Collins' own conduct, in violation of his own contractual obligations.

We agree with appellants' premise that there is no such thing as an indissoluble partnership only in the sense that there always exists the power, as opposed to the right, of dissolution. But legal right to dissolution rests in equity, as does the right to relief from the provisions of any legal contract. The jury finding that there is not a reasonable expectation of profit from the L–C Cafeteria under the continued management of Lewis, must be read in connection with their findings that Lewis is competent to manage the business of L–C Cafeteria, and that but for the conduct of Collins there would be a reasonable expectation of profit therefrom. In our view those are the controlling findings upon the issue of dissolution. It was Collins' obligation to furnish the money; Lewis' to furnish the management, guaranteeing a stated minimum repayment of the money. The jury has found that he was competent, and could reasonably have performed his obligation but for the conduct of Collins. We know of no rule which grants Collins, under such circumstances, the right to dissolution of the partnership. The rule is stated in Karrick v. Hannaman, 168 U.S. 328, 18 S.Ct. 135, 138, 42 L.Ed. 484, as follows: "A court of equity, doubtless, will not assist the partner breaking his contract to procure a dissolution of the partnership, because, upon familiar principles, a partner who has not fully and fairly performed the partnership agreement on his part has no standing in a court of equity to enforce any rights under the agreement." It seems to this Court that the proposition rests upon maxims of equity, too fundamental in our jurisprudence to require quotation.

The basic agreement between Lewis and Collins provided that Collins would furnish money in an amount sufficient to defray the cost of building, equipping and opening the L–C Cafeteria for operation. As a part of the agreement between Lewis and Collins, Lewis executed, and delivered to Collins, a mortgage upon Lewis' interest in the partnership "until the indebtedness incurred by the said Carr P. Collins * * * has been paid in full out of income derived from the said L–C Cafeteria, Houston, Texas." * * *

Collins' right to foreclose [the mortgage on Lewis' interest] depends upon whether or not Lewis has met his basic obligation of repayment at the rate agreed upon. Appellees contend, we think correctly, that he has, in the following manner: the evidence shows that Collins advanced a total of $636,720 for the purpose of building, equipping and opening the cafeteria for business. The proof also shows that Lewis contended that the actual cost exceeded that amount by over $30,000. The litigants differed in regard to such excess, it being Collins' contention that it represented operating expense rather than cost of building, equipping and opening the cafeteria. The jury heard the conflicting proof relative to these contentions, and resolved the question by their answer to Special Issue 20, whereby they found that the minimum cost of building, equipping and opening the cafeteria for operation amounted to $697,603.36. Under the basic agreement of the partners, therefore, this excess was properly Collins' obligation. Upon the refusal of

Collins to pay it, Lewis paid it out of earnings of the business during the first year of its operation. Thus it clearly appears that Lewis met his obligation, and the trial court properly denied foreclosure of the mortgage.

In their brief, appellants repeatedly complain that they should not be forced to endure a continuing partnership wherein there is no reasonable expectation of profit, which they say is the effect of the trial court's judgment. The proper and equitable solution of the differences which arise between partners is never an easy problem, especially where the relationship is as involved as this present one. We do not think it can properly be said, however, that the judgment of the trial court denying appellants the dissolution which they seek forces them to endure a partnership wherein there is no reasonable expectation of profit. We have already pointed out the ever present inherent power, as opposed to the legal right, of any partner to terminate the relationship. Pursuit of that course presents the problem of possible liability for such damages as flow from the breach of contract. The alternative course available to appellants seems clearly legible in the verdict of the jury, whose services in that connection were invoked by appellants.

Judgment affirmed.

Notes

(1) The principal case arose before Texas enacted its version of the Uniform Partnership Act. Would the result have been the same under that Act? See UPA §§ 31(1)(b), 31(2), 38(2).

(2) Assuming the case had arisen under the Uniform Partnership Act, would Collins' rights have been different if he could have dissolved the partnership under § 31(1)(b) rather than under § 32? In what way?

(3) Apparently Collins and Lewis are locked into a partnership that is, as a practical matter, not dissolvable. What happens next?

It is an observable fact of the modern business world that most partnership dissolutions are not followed by a period of winding up and termination even when there is no agreement to continue the business. Rather the partnership business is continued by one or more of the former partners, perhaps with the infusion of new blood, while the interest of any partners falling by the wayside is liquidated by the continuing business in some way. The former partners may consent to the continuation or merely accept the fact that it has continued. The reason for this is that usually the continuation of the business is more sensible, as a matter of simple business economics, than a piece-meal liquidation and sale of the business assets.

CAUBLE v. HANDLER

Texas Court of Civil Appeals, 1973.
503 S.W.2d 362, writ ref'd n.r.e.

BREWSTER, JUSTICE.

This is a suit brought by the administratrix of the estate of a deceased partner against the surviving partner for an accounting of the partnership assets. No jury was involved and the trial court did not file findings of fact and conclusions of law. Tom Handler, the defendant, was the surviving partner and Thomas Cauble was the deceased partner. The partnership was engaged in selling at retail furniture and appliances and each partner owned a 50% interest.

The trial court awarded the plaintiff, the administratrix of the estate of the deceased partner, a judgment against the surviving partner for $20.95 plus six per cent interest thereon from February 2, 1973, the date of the judgment. The judgment also awarded the court appointed auditor a fee in the sum of $1,800.00 for his services in auditing the partnership accounts, taxed the item as court costs, and then taxed the entire court costs against plaintiff. It is from this judgment that plaintiff is appealing. We will refer herein to the parties as they appeared in the court below.

We reverse and remand the case for a new trial.

The plaintiff's first point is that the trial court erred in basing its judgment upon the book value of the partnership assets that were arbitrarily established by defendant. Her eighth point of error is that the court erred in refusing to consider the cash market value of the partnership assets in arriving at its judgment.

We sustain both of these points of error.

It is apparent from the record that the trial court determined the value of the partnership inventory by using the cost or book value thereof. Thomas Cauble died on May 18, 1971. * * * Handler kept the partnership books and took a physical inventory that was used by the partnership tax man in preparing [the] final partnership income tax return. In preparing the inventory Handler testified that he priced each item in the inventory "According to the invoices, according to cost." Again he stated: "Take the count first and then you * * * go back to the invoice and pick up the amount."

The value of the partnership inventory, arrived at as above indicated, was used by the accountant in preparing the final income tax return and was used by the court in determining the value of the plaintiff's interest in the partnership at the date of Cauble's death.

The court erred when he used the cost price or book value of the partnership assets in determining the value of the inventory. The following is from the opinion in the case of Johnson v. Braden, 286 S.W. 2d 671 (San Antonio, Tex.Civ.App., 1956, no writ hist.), at page 672: "The judgment must be reversed. Market values of the company assets are wholly absent from the record, and Johnson, on cross-examination, demonstrated that the plaintiff's audit was based on book values. *It should have been based on market value.*" (Emphasis ours.)

See also * * * Hurst v. Hurst, 1 Ariz.App. 227, 401 P.2d 232 (1965). This Hurst case holds that book values are simply arbitrary values and cannot be used. The case also holds that the amount for which the partnership assets were sold four years after the date of dissolution is also not proper evidence to be considered on the issue of market value of the partnership property at date of dissolution. * * *

Much of plaintiff's argument under her first three points of error is devoted to her contention that the trial court erred in failing and refusing to allow her a share of the profit made by Handler by continuing the partnership business between date of dissolution and date of judgment.

We sustain this contention.

The undisputed evidence shows that Handler continued to operate and to control the partnership business after the death of Cauble and down to the trial date, and that he used and sold the assets of the partnership during all that period. The record does not show that this was done with the consent of the administratrix of the deceased's estate.

Exhibit E of the court appointed auditor's report was offered into evidence and it showed that during the period from May 19, 1971, to May 21, 1972, Handler made a net profit of $40,163.42 out of operating the partnership business after dissolution. The fact that this net profit was made is undisputed. As demonstrated above this auditor's report was legitimate evidence of the amount of those profits.

The defendant * * * admits that plaintiff tried this case on the theory that she was entitled to recover, after the accounting, one-half of the value of the partnership assets, plus a share of the profits from the date of Cauble's death to date of judgment.

The trial court, in its judgment, refused to allow the plaintiff to recover one-half of the profits that were made by Handler after the dissolution of the partnership by his continued operation of the business. Instead the trial court awarded plaintiff a recovery of some interest in the amount of $3,764.89.

It is section 38(1) of [UPA] that gave the representative of the estate of the deceased partner the right to elect, if she so desired, to have the partnership assets liquidated, the debts paid, and the share of each partner in the surplus paid to him in cash.

The plaintiff in this case did not elect to have this done.

If that election is made it many times results in the sacrifice of going concern values. See "Law of Partnership" by Crane and Bromberg, page 474, note 43.

The following quotation explains the several elections that were open to the plaintiff under the fact situation that we have here. It is from "Law of Partnership" by Crane and Bromberg, Section 86(c), pages 495–496, and is as follows:

"If a partnership is seasonably wound up after dissolution, profits and losses during the liquidation are shared by the partners in proportion to their pre-dissolution ratios, unless they have agreed otherwise. * * *

"*The situation changes if the business is not wound up, but continued, whether with or without agreement.* In either case, the noncontinuing partner (or his representative) has a first election between two basic alternatives, either of which can be enforced in an action for an accounting. He can force a liquidation, taking his part of the proceeds and thus sharing in profits and losses after dissolution. Alternatively, he can permit the business to continue (or accept the fact that it has continued) and claim as a creditor (though subordinate to outside creditors) the value of his interest at dissolution. This * * * means he is unaffected by later changes in those values. *If he takes the latter route, he has a second election to receive in addition* either interest * * * *or profits from date of dissolution.* This second election shields him from losses, * * *

"The second election may seem one-sided. It serves as 'a species of compulsion * * * to those continuing the business * * * to hasten its orderly winding up.' In part it is compensation to the outgoing partner for his liability on partnership obligations existing at dissolution; this liability continues until satisfaction, which would normally occur in the process of winding up. * * *

"The second election rests partly on the use of the outgoing partner's assets in the conduct of the business * * * his right to profits ends when the value of his interest is properly paid to him." (Emphasis ours.)

[UPA] Section 42 * * * gives the representative of the estate of a deceased partner a right to share in the profits, if he elects to do so, if the other partner continues to operate the business after dissolution.

The great weight of authority is to the effect that Sec. 42, giving the option to take profits to the non-continuing partner is applicable regardless of whether the business is continued with or without the consent of the non-continuing partner or the representative of his estate. For a full discussion of this see the law review article in 63 Yale Law Journal 709, entitled "Profit Rights and Creditors' Priorities After a Partner's Death or Retirement: Section 42 of the UPA" and the additional article on this subject in 67 Harvard Law Review 1271.

It is manifestly clear that the plaintiff in this case elected, as she had a right to do under Sec. 42 to have the value of Cauble's partnership interest at the date of dissolution ascertained and to receive from the surviving partner, Handler, as an ordinary creditor, an amount equal to the value of Cauble's interest in the dissolved partnership at date of dissolution, plus the profits attributable to his right in the property of the dissolved partnership.

The following proceedings that occurred during the trial show that this election was made by plaintiff:

"THE COURT: You think they're making an election for the profits, is that correct, sir?

"MR. OWENS: The way they've been introducing their evidence and talking here I presume they have.

"MR. SCHATTMAN: That's correct.

"THE COURT: If you have not done so that is your election?

"MR. SCHATTMAN: Right.

"THE COURT: All right, then that disposes of that point."

Although the undisputed evidence showed that Handler made over $40,163.42 by operating the partnership business after dissolution the Court refused to allow plaintiff to recover from Handler the Cauble estate's share of those profits, which plaintiff had a right to do. In lieu of profits, which plaintiff elected to recover, the Court awarded her six per cent interest on what he found to be the cost or book value of the Cauble interest in the partnership at date of dissolution. This interest amounted to $3,764.89, which sum was considerably less than a one-half interest in the $40,163.42 in profits that Handler made out of his operation of the partnership business after dissolution.

This error was obviously prejudicial to plaintiff.

In plaintiff's fifth point of error she contends that the trial court erred in taxing all the costs incurred in connection with the accounting case, including the court appointed auditor's fee of $1,800.00, against the plaintiff. * * *

The record does not reveal the court's reason for taxing all the court costs, including the $1,800.00 court appointed auditor's fee, against just one of the two partners involved in this accounting suit. * * *

We recognize that the trial court does have a broad discretion in taxing the costs in a case like this and there are occasions where the costs have been taxed against just one partner. But, as a general rule, the costs that are incurred in an accounting case are ordered paid out of the partnership estate. This results in the costs being paid by the partners in proportion to their interest in the business.

It would seem that in the ordinary case both partners would benefit by having the state of the account between them legally adjudicated so that the partnership can be terminated. One partner is not obligated to accept the adverse party's word for the state of the partnership account. * * *

Reversed and remanded for a new trial.

Notes

(1) In addition to the basic elections provided by the Uniform Partnership Act described in the principal case, the Act also provides answers for a number of other questions that may arise when a partnership business is simply continued after dissolution. For example:

(a) What are the rights of creditors of the old partnership with respect to the assets of the continuing business? See UPA § 41.

(b) In view of the agency that exists between partners, what must a retiring partner do to avoid liability for subsequent partnership obligations? See UPA § 35(1)(b).

(c) If a creditor knows that a partner has retired and deals with the successor partnership, does that release the retired partner from preretirement partnership obligations? See UPA § 36(2).

(2) The proposed Revised Uniform Partnership Act preserves the § 38(1) right of a withdrawing partner to compel a winding up but eliminates entirely the § 42 election. Section 32 of this proposed statute substitutes a more precise definition of what the partner is to receive when the partnership is not wound up: the "fair market value" of the partner's interest is defined to be "the amount that would have been distributable to that person in a winding up of the partnership." That amount, in turn, is to be the greater of "(1) liquidation value or (2) value based on sale of the entire business as a going concern without the withdrawing partner" on the basis "of the price that would be paid between a willing buyer and a willing seller, neither being under any compulsion to buy or sell, with the knowledge of all relevant facts." Finally, "[i]n the case of a partner in a partnership in which capital is a material income-producing factor, regularly scheduled distributions shall continue to be made to the former partner or his successor in interest." A. Bromberg and L. Ribstein, Bromberg and Ribstein on Partnership (1989 Supp.) at 153. Is this a satisfactory substitute for UPA §§ 38(1) and 42? For example, what about a partnership that makes substantial distributions on an erratic basis?

(3) In general, the dissolution provisions of the UPA are complicated because they deal with a number of possible variations and a number of possible problems. They are also arranged in a sequence which complicates the process of tracing through how each specific situation should be handled. The provisions of the proposed RUPA are a modest improvement in this regard.

ADAMS v. JARVIS

Supreme Court of Wisconsin, 1964.
23 Wis.2d 453, 127 N.W.2d 400.

Action for declaratory judgment construing a medical partnership agreement between three doctors. Plaintiff-respondent withdrew from the partnership seven years after it was formed. * * *

The dispute concerns the extent of the plaintiff's right to share in partnership assets, specifically accounts receivable. The relevant portions of the agreement provide:

"12. Books of Account. Proper books of account shall be kept by said partners and entries made therein of all matters, transactions, and things as are usually entered in books of account kept by persons engaged in the same or similar business. Such books and all partnership letters, papers and documents shall be kept at the firm's office and each partner shall at all times have access to examine, copy, and take extracts from the same.

"13. Fiscal Year—Share of Profits and Losses. The partnership fiscal year shall coincide with the calendar year. Net profits and losses of the partnership shall be divided among the individuals in the same proportion as their capital interests in the partnership, except as hereinafter provided for partners who become incapacitated or have withdrawn from the partnership, or the estates of the deceased partners. * * *

"15. Conditions of Termination. Partnership shall not terminate under certain conditions. The incapacity, withdrawal or death of a partner shall not terminate this partnership. Such partner, or the estate or heirs of a deceased partner shall continue to participate in partnership profits and losses, as provided in this agreement, but shall not participate in management, the making of partnership decisions, or any professional matters. On the happening of any of the above events, the books of the partnership shall not be closed until the end of the partnership fiscal year.

"16. Withdrawal. No withdrawal from the firm shall be effective until at least thirty (30) days have elapsed from the date on which written notice of such intention is given the other partners by registered mail to their last known address.

"As used herein 'withdrawal' shall refer to any situation in which a partner leaves the partnership, at a time when said partnership is not dissolving, pursuant to a written agreement of the parties to do so. The withdrawing partner shall be entitled to receive from the continuing partners the following:

"(1) Any balance standing to his credit on the books of the partnership;

"(2) That proportion of the partnership profits to which he was entitled by this agreement in the fiscal year of his withdrawal, which the period from the beginning of such year to the effective date of withdrawal shall bear to the whole of the then current fiscal year. Such figure shall be ascertained as soon as practicable after the close of the current fiscal year and shall be payable as soon as the amount thereof is ascertained. All drawings previously made during the then fiscal year shall be first charged against the share in net partnership profits as above computed. If there shall have been losses for such fiscal year, or overdrawings, or losses and the whole of any overdrawings or loans, shall be determined and charged against his capital account, and if in excess thereof, shall be paid by him or his estate promptly after the close of the fiscal year, plus

"(3) The amount of his capital account on the effective date of his withdrawal (after deduction of any losses required to be paid in subdivision (2) above).

"In the event such withdrawing partner dies prior to receiving any or all of the above payments, his personal representative, heirs or assigns shall receive the same payments at the same time as those to which he would have been entitled by the terms had he lived. Payment of the items set forth in subdivisions (1) and (3) above shall be made according to and evidenced by a promissory note, executed by the remaining partners, payable in twelve (12) equal quarterly installments, the first of which shall be payable at the end of the six (6) months following the effective date of such withdrawal. Acceleration of said note shall be permitted at the sole discretion of the two remaining partners. Such note shall bear interest at Two (2) Per Cent, payable with each installment.

"It is further agreed that in the event of the withdrawal of any partner or partners, any and all accounts receivable for any current year and any and all years past shall remain the sole possession and property of the remaining member or members of THE TOMAHAWK CLINIC. ＊ ＊ ＊

"18. Dissolution. Should this partnership be dissolved by agreement of the parties, all accounts and notes shall be liquidated and all firm assets sold or divided between the partners at agreed valuations. The books of the partnership shall then be closed and distribution made in proportion to the capital interests of the partners as shown by the partnership books. No drawings should be paid once the partnership has begun to wind up its affairs, although liquidating dividends based on estimates may be paid from time to time. No dissolution shall be effective until the end of the then fiscal year, and until ninety (90) days have elapsed from the date on which written agreement to such dissolution shall have been executed by the parties hereto.

"This agreement shall be binding not only upon the parties hereto, but also upon their heirs, executors, administrators, successors, and assigns, and the wives of said partners have signed this agreement as witnesses, after being advised of the terms of this agreement."

The trial court decided that the withdrawal of the plaintiff worked a dissolution of the partnership under [UPA §§ 29, 30]; that the partnership assets should be liquidated and applied to the payment of partnership interests according to the scheme set forth in [UPA § 38] for the reason that paragraphs 15 and 16 of the partnership agreement did not apply in the case of a statutory dissolution; that plaintiff's interest was one-third of the net worth, including therein accounts receivable of the partnership as of May 31, 1961; that plaintiff should recover from defendants the value of his partnership interest; and gave judgment accordingly, but retained jurisdiction for supplementary proceedings. Defendants appeal.

BEILFUSS, JUSTICE.

1. Does a withdrawal of a partner constitute a dissolution of the partnership under [UPA §§ 29, 30], notwithstanding a partnership agreement to the contrary?

2. Is plaintiff, as withdrawing partner, entitled to a share of the accounts receivable?

WITHDRAWAL

* * * [The court quotes UPA §§ 29, 30.]

The partnership agreement as set forth above (paragraph 15) specifically provides that the partnership shall not terminate by the withdrawal of a partner. We conclude the parties clearly intended that even though a partner withdrew, the partnership and the partnership business would continue for the purposes for which it was organized. Paragraph 18 of the agreement provides for a dissolution upon agreement of the parties in the sense that the partnership would cease to function as such subject to winding up of its affairs.

While the withdrawal of a partner works a dissolution of the partnership under the statute as to the withdrawing partner, it does not follow that the rights and duties of remaining partners are similarly affected. The agreement contemplates a partnership would continue to exist between the remaining partners even though the personnel constituting the partnership was changed.

Persons with professional qualifications commonly associate in business partnerships. The practice of continuing the operation of the partnership business, even though there are some changes in partnership personnel, is also common. The reasons for an agreement that a medical partnership should continue without disruption of the services rendered is self evident. If the partnership agreement provides for continuation, sets forth a method of paying the withdrawing partner his agreed share, does not jeopardize the rights of creditors, the agreement is enforceable. The statute does not specifically regulate this type of withdrawal with a continuation of the business. The statute should not be construed to invalidate an otherwise enforceable contract entered into for a legitimate purpose.

The provision for withdrawal is in effect a type of winding up of the partnership without the necessity of discontinuing the day-to-day business. [UPA § 38] contemplates a discontinuance of the day-to-day business but does not forbid other methods of winding up a partnership.

The agreement does provide that Dr. Adams shall no longer actively participate and further provides for winding up the affairs insofar as his interests are concerned. In this sense his withdrawal does constitute a dissolution. We conclude, however, that when the plaintiff, Dr. Adams, withdrew, the partnership was not wholly dissolved so as to require complete winding up of its affairs, but continued to exist under the terms of the agreement. The agreement does not offend the statute and is valid.

ACCOUNTS RECEIVABLE

* * * [The Court quotes UPA § 38(1).]

The trial court concluded that the withdrawal constituted a statutory dissolution; that partnership assets shall be liquidated pursuant to the statute and that the plaintiff was entitled to a one-third interest in the accounts receivable.

[UPA § 38(1)], applies only "unless otherwise agreed." The distribution should therefore be made pursuant to the agreement.

Paragraphs 15 and 16 of the contract as set forth above provide for the withdrawal of a partner and the share to which he is entitled. Subject to limitations not material here, paragraph 16 provides that a withdrawing partner shall receive (1) any balance to his credit on partnership books, (2) his proportionate share of profits calculated on a fiscal year basis, and (3) his capital account as of the date of his withdrawal. Paragraph 16 further provides that in event of withdrawal "any and all accounts receivable for any current year and any and all years past shall remain the sole possession and property of the remaining member or members of THE TOMAHAWK CLINIC."

The plaintiff contends that provision of the agreement denying him a share of the accounts receivable works a forfeiture and is void as being against public policy.

We conclude the parties to the agreement intended accounts receivable to be restricted to customer or patient accounts receivable.

The provision of the agreement is clear and unambiguous. There is nothing in the record to suggest the plaintiff's bargaining position was so unequal in the negotiations leading up to the agreement that the provision should be declared unenforceable upon the grounds of public policy. Legitimate business and good will considerations are consistent with a provision retaining control and ownership of customer accounts receivable in an active functioning professional medical partnership. We hold the provision on accounts receivable enforceable.

Because of our determination that the partnership agreement is valid and enforceable the judgment of the trial court insofar as it decrees a dissolution of the partnership and a one-third division of the accounts receivable to the plaintiff must be reversed and remanded to the trial court with directions to enter judgment in conformity with this opinion.

The trial court properly retained jurisdiction for the purpose of granting supplementary relief to plaintiff to enforce a distribution to the plaintiff. The trial court may conduct such proceedings as are necessary to effectuate a distribution pursuant to the agreement.

The parties have stipulated that the plaintiff ceased to be an active partner as of June 1, 1961. The agreement provides that the partnership fiscal year shall coincide with the calendar year. It further provides that his share of the partnership profits upon withdrawal shall be calculated upon the whole year and in proportion to his participation of the whole fiscal year. He is, therefore, entitled to $5/12$ of $1/3$, or $5/36$ of the profits for the fiscal year ending December 31, 1961.

Such of the accounts receivable as were collected during the year 1961 do constitute a part of the profits for 1961. The plaintiff had no part of the management of the partnership after June 1, 1961; however, his eventual distributive share of profits is dependent, in some degree, upon the management of the business affairs and performance of the continuing partners for the remainder of the fiscal year. Under these circumstances the continuing partners stand in a fiduciary relationship to the withdrawing partner and are obligated to conduct the business in a good faith manner including a good faith effort to liquidate the accounts receivable consistent with good business practices.

Judgment reversed with directions to conduct supplementary proceedings to determine distributive share of plaintiff and then enter judgment in conformity with this opinion.

Notes

(1) If the business is to be continued after dissolution, a critical problem that must be addressed in the partnership agreement is how the interest of the departed partners is to be liquidated. As the principal case holds, such an agreement will be enforced in lieu of rights otherwise given by statute in the absence of agreement.

(2) What was the potential problem with year-end accounts receivable that caused the court in the next-to-last paragraph of its opinion to refer to the partners' fiduciary duties to each other?

(3) The manner of liquidating a former partner's interest in The Tomahawk Clinic set forth in the partnership agreement probably worked reasonably fairly, given the economics of most medical practices. Would you recommend that similar provisions be used in say, a law partnership specializing in plaintiff personal injury litigation?

(4) A drafter of a continuation agreement must resolve several basic questions that are not unlike the problems faced by a drafter of share transfer restrictions in closely held corporations. See, pp. 501–506, infra. Generally, fair treatment of the retiring interest is the ultimate aim; there is often an element of Russian roulette in drafting these provisions since clauses are usually reciprocal and it cannot be determined in advance which partner will be the first to withdraw. How were the following matters handled by the agreement in Adams v. Jarvis?

(a) First, a determination must be made as to the types of dissolution which trigger the clause. The most common provision covers death or retirement, but other types of dissolution, such as expulsion or bankruptcy may also be covered.

(b) Second, what is to happen to the outgoing interest? There are several alternatives which have widely varying income tax consequences. The other partners may simply purchase the interest. They may arrange to have the interest purchased by an acceptable third person. Or the partnership may purchase the interest. Or the assets of the partnership may be sold as a unit to the remaining partners who are to continue the business. Or the outgoing interest may continue to share in future earnings on a more or less permanent basis.

(c) Third, is the disposition to be optional or mandatory from the standpoint of the remaining partners? In other words, may the remaining partners elect to terminate, ignoring the provision in the agreement?

(d) Fourth, how much is the withdrawing interest to receive? Valuation is usually a complex task and there is no one best method. Much depends on the nature of the business. Appraisal of each asset by an independent appraiser may be most appropriate in the case of a real estate partnership, but hopelessly inadequate in a law firm where most of the assets are represented by contingent work in progress. What would be a fair basis for valuing an interest in a large law firm?

The following suggestions cover the most popular techniques of valuation:

   (i) A fixed sum, usually with provision for periodic adjustment;

  (ii) Book value, perhaps with supplemental appraisals of real estate, marketable securities, and inventory (which may be written down for tax purposes);

 (iii) Appraisal;

 (iv) Capitalization of earnings in the past;

  (v) A fraction of future earnings over a specified period of time, often with provision of specific accounting rules to determine profits;

 (vi) Negotiation after the fact, perhaps with a provision for arbitration if agreement cannot be reached; and

(vii) A right of first refusal to meet the best offer obtainable elsewhere by the withdrawing interest.

(e) Fifth, is the payment to be made in a lump sum, or over a period of time?

(f) Sixth, how is the cash to be raised to meet the required payments? If a lump sum payment is required, life insurance may be the answer, or the business may create a reserve by regularly setting aside a portion of earnings, despite the unfavorable tax consequences. Borrowing may be possible. If the payment is to be made over a period of time, funds may be generated from the regular operations of the business.

(g) Seventh, may the retiring interest compete with the partnership interest? If not, how much of the consideration is to be allocated to the covenant not to compete? This allocation is important for Federal income tax purposes.

(h) Eighth, should the retiring interest have power to inspect books and records or demand an audit?

(5) Even where it is desired to wind up a business on the dissolution of a partnership, e.g. on the retirement of a senior partner, it may be desirable to establish a pattern for the liquidation in the agreement rather

than relying on the skeletal provisions of the UPA. In this way, property may be distributed as desired, good will realized, etc.

MEEHAN v. SHAUGHNESSY

Supreme Court of Massachusetts, 1989.
404 Mass. 419, 535 N.E.2d 1255.

Before HENNESSEY, C.J., and WILKINS, LIACOS, LYNCH and O'CONNOR, JJ.

HENNESSEY, CHIEF JUSTICE.

* * * Parker, Coulter, Daley & White is a large partnership which specializes in litigation on behalf of both defendants and plaintiffs. Meehan joined the firm in 1959, and became a partner in 1963; his practice focuses primarily on complex tort litigation, such as product liability and aviation defense work. Boyle joined Parker Coulter in 1971, and became a partner in 1980; he has concentrated on plaintiffs' work. Both have developed outstanding reputations as trial lawyers in the Commonwealth. Meehan and Boyle each were active in the management of Parker Coulter. They each served, for example, on the partnership's executive committee and, as members of this committee, were responsible for considering and making policy recommendations to the general partnership. Boyle was also in charge of the "plaintiffs department" within the firm, which managed approximately 350 cases. At the time of their leaving, Meehan's interest in the partnership was 6% and Boyle's interest was 4.8%.

Meehan and Boyle had become dissatisfied at Parker Coulter. On June 27, 1984, after unsuccessfully opposing the adoption of a firm-wide pension plan, the two first discussed the possibility of leaving Parker Coulter. Another partner met with them to discuss leaving but told them their proposed firm would not be suitable for his type of practice. On July 1, Meehan and Boyle decided to leave Parker Coulter and form their own partnership.

Having decided to establish a new firm, Meehan and Boyle then focused on whom they would invite to join them. The two spoke with Cohen, a junior partner and the de facto head of Parker Coulter's appellate department, about joining the new firm as a partner. They arranged to meet with her on July 5, and told her to keep their conversations confidential. The day before the July 5 meeting, Boyle prepared two lists of what he considered to be his cases. The lists contained approximately eighty to 100 cases, and for each case indicated the status, fee arrangement, estimated settlement value, and potential fee to [the new firm]. Boyle gave these lists to Cohen for her to examine in preparation for the July 5 meeting.

At the July 5 meeting, Meehan and Boyle outlined to Cohen their plans for the new firm, including their intent to offer positions to [associate Steven H.] Schafer, Peter Black (Black), and Warren Fitzgerald (Fitzgerald), who were associates at Parker Coulter. Boyle stated that he hoped the clients he had been representing would go with him to the new firm; Meehan said he would take the aviation work he had at Parker Coulter with him. Both stated that they felt others at Parker Coulter were getting paid as much as or more than they were, but were not working as hard. Cohen decided to consider the offer from Meehan and Boyle, and agreed to keep the plans confidential until formal notice of the separation was given to the partnership. Although the partnership agreement required a notice period of three months, the three decided to give only thirty days' notice. They chose to give shorter notice to avoid what they believed would be an uncomfortable situation at the firm, and possible retaliatory measures by the partnership. Meehan and Boyle had agreed that they would leave Parker Coulter on December 31, 1984, the end of Parker Coulter's fiscal year.

During the first week of August, Cohen accepted the offer to join the new firm as a partner. [The new firm was then named Meehan, Boyle & Cohen, P.C. (MBC).] Her primary reason for leaving Parker Coulter to join MBC was that she enjoyed working with Meehan and Boyle.

In July, 1984, Boyle offered a position at MBC to Schafer, who worked closely with Boyle in the plaintiffs department. Boyle told Schafer to organize his cases, and "to keep an eye towards cases to be resolved in 1985 and to handle these cases for resolution in 1985 rather than 1984." He also told Schafer to make a list of cases he could take with him to MBC, and to keep all their conversations confidential.

Late in the summer of 1984, Meehan asked Black and Fitzgerald to become associates at MBC. Fitzgerald had worked with Meehan in the past on general defense work, and Black worked with Meehan, particularly in the aviation area. Meehan was instrumental in attracting Black, who had previously been employed by U.S. Aviation Underwriters (USAU), to Parker Coulter. Although Black had already considered leaving Parker Coulter, he was concerned about whether USAU would follow him to a small firm like MBC, and wanted to discuss his leaving Parker Coulter with the vice president of USAU. In October, 1984, Black and Meehan met with the USAU vice president in New York. They later received assurances from him that he would be interested in sending USAU business to the proposed new firm. Black then accepted the offer to join MBC. Fitzgerald also accepted. Schafer, Black, and Fitzgerald were the only associates Meehan, Boyle, and Cohen approached concerning the new firm.

During July and the following months, Meehan, Boyle, and Cohen made arrangements for their new practice apart from seeking associates. They began to look for office space and retained an architect. In early fall, a lease was executed on behalf of MBC in the name of MBC Realty Trust. They also retained an attorney to advise them on the formation of the new firm.

Boyle was assigned the task of arranging financing. He prepared a personal financial statement and obtained a bank loan in September,

1984. During that fall, two other loans were made on MBC's credit. Cohen, at the request of an accountant, had been trying to develop projections of MBC's expected revenue in order to obtain long-term financing. The accountant requested a list of cases with indications as to MBC's expected fees for this purpose. In November, Boyle updated and revised the list of cases he expected to take to MBC which he had compiled in July. The November list contained approximately 135 cases. The increase in Boyle's caseload from July to November resulted in part from the departure of a Parker Coulter attorney in early September, 1984. Boyle was in charge of reassigning the cases this attorney worked on. Although another attorney requested transfer of some of these cases, Boyle assigned none to that attorney, and assigned most of the cases to himself and Schafer. Meehan, Cohen, and Black also prepared lists of cases which they anticipated they would remove, and included the potential fee each case would generate for MBC.

Toward the end of November, Boyle prepared form letters to send to clients and referring attorneys as soon as Parker Coulter was notified of the separation. He also drafted a form for the clients to return to him at his home address authorizing him to remove cases to MBC. An outside agency typed these materials on Parker Coulter's letterhead. Schafer prepared similar letters and authorization forms.

While they were planning their departure, from July to approximately December, Meehan, Boyle, Cohen, Schafer, Black, and Fitzgerald all continued to work full schedules. They settled cases appropriately, made reasonable efforts to avoid continuances, tried cases, and worked on discovery. Each generally maintained his or her usual standard of performance.

Meehan and Boyle had originally intended to give notice to Parker Coulter on December 1, 1984. Rumors of their leaving, however, began to circulate before then. During the period from July to early fall, different Parker Coulter partners approached Meehan individually on three separate occasions and asked him if the rumors about his leaving were true. On each occasion, Meehan denied that he was leaving. On November 30, 1984, a partner, Maurice F. Shaughnessy (Shaughnessy), approached Boyle and asked him whether Meehan and Boyle intended to leave the firm. Shaughnessy interpreted Boyle's evasive response as an affirmation of the rumors. Meehan and Boyle then decided to distribute their notice that afternoon, which stated, as their proposed date for leaving, December 31, 1984. A notice was left on the desk of each partner. When Meehan, Boyle, and Cohen gave their notice, the atmosphere at Parker Coulter became "tense, emotional and unpleasant, if not adversarial."

On December 3, the Parker Coulter partners appointed a separation committee and decided to communicate with "important sources of business" to tell them of the separation and of Parker Coulter's desire to continue representing them. Meehan and Boyle asked their partners for financial information about the firm, discussed cases and clients with them, and stated that they intended to communicate with clients and referring attorneys on the cases in which they were involved. Sometime during the week of December 3, the partners sent Boyle a list of cases and requested that he identify the cases he intended to take with him.

Boyle had begun to make telephone calls to referring attorneys on Saturday morning, December 1. He had spoken with three referring attorneys by that date and told them of his departure from Parker Coulter and his wish to continue handling their cases. On December 3, he mailed his previously typed letters and authorization forms, and by the end of the first two weeks of December he had spoken with a majority of referring attorneys, and had obtained authorizations from a majority of clients whose cases he planned to remove to MBC.

Although the partners previously were aware of Boyle's intention to communicate with clients, they did not become aware of the extent of his communications until December 12 or 13. Boyle did not provide his partners with the list they requested of cases he intended to remove until December 17. Throughout December, Meehan, Boyle, and Schafer continued to communicate with referring attorneys on cases they were currently handling to discuss authorizing their transfer to MBC. On December 19, 1984, one of the partners accepted on behalf of Parker Coulter the December 31 departure date and waived the three-month notice period provided for by the partnership agreement. Meehan, Boyle, and Cohen formalized their arrangement as a professional corporation on January 1, 1985.

MBC removed a number of cases from Parker Coulter. Of the roughly 350 contingent fee cases pending at Parker Coulter in 1984, Boyle, Schafer, and Meehan removed approximately 142 to MBC. Meehan advised Parker Coulter that the 4,000 asbestos cases he had attracted to the firm would remain, and he did not seek to take certain other major clients. Black removed thirty-five cases; Fitzgerald removed ten; and Cohen removed three. A provision in the partnership agreement in effect at the separation provided that a voluntarily retiring partner, upon the payment of a "fair charge," could remove "any matter in which the partnership had been representing a client who came to the firm through the personal effort or connection of the retiring partner," subject to the right of the client to stay with the firm. Approximately thirty-nine of the 142 contingent fee cases removed to MBC came to Parker Coulter at least in part through the personal efforts or connections of Parker Coulter attorneys other than Meehan, Boyle, Cohen, Schafer, Black, or Fitzgerald. In all the cases removed to MBC, however, MBC attorneys had direct, existing relationships with the clients. In all the removed cases, MBC attorneys communicated with the referring attorney or with the client directly by telephone or letter. In each case, the client signed an authorization.

Schafer subsequently separated his practice from MBC's. He took with him a number of the cases which had been removed from Parker Coulter to MBC.

Based on these findings, the judge determined that the MBC attorneys did not manipulate cases, or handle them differently as a result of their decision to leave Parker Coulter. He also determined that Parker Coulter failed to prove that the clients whose cases were removed did not freely choose to have MBC represent them. Consequently, he concluded that Meehan and Boyle neither violated the partnership agreement nor breached the fiduciary duty they owed to their partners. In addition, the judge also found that Meehan and Boyle did not tortiously interfere with Parker Coulter's relations with clients or employees. He similarly rejected Parker Coulter's claims against Cohen and Schafer. * * *

The Parker Coulter partnership agreement provided for rights on a dissolution caused by the will of a partner which are different from those [UPA] provides.[14] Because going concerns are typically destroyed in the dissolution process of liquidation and windup, see J. Crane & A. Bromberg, Partnership 419 (1968), the agreement minimizes the impact of this process. The agreement provides for an allocation to the departing partner of a share of the firm's current net income, and a return of his or her capital contributions. In addition, the agreement also recognizes that a major asset of a law firm is the expected fees it will receive from unfinished business currently being transacted. Instead of assigning a value to the departing partner's interest in this unfinished business, or waiting for the unfinished business to be "wound up" and liquidated, which is the method of division [UPA] provides, the agreement gives the partner the right to remove any case which came to the firm "through the personal effort or connection" of the partner, if the partner compensates the dissolved partnership "for the services to and expenditures for the client."[15] Once the partner has removed a case, the agreement provides that the partner is entitled to retain all future fees in the case, with the exception of the "fair charge" owed to the dissolved firm.[16]

14. [By the Court] [UPA] is intended to be a type of "form contract." See 1 A.R. Bromberg & L.E. Ribstein, Partnership § 1.01(d) (1988). Parties are therefore allowed the freedom to provide for rights at dissolution and during the wind-up period which are different from those provided for in the statute. See [UPA] § 38(1).

15. [By the Court] The agreement expressly protects a client's right to choose his or her attorney, by providing that the right to remove a case is "subject to the right of the client to direct that the matter be retained by the continuing firm of remaining partners."

16. [By the Court] The agreement provides that this "fair charge" is a "receiva-ble account of the earlier partnership . . . and [is] divided between the remaining partners and the retiring partner on the basis of which they share in the profits of the firm at the time of the withdrawal." This fair charge is thus treated as an asset of the former partnership. Because the partnership, upon the receipt of the fair charge, gives up all future rights to income from the removed case, the partnership's collective interest in the case is effectively "wound up." The fair charge, therefore, is a method of valuing the partnership's unfinished business as it relates to the removed case.

Although the provision in the partnership agreement which divides the dissolved firm's unfinished business does not expressly apply to the removal of cases which did not come to Parker Coulter through the efforts of the departing partner, we believe that the parties intended this provision to apply to these cases also. We interpret this provision to cover these additional cases for two reasons. First, according to the Canons of Ethics and Disciplinary Rules Regulating the Practice of Law, a lawyer may not participate in an agreement which restricts the right of a lawyer to practice law after the termination of a relationship created by the agreement. One reason for this rule is to protect the public. The strong public interest in allowing clients to retain counsel of their choice outweighs any professional benefits derived from a restrictive covenant. Thus, the Parker Coulter partners could not restrict a departing partner's right to remove any clients who freely choose to retain him or her as their legal counsel. Second, we believe the agreement's carefully drawn provisions governing dissolution and the division of assets indicate the partners' strong intent not to allow the provisions of [the UPA] concerning liquidation and windup to govern any portion of the dissolved firm's unfinished business. Therefore, based on the partners' intent, and on the prohibition against restrictive covenants between attorneys, we interpret the agreement to provide that, upon the payment of a fair charge, any case may be removed regardless of whether the case came to the firm through the personal efforts of the departing partner. This privilege to remove, as is shown in our later discussion, is of course dependent upon the partner's compliance with fiduciary obligations.

Under the agreement, therefore, a partner who separates his or her practice from that of the firm receives (1) the right to his or her capital contribution, (2) the right to a share of the net income to which the dissolved partnership is currently entitled, and (3) the right to a portion of the firm's unfinished business, and in exchange gives up all other rights in the dissolved firm's remaining assets. As to (3) above, "unfinished business," the partner gives up all right to proceeds from any unfinished business of the dissolved firm which the new, surviving firm retains. Under the agreement, the old firm's unfinished business is, in effect, "wound up" immediately; the departing partner takes certain of the unfinished business of the old, dissolved Parker Coulter on the payment of a "fair charge," and the new, surviving Parker Coulter takes the remainder of the old partnership's unfinished business.[17] The two entities surviving after the dissolution possess "new business," unconnected with that of the old firm, and the former partners no longer have a continuing fiduciary obligation to windup for the benefit of each other the business they shared in their former partnership.

17. [By the Court] A more equitable provision would require that the new, surviving partnership also pay a "fair charge" on the cases it takes from the dissolved partnership. This "fair charge" from the new firm, as is the "fair charge" from the departing partner, would be an asset of the dissolved partnership, in which the departing partner has an interest.

In sum, * * * the partners have fashioned a division method which immediately winds up unfinished business, allows for a quick separation of the surviving practices, and minimizes the disruptive impact of a dissolution. * * *

We now consider Parker Coulter's claims of wrongdoing. Parker Coulter claims that the judge erred in finding that Meehan, Boyle, Cohen, and Schafer fulfilled their fiduciary duties to the former partnership. In particular, Parker Coulter argues that these attorneys breached their duties (1) by improperly handling cases for their own, and not the partnership's benefit, (2) by secretly competing with the partnership, and (3) by unfairly acquiring from clients and referring attorneys consent to withdraw cases to MBC.[18] We do not agree with Parker Coulter's first two arguments but agree with the third. We first address the claims against Meehan and Boyle, and then turn to those against Cohen and Schafer.

It is well settled that partners owe each other a fiduciary duty of "the utmost good faith and loyalty." As a fiduciary, a partner must consider his or her partners' welfare, and refrain from acting for purely private gain. Partners thus "may not act out of avarice, expediency or self-interest in derogation of their duty of loyalty." *Donahue v. Rodd Electrotype Co. of New England, Inc.*, 367 Mass. 578, 593, 328 N.E.2d 505 (1975). Meehan and Boyle owed their copartners at Parker Coulter a duty of the utmost good faith and loyalty, and were obliged to consider their copartners' welfare, and not merely their own.

Parker Coulter first argues that Meehan and Boyle violated their fiduciary duty by handling cases for their own benefit, and challenges the judge's finding that no manipulation occurred.[19] * * *

We have reviewed the record, and conclude that the judge was warranted in determining that Meehan and Boyle handled cases no differently as a result of their decision to leave Parker Coulter, and that they thus fulfilled their fiduciary duty in this respect.

Parker Coulter next argues that the judge's findings compel the conclusion that Meehan and Boyle breached their fiduciary duty not to

---

18. [By the Court] Parker Coulter does not claim that Meehan and Boyle wrongfully dissolved the partnership by leaving prematurely. The partnership agreement, although providing that the firm "shall continue indefinitely," required that a partner who leaves to continue practicing elsewhere give three-months' advance notice. This, therefore, may not have been a purely "at will" partnership which a partner has a right to dissolve at any time without triggering the remedies of [UPA] § 38(2). See [UPA] §§ 31(1), 38. Here, Parker Coulter waived compliance with the agreement's three-month notice provision. Meehan and Boyle, therefore, dissolved the partnership "[w]ithout violation of the agreement between the partners." [UPA] § 31.

19. [By the Court] The judge found, specifically, that: "MBC, Schafer, Black and Fitzgerald worked full schedules from July to November 30, 1984, and some beyond. There was no manipulation of the cases nor were the cases handled differently as a result of the decision by MBC to leave Parker Coulter. They tried cases, worked on discovery, settled cases and made reasonable efforts to avoid continuances, to try their cases when reached, and settle where appropriate and in general maintain the same level of industry and professionalism that they had always demonstrated."

compete with their partners by secretly setting up a new firm during their tenure at Parker Coulter. We disagree. We have stated that fiduciaries may plan to compete with the entity to which they owe allegiance, "provided that in the course of such arrangements they [do] not otherwise act in violation of their fiduciary duties." *Chelsea Indus. v. Gaffney,* 389 Mass. 1, 10, 11–12, 449 N.E.2d 320 (1983). Here, the judge found that Meehan and Boyle made certain logistical arrangements for the establishment of MBC. These arrangements included executing a lease for MBC's office, preparing lists of clients expected to leave Parker Coulter for MBC, and obtaining financing on the basis of these lists. We believe these logistical arrangements to establish a physical plant for the new firm were permissible under *Chelsea Indus.,* especially in light of the attorneys' obligation to represent adequately any clients who might continue to retain them on their departure from Parker Coulter. Canons of Ethics and Disciplinary Rules Regulating the Practice of Law, Canon 7. There was no error in the judge's determination that this conduct did not violate the partners' fiduciary duty.[20]

Lastly, Parker Coulter argues that the judge's findings compel the conclusion that Meehan and Boyle breached their fiduciary duties by unfairly acquiring consent from clients to remove cases from Parker Coulter. We agree that Meehan and Boyle, through their preparation for obtaining clients' consent, their secrecy concerning which clients they intended to take, and the substance and method of their communications with clients, obtained an unfair advantage over their former partners in breach of their fiduciary duties.

A partner has an obligation to "render on demand true and full information of all things affecting the partnership to any partner." [UPA] § 20. On three separate occasions Meehan affirmatively denied to his partners, on their demand, that he had any plans for leaving the partnership. During this period of secrecy, Meehan and Boyle made preparations for obtaining removal authorizations from clients. Meehan traveled to New York to meet with a representative of USAU and interest him in the new firm. Boyle prepared form letters on Parker Coulter's letterhead for authorizations from prospective MBC clients. Thus, they were "ready to move" the instant they gave notice to their partners.

On giving their notice, Meehan and Boyle continued to use their position of trust and confidence to the disadvantage of Parker Coulter. The two immediately began communicating with clients and referring attorneys. Boyle delayed providing his partners with a list of clients he intended to solicit until mid-December, by which time he had obtained authorization from a majority of the clients.

20. [By the Court] Parker Coulter also argues that Meehan and Boyle impermissibly competed with the firm by inducing its employees to join MBC. Because Parker Coulter identifies no specific loss resulting from this claimed breach, see, e.g., *Chelsea Indus., supra* 389 Mass. at 19 n. 23, 449 N.E.2d 320, (costs of retraining new employees), we need not address this issue.

Finally, the content of the letter sent to the clients was unfairly prejudicial to Parker Coulter. The ABA Committee on Ethics and Professional Responsibility, in Informal Opinion 1457 (April 29, 1980), set forth ethical standards for attorneys announcing a change in professional association.[21] Because this standard is intended primarily to protect clients, proof by Parker Coulter of a technical violation of this standard does not aid them in their claims. We will, however, look to this standard for general guidelines as to what partners are entitled to expect from each other concerning their joint clients on the division of their practice. The ethical standard provides that any notice explain to a client that he or she has the right to decide who will continue the representation. Here, the judge found that the notice did not "clearly present to the clients the choice they had between remaining at Parker Coulter or moving to the new firm." By sending a one-sided announcement, on Parker Coulter letterhead, so soon after notice of their departure, Meehan and Boyle excluded their partners from effectively presenting their services as an alternative to those of Meehan and Boyle.

Meehan and Boyle could have foreseen that the news of their departure would cause a certain amount of confusion and disruption among their partners. The speed and preemptive character [22] of their campaign to acquire clients' consent took advantage of their partners' confusion. By engaging in these preemptive tactics, Meehan and Boyle violated the duty of utmost good faith and loyalty which they owed their partners. Therefore, we conclude that the judge erred in deciding that Meehan and Boyle acted properly in acquiring consent to remove cases to MBC.

We next consider Parker Coulter's claims against Cohen and Schafer. We have determined that "[e]mployees occupying a position of trust and confidence owe a duty of loyalty to their employer and must protect the interests of their employer." *Chelsea Indus., supra,* 389

---

21. [By the Court] These standards provide the following guidelines for notice to clients:

"(a) the notice is mailed; (b) the notice is sent only to persons with whom the lawyer had an active lawyer-client relationship immediately before the change in the lawyer's professional association; (c) the notice is clearly related to open and pending matters for which the lawyer had direct professional responsibility to the client immediately before the change; (d) the notice is sent promptly after the change; (e) the notice does not urge the client to sever a relationship with the lawyer's former firm and does not recommend the lawyer's employment (although it indicates the lawyer's willingness to continue his responsibility for the matters); (f) the notice makes it clear that the client has the right to decide who will complete or continue the

matters; and (g) the notice is brief, dignified, and not disparaging of the lawyer's former firm." See also ABA Committee on Ethics and Professional Responsibility Informal Opinion 1466 (Feb. 12, 1981) (extending Informal Opinion 1457 to departing associates as well as partners).

22. [By the Court] We repeatedly * * * refer to "preemptive conduct" of Meehan and Boyle, as well as their "breach of duty." Undoubtedly these are accurate descriptions, but we do not wish to leave the impression that the MBC attorneys were unfair in the totality of their conduct in departing from the firm. For instance, * * * Meehan and Boyle left undisturbed with their partners, and made no attempt to claim, a very large amount of business which Meehan had attracted to Parker Coulter.

Mass. at 11, 449 N.E.2d 320. Cohen was a junior partner, and acting head of Parker Coulter's appellate department. Schafer was an associate responsible for a substantial case load. Both had access to clients and information concerning clients and therefore occupied positions of trust and confidence. We conclude that their participation in the preemptive tactics of Meehan and Boyle violated the duty they owed the partnership. *   *   *

Before we examine the consequences of the MBC attorneys' breach of duty, we briefly outline what is at stake. If there had been no breach of duty, the assets of the partnership upon dissolution would be divided strictly according to the partnership agreement. Under the agreement, Meehan and Boyle would be entitled to the return of their capital contributions and their share of the dissolved firm's profits. They would also possess the right to remove cases from the old partnership, and to retain all future fees generated by these cases in excess of the fair charge owed to the partnership for work performed there on the removed cases. Because the fair charge is an asset of the dissolved firm under the agreement, Meehan and Boyle would share in this amount according to their respective interests in the former partnership. Thus, of the fair charges returned to their former partnership, Meehan and Boyle would receive their combined 10.8% partnership share, and their former partners would receive the remainder.

Parker Coulter essentially argues that, because of their breach of fiduciary duty, Meehan and Boyle forfeit all rights under the partnership agreement. Thus, Parker Coulter contends, Meehan and Boyle are not entitled to their capital contributions or their share of the dissolved partnership's profits. More importantly, according to Parker Coulter, because of their breach Meehan and Boyle have lost the right to retain any fees generated by the cases they removed. Instead, Parker Coulter claims, these fees are owed to them directly. *   *   * Finally, Parker Coulter contends that the MBC attorneys have forfeited all rights to the compensation they received from July through December, 1984. We reject this extreme remedy. *   *   *

For Parker Coulter to recover any amount in addition to what it would be entitled to receive upon dissolution under the partnership agreement or the statute, there must be a causal connection between its claimed losses and the breach of duty on the part of the MBC attorneys. We have concluded that the MBC attorneys unfairly acquired consent from clients. Parker Coulter, therefore, is entitled to recover only those amounts which flow from this breach of duty.

There is no conceivable connection between the attorneys' breach of duty and Parker Coulter's claims to the capital contributions and profit shares of Meehan and Boyle. *   *   * These amounts are not a form of liquidated damages to which partners can resort in the event of a breach. We conclude, therefore, that Parker Coulter is not entitled to recover these amounts. The judge correctly found that Meehan and Boyle are entitled to a return of their capital contributions (their interest, as determined by the judge, in the partners' reserve account and the partners' capital account), and to the receipt of a portion of the old firm's profits (their interest in the income earned but not distributed account).

We similarly reject Parker Coulter's claims that the MBC attorneys should be required to forfeit all compensation during the period of their breach. Parker Coulter is correct in stating that a fiduciary "can be required to forfeit the right to retain or receive his compensation for conduct in violation of his fiduciary duties." *Chelsea Indus. v. Gaffney*, 389 Mass. 1, 12, 449 N.E.2d 320 (1983). Parker Coulter fails to consider, however, that a fiduciary may be required "to repay only that portion of his compensation, if any, that was in excess of the worth of his services to his employer." *Chelsea Indus., supra*. Here, the judge found that throughout the period in question the MBC attorneys worked as hard, and were as productive as they had always been. This finding was warranted, and is unchallenged by Parker Coulter. In these circumstances, we conclude that the value of the MBC attorneys' services was equal to their compensation. Parker Coulter, therefore, is not entitled to this relief. * * *

In these circumstances, it is appropriate to place on the party who improperly removed the case the burden of proving that the client would have consented to removal in the absence of any breach of duty. * * * [Thus] Meehan and Boyle had the burden of proving no causal connection between their breach of duty and Parker Coulter's loss of clients. Cf. *Energy Resources Corp. v. Porter*, 14 Mass.App.Ct. 296, 302, 438 N.E.2d 391 (1982) (fiduciary who secretly acquires corporate opportunity barred from asserting that corporation would have been unable to exploit opportunity). Proof of the circumstances of the preparations for obtaining authorizations and of the actual communications with clients was more accessible to Meehan and Boyle than to Parker Coulter. Furthermore, requiring these partners to disprove causation will encourage partners in the future to disclose seasonably and fully any plans to remove cases. This disclosure will allow the partnership and the departing partner an equal opportunity to present to clients the option of continuing with the partnership or retaining the departing partner individually.[23]

We remand the case to the Superior Court for findings consistent with our conclusion that the MBC attorneys bear the burden of proof. * * *

To guide the judge on remand in his reexamination of the record and his subsidiary findings, we briefly outline factors relevant to determining whether a client freely chose MBC and, thus, whether the

---

23. [By the Court] As between the attorneys, a mutual letter, from both the partnership and the departing partner, outlining the separation plans and the clients' right to choose, would be an appropriate means of opening the discussion between the attorneys and their clients concerning the clients' choice of continuing representation.

MBC attorneys met their burden of disproving a causal relationship between their preemptive tactics and the removal of the case. * * *

Although the record contains no evidence as to the actual preference of a particular client, expressed and unaffected by the MBC attorneys' improper communications, the record is replete with circumstantial evidence bearing on this issue. * * *

In those cases, if any, where the judge concludes, * * * that Meehan and Boyle have met their burden, we resolve the parties' dispute over fees solely under the partnership agreement. Under the agreement's terms, as we have interpreted them, Meehan and Boyle owe a fair charge to their former partnership for its "services to and expenditures for" the clients in these matters. Meehan and Boyle are entitled to their combined 10.8% partnership share of this amount, and their former partners are entitled to the remainder. We agree with the judge that a "fair charge" on a removed case consists of the firm's unreimbursed expenses plus the rate billed per hour by members of the firm multiplied by the hours expended on the case.[24] In fixing this hourly rate, the firm made a determination that the time charged was reasonable and fair compensation for the services rendered. We conclude, therefore, that, in accordance with the partnership agreement, Meehan and Boyle must reimburse their former partnership for time billed and expenses incurred at that firm on all cases which were fairly removed. We further conclude that, under the agreement, Meehan and Boyle have the right to retain all fees generated by these cases in excess of the fair charge.

We now address the correct remedy in those cases, if any, which the judge determines Meehan and Boyle unfairly removed. In light of a conclusion that Meehan and Boyle have failed to prove that certain clients would not have preferred to stay with Parker Coulter, granting Parker Coulter merely a fair charge on these cases pursuant to the partnership agreement would not make it whole. We turn, therefore, to [the UPA. The Court quotes § 21.] * * *

Meehan and Boyle breached the duty they owed to Parker Coulter. If the judge determines that, as a result of this breach, certain clients left the firm, Meehan and Boyle must account to the partnership for any profits they receive on these cases pursuant to [the UPA] in addition to paying the partnership a fair charge on these cases pursuant to the agreement. The "profit" on a particular case is the amount

---

24. [By the Court] MBC attorneys removed from Parker Coulter a number of insurance company cases, where the fee is determined on an hourly basis, and a number of contingent fee cases, where the fee does not depend on the time involved. Deciding that billable hours is a fair charge on contingent fee cases has two effects which are arguably unfair both to Parker Coulter and to MBC. If the client is unsuccessful, MBC will nonetheless have reimbursed Parker Coulter for services which generated no contingent fee. Conversely, if the client is successful, MBC will retain all the potential "windfall" of the amount by which the contingent fee exceeds MBC's investment of time in the case and its payment of a fair charge to Parker Coulter. Treating a contingent fee case as if the fee were determined on an hourly basis is justified here, however, because the parties did not bargain otherwise.

by which the fee received from the case exceeds the sum of (1) any reasonable overhead expenses MBC incurs in resolving the case, and (2) the fair charge it owes under the partnership agreement. We emphasize that reasonable overhead expenses on a particular case are not the equivalent of the amount represented by the hours MBC attorneys have expended on the case multiplied by their hourly billing rate. Reasonable overhead expenses are to include only MBC's costs in generating the fee, and are not to include any profit margin for MBC. We treat this profit on a particular case as if it had been earned in the usual course of business of the partnership which included Meehan and Boyle as partners. Failing to treat this profit as if it had been earned by Meehan or Boyle while at their former partnership would exclude Meehan and Boyle from participating in the fruits of their labors and, more importantly, would provide Parker Coulter with an unjustified windfall. Parker Coulter would receive a windfall because there is no guarantee that the profit would have been generated had the case not been handled at MBC. Meehan's and Boyle's former partners are thus entitled to their portion of the fair charge on each of the unfairly removed cases (89.2%), and to that amount of profit from an unfairly removed case which they would have enjoyed had the MBC attorneys handled the case at Parker Coulter (89.2%). * * *

The judgment below is reversed and the case is remanded to the Superior Court (1) for findings, in accordance with the factors we have identified, as to which cases were unfairly removed, (2) for a further evidentiary hearing to determine the reasonable overhead and thus the "profits" on the cases, if any, which were unfairly removed, and (3) for entry of a new judgment dispositive of all issues.

SO ORDERED.

Notes

(1) The Parker Coulter agreement relating to the withdrawal of partners differs significantly from the provisions in the partnership agreement of the Tomahawk Clinic. What considerations dictated the use the Parker Coulter type of agreement for a large law partnership and the Tomahawk Clinic type of agreement for a small medical partnership?

(2) Assume that after several years as partner in the law firm you join after law school, you decide to strike out on your own. Assuming that the partnership agreement is similar to that of Parker Coulter, what should you do in order to make sure that your withdrawal does not violate the partnership agreement?

(3) Consider the following situation: Rosenfeld, Meyer, and Susman is a 19–partner law firm; the firm is an at-will partnership without a written partnership agreement; each partner's profit percentage is fixed by a committee at the beginning of each year. In 1968 it was retained by a client to bring a major antitrust case under a one-third contingent fee arrangement. Since the case involved extensive discovery and would take several years to complete, the fee arrangement contemplated that the

client would make certain annual payments to the firm to cover a portion of the firm's costs, these payments ultimately to be offset against the firm's share of any recovery. Cohen and Riordan, two partners with extensive trial experience were assigned responsibility for the antitrust case and they worked on the case full-time for six years. During this period they received shares of general partnership income even though they produced virtually no revenue. By 1974 it had become clear that the antitrust case would be settled for more than $20,000,000. May Cohen and Riordan dissolve the partnership and form a new law firm in the expectation that it would be retained by the client to pursue the antitrust case? Does Rosenfeld, Meyer and Susman have a claim against Cohen and Riordan if the client exercises its unquestioned power to terminate its representation by the Rosenfeld firm and retain Cohen and Riordan? Is this a "wrongful dissolution"? Can there be a "wrongful dissolution" of a partnership at will under the UPA? Or should the issue be resolved under UPA § 21? See Rosenfeld, Meyer & Susman v. Cohen, 146 Cal.App.3d 200, 194 Cal.Rptr. 180 (1983). The departure of Cohen and Riordan, of course, automatically dissolved Rosenfeld, Meyer & Susman, thereby requiring a determination under the UPA of the value of the partnership interests in that law firm at the time of the split-up. In 1987, the court of appeals resolved a number of complex issues arising from this litigation, Rosenfeld, Meyer & Susman v. Cohen, 191 Cal.App.3d 1035, 237 Cal.Rptr. 14 (1987), and remanded Rosenfeld, Meyer & Susman's suit for an accounting for trial. Clearly, resolution of disputes arising from a law firm break-up are as difficult under the UPA default provisions as they are under Parker Coulter's carefully-crafted partnership agreement.

(4) See generally R. Hillman, Law Firm Breakups: The Law and Ethics of Grabbing and Leaving (1990).

GELDER MEDICAL GROUP v. WEBBER

Court of Appeals of New York, 1977.
41 N.Y.2d 680, 394 N.Y.S.2d 867, 363 N.E.2d 573.

BREITEL, CHIEF JUDGE.

In an action by a medical partnership for a permanent injunction to enforce a restrictive covenant not to compete, defendant physician appeals. He had been expelled as a partner pursuant to the partnership agreement. Special Term granted the injunction on summary judgment under CPLR 3212, and dismissed defendant's counterclaim for a declaratory judgment and damages resulting from plaintiff's alleged breach of the partnership agreement. A divided Appellate Division affirmed.

At issue is whether a partner who has been forced out of a partnership as permitted by the partnership agreement may be held to his covenant not to compete within a restricted radius of 30 miles for a five-year period.

There should be an affirmance. Having joined a partnership governed by articles providing for the expulsion without cause of a member on terms that are not oppressive, and including a reasonable restrictive covenant, defendant may not complain of its enforcement.

The Gelder Medical Group, a partnership engaged in practicing medicine and surgery in Sidney, New York, was first formed in 1956. Some 17 years later, defendant Dr. Webber, then 61 years old and a newcomer to Sidney, a village of 5,000 population, was admitted to the small partnership following a one-year trial period in which he was employed by the group as a surgeon. Previously, after having entered the field of surgery, he had drifted from one professional association to another in two different provinces of Canada and in at least four different States of this country in the northeast and midwest. He came to the group from Columbus, Indiana.

As had the other members of the group who had joined since its inception, and critical to plaintiff's complaint, Dr. Webber had agreed that he "will not for five years after any [voluntary or involuntary] termination of his association with said Gelder Medical Group, practice his profession within a radius of 30 miles of the Village of Sidney, as a physician or surgeon ∗ ∗ ∗ without the consent, in writing, of said Gelder Medical Group." The partnership agreement also provided a procedure for the involuntary withdrawal of partners. Thus, it was, in pertinent part, provided that "In the event that any member is requested to resign or withdraw from the group by a majority vote of the other members of the group, such notice shall be effective immediately and his share of the profits to the date of termination shall be computed and he shall be paid in full to the date of termination of his employment pursuant to his agreement with the association."

Dr. Webber's association turned out to be unsatisfactory to his partners. His conduct, both professional and personal, assertedly became abrasive and objectionable to his partners and their patients, a cause of "intolerable" embarrassment to the group. Revealing is a letter of a psychiatrist who, after his formal termination, examined Dr. Webber a number of times on the referral of the partnership. In the psychiatrist's words, Dr. Webber initially "appeared clinically with what would be termed an adjustment reaction of adult life with anxiety and depression". While the psychiatrist concluded that the adjustment reaction soon cleared, he summed up his description of Dr. Webber as a perfectionist who was a "rather idealistic sincere, direct, frank individual who quite possibly could be perceived at times as being somewhat blunt." In fact, Dr. Webber, in one of his affidavits, conceded, commendably, that he is probably "more of a perfectionist and idealist than he should be."

Although during the association difficulties were from time to time discussed with Dr. Webber, the unhappy relationship persisted. In October, 1973, the discord culminated with the group's unanimous decision to terminate Dr. Webber's association with the partnership. After Dr. Webber refused to withdraw voluntarily, the group, in writing, formally notified him of the termination. It was effective immediately, and, on the basis of an accounting, Webber was paid $18,568.41 in full compliance with the articles of agreement which, it is notable, provided for voluntary or involuntary termination on substantially the same terms. But that did not end the unpleasantness.

In about two months, the expelled partner, disregarding the restrictive covenant, resumed his surgical practice as a single practitioner in Sidney. The group, to protect its practice, promptly brought this action to enjoin Dr. Webber's violation of the restrictive covenant and obtained a temporary injunction. Dr. Webber instituted his own action for a declaratory judgment and for damages in allegedly wrongfully expelling him. The actions were consolidated.

The plain meaning and intended effect of the restrictive covenant and the provisions for expulsion are not now in dispute. Dr. Webber urges, however, that the court superimpose a good faith requirement on the partnership's right to expel and to enforce the restrictive covenant. Also urged is the inevitable argument that the restrictive covenant is unreasonable under the circumstances.

The applicable law is straightforward. Covenants restricting a professional, and in particular a physician, from competing with a former employer or associate are common and generally acceptable (see, e.g., Karpinski v. Ingrasci, 28 N.Y.2d 45, 47–49, 320 N.Y.S.2d 1, 2–5, 268 N.E.2d 751, 752–753. As with all restrictive covenants, if they are reasonable as to time and area, necessary to protect legitimate interests, not harmful to the public, and not unduly burdensome, they will be enforced.

Similarly common and acceptable are provisions in a partnership agreement to provide for the withdrawal or expulsion of a partner. While there is no common-law or statutory right to expel a member of a partnership, partners may provide, in their agreement, for the involuntary dismissal, with or without cause, of one of their number.

Turning to the Gelder Group agreement, no acceptable reason is offered for limiting the plainly stated provisions for expulsion, freely subscribed to by Dr. Webber when he joined the group, and none is perceived. When, as here, the agreement provides for dismissal of one of their number on the majority vote of the partners, the court may not frustrate the intention of the parties at least so long as the provisions for dismissal work no undue penalty or unjust forfeiture, overreaching, or other violation of public policy.

Assuming, not without question, that bad faith might limit the otherwise absolute language of the agreement, the record does not reveal bad faith. Embarrassing situations developed, affecting the physicians and their patients, as a result of Dr. Webber's conduct, however highly motivated his conduct might have been. It was as important, therefore, in the group's eyes, as anything affecting survival of the group that it be disassociated from the new member's conflict-producing conduct. Indeed, at the heart of the partnership concept is the principle that partners may choose with whom they wish to be associated.

Even if bad faith on the part of the remaining partners would nullify the right to expel one of their number, it does not follow that under an agreement permitting expulsion without cause the remaining partners have the burden of establishing good faith. To so require would nullify the right to expel without cause and frustrate the obvious intention of the agreement to avoid bitter and protracted litigation over the reason for the expulsion. Obviously, no expulsion would ever occur without some cause, fancied or real, but the agreement provision is addressed to avoiding the necessity of showing cause and litigating the issue. On the other hand, if an expelled partner were to allege and prove bad faith going to the essence, a different case would be presented. As with any contractual agreement, in the time-honored language of the law, there is an implied term of good faith. In his affidavits Dr. Webber has not shown even a suggestion of evil, malevolent, or predatory purpose in the expulsion. Hence, he raises no triable issue on this score.

Insofar as the restrictive covenant is concerned, its reasonableness must be measured by the circumstances and context in which enforcement is sought. * * * [The Court concluded that the covenant was reasonable].

Hence, defendant's attempts to free himself from the covenant not to compete, which, it is notable, will expire by its own provisions in less than two years, must be rejected. It is true, as the group stated in its letter of termination to Dr. Webber, that the termination was a tragedy which it regretted. But the expulsion clause was designed to function when the conflict between the group and one of its members was insoluble, and the necessity for its use must always be unfortunate. Such use is free of fault to remedy an intolerable situation, a situation which would not be less intolerable because the "blame" for its occasion could be pointed in one direction rather than another.

Accordingly, the order of the Appellate Division should be affirmed, with costs.

JASEN, GABRIELLI, JONES, WACHTLER, FUCHSBERG and COOKE, JJ., concur.

Order affirmed.

Notes

(1) Consider UPA §§ 31(1)(d), 38(2). What is the relationship between "wrongful dissolution" and "expulsion"? Could the Gelder group have viewed Webber's conduct as a wrongful dissolution? Does "expulsion" have any meaning in partnerships at will? Consult Hillman, Misconduct as a Basis for Excluding or Expelling a Partner: Effecting Commercial Divorce and Securing Custody of the Business, 78 N.W.L.Rev. 527 (1983).

(2) Does the UPA contemplate that a partner may be expelled "without cause"? See UPA § 31(1)(d). What, then, does the phrase "bona fide" mean in this section? The proposed Revised Uniform Partnership Act does not change this wording, relying on case law that holds that neither good faith nor good cause need be shown under UPA § 31(1)(d). The RUPA adds provisions for judicial expulsion following a finding of bad faith similar to that contemplated under UPA §§ 32(1)(c) and (d). A. Bromberg and L. Ribstein, Bromberg and Ribstein on Partnerships (1989 Supp.) at 131.

(3) Many law firms have adopted formal retirement policies for partners who reach a designated age: the traditional age of 65 is increasingly being increased to 70 or even 75. Voluntary retirement may generally be made available as early as age 60. See generally Maskaleris, How Law Firms Handle Retirement, 71 A.B.A.J. 60 (Feb.1985). The rights of a retiring partner are of course specified in the partnership agreement; a retired partner is often given the honorary "of counsel" designation, and may be provided office space and secretarial assistance after retirement. As a legal matter under the UPA, should a mandatory retirement be viewed as an expulsion, a dissolution, or what?

(4) May a law firm "expel" a 63 year old partner without cause as permitted by the partnership agreement, in order to avoid paying a pension when the partner reaches the age of 65?

I. INADVERTENT PARTNERSHIPS

A recurring issue in partnership law is whether an arrangement between persons may unintentionally constitute a partnership so that a creditor who dealt with A may force B to pay its claim. At common law, a sharing of profits was often deemed conclusive of the existence of a partnership. Consider UPA §§ 6, 7, 16. Section 7(4) states that such sharing is "prima facie evidence" of a partnership except that in certain cases "no such inference shall be drawn." May "prima facie evidence" be rebutted? If so, what kind of "evidence" might do so? If no "inference" of partnership is to be drawn in certain situations, does that mean no partnership exists, or does it mean that a partnership might be found to exist on the basis of other information? If so, what information? Finally, what is the significance of the co-ownership requirement in § 6 in this context? Does this definition help in determining when an arrangement is a partnership as compared to something else? Is § 7 more helpful than § 6?

Notes

The proposed Revised Uniform Partnership Act makes substantial changes in UPA §§ 6 and 7 in an effort to give more guidance as to the existence of the partnership relation. The RUPA eliminates the presumption concept of § 7(4) and draws a distinction between "mere passive coownership" and "shared control," the latter being the "essence of partnership." A. Bromberg and L. Ribstein, Bromberg and Ribstein on Partnership (1989 Supp.) 54. Do these phrases provide more guidance than UPA §§ 6 and 7?

MARTIN v. PEYTON

Court of Appeals of New York, 1927.
246 N.Y. 213, 158 N.E. 77.

ANDREWS, J.   Much ancient learning as to partnership is obsolete. Today only those who are partners between themselves may be charged for partnership debts by others.   [UPA § 7] There is one exception. Now and then a recovery is allowed where in truth such relationship is absent.   This is because the debtor may not deny the claim.   [UPA § 16]

Partnership results from contract, express or implied.   If denied, it may be proved by the production of some written instrument, by testimony as to some conversation, by circumstantial evidence.   If nothing else appears, the receipt by the defendant of a share of the profits of the business is enough.   [UPA § 7]

Assuming some written contract between the parties, the question may arise whether it creates a partnership.   If it be complete, if it expresses in good faith the full understanding and obligation of the parties, then it is for the court to say whether a partnership exists.   It may, however, be a mere sham intended to hide the real relationship. Then other results follow.   In passing upon it, effect is to be given to each provision.   Mere words will not blind us to realities.   Statements that no partnership is intended are not conclusive.   If as a whole a contract contemplates an association of two or more persons to carry on as co-owners a business for profit, a partnership there is.   [UPA § 6] On the other hand, if it be less than this, no partnership exists.   Passing on the contract as a whole, an arrangement for sharing profits is to be considered.   It is to be given its due weight.   But it is to be weighed in connection with all the rest.   It is not decisive.   It may be merely the method adopted to pay a debt or wages, as interest on a loan or for other reasons.

An existing contract may be modified later by subsequent agreement, oral or written.   A partnership may be so created where there was none before.   And again, that the original agreement has been so modified may be proved by circumstantial evidence—by showing the conduct of the parties.

In the case before us the claim that the defendants became partners in the firm of Knauth, Nachod & Kuhne, doing business as bankers and brokers, depends upon the interpretation of certain instruments.   There is nothing in their subsequent acts determinative of or indeed material upon this question.   And we are relieved of questions that sometimes arise.   "The plaintiff's position is not," we are told, "that the agreements of June 4, 1921, were a false expression or incomplete expression of the intention of the parties.   We say that they express defendants' intention and that that intention was to create a relationship which as a matter of law constitutes a partnership."   Nor may the claim of the plaintiff be rested on any question of estoppel.

"The plaintiff's claim," he stipulates, "is a claim of actual partnership, not of partnership by estoppel, and liability is not sought to be predicated upon [§ 16] of the [Uniform] Partnership [Act]."

Remitted then, as we are, to the documents themselves, we refer to circumstances surrounding their execution only so far as is necessary to make them intelligible. And we are to remember that although the intention of the parties to avoid liability as partners is clear, although in language precise and definite they deny any design to then join the firm of K.N. & K.; although they say their interests in profits should be construed merely as a measure of compensation for loans, not an interest in profits as such; although they provide that they shall not be liable for any losses or treated as partners, the question still remains whether in fact they agree to so associate themselves with the firm as to "carry on as co-owners a business for profit."

In the spring of 1921 the firm of K.N. & K. found itself in financial difficulties. John R. Hall was one of the partners. He was a friend of Mr. Peyton. From him he obtained the loan of almost $500,000 of Liberty bonds, which K.N. & K. might use as collateral to secure bank advances. This, however, was not sufficient. The firm and its members had engaged in unwise speculations, and it was deeply involved. Mr. Hall was also intimately acquainted with George W. Perkins, Jr., and with Edward W. Freeman. He also knew Mrs. Peyton and Mrs. Perkins and Mrs. Freeman. All were anxious to help him. He therefore, representing K.N. & K., entered into negotiations with them. While they were pending a proposition was made that Mr. Peyton, Mr. Perkins, and Mr. Freeman, or some of them, should become partners. It met a decided refusal. Finally an agreement was reached. It is expressed in three documents, executed on the same day, all a part of the one transaction. They were drawn with care and are unambiguous. We shall refer to them as "the agreement," "the indenture," and "the option."

We have no doubt as to their general purpose. The respondents were to loan K.N. & K. $2,500,000 worth of liquid securities, which were to be returned to them on or before April 15, 1923. The firm might hypothecate them to secure loans totaling $2,000,000, using the proceeds as its business necessities required. To insure respondents against loss K.N. & K. were to turn over to them a large number of their own securities which may have been valuable, but which were of so speculative a nature that they could not be used as collateral for bank loans. In compensation for the loan the respondents were to receive 40 per cent. of the profits of the firm until the return was made, not exceeding, however, $500,000, and not less than $100,000. Merely because the transaction involved the transfer of securities and not of cash does not prevent its being a loan, within the meaning of section 11. The respondents also were given an option to join the firm if they, or any of them, expressed a desire to do so before June 4, 1923.

Many other detailed agreements are contained in the papers. Are they such as may be properly inserted to protect the lenders? Or do they go further? Whatever their purpose, did they in truth associate the respondents with the firm so that they and it together thereafter carried on as co-owners a business for profit? The answer depends upon an analysis of these various provisions.

As representing the lenders, Mr. Peyton and Mr. Freeman are called "trustees." The loaned securities when used as collateral are not to be mingled with other securities of K.N. & K., and the trustees at all times are to be kept informed of all transactions affecting them. To them shall be paid all dividends and income accruing therefrom. They may also substitute for any of the securities loaned securities of equal value. With their consent the firm may sell any of its securities held by the respondents, the proceeds to go, however, to the trustees. In other similar ways the trustees may deal with these same securities, but the securities loaned shall always be sufficient in value to permit of their hypothecation for $2,000,000. If they rise in price, the excess may be withdrawn by the defendants. If they fall, they shall make good the deficiency.

So far, there is no hint that the transaction is not a loan of securities with a provision for compensation. Later a somewhat closer connection with the firm appears. Until the securities are returned, the directing management of the firm is to be in the hands of John R. Hall, and his life is to be insured for $1,000,000, and the policies are to be assigned as further collateral security to the trustees. These requirements are not unnatural. Hall was the one known and trusted by the defendants. Their acquaintance with the other members of the firm was of the slightest. These others had brought an old and established business to the verge of bankruptcy. As the respondents knew, they also had engaged in unsafe speculation. The respondents were about to loan $2,500,000 of good securities. As collateral they were to receive others of problematical value. What they required seems but ordinary caution. Nor does it imply an association in the business.

The trustees are to be kept advised as to the conduct of the business and consulted as to important matters. They may inspect the firm books and are entitled to any information they think important. Finally, they may veto any business they think highly speculative or injurious. Again we hold this but a proper precaution to safeguard the loan. The trustees may not initiate any transaction as a partner may do. They may not bind the firm by any action of their own. Under the circumstances the safety of the loan depended upon the business success of K.N. & K. This success was likely to be compromised by the inclination of its members to engage in speculation. No longer, if the respondents were to be protected should it be allowed. The trustees therefore might prohibit it, and that their prohibition might be effective, information was to be furnished them. Not dissimilar agreements have been held proper to guard the interests of the lender.

As further security each member of K.N. & K. is to assign to the trustees their interest in the firm. No loan by the firm to any member is permitted and the amount each may draw is fixed. No other distribution of profits is to be made. So that realized profits may be calculated the existing capital is stated to be $700,000, and profits are to be realized as promptly as good business practice will permit. In case the trustees think this is not done, the question is left to them and to Mr. Hall, and if they differ then to an arbitrator. There is no obligation that the firm shall continue the business. It may dissolve at any time. Again we conclude there is nothing here not properly adapted to secure the interest of the respondents as lenders. If their compensation is dependent on a percentage of the profits, still provision must be made to define what these profits shall be.

The "indenture" is substantially a mortgage of the collateral delivered by K.N. & K. to the trustees to secure the performance of the "agreement." It certainly does not strengthen the claim that the respondents were partners.

Finally we have the "option." It permits the respondents, or any of them, or their assignees or nominees to enter the firm at a later date if they desire to do so by buying 50 per cent. or less of the interests therein of all or any of the members at a stated price. Or a corporation may, if the respondents and the members agree, be formed in place of the firm. Meanwhile, apparently with the design of protecting the firm business against improper or ill-judged action which might render the option valueless, each member of the firm is to place his resignation in the hands of Mr. Hall. If at any time he and the trustees agree that such resignation should be accepted, that member shall then retire, receiving the value of his interest calculated as of the date of such retirement.

This last provision is somewhat unusual, yet it is not enough in itself to show that on June 4, 1921, a present partnership was created, nor taking these various papers as a whole do we reach such a result. It is quite true that even if one or two or three like provisions contained in such a contract do not require this conclusion, yet it is also true that when taken together a point may come where stipulations immaterial separately cover so wide a field that we should hold a partnership exists. As in other branches of the law, a question of degree is often the determining factor. Here that point has not been reached.

The judgment appealed from should be affirmed, with costs.

CARDOZO, C.J., and POUND, LEHMAN, KELLOGG, and O'BRIEN, JJ., concur.

Notes

(1) The indenture in Martin v. Peyton contained the following provision:

> The parties of the first part shall not be interested in 'profits' as such. Their interest in profits shall be construed merely as a measure of compensation for loaning said active securities to said firm and granting permission to the firm to hypothecate the same, and for the services to be rendered by the Trustees. The parties of the first part shall not be responsible for any losses that may be made by said firm. The parties of the first part shall not in any way be deemed or treated or held as partners in said firm. No one of the parties of the first part shall be under any partnership liability or obligation. It is not the intention of any of the parties of the first part to assume any of the liabilities of the said firm * * *

220 N.Y.S. 29, at 34 (1927). To what extent should provisions of this nature be given effect as against third parties?

(2) Many modern financing arrangements involve a sharing of profits. Leases of stores in shopping centers often contain provisions for increasing the rent based on increased sales or, more rarely, profits. A large institutional investor making a loan for a real estate venture may insist on a "piece of the action." Elaborate provisions are necessary to protect the investor's interest in such arrangements. For example, in a percentage rent shopping center lease, the lease may permit the landlord to establish (uniform) hours of operation, advertising programs, and the like. The lessee may be required to open its books on demand, to keep its store fully stocked and staffed, and so forth. Is there any danger that such arrangements may be deemed to constitute a partnership rather than a lease?

SMITH v. KELLEY

Appellate Court of Kentucky, 1971.
465 S.W.2d 39.

CLAY, COMMISSIONER.

Appellant brought this suit for a partnership accounting. The Chancellor adjudged no partnership existed and dismissed appellant's claim. Appellant contends on appeal that the judgment is "erroneous".

With one exception, there is little dispute about the facts. In 1964 appellees Kelley and Galloway were partners in an accounting business. Appellant left another firm and came to work for them. For three and one-half years appellant drew $1,000 a month, plus $100 a month for travel expenses. At the end of each year he was paid a relatively small additional sum as a bonus out of the profits of the business. Not until appellant left the Kelley–Galloway firm in 1968 did he make any claim that he was entitled to a fixed percentage of the profits. In this lawsuit he asserts he had a twenty-percent interest therein.

There was no writing evidencing a partnership agreement. However, during the years appellant worked for the firm he was held out to the public as a partner. In a contract entered into between Kelley, Galloway, appellant and a third party, appellant was designated a partner. Partnership tax returns listed him as such; so did a statement filed with the Kentucky Board of Accountancy. In a suit filed in the circuit court against a third party he was designated a partner.

On the other hand, Kelley, Galloway and another employee of the firm testified there was no agreement that Smith would be a partner or have a right to share in the profits; he made no contribution to the assets of the partnership; he took no part in the management; he had no authority to hire or fire employees or to make purchases for the firm; he did not sign any notes when the firm was borrowing money; and he was not obligated to stand any losses of the firm.

A partnership is a contractual relationship and the intention to create it is necessary. As to third parties, a partnership may arise by estoppel, but our question is whether the parties intended to and did create such a relationship as would entitle appellant to share in the profits.

The Chancellor found that the original partners had at no time agreed that appellant would be entitled to share in a percentage of the profits. This was a matter of credibility and the Chancellor, who heard the evidence, chose to believe appellees. His finding on this point was not clearly erroneous and would seem to be dispositive of the case. In addition however, the conduct of the parties over a three-and-one-half-year period confirms the conclusion that, though appellant was held out to the public as a partner, between themselves a partnership relationship was not intended to be and was not created. We find no error in the court's findings of fact or conclusions of law.

Appellant relies on Guthrie v. Foster, 256 Ky. 753, 76 S.W.2d 927 (1934), wherein the Chancellor's finding that a partnership existed was based on certain facts similar to those we have in this case. However, there were other considerations in the cited case that do not appear here and it is not controlling.

We have examined the Uniform Partnership Act, and particularly [§§ 6, 7(1), 7(4), 18(a), 18(e), 18(g)], and find the trial court's decision took cognizance of the essential elements of a partnership therein prescribed.

The judgment is affirmed.

Notes

(1) Is the question involved in this case essentially the same question involved in Martin v. Peyton?

(2) Would Smith have been liable if one of Kelley's customers sued the partnership and Smith for malpractice by Kelley? See UPA § 16.

Chapter Three

SELECTION AND DEVELOPMENT
OF BUSINESS FORMS

A. SELECTION OF BUSINESS FORM

A fundamental question often faced by attorneys is whether or not to recommend to a client that the business be conducted in corporate form or as a partnership, limited partnership or proprietorship. (For this purpose a proprietorship may be considered as a one-person firm analogous to a partnership.) Superficially, it might appear that the advantages of limited liability are so great that all businesses should be incorporated if they may legally be conducted in corporate form. Surprisingly, many experienced attorneys tend toward the opposite conclusion.

> "When in doubt, do not incorporate. Many small corporations are formed inadvisedly. The corporate form of doing business is probably disadvantageous for a small, new venture." Seward and Nauss, Basic Corporate Practice 1 (2d Ed., 1977).

The choice of the best business form for a specific business obviously depends in part on the nature of the business. Consider several typical small businesses:

(1) A retail furniture, clothing, appliance or hardware store;

(2) A law firm;

(3) A restaurant and bar;

(4) An automobile distributorship;

(5) An apartment complex;

(6) An advertising, insurance or employment agency; and

(7) A wholesale supply firm.

A variety of factors must be taken into account when selecting the appropriate business form. Of the various factors discussed below, the second, third, and fourth (liability concerns, tax treatment, and the desire for flexibility and simplicity) are apt to predominate.

119

1. LEGAL RESTRICTIONS

Certain professions, such as law, medicine and dentistry, traditionally have been required for ethical reasons to be conducted as a partnership or proprietorship. The development of so-called "professional corporations" or "professional associations," by which members of these professions may obtain the tax benefits of incorporation, is discussed in part C of this Chapter.

Most states now provide that a corporation may be formed under general corporation statutes for "any lawful purpose" with narrow, specifically enumerated exceptions (that often do not appear in the state's general corporation statute). The most common exceptions involve corporations formed to carry on certain businesses that are subject to special incorporation and regulatory statutes: banks, insurance companies, savings and loan companies, railroads, and public utilities. Several states also use their general corporation statutes to further perceived state policies, such as limiting the power of corporations to acquire farmland. Generally, however, corporations may engage in any business to the same extent as individuals. The RMBCA contains no restrictions on the businesses that a corporation may engage in; see, however, RMBCA § 3.01(b).

2. LIMITED LIABILITY

As a practical matter, how significant is limited liability to each of the small businesses described above?

What about tort liability, e.g. for malpractice in a law partnership or for an accident involving a delivery truck owned by a wholesale or retail business? An individual or partner can of course obtain considerable protection against individual liability by the purchase of insurance. Do corporations purchase less insurance than partnerships? Why do they purchase insurance at all? To what extent does insurance fail to give complete protection to a partner or individual?

What about liability on important contracts such as bank loans, inventory purchases on credit, leases, and the like? Some lenders almost routinely require substantial shareholders in closely held corporations to personally guarantee the corporate obligations; in these situations, the advantage of limited liability largely disappears. Many suppliers rely upon security interests on inventory or liens on property to assure corporate performance and do not seek personal guarantees; the corporate form may provide some protection against personal liability on such obligations. As a practical matter, however, many suppliers do not pursue personal liability after seizing the inventory or property of partnerships or proprietorships, where personal liability exists. Landlords may rely on security deposits in a similar fashion. Thus, in these areas the protections of limited liability may not be as important as first appear.

There remains, however, a variety of business liabilities that may cumulatively be substantial and for which the corporate form provides protection: e.g. tax claims, wage claims, warranty claims, claims of service providers such as accountants and lawyers, and claims of small suppliers. If it is important to conduct business in partnership or proprietorship form, some protection may be given against personal liability on such claims, as a practical matter, by careful oversight of business activities engaged in by agents, employees and partners. In particular, a timely decision to close down a marginal partnership or proprietorship business may significantly reduce exposure to excessive and unacceptable liabilities.

Inactive investors are particularly likely to be risk adverse and unwilling to accept risk of exposure to liability for business obligations. Of course, there exists a wide variety of investment opportunities in modern society that carry with them no risk of liability (and may also have the advantage of instant liquidity), so this attitude is understandable.

Large businesses are usually incorporated. Why is this? Is it because large businesses have large liabilities?

3. FEDERAL INCOME TAXATION

The Federal income tax laws are usually the most significant single factor in determining the form of business organization. A complete discussion of the impact of income taxation on business forms must await courses in Federal Income Taxation and Business Planning, but a knowledge of the fundamentals of the subject is essential.

Initially, all businesses compute income for tax purposes in the same manner, deducting expenses of doing business from receipts in order to compute taxable income. After determination of taxable income, however, partnerships and corporations are subject to different rules of taxation; these different rules largely drive the selection of business form for specific enterprises.

R. HAMILTON, FUNDAMENTALS OF MODERN BUSINESS *
Pages 294–295 (1989).

Corporations are generally treated as separate taxable entities under the Internal Revenue Code with their own sets of rules and own tax schedules. Partnerships, on the other hand, are not treated as separate taxable entities. Rather, partnerships file information returns showing the results of operations and allocating the profit or loss among the partners. The partners then must include the income or loss in their own personal returns, whether or not any monies are in fact distributed to them. This method of taxation is usually called *pass through* or *conduit* taxation. [A variety of] limitations on deductions of passive losses and investment interest * * * applicable to [individuals

* Reprinted with permission of Little, Brown & Company.

are also applicable to] investment interest or passive losses incurred by the partnership: In other words, the same individual limitations on deductibility exist whether the investment is made individually or in the form of a partnership.

* * * Under the 1986 Act, corporations are [generally] subject to tax on income at the following rates:

Taxable income	Tax rate
Not over $50,000	15%
Over $50,000, under $75,000	25%
Over $75,000	34%

An additional 5 percent surtax is imposed on a corporation's taxable income in excess of $100,000 to phase out the lower graduated rates for income under $75,000. * * * The effect is that corporations with incomes from $100,000 to $335,000 pay at the [marginal] rate of 39 percent; above $335,000, all corporations pay a flat tax at a 34 percent rate for all of their income. * * *

Notes

(1) It is important to distinguish between *marginal* tax rates and *effective* tax rates. The *marginal* tax rate applicable to a corporation with exactly $75,000 of income is 34 per cent because that is the rate applicable to each additional dollar of income the corporation earns over $75,000. However, the *effective* tax rate on such income is 18 per cent since its tax bill on exactly $75,000 of income is $13,750 (15 per cent of $50,000 plus 25 per cent of $25,000). A corporation with precisely $100,000 of taxable income owes $22,250; that is an effective rate of 22.25 per cent, but the marginal rate on each additional dollar of income is 39 or 34 per cent. The corporate tax structure for lower income corporations (those with less than $100,000 of income) is mildly progressive; it is "progressive" because additional income is taxed at increasingly higher effective rates, but the progression is mild since there are only three steps and the maximum marginal rate is "only" 34 per cent.

(2) A tax structure is "regressive" if lower amounts of income are taxed at higher rates than higher amounts of income. When a corporation's income exceeds $100,000 it becomes subject to the 5 per cent surtax (so that the marginal rate becomes 39 per cent); this rate remains in effect until corporate income exceeds $335,000, when the surtax ends and the marginal rate reverts to 34 per cent. This decline of marginal rates at the $335,000 level may be viewed as regressive even though the effective rate of taxation on corporate income can never exceed 34 per cent at any level of income. This regressive feature of the Internal Revenue Code was introduced by the Tax Reform Act of 1986.

(3) Corporations subject to the foregoing tax rates are called C corporations because the corporation income tax described in the text is set forth in subchapter C of the Internal Revenue Code.

(4) Corporations with fewer than 35 shareholders that meet certain other very detailed requirements may elect to be taxed under subchapter S

rather than subchapter C of the Internal Revenue Code; corporations making that election are called S corporations. S corporations are taxed on a modified conduit basis similar to that applicable to partnerships: the corporation files a return showing the earnings allocable to each shareholder, who must include that amount in his or her personal income tax return. That amount is includible whether or not any distributions are made by the corporation. The tax treatment of S corporations is not identical to that of a partnership in all respects: in some situations an S corporation may itself become subject to income taxation to a limited extent. Nevertheless, an S corporation does have the basic feature of conduit or pass through taxation that is typical of partnership and proprietorship forms of business.

(5) The S corporation election is a tax election and not a corporate law election: an S corporation possesses all of the normal attributes of a corporation under state law, but is taxed in a different way than C corporations.

(6) To be eligible for S corporation treatment, a corporation, in addition to meeting the maximum 35 shareholder requirement, may not have shareholders who are nonresident aliens, corporations, or other artificial entities, may not own a controlling interest in any other corporation, and may not have issued more than one class of stock (except for classes of common stock that differ only in voting rights). There is no maximum size limitation for S corporations, though doubtless most of them are very small. These various requirements are fleshed out in considerable detail in the Internal Revenue Code and the regulations issued thereunder.

(money)

Individual income tax rates are considerably more complex than the corporate rate schedule described above. There are three different rate schedules based primarily on marital status, plus elaborate sets of tax tables for use by persons with relatively small amounts of income derived solely from employment. In addition, there are a variety of personal exemptions, deductions, and credits that Congress has in its wisdom made available to individual taxpayers. For purposes of observing the interaction of personal and corporate tax rates upon business income, however, a detailed consideration of this complex structure is unnecessary. It is simplest to use the most generally applicable tax schedule, married taxpayers filing joint returns, in 1989:

If taxable income is:	The tax is:
Not over $29,750	15% of taxable income
Over $29,750 but not over $71,900	$4,462 + 28% of excess over $29,750
Over $71,900 but not over $149,250	$16,264.50 + 33% of excess over $71,900
Over $149,250	28% or 33% of taxable income [1]

1. [By the Editor] Taxable income in excess of $149,250 is subject to an additional surcharge of 5 per cent until the effect of the taxpayers' personal exemptions are eliminated. Thus the 33 per cent marginal rate actually continues above the $149,750 taxable income level. Since, however, the number of personal exemptions (of $2,000 each in 1989 for husband, wife and dependent relatives) is dependent on the person-

Other individual tax rate schedules all involve higher tax rates than the schedule for married taxpayers filing joint returns.

Notes

(1) Where do the strange numbers, $4,462 and $16,264.50 come from? Hint: What is the tax on precisely $29,750 of taxable income? On $71,900?

(2) Before 1987, the personal income tax rate schedule was consistently progressive with very high marginal rates on large incomes. The highest marginal rate was 70 per cent as late as 1980, and for some periods during and after World War II, the highest marginal rate was above 90 per cent. One of the major changes made by the 1986 Tax Reform Act was the elimination of most of this progressivity, and the substitution of a much lower maximum rate combined with the same kind of marginal regressivity caused by the 5 per cent surtaxes that also appears in the corporate income tax rate structure.

When personal and corporate income tax rates are compared, the differences at first blush seem modest or insignificant. Both individual and corporate rates start at 15 per cent of taxable income; that rate remains steady for corporations until taxable income exceeds $50,000 while the individual rate jumps to a higher bracket at $29,750. Similarly, the highest tax rates for very large incomes is 39 or 34 per cent for corporations, and 33 or 28 per cent for individuals. However, despite these superficial similarities, the tax treatment of businesses and investors continues to be the most significant single determinant of business form. Tax planning for businesses is driven by several basic considerations:

First, everyone has to pay, or at least account to the United States by filing returns for, income taxes. The risks of unlimited liability when business is engaged in as a partnership may or may not materialize depending on what happens in the future; but liability for taxes is a certainty, not a possibility.

Second, taxpayers quite legitimately expect to minimize their tax liability to the extent they may legally do so. There is a basic distinction between legitimate tax avoidance on the one hand and tax evasion that may lead to fraud penalties, or worse, on the other.[2] The selection of business forms in order to take advantage of differences in

---

al circumstances of the taxpayers it cannot be reflected in the above table.

2. [By the Editor] The claiming of personal exemptions for household pets is an example of tax evasion. While this distinction may seem obvious, the line between legitimate avoidance and improper evasion is often shadowy. The Internal Revenue Service, for example, possesses statutory power to compel accounting changes so as "to clearly reflect income" (Internal Reve-

nue Code § 446) that may result in significant tax liability arising from apparently proper tax avoidance transactions. The Service may also take advantage of court-created doctrines relating to "step transactions." These doctrines permit the Internal Revenue Service to treat a series of transactions as a single transaction resulting in significant tax liabilities arising from apparently proper tax avoidance transactions.

tax schedules or the S corporation election is clearly permissible tax avoidance.

Third, in tax planning one must usually concentrate on the marginal rate of taxation, not the effective rate. As a practical matter, most individuals considering an investment in a business venture will already have income from other sources that exceeds $29,750, so that every dollar of income obtained from the business venture will be taxed at 28 or 33 per cent; the 15 per cent individual tax rate is simply irrelevant in most situations.[3]

Fourth, in selecting the form of business, the total tax liabilities of both business and owners must be taken into account. In comparing the tax consequences of conducting a business in corporate or partnership form, it is essential to recognize that the corporate rate is not in lieu of, but is in addition to, the tax on the ultimate shareholders. A naive comparison of corporate and individual rate schedules similar to that described above misses a fundamental point. If the corporation has taxable income of precisely $75,000, the corporation must pay a corporate income tax of $13,750, leaving $61,250; if the corporation then distributes the $61,250 to its shareholders, all of whom are in the 33 per cent bracket, the shareholders will owe another $20,212.50, for a total tax bill at both levels of $33,962.50. The effective combined tax rate on $75,000 of income is 45 per cent. In contrast, if the business were conducted as a proprietorship, partnership, or S corporation, the maximum aggregate tax would be calculated at the rate of either 33 or 28 per cent, or a total tax bill of either $21,750 or $24,750. In other words, on the assumption that all income is to be distributed to shareholders, the failure to obtain conduit or pass through tax treatment results in more than $10,000 in additional federal income taxes in a single year!

Under current tax rates, it is almost always advantageous to conduct a small business in a form that permits conduit tax treatment. Indeed, if the corporate and individual taxpayers are both at the highest marginal rates, 34 per cent and 28 per cent respectively, the combined tax rate on a C corporation and its shareholders (assuming the distribution of all income) is 52.48 per cent. The maximum rate on individuals is 28 per cent. There is thus a 24.48 per cent differential or bias against C corporation tax status.

It is instructive at this point to consider briefly pre–1986 tax strategies and how they were affected by the 1986 Tax Reform Act. Before 1987, corporate rates were lower than individual rates at most levels of income; as a result, profitable corporations paid the least tax if they elected C corporation status and adopted a policy of not paying

3. [By the Editor] The same is not true of a newly formed corporation. That entity will always be taxed at the 15 per cent rate for its income up to $75,000, though the 5 per cent surtax will wipe out the benefit of that lower tax rate after the corporation's taxable income grows. Since new businesses may be placed in new corporations, multiple use of the 15 per cent bracket may be available in many situations.

dividends that were taxable as such to shareholders. To minimize tax bills before the 1986 Tax Reform Act, therefore, profitable corporations often accumulated large amounts of undistributed earnings.[4] Of course, at some point something had to be done to permit the owners to enjoy the fruits of their successful enterprise. One widely followed strategy was to accumulate the maximum amount possible within the corporation at the favorable corporate rates and then sell all the stock in the business at a price that presumably reflected the accumulated income within the corporation. Properly structured, the gain on the sale of the stock would be taxed at favorable capital gains tax rates.[5] This basic strategy was so common in pre–1986 Tax Act strategy that it had its own name: the "accumulation/bail out" strategy. Its success was based ultimately on the combined effect of the favorable income tax rate on corporations coupled with the equally favorable tax rate applicable to capital gains.

The 1986 Tax Reform Act basically reversed this strategy by one hundred eighty degrees. Since corporate marginal rates are higher than individual marginal rates, net tax savings are maximized if income is taken directly by the owners of the business either by electing S corporation treatment or by conducting business in a form that provides conduit tax treatment. With the repeal of the special capital gains tax, the possibility of "bailing out" earnings has been eliminated. Even if the favorable treatment of capital gains is restored as President Bush has proposed, it is unlikely that this strategy would yield favorable tax results given the generally higher tax rate applicable to C corporations and other technical changes made in the Tax Reform Act of 1986.

A second strategy, that enabled a corporation under pre–1986 Act tax rates to minimize the impact of double taxation of corporate income, involved "zeroing out" a C corporation's taxable income. This strategy relied on the fact that, while distributions in the form of dividends are not deductible by corporations, payments to shareholders in the form of salary, rent, and interest are deductible by the corporation (so long as the payments are reasonable in amount).[6] The distribu-

---

4. [By the Editor] The Internal Revenue Code contains a penalty tax aimed at unreasonable accumulations of income in a corporation to avoid the taxation of dividends to shareholders. While this tax did limit the strategy described in the text, it was only applicable to large accumulations unrelated to the reasonable needs of the enterprise, and could often be avoided as a practical matter. This penalty tax has become much less important as a result of the 1986 Tax Reform Act.

5. [By the Editor] The calculation of tax on a sale or exchange of property was (and still is) fairly complex and need not be described in detail. A maximum tax of 25 per cent was imposed on long term capital

gains during most of the period since World War II. At the same time the marginal rate on ordinary income was generally 70 per cent or even higher, so that there was a strong incentive to structure transactions to provide long term capital gains rather than ordinary income.

6. [By the Editor] The suggestion was sometimes made that the corporation should not pay dividends but provide living benefits indirectly or secretly: the corporation might pay shareholders' grocery bills or provide automobiles at no expense to shareholders. Some such suggestions moved across the shadowy line between permissible tax avoidance and improper tax evasion. Also, if the Internal Revenue

tion of income in the form of salary, rent, and interest to shareholders thus eliminated the corporate tax on that income and in effect shifted it to the shareholders, since such payments were taxable as ordinary income to the shareholders who receive them. The effect was to reduce the taxable income of the corporation and increase the taxable income of the shareholder by the amount of the deductible payments. Theoretically, "zeroing out", when carried to its ultimate conclusion, could result in the reduction of corporate income to zero by transferring all the income to shareholders. While this resulted in the loss of the favorable corporate income tax rate, it might be advantageous depending on the marginal rates applicable to the corporation and to the owners. However, the process of "zeroing out" was not precise and often not pursued to the ultimate: if the corporation were extremely successful, it might not be optimal from a tax standpoint to shift all the taxable income to shareholders and, indeed, it might not be possible to sustain as reasonable deductions equal to the corporation's income.[7] As a result, under pre–1986 tax rates, the "zeroing out" process was often not carried to its ultimate, but the payments were structured so as broadly to minimize the combined corporation/shareholders tax obligations. Partial "zeroing out" might be combined with the accumulation/bail out strategy.

In a sense, the election of S corporation treatment constitutes total "zeroing out." In the case of highly profitable corporations under the pre–1986 Tax Reform Act rates, the S corporation election, even when available, was usually unattractive from a tax standpoint because of the significantly higher marginal rates applicable to individuals as compared to C corporations. Under the rates applicable under the 1986 Tax Reform Act at the present time, election of S corporation status is almost always advantageous where it is available; where it is not, zeroing out the corporate income to the maximum extent feasible—to zero if possible—is almost always advantageous. "Zeroing out", in short, remains a highly attractive strategy under the 1986 Tax Reform Act only where the S corporation election is unavailable.

A final strategy popular in the pre–1986 Tax Act period involved businesses which expected losses at least temporarily. In this situation, it was highly attractive to have the business be taxed on a conduit or pass through basis, since that enabled the shareholders to take advantage of the losses to shield other income from taxation. In effect, the loss business served as a kind of tax shelter for its shareholders. A common pattern then was initially to conduct the business as a partnership or proprietorship until it became profitable and then incorporate, or to elect S corporation status during the period losses continued and

Service learned that such benefits were being provided (as it might, for example, from an audit of the corporate books), it would, at the least, insist that the benefits be taxed to the individual shareholders as informal dividends.

7. [By the Editor] A more serious problem often was that distributions in these forms sometimes led to friction within the corporate family since payments may not be made in proportion to shareholdings.

then revoke that election when the corporation became profitable. The accumulation/bail out strategy would then be followed. While the use of losses to shelter income from tax under the 1986 Tax Reform Act may be possible in some situations, the 1986 Tax Act imposed significant restrictions on the deductibility of passive losses in an effort to stamp out "abusive" tax shelters and these restrictions prevent the widespread use of loss businesses as tax shelters. Further, under the 1986 Tax Reform Act there is no point at which the assumption of C corporation status becomes attractive from a tax standpoint.

In summary, under the rates in effect under the 1986 Tax Reform Act, unlike earlier periods, the name of the game is to take advantage, whenever possible, of conduit or pass-through taxation. When that is not possible, zero out as much as possible. Taxation as a C corporation is to be avoided whenever possible.

Notes

(1) The tax treatment of corporations has been the subject of considerable theoretical discussion, both historically and at the present time. One basic problem is that it is unclear where the ultimate incidence of the corporate income tax falls, whether on consumers, employees, shareholders, or other businesses. At the beginning of President Reagan's second term in 1985 there was a brief flirtation with the idea that the corporate income tax should be abolished; however, as the compromises that eventually became the Tax Reform Act of 1986 were hammered out, this idea was abandoned. Instead, there was increased reliance on the corporate income tax as a revenue raiser, as investment tax credits, accelerated depreciation deductions, and similar revenue reducing items were either eliminated entirely or cut back. To some extent these changes were offset by unanticipated consequences of the changes in tax rates.

(2) American Law Institute, Federal Income Tax Project, Reporter's Study Draft * (June 1, 1989), 48–50:

The most significant thing about the 1986 tax act is the dramatic reduction achieved in top marginal rates. The top nominal rate for individuals was reduced from 50 to 28 percent, and the basic corporate rate was lowered from 46 percent to 34. * * *

These reductions were paid for partly by eliminating the capital gain preference. The result of this was to *raise* the "top" rate of tax on capital gains from 20 to 28.

Individual rate reductions were paid for even more by shifting tax burdens from individual to corporate taxpayers. The increase in corporate tax was mostly a matter of cutting back on investment incentives; corporate rates were actually reduced. But the "top" corporate rate was reduced only from 46 to 34, with the result that the top corporate rate is now significantly above the top individual rate, apparently for the first time since the 16th Amendment.[8] This development has come to be called rate inversion.

The way the income tax appears to have worked in the past, with respect to corporations, has been that capital devoted to growing businesses was attracted into corporate solution, either by accumulation or even by contribution, partly in order to secure the benefit of lower immediate rates. A corporation could accumulate profits faster than a top bracket individual with the same pre-tax income just because of this difference in rates. In exchange for this reduction in immediate tax, the government would enjoy a combination of increased capital base for the corporate income tax and the prospect of two rounds of tax whenever earnings became sufficient to support dividend distributions.

This mode of operation is obviously threatened by the current phenomenon of rate inversion, since the reason is gone for putting funds into corporate solution, or even letting them accumulate. Top bracket individuals will now do better to hold everything they can out of corporate solution and pay immediate taxes at the individual instead of the corporate level. This is particularly serious for the whole scheme of tax reform, since the government has counted on increased corporate tax revenue to pay for individual rate reductions, and that increased corporate tax revenue will not be forthcoming in the long run if the higher rate on corporations drives capital out, or keeps it out, of corporate solution. * * *

The American Law Institute has traditionally not made proposals with respect to tax rates, and that tradition is followed here insofar as formal proposals are concerned. But [we believe] the normal relationship between corporate and individual rates is one in which the corporate rate is significantly below the top individual rates, and a restoration of that normal relationship is greatly to be desired. * * *

There is another, older vision of what is wrong with our present taxation of corporate income. In that view, the basic trouble is the imposition of a double tax on corporate income in the first place. The cure, therefore, is to reduce the incidence of double taxation * * *.

Double taxation of distributed corporate earnings could be curtailed by any of several schemes, all of which go under the name of *integration*. Corporate shareholders might be taxed directly on their shares of corporate income, like partners. More likely, corporate dividends could be relieved of double taxation either by giving a corporate deduction (for all dividends, not subject to a limit * * * or even more likely by giving shareholders credit for their shares of corporate taxes paid on the income from which their dividends are paid. A deduction for all dividends would eliminate the corporate tax

---

8. [By the Author] From 1909 until 1913 the corporate rate was higher since we only had a corporate income tax. Determining whether the top corporate rate ever exceeded the top individual rate thereafter, until the 1986 Act, would apparently require close examination and evaluation of excess profits provisions during the wars.

on income distributed as dividends, leaving it subject only to investor tax; a credit would leave the corporate tax in place but turn it into a withholding device, leaving the ultimate determination of tax to be made at the shareholder level in either case. The credit approach is said to have the advantage of facilitating retention of corporate income taxes on income distributed to shareholders who cannot use the credit, particularly tax-exempts and foreigners.

Corporate tax integration has been extensively studied, inside and outside the government. It has been adopted, in various forms, in most advanced economies throughout the world today. Partial dividend integration has been proposed here, in different forms, on several occasions.

An integrationist is likely to look at the distribution of burdens represented by our present system, and conclude that the corporate income tax, in its unintegrated form, casts an excess, unjustified burden on corporate shareholders, that ought to be lifted. * * *

But whatever the chief aim of integration, its effect on the biases and distortions described herein would be altogether salutary. * * *

(3) Do you agree that the double taxation feature of current corporate/ shareholder tax law should be eliminated? For interesting analyses of the basic fundamentals of the corporate tax structure and the double taxation issue, see Faber, Taxation of Corporations and Shareholders: Premises of the Present System, 22 San Diego L.Rev. 5 (1985); Warren, Corporate Integration Proposals and ACRS, 22 San Diego L.Rev. 325 (1985).

4. INFORMALITY, FLEXIBILITY, COST

The factors discussed above—limited liability and the impact of federal income taxation—are probably the two most significant single factors in determining the most suitable form of business association for most specific ventures. Where, however, a brand new venture is just starting out on uncharted seas with no prior experience and with very limited capital, the advantages of the partnership (or proprietorship) form in terms of simplicity, flexibility, informality, and cost are likely to be stressed.

A partnership may be conducted with little regard to formalities, meetings, records, and the like. Partners may get together and make business decisions with a minimum of fuss. In contrast, most corporation statutes assume that certain formalities, such as meetings, elections, consents, and the like will be followed by every corporation. Indeed, the requirement of having "directors" and a "president" often seems somewhat ludicrous in closely held corporations. The consequence of a failure to follow corporate requirements (which are likely to be considered silly play-acting by businessmen) are not specified in the RMBCA, but could conceivably result in loss of the advantages of corporateness. As discussed in Chapter 8 below, however, some states have relaxed the statutory requirements with respect to the closely held corporation.

A corporation is also more expensive to operate than a partnership. A corporation must pay an annual franchise tax based on its income, net worth, or capitalization, or a combination of the foregoing. A partnership is not of itself liable for such tax. A partnership may freely conduct business in several states without formally qualifying to transact business in each. Not so with a corporation. See RMBCA §§ 15.01–15.02. Qualification to do business in another state requires the assistance of an attorney, and results in the corporation being subject to tax in that state without any reduction in taxes in the state of incorporation. The corporation is also liable to suit in the state of qualification. If a corporation does business without first qualifying, it may find the courts of that state closed to it, RMBCA § 15.02, and may be subject to other penalties as well.

Because of the additional legal requirements applicable to corporations, such a form of enterprise probably incurs greater expenses and legal fees in operation than a partnership. There are, however, complexities in the partnership statutes, and particularly in the Internal Revenue Code provisions applicable to partnerships, which may to some extent offset this advantage. See Int.Rev.Code of 1954, § 701, et seq.

Partnerships are also usually cheaper to form than corporations. Incorporation requires legal assistance, the drafting of certain formal papers, and the payment of a filing fee; a partnership may be created simply by an informal agreement between the parties without the presence of an attorney. Of course, if an attorney does prepare a written partnership agreement, the cost of formation will increase substantially, and may well approximate the costs of forming a corporation. A corporation also usually purchases a minute book, prints share certificates, and acquires a seal. A partnership need incur none of these expenses. Further, in several states there is a minimum capitalization requirement for corporations (usually $1,000) but none for partnerships. Of course, in the last analysis the costs of formation are incurred only once, so that such costs are unlikely to be determinative except possibly in the most marginal business enterprise.

5. MISCELLANEOUS FACTORS

Three final factors influencing the choice between the corporate and partnership forms of business are continuity of life, centralization of management, and free transferability of interest. These factors, however, are rarely of critical importance in the selection of the most appropriate form of business, in part because sophisticated advance planning will solve most problems in these areas that otherwise might arise.

(i) Continuity of Life

A corporation has "perpetual duration and succession in its corporate name," RMBCA § 3.02, whereas a partnership is subject to abrupt and unexpected dissolution, UPA §§ 31, 32. A sharp distinction, however, should be drawn between legal continuity and economic continuity. If the key shareholder and manager of a small corporate business should die, it may be impractical to continue the business despite the "perpetual duration" of a corporation. There simply may be no one to run the business. On the other hand, the death or bankruptcy of an inactive partner may constitute a "dissolution" of a partnership in a technical sense without in any way impairing the earning capacity or survivability of the business. In such instances the business is likely to be continued by the surviving partners much as before, with some provision being made for the interest of the inactive partner. In a larger partnership, e.g., a large law firm, the withdrawal of even several active partners is unlikely to affect the continuity of the business.

Certainly, one of the major areas of concern for counsel drafting a partnership agreement is the death, withdrawal or expulsion of a partner. Professor A.R. Bromberg, in Partnership Dissolution—Causes, Consequences, and Cures, 43 Tex.L.R. 631, at 668 (1965), concludes that proper contractual provisions can usually ensure that dissolution will not force termination of the business. As he puts it, "with [advance agreement], the partnership may be given virtually as much continuity as a corporation." If in the case of our furniture store partnership, the agreement provided that the business should continue on the death of a partner, and payments should be made to the partner or his estate or his beneficiaries, what are the problems that must be considered in the event of the death of A? Of B? In the case of the large law firm, the partnership agreement may impose liquidated damages or forfeitures on a partner who withdraws that are so onerous that the withdrawal itself may be deterred.

(ii) Centralization of Management

Consider the language of RMBCA § 8.01(b). This language establishes the primacy of the board of directors with respect to the management of the business and affairs of the corporation. Earlier versions of the Model Business Corporation Act did not contain the qualifications and exceptions of section 8.01. The first sentence of section 35 of the 1960 Model Act, for example, stated without qualification that "the business and affairs of a corporation shall be managed by a board of directors." The phrase "except as may be otherwise provided in the articles of incorporation" was added in 1969 to permit the very small, closely held corporation to dispense with the board of directors and permit the shareholders to manage the corporation directly, and was made only after "prolonged consideration." The option for the closely held corporation to dispense with a board of directors is now codified in RMBCA § 8.01(c), but it is clear that centralization of management is still contemplated since the articles of incorporation must specify "who will perform some or all of the duties of a board of directors." [9] In

---

9. [By the Editor] Section 8.01(b) also recognizes that the power of management of the board of directors is subject to limitation expressly set forth in the articles of

1975, the language of then section 35 was further amended to include language, now appearing in § 8.01(b), that the business and affairs of the corporation may be managed "under the authority of" (rather than "by") the board of directors. The purpose of this change was to recognize that outside directors of huge publicly held corporations could not reasonably be expected to manage the detailed affairs of such a corporation. See 30 Bus.Law. 501, 504–505 (1975). It is clear, however, that in even these large corporations the directors may delve into whatever areas of corporate management they desire—in other words, the general power still resides in the board of directors. The changes described above may blur to some extent the basic notion still set forth in section 8.01 that the power to manage the business and affairs of a corporation is vested in its board of directors or other centralized authority and not in its owners—the shareholders. The board of directors, further, may be composed partially or wholly of persons who are not shareholders, and there is no requirement that the board contain representatives of various groups or factions of shareholders. See RMBCA § 8.02, second sentence. These provisions should be contrasted with UPA § 18(e), which seems to adopt a pluralistic approach, vesting power to manage in the partners—the owners—as a group, rather than in a centralized board.

In what circumstances might it be desirable to have a board of directors consisting partially or wholly of nonshareholders?

In many corporations, particularly the larger ones, the actual management of the business is conducted by officers or employees organized in a heirarchical fashion and headed by a single individual, usually called the Chief Executive Officer, or "CEO." The board of directors' role then becomes one of oversight rather than of direct management; the board's ultimate power is the power to select and discharge the CEO and set his or her compensation.

Is it possible to provide a similar degree of centralized management in a partnership by agreement? What about the introductory clause to section 18 of the Uniform Partnership Act to the effect that the section governs the "rights and duties of the partners in relation to the partnership * * * subject to any agreement between them"? What is the legal effect of a partnership agreement giving X "centralized management": e.g. "X shall have the sole power to manage the business and affairs of the partnership and Y shall have no power to manager the business or bind the partnership"? Compare UPA §§ 9(1), 13, 14, 15. If, despite such a provision, Y obtains a loan from a bank in the partnership name, is the partnership liable to the bank even though Y subsequently misappropriates the money? Does X thereafter

incorporation. Even though the 1969 amendment described in the text was added for the purpose of assisting the closely held corporation, it also had the incidental effect of expressly recognizing the validity of restrictions on the powers of board of directors that are set forth in the articles of incorporation. This incidental effect was recognized as having value and was preserved in section 8.01(b). The issue discussed in this note is further discussed in Chapter 8.

have any claim over against Y? What would be the situation if X manages the business for his sole benefit, e.g. by paying himself a "salary" equal to the profits each month? Is Y totally at the mercy of X as a result of the partnership agreement? On a more realistic level, consider the internal management of a large law firm with 150 or so partners. The day-to-day business affairs of the firm are usually handled by a single partner (who is expected to devote the bulk or all of his or her time to this task), subject to the general direction, advice, and assistance of a committee of senior partners. These relationships may be formalized by specific provisions in the partnership agreement. The close analogy to the corporate management structure described above should be obvious.

(iii) Free Transferability of Interest

Shares of stock in a corporation are in theory freely transferable, whereas there are serious difficulties in transferring interests in partnerships. See UPA § 27. However, in practice, this distinction is again often more apparent than real. There is no market for the shares of a closely held corporation, and the only persons likely to be interested in buying the shares are those with an economic interest in the venture. This is particularly apt to be true if the shares represent only a minority interest and the shareholder is precluded from participating in management because of the antagonism of the majority shareholders. A shareholder who wants to sell under those circumstances may be at the mercy of the other shareholders who need not offer a very generous price. In this respect the shareholder may be worse off than a partner in a partnership (who has a residual power to compel dissolution). Further, shareholders in a close corporation will usually wish to remain close. They will wish to exercise a veto power over who may participate in the venture. For this reason, counsel often are requested to draft option or buy-sell agreements between shareholders which have the effect of keeping shares from being freely transferable. See RMBCA § 6.27, discussed in Chapter 8, Section B, below.

Free transferability of corporate shares may be of importance if the shareholders are considering "going public" in the future, and, of course, is a basic ingredient of publicly held corporations, such as General Motors.

Notes

(1) Would you recommend that the AB Furniture Store incorporate or operate as a partnership? If it incorporates, should it elect to be taxed as an S Corporation?

(2) Assume that you have represented A on legal matters for several years but you have never represented B. B does not have a lawyer. When A asks you to give advice on the best form of business for the furniture store, B indicates that he relies on your judgment and will accept your

recommendation. Some of the decisions you make may have an adverse effect on B. Do you have any obligation to B? Does he become your client also if you give him legal advice? Are you "counsel for the venture"? Consider Model Rules of Professional Conduct, Rule 1.7:

> (a) A lawyer shall not represent a client if the representation of that client will be directly adverse to another client, unless:
>
>> (1) the lawyer reasonably believes the representation will not adversely affect the relationship with the other client; and
>>
>> (2) each client consents after consultation.
>
> (b) A lawyer shall not represent a client if the representation of that client may be materially limited by the lawyer's responsibilities to another client or to a third person, or by the lawyer's own interests, unless:
>
>> (1) the lawyer reasonably believes the representation will not be adversely affected; and
>>
>> (2) the client consents after consultation. When representation of multiple clients in a single matter is undertaken, the consultation shall include explanation of the implications of the common representation and the advantages and risks involved.

Does that rule apply to your situation? If so, how do you explain "the implications of the common representation and the advantages and risks involved" to B?

B. THE MODERN LIMITED PARTNERSHIP

The limited partnership is a form of business that has some characteristics of both a corporation and a partnership. Traditionally, this form of enterprise did not receive a great deal of attention. The drafters of the original 1916 Uniform Limited Partnership Act obviously assumed that a limited partnership was a small local business in which risk capital was contributed by local investors. The possibility of interstate operations was not referred to anywhere in the ULPA, and the requirement in many states that limited partnership instruments be filed in county offices was clearly based on this assumption. Further, the filing and execution requirements set forth in that Act required executions by all limited and general partners, and therefore were only practicable if the number of limited and general partners was small.[10] The same assumption underlay the early case law and legal thinking about limited partnerships, which subjected them to the same rules as general partnerships. For example, limited partnerships are still generally not subject to corporate franchise taxes, and, until the 1970s, were not required to qualify to transact business in a foreign jurisdiction if they engaged in business in that jurisdiction.

---

10. [By the Editor] As the number of limited partners grew, attorneys were successful in devising techniques to overcome these onerous execution requirements. The most widely used was a power of attorney executed by each limited partner at the time he or she made the investment authorizing one of the general partners to execute future amendments to the limited partnership certificate on his or her behalf.

The principal reason for the development of larger limited partnerships was that this form of business permits the combination of conduit or pass through tax treatment for federal income tax purposes with a large number of passive investors each with limited liability. The so-called "tax shelters" that proliferated throughout the 1970s and early 1980s were almost always organized in the form of limited partnerships so that the investors could take advantage of the losses generated by the business to shelter income from other sources from federal income tax. An oil drilling venture, for example, might have hundreds or thousands of limited partners, millions of dollars of assets and liabilities, and operate in a number of different states or foreign countries as it busily generated tax losses for its investors. Obviously, legal principles created on the assumption that the typical limited partnership was a local hardware store with two general partners and three limited partners are going to be strained when applied to such an ungainly creature.

The development and growth of large limited partnerships pointed up the inadequacies of the 1917 Uniform Limited Partnership Act, led indirectly to the decision to develop a new limited partnership statute, and brought into increasing question the earlier view that limited partnerships should be uniformly treated as a species of partnership. The reality that modern limited partnerships resemble corporations more closely than general partnerships creates problems for the practicing attorney:

> All of us who are practitioners or students of business law are aware of, and often frustrated by, the fact that business practice almost always develops more rapidly than business law. As a result, business lawyers often must grapple with important questions in the context of laws premised on the business practices of by-gone days.
>
> Lawyers who counsel limited partnership clients are especially vexed by this time warp. Both the Uniform Limited Partnership Act (ULPA) and the Revised Uniform Limited Partnership Act (RULPA) seem to have been drafted on the assumption that a limited partnership is a small, if not intimate, business association, each member of which knows the other members and cares about the identity of the other members. While this assumption may well have once been correct, limited partnerships today often have hundreds (and sometimes thousands) of partners. Many limited partnerships have registered limited partnership interests with the Securities and Exchange Commission and limited partnership interests are now traded on national securities exchanges and in the over-the-counter market. As one would expect, rules that may be sensible for limited partnerships with a few partners become unworkable when applied to limited partnerships with many partners.

Basile, Admission of Additional and Substitute General Partners to a Limited Partnership: A Proposal for Freedom of Contract, 1984 Ariz. St.L.J. 235, 235–6. Professor Basile's complaint about the RULPA was basically limited to section 401 that, before its amendment in 1985, permitted the addition or substitution of general partners only with the unanimous consent of all limited partners, and did not recognize the possibility of advance consent as an alternative method of admitting general partners in the partnership agreement.

See also RULPA § 1105.

The development of the RULPA, the amendments to it adopted between 1975 and 1985, and the numerous non-conforming amendments adopted by various states, all attest to the complexity of melding together traditional views of the limited partnership, federal tax rules, the need for some protections for passive investors in large limited partnerships, and working rules that take into account the practical necessities of managing a widely held, large and diverse economic enterprise.

The enactment of the 1986 Tax Reform Act, with its lower tax rates for individuals than for corporations, naturally accelerated the trend toward wider use of the limited partnership. And, rather predictably, this caused a backlash.

ADLER, MASTER LIMITED PARTNERSHIPS *
40 U.Fla.L.Rev. 755, 756–758, 763–765, 774, 777, 779, 783–785 (1988).

In 1981, a new breed of partnership was born—a master limited partnership. Although the parameters of this new species are not yet clearly defined, widespread consensus exists that these large, publicly traded partnerships do not fit cleanly within the structure of the partnership rules in [the Internal Revenue Code]. The debate over the proper treatment of master limited partnerships resulted in the enactment of a provision in the Revenue Act of 1987 that will cause certain "publicly traded partnerships" to be taxed as corporations. * * *

The term "master limited partnership" arose as a description of the method by which these large publicly traded partnerships were first developed. An independent oil company formed the first master limited partnership in 1981. The company consolidated thirty pre-existing drilling and exploration limited partnerships into one "master" limited partnership. The partners of the drilling and exploration partnerships contributed their partnership interests to a new limited partnership in return for limited partnership interests in the new entity. This method of forming a master limited partnership is called a "roll up" and is generally used to combine several smaller limited partnerships into one large partnership. The definition of master limited partnerships has expanded over the past seven years, and "master limited partnership" now refers more generally to large partnerships that are widely held and whose ownership interests are frequently traded.

Master limited partnerships can also be formed in rollout transactions, acquisition transactions, liquidation transactions, and initial formations. A rollout transaction generally involves a corporate sponsor that contributes assets to a limited partnership in return for partnership interests. The corporate general partner then sells the limited partnership interests. An acquisition transaction is similar to the rollout master limited partnership except that instead of contributing assets, the corporate sponsor acts as the general partner in a limited partnership that sells its interests to the public. The new limited partnership then purchases assets from either the corporate sponsor or an unrelated party. Liquidation transactions involve the contribution of all of the corporate sponsor's assets to a limited partnership in return for partnership interests that are then distributed to the corporate shareholders in complete liquidation.

Between 1981 and 1987, the number of master limited partnerships grew markedly. The Department of the Treasury found that from 1981 through 1985, forty-eight master limited partnerships had been formed and were being traded on established exchanges. In 1986 alone, thirty-eight additional exchange-traded master limited partnerships were formed, and in the first six months of 1987, another forty had been marketed.

In addition to burgeoning numbers of master limited partnerships, these entities were changing qualitatively as well. Prior to 1986, most master limited partnerships held real estate and oil and gas property. Since then, the number of non-real estate and non-oil and gas master limited partnerships has increased significantly. Among the new master limited partnership offerings were such established businesses as Burger King, Mauna Loa Macadamia, and the Boston Celtics. * * *

Prior to the Revenue Act of 1987, the Kintner regulations set forth the test of whether a master limited partnership would be treated as an association taxable as a corporation or as a partnership.[11] These regulations identify six characteristics that are "found in a pure corporation which, taken together, distinguish it from other organizations." These characteristics are: "(i) associates, (ii) an objective to carry on a business and divide the gains therefrom, (iii) continuity of life, (iv) centralization of management, (v) liability for corporate debts limited to corporate property, and (vi) free transferability of interests." A partnership will be treated as an association taxable as a corporation if it "more nearly resembles a corporation than a partnership." Because both corporations and partnerships have as common characteristics associates and an objective to carry on a business and divide the gains therefrom, those traits will be disregarded in determining whether the partnership will be taxed as a corporation. If a partnership lacks two of the four remaining characteristics, its status as a partnership will be respected for tax purposes. Most limited partnerships, including mas-

11. [By the author] Treas.Reg. § 301.7701–2 (as amended in 1983).

ter limited partnerships, do not possess the characteristic of continuity of life because death, insanity, or bankruptcy of the general partner will cause the termination of the partnership. In addition, liability for partnership debts is not limited to partnership property if the general partner is not a "dummy" or has a substantial amount of assets.[12]

Master limited partnerships can fulfill the necessary requirements to avoid being treated as associations taxable as corporations rather easily. Most states have adopted partnership laws that provide for the termination of the partnership on the death, insanity, or bankruptcy of the general partner. Case law has held that even if the limited partners can replace the general partner, the possibility that the partnership could terminate under state law precludes the partnership from having the characteristic of continuity of life. Furthermore, a general partner that either has a substantial amount of assets or plays an active managerial role in the partnership business will be considered as having unlimited liability. The classification rules consider only the above-listed characteristics, and the determination does not turn on whether the partnership interests are publicly traded. Through careful planning, many businesses could, in effect, choose whether to be treated as partnerships by forming a master limited partnership that complied with a state's uniform limited partnership act or as a corporation merely by incorporating under state law. * * *

Large partnerships that are listed and publicly traded on established securities markets are, in many respects, indistinguishable from publicly traded corporations. The partners of a master limited partnership are generally investors that are not concerned with the identity of the other partners; rather, they view investment in these partnerships much the same way they view corporate stock. Commentators and planners have noted that "[t]here is . . . another type of business entity, the [publicly traded] limited partnership, which can be structured essentially to embody the salient features of a corporation from the investor's point of view."[13] Master limited partnerships, therefore, are competing for the same capital investment as corporations but can promise higher yields because of the competitive edge created by the tax advantages of operating in partnership form. * * *

Congress responded to the concerns and complexities raised by master limited partnerships in the Revenue Act of 1987.[14] The major thrust of the changes in the Revenue Act is to treat certain "publicly traded partnerships" as corporations.[15] Generally, publicly traded partnerships are defined as any partnership with interests that are "traded on an established securities market," or has interests that "are readily tradeable on a secondary market (or the substantial equivalent thereof)."[16] * * * On the first day a partnership is treated as a corpora-

---

12. [By the author] *Id.* § 301.7701–2.

13. [By the author] Million & Bolding [Metamorphosis: Liquidation of the Corporation into a Publicly Traded Limited Partnership, 38 Bus.Law.], at 1487.

14. [By the author] Revenue Act of 1987, Pub.L.No. 100–203.

15. [By the author] I.R.C. § 7704(a).

16. [By the author] *Id.* § 7704(b).

tion, the partnership will be considered to have transferred all its assets to a newly formed corporation in exchange for its stock and distributed the stock to the partners in liquidation of their partnership interests.

* * *

By selecting public trading as the dividing line, Congress has undercut its own efforts at correcting the tax equity and neutrality problems. Congress has chosen public trading as the sole characteristic that makes the Burger King master limited partnership qualitatively different from a Mom and Pop burger stand that operates as a general partnership. Neither the statutory language nor the legislative history presents a convincing argument that public trading is the characteristic that differentiates the two.

The justification for treating publicly traded partnerships as corporations for tax purposes is that they are essentially no different from corporations. Using public trading as the overriding factor in classifying partnerships as corporations, however, ignores the wide diversity among corporations. Most corporations are not publicly traded, but they still incur a corporate-level tax. * * *

The Revenue Act of 1987 granted certain master limited partnerships a ten year reprieve from the recharacterization as corporations. In order to qualify, master limited partnerships must have been publicly traded on December 17, 1987 * * *. The Code continues to treat these "existing partnerships" as partnerships until December 31, 1997. All other publicly traded partnerships will be taxed as corporations for taxable years beginning after December 31, 1987. To prevent "existing partnerships" from manipulating their status, an existing partnership that adds a substantial new line of business will no longer be treated as an existing partnership and will be taxed as a corporation. A substantial new line of business, however, "does not include a line of business that was specifically described as a proposed business activity of the partnership . . . in a registration statement . . . filed . . . with the SEC on or before December 17, 1987." [17] * * *

[Also,] the new section 7704 excepts from corporate treatment a large segment of publicly traded partnerships. Oil and gas and real estate partnerships make up from one-third to one-half of all existing master limited partnerships. These partnerships will maintain their partnership status indefinitely. The Code will continue to treat existing partnerships as partnerships for ten years. However, no additional guidance has been given on how to address the accounting, record keeping, and fungibility problems associated with the taxation of these partnerships. This leaves one of the major problems associated with master limited partnerships completely unanswered. * * *

17. [By the author] [H.Rep. No. 495, 100th Cong. 1st. Sess. 947], at 950.

DELANEY v. FIDELITY LEASE LTD.

Supreme Court of Texas, 1975.
526 S.W.2d 543.

DANIEL, JUSTICE.

The question here is whether limited partners in a limited partnership become liable as general partners if they "take part in the control of the business" while acting as officers of a corporation which is the sole general partner of the limited partnership. The trial court, by summary judgment, held that under such circumstances the limited partners did not become liable as general partners. The court of civil appeals affirmed with a dissent and a concurring opinion. 517 S.W.2d 420. We reverse and remand the case for trial on the merits.

Fidelity Lease Limited is a limited partnership organized under the Texas Uniform Limited Partnership Act, to lease restaurant locations. It is composed of 22 individual partners, and a corporate general partner, Interlease Corporation. Interlease's officers, directors and shareholders were W.S. Crombie, Jr., Alan Kahn, and William D. Sanders, who were also limited partners of Fidelity. In February of 1969, plaintiffs Delaney, et al. entered into an agreement with the limited partnership, Fidelity, acting by and through its corporate general partners, Interlease, to lease a fast-food restaurant to the partnership.[18] In accordance therewith, plaintiffs built the restaurant, but Fidelity failed to take possession or pay rent.

Plaintiffs brought suit for damages for breach of the lease agreement, naming as defendants the limited partnership of Fidelity Lease Limited, its corporate general partner Interlease Corporation, and all of its limited partners. On plaintiffs' motion the cause against the limited partners individually, insofar as it relates to their personal capacities and liabilities, was severed from the cause against Fidelity and Interlease. In this severed cause, the trial court granted a take nothing summary judgment for the limited partners. Plaintiffs appealed only as to limited partners Crombie, Kahn, and Sanders. Plaintiffs sought to hold these three individuals personally liable under Section [7 of ULPA] alleging that they had become general partners by participating in the management and control of the limited partnership.

Pertinent portions of the * * * Uniform Limited Partnership Act provide:

18. [By the Editor] According to the Court of Appeals, the lease was executed in the following form: " 'FIDELITY LEASE, LTD., a limited partnership acting by and through INTERLEASE CORPORATION, General Partner, * * * hereinafter called 'LESSEE,' * * *.' The lease was executed by the lessee, Fidelity Lease, Ltd., by the General Partner, Interlease Corporation, by W.S. Crombie, Jr., President. The acknowledgment to the lease is by W.S. Crombie, Jr., as President of Interlease Corporation, who acknowledged to the notary that the same was the act of said Interlease Corporation and that he executed the same as the act of the corporation and in the capacity therein stated."

"Sec. [7]   A limited partner shall not become liable as a general partner unless, in addition to the exercise of his rights and powers as a limited partner, he *takes part in the control of the business.*

"Sec. [12]   (a) A person may be a general partner and a limited partner in the same partnership at the same time.

"(b) A person who is a general, and also at the same time a limited partner, shall have all the rights and powers and be subject to all the restrictions of a general partner; except that, in respect to his contribution, he shall have the rights against the other members which he would have had if he were not also a general partner."   (Emphasis added.)

It was alleged by plaintiffs, and there is summary judgment evidence, that the three limited partners controlled the business of the limited partnership, albeit through the corporate entity.   The defendant limited partners argue that they acted only through the corporation and that the corporation actually controlled the business of the limited partnership.   In response to this contention, we adopt the following statements in the dissenting opinion of Chief Justice Preslar in the court of civil appeals:

"I find it difficult to separate their acts for they were at all times in the dual capacity of limited partners and officers of the corporation. Apparently the corporation had no function except to operate the limited partnership and Appellees were obligated to their other partners to so operate the corporation as to benefit the partnership.   Each act was done then, not for the corporation, but for the partnership. Indirectly, if not directly, they were exercising control over the partnership.   Truly 'the corporation fiction' was in this instance a fiction." 517 S.W.2d at 426–27.

Thus, we hold that the personal liability, which attaches to a limited partner when "he takes part in the control of the business," cannot be evaded merely by acting through a corporation.

The defendant limited partners also contend that the "control" test enumerated in Section [7] for the purpose of inflicting personal liability should be coupled with a determination of whether the plaintiffs relied upon the limited partners as holding themselves out as general partners.   Thus, they argue that, before personal liability attaches to limited partners, two elements must coincide: (1) the limited partner must take part in the control of the business; and (2) the limited partner must have held himself out as being a general partner having personal liability to an extent that the third party, or plaintiff, relied upon the limited partners' personal liability.   They observe that there is no question in this case but that the plaintiffs were in no way misled into believing that these three limited partners were personally liable on the lease, because the lease provided that the plaintiffs were entering into the lease with "Fidelity Lease, Ltd., a limited partnership acting by and through Interlease Corporation, General Partner."

We disagree with this contention. Section [7] simply provides that a limited partner who takes part in the control of the business subjects himself to personal liability as a general partner. The statute makes no mention of any requirement of reliance on the part of the party attempting to hold the limited partner personally liable. * * *

Accordingly, the cause of action against the defendants Crombie, Kahn, and Sanders is severed, and as to that portion of the case the judgments of the lower courts are reversed and such cause as to them is remanded for trial in accordance with this opinion. As to the remainder of the case, the judgment of the trial court is affirmed.

Notes

(1) Why did the persons interested in Fidelity Lease Limited create such a complex arrangement? In 1969, when the Fidelity Lease Limited transaction was entered into, the Subchapter S election was available only to corporations with ten or fewer shareholders. Is that relevant?

(2) The power of a corporation to serve as a general partner in a limited partnership was in doubt under the 1917 Uniform Limited Partnership Act and the corporation statutes of most states before about 1970. Under the RULPA and RMBCA there is no doubt that the rule in *Delaney* has been rendered obsolete by statute. See RULPA §§ 101(5), 101(11), 402(6), 402(9), RMBCA § 3.02(9). May a limited partner serve as a director or officer of the general partner without fear of liability under the RULPA? See RULPA § 303.

(3) Recall that the "Kintner regulations" (summarized in Professor Adler's article) list as an important partnership characteristic, that liability for partnership debts not be limited to business assets. Isn't the use of corporate general partners—now virtually universal in large limited partnerships—inconsistent with that characteristic? Consider Rev.Proc. 72–13, 1972–1 CB 735:

> The purpose of this Revenue Procedure is to specify the conditions that must be present before the Internal Revenue Service will consider issuing advance rulings concerning classification of organizations as partnerships, for Federal tax purposes under existing regulations * * * where they are formed as limited partnerships and a corporation is the *sole* general partner. The decision whether the organization may be classified as a partnership under existing regulations will depend on all the facts and circumstances. * * *
>
> The Service will consider a request for a ruling on the classification of an organization as a partnership where it is formed as a limited partnership and a corporation is the *sole* general partner under the following conditions:
>
> .01 The limited partners will not own, directly or indirectly, individually or in the aggregate, more than 20 percent of the stock of the corporate general partner * * *
>
> .02 If the corporate general partner has an interest in only one limited partnership and the total contributions to that Partnership are

less than $2,500,000, the net worth of the corporate general partner at all times will be at least 15 percent of such total contributions or $250,000, whichever is the lesser; if the total contributions to that partnership are $2,500,000 or more, the net worth of the corporate general partner at all times will be at least 10 percent of such total contributions. * * *

.05 The purchase of a limited partnership interest by a limited partner does not entail either a mandatory or discretionary purchase or option to purchase any type of security of the corporate general partner or its affiliates.

.06 The organization and operation of the limited partnership must be in accordance with the applicable state statute relating to limited partnerships.

Most passive investors are unwilling to make an investment if the tax consequences are uncertain. As a result, an advance ruling is usually essential, and the standards of Rev.Proc. 72–13 become, de facto, the minimum standards for financing the corporate general partner. Do these standards provide for an adequate amount of "unlimited liability" to justify treating the limited partnership as possessing that essential characteristic of partnership?

MOUNT VERNON S. & L. ASS'N. v. PARTRIDGE ASSOCIATES

United States District Court, District of Maryland, 1987.
679 F.Supp. 522.

[The Federal Savings & Loan Association (FSLIC) brought suit on behalf of Mount Vernon S & L to hold MIW Investors of Washington (MIW), a limited partner in Partridge Associates, personally liable on an obligation of the limited partnership. A corporation, American Housing, Inc., was the general partner of Partridge Associates. MIW created Partridge Associates in order to "turn around" a real estate venture that had gone sour. MIW owned a 50 percent limited partnership interest in Partridge and participated in periodic operational meetings concerning the project.]

MOTZ, DISTRICT JUDGE.

* * * FSLIC contends that MIW has unlimited liability for Partridge Associates' obligations because MIW took part in the control of the business of the partnership. Theoretically, a threshold question is presented whether this case is governed by the "old" Uniform Limited Partnership Act, which was in effect in Maryland when Partridge Associates was formed and which governed Partridge Associates at the time of the occurrence of the events giving rise to this action, or under the "new" Revised Uniform Limited Partnership Act, which became applicable to partnerships formed under the old Act on July 1, 1985. However, this Court believes that insofar as the statutory provisions here involved are concerned, the new Act merely clarifies

what was inchoate in the old.   Therefore, this threshold question need not be resolved.

Section 7 of the old Act * * * provided as follows:

A limited partner shall not become liable as a general partner unless, in addition to the exercise of his rights and powers as a limited partner, he takes part in the control of the business.

Some courts held that, under this section, a limited partner could not be held liable as a general partner unless he had led the plaintiff to believe that he was a general partner. *See, e.g., Frigidaire Sales Corp. v. Union Properties, Inc.,* 88 Wash.2d 400, 562 P.2d 244 (1977) (en banc). These cases drew support from an official comment to Section 1 of the old Act that "no public policy requires a person who contributes to the capital of a business . . . to become bound for the obligations of the business; provided creditors have no reason to believe that the times their credits were extended that such person was so bound." At least one other court held, however, that reliance by the plaintiff was not an element of control under the old Act. *See Delaney v. Fidelity Lease Ltd.,* 526 S.W.2d 543, 545 (Tex.1975).

Although undoubtedly in conflict with one another, these two dichotomous lines of authority can be explained by recognizing that the different courts had different focuses.   Those which required reliance as an element of control were concentrating upon the external relationship between the plaintiff and the limited partner, and were concerned with the equities arising from that relationship.   The *Delaney* Court, in contrast, appears to have been concerned about the broader public policy of requiring those who choose to accept the benefits of the limited partnership form to preserve the integrity of the partnership's internal relationships.   This distinction is made explicit in the new Act. Under Section 303(a) * * * [of RULPA] a limited partner who disregards the limited partnership form to such an extent that he becomes substantially the same as a general partner has unlimited liability regardless of a plaintiff's knowledge of his role.   At the same time, a limited partner may have unlimited liability for exercising less than a general partner's power if the fact that he acted as more than a limited partner was actually known to the plaintiff.

Against this background it is too facile simply to say that "control" is a question of fact which must be resolved by the fact-finder.   Such an approach begs the question of what "control" means.   Rather, analysis must first proceed by asking whether Mount Vernon had actual knowledge that MIW was acting as something more than a limited partner. FSLIC has presented no evidence to prove that fact.   There is no indication whatsoever that Russell [the then President of Mount Vernon] was led into the Partridge transaction by knowledge of MIW's participation in the partnership, and Donald Eversoll, the then chairman of the Board of Mount Vernon, has testified that he did not learn of the Partridge transaction until November, 1982, long after Mount Vernon had entered * * * [into that transaction.]   Furthermore, the documents promoting the Partridge venture to which FSLIC points as mentioning MIW's participation clearly identify MIW as a limited partner.

Therefore, it must then be asked, as phrased in the new Act, whether MIW's "participation in the control of . . . [Partridge Associates] . . . was substantially the same as the exercise of the powers of a general partner." As to this question, FSLIC properly maintains that the record is clear that MIW originated the basic concept of Partridge Associates in order to breathe life into a dormant loan. Further, the affidavit of Michael J. Ferraguto, Jr., the president of an American Housing subsidiary which did construction for the Partridge project, does establish that MIW's president attended and participated in periodic operational meetings concerning the progress of the project. However, the law does not confine the role of a limited partner to that of a passive investor, as in a conventional syndication. To the contrary, as is expressly recognized in the new Act, [RMBCA § 303(b)] and as was implicit in the old, *see Silvola v. Rowlett*, 129 Colo. 522, 272 P.2d 287 (1954) (en banc), a limited partner may be actively involved in the day to day operation of the partnership's affairs, provided that he does not have ultimate decision making responsibility. Thus, the question is not whether MIW provided advice and counsel to Partridge Associates (which, undoubtedly, it did in light of its long association with the Partridge project) but whether it exercised at least an equal voice in making partnership decisions so as, in effect, to be a general partner. On that issue FSLIC has presented no evidence, and summary judgment against it is therefore proper.

[The Court declined to grant summary judgment on FSLIC's claim against Partridge Associates and American Housing, Inc., ordering the case set for trial.]

Notes

(1) The "take part in the control of the business" test of the original ULPA has been applied in a variety of different contexts. For example:

(a) In Silvola v. Rowlett, 129 Colo. 522, 272 P.2d 287 (1954), discussed in the principal case, a limited partner was held not generally liable for partnership obligations even though he "express[ed] opinions as to the advisability of transactions when his suggestions or opinion was sought by the general partner."

(b) What if the limited partner also acts as an employee or agent of the limited partnership? As a surety on bank indebtedness? What if he retains the power to approve or disapprove amendments to the limited partnership agreement or fundamental changes in the nature of the limited partnership's business? The answer of the RULPA to these various questions appears in § 303. Under the ULPA the test appeared to depend on whether the limited partner had actually exercised the power he had reserved. For example, in Rathke v. Griffith, 36 Wn.2d 394, 218 P.2d 757 (1950), a limited partner was named to the "board of directors" of the limited partnership but did not actually participate in the day-to-day decisions of the business. Even though the limited partner had also signed a few documents on behalf of the limited partnership, the court refused to hold the limited partner liable to creditors who were unaware of such documents. What about the power of a limited partner to draw checks if he does not actually exercise the power? Cf. Grainger v. Antoyan, 48 Cal. 2d 805, 313 P.2d 848 (1957).

(c) May a person create a trust for children, make the trust a limited partner in a partnership and then direct the day-to-day affairs of the partnership as an employee—a "general manager?" See Plasteel Products Corp. v. Eisenberg, 170 F.Supp. 100, 102–103 (D.Mass.1959), affirmed on other grounds 271 F.2d 354 (1st Cir.1959). If this arrangement is "looked through," is the trust a general partner or is the general manager a partner rather than an employee? Does it make any difference if the general partner has power to remove the general manager?

(d) May limited partners retain the power to remove the general partner and substitute another person in that position? See RULPA § 303(b)(6)(v).

(e) Assume that a limited partnership agreement provides:

No additional contributions have been agreed to be made. However, additional contributions are required if the General Partner determines that the partnership requires additional funds to meet the obligations of the partnership.

If the limited partnership becomes insolvent, may a creditor compel the general partner to call for additional contributions from the limited partners or hold them liable directly on the theory that the general partner should have made a call but did not? For a negative answer see Northampton Vly. Constr. v. Horne–Lang Assoc., 310 Pa.Super. 559, 456 A.2d 1077 (1983). Could a bankruptcy trustee exercise the power of the general partner in this regard?

(2) Commissioner's Comment to RULPA § 303 states:

* * * The first sentence of Section 303(a) differs from the text of Section 7 of the 1916 Act in that it speaks of participating (rather than taking part) in the control of the business; this was done for the sake of consistency with the second sentence of Section 303(a), not to change the meaning of the text. It is intended that judicial decisions interpreting the phrase "takes part in the control of the business" under the prior uniform law will remain applicable to the extent that a different result is not called for by other provisions of Section 303 and other provisions of the Act. The second sentence of Section 303(a) reflects a wholly new concept in the 1976 Act that has been further modified in the 1985 Act. It was adopted partly because of the difficulty of determining when the "control" line has been overstepped, but also (and more importantly) because of a determination that it is not sound public policy to hold a limited partner who is not also a general partner liable for the obligations of the partnership except to persons who have done business with the limited partnership reasonably believing, based on the limited partner's conduct, that he is a general

partner. Paragraph (b) is intended to provide a "safe harbor" by enumerating certain activities which a limited partner may carry on for the partnership without being deemed to have taken part in control of the business. This "safe harbor" list has been expanded beyond that set out in the 1976 Act to reflect case law and statutory developments and more clearly to assure that limited partners are not subjected to general liability where such liability is inappropriate. * * *

6 U.L.A.Ann. (1990 Supp.) at 308.

(3) In addition to § 7 of ULPA applied in *Delaney*, the original ULPA also imposed further restrictions on limited partners. Section 4 provided that the contributions of a limited partner may be "cash or other property, but not services." Compare RULPA § 501. Section 4 did not identify the consequences of a limited partner agreeing to contribute services to a limited partnership. Section 5 of ULPA provided:

(1) The surname of a limited partner shall not appear in the partnership name, unless

(a) It is also the surname of a general partner, or

(b) Prior to the time when the limited partner became such the business had been carried on under a name in which his surname appeared.

(2) A limited partner whose name appears in a partnership name contrary to the provisions of paragraph (1) is liable as a general partner to partnership creditors who extend credit to the partnership without actual knowledge that he is not a general partner.

Compare RULPA § 102(2). What is the consequence under the RULPA of the use of the name of a limited partner in the name of a limited partnership? Is a "name" and a "surname" the same thing?

(4) What theory appears to underlie the restrictions on limited partners in the ULPA? In the RULPA?

(5) Inadvertent general partnership liability may be imposed on limited partners if a general partner falsely represents to investors that a limited partnership certificate has been or will be filed, but no such filing occurs. ULPA § 11 addressed this problem:

A person who has contributed to the capital of a business conducted by a person or partnership erroneously believing that he has become a limited partner in a limited partnership, is not, by reason of his exercise of the rights of a limited partner, a general partner with the person or in the partnership carrying on the business, or bound by the obligations of such person or partnership; provided that on ascertaining the mistake he promptly renounces his interest in the profits of the business, or other compensation by way of income.

Precisely what should such an investor do after discovering there has been no filing? Can he or she wait a month or so to see whether the venture will "pan out"? In Vidricksen v. Grover, 363 F.2d 372 (9th Cir.1966), a physician learned in March that a Chevrolet car agency business in which he had invested had never filed a certificate. A renunciation was filed in September. Commenting that "the shoemaker strayed from his last," the

Court held the physician to be a general partner. See also Direct Mail Specialist v. Brown, 673 F.Supp. 1540 (D.Mont.1987). For cases involving a happier result see Graybar Elec. Co. v. Lowe, 11 Ariz.App. 116, 462 P.2d 413 (1969); Voudouris v. Walter E. Heller & Co., 560 S.W.2d 202 (Tex.Civ. App.1977). The leading case stating that the purpose of ULPA § 11 is broadly remedial is Giles v. Vette, 263 U.S. 553, 44 S.Ct. 157, 68 L.Ed. 441 (1924).

(6) Under ULPA § 11 [note 5, above] precisely what does a putative limited partner renounce? Does that mean the partner gets his or her invested capital back but without interest? Does RULPA § 304(a)(2) provide any greater guidance? May a putative limited partner personally prepare, execute, and file a certificate of limited partnership or a certificate of amendment under RULPA § 304(a)(1)? See RULPA § 204. Why not permit a putative limited partner to file a certificate stating in effect "I am only a limited partner" if the general partners fail to execute an appropriate certificate on request?

(7) Modern limited partnership agreements are complex and formidable documents based on tax considerations as much as substantive partnership law. For a carefully prepared example of such a document, see Partnership Law Committee (Corporation, Banking and Business Law Section, State Bar of Texas), Limited Partnership: Model Agreement and Certificate with Commentaries, 26 S.Tex.L.J. 25 (1985). This agreement involves a real estate venture in which the limited partners provide substantially all the capital with a shift of payment ratios between the general and the limiteds when the limited partners have received "payout," i.e. cash payments equal to their aggregate capital contributions. Such complex payout patterns are common in modern limited partnership agreements.

(8) Del.Gen.Corp.L. § 263 authorizes mergers or consolidations of limited partnerships with corporations. A corporation and a limited partnership "may merge with or into a corporation * * * or they may merge with or into a limited partnership * * * or they may consolidate into a new corporation or limited partnership formed by the consolidation * * *." Is there any problem, legally or conceptually, with allowing transactions of this type? Could a statute authorize a general partnership and corporation to merge? A proprietorship and a corporation? If a corporation is the surviving party to a merger with a limited partnership, who is liable on the prior obligations of the limited partnership? What about subsequent obligations?

C. THE PROFESSIONAL CORPORATION

The forms of business organization discussed above—the partnership or proprietorship, the limited partnership, and the corporation—constitute the most common forms of business organization, and are those customarily considered when evaluating alternative forms of business organization. Other forms do exist, however, and should be at least briefly mentioned. Some of these, such as the joint stock company and the "Massachusetts trust" are largely of historical interest, though some businesses so organized may still be operating in some states. Others, such as the mining partnership, are specially tailored variations of the traditional forms of organization to meet the peculiar needs of a specific industry.

By far the most significant factor in the creation of new or variant forms of business organization today is the Federal Internal Revenue Code. Mention has previously been made of the master limited partnership and the S corporation election. Special tax treatment has also been extended to investment companies (the ubiquitous "mutual funds" and "money market funds" being the most important examples), and a variety of other specialized enterprises such as real estate investment trusts (REITs) and domestic international sales corporations (DISCs). At another level, practically every state has adopted statutes to permit attorneys and other professionals to form "professional corporations" or "professional associations." These are new forms of business organization created by states to give certain citizens the benefit of a tax treatment not otherwise available to them. These statutes are of considerable practical importance to attorneys, in part because they usually may utilize them in the independent practice of law.

The tax advantages of professional incorporation were sharply restricted by the "Tax Equity and Fiscal Responsibility Act of 1982" (TEFRA). Before describing the changes made by this statute and the limited (but real) benefits that professional incorporation continue to provide after TEFRA, it is helpful to outline the original justification for inventing these new forms of business organization. If nothing else, this story is another dramatic illustration of the pervasive impact that the principles of federal income taxation have on business forms generally.

The Internal Revenue Code encourages employers to provide employees generally with certain fringe benefits by granting favorable tax treatment for those benefits. In the present context, we are not talking about stock options and other devices to provide benefits to top level corporate management in publicly held corporations, but primarily about retirement benefits designed for virtually all permanent employees of any type of business: secretaries, clerks, blue collar employees, and the like. Historically, the most important of these tax-favored benefits was the "qualified" pension or profit-sharing retirement plan. The desire of certain taxpayers to take advantage of those plans led to the invention of the professional corporation.

In qualified retirement plans, employers make contributions to specially created trusts for the exclusive benefit of their employees; the amount of the contributions is based on a formula usually dependent either on the employer's profits or the employee's salary (a defined contribution plan) or on an actuarial or some other type of computation to provide a pension of a specified amount upon retirement (a defined benefit plan). The tax benefits of "qualified" plans are the following: (1) the employer is given an immediate deduction for the amount of its contribution, (2) the investment income of the plan is not itself subject to tax to either the employer or the employee, and (3) the employee is not taxed on either the contributions or income until payments are received, usually upon retirement or death. Since these plans permit substantial annual contributions (up to 25 per cent of the direct compensation paid to the employee each year, or in some cases considerably more), they permit the accumulation of substantial nest-eggs on a tax free basis, and have obvious social implications since they strongly encourage the creation of privately financed retirement plans in addition to the social security system.

Qualified retirement plans were particularly attractive to highly compensated employees subject to the progressive income tax rates in effect before the 1986 Tax Reform Act. For these employees the shifting of taxable income from high income pre-retirement years to lower income post-retirement years promised a substantial tax saving independent of the tax-free build up of earnings within the retirement plan before retirement.

In order to qualify for this favorable tax treatment, a plan has to meet certain specified requirements: it may not discriminate in favor of higher paid employees, it must provide prompt vesting of benefits (so that employees who quit before retirement may take their retirement benefits with them), and it must ensure that the plan assets do not fall under the direct control of the employer. While many of these plans are contributory, i.e. they require the employee to contribute something to the plan as well as the employer, the favored tax treatment is not dependent on this factor.

Qualified retirement plans are attractive to the owners of a business for exactly the same reasons they are attractive to employees generally. The owner of a business, however, is in a somewhat different position from other employees: he or she not only controls the size of the plan, but also can distribute profits to himself or herself and use these funds to provide privately financed pension or retirement benefits. As compared to a qualified plan, this is singularly unattractive since the owner has to pay income tax on the distribution and thus is buying retirement benefits with after-tax dollars while a qualified plan permits the use of before-tax dollars, and gives the corporation a deduction besides. The substantial advantages of qualified plans thus often make it desirable for partners and sole owners of a business to be considered "employees" for tax purposes. The Internal Revenue Service, however, long ago took the position that a partner cannot be an employee of the partnership on the theory that a partner is an owner with the power of direction and control, not an employee. In most businesses, if the desire to create a qualified retirement plan primarily for the benefit of the owners is strong enough, the obvious solution is to incorporate the business and "employ" the former owners. Indeed, many small businesses are incorporated in large part for this reason. State law and professional canons of ethics, however, traditionally prohibit certain professions—principally, law, medicine and dentistry—from doing business in corporate form. While these prohibitions were based on considerations that really have nothing to do with how the income of a business should be taxed, the Internal Revenue Service drew from them the conclusion that professionals in those fields should be taxed as partners and should not be permitted to claim employee-type benefits for themselves. Of course, a partnership could employ secretaries and the like and form a qualified plan to give them these tax-free benefits; the issue was whether the partners themselves could get the same benefits.

The Internal Revenue Service waged a long, rear-guard action to prevent professionals from obtaining corporate tax treatment. Its motive in this regard was presumably the preservation of the public fisc, as well as implementation of its view of the presumed intention of Congress. The Kintner regulations (described briefly in the previous section) defining when an entity possessed sufficient corporate characteristics to obtain corporate tax treatment were amended at least twice, apparently with the sole intention of denying such tax benefits to professionals. The IRS threw in the sponge on this issue reluctantly only after suffering a series of judicial setbacks as to the validity of its regulations when applied to state-authorized professional corporations.

Of course, lawyers, doctors, and dentists are not without political clout at both federal and state levels. In response to claims of discrimination against the self-employed professional, Congress in 1962 enacted legislation that specifically permitted owners of unincorporated businesses to create limited self-employed qualified retirement plans, called "Keogh plans." These plans were much less attractive than corporate retirement plans, however, primarily because tax deductions were originally permitted for only $2,500 in contributions; this was increased to $7,500 per year in 1973, but it was still significantly less than what could be contributed under regular employee benefit plans. The Keogh plan, incidentally, is not related to the better known "Individual Retirement Account" or "I.R.A.") Much more promising was the enactment by states of professional incorporation or professional association statutes, and amendments to codes of ethics, which permitted professionals to conduct their practices in corporate form. After 1969, when the IRS finally agreed to recognize professional corporations as corporations for tax purposes, all states rushed to provide this option for their professionals, which, after all, was primarily at the expense of the United States Treasury.

By 1982, however, the mood of Congress with respect to professional incorporation had hardened into the conclusion that, rather than equalizing the tax benefits between different types of self-employed taxpayers, professional incorporation had become primarily a tax avoidance device that permitted professional taxpayers to avoid their "fair share" of the tax burden. Two practices that developed during the 1970's largely shaped this view:

(1) The first was the widespread use of "defined benefit" pension plans by high bracket professionals who were utilizing professional corporations for the first time relatively late in their professional careers. [As described earlier, a defined benefit plan seeks to ensure participants a retirement benefit of a stated amount (usually dependent on their recent income). For a person in his or her early fifties, say, a defined benefit plan requires very large contributions in the relatively few years remaining before retirement in order to fund post-retirement income of the specified amount. In recognition of this, the Internal Revenue Code in (and before) 1980 allowed deductions of whatever was actuarially necessary in order to fund a defined benefit plan so long as the maximum benefit did not exceed $124,500 per year.] Defined benefit plans often led to very large tax-deductible contributions for the benefit of senior, high income, high bracket, taxpayers: an attorney or physician with, say, $400,000 per year of income might contribute (and deduct) well over half his taxable income each year until retirement to fund his pension. Because of progressive income tax rates, the resulting saving in tax often approached or even exceeded 50 percent of the contribution. Furthermore, it was not uncommon for such people to borrow additional sums each year for living expenses (needed because of the very large retirement plan contributions) and then deduct the interest on those loans. The result was that some professionals were saving very large amounts on a tax free basis for retirement while retaining a very expensive life style.

(2) The second major practice widely viewed as unacceptable tax avoidance was having individual professionals in a single law or medical practice each form their own professional corporation and associate with the other professionals through a "partnership of corporations and individuals." In other words, a successful attorney might form his or her own professional corporation, with the professional being the sole employee and with its defined benefit pension plan created to maximize the professional's tax benefits. That professional corporation in turn might be a partner in the law firm in which the attorney was previously a partner on an individual basis. This "partnership of corporations" approach had at least two advantages: (1) it permitted each professional to tailor his or her own retirement plan to the needs of that individual rather than creating a single retirement plan covering all the professionals in the firm, and (2) it made it unnecessary to cover lower paid employees of the law firm in the retirement plans created primarily to benefit the partners. The secretaries, messengers, paralegals, and associates in the law firm, for example, would be employees of the "partnership" and not employees of the professional corporations themselves. Do you think that this innovative use of multiple business forms is subject to attack either on tax policy grounds or on the basis of substantive corporation/partnership principles? In any event, the Tax Court, in Keller v. Commissioner, 77 T.C. 1014 (1981), generally authorized this practice when it rejected an attack by the Internal Revenue Service against the substitution of a one-person professional corporation

for the individual pathologist in a partnership; the IRS unsuccessfully argued that the substitution served no meaningful business purpose and was entered into solely to secure tax benefits that would not otherwise be available.

The response by Congress to these perceived abuses in TEFRA was basically simple: it reduced the maximum deductions permitted for defined benefit plans, increased the maximum deductions permitted for Keogh plans, and then applied the same maxima consistently to both Keogh plans and qualified retirement plans maintained on behalf of corporate employees. Thus, in a single stroke, the principal benefit of professional incorporation was eliminated, since the professional can, by conducting business in partnership form and creating a Keogh plan, obtain the same retirement income benefits that could be obtained through a professional corporation. Members of Congress clearly believed that these provisions of TEFRA spelled the death knell for the professional corporation.[19]

In one respect, the predictions of the demise of the professional corporation turned out to be premature. Most persons who formed professional corporations prior to TEFRA have not returned to individual practice, and there has even been modest growth in the number of professional corporations. On the other hand, the free and easy period of rapid growth of professional corporations has ended.

Some minor tax benefits are available from professional incorporation, despite TEFRA. One minor fringe benefit employers may provide employees (on a tax deductible/non-includible basis) is group-term life insurance in an amount of $50,000 per employee, or less. A death benefit of up to $5,000 may also be provided. A partner or a self-employed person can only provide similar insurance or benefits with after-tax dollars. A second, somewhat more important, benefit is that employers may make tax deductible payments to accident or health plans for employees that are not taxable income to the employees. The importance of this fringe benefit has increased as medical insurance costs have continued to increase, and as Congress has limited the deduction for medical expenses (by raising the minimum deductible from three to five per cent of adjusted gross income and also by

---

19. [By the Editor] The Conference Committee Report describing these provisions of TEFRA states:

* * * The conferees intend that the provisions overturn the results reached in cases like Keller v. Commissioner, 77 T.C. 1014 (1981), where the corporation served no meaningful business purpose other than to secure tax benefits which would not otherwise be available.
* * *

The conferees understand that a number of personal service corporations may wish to liquidate when the parity provi-

sions of the conference agreement take effect. Therefore, a transitional rule is provided under which personal service corporations may, during 1983 or 1984, complete a one-month liquidation under section 333 of the Code without the risk that the corporation would incur tax on its unrealized receivables. Of course, the income represented by unrealized receivables will retain its character as ordinary income and will be fully recognized by the distributee shareholder upon subsequent collection or other disposition.

eliminating all deductions for medical insurance premiums except through the deduction for medical expenses.)[20]

In addition to these tax benefits, there may be nontax benefits of professional incorporation.

FIRST BANK & TRUST CO. v. ZAGORIA

Supreme Court of Georgia, 1983.
250 Ga. 844, 302 S.E.2d 674.

CLARKE, JUSTICE.

We granted certiorari in this case to address the following question: Where an attorney, who is a shareholder of a professional corporation engaged in the practice of law, issues checks to clients in connection with real estate and other loan closings, and these checks are dishonored because withdrawals from the corporate checking account on which they were drawn left insufficient funds therein, does another attorney, who is a shareholder of the corporation but who was not personally involved in the closings or withdrawals, become personally liable for the dishonored checks? The Court of Appeals answered this question in the negative. Zagoria v. DuBose Enterprises, Inc., 163 Ga. App. 880, 296 S.E.2d 353 (1982). For reasons which follow, we reverse.

Zagoria and Stoner are the only shareholders of a professional corporation entitled Zagoria and Stoner, P.C. While acting as closing attorney Zagoria issued the checks and withdrew funds from the account so as to cause the checks to be dishonored. The question is whether Stoner shares personal liability for these acts. He contends he is protected because he is not Zagoria's partner but merely a fellow shareholder in a corporation.

The fact that a corporation is a legal entity separate and apart from its shareholders is so well recognized that it needs no elaboration. It is equally well recognized that a corporation's shareholders are generally insulated from personal liability for corporate debts. However, there is no clear authority enunciating whether such a limitation of liability exists for a professional corporation organized for the purpose of practicing the legal profession. The courts in other jurisdictions have reached varying conclusions. See Petition of Bar Association, 55 Haw. 121, 516 P.2d 1267 (Haw.1973); Matter of Rhode Island Bar Association, 106 R.I. 752, 263 A.2d 692 (1970); Re Florida Bar, 133 So. 2d 554, 4 A.L.R.3d 375 (Fla.1961).

20. [By the Editor] The discussion in the text does not cover all possible tax benefits that may be obtained from the corporate form despite TEFRA. For example, a corporation may choose a different fiscal year than its shareholders; different fiscal years may permit a limited deferring of taxable income by the individual taxpayer in some circumstances. Additionally, limited borrowing is permissible by an employee from a corporate qualified pension or profit sharing plan; no borrowing is permitted from a Keogh plan. Some minor fringe benefits not discussed in the text may also be available from the corporate form. These tax-related differences all tend to favor incorporation over partnership-plus-Keogh plan.

We do not view this case as one in which we need to interpret the statute providing for the creation and operation of professional corporations. We rather view this case as one which calls for the exercise of this court's authority to regulate the practice of law. This court has the authority and in fact the duty to regulate the law practice and in the past two decades we have been diligent in our exercise of this duty.

The diligence of this court has been directed toward the assurance that the law practice will be a professional service and not simply a commercial enterprise. The primary distinction is that a profession is a calling which demands adherence to the public interest as the foremost obligation of the practitioner.

The professional corporation statute should be interpreted with this thought in mind. The legislature has the clear right to enact technical rules for the creation and operation of professional corporations, but it cannot constitutionally cross the gulf separating the branches of government by imposing regulations upon the practice of law.

By enacting the professional corporation statute the legislature performed a useful and constitutional act. A professional corporation has numerous legitimate business purposes. By conducting a law practice through the structure of a professional corporation, its shareholders realize the advantages of more orderly business operations, greater ease in acquiring, holding and transferring property, and more continuity of its existence. Additionally, a professional corporation affords to its shareholders insulation against liability for obligations which do not arise as a result of a breach of a lawyer's obligation to his client or an act of professional malpractice. The shareholders of a professional corporation have the same insulation from liability as shareholders of other corporations with respect to obligations of a purely business and nonprofessional nature. However, the influence of the statute upon the professional corporation cannot extend to the regulation of the law practice so as to impose a limitation of liability for acts of malpractice or obligations incurred because of a breach of a duty to a client.

The professional nature of the law practice and its obligations to the public interest require that each lawyer be civilly responsible for his professional acts. A lawyer's relationship to his client is a very special one. So also is the relationship between a lawyer and the other members of his or her firm a special one. When a client engages the services of a lawyer the client has the right to expect the fidelity of other members of the firm. It is inappropriate for the lawyer to be able to play hide-and-seek in the shadows and folds of the corporate veil and thus escape the responsibilities of professionalism. * * *

We hold that when a lawyer holds himself out as a member of a law firm the lawyer will be liable not only for his own professional misdeeds but also for those of the other members of his firm. We make no distinction between partnerships and professional corporations in this respect. We cannot allow a corporate veil to hang from the cornices of professional corporations which engage in the law practice.

Judgment reversed.

All the Justices concur.

Notes

(1) The court in *Zagoria* refers to several non-tax advantages of incorporation such as "the advantages of more orderly business operations" and "more continuity of existence." Are these benefits that inhere in the corporate form? Might not they be obtained in a well-run partnership just as easily?

(2) Professional incorporation statutes have to address several problems which are not present in business corporations generally. For example, there is the question whether such a corporation should be permitted to go into more than one line of business. Is there any reason why a professional corporation that is primarily engaged in the practice of law should be prohibited from owning and managing the office building in which its offices are located? What about combining law with a private detective business? With the practice of dentistry (through a qualified dentist, of course)? May a professional corporation have shareholders who are not themselves members of the specific profession? It is unethical in many professions for the professional to share fees with non-professionals. If this is the case, what happens when a shareholder in a professional corporation dies? When the sole shareholder of a one-person professional corporation dies? There is also the question of the name; codes of ethics of many professions impose limitations on names: it would hardly do, for example, to permit a law corporation named "Exceptionally Large Judgments Guaranteed, Inc." What about a dentist who wishes to incorporate his practice under the name "The Smile Clinic, Inc."? Questions such as the foregoing can only be answered definitively by examination of the precise language of the professional corporation statute, and of the applicable code of ethics adopted in the jurisdiction in question. There is a great diversity in the statutes, and many of them do not provide firm answers to such questions. While the amount of non-tax litigation dealing with professional corporations is increasing, many questions in many states still do not have definitive answers. Is this lack of definiteness or specificity a reason to avoid incorporation? The numerous variations in professional corporation statutes from state to state are detailed in books such as the C.C.H. Professional Corporation Handbook.

(3) The issue of limited liability addressed in *Zagoria* has arisen in several cases, and the answers reached by courts are not uniform. Applying basically the same public policy arguments with respect to attorneys, the Ohio Supreme Court concluded that shareholders in a professional law corporation were liable for all obligations of the corporation, including liability on a lease, in the same way as if they were partners. South High Development Ltd. v. Weiner, Lippe, & Crowley Co., L.P.A., 4 Ohio St.3d 1, 445 N.E.2d 1106 (1983). Did the court in *Zagoria* reach the same conclusion? On the other hand, in Schnapp, Hochberg & Sommers v. Nislow, 106

Misc.2d 194, 431 N.Y.S.2d 324 (1980), the court held a shareholder not liable on a sublease. Several other courts have similarly held shareholders in a professional corporation not liable on corporate obligations unrelated to the professional services rendered by the shareholders or corporate employees. Lyon v. Barrett, 89 N.J. 294, 445 A.2d 1153 (1982) [workers' compensation claim brought by legal secretary]; We're Associates Co. v. Cohen, Stracher & Bloom, P.C., 65 N.Y.2d 148, 490 N.Y.S.2d 743, 480 N.E.2d 357 (1985) [ordinary business debts]. In Birt v. St. Mary Mercy Hosp. of Gary, Inc., 175 Ind.App. 32, 370 N.E.2d 379 (1977), the court went further and held a shareholder of a medical professional corporation not liable for the malpractice of a co-shareholder, though in dicta the court made clear its belief that a shareholder would be liable not only for his own personal negligence but also for the acts of corporate employees under his or her general direction and control. The Birt case, unlike *Zagoria,* rested primarily on the language of the Indiana Medical Professional Corporation Act rather than on broad policy notions.

(4) Should not the question of the scope of limited liability in a professional corporation be resolved by the statute under which the corporation is formed? The professional corporation statutes were enacted simply as tax saving devices; nevertheless, the statutes of many states quietly build in a measure of limited liability with respect to claims similar to those involved in *Birt* and *Nislow.* The diversity of state law on this important issue led the Committee on Corporate Laws to recommend alternative provisions in § 34 of the Model Professional Corporation Supplement:

(a) Each individual who renders professional services as an employee of a domestic or foreign professional corporation is liable for a negligent or wrongful act or omission in which he personally participates to the same extent as if he rendered the services as a sole practitioner. An employee of a domestic or foreign professional corporation is not liable, however, for the conduct of other employees of the corporation unless he is at fault in appointing, supervising, or cooperating with them.

(b) A domestic or foreign professional corporation whose employees perform professional services within the scope of their employment or of their apparent authority to act for the corporation is liable to the same extent as its employees.

ALTERNATIVE 1

(c) Except as otherwise provided by statute, the personal liability of a shareholder of a domestic or foreign professional corporation is no greater in any respect than the liability of a shareholder of a corporation incorporated under the [Model] Business Corporation Act.

ALTERNATIVE 2

(c) Except as otherwise provided by statute, if a domestic or foreign professional corporation is liable under subsection (b), every shareholder of the corporation is liable to the same extent as if he were a partner in a partnership and the services creating liability were rendered on behalf of the partnership.

ALTERNATIVE 3

(c) If a domestic or foreign professional corporation is liable under subsection (b), every shareholder of the corporation is liable to the same extent as if he were a partner in a partnership and the services creating liability were rendered on behalf of the partnership:

(1) except as otherwise provided by statute; or

(2) unless the corporation has provided security for professional responsibility under subsection (d) and the liability is satisfied to the extent provided by the security.

3 Mod.Bus.Corp.Ann. (3d Ed.), 1911.

(5) The continued existence of professional corporations despite TEFRA appears to be based largely on the benefits of limited liability. Indeed, a number of law firms have incorporated as a single entity with each former partner becoming a "shareholder." Presumably these incorporations are motivated by the potential limitation of liability that the professional corporation promises.

(6) Is not the basic lesson of the professional corporation experience that courts and legislatures are willing to accept business forms at their face value rather than looking at the underlying economic reality? Is there any justification for whatever differences in treatment exist between professionals who incorporate and those who conduct business in more traditional forms?

Chapter Four

THE DEVELOPMENT OF CORPORATION LAW IN THE UNITED STATES

In post-revolutionary America, state legislatures assumed the powers of the Crown to award charters. For many years, this power was exercised sparingly, usually limited to ventures of a public or quasi-public nature. Charters often contained numerous restrictions. Perhaps as a result of the English heritage (which often combined corporate charters with grants of monopoly power), corporations were viewed with suspicion and mistrust. Also, since charters were issued on a case-by-case basis by the legislature, such decisions were directly involved in the political process.

Industrialization and the development of very large business entities during the Nineteenth Century spelled the end of that era. The corporation proved to be an ideal vehicle for the development of large business entities since it combined firm, centralized direction with limited financial commitment by a theoretically limitless number of passive investors. As commerce developed during the Nineteenth Century, the charters issued to corporations became increasingly standardized, and the restrictions became less onerous. The enactment of the first general and unlimited corporation statute by New Jersey, closely followed by Delaware, touched off an unseemly race between states, which is vividly described in the following excerpt.

LOUIS K. LIGGETT CO. v. LEE
Supreme Court of the United States, 1933.
288 U.S. 517, 548–566, 53 S.Ct. 481, 490–496, 77 L.Ed. 929.

MR. JUSTICE BRANDEIS, dissenting. * * *

* * * The prevalence of the corporation in America has led men of this generation to act, at times, as if the privilege of doing business in

corporate form were inherent in the citizen; and has led them to accept the evils attendant upon the free and unrestricted use of the corporate mechanism as if these evils were the inescapable price of civilized life, and, hence, to be borne with resignation. Throughout the greater part of our history a different view prevailed. Although the value of this instrumentality in commerce and industry was fully recognized, incorporation for business was commonly denied long after it had been freely granted for religious, educational, and charitable purposes. It was denied because of fear. Fear of encroachment upon the liberties and opportunities of the individual. Fear of the subjection of labor to capital. Fear of monopoly. Fear that the absorption of capital by corporations, and their perpetual life, might bring evils similar to those which attended mortmain. There was a sense of some insidious menace inherent in large aggregations of capital, particularly when held by corporations. So at first the corporate privilege was granted sparingly; and only when the grant seemed necessary in order to procure for the community some specific benefit otherwise unattainable. The later enactment of general incorporation laws does not signify that the apprehension of corporate domination had been overcome. The desire for business expansion created an irresistible demand for more charters; and it was believed that under general laws embodying safeguards of universal application the scandals and favoritism incident to special incorporation could be avoided. The general laws, which long embodied severe restrictions upon size and upon the scope of corporate activity, were, in part, an expression of the desire for equality of opportunity.

(a) Limitation upon the amount of the authorized capital of business corporations was long universal. The maximum limit frequently varied with the kinds of business to be carried on, being dependent apparently upon the supposed requirements of the efficient unit. Although the statutory limits were changed from time to time, this principle of limitation was long retained. Thus in New York the limit was at first $100,000 for some businesses and as little as $50,000 for others. Until 1881 the maximum for business corporations in New York was $2,000,000; and until 1890, $5,000,000. In Massachusetts the limit was at first $200,000 for some businesses and as little as $5,000 for others. Until 1871 the maximum for mechanical and manufacturing corporations was $500,000; and until 1899, $1,000,000. The limit of $1,000,000 was retained for some businesses until 1903.

In many other states, including the leading ones in some industries, the removal of the limitations upon size was more recent. Pennsylvania did not remove the limits until 1905. * * * Michigan did not remove the maximum limit until 1921. * * * Missouri did not remove its maximum limit until 1927. Texas still has such a limit for certain corporations.

(b) Limitations upon the scope of a business corporation's powers and activity were also long universal. At first, corporations could be formed under the general laws only for a limited number of purposes—usually those which required a relatively large fixed capital, like transportation, banking and insurance, and mechanical, mining, and manufacturing enterprises. Permission to incorporate for "any lawful purpose" was not common until 1875; and until that time the duration of corporate franchises was generally limited to a period of 20, 30, or 50 years. All, or a majority, of the incorporators or directors, or both, were required to be residents of the incorporating state. The powers which the corporation might exercise in carrying out its purposes were sparingly conferred and strictly construed. Severe limitations were imposed on the amount of indebtedness, bonded or otherwise. The power to hold stock in other corporations was not conferred or implied. The holding company was impossible.

(c) The removal by the leading industrial states of the limitations upon the size and powers of business corporations appears to have been due, not to their conviction that maintenance of the restrictions was undesirable in itself, but to the conviction that it was futile to insist upon them; because local restriction would be circumvented by foreign incorporation. Indeed, local restriction seemed worse than futile. Lesser states, eager for the revenue derived from the traffic in charters, had removed safeguards from their own incorporation laws.[1] Companies were early formed to provide charters for corporations in states where the cost was lowest and the laws least restrictive.[2] The states

1. [By the Justice] The traffic in charters quickly became widespread. In 1894 Cook on Stock and Stockholders (3d Ed.) Vol. II, pp. 1604, 1605, thus described the situation: "New Jersey is a favorite state for incorporations. Her laws seem to be framed with a special view to attracting incorporation fees and business fees from her sister states and especially from New York, across the river. She has largely succeeded in doing so, and now runs the state government very largely on revenues derived from New York enterprises."

* * *

In 1906 John S. Parker thus described the practice, in his volume Where and How—A Corporation Handbook (2d Ed.) p. 4: "Many years ago the corporation laws of New Jersey were so framed as to invite the incorporation of companies by persons residing in other states and countries. The liberality and facility with which corporations could there be formed were extensively advertised, and a great volume of incorporation swept into that state. * * *

"The policy of New Jersey proved profitable to the state, and soon legislatures of other states began active competition. * * *

"Delaware and Maine also revised their laws, taking the New Jersey act as a model, but with lower organization fees and annual taxes. Arizona and South Dakota also adopted liberal corporation laws, and contenting themselves with the incorporation fees, require no annual state taxes whatever.

"West Virginia for many years has been popular with incorporators, but in 1901, in the face of the growing competition of other states, the legislature increased the rate of annual taxes." And West Virginia thus lost her popularity. See Conyngton and Bennett, Corporation Procedure (Rev.Ed. 1927), p. 712. On the other hand, too drastic price cutting was also unprofitable. The bargain prices in Arizona and South Dakota attracted wild cat corporations. Investors became wary of corporations organized under the laws of Arizona or South Dakota and both states fell in disrepute among them and consequently among incorporators. See Conyngton on Corporate Organizations (1913) c. 5.

2. [By the Justice] Thus, in its pamphlet "Business Corporations Under the Laws of Maine" (1903), the Corporation Trust Company enumerated among the advantages of the Maine laws: The comparatively low organization fees and annual taxes; the absence of restrictions upon capital stock or corporate indebtedness; the

joined in advertising their wares.[3] The race was one not of diligence but of laxity. Incorporation under such laws was possible: and the great industrial States yielded in order not to lose wholly the prospect of the revenue and the control incident to domestic incorporation.

The history of the changes made by New York is illustrative. The New York revision of 1890, which eliminated the maximum limitation on authorized capital, and permitted intercorporate stockholding in a limited class of cases, was passed after a migration of incorporation from New York, attracted by the more liberal incorporation laws of New Jersey. But the changes made by New York in 1890 were not sufficient to stem the tide. In 1892, the Governor of New York approved a special charter for the General Electric Company, modelled upon the New Jersey act, on the ground that otherwise the enterprise would secure a New Jersey charter. Later in the same year the New York corporation law was again revised, allowing the holding of stock in other corporations. But the New Jersey law still continued to be more attractive to incorporators. By specifically providing that corporations might be formed in New Jersey to do all their business elsewhere, the state made its policy unmistakably clear. Of the seven largest trusts existing in 1904, with an aggregate capitalization of over two and a half billion dollars, all were organized under New Jersey law; and three of these were formed in 1899. During the first seven months of that year, 1336 corporations were organized under the laws of New Jersey, with an aggregate authorized capital of over two billion dollars. The Comptroller of New York, in his annual report for 1899, complained that "our tax list reflects little of the great wave of organization that has swept over the country during the past year and to which this state contributed more capital than any other state in the Union." "It is time," he declared, "that great corporations having their actual headquarters in this State and a nominal office elsewhere, doing nearly all of their business within our borders, should be brought within the jurisdiction of this State not only as to matters of taxation but in

authority to issue stock for services as well as property, with the judgment of the directors as to their value conclusive; and, significantly enough, "the method of taxation, which bases the annual tax upon the stock issued, does not necessitate inquiry into or report upon the intimate affairs of the corporation." * * * See, also, the Red Book on Arizona Corporation Laws (1908), published by the Incorporating Company of Arizona, especially page 5:

"The remoteness of Arizona from the Eastern and Southern States has in a measure delayed the promulgation of the generousness of its laws. New Jersey, Delaware and West Virginia have become widely known as incorporating states. More recently Arizona, [South] Dakota, New Mexico and Nevada have come into more or less prominence by the passage of laws with liberal features."

3. [By the Justice] Thus, in an official pamphlet containing the corporation laws of Delaware (1901), the secretary of state wrote in the preface: "It is believed that no state has on its statute books more complete and liberal laws than these"; and the outstanding advantages were then enumerated. * * * See, also, "The General Corporation Act of New Jersey" (1898), edited by J.B. Dill, issued by the secretary of state: "Since 1875 it has been the announced and settled policy of New Jersey to attract incorporated capital to the State. * * *" P. xvii. * * *

respect to other and equally important affairs." In 1901 the New York corporation law was again revised. * * *

Third. Able, discerning scholars have pictured for us the economic and social results of thus removing all limitations upon the size and activities of business corporations and of vesting in their managers vast powers once exercised by stockholders—results not designed by the states and long unsuspected. They show that size alone gives to giant corporations a social significance not attached ordinarily to smaller units of private enterprise. Through size, corporations, once merely an efficient tool employed by individuals in the conduct of private business have become an institution—an institution which has brought such concentration of economic power that so-called private corporations are sometimes able to dominate the state. The typical business corporation of the last century, owned by a small group of individuals, managed by their owners, and limited in size by their personal wealth, is being supplanted by huge concerns in which the lives of tens or hundreds of thousands of employees and the property of tens or hundreds of thousands of investors are subjected, through the corporate mechanism, to the control of a few men. Ownership has been separated from control; and this separation has removed many of the checks which formerly operated to curb the misuse of wealth and power. And, as ownership of the shares is becoming continually more dispersed, the power which formerly accompanied ownership is becoming increasingly concentrated in the hands of a few. The changes thereby wrought in the lives of the workers, of the owners and of the general public are so fundamental and far-reaching as to lead these scholars to compare the evolving "corporate system" with the feudal system; and to lead other men of insight and experience to assert that this "master institution of civilised life" is committing it to the rule of a plutocracy. * * *

The problems discussed by Mr. Justice Brandeis largely relate to the role of large corporations with many shareholders rather than the small, closely held corporation that might operate a retail store. The competition for the corporation business of larger corporations continues. Delaware particularly has found it profitable to maintain a hospitable climate for corporations. The success of this small state in attracting and retaining the incorporation business has been the subject of considerable study.

COMMENT, LAW FOR SALE: A STUDY OF THE DELAWARE CORPORATION LAW OF 1967

117 U.Pa.L.Rev. 861, 863–864, 866–869 (1969) *

The three groups responsible for the 1899 law are still active in shaping Delaware's corporation law. They are the corporation service companies, which have grown considerably since their inception in 1899; the legislature, which seems to have become more docile; and the Delaware bar, which consists of approximately 500 lawyers, about 425 of whom practice in Wilmington. Approximately twenty-five of these Wilmington lawyers comprise the full-time corporate bar. It is a very friendly bar, considered by outsiders to be quite competent in dealing with the Delaware corporation law, and headed by three firms—Morris, Nichols, Arsht & Tunnell, Richards, Layton & Finger, and Potter, Anderson & Corroon.

The 1963 statute calling for a revision of Delaware's corporation law empowered the Secretary of State, Elisha Dukes, to spend the appropriated money [Ed.—$25,000] "for consultants and assistance in such manner as will, in his discretion, most expeditiously accomplish" the revision. He decided to form the Delaware Corporation Law Revision Commission, made up of himself and nine others. * * *

Several decisions were made quickly. The first problem was whether to scrap the existing statute and start over again or simply to amend and revise the present one. * * * The Commission decided to preserve as much of the present wording as possible so as to keep the body of precedents that had been built up over the years. This is not, of course, an unsound decision for a legislative draftsman to make. Statutes should be written to make their meaning as clear as possible, and using phrases which have already been interpreted furthers this goal. But the decision not to scrap the existing statute may have been made with other considerations in mind. A wealth of judicial decisions helps Delaware attract corporations; to do away with this body of precedent could very well lessen Delaware's salability. Thus the "comprehensive revision" of an 1899 bill began by rejecting thorough change of what can only be termed a tortured statute. Delaware began its business by borrowing New Jersey's wording so as to insure settled judicial interpretation, and it was not about to tamper lightly with part of the formula for its success.

For a similar reason, it was also decided that the revision should not follow the Model Act. The reason was stated simply by Mr. Jackman, President of the United States Corporation Company, who "emphasized that Delaware should not adopt the Model Act because we do not want to be a 'me too' state in view of the fact that in the past most of the other States had copied our laws and that we should be a leader not a follower." * * *

The new statute was not written as rapidly as had been planned. The ten-member Commission proved unwieldy, so Chief Justice Southerland split up assignments among the members. A drafting committee of three was formed—Corroon, Canby, and Arsht. Through late 1966 and early 1967 they met to draft the actual statute, usually meeting on Saturdays in Arsht's office. Their job was far from mechanical. They considered many things the entire Commission never did, and felt they had broad authority and full responsibility.[4] Although they rejected some of Folk's recommendations, and although he never attended any of their meetings, much of his wording was adopted *in toto,* a result which seems to frighten him.

Since the product being manufactured is a law, the legislature (remember the legislature?) is supposed to have something to do with it. But it is clear that this was not the case. Simply stated, the Commission never expected the legislature to do anything with this law except pass it. One member of the Commission referred to the legislature as "just a bunch of farmers." Corroon did attend a caucus of Democratic Senators, and Canby did attend a caucus of Republican Senators. But Corroon was out in fifteen minutes, Canby in three, and neither was asked any questions about the law. The legislature did have one concern (besides tax revenues)—jobs. While it makes little sense to have certificates of incorporation filed with the Secretary of State *and* with county Recorders, to eliminate the Recorders would mean putting people out of jobs and the legislature might not have accepted that. So at the fourth meeting of the Commission, we find that "[i]t was moved by Mr. Jackman and seconded by Judge Herrmann that recordation as presently practiced should be continued * * *." There is no evidence that the legislature had any other influence on the actual content of the law.

The bill was passed unanimously by the legislature and became effective on July 3, 1967; amendments were worked through their "normal" course, the Delaware Bar Association's Committee on Corporation Law, and became effective on January 2, 1968. There were no official documents explaining the statute's provisions, no legislative hearings, and no publications by the Revision Commission. Folk's Report, Review of the Delaware Corporation Law, may not prove

---

4. [By the Editor] Mr. Arsht later described this portion of the statutory development process as follows:

"A drafting subcommittee, consisting of myself and Messrs. Canby and Corroon, assisted by three young lawyers from our respective law firms who had also been serving as law clerks for the Revision Committee, began the task of putting the Revision Committee's decisions into bill form. As soon as this project began it became clear that much work remained to be done and that a satisfactory bill could not be drafted without making numerous substantive decisions that the full Committee had not made and reversing some that it had made. In making the necessary changes, the subcommittee looked again to the Folk Report, to the minutes of the Revision Committee and to other sources such as the Model Business Corporation Act for guidance.

After meeting each Saturday for the better part of a year, the subcommittee presented a draft bill to the full Revision Committee for its consideration. The Revision Committee unanimously approved the draft bill without change. Subsequently, the proposed bill was approved by the Bar Association and the legislature and became effective July 3, 1967."

Arsht, A History of Delaware Corporation Law, 1 Del.J.Corp.Law 1, 16 (1976). Compare Seligman, A Brief History of Delaware's General Corporation Law of 1889, 1 Del.J.Corp.Law, 249, 282 (1976):

"Ultimately, the revisions to the Delaware General Corporation Law, the most influential business statute in the country, the closest thing we have to a national corporate law, were drafted in the law office of one S. Samuel Arsht."

extremely helpful on key points and, in any event, it may be hard to find. The Commission originally made only one copy publicly available (in the New Castle County Law Library), but xerographic reproductions can now be bought from the Corporation Service Company for $25.00. Despite the fact that the Commission had about $15,000 left over, Secretary of State Dukes did not want to spend the money to reproduce the report. Thus, the participants are left free to write their own "legislative history," an invaluable opportunity for a lawyer. This can be done through writing books and articles "explaining" the law, or through argument in litigation.

It is difficult to believe that the process just described represents the way legislation should be drafted. State legislatures may not be noted for thoroughgoing consideration of proposed bills, but the Delaware legislature's lack of concern seems extraordinary. The legislature simply abdicated its responsibility to consider the merits of its corporation law. It made no attempt to go outside the Commission and determine whether the statute served that "public interest" a legislature is supposed to represent. It was content to leave its work entirely to an appointed commission. It was content to leave this commission free to do what it pleased; and it pleased to solicit the views only of corporate interests and then to write a statute without one official word to guide future interpretation.

Notes

(1) Arsht, A History of Delaware Corporation Law, 1 Del.J.Corp.Law 1, 17–18 (1976):

> The present position of Delaware's General Corporation Law as the most popular of such laws in the United States is attributable to many factors, some of which have their roots in the distant past. The authors of a number of recent articles critical of the General Corporation Law,[5] to the extent they have traced the history of corporation law in Delaware, have alluded to sinister motives and methods in its development. It is not the thesis of this article to rebut such allegations and the arguments for federal chartering, nor is it my purpose to deny that the motivation for change in Delaware's corporation laws over their 189–year history is unrelated to the interests of American business and industry. On the other hand, I do not believe that enough emphasis has been given to the positive aspects of the development of the Delaware law. * * *

> Following the enactment of technical amendments to the corporation law in 1968, the Revision Committee's work came to an end and the Delaware Bar Association's standing committee on the General Corporation Law resumed its traditional role as the initiator of amendments to the law. Although the Bar Association has had a standing

5. [By the Author] Cary, A Proposed Federal Corporate Minimum Standards Act, 29 Bus.Law 1101 (1975); Cary, Federalism and the Corporate Law: Reflections Upon Delaware, 83 Yale L.J. 663 (1974); Law for Sale: A Study of the Delaware Corporation Law of 1967, 117 U.Pa.L.Rev. 861 (1969).

committee on the General Corporation Law during my forty plus years at the bar, the Committee is now quite large when compared to its predecessors in the years prior to the 1967 revision. At present, the Committee includes twenty-three private practitioners from all three Delaware counties and inside counsel from two large Delaware-based corporations. In addition, representatives of the Corporation Department of the Secretary of State's office and of the corporation service companies regularly attend Committee meetings.

In discharging their responsibility to improve the corporation law, Committee members draw on their own experience as practitioners, on suggestions received by them from corporate attorneys throughout the United States and on experience gained as members of American Bar Association committees such as the Committee on Corporate Laws and the Committee on Securities Laws.

It has been the practice of the Committee since 1967 to seek amendments to the corporation law on a yearly basis.[6] Amendments proposed by the Committee are first approved by the Bar Association and then submitted to the legislature in bill form.[7] Within the Committee, suggested changes in the law are, in most cases, first raised by a letter from a Committee member to the Chairman. The Chairman then places the suggested change on the agenda for a forthcoming meeting. If the change is one of substance rather than a minor change in language and if the Committee does not disapprove the suggested change on initial consideration, the Chairman usually names a subcommittee to draft a suggested revision to the statute. On a major substantive change, the subcommittee will meet separately from the full Committee and work through numerous drafts before presenting its proposal to the full Committee.

(2) Seligman, A Brief History of Delaware's General Corporation Law of 1899, 1 Del.J.Corp.Law, 249, 282–283 (1976):

> [The revised Delaware General Corporation Law] became effective on July 3, 1967. It was an immediate financial success. According to the January 12, 1969 *New York Times,*
>
>> Delaware began chartering new companies at a record-breaking clip after it revised and liberalized its corporation laws to meet modern needs. Before the revisions were made in July 1967, Delaware was signing up new corporations at an average of 300 a

---

6. [By the Author] Some members of the Committee have suggested that the yearly amendment process may detract from the perceived stability of the Delaware General Corporation Law.

7. [By the Author] Beginning with the proposed 1973 amendments to the General Corporation Law, the Committee prepared a brief commentary for distribution to the members of the Bar Association and, in turn, to the legislature. In 1973 several corporation service companies asked the Committee for permission to publish the commentary for distribution to the corporate bar throughout the United States. The Committee granted those requests with the proviso that publication of the text of the commentary reflect that it is the product of the Committee on the General Corporation Law. Unlike the comments accompanying the Delaware version of the Uniform Commercial Code, the Committee's commentary is not official nor was it intended to be. Its purpose is to aid in the legislative process and not to function as a definitive guide to statutory construction.

month. * * * [Delaware is now] chartering new corporations at a record rate of 800 a month. * * *

The article concluded with Secretary of State Dukes' statement. "The franchise tax will bring the state about $21 million in the fiscal year ending June 30."

That was just the beginning. By 1971 corporation franchise taxes and related corporate income represented $55.5 million out of $246 million in state revenue collections, approximately 23 percent of the total—the result of a stampede of the leading industrial corporations to Delaware. Of *Fortune* magazine's 1000 largest industrial corporations, 134 reincorporated or incorporated for the first time in Delaware in the years 1967–1974. This meant that by late 1974, Delaware was "home" for 448 of the 1,000 largest corporations—including 52 of the largest 100, and 251 out of the largest 500. These 448 corporations accounted for over 52 percent of the sales of the largest 1,000 manufacturers.

A 1974 Report to the Governor of Delaware further highlighted the special relationship between Delaware and the largest corporations. Although Delaware had chartered 76,000 corporations by June, 1974, franchise tax revenues received from the largest 556 corporations equalled 64 percent of all franchise tax revenues; revenues received from the largest 950 corporations equalled nearly 80 percent of the total.

(3) All this does not entirely explain Delaware's spectacular success in the incorporation business. Mr. Seligman suggests that the advantage of Delaware lies "not [in] her statute alone, but rather [in] the manner in which her judiciary interprets it." Id. at 284. In reaching this conclusion Mr. Seligman relies primarily on an earlier article by Professor William Cary, a former chairman of the SEC, who, after reviewing a number of Delaware decisions, concludes that "there is no public policy left in Delaware corporate law except the objective of raising revenue. * * * [C]onsciously or unconsciously, fiduciary standards and standards of fairness generally have been relaxed. In general, the judicial decisions can best be reconciled on the basis of a desire to foster incorporation in Delaware." Cary, Federalism and Corporate Law, Reflections Upon Delaware, 83 Yale L.J. 663, 670, 684 (1974). Professor Cary attributes this attitude to the relationship between the Delaware bench, bar, and state government: *

What is striking about the membership of the court in the last 23 years is that almost all the justices were drawn from the group responsible for the 1967 revision of the corporation law. In fact, two of them were members of the Commission. A majority of the justices practiced law in the firms which represent the important corporations registered in Delaware. Justices Southerland and Wolcott had been partners in a distinguished firm. Justice Tunnell eventually joined another, and Justice Herrmann was the senior partner of still another bearing his name. Three left the bench, two of them to return to leading firms in Delaware, and one to become Governor. With the

* Reprinted by permission of The Yale Law Journal Company and Fred B. Rothman & Company from *The Yale Law Journal*, Vol. 83, pp. 690–2.

exception of Justice Carey, who served from 1945 on the bench in various roles, all but two of the justices have been directly involved in major political positions in the state. The three chief justices have been chronologically (1) Attorney General, (2) Secretary of State and Governor, and (3) the Democratic candidate for Attorney General. Two other justices were Chairman of the State Planning Commission and attorney for the Delaware Senate. The whole process is reminiscent of musical chairs. In such a small state as Delaware, with a population of 548,000 and a bar of 733, of whom 423 are in private practice, we have in microcosm the ultimate example of the relationship between politics, the bar, and the judiciary. There is certainly nothing "wrong" or surprising about these relationships. Yet it is clear that Delaware may be characterized as a tight little club in which the corporate bar cites unreported decisions before the courts in which they practice. Thus major participation in state politics and in the leading firms inevitably would align the Delaware judiciary solidly with Delaware legislative policy. Indeed, as outstanding members of the bar they may have contributed to its formulation before they became judges and at any rate might be disloyal to their state to pursue any other course.

This is harsh criticism and it is not surprising that defenders of the Delaware Corporation Act reacted sharply and with outrage: E.g. Arsht, Reply to Professor Cary, 31 Bus.Law. 1113 (1976):

Professor Cary premises his advocacy of a Federal Corporate Minimum Standards Act upon the alleged deficiencies of state law, particularly focusing upon Delaware, its statutes, bench and bar. I submit that Professor Cary's analysis of the Delaware experience is biased, unscholarly and wholly unfair. If his articles had to measure up to the required standards of an SEC disclosure document, they would be found woefully deficient.

(4) B. Manning, The State Competition Debate in Corporate Law—Panel Response, 8 Cardozo L.Rev. 779, 785–6 (1987):

We, as practitioners, do not go to Delaware to incorporate and to litigate primarily because the law is "favorable" (whatever that may mean). We go to Delaware because there is a vast corpus of sophisticated law there and a lot of people in the right positions who know what it is all about.

I happen to be particularly fond of the State of Idaho. I have a home and spend a good bit of time there. I am prepared to rise to the defense of that great state for a good many purposes. But even I would not argue that one should choose that jurisdiction for litigation of a complex question of corporation law. In the forum of Delaware, I may lose, I may win, I may have a bad day, or whatever. But when people from my law firm go to Delaware, or when I talk on the phone to the Delaware Secretary of State's office, we are confident that we will encounter someone who already knows what a preemptive right is, and we will not have to start from zero.

Why, as a lawyer, am I inclined to recommend to a client that his new company be formed in Delaware? My answer is more grounded in that jurisdiction's unique human capital that in anything else. In Delaware, I will be dealing with pros. In many circumstances, speed of administrative and legal response will be important and in Delaware I will find that. And if one able Delaware corporation lawyer should be barred by a conflicting engagement from helping me, I know I will have available an array of other talented, experienced counsel to choose from.

Further, my Delaware counsel and I will have a wide ranging and sophisticated body of corporation law—a jurisprudence if you will—to bring to bear on almost any problem that will arise. No other jurisdiction can provide so much. And that is why Delaware is, in fact, national, and why its own gravitational pull tends to attract more companies each year and thereby further reinforce its preeminence.

(5) R. Winter, Government and the Corporation, 9–10 (1978):

Rejecting full federal chartering as "politically unrealistic," Cary calls for federal minimum-standards legislation. He claims this legislation, designed to "raise" the standards of management conduct, would increase public confidence—and investment—in American corporations. This last claim, it is absolutely critical to note, is not that an overriding social goal is sacrificed by state law but that Delaware is preventing *private* parties from optimizing their *private* arrangements.

With all due respect to Cary and to the almost universal academic support for his position, it is implausible on its face. The plausible argument runs in exactly the opposite direction. (1) If Delaware permits corporate management to profit at the expense of shareholders and other states do not, then earnings of Delaware corporations must be less than earnings of comparable corporations chartered in other states; therefore, shares in the Delaware corporations must trade at lower prices. (2) Corporations with lower earnings will be at a disadvantage in raising debt or equity capital. (3) Corporations at a disadvantage in the capital market will be at a disadvantage in the product market, and their share price will decline, thereby increasing chances of a takeover that would replace management. To avoid this result, corporations must seek legal systems more attractive to capital. (4) States desiring corporate charters will thus try to provide legal systems that optimize the shareholder-corporation relation. * * *

(6) Fischel, The "Race to the Bottom" Revisited: Reflections on Recent Developments in Delaware's Corporation Law, 76 Nw.U.L.Rev. 913, 917, 920–21 (1982) *:

The difficulty with * * * the "race to the bottom" thesis itself is that [it is] based on a model of shareholder irrationality. Why, given the infinite number of alternative investment opportunities, do shareholders voluntarily * * * invest in firms located in Delaware, given its alleged promanagement bias which supposedly exacerbates the detriment to shareholders caused by the separation of ownership and control? The extreme unlikelihood that investors would behave in this irrational manner suggests that the Berle–Means–Cary thesis is based on an erroneous premise regarding the structure of the modern publicly held corporation. * * *

The "race to the bottom" thesis can be tested empirically. If the popularity of Delaware as a state of incorporation and reincorporation is attributable to the ease with which managers can exploit shareholders then the negative effect which such exploitation would have upon the firm's income stream would be reflected in lower stock prices. To take the extreme case, stock prices of firms incorporated in Delaware would be zero if Delaware law allowed managers to divert all corporate funds to themselves. If, on the other hand, the primacy of Delaware is attributable to a permissive corporation statute, as interpreted by judicial decisions, that allows private parties to maximize their joint welfare by contract, then stock prices should reflect this fact as well.

In the one empirical study that has tested this proposition, economists Peter Dodd and Richard Leftwich measured the effect on stock prices when a firm reincorporates in Delaware. Dodd and Leftwich found that stockholders of firms reincorporating in Delaware earn positive abnormal returns of 30.25% over the twenty-five month period preceding and including the month of the change.[8] They found no evidence of any negative market reaction either before or after reincorporation.

The Dodd–Leftwich study is a powerful empirical refutation of the "race to the bottom" thesis and, more generally, of the attack on the separation of ownership and control in the large publicly held corporation. It suggests that managers make the decision where to incorporate with the objective of maximizing shareholders' welfare. To put the point differently, it refutes the underlying assumption of the Cary thesis that shareholders will be exploited in the absence of federal regulation of the corporation.

(7) Are you satisfied by the economists' analysis? Are studies based on stock prices an appropriate measure for evaluating the "race to the bottom" thesis? Are there social policies other than investor profit-maximization involved? Consider also the following commentary:

Winter's critique is devastating to Cary's analysis because Cary completely overlooked the interaction of markets on managers' incentives. Yet Cary's position cannot be entirely dismissed: More sophisticated proponents of national chartering can move to another line of attack by maintaining that there is a true difference in opinion that turns upon Cary's and Winter's assessments of the disciplining effect of markets on managers. Winter can assume away the agency problem because of his view that the capital market is efficient such that information concerning the impact of different legal regimes is publicly

---

8. [By the Editor] Dodd & Leftwich, The Market for Corporation Charters: "Unhealthy Competition" versus Federal Regulation, 53 J.Bus. 259, 275 (1980). For a later study see Baysinger & Butler, The Role of Corporate Law in the Theory of the Firm, 28 J.Law & Econ. 179 (1985), which suggests that corporations with large numbers of diffuse shareholders tend to incorporate in the "liberal" states such as Delaware, while corporations with more concentrated shareholders tend to incorporate in the "strict" states (of which California and Texas are examples).

available and fully assimilated into stock prices. In contrast, support for national chartering presupposes a market that is, at best, only weakly efficient, such that it does not digest information concerning legal rules. In addition, even if stock prices accurately reflect the value of different legal regimes, if product markets are not competitive or the costs of takeovers are substantial, then a manager's livelihood may not be jeopardized by the choice of a non-value-maximizing incorporation state. When the debate is phrased in this way, the disagreement is over an empirical question concerning market efficiency, for which, in principle, there is a clean answer.

Romano, The State Competition Debate in Corporate Law, 8 Cardozo L.Rev. 709, 711–712 (1987).

(8) Does the economic analysis answer Professor Cary's basic charge about the Delaware courts? Because of the importance of Delaware as the preferred state of incorporation for publicly held corporations, the Delaware Supreme Court is probably the most powerful commercial court in the United States today. In the chapters that follow, a number of decisions by Delaware courts are included. The reader should reserve final judgment on the merits of this criticism until after reading these opinions, and particularly the opinions since 1974. After all, it is reasonable to assume that members of the Delaware bench have read the foregoing criticisms, and it is hard to believe that any conscientious judge would not be influenced by their general tenor.

BRANSON, COUNTERTRENDS IN CORPORATION LAW: MODEL BUSINESS CORPORATION ACT REVISION, BRITISH COMPANY LAW REFORM, AND PRINCIPLES OF CORPORATE GOVERNANCE AND STRUCTURE

68 Minn.L.Rev. 53, 62–63, 67–70 (1983).*

The proposed Revised Model Business Corporation Act (RMA)[9] has features which represent an improvement over prior MBCA versions. The proposed statute's organization alone is an improvement. Some of its substantive provision, as well, seem to provide workable, creative solutions, even in an absolute sense.

Even so, in order to evaluate the RMA, "you must," in Justice Holmes' words, "look at it as a bad man, who cares only for the material consequences * * * knowledge enables him to predict" and "not as a good one, who finds his reasons for conduct * * * in the vaguer sanctions of conscience."[10] The RMA's drafters predicate the overwhelming majority of their revisions on a need for yet more flexibility, and apparently find justification for those revisions in no-

---

* Copyright (1983) by the Minnesota Law Review.

9. [By the Editor] Professor Branson was working from an intermediate version of the RMBCA, now called the "Exposure Draft." His comments, however, are

equally pertinent to the RMBCA, as finally approved.

10. [By the Author] O.W. Holmes, *The Path of the Law,* in COLLECTED LEGAL PAPERS 171 (1920).

tions of good faith, fiduciary duty, and "the vaguer sanctions of conscience" in those to whom they would entrust that flexibility. * * *

[S]hareholders have never had complete protection against a squeeze or freeze-out by means of a share issuance. Fifteen years ago, however, the shareholders did have several statutory and common law shields, none of which afforded complete protection. In combination, though, the protection afforded would in most cases prevent management from achieving nefarious ends. Tomorrow under the RMA, or even today under the MBCA, all or most of these shareholder protections are gone. In addition, the RMA will give corporate management a proliferating choice of swords to use, although, perhaps, no one of them may be capable of striking a death blow to the minority. In combination, though, the RMA provisions give, and have as an avowed aim the bestowal of, an almost infinite range of choices for corporate management to use for good or for evil as they wish. * * *

Many other RMA provisions also purposefully eliminate all substantive or other control over corporate entities.[11] Some of these provisions have surface appeal. Others run flatly counter to well-developed state or federal policy.[12] * * *

All of this elimination is done in the name of flexibility. Repeatedly, the RMA official comments reason that this or that relaxation or elimination of a formerly required procedure or substantive command is required because "flexibility" is needed and "discretion" is necessary. Curiously, in their comments the RMA drafters use the passive voice. The question that arises is flexibility and discretion for whom. The answer is flexibility and discretion for corporate managements and, secondarily, for their counsel. At a minimum, the RMA could forthrightly use the active voice in telling legislators and opinionmakers that it is management who purportedly needs additional flexibility.

The RMA is a lawyers' product. Members of the ABA Committee on Corporate Laws are corporate lawyers. When faced with a choice between substantive commands or "flexible" organizational guidelines, they consider the former but adopt the latter. They do so not because of any ulterior motive, but rather because they understandably believe

11. [By the Author] See e.g., RMA §§ 2.03 (secretary of state or analogous official no longer required to ascertain upon filing if articles of incorporation conform to law), [6.02(a)] (directors may be granted blank check authority to determine relative rights and preferences of new issuances of preferred shares), 6.40(d) (directors have power to revalue corporate assets for purposes of declaring a dividend or making other distributions), 11.03(g) (in surviving corporation, no shareholder vote required on merger if merger will not cause more than 20% increase in shares outstanding).

12. [By the Author] See e.g., RMA § 7.28 (elimination of cumulative voting).

* * * Seven state constitutions mandate cumulative voting. Ten other states statutorily mandate cumulative voting in all corporations. See § 3.02[16] comment (permitting corporate "contributions * * * that may not be charitable such as for political purposes or to influence elections"). Federal law, of course, makes criminal direct corporate contributions to political campaigns. See 2 U.S.C.A. § 441b, *construed in* Cort v. Ash, 422 U.S. 66, 95 S.Ct. 2080, 45 L.Ed.2d 26 (1975). Indirect corporate support for elections, such as through political action committees, is also currently a matter of some debate.

the corporate bar to be comprised of persons of rectitude and ability. Naturally, such individuals would not allow the flexibility the statute grants to be used for mean or sharp dealing. Coincidently, however, that flexibility also may make easier counsel's task of advising management, structuring a transaction, or authoring an opinion letter. Under older MBCA versions, attorneys sometimes found it difficult to defend the legality of a transaction because a substantive prohibition or command directly or indirectly impinged on the transaction. Yet the RMA drafters fail to heed Justice Holmes's admonition to approach and evaluate the proposed statute from the perspective of a "bad man." Undoubtedly, there exist some members of the corporate bar with only a modicum, or less, of integrity. There are also corporate managers whom even the "vaguer sanctions of conscience" do not affect. * * *

In truth, though, the seemingly infinite flexibility the RMA will grant is not infinite. Corporate directors have independent fiduciary duties of care and loyalty. Time and again the RMA official comments, and occasionally the proposed statute itself, remind the reader that exercise of this flexibility remains subject to fiduciary duty. * * *

Considered together with the ever-escalating degree of flexibility the statute grants, all of this RMA effort to remind of fiduciary duty * * * [makes it appear] that the entire edifice of corporate law has begun to totter on the head of a pin. Every issue comes directly or indirectly to fiduciary duty. Moreover, that fiduciary duty is not the strict common law variety which even at its best produced inconsistent results. Instead, it has become a much weakened statutory variety designed, in the main, as a safe harbor into which corporate managements may sail.

HAMILTON, REFLECTIONS OF A REPORTER
63 Tex.L.Rev. 1455, 1455–6, 1459, 1464–9 (1986).*

For the last five years I have served as the Reporter for the project that led to the development of the Revised Model Business Corporation Act (RMBCA). This new Act * * * is a model statute designed for use by states in revising and updating their corporation statutes. It is intended to be a "convenient guide for revision of state business corporation statutes, reflecting current views as to the appropriate accommodation of the various commercial and social interests involved in modern business corporations." [13] The initial reception of the new Act has been extremely favorable: it has already formed the basis of a major statutory revision in Virginia and is under active consideration in approximately fifteen other states. It appears likely that the new Model Act will be at least as influential as the original Model Business Corporation Act (MBCA) published in 1950.[14] * * *

* Published originally in 63 Texas Law Review 1455, 1455–70 (1985). Copyright 1985 by the Texas Law Review Association. Reprinted by permission.

13. [By the Author] Revised Model Business Corp. Act (1985).

14. [By the Author] According to the Model Business Corp. Act Annot. (2d ed. 1971), the 1950 Act served as the basis of codification for the corporation statutes of nine states from 1950 to 1959 and eleven

The Committee on Corporate Laws of the ABA's Section on Corporation, Banking, and Business Law has complete responsibility for developing and updating the MBCA. This Committee is unusual in several respects. Unlike practically all other ABA standing committees, its membership is closed and is currently limited to twenty-five persons; membership is by invitation only. Furthermore, the Committee on Corporate Laws has authority to make final decisions with reference to the MBCA solely on its own motion without prior approval from the Section on Corporation, Banking, and Business Law or the ABA's Board of Governors. * * *

The Committee on Corporate Laws is widely viewed as one of the most prestigious committees in the Section on Corporation, Banking, and Business Law: no attempt has been made, however, to require it to be representative of all the various constituencies that might have an interest in state corporation laws. In the early years of the Committee's history, it was considerably less representative than now: until the early 1970s, the members were almost exclusively lawyers from a handful of big cities and from major firms whose clients were predominantly large, publicly held corporations. It was, in short, management- and defense-oriented. Members, furthermore, were appointed for indefinite terms. As a result, the Committee experienced relatively little turnover in membership. As late as 1974, the Committee was described as follows: "[M]anagement lawyers apparently filled every one of the Committee's seats during the twenty-year period ending in 1969; filled all but one seat from 1969 through 1972, and still fill virtually all the Committee's seats even today." [15]

While the present Committee continues to have a strong predominance of management-oriented attorneys, diversification has occurred. Members serve for six-year terms and are rotated off the Committee at the conclusion of their terms. One or two attorneys who principally represent plaintiffs in derivative litigation and two or three law professors regularly serve on the Committee.[16] Diversity of viewpoints has also been enhanced by appointing attorneys from smaller cities and in a more geographically diverse manner. However, even with these changes, corporate attorneys from large firms continue their numerical dominance of the Committee on Corporate Laws membership. * * *

Professor Eisenberg's 1974 article, the first external examination of the procedures followed by the Committee on Corporate Laws in revising the MBCA, made serious and fundamental criticisms. The Committee did not regularly follow basic notice-and-comment procedures, which prevented interested persons from commenting upon proposed changes. Further, even when notice of proposed changes was given,

additional states from 1960 through 1969. * * *

15. [By the Author] Eisenberg, *The Model Business Corporation Act and the Model Business Corporation Act Annotated,* 29 Bus.Law. 1407, 1410 (1974).

16. [By the Author] It should be noted that I was invited to join the Committee in 1977 and served until 1983. Since then my only association with the Committee has been in my capacity as Reporter for the Revised Model Business Corporation Act.

the Committee appeared to exhibit little interest in obtaining public comment or willingness to consider carefully comments that were made.[17] Promptly following that critical analysis, however, the Committee made procedural changes and since then has consistently published proposed changes to the Model Act in *The Business Lawyer* with requests for comment. Final changes are promulgated only after consideration of all comments received. * * *

There is a widespread belief that an academic Reporter has broad power in major revision or codification projects to determine what is included and what is excluded. The committee or governing authority has ultimate power, but, in reality, the real power rests in the capable hands of the Reporter. Whatever may be the case in other projects, that is an inaccurate perception of the relation I had with the Committee on Corporate Laws. That Committee was fully in charge of all decisions. Preliminary drafts were prepared by me and screened by subcommittees that sometimes did not reflect the sentiment of the full Committee; statutory provisions or official comments, after being hammered out in extended (and sometimes excruciating) debate, were included only with the express and considered judgment of the Committee. The RMBCA is the product of the Committee, and not of my own views.

There were several reasons for the dominance of the Committee in this project. For one thing, the Committee participants were very capable. Each was a successful practitioner with many years of experience in the best corporate practice; the members are accustomed to dealing squarely with major transactions and difficult issues. They were not deferential, to say the least, to the views of a mere academic on issues they have been dealing with for years. Second, most Committee members welcomed the opportunity to put aside the parochial interests of their clients and develop the "best" principles.[18] Discussions were spirited, the level of interest was high, and the willingness to spend time away from the meeting room to review drafts, prepare memoranda, or write substitute sections was remarkable. No one will ever know the number of uncompensated hours spent on this project by these leading attorneys, but the total must run into the tens of thousands of hours. In short, the Committee controlled the product because its members were intelligent, they had broad practical experi-

---

17. Professor Eisenberg stated:

[T]he severe imbalance in the Committee's composition has been compounded, over the years, by the Committee's failure to adopt adequate procedures for circulating draft provisions among relevant sectors of the profession for comment. The values of such circulation hardly need explication and the procedure is so common in projects of this kind that one would think it rou-

tine. Yet until recently the Committee failed to do anything of the sort.

Id.

18. [By the Author] This was probably not uniformly true: in a few instances, I sensed that positions taken at meetings or in memoranda might have been influenced by the interests of clients or, in the case of corporate general counsels, by their employers. These positions generally did not survive the review process that led to the final statute.

ence, they were very interested in the project, and they worked hard. * * *

Because most Committee members had backgrounds in large-firm corporate practice, one might be tempted to dismiss the RMBCA as an exercise in improving "flexibility" so that corporate management can do what it wishes as efficiently as possible.[19] I believe this is a misleading oversimplification. The Committee members generally *were* trying to develop the "best" statute they could in a jurisprudential sense. They were trying to meld principles of fairness and equity with a system of management that permitted efficiency in operation.

In approaching this task, two factors strongly influenced the Committee members' perspectives on the issues that arose. The first was that they had a wealth of practical experience which no academic could reasonably hope to match. As a result, issues were not approached as theoretical or logical questions but as real-life problems. The second was the geographic diversity of the Committee members. This diversity allowed attorneys from more than ten states to bring their experience to bear on statutory issues that arose. Furthermore, their experience involved practical application of various corporate statutes to numerous diverse situations. From the vantage of these perspectives, a provision superficially desirable in one setting could be seen as increasing the complexity of transactions in a variety of other situations. The weighing of these advantages and disadvantages obviously involved practical questions about the frequency of events. After listening to and participating in this process, on a number of occasions I was persuaded that provisions I had openly criticized in class and in published writing had more support in fact than I had previously supposed.[20] * * *

19. [By the Author] Indeed, one early assessment of the Exposure Draft takes precisely this position. Branson, Countertrends in Corporation Law: Model Business Corporation Act Revision, British Company Law Reform, and Principles of Corporate Governance and Structure, 68 Minn.L.Rev. 53 (1983). * * *

20. [By the Author] A good example of this is the provision in most indemnification statutes that a director is entitled to indemnification as a matter of right if he or she "is successful on the merits *or otherwise*." The "or otherwise" language, from an academic viewpoint, is objectionable because it may require indemnification of a director who has a valid procedural defense—for example, that the statute of limitations has run—even though his conduct concededly violates every conceivable duty that directors or officers owe to a corporation. Accepting this reasoning, the California statute does not contain the "or otherwise" phrase. Cal.Corp.Code § 317(d) (West Supp.1985). When revisions to the indemnification statutes were being considered in 1980, I unsuccessfully urged the committee to follow the California approach on the grounds that the statute should not condone indemnification that violates basic concepts of public policy. The argument against its elimination was a very practical one: if a director has a valid procedural defense, he or she should not be required to go through the expense of preparing for what was essentially a second trial in order to establish his or her right to indemnification. The implicit premise was that the cost of all such second proceedings exceeds the injuries suffered by corporations when a procedural defense shields improper conduct. It was also argued that the cost of the second proceeding might adversely affect the litigation decision of a defendant with a valid procedural defense and a plausible substantive defense. While I do not agree that these arguments carry the day, I believe the issue is a much closer one than I originally thought.

In drafting a new corporate statute it is necessary to determine what goals the statute is designed to achieve. Traditionally, the watchwords of the Model Act have been "flexibility" and "modernization." From this perspective, corporation statutes should be designed to assure efficiency and economy of management and to avoid unnecessary costs. In contrast, some academics have criticized most modern corporation statutes on the ground that they are too "permissive"—that they do not provide adequate protection for interests other than incumbent corporate management. This view would make the basic goal of corporation statutes the "protection of shareholders" or "strong" regulatory goals.[21]

Economists have developed quite a different theory of state corporation statutes.[22] According to them, the purpose of a corporation statute is to serve as a substitute for private contract: in other words, a corporation statute should not be regulatory at all, but, instead, should be an efficiency-creating device that avoids costs associated with drafting and redrafting recurrent provisions by codifying these provisions. Because a corporation may incorporate in any state, differing state corporation statutes give each corporation the opportunity to select those provisions most suitable to its needs.[23]

The economist's approach toward corporation statutes is certainly not the theory on which the RMBCA was drafted. This theory was never expressly considered or explored by the Committee on Corporate Laws during the drafting process. Further, I suspect that most practicing attorneys would not accept the underlying premise of this argument that corporations are purely contractual in nature. Contract-type

---

21. [By the Author] There are many provisions in modern corporation statutes that arguably fail to provide adequate protection to minority interests in unregistered corporations. As Reporter, I raised many of these issues, among them the modest proposal to extend minimal proxy disclosure requirements to unregistered corporations to cover, for instance, recommendations on issues management knows will arise at an annual meeting. This suggestion and other similar ones were rejected in large part because the Model Act had never contained analogous provisions, the need for them had not been demonstrated, and most states had not seen fit to adopt them. The response to suggestions such as these was sometimes sympathetic ("We will study that idea further") but more often negative ("In my experience, cumulative voting is almost always a nuisance and usually has no effect on what happens"). Sometimes suggestions such as these were rejected on the ground of precedent ("We talked about that several years ago [i.e. before I had joined the committee] and there was no interest in including such provisions"). However, given the history

of the Committee, it is possible that some of these suggestions may be considered further at a later date.

On the other hand, in order not to give a misleading impression, many new suggestions I made on various issues were accepted. They appear, for example, in relaxation of involuntary dissolution requirements for deadlocked corporations, for liability for preincorporation transactions, and for requiring shareholders' lists to be available before meetings of shareholders. In these instances, support seemed to turn on whether Committee members had experienced situations where such provisions would have been useful.

22. [By the Author] R. Winter, Government and the Corporation (1978); Fischel, The Corporate Governance Movement, 35 Vand.L.Rev. 1259 (1982).

23. [By the Author] Statements such as this regularly appear in the market-dominated economics literature; it is certainly true of a large corporation active in many states but may not be true of a small corporation active only in one state.

arguments were raised by Committee members in a number of contexts, * * * [b]ut all members appeared to recognize that although corporation law obviously does have contractual aspects, some regulation was necessary. The Committee generally accepted, for example, that some actions authorized by articles of incorporation or other corporate documents can and should be subject to judicial invalidation. The powers and duties of corporate officers and directors are only partially contractual, and some duties may not be contracted away by simple agreement. * * * [Further,] numerous RMBCA provisions embody clearly regulatory purposes and expressly exclude or simply do not contemplate an election of nonapplicability. Examples of provisions of this type include: shareholders' inspection rights; power of directors to change the size of the board without shareholder approval; the requirement that every corporation provide certain minimum financial statements to each shareholder; availability of a list of shareholders before each meeting; and the grant of voting rights to nonvoting shares in connection with certain adverse fundamental transactions. None of these provisions are contractual because they cannot be eliminated by provisions in the articles of incorporation or bylaws.

Given a regulatory premise for corporation statutes, opinions will differ about whether the RMBCA pursues "flexibility" and "modernization" too aggressively, at the cost of "shareholder protection." My own view is that the new Act strikes a plausible balance between the two goals, though I personally disagree with some of the choices made by the Committee.

The advantages of many traditional "shareholder protection" devices urged by proponents of a regulatory statute are more apparent than real. The devices that might be cited as falling within this category include cumulative voting, preemptive rights, shareholder approval of certain transactions, and many traditional restrictions on the issuance of shares, such as the prohibition against issuing shares for promissory notes or future services. The protection afforded by these traditional "shareholder protection" devices is illusory because they do not prevent harmful transactions if the corporation is willing to structure the transaction in a manner that circumvents the statute. To dismiss such provisions as harmless and simply view them as ineffective regulatory devices however, would be a mistake: they have a real capacity for harm because a statute may, by containing such provisions, create the impression that it affords greater protection than really exists. * * *

ATLANTIC RICHFIELD COMPANY

NOTICE OF ANNUAL MEETING OF SHAREHOLDERS

May 7, 1985.

To the Preference and Common Shareholders:

The Annual Meeting of Shareholders of Atlantic Richfield Company (the "Company") will be held in the Grand Ballroom of the Beverly Wilshire Hotel, 9500 Wilshire Boulevard, Beverly Hills, California, on Tuesday, May 7, 1985, at 10:00 a.m., local time, for the following purposes, as more fully described in the attached Proxy Statement:
* * *

(3) To consider and act upon a proposal to approve the Agreement and Plan of Merger pursuant to which the Company shall change its state of incorporation from Pennsylvania to Delaware by merging into a wholly owned Delaware subsidiary; * * *

PROXY STATEMENT

March 18, 1985

The accompanying proxy is solicited by the Board of Directors of Atlantic Richfield Company. The proxy may be revoked by the shareholder at any time prior to its use by giving notice of such revocation either personally or in writing to the Secretary of the Company. The persons named in the accompanying proxy will vote as set forth herein with respect to the election of directors. With respect to the proposal * * * to merge the Company into a wholly owned Delaware subsidiary * * * they will vote or abstain as directed by the proxy, or, in the absence of such direction, will vote for the proposal. As to other items of business which may come before the meeting, they will vote in accordance with their best judgment. * * *

GENERAL DISCUSSION OF PROPOSAL * * * TO REINCORPORATE IN DELAWARE

There has been a recent trend toward the accumulation of substantial stock positions in public companies by certain parties as a prelude to proposing a takeover, restructuring or sale of all or part of the company or other similar extraordinary corporate action. Such actions are often undertaken without advance notice to, or consultation with, management of the company. In many cases, the purchaser seeks representation on the company's board of directors in order to increase the likelihood that its proposal will be implemented by the company or its interests will be served. If the company resists the efforts of the purchaser to obtain representation on the company's board, the purchaser may commence a proxy contest to have its nominees elected to the board in place of certain directors or of the entire board. In some cases, the purchaser may not be truly interested in taking over the company but uses the threat of a proxy fight and/or a bid to take over the company as a means of either forcing the company to repurchase its equity position at a substantial premium over market price or obtaining for itself a special benefit which will not be available to all of the company's shareholders.

The Board believes these tactics are generally not in the best interests of all of the shareholders. * * * The proposal to reincorporate in Delaware being submitted to shareholders at the Annual Meeting would tend to deter a proxy contest, the removal of the incumbent Board or the assumption of control of the Company and is intended to encourage persons interested in acquiring the Company to negotiate with the Board of Directors. * * * The Board recognizes that to the extent the proposals may discourage accumulations of large blocks of Common Stock * * * or tender offers for less than all of the Common Stock, incumbent directors are more likely to retain their positions and shareholders may not have the opportunity to sell their stock at an increased market price which typically results from this kind of activity. However, the Board believes that the overall benefits from these proposals more than outweigh these factors. * * *

PROPOSAL TO REINCORPORATE IN DELAWARE

General

The holders of the Company's Common and Preference Stocks are asked to consider and vote upon the adoption and approval of the Agreement and Plan of Merger (the "Agreement of Merger"). * * * Pursuant to the Agreement of Merger, the Company will be merged (the "Merger") into a wholly owned subsidiary, Atlantic Richfield Delaware Corporation (the "Delaware Company"), in order to change the state of incorporation of the Company from Pennsylvania to Delaware. On the date the Merger is consummated, each share of Common Stock, par value $2.50, Cumulative Preferred Stock, 3.75% Series B, par value $100.00, $3.00 Cumulative Convertible Preference Stock, par value $1.00, and $2.80 Cumulative Convertible Preference Stock, par value $1.00 (collectively, the "Company Capital Stock"), will be automatically converted into a corresponding share of stock of the Delaware Company (collectively, the "Delaware Company Capital Stock").

As a result of the conversion of Company Capital Stock into Delaware Company Capital Stock, the shareholders of the Company will automatically become stockholders of the Delaware Company. On the Effective Date, * * * the separate existence of the Company, except insofar as it may be continued by operation of law, will terminate and cease. * * *

After the Merger, the daily business operations of the Company will continue to be conducted as at present, with its principal executive offices at the same location in Los Angeles and with the same management. The consolidated financial condition and results of operations of the Delaware Company on the Effective Date will be identical to those of the Company immediately prior to the Merger. * * *

Principal Reasons for and Effects of the Merger

Your Board of Directors chose Delaware as the state of reincorporation for several reasons. For many years Delaware has followed a policy of encouraging incorporation in that state, and in furtherance of that policy, has adopted comprehensive, modern and flexible corporate laws which are periodically updated and revised to meet changing business needs. As a result, many major corporations are now incorporated in Delaware. The Delaware courts have developed considerable expertise in dealing with corporate issues, and a substantial body of case law has developed construing Delaware law and establishing public policies with respect to Delaware corporations, thereby providing greater predictability with respect to corporate legal affairs.

In the view of the Board of Directors, one of the principal advantages of the Merger will be the elimination of cumulative voting in the election of directors by holders of Common Stock. * * * Under cumulative voting, a shareholder's total vote (which is equal to the number of votes such shareholder is entitled to cast multiplied by the number of directors to be elected in that election) may be cast entirely for one candidate or distributed among two or more candidates. With this voting process, which is currently used in the election of the Company's directors, it is possible for representation on the Board of Directors to be obtained by an individual shareholder or a group of shareholders holding Voting Stock with far less than a majority of the voting rights. Such a shareholder or group may have interests and goals which are not consistent with, and indeed might be in conflict with, those of a majority of the shareholders. The Board of Directors believes that the presence on the Board of one or more directors representing such a special constituency could disrupt and impair the efficient management of the Company. * * *

If the Merger is effected, the holders of shares representing more than 50% of the votes which may be cast by the Delaware Company Voting Stock will be able * * * to elect all of the directors to be elected at any meeting held to elect directors. Many large, widely-held companies use this method of choosing directors and the Board of Directors considers this an appropriate method of choosing directors of the Delaware Company. The Merger will therefore have the effect of eliminating the ability of a holder of Common Stock to elect one or more directors at any meeting unless such holder can obtain a majority of the votes represented by the shares of Voting Stock present at the meeting. * * *

Other changes resulting from the Merger include (i) eliminating the right of stockholders to call special meetings and to propose amendments to the Certificate of Incorporation, (ii) requiring a Two–Thirds

Stockholder Vote to amend or repeal, or adopt a provision inconsistent with, the present classification of the Company's Board of Directors, and (iii) certain other provisions relating to the Board of Directors and the conduct of the business of the Company. * * *

Other important consequences of the Merger will be that (i) the provision classifying the Board of Directors into three classes (which provision is currently contained in the Company's by-laws) will be moved to the Certificate of Incorporation of the Delaware Company and (ii) certain other new provisions of the Certificate of Incorporation will restrict the ability of a person who acquires control of a majority of the Delaware Company's voting power from repealing or otherwise circumventing the classified Board structure.

Under Delaware law, cause is required for removal of the Delaware Company's directors and the Certificate of Incorporation will require a Two–Thirds Stockholder Vote to so remove directors; under Pennsylvania law all directors or a class thereof may be removed with or without cause by an absolute majority of votes entitled to be cast in an election of directors. An individual director may also be so removed, unless the number of votes cast against his removal would be sufficient, if cumulatively voted, to elect one director. The Board of Directors will have the sole authority pursuant to the Certificate of Incorporation to fill any vacancies or newly created directorships on the Board and will determine the size of the Board. Furthermore, a Two–Thirds Stockholder Vote (rather than a simple majority) will be required to amend or repeal, or to adopt any provision inconsistent with, the provisions in the Certificate of Incorporation relating to the Board of Directors, and a similar vote will be required for stockholders to amend or repeal, or to adopt any provision inconsistent with, the By–Laws. As a result, it will be more difficult to change the composition of the Board of Directors, and the holders of a majority of the Delaware Company Common Stock might not be able to elect a majority of the Delaware Company's directors until two or more annual meetings have been held. Although there have been no problems with respect to continuity or stability of the Board of Directors in the past, the Board believes that the longer time required to displace a classified Board will help to ensure the continuity and stability of the Company's management and policies in the future, since a majority of the directors at any given time will ordinarily have prior experience as directors of the Company. * * *

* * *

Notes

(1) The importance of the law of the state of incorporation is greatly enhanced by the so-called "internal affairs rule," which provides that foreign courts will apply the law of the state of incorporation to issues relating to the internal affairs of a foreign corporation. Consult RMBCA § 15.05(c). See generally Kozyris, Corporate Wars and Choice of Law, 1985 Duke L.J. 1; De Mott, Perspectives on Choice of Law for Corporate Internal Affairs, 48 Law & Contem.Prob., 161 (Summer 1985).

(2) California is the principal state that has adopted a relatively stringent corporation statute and then sought to apply it against corporations formed in other states but whose principal business activities are in California. West's Ann.Cal.Corp.Code § 2115 requires corporations with "specified minimum contacts" in California to comply with designated provisions of the California statute: among others, sections dealing with cumulative voting, limitations on distributions, inspection rights of shareholders, and dissenters' rights. The section is not applicable to corporations with shares listed on national securities exchanges, and thus would not apply to Atlantic Richfield. The constitutionality of this approach has not been definitively resolved. Wilson v. Louisiana–Pacific Resources, Inc., 138 Cal.App.3d 216, 187 Cal.Rptr. 852 (1982) upheld the imposition of the California cumulative voting provisions upon a Utah corporation that was subject to § 2115; the California shareholders' inspection statute was applied to a foreign corporation in Valtz v. Penta Investment Corp., 139 Cal.App.3d 803, 188 Cal.Rptr. 922 (1983). But see Arden–Mayfair, Inc. v. Louart Corporation, 385 A.2d 3 (Del.Ch.1978), holding the California statute inapplicable under "generally recognized choice of law principles" and discussing an unreported California lower court decision holding § 2115 unconstitutional.

MANNING, THE SHAREHOLDER'S APPRAISAL REMEDY: AN ESSAY FOR FRANK COKER

72 Yale L.J. 223, 245, n. 37 (1962).*

One result of this break-through is that corporation law, as a field of intellectual effort, is dead in the United States. When American law ceased to take the "corporation" seriously, the entire body of law that had been built upon that intellectual construct slowly perforated and rotted away. We have nothing left but our great empty corporation statutes—towering skyscrapers of rusted girders, internally welded together and containing nothing but wind. But that is a broader thesis best saved for another day.

Those of us in academic life who have specialized in corporation law face technological unemployment, or at least substantial retooling. There is still a good bit of work to be done to persuade someone to give a decent burial to the shivering skeletons. And there will be plenty of work overseas for a long time to come, for in Latin America, and to a lesser extent on the Continent, the "corporation" yet thrives and breeds as it did in this country eighty years ago.

Notes

(1) In contrast with Manning's gloomy assessment, consider Eisenberg, The Modernization of Corporate Law: An Essay for Bill Cary, 37 Miami L.Rev. 187, 209 (1983):

* Reprinted by permission of The Yale Law Journal Company and Fred B. Rothman & Company from *The Yale Law Journal*, Vol. 72, p. 245.

Within the last ten years or so, there has been a remarkable amount of ferment in the area of corporate law. For the moment, the American Law Institute's *Principles of Corporate Governance: Analysis and Recommendations* is at center stage, but the ferment precedes that project. In 1977, the Business Roundtable issued its statement on *The Role and Composition of the Board of Directors of the Large Publicly Owned Corporation.*[24] In 1977 and 1978, the ALI, the American Bar Association's Section of Corporation, Banking and Business Law, and the ALI–ABA Committee on Continuing Professional Education, jointly convened four important regional conferences on corporate law.[25] In 1978, the American Assembly issued a report on *Corporate Governance in America,*[26] and the ABA Section issued the *Corporate Director's Guidebook.*[27] In 1979, the ABA Section issued a follow-up guidebook, *The Overview Committees of the Board of Directors.*[28]

This ferment was precipitated in large part by several developments in the mid–1970's. One was the general reexamination of our institutions that followed in the wake of Watergate. An element of Watergate was the revelation that some of our largest corporations had been engaged in widespread violation of domestic law, and some others had paid bribes to persons at the highest levels of foreign governments and thereby recklessly endangered our national security by putting at risk the political stability of our closest allies. In the short term, these disclosures led to the Foreign Corrupt Practices Act of 1977.[29] In the long term, they needlessly shook the public's confidence in one of the pillars of legitimacy of the American corporate system—the premise (which I regard as correct that placing control of the factors of production and distribution in the hands of privately appointed managers maximizes our national wealth without entailing substantial nonfinancial costs.

A second development precipitating the current reexamination of corporate law appears to have been a growing realization by the profession that such a reexamination was needed sooner or later, and was best conducted now, in an atmosphere of relative calm. The priority of this need was accentuated by the publication in 1974 of Bill Cary's article *Federalism and Corporate Law: Reflections Upon Delaware,* * * *

Whatever factors have motivated the present reexamination of corporate law, it is clear that the reexamination is long overdue. The

---

24. [By the Author] The Business Roundtable, The Role and Composition of the Board of Directors of the Large Publicly Owned Corporation, 33 Bus.Law 2083 (1978).

25. [By the Author] See Commentaries on Corporate Structure and Governance: The ALI–ABA Symposiums 1977–1978 (D. Schwartz ed. 1979) (edited transcripts of the four conferences).

26. [By the Author] Corporate Governance in America (1978) (54th American Assembly).

27. [By the Author] Committee on Corporate Laws, ABA Section of Corporation, Banking & Business Law, Corporate Directors' Guidebook, 33 Bus.Law 1591 (1978).

28. [By the Author] Committee on Corporate Laws, ABA Section of Corporation, Banking & Business Law, The Overview Committees of the Board of Directors, 34 Bus.Law 1837 (1979).

29. [By the Author] Pub.L. No. 95–213, 91 Stat. 1494 (codified at 15 U.S.C. §§ 78a note, 78m, 78dd–1, 78dd–2, 78ff (1982)).

American corporate system is a complex economic machine, and statutory corporate law is one of the important subsystems on which the machine is based. Some components of that subsystem are badly in need of modernization. Modernization always entails some present costs, but typically they are much less than the future costs of obsolescence.

(2) The American Law Institute's Corporate Governance Project referred to in the excerpt from Professor Eisenberg, is presently scheduled to continue through 1991. It has been awash in controversy. See, e.g. Symposium on the ALI Corporate Governance Project, 37 Miami L.Rev. 169–349 (1983); id., 52 Geo.Wash.L.Rev. 495–871 (1984); Symposium on Corporate Governance, 8 Cardozo L.Rev. 657 (1987).

(3) The emphasis on *state* corporation law in this chapter should not be misinterpreted. A significant portion of the modern law of corporations is federal in origin. There is already a significant amount of federal regulation based primarily on two New Deal era statutes, the Securities Act of 1933 and the Securities Exchange Act of 1934. In a sense, of course, these statutes were a response to the perceived inadequacy of state regulation of corporations in the period before the Great Depression, but they did not create a pervasive scheme of federal regulation. The relationship between federal and state law has not always been stable. During the 1960s and early 1970s there was a trend toward the gradual expansion of federal law at the expense of state law under these two statutes, largely based on expansive construction of antifraud concepts in the 1934 Act and Rule 10b–5 promulgated thereunder. As a result of several restrictive United States Supreme Court opinions in the late 1970s (see chapter 13, infra), however, this trend toward the federalization of broad areas of corporation law stopped abruptly. Again, in the early 1980s another trend toward federalization of state corporation law developed from the conservative "law and economics" movement's theory that there existed a national market for "corporate control" of publicly held corporations with which states were powerless to interfere. The United States abruptly dismantled this theory in CTS Corporation v. Dynamics Corp. of America, 481 U.S. 69, 107 S.Ct. 1637, 95 L.Ed.2d 67 (1987). Justice Powell's majority opinion contains the following articulation of the traditional role of states in the regulation of state-created publicly held corporations:

We think the Court of Appeals failed to appreciate the significance for Commerce Clause analysis of the fact that state regulation of corporate governance is regulation of entities whose very existence and attributes are a product of state law. As Chief Justice Marshall explained:

"A corporation is an artificial being, invisible, intangible, and existing only in contemplation of law. Being the mere creature of law, it possesses only those properties which the charter of its creation confers upon it, either expressly, or as incidental to its very existence. These are such as are supposed best calculated to effect the object for which it was created." Trustees of Dartmouth College v. Woodward, 4 Wheat. 518, 636, 4 L.Ed. 518 (1819).

Every State in this country has enacted laws regulating corporate governance. By prohibiting certain transactions, and regulating others, such laws necessarily affect certain aspects of interstate commerce. This necessarily is true with respect to corporations with shareholders in States other than the State of incorporation. Large corporations that are listed on national exchanges, or even regional exchanges, will have shareholders in many States and shares that are traded frequently. The markets that facilitate this national and international participation in ownership of corporations are essential for providing capital not only for new enterprises but also for established companies that need to expand their businesses. This beneficial free market system depends at its core upon the fact that a corporation—except in the rarest situations—is organized under, and governed by, the law of a single jurisdiction, traditionally the corporate law of the State of its incorporation.

These regulatory laws may affect directly a variety of corporate transactions. Mergers are a typical example. In view of the substantial effect that a merger may have on the shareholders' interests in a corporation, many States require supermajority votes to approve mergers. See, e.g., MBCA § 73 (requiring approval of a merger by a majority of all shares, rather than simply a majority of votes cast); RMBCA § 11.03 (same). By requiring a greater vote for mergers than is required for other transactions, these laws make it more difficult for corporations to merge. State laws also may provide for "dissenters' rights" under which minority shareholders who disagree with corporate decisions to take particular actions are entitled to sell their shares to the corporation at fair market value. See, e.g., MBCA § 80–81; RMBCA § 13.02. By requiring the corporation to purchase the shares of dissenting shareholders, these laws may inhibit a corporation from engaging in the specified transactions.[30]

It thus is an accepted part of the business landscape in this country for States to create corporations, to prescribe their powers, and to define the rights that are acquired by purchasing their shares. A State has an interest in promoting stable relationships among parties involved in the corporations it charters, as well as in ensuring that investors in such corporations have an effective voice in corporate affairs.

---

30. [By the Court] Numerous other common regulations may affect both non-resident and resident shareholders of a corporation. Specified votes may be required for the sale of all of the corporation's assets. See MBCA § 79; RMBCA § 12.02. The election of directors may be staggered over a period of years to prevent abrupt changes in management. See MBCA § 37; RMBCA § 8.06. Various classes of stock may be created with differences in voting rights as to dividends and on liquidation. See MBCA § 15; RMBCA § 6.01(c). Provisions may be made for cumulative voting. See MBCA § 33, par. 4; RMBCA § 7.28.

Corporations may adopt restrictions on payment of dividends to ensure that specified ratios of assets to liabilities are maintained for the benefit of the holders of corporate bonds or notes. See MBCA § 45 (noting that a corporation's articles of incorporation can restrict payment of dividends); RMBCA § 6.40 (same). Where the shares of a corporation are held in States other than that of incorporation, actions taken pursuant to these and similar provisions of state law will affect all shareholders alike wherever they reside or are domiciled. * * *

481 U.S. at 87–91. 107 S.Ct. at 1649–1651. The modern law of corporations is thus an amalgam of federal and state law principles: today it appears unlikely that one will supplant the other or that proposals for enhancement of the federal role (such as for federal incorporation or for viewing the corporation as a contract subject to the Contracts clause of the United States Constitution,[31]) stand any real chance of enactment or acceptance. Indeed, as described in chapter 12, below, it is likely that after CTS the trend is in the opposite direction.

31. [By the Editor] This argument has recently been put forth in Butler and Ribstein, State Anti–Takeover Statutes and the Contract Clause, 57 Cinc.L.Rev. 611 (1988); Ribstein, Takeover Defenses and the Corporate Contract, 78 Geo.L.J. 71 (1989); Butler and Ribstein, The Contract Clause and the Constitution, 55 Brooklyn L.Rev. 767 (1989). The Brooklyn Law Review article is the centerpiece of a symposium devoted to this thesis. The other participants were critical of this thesis, which does seem to be an obvious attempt to make an end run around the CTS opinion. The strongest criticism in this symposium appears in Bard, Advocacy Masquerading as Scholarship or, Why Legal Scholars Cannot Be Trusted, 55 Brooklyn L.Rev. 853 (1989).

Chapter Five

THE FORMATION OF A CLOSELY HELD CORPORATION

A. WHERE TO INCORPORATE

Selection of the state of incorporation involves an appraisal of two factors: (a) a dollars-and-cents analysis of the relative cost of incorporating, or qualifying as a foreign corporation, under the statutes of the states under consideration, and (b) a consideration of the advantages and disadvantages of the substantive corporation laws of these states. As a practical matter the choice often comes down to the jurisdiction where the business is to be conducted, or Delaware, the most popular outside jurisdiction.

If the corporation is closely held and its business is to be conducted largely or entirely within a single state, local incorporation is almost always to be preferred. (a) The cost of forming a Delaware corporation and qualifying it to transact business in another state will be greater than forming a local corporation in that state. In addition, the probable cost of legal assistance in forming a Delaware corporation must be considered. (b) The cost of operating a Delaware corporation also will be greater than the cost of operating a local corporation. Income and franchise taxes are usually the same for both domestic and qualified foreign corporation, but again the Delaware taxes must be added. (c) Another substantial disadvantage of Delaware incorporation is the possibility of being forced to defend a suit in a distant state rather than where the corporation has its principal place of business. (d) While the Delaware statute may offer some flexibility not available in other states, most desired control arrangements can be worked out under most states' current statutes. Several states, for example, give specific statutory recognition to the close corporation. These statutes are discussed in Chapter 8, Section F, below.

How does an attorney in, say, California, go about forming a Delaware corporation? One possibility, of course, is to make a crash study of the statutory and case law of the unfamiliar state, but there

190

are obvious risks in that as well as a substantial (and perhaps uncompensated) expenditure of time. Another possibility is to contact a Delaware attorney, though that may raise a question in the client's mind as to whether an attorney is needed in California. A third, and often most attractive, possibility is to use the services of a "corporation service company." For a fee, these companies provide a variety of services, including incorporation, qualification as a foreign corporation, post-corporate filings, provision of a registered office and registered agent, corporate staffing of inactive (usually nameholder) corporations, and conducting of meetings. One such corporation offers such services "for any state, the District of Columbia, Puerto Rico, the Virgin Islands, Canada, any Canadian province, the Bahama Islands, Liberia, or Panama." The services provided with respect to incorporation of a new domestic corporation are described in a promotional brochure:

> There is no easier, more systematic, more economical way for a lawyer to handle the detail work connected with incorporation—leaving the lawyer free to concentrate on the law work involved—than through the use of C T Information and services. * * *

> * * * C T, at your specific direction (and only at your direction) as Counsel for the Corporation, will:

- Check availability of corporate name wherever the corporation proposes to do business.
- Reserve the name approved, if desired, where permitted.
- Type charter and by-laws according to your specifications.
- Compile supplementary incorporation papers.
- Furnish incorporators, temporary directors and, in some instances, shareholders.
- Furnish statutory agent and/or office.
- Type minutes of organization meetings.
- Submit all papers to you for personal approval.
- Furnish an itemized estimate of all fees, taxes, other disbursements and charges.
- Prepare checks and letters of transmittal to state officials.
- File approved papers with proper state department or departments.
- Arrange for publication, recording where required.
- Obtain certified copies of documents if desired.
- Give you prompt notice of completion of filings.
- Forward evidence of filing issued by state.
- Hold organizational meetings required and furnish minutes of the meetings held.
- Provide you, for your files, with conformed copies of all typed papers and forms.

It's that easy. You direct, approve and control every step. C T handles the details—the clerical work—for a moderate charge.

* * * The different types of process which may be served on a corporation's statutory agent or office are many and varied. Nor is it unusual for a single Complaint to contain a number of counts with the plaintiff seeking more than monetary damages—a plea for a temporary injunction on short notice, for example. It is information you would want to know about at once.

The handling of such papers is not a responsibility very many lawyers are happy to see delegated to a corporation's salesman, office manager or other company employee. Thousands of lawyers prefer the experienced statutory agents provided as part of the C T System of Corporation Protection. * * *

CORPORATE STAFFING

For inactive nameholder (namesaver) corporations and approved conduit corporations, C T can handle the complex, time-consuming details connected with maintaining the corporation's good standing in its state of incorporation and all foreign states in which it is qualified. For more information, ask your local C T office for a copy of our Corporate Staffing brochure.

STOCKHOLDERS' MEETING SERVICES

* * * C T assists at more corporate stockholders' meetings— regular, special and contested—than most other organizations combined. * * *

B. HOW TO INCORPORATE

The process of corporate formation in most states is essentially a very simple one, and much (though not all) of it may be performed by a legal secretary. There are two significant pitfalls in the corporation-formation process. The first is the danger of overlooking some obvious matter. This danger can be largely avoided by the routine use of a decent checklist of steps to be followed. The second danger is the use of "boiler-plate" forms which may contain some provision that was suitable for the last corporation but is egregiously inappropriate for this corporation. Some corporations may be stamped from a single mold and be perfectly satisfactory, but many cannot. Depending on such matters as the nature of the business, the agreements between the shareholders, and the degree of trust and confidence between them, some individual tailoring may be necessary. Read RMBCA §§ 2.01–2.03, 2.05–2.06. The formal requirements for filing of documents are set forth in RMBCA, chapter one, particularly §§ 1.20–1.26. These minimal requirements are similar to those adopted by a substantial number of states, and the trend is towards limiting the procedures for forming a corporation to those specified in the RMBCA. Generally, the trend in most states is towards the simplification of the process of incorporation wherever possible, and "incorporation by postcard" is feasible in some states. However, about a dozen states still require the filing or recording of the articles of incorporation in one or more counties as well as with a state official. About a half-dozen states still require publication of the articles of incorporation as well as filing with a state official. Double filing and/or publication of the articles appear to serve little purpose. Why are they preserved in face of the general trend toward simplification?

Consider again RMBCA §§ 2.02, 1.20. Would the following document, submitted to the secretary of state with the appropriate fee (a) be accepted for filing under the RMBCA, and (b) result in the formation of a corporation?

ARTICLES OF INCORPORATION

1. The name of the corporation is AB Furniture Store, Inc.

2. The corporation is authorized to issue 1,000 shares of stock.

3. The street address of the corporation's registered office is 125 Main Street, City of _____, State of _____ and the name of the corporation's registered agent at that address is Robert B_____.

4. The name and address of the incorporator is Robert B_____, 125 Main Street, City of _____, State of _____.

/s/ Robert B_____

Robert B_____, Incorporator

Whatever minor technical defects may exist in this form, incorporation under the RMBCA appears to be a very simple process that hardly requires the services of an attorney (if a "plain vanilla" corporation such as that described above is desired).[1] This apparent simplicity is somewhat deceptive since articles of incorporation usually will have to contain express provisions on additional topics if the desires of the interested parties are to be fully carried out. Consider, for example, section 6.01 in the situation where it is contemplated that the corporation will issue shares of stock of more than one class. The Official Comment to RMBCA § 2.02 contains a two-page list of provisions "that may be elected only in the articles of incorporation" and a shorter list of provisions "that may be elected either in the articles of incorporation or the bylaws."

1. [By the Editor] Also, it should be obvious that modern articles of incorporation provide relatively little useful information to third persons about the owners of the corporation, its assets, or the nature of its business. For example, the incorporator, "Robert B_____," might be an attorney, an employee of a law firm, or an employee of a corporation service company. Somewhat more meaningful information may sometimes be obtained from other filed documents. See for example, RMBCA § 16.22.

Notes

(1) So far as formal requirements for filing are concerned, a document must be accompanied by "one exact or conformed copy." RMBCA § 1.20(i). In addition, the correct filing fee and "any franchise tax, license fee, or penalty required by this Act of other law" must accompany the document. Id. Many states also require that a document, to be eligible for filing with the secretary of state, be acknowledged or verified, steps that usually involve presentment to a public notary and the attachment of his or her acknowledgement and notarial seal. Earlier versions of the Model contained such requirements for articles of incorporation and most other documents filed with the secretary of state, but the RMBCA eliminated them because "these requirements serve little purpose in connection with documents filed under corporation statutes." Official Comment to RMBCA § 1.20. See, however, § 1.29.

(2) The processing of filed documents by the secretary of state is described in § 1.25. The date the existence of the corporation so formed begins is described in § 2.03, as is the legal effect of the decision by the secretary of state to file the document. Chapter One of the RMBCA does not reflect a very expansive approach to the powers of the office of secretary of state. For example, the secretary of state may not prescribe a mandatory form for articles of incorporation [§ 1.21(b)], but its filing duty is expressly defined as "ministerial" [§ ...] and it is expressly commanded to file a document if it "satisfies the requirements of section 1.20" [RMBCA § 1.25(a)]. The Official Comment to RMBCA § 1.25 expands upon this language:

> This language should be contrasted with earlier versions of the Model Act (and many state statutes) that required the secretary of state to ascertain whether the document "conformed with law" before filing it. The purpose of this change is to limit the discretion of the secretary of state to a ministerial role in reviewing the contents of documents. If the document submitted is in the form prescribed and contains the information required by section 1.20 and the applicable provision of the Model Act, the secretary of state under section 1.25 must file it even though it contains additional provisions the secretary of state may feel are irrelevant or not authorized by the Model Act or by general legal principles.

This restrictive view of the powers of the secretary of state rests on the experience of attorneys in a number of states where the office of secretary of state viewed its powers broadly, purported to adopt rules or regulations in addition to the requirements of the corporation statute,[2] and often conducted wide-ranging review of the propriety of specific provisions of documents filed with it. One can envision the frustration of an attorney who, after negotiating a complex provision for inclusion in a proposed

---

2. [By the Editor] In this connection, consider also RMBCA § 1.30. Contrast this narrow grant of authority with section 139 of the 1969 Model Act, which granted the secretary of state the power and authority "reasonably necessary to enable him to administer this Act efficiently and to perform the duties therein imposed upon him."

articles of incorporation (or other document), is faced with the task of persuading a relatively low-level employee in the office of the secretary of state that the provision is consistent with the secretary of state's view of the meaning of the corporation statute.

Of course, the office of secretary of state has considerable political "clout" in the legislatures of most states, and therefore these provisions may not be accepted in some states. In Virginia, the first state to largely adopt the RMBCA, for example, § 1.25 was simply not adopted.

(3) There is a great deal of history and some substantive complexity behind the requirements for articles of incorporation that now appear (or no longer appear) in the RMBCA. The following notes describe some of this history.

(4) *Names.* Consider, for example, the requirement that the corporation have a name, and the requirements relating to that name in RMBCA § 4.01. Consider also RMBCA §§ 4.02, 4.03.

(a) The critical language in § 4.01(b) is that a corporate name "must be distinguishable upon the records of the secretary of state" from other corporate names. Earlier versions of the Model Business Corporation Act required that a corporate name "not be the same as, or deceptively similar to, the name" of an existing corporation. MBCA (1969 Ed.) § 8. Many secretaries of state construed this or similar language to require a determination whether the proposed name constituted unfair competition with existing corporations. The Official Comment to § 4.01 states that "confusion in an absolute or linguistic sense is the appropriate test under the Model Act, not the competitive relationship between the corporations, which is the test for fraud or unfair competition." The Official Comment adds that "the secretary of state does not generally police the unfair competitive use of names and, indeed, usually has no resources to do so," and that he or she typically does not know what businesses a corporation is actually engaged in or the names a corporation may be using in conducting those businesses. In enforcing whatever statutory standard is applicable, the secretary of state "simply maintains an alphabetical list of 'official' corporate names as they appear from corporate records and makes his decision * * * by comparing the proposed name with those on the list." Official Comment to § 4.01.

(b) Is the new test a desirable one for determining name availability? The "distinguishable on the records of the secretary of state" language was taken directly from the Delaware statute. In Trans–Americas Airlines, Inc. v. Kenton, 491 A.2d 1139 (Del.1985), Transamerica Corporation, the nationally-known conglomerate, had long associated the name "Transamerica" with the activities of a wholly owned subsidiary named "Trans International Airlines, Inc.," which operated a worldwide air charter service. This association took the form of national advertising by Transamerica and the use of the word "Transamerica" on many of the airplanes operated by the subsidiary. An entirely unrelated corporation was permitted by the Delaware Secretary of State (and the Delaware Supreme Court) to change its name from "Trans–Americas Airlines, Inc." to "Transamerica Airlines, Inc." over the strenuous objection of Transamerica. The court held that "Transamerica Airlines, Inc." was plainly "distinguishable upon the records" of the secretary of state from the names "Transamerica Corporation" and "Trans International Airlines, Inc.," and that the statute did not authorize the secretary of state to reject a name on the ground that it was "confusingly similar" to a name or names already in use.

(c) Because of the wide-spread adoption of earlier versions of the Model Act, the statutes of many states today contain a "deceptively similar" standard (though sometimes phrased in different words) that makes it clear that prevention of unfair competition is at least partially the objective of corporate name regulation. The extent to which secretaries of state actually attempt to police against unfair competition apparently varies widely from state to state. Many secretaries of state have also evolved "house rules" about name availability that may lead to rather peculiar results. For example, in Texas (which has a "deceptively similar" statute) the names "AGX Corporation" and "A*G*X Corporation" would be viewed as "deceptively similar" but the names "AAA Corporation" and "AAAA Corporation" would not.

(d) As noted in RMBCA § 4.01(e), corporations may generally conduct business under an assumed or fictitious name to the same extent that an individual may. [The general test for the lawfulness of doing business under an assumed or fictitious name is that it is proper to do so so long as the purpose is not to defraud. See e.g. United States v. Dunn, 564 F.2d 348, 354, n. 12 (9th Cir.1977).] Many states, however, have "assumed name" statutes requiring a person conducting business under an assumed or fictitious name to make a public filing disclosing his or her real identity. The use of assumed or fictitious names by corporations is usually not a matter of record with the secretary of state, since filing is normally in local offices rather than statewide. See also RMBCA § 15.06(a)(2). As a result, no matter what the secretary of state does, unfair competition through the use of unfairly similar assumed or fictitious names may readily occur. Of course, injured businesses may have common law or statutory causes of action against such competition independent of the provisions of the corporation statutes.

(e) Despite this, there is a fair amount of litigation over corporate names as they are filed with the secretary of state. Most of that litigation is presumably based on the presence or fear of unfair competition by existing businesses.

(f) What purposes are served by "reserved names" (RMBCA § 4.02) and "registered names" (RMBCA § 4.03)?

(5) *Duration.* Section 3.02 of the Revised Model Business Corporation Act automatically grants every corporation "perpetual duration and succession in its corporate name," unless its articles of incorporation provide otherwise. Earlier versions of the Model Act required that the articles of incorporation affirmatively set forth "the period of duration, which may be perpetual." MBCA (1969 Ed.) § 54(b); see also id. § 4(a). Many state corporation acts today contain provisions similar to the 1969 Act. Since almost all corporations elected perpetual status under these provisions, the Revised Model Act provision making duration perpetual unless a shorter period is established in the articles of incorporation does not reflect a

significant change. Why might a corporation with less than a perpetual duration ever be created?

(6) *Purposes.* Historically, a great deal of importance was attached to the statement of purposes in the articles of incorporation. It "is undoubtedly the most important part of the corporate charter, for this clause, together with the general act under which it is drawn, is the true measure of the powers of the corporation." Berkhoff, The Object Clause in Corporate Articles, 4 Wis.L.Rev. 424 (1924). During the nineteenth and early twentieth centuries, corporations were formed for a specific "purpose" that had to be "fully stated;" general purpose and multiple purpose clauses were not accepted in many states. As a result, a great deal of litigation involved the question whether a corporation had exceeded its purpose in some transaction. See the discussion of *ultra vires* in part C in this Chapter. This problem has just about disappeared under modern statutes. See RMBCA § 3.01(a). Indeed, the disappearance of litigation over the scope of purpose clauses is one of the more visible and sensible changes in corporation law in the last half-century.

(a) The first step in this development was recognition that a corporation may list multiple purposes without any limitation on the number of purposes specified and without any obligation that the corporation actually pursue all the purposes contained in its articles. The result was that formbooks were developed that contained hundreds of possible purposes clauses. A couple chosen at random from an old Pennsylvania formbook give their flavor:

(i) To clean by chemical, machinery or other means, boilers, tanks, heat exchangers, cooling towers, coils, condensers, piping, evaporators, kettles, compressor jackets, innercoolers, aftercoolers, wells, water softeners, filters, septic tanks, all pressure vessels and heat exchange attachments; to manufacture, repair and maintain any and all types of heat exchange or pressure vessels, together with all attachments pertaining thereto.

(ii) To carry on the business of brewers and maltsters in all its branches.

To manufacture, brew, buy, sell, deal in, distribute, store, warehouse, and export malt, beers, ales, alcohol and other spirituous and fermented and distilled products and by-products thereof and all kinds of brewery products and by-products, and such other commodities as are or may be handled, used and employed in and about such manufacture, distribution and sale.

To carry on the business of distillers in all its branches and to manufacture, buy, sell and deliver in any and all such commodities and products as are or may be handled, used and employed in and about such business.

To manufacture, buy, sell, deal in, distribute and store ice and refrigerated products.

To build, construct, purchase or lease, or otherwise acquire, and to own, hold, operate, sell, lease or otherwise dispose of breweries, factories, plants, warehouses, works and machinery, and any and all other property and things of whatsoever kind and character, real, personal or mixed, tangible or intangible, including good will necessary or desirable in connection with any of the objects hereinbefore or hereinafter set forth.

15 Purdon's Penna.Forms, 15 P.S. § 1201, Forms 51, 55.

Such clauses were generally drafted on the theory that they should be as broad as possible consistently with the idea of describing some line or kind of business. Since the number of purposes was unlimited, furthermore, it was possible to string together a large number of such clauses to produce an impressively long and unreadable articles of incorporation. Purpose clauses in this era often ran pages in length but usually gave little or no information as to what precise business the corporation planned to engage in.

(b) The next step, quite logically, was to eliminate the excessive verbiage of purposes clauses by permitting incorporation "for the transaction of any lawful business," or similar language that did not require specification of particular lines or kinds of business. These clauses, however, were not quickly accepted; their use did not become widespread until the second half of the twentieth century. The 1969 Model Act permitted this streamlined language (which, after all, did little more than what a long statement of specific purposes did), but it continued to require an affirmative statement of the purposes of the corporation in the articles of incorporation "which may be stated to be, or to include, the transaction of any or all lawful business for which corporations may be incorporated under this Act." MBCA (1969 Ed.) § 54(c). Where such general statements of purpose were acceptable, they were usually used as a routine matter in virtually every articles of incorporation. Thus, the decision reflected in RMBCA § 3.01(a) to eliminate purposes clauses unless a narrow purpose is desired was analogous to the similar decision made in connection with the duration clause.

(c) Why might articles of incorporation today ever include a narrow purposes clause? There are several possible explanations: (1) some types of corporations may be engaged in businesses subject to state regulation that permits incorporation under general business statutes [see RMBCA § 3.01(b)] but requires limitations on corporate activities; (2) some persons may be uncomfortable with the totally silent version of the articles of incorporation permitted by the RMBCA, preferring that some statement of at least the principal business of the corporation appear in the articles of incorporation (without restricting the corporation to that business); and (3) in closely held corporations, a limited purposes clause may be used where one or more persons interested in the corporation (but not in control of its affairs) wish to restrict the lines of business the corporation may enter. Other justifications may exist as well.

(7) *Powers.* Historically, one often encountered provisions in articles of incorporation that dealt with corporate "powers" as well as corporate "purposes." The distinction between "powers" and "purposes" is not self-evident; it can best be appreciated by comparing the list of "general powers" in RMBCA § 3.02 with a "purpose" such as operating a furniture store. The distinction between "purposes" and "powers" certainly was not

understood by many practitioners, since articles of incorporation clauses dealing with "powers" were often indiscriminately mixed in with "purposes." A useful psychological device that aids in distinguishing "powers" from "purposes" is mentally to precede each statement with the phrase "to engage in the business of * * *" and then to use the present participle form of the applicable verb. Thus, instead of saying, "The purpose for which the corporation is organized is to operate a retail furniture store," say "The purpose for which the corporation is organized is *to engage in the business of* operating a retail furniture store." By transposing the verb form from the infinitive to the present participle form, the distinction between powers such as "to sue and be sued" and purposes such as "to operate a furniture store" becomes accentuated.

(a) Is it necessary or desirable to make any references to corporate powers in a modern articles of incorporation? Consider RMBCA § 2.02(c). Most attorneys agree that it is preferable to take this subsection at face value, at least in states where the statutory powers are sufficiently broad to encompass various acts that raised *ultra vires* problems in an earlier era, such as the power of a corporation to enter into a general partnership or to guarantee the debts of customers or third persons. A listing of powers will be partial rather than complete, and inclusion of express powers may give rise to an inference that it was intended that unlisted powers be denied. Adverse inferences may also arise from any variation between the language of the statute and the listed powers. Where, however, a question exists under the law of a state whether corporations generally possess a specific power, an appropriate provision in the articles may resolve all doubt and avoid possible problems. Thus, it is necessary to examine the substantive issue whether corporations in the specific state have specified powers.

(b) Today, all statutes contain a list of general powers analogous to those found in RMBCA § 3.02. In addition, provisions relating to specific powers may be "tucked away" in substantive provisions themselves. See, e.g. RMBCA § 8.51. Section 3.02 contains several changes from earlier versions of similar sections in earlier Model Acts. Perhaps most important is the addition of the introductory phrase "has *the same powers as an individual* to do all things necessary or convenient to carry out its business and affairs." (Emphasis added) Relatively few state statutes contain similar language. If this language really is effective in giving corporations the same powers as an individual, why is it necessary or desirable for the section also to contain a relatively long traditional list of specific powers found in varying form in most state corporation statutes?

Section 3.02 of the Revised Act begins with the phrase "[u]nless its articles of incorporation provide otherwise." Why might it be desired to preclude a corporation from exercising specific powers? Consider, for example, § 3.02(15), which according to the Official Comment was included in addition to § 3.02(13) to permit "contributions for purposes that may not be charitable, such as for political purposes or to influence elections." Might an investor wish to preclude such contributions? What other kinds of restrictions on powers might a cautious investor wish to impose on a corporation in which he or she is making an investment as a minority shareholder?

(8) *Registered office and registered agent.* The designation of a registered office and registered agent, and the statutory provisions relating thereto, see RMBCA §§ 5.01–5.04, are designed to ensure that every corporation has publicly stated a current place where it may be found for purposes of service of process, tax notices, and the like. Often a corporation designates its registered office to be its principal business office. In such a case, the registered agent usually is a corporate officer or employee. The principal disadvantage of this is the possibility that legal documents or communications may be mixed in with routine business mail and not receive the attention they deserve. For this reason, many attorneys suggest that they be designated as registered agent and their office be designated as the registered office. Corporation service companies also routinely provide registered offices and registered agents for a fee.

The provisions of the RMBCA deal with several mundane questions that may arise in connection with registered offices and registered agents. For example: (a) What happens when a process server goes to the designated street address and finds no office and/or no registered agent on which process may be served? (b) How can a corporation service company effectively discontinue acting as a registered agent when its annual fee is not paid? (c) What is to prevent a person from being named a registered agent without his knowledge or consent? (d) Assume that a corporate service company wishes to change the location of its office in a major city; its old address is the registered office for several thousand corporations. Can it change its office address without seeking the consent of every corporation for which it maintains a registered office? Does it have to obtain the signature of corporate officers for every one of those corporations?

(9) *"Initial directors" and "incorporators."* Under earlier versions of the Model Act the organization of the corporation was accomplished by "initial directors" named in the articles of incorporation; the "incorporators" executed the articles of incorporation but did not meet. MBCA (1969 Ed.) § 57. A number of states, however, provided that the incorporators were to complete the organization of the corporation, and therefore did not require that initial directors be named in the articles of incorporation. RMBCA § 2.05 in effect gives the drafter of articles of incorporation an option as to how the organization of the corporation is to be completed. Factors that might be considered in this regard include (a) will it be necessary for shareholders to meet shortly after the formation of the corporation to elect permanent directors and conduct other business, and (b) do the real parties in interest desire anonymity?

Should an attorney serve as incorporator or initial director? In most states it is clear that no liability attaches to the role of incorporator; the same may not necessarily be true of the position of director, which as discussed in a later chapter, may carry with it certain fiduciary duties and potential liabilities. Some cautious attorneys refuse as a matter of principle to serve as directors of corporations they form, though there appears to be no ethical objection to doing so.

(10) *The number of incorporators, directors or shareholders.* As Blackstone noted, "Three make a corporation." Until very recent times, statutes

required that there be at least three incorporators and three directors. Further, there were often residency requirements, shareholding requirements, and the like. So far as incorporators are concerned, the trend is clearly to reduce the minimum number to one and to allow corporations or other artificial entities to serve as incorporators; all but a handful of states now follow the Revised Model Act in this regard. Of course, in view of the limited role of incorporators, this result is probably reasonable.

What about a minimum number of shareholders and directors? There apparently has never been in recent history a requirement that a corporation have at least three shareholders. One North Carolina case that appears to have so held, Park Terrace v. Phoenix Indemnity Company, 243 N.C. 595, 91 S.E.2d 584 (1956), was promptly overruled by statute. Assuming this is so, what then about directors? See RMBCA § 8.03(a). About twenty states still require a board of at least three directors, though a number of these states permit a corporation with one or two shareholders to reduce the size of the board to the number of shareholders. As a matter of policy, should the privilege of having a board of one or two persons be limited to corporations with one or two shareholders, or should it be extended to all corporations? Is there anything magical about the number three? Assume that you are practicing in a state that continues to require at least three directors. If you are forming a corporation which will have only one shareholder, who should be the directors? Is there any device by which their loyalty to the single shareholder can be assured? Consider, for example, RMBCA § 8.08. Assume that after a few years of operation, the sole shareholder wishes to begin making gifts of shares of stock to her three minor children. If she is in a state that allows a board with one member only in corporations with one shareholder, will she have to add two directors to the board?

(11) *Initial Capital.* One interesting aspect of the articles of incorporation set forth above is that there is no reference to dollars: no dollar figure is associated with the shares of stock (i.e. no minimum issuance price is established) and no minimum capitalization of the corporation is set forth.

The matter of the issuance price for shares is discussed in Chapter Seven and discussion of that issue is deferred until then.

Shouldn't a new corporation be required to have at least some minimum amount of capital before it is launched into the business world? Until relatively recently there was such a requirement. Prior to 1969, the Model Act prohibited a corporation from transacting any business or incurring any indebtedness "until there has been paid in for the issuance of shares consideration of the value of at least one thousand dollars." [MBCA (1966 Ed.) § 51.] The articles of incorporation also had to contain a recitation to the same effect. [Id. § 48(g).] Similar provisions continue to appear in the statutes of some states. Since there is no public disclosure or public review of the sale of shares by closely held corporations in most states, there was little attempt to enforce these minimum capitalization requirements by holding up the certificate of incorporation, though some states did require the submission of an affidavit or certificate that the required amount had been contributed. Much more important was the question whether initial or subsequent directors who acquiesced in the conduct of business before the minimum capital was in fact paid in might be personally liable either for the $1,000 or for all debts of the corporation incurred before the required capital was paid in. The Model Act [MBCA (1966 Ed.) § 43(e)] minimized the potential impact of the minimum capitalization requirement by providing that directors who assent to the commencement of business are "jointly and severally liable to the corporation for such part of one thousand dollars as shall not have been received before commencing business, but such liability shall be terminated when the corporation has actually received one thousand dollars as consideration for the issuance of shares." Not all states followed this provision. In Tri–State Developers, Inc. v. Moore, 343 S.W.2d 812 (Ky.1961), a corporation began business with $500 rather than the required minimum of $1,000. In upholding a judgment for $10,180.34 under such a statute, the court said:

> The state extends to the members of a corporation organized under Chapter 271 personal immunity from corporate liabilities, but only if and when the requirements of KRS 271.095 are satisfied. Those requirements are quite minimal. Anyone can launch a corporate enterprise with $1,000. It may seem harsh that personal immunity should be withheld for a mere $1,000 (in this case $500), but that is a legislative prerogative, and we can find no lesser meaning in the plain words of the statute. One may start business on a shoestring in Kentucky, but if it is a corporate business the shoestring must be worth $1,000.

Kentucky eliminated entirely the minimum capital requirement in 1972. See Ky.Rev.Stat. § 271A.270. Do you think that the Committee on Corporate Laws of the MBCA made a wise decision when it eliminated all reference to minimum capitalization? Considering today's prices and today's conditions, shouldn't the move be in the opposite direction? Or is this simply another illustration of the race of laxity?

What happens after the articles of incorporation are filed? See RMBCA §§ 2.05, 2.06. In addition to preparing and filing the articles of incorporation, attorneys often handle a number of other routine details in connection with the formation of a corporation. They may:

(1) Prepare the corporate by-laws;

(2) Prepare the notice calling the meeting of the initial board of directors, minutes of this meeting, and waivers of notice if necessary;

(3) Obtain a corporate seal and minute book for the corporation;

(4) Obtain blank certificates for the shares of stock, arrange for their printing or typing, and ensure that they are properly issued;

(5) Arrange for the opening of the corporate bank account; and

(6) Prepare employment contracts, voting trusts, pooling agreements, share transfer restrictions, and other special arrangements which are to be entered into with respect to the corporation and its shares.

It was thereupon resolved that Ms. Brown should be reimbursed for such expenses in the total sum of $377.20 and the treasurer was instructed to pay Ms. Brown such sum as soon as possible out of corporate funds.

On motion duly made, seconded and unanimously adopted, it was

RESOLVED that the _____ Bank be chosen as the depository of the funds of the corporation, and the _____ and the _____ were each authorized to draw checks on the corporation's bank account in such bank. A form of resolution furnished by such bank was then presented to the meeting and, after being read and fully understood, such form of resolution was adopted and is attached to these minutes as an exhibit.

There being no further business, on motion duly made, seconded and unanimously adopted, the meeting was adjourned.

_____
Secretary

We consent to the foregoing actions

_____

_____

_____

WAIVER

[Alternate form]

We, the undersigned, being all the original directors of ABC Corporation named in the articles of incorporation, do hereby waive notice and the call by the incorporators of said corporation of the organization meeting of the directors of said corporation, and agree that the organization meeting shall be held at _____, in the city of _____, _____ _____ o'clock __.M. on the _____ day of _____, 19__.

_____

_____

_____

Notes

(1) Under the RMBCA, there may be only one initial director or one incorporator who organizes the corporation. Where only a single person is acting, much of the "playacting" flavor of these minutes should disappear and a simpler formulation followed, e.g. "The original director determined that . . ." On the other hand, many attorneys continue to draft minutes that have a "playacting" flavor even though only one person is acting.

(2) Most of the miscellaneous matters relating to the launching of a new corporation are accomplished at a meeting of the incorporators or initial directors. The attorney will normally draft the minutes of this meeting; also, in some circumstances it may be necessary to have a meeting of the shareholders to elect permanent directors; the attorney normally drafts the minutes of this meeting also.

(3) If the corporation is small and closely held, it is not necessary to actually hold meetings of incorporators, directors, or shareholders. See RMBCA §§ 2.05, 7.04, 8.21. A consent signed by all the incorporators, directors, or shareholders is effective as a legal matter. If the consent procedure is not utilized (as may be the case, for example, where one individual is absent, or where the number of persons involved is large), it is generally desirable to actually hold a meeting, using the minutes as a form of script. Some attorneys object to the playacting nature of such a meeting, but there is some question of validity of actions taken without a meeting and without taking advantage of the consent procedure. Of course, the consent procedure should be followed where a single incorporator or initial director is acting.

(4) At the very early stages of corporate formation, there is unlikely to be significant disagreement, dissent, or controversy.

C. THE DECLINE OF THE DOCTRINE OF *ULTRA VIRES*

A classic English case presents the doctrine of *ultra vires* in its full rigor and glory. In Ashbury Railway Carriage & Iron Co. v. Riche, 33 N.S. Law Times Rep. 450 (1875), the charter of a corporation authorized it to "sell or lend all kinds of railway plant, to carry on the business of mechanical engineers and general contractors, &c." The corporation entered into contracts with one Riche to purchase a concession to construct and operate a railway line in Belgium. Riche was apparently to construct the railroad line, and the corporation was to raise the necessary capital. After partial performance, the corporation repudiated the contract. The House of Lords concluded that the corporation was not liable to Riche because owning and operating a railway line was *ultra vires*. Lord Chancellor Cairns declared:

> * * * In a case such as your Lordships have now to deal with, it is not a question whether the contract sued upon involves that which is *malum prohibitum* or *malum in se,* or is a contract contrary to public policy, and illegal in that sense. I assume the contract in itself to be perfectly legal; to have nothing in it obnoxious to any of the powers involved in the expressions which I have used. The question is not the illegality of the contract, but the competency and power of the company to make the contract. I am of opinion that this contract was, as I have said, entirely beyond the objects of the memorandum of association. If so it was thereby placed beyond the powers of the company to make the contract. If so it is not a question whether the contract ever was ratified or not ratified. If it was a contract void at its beginning it was void for this reason—because the company could not make the

contract. If every shareholder of the company had been in this room, and every shareholder of the company had said, "That is a contract which we desire to make, which we authorize the directors to make, to which we sanction the placing the seal of the company," the case would not have stood in any different position to that in which it stands now. The company would thereby by unanimous assent have been attempting to do the very thing which by the Act they were prohibited from doing.

Several things may be noted about this case. First, while it involves a purposes clause that is narrower than the activities actually engaged in by the corporation, the activities themselves were not inherently unlawful or beyond the powers of corporations generally. Presumably, the corporation could have amended its memorandum of association to permit it to operate a Belgian railroad. Modern practice in drafting articles of incorporation greatly reduces but does not eliminate the possibility that such a case will arise in the future. Such a case is unlikely ever to arise under either a general "all lawful business" purposes clause, but conceivably might arise if a narrow purposes clause is included in articles of incorporation. Second, the result of the case hardly seems reasonable or fair. After entering into what appears to be an entirely reasonable business contract, and presumably receiving benefits thereunder, the corporation is permitted to avoid the contract on the basis of a defense that was entirely within its power to correct. Third, the argument that corporations simply are unable to commit *ultra vires* acts threatens to be very unsettling. It might be used, for example, to set aside completed transactions, including sales of goods and land, that the corporation now regrets. It also would appear to be a handy defense for the corporation to avoid liability to injured plaintiffs in torts cases. Thus, almost from the first, the law of *ultra vires* became, in effect, a judicial attempt to avoid the harsh and undesirable but apparently logically compelled consequences of a judicially-created doctrine.

Some courts avoided the *ultra vires* doctrine by construing purposes clauses broadly and finding implied purposes from the language used. A famous example is the conclusion by the United States Supreme Court that a railway company might engage in the business of leasing and running a seaside resort hotel. Jacksonville M.P.Ry. & Nav. Co. v. Hooper, 160 U.S. 514, 16 S.Ct. 379, 40 L.Ed. 515 (1896). Other doctrines that have found acceptance include estoppel, unjust enrichment, including quasi-contract, and waiver. In particular, these doctrines were applied to ensure that completed transactions would not be disturbed, and to permit tort claimants to recover for injuries suffered as a consequence of the corporation's conduct of an *ultra vires* business. *Ultra vires* continued to be applied, however, in connection with executory agreements and, when all is said and done, the doctrine was an undesirable one, involving harsh and erratic consequences.

In the *Ashbury Railway* case could the House of Lords have concluded that constructing and operating a Belgian railroad was subsumed under the purpose of carrying on a "general contractors" business? This argument was strongly pressed by the plaintiff, but was rejected by the House of Lords.

One superficially plausible justification for the doctrine arises from the fact that articles of incorporation are on public file; it seems reasonable to argue that one is charged with notice of whatever unexpected provision might appear in public documents. From a business standpoint, that argument is unrealistic: it assumes people will check articles of incorporation when in fact they do not, and that when they do check the articles, they will make business judgments based on a reading of what often is essentially boiler-plate legalese. Whatever the merits of the notion of being charged with notice of public documents in different contexts, the decline and elimination of the *ultra vires* doctrine prove that it should not be applied to purposes clauses of articles of incorporation.

711 KINGS HIGHWAY CORP. v. F.I.M.'S MARINE REPAIR SERV. INC.

Supreme Court of New York, 1966.
51 Misc.2d 373, 273 N.Y.S.2d 299.

VICTOR L. ANFUSO, JUSTICE.

Defendant corporation moves pursuant to CPLR 3211, subdiv. [a], par. 7 for judgment dismissing the complaint for legal insufficiency or in the alternative for summary judgment pursuant to CPLR 3212.

The verified complaint alleges that on or about April 20, 1965 the plaintiff, owner of premises known as 711–715 Kings Highway in the County of Kings, City of New York, entered into a written lease agreement with defendant whereby plaintiff leased the aforesaid premises to defendant for a period of 15 years commencing July 1, 1966; that with the exception of a security deposit of $5,000 paid by defendant to plaintiff pursuant to the lease agreement, which sum plaintiff now tenders or offers to return to defendant, the lease remains wholly executory; that under the terms of the lease the demised premises were to be used as a motion picture theatre; that the purposes for which the defendant corporation was formed were restricted generally to marine activities including marine repairs and the building and equipment of boats and vessels, as set forth in the certificate of incorporation; that the execution of the subject lease calling for defendant's use of the demised premises as a motion picture theatre, and the conduct and operation of a motion picture theatre, and the conduct and operation of a motion picture theatre business for profit by the defendant are acts which fall completely outside the scope of the powers and authority conferred by the defendant's corporate charter, thereby rendering invalid the lease agreement entered into by the parties. The complaint then prays for a declaratory judgment declaring the lease to be invalid or in the alternative for rescission and further that the defendant be enjoined from performing, or exercising any rights, under the lease.

In the opinion of the court Section 203 of the New York Business Corporation Law embraces the situation presented by the factual allegations of the complaint and requires a dismissal of the complaint for failure to state a cause of action. This section provides as follows: That no act of a corporation and no transfer of property to or by a corporation, otherwise lawful, shall be invalid by reason of the fact that the corporation was without capacity or power to do such act or engage in such transfer except that such lack of capacity or power may be asserted (1) in an action brought by a shareholder to enjoin a corporate act or (2) in an action by or in the right of a corporation against an incumbent or former officer or director of the corporation or (3) in an action or special proceeding brought by the Attorney General. It is undisputed that the present case does not fall within the stated exceptions contained in Section 203. It is accordingly clear from the language of the statutory provision hereinabove referred to that there is no substance to plaintiff's argument, in opposition to the instant motion, which is predicated on a want of corporate power to do an act or enter into an agreement beyond the express or implied powers of the corporation conferred by the corporate charter.

Neither is there merit to the plaintiff's contention that Section 203 applies only where ultra vires is raised as a defense. Notwithstanding the fact that this section is entitled "Defense of ultra vires" it seems that except in the three stated situations set forth in the section, which are not applicable to the instant case, ultra vires may not be invoked as a sword in support of a cause of action any more than it can be utilized as a defense. To hold otherwise would render meaningless those provisions in Section 203 which permit ultra vires to be invoked in support of the actions or proceedings set forth as exceptions to the general language of this section.

Finally plaintiff's contention that the ultra vires doctrine still applies fully to executory contracts must be rejected. By virtue of Section 203 the doctrine may not be invoked even though the contract which is claimed to be ultra vires is executory, as in the instant case. See Revisers' Notes and Comments on Section 203 of the Business Corporation Law.

Accordingly the defendant's motion for judgment dismissing the complaint for insufficiency is granted. So much of the defendant's motion as seeks in the alternative summary judgment based on the amendment of defendant's certificate of incorporation subsequent to the commencement of the instant action, so as to include in the powers granted to the corporation the power to exhibit motion pictures, need not be considered in view of the determination herein made on the motion to dismiss for insufficiency.

Notes

(1) Consider RMBCA § 3.04. Does this give the court the needed flexibility to protect legitimate and reasonable business relationships on

the one hand while protecting shareholders who may have relied on a narrow purposes clause as protection against undesired business expansion on the other?

(2) Do not RMBCA §§ 3.04(b)(1) and (c) give shareholders greater rights to set aside executory transactions than the corporation itself? Might not a corporation, having entered into a disadvantageous *ultra vires* transaction, enlist a shareholder to intervene and seek the cancellation of the contract? Of course, if it is advantageous for the corporation to avoid a transaction, it probably will be advantageous from the standpoint of the shareholder also, since it will increase the value of the shares. In Inter–Continental Corp. v. Moody, 411 S.W.2d 578 (Tex.Civ.App.—Houston, 1966), writ ref'd n.r.e., a shareholder intervened in a suit brought against the corporation on an *ultra vires* promissory note, and sought to enjoin payment of the note. In permitting the intervention, the court said:

> Upon the above evidence it may well be concluded that the intervening stockholder was acting in his own interest at the urging of another stockholder * * *. The mere fact that a corporation representative may have given notice of the suit and suggested it might be wise for the stockholder to intervene does not make such stockholder an agent of the corporation. As a practical matter today when corporate stock is so widely held by different persons in varying and small amounts, the average stockholder can hardly be expected to keep himself informed of corporate operations except for information afforded him by corporate representatives or those associated with them. There might in some particular case be facts establishing such an agency so that in a trial on the merits he would not be entitled to the relief sought. However, whether the stockholder is in fact but the agent of the corporation is to be determined at a trial on the merits. We note that under all facts shown here no such agency is established, * * *. We do not know what a fuller development of the facts will show. In this connection we think it material to show who is paying Mr. Hicks' attorney's fee. He may be required to disclose this though it may not be required that he show the amount.

> If on trial the trier of the facts, on evidence of probative force, finds that Richardson is but the agent of Inter–Continental, then he would not be entitled to the relief sought. If intervenor is found not to be the mere agent of Inter–Continental, then he will be entitled to * * * some relief * * *. [A]ppellee will be entitled to a judgment against the corporation, not for the full amount of the note, but only to the extent that the stockholder is held not to be entitled to relief. This is not because of a right in the corporation, but because of the rights of the stockholder.

Does the court's cryptic comment mean that the corporation can resist payment of the note only in proportion to the shareholder's relative interest in the corporation? If not, what did the court mean?

THEODORA HOLDING CORP. v. HENDERSON

Court of Chancery of Delaware, 1969.
257 A.2d 398.

MARVEL, VICE CHANCELLOR:

Plaintiff, which was formed in May of 1967 by the defendant Girard B. Henderson's former wife, Theodora G. Henderson, is the holder of record of 11,000 of the 40,500 issued and outstanding shares of common stock of the defendant Alexander Dawson, Inc. It sues derivatively as well as on its own behalf for an accounting by the individual defendants for the losses allegedly sustained by the corporate defendant and the concomitant improper gains allegedly received by the individual defendants as a result of certain transactions of which plaintiff complains. * * *

The individual defendant Henderson by reason of the extent of his combined majority holdings of common and preferred stock of Alexander Dawson, Inc., each class of which has voting rights, exercises effective control over the affairs of such corporation, the net worth of the assets of which, at the time of the filing of this suit, was approximately $150,000,000.

It is claimed and the evidence supports such contention that on December 8, 1967, the defendant Girard B. Henderson, by virtue of his voting control over the affairs of Alexander Dawson, Inc., caused the board of directors of such corporation to be reduced in number from eight to three persons, namely himself, the defendant Bengt Ljunggren,[3] an employee of the corporate defendant, and Mr. Henderson's daughter, Theodora H. Ives. It is alleged that thereafter the defendant Girard B. Henderson (over the objection of the director, Mrs. Ives) caused the board and the majority of the voting stock of Alexander Dawson, Inc., improperly to contribute stock held by it in the approximate value of $550,000 to the Alexander Dawson Foundation, a charitable trust, the affairs of which were then controlled and continue to be controlled by Mr. Henderson. * * *

Alexander Dawson, Inc. has functioned as a personal holding company since 1935 when Mr. Henderson's mother exchanged a substantial number of shares held by her in a company which later became Avon Products, Inc., for all of the shares of her own company known as Alexander Dawson, Inc. Mr. Henderson and a brother later succeeded to their mother's interest in Alexander Dawson, Inc., the brother thereafter permitting his shares to be redeemed by the corporation. As noted earlier, Mr. Henderson, by reason of his combined holdings of common and preferred stock of the corporate defendant, is in clear control of the affairs of such corporation, which, for the most part, has

---

3. [By the Court] Mr. Ljunggren, whose forte appears to be that of public relations, joined Alexander Dawson, Inc. in 1966 at a salary of $12,000 per annum. He has since been rewarded with substantial raises and bonuses which have more than doubled his starting salary.

been operated informally by Mr. Henderson with scant regard for the views of other board members. Some seventy-five percent of its assets consist of shares of Avon Products, Inc. stock, there having been some diversification, particularly in 1967, largely through the urging of officers of the United States Trust Company of New York who have served as advisors. Through exercise of such control, Mr. Henderson has, since 1957, caused the corporate defendant to donate varying amounts to a charitable trust organized in that year by Mr. Henderson, namely the Alexander Dawson Foundation. In 1957, $10,610 was donated to such trust. From 1960 to 1966 (except for the year 1965) gifts were in the range of approximately $63,000 to $70,000 or higher in each year other than 1963 when $27,923 was donated. In 1966, however, a gift in the form of a large tract of land in Colorado, having a value of some $467,750, was made. All of these gifts through 1966 were unanimously approved by all of the stockholders of Alexander Dawson, Inc., including Mrs. Theodora G. Henderson. The gift now under attack, namely one of the shares of stock of [sic: owned by (?)] the corporate defendant having a value of some $528,000, was made to the Alexander Dawson Foundation in December of 1967. Such gift was first proposed by Mr. Henderson in April, 1967 before the board of the corporate defendant was reduced in number from eight to three. However, director reaction was thereafter confused, one of the directors, Mrs. Henderson's daughter, Theodora H. Ives, having expressed a desire that a corporate gift also be made to her own charitable corporation and that of her mother, Theodora G. Henderson. Accordingly, the matter was not pressed by Mr. Henderson until late December when the reduced board had taken over management of the corporate defendant. It is claimed and admitted that such gift had an effect on the equity and dividends of shareholders of the corporate defendant although the tax consequences of such gift clearly soften the apparent impact of such transaction. It is significant, however, as noted above, that the 1966 corporate gift, consisting of a ranch located in Colorado, had been approved by all of the directors and stockholders of the corporate defendant, and that the gift here under attack was apparently intended to be a step towards consummation of the purpose behind such grant of land, namely to provide a fund for the financing of a western camp for underprivileged boys, particularly members of the George Junior Republic, a self-governing institution which has served the public interest for some seventy-five years at a school near Freeville, New York. Thus, in the summer of 1967, a small group of underprivileged children had enjoyed the advantages of such camp in a test of the feasibility of such an institution. However, it is apparently Mr. Henderson's intention to continue and expand his interest in such camp where he maintains an underground home which he occupies at a $6,000 rental per annum, such house being occupied by him during some three months of the year. * * *

The next matter to be considered is the propriety of the December 1967 gift made by Alexander Dawson, Inc. to the Alexander Dawson

Foundation of shares of stock of [sic: owned by (?)] the corporate defendant having a value in excess of $525,000, an amount within the limits of the provisions of the federal tax law having to do with deductible corporate gifts, Internal Revenue Code of 1954 §§ 170(b)(2), 545(b)(2).

Title 8 Del.C. § 122 provides as follows:

"Every corporation created under this chapter shall have power to—

* * *

   (9) Make donations for the public welfare or for charitable, scientific or educational purposes, and in time of war or other national emergency in aid thereof."

There is no doubt but that the Alexander Dawson Foundation is recognized as a legitimate charitable trust by the Department of Internal Revenue. It is also clear that it is authorized to operate exclusively in the fields of " * * * religious, charitable, scientific, literary, or educational purposes, or for the prevention of cruelty to children or animals * * *." Furthermore, contemporary courts recognize that unless corporations carry an increasing share of the burden of supporting charitable and educational causes that the business advantages now reposed in corporations by law may well prove to be unacceptable to the representatives of an aroused public. The recognized obligation of corporations towards philanthropic, educational and artistic causes is reflected in the statutory law of all of the states, other than the states of Arizona and Idaho.

In A.P. Smith Mfg. Co. v. Barlow, 13 N.J. 145, 98 A.2d 681, 39 A.L.R.2d 1179, appeal dismissed, 346 U.S. 861, 74 S.Ct. 107, 98 L.Ed. 373, a case in which the corporate donor had been organized long before the adoption of a statute authorizing corporate gifts to charitable or educational institutions, the Supreme Court of New Jersey upheld a gift of $1500 by the plaintiff corporation to Princeton University, being of the opinion that the trend towards the transfer of wealth from private industrial entrepreneurs to corporate institutions, the increase of taxes on individual income, coupled with steadily increasing philanthropic needs, necessitate corporate giving for educational needs even were there no statute permitting such gifts, and this was held to be the case apart from the question of the reserved power of the state to amend corporate charters. The court also noted that the gift tended to bolster the free enterprise system and the general social climate in which plaintiff was nurtured. And while the court pointed out that there was no showing that the gift in question was made indiscriminately or to a pet charity in furtherance of personal rather than corporate ends, the actual holding of the opinion appears to be that a corporate charitable or educational gift to be valid must merely be within reasonable limits both as to amount and purpose.

The New Jersey statute in force and effect at the time of the Smith case gift provided that directors might cause their corporation to contribute for charitable and educational purposes and the like

" * * * such reasonable sum or sums as they may determine * * * " provided, however, that such contributions might not be made in situations where the proposed donee owned more than 10% of the voting stock of the donor and provided further that such gifts be limited to 5% of capital and surplus unless " * * * authorized by the stockholders."

Whether or not these statutory limitations on corporate giving were the source of the limiting language of the New Jersey Supreme Court is not clear, the point being that the Delaware statute contains no such limiting language and therefor must, in my opinion, be construed to authorize any reasonable corporate gift of a charitable or educational nature. Significantly, Alexander Dawson, Inc. was incorporated in Delaware in 1958 after 8 Del.C. § 122(9) was cast in its present form, therefor no constitutional problem arising out of the effect on a stockholder's property rights of the State's reserved power to amend corporate charters is presented.

I conclude that the test to be applied in passing on the validity of a gift such as the one here in issue is that of reasonableness, a test in which the provisions of the Internal Revenue Code pertaining to charitable gifts by corporations furnish a helpful guide. The gift here under attack was made from gross income and had a value as of the time of giving of $528,000 in a year in which Alexander Dawson, Inc.'s total income was $19,144,229.06, or well within the federal tax deduction limitation of 5% of such income. The contribution under attack can be said to have "cost" all of the stockholders of Alexander Dawson, Inc. including plaintiff, less than $80,000, or some fifteen cents per dollar of contribution, taking into consideration the federal tax provisions applicable to holding companies as well as the provisions for compulsory distribution of dividends received by such a corporation. In addition, the gift, by reducing Alexander Dawson, Inc.'s reserve for unrealized capital gains taxes by some $130,000, increased the balance sheet net worth of stockholders of the corporate defendant by such amount. It is accordingly obvious, in my opinion, that the relatively small loss of immediate income otherwise payable to plaintiff and the corporate defendant's other stockholders, had it not been for the gift in question, is far out-weighed by the overall benefits flowing from the placing of such gift in channels where it serves to benefit those in need of philanthropic or educational support, thus providing justification for large private holdings, thereby benefiting plaintiff in the long run. Finally, the fact that the interests of the Alexander Dawson Foundation appear to be increasingly directed towards the rehabilitation and education of deprived but deserving young people is peculiarly appropriate in an age when a large segment of youth is alienated even from parents who are not entirely satisfied with our present social and economic system. * * *

Notes

(1) N. Lattin, Lattin on Corporations (2d Ed.1971) 206:

There are some powers, however, not easily implied as reasonably incidental to the pursuit of charter objectives. Such are contracts of suretyship and guaranty, the purchase of shares in other corporations or the purchase of its own shares, the carrying on as a member of a partnership either with a natural person or another corporation or other business association, the making of gifts to charitable or educational institutions, the building of homes for corporate employees or the financing of the same for them, or the building of entire villages with banking, educational, religious and recreational facilities for employees as well as other facilities necessary or convenient for the running of a municipality. Powers have been implied in appropriate cases to permit all of the above activities but they have not been easily implied and more often have most of such powers been denied unless statutory or charter authorization is shown.

Reliance on implied corporate powers to authorize questionable corporate actions of the type described by Professor Lattin is basically unsatisfactory. Litigation over whether a corporation has power to engage in some action is as unproductive as litigation over whether or not such action is in furtherance of the corporate purpose. Section 3.04 provides that the validity of corporate action may not be challenged on the ground that the corporation "lacks or lacked power to act." Under this phrase, according to the Official Comment, "it makes no difference whether a limitation in articles of incorporation is considered to be a limitation on a purpose or a limitation on a power; both are equally subject to § 3.04." In addition, modern corporate statutes purport to specifically authorize the major types of questionable actions described by Professor Lattin under general powers clauses similar to RMBCA § 3.02 or other sections of the statute. That, however, does not completely solve all problems.

(2) The "black letter" rule has long been that corporations are state creations with limited powers granted by the states. Head & Amory v. Providence Insurance Co., 6 U.S. (2 Cranch) 127, 169, 2 L.Ed. 229 (1804). In First National Bank v. Bellotti, 435 U.S. 765, 98 S.Ct. 1407, 55 L.Ed.2d 707 (1978) and Consolidated Edison Co. v. Public Service Commission, 447 U.S. 530, 100 S.Ct. 2326, 65 L.Ed.2d 319 (1980), the Supreme Court recognized that corporate political speech had constitutional protection. In both instances the speech was viewed as involving public controversial issues not directly affecting the property, business, or assets of the corporation. At the time of these decisions applicable state law did not permit, and indeed purported to prohibit expressly, corporate expenditures to influence elections or public sentiment on matters unrelated to the business of the corporation. Where did the corporations obtain the basic power to exercise these constitutional rights found by the Supreme Court? Does RMBCA § 3.02(15) authorize those expenditures?

(3) Is there risk in broadly authorizing corporate powers in statutes such as RMBCA § 3.02 without any kind of restriction or limitation? Or

does the holding in *Theodora Holding Corporation* itself provide a suitable restriction?

(4) Charitable contributions by corporations, particularly publicly held corporations, have been the subject of some criticism. Are you impressed by the argument that the function of business corporations is profit, and that charitable contributions are inconsistent with that function since they involve gifts of corporate assets? A related argument is that shareholders, rather than corporate management, should be permitted to decide which charities to support since that choice is essentially a personal rather than a business related one. Do you agree? Should a distinction be drawn between charitable contributions that may benefit the corporation directly (e.g., General Motors making contributions to support hospitals in areas close to General Motors plants), and more general contributions, e.g., to Harvard University? Would it affect your evaluation of this issue if the General Motors' executive with authority to decide which charities receive GM's contributions had a daughter at Harvard?

D. PREMATURE COMMENCEMENT OF BUSINESS

1. PROMOTERS

The term "promoter" includes a "person who, acting alone or in conjunction with one or more other persons, directly or indirectly takes initiative in founding and organizing the business or enterprise of an issuer."[4] A promoter is often referred to as the "founder" or "organizer" of an enterprise. S.E.C. Rule 405, 17 C.F.R. 230.405. The formation of a business enterprise largely involves business rather than legal problems. If the new business needs a plant, the promoter must locate one and rent or buy it. If a key person is essential for the success of the venture, the promoter must negotiate a contract of employment with him. If a distributive network for the business' product or a source of raw materials is necessary, the promoter must make the necessary arrangements. In any event, capital must be raised, either through the sale of equity interests in the business, or through loans, or commonly, a combination of both.

One aspect of the promoter's duties is to arrange for the formation of the corporation to conduct the business. The process of incorporation, however, as described in a preceding section, is now so simple and routine that this is usually considered a small and relatively unimportant part of the promoter's role.

Some opprobrium may attach to the word "promoter." In the sense the word is used here, however, a promoter is usually an individual engaging in a useful and desirable economic function.

---

4. [By the Editor] According to Rule 405, the term "promoter" also includes a person "who, in connection with the founding and organizing of the business or enterprise of an issuer, directly or indirectly receives in consideration of services or property, or both services and property, ten per cent or more of any class of securities or ten per cent or more of the proceeds from any class of securities."

FRICK v. HOWARD

Supreme Court of Wisconsin, 1964.
23 Wis.2d 86, 126 N.W.2d 619.

[Editor: On January 24, 1958 Preston entered into a contract to purchase certain real estate for $240,000. On April 1, 1958 he formed a corporation, Pan American Motel, Inc., which issued one share of stock to him for the nominal value of $1,000. He completed the purchase of the real estate on August 29, 1958, and three days later the corporation offered him $350,000 for the land. In connection with this sale, the corporation issued Preston a note and mortgage for $110,000.

[After purchasing the land, Pan American Motel, Inc., secured additional financing and constructed a motel on the land, which it operated for about two years. In 1961, it issued a substitute note and mortgage to Preston in the amount of $145,000. In December, 1961, when payments on the note were current, Preston assigned the note and mortgage to plaintiff for $72,500. The corporation defaulted on the note in January, 1962, and a receiver for the corporation was appointed later that month.

[The plaintiff brought suit to foreclose the mortgage. The trial court entered judgment for the plaintiff for the amount of $77,159.57, based on the amount he invested in the mortgage, and the receiver appeals.]

BEILFUSS, JUSTICE. * * *

Did Preston, as a promoter, breach a fiduciary duty to the corporation? It appears without dispute that Preston was the organizer and promoter of the Pan American Motel, Inc.

* * * At the time the offer to purchase was made by the corporation Preston was, as far as the record reveals, the sole stockholder and completely dominated the affairs of the corporation. There was a board of directors consisting of Preston and two others but the record does not show they owned any stock or that they were in any way independent of Preston. On April 1, 1959 the note of $110,000 and mortgage were signed by Preston as president of the corporation and by Frank J. Mack as secretary payable to Preston and his wife.

The trial court found that Preston committed a fraud upon the corporation but that the transaction was not secret.

The fact that the transaction was not secret does not in all instances relieve a promoter of his fiduciary obligation to the corporation.

"The promoters may deal with the corporation, but they must deal fairly, the burden of proof and fairness being on them. When they deal with the corporation, it must have independent directors; and the promoters cannot also be directors or dominate them as representatives of the other adversely interested parties.

"Perfect candor, full disclosure, good faith, in fact, the utmost good faith, and the strictest honestly [sic] are required of promoters, and their dealings must be open and fair, or without undue advantage taken.

"It is the duty of the promoters to retain in their hands the property which is to constitute corporate assets until the corporation is formed, to cause it to be formed within a reasonable time, and then to turn over to it the assets so held * * *."

"As a result of the fiduciary relation or relation of trust and confidence sustained by a promoter, an unfair advantage taken or secret profit gained thereby is a fraud. * * *" 1 Fletcher, Cyc. Corp. (perm. ed.), pp. 730–733, secs. 192, 193. * * *

The fact that the land may or may not have been worth more than $240,000 cannot override Preston's fiduciary obligation as a promoter of the corporation. In this instance where he completely dominated the corporation at the time of the transaction it was his fiduciary obligation to give the corporation the benefit of his bargain, if it was one. If Preston had provided the corporation with a board of directors who could have acted independently and at arm's length the situation might have been different. For Preston to obtain a profit of $110,000 for himself under the circumstances herein is unconscionable and a violation of his fiduciary obligation and as such a fraud upon the corporation.

That the transaction constituted a fraud on creditors, existing and subsequent, is all the more apparent when it is considered that Preston attempted to elevate himself to the position of a secured creditor by the note and mortgage of April 1, 1959. If the transaction had been fair and above board the best that Preston could have claimed was a contribution to capital because of the top-heavy debt structure already existing. We, therefore hold there was no valid consideration for the note and mortgage of April 1, 1959 in the amount of $110,000 and that the corporation, subsequent stockholders, creditors, or the receiver for their benefit can assert this defense.

Frick, the assignee of Preston, contends that the land sale transaction was subsequently ratified by the corporation and, therefore, the defense of constructive fraud by the promoter is no longer available. The burden of proof to show ratification and to show that it was the act of an independent board of directors was upon Preston's assignee. He has not met this burden. In any event the creditors cannot be bound by a ratification in which they had no voice.

Can the defense of want of consideration of the original note securing the assigned mortgage be asserted in an action to foreclose the mortgage where the replacement note was non-negotiable upon its face? The plaintiff takes no issue with the finding by the court that the note assigned to him by Preston was non-negotiable but contends that he was a holder for value without notice of infirmities. * * *

The foreclosure of the mortgage is a proceeding in equity. The plaintiff, Frick, received an assignment of a mortgage which upon its face provided it was secured by a note described in the mortgage. The mortgage provided it was secured by a note of even date. The note that he did receive was not of even date and was by terms upon its face non-negotiable. He paid $72,500 for a note of $145,000. Under these facts Frick had the constructive notice of the infirmities of the original note of 1959. He was not a bona fide holder for value of the note which the mortgage secured. Equity will not bar the defense of want of the consideration for the original debt.

Does a receiver of a corporation under an assignment for benefit of creditors have the right to assert a defense in an action to foreclose a mortgage given by the corporation? We have heretofore determined that the $110,000 profit by Preston constituted a promoter's fraud upon the corporation and, therefore, there was no consideration for the $110,000 note. The persons most affected by the fraud on the corporation if permitted would be the subsequent stockholders and creditors.

The obligation of receiver is to protect the interest of the creditors. * * * [T]he receiver has the title that the corporation had to its property and may avoid any transfer which any creditor may have avoided unless the transfer was to a bona fide holder for value prior to the filing of the petition. Inasmuch as we have held that Frick was not a bona fide holder for value and that there was no consideration for the note of $110,000, the receiver may resist the foreclosure and assert the defense.

We do not decide whether or not Frick has a claim as a general creditor for part of the $145,000 note for the reason that the issue has not been presented to us.

Judgment reversed with directions to dismiss the complaint.

Notes

(1) Consider the situation after Preston resold the land to the corporation of which he was sole shareholder, at a profit of $110,000. Has anyone been injured? Could the transaction have been attacked by anyone if the corporation had remained solvent? Despite the broad language quoted by the Court, is not the vice of this transaction the possibility that subsequent shareholders or creditors might be injured? If so, is not the problem one of disclosure rather than fiduciary duty to the corporation?

(2) Other than general creditors or their representatives (e.g. Frick v. Howard), who may attack transactions between a promoter and the corporation on the ground the transaction violates the promoter's fiduciary duty? At least the following possibilities exist:

(a) *Co-promoters.* It is clear that a promoter is in a fiduciary relationship with his or her co-promoters, Geving v. Fitzpatrick 56 Ill.App.3d 206, 371 N.E.2d 1228 (1978), though when the venture is incorporated, complications may arise from the injection of the corporation into the picture, and the substitution of corporate relationships for joint venture relationships.

(b) *Subsequent shareholders.* Another class of persons who may be injured by promoters' transactions are persons who subsequently invest in the enterprise, unaware of the transaction in question. If the subsequent shareholder has dealt directly with the promoter in connection with the purchase of the securities, there is little doubt that the promoter is liable for fraud in the event of misrepresentation, or for mere nondisclosure of a material fact under Rule 10b–5, 17 C.F.R. § 240.10b–5, promulgated by the S.E.C. under § 10 of the Securities Exchange Act of 1934.

(c) *The Corporation.* Historically, a great volume of litigation arose in connection with attempts by the corporation, after it came under the control of subsequent investors or other persons, to attack transactions entered into between the promoter and the corporation. Confusion as to the existence of a corporate cause of action has persisted because of the conflicting reasoning of the United States Supreme Court and of the Supreme Court of Massachusetts in two leading cases arising out of the same promotional scheme. The promoters had sold property to the corporation formed by them for shares with a par value equal to about three times what they had paid for the property, and about twice what the property was worth at the time of the transfer. The United States Supreme Court in Old Dominion Copper Mining & Smelting Co. v. Lewisohn, 210 U.S. 206, 28 S.Ct. 634, 52 L.Ed. 1025 (1908), an action by the corporation against one of the principal promoters, argued that since the promoters and the shareholders were identical at the time of the transaction, there were no members of the corporation who were not informed of the facts, that corporate assent was therefore given with full knowledge and, that as a result, there was no breach of duty or wrong to the corporation. It was immaterial, the court said, that thereafter outsiders subscribed for shares in ignorance of the true facts because "of course, legally speaking, a corporation does not change its identity by adding a cubit to its stature." In Old Dominion Copper Mining & Smelting Co. v. Bigelow, 203 Mass. 159, 89 N.E. 193 (1909), an action by the corporation against the other principal promoter, on the other hand, the Massachusetts court argued that promoters stand in the same fiduciary position to the corporation when uninformed shareholders are expected to be brought in after the wrong has been perpetrated as they do when there are current shareholders to whom no disclosure is made. While a wrong is committed immediately against the corporation, there is no one to enforce the remedy until the new shareholders come in. While both cases are often cited, the views of the Massachusetts court appear to have gained ascendancy where the promoters plan to invite the public to become subscribers for shares. See Northridge Cooperative Section No. 1, Inc. v. 32nd Avenue Const. Corp., 2 N.Y.2d 514, 161 N.Y.S.2d 404, 141 N.E.2d 802 (1957).

(3) In recent years, litigation involving promoters' fraud has declined. This is partly due to the Federal Securities Act of 1933, which makes it unlawful to use means of interstate commerce or the mails to sell publicly a security unless a registration statement has been filed with the S.E.C. setting forth required information. Among the required disclosures are the following:

(d) *Transactions with promoters.* Registrants that have been organized within the past five years and that are filing a registration statement * * * shall:

(1) State the names of the promoters, the nature and amount of anything of value (including money, property, contracts, options or rights of any kind) received or to be received by each promoter, directly or indirectly, from the registrant and the nature and amount of any assets, services or other consideration therefore received or to be received by the registrant; and

(2) As to any assets acquired or to be acquired by the registrant from a promoter, state the amount at which the assets were acquired or are to be acquired and the principle followed or to be followed in determining such amount and identify the persons making the determination and their relationship, if any, with the registrant or any promoter. If the assets were acquired by the promoter within two years prior to their transfer to the registrant, also state the cost thereof to the promoter. * * *

If the information called for by [this Item] is being presented in a registration statement filed pursuant to the Securities Act or the Exchange Act, information shall be given for the periods specified in this Item and, in addition, for the two fiscal years preceding the registrant's last fiscal year. * * *

17 C.F.R. § 229.404(d). Many state Blue Sky laws also require similar disclosure.

STANLEY J. HOW & ASSOCIATES, INC. v. BOSS

United States District Court Southern District of Iowa, 1963.
222 F.Supp. 936.

[Editor: This was an action to recover on a contract for the performance of architectural services. The plaintiff alleged that it had performed the required services and was entitled to a fee of $38,250, of which it had received only $14,500. It seeks to collect the difference from Boss, a promoter of a corporation. The pertinent parts of the contract (with italics added) are as follows:

This agreement made as of the twentieth (20th) day of April in the year Nineteen Hundred and Sixty–One by and between *Boss Hotels Company, Inc. hereinafter called the Owner,* and Stanley J. How and Associates, Inc. hereinafter called the Architect * * *.

The Owner agrees to pay the Architect for such services a fee of six (6) per cent of the construction cost of the Project, with other payments and reimbursements as hereinafter provided.

The Owner and the Architect each binds himself, his partners, successors, legal representatives and assigns to the other party to this Agreement and to the partners, successors, legal representatives and assigns of such other party in respect to all covenants of this Agreement.

Except as above, neither the Owner nor the Architect shall assign, sublet or transfer his interest in this Agreement without written consent of the other.

IN WITNESS WHEREOF the parties hereto have made and executed this Agreement the day and year first above written.

Owner: /s/ Edw. A. Boss

By: Edwin A. Boss, agent for a Minnesota corporation to be formed who will be the obligor.

Architect:

Stanley J. How and Associates, Inc.

/s/ Stanley J. How.

This contract is the Standard Form of Agreement Between Owner and Architect printed by the American Institute of Architects. The blanks were originally filled in by a representative of the plaintiff; as originally prepared, the signature clause as well as the caption referred to "Boss Hotels Co., Inc." as the "owner." However, when the contract was presented to Boss, he erased the words "Boss Hotel Co., Inc." and inserted the language "By: Edwin A. Boss, agent for a Minnesota corporation to be formed who will be the obligor." He then asked Mr. How, "Is this all right?" or "Is this acceptable, this manner of signing?" or words to that effect. How said "Yes," and the contracts were then signed by defendant and Stanley J. How. Defendant caused an Iowa corporation named Minneapolis–Hunter Hotel Co. to be formed to construct the project. The checks sent to plaintiff for partial payments under the contract bore the name of this corporation. The project was ultimately abandoned after a substantial amount of architectural work had been performed under the contract.]

HANSON, DISTRICT JUDGE.

* * * To what extent [the Minneapolis–Hunter Hotel Co.] actually came into being is not clear in the record. No corporate charter, by-laws, or resolutions were offered into evidence. At any rate, if this new corporation exists, there are no assets in it to pay the amount due on the contract.

There really is not much debate as to what the law is on the questions raised. Both parties site [sic] King Features Syndicate, Dept. of Hearst Corp. International News Service Division v. Courrier, 241 Iowa 870, 43 N.W.2d 718, 41 A.L.R.2d 467, for the proposition that a promoter, though he may assume to act on behalf of the projected corporation and not for himself, will be personally liable on his contract unless the other party agreed to look to some other person or fund for payment. * * *

[The court then summarizes Comment b to Section 326 of the Restatement of Agency. This comment, as revised in the Restatement of Agency, Second, reads:

b. *Promoters.* The classic illustration of the rule stated in this Section is the promoter. When a promoter makes an agreement with another on behalf of a corporation to be formed, the following alternatives may represent the intent of the parties:

(1) They may understand that the other party is making a revocable offer to the nonexistent corporation which will result in a contract if the corporation is formed and accepts the offer prior to withdrawal. This is the normal understanding.

(2) They may understand that the other party is making an irrevocable offer for a limited time. Consideration to support the promise to keep the offer open can be found in an express or limited promise by the promoter to organize the corporation and use his best efforts to cause it to accept the offer.

(3) They may agree to a present contract by which the promoter is bound, but with an agreement that his liability terminates if the corporation is formed and manifests its willingness to become a party. There can be no ratification by the newly formed corporation, since it was not in existence when the agreement was made.

(4) They may agree to a present contract on which, even though the corporation becomes a party, the promoter remains liable either primarily or as surety for the performance of the corporation's obligation.

Which one of these possible alternatives, or variants thereof, is intended is a matter of interpretation on the facts of the individual case.]

[The third] possible interpretation is not very important in this case because a novation was not pleaded or argued. * * *

In the present case, the contract was signed: "Edwin A. Boss, agent for a Minnesota corporation to be formed who will be the obligor." The defendant argues that this is an agreement that the new corporation is solely liable. The problem here is what is the import of the words "who will be the obligor." It says nothing about the present obligor. The words "will be" connote something which will take place in the future.

* * *

About the closest case to the present in terms of signature is O'Rorke v. Geary, 207 A. 240, 56 A. 541, where the contract was signed "D.J. Geary for a bridge company to be organized and incorporated as party of the second part." The payments were to be made monthly and work was to be done before it was possible for the corporation to make the payments. The court held the promoter personally liable.

In White & Bollard, Inc. v. Goodenow, 58 Wash.2d 180, 361 P.2d 571, a case cited by both parties, the contract was signed: "Melvin D. Lurie, an agent for a corporation to be formed." The court said this language meant that Melvin D. Lurie was bound by the contract but in dicta states that if the corporation was formed this was also an agreement to allow the corporation to assume the liability of Melvin D. Lurie. The defendant cites this case only to distinguish it by saying that the present contract contains the additional words: "who will be the obligor." However, these words only tend to make clear what the court implied in the Goodenow case. It cannot be said that they express any clear intention to do more than that. In O'Rorke v. Geary, supra, language almost identical to that used in White & Bollard, Inc. v. Goodenow was said not to be an agreement for a novation. O'Rorke v. Geary is more similar factually to the present case than is White & Bollard, Inc. v. Goodenow.

These cases show that this is a situation where the parties used ambiguous words to describe their intentions. To resolve this ambiguity, it is helpful to resort to the usual rules of interpretation of ambiguous contracts. * * *

Mr. How's testimony and his business record, Exhibit K, show that he did not intend that the new corporation was the sole obligor on the contract. He stated that he believed Boss Hotel Co., Inc. or Boss Hotels was liable on the contract. This is not inconsistent with thinking Mr. Boss was liable on the contract but it is inconsistent with intending that the new corporation was to be solely liable on the contract. Promoters other than the one signing the contract may be liable on the contract also. In this case, Boss Hotel Co., Inc. was not made a party but this does show a reason why Mr. How might state that he felt Boss Hotel Co., Inc. was liable on the contract. The oral testimony on this point was only generally to the effect that the parties agreed that the contract was all right as written, but did tend to support the conclusion that Mr. Boss was intended to be the present obligor on the contract. * * *

It might well be that the parties were thinking about an understanding such as the [third] type wherein there would be a future novation. However, the defendant didn't feel this was the situation. He did not plead or argue novation or agreement to that effect. Therefore, the only issue was whether the contract was a continuing offer to the then nonexistent corporation or was an agreement that Mr. Boss was a present obligor. While the agreement was not completely clear, the words "who will be the obligor" are not enough to offset the rule that the person signing for the nonexistent corporation is normally to be personally liable. This is especially true when considered in the light of other circumstances of this case and would be true even without the inference that the law puts on this situation. * * *

The defendant argues that a practical construction has been put on the contract to the effect the plaintiff agreed to look solely to the credit of the new corporation. For this construction, the defendant relies upon the fact that the two checks which were given to Mr. Boss carried the letterhead of the new corporation and were signed by Edwin Hunter. * * * This would be an attempt to penalize the plaintiff for being patient and not demanding strict compliance. The court feels there was no waiver of rights and none was pleaded. * * *

In this case, the defendant was the principal promoter, acting for himself personally and as President of Boss Hotels, Inc. The promoters abandoned their purpose of forming the corporation. This would make the promoter liable to the plaintiff unless the contract be construed to mean: (1) that the plaintiff agreed to look solely to the new corporation for payment, and (2) that the promoter did not have any duty toward the plaintiff to form the corporation and give the corporation the opportunity to assume and pay the liability. * * *

At the time the specifications and drawings were completed, the amount owed the plaintiff was 75% of 6% of $850,000.00 (the reasonable cost estimate). This would amount to $38,250.00. $14,500.00 of this amount has been paid leaving an amount of $23,750.00 due to the plaintiff.

Accordingly the court concludes that the plaintiff, Stanley J. How & Associates, Inc., should have and recover judgment against the defendant, Edwin A. Boss, in the sum of $23,750.00, with interest and costs and, accordingly, a judgment will be entered. * * *

QUAKER HILL, INC. v. PARR

Supreme Court of Colorado, 1961.
148 Colo. 45, 364 P.2d 1056.

DOYLE, JUSTICE.

The plaintiff in error, to which we will refer as Quaker Hill or plaintiff, was plaintiff in the trial court in an action to recover the sum of $14,503.56 from defendants, defendants in error here. Judgment was in favor of the defendants, and Quaker Hill seeks review.

In May, 1958, the plaintiff, a New York corporation with offices in Newark, New York, sold a large quantity of nursery stock to the Denver Memorial Nursery, Inc. A sales contract, together with a promissory note was executed on May 19, 1958, and the Denver Memorial Nursery, Inc. was named as the contracting party in the sales contract and as the maker of the promissory note. The form of the signature on the note was as follows:

"Denver Memorial Nursery, Inc.

E.D. Parr, Pres.

James P. Presba, Sc'y.–Treas."

The contract shows the Denver Memorial Nursery, Inc. as purchaser and is signed:

"E.D. Parr, Pres."

From the evidence it appears that in the year 1958, prior to this transaction, Parr, Presba and others formed a corporation having the name "Denver Memorial Gardens, Inc." Its purpose was to operate a cemetery. In May of 1958 Parr and Presba, while in the course of negotiations with plaintiff to purchase nursery stock, undertook to organize a separate corporation called "Denver Memorial Nursery, Inc." On May 14, 1958, an order was signed by Parr on behalf of Denver Memorial Nursery, Inc. which, to the knowledge of plaintiff, was not yet formed, that fact being noted in the contract. Subsequently another order dated May 16, 1958, together with the mentioned note, was executed and was delivered to the plaintiff, together with a down payment in the amount of $1,000. Under the contract the balance of the purchase price was not due until the end of the year. The nursery stock was shipped immediately and arrived on May 26, 1958. It was temporarily planted with the assistance of plaintiff. After this temporary planting had occurred, a substitute order was sent to Quaker Hill which was similar in all respects to the previous order except that it contained the name "Mountain View Nurseries" instead of "Denver Memorial Nursery, Inc." as the purchaser. During the course of the ensuing winter and spring and prior to the due date of the balance of the purchase price, the nursery stock all died. The contract contained a guarantee providing for replacement of stock which died.

The Denver Memorial Nursery, Inc. was never formed. Because of name confusion, this corporation was called Mountain View Nurseries, Inc. Its articles were executed on May 27, 1958, and were subsequently filed with the Secretary of State. Neither the Denver Memorial Nursery, Inc. nor the Mountain View Nurseries, Inc. ever functioned as going concerns.

The explanation given at the trial for failure to form the corporation prior to entering into the first contract stemmed from insistence of Quaker Hill that the deal be consummated at once because the growing season was rapidly passing. Barker, who was salesman for Quaker Hill at the time of the sale, testified that the transaction was consummated in this form as a result of his insistence.

After Mountain View Nurseries, Inc. was formed, a new note and contract, prepared by the Division Manager of plaintiff and containing the name "Mountain View Nurseries, Inc." as contracting party, was submitted to defendants, signed in the name of Mountain View Nurseries, Inc. and returned to plaintiff. The plaintiff company thereafter used the designation "Mountain View Nurseries" in its communications. The present action seeks to subject defendants to *personal* liability in view of the defunct financial condition of the corporation, based upon the fact that the corporation was not formed at the time the contract was made and on the further ground that the defendants as promoters were individually liable. * * *

In summary, the facts disclose that Quaker Hill, a New York corporation acting through a local agent, made a sale to a corporation to be formed, and later accepted still another corporation after formation of the latter. The contract imposed no obligation on defendants to form the corporation nor did it name them as obligors on the note or as promisees in the contract. The question is whether under these circumstances personal liability can be imposed.

In urging that the trial court erred and that the cause should be reversed, plaintiff argues:

1. That promoters who enter a contract in the name of a proposed corporation are personally liable in the absence of an agreement that they should not be liable.

2. That the subsequent formation of a corporation and the ratification of the contract does not operate to release the promoters.

3. That the failure of the nursery stock, the subject matter of this contract, is not a defense because the contractual remedy was replacement.

4. That there should be liability on a quantum meruit basis.

The general principle which plaintiff urges as applicable here is that promoters are personally liable on their contracts, though made on behalf of a corporation to be formed. * * * A well recognized exception to this general rule, however, is that if the contract is made on behalf of the corporation and the other party agrees to look to the corporation and not to the promoters for payment, the promoters incur no personal liability.

In the present case, according to the trial court's findings, the plaintiff, acting through its agent, was well aware of the fact that the corporation was not formed and nevertheless urged that the contract be made in the name of the proposed corporation. There is but little evidence indicating intent on the part of the plaintiff to look to the defendants for performance or payment. The single fact supporting plaintiff's theory is the obtaining of an individual balance sheet. On the contrary, the entire transaction contemplated the corporation as the contracting party. Personal liability does not arise under such circumstances. See 41 A.L.R.2d 477, where the annotation recognizes the noted exception that personal liability does not attach where the contracting party is shown to be looking solely to the corporation for payment and not to the promoters or officers. * * *

In the case at bar, the findings of the trial court clearly establish intent on the part of the plaintiff to contract with the corporation and not with the individual defendants.

The curious form of this transaction is undoubtedly explainable on the basis of the long distance dealing, the great rush to complete it, the heavy emphasis on completion of the sale rather than on securing payment or a means of payment. No effort was made to expressly obligate the defendants and this present effort must be regarded as pure afterthought.

Being convinced that the trial court's determination was proper under the circumstances, we conclude that the judgment should be and it is affirmed.

Notes

(1) In Coopers and Lybrand v. Fox, 758 P.2d 683 (Colo.App.1988), Garry Fox was in the process of forming a new business to be called "Fox and Partners, Inc." On November 3, 1981 he met with a representative of Coopers and Lybrand and arranged for a tax opinion and other accounting services. Articles of incorporation were filed on December 4, 1981. After rendering the services, Coopers and Lybrand sent a bill for $10,827 to "Mr.

Garry R. Fox, Fox and Partner, Inc." When the bill was not paid, suit was brought against Garry Fox individually. The Court held that Fox was not entitled to the protection provided by Quaker Hill, Inc. v. Parr:

> As a general rule, promoters are personally liable for the contracts they make, though made on behalf of a corporation to be formed. The well-recognized exception to the general rule of promoter liability is that if the contracting party knows the corporation is not in existence but nevertheless agrees to look solely to the corporation and not to the promoter for payment, then the promoter incurs no personal liability. *Quaker Hill, Inc. v. Parr.* In the absence of an express agreement, the existence of an agreement to release the promoter from liability may be shown by circumstances making it reasonably certain that the parties intended to and did enter into the agreement.

> Here, the trial court found there was *no* agreement, either express or implied, regarding Fox's liability. Thus, in the absence of an agreement releasing him from liability, Fox is liable.

> Coopers also contends that the trial court erred in ruling, in effect, that Coopers had the burden of proving any agreement regarding Fox's personal liability for payment of the fee. We agree. Release of the promoter depends on the intent of the parties. As the proponent of an alleged agreement to release the promoter from liability, the promoter has the burden of proving the release agreement. * * * The trial court found that there was no agreement regarding Fox's liability. Thus, Fox failed to sustain his burden of proof, and the trial court erred in granting judgment in his favor.

> It is undisputed that the defendant, Garry J. Fox, engaged Coopers' services, that G. Fox and Partners, Inc., was not in existence at that time, that Coopers performed the work, and that the fee was reasonable. The only dispute, as the trial court found, is whether Garry Fox is liable for payment of the fee. We conclude that Fox is liable, as a matter of law, under the doctrine of promoter liability.

Does this holding help to reconcile *Quaker Hill* and *Stanley J. How?*

(2) How explicit does the agreement to look only to the not-yet-formed corporation have to be? Consider the following:

> We do not believe the agreement to release a promoter from liability must say in so many words, "I agree to release." Where the promoter cannot show an express agreement, existence of the agreement to release him from liability may be shown by circumstances. Of course, where circumstantial evidence is relied on, the circumstances must be such as to make it reasonably certain that the parties intended to and did enter into the agreement. * * * From its oral opinion it is clear that the trial court relied on three considerations in holding that the parties agreed to release Goodman from the contract: (1) DDS knew of the corporation's nonexistence; (2) Goodman told Doman that he was forming a corporation to limit his personal liability; and (3) the progress payments were made to the corporation.

> The fact that DDS knew of the corporation's nonexistence is not dispositive in any way of its intent. The rule is that the contracting

party may know of the nonexistence of the corporation *but nevertheless* may agree to look solely to the corporation. The fact that a contracting party knows that the corporation is nonexistent does not indicate any agreement to release the promoter. To the contrary, such knowledge alone would seem to indicate that the members of DDS intended to make Goodman a party to the contract. They could not hold the corporation, a nonexistent entity, responsible and of course they would expect to have recourse against someone (Goodman) if default occurred. This consideration also relates to another factor the trial court apparently had in mind—that the members of DDS were all educated people. Goodman argues that as such they should have expressly requested that he be personally liable. This was unnecessary because under the law as set out above, Goodman was liable until the partners of DDS agreed otherwise. Thus, they were not required to specify personal liability.

The fact that Goodman expressed a desire to form the corporation to limit his liability also is not dispositive of the intentions of the members of DDS. No one from DDS objected to his incorporating but this failure to object does not indicate an affirmative assent to limit Goodman's personal liability. Apparently Goodman believed that incorporation would automatically limit his liability thus misunderstanding the rules regarding promoter liability. * * * The only other evidence of the parties' intent to make the corporation the sole party to the contract is that the progress payments were made payable to the corporation. However, they were so written only at the instruction of Goodman and in fact the first check written by DDS after the signing of the contract was written to the corporation *and* Goodman as an individual. This evidence does not show by reasonable certainty that DDS intended to contract only with the corporation.

Goodman v. Darden, Doman & Stafford Assoc., 100 Wn.2d 476, 670 P.2d 648, 652–3 (1983). Three Justices dissented.

(3) Is it not a fair inference from the circumstances surrounding the execution of the contract in the case of Stanley J. How & Associates v. Boss that both parties probably contemplated that the architect was to look solely to some corporation for payment, that neither party thought that Boss was to be *personally* liable, and that therefore the holding of the court in effect gives the plaintiff an unjustified windfall? In light of this reasoning, how persuasive is the court's reliance on O'Rorke v. Geary and other cases holding that where performance is called for before the corporation is formed, there is an inference that the promoter intended to be personally liable?

(4) Assume that Quaker Hill, Inc. defaulted on its obligation to deliver the nursery stock before any corporation was formed. Could Parr act as plaintiff in a suit against Quaker Hill for breach of contract? Or would he have to form a "shell" corporation for the sole purpose of bringing suit? Or should Quaker Hill's default be deemed the revocation of a mere offer so that no contractual liability exists?

(5) Presumably, it would have been entirely feasible for Boss to have formed a new corporation to construct the project under the corporation

laws of either Minnesota or Iowa. If he had done so, and thereafter the contract had been entered into in the name of the new corporation, the possibility of a successful suit by the architect against Boss personally would have been very slight. Is the same true in Quaker Hill v. Parr? The fact that cases involving promoter liability on contracts continue to rise with some regularity probably indicates that many promoters do not have legal advice in the early stages of the promotion, since presumably an attorney would insist that basic rights and obligations be expressed reasonably clearly, and that some provision should be made for obvious contingencies such as a total failure of the promotion. An attorney representing the promoter would normally recommend that a corporation be formed and that all contracts be taken in the name of the corporation exclusively. Alternatively, the attorney might recommend that the agreement expressly provide that the other party should look only to the corporation for payment. Of course, counsel for the other party would doubtless recommend that the promoter expressly assume personal responsibility for performance of the contract.

(6) Are additional theories available to hold a promoter personally liable when he or she executes a contract in the name of a corporation but the corporation in fact has not been formed? See H. Henn and J. Alexander, Laws of Corporations (3d Ed.1983), 249, n. 13:

> When a promoter agrees in behalf of the corporation, the promoter might be liable to the third person on several theories other than as an intended party to the contract. If the promoter gives the third person the impression that the promoter as agent is agreeing in behalf of an *existing* corporation, the promoter might be liable: (a) For breach of implied warranty of the existence of the principal; or (b) For breach of implied warranty of authority from the principal. If the promoter makes it clear that the promoter is acting in behalf of a corporation *to be* formed, the otherwise implied warranties of the existence of the principal or of authority from the principal would be negatived. However, the promoter might be liable, if the corporation is not formed, for: (a) Misrepresentation that the corporation was being formed; (b) Breach of promise to form the corporation; or (c) Breach of warranty that the corporation would be formed. See Weiss v. Baum, 218 App. Div. 83, 217 N.Y.S. 820 (2d Dep't 1926). *   *   *

Consider Res. Agency 2d, §§ 329, 330 [Appendix One]. What difference does it make whether the theory of liability is on the contract itself, for breach of implied warranty, or in tort for fraud? Possible differences may arise in connection with the applicable statute of limitations, the measure of recovery, and other factors as well.

(7) A "headcount" of the numerous cases involving the personal liability of promoters would probably show that a majority of the cases hold the defendant-promoter personally liable on one theory or another. Prediction of result in a specific case, however, is hazardous.

McARTHUR v. TIMES PRINTING CO.

Supreme Court of Minnesota, 1892.
48 Minn. 319, 51 N.W. 216.

MITCHELL, J. The complaint alleges that about October 1, 1889, the defendant contracted with plaintiff for his services as advertising solicitor for one year; that in April, 1890, it discharged him, in violation of the contract. The action is to recover damages for the breach of the contract. * * * Upon the trial there was evidence reasonably tending to prove that in September, 1889, one C.A. Nimocks and others were engaged as promoters in procuring the organization of the defendant company to publish a newspaper; that, about September 12th, Nimocks, as such promoter, made a contract with plaintiff, in behalf of the contemplated company, for his services as advertising solicitor for the period of one year from and after October 1st,—the date at which it was expected that the company would be organized; that the corporation was not, in fact, organized until October 16th, but that the publication of the paper was commenced by the promoters October 1st, at which date plaintiff, in pursuance of his arrangement with Nimocks, entered upon the discharge of his duties as advertising solicitor for the paper; that after the organization of the company he continued in its employment in the same capacity until discharged, the following April; that defendant's board of directors never took any formal action with reference to the contract made in its behalf by Nimocks, but all of the stockholders, directors, and officers of the corporation knew of this contract at the time of its organization, or were informed of it soon afterwards, and none of them objected to or repudiated it, but, on the contrary, retained plaintiff in the employment of the company without any other or new contract as to his services.

There is a line of cases which hold that where a contract is made in behalf of, and for the benefit of, a projected corporation, the corporation, after its organization, cannot become a party to the contract, either by adoption or ratification of it. This, however, seems to be more a question of name than of substance; that is, whether the liability of the corporation, in such cases, is to be placed on the grounds of its adoption of the contract of its promoters, or upon some other ground, such as equitable estoppel. This court, in accordance with what we deem sound reason, as well as the weight of authority, has held that, while a corporation is not bound by engagements made on its behalf by its promoters before its organization, it may, after its organization, make such engagements its own contracts. And this it may do precisely as it might make similar original contracts; formal action of its board of directors being necessary only where it would be necessary in the case of a similar original contract. That it is not requisite that such adoption or acceptance be express, but it may be inferred from acts or acquiescence on part of the corporation, or its authorized agents, as any similar original contract might be shown. * * * That the contract in this case was of that kind is very clear; and the acts and acquiescence of the corporate officers, after the organization of the company, fully justified the jury in finding that it had adopted it as its own.

The defendant, however, claims that the contract was void under the statute of frauds, because, "by its terms, not to be performed within one year from the making thereof," which counsel assumes to be September 12th,—the date of the agreement between plaintiff and the promoter. This proceeds upon the erroneous theory that the act of the corporation, in such cases, is a ratification, which relates back to the date of the contract with the promoter, under the familiar maxim that "a subsequent ratification has a retroactive effect, and is equivalent to a prior command." But the liability of the corporation, under such circumstances, does not rest upon any principle of the law of agency, but upon the immediate and voluntary act of the company. Although the acts of a corporation with reference to the contracts made by promoters in its behalf before its organization are frequently loosely termed "ratification," yet a "ratification," properly so called, implies an existing person, on whose behalf the contract might have been made at the time. There cannot, in law, be a ratification of a contract which could not have been made binding on the ratifier at the time it was made, because the ratifier was not then in existence. What is called "adoption," in such case, is, in legal effect, the making of a contract of the date of the adoption, and not as of some former date. The contract in this case was, therefore, not within the statute of frauds. The trial court fairly submitted to the jury all the issues of fact in this case, accompanied by instructions as to the law which were exactly in the line of the views we have expressed; and the evidence justified the verdict. * * *

Order affirmed.

Notes

(1) The position taken in the principal case, that a corporation is not liable on a promoter's contract unless it expressly or impliedly adopts (or "ratifies") it, appears to be generally accepted, though the issue has arisen in only a few litigated cases. For an example of implied adoption, see Stolmeier v. Beck, 232 Neb. 705, 441 N.W.2d 888 (1989) [subsequently-formed corporation was obligated to return funds to an investor since funds were later used by the corporation in operation of its business]. In Framingham Sav. Bank v. Szabo, 617 F.2d 897 (1st Cir.1980) the Court applied the "extreme minority" rule of Massachusetts that a newly formed corporation "could not become bound to the contract by ratification or adoption of the putative agent's bargain. Rather, to bind itself the corporation must introduce 'into the transaction such elements as would be sufficient foundation for a new contract.' * * * The corporation can become liable on the terms of the original contract, but only if its post-incorporation acts are sufficient independently to bind it to a new contract." 617 F.2d at 898. Considering that corporations act only through agents, do you think results will often differ if a court applies the general rule or the "extreme minority" rule applied in Massachusetts?

(2) Both the general rule and the narrower rule applied in Massachusetts require newly formed corporations to do something before they are bound on contracts made on their behalf by promoters. Can this requirement be justified on policy grounds as well as conceptual grounds? Why not adopt a rule that newly formed corporations automatically become bound on all contracts entered into on their behalf by promoters?

(3) If the corporation adopts a contract, is the promoter thereafter relieved of liability on it? In other words, is there a novation? In Decker v. Juzwik, 255 Iowa 358, 121 N.W.2d 652, 659 (1963), the court, holding that a novation occurred, stated:

> The question is not without difficulty, for it is the general rule that promoters are personally liable on contracts which they have entered into personally, even though they have contracted for the benefit of the projected corporation, and although the corporation has been formed and has received the benefit of the contract, and they are not discharged from liability by the subsequent adoption of the contract by the corporation when formed, *unless* there is a novation or other agreement to such effect. * * * It is not greatly disputed that plaintiffs looked to the new corporation for payment of this obligation and although it was not expressed, the intention was quite evident that payments were to come from the corporation on a stated basis and that plaintiffs did accept that method of payment rather than look to the promoters for payment. The question is largely one of fact.

Compare 2 Williston on Contracts (3d Ed.) § 306, p. 431 (1959): "But it seems more nearly to correspond with the intentions of the parties to suggest that when the corporation assents to the contract, it assents to take the place of the promoter—a change of parties to which the other side of the contract assented in advance."

(4) A peculiar problem arises in connection with a contract between a promoter and an attorney, pursuant to which the attorney agrees to form the corporation. If a straightforward theory of implied adoption is followed, the mere existence of the corporation constitutes acceptance of the benefits of the attorney's services, and an agreement to pay whatever fee is set forth in the contract. However, in Kridelbaugh v. Aldrehn Theatres Co., 195 Iowa 147, 191 N.W. 803 (1923), the court refused to follow this logic: "This is not a case in which the corporation can accept or refuse the benefits of a contract. Under the instant record it had no choice. Like a child at its birth, it must be born in the manner provided. There is no volition on its part." See also David v. Southern Import Wine Co., 171 So. 180, 182 (La.App.1936): "A corporation brought into existence—given its life—by the service of an attorney may not be heard to say that the service was unauthorized because rendered prior to incorporation. When the benefit of such service is received and accepted by the corporation, it cannot be heard to question the authority through which the service was employed. It may be that in such case the corporation may not be held to the express terms of a contract for such employment; in other words, it may not be held to the contract itself, but it may not repudiate the service entirely and yet reap the benefits therefrom. It may repudiate the contract price if a price has been agreed upon, but it may not refuse to pay for

the service on the basis of the value of the benefits received; in other words on a quantum meruit." Of course, an informal adoption will be given effect if it appears to be truly voluntary. See, e.g. Indianapolis Blue Print & Mfg. Co. v. Kennedy, 215 Ind. 409, 412, 19 N.E.2d 554, 555 (1939).

2. DEFECTIVE INCORPORATION

ROBERTSON v. LEVY

Court of Appeals, District of Columbia, 1964.
197 A.2d 443.

HOOD, CHIEF JUDGE.

On December 22, 1961, Martin G. Robertson and Eugene M. Levy entered into an agreement whereby Levy was to form a corporation, Penn Ave. Record Shack, Inc., which was to purchase Robertson's business. Levy submitted articles of incorporation to the Superintendent of Corporations on December 27, 1961, but no certificate of incorporation was issued at this time. Pursuant to the contract an assignment of lease was entered into on December 31, 1961, between Robertson and Levy, the latter acting as president of Penn Ave. Record Shack, Inc. On January 2, 1962, the articles of incorporation were rejected by the Superintendent of Corporations but on the same day Levy began to operate the business under the name Penn Ave. Record Shack, Inc. Robertson executed a bill of sale to Penn Ave. Record Shack, Inc. on January 8, 1962, disposing of the assets of his business to that "corporation" and receiving in return a note providing for installment payments signed "Penn Ave. Record Shack, Inc. by Eugene M. Levy, President." The certificate of incorporation was issued on January 17, 1962. One payment was made on the note. The exact date when the payment was made cannot be clearly determined from the record, but presumably it was made after the certificate of incorporation was issued. Penn Ave. Record Shack, Inc. ceased doing business in June 1962 and is presently without assets. Robertson sued Levy for the balance due on the note as well as for additional expenses incurred in settling the lease arrangement with the original lessor. In holding for the defendant the trial court found that [section 139 of the 1950 Model Act], relied upon by Robertson, did not apply and further that Robertson was estopped to deny the existence of the corporation.

The case presents the following issues on appeal: Whether the president of an "association" which filed its articles of incorporation, which were first rejected but later accepted, can be held personally liable on an obligation entered into by the "association" before the certificate of incorporation has been issued, or whether the creditor is "estopped" from denying the existence of the "corporation" because, after the certificate of incorporation was issued, he accepted the first installment payment on the note.

The Business Corporation Act of the District of Columbia, Code 1961, is patterned after the Model Business Corporation Act which is largely based on the Illinois Business Corporation Act of 1933. On this appeal, we are concerned with an interpretation of sections [50 and 139 of the 1950 Model Act]. Several states have substantially enacted the Model Act, but only a few have enacted both sections similar to those under consideration. A search of the case law in each of these jurisdictions, as well as in our own jurisdiction, convinces us that these particular sections of the corporation acts have never been the subject of a reported decision.

For a full understanding of the problems raised, some historical grounding is not only illuminative but necessary. In early common law times private corporations were looked upon with distrust and disfavor. This distrust of the corporate form for private enterprise was eventually overcome by the enactment of statutes which set forth certain prerequisites before the status was achieved, and by court decisions which eliminated other stumbling blocks. Problems soon arose, however, where there was substantial compliance with the prerequisites of the statute, but not complete formal compliance. Thus the concepts of de jure corporations, de facto corporations, and of "corporations by estoppel" came into being.

Taking each of these in turn, a de jure corporation results when there has been conformity with the mandatory conditions precedent (as opposed to merely directive conditions) established by the statute. A de jure corporation is not subject to direct or collateral attack either by the state in a *quo warranto* proceeding or by any other person.

A de facto corporation is one which has been defectively incorporated and thus is not de jure. The Supreme Court has stated that the requisites for a corporation de facto are: (1) A valid law under which such a corporation can be lawfully organized; (2) An attempt to organize thereunder; (3) Actual user of the corporate franchise. Good faith in claiming to be and in doing business as a corporation is often added as a further condition. A de facto corporation is recognized for all purposes except where there is a direct attack by the state in a *quo warranto* proceeding. The concept of de facto corporation has been roundly criticized.[5]

Cases continued to arise, however, where the corporation was not de jure, where it was not de facto because of failure to comply with one of the four requirements above, but where the courts, lacking some clear standard or guideline, were willing to decide on the equities of the case. Thus another concept arose, the so-called "corporation by estoppel." This term was a complete misnomer. There was no corporation, the acts of the associates having failed even to colorably fulfill the statutory requirements; there was no estoppel in the pure sense of the word because generally there was no holding out followed by reliance on the part of the other party. Apparently estoppel can arise whether

---

5. [By the Court] Ballantine § 20 ("a baffling and discouraging maze,"); Stevens, Corporations, pp. 135–6 (1949) ("inaccurate and confusing,"); Frey, Legal Analysis and the De Facto Doctrine, 100 U.Pa.L.Rev. 1153, 1180 (1952) ("legal conceptualism at its worst,").

or not a de facto corporation has come into existence. Estoppel problems arose where the certificate of incorporation had been issued as well as where it had not been issued, and under the following general conditions: where the "association" sues a third party and the third party is estopped from denying that the plaintiff is a corporation; where a third party sues the "association" as a corporation and the "association" is precluded from denying that it was a corporation; where a third party sues the "association" and the members of that association cannot deny its existence as a corporation where they participated in holding it out as a corporation; where a third party sues the individuals behind the "association" but is estopped from denying the existence of the "corporation"; where either a third party, or the "association" is estopped from denying the corporate existence because of prior pleadings.

One of the reasons for enacting modern corporation statutes was to eliminate problems inherent in the de jure, de facto and, estoppel concepts. Thus sections [50 and 139 of the Model Business Corporation Act] were enacted as follows:

[Section 50. Effect of issuance of certificate of incorporation]

Upon the issuance of the certificate of incorporation, the corporate existence shall begin, and such certificate of incorporation shall be conclusive evidence that all conditions precedent required to be performed by the incorporators have been complied with and that the corporation has been incorporated under this Act, except in a proceeding to cancel or revoke the certificate of incorporation or for involuntary dissolution of the corporation.

[Section 139. Unauthorized assumption of corporate powers]

All persons who assume to act as a corporation without authority so to do shall be jointly and severally liable for all debts and liabilities incurred or arising as result thereof.

The first portion of section [50] sets forth a *sine qua non* regarding compliance. No longer must the courts inquire into the equities of a case to determine whether there has been "colorable compliance" with the statute. The corporation comes into existence only when the certificate has been issued. Before the certificate issues, there is no corporation de jure, de facto or by estoppel. After the certificate is issued under section [50], the de jure corporate existence commences. Only after such existence has begun can the corporation commence business through compliance with section [§ 48(g) of the 1950 version of the Model Act] by paying into the corporation the minimum capital, and with section [51 of that Act], which requires that the capitalization be no less than $1,000. These latter two sections are given further force and effect by [a non-Model Act section] which declares that directors of a corporation are jointly and severally liable for any assets distributed or any dividends paid to shareholders which renders the corporation insolvent or reduces its net assets below its stated capital.

The authorities which have considered the problem are unanimous in their belief that [MBCA § 50] and [MBCA § 139] have put to rest de facto corporations and corporations by estoppel. Thus the Comment to section 50, * * * after noting that de jure incorporation is complete when the certificate is issued, states that:

> "Since it is unlikely that any steps short of securing a certificate of incorporation would be held to constitute apparent compliance, the possibility that a de facto corporation could exist under such a provision is remote." [6]

Similarly, Professor Hornstein in his work on Corporate Law and Practice (1959) observes at § 29 that: "Statutes in almost half the jurisdictions have virtually eliminated the distinction between de jure and de facto corporations [citing § 139 of the Model Act]." * * *

The portion of [§ 50] which states that the certificate of incorporation will be "conclusive evidence" that all conditions precedent have been performed eliminates the problems of estoppel and de facto corporations once the certificate has been issued. The existence of the corporation is conclusive evidence against all who deal with it. Under [§ 139], if an individual or group of individuals assumes to act as a corporation before the certificate of incorporation has been issued, joint and several liability attaches. We hold, therefore, that the impact of these sections, when considered together, is to eliminate the concepts of estoppel and de facto corporateness under the Business Corporation Act of the District of Columbia. It is immaterial whether the third person believed he was dealing with a corporation or whether he intended to deal with a corporation.[7] The certificate of incorporation provides the cut off point; before it is issued, the individuals, and not the corporation, are liable.

Turning to the facts of this case, Penn Ave. Record Shack, Inc. was not a corporation when the original agreement was entered into, when the lease was assigned, when Levy took over Robertson's business, when operations began under the Penn Ave. Record Shack, Inc. name, or when the bill of sale was executed. Only on January 17 did Penn Ave. Record Shack, Inc. become a corporation. Levy is subject to personal liability because, before this date, he assumed to act as a corporation without any authority so to do. Nor is Robertson estopped from denying the existence of the corporation because after the certificate

---

6. [By the Editor] The comment to the 1969 version of the Model Act was even more unambiguous:

> "Under the unequivocal provisions of the Model Act, any steps short of securing a certificate of incorporation would not constitute apparent compliance. Therefore a de facto corporation cannot exist under the Model Act."

Model Bus.Corp.Act Ann.2d, § 56, ¶ 2.

The comment to section 146 (identical to section 139 of the 1950 Act) added "Aboli-

tion of the concept of de facto incorporation, which at best was fuzzy, is a sound result. No reason exists for its continuance under general corporate laws, where the process of acquiring de jure incorporation is both simple and clear. The vestigial appendage should be removed."

7. [By the Court] In the present case, Robertson admitted intending to deal with a corporation.

was issued he accepted one payment on the note. An individual who incurs statutory liability on an obligation under [§ 139] because he has acted without authority, is not relieved of that liability where, at a later time, the corporation does come into existence by complying with section [§ 50]. Subsequent partial payment by the corporation does not remove this liability.

The judgment appealed from is reversed with instructions to enter judgment against the appellee on the note and for damages proved to have been incurred by appellant for breach of the lease.

Reversed with instructions.

Notes

(1) Several decisions in states that have adopted both sections 50 and 139 of the 1969 Model Business Corporation Act accept the result reached in Robertson v. Levy, holding that there can be no limited liability before articles of incorporation are filed. Booker Custom Packing Co., Inc. v. Sallomi, 149 Ariz. 124, 716 P.2d 1061 (App.1986); Thompson & Green Mach. v. Music City Lumber, 683 S.W.2d 340 (Tenn.App.1984); Bowers Building Co. v. Altura Glass Co., Inc., 694 P.2d 876 (Colo.App.1984); Cahoon v. Ward, 231 Ga. 872, 204 S.E.2d 622 (1974); Timberline Equipment Co., Inc. v. Davenport, 267 Or. 64, 514 P.2d 1109 (1973).

(2) In Sherwood & Roberts–Oregon, Inc. v. Alexander, 269 Or. 389, 525 P.2d 135 (1974), the court refused to apply §§ 50 and 139 when no attempt was made at all to incorporate. The court further held that the promoters were not liable on the ground that the third person had agreed not to look to the promoter for payment of the note that had been executed in the name of the nonexistent corporation. See also Frontier Refining Co. v. Kunkel's, Inc., 407 P.2d 880 (Wyo.1965).

(3) When applying §§ 50 and 139 should a distinction be drawn between active participants and inactive investors? Can such a distinction be justified under the common law of de facto corporations? Under the language of § 139? What does "assume to act" mean in that section? Does it refer to all participants in an active promotion? Only the active promoter? Consider the following analysis:

We find the language ambiguous. Liability is imposed on "[a]ll persons who assume to act as a corporation." Such persons shall be liable "for all debts and liabilities incurred or arising as a result thereof."

We conclude that the category of "persons who assume to act as a corporation" does not include those whose only connection with the organization is as an investor. On the other hand, the restriction of liability to those who personally incurred the obligation sued upon cannot be based upon logic or the realities of business practice. When several people carry on the activities of a defectively organized corporation, chance frequently will dictate which of the several active principals directly incurs a certain obligation or whether an employee, rather than an active principal, personally incurs the obligation.

We are of the opinion that the phrase, "persons who assume to act as a corporation" should be interpreted to include those persons who have an investment in the organization and who actively participate in the policy and operational decisions of the organization. Liability should not necessarily be restricted to the person who personally incurred the obligation.

Timberline Equipment Co., Inc. v. Davenport, 267 Or. 64, 72–76, 514 P.2d 1109, 1113–1114 (1973).

(4) Consider RMBCA § 2.04. Does this provision change the result in Robertson v. Levy? Does it change the construction of § 139 of the MBCA in the *Timberline* case described in the last note?

(5) Before the development of the Model Act provisions set forth in the principal case, there was a tendency to hold all participants in a corporation that was neither de facto nor de jure personally liable. See H. Henn and J. Alexander (3d Ed) at 343:

Under the old rule, all of the associates were held liable as partners, the theory being that the associated group was either a corporation or a partnership with its mutual agency. This viewpoint failed to take into account the differentiation between active and inactive members of the group, as well as the objection that the shareholders did not intend to act as a partnership.

The more modern approach has been to examine each situation and thereby determine whether the too-defectively-incorporated enterprise should be treated as a partnership. Associates who assumed an inactive role and who believed that they were members of a valid corporation ought not to be held liable as partners. Factors such as vesting authority in a "board of directors" and the absence of any holding out as partners (which might give rise to estoppel) assume importance under the modern view.

There are other theories upon which associates may be held liable by creditors. For instance, there is a possibility that an action may lie for breach of an implied warranty of authority or existence of principal brought against those who have acted on behalf of the supposed corporation. The same is true of an action based on a theory of joint venture against those who have acted or who have authorized or ratified such acts (there being no, or at most a, limited implied mutual agency in a joint venture).

CANTOR v. SUNSHINE GREENERY, INC.

Superior Court of New Jersey, 1979.
165 N.J.Super. 411, 398 A.2d 571.

Before JUDGES MICHELS and LARNER.

The opinion of the court was delivered by LARNER, J.A.D.

This appeal involves the propriety of a personal judgment against defendant William J. Brunetti for the breach of a lease between plaintiffs and a corporate entity known as Sunshine Greenery, Inc., and more particularly whether there was a *de facto* corporation in existence at the time of the execution of the lease.

Plaintiffs brought suit for damages for the breach of the lease against Sunshine Greenery, Inc. and Brunetti. Default judgment was entered against the corporation and a nonjury trial was held as to the liability of the individual. The trial judge in a letter opinion determined that plaintiffs were entitled to judgment against Brunetti individually on the theory that as of the time of the creation of the contract he was acting as a promoter and that his corporation, Sunshine Greenery, Inc., was not a legal or *de facto* corporation.

The undisputed facts reveal the following: Plaintiffs prepared the lease naming Sunshine Greenery, Inc. as the tenant, and it was signed by Brunetti as president of that named entity. Mr. Cantor, acting for plaintiffs, knew that Brunetti was starting a new venture as a newly formed corporation known as Sunshine Greenery, Inc. Although Cantor had considerable experience in ownership and leasing of commercial property to individuals and corporations, he did not request a personal guarantee from Brunetti, nor did he make inquiry as to his financial status or background. Without question, he knew and expected that the lease agreement was undertaken by the corporation and not by Brunetti individually, and that the corporation would be responsible thereunder.

At the time of the signing of the lease on December 16, 1974 in Cantor's office, Brunetti was requested by Cantor to give him a check covering the first month's rent and the security deposit. When Brunetti stated that he was not prepared to do so because he had no checks with him, Cantor furnished a blank check which was filled out for $1,200, with the name of Brunetti's bank and signed by him as president of Sunshine Greenery, Inc. The lease was repudiated by a letter from counsel for Sunshine Greenery, Inc. dated December 17, 1974, which in turn was followed by a response from Cantor to the effect that he would hold the "client" responsible for all losses. The check was not honored because Brunetti stopped payment, and in any event because Sunshine Greenery, Inc. did not have an account in the bank.

The evidence is clear that on November 21, 1974 the corporate name of Sunshine Greenery, Inc. had been reserved for Brunetti by the Secretary of State, and that on December 3, 1974 a certificate of incorporation for that company was signed by Brunetti and Sharyn N. Sansoni as incorporators. The certificate was forwarded by mail to the Secretary of State on that same date with a check for the filing fee, but for some unexplained reason it was not officially filed until December 18, 1974, two days after the execution of the lease.[8]

---

8. [By the Court] We note that the letter enclosing the certificate of incorporation is addressed to "Mortimer G. Newman, Jr., Secretary of State, State House Annex, Trenton, New Jersey." Whether this misidentification of the person holding the office of Secretary of State accounts for the filing delay we are unable to say from the record.

In view of the late filing, Sunshine Greenery, Inc. was not a *de jure* corporation on December 16, 1974 when the lease was signed. See N.J. S.A. 14A:2–7(2). Nevertheless, there is ample evidence of the fact that it was a *de facto* corporation in that there was a *bona fide* attempt to organize the corporation some time before the consummation of the contract and there was an actual exercise of the corporate powers by the negotiations with plaintiffs and the execution of the contract involved in this litigation. When this is considered in the light of the concession that plaintiffs knew that they were dealing with that corporate entity and not with Brunetti individually, it becomes evident that the *de facto* status of the corporation suffices to absolve Brunetti from individual liability. Plaintiffs in effect are estopped from attacking the legal existence of the corporation collaterally because of the nonfiling in order to impose liability on the individual when they have admittedly contracted with a corporate entity which had *de facto* status. In fact, their prosecution of the claim against the corporation to default judgment is indicative of their recognition of the corporation as the true obligor and theoretically inconsistent with the assertion of the claim against the individual.

The trial judge's finding that Sunshine Greenery, Inc. was not a *de facto* corporation is unwarranted under the record facts herein. The mere fact that there were no formal meetings or resolutions or issuance of stock is not determinative of the legal or *de facto* existence of the corporate entity, particularly under the simplified New Jersey Business Corporation Act of 1969, which eliminates the necessity of a meeting of incorporators. See N.J.S.A. 14A:2–6 and Commissioners' Comment thereunder. The act of executing the certificate of incorporation, the *bona fide* effort to file it and the dealings with plaintiffs in the name of that corporation fully satisfy the requisite proof of the existence of a *de facto* corporation. To deny such existence because of a mere technicality caused by administrative delay in filing runs counter to the purpose of the *de facto* concept, and would accomplish an unjust and inequitable result in favor of plaintiffs contrary to their own contractual expectations. * * *

Since the trial judge erred in negating the *de facto* existence of the corporation herein, the consequent imposition of individual liability on the thesis that Brunetti was a "promoter" is also unwarranted. Since plaintiffs looked to the corporation for liability on the lease, and since we find that Sunshine Greenery, Inc. had a *de facto* existence, there can be no personal liability of Brunetti on the theory that he was a "promoter."

In view of the foregoing, the judgment entered against defendant William J. Brunetti is reversed and set aside, and the matter is remanded to the Law Division to enter judgment on the complaint in favor of William J. Brunetti.

Notes

(1) Can you see any factual differences between this case and Robertson v. Levy that might justify the difference in result?

(2) One obvious basis for reconciling the two cases is the difference in statutory provisions in the District of Columbia and New Jersey. As indicated in *Robertson,* the critical provisions in the District of Columbia were drawn directly from §§ 50 and 139 of the 1950 Model Act. New Jersey is not basically a Model Act jurisdiction; the relevant portion of section 14A:2–7(2) reads as follows:

> * * * The corporate existence shall begin upon the effective date of the certificate, which shall be the date of the filing or such later time, not to exceed 90 days from the date of filing, as may be set forth in the certificate. Such filing shall be conclusive evidence that all conditions precedent required to be performed by the incorporators have been complied with and, after the corporate existence has begun, that the corporation has been incorporated under this act, except as against this State in a proceeding to cancel or revoke the certificate of incorporation or for involuntary dissolution of the corporation.

New Jersey has not enacted anything comparable to § 139 of the 1969 Model Act. Despite this, the Commissioner's Comment to the New Jersey statute states that "the last sentence of subsection 14A:2–7(2) * * * is adapted from section 50 of the Model Act. Such a provision, * * * virtually eliminates the distinction between *de jure* and *de facto* corporations * * *." This comment was not cited or referred to by the Court in *Cantor.*

(3) Every state has enacted a provision somewhat similar to § 50 of the 1969 Model Act, defining when the corporate existence commences. Only about 20 Model Act states enacted provisions similar to § 139 of that Act. If Robertson v. Levy were to arise in a jurisdiction that had enacted § 50 but not § 139, how should the case be decided?

(4) Would RMBCA § 2.04 change the result reached in the principal case?

CRANSON v. INTERNATIONAL BUSINESS MACHINES CORP.

Court of Appeals of Maryland, 1964.
234 Md. 477, 200 A.2d 33.

HORNEY, JUDGE.

On the theory that the Real Estate Service Bureau was neither a *de jure* nor a *de facto* corporation and that Albion C. Cranson, Jr., was a partner in the business conducted by the Bureau and as such was personally liable for its debts, the International Business Machines Corporation brought this action against Cranson for the balance due on electric typewriters purchased by the Bureau. At the same time it moved for summary judgment and supported the motion by affidavit. In due course, Cranson filed a general issue plea and an affidavit in opposition to summary judgment in which he asserted in effect that the Bureau was a *de facto* corporation and that he was not personally liable for its debts.

The agreed statement of facts shows that in April 1961, Cranson was asked to invest in a new business corporation which was about to be created. Towards this purpose he met with other interested individuals and an attorney and agreed to purchase stock and become an officer and director. Thereafter, upon being advised by the attorney that the corporation had been formed under the laws of Maryland, he paid for and received a stock certificate evidencing ownership of shares in the corporation, and was shown the corporate seal and minute book. The business of the new venture was conducted as if it were a corporation, through corporate bank accounts, with auditors maintaining corporate books and records, and under a lease entered into by the corporation for the office from which it operated its business. Cranson was elected president and all transactions conducted by him for the corporation, including the dealings with I.B.M., were made as an officer of the corporation. At no time did he assume any personal obligation or pledge his individual credit to I.B.M. Due to an oversight on the part of the attorney, of which Cranson was not aware, the certificate of incorporation, which had been signed and acknowledged prior to May 1, 1961, was not filed until November 24, 1961. Between May 17 and November 8, the Bureau purchased eight typewriters from I.B.M., on account of which partial payments were made, leaving a balance due of $4,333.40, for which this suit was brought.

The fundamental question presented by the appeal is whether an officer [9] of a defectively incorporated association may be subjected to personal liability under the circumstances of this case. We think not.

Traditionally, two doctrines have been used by the courts to clothe an officer of a defectively incorporated association with the corporate attribute of limited liability. The first, often referred to as the doctrine of *de facto* corporations, has been applied in those cases where there are elements showing: (1) the existence of law authorizing incorporation; (2) an effort in good faith to incorporate under the existing law; and (3) actual user or exercise of corporate powers. The second, the doctrine of estoppel to deny the corporate existence, is generally employed where the person seeking to hold the officer personally liable has contracted or otherwise dealt with the association in such a manner as to recognize and in effect admit its existence as a corporate body.

It is not at all clear what Maryland has done with respect to the two doctrines. There have been no recent cases in this State on the subject and some of the seemingly irreconcilable earlier cases offer little to clarify the problem.[10] * * *

9. [By the Court] Although we are concerned with the liability of an "officer" in this case, the principles of law stated herein might under other circumstances be applicable to a determination of the liability of a member or shareholder of a defectively organized corporation.

10. [By the Court] Apparently because it was not requested to do so, the lower

[Discussion of Maryland cases omitted].

When summarized, the law in Maryland pertaining to the *de facto* and estoppel doctrines reveals that the cases seem to fall into one or the other of two categories. In one line of cases, the Court, choosing to disregard the nature of the dealings between the parties, refused to recognize both doctrines where there had been a failure to comply with a condition precedent to corporate existence, but, whenever such non-compliance concerned a condition subsequent to incorporation, the Court often applied the estoppel doctrine. In the other line of cases, the Court, choosing to make no distinction between defects which were conditions precedent and those which were conditions subsequent, emphasized the course of conduct between the parties and applied the estoppel doctrine when there had been substantial dealings between them on a corporate basis. * * * [Insofar as two Maryland cases hold] that the doctrine of estoppel cannot be invoked unless a corporation has at least *de facto* existence, both cases * * * should be, and are hereby, overruled to the extent of the inconsistency. There is, as we see it, a wide difference between creating a corporation by means of the *de facto* doctrine and estopping a party, due to his conduct in a particular case, from setting up the claim of no incorporation. Although some cases tend to assimilate the doctrines of incorporation *de facto* and by estoppel, each is a distinct theory and they are not dependent on one another in their application. Where there is a concurrence of the three elements necessary for the application of the *de facto* corporation doctrine, there exists an entity which is a corporation *de jure* against all persons but the state. On the other hand, the estoppel theory is applied only to the facts of each particular case and may be invoked even where there is no corporation *de facto*. Accordingly, even though one or more of the requisites of a *de facto* corporation are absent, we think that this factor does not preclude the application of the estoppel doctrine [11] in a proper case, such as the one at bar.

I.B.M. contends that the failure of the Bureau to file its certificate of incorporation debarred *all* corporate existence. But, in spite of the fact that the omission might have prevented the Bureau from being either a corporation *de jure* or *de facto*,[12] we think that I.B.M. having

court did not undertake to prepare and file a memorandum of its reasons for deciding the problem as it did. But, inexcusably, the briefs were for the most part of no practical use to this Court in arriving at a decision of the intricate question of law presented by the appeal. While the appellant cited three Maryland cases for the proposition that a *de facto* corporation was created and the appellee cited one Maryland case for the proposition that a corporation cannot be created by estoppel, neither made an attempt to analogize or distinguish the numerous other Maryland cases touching the problem.

11. [By the Court] A third doctrine, called the modern "enterprise-entity theory," which in many respects is not unlike the estoppel theory applied in Maryland, is described in 1 Oleck, Modern Corporation Law, § 592. * *

12. [By the Court] Those states which recognize the *de facto* doctrine are not in accord as to whether a corporation *de facto* may be created in spite of the failure to file the necessary papers. Some courts, without making clear in every instance whether a *de facto* corporation was meant or not, have stated that failure to file the required

dealt with the Bureau as if it were a corporation and relied on its credit rather than that of Cranson, is estopped to assert that the Bureau was not incorporated at the time the typewriters were purchased. * * *

Since I.B.M. is estopped to deny the corporate existence of the Bureau, we hold that Cranson was not liable for the balance due on account of the typewriters.

Judgment reversed; the appellee to pay the costs.

Notes

(1) What is the difference in factual pattern that results in *Robertson* and *Cantor* being classified as "corporation de facto" cases while *Cranson* is classified as a "corporation by estoppel" case? Do these types of cases differ from cases such as Quaker Hill v. Parr (see p. 225, supra), which are classified as "promoters' transactions" cases?

(2) Can you see any factual differences between *Robertson* and *Cranson* that might justify the difference in result? In Harry Rich Corp. v. Feinberg, 518 So.2d 377 (Fla.App.1987), Feinberg found himself in essentially the same position that Cranson did in the principal case. Florida had adopted § 139 of the 1969 Model Business Corporation Act; the court, however, held that Feinberg was not liable under that section since "assume to act" should be construed to permit recovery "only where the individual acts with actual or constructive knowledge that no corporation exists." 518 So.2d, at 381. The court also relied on a non-Model Act statute enacted in Florida that prohibits a defectively formed corporation from using its lack of legal organization as a defense against claims brought by third persons.

(3) The court in the *Cranson* case treated the question as one involving only Maryland case law, and in this regard it made a rather caustic reference to the inadequacy of the briefs before it. Neither the court nor the attorneys apparently considered the possibility that Maryland statutory law might be relevant. At least, there is no reference to Maryland statutory law in the court's opinion. When *Cranson* was decided, Maryland had not yet adopted its version of the old Model Business Corporation Act. However, Art. 23, § 131(b) of the Maryland corporation statute [Md.Code 1957], provided:

> Upon acceptance for record by the Department of any articles of incorporation, the proposed corporation shall, according to the purposes, conditions and provisions contained in such articles of incorporation, become and be a body corporate by a name therein stated. Such acceptance for the record shall be conclusive evidence of the formation of the corporation except in a direct proceeding by the State for the forfeiture of the charter.

papers prevented the organizations from becoming a corporation and have held in effect that the persons acting as a corporation are a mere association or partnership. Other courts, without expressly deciding whether a *de facto* corporation was created, hold that the statutes of the state imply corporate existence prior to the filing of articles of incorporation. Still other courts hold that a *de facto* existence is not precluded by failure to file the articles of incorporation.

Do the differences between the D.C. and Maryland statutes explain the difference in result between Robertson v. Levy and Cranson v. I.B.M.?

(4) If the suit in Cranson v. I.B.M. was based on a tort rather than on a contract, is there any possible way for Cranson to avoid liability? Does it make any difference, as the court notes, that I.B.M. was seeking to hold Cranson as an "officer" rather than as a "member" or "shareholder"?

(5) In Goodwyne v. Moore, 170 Ga.App. 305, 316 S.E.2d 601 (1984), a promissory note was executed in the form "C & N Industries, Inc., by Charles Goodwyne, Pres." The plaintiffs thereafter accepted payments made by "C & N Industries, Inc." and issued receipts for those payments addressed to that corporation. Following default on the remaining payments, an attempt was made to hold Goodwyne individually liable. It turned out that at the time the note was executed there was no corporation named "C & N Industries, Inc." in existence. Goodwyne, however, had earlier formed a corporation under the name "C & N Bottle Shop, Inc.," and four days before signing the promissory note had also obtained a certificate reserving the name "C & N Industries, Inc." Two months after the execution of the promissory note, "C & N Bottle Shop, Inc." filed articles of amendment changing its name to "C & N Industries, Inc." The court held that the plaintiffs had "admitted the legal existence of C & N Industries, and are estopped from denying its legal existence in a suit to enforce the note." Two other Georgia cases reach the same result on roughly analogous facts. In Pinson v. Hartsfield Intern. Comm. Ctr., Ltd., 191 Ga.App. 459, 382 S.E.2d 136 (1989), Pinson was held not personally liable on a lease executed in the name "Pinson Air Freight, Inc." when there was no corporation by that name; Pinson's corporation was actually named "Pinson Air Freight of Chattanooga, Inc." In Hawkins v. Turner, 166 Ga.App. 50, 303 S.E.2d 164 (1983), Hawkins was held not liable on a contract executed in the name "Hawkins Plumbing Co., Inc." when he was an officer and major shareholder in a corporation named "Hawkins Heating & Plumbing Co." In both of these cases there was evidence of a considerable degree of casualness on the part of Pinson and Hawkins in other transactions as to the name of the corporation, and as to whether the business was owned on an individual or corporate basis.

(6) Are cases described in the preceding note distinguishable from yet another Georgia case, Echols v. Vienna Sausage Mfg. Co., 162 Ga.App. 158, 290 S.E.2d 484 (1982). In this case the individual was held personally liable on a "corporate" obligation; he had reserved the corporate name but had not taken any additional steps to complete the incorporation at the time of the transaction in question.

MATTER OF WHATLEY

United States Court of Appeals, Fifth Circuit, 1989.
874 F.2d 997.

Before GARZA, JOLLY and JONES, Circuit Judges.

EDITH H. JONES, CIRCUIT JUDGE:

In this lien priority dispute between competing creditors, two questions are at issue: whether the debtor Whatley Farms, Inc. is a corporation under Mississippi law and whether Whatley Farms, Inc. ever obtained rights in the collateral (in this case farming equipment) which it pledged as security to the Small Business Administration ("SBA"). If either question is answered in the negative, a subsequent lienholder Guaranty Bank & Trust Company (the "bank") will prevail. The bankruptcy court determined that the SBA, although first in time, did not have a valid security interest in the farming equipment. The district court affirmed. Concluding that the bankruptcy court erred as a matter of law, we REVERSE.

FACTS

The facts are undisputed. On October 28, 1975, the Secretary of State of Mississippi issued a certificate of incorporation to the debtor, Whatley Farms, Inc. ("Whatley Farms"). John W. Whatley and his wife, Ruby G. Whatley were listed as the incorporators.[13] The certificate of incorporation and proof of publication were duly filed in the Office of the Chancery Clerk, Humphreys County.

The farming equipment used by the Whatleys in their agricultural operations was depreciated annually on the corporate tax return and considered by the corporation's accountant as a corporate asset from the inception of the corporation. No formal bill of sale ever transferred the equipment from the Whatleys to the corporation, however. Between 1976 and 1980, John Whatley purchased farming equipment in his personal name and financed such purchases with personal loans through Guaranty Bank. After its incorporation, Whatley Farms opened a corporate checking account with the Cleveland State Bank, Cleveland, Mississippi and used the account regularly in its business activities. The funds in this account were used for payment of obligations to Guaranty Bank on several occasions.

In 1981, the Whatleys relocated their farming business, including the farming equipment, from Humphreys County, in western Mississippi, across the state to Kemper County. On November 11, 1981, Whatley Farms borrowed $158,600.00 from the SBA and executed a security agreement and UCC–1 financing statement providing for a floating lien on all machinery and equipment excluding automotive, including, but not limited to, certain items of property described on a list appended to the UCC–1 financing statement. This statement was filed in Kemper County.

In April 1983 the Whatleys moved back to Humphreys County along with their farming equipment. On May 23, 1983 John Whatley obtained a personal loan from Guaranty Bank for which he granted the bank a security interest in much of the same farming equipment listed in the SBA's financing statement. The bank's financing statement listed the farming equipment as belonging to John Whatley; it purported to cover "all equipment" of John Whatley's farming operations.

---

13. [By the Court] The Whatleys were not sophisticated in setting up a corpora- tion and relied heavily on their accountant for advice.

Significantly, at the time that these loans were made Mississippi did not require duplicate filings of the financing statements both in the county of residence and with the secretary of state. Filing in the county of residence was legally sufficient. The SBA's financing statement was thus properly filed under Mississippi law in Kemper County, but was never filed with the secretary of state. Likewise, the bank properly filed its financing statement only in Humphreys County. Both the bank and the SBA have acted in good faith.

On April 23, 1984, John W. Whatley and Ruby L. Whatley filed a voluntary Chapter 11 petition with the bankruptcy court. On June 5, 1984, Whatley Farms filed its voluntary Chapter 11 petition. A priority dispute arose between the SBA and Guaranty Bank. * * *

ANALYSIS

The bankruptcy court's logic is simple. Whatley Farms was not legally organized under the laws of Mississippi because it did not comply with certain corporate formalities. Not having a legal existence, Whatley Farms could not hold legal title to the equipment pledged to the SBA and never actually owned that equipment. The court therefore held that Whatley Farms could not grant a security interest in the equipment to the SBA because it was not a legal entity and did not own the equipment.

We disagree with each of these conclusions as follows: Whatley Farms, Inc. is a *de facto* corporation under Mississippi law. As such, it could own the farm equipment it continuously depreciated for tax purposes. * * *

I. DE FACTO CORPORATE STATUS

Mississippi law recognizes the concept of *de facto* corporations.[14] In *Allen v. Thompson,* 248 Miss. 544, 158 So.2d 503 (1963), the Mississippi Supreme Court established three necessary conditions for *de facto* corporate status: (1) a valid law under which the entity could be incorporated, (2) a bona fide attempt to organize a corporation under the law, and (3) an actual exercise of corporate powers.[15] Peculiarly, neither the bankruptcy court nor the district court applied Mississippi's test for *de facto* status to the facts of this case. The issue was not waived. Since the facts are undisputed, we may undertake the task ourselves in the interest of judicial economy.

14. [By the Court] Some states, upon the adoption of the Model Corporation Act, have abandoned the concept of *de facto* corporations. *See, e.g., Timberline Equipment Co. v. Davenport,* 267 Or. 64, 514 P.2d 1109 (1973) (*de facto* doctrine no longer exists). SBA argues that evidence of Whatley Farms's certificate of incorporation should be conclusive proof of corporate existence in Mississippi. This may be true, but no Mississippi case directly supports that proposition. Because we conclude that Whatley Farms is at least a *de facto* corporation, we need not address how definitive a certificate of incorporation may be.

15. [By the Court] Generally, a *de facto* corporation possesses all of the powers and rights (as well as the duties and liabilities) of a *de jure* corporation. The most significant distinction between the two is that the status of a *de facto* corporation is subject to a direct challenge by the State.

Sections 79–3–101 through 79–3–113 of the Mississippi Code, Miss. Code Ann. (1972), satisfy the first requirement,[16] that there be a law enabling the company to incorporate. * * * The record also reflects a bona fide attempt to organize the corporation. No simple or talismanic test exists to determine whether a corporation has satisfied this condition. Rather, we must examine all of the pertinent facts. The test is neither complete performance nor even substantial compliance; however, there must be evidence of at least a colorable attempt to comply with the statutory requirements by taking some of the statutory steps toward incorporation.

The bank argues that the following undisputed facts preclude a finding of *de facto* corporate status: (1) the failure to pay $1,000.00 into the corporation as initial paid-in capital and the related failure to issue any stock, as required by Miss.Code Ann. § 79–3–111, (2) the failure to hold an initial organizational meeting of the board of directors, as required by Miss.Code Ann. § 79–3–113, (3) the failure to adopt bylaws, and (4) the failure to hold annual shareholders' meetings. To this list may be added the absence of corporate bylaws or of signed minutes for any directors or shareholders' meetings.

On the other hand, Whatley Farms had corporate officers. John W. Whatley was president, Ruby Whatley held the dual positions of secretary and treasurer, and the Whatleys' son John served as vice-president. Whatley Farms also filed a certificate of incorporation with the proper authority, the Office of the Chancery Clerk for Humphreys County. Section 79–3–109, quoted above, indicates the critical significance of this fact. Under Mississippi law, such a filing is conclusive evidence that the necessary conditions precedent have been complied with, except as against a challenge brought by the state in a direct proceeding.[17]

Although there appears to be no Mississippi case precisely on point, we are confident that Mississippi would find a bona fide attempt to organize Whatley Farms, Inc. The facts relied upon by the bank, taken individually or collectively, do not refute our conclusion. First, the Mississippi statutes do not require that a corporation adopt bylaws.

* * *

16. [By the Court] Mississippi has subsequently repealed §§ 79–3–109 through 79–3–117 effective January 1, 1988. Our decision is based on the Mississippi statutes then applicable.

17. [By the Court] The Model Corporation Act suggests a preference for holding certificates of incorporation to be conclusive evidence of incorporation. *See* Model Business Corp.Act § 56 (1977). *See also,* S. FitzGibbon & D. Glazer, *Legal Opinions on Incorporation, Good Standing and Qualification To Do Business,* 41 Bus.Law. 461 (1986). *See* 8 Fletcher, [Cyclopedia of the Law of Private Corporations], § 3762.1 ("the provision which establishes corporate existence by the filing of the certificate largely supersedes the necessity of resorting to the common law doctrines of *de facto* corporations . . . where there is some defect or irregularity in the incorporation papers or proceedings leading up to the issue of the certificate").

Likewise, Mississippi courts have held on several occasions that failure to comply with the paid-in capital requirement does not, of itself, preclude a finding of *de facto* corporate status. * * *

In a similar vein, the Mississippi Supreme Court has held that a corporation's failure to comply with its own bylaws does not necessarily imperil the corporate existence. In *Smith v. Natchez Steamboat Co.,* 1 How. (2 Miss.) 479 (1837), the court held that neither the failure to hold shareholders' meetings as required in the bylaws, nor the additional failure to elect officers at times specified in the bylaws, would require the dissolution of the corporation. In fact, Miss.Code Ann. § 79–3–53 (1972) specifically states that "[f]ailure to hold the annual meeting at the designated time shall not work a forfeiture or dissolution of the corporation."

In analyzing the facts of this case, we are mindful that

> [s]ubstantial compliance with the [incorporation] statutes is not necessarily required for *de facto* corporate existence. There must, however, be at least a colorable compliance with statutory requirements by taking some of the statutory steps. * * *

> The nature and character of the informality or defect is immaterial so far as *de facto* existence is concerned, provided, notwithstanding such defect, it is apparent that there was an attempt in good faith to create a corporation and that in like good faith there has been an assumption and exercise of corporate functions.

18A Am.Jur.2D *Corporations* § 244. * * *

We conclude that Whatley Farms attempted in good faith to incorporate and has therefore satisfied its requirement under the second prong of the test for *de facto* corporate status.

The third prong of the test is whether Whatley Farms actually exercised corporate powers. "The signing of a certificate of incorporation, though an element to be considered, does not create a *de facto* corporation, unless, after that step is taken, the incorporators do an act which shows that they are using corporate powers they have attempted to assume." 18A Am.Jur.2D § 247. * * *

The bankruptcy court found that Whatley Farms's corporate minute book contained unsigned minutes for a special board of directors meeting in April 1976 and a resolution of the stockholders and directors dated May 24, 1984. In addition, a resolution dated November 11, 1981 authorized the corporation to apply to the SBA for a loan not to exceed $158,600.00 and to pledge the corporate assets as security for the loan. Whatley Farms continuously filed corporate tax returns and did business through a corporate bank account. As far as can be determined, John W. Whatley and his family continued to be officers of the company. The test for user must be applied in light of the particular circumstances of each case. We are persuaded that, despite their spotty compliance with corporate formalities, the Whatleys "used"

Whatley Farms's corporate existence sufficiently to justify its status as a *de facto* corporation.[18] * * *

[The court concluded that the SBA's lien had priority over the lien of Guaranty Bank & Trust Co.]

Notes

(1) Is not this a misapplication of the de facto corporation doctrine in the light of § 50 of the 1969 Model Business Corporation Act? If articles of incorporation are properly filed, as they appear to have been in the principal case, is not that the end of the matter so far as persons other than the state are concerned?

(2) The failure to follow post-incorporation formalities may sometimes be relevant to the question whether shareholders should be held liable on corporate obligations on a theory, usually known as "piercing the corporate veil," which is discussed in the following chapter. Judge Jones discusses this doctrine briefly in n. 18 of her opinion, and disclaims its applicability to this case on the ground that the doctrine applies only to the liability of shareholders for corporate obligations. If so, why should not the de facto corporation doctrine also be inapplicable for the same reason? In either event, doesn't it seem a bit incongruous for a doctrine addressing shareholder liability to be applied in order to determine the priority of liens between two innocent parties?

(3) The concept of a *de facto* corporation also appears in at least one other context. The franchise tax statutes of many states provide for administrative forfeiture of the charter for non-payment of taxes. Some statutes also provide for reinstatement of the charter upon correction of all delinquencies. Of course, many corporations fail to pay franchise taxes from inadvertence and continue actively in business despite the dissolution. A corporation whose charter has been forfeited has been described as a "de facto corporation"—i.e. only the state may attack it. It should be added that franchise tax statutes often provide sanctions during the period the charter is forfeited. Officers, directors, and shareholders may be made personally liable for obligations incurred by the corporation, the courts of the state may be closed to the corporation, and there may be civil or criminal penalties levied. In Moore v. Occupational Safety & Health Review Comm'n, 591 F.2d 991 (4th Cir.1979), officers of Life Science Products Company were held personally liable for penalties imposed on the corporation for kepone contamination occurring after the corporation was administratively dissolved for temporary nonpayment of franchise taxes. Consult generally Comment, Dissolution and Suspension as Remedies for Corporate Franchise Tax Delinquency: a Comparative Analysis, 41 N.Y. U.L.Rev. 602 (1966).

18. [By the Court] This is not a case involving the doctrine of piercing the corporate veil. That equitable doctrine is not appropriate or applicable to a standard dispute over the priority of liens. The corporate veil may occasionally be pierced where the provisions of applicable incorporation statutes have been literally satisfied. The doctrine is most frequently applied to circumvent the limited liability that the shareholders would otherwise enjoy.

(4) As noted previously, the statutes of many states contain procedural and substantive requirements for forming a corporation in addition to the filing of articles of incorporation with a central state authority. The most common such requirements are that a corporation have a minimum capitalization before commencing business, and that the articles of incorporation be recorded in a local county office. A few states also require newspaper publication of the articles. The effect of a failure to comply with one or more of these requirements is sometimes specified in the statute; more often, however, the statute is silent and the courts must decide whether the failure to comply means that investors in the enterprise lose their shield of limited liability.

(5) Professor Alexander Frey, of the University of Pennsylvania Law School, attempted to classify all *de facto* corporation cases arising prior to 1952 on the basis of the nature of the defect, whether there had been dealings on a corporate basis (roughly, whether the suit was based on contract or tort), and whether the suit sought to hold active or inactive investors personally liable. The year 1952 antedates the statutes discussed in this section so that most of the cases classified by Professor Frey involved the common law de facto corporation doctrine. The following table is the result of Professor Frey's analysis. Does it shed any light on what is really going on in this area?

ANALYSIS OF CASES CONCERNING INDIVIDUAL LIABILITY OF MEMBERS OF
DEFECTIVELY INCORPORATED ASSOCIATIONS

Nature of Defect	Dealings on Corporate Basis				Totals	Dealings Not On Corporate Basis				Totals	Total Cases
	Inactive Associates Liable	Inactive Associates Not Liable	Managing Associates Liable	Managing Associates Not Liable	Non-Liability v. Liability	Inactive Associates Liable	Inactive Associates Not Liable	Managing Associates Liable	Managing Associates Not Liable	Non-Liability v. Liability	Non-Liability v. Liability
Articles Not Recorded at All	10	9	4	2	14–11	3	0	6	1	9–1	23–12
No Attempt to Incorporate	4	2	7	0	11–2	2	0	2	0	4–0	15–2
Articles Not Recorded with Secretary of State	5	6	2	3	7–9	0	0	0	0	0–0	7–9
Articles Not Recorded Locally	2	7	0	4	2–11	2	0	3	0	5–0	7–11
Insufficient Capital Paid In	3	9	8	13	11–22	4	0	1	0	5–0	16–22
Miscellaneous	12	30	12	25	24–55	4	0	3	1	7–1	31–56
Total Cases	36	63	33	47	69–110	15	0	15	2	30–2	99–112

Source: Frey, Legal Analysis and the De Facto Doctrine, 100 U.Pa.L.Rev. 1153, 1174 (1952).[*]

[B2963]

Chapter Six

DISREGARD OF THE CORPORATE ENTITY

BARTLE v. HOME OWNERS COOPERATIVE

Court of Appeals of New York, 1955.
309 N.Y. 103, 127 N.E.2d 832.

FROESSEL, JUDGE.

Plaintiff, as trustee in bankruptcy of Westerlea Builders, Inc., has by means of this litigation attempted to hold defendant liable for the contract debts of Westerlea, defendant's wholly owned subsidiary. Defendant, as a co-operative corporation composed mostly of veterans, was organized in July, 1947, for the purpose of providing low-cost housing for its members. Unable to secure a contractor to undertake construction of the housing planned, Westerlea was organized for that purpose on June 5, 1948. With building costs running considerably higher than anticipated, Westerlea, as it proceeded with construction on some 26 houses, found itself in a difficult financial situation. On January 24, 1949, the creditors, pursuant to an extension agreement, took over the construction responsibilities. Nearly four years later, in October, 1952, Westerlea was adjudicated a bankrupt. Meanwhile, defendant had contributed to Westerlea not only its original capital of $25,000 but additional sums amounting to $25,639.38.

Plaintiff's principal contention on this appeal is that the courts below erred in refusing to "pierce the corporate veil" of Westerlea's corporate existence; as subordinate grounds for recovery he urged that the defendant equitably pledged its assets toward the satisfaction of the debts of the bankrupt's creditors, and that the doctrine of unjust enrichment should apply.

The trial court made detailed findings of fact which have been unanimously affirmed by the Appellate Division, 285 App.Div. 1113, 140 N.Y.S.2d 512, which are clearly supported by the evidence, and by which we are bound. It found that while the defendant, as owner of the stock of Westerlea, controlled its affairs, the outward indicia of

253

these two separate corporations was at all times maintained during the period in which the creditors extended credit; that the creditors were in no wise misled; that there was no fraud; and that the defendant performed no act causing injury to the creditors of Westerlea by depletion of assets or otherwise. The trial court also held that the creditors were estopped by the extension agreement from disputing the separate corporate identities.

We agree with the courts below. The law permits the incorporation of a business for the very purpose of escaping personal liability. Generally speaking, the doctrine of "piercing the corporate veil" is invoked "to prevent fraud or to achieve equity", International Aircraft Trading Co. v. Manufacturers Trust Co., 297 N.Y. 285, 292, 79 N.E.2d 249, 252. But in the instant case there has been neither fraud, misrepresentation nor illegality. Defendant's purpose in placing its construction operation into a separate corporation was clearly within the limits of our public policy.

The judgment appealed from should be affirmed, without costs.

VAN VOORHIS, JUDGE (dissenting).

The judgment of the Appellate Division should be reversed on the law, as it seems to me, and plaintiff should have judgment declaring defendant to be liable for the debts of the bankrupt, Westerlea Builders, Inc., and that defendant holds its real property subject to the claims of creditors of Westerlea. Not only is Westerlea a wholly owned subsidiary of defendant Home Owners, having the same directors and management, but also and of primary importance, business was done on such a basis that Westerlea could not make a profit. Home Owners owned a residential subdivision; Westerlea was organized as a building corporation to erect homes for stockholders of Home Owners upon lots in this tract. Home Owners arranged with Westerlea for the construction of houses and then would sell the lots on which such houses had been erected to Home Owners' stockholders—at prices fixed by Home Owners' price policy committee in such amounts as to make no allowance for profit by Westerlea. The object was to benefit Home Owners' stockholders by enabling them to obtain their houses at cost, with no builder's profit.

The consequence is that described by Latty, Subsidiaries and Affiliated Corporations at pages 138–139: "The subsidiaries had, to begin with, nothing, made nothing, and could only end up with nothing. It is not surprising that the parent was held liable in each case." And again: "This set-up is often, though not necessarily, found in combination with a scheme whereby the corporation cannot possibly make profits (or can at the most make only nominal profits), and whereby all the net income in the course of the corporation's business is drained off as operating charges of one sort or another. The presence of this additional factor should remove any doubt that may remain as to the right of the creditor of the corporation not to be limited to the corporate assets for the satisfaction of his debt."

In the present instance, Westerlea was organized with a small capital supplied by Home Owners, which soon became exhausted. Thereafter, it had no funds and could acquire none over and beyond the actual cost of the houses which it was building for stockholders of Home Owners. Those stockholders obtained the entire benefit of Westerlea's operations by obtaining these houses at cost. Not only was Westerlea allowed no opportunity to make money, but it was placed in a position such that if its business were successful and times remained good, it would break even, otherwise it would inevitably become insolvent. The stockholders of Home Owners became the beneficiaries of its insolvency. This benefit to the stockholders of Home Owners was analogous to dividends, at least it was something of value which was obtained by them from Home Owners by virtue of their stock ownership. Under the circumstances, this benefit to its stockholders was a benefit to Home Owners as a corporation.

It follows that Westerlea was merely an agent of Home Owners to construct houses at cost for Home Owners stockholders, and therefore Home Owners is rendered liable for Westerlea's indebtedness.

CONWAY, C.J., and DESMOND, DYE, FULD and BURKE, JJ., concur with FROESSEL, J.

VAN VOORHIS, J., dissents in an opinion.

Judgment affirmed.

DEWITT TRUCK BROKERS v. W. RAY FLEMMING FRUIT CO.

United States Court of Appeals, Fourth Circuit, 1976.
540 F.2d 681.

Before RUSSELL and WIDENER, CIRCUIT JUDGES, and THOMSEN, SENIOR DISTRICT JUDGE.[1]

DONALD RUSSELL, CIRCUIT JUDGE:

In this action on debt, the plaintiff seeks, by piercing the corporate veil under the law of South Carolina, to impose individual liability on the president of the indebted corporation individually.[2] The District Court, making findings of fact which may be overturned only if clearly erroneous, pierced the corporate veil and imposed individual liability. The individual defendant appeals. We affirm.

At the outset, it is recognized that a corporation is an entity, separate and distinct from its officers and stockholders, and that its debts are not the individual indebtedness of its stockholders. This is expressed in the presumption that the corporation and its stockholders are separate and distinct. And this oft-stated principle is equally applicable, whether the corporation has many or only one stockholder. But this concept of separate entity is merely a legal theory, "introduced

---

1. [By the Court] Sitting by designation.   2. [By the Court] The corporate defendant, it is conceded, is not responsive to judgment.

for purposes of convenience and to subserve the ends of justice," and the courts "decline to recognize [it] whenever recognition of the corporate form would extend the principle of incorporation 'beyond its legitimate purposes and [would] produce injustices or inequitable consequences.'" Krivo Industrial Supp. Co. v. National Distill. & Chem. Corp. (5th Cir.1973), 483 F.2d 1098, 1106. Accordingly, "in an appropriate case and in furtherance of the ends of justice," the corporate veil will be pierced and the corporation and its stockholders "will be treated as identical." 18 Am.Juris.2d at 559.

This power to pierce the corporate veil, though, is to be exercised "reluctantly" and "cautiously" and the burden of establishing a basis for the disregard of the corporate fiction rests on the party asserting such claim. Coryell v. Phipps (5th Cir.1942), 128 F.2d 702, 704, aff., 317 U.S. 406, 63 S.Ct. 291, 87 L.Ed. 363 (1943).

The circumstances which have been considered significant by the courts in actions to disregard the corporate fiction have been "rarely articulated with any clarity." Swanson v. Levy (9th Cir.1975), 509 F.2d 859, 861–2. Perhaps this is true because the circumstances "necessarily vary according to the circumstances of each case," and every case where the issue is raised is to be regarded as "*sui generis* [to] ∗ ∗ ∗ be decided in accordance with its own underlying facts." Since the issue is thus one of fact, its resolution "is particularly within the province of the trial court" and such resolution will be regarded as "presumptively correct and [will] be left undisturbed on appeal unless it is clearly erroneous."

Contrary to the basic contention of the defendant, however, proof of plain fraud is not a necessary element in a finding to disregard the corporate entity. This was made clear in Anderson v. Abbott (1944), 321 U.S. 349, 362, 64 S.Ct. 531, 538, 88 L.Ed. 793, reh. denied, 321 U.S. 804, 64 S.Ct. 845, 88 L.Ed. 1090 (1944), where the Court, after stating that "fraud" has often been found to be a ground for disregarding the principle of limited liability based on the corporate fiction, declared:

     "∗ ∗ ∗ The cases of fraud make up part of that exception [which allow the corporate veil to be pierced, citing cases]. *But they do not exhaust it.* An obvious inadequacy of capital, measured by the nature and magnitude of the corporate undertaking, has frequently been an important factor in cases denying stockholders their defense of limited liability." (Italics added.) ∗ ∗ ∗

Nor is there any basis for assuming the rule in South Carolina, which is controlling in this diversity case, to be different from the general rule declaring fraud not to be a necessary predicate for piercing the corporate veil. In fact, the South Carolina court has stated the doctrine for disregarding the corporate entity in terms similar to the general rule earlier phrased. ∗ ∗ ∗

On the other hand, equally as well settled as is the principle that plain fraud is not a necessary prerequisite for piercing the corporate veil is the rule that the mere fact that all or almost all of the corporate stock is owned by one individual or a few individuals, will not afford sufficient grounds for disregarding corporateness. But when substantial ownership of all the stock of a corporation in a single individual is combined with other factors clearly supporting disregard of the corporate fiction on grounds of fundamental equity and fairness, courts have experienced "little difficulty" and have shown no hesitancy in applying what is described as the "alter ego" or "instrumentality" theory in order to cast aside the corporate shield and to fasten liability on the individual stockholder. Iron City S. & G. Div. of McDonough Co. v. West Fork Tow. Corp., [N.D.W.Va., 1969] 298 F.Supp. at 1098.

But, in applying the "instrumentality" or "alter ego" doctrine, the courts are concerned with reality and not form, with how the corporation operated and the individual defendant's relationship to that operation. One court has suggested that courts should abjure "the mere incantation of the term 'instrumentality' " in this context and, since the issue is one of fact, should take pains to spell out the specific factual basis for its conclusion. Kirvo Industrial Supp. Co. v. National Distill. & Chem. Corp., supra, 483 F.2d at 1103. And the authorities have indicated certain facts which are to be given substantial weight in this connection. One fact which all the authorities consider significant in the inquiry, and particularly so in the case of the one-man or closely-held corporation, is whether the corporation was grossly undercapitalized for the purposes of the corporate undertaking. Henn, Law of Corporations 2d Ed. (1970), at 257; Anderson v. Abbott, supra, 321 U.S. at 362, 64 S.Ct. 531; Stone v. Eacho, [4th Cir.1942], 127 F.2d at 288; Luckenback S.S. Co. v. W.R. Grace & Co. (4th Cir.1920), 267 F. 676, 681, cert. denied, 254 U.S. 644, 41 S.Ct. 14, 65 L.Ed. 454 (1920); Arnold v. Phillips (5th Cir.1941), 117 F.2d 497, 502, cert. denied, 313 U.S. 583, 61 S.Ct. 1102, 85 L.Ed. 1539 (1940); Mull v. Colt Co. (S.D.N.Y.1962), 31 F.R.D. 154, 163; Automotriz Del Golfo De Cal. v. Resnick (1957), 47 Cal. 2d 792, 306 P.2d 1, 63 A.L.R.2d 1042, 1048, with annotation.[3] And, "[t]he obligation to provide adequate capital begins with incorporation and is a continuing obligation thereafter * * * during the corpora-

---

3. [By the Court] * * * In *Mull*, supra, 31 F.R.D. at 163, the Court quoted from Ballentine, Corporations, 303 (rev. ed. 1946):

" * * * It is coming to be recognized as the policy of the law that shareholders should in good faith put at the risk of the business unincumbered capital reasonably adequate for its prospective liabilities. If the capital is illusory or trifling compared with the business to be done and the risks of loss, this is a ground for denying the separate entity privilege."

In Note, Disregard of the Corporate Entity: Contract Claims, 28 Ohio S.L.J. 441 (1967), the author argues that under capitalization as a factor in determining whether to pierce the corporate veil should be inapplicable in contract cases; cf., however, Note, Limited Liability: A Definite Judicial Standard for the Inadequate Capitalization Problem, 47 Temple L.Q. 32 (1974). The reasoning is that when one extends credit or makes any other contractual arrangement with a corporation, it is to be assumed he acquaints himself with the corporation's capitalization and contracts on such basis, and not on the individual credit of the dominant stockholder. In this case, however, that reasoning would be inapplicable, since the plaintiff did not rely on the corporation's capitalization but received an assurance from Flemming of personal liability.

tion's operations." Other factors that are emphasized in the application of the doctrine are failure to observe corporate formalities,[4] non-payment of dividends, the insolvency of the debtor corporation at the time, siphoning of funds of the corporation by the dominant stockholder,[5] non-functioning of other officers or directors, absence of corporate records, and the fact that the corporation is merely a facade for the operations of the dominant stockholder or stockholders. The conclusion to disregard the corporate entity may not, however, rest on a single factor, whether undercapitalization, disregard of corporation's formalities, or what-not, but must involve a number of such factors; in addition, it must present an element of injustice or fundamental unfairness. But undercapitalization, coupled with disregard of corporate formalities, lack of participation on the part of the other stockholders, and the failure to pay dividends while paying substantial sums, whether by way of salary or otherwise, to the dominant stockholder, all fitting into a picture of basic unfairness, has been regarded fairly uniformly to constitute a basis for an imposition of individual liability under the doctrine. * * *

If these factors, which were deemed significant in other cases concerned with this same issue, are given consideration here, the finding of the District Court that the corporate entity should be disregarded was not clearly erroneous. Certainly the corporation was, in practice at least, a close, one-man corporation from the very beginning. Its incorporators were the defendant Flemming, his wife and his attorney. It began in 1962 with a capitalization of 5,000 shares, issued for a consideration of one dollar each. In some manner which Flemming never made entirely clear, approximately 2,000 shares were retired. At the times involved here Flemming owned approximately 90% of the corporation's outstanding stock, according to his own testimony, though this was not verified by any stock records. Flemming was obscure on who the other stockholders were and how much stock these other stockholders owned, giving at different times conflicting statements as to who owned stock and how much. His testimony on who were the officers and directors was hardly more direct. He testified that the corporation did have one other director, Ed Bernstein, a resident of New York. It is significant, however, that, whether

---

4. [By the Court] House of Koscot Dev. Corp. v. American Line Cosmetics, Inc. (5th Cir.1972), 468 F.2d 64, 66–7 (" * * * Turner ignored normal corporate formalities * * * "); Lakota Girl Scout C., Inc. v. Havey Fund–Rais. Man., Inc. (8th Cir. 1975), 519 F.2d 634, 638 (" * * * corporate formalities [were] not followed * * * "). While disregard of corporate formalities is a circumstance to be considered, it is generally held to be insufficient in itself, without some other facts, to support a piercing of the corporate veil.

Cf., Zubik v. Zubik (3d Cir.1967), 384 F.2d 267, 271, cert. denied, 390 U.S. 988, 88 S.Ct. 1183, 19 L.Ed.2d 1291 (1968), n. 4, where the Court stated that "[i]n the context of an attempt by an outside party to pierce the corporate veil of such a closely-held corporation, the informalities are considered of little consequence." * * *

See, however, Harrison v. Puga (1971), 4 Wash.App. 52, 480 P.2d 247, 254, where the Court said that if the defendants disregarded the corporate formalities, they could hardly complain if the court did likewise.

5. [By the Court] Chatterley v. Omnico, 26 Utah 2d 88, 485 P.2d 667, 670.

Bernstein was nominally a director or not, there were no corporate records of a real directors' meeting in all the years of the corporation's existence and Flemming conceded this to be true. Flemming countered this by testifying that Bernstein traveled a great deal and that his contacts with Bernstein were generally by telephone. The evidence indicates rather clearly that Bernstein was * * * "nothing more than [a] figurehead[s]," who had "attended no directors meeting," and even more crucial, never received any fee or reimbursement of expenses or salary of any kind from the corporation.

The District Court found, also, that the corporation never had a stockholders' meeting. * * * It is thus clear that corporate formalities, even rudimentary formalities, were not observed by the defendant.

Beyond the absence of any observance of corporate formalities is the purely personal matter in which the corporation was operated. No stockholder or officer of the corporation other than Flemming ever received any salary, dividend, or fee from the corporation, or, for that matter, apparently exercised any voice in its operation or decisions. In all the years of the corporation's existence, Flemming was the sole beneficiary of its operations and its continued existence was for his exclusive benefit. During these years he was receiving from $15,000 to $25,000 each year from a corporation, which, during most of the time, was showing no profit and apparently had no working capital. Moreover, the payments to Flemming were authorized under no resolution of the board of directors of the corporation, as recorded in any minutes of a board meeting. Actually, it would seem that Flemming's withdrawals varied with what could be taken out of the corporation at the moment: If this amount were $15,000, that was Flemming's withdrawal; if it were $25,000, that was his withdrawal. * * *

That the corporation was undercapitalized, if indeed it were not without any real capital, seems obvious. Its original stated "risk capital" had long since been reduced to approximately $3,000 by a reduction in the outstanding capital, or at least this would seem to be inferable from the record, and even this, it seems fair to conclude, had been seemingly exhausted by a long succession of years when the corporation operated at no profit. The inability of the corporation to pay a dividend is persuasive proof of this want of capital. In fact, the defendant Flemming makes no effort to refute the evidence of want of any capital reserves on the part of the corporation. It appears patent that the corporation was actually operating at all times involved here on someone else's capital. This conclusion follows from a consideration of the manner in which Flemming operated in the name of the corporation during the year when plaintiff's indebtedness was incurred.

The corporation was engaged in the business of a commission agent, selling fruit produce for the account of growers of farm products such as peaches and watermelons in the Edgefield, South Carolina, area. It never purported to own such products; * * * it (always acting through Flemming) sold the products as agent for the growers.

Under the arrangement with the growers, it was to remit to the grower the full sale price, less any transportation costs incurred in transporting the products from the growers' farm or warehouse to the purchaser and its sales commission. An integral part of these collections was * * * represented by the plaintiff's transportation charges. Accordingly, during the period involved here, the corporation had as operating funds seemingly only its commissions and the amount of the plaintiff's transportation charges, for which the corporation had claimed credit in its settlement with its growers. At the time, however, Flemming was withdrawing funds from the corporation at the rate of at least $15,000 per year; and doing this, even though he must have known that the corporation could only do this by withholding payment of the transportation charges due the plaintiff, which in the accounting with the growers Flemming represented had been paid the plaintiff. And, it is of some interest that the amount due the plaintiff for transportation costs was approximately the same as the $15,000 minimum annual salary the defendant testified he was paid by the corporation. Were the opinion of the District Court herein to be reversed, Flemming would be permitted to retain substantial sums from the operations of the corporation without having any real capital in the undertaking, risking nothing of his own and using as operating capital what he had collected as due the plaintiff. Certainly, equity and fundamental justice support individual liability of Flemming for plaintiff's charges, payment for which he asserted in his accounting with the growers that he had paid and for which he took credit on such accounting. This case patently presents a blending of the very factors which courts have regarded as justifying a disregard of the corporate entity in furtherance of basic and fundamental fairness.

Finally, it should not be overlooked that at some point during the period when this indebtedness was being incurred—whether at the beginning or at a short time later is not clear in the record—the plaintiff became concerned about former delays in receipt of payment for its charges and, to allay that concern, Flemming stated to the plaintiff, according to the latter's testimony as credited by the District Court, that "he (i.e., Flemming) would take care of [the charges] personally, if the corporation failed to do so * * *." On this assurance, the plaintiff contended that it continued to haul for the defendant. The existence of this promise by Flemming is not disputed. * * * This assurance was given for the obvious purpose of promoting the *individual* advantage of Flemming. This follows because the only person who could profit from the continued operation of the corporation was Flemming. When one, who is the sole beneficiary of a corporation's operations and who dominates it, as did Flemming in this case, induces a creditor to extend credit to the corporation on such an assurance as given here, that fact has been considered by many authorities sufficient basis for piercing the corporate veil. Weisser v. Mursam Shoe Corporation (2d Cir.1942), 127 F.2d 344, 145 A.L.R. 467. The only argument against this view is bottomed on the statute of frauds. But reliance on such statute is often regarded as without merit in a case where the promise or assurance is given "at the time or before the debt is created," for in that case the promise is original and without the statute. Goldsmith v. Erwin (4th Cir.1950), 183 F.2d 432, 435–6, 20 A.L.R.2d 240, with annotation. A number of courts, including South Carolina, however, have gone further and have held that, where the promisor owns substantially all the stock of the corporation and seeks by his promise to serve his personal pecuniary advantage, the question whether such promise is "within the statute of frauds" is a fact question to be resolved by the trial court and this is true whether the promise was made before the debt was incurred or during the time it was being incurred. Amer. Wholesale Corp. v. Mauldin (1924), 128 S.C. 241, 244–5, 122 S.E. 576. This is that type of case and may well have been resolved on this issue.

For the reasons stated, we conclude that the findings of the District Court herein are not clearly erroneous and the judgment of the District Court is

Affirmed.

Notes

(1) The rhetoric and reasoning in these opinions are typical of "piercing the corporate veil" cases. Many such cases are long on rhetoric and short on reasoning. Indeed, perhaps in no other area are courts more prone to decide real life disputes by verbal characterizations, epithets, and metaphors: "mere adjunct," "agent," "alias," "alter ego," "alter idem," "arm," "blind," "branch," "buffer," "cloak," "coat," "corporate double," "instrumentality," "mouthpiece," "name," "nominal identity," "phrase," "puppet," "screen," "sham," "simulacrum," "snare," "stooge," "subterfuge," or "tool," to select a few. Various terms are often combined in artful phraseology. P. Blumberg, The Law of Corporate Groups: Procedural Law (1983), 8:

> This is jurisprudence by metaphor or epithet. It does not contribute to legal understanding because it is an intellectual construct, divorced from business realities. The metaphors are no more than conclusory terms, affording little understanding of the considerations and policies underlying the court's action and little help in predicting results in future cases.

> Such courts state that the corporate entity is to be disregarded because the corporation is, for example, a mere "alter ego." But they do not inform us why this is so, except in very broad terms that provide little general guidance. As a result, we are faced with hundreds of decisions that are irreconcilable and not entirely comprehensible. Few areas of the law have been so sharply criticized by commentators.

(2) Consider the following attempt to rationalize the principles underlying the "piercing the corporate veil" concept:

> A somewhat more meaningful analysis of this problem may be undertaken. First, no conceptual problems emerge when liability is

imposed upon shareholders under conventional theories of agency or tort law. To argue that the corporate veil is "pierced" in such cases is both unnecessary and confusing. If the shareholder is acting as a principal in his own name, he is clearly liable on the obligation. Moreover, if the corporation can be considered his agent under accepted principles of agency law, the shareholder-principal is liable on a contract because he is a principal, not because he is a shareholder in a corporation whose "veil has been pierced." Similarly, if the shareholder himself commits a tort while acting as agent for his corporation, it is the substantive law of agency that imposes liability for the act on the shareholder. * * *

Secondly, a major consideration in determining whether the shareholders or the third party should bear the loss is whether the third party dealt voluntarily with the corporation or whether he is an involuntary creditor, typically a tort claimant. In a contract case, the plaintiff has usually dealt in some way with the corporation and should be aware that the corporation lacks substance. In the absence of some sort of deception, the creditor more or less assumed the risk of loss when he dealt with a "shell"; if he was concerned, he should have insisted that some solvent third person guarantee the performance by the corporation. In tort cases, on the other hand, there is usually no element of voluntary dealing, and the question is whether it is reasonable for businessmen to transfer a risk of loss or injury to members of the general public through the device of conducting business in the name of a corporation that may be marginally financed. The issues of public policy raised by tort claims bear little relationship to the issues raised by a contract claim. It is astonishing to find that this fundamental distinction is only dimly perceived by many courts, which indiscriminately cite and purport to apply, tort precedents in contract cases and vice versa.

Hamilton, The Corporate Entity, 49 Tex.L.Rev. 979, 983–985 (1971).* Certainly, a nominally-capitalized corporation may be an ideal device for allocating the risk of loss between the parties. If X extends credit to a venture operated by A, the risk of loss is normally on A; however, if it is agreed that X is to look only to the profits of the venture rather than to A personally, a nominally capitalized corporation to operate the venture allocates the risk as desired.

(3) In light of the analysis in the last note, consider again the facts of the two principal cases. Both are contract cases in which the plaintiff is suing the shareholder on prior commercial dealings with a corporate "shell." Why is the "assumption of risk" argument more persuasive to the Court in *Bartle* than to the Court in *DeWitt?*

(4) In *DeWitt* the Court relied on certain factors that are not present in *Bartle,* or at least are not referred to by the Court in *Bartle.* These factors appear in various combinations in numerous cases.

(a) For example, in *DeWitt* the Court relied in part on the fact that the Fruit Company failed to follow corporate formalities, including the holding

* Published originally in 49 Texas Law Review 979, 979–1009 (1971). Copyright 1971 by the Texas Law Review Association. Reprinted by permission.

of meetings, the designation of directors, and so forth. How persuasive is this? Consider Hamilton, The Corporate Entity, 49 Tex.L.Rev. 979, 989–991 (1971) *:

> Anyone reading * * * cases dealing with shareholder liability for corporate obligations will be struck by the emphasis of the courts on failure to follow the requisite corporation formalities as a ground for imposing shareholder liability. In most opinions, a failure to follow normal corporate routine appears a most significant consideration in deciding whether a corporation is the "alter ego" of the shareholder or whether the "corporate veil should be pierced." * * *

> It is difficult to see, as a matter of logic, why corporate confusion and informality have been given the importance that they have. In most cases, the confusion and informality are not related to the claim advanced by either tort or contract plaintiffs. As a matter of fact, evidence of informality or commingling of affairs is first sought long after the transaction giving rise to the particular litigation took place. A judgment against shareholders based on these activities, which are unrelated to the plaintiff's claim, is a windfall. * * * One possible theory underlying these holdings is that the shareholder is liable because he should not be permitted first to ignore the rules of corporate behavior and then to claim the advantage of the corporate shield. In other words, the apparent theory is to punish an errant shareholder. The cases, however, do not articulate this theory, and there seems to be little reason to punish errant shareholders unless their actions are directed toward defrauding another party.

> The use of confusion as an important part of the test for determining whether the corporation's separate existence will be recognized also tends to create a trap for the unwary shareholder in the closely held corporation. Shareholders in a small business often find managing the business a full-time occupation; formal corporate affairs are put off or ignored because there is full agreement in fact by all interested parties regarding what should be done and who should do it. Also, the play-acting aspects of corporate meetings, elections, and the like, may strike businessmen as rather silly. Insistence by an attorney that formal corporate procedures be followed may be dismissed as a subtle attempt at an additional fee. This attitude invites disaster.

> When failure to follow appropriate corporate procedures tends to injure third persons, there can be little objection to holding the shareholder liable. Procedures within the corporation may be so undifferentiated that a person may believe he is dealing with a shareholder individually when he is dealing with the corporation. Similarly, intermingled personal and corporate assets may disappear into the personal coffers of the shareholder to the detriment of corporate creditors.

One well reasoned case that refuses to find shareholder liability despite considerable evidence of confusion is Zubik v. Zubik, 384 F.2d 267 (3d Cir. 1967).

* Published originally in 49 Texas Law Review 979, 979–1009 (1971). Copyright 1971 by the Texas Law Review Association. Reprinted by permission.

Is it sound to argue that public policy requires attention to be paid to corporate formalities, and that ignoring the corporate entity where formalities have been omitted furthers this policy? Or should liability be imposed only to protect creditors who may have been mislead or injured in some way? Many courts adopt this latter position.

(b) A second factor relied upon by the Court in *DeWitt* was the inadequate capitalization of the Fruit Company coupled with its asset distribution policy: it apparently made distributions to Flemming personally out of funds that were earmarked for the payment of plaintiff's transportation charges on the Fruit Company's statements of account with growers. Whether or not this constitutes "plain fraud" is probably open to question; certainly, however, it was an unusual or abnormal manner of operation that effectively disabled the Fruit Company from paying the plaintiff. Presumably such a diversion might be attacked as a fraud on creditors; in addition, the force of theoretical arguments that the Fruit Company was a "separate legal person" may well unravel in the light of such inequitable conduct. Consider, however, the conduct involved in *Bartle* as described in the dissent. If that description is accurate, is that conduct any less objectionable than what was done in *DeWitt*?

(c) In *DeWitt*, Flemming at some point made an oral promise that he would pay the plaintiff's transportation charges personally if necessary. Despite the Court's discussion, is not the statute of frauds a bar to a direct suit on that promise? If so, can one avoid the statute of frauds by arguing that the oral promise should permit the court to pierce the corporate veil? The argument about risk allocation in the foregoing note does not address this aspect of *DeWitt*; in some cases, however, such an oral promise may arguably mislead or trick the third person into dealing with the corporate "shell". Arguably, Weisser v. Mursam Shoe Corp., 127 F.2d 344 (2d Cir. 1942), relied upon by the Court in *DeWitt* is such a case:

> In 1926, Murray Rosenberg approached the plaintiffs to negotiate the terms of a lease of certain premises in Paterson, New Jersey. Their version of the negotiations is as follows: "When we had agreed upon the terms of the lease, Murray M. Rosenberg told us that the tenant was to be the Mursam Shoe Corporation. I asked him who was the Mursam Shoe Corporation. Murray M. Rosenberg represented to me that the name Mursam was an abbreviation for Murray and Samuel, and that he and his brother were the corporation and 'stood behind' the lease. He told us that the store to be opened at the leased premises by them, was to be part of the chain of stores which he and his brother were then operating. Relying upon these representations, the plaintiffs entered into a lease with Mursam for a term of fifteen years." The Mursam Shoe Corporation was organized by the Rosenbergs the day the lease was signed and sealed by the plaintiffs, and two days later it signed and sealed the lease as tenant. According to its books, the original capital investment in Mursam was $1; apart from paying legal and similar fees arising out of the organization of Mursam, the Rosenbergs paid nothing for their stock, and it does not appear that subsequently they made any contributions to capital. Mursam was, therefore, a corporation without assets. Its obligation under the lease was $10,000 annually, for the first five years, $11,000

for the next five and $12,000 for the last five years, or $165,000 for the entire term.

For fourteen years Mursam met its obligations on this lease. It was able to do so because of payments made to it by Murray M. Rosenberg, Inc., which occupied the leased premises under short term subleases. In March 1940, Murray M. Rosenberg, Inc., terminated the sublease then in effect (made February 1, 1939), which was of unspecified duration on a monthly basis, and vacated the premises. Mursam having no assets, this action for damages caused by breach of the lease by failing to pay rent was brought against the other individual and corporate defendants as well.

On these facts, the court concluded that it was error to grant summary judgment in favor of the Rosenbergs, and that the statute of frauds was not a defense available to the Rosenbergs. In both this case and *DeWitt* the plaintiff could easily have declined credit or refused to enter into the lease unless the guarantee was in writing. If they fail to do so, why should they be able to recover despite the statute of frauds?

(5) *Bartle* and *DeWitt* differ in one less obvious respect as well. In *Bartle* the defendant is another corporation, while in *DeWitt* the defendant is an individual, Flemming. Cases where a parent corporation is being held liable for the debts of a subsidiary have quite a different flavor than cases where an individual is the defendant.

Some cases suggest that different tests should apply depending on whether the shareholder-defendant is an individual or a corporation. When a corporation is the defendant, only a larger corporate entity is being held responsible for the debt; but when an individual is the defendant, personal liability extending to non-business assets is being imposed. Whatever the merits of this suggestion as a basis for decision, courts are probably more willing to "pierce the corporate veil" when the defendant is a corporation rather than an individual. Courts are particularly likely to find the broader business entity liable under the following circumstances:

(a) when the business affairs of the two corporations are interwined, and the separate corporate formalities of the subsidiary are not followed;

(b) when the subsidiary and parent are operating portions of a single business, and the subsidiary is undercapitalized; or

(c) when the subsidiary is being operated in an "unfair manner," e.g., by funneling profits to the parent.

Many cases treat the lack of clear delineation between the parent's affairs and the subsidiary's affairs as determinative of liability. * * * An additional basis of liability often arises when the individual acting for the subsidiary is * * * [also] an agent of the parent; unless his status is clearly stated when he acts, the argument may be made that he was acting on behalf of the parent rather than the subsidiary. The probability of parental liability on these theories increases significantly when there are close relationships, informality of operation, and overlapping of personnel employed by the corporations.

    In addition, in contract cases, failure to delineate between operations of the parent and the subsidiary may mislead creditors into believing they are dealing with the broader corporate entity. Most cases, however, make no attempt to explain why liability should result from intermingling of affairs and simply impose liability whenever intermingling is present on a wide scale. Consequently, if the advantage of limited liability is to be preserved, it is very important to draw the necessary distinction between parent and subsidiary. * * *

Hamilton, The Corporate Entity, 49 Tex.L.Rev. 979, 992–993 (1971).*

    (6) Professor Phillip Blumberg, in his multi-volume treatise on piercing the corporate veil entitled *The Law of Corporate Groups* refers to "three variants" on the piercing the corporate veil jurisprudence: the "instrumentality" doctrine, the "alter ego" doctrine, and the "identity" doctrine. P. Blumberg, The Law of Corporate Groups: Substantive Law, § 6.01 (1987). The "instrumentality" doctrine embraces three factors: "excessive exercise of control; wrongful or inequitable conduct; and causal relationship to the plaintiff's loss." Id., § 6.02. The "alter ego" doctrine holds that piercing is proper when "(1) such unity of ownership and interest exists that the two affiliated corporations have ceased to be separate and the subsidiary has been relegated to the status of the 'alter ego' of the parent; and (2) where recognition of them as separate entities would sanction fraud or lead to an inequitable result." Id., § 6.03. The "identity" doctrine "is such a diffuse and relatively useless approach that it does not deserve extended discussion. * * * [The standard is] 'that there was such a unity of interest and ownership that the independence of the corporations had in effect ceased or had never begun, an adherence to the fiction of separate entity would serve only to defeat justice and equity by permitting the economic entity to escape liability arising out of an operation of one corporation for the benefit of the whole enterprise.' " Id., § 6.04 [quoting from Zaist v. Olson, 154 Conn. 563, 227 A.2d 552, 558 (1967)]. Professor Blumberg adds that "[i]n spite of different formulations, the doctrines are essentially the same, and most courts generally regard the doctrines as interchangeable." Id., § 6.01. These "doctrines" are likely to be relied upon in both tort and contract cases and in suits against either individual or corporate shareholders.

    (7) For an interesting discussion of the economists' analysis of the piercing the corporate veil concept, see Easterbrook and Fischel, Limited Liability and the Corporation, 52 U.Chi.L.Rev. 89 (1985). This article considers, among other things, the contract/tort and parent/subsidiary distinctions discussed above. See also Landers, A Unified Approach to Parent, Subsidiary and Affiliate Questions in Bankruptcy, 42 U.Chi.L.Rev. 589 (1975); Posner, The Rights of Creditors of Affiliated Corporations, 43 U.Chi.L.Rev. 499 (1976); Landers, Another Word on Parents, Subsidiaries and Affiliates in Bankruptcy, 43 U.Chi.L.Rev. 527 (1976).

WALKOVSKY v. CARLTON
Court of Appeals of New York, 1966.
18 N.Y.2d 414, 276 N.Y.S.2d 585, 223 N.E.2d 6.

FULD, JUDGE.

This case involves what appears to be a rather common practice in the taxicab industry of vesting the ownership of a taxi fleet in many corporations, each owning only one or two cabs.

The complaint alleges that the plaintiff was severly injured four years ago in New York City when he was run down by a taxicab owned by the defendant Seon Cab Corporation and negligently operated at the time by the defendant Marchese. The individual defendant, Carlton, is claimed to be a stockholder of 10 corporations, including Seon, each of which has but two cabs registered in its name, and it is implied that only the minimum automobile liability insurance required by law (in the amount of $10,000) is carried on any one cab. Although seemingly independent of one another, these corporations are alleged to be "operated * * * as a single entity, unit and enterprise" with regard to financing, supplies, repairs, employees and garaging, and all are named as defendant.[6] The plaintiff asserts that he is also entitled to hold their stockholders personally liable for the damages sought because the multiple corporate structure constitutes an unlawful attempt "to defraud members of the general public" who might be injured by the cabs.

The defendant Carlton has moved, pursuant to CPLR 3211(a)7, to dismiss the complaint on the ground that as to him it "fails to state a cause of action". The court at Special Term granted the motion but the Appellate Division, by a divided vote, reversed, holding that a valid cause of action was sufficiently stated. The defendant Carlton appeals to us, from the nonfinal order, by leave of the Appellate Division on a certified question.

The law permits the incorporation of a business for the very purpose of enabling its proprietors to escape personal liability (see e.g., Bartle v. Home Owners Co-op., 309 N.Y. 103, 106, 127 N.E.2d 832, 833) but, manifestly, the privilege is not without its limits. Broadly speaking, the courts will disregard the corporate form, or, to use accepted terminology, "pierce the corporate veil", whenever necessary "to prevent fraud or to achieve equity". (International Aircraft Trading Co. v. Manufacturers Trust Co., 297 N.Y. 285, 292, 79 N.E.2d 249, 252.) In determining whether liability should be extended to reach assets beyond those belonging to the corporation, we are guided, as Judge Cardozo noted, by "general rules of agency." (Berkey v. Third Ave. Ry. Co., 244 N.Y. 84, 95, 155 N.E. 58, 61, 50 A.L.R. 599.) In other words whenever anyone uses control of the corporation to further his own rather than the corporation's business, he will be liable for the corporation's acts "upon the principle of *respondeat superior* applicable even

---

6. [By the Court] The corporate owner of a garage is also included as a defendant.

where the agent is a natural person". Such liability, moreover, extends not only to the corporation's commercial dealings (see, e.g., * * * Weisser v. Mursam Shoe Corp., 2 Cir., 127 F.2d 344, 145 A.L.R. 467) but to its negligent acts as well. (See Berkey v. Third Ave. Ry. Co., 244 N.Y. 84, 155 N.E. 58, supra * * * Mangan v. Terminal Transp. System, 247 App.Div. 853, 286 N.Y.S. 666, mot. for lv. to app. den. 272 N.Y. 676, 286 N.Y.S. 666.)

In the Mangan case (247 App.Div. 853, 286 N.Y.S. 666, mot. for lv. to app. den. 272 N.Y. 676, 286 N.Y.S. 666, supra), the plaintiff was injured as a result of the negligent operation of a cab owned and operated by one of four corporations affiliated with the defendant Terminal. Although the defendant was not a stockholder of any of the operating companies, both the defendant and the operating companies were owned, for the most part, by the same parties. The defendant's name (Terminal) was conspicuously displayed on the sides of all of the taxis used in the enterprise and, in point of fact, the defendant actually serviced, inspected, repaired and dispatched them. These facts were deemed to provide sufficient cause for piercing the corporate veil of the operating company—the nominal owner of the cab which injured the plaintiff—and holding the defendant liable. The operating companies were simply instrumentalities for carrying on the business of the defendant without imposing upon it financial and other liabilities incident to the actual ownership and operation of the cabs.

In the case before us, the plaintiff has explicitly alleged that none of the corporations "had a separate existence of their own" and, as indicated above, all are named as defendants. However, it is one thing to assert that a corporation is a fragment of a larger corporate combine which actually conducts the business. (See Berle, The Theory of Enterprise Entity, 47 Col.L.Rev. 343, 348–350.) It is quite another to claim that the corporation is a "dummy" for its individual stockholders who are in reality carrying on the business in their personal capacities for purely personal rather than corporate ends. Either circumstance would justify treating the corporation as an agent and piercing the corporate veil to reach the principal but a different result would follow in each case. In the first, only a larger *corporate* entity would be held financially responsible (see, e.g., Mangan v. Terminal Transp. System, 247 App.Div. 853, 286 N.Y.S. 666, mot. for lv. to app. den. 272 N.Y. 676, 286 N.Y.S. 666, supra * * *) while, in the other the stockholder would be personally liable. (See, e.g., * * *; Weisser v. Mursam Shoe Corp., 2 Cir., 127 F.2d 344, 145 A.L.R. 467, supra.) Either the stockholder is conducting the business in his individual capacity or he is not. If he is, he will be liable; if he is not, then, it does not matter—insofar as his personal liability is concerned—that the enterprise is actually being carried on by a larger "enterprise entity". (See Berle, The Theory of Enterprise Entity, 47 Col.L.Rev. 343.)

At this stage in the present litigation, we are concerned only with the pleadings and, * * * [r]eading the complaint in this case most

finding

favorably and liberally, we do not believe that there can be gathered from its averments the allegations required to spell out a valid cause of action against the defendant Carlton.

The individual defendant is charged with having "organized, managed, dominated and controlled" a fragmented corporate entity but there are no allegations that he was conducting business in his individual capacity. Had the taxicab fleet been owned by a single corporation, it would be readily apparent that the plaintiff would face formidable barriers in attempting to establish personal liability on the part of the corporation's stockholders. The fact that the fleet ownership has been deliberately split up among many corporations does not ease the plaintiff's burden in that respect. The corporate form may not be disregarded merely because the assets of the corporation, together with the mandatory insurance coverage of the vehicle which struck the plaintiff, are insufficient to assure him the recovery sought. If Carlton were to be held individually liable on those facts alone, the decision would apply equally to the thousands of cabs which are owned by their individual drivers who conduct their businesses through corporations organized pursuant to section 401 of the Business Corporation Law, Consol.Laws, c. 4 and carry the minimum insurance required by subdivision 1 (par. [a]) of section 370 of the Vehicle and Traffic Law, Consol. Laws, c. 71. These taxi owner-operators are entitled to form such corporations (cf. Elenkrieg v. Siebrecht, 238 N.Y. 254, 144 N.E. 519, 34 A.L.R. 592), and we agree with the court at Special Term that, if the insurance coverage required by statute "is inadequate for the protection of the public, the remedy lies not with the courts but with the Legislature." It may very well be sound policy to require that certain corporations must take out liability insurance which will afford adequate compensation to their potential tort victims. However, the responsibility for imposing conditions on the privilege of incorporation has been committed by the Constitution to the Legislature and it may not be fairly implied, from any statute, that the Legislature intended, without the slightest discussion or debate, to require of taxi corporations that they carry automobile liability insurance over and above that mandated by the Vehicle and Traffic Law.[7]

This is not to say that it is impossible for the plaintiff to state a valid cause of action against the defendant Carlton. However, the simple fact is that the plaintiff has just not done so here. While the complaint alleges that the separate corporations were undercapitalized and that their assets have been intermingled, it is barren of any "sufficiently particular[ized] statements" that the defendant Carlton and his associates are actually doing business in their individual

---

7. [By the Court] There is no merit to the contention that the ownership and operation of the taxi fleet "constituted a breach of hack owners regulations as promulgated by [the] Police Department of the City of New York". Those regulations are clearly applicable to individual owner-operators and fleet owners alike. They were not intended to prevent either incorporation of a single-vehicle taxi business or multiple incorporation of a taxi fleet.

capacities, shuttling their personal funds in and out of the corporations "without regard to formality and to suit their immediate convenience." (Weisser v. Mursam Shoe Corp., 2 Cir., 127 F.2d 344, 345, 145 A.L.R. 467, supra.) Such a "perversion of the privilege to do business in a corporate form" (Berkey v. Third Ave. Ry. Co., 244 N.Y. 84, 95, 155 N.E. 58, 61, 50 A.L.R. 599, supra) would justify imposing personal liabilty on the individual stockholders. Nothing of the sort has in fact been charged, and it cannot reasonably or logically be inferred from the happenstance that the business of Seon Cab Corporation may actually be carried on by a larger corporate entity composed of many corporations which, under general principles of agency, would be liable to each other's creditors in contract and in tort.[8]

In point of fact, the principle relied upon in the complaint to sustain the imposition of personal liability is not agency but fraud. Such a cause of action cannot withstand analysis. If it is not fraudulent for the owner-operator of a single cab corporation to take out only the minimum required liability insurance, the enterprise does not become either illicit or fraudulent merely because it consists of many such corporations. The plaintiff's injuries are the same regardless of whether the cab which strikes him is owned by a single corporation or part of a fleet with ownership fragmented among many corporations. Whatever rights he may be able to assert against parties other than the registered owner of the vehicle come into being not because he has been defrauded but because, under the principle of *respondeat superior,* he is entitled to hold the whole enterprise responsible for the acts of its agents.

In sum, then, the complaint falls short of adequately stating a cause of action against the defendant Carlton in his individual capacity.

The order of the Appellate Division should be reversed, with costs in this court and in the Appellate Division, the certified question answered in the negative and the order of the Supreme Court, Richmond County, reinstated, with leave to serve an amended complaint.

KEATING, JUDGE (dissenting).

The defendant Carlton, the shareholder here sought to be held for the negligence of the driver of a taxicab, was a principal shareholder and organizer of the defendant corporation which owned the taxicab. The corporation was one of 10 organized by the defendant, each containing two cabs and each cab having the "minimum liability" insurance coverage mandated by section 370 of the Vehicle and Traffic

---

8. [By the Court] In his affidavit in opposition to the motion to dismiss, the plaintiff's counsel claimed that corporate assets had been "milked out" of, and "siphoned off" from the enterprise. Quite apart from the fact that these allegations are far too vague and conclusory, the charge is prema-ture. If the plaintiff succeeds in his action and becomes a judgment creditor of the corporation, he may then sue and attempt to hold the individual defendants accountable for any dividends and property that were wrongfully distributed.

Law. The sole assets of these operating corporations are the vehicles themselves and they are apparently subject to mortgages.[9]

From their inception these corporations were intentionally under-capitalized for the purpose of avoiding responsibility for acts which were bound to arise as a result of the operation of a large taxi fleet having cars out on the street 24 hours a day and engaged in public transportation. And during the course of the corporations' existence all income was continually drained out of the corporations for the same purpose.

The issue presented by this action is whether the policy of this State, which affords those desiring to engage in a business enterprise the privilege of limited liability through the use of the corporate device, is so strong that it will permit that privilege to continue no matter how much it is abused, no matter how irresponsibly the corporation is operated, no matter what the cost to the public. I do not believe that it is.

Under the circumstances of this case the shareholders should all be held individually liable to this plaintiff for the injuries he suffered. At least the matter should not be disposed of on the pleadings by a dismissal of the complaint. "If a corporation is organized and carries on business without substantial capital in such a way that the corporation is likely to have no sufficient assets available to meet its debts, it is inequitable that shareholders should set up such a flimsy organization to escape personal liability. The attempt to do corporate business without providing any sufficient basis of financial responsibility to creditors is an abuse of the separate entity and will be ineffectual to exempt the shareholders from corporate debts. It is coming to be recognized as the policy of law that shareholders should in good faith put at the risk of the business unincumbered capital reasonably adequate for its prospective liabilities. If capital is illusory or trifling compared with the business to be done and the risks of loss, this is a ground for denying the separate entity privilege." (Ballantine, Corporations [rev. ed., 1946], § 129, pp. 302–303.)

 * * * [Judge Keating here summarizes Minton v. Cavaney, the following principal case, and Anderson v. Abbott, 321 U.S. 349, 64 S.Ct. 531, 88 L.Ed. 793 (1944).]

The policy of this State has always been to provide and facilitate recovery for those injured through the negligence of others. The automobile, by its very nature, is capable of causing severe and costly injuries when not operated in a proper manner. The great increase in the number of automobile accidents combined with the frequent financial irresponsibility of the individual driving the car led to the adoption of section 388 of the Vehicle and Traffic Law which had the effect of imposing upon the owner of the vehicle the responsibility for its negligent operation. It is upon this very statute that the cause of

---

9. [By the Judge] It appears that the medallions, which are of considerable value, are judgment proof. (Administrative Code of City of New York, § 436–2.0.)

action against both the corporation and the individual defendant is predicated.

In addition the Legislature, still concerned with the financial irresponsibility of those who owned and operated motor vehicles, enacted a statute requiring minimum liability coverage for all owners of automobiles. The important public policy represented by both these statutes is outlined in section 310 of the Vehicle and Traffic Law. That section provides that: "The legislature is concerned over the rising toll of motor vehicle accidents and the suffering and loss thereby inflicted. The legislature determines that it is a matter of grave concern that motorists shall be financially able to respond in damages for their negligent acts, so that innocent victims of motor vehicle accidents may be recompensed for the injury and financial loss inflicted upon them."

The defendant Carlton claims that, because the minimum amount of insurance required by the statute was obtained, the corporate veil cannot and should not be pierced despite the fact that the assets of the corporation which owned the cab were "trifling compared with the business to be done and the risks of loss" which were certain to be encountered. I do not agree.

The Legislature in requiring minimum liability insurance of $10,000, no doubt, intended to provide at least some small fund for recovery against those individuals and corporations who just did not have and were not able to raise or accumulate assets sufficient to satisfy the claims of those who were injured as a result of their negligence. It certainly could not have intended to shield those individuals who organized corporations, with the specific intent of avoiding responsibility to the public, where the operation of the corporate enterprise yielded profits sufficient to purchase additional insurance. Moreover, it is reasonable to assume that the Legislature believed that those individuals and corporations having substantial assets would take out insurance far in excess of the minimum in order to protect those assets from depletion. Given the costs of hospital care and treatment and the nature of injuries sustained in auto collisions, it would be unreasonable to assume that the Legislature believed that the minimum provided in the statute would in and of itself be sufficient to recompense "innocent victims of motor vehicle accidents * * * for the injury and financial loss inflicted upon them".

The defendant, however, argues that the failure of the Legislature to increase the minimum insurance requirements indicates legislative acquiescence in this scheme to avoid liability and responsibility to the public. In the absence of a clear legislative statement, approval of a scheme having such serious consequences is not to be so lightly inferred. * * *

What I would merely hold is that a participating shareholder of a corporation vested with a public interest, organized with capital insufficient to meet liabilities which are certain to arise in the ordinary course of the corporation's business, may be held personally responsible for such liabilities. Where corporate income is not sufficient to cover the cost of insurance premiums above the statutory minimum or where initially adequate finances dwindle under the pressure of competition, bad times or extraordinary and unexpected liability, obviously the shareholder will not be held liable.

The only types of corporate enterprises that will be discouraged as a result of a decision allowing the individual shareholder to be sued will be those such as the one in question, designed solely to abuse the corporate privilege at the expense of the public interest.

For these reasons I would vote to affirm the order of the Appellate Division.

DESMOND, C.J., and VAN VOORHIS, BURKE and SCILEPPI, JJ., concur with FULD, J.

KEATING, J., dissents and votes to affirm in an opinion in which BERGAN, J., concurs.

Notes

(1) Following the decision, Walkovsky amended his complaint to allege that Carlton was "conducting the business of the taxicab fleet in [his] individual capacity." This complaint was upheld on motion to dismiss for failure to state a cause of action, one judge dissenting. Walkovsky v. Carlton, 29 A.D.2d 763, 287 N.Y.S.2d 546 (1968), affirmed 23 N.Y.2d 714, 296 N.Y.S.2d 362, 244 N.E.2d 55 (1968). The case then was settled.

(2) The majority in the original Walkovsky opinion rejects the policy argument made by the dissent, on the ground that it raises a legislative rather than a judicial question, and that the legislature has acted. What would the majority's response be if the state did not impose any minimum insurance requirement?

(3) Should the ten corporations owned by Carlton each be liable for Walkovsky's injury even though Carlton himself may not be? On what theory? Compare Berle, The Theory of Enterprise Entity, 47 Colum.L.Rev. 343, 348 (1947):

> Another illustration of judicial erection of a new entity occurs in situations where the corporate personality (as embodied in its charter, books and so forth) does not correspond to the actual enterprise, but merely to a fragment of it. The result is to construct a new aggregate of assets and liabilities. Typical cases appear where a partnership or a central corporation owns the controlling interest in one or more other corporations, but has so handled them that they have ceased to represent a separate enterprise and have become, as a business matter, more or less indistinguishable parts of a larger enterprise. The decisions disregard the paper corporate personalities and base liability on the assets of the enterprise. The reasoning by which courts reach this result varies: it is sometimes said that one corporation has become a mere "agency" of another; or that its operations have been so intermingled that it has lost its identity; or that the business arrangements indicate that it has become a "mere instrumentality."

(4) Easterbrook and Fischel, Limited Liability and the Corporation, 52 U.Chi.L.Rev. 89, 111 (1985):

> [Parent corporations should not always] be liable for the debts of those in which they hold stock. Far from it. Such general liability would give unaffiliated firms a competitive advantage. Think of the taxicab business. Taxi firms may incorporate each cab or put just a few cabs in a firm. If courts routinely pierced this arrangement and put the assets of the full venture at risk for the accidents of each cab, then "true" single-cab firms would have lower costs of operation because they alone could cut off liability. That would create a perverse incentive because, as we have emphasized, larger firms are apt to carry more insurance. Potential victims of torts would not gain from a legal rule that promoted corporate dis-integration. As a result, courts properly disregard the corporate form only when the corporate arrangement has increased risks over what they would be if firms generally were organized as separate ventures.

Do you agree? Do Easterbrook and Fischel correctly state "the law" in the last sentence that is quoted?

(5) Is the motive of the shareholder relevant in deciding to incorporate? What if the business is a very risky one, and the owner incorporates solely for the purpose of avoiding personal liability? In Western Rock Co. v. Davis, 432 S.W.2d 555 (Tex.Civ.App.—Fort Worth, 1968), a marginally financed corporation engaged in extensive blasting operations in a rock quarry near Jacksboro, Texas causing property damage. The court held the individual shareholders personally liable. As in most "corporate veil" cases, however, the court referred to numerous facts without stating which were decisive: the shareholders had individually participated in the blasting, and the business of the corporation was conducted in such a way that all assets would be promptly siphoned off to the principal shareholder through rental payments for the assets needed by the corporation.

MINTON v. CAVANEY

Supreme Court of California, 1961.
15 Cal.Rptr. 641, 364 P.2d 473.

TRAYNOR, JUSTICE.

The Seminole Hot Springs Corporation, hereinafter referred to as Seminole, was duly incorporated in California on March 8, 1954. It conducted a public swimming pool that it leased from its owner. On June 24, 1954 plaintiffs' daughter drowned in the pool, and plaintiffs recovered a judgment for $10,000 against Seminole for her wrongful death. The judgment remains unsatisfied.

On January 30, 1957, plaintiffs brought the present action to hold defendant Cavaney personally liable for the judgment against Seminole. Cavaney died on May 28, 1958 and his widow, the executrix of his estate, was substituted as defendant. The trial court entered judgment for plaintiffs for $10,000. Defendant appeals.

Plaintiffs introduced evidence that Cavaney was a director and secretary and treasurer of Seminole and that on November 15, 1954, about five months after the drowning, Cavaney as secretary of Seminole and Edwin A. Kraft as president of Seminole applied for permission to issue three shares of Seminole stock, one share to be issued to Kraft, another to F.J. Wettrick and the third to Cavaney. The commissioner of corporations refused permission to issue these shares unless additional information was furnished. The application was then abandoned and no shares were ever issued. There was also evidence that for a time Seminole used Cavaney's office to keep records and to receive mail. Before his death Cavaney answered certain interrogatories. He was asked if Seminole "ever had any assets"? He stated that "insofar as my own personal knowledge and belief is concerned said corporation did not have any assets." Cavaney also stated in the return to an attempted execution that "[I]nsofar as I know, this corporation had no assets of any kind or character. The corporation was duly organized but never functioned as a corporation."

Defendant introduced evidence that Cavaney was an attorney at law, that he was approached by Kraft and Wettrick to form Seminole, and that he was the attorney for Seminole. Plaintiffs introduced Cavaney's answer to several interrogatories that he held the post of secretary and treasurer and director in a temporary capacity and as an accommodation to his client.

Defendant contends that the evidence does not support the court's determination that Cavaney is personally liable for Seminole's debts and that the "alter ego" doctrine is inapplicable because plaintiffs failed to show that there was " '(1) * * * such unity of interest and ownership that the separate personalities of the corporation and the individual no longer exist and (2) that, if the acts are treated as those of the corporation alone, an inequitable result will follow.' " Riddle v. Leuschner, 51 Cal.2d 574, 580, 335 P.2d 107, 110; Automotriz Del Golfo De California S.A. De C.V. v. Resnick, 47 Cal.2d 792, 796, 306 P.2d 1, 63 A.L.R.2d 1042; Minifie v. Rowley, 187 Cal. 481, 487, 202 P. 673.

The figurative terminology "alter ego" and "disregard of the corporate entity" is generally used to refer to the various situations that are an abuse of the corporate privilege. Ballantine, Corporations (rev. ed. 1946) § 122, pp. 292–293. The equitable owners of a corporation, for example, are personally liable when they treat the assets of the corporation as their own and add or withdraw capital from the corporation at will; when they hold themselves out as being personally liable for the debts of the corporation; or when they provide inadequate capitalization and actively participate in the conduct of corporate affairs.

In the instant case the evidence is undisputed that there was no attempt to provide adequate capitalization. Seminole never had any substantial assets. It leased the pool that it operated, and the lease was forfeited for failure to pay the rent. Its capital was " 'trifling compared with the business to be done and the risks of loss * * *.' " Automotriz Del Golfo De California S.A. De C.V. v. Resnick, supra, 47 Cal.2d 792, 797, 306 P.2d 1, 4. The evidence is also undisputed that Cavaney was not only the secretary and treasurer of the corporation but was also a director. The evidence that Cavaney was to receive one-third of the shares to be issued supports an inference that he was an equitable owner, and the evidence that for a short time the records of the corporation were kept in Cavaney's office supports an inference that he actively participated in the conduct of the business. The trial court was not required to believe his statement that he was only a "temporary" director and officer "for accommodation." In any event it merely raised a conflict in the evidence that was resolved adversely to defendant. Moreover, section 800 of the Corporations Code provides that " * * * the business and affairs of every corporation shall be controlled by a board of not less than three directors." Defendant does not claim that Cavaney was a director with specialized duties. It is immaterial whether or not he accepted the office of director as an "accommodation" with the understanding that he would not exercise any of the duties of a director. A person may not in this manner divorce the responsibilities of a director from the statutory duties and powers of that office.

There is no merit in defendant's contentions that the "alter ego" doctrine applies only to contractual debts and not to tort claims; that plaintiffs' cause of action abated when Cavaney died, or that the judgment in the action against the corporation bars plaintiffs from bringing the present action. Defendant Cavaney waived the defense of the statute of limitations by failing to plead that defense in the answer to the complaint or by specifying the statute of limitations as a ground of its general demurrer.

In this action to hold defendant personally liable upon the judgment against Seminole plaintiffs did not allege or present any evidence on the issue of Seminole's negligence or on the amount of damages sustained by plaintiffs. They relied solely on the judgment against Seminole. Defendant correctly contends that Cavaney or his estate cannot be held liable for the debts of Seminole without an opportunity to relitigate these issues. Cavaney was not a party to the action against the corporation, and the judgment in that action is therefore not binding upon him * * *

The judgment is reversed.

GIBSON, C.J., and PETERS, WHITE and DOOLING, JJ., concur.

SCHAUER, JUSTICE (concurring and dissenting).

I concur in the judgment of reversal on the ground that (as stated in the majority opinion) "In this action to hold defendant personally liable upon the judgment against Seminole plaintiffs did not allege or present any evidence on the issue of Seminole's negligence or on the amount of damages sustained by plaintiffs. They relied solely on the judgment against Seminole. Defendant correctly contends that Cavaney or his estate cannot be held liable for the debts of Seminole without an opportunity to relitigate these issues. Cavaney was not a party to the action against the corporation, and the judgment in that action is therefore not binding upon him * * *."

I dissent from any implication that *mere professional activity by an attorney at law, as such,* in the organization of a corporation, can constitute any basis for a finding that the corporation is the attorney's alter ego or that he is otherwise personally liable for *its* debts, whether based on contract or tort. That in such circumstances an attorney does not incur any personal liability for debts of the corporation remains true whether or not the attorney's professional services include the issuance to him of a qualifying share of stock, the attendance at and participation in an organization meeting or meetings, the holding and exercise for such preliminary purposes, in the course of his professional services, of an office or offices, whether secretary or treasurer or presiding officer or any combination of offices in the corporation.

The acts and services performed in *organizing* a corporation do not constitute the carrying on of business *by a corporation.* In this respect a corporation cannot properly be regarded as organized and ready to even begin carrying on business until at least qualifying shares of stock have been issued, a stockholders' meeting held, bylaws adopted and directors and officers elected. Furthermore, a permit from the Commissioner of Corporations must have been secured and minimum requirements of that agency met before the corporation can secure assets for which its stock may issue (possibly to be impounded on conditions) and without which it cannot (at least normally) commence business. The scope of a lawyer's services in corporate organization may often include advice and direction as to the legal architecture of financial structures but does not, as such, encompass responsibility for securing assets.

In the process of developing an idea of a person or persons into an embryonic corporation and finally to full legal entity status with a permit issued, directors and officers elected, and assets in hand ready to begin business, there may often be delays. In such event a qualifying share of stock may stand in the name of the organizing attorney for substantial periods of time. In none of the activities indicated is the corporation actually engaging in business. And the lawyer who handles the task of determining and directing and participating in the steps appropriate to transforming the idea into a competent legal entity *ready to engage in business* is not an alter ego of the corporation. By his professional acts he has not been engaging in business in the name of the corporation; he has been merely practicing law.

McComb, J., concurs.

Notes

(1) Can the decisions in the last two principal cases be reconciled? Given the amorphous doctrine being applied, is there any reason to attempt to do so?

(2) The foregoing four principal cases give a flavor of the classic "piercing the corporate veil" jurisprudence. The balance of this note discusses recent developments in a rather selective fashion. As of about 1980, it was probably fair to say that there appeared to exist a national jurisprudence on piercing the corporate veil. Cases usually involved contract rather than tort issues and courts usually cited cases from various jurisdictions without discrimination in their attempts to apply whatever standards and doctrines that exist in this area to the specific facts before them. Further, many courts, like the New York court in Walkovsky v. Carlton, did not recognize any distinction between tort and contract cases, and cited both types of cases indiscriminately. Recent developments appear to have increased rather than decreased the uncertainty and diversity in this area.

(3) The Texas law of piercing the corporate veil took a rather bizarre turn in 1986. In Castleberry v. Branscum, 721 S.W.2d 270 (Tex.1986), a case that was decided by a five-to-four vote, the court rewrote the traditional piercing rhetoric so broadly that it appeared likely that thereafter shareholders' protection from liability on both contract and tort corporate obligations had become entirely dependent on a jury's determination that the transaction met some undefined and abstract standard of fairness:

(a) The court held that the "corporate veil may be pierced" whenever the corporate fiction is used "as a means of perpetrating a fraud" or as "a sham to perpetrate a fraud." In this connection, either "actual fraud" or "constructive fraud" was held to be sufficient; the difference between "actual" and "constructive" fraud is that "actual fraud usually involves dishonesty of purpose or intent to deceive, whereas constructive fraud is the breach of some legal or equitable duty which, irrespective of moral guilt, the law declares fraudulent because of its tendency to deceive others, to violate confidence, or to injure public interests." Archer v. Griffith, 390 S.W.2d 735, 740 (Tex.1964). Furthermore, all distinction between tort and contract claimants (a distinction which several earlier Texas opinions had accepted) was rejected; in either type of case, plaintiffs may hold shareholders personally liable if they can establish "a sham to perpetrate a fraud," which involves, the court stated, "a flexible fact-specific approach focusing on equity."

(b) The issue whether the corporate veil should be pierced is a question of fact for the jury rather than a question of law for the judge. Of course, the plaintiff must present evidence sufficient to permit the issue to be submitted to the jury, but once that threshhold showing has been made, the issue is purely one of fact.

(c) Piercing the corporate veil, as a doctrine, may be subdivided into a multi-tiered classification comprised of seven or eight independent categories. However, the classification created by the court was highly confusing, with overlapping requirements and vague definitional provisions. More importantly, "alter ego" was itself defined to be a "totally separate and independent legal principle" from the listed categories. Alter ego involves "such unity between corporation and individual that the separateness of the corporation has ceased and holding only the corporation liable would result in injustice."

(4) The *Castleberry* opinion caused grave concern within the Texas business community since it created an apprehension that it might no longer be safe to conduct business in corporate form in Texas. These concerns, in turn, almost immediately gave rise to calls for legislative correction. In 1989 the Texas Legislature enacted such a statute, apparently the first legislative attempt to codify, or partially codify, the piercing the corporate veil doctrine. V.A.T.S.Bus.Corp.Act, art. 2.21 was amended to read as follows:

> A. A holder of shares, an owner of any beneficial interest in shares, or a subscriber for shares * * * shall be under no obligation to the corporation or to its obligees with respect to: * * *
>
> (2) any contractual obligation of the corporation on the basis of actual or constructive fraud, or a sham to perpetrate a fraud, unless the obligee demonstrates that the holder, owner, or subscriber caused the corporation to be used for the purpose of perpetrating and did perpetrate an actual fraud on the obligee primarily for the direct personal benefit of the holder, owner, or subscriber; or
>
> (3) any contractual obligation of the corporation on the basis of the failure of the corporation to observe any corporate formality, including without limitation: (a) the failure to comply with any requirement of this Act or of the articles of incorporation or bylaws of the corporation; or (b) the failure to observe any requirement prescribed by this Act or by the articles of incorporation or bylaws for acts to be taken by the corporation, its board of directors, or its shareholders.

Do you believe this statute limits too narrowly the scope of the piercing the corporate veil doctrine? What law in Texas should apply to piercing issues in tort cases under this legislation? *Castleberry?* The former "general" law of piercing the corporate veil?

(5) A decision such as *Castleberry,* and the Texas statute enacted in 1989, makes clear that states may develop different rules with respect to piercing the corporate veil. This in turn raises the question of the choice of law that should be applied in cases involving migratory corporations. Consider, for example, a Delaware corporation that transacts all of its business in Illinois; its shares are owned by Illinois residents and the decision to incorporate in Delaware was based on the perceived benefits of Delaware law. If this corporation enters into a contract with citizens of Illinois who later bring suit in an Illinois court for breach of contract, naming the shareholders as co-defendants, should the court apply Illinois or Delaware "veil piercing" principles in determining the liability of the shareholders? There is a plausible argument that Delaware law should apply, since the relationship of shareholders to their corporation may be viewed as a matter of "internal affairs" of the corporation to be governed by the law of the state of incorporation. Proceeding on this theory, Texas

in 1989 also amended its Business Corporation Act to make clear that *Castleberry* should never apply to a qualified foreign corporation:

> Art. 8.02 A.   A foreign corporation which shall have received a certificate of authority under this Act shall * * * enjoy the same, but no greater, rights and privileges as a domestic corporation * * *; provided, however, that only the laws of the jurisdiction of incorporation of a foreign corporation shall govern (1) the internal affairs of the foreign corporation, including but not limited to the rights, powers, and duties of its board of directors and shareholders and matters relating to its shares, and (2) the liability, if any of shareholders of the foreign corporation for the debts, liabilities, and obligations of the foreign corporation for which they are not otherwise liable by statute or agreement."

The choice of law issue in piercing cases has been discussed in a handful of opinions.   The sparse case law tends to support the "internal affairs" principle, at least in contract cases.   See generally, P. Blumberg, The Law of Corporate Groups—Substantive Law, Chapter 27.   In many of the cases that discuss the choice of law issue, however, the court indicates it can find no substantive difference between the laws of the two relevant states, and apply "general" veil piercing concepts without deciding which state law is applicable.

(6) The traditional choice-of-law rule in tort cases is to apply the law of the state in which the tort occurred.   In § 145 of the second Restatement of Conflicts of Law, it is suggested that the local law of the state which has the "most significant relationship to the occurrence and the parties" should apply.   Assume that a Delaware corporation owned entirely by Illinois residents and doing business solely in Illinois commits a tort in Illinois that injures an Illinois resident.   If suit is brought in Illinois, should not § 145 of the second Restatement "trump" the "internal affairs" rule and require the application of Illinois piercing principles?   Would it make any difference if Illinois veil-piercing law gives no indication that it views tort cases differently from contracts cases?   What would be the result if Texas rather than Illinois were involved?   Would not article 8.02 of the Texas Business Corporation Act compel the application of Delaware law despite the fact that Delaware has virtually no relationship with the case?

(7) To the extent the "internal affairs" rule dictates that the law of the state of incorporation determines principles relating to "piercing the corporate veil," attention should be focused on the case law of Delaware.   That is relatively easy to do since there are almost no Delaware cases on the "piercing" issue.   Indeed, the two leading Delaware cases, Pauley Petroleum, Inc. v. Continental Oil Co., 43 Del.Ch. 366, 231 A.2d 450 (1967), affirmed 43 Del.Ch. 516, 239 A.2d 629 (1968), and Buechner v. Farbenfabriken Bayer Aktiengesellschaft, 38 Del.Ch. 490, 154 A.2d 684 (1959), do not involve shareholder liability for corporate indebtedness, but rather issues of jurisdiction in parent/subsidiary relationships.

(8) In United States v. Pisani, 646 F.2d 83 (3d Cir.1981), the United States sought to recover $151,413 in overpayments from a provider of services under the Medicare Program.   The United States also brought suit

against the provider's sole shareholder on a piercing the corporate veil theory. The Court stated:

> This court must first determine whether federal or New Jersey law controls the issue of Pisani's individual liability for overpayments to the corporation. We hold that federal law applies under *Clearfield Trust Co. v. United States,* 318 U.S. 363, 63 S.Ct. 573 (1943). "[F]ederal law governs questions involving the rights of the United States arising under nationwide federal programs." *United States v. Kimbell Foods, Inc.,* 440 U.S. 715, 726, 99 S.Ct. 1448, 1457 (1979). * * *
>
> In deciding what law to adopt as the federal rule for this case, this court could adopt New Jersey law or fashion a uniform federal rule of decision. *See Kimbell Foods,* 440 U.S. at 728, 99 S.Ct. at 1458. Several factors are relevant to this choice. First is whether a need for national uniformity exists. Second is the extent to which "a federal rule would disrupt commercial relationships predicated on state law." *Id.* at 729, 99 S.Ct. at 1459. Finally, and most important here, "we must also determine whether application of state law would frustrate specific objectives of the federal programs. If so, we must fashion special rules solicitous of those federal interests." *Id.* at 728, 99 S.Ct. at 1458.
>
> We hold that here a uniform federal rule is needed since state law could frustrate specific objectives of the Medicare program.[10] * * *
>
> We do not reach the issue whether New Jersey law would permit piercing the corporate veil here. We have not found or been referred to any New Jersey cases which explicitly adopt the alter ego theory, relied on by the district court, in the absence of fraud. New Jersey law thus might be more restrictive than the cases relied on by the trial court. In any event, we believe it is undesirable to let the rights of the United States in this area change whenever state courts issue new decisions on piercing the corporate veil.
>
> To fashion a federal rule, we turn to cases which articulate the alter ego theory.[11] *DeWitt Truck Brokers v. W. Ray Flemming Fruit Co.,* 540 F.2d 681 (4th Cir.1976), sets out in detail the relevant factors.
>
> * * *

Other courts have generally accepted the basic holding of this case, that a federal standard for piercing the corporate veil is appropriate in cases involving federal programs. See particularly United States v. Golden

---

10. [By the Court] *Cf. Audit Services, Inc. v. Rolfson,* 641 F.2d 757 (9th Cir.1981) (federal law governs piercing corporate veil to recover unpaid pension contributions, even though United States is not a party); *Seymour v. Hull & Moreland Engineering,* 605 F.2d 1105, 1110–11 (9th Cir.1979) (same).

11. [By the Court] *Zubik v. Zubik,* 384 F.2d 267 (3d Cir.1967), *cert. denied,* 390 U.S. 988, 88 S.Ct. 1183, 19 L.Ed.2d 1291 (1968), stated that the corporate existence could be disregarded to "prevent fraud, illegality, or injustice, or when recognition of the corporate entity would defeat public policy. . . ." *Id.* at 272. It did not explicitly adopt the alter ego theory, and it apparently relied at least partially on federal rather than state law. *Id.* at 273. *Zubik,* however, involved a corporate tort and the court recognized that business transactions often involve much stronger cases for piercing the veil of an undercapitalized corporation. *Id.* A party to a contract may have relied on conduct by the defendant shareholder, while tort plaintiffs like those in *Zubik* usually never knew the shareholder, much less relied on his conduct or representations.

Acres, Inc., 702 F.Supp. 1097 (D.Del.1988), affirmed without opinion, 879 F.2d 857 (3d Cir.1989). See also United States v. Jon–T Chemicals, Inc., 768 F.2d 686 (5th Cir.1985), where the court concluded that the pre-Castleberry Texas rules of alter ego were indistinguishable from the federal rules, and "we cite federal and state cases interchangeably."

STARK v. FLEMMING

United States Court of Appeals, Ninth Circuit, 1960.
283 F.2d 410.

[Editor: The Secretary of Health, Education and Welfare ruled that Mrs. Stark was not entitled to old-age benefits. The District Court affirmed, 181 F.Supp. 539 (N.D.Cal.1959).]

PER CURIAM.

* * * Appellant placed her assets—a farm and a duplex house—in a newly organized corporation. Then she began to draw $400 per month as salary. The Secretary has found the corporation was a sham. There is no doubt that the corporation was set up to qualify appellant in a short time for social security payments.

But here there seems to have been proper adherence to the normal corporate routines. And it is difficult to understand how the corporate arrangement would not have to be respected by others than the Secretary. And we think he must respect it, too.

Congress could have provided that the motivation to obtain social security by organizing a corporation would defeat the end. It did not.

The Secretary is justified in taking exception to the amount paid Mrs. Stark for her services by which she sought to qualify herself for the maximum amount of social security payments. The salary left little or nothing for a return on capital, and the capital was substantial.

So we think the Secretary is entitled to make an objective reappraisal of the salary to determine what would have been a reasonable salary for Mrs. Stark for the services she performed. One legitimate approach would be: What would a commercial farm agency in the vicinity of the farm have charged? And what would a rental agency in the vicinity of the duplex have charged for the same service? And perhaps she might be allowed slightly more than such agencies. It is not for us to review such determinations within reasonable limits. When the Secretary determines a reasonable salary, then the amount of social security payments can be readily computed.

We, therefore, hold that the district court's judgment should be vacated and that the case should go back through the district court for direction to the Secretary to reevaluate the case on an approach consistent with what we have indicated herein.

Reversed.

ROCCOGRANDI v. UNEMPLOYMENT COMP. BD. OF REVIEW

Superior Court of Pennsylvania, 1962.
197 Pa.Super. 372, 178 A.2d 786.

MONTGOMERY, JUDGE.

The appellants are all members of a family who are involved in the wrecking business together. Each owns 40 shares of stock in the company which has 205 outstanding shares, and all three are officers of the company. The officers of the company, during periods of insufficient work to employ all the members of the family, hold a meeting and by majority vote decide which members shall be "laid off". It was decided by majority vote of all the stockholders that the appellants would be "laid off" because it was their respective turns. Immediately thereafter claims for unemployment compensation benefits were filed by the three appellants. The Bureau of Employment Security denied the claims on the grounds that the appellants were self-employed. Upon appeal the referee reversed the bureau and held the appellants to be entitled to benefits. The Board of Review reversed the referee's decision, holding that the appellants had sufficient control to lay themselves off and that they did just that. Therefore the appellants were self-employed and must be denied eligibility for benefits under section 402(h) and section 402(b)(1) of the law, 43 P.S. § 802(b)(1), (h).

This case is ruled by De Priest Unemployment Compensation Case, 196 Pa.Super. 612, 177 A.2d 20, in which this Court held that the corporate entity may be ignored in determining whether the claimants, in fact, were "unemployed" under the act, or were self-employed persons whose business merely proved to be unremunerative during the period for which the claim for benefits was made.

Decisions affirmed.

Notes

(1) Does the question raised by these two cases relate to the nature of corporateness, or does it merely involve an interpretation of the Federal Social Security Act or Pennsylvania Unemployment Compensation Act? If the former, is the question the same as in the cases discussed earlier involving whether a shareholder should be liable for the debts of the corporation?

(2) State unemployment compensation statutes provide an exemption from contributions for employers who employ less than a minimum number of employees, often eight. May an employer avoid liability under these statutes by splitting his business among several different corporations so that each corporation has less than the minimum number of employees? See State v. Dallas Liquor Warehouse No. 4, 147 Tex. 495, 217 S.W.2d 654 (1949).

UNITED STATES v. KAYSER–ROTH CORPORATION

United States District Court, District of Rhode Island, 1989.
724 F.Supp. 15.

FRANCIS J. BOYLE, CHIEF JUDGE.

In the somnolent village of Forestdale, Rhode Island, the ground waters run deep. Unfortunately, the waters also contain pollutants. Having long been home to machining and textile manufacturing industries, Forestdale found itself a victim of its own hospitality. Trichloroethylene, sometimes a by-product of those industries, had filtered into Forestdale's private and public residential water wells. The Government alleges that Stamina Mills, Inc., a defunct textile operation, was a source of the contaminant.

In a slight twist on a biblical passage, the Court in this case must also decide whether the sins of the son should be visited upon the father. *Cf.* Exodus 20:5. Specifically, the issue is whether Kayser–Roth Corporation, the parent corporation and sole shareholder of Stamina Mills, Inc., is responsible for clean-up and response costs generated at least in part by a spill of a hazardous substance on its subsidiary's property in 1969. The answer to that query requires not only a journey through the labyrinth of the Comprehensive Environmental Response, Compensation and Liability Act ("CERCLA"), but thorough examination of the relationship between the related corporations as well.

FACTS

RELEASE AND RESPONSE

Stamina Mills, Inc. was a textile manufacturing operation in North Smithfield, Rhode Island from approximately 1952 to 1975. The mill building had been on the site since some time in the last century. It is located on the north side of the Branch River. The Branch River flows west to east at the site. The company employed a soap scouring system to remove oil and dirt from newly-woven fabric. Because of complaints involving discharge into and pollution of the Branch River, Stamina Mills replaced the soap scouring system with one that used trichloroethylene ("TCE") in March 1969. Tanker trucks delivered the TCE which was pumped into a storage tank. During one delivery before November 1969, a mishap occurred; a tanker driver improperly attached a hosing coupling and spilled an indeterminate number of gallons of TCE. In addition to this accidental release of TCE, there is evidence that Stamina Mills would deposit used quantities of TCE bottoms in a landfill on its property. One witness, a Rhode Island Department of Health employee, testified that he saw a truck back up to the landfill and dump a purplish fluid with oily texture. The same witness also stated that the odor of TCE emanated from Stamina Mills' building.

In August 1979, ten years after Stamina Mills began to use TCE, the Rhode Island Department of Health conducted a survey of drinking water supplies in the Forestdale area, which is generally north and northwest of the Stamina property. The survey found that residential wells north of the Stamina Mills site had elevated levels of TCE. In September 1982, the Environmental Protection Agency ("EPA") completed a hydrogeological study of the area which concluded that the Stamina Mills site was a source of the contaminant. The study found a hydraulic connection between the Stamina Mills site and the residential wells. Although the flow of water through the bedrock aquifer was from north to south, normal pumping of the residential wells would reverse the flow. Consequently, the site was added to the National Priorities List the following September, making Superfund monies available for response actions. * * *

The EPA conducted remedial measures at both the Stamina Mills site and the residential wells. The parties have stipulated that the EPA incurred $660,612.71 in costs related to removal and enforcement activities. In addition, the parties have agreed that the Department of Justice (DOJ) spent $185,879.62 for enforcement activities. The record fails to reflect any distinction between costs related to "on-site" clean-up (at the Stamina Mills site) and "off-site" clean-up (at the residential wells).

CORPORATE RELATIONSHIPS

Stamina Mills, Inc. has expired. Its parent corporation, or more accurately, the parent's successor, remains in the form of the Kayser–Roth Corporation. Before Stamina Mills' dissolution, the two corporations shared a common history. * * * [In 1966, Kayser–Roth became the sole shareholder of Stamina Mills in a merger transaction by which Kayser–Roth acquired all the stock of Stamina Mills' parent. In the same transaction it also became the sole shareholder of Crown Mfg.] Kayser–Roth was therefore the owner of all the capital stock of both Crown Mfg. and Stamina Mills. Both subsidiaries, along with many other corporations, were part of Kayser–Roth's "Crown Division", a designation created for internal organization purposes only. Kayser–Roth remained the sole stockholder of Stamina Mills until its dissolution on December 31, 1977. Pursuant to the dissolution plan, Kayser–Roth received Stamina Mills' assets and assumed "all liabilities and obligations" of Stamina Mills.

As might well be expected, the two corporations shared common officers nominated and appointed by Kayser–Roth. * * * Moreover, and probably of greater significance, Kayser–Roth and Stamina Mills shared common directors, again nominated and appointed by Kayser–Roth, including Chester H. Roth, Alfred P. Slaner, Norman A. Jackson, Harold L. Glasser, David J. Roth, and James I. Spiegel. These individuals were officers of Kayser–Roth at the time they were also directors of Stamina Mills.

Kayser–Roth and its Crown Mfg. Division exerted practical total influence and control over Stamina Mills' operations. Kayser–Roth required Stamina Mills, after obtaining Crown Mfg. Division's approval, to obtain Kayser–Roth's approval in almost all its activities including purchase or movement of capital assets; leasing, buying, or selling real estate; borrowing money; and its budgets. The fiscal operations were completely in the control of Kayser–Roth including accounting supervision, payment of bills, collection of accounts receivable and executive compensation. Stamina Mills' officers did participate in union negotiations but this was simply a bargaining ploy since Kayser–Roth had to approve the ultimate collective bargaining agreement. Three former presidents of Stamina Mills each testified that they played little or no role in major decisions affecting Stamina Mills, except with respect to the local details of operating the factory. Kayser–Roth essentially was in charge in practically all of Stamina's operational decisions, including those involving environmental concerns. Kayser–Roth made the ultimate decision to acquire the dry cleaning process using TCE. Moreover, Kayser–Roth issued a directive requiring Stamina Mills to notify the Kayser–Roth Legal Department of any correspondence with courts or governmental agencies regarding environmental matters. The only autonomy given the officers of Stamina Mills was that absolutely necessary to operate the facility on-site from day to day such as hiring and firing hourly employees and ordering inventory. Stamina was in fact and effect the serf of Kayser–Roth.

LAW

CERCLA, enacted in 1980, allocates responsibility for the clean-up of releases and threatened releases of hazardous materials into the environment. 42 U.S.C. §§ 9601–9675.[12] A responsible party is strictly, jointly and severally liable for costs incurred for removal or remedial action as well as for damages for injury to or loss of natural resources. *Id.* at § 9607(a). Because CERCLA liability is strict, a party will be held responsible upon proof that: (1) a release or threat of a release of a hazardous substance occurred; (2) the government or other authorized party incurred response costs as a result of the release, and (3) the party falls into one of the four categories of responsible parties. *Id.* The four categories are: (1) the current owner or operator of the site; (2) any former owner or operator of the site at the time of the release or threatened release; (3) a transporter of hazardous materials which are released; and (4) a generator of hazardous waste. *Id.* The Government claims that Kayser–Roth and Crown Mfg. were owners and operators of Stamina Mills at the time of the TCE release.

CERCLA's definition of "owner or operator" is not especially illuminating. In terms of an expanded definition, it states that "in the

---

12. [By the Court] CERCLA as initially enacted encompassed 42 U.S.C. §§ 9601–9657. In 1986, the Superfund Amendments and Reauthorization Act (SARA) was passed, which provided additional funding and repealed certain sections while adding certain other sections. *See* 95 Pub.L. No. 99–499, 100 Stat. 1613 (1986). The statute, as amended, now comprises 42 U.S.C. §§ 9601–9675.

case of an onshore facility . . ., any person owning or operating such facility" qualifies as an owner or operator. 42 U.S.C. § 9601(20)(A)(ii). The term "person" expressly includes corporations. *Id.* at § 9601(21). CERCLA does provide that the term "owner or operator" does not include "a person, who, without participating in the management of a . . . facility, holds indicia of ownership primarily to protect his security interest in the . . . facility." *Id.* at 9601(20)(A). Courts have generally concluded that these provisions confer a subsidiary's liability upon its parent in two situations. The first occurs when the parent dominates the subsidiary to such an extent that the corporate form ought to be ignored and the corporate veil pierced. The second situation takes place where a stockowner participates directly in the management of a facility, although not to the extent that allows a piercing of the corporate veil.   *   *   *

LIABILITY WITHOUT PIERCING THE CORPORATE VEIL

A parent corporation that controls the management and operations of its wholly owned subsidiary can be held responsible for its subsidiary's CERCLA liability without piercing the corporate veil. *E.g., Idaho v. Bunker Hill Co.,* 635 F.Supp. 665, 671–72 (D.Idaho 1986). *Cf. New York v. Shore Realty Corp.,* 759 F.2d 1032, 1052 (2d Cir.1985) (individual stockholder liable as operator); *But see Joslyn Corp. v. T.L. James & Co.,* 696 F.Supp. 222, 224–25 (W.D.La.1988) (parent corporation cannot be held liable under CERCLA unless corporate veil is pierced). While courts have reached this conclusion by finding that the parent corporation was a de facto operator of the subsidiary, they have used two slightly different approaches.

One line of cases holds that a stockholder who manages the corporation may incur CERCLA operator liability. *E.g., Shore Realty,* 759 F.2d at 1052; *United States v. Northeastern Pharmaceutical and Chemical Co.,* 579 F.Supp. 823, 848 (W.D.Mo.1984), *aff'd,* 810 F.2d 726 (8th Cir.1986). These cases note that the definition of operator or owner excludes "a person, who without participating in the management of a . . . facility, holds indicia of ownership primarily to protect his securing interest in the . . . facility." 42 U.S.C. § 9601(20)(A). Reasoning that this exception implies that a person who holds indicia of a corporation's ownership and who participates in its management can be an owner or operator, the courts have concluded that stockholders participating in management can be liable. *Shore Realty,* 759 F.2d at 1052; *Northeastern Pharmaceutical,* 579 F.Supp. at 848.

Other cases support a second theory. A stockholder, parent corporation, or any person associated with a facility whether he or she has any ownership interest or not, may be held liable if that person (including a corporate entity) controls the management and operation of the polluting corporation. This approach focuses primarily on control.

Federal common law is emerging to determine whether a parent corporation, individual stockholder, or sister subsidiary for that matter, may be held directly liable as an operator. *See Northeastern Pharmaceutical*, 810 F.2d at 743–44 (individual stockholder); *Shore Realty*, 759 F.2d at 1052 (individual stockholder); *Vermont v. Staco, Inc.*, 684 F.Supp. 822, 831 (D.Vt.1988) (sister subsidiary); *Bunker Hill*, 635 F.Supp. at 672 (parent corporation). To be held directly liable as an operator, courts have considered a number of factors including: whether the person or corporation had the capacity to discover in a timely fashion the release or threat of release of hazardous substances; whether the person or corporation had the power to direct the mechanisms causing the release; and whether the person or corporation had the capacity to prevent and abate damages. * * *

PARENT LIABILITY: PARENT AS OPERATOR

* * * The evidence establishes that Kayser–Roth was indeed an operator for purposes of CERCLA. Kayser–Roth exercised pervasive control over Stamina Mills through, among other things: 1) its total monetary control including collection of accounts payable; 2) its restrictions on Stamina Mills' financial budget; 3) its directive that subsidiary-governmental contact, including environmental matters, be funneled directly through Kayser–Roth; 4) its requirement that Stamina Mills' leasing, buying or selling of real estate first be approved by Kayser–Roth; 5) its policy that Kayser–Roth approve any capital transfer or expenditures greater than $5,000; and finally, 6) its placement of Kayser–Roth personnel in almost all Stamina Mills' director and officer positions, as a means of totally ensuring that Kayser–Roth corporate policy was exactly implemented and precisely carried out. These are only examples of Kayser–Roth's practical total control over Stamina Mills' operations.

Illustrative of Kayser–Roth's control are its actions with regard to environmental matters affecting Stamina Mills. Kayser–Roth had the power to control the release or threat of release of TCE, had the power to direct the mechanisms causing the release, and had the ultimate ability to prevent and abate damage. Kayser–Roth knew that Stamina Mills employed a scouring system that used TCE; indeed, Kayser–Roth approved the installation of that system after mandating that a cost-benefit study be made by Stamina Mills. Kayser–Roth not only had the capacity to determine the use of TCE but also was able to direct Stamina Mills on how the TCE should have been handled.[13] There are other examples of Kayser–Roth's participation in Stamina Mills' environmental decision-making. Evidence was introduced that Kayser–Roth issued a directive to its subsidiaries, including Stamina Mills, requiring that Kayser–Roth's Legal Department be notified of any governmental agency or court contact regarding environmental matters. Furthermore, when Stamina Mills was sued in 1974 by the United States for an illegal waste water discharge into the Branch

---

13. [By the Court] Actual knowledge of the release is not required for CERCLA liability; CERCLA is a strict liability scheme. *O'Neil v. Picillo*, 883 F.2d at 182 n. 9.

River, the final decision on settlement was made by Kayser–Roth's directors.

Although not singularly determinative on the issue of operator liability, these factors along with Kayser–Roth's other acts of pervasive control over Stamina Mills, warrant a finding that Kayser–Roth was an "operator" for CERCLA purposes within the provisions of 42 U.S.C. § 9607(a).

PARENT LIABILITY: PIERCING THE CORPORATE VEIL

CERCLA liability based upon piercing the corporate veil is a species of owner, rather than operator, liability. While an owner may be, in most cases, an operator, the converse is not necessarily true. Imputing CERCLA liability upon a parent corporation by piercing the corporate veil is, in essence, concluding that the parent is an owner for CERCLA's purposes. " 'The effect of piercing a corporate veil is to hold *the owner* . . . liable. The rationale for piercing the corporate veil is that the corporation is something less than a bona fide independent entity.' " *Northeastern Pharmaceutical,* 810 F.2d at 744 (quoting *Donsco, Inc. v. Casper Corp.,* 587 F.2d 602, 606 (3d Cir.1978)) (emphasis added). [The court preliminarily concludes that federal rather than state law controls the piercing of the corporate veil in CERCLA cases. The court notes, however, that "this federal common law borrows heavily from state law," and that the "considerations do not radically differ from Rhode Island law."] Upon analysis of the factors relevant to piercing Stamina Mills' veil, and mindful of the liberal construction CERCLA must be afforded so as not to frustrate probable legislative intent, the Court concludes that Kayser–Roth is an owner for CERCLA's purposes. * * *

Kayser–Roth has exhibited overwhelming pervasive control over Stamina Mills. Many of the same factors used in holding Kayser–Roth liable as an operator are relevant. Kayser–Roth's control over environmental matters; its policy of approving all capital expenditures of greater than $5,000; its stranglehold on income and expenses; its practice of placing Kayser–Roth personnel in Stamina Mills' director positions, thereby precluding other Stamina Mills executives from significant daily decision-making; and its overwhelming control over Stamina Mills' financial and operational structure add flesh to the skeletal proposition that Kayser–Roth's corporate existence should be disregarded.[14] Accordingly, Stamina Mills' veil should be pierced to hold Kayser–Roth liable, not only because public convenience, fairness, and equity dictate such a result, but also due to the all encompassing control which Kayser–Roth had over Stamina Mills as, in fact and deed, an owner. Any other result would provide too much solace to deliberate polluters, who would use this device as an escape. * * *

14. [By the Court] One version of the "Golden Rule" is that he who has the Gold rules. The circumstances comport completely with this version of the "Golden Rule."

Accordingly, Kayser–Roth is found liable for $846,492.33. In addition, the Government shall within 10 days prepare and present a form of declaratory judgment holding Kayser–Roth liable for future response costs related to on-site and off-site clean-up.

SO ORDERED.

Notes

(1) Given the definition of "operator" in CERCLA, is there any need to get into the piercing the corporate veil issue?

(2) Should the issue of Kayser–Roth's liability for the cost of the clean-up of the site be based on the law of parent-subsidiary obligations on contracts entered by the subsidiary? On torts committed by the subsidiary? Or is this a *sui generis* issue of parent liability?

PEPPER v. LITTON
Supreme Court of the United States, 1939.
308 U.S. 295, 60 S.Ct. 238, 84 L.Ed. 281.

[Editor: Pepper sued the Dixie Splint Coal Company for an accounting of royalties due Pepper under a lease. While this case was pending, Litton, the sole shareholder of Dixie Splint, caused Dixie Splint to confess a judgment in favor of Litton based on alleged claims for back salary. After Pepper obtained a judgment, Litton caused execution to be issued on his judgment; Litton purchased the corporate assets at the resulting sale, and then caused Dixie Splint to file a voluntary petition in bankruptcy. The trustee in bankruptcy brought suit in state court to have the judgment obtained by Litton set aside and the execution sale quashed; the trustee lost. Smith v. Litton, 167 Va. 263, 188 S.E. 214 (1936). Litton then filed a claim in the bankruptcy court based on the portion of the judgment not satisfied by the proceeds of the execution sale. The District Court disallowed Litton's claim in its entirety and directed that the trustee should recover for the benefit of the bankrupt's estate the property purchased by Litton at the execution sale. The Court of Appeals reversed on the ground that the state court decision was res judicata.]

MR. JUSTICE DOUGLAS, delivered the opinion of the Court.

This case presents the question of the power of the bankruptcy court to disallow either as a secured or as a general or unsecured claim a judgment obtained by the dominant and controlling stockholder of the bankrupt corporation on alleged salary claims. * * *

The findings of the District Court, amply supported by the evidence, reveal a scheme to defraud creditors reminiscent of some of the evils with which 13 Eliz. c. 5 was designed to cope. But for the use of a so-called "one-man" or family corporation, Dixie Splint Coal Company, of which respondent was the dominant and controlling stockholder, that scheme followed an ancient pattern. * * *

In the first place, res judicata did not prevent the District Court from examining into the Litton judgment and disallowing or subordinating it as a claim. * * *

In the second place, even though we assume that the alleged salary claim on which the Litton judgment was based was not fictitious but actually existed, we are of the opinion that the District Court properly disallowed or subordinated it.

Courts of bankruptcy are constituted by §§ 1 and 2 of the bankruptcy act, 30 Stat. 544, 11 U.S.C.A. §§ 1(8), 11, and by the latter section are invested "with such jurisdiction at law and in equity as will enable them to exercise original jurisdiction in bankruptcy proceedings." Consequently this Court has held that for many purposes "courts of bankruptcy are essentially courts of equity, and their proceedings inherently proceedings in equity". Local Loan Co. v. Hunt, 292 U.S. 234, 240, 54 S.Ct. 695, 697, 78 L.Ed. 1230, 93 A.L.R. 195. * * *

That equitable power also exists in passing on claims presented by an officer, director, or stockholder in the bankruptcy proceedings of his corporation. The mere fact that an officer, director, or stockholder has a claim against his bankrupt corporation or that he has reduced that claim to judgment does not mean that the bankruptcy court must accord it pari passu treatment with the claims of other creditors. Its disallowance or subordination may be necessitated by certain cardinal principles of equity jurisprudence. A director is a fiduciary. Twin–Lick Oil Company v. Marbury, 91 U.S. 587, 588, 23 L.Ed. 328. So is a dominant or controlling stockholder or group of stockholders. Southern Pacific Company v. Bogert, 250 U.S. 483, 492, 39 S.Ct. 533, 537, 63 L.Ed. 1099. Their powers are powers in trust. See Jackson v. Ludeling, 21 Wall. 616, 624, 22 L.Ed. 492. Their dealings with the corporation are subjected to rigorous scrutiny and where any of their contracts or engagements with the corporation is challenged the burden is on the director or stockholder not only to prove the good faith of the transaction but also to show its inherent fairness from the viewpoint of the corporation and those interested therein. Geddes v. Anaconda Copper Mining Company, 254 U.S. 590, 599, 41 S.Ct. 209, 212, 65 L.Ed. 425. The essence of the test is whether or not under all the circumstances the transaction carries the earmarks of an arm's length bargain. If it does not, equity will set it aside. While normally that fiduciary obligation is enforceable directly by the corporation, or through a stockholder's derivative action, it is, in the event of bankruptcy of the corporation, enforceable by the trustee. For that standard of fiduciary obligation is designed for the protection of the entire community of interests in the corporation—creditors as well as stockholders.

As we have said, the bankruptcy court in passing on allowance of claims sits as a court of equity. Hence these rules governing the fiduciary responsibilities of directors and stockholders come into play on allowance of their claims in bankruptcy. [I]n the exercise of its equitable jurisdiction the bankruptcy court has the power to sift the circumstances surrounding any claim to see that injustice or unfairness is not done in administration of the bankrupt estate. And its duty so to do is especially clear when the claim seeking allowance accrues to the benefit of an officer, director, or stockholder. That is clearly the power and duty of the bankruptcy courts under the reorganization sections. In Taylor v. Standard Gas & Electric Co., 306 U.S. 307, 59 S.Ct. 543, 83 L.Ed. 669, this Court held that the claim of Standard against its subsidiary (admittedly a claim due and owing) should be allowed to participate in the reorganization plan of the subsidiary only in subordination to the preferred stock of the subsidiary. This was based on the equities of the case—the history of spoliation, mismanagement, and faithless stewardship of the affairs of the subsidiary by Standard to the detriment of the public investors. Similar results have properly been reached in ordinary bankruptcy proceedings. Thus, salary claims of officers, directors, and stockholders in the bankruptcy of "one-man" or family corporations have been disallowed or subordinated where the courts have been satisfied that allowance of the claims would not be fair or equitable to other creditors. And that result may be reached even though the salary claim has been reduced to judgment. It is reached where the claim asserted is void or voidable because the vote of the interested director or stockholder helped bring it into being or where the history of the corporation shows dominancy and exploitation on the part of the claimant. It is also reached where on the facts the bankrupt has been used merely as a corporate pocket of the dominant stockholder, who, with disregard of the substance or form of corporate management, has treated its affairs as his own. And so-called loans or advances by the dominant or controlling stockholder will be subordinated to claims of other creditors and thus treated in effect as capital contributions by the stockholder not only in the foregoing types of situations but also where the paid-in capital is purely nominal, the capital necessary for the scope and magnitude of the operations of the company being furnished by the stockholder as a loan.

Though disallowance of such claims will be ordered where they are fictitious or a sham, these cases do not turn on the existence or nonexistence of the debt. Rather they involve simply the question of order of payment. At times equity has ordered disallowance or subordination by disregarding the corporate entity. That is to say, it has treated the debtor-corporation simply as a part of the stockholder's own enterprise, consistently with the course of conduct of the stockholder. But in that situation as well as in the others to which we have referred, a sufficient consideration may be simply the violation of rules of fair play and good conscience by the claimant; a breach of the fiduciary standards of conduct which he owes the corporation, its stockholders and creditors. * * *

On such a test the action of the District Court in disallowing or subordinating Litton's claim was clearly correct. Litton allowed his salary claims to lie dormant for years and sought to enforce them only when his debtor corporation was in financial difficulty. Then he used them so that the rights of another creditor were impaired. Litton as an insider utilized his strategic position for his own preferment to the damage of Pepper. Litton as the dominant influence over Dixie Splint Coal Company used his power not to deal fairly with the creditors of that company but to manipulate its affairs in such a manner that when one of its creditors came to collect her just debt the bulk of the assets had disappeared into another Litton company. Litton, though a fiduciary, was enabled by astute legal manoeuvering to acquire most of the assets of the bankrupt not for cash or other consideration of value to creditors but for bookkeeping entries representing at best merely Litton's appraisal of the worth of Litton's services over the years.

This alone would be a sufficient basis for the exercise by the District Court of its equitable powers in disallowing the Litton claim. But when there is added the existence of a "planned and fraudulent scheme", as found by the District Court, the necessity of equitable relief against that fraud becomes insistent. No matter how technically legal each step in that scheme may have been, once its basic nature was uncovered it was the duty of the bankruptcy court in the exercise of its equity jurisdiction to undo it. Otherwise, the fiduciary duties of dominant or management stockholders would go for naught; exploitation would become a substitute for justice; and equity would be perverted as an instrument for approving what it was designed to thwart. * * *

In view of these considerations we do not have occasion to determine the legitimacy of the "one-man" corporation as a bulwark against the claims of creditors.[15]

Accordingly the judgment of the Circuit Court of Appeals is reversed and that of the District Court is affirmed.

Reversed.

Notes

(1) The doctrine applied in Pepper v. Litton is usually referred to as the "Deep Rock" doctrine, after the name of the corporation involved in Taylor v. Standard Gas & Electric Co., discussed in Pepper v. Litton. Could the court have "pierced the corporate veil" of Dixie Splint Coal Co. and avoided Litton's claim on the theory that one cannot owe a debt to oneself? If the latter approach had been followed, Litton may have been personally liable for all of Dixie Splint's debts. What tests should the court use in determining which approach to follow? Is it simply a matter of relative

15. [By the Court] On this point the District Court said: "An examination of the facts disclosed here shows the history of a deliberate and carefully planned attempt on the part of Scott Litton and Dixie Splint Coal Company to avoid the payment of a just debt. I speak of Litton and Dixie Splint Coal Company because they are in reality the same. In all the experience of the law, there has never been a more prolific breeder of fraud than the one-man corporation. It is a favorite device for the escape of personal liability. This case illustrates another frequent use of this fiction of corporate entity, whereby the owner of the corporation, through his complete control over it, undertakes to gather to himself all of its assets to the exclusion of its creditors."

(and subjective) degrees of bad faith or improper conduct? The absence of reasonably objective tests in this area has led to considerable confusion and some inconsistency in result.

(2) Section 510(c) of the Bankruptcy Act of 1978, 11 U.S.C.A. § 510(c), provides that " * * * after notice and hearing the court may * * * under principles of equitable subordination, subordinate for purposes of distribution all or part of an allowed claim to all or part of another allowed claim or all or part of an allowed interest to all or part of another allowed interest * * *." H.R.Rep. 595 (95th Cong. 1st Sess.), 359 states that "this section [was] intended to codify case law, such as Pepper v. Litton, * * *."

(3) Obligations running from a corporation to a controlling shareholder may arise in several different ways. For example, a shareholder may desire to put in a portion of his initial capital contribution in the form of debt to minimize the double taxation problem. How should such debt be treated in bankruptcy? See Arnold v. Phillips, 117 F.2d 497 (5th Cir.1941); Small v. Williams, 313 F.2d 39 (4th Cir.1963). Or, a shareholder may take preferred stock or debt in order to equalize the distribution of voting power and the original contributions of the shareholders. How should such debt be treated in bankruptcy? See Obre v. Alban Tractor Co., 228 Md. 291, 179 A.2d 861 (1962). Or, a shareholder may lend his corporation money in an unsuccessful attempt to save it from financial disaster. How should such debt be treated in bankruptcy? See Arnold v. Phillips, supra, at 501–502:

> The two series of advances differ materially as respects their nature and purpose. Those made before the enterprise was launched were, as the district court found, really capital. Although the charter provided for no more capital than 50,000, what it took to build the plant and equip it was a permanent investment, in its nature capital. There was no security asked or given. Arnold saw that he could not proceed with his enterprise unless he enlarged the capital. There can be little doubt that what he contributed to the plant was actually intended to be capital, notwithstanding the charter was not amended and demand notes were taken. The district court was justified in concluding as a matter of fact that the advances during the first year were capital, a sort of interest-bearing redeemable stock; and that as a matter of law these contributions could not, as against corporate creditors, either precedent or subsequent, be turned into secured debts by afterwards taking and recording a trust deed to secure them. There was no debt to be secured.

> After two years of prosperity, with the original capital thus enlarged demonstrated to be sufficient, with a book surplus of nearly $100,000 after payment of large salaries and dividends in the form of interest, there arose a situation very different from that in the beginning. Adversity then occurring raised a problem not different from that which commonly faces a corporation having losses. It may borrow to meet its needs. Had this corporation borrowed of a bank upon the security of the plant, the debt would no doubt be valid. What would render it invalid when Arnold furnished the money? As to each of these later advances, it is testified without contradiction that it was made after consultation with Otto, the Secretary and Treasurer, and

on the security of the deed of trust. The money went to relieve the needs of the business exactly as it would have done if a bank had advanced it. No other creditor was prejudiced or misled. There are no circumstances which discredit the testimony. They were truly loans and not new capital. With additional clearness all this is true as to the advances made after May 4, 1938, when Arnold was no longer a stockholder or officer at all.

Chapter Seven

FINANCIAL MATTERS AND THE CLOSELY HELD CORPORATION

A. THE SOURCES OF CAPITAL FOR THE CLOSELY HELD BUSINESS

R. HAMILTON, FUNDAMENTALS OF MODERN BUSINESS

Pp. 325, 330–335 (1989).

Most newly formed and ultimately successful businesses go through several different stages of development. The financing * * * needs of the business vary significantly depending on the stage of development. Obviously not all businesses go through each of these stages, but they are sufficiently typical to justify discussion. The three stages discussed here may be described as the start-up stage, the established business stage, and the publicly held stage. * * *

There are [three principal] * * * sources of financing for a start-up business.

1. The entrepreneur may use his or her personal funds to finance the business. This may involve prior savings or current earnings from unrelated employment or activity to finance the new business. It is not uncommon for an entrepreneur to invest all available family funds in the new business: savings set aside for a rainy day, for medical expenses, for education of small children, for vacations, for the purchase of a new home, and for what-have-you. Where the business ultimately succeeds, this strategy usually maximizes the value of the business to the entrepreneur. However, where it does not, the entrepreneur's personal and family financial picture will certainly be adversely affected to some extent, and may be devastated.

Modern portfolio theory recommends that investments generally should be diversified. The owner of a typical start-up business rarely is in a position to diversify investments—indeed, the investment of all

available funds in the new business is the opposite of diversification.
* * *

2.   A second major source of financing for a start-up business is capital borrowed by the entrepreneur from commercial sources.   The entrepreneur may be able to borrow funds on the basis of a signature loan from a bank or commercial lending agency.   More likely, security will have to be given for such a loan, perhaps a second mortgage on the family residence.   The cash surrender value of ordinary life insurance policies may be borrowed to invest in the new business.   Some start-up entrepreneurs rely on personal credit cards to obtain additional loan funds at interest rates in excess of 18 percent per year.   Such an entrepreneur may have eight or ten bank credit cards each with an independent line of credit that in the aggregate may provide borrowing power in excess of $25,000 in a single month.   * * *

Once the business is underway, a fair amount of credit can usually be raised through anticipation of the receipts of the business itself. Inventory may be purchased on credit to be repaid (hopefully) out of the sale of the inventory.   Accounts receivable may be assigned as security for a continuing loan arrangement.   Of course, the entrepreneur is usually personally liable on this debt, but the issue under discussion here is not what happens if the business fails, but how the business is to get the capital desperately needed for it to stay in business.

Since the liquid assets of the entrepreneur are often limited, most of the capital of the start up business may be in the form of debt.   Most of this debt is short-term, carrying relatively high interest rates and short repayment dates.   The business must generate a sufficient cash flow to service this debt which may be a major obstacle to future growth, though if the business appears to be a success the debt may usually be rolled over by borrowing new debt to pay off the old when it matures.

3.   The third major source of financing for a start-up business is from relatives, friends, and acquaintances.   Sometimes individuals involved with the business as satisfied customers, suppliers, or employees may express an interest in investing in, or be prevailed upon to invest in, the business.   The major problem with this type of financing is apt to be uncertainty as to the precise legal relationship between the provider of the capital and the proprietorship.   When nonrelatives invest in a business, they usually intend to purchase an interest in the ownership of the business and not simply make a loan to a business. The entrepreneur, on the other hand, is not happy at the idea of giving up a part of his or her business.   Since these arrangements are often informal, entered into without the advice of a lawyer, there may be no definitive resolution of the underlying disagreement as to whether the transaction is a loan or a purchase of an interest in the business. Where a definitive understanding is reached that the investment in-

volves an equity interest,[1] the entrepreneur should normally insist on a provision that permits the reacquisition on a reasonable basis of that interest if there is a disagreement as to goals or policy. Otherwise, the entrepreneur may find it necessary to pay a premium price (largely caused by the entrepreneur's efforts) to reacquire the equity interests granted at an earlier time.

Much the same uncertainty may exist as to funds supplied by relatives, though it is more likely that an indefinite loan, or even an outright gift, was intended than is the case with capital provided by nonrelatives. In this context, an indefinite loan is one in which there are not definite terms of repayment: Typically there is a vague understanding that the loan is to be repaid when the business is able to do so.

*   *   *

An established [closely held] business has sources of debt and equity financing not available to a start-up business. Because it has a credit history and a credit rating, it usually may borrow funds on its own credit without involving the shareholders. In addition, new sources of debt and equity capital may be open to the business with an established track record.

1. *Internally generated funds.* A successful and established business has the capacity of generating significant amounts of funds internally. Earnings may be set aside and accumulated over a period of several years to finance expansion or the development of new manufacturing facilities. However, a significant positive cash flow may be generated even without substantial earnings if the corporation claims accelerated depreciation or other deductions that do not require cash outlays. Internally generated funds represent equity capital.

2. *Lines of credit.* An established business may create lines of credit at one or more commercial banks that provide access to working capital as needed for the day-to-day activities of the business. Lines of credit are established in advance, up to specific maxima, and may be drawn upon simply by writing checks. Interest is payable only on funds actually drawn upon. Similarly, an established business may enter into regular inventory financing plans, assignments of accounts receivable, and the like, which permit the business access to cash immediately rather than tying up working capital in accounts receivable and inventory.

3. *Government assistance or government guaranteed loans.*

*   *   *

4. *Venture capital funds.* An important source of capital for developing businesses that have economic promise are venture capital funds. These funds pool equity or risk capital from a variety of sources in order to provide capital to promising small businesses. These funds

---

1. [By the Editor] "Equity" in this context is synonymous with "ownership:" the market value of a piece of property minus liabilities attached to the property equals the "owner's equity" in the property. In this context, "equity" has nothing to do with its historical or traditional legal meaning.

actively seek out promising businesses in which to make substantial equity/debt investments. For many businesses struggling to develop sufficient capital resources to expand, joint venture funds are the answer, since the relationship is a continuing one, and the joint venture fund may provide additional capital at a later date. The cost of this type of financing is not cheap, however. * * *

5. *Private placements of debt.* Well-established businesses may be able to borrow large amounts of funds from a small number of institutional investors such as insurance companies, pension funds, and similar organizations. These loans are usually secured by liens on real estate or substantial machinery or equipment, or on all of the assets of the corporation. They are known as private placements since they are effected without registration of the securities for public sale under the Securities Act of 1933 or state blue sky laws. These loans may be for very long terms: They may provide for adjustments in interest rates based on market rates or permit the institutional investor to convert into an equity position if the business goes public.

A company that is sufficiently established to raise funds through a private placement is unlikely to be interested in dealing with venture capital funds, since such funds usually insist on receiving a major portion of the company's equity as the price for providing capital.

6. *Private sales of equity interests.* An established company may raise equity capital by sales of common stock to a limited group of investors. However, direct sales of corporate shares to investors located by officers or directors of the corporation may be inefficient and distracting: The loss of executive time and attention from the business must be factored in. Further, such attempts run a significant risk of inadvertant violations of federal or state securities laws. As in the case of private debt placements, such sales must be carefully structured to avoid registration under the Securities Act of 1933 and state blue sky laws. * * *

7. *Registered public offerings of equity securities.* An established business may consider going public to raise capital by selling equity securities to members of the general public. This is a serious and substantial step that should be taken only after careful consideration.
* * *

B. TYPES OF EQUITY SECURITIES

There is a recognized nomenclature for equity securities issued by corporations. The following brief discussion is essential background for those unfamiliar with this nomenclature; it also illustrates that while the language is sometimes arcane, the underlying ideas are not complicated.

It is helpful to begin with the concept of common shares or common stock. Most corporation statutes do not attempt to define this basic concept. The Revised Model Business Corporation Act defines "shares" to be "the units into which the proprietary interests in a corporation are divided," RMBCA § 1.40(21), but does not expressly define "common shares." The RMBCA does indirectly identify, however, two fundamental characteristics of common shares in §§ 6.01(b) and 6.03(c):

> (1) They are entitled to vote for the election of directors and on other matters coming before the shareholders, and

> (2) They are entitled to the net assets of the corporation (after making allowance for debts), when distributions are made in the form of dividends or liquidating distributions.

RMBCA § 6.01(b) permits these essential attributes of common shares to be placed in different classes of shares, but requires that one or more classes with these attributes must always be authorized. Section 6.03(c) adds that at least one share of each class with each of these basic attributes must always be outstanding. The reasons for these abstruse provisions are described below.

"Common shares" may be defined in other ways as well. The United States Supreme Court identified the characteristics usually associated with common stock as (i) the right to receive dividends contingent upon an apportionment of profits, (ii) negotiability, (iii) the ability to be pledged or hypothecated, (iv) the conferring of voting rights in proportion to the number of shares owned, and (v) the capacity to increase in value. United Housing Foundation, Inc. v. Forman, 421 U.S. 837, 95 S.Ct. 2051, 44 L.Ed.2d 621 (1975). This definition was set forth in a case involving the issue whether a "share of stock" that 'entitled the owner to lease an apartment in a housing cooperative was a "security"; housing cooperative shares possess virtually none of the enumerated characteristics.

Whatever the niceties of definition, common shares are usually viewed as representing the residual ownership interest in the corporation. The financial interests of common shares in the corporation are open-ended in the sense that as the business prospers and the corporate assets increase, the additional assets are allocable to the holders of the common shares, and those shares should increase in value. Dividend payments to common shareholders, however, are within the discretion of the board of directors. Whether a dividend should be paid, and if so, how much, are issues within the business judgment of directors, and shareholders typically have no legal basis for complaint if dividends on the common shares are omitted over extended periods of time. Holders of common shares have other rights as well: a right to inspect books and records (see RMBCA § 16.02), a right to sue on behalf of the corporation to right a wrong committed against it (see RMBCA § 7.40–7.47), a right to financial information (see RMBCA § 16.20), and so forth. But the fundamental rights of the common shareholders, as the residual owners, appear to be those identified in sections 6.01(b) and 6.03(c): the right to vote and the right to receive excess assets, either during the life of the corporation or upon its dissolution.

Where a corporation has only one class of shares outstanding, that class obviously has the voting and distributional rights described above. They are common shares, even though they may be described in the articles of incorporation as "capital stock" or simply "stock" or "shares." The RMBCA (as did earlier versions of the Model Act) consistently uses the word "shares" rather than "stock" in describing equity security interests, but the Official Comment to section 6.01 points out that "no specific designation is required by the Model Act."

Many corporations begin their life with only a modest amount of capital raised by the sale of stock. As noted earlier, the statutes in some states prescribe a minimum initial capitalization—often $1,000. The Model Act contained such a requirement until 1969 when it was eliminated on the grounds "that the protection sought to be achieved was illusory and that the provision served no useful purpose." 2 Mod. Bus.Corp.Act Ann.2d § 56, ¶ 2. The RMBCA does not contain a minimum capital requirement.

Under § 2.02(a)(2) of the RMBCA the articles of incorporation must set forth "the number of shares the corporation is authorized to issue." This provision is incomplete, however, since section 6.01(a) provides that, if more than one class of shares is authorized, the articles of incorporation must prescribe "the classes of shares and the number of shares of each class" that the corporation is authorized to issue; in addition the articles of incorporation "must prescribe a distinguishing designation for each class, and, prior to the issuance of shares of a class, the preferences, limitations, and relative rights of that class must be described" in the articles of incorporation. If only one class of shares is authorized, it is not necessary to say anything about what the rights of that class are.

What other types of shares might a corporation wish to issue? The traditional distinction is between common shares on the one hand and "preferred" shares on the other. "Preferred" means that the shares are entitled to a preference or priority in payment as against the holders of common shares. This priority may be either in the payment of dividends or the making of distributions in liquidation of a corporation, or very commonly, in both. A "priority" or "preference" simply means that the preferred shares are entitled to a specified distribution before anything can be paid on the common shares. For example, if a class of preferred shares is entitled to a dividend preference of $5 per year, that means only that nothing can be paid to the holders of common shares until the preferred is first paid its $5 per share. Preferred shares are often described by reference to the amount of their dividend preference, or by the percentage such preference bears to the stock's par or stated value. Thus, a "$5.00 preferred" has a dividend preference of $5.00 per year, while a "5% preferred" has a dividend preference equal to five per cent of the share's par value.

The precise scope of the rights of a preferred shareholder is traditionally established by the detailed provisions in the articles of incorporation creating that class of shares. These provisions are usually called the "preferred shareholder's contract", and may not be amended without the consent of some statutorily designated fraction of the preferred shareholders themselves. Rights and privileges usually given to publicly traded preferred shares include the following:

The dividend preference of preferred shares may be cumulative, noncumulative, or partially cumulative. A cumulative dividend simply means that if the dividend is not paid in any year it accumulates and must be paid (along with the following years' unpaid cumulative dividends) before any dividend may be paid on the common in a later year. A noncumulative dividend, if not paid in any year, simply disappears and the following year is a new ball game. A partially cumulative dividend typically is cumulative to the extent there are earnings in the year, and noncumulative with respect to any excess dividend preference. Unpaid cumulative dividends are not debts of the corporation, but a right of priority in future distributions. Unlike interest on a debt, dividends on preferred shares may be paid only from funds that are legally available for the payment of dividends. Many state statutes, however, liberally permit the payment of cumulative preferred dividends from various capital accounts. Typically, publicly traded preferred shares have cumulative dividend rights.

Preferred shares are usually nonvoting shares (though many exceptions exist, particularly in closely held corporations). In order to provide some protection for preferred shareholders, it is customary to provide that nonvoting preferred shares obtain a right to vote for the election of a specified number of directors if preferred dividends have been omitted for a specified period.

Preferred shares usually have a liquidation preference as well as a dividend preference. The liquidation preference is often fixed at a specified price per share, payable upon the dissolution of the corporation before anything may be paid to the common shares. Like preferred dividends, a liquidation preference is not a debt but a claim to priority if funds are available. The amount of the liquidation preference is usually a fixed amount, so that the preferred does not share in any general appreciation in value of the corporation's assets.

Preferred shares may be made redeemable at the option of the corporation at a price fixed by the articles of incorporation. Typically, the redemption price is set somewhat in excess of the amount of the share's liquidation preference. For example, preferred shares which are entitled to receive $100.00 per share on liquidation may be made redeemable at any time for $105.00.

Preferred shares may be made convertible at the option of the holder into common shares at a fixed ratio specified in the articles of incorporation; convertible preferred is attractive when the common shares are publicly traded, so that an active market exists for the conversion securities. A conversion privilege allows the holders of the preferred shares to obtain a part of the long term appreciation of the corporation's assets if the holders are willing to give up their preferred rights by converting their shares into common shares. Typically, the conversion ratio is established so that the common must appreciate substantially in price before it is profitable to convert the preferred. When the price of the common rises above this level, the preferred shares fluctuate in price with the common. Convertible shares are also usually redeemable, but typically the privilege to convert continues for a limited period of time after the call for redemption. A conversion is described as "forced" when shares are called for redemption at a time when the market value of the shares obtainable on conversion exceeds the redemption price.

Preferred shares may also have certain financial protections, such as sinking fund provisions, which require the corporation to set aside a certain amount each year to redeem a specified portion of the preferred stock issue. In addition, convertible preferred usually contain elaborate provisions protecting the conversion privilege from dilution in case of share dividends, share splits, or the issuance of additional common shares.

The preferred shares described above are non-participating. Non-participating shares are entitled to the specified dividend payment and the specified liquidation preference, and nothing more no matter how profitable the corporation. "Participating preferred" shares are entitled to the specified dividend, and after the common shares receive a specified amount, they may share with the common in any additional distributions. Such shares combine some of the features of common and preferred. They are sometimes referred to as "Class A common" or by a similar designation that shows that their right to participate is open-ended and therefore that they have one of the major attributes of common shares. Preferred shares that are participating in dividend distributions usually have liquidation preferences that are tied in some way to the amounts receivable by the common shares on liquidation.

A corporation may issue different classes of preferred shares. A corporation, for example, may issue "Class A preferred" and "Class B preferred" with different dividend rates, different rights on dissolution, and different priorities. The Class A preferred may be junior to the Class B in terms of priorities or it may be superior to or on a parity with the Class B. Both are "senior" securities, however, because both have preferential rights over common shares.

RMBCA § 6.02(a)(2) refers to "one or more series within a class." The concept of a "series" arose because of problems of raising substantial amounts of capital over periods of time through the issuance of preferred shares. In preferred share financing it is often advantageous to tailor the price, dividend, and other terms of the issue to the market conditions current at the time of issue. It was inconvenient and expensive to amend the articles of incorporation to create a new class of preferred shares whenever a new issue was to be sold; as a result, a number of states authorized the creation of a "class" of preferred shares that contained no financial terms but authorized the board of directors to carve out different "series" of shares from within the class, and designate the financial terms of each series when it was issued. Preferred shares for which the board of directors is authorized to establish terms are often called "blank shares." RMBCA § 6.02 is a somewhat broader "blank shares" provision since it authorizes the board to establish "classes" as well as "series." In practice, however, there is usually no economic difference between a "class" of preferred shares and a "series within a class" of preferred shares: both have unique financial terms, but all shares within the "class" or "series" have identical preferences, limitations and relative rights [see RMBCA § 6.02(c)]. As noted in the Official Comment to RMBCA § 6.02, the labels "class" and "series" are "often a matter of convenience"; it does not seem sensible to limit the power of directors merely because of historical nomenclature.

The terms of one or more "series" may also be specified in the articles of incorporation if that is desired. However, the term "series" is still most widely used in connection with preferred shares, the financial terms of which may be established by the board of directors following procedures similar to those set forth in RMBCA § 6.02.

Section 6.01 of the RMBCA, like all state statutes, also authorize the creation of classes of common shares by appropriate provision in the articles of incorporation; such classes may vary in terms of management, financial or voting rights. For example, classes of non-voting common shares, classes with multiple or fractional votes per share, classes entitled to twice the dividend of another class, classes entitled to a preference or priority in distributions to another class, classes entitled to elect a specified number of directors, are all permissible. Different classes of common shares are also often designated by alphabetical reference, e.g. "Class A common shares," or sometimes by description, e.g. "nonvoting common stock." Classes of common shares are widely used as planning devices in closely held corporations (as are classes of preferred stock).

From the foregoing description, it should be clear that the precise line between "preferred" and "common" shares, at the margin at least, was always a shadowy one. There might be little or no difference, for example, between a "participating preferred" and a "class A common" except the title. Developments during the 1970s and early 1980s also tended to blur this distinction (as well as the distinction between "debt securities" and preferred shares). Extremely high interest rates during this period led to the development of novel financing devices. This period, for example, saw the development of "flexible rate" preferred, where the dividend was tied to interest rates or some other objective criteria, or left discretionary with the board of directors. It also saw the development of preferred shares redeemable at the option of the holder, a security that has some characteristics of demand indebtedness.

Faced with these developments, the drafters of the Revised Model Business Corporation Act, in § 6.01, made a significant philosophical break with the past by studiously avoiding the words "preferred shares" and "common shares", and by establishing a scheme of consummate generality designed to accommodate the most innovative and ingenious creator of new classes or types of shares.

When considering classes of debt or equity securities, not too much weight should be given to the name. A class may be described as a "senior preferred" and yet be subordinate to virtually all other classes of shares with much more modest titles. Modern equity and debt issues often have unique or fanciful names, such as "senior reset preferred stock" or "preferred equity redemption cumulative stock" ("PERCS") that give little or no clue as to either the nature of the securities involved or their investment quality.

Notes

(1) May a corporation create a class of preferred shares that is redeemable at the option of the holder? Such shares have some of the characteristics of a demand note, and have been widely used as a financing device during the 1980s. They are not (or arguably may not be) permitted by the statutes of some states.

(2) What about creating common shares that are redeemable at the option of the holder? Is there any possible evil that might arise from such shares? Some states also prohibit this kind of security, except in specified limited circumstances. One well-known example of such shares are shares of "mutual funds" that stand ready at any time to redeem their outstanding shares at net asset value.

(3) What about creating common shares that are callable at the option of the corporation? The great majority of states impose limitations on this type of security or prohibit it entirely. In older versions of the Model Act a right of redemption at the corporation's option could be created only in connection with shares with preferential rights; several states authorize callable or redeemable common shares only if there is another class of common shares that is not callable or redeemable. E.g. West's Ann.Cal. Corp.Code § 402; N.Y.—McKinney's Bus.Corp.Law § 512(c). What possible evils might be created if the corporation had the power generally to "call" common shares at a predetermined price?

(4) Most state statutes also prohibit shares with "upstream conversion" rights, that is the right of common shares to convert to preferred shares, or of either common or preferred shares to convert to debt securities or interests. What possible evils might arise if shareholders generally had the power to convert their equity interests into senior securities or into debt?

(5) The RMBCA permits the creation of all types of shares referred to in the previous paragraphs without restriction or limitation. Indeed, the RMBCA goes even further in some respects, permitting, for example, the creation of shares that are redeemable at the option of a third person, e.g. the holders of other classes of shares, or the creation of shares that are

redeemable at a price "determined in accordance with a designated formula or by reference to extrinsic data or events." RMBCA § 6.01(c)(2). Is this total freedom a good idea? It may be justified on several grounds: (1) there is no evidence of demonstrated harm caused by these types of securities in states that permit their use; (2) the rights of classes of shares are determined in part by contractual negotiation and an absence of restriction may be justified on the ground of "freedom of contract"; (3) essentially the same results may usually be attained by contractual commitments between investors and the corporation independent of the articles of incorporation, and there seems to be no reason why persons cannot place their commitments in the articles of incorporation if they wish; and (4) upstream conversions and similar transactions are potentially less damaging to creditors and other senior security holders than the redemption of shares for cash. Whatever the force of this reasoning, it is likely that individual states will continue to retain a variety of restrictions on the creation of specific rights in classes of shares for the indefinite future.

C. ISSUANCE OF SHARES: HEREIN OF SUBSCRIPTIONS, PAR VALUE AND WATERED STOCK

1. SHARE SUBSCRIPTIONS AND AGREEMENTS TO PURCHASE SECURITIES

Historically, the traditional method of raising capital for a new venture was by preincorporation subscriptions pursuant to which persons agreed to purchase a specified number of shares contingent upon a specified amount of capital being raised. In an agrarian society, one can envision promoters of a new mill going from farm to farm seeking to persuade shrewd and cautious farmers to subscribe for shares in the new venture that promised to be of benefit to them. The common law of subscription agreements grappled with a number of problems arising from raising capital in this fashion, including the revocability of subscriptions before acceptance, the basis on which calls are to be made, and the remedies available to the new corporation if the subscription was not paid. These issues are now usually resolved in an unambiguous way by statute. See RMBCA § 6.20.

 The use of preincorporation subscription agreements declined in importance with the development of the modern investment banking industry, which permitted large amounts of capital to be raised on a nation-wide basis. Their public use was rendered impractical by the enactment of the state blue sky laws and the Federal Securities Act of 1933. These statutes required an expensive registration process for new issues of securities; the definition of "security" in these statutes was sufficiently broad that both the initial seeking of subscriptions and the later issuance of shares would require registration.

Subscription agreements may be used to a limited extent in connection with the capitalization of a closely held business with a small number of investors. Modern practice, however, is to use simple contractual agreements to purchase securities rather than a formal subscription agreement. In the words of the annotation to the 1969 Model Business Corporation Act, "today financing by subscription is the exception." Mod.Bus.Corp.Act Ann.2d § 17, ¶ 2.

2. AUTHORIZATION AND ISSUANCE OF COMMON SHARES UNDER THE REVISED MODEL ACT

Assume that a corporation has been formed under the RMBCA, and that it is desired to create only a single class of common shares. These shares, or some of them, are to be issued equally to two persons, A and B, for an aggregate consideration of $10,000 in cash or for specified property, the value of which is uncertain but probably about $10,000. How many shares should be authorized, how many shares should be issued, and what price should be established as the issue price for such shares?

Under the RMBCA, the answers to these questions are so simple and direct that they do not merit extended consideration. From the standpoint of A and B the number of shares to be issued and the price may be set at any combination that totals $10,000. It may be 5,000 shares each at $1 per share, 500 shares each at $10 per share, 50 shares each at $100 per share, 5 shares each at $1,000 per share, or any combination in between. It is important that the price be the same for both A and B if they are to be equally treated, but the number of shares and the corresonding price may be set at any level. Further, the number of authorized shares must at least equal the number it is planned to issue; however, since it is always possible that more capital may be needed at a later date, the authorization of some excess shares may be sensible. On the other hand, it may not be desirable to authorize vastly more shares than it is planned to issue for a couple of reasons. First, limiting the number of shares may protect minority shareholders. The majority may be able to issue authorized but unissued shares more easily than they can secure an amendment to the articles of incorporation increasing the authorized shares. Since, as will subsequently appear, the issuance of shares in some situations may harm the minority's interest, greater protection is generally given the minority if only the number of shares actually to be issued are authorized. Second, many states impose taxes based on authorized shares: authorizing unnecessary shares may simply increase one's taxes. On balance, most attorneys recommend that some shares be authorized in excess of what is proposed to be issued, even if there is some additional tax cost.

The A–B example set forth above is elementary because A and B both are contributing cash or property. The problem involved in incorporating the AB Furniture Store is obviously more complicated because B is contributing only services, and it is unclear how his services should be balanced against A's capital. This problem is discussed more fully below.

3. PAR VALUE AND STATED CAPITAL

In about 35 states, the articles of incorporation must state the "par value" of the shares of each class (or state that the shares are issued "with no par value" or "without par value"). The remaining states, like the RMBCA, have eliminated the concept of par value, and the current trend is toward the elimination of this concept as an historical anomaly. Par value provisions involve archaic and confusing concepts. These provisions in turn involve common law concepts of legal capital and watered stock and, in most jurisdictions, form the basis for restrictions on dividends, corporate share repurchases, and other transactions involving a direct or indirect distribution of corporate assets to shareholders.

The Statutory Supplement (pages 150–163) contains the provisions of the 1969 Model Business Corporation Act relating to par value. The discussion below is tied to these individual provisions, the text of which should be carefully examined. While not all state statutes adopted the 1969 Model Act par value provisions, they are typical of these statutes, and raise the basic problems that must be considered under all state statutes that retain these concepts.

Perhaps one final preliminary comment should be made. Simply because the statutory par value provisions appear on their face to be logical and regulatory in nature, they are not necessarily so.

Consider MBCA (1969), §§ 54(d), 15 (second sentence), 18, 21. As these statutory provisions make clear, par value is established in the articles of incorporation as a fundamental part of the description of the shares. It is whatever amount designated as par value by the drafter; it may be one mil, one cent, one dollar, ten dollars, or some other amount. Originally, par value had considerable importance because it was widely viewed as the amount for which shares would be issued: shares with a par value of one hundred dollars per share could be subscribed for at one hundred dollars per share with confidence that all other identical shares would also be issued for $100. In effect, par value originally ensured proportionality of treatment of widely dispersed shareholders, increased confidence in the resale market that the shares had real value (and were not "mere pieces of paper"), and assured the population in general that corporations had in fact been capitalized as advertised by the par values of the shares they issued.

It did not take long, however, for unscrupulous promoters to turn this practice to their own advantage. In the leading case of Hospes v. Northwestern Mfg. & Car Co., 48 Minn. 174, 50 N.W. 1117 (1892), for example, the Court summarized the allegations of the complaint as follows:

> Briefly stated, the allegations of the complaint are that on May 10, 1882, Seymour, Sabin & Co. owned property of the value of several million dollars, and a business then supposed to be profitable. That, in order to continue and enlarge this business, the parties interested in Seymour, Sabin & Co., with others, organized the car company, to

which was sold the greater part of the assets of Seymour, Sabin & Co. at a valuation of $2,267,000, in payment of which there were issued to Seymour, Sabin & Co. shares of the preferred stock of the car company of the par value of $2,267,000, it being then and there agreed by both parties that this stock was in full payment of the property thus purchased. It is further alleged that the stockholders of Seymour, Sabin & Co., and the other persons who had agreed to become stockholders in the car company, were then desirous of issuing to themselves, and obtaining for their own benefit, a large amount of common stock of the car company, "without paying therefor, and without incurring any liability thereon or to pay therefor;" and for that purpose, and "in order to evade and set at naught the laws of this state," they caused Seymour, Sabin & Co. to subscribe for and agree to take common stock of the car company of the par value of $1,500,000. That Seymour, Sabin & Co. thereupon subscribed for that amount of the common stock, but never paid therefor any consideration whatever, either in money or property. That thereafter these persons caused this stock to be issued to D.M. Sabin as trustee, to be by him distributed among them. That it was so distributed without receipt by him or the car company from any one of any consideration whatever, but was given by the car company and received by these parties entirely "gratuitously." * * *

The common stock issued by the Car Company is a species of "watered stock", since the corporation did not receive the par value for the stock when it was issued. What should be done about this? Is there a danger that innocent creditors might rely on the fact that shares with a specified par value are outstanding and assume that the corporation had at least the specified amount of capital? The Court believed that this was a potential problem, and concluded that under some circumstances the recipients of watered shares should be required to pay in the par value even though they had never agreed to do so. The Court, however, had some difficulty with the rationale:

[The plaintiff] plants itself upon the so-called "trust-fund" doctrine that the capital stock of a corporation is a trust fund for the payment of its debts; its contention being that such a "bonus" issue of stock creates, in case of the subsequent insolvency of the corporation, a liability on part of the stockholder in favor of creditors to pay for it, notwithstanding his contract with the corporation to the contrary.

This "trust fund" doctrine, commonly called the "American doctrine," has given rise to much confusion of ideas as to its real meaning, and much conflict of decision in its application. To such an extent has this been the case that many have questioned the accuracy of the phrase, as well as doubted the necessity or expediency of inventing any such doctrine. * * * The phrase that "the capital of a corporation constitutes a trust fund for the benefit of creditors" is misleading. Corporate property is not held in trust, in any proper sense of the term. A trust implies two estates or interests,—one equitable and one legal; one person, as trustee, holding the legal title, while another, as the *cestui que trust,* has the beneficial interest. Absolute control and power of disposition are inconsistent with the idea of a trust. The capital of a corporation is its property. It has the whole beneficial interest in it, as well as the legal title. It may use the income and profits of it, and sell and dispose of it, the same as a natural person. It is a trustee for its creditors in the same sense and to the same extent as a natural person, but no further. * * *

Another proposition which we think must be sound is that creditors cannot recover on the ground of contract when the corporation could not. Their right to recover in such cases must rest on the ground that the acts of the stockholders with reference to the corporate capital constitutes a fraud on their rights. We have here a case where the contract between the corporation and the takers of the shares was specific that the shares should not be paid for. * * * In such a case the creditors undoubtedly may have rights superior to the corporation, but these rights cannot rest on the implication that the shareholder agreed to do something directly contrary to his real agreement, but must be based on tort or fraud, actual or presumed. In England, since the act of 1867, there is an implied contract created by statute that "every share in any company shall be deemed and be taken to have been issued and to be held subject to the payment of the whole amount thereof in cash." This statutory contract makes every contrary contract void. Such a statute would be entirely just to all, for every one would be advised of its provisions, and could conduct himself accordingly. And in view of the fact that "watered" and "bonus" stock is one of the greatest abuses connected with the management of modern corporations, such a law might, on grounds of public policy, be very desirable. But this is a matter for the legislature, and not for the courts. We have no such statute * * *.

It is well settled that an equity in favor of a creditor does not arise absolutely and in every case to have the holder of "bonus" stock pay for it contrary to his actual contract with the corporation. Thus no such equity exists in favor of one whose debt was contracted prior to the issue, since he could not have trusted the company upon the faith of such stock. Handley v. Stutz, 139 U.S. 435, 11 Sup.Ct.Rep. 530. It does not exist in favor of a subsequent creditor who has dealt with the corporation with full knowledge of the arrangement by which the "bonus" stock was issued, for a man cannot be defrauded by that which he knows when he acts. It has also been held not to exist where stock has been issued and turned out at its full market value to pay corporate debts. The same has been held to be the case where an active corporation, whose original capital has been impaired, for the purpose of recuperating itself issues new stock, and sells it on the market for the best price obtainable, but for less than par, (Handley v. Stutz, supra) although it is difficult to perceive, in the absence of a statute authorizing such a thing, (of which every one dealing with the corporations is bound to take notice) any difference between the original stock of a new corporation and additional stock issued by a "going concern." It is difficult, if not impossible, to explain or reconcile these cases upon the "trust-fund" doctrine, or, in the light of them, to predicate the liability of the stockholder upon that doctrine. But by putting it upon the ground of fraud, and applying the old and familiar rules of law on that subject to the peculiar nature of a corporation and the relation which its stockholders bear to it and to the public, we have at once rational and logical ground on which to stand. The capital of a corporation is the basis of its credit. It is a substitute for the individual liability of those who own its stock. People deal with it and give it credit on the faith of it. They have a right to assume that it has paid in capital to the amount which it represents itself as having; and if they give it credit on the faith of that representation, and if the representation is false, it is a fraud upon them; and, in case the corporation becomes insolvent, the law, upon the plainest principles of common justice, says to the delinquent stockholder, Make that representation good by paying for your stock. It certainly cannot require the invention of any new doctrine in order to enforce so familiar a rule of equity. It is the misrepresentation of fact in stating the amount of capital to be greater than it really is that is the true basis of the liability of the stockholder in such cases; and it follows that it is only those creditors who have relied, or who can fairly be presumed to have relied, upon the professed amount of capital, in whose favor the law will recognize and enforce an equity against the holders of "bonus" stock. This furnishes a rational and uniform rule, to which familiar principles are easily applied, and which frees the subject from many of the difficulties and apparent inconsistencies into which the "trust-fund" doctrine has involved it; and we think that, even when the trust-fund doctrine has been invoked, the decision in almost every well-considered case is readily referable to such a rule.

The Court then concluded that subsequent creditors should not be required to allege and prove affirmatively that they relied on the capital represented by the bonus shares, but that lack of reliance might be a defense. In other words, the capitalization of a corporation as established by the par values of its issued shares was a public representation on which subsequent creditors might rely and enforce, unless the corporation could establish that the creditors extended credit knowing the represented capital was not there. Finally, the Court concluded that the particular plaintiff involved in the Hospes case (a newly formed corporation that had bought up claims against the original car company at significant discounts) had not sufficiently alleged its own bona fides to be allowed to maintain suit.

Notes

(1) The shares issued by the Car Company in the Hospes case are usually described as "bonus shares", because nothing was paid for them. "Watered shares" are technically shares issued for property worth less than their par value, while "discount shares" are shares issued for less than par. All three types are often lumped under the single phrase "watered stock." As indicated in *Hospes,* recipients of such shares are potentially liable to subsequent creditors of the corporation.

(2) In *Hospes* the Court stated that watered stock "is one of the greatest abuses connected with the management of modern corporations." Of course, the Court was speaking as of 1892. Was that true even then? In that connection draw up a balance sheet for the Car Company. Is it not clear that fundamental accounting principles require the creation of some fictional assets to balance things off? Is the risk of fraud increased by the presence of fictional assets on a balance sheet?

(3) Bing Crosby Minute Maid Corp. v. Eaton, 46 Cal.2d 484, 488, 297 P.2d 5, 8 (1956):

> The liability of a holder of watered stock has been based on one of two theories: the misrepresentation theory or the statutory obligation theory. The misrepresentation theory is the one accepted in most jurisdictions. The courts view the issue of watered stock as a misrepresentation of the corporation's capital. Creditors who rely on this misrepresentation are entitled to recover the "water" from the holders of the watered shares. * * *

> Statutes expressly prohibiting watered stock are commonplace today. * * * In some jurisdictions where they have been enacted, the statutory obligation theory has been applied. * * * Under that theory the holder of watered stock is held responsible to creditors whether or not they have relied on an over-valuation of corporate capital.

To what extent did the 1969 Model Business Corporation Act adopt the "statutory obligation" theory? That question requires that MBCA (1969) § 25 be read in close conjunction with the first two paragraphs of § 18. Under these sections is there watered share liability if—

(a) The directors fraudulently recite that property is worth $2,000 when it is really worth only $1,000, and then issue shares with a par value of $2,000 for it?

(b) The directors reasonably and nonfraudulently recite that property is worth $1,000, but then issue shares with a par value of $2,000 for it? As a practical matter the last paragraph of MBCA § 19 eliminates many potential problems in this area.

(4) In most states, problems of "watered stock" may be avoided if the corporation reacquires its own shares after they have been lawfully issued. Such shares are viewed as being "issued" and held in the corporation's treasury. These shares (called "treasury shares") have an intermediate status under most statutes: they are not viewed as "outstanding" for purposes of dividends, quorum and voting purposes, but are viewed as "issued" so that their "reissuance" does not violate the restrictions imposed by the par value statutes. Basically, the assumption is that treasury shares will be resold and are only temporarily in the corporation's hands. Since the treasury shares had originally been issued lawfully, they are still lawfully issued while in the corporation's treasury and can be resold for less than par value. RMBCA § 6.31 eliminates the concept of treasury shares (for reasons to be discussed later) and treats reacquired shares as authorized but unissued shares. States with par value statutes, however, still retain the concept of treasury shares.

(5) The notion that funds paid in for stock constitute a "trust fund" for creditors has a strange fascination for many courts. See e.g. Wood v. Dummer, 30 Fed.Cas. 435, No. 17,944 (C.C.D.Me.1824). While most of these cases are old, the language appears in some fairly recent decisions, and it is possible that it may influence decisions in some cases. The idea that corporate capital constitutes a "trust fund" is, of course, a total fiction for the reasons recognized in the quoted excerpts from *Hospes*.

4. ELIGIBLE AND INELIGIBLE CONSIDERATION FOR SHARES

Consider MBCA (1969) § 19. The idea that only the actual receipt of certain types of property or services by a corporation will support the issuance of shares is not technically a part of the par value structure, but it is closely aligned with it and must be taken into account whenever shares are being issued under a traditional statute. In the AB Furniture Store, if B receives shares with a par value in exchange for a promise for services in the future, does he have a potential "watered stock" liability under §§ 19 and 25? If so, what arrangements may be made for the issuance of B's shares to avoid this potential liability? What if the issuance is held back until some services are performed? May the directors allocate all the shares to the services already performed under section 18 and thereby avoid the creation of this liability?

What purpose is served by § 19? There are at least two possibilities: first, it was designed to protect creditors of the corporation who may rely on its capital in extending credit, since it attempts to assure that there is something "real" which can be levied against and sold; second, it may protect other investors (who invest "real" assets such as money or property) from dilution of their interests.

Obviously, in some circumstances a contract to perform services may have considerable value. If Jane Fonda enters into a contract to perform in a film, the producer could presumably borrow large sums solely on the strength of the Fonda contract. If Ms. Fonda is to receive a twenty-five per cent interest in the corporation producing the film, can the corporation issue shares to her reflecting that interest when she signs the contract? If not, how can she be given the interest that her contract entitles her to at the outset of the filming?

Consider, on the other hand, John Q. Promoter, who sells 75 per cent of his newly formed corporation's shares to outsiders for cash, and issues the remaining 25 per cent to himself in exchange for his contract to perform services of an indefinite nature in the future. The investors determine that Promoter's future services are of no benefit to the corporation. Section 19 of the 1969 MBCA may permit the corporation to cancel the shares issued to Promoter, thus allowing the investors to avoid dilution of their interests in the corporation. Is there any basis for attacking such a transaction on grounds other than § 19?

Shares issued for a promissory note are also prohibited by MBCA (1969) § 19. Again it is possible to divine an intention either to protect creditors of the corporation or to protect other investors who contribute cash while the promoter puts in an uncollectible promissory note. Courts have held that if a corporation does issue shares for a promissory note in violation of this section, the corporation may nevertheless enforce the note; the corporation, however, may be able to cancel the offending shares for failing to comply with § 19. Presumably, a note executed by John D. Rockefeller is "as good as gold," and yet shares cannot be issued to John D. in exchange for that note. On the other hand, if John D.'s note is owned by a third person, Pam Smith, may Smith be issued shares in consideration of John D.'s note?

Another problem may be raised by the language in MBCA (1969) § 19: "other property, tangible or intangible." What about claimed secret processes, formulas, conditional or contingent contract rights, "good will", capitalized research costs that have not yet led to a marketable product, and other intangible "property"? Such property is not only difficult to value; its very existence may be so ephemeral as not to constitute "property" at all in the eyes of some courts, at least for purposes of § 19. There are a reasonably large number of decisions in which this question has been raised, usually in the context of seeking to cancel shares issued in exchange for such "property."

While statutes are less than crystal-clear on the matter, a good argument can be made that it is proper to resell treasury shares for a consideration that is not eligible consideration for the issuance of new shares under MBCA § 19. One court that reached the opposite conclusion, Public Inv. Ltd. v. Bandeirante Corp., 740 F.2d 1222 (D.C.Cir.1984), was apparently influenced by the unfortunate consequences of the transaction under consideration; the result reached is probably not consistent with generally understood principles relating to treasury shares.

Notes

(1) What about issuing shares for a promise to pay money in the future that is not evidenced by a promissory note? Is not that literally permitted by MBCA (1969) § 19? The New York analogue to this section uses the phrase "obligations of the subscriber for future payments" rather than "promissory notes." McKinney's N.Y.Bus.Corp.Law § 504(b). What about a *secured* promissory note? General Bonding & Cas. Ins. Co. v. Moseley, 110 Tex. 529, 222 S.W. 961 (1920) held that a note secured by a valid first trust lien on real estate was permissible consideration; cf. also American Radiator & Standard Sanitary Corp. v. United States, 155 Ct.Cl. 515, 295 F.2d 939 (1961).

(2) As indicated in the text, these restrictions on eligible consideration for shares are not technically part of the par value structure. A state may abolish par value and yet decide to retain these traditional restrictions on eligible consideration (as California, for example, has done). Indeed, in a

few states, language similar to MBCA (1969) § 19 appears in the state constitution; in these states it will be presumably possible to abolish par value so long as these restrictions are retained.

(3) Consider RMBCA §§ 6.21(b), 6.21(d), 6.21(e), 16.21(b). Does § 16.21(b) provide adequate protection against a transaction like that of John Q. Promoter referred to in the text? In many cases, of course, the corporation will elect to follow the escrow procedure suggested in § 6.21(e), thereby avoiding possible dilution.

(4) The Official Comment to § 6.21 states that the term "benefit" should be "broadly construed to include, for example, a reduction of a liability, a release of a claim, or benefits obtained by a corporation by contribution of its shares to a charitable organization or as a prize in a promotion."

(5) The Official Comment to § 6.21 also states that "in the realities of commercial life, there is sometimes a need for the issuance of shares for contract rights or * * * intangible property or benefits." Do you agree? If you were drafting a new corporation statute, would you follow § 6.21 in this regard, or would you retain some or all of old § 19?

5. PAR VALUE IN MODERN PRACTICE

The early practice of creating shares with a par value equal to the proposed issuance price long ago fell into disuse. As a result, par value serves only a minor function and is in no way an indication of the price at which the shares are issued. There is, however, one significant carryover from the earlier practice: to avoid watered stock liability the issuance price for shares of stock with par value must always be equal to or greater than par value. Today, the practice most often followed is to use "nominal" par value, that is one cent, ten cents, or one dollar per share when the shares are issued for several dollars or more per share. The use of no par shares—for reasons discussed below—is a distant second.

Several factors caused the gradual movement away from par value as a representation of the purchase price of shares and the development of nominal par value shares. Doubtless, concern about watered stock liability, particularly where property of uncertain value is being contributed, was a factor. If high par value shares are given in exchange for such property, arguments may later arise that the property was not worth the par value of the shares received and the recipients might be sued for the difference. Another factor was the possible loss of flexibility of pricing shares. When a secondary market for previously issued shares develops, a corporation raising capital by selling shares in effect competes with that market. A corporation issuing shares with a par value of $100 may not be able to reduce the price below that figure and may have to stop selling shares if the market price of the previously-issued shares dropped below $100 per share. (At that point interested investors could get a better price by buying previously issued shares in the secondary market than they could from the corporation which may be locked into the $100 price by the par value).

Still another factor was that nominal par shares increase corporate flexibility in making distributions in the future. Consider MBCA (1969) § 21, and its possible application to "high par," "nominal par," and "no par" alternatives when forming a corporation. Consider the following alternatives:

(i) The corporation issues 10 shares of $100 par value stock for $1,000 in cash.

(ii) The corporation issues 10 shares of $1 par value stock for $1,000 in cash.

(iii) The corporation issues 10 shares of no par value stock for $1,000 in cash.

The appropriate accounting for alternatives (i) and (ii) are as follows:

Alternative (i)

Assets		Liabilities	0
Cash	1000	Capital accounts	
		Stated Capital	1000
		Capital Surplus	0
	1000		1000

Alternative (ii)

Assets		Liabilities	0
Cash	1000	Capital accounts	
		Stated Capital	10
		Capital Surplus	990
	1000		1000

In connection with alternative (iii), MBCA (1969) § 21 provides that the entire $1,000 should be treated as stated capital unless the directors determine to allocate to capital surplus "any portion of the consideration received for the issuance of such shares." (Does "any portion" include "all"?) Not all states gave the directors total freedom to allocate the proceeds from no par shares to capital surplus. Some states do not permit such allocation at all [in which case, alternative (iii) becomes identical to alternative (i)], while others permit only a partial allocation. Before 1985, Texas, for example, permitted allocation of only 25 per cent of the consideration to capital surplus. V.A. T.S.Bus.Corp.Act, art. 2.17B (1980). Assuming that such a restriction is applicable, and the directors elect to classify the maximum amount possible to capital surplus, alternative (iii) becomes:

Alternative (iii)

Assets		Liabilities	0
Cash	1000	Capital accounts	
		Stated Capital	750
		Capital Surplus	250
	1000		1000

Now, a logical question is what difference does it make if the capital contribution is recorded as stated capital or capital surplus? Rather surprisingly, it does make a difference, which can best be appreciated if a balance sheet is drawn up after the corporation (financed as suggested in alternative (ii)) (1) has borrowed $1,000 from a bank, and (2) has had two years of operations during which it has earned and accumulated an aggregate of $2,000 from its earnings. Further, for simplicity, it will be assumed that all of the assets are held by the corporation in the form of cash. The balance sheet looks like this:

Assets		Liabilities	$1,000
Cash	$4,000	Capital accounts	
		Earned Surplus	$2,000
		Stated Capital	10
		Capital Surplus	990
	$4,000		$4,000

At this point the shareholders decide they want to distribute to themselves some or all of the $4,000. If the balance sheet is to continue to balance, every dollar taken from the left-hand column must obviously be reflected by the reduction of a right-hand column entry. The significance of the right-hand entries is that they in effect limit or monitor the distribution of assets from the left-hand column. The distributions permitted by a corporation should be evaluated in accordance with MBCA (1969) §§ 45, 46, and 6.

Under these statutes, capitalizing a corporation with large amounts of capital surplus gave that corporation greater freedom and flexibility to make distributions or reacquire its own shares than it would have had if it were capitalized with large amounts of stated capital. In the above examples, the corporation, no matter how capitalized, could use the $2,000 of earned surplus to reacquire shares or make a distribution to shareholders. However, the corporation capitalized solely with stated capital (alternative (i)) would be limited to that amount; the corporation created with no par shares (alternative (iii)) would have available for distribution an additional $250 of capital surplus, for total potential distributions of $2250; the corporation capitalized most flexibly (alternative (ii)) could legally distribute $2990 out of its assets (subject, however, to the general insolvency tests in the 1969 Model Act). Admittedly, this increase in flexibility does not seem to be of earthshaking significance, and indeed may raise policy questions about whether corporations should have the freedom to distribute virtually all their capital as permitted in alternative (ii). However, why should the persons creating a corporation needlessly impose any restriction on a corporation's freedom?

Where the consideration for no par shares may be allocated to capital surplus without limitation (as permitted by § 18 of the 1969 MBCA), either no par or nominal par shares give the same amount of freedom. No par shares, however, never gained the popularity and widespread use of nominal par shares. One factor that in the past undoubtedly encouraged the use of nominal par shares, and discouraged the use of both high par and no par, was the Federal excise tax statute, repealed in 1965, that imposed a documentary stamp tax on issues and transfers of securities. This tax was based on "the par or face value of each certificate" of par value stock and "the actual value of each certificate" of no-par stock. Internal Revenue Code of 1954, § 4301, repealed by Pub.L. 89–44, Tit. IV, § 401(a), 79 Stat. 148 (1965). While this tax is no longer in effect, its influence may linger in the habits and practices of attorneys. Further, several states continue to measure their taxes on a similar basis, and if so, the use of low par is virtually mandatory to minimize tax obligations.

Is there any public relations value in the use of high par value stock? Is such stock desirable in order to ensure protection to creditors? Of course, from the creditors' standpoint, assets reflected as stated capital are somewhat preferable to assets reflected as capital surplus since they are more "locked in" and unavailable for distribution to shareholders. Consider, however, MBCA (1969) §§ 58(d), (e), (h), and (i).

Notes

(1) Why are restrictions placed on the power of a corporation to reacquire its own shares? Do such reacquisitions differ in degree or kind from the acquisition by a corporation of shares in another corporation? The close relation between corporate distributions or dividends on the one hand and corporate reacquisitions of its own shares on the other is implicit in the provisions of both § 6 of the 1969 MBCA and § 6.40 of the RMBCA which impose essentially the same kinds of legal restrictions on both kinds of transactions. Their close relationship is highlighted even more by RMBCA § 1.40(6), which defines a "distribution" to include a "purchase, redemption or other acquisition of shares." See generally, Part H, page 406 infra.

(2) What was the relationship of "stated capital" in the foregoing statutes to the requirement, formerly almost universal but now deleted from most statutes, that a corporation may not commence business unless it has a specified amount of capital? Even though "stated capital" was viewed as "locked in" the corporation more tightly than capital surplus, the minimum capitalization requirement was usually tested simply by the capital "paid in for shares" without regard to its classification as stated capital or capital surplus. In this connection, of course, the precise language of specific state statutes would have to be examined.

T. FIFLIS, H. KRIPKE, & P. FOSTER, ACCOUNTING FOR BUSINESS LAWYERS

(3d Ed., 1984), pp. 431–433.

Whatever the policy grounds for the rule that par or stated value must be paid-in to the corporation on issuance of its shares, we have seen that it virtually has been eliminated as a practical problem.

A corollary to that requirement is the typical statutory provision or case law holding that dividends or other voluntary distributions [2] should not be paid to shareholders if the result would be to reduce the corporation's net assets below the aggregate par or stated value of issued shares. This rule had its genesis in Wood v. Dummer,[3] where Mr. Justice Story said that the capital of a corporation was a "trust fund" for creditors. The basic concept of Wood v. Dummer has survived thus far to some extent in the law of every state—namely, that the capital of a corporation is to be preserved for the benefit of creditors. See Comment, 49 Yale L.J. 492 (1940). Without such a restriction on distributions a brand new corporation could issue, say one share of $10 par stock for a consideration of $10 in cash, and then turn around and declare and pay a $10 dividend, thus nullifying the rule requiring par or stated value to be paid-in. * * *

What protection does this give creditors? Two points may be made. First, a prospective creditor who inspects the balance sheet of a corporation and finds a low par or stated capital and most of the net worth embodied in capital surplus should know * * * that corporation laws to some extent permit the distribution of capital surplus as well as earned surplus to stockholders, giving creditors no protection beyond the legal capital consisting of par or stated capital.

Not equally well-known is the fact that just as lawyers minimized the effect of the rule that the legal capital must be paid-in to the corporation, by use of low par or low stated value no-par stock, so too they minimized the effect of the rule limiting distributions out of legal capital by various techniques permitting reduction of legal capital without creditors' approval. The conclusion is that corporation law provides creditors with very little actual protection, despite Wood v. Dummer.

As a result creditors today do not rely upon statutory protection against shareholder distributions. Trade creditors rely instead on security interests or careful monitoring of their receivables while commercial lenders require disclosure of financial data, security interests, and contractual limitations on distributions. It is in the areas of disclosure and statutory and contractual limitations that the practitioner must understand the accounting in order to serve his clients properly.

Notes

(1) Official Comment to § 6.21 of the RMBCA (1984):

The financial provisions of the Model Act reflect a modernization of the concepts underlying the capital structure and limitations on distri-

---

2. [By the Authors] Many types of informal dividends may be paid to shareholders, especially in close corporations; e.g., payment of shareholders' personal expenses, such as for an automobile or pleasure trip, excessive salaries, etc. For a collection of early cases, see E. Dodd & R. Baker, Cases and Materials on Corpora-

tions 1177–80 (2d ed. 1951), incidentally stating that the courts frequently fail to note the applicability of dividend restrictions in those situations.

3. [By the Authors] 30 Fed.Cas. 435 (C.C.D.Me.1824).

butions of corporations. * * * Practitioners and legal scholars have long recognized that the statutory structure embodying "par value" and "legal capital" concepts is not only complex and confusing but also fails to serve the original purpose of protecting creditors and senior security holders from payments to junior security holders. Indeed, to the extent security holders are led to believe that it provides this protection, these provisions may be affirmatively misleading. The Model Act has therefore eliminated these concepts entirely and substituted a simpler and more flexible structure that provides more realistic protection to these interests. Major aspects of this new structure are:

(1) the provisions relating to the issuance of shares set forth in this and the following sections;

(2) the provisions limiting distributions by corporations set forth in section 6.40 * * *; and

(3) the elimination of the concept of treasury shares described in the Official Comment to § 6.31.

* * * Since shares need not have a par value, under section 6.21 there is no minimum price at which specific shares must be issued and therefore there can be no "watered stock" liability for issuing shares below an arbitrarily fixed price. The price at which shares are issued is primarily a matter of concern to other shareholders whose interests may be diluted if shares are issued at unreasonably low prices or for overvalued property. This problem of equality of treatment essentially involves honest and fair judgments by directors and cannot be effectively addressed by an arbitrary doctrine establishing a minimum price for shares such as "par value" provided under older statutes.

(2) It is important to distinguish conceptually between "no par shares" in states that retain the par value structure, and shares issued in states that, like the RMBCA, have eliminated par value. The issuance of "no par shares" in par value states affects the stated capital and capital surplus accounts, may create a watered stock liability in certain circumstances, and may affect the distributions a corporation may lawfully make. States that have eliminated the par value structure have eliminated the watered stock concept and have also generally eliminated the mandatory capital accounts. They have also established different rules relating to when distributions lawfully may be made.

(3) Of course, it is not strictly true that the RMBCA has "eliminated" the concept of par value. See RMBCA § 2.02(b)(2)(iv). The Official Comment explains that optional par value provisions may be of use "to corporations which are to be qualified in foreign jurisdictions if franchise or other taxes are computed upon the basis of par value." In addition, optional par value may also be given effect "essentially as a matter of contract" between the parties. In other words, the par value rules described in this chapter may be elected by the participants in a corporation, if they so desire, by creating a par value for shares in the articles of incorporation.

(4) Where a corporation formed in a state that has abolished par value contemplates multi state operations, lawyers usually recommend that an

optional par value be adopted to minimize tax consequences if the corporation becomes subject to taxation in a state that uses par value as a measure of tax liability.

(5) Issues involving the legality of distributions, dividends or reacquisition or redemption of shares under the Revised Model Business Corporation Act and other statutes, are considered further in subsequent sections. See Part I of this chapter.

D. DEBT FINANCING

Evidences of indebtedness usually referred to as securities are bonds and debentures. Both involve unconditional promises to pay a stated sum in the future, and to pay interest periodically until then. Technically, a debenture is an unsecured corporate obligation while a bond is secured by a lien or mortgage on corporate property. However, the word "bond" is often used indiscriminately to cover both bonds and debentures. Bonds and debentures historically were payable to bearer; interest coupons reflecting the periodic obligation to pay interest were attached. A registered bond is one that has been registered in the name of a specific individual and from which the coupons have been removed; interest is paid directly to the registered owner. Virtually all new bonds are issued today in registered form. Of course, registered bonds are freely transferable.[4]

In recent years novel types of debt instruments have been created, and new words have entered the common vocabulary. Zero coupon bonds, often called "zeroes," pay no interest at all; they sell at a substantial discount from face value and upon maturity the holder receives the face value. The entire difference between original issue price and face value represents interest payable upon the maturity of the "zero." For income tax purposes, however, a holder of a "zero" must include in taxable income an allocable portion of the discount even though it is not to be received until some time in the distant future; as a result, "zeroes" are attractive investments primarily for tax exempt or tax deferred entities. Junk bonds, widely used in takeovers, are simply below investment-grade debt instruments. Many other novel variations exist. See generally R. Hamilton, Fundamentals of Modern Business, §§ 18.18–18.22.

---

4. [By the Editor] Other typical characteristics of debt securities are: (1) Interest payments are usually fixed obligations, due in any event, and expressed as a percentage of the face amount of the security. However, so-called income bonds, in which the obligation to pay interest is conditioned on adequate corporate earnings, are also known. Somewhat rarer are so-called participating bonds, where the interest obligation increases with corporate earnings. (2) Debt securities are usually subject to redemption, permitting the corporation to pay off the obligation before it is due, often at a premium over the face value. (3) Debt securities may be subordinated to the payment of other obligations. (4) Debt securities may be convertible into other classes of stock, usually common stock. Convertible debentures are treated as equity securities for many purposes. See, e.g., 15 U.S. C.A. § 78c(a)(11). (5) Some states authorize holders of bonds or debentures to participate in the selection of the board of directors upon specified contingencies. Many of these characteristics are also present in preferred shares.

Preferred and common shares are referred to as "equity securities" while bonds and debentures are referred to as "debt securities." The distinction between "equity" and "debt" underlies much of the modern law and practice relating to corporation finance. At the simplest level the distinction is easy to grasp. A "debt" is something that must be repaid: it is the result of a "loan," the person making the loan is a "creditor," and if periodic payments are made, they are "interest." On the other hand, "equity" represents an ownership interest in the business itself. One thinks in terms of "shareholders," shares of "capital stock," voting, and "dividends" rather than "interest."

As has previously been indicated, the distinction between debt and equity may not be at all clear in many situations. The ambivalent nature of preferred shares redeemable at the option of the holder has previously been commented upon. Also, as a matter of economics, how does a subordinated 100 year income debenture differ from a class of plain vanilla preferred shares? It is obviously possible to create a variety of mixed or "hybrid" securities that have some of the characteristics of debt and some of equity.[5]

It is usually advantageous to engage to some extent in debt financing. The notion that the best business is a debt-free business, while sounding attractive, is not consistent either with the minimization of income taxes or with the maximization of profits. A sharp distinction must be drawn, however, between debt owed to third persons, and debt owed to shareholders.

1. THE CONCEPT OF LEVERAGE

Debt owed to third persons creates leverage. Leverage is favorable to the borrower when the borrower is able to earn more on the borrowed capital than the cost of the borrowing. The entire excess is allocable to the equity accounts of the corporation, thereby increasing the rate of return on the equity invested in the corporation. An example should help to make this clear. Assume that a corporation has a total invested capital of $500,000. Let us consider the earnings per share on two alternative assumptions: (a) all this capital is invested as equity capital, e.g., 50,000 shares sold at $10.00 per share, and (b) half is borrowed on a long term basis, and the other half is contributed capital, e.g., 25,000 shares sold at $10.00 per share.

ALTERNATIVE A

Assumed net earnings	$25,000	$100,000	$150,000	$200,000
Number of shares	50,000	50,000	50,000	50,000
Earnings per share	$ 0.50	$ 2.00	$ 3.00	$ 4.00

ALTERNATIVE B

Assumed net earnings	$25,000	$100,000	$150,000	$200,000
Interest on bonds (8% on $250,000)	$20,000	$ 20,000	$ 20,000	$ 20,000

---

5. [By the Editor] The use of such securities is often questionable as a business matter, however, because of lack of certainty as to how the instruments will be treated for tax purposes. Also, unusual securities may be difficult to market publicly.

ALTERNATIVE B—Cont'd

Earnings allocable to common [6]	$ 5,000	$ 80,000	$130,000	$180,000
Number of shares	25,000	25,000	25,000	25,000
Earnings per share	$ 0.20	$ 3.20	$ 5.20	$ 7.20

In alternative B, the interest represents a fixed cost, a charge for obtaining the use of $250,000 of capital. When earnings are low, debt service takes up most of the earnings: in the hypothetical above, if earnings drop below $20,000, alternative B will show losses while alternative A continues to show modest profits until earnings drop to zero. When earnings increase above $20,000, however, the per share earnings under alternative B rise much more rapidly than alternative A even though the shares are otherwise identical. In effect in alternative B the common shareholders are getting $500,000 to work for them even though they contributed only $250,000 at the cost of the fixed interest charge which they must meet out of their own capital if necessary. Even this fixed charge is partially offset by the tax saving resulting from the deductibility of the interest.[7] This is leverage, a device well understood by real estate syndicates and promoters who seek to obtain the largest possible mortgage and the smallest possible equity investment of their own. The risk, of course, is that the income from the project may not be sufficient to cover the fixed charges, and the investors may quickly be wiped out.[8]

Since World War II, the United States has suffered a period of prolonged inflation. If inflation continues even at diminished levels, debt financing is also attractive because the loans will ultimately be repaid with inflated dollars. Of course, the competition for loans in such circumstances may cause high interest charges which will offset, either wholly or partially, this advantage of debt financing.

Leverage can generally be obtained only by the use of other people's money.[9]

6. [By the Editor] Computed simply by subtraction and without regard to reduction in income taxes as a result of the increased interest deduction.

7. [By the Editor] Non-participating preferred stock owned by third persons also creates leverage, which technically is a phenomenon of a senior, limited position rather than of debt. However, the tax advantage of debt—the deductability of the interest—is lost if preferred stock is used, with the result that most leverage situations created today involve the issuance of debt. On the other hand, a corporation is entitled to a credit for dividends received, including dividends paid upon preferred stock.

8. [By the Editor] An economist might show impatience with an example such as that set forth in the text. Assuming that both the common shares and the bonds are publicly traded (and with certain further simplifying assumptions), the economist would argue that the total value of the securities issued by the enterprise (the aggregate market value of all issued common shares plus all issued bonds) would be independent of the amount of debt in the capital structure of the enterprise. In other words, any increase in value of the common stock by reason of the corporation's capital structure would be offset by a decrease in the market price for the bonds. Even if this principle, first set forth by Miller and Modigliani, is abstractly accepted, a leveraged capital structure such as set forth in the example may benefit common shareholders at the expense of the debtholders. Also, this relationship may not be visible to the holders of the bonds where the assumptions are not fully true, for example, where the debt is not publicly or widely held.

9. [By the Editor] Some leverage may also be obtained if loans by shareholders are made on a basis other than in proportion to their shareholdings.

2. TAX ADVANTAGES OF DEBT

There are usually tax advantages for shareholders who are individuals to lend to the corporation a portion of their investment in the corporation rather than to contribute it outright. Interest payments on debt are deductible by the borrower whereas dividend payments on equity securities are not.[10] Of course, if the corporation files an S Corporation election, all corporate income is "passed through" to shareholders, but indebtedness is useful to "zero out" corporate income where that election is unavailable or is not made. Further, repayment of a debt is a non-taxable return of capital while a purchase or redemption of equity securities by the corporation may be a fully taxable dividend. When a shareholder lends a portion of his or her investment to the corporation the shareholder is in effect reserving the option of recovering this portion tax free at some later date if the corporation is successful.

A further advantage of debt rather than equity is that if the venture fails, a business bad debt may be a fully-deductible ordinary loss while the loss from worthless shares of stock is a capital loss which is deductible only to a limited extent. However, Internal Revenue Code of 1954, § 1244 permits losses from worthless shares to be treated as ordinary losses in many situations.

These advantages of debt financing tend to minimize the double tax problem of the corporate form of business enterprise discussed earlier. If subchapter S, which eliminates the double tax problem, is elected, there is little or no tax advantage in holding debt rather than equity.

There are only minor similar tax advantages in debt owed to persons other than shareholders.[11]

10. [By the Editor] On the other hand, a shareholder that is a corporation might prefer to make an equity investment in order to take advantage of the dividend-receipt credit even though that causes the "borrower" to lose the benefit of the interest deduction.

There are also technical differences between interest payments and dividends. For example, dividends are taxable to the provider of capital only if the corporation has earnings and profits, while interest is taxable in any event.

11. [By the Editor] Shareholders in a corporation may prefer to use outside loans rather than personal loans to provide the necessary capital for the corporation on the theory that this will ensure the deductibility of the interest payments by the corporation and the shareholder will have assets available to earn offsetting income. However, as a practical matter, close corporations usually are able to borrow risk capital from outside sources only on the strength of personal guarantees by shareholders. The Internal Revenue Service has sometimes attempted to treat a share-holder guaranteed loan as a personal loan to the shareholder followed by a contribution of the proceeds to the corporation (thereby denying the corporation an interest deduction for the payments made to the outside source and leaving the shareholder's taxable income unaffected since the dividend offsets the interest payment). See e.g. Murphy Logging Co. v. United States, 378 F.2d 222 (9th Cir.1967). The propriety of such rearranging of a transaction (which in some situations may favor the taxpayer rather than the Commissioner) is discussed in Moore and Sorlien, Adventures in Subchapter S and Section 1244, 14 Tax L.Rev. 453, 493, n. 108 (1959). See also Plantation Patterns, Inc. v. Commissioner, 462 F.2d 712 (5th Cir.1972). The same issue arises in another context in S corporations. See Estate of Leavitt v. Commissioner, 875 F.2d 420 (4th Cir.1989) [shareholders in S corporation unsuccessfully argued that third party debt guaranteed by them should increase basis of stock to permit them to take advantage of corporate losses in excess of contributed capital]; Selfe v. United States, 778 F.2d 769 (11th

SLAPPEY DRIVE INDUS. PARK v. UNITED STATES

United States Circuit Court, Fifth Circuit, 1977.
561 F.2d 572.

Before TUTTLE, GOLDBERG and RONEY, CIRCUIT JUDGES.

GOLDBERG, CIRCUIT JUDGE.

This tax refund suit involves seven closely held real estate development corporations that Spencer C. Walden, Jr. organized and manages. The first issue, the one most extensively debated by the parties, is whether certain purported debts that the corporations owed their shareholders should be treated for tax purposes as contributions to capital. * * * The district court, Cairo Developers, Inc. v. United States, D.C., 381 F.Supp. 431, resolved each issue in the government's favor. We affirm.

I. FACTS

Spencer C. Walden, Jr. is a successful real estate developer in Albany, Georgia, a city of some 100,000 located less than 50 miles southeast of Plains. Acting primarily through the partnership of Walden & Kirkland, Walden has developed numerous residential subdivisions and various commercial properties. This case concerns a subset of his activities.

Among the properties Walden has developed are several tracts originally owned by his father-in-law, J.T. Haley, and Haley's descendants.[12] With Walden directing organizational efforts, members of the Haley family formed six corporations over a fifteen year period.

* * *

Cir.1985); In re Lane, 742 F.2d 1311 (11thCir.1984); Blum v. Commissioner, 59 T.C. 436 (1972). In these cases, where the taxpayers are claiming that their guarantees constitute investments of capital by them, there is a strong flavor of judicial skepticism about whether the taxpayers would make the same argument if the venture had been successful with the result that payments on that debt constituted constructive income to them.

Tax advantages may also arise in complex transactions through the substitution of debt owed to third person for equity securities owned by such person.

12. [By the Court] The following chart illustrates the relationships:

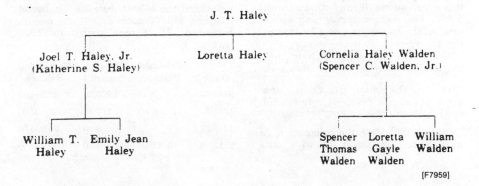

[F7959]

Walden was the moving force behind each of these corporations. He was president of each enterprise, and his partnership, Walden & Kirkland, handled their development work. * * *

* * * We develop the facts * * * by discussing the corporations in the order of their incorporation,[13] referring to the contested transfers by alphabetical labels.

Pecan Haven. Pecan Haven was formed in June 1947. The shareholders were Walden (1 share), his wife Cornelia Haley Walden (59 shares) and her twin sister Loretta Haley (60 shares). They paid $12,000 for their shares. Pecan Haven developed several tracts obtained from Loretta and Cornelia and later developed a tract purchased from their father J.T. Haley.

Transfer A occurred July 26, 1960. Spencer Walden transferred 69.435 acres to the corporation in exchange for its $65,000 five-year 3% installment notes. Appellants assert that the corporation's book net worth at that time was $83,000 and that its "true" net worth, taking into account the appreciated value of its real estate holdings, was $476,000. The corporation failed to make timely payments of principal or interest, and $20,000 remains outstanding.[14]

Lake Park. J.T. Haley's three children—Joel T. Haley, Jr., Cornelia and Loretta—organized Lake Park in November 1950 intending to develop lands they held jointly. They took equal shares of the corporation's stock, for which they paid a total of $28,000. The corporate books reflected the contributions as $9,000 paid-in capital and $19,000 paid-in surplus. The corporation immediately acquired land from its shareholders that it developed.

13. [By the Court] This appeal actually involves twelve separate refund suits, one brought by each of the seven corporations and five brought individually by shareholding members of the Haley family. * * * The tax years in question are those ending in 1961 through 1965, though some of the actions involve fewer years. The taxes contested in these suits total about $350,000 plus interest, and the amount of tax liability affected in these and other years will presumably run much higher.

Because the facts are crucial in cases of this type, we set them forth in plentiful detail. Our discussion may rank with any drug on the market as a cure for insomnia, though we trust that our version of "the Waldens" will prove more lively than a current Thursday night television series.

14. [By the Editor: The Court's appendix contains the following detailed information about "Transfer A."]

On July 26, 1960, the corporation gave its note for $65,000 at 3% with install-

ments of $12,500 due July 26 of each year from 1961 through 1964 and the final payment of $15,000 due July 26, 1965. The corporation has made the following payments:

Date	Principal Payment	Interest Payment	Remaining Balance
9/1/61	12,500.00	1,950.00	52,500.00
6/8/62	12,500.00	1,575.00	40,000.00
9/22/64		2,606.64	40,000.00

On September 22, 1964, the corporation refinanced the $40,000 balance. It issued four new $10,000 notes at 3%, one due on September 21 of each year from 1965 through 1968.

Date	Principal Payment	Interest Payment	Remaining Balance
9/15/70		1,200.00	40,000.00
10/5/70	10,000.00	1,503.45	30,000.00
11/16/71		3,600.00	30,000.00
2/17/72	10,000.00	491.50	20,000.00

Transfer B occurred September 7, 1954. The shareholders transferred 100 acres to the corporation in exchange for $10,000 cash and a $40,000 demand note bearing 4% interest. Appellants contend that at the time of the transfer the corporation's net worth was $50,000 and that its "true" net worth was $78,000. Lake Park made irregular principal payments and retired the note in 1959. The corporation did not pay interest as provided in the note, making only a single $2,500 interest payment in 1956.[15] * * * [Descriptions of similar transactions involving the other corporations are omitted.]

Overview. We may assume, as appellants contend, that in each ostensible sale of property to a corporation the price reflected the fair market value.[16] Nonetheless, the recurring pattern in regard to all the loans has been the corporations' failure to adhere to the announced repayment schedules. Although the corporations did make some principal and interest payments, in not a single case did the payments conform to the terms included in the notes. In addition, Spencer Walden's deposition testimony makes clear that the creditor-shareholders viewed their situation not at all as normal creditors would. The shareholders entered no objections to the passing of payment dates and requested payments only when the corporations had "plenty of cash." In explaining the willingness to tolerate delinquencies even when interest was not being paid, Walden candidly stated that the individuals were more concerned with their status as shareholders than in their status as creditors.

II. DEBT–EQUITY

The tax code provides widely disparate treatment of debt and equity. In regard to a typical transfer at issue here, involving an individual's transfer of property to his corporation in exchange for the instrument in question, the classification as debt or equity may affect the taxation of the original transaction, the resulting bases and hence the taxation of subsequent transfers, and the taxation of payments the corporation makes to the shareholder with respect to the instrument.[17]

---

15. [By the Editor: Detailed information about "Transfer D" is also set forth in the Court's appendix.]

On September 7, 1954, the corporation gave its demand note for $40,000 at 4%. The corporation has made the following payments:

Date	Principal Payment	Interest Payment	Remaining Balance
12/31/55	1,802.17		38,197.83
6/27/56		2,500.00	38,197.83
4/3/57	1,000.00		37,197.83
4/15/57	1,500.00		35,697.83
5/24/57	4,750.00		30,947.83
5/31/58	10,000.00		20,947.83
12/9/58	947.83		20,000.00
1/31/59	20,000.00		—0—

16. [By the Court] We note also that the ostensible lenders took no security interests in the transferred property or otherwise and that, with a single exception, the debts at issue were not subordinated to other corporate obligations.

17. [By the Court] The corporation may deduct interest on indebtedness, see I.R.C. § 163, but if the transaction is characterized as equity, ostensible interest payments become non-deductible dividends. In general, the recipient is not taxable on loan principal payments but is taxable if the transaction constitutes equity; in that instance the purported principal payments come in for dividend treatment. See I.R.C. § 316.

In the case at bar debt classification would greatly benefit the taxpayers.

Unfortunately, the great disparity in the tax treatment of debt and equity does not derive from a clear distinction between those concepts. The problem is particularly acute in the case of close corporations, because the participants often have broad latitude to cast their contributions in whatever form they choose. Taxpayers have often sought debt's advantageous tax treatment for transactions that in substance more closely resembled the kind of arrangement Congress envisioned when it enacted the equity provisions. Thus the labels that parties attach to their transactions provide no guarantee of the appropriate tax treatment. See, e.g., Tyler v. Tomlinson, 414 F.2d 844, 850 (5th Cir. 1969); Berkowitz v. United States, 411 F.2d 818, 820 (5th Cir.1969).

Articulating the essential difference between the two types of arrangement that Congress treated so differently is no easy task. Generally, shareholders place their money "at the risk of the business" while lenders seek a more reliable return. See Midland Distributors, Inc. v. United States, 481 F.2d 730, 733 (5th Cir.1973); Dillin v. United States, 433 F.2d 1097, 1103 (5th Cir.1970). That statement of course glosses over a good many considerations with which even the most inexperienced investor is abundantly familiar. A purchaser of General Motors stock may bear much less risk than a bona fide lender to a small corporation.

Nevertheless, the "risk of the business" formulation has provided a shorthand description that courts have repeatedly invoked. Contributors of capital undertake the risk because of the potential return; in the form of profits and enhanced value, on their underlying investment. Lenders, on the other hand, undertake a degree of risk because of the expectancy of timely repayment with interest. Because a lender unrelated to the corporation stands to earn only a fixed amount of interest, he usually is unwilling to bear a substantial risk of corporate failure or to commit his funds for a prolonged period. A person ordinarily would not advance funds likely to be repaid only if the venture is successful without demanding the potential enhanced return associated with an equity investment. See Curry v. United States, 396 F.2d 630, 634 (5th Cir.), cert. denied, 393 U.S. 967, 89 S.Ct. 401, 21 L.Ed.2d 375 (1968); DuGro Frozen Foods, Inc. v. United States, 481 F.2d 1271, 1272 (5th Cir. 1973).

These considerations provide only imperfect guidance when the issue relates to a shareholder's purported loan to his own corporation, the usual situation encountered in debt-equity cases. It is well established that shareholders may loan money to their corporations and achieve corresponding tax treatment. See United States v. Snyder Bros. Co., 367 F.2d 980, 983 (5th Cir.1966), cert. denied, 386 U.S. 956, 87 S.Ct. 1021, 18 L.Ed.2d 104 (1967); Rowan v. United States, 219 F.2d 51 (5th Cir.1955). When making such loans they could hardly be expected to ignore their shareholder status; their motivations will not match those of potential lenders who have no underlying equity interest. The "risk of the business" standard, though, continues to provide a backdrop for our analysis. While we should not expect a creditor-shareholder to evidence motivations and behavior conforming perfectly to those of a mere creditor, neither should we abandon the effort to determine whether the challenged transaction is in substance a contribution to capital masquerading as debt.

Rather than attempt to measure concrete cases against an abstract formulation of the overriding test, we have identified numerous observable criteria that help place a given transaction on one side of the line or the other. We have always recognized, however, that the various factors are not equally significant. "The object of the inquiry is not to count factors, but to evaluate them." Tyler v. Tomlinson, 414 F.2d 844, 848 (5th Cir.1969). Each case turns on its own facts; differing circumstances may bring different factors to the fore. See In re Indian Lake Estates, Inc., 448 F.2d 574, 579 (5th Cir.1971); Tomlinson v. The 1661 Corp., 377 F.2d 291, 295 (5th Cir.1967).

With that preliminary caveat, we note the factors that prior cases have identified:

(1) the names given to the certificates evidencing the indebtedness;

(2) the presence or absence of a fixed maturity date;

(3) the source of payments;

(4) the right to enforce payment of principal and interest;

(5) participation in management flowing as a result;

(6) the status of the contribution in relation to regular corporate creditors;

(7) the intent of the parties;

(8) "thin" or adequate capitalization;

(9) identity of interest between creditor and stockholder;

(10) source of interest payments;

(11) the ability of the corporation to obtain loans from outside lending institutions;

(12) the extent to which the advance was used to acquire capital assets; and

(13) the failure of the debtor to repay on the due date or to seek a postponement.

Estate of Mixon v. United States, 464 F.2d 394, 402 (5th Cir.1972).[18] As indicated above, these factors are but tools for discerning whether a

---

18. [By the Court] The list is not exhaustive; our cases undoubtedly mention considerations that have yet to take a number. Congress has recently authorized the Secretary to promulgate regulations setting forth appropriate factors. See I.R.C. § 385. For the time being, however, we must rely on our own pronouncements.

transaction more closely resembles the type arrangement for which Congress provided debt or equity treatment.[19]

In the case at bar the most telling of the *Mixon* factors is the corporate debtors' consistent failure to repay the debts on the due dates or to seek postponements. More generally, that failure and the corresponding absence of timely interest payments combine with Walden's testimony regarding the parties' view of their relationships to make clear that these transactions were in substance not at all the type arrangements for which debt treatment is appropriate.

The individuals' failure to insist upon timely repayment or satisfactory renegotiation indicates that the compensation they sought went beyond the announced interest rate, for an investor would not ordinarily undertake such a risk for so limited a return. The failure to insist that the corporations pay the interest that the agreements provided underscores the inference; "a true lender is concerned with interest." Curry v. United States, 396 F.2d 630, 634 (5th Cir.), cert. denied, 393 U.S. 967, 89 S.Ct. 401, 21 L.Ed.2d 375 (1968). When a corporate contributor seeks no interest, it becomes abundantly clear that the compensation he seeks is that of an equity interest: a share of the profits or an increase in the value of his shareholdings.

Walden's testimony confirms these conclusions. He acknowledged that the individuals sought payments of principal or interest only when the corporations had "plenty of cash" and that the investors did so because they were more concerned with their status as shareholders than as creditors. That statement of how the individuals viewed their situation corresponds almost perfectly to the classic equity situation. A corporation normally declares dividends only when it has "plenty of cash." Shareholders ordinarily acquiesce in such dividend policies because their primary concern is the health and long-term success of the enterprise. Walden's statement indicates that the individuals here possessed precisely those motivations and that they believed it appropriate for the corporations to decide when to make payments on the same basis that corporations customarily make dividend decisions. The taxpayers' pattern of conduct belies any intention to structure their affairs as parties to a debt transaction ordinarily would. In the circumstances here, these factors indicate that all the transactions should be characterized for tax purposes as equity arrangements.

In reaching this conclusion we have not ignored the other factors our cases have identified. Appellants place particular reliance on the intent of the parties. Here, appellants contend, the form in which the parties cast the transactions conclusively demonstrates their intent to create a debt relationship. In relying so heavily on this factor, however, appellants misconceive its import. The question is not whether the parties intended to call their transaction "debt" and thus to achieve

---

19. [By the Court] The issue is primarily one of law. We must uphold the district court's findings of basic facts unless clearly erroneous, but the ultimate characterization of the transactions as debt or equity receives no such protection.

advantageous tax treatment; that a person wants to pay less tax rather than more provides little basis for discerning how much tax Congress decided he should pay. Instead, the relevant inquiry is the actual manner, not the form, in which the parties intended to structure their relationship. If the intended structuring accords with the type arrangement that qualifies for taxation as debt, that intent supports a finding of debt. Here, however, the parties intended to structure their relationship in a manner placing funds at the prolonged risk of the businesses; they intended decisions whether to make payments on the advances to be based on the criteria usually associated with dividend decisions. To the extent that intent is relevant, it favors equity classification.[20] * * *

Another factor from *Mixon* that sometimes proves most instructive is the identity of interest between creditor and stockholder. Courts and commentators have often discussed this criterion under the rubric "proportionality." When each shareholder owns the same proportion of the company's stock as he does of the ostensible shareholder debt, the parties' framing of the transaction contributes little to the analysis. In that situation the owners' decision regarding how much of their contribution to cast as equity and how much as debt does not affect the distribution of control over the company. Non-tax considerations may play little role in the choice, and reviewing courts accordingly must scrutinize carefully the resulting transaction. When, on the other hand, an individual holds different percentages of the corporation's stock and shareholder debt, the casting of debt in that form ordinarily will affect substantial non-tax interests. There is thus reason to believe that the parties' debt characterization has substance as well as form.[21]

Appellants argue in the case at bar that many of the challenged transfers exhibited imperfect proportionality and that some displayed none at all. While that argument would carry weight in the usual case, it has little force here. The disproportional holdings all occurred among close relatives. Although we do not treat the various shareholding members of the J.T. Haley family as an indivisible unit, neither do we treat them as unrelated individuals. For all that appears in this record, relations among the various family members were completely

---

20. [By the Court] Walden testified that the corporations intended to repay the indebtedness. Even accepting that testimony as true, the parties' conduct makes clear that they intended to repay only after a prolonged period, at which time repayment would be likely only if the enterprises had proved successful. Thus they intended to repay in the same sense that corporations might intend their dividends eventually to total up to the original price of the stock. Walden's testimony in this regard provides only the barest support for debt classification.

21. [By the Court] Even when a corporation incurs bona fide debt, of course, the opportunity to advance the funds and earn the corresponding return provides both tax and other advantages to the shareholder. Individual shareholders may therefore insist upon receiving their share of such advantages. Thus "proportionality" justifies courts in applying careful examination of the transactions but is not necessarily inconsistent with a finding of bona fide debt.

harmonious. Because shareholding family members were thus less likely to attribute major significance to departures from strict equality in their positions, the instances of disproportionate debt and equity holdings provide a much weaker inference than they ordinarily would that the ostensible debt was in fact what it purported to be.

Finally, appellants strenuously urge that the level of the corporations' capitalization does not undermine their position. We have not, however, based our decision on the inadequacy of the corporate capitalization. While some of the purported loans were made to corporations with woefully inadequate capital, others were not. In some cases, as the taxpayers note, capitalization was adequate.[22] These facts strengthen our conclusion as to some transactions, weaken it for others. They do not, however, suffice to change the conclusion we have derived from the parties' pattern of conduct and from Walden's testimony.[23]

Because the parties to the transactions in question intended to conduct and did conduct their affairs in a manner that the tax code labels equity rather than debt, taxation of the transactions as equity is appropriate. Contrary to appellants' assertions, in reaching that result we do not disapprove their decisions concerning how to organize the corporations, and we do not substitute our business judgment for theirs. We merely announce the tax consequences that attach to their decisions. While appellants are correct that they were free to decide without our supervision how much of the corporate financing to derive from loans and how much from capital contributions, they were not free to decide for themselves what tax consequences would attach to their conduct. * * *

Affirmed.

Notes

(1) The number of citations to cases arising within a single circuit indicates that the issue involved in the principal case is a recurring one.

22. [By the Court] Taxpayers urge that these businesses involved little risk and therefore needed little capital. * * * The ventures incurred development expenses running into six figures and required as much as two or three years to begin receiving any revenues by selling lots. These considerations demonstrate the inadequacy of, for example, the initial capitalizations of $5,100 * * * [to] $21,000. * * * Thus the capitalization factor favors the government with respect to transfers made to those corporations upon their formation.

23. [By the Court] The Mixon factors not discussed in text carry little weight in this case. The source of principal and interest payments and the questionable availability of similar loans from outside lenders provide slight support to the government. That most of the obligations possessed fixed maturity dates would favor appellants had they not consistently ignored those dates. Similarly, the individuals' legal right to enforce payment does not aid appellants in light of the apparent understanding, as manifested in observable behavior, that they would not enforce those rights. The lenders already controlled corporate management; that they derived no more control as a result of the ostensible loans does not cut against the equity classification. See Dillin v. United States, 433 F.2d 1097, 1101 (5th Cir.1970). Finally, that appellants did not subordinate their loans to other corporate obligations, provides slight support for appellants but does not undermine the conclusion we have drawn from the more significant indicia discussed in text.

argument

Generally, in these cases the taxpayer consistently contends that obligations should be treated as debt while the Internal Revenue Service contends for equity securities treatment.

(2) In Texas Farm Bureau v. United States, 732 F.2d 437, 438–9 (5th Cir.1984), the court said *Slappey Drive* involves the development of "a set of objective factors to aid courts in making the determination whether the particular transaction creates debt. Furthermore, * * * debt-equity determination is ordinarily a question of law to be decided by the court. Although in some situations intent may play an important role in debt-equity determinations, courts look to intent only when other relevant objective factors regarding the transaction fail to clearly indicate either debt or equity. * * * Our high technology age has yet to produce an accurate, dependable means for determining a man's subjective beliefs. At least until such a development occurs, reliance on more objective types of evidence is generally desirable."

(3) The Tax Reform Act of 1969 authorized the Service to prescribe regulations on the issue whether an interest in a corporation "is to be treated * * * as stock or indebtedness." I.R.C. § 385, added by P.L. 91–172, § 415(a) (1969). The Service issued regulations implementing this section only in December, 1980, in the waning days of the Carter administration. The Reagan administration promptly suspended the effective date of these regulations, and after a long delay, withdrew them, announcing that no further attempt would be made to adopt regulations on this subject. T.D. 7920, 1983–2 C.B. 69. Why do you think (a) it took a decade to develop regulations on this subject, and (b) the Reagan administration gave up on attempts to create regulations under section 385?

(4) A "debt/equity ratio" is the mathematical ratio between a corporation's liabilities and the shareholders' equity. For example, a corporation with $10,000 of equity that borrows $100,000 has a debt/equity ratio of 10/1. This ratio may be calculated on an aggregate or overall liabilities basis (taking into account debts and obligations owed to persons other than shareholders) or on an "inside" basis (taking into account only debts owed to shareholders). The regulations proposed in 1980 under section 385 but later withdrawn would have provided that debt was not "excessive" if the corporation's "outside" ratio was less than 10/1 and its "inside" ratio was less than or equal to 3/1. Is this a sensible way to create a "safe harbor" for shareholder-created debt? Would such a "safe harbor" be desirable?

(5) At one time, it was thought that under the case law an inside debt/equity ratio of 4/1 or higher would be decisive in reclassifying the debt as equity. This ratio test, originally based on a statement in John Kelley Co. v. Commissioner, 326 U.S. 521, 66 S.Ct. 299, 90 L.Ed. 278 (1946), was generally rejected by courts in favor of a more flexible approach epitomized by the discussion in the principal case.

(6) A corporation with a high debt/equity ratio is sometimes referred to as a "thin corporation."

(7) The issue whether debt should be reclassified as equity for tax purposes arises in other contexts as well. It may be recalled that a corporation eligible to be taxed as an S corporation may have only one class of stock. See p. 123 supra. If an S corporation issues debt to shareholders

that might be reclassified as equity under *Slappey Drive,* is that corporation's S corporation status at risk? The Service first took a rather literalistic approach, arguing that "administrative complexities" compelled disallowance of S corporation status in all reclassification cases. Some courts accepted this view, but others did not, holding the regulations invalid. The leading case so holding was Portage Plastics Co., Inc. v. United States, 486 F.2d 632 (7th Cir.1973). In 1982, Congress largely solved this problem by creating a "safe harbor" for "straight debt," the existence of which does not disqualify a corporation from the S corporation election. I.R.C. § 1361(c)(5) defines "straight debt" as debt that involves a written unconditional promise to pay a sum certain in money if (a) interest rates and interest payment dates are not contingent on profits, the borrower's discretion, or similar factors, (b) there is no direct or indirect convertibility into stock, and (c) the creditor is an eligible shareholder under Chapter S.

There was an irony in the attempts by the IRS to disqualify corporations from S corporation treatment on the basis of the existence of reclassifiable debt interests, since this special tax election was originally created to eliminate the double tax treatment that gives rise to the incentive for shareholders to create thin corporations to begin with. For another decision that appears to use the one class of stock requirement to defeat the legislative purpose, see Paige v. United States, 580 F.2d 960 (9th Cir.1978), holding that different treatment of cash and property contributions required by the California Department of Corporations created two classes of stock and disqualified the corporation from electing S corporation treatment.

3. DEBT AS A PLANNING DEVICE

The advantages of debt as a planning device in closely held corporations are well illustrated by Obre v. Alban Tractor Co., 228 Md. 291, 179 A.2d 861 (1962). Obre and Nelson formed a new corporation, Annel Corporation, to engage in the dirt moving and road building business. Obre agreed to contribute to the corporation equipment and cash worth $65,548.10 while Nelson agreed to contribute $10,000 in cash and equipment. The equipment values were based on an independent appraisal. The parties agreed that control was to be shared equally from the outset. Acting upon the advice of "a well-known and reputable firm of certified public accountants," the parties capitalized the corporation as follows:

Obre $10,000 par value voting common stock
        $20,000 par value non-voting preferred stock
        $35,548.10 unsecured promissory note
Nelson $10,000 par value voting common stock

The venture was an economic failure, shortly ending up in a state insolvency proceeding. In this proceeding Obre successfully claimed the right to participate as an unsecured creditor to the extent of his $35,548.10 unsecured note. The unpaid trade creditors argued that a "subordinating equity" principle required that this note be treated as equity—a capital contribution—rather than as a valid debt. The court rejected this argument, stating that there was no showing of under-capitalization, fraud, misrepresentation, or estoppel. In deciding that Annel Corporation was not undercapitalized, the court treated Obre's preferred stock as an equity investment so that the corporation had begun business with $40,000 of equity and only $35,548.10 of debt. The court held that there was no showing that $40,000 of equity capital was inadequate for a business such as Annel Corporation's. The court also relied on the fact that Obre's "loan" to the corporation was either known to the creditors or could easily have been discovered by examining public state tax filings, by requesting a financial statement, or by obtaining a credit report.

Notes

(1) The "subordinating equity" concept is essentially the Deep Rock doctrine in a state law context. Do you think the trade creditors might have been more successful if they had placed Annel Corporation in federal bankruptcy proceedings?

(2) Was the Annel Corporation adequately capitalized? Isn't it reasonably clear that even $75,548.10 was not enough capital and that $40,000 was inadequate? Should this be a matter of proof or of presumption?

(3) Why did those certified public accountants recommend that a significant portion of Obre's contribution be in the form of debt rather than simply having a preferred stock investment of $55,548.10?

E. PLANNING THE CAPITAL STRUCTURE FOR THE CLOSELY HELD CORPORATION

Attorneys are often requested to review and make recommendations about the proposed capital structure of newly formed closely held ventures. Usually, the capital structure will be an integral part of broader control considerations in which individual participants attempt to ensure their continued right to participate in the venture and the attorney reviews the entire "package" as a single unit. Tax considerations may also be of critical importance. In reviewing proposed capital structures, an attorney will generally have several basic goals, including:

(1) Will the structure "work;" i.e., will it stand up in the event of later disagreement and possible legal attack?

(2) Will the structure actually provide the desired result? For example, a person desiring a guaranteed, unconditional periodic payment who is asked to accept preferred stock should be made aware that the directors may usually forego declaring dividends on the preferred if they so desire.

(3) Will the desired tax treatment be available, or more likely, is the structure created one that makes the desired tax treatment probable if not certain?

(4) Might the structure give rise to unexpected liabilities? The most likely sources of unexpected liabilities are the possible application of the concepts of par value and watered stock (in states that still recognize such concepts) and, possibly, the ubiquitous doctrine of piercing the corporate veil.

(5) Are his or her clients' financial contributions reasonably protected and reasonably fairly treated in the event of unexpected or calamitous occurrences causing the sudden and premature termination of the venture?

This listing is only partial. Depending on the circumstances, participants will usually have additional concerns about the capital structure. For example, a person planning on contemplated periodic payments for living expenses may wish to have assurance that corporate matters are handled conservatively and not in a way that may jeopardize future distributions. Other persons may wish to have a major voice in fiscal management and future plans to raise additional capital which may affect their roles in the venture. Considerations about capital structure obviously shade over into questions relating to control over the venture in general, and indeed should be addressed as part of the broader considerations of control.

Notes

(1) These various factors may be illustrated by an analysis of the AB Furniture Store, where A is to contribute $100,000 in cash and B is to render services in exchange for a "salary" and a 50 per cent interest in the business. Assuming that the corporation is formed under the 1969 Model Act consider the following alternatives:

(a) At the outset of the venture, 1,000 shares of stock, par value of $100 per share, are simply issued to A and to B. Does B have a watered stock liability? What about MBCA (1969) § 19, second paragraph?

(b) At the outset of the venture, 100 shares of stock, $1 par value, are issued to A for $100,000; 100 shares are issued to B only after he has performed services for two years in consideration of such services. Does this avoid the § 19 and watered stock problems? What happens if A decides to close out the business after eighteen months? Where does B stand? [B, however, may have a breach of contract action against A if A wrongfully excludes B from the venture in violation of the agreement.]

(c) At the outset of the venture, 100 shares of stock, par value of $1, are issued to A for $100,000; B executes a promissory note for $100,000, payable in two years out of future services, and B is issued 100 shares in exchange for that note. Again consider MBCA (1969) § 19. As indicated earlier, some states permit shares to be issued in exchange for a promissory note; in those states B presumably would be simultaneously a shareholder and a debtor.

(d) At the outset of the venture, shares of common stock are issued to A and B at different prices. For example, using $1.00 par value shares, 100 shares are issued to A for $100,000 and 100 shares to B are issued to B for

$100. B actually pays the $100. So long as there is full disclosure, is there anything improper in issuing otherwise identical shares for different prices? However, even if this is proper, what happens if there is a fire shortly after the venture is begun, covered by insurance, and the parties decide to liquidate and distribute the insurance proceeds? Would not B be entitled to $50,000, even though he invested only $100? There is also an income tax problem from B's standpoint, since the bargain purchase of shares will probably be treated as compensation to B which is fully taxable in the year in which he receives the shares. This income tax problem is involved in some of the other alternatives as well including alternatives (b) and (c).

(e) At the outset of the venture, two classes of common shares are created with identical rights per share on dissolution, but with different voting rights:

(i) Class A common, par value $1.00 per share, one vote per share, 10,000 shares issued to A for $10.00 per share, or a total of $100,000.

(ii) Class B common, par value $1.00 per share, one thousand votes per share, 10 shares issued to B for $10.00 per share, or a total of $100.

If this technique were followed, how should the relative dividend rights of the two shares be established? [If dividend rights differ, which will probably be the case, the S corporation election is unavailable.] Generally, the RMBCA permits multiple or fractional votes per share; some state statutes, however, permit only single votes per share. Obviously, essentially the same structure could be created with fractional votes per share.

(f) At the outset of the venture, a single class of shares is created with a par value of $1.00 per share, and 10 shares are issued to A for $100 and 10 shares are issued to B for $100. A then lends the corporation $99,800 to complete the capitalization. Would that loan qualify for the "straight debt" safe harbor for the S corporation election (see p. 334, supra)? What should be the terms of repayment? Of interest? Is it fair to B to require that a commercial rate of interest be paid to A?

(g) At the outset of the venture, two classes of shares, preferred and common, are created each with a par value of $1.00 per share; 10 shares of common stock are issued to A for $100, 10 shares of common stock are issued to B for $100, and 9,980 shares of preferred are issued to A at $10 per share for $99,800, completing the capitalization. How should the dividend right of the preferred be established? Why is this alternative less attractive than others?

(h) Combine alternatives (f) and (g) as follows: at the outset of the venture, two classes of shares, preferred and common, are created each with a par value of $1.00 per share; ten shares of common are issued to A and B for $100 each; A is also issued 5,000 shares of preferred for $50,000 and lends the corporation the remaining $49,800, completing the capitalization. Is this an improvement over both alternatives (f) and (g)? Does this solution make the corporation ineligible for the S corporation election? Does it resemble the structure proposed by that "well-known and reputable firm of certified public accountants" in *Obre?*

(i) Combine alternatives (d) and (f) as follows: at the outset of the venture one class of common stock with a par value of $1.00 per share is created and ten shares are issued to A for $50,000 and ten shares to B for $100. A then lends the corporation the remaining $49,900. Is this the best solution?

(2) What difference would the enactment of the RMBCA make in the above alternatives? The elimination of par value and the restrictions on eligible consideration obviously simplify several of the alternatives, but the choices involving different classes of common shares and the mixing of debt and preferred shares in the capital structure are basically unaffected. It would be possible under the RMBCA to have B sign a two-year employment contract and issue all shares immediately. This, however, is not without its disadvantages. First, there may be a bunching of B's income for tax purposes in the year the corporation is formed. Second, what is the corporation to do with the employment contract if the fire described in example 1(d) above occurs? Sell it? To whom and for how much? B's shares have been properly issued so that B is entitled to share ratably with A in the assets; A might quite justifiably object if no attempt is made to realize upon this "asset."

(3) In the AB Furniture Store, A is a passive investor, putting in capital but not participating in the day-to-day affairs of the store. As indicated above, such investors often demand, and are entitled to receive, some sort of return on their investment. The choice of "how much" and "when" are obviously sensitive business decisions that must be negotiated. From the standpoint of the venture, if the S corporation election is unavailable, it is usually advantageous that such payments be in deductible form rather than as nondeductible dividends on, say, a special class of preferred shares. On the other hand, it is also usually desirable to give the corporation the option to defer or omit such payments if business demands dictate. That, of course, means that the debt is no longer within the "straight debt" safe harbor for the S corporation election. On such issues it is not uncommon for different participants to have different and inconsistent goals which must be accommodated, adjusted or compromised before the venture can begin.

(4) In many of the above alternatives, the interests of A and B are potentially, if not actually, adverse. If B is without a lawyer, an attorney representing A faces essentially the same ethical problems that must be addressed when considering the more basic question of the form of the enterprise. See chapter 3, section A, pages 134–5, supra. As indicated there, B is very likely to resist retaining a lawyer for reasons of cost, and may wish to rely on A's lawyer to represent his interests as well as A's. If you were A's lawyer in this situation, would you feel comfortable in giving B advice as well as A? Are the problems associated with par value/classes of stock/watered stock/S corporation election/Deep Rock, and other issues arising in the capitalization areas of such complexity that you should insist B retain his own lawyer?

F.   PUBLIC OFFERINGS

Whenever a corporation makes an offering of shares, consideration must be given to the possible application of the state and federal securities laws. If the offering is made to only a few persons, one or more exemptions will often be available, though that cannot be absolutely guaranteed simply by the size of the offering; if the offering is made in a public manner or to numerous persons, there is a presumption that compliance with the securities laws will be necessary unless an exemption is clearly available. The balance of this subsection deals with the following statute, the sequence of sections of which has been rearranged to simplify the reader's understanding of its basic structure. The materials following this statute contain references to the statutory provisions quoted here:

SECURITIES ACT OF 1933
15 U.S.C.A. §§ 77a–77aa.

Sec. 5.   (a) Unless a registration statement is in effect as to a security, it shall be unlawful for any person, directly or indirectly—

(1) to make use of any means or instruments of transportation or communication in interstate commerce or of the mails to sell such security through the use or medium of any prospectus or otherwise; or

(2) to carry or cause to be carried through the mails or in interstate commerce, by any means or instruments of transportation, any such security for the purpose of sale or for delivery after sale. * * *

Sec. 12.   Any person who—

(1) offers or sells a security in violation of section 5, or

(2) offers or sells a security (whether or not exempted by the provisions of section 3, * * * by the use of any means or instruments of transportation or communication in interstate commerce or of the mails, by means of a prospectus or oral communication, which includes an untrue statement of a material fact or omits to state a material fact necessary in order to make the statements, in the light of the circumstances under which they were made, not misleading (the purchaser not knowing of such untruth or omission), and who shall not sustain the burden of proof that he did not know, and in the exercise of reasonable care could not have known, of such untruth or omission,

shall be liable to the person purchasing such security from him, who may sue either at law or in equity in any court of competent jurisdiction, to recover the consideration paid for such security with interest thereon, less the amount of any income received thereon, upon the tender of such security, or for damages if he no longer owns the security. * * *

Sec. 17. (a) It shall be unlawful for any person in the offer or sale of any securities by the use of any means or instruments of transportation or communication in interstate commerce or by the use of the mails, directly or indirectly—

(1) to employ any device, scheme, or artifice to defraud, or

(2) to obtain money or property by means of any untrue statement of a material fact or any omission to state a material fact necessary in order to make the statements made, in the light of the circumstances under which they were made, not misleading, or

(3) to engage in any transaction, practice, or course of business which operates or would operate as a fraud or deceit upon the purchaser.

(b) It shall be unlawful for any person, by the use of any means or instruments of transportation or communication in interstate commerce or by the use of the mails, to publish, give publicity to, or circulate any notice, circular, advertisement, newspaper, article, letter, investment service, or communication which, though not purporting to offer a security for sale, describes such security for a consideration received or to be received, directly or indirectly, from an issuer, underwriter, or dealer, without fully disclosing the receipt, whether past or prospective, of such consideration and the amount thereof.

(c) The exemptions provided in section 3 shall not apply to the provisions of this section.

Sec. 3. (a) Except as hereinafter expressly provided, the provisions of this subchapter shall not apply to any of the following classes of securities: * * *

(11) Any security which is a part of an issue offered and sold only to persons resident within a single State or Territory, where the issuer of such security is a person resident and doing business within, or, if a corporation, incorporated by and doing business within, such State or Territory. * * *

(b) The Commission may * * * add any class of securities to the securities exempted as provided in this section, if it finds that the enforcement of this title with respect to such securities is not necessary in the public interest and for the protection of investors by reason of the small amount involved or the limited character of the public offering; but no issue of securities shall be exempted under this subsection where the aggregate amount at which such issue is offered to the public exceeds $5,000,000. [The Small Business Investment Incentive Act of 1980 increased the maximum dollar amount in this subsection from $2,000,000 to $5,000,000.] * * *

Sec. 4. The provisions of section 5 shall not apply to—

(1) transactions by any person other than an issuer, underwriter, or dealer.

(2) transactions by an issuer not involving any public offering.

* * *

(6) transactions involving offers or sales by an issuer solely to one or more accredited investors, if the aggregate offering price of an issue of securities offered in reliance on this paragraph does not exceed the amount allowed under section 3(b) of this title, if there is no advertising or public solicitation in connection with the transaction by the issuer or anyone acting on the issuer's behalf, and if the issuer files such notice with the Commission as the Commission shall prescribe. [Subsection (6) was added by The Incentive Act of 1980.] * * *

Sec. 2. When used in this subchapter, unless the context otherwise requires—

(1) The term "security" means any note, stock, treasury stock, bond, debenture, evidence of indebtedness, certificate of interest or participation in any profit-sharing agreement, collateral-trust certificate, preorganization certificate or subscription, transferable share, investment contract, voting-trust certificate, certificate of deposit for a security, fractional undivided interest in oil, gas, or other mineral rights, any put, call, straddle, option, or privilege on any security, certificate of deposit, or group or index of securities (including any interest therein or based on the value thereof), or any put, call, straddle, option, or privilege entered into on a national securities exchange relating to foreign currency, or, in general, any interest or instrument commonly known as a "security," or any certificate of interest or participation in, temporary or interim certificate for, receipt for, guarantee of, or warrant or right to subscribe to or purchase, any of the foregoing. * * *

(11) The term "underwriter" means any person who has purchased from an issuer with a view to, or offers or sells for an issuer in connection with, the distribution of any security * * *. As used in this paragraph the term "issuer" shall include, in addition to an issuer, any person directly or indirectly controlling or controlled by the issuer, or any person under direct or indirect common control with the issuer.

(12) The term "dealer" means any person who engages either for all or part of his time, directly or indirectly, as agent, broker, or principal, in the business of offering, buying, selling, or otherwise dealing or trading in securities issued by another person. * * *

(15) The term "accredited investor" shall mean—

(i) a bank as defined in section 3(a)(2) of the Act whether acting in its individual or fiduciary capacity; an insurance company as defined in section 2(13) of the Act; an investment company registered under the Investment Company Act of 1940 or a business development company as defined in section 2(a)(48) of that Act; a Small Business Investment Company licensed by the Small Business Administration; or an employee benefit plan, including an individual retirement account, which is subject to the provisions of the Employee Retirement Income Security Act of 1974, if the investment decision is made by a plan fiduciary, as defined in section 3(21) of such Act, which is either a bank, insurance company, or registered investment adviser; or

(ii) any person who, on the basis of such factors as financial sophistication, net worth, knowledge, and experience in financial matters, or amount of assets under management qualifies as an accredited investor under rules and regulations which the Commission shall prescribe. [Subsection (15) was added by the Small Business Investment Incentive Act of 1980.] * * *

Notes

(1) The Securities Act of 1933 is an involuted and complex statute that is studied in depth in advanced law school courses. Significant portions of this statute not reproduced above include:

(a) Sections 6 through 10, and Schedule A, which describe the procedure for registration and the information required to be included in a registration statement;

(b) Section 11, which provides for personal liability for signers of registration statements for false statements in them, subject to complex defenses; and

(c) Sections 19 and 20, which provide for criminal penalties for knowing violation of the Act and for injunctive remedies where appropriate.

(2) Registration statements are filed with the Securities and Exchange Commission in Washington, D.C. The SEC has promulgated a "short form" registration process under its exemptive authority under section 3(b) for offerings of up to $5,000,000 which are filed with the SEC's regional offices. This regulation, known universally as "Reg A", is basically a short-form registration procedure, though technically it is a section 3(b) exemption. The importance of Reg A filings has declined with the development of newer small offering exemptions discussed below.

(3) Section 5(a), it should be noted, permits sales only after a registration statement is "in effect." The S.E.C. is charged with the responsibility of reviewing registration statements filed with it and permitting a statement to become effective only after assuring that disclosure requirements are met. Because of heavy work loads and changes in regulatory philosophy, the degree of detailed review of registration statements performed by the S.E.C. staff has declined in recent years, though of course the civil and criminal responsibility of filing parties has not been affected.

(4) The Securities Act of 1933 is a full disclosure statute. The S.E.C. is not authorized to make a judgment about the investment quality of a security; if all negative factors have been fully and adequately disclosed, the registration statement must be permitted to become effective even if

the S.E.C. believes there is no chance that investors can ever realize anything but the loss of their investment. In this respect, federal securities regulation differs from the regulatory philosophy of some state statutes, which provide for "merit review" of the investment quality of securities offered within the state. The Texas statute, for example, requires the Securities Commissioner to determine that the terms of an issue are "fair, just, and equitable" before the issue may be sold in Texas. Vernon's Ann. Tex.Civ.Stat. art. 581–10A.

(5) The Securities Act of 1933 was the product of the early New Deal era, and its roots lie in the frenetic years of the 1920s and the collapse of securities values generally during the early years of the great depression. As one Congressional Report noted:

> Fully half or $25,000,000,000 worth of securities floated during * * * [the 1920s] have been proved to be worthless. * * * The flotation of such a mass of essentially fraudulent securities was made possible because of the complete abandonment by many underwriters and dealers in securities of those standards of fair, honest and prudent dealing that should be basic to the encouragement of investment in any enterprise.

H.R.Rep. No. 85, 73rd Cong., 1st Sess. (1933), p. 2. Losses in the late 1920s and early 1930s were not limited to securities, of course. Real estate, art works, and practically everything else declined precipitously in value during this period. Securities were viewed as a compelling case for regulation for several reasons: the securities markets were viewed as central in the American capitalistic economy; securities are different from most tangible commodities and real estate in that they are intangibles, represented by pieces of paper that have no intrinsic value; also, the abuses in the securities markets of the 1920s were viewed as the continuation of a pattern of abuse that was evident in the late 1800s and could be traced back much further.

(6) State regulation of securities issues generally predates the Securities Act of 1933. State statutes on this subject are called "blue sky laws" because of a Kansas promoter in the early years of this century who was reputedly selling "lots in the blue sky in fee simple absolute." See Mulvy, Blue Sky Law, 36 Can.L.Times 37 (1916). These statutes generally require registration of new issues proposed to be sold within the state. A national issue of securities therefore requires registration in 50 states as well as under the 1933 Act. This process, known as "blue skying an issue," is practical because states generally permit "registration by coordination" or "registration by notification" (by seasoned issuers), relying primarily on the Federal system of disclosure.

————

For most small corporations it is essential that capital-raising be structured so as to *avoid* the registration requirements of the Federal Securities Act of 1933. Registration of an issue by an "unseasoned company," i.e. one whose shares are not widely traded in the public markets and that has never previously filed a registration statement under the 1933 Act, is an expensive, complex and often messy process. R. Hamilton, Fundamentals of Modern Business (1989) pp. 334–335:*

A registered public sale of securities will usually involve the use of professional securities underwriters and securities firms to distribute the securities to the investing public. An underwriter is a person or organization that acquires shares for resale or who arranges the direct sale of shares by the issuer. Investment bankers and securities firms regularly underwrite new securities issues on a commercial basis. Large issues are "syndicated" or broken up among a number of securities firms and sold by them to investors. There is a precept in the securities business that "shares are sold not bought" and that professional selling assistance is essential for most successful floatations of new securities. The flip side, of course, is that underwriting fees and sales commissions add significantly to the cost of the public offering. Nevertheless professional assistance may be a bargain in the long run, since a do-it-yourself public offering may not raise enough capital. * * *

There are significant advantages to a public offering. A successful public offer may create a market for the shares of the corporation: The entrepreneur may later use this market to liquidate a portion of his or her investment in the business. Further, very large amounts of capital may be raised through a public offering. * * *

There are significant disadvantages as well. The cost of a public offering for an "unseasoned" company (one that has not previously made a public offering) is so substantial that a public offering of at least $10,000,000 is necessary to justify the expense. Further, there are substantial disclosure obligations with respect to previous transactions that the entrepreneur may prefer not be made public. Finally, a public company takes on disclosure and other legal obligations that add to the cost of operation and limit the amount of information about future developments that may be kept confidential. Whether or not these disadvantages outweigh the advantages cannot be answered in the abstract.

Notes

(1) The principal costs of a public offering are brokerage and underwriting commissions, attorneys' fees for preparation of offering materials, accountants' fees for a special audit and for review of offering materials, printing costs, and filing fees for the SEC, state securities commissions (or other Blue Sky agencies), and the National Association of Securities Dealers.

(2) A company making an initial public offering (usually referred to as an IPO) must create financial statements that are prepared in accordance with Regulation S–X for its previous five years. Most closely held companies find that their existing financial statements, while perhaps entirely suitable for their own needs while closely held, must be significantly

* Reprinted with permission of Little, Brown and Company.

revised to meet the requirements of Regulation S–X. Recalculation over a five year period is often difficult and expensive, sometimes complicated by the absence of complete financial records.

(3) Securities registration from the standpoint of the attorney is a highly specialized and complex matter. The "corporate check" required for an IPO usually involves the cooperation of two sets of attorneys: those representing the issuer and those representing the underwriter. Because the 1933 Act imposes substantial civil liabilities for the use of prospectuses or other selling documents that contain untrue statements of material fact (or omit a statement needed to make the statements made not misleading), the attorneys must examine carefully the background of prior transactions, determine whether disclosure may be required of transactions between the issuer and the managers, determine whether prior issues of securities were lawfully made pursuant to an available exemption, and so forth. The process by which attorneys verify the accuracy and completeness of registration statements is usually referred to as a "due diligence" investigation. A sloppily prepared or incomplete registration statement may subject the attorneys to personal liability to investors as well as causing damage to their reputations if they are named as parties in a securities fraud or disciplinary proceeding. The number of suits filed against attorneys under the 1933 Act is surprisingly large, and this type of practice is viewed as a high risk practice. Insurers may be reluctant to write malpractice insurance for securities attorneys in solo practice or with small firms. This, plus the fact that the SEC disclosure requirements are complex, means that lawyers generally should not attempt an IPO unless they are specialists in this area or they obtain the assistance of specialized counsel.

SECURITIES AND EXCHANGE COMM'N v. RALSTON PURINA CO.

Supreme Court of the United States, 1953.
346 U.S. 119, 73 S.Ct. 981, 97 L.Ed. 1494.

MR. JUSTICE CLARK, delivered the opinion of the Court.

Section [4(2)] of the Securities Act of 1933 exempts "transactions by an issuer not involving any public offering" from the registration requirements of § 5. We must decide whether Ralston Purina's offerings of treasury stock to its "key employees" are within this exemption. On a complaint brought by the Commission under § 20(b) of the Act seeking to enjoin respondent's unregistered offerings, the District Court held the exemption applicable and dismissed the suit. The Court of Appeals affirmed. The question has arisen many times since the Act was passed; an apparent need to define the scope of the private offering exemption prompted certiorari. 345 U.S. 903, 73 S.Ct. 643.

Ralston Purina manufactures and distributes various feed and cereal products. Its processing and distribution facilities are scattered throughout the United States and Canada, staffed by some 7,000 employees. At least since 1911 the company has had a policy of encouraging stock ownership among its employees; more particularly, since 1942 it has made authorized but unissued common shares available to some of them. Between 1947 and 1951, the period covered by the record in this case, Ralston Purina sold nearly $2,000,000 of stock to employees without registration and in so doing made use of the mails.

In each of these years, a corporate resolution authorized the sale of common stock "to employees * * * who shall, without any solicitation by the Company or its officers or employees, inquire of any of them as to how to purchase common stock of Ralston Purina Company." A memorandum sent to branch and store managers after the resolution was adopted, advised that "The only employees to whom this stock will be available will be those who take the initiative and are interested in buying stock at present market prices." Among those responding to these offers were employees with the duties of artist, bakeshop foreman, chow loading foreman, clerical assistant, copywriter, electrician, stock clerk, mill office clerk, order credit trainee, production trainee, stenographer, and veterinarian. The buyers lived in over fifty widely separated communities scattered from Garland, Texas, to Nashua, New Hampshire and Visalia, California. The lowest salary bracket of those purchasing was $2,700 in 1949, $2,435 in 1950 and $3,107 in 1951. The record shows that in 1947, 234 employees bought stock, 20 in 1948, 414 in 1949, 411 in 1950, and the 1951 offer, interrupted by this litigation, produced 165 applications to purchase. No records were kept of those to whom the offers were made; the estimated number in 1951 was 500.

The company bottoms its exemption claim on the classification of all offerees as "key employees" in its organization. Its position on trial was that "A key employee * * * is not confined to an organization chart. It would include an individual who is eligible for promotion, an individual who especially influences others or who advises others, a person whom the employees look to in some special way, an individual, of course, who carries some special responsibility, who is sympathetic to management and who is ambitious and who the management feels is likely to be promoted to a greater responsibility." That an offering to all of its employees would be public is conceded.

The Securities Act nowhere defines the scope of § [4(2)'s] private offering exemption. Nor is the legislative history of much help in staking out its boundaries. The problem was first dealt with in § 4(1) of the House Bill, H.R. 5480, 73d Cong., 1st Sess., which exempted "transactions by an issuer not with or through an underwriter; * * *." The bill, as reported by the House Committee, added "and not involving any public offering." H.R.Rep. No. 85, 73d Cong., 1st Sess. 1. This was thought to be one of those transactions "where there is no practical need for * * * [the bill's] application or where the public benefits are too remote." Id., at 5. The exemption as thus delimited became law. It assumed its present shape with the deletion of "not with or through an underwriter" by § 203(a) of the Securities Exchange Act of 1934, 48 Stat. 906, a change regarded as the elimination of superfluous language. H.R.Rep. No. 1838, 73d Cong., 2d Sess. 41.

Decisions under comparable exemptions in the English Companies Acts and state "blue sky" laws, the statutory antecedents of federal securities legislation have made one thing clear—to be public, an offer need not be open to the whole world. In Securities and Exchange Comm. v. Sunbeam Gold Mines Co., 9 Cir., 1938, 95 F.2d 699, 701, this point was made in dealing with an offering to the stockholders of two corporations about to be merged. Judge Denman observed that:

> "In its broadest meaning the term 'public' distinguishes the populace at large from groups of individual members of the public segregated because of some common interest or characteristic. Yet such a distinction is inadequate for practical purposes; manifestly an offering of securities to all redheaded men, to all residents of Chicago or San Francisco, to all existing stockholders of the General Motors Corporation or the American Telephone & Telegraph Company, is no less 'public', in every realistic sense of the word, than an unrestricted offering to the world at large. Such an offering, though not open to everyone who may choose to apply, is none the less 'public' in character, for the means used to select the particular individuals to whom the offering is to be made bear no sensible relation to the purposes for which the selection is made. * * * To determine the distinction between 'public' and 'private' in any particular context, it is essential to examine the circumstances under which the distinction is sought to be established and to consider the purposes sought to be achieved by such distinction."

The courts below purported to apply this test. The District Court held, in the language of the Sunbeam decision, that "The purpose of the selection bears a 'sensible relation' to the class chosen," finding that "The sole purpose of the 'selection' is to keep part stock ownership of the business within the operating personnel of the business and to spread ownership throughout all departments and activities of the business." The Court of Appeals treated the case as involving "an offering, without solicitation, of common stock to a selected group of key employees of the issuer, most of whom are already stockholders when the offering is made, with the sole purpose of enabling them to secure a proprietary interest in the company or to increase the interest already held by them."

Exemption from the registration requirements of the Securities Act is the question. The design of the statute is to protect investors by promoting full disclosure of information thought necessary to informed investment decisions. The natural way to interpret the private offering exemption is in light of the statutory purpose. Since exempt transactions are those as to which "there is no practical need for * * * [the bill's] application," the applicability of § [4(2)] should turn on whether the particular class of persons affected need the protection of the Act. An offering to those who are shown to be able to fend for themselves is a transaction "not involving any public offering."

The Commission would have us go one step further and hold that "an offering to a substantial number of the public" is not exempt under

§ [4(2)]. We are advised that "whatever the special circumstances, the Commission has consistently interpreted the exemption as being inapplicable when a large number of offerees is involved." But the statute would seem to apply to a "public offering" whether to few or many. It may well be that offerings to a substantial number of persons would rarely be exempt. Indeed nothing prevents the commission, in enforcing the statute, from using some kind of numerical test in deciding when to investigate particular exemption claims. But there is no warrant for superimposing a quantity limit on private offerings as a matter of statutory interpretation.

The exemption, as we construe it, does not deprive corporate employees, as a class, of the safeguards of the Act. We agree that some employee offerings may come within § [4(2)], e.g., one made to executive personnel who because of their position have access to the same kind of information that the act would make available in the form of a registration statement. Absent such a showing of special circumstances, employees are just as much members of the investing "public" as any of their neighbors in the community. Although we do not rely on it, the rejection in 1934 of an amendment which would have specifically exempted employee stock offerings supports this conclusion. The House Managers, commenting on the Conference Report, said that "the participants in employees' stock-investment plans may be in as great need of the protection afforded by availability of information concerning the issuer for which they work as are most other members of the public." H.R.Rep. No. 1838, 73d Cong., 2d Sess. 41.

Keeping in mind the broadly remedial purposes of federal securities legislation, imposition of the burden of proof on an issuer who would plead the exemption seems to us fair and reasonable. Agreeing, the court below thought the burden met primarily because of the respondent's purpose in singling out its key employees for stock offerings. But once it is seen that the exemption question turns on the knowledge of the offerees, the issuer's motives, laudable though they may be, fade into irrelevance. The focus of inquiry should be on the need of the offerees for the protections afforded by registration. The employees here were not shown to have access to the kind of information which registration would disclose. The obvious opportunities for pressure and imposition make it advisable that they be entitled to compliance with § 5.

Reversed.

THE CHIEF JUSTICE and MR. JUSTICE BURTON dissent.

Notes

(1) Assume that a corporation seeking to take advantage of the non-public offering exemption inadvertently makes one offer to a person who needs the protection of the Securities Act under the *Ralston Purina* test. Is the exemption thereby totally lost and full scale registration required? For an affirmative answer, see Securities and Exchange Comm'n v. Conti-

nental Tobacco Co. of South Carolina, 463 F.2d 137 (5th Cir.1972), though the case actually involves offers to several such persons.

(2) Could Ralston–Purina have avoided the impact of the holding in this case by structuring its stock sale plan in the form of a sale to a corporate officer (such as the president or a vice president) who clearly did not need the protection of the Act, and then having that officer sell shares to employees who asked about the possibility of stock purchases? Consider the definition of "underwriter" in section 2(11) [page 341 supra]. How can a person who acquires shares in a legitimate section 4(2) transaction, ever safely resell those shares in light of this definition? The SEC has adopted Rule 144, 17 C.F.R. § 230.144, to establish guidelines for resales of unregistered shares [often called "restricted stock"] by investors without concern that the seller may be deemed to be an "underwriter" under section 2(11). Rule 144 basically establishes a two year holding requirement; this Rule is complex, however, and cannot be simply summarized. Rule 144 is not exclusive so that resales in some circumstances within the two year period may be consistent with the original non-public offering exemption even though they do not comply with Rule 144. [Rule 144 probably would not permit the president or vice president to offer shares in the hypothetical set forth above.]

(3) In 1988, the SEC proposed Regulation 144A, which permits offers and sales of restricted securities without regard to holding periods to institutional investors with portfolios of $100,000,000 or more. The securities remain restricted in the hands of the purchaser, though, of course, further sales under Rule 144A would be permitted. SEC Rel. No. 33–6808 (1988); reproposed, SEC Rel. No. 33–6839 (1989). For a description of the background of the Rule 144A problem, see Schneider, Section 4(1½)— Private Resales of Restricted Securities, 49 Ohio St.L.J. 501 (1988).

(4) Consider the problem of section 2(11) from the standpoint of the corporation. If it verifies that all the offerees meet the test of *Ralston Purina,* has it not inadvertently violated the 1933 Act if one of the offerees is a section 2(11) underwriter who reoffers the shares to a person who does not meet the *Ralston Purina* standard? Is such a subsequent resale exempt by reason of section 4(1) in light of the fact that the seller is an "underwriter"? The excerpts from Regulation D following this note describe protections the issuer may avail itself of to avoid such inadvertent violations of the Securities Act.

SECURITIES ACT RELEASE NO. 33–6389

47 Fed.Reg. 11251 (1982).

SUMMARY

The Commission announces the adoption of a new regulation governing certain offers and sales of securities without registration under the Securities Act of 1933 and a uniform notice of sales form to be used for all offerings under the regulation. The regulation replaces three exemptions and four forms, all of which are being rescinded. The new regulation is designed to simplify and clarify existing exemptions, to expand their availability, and to achieve uniformity between federal and state exemptions in order to facilitate capital formation consistent with the protection of investors.   * * *

I. BACKGROUND

Regulation D is the product of the Commission's evaluation of the impact of its rules and regulations on the ability of small businesses to raise capital. This study has revealed a particular concern that the registration requirements and the exemptive scheme of the Securities Act impose disproportionate restraints on small issuers. * * *

Coincident with the Commission's small business program, Congress enacted the Small Business Investment Incentive Act of 1980 (the "Incentive Act") [94 Stat. 2275 (codified in scattered sections of 15 U.S.C.)]. The Incentive Act included three changes to the Securities Act: the addition of an exemption in Section 4(6) for offers and sales solely to accredited investors, the increase in the ceiling of Section 3(b) from $2,000,000 to $5,000,000, and the addition of Section 19(c) which, among other things, authorized "the development of a uniform exemption from registration for small issuers which can be agreed upon among several States or between the States and the Federal Government." * * *

Commentary to the Commission criticized the complexity of the exemptive scheme as it relates to all issuers. * * *

REGULATION D—RULES GOVERNING THE LIMITED OFFER AND SALE OF SECURITIES WITHOUT REGISTRATION UNDER THE SECURITIES ACT OF 1933

17 C.F.R. § 230.501 et seq. (1989).

PRELIMINARY NOTES

1. The following rules relate to transactions exempted from the registration requirements of section 5 of the Securities Act of 1933 (the "Act"). * * *

2. Nothing in these rules obviates the need to comply with any applicable state law relating to the offer and sale of securities. Regulation D is intended to be a basic element in a uniform system of Federal–State limited offering exemptions consistent with the provisions of sections 18 and 19(c) of the Act. * * *

6. In view of the objectives of these rules and the policies underlying the Act, regulation D is not available to any issuer for any transaction or chain of transactions that, although in technical compliance with these rules, is part of a plan or scheme to evade the registration provisions of the Act. In such cases, registration under the Act is required. * * *

§ 230.501 Definitions and terms used in Regulation D

As used in Regulation D (§§ 230.501–230.508), the following terms shall have the meaning indicated:

(a) *Accredited investor.* "Accredited investor" shall mean any person who comes within any of the following categories, or who the issuer reasonably believes comes within any of the following categories, at the time of the sale of the securities to that person:

(1) Any bank * * * or any savings and loan association or other institution * * * whether acting in its individual or fiduciary capacity; any [registered] broker or dealer * * * any insurance company * * * any investment company * * * or a business development company * * * any Small Business Investment Company [or certain employee benefit plans]. * * *

(3) Any organization described in section 501(c)(3) of the Internal Revenue Code, corporation, Massachusetts or similar business trust, or partnership, not formed for the specific purpose of acquiring the securities offered, with total assets in excess of $5,000,000;

(4) Any director, executive officer, or general partner of the issuer of the securities being offered or sold, or any director, executive officer, or general partner of a general partner of that issuer;

(5) Any natural person whose individual net worth, or joint net worth with that person's spouse, at the time of his purchase exceeds $1,000,000;

(6) Any natural person who had an individual income in excess of $200,000 in each of the two most recent years or joint income with that person's spouse in excess of $300,000 in each of those years and has a reasonable expectation of reaching the same income level in the current year;

(7) Any trust, with total assets in excess of $5,000,000, not formed for the specific purpose of acquiring the securities offered, whose purchase is directed by a sophisticated person as described in § 230.506(b)(2)(ii); and

(8) Any entity in which all of the equity owners are accredited investors. * * *

(e) *Calculation of number of purchasers.* For purposes of calculating the number of purchasers under §§ 230.505(b) and 230.506(b) only, the following shall apply:

(1) The following purchasers shall be excluded:

(i) Any relative, spouse or relative of the spouse of a purchaser who has the same principal residence as the purchaser;

(ii) Any trust or estate in which a purchaser and any of the persons related to him as specified in paragraph (e)(1)(i) or (e)(1)(iii) of this section collectively have more than 50 percent of the beneficial interest (excluding contingent interests);

(iii) Any corporation or other organization of which a purchaser and any of the persons related to him as specified in paragraph (e)(1)(i) or (e)(1)(ii) of this section collectively are beneficial owners of more than 50 percent of the equity securities (excluding directors' qualifying shares) or equity interests; and

(iv) Any accredited investor. * * *

§ 230.502 General conditions to be met

The following conditions shall be applicable to offers and sales made under Regulation D (§§ 230.501–230.508):

(a) *Integration.* All sales that are part of the same Regulation D offering must meet all of the terms and conditions of Regulation D. Offers and sales that are made more than six months before the start of a Regulation D offering or are made more than six months after completion of a Regulation D offering will not be considered part of that Regulation D offering, so long as during those six month periods there are no offers or sales of securities by or for the issuer that are of the same or a similar class as those offered or sold under Regulation D, * * *

Note: The term "offering" is not defined in the Act or in Regulation D. If the issuer offers or sells securities for which the safe harbor rule in paragraph (a) of this § 230.502 is unavailable, the determination as to whether separate sales of securities are part of the same offering (i.e. are considered "integrated") depends on the particular facts and circumstances. Generally, transactions otherwise meeting the requirements of an exemption will not be integrated with simultaneous offerings being made outside the United States effected in a manner that will result in the securities coming to rest abroad.

The following factors should be considered in determining whether offers and sales should be integrated for purposes of the exemptions under Regulation D:

(a) Whether the sales are part of a single plan of financing;

(b) Whether the sales involve issuance of the same class of securities;

(c) Whether the sales have been made at or about the same time;

(d) Whether the same type of consideration is received; and

(e) Whether the sales are made for the same general purpose.

(b) *Information requirements* —(1) *When information must be furnished.* If the issuer sells securities under § 230.505 or § 230.506 to any purchaser that is not an accredited investor, the issuer shall furnish the information specified in paragraph (b)(2) of this section to such purchaser a reasonable time prior to sale. * * *

(c) *Limitation on manner of offering.* Except as provided in § 230.504(b)(1), neither the issuer nor any person acting on its behalf shall offer or sell the securities by any form of general solicitation or general advertising, including, but not limited to, the following:

(1) Any advertisement, article, notice or other communication published in any newspaper, magazine, or similar media or broadcast over television or radio; and

(2) Any seminar or meeting whose attendees have been invited by any general solicitation or general advertising.

(d) *Limitations on resale.* Except as provided in § 230.504(b)(1), securities acquired in a transaction under Regulation D shall have the status of securities acquired in a transaction under section 4(2) of the Act and cannot be resold without registration under the Act or an exemption therefrom. The issuer shall exercise reasonable care to assure that the purchasers of the securities are not underwriters within the meaning of section 2(11) of the Act, which reasonable care may be demonstrated by the following:

(1) Reasonable inquiry to determine if the purchaser is acquiring the securities for himself or for other persons;

(2) Written disclosure to each purchaser prior to sale that the securities have not been registered under the Act and, therefore, cannot be resold unless they are registered under the Act or unless an exemption from registration is available; and

(3) Placement of a legend on the certificate or other document that evidences the securities stating that the securities have not been registered under the Act and setting forth or referring to the restrictions on transferability and sale of the securities.

While taking these actions will establish the requisite reasonable care, it is not the exclusive method to demonstrate such care. Other actions by the issuer may satisfy this provision. * * *

§ 230.504 Exemption for limited offerings and sales of securities not exceeding $1,000,000

(a) *Exemption.* Offers and sales of securities that satisfy the conditions in paragraph (b) of this section * * * shall be exempt from the provisions of section 5 of the Act under section 3(b) of the Act.

(b) *Conditions to be met* —(1) *General Conditions.* To qualify for exemption under this § 230.504, offers and sales must satisfy the terms and conditions of §§ 230.501 and 230.502, except that the provisions of § 230.502(c) and (d) shall not apply to offers and sales of securities under this § 230.504 that are made:

(i) Exclusively in one or more states each of which provides for the registration of the securities and requires the delivery of a disclosure document before sale and that are made in accordance with those state provisions; or

(ii) In one or more states which have no provision for the registration of the securities and the delivery of a disclosure document before sale, if the securities have been registered in at least one state which provides for such registration and delivery before sale, offers and sales are made in the state of registration in accordance with such state provisions, and such document is in fact delivered to all purchasers in the states which have no such procedure before the sale of the securities.

(2) *Specific condition*—(i) *Limitation on aggregate offering price.* The aggregate offering price for an offering of securities * * * shall not exceed $1,000,000, less the aggregate offering price for all securities sold within the twelve months before the start of and during the offering of securities under this § 230.504 in reliance on any exemption under section 3(b) of the Act or in violation of section 5(a) of the Act, provided that no more than $500,000 of such aggregate offering price is attributable to offers and sales of securities without registration under a state's securities laws. * * *

§ 230.505 Exemption for limited offers and sales of securities not exceeding $5,000,000

(a) *Exemption.* Offers and sales of securities that satisfy the conditions in paragraph (b) of this section by an issuer that is not an investment company shall be exempt from the provisions of section 5 of the Act under section 3(b) of the Act.

(b) *Conditions to be met*—(1) *General conditions.* To qualify for exemption under this section, offers and sales must satisfy the terms and conditions of §§ 230.501 and 230.502.

(2) *Specific conditions*—(i) *Limitation on aggregate offering price.* The aggregate offering price for an offering of securities under this § 230.505, as defined in § 203.501(c), shall not exceed $5,000,000, less the aggregate offering price for all securities sold within the twelve months before the start of and during the offering of securities under this section in reliance on any exemption under section 3(b) of the Act or in violation of section 5(a) of the Act. * * *

(ii) *Limitation on number of purchasers.* There are no more than or the issuer reasonably believes that there are no more than 35 purchasers of securities from the issuer in any offering under this section. * * *

§ 230.506 Exemption for limited offers and sales without regard to dollar amount of offering

(a) *Exemption.* Offers and sales of securities by an issuer that satisfy the conditions in paragraph (b) of this section shall be deemed to be transactions not involving any public offering within the meaning of section 4(2) of the Act.

(b) *Conditions to be met*—(1) *General conditions.* To qualify for an exemption under this section, offers and sales must satisfy all the terms and conditions of §§ 230.501 and 230.502.

(2) *Specific Conditions*—(i) *Limitation on number of purchasers.* There are no more than or the issuer reasonably believes that there are

no more than 35 purchasers of securities from the issuer in any offering under this section. * * *

(ii) *Nature of purchasers*. Each purchaser who is not an accredited investor either alone or with his purchaser representative(s) has such knowledge and experience in financial and business matters that he is capable of evaluating the merits and risks of the prospective investment, or the issuer reasonably believes immediately prior to making any sale that such purchaser comes within this description. * * *

§ 230.508 Insignificant deviations from a term, condition or requirement of Regulation D

(a) A failure to comply with a term, condition or requirement of § 230.504, § 230.505 or § 230.506 will not result in the loss of the exemption from the requirements of section 5 of the Act for any offer or sale to a particular individual or entity, if the person relying on the exemption shows:

(1) The failure to comply did not pertain to a term, condition or requirement directly intended to protect that particular individual or entity; and

(2) The failure to comply was insignificant with respect to the offering as a whole, provided that any failure to comply with paragraph (c) of § 230.502, paragraph (b)(2)(i) of § 230.504, paragraphs (b)(2)(i) and (ii) of § 230.505 and paragraph (b)(2)(i) of § 230.506 shall be deemed to be significant to the offering as a whole; and

(3) A good faith and reasonable attempt was made to comply with all applicable terms, conditions and requirements of § 230.504, § 230.505 or § 230.506. * * *

Notes

(1) In its initial release of Regulation D, SEC Rel. 33–6389, 47 Fed.Reg. 11251 (1982), the SEC explained the purpose of rule 504 as follows:

> Rule 504 * * * removes restrictions on the manner of offering and on resale if an offering is conducted exclusively in states where it is registered and where a disclosure document is delivered under the applicable state law. * * * Rule 504 does not prescribe specific disclosure requirements. Rule 504 is an effort by the Commission to set aside a clear and workable exemption for small offerings by small issuers to be regulated by state "Blue Sky" requirements and to be subject to federal antifraud provisions and civil liability provisions such as Section 12(2). Therefore, the exemption is not available to issuers that are subject to the reporting obligations of the Securities Exchange Act of 1934 * * *.

(2) Regulation D was also designed to implement the statutory command to the SEC to develop uniform exemptions from registration for both federal and state regulatory agencies. Again, SEC Rel. 33–6389, explains:

> In conjunction with the proposal and adoption of Regulation D, the Commission, through its Division of Corporation Finance, has coordi-

nated with the North American Securities Administrators Association ("NASAA"),[24] through its Subcommittee on Small Business Financing ("NASAA Subcommittee"), * * *

The objective of this process has been to develop a basic framework of limited offering exemptions that can apply uniformly at the federal and state levels. Regulation D is intended to be the principal element of this framework. * * * Rules 505 and 506, and applicable definitions, terms and conditions in Rules 501–503, are intended to be uniform federal-state exemptions.

In October 1981, NASAA formally adopted a uniform limited offering exemption as an official policy guideline. This exemption, which had two alternatives, was based on proposed Rule 505 of Regulation D but differed from that provision in certain respects. Subsequent to the endorsement of the uniform exemption and considering the public comment received, the NASAA Subcommittee and the Division of Corporation Finance coordinated to minimize differences in the NASAA policy guideline and Regulation D. The Commission understands that, following its adoption of Regulation D, the NASAA Subcommittee will recommend adoption by NASAA of modifications to its uniform limited offering exemption to provide for a uniform exemptive system. This system will endorse Rule 505 with certain additional terms as one option, and Rules 505 and 506 with no changes as a second option.

(3) Rule 508 was added in 1989, SEC Rel. No. 33–6825, 54 Fed.Reg. 11369 (1989), to "alleviate the draconian consequences of an innocent and insignificant defect in perfecting an exemption from registration." Keller, Securities Exemptions: The Saga of a Substantial Compliance Defense, Insights, Vol. 3, No. 8, p. 11 (Aug. 1989).* The author observes:

In my judgment, the substantial compliance revision will not create a significant change in practice. Nor should it result in any slackening of rigor in attempting to comply with the requirements of Regulation D and ULOE [Uniform Limited Offering Exemption]. There may be some situations where the revision may be beneficial in connection with completing a transaction—for example, when a non-accredited investor emerges late in the deal and the offering can proceed by providing the requisite information only to him * * *

It is important to keep in mind that Rule 508 is self-executing and will give issuers and their counsel broad latitude to make a good faith determination whether relief under the rule is available. These principles will come into play and be helpful when counsel responds to the auditors, when opinions are rendered on subsequent rounds of financing regarding the exempt status of prior rounds, * * * and when the disclosure for subsequent financings has to be formulated.

---

24. [By the Commissioner] NASAA is a voluntary organization composed of securities regulatory agencies of 49 states, the Commonwealth of Puerto Rico, and Guam, as well as Mexico and 13 provinces of Canada.

* Insights: The Corporate & Securities Law Advisor. Copyright by Prentice Hall Law & Business.

The substantial compliance revisions also add a general benefit to securities jurisprudence that is somewhat less easy to define. For the first time, in a body of law that requires exemptions to be strictly construed and the burden of establishing them to be on the claiming party, a concept of substantial compliance and relief from technical violations is introduced. Also, for the first time in the case of transactional exemptions, there is the concept that only the injured party may be entitled to relief and that the entire transaction is not necessarily jeopardized. In addition, and perhaps most importantly, the substantial compliance rule invites a court to apply equitable considerations in determining what relief fits the crime.

See also Schneider, A Substantial Compliance ("I & I") Defense and Other Changes are Added to SEC Regulation D, 44 Bus.Law. 1207 (1989).

SECURITIES ACT RELEASE NO. 33–5450
39 Fed.Reg. 2353 (1974).

BACKGROUND AND PURPOSE

Section 3(a)(11) was intended to allow issuers with localized operations to sell securities as part of a plan of local financing. Congress apparently believed that a company whose operations are restricted to one area should be able to raise money from investors in the immediate vicinity without having to register the securities with a federal agency. In theory, the investors would be protected both by their proximity to the issuer and by state regulation. Rule 147 reflects this Congressional intent and is limited in its application to transactions where state regulation will be most effective. The Commission has consistently taken the position that the exemption applies only to local financing provided by local investors for local companies. To satisfy the exemption, the entire issue must be offered and sold exclusively to residents of the state in which the issuer is resident and doing business. An offer or sale of part of the issue to a single non-resident will destroy the exemption for the entire issue.

Certain basic questions have arisen in connection with interpreting section 3(a)(11). They are:

1. What transactions does the section cover;

2. What is "part of an issue" for purposes of the Section;

3. When is a person "resident within" a state or territory for purposes of the section; and

4. What does "doing business within" mean in the context of the Section?

The courts and the Commission have addressed themselves to these questions in the context of different fact situations, and some general guidelines have been developed. Certain guidelines were set forth by the Commission in Securities Act Release No. 4434 and, in part, are reflected in Rule 147. However, in certain respects, as pointed out below, the rule differs from past interpretations.

The Transaction Concept

Although the intrastate offering exemption is contained in section 3 of the Act, which section is phrased in terms of exempt "securities" rather than "transactions", the legislative history and Commission and judicial interpretations indicate that the exemption covers only specific transactions and not the securities themselves. Rule 147 reflects this interpretation.

The "Part of an Issue" Concept

The determination of what constitutes "part of an issue" for purposes of the exemption, i.e. what should be "integrated", has traditionally been dependent on the facts involved in each case. * * * [The Commission refers to the same factors that are discussed in Rule 230.502, page 352, supra.]

The "Person Resident Within" Concept

The object of the section 3(a)(11) exemption, i.e., to restrict the offering to persons within the same locality as the issuer who are, by reason of their proximity, likely to be familiar with the issuer and protected by the state law governing the issuer, is best served by interpreting the residence requirement narrowly. In addition, the determination of whether all parts of the issue have been sold only to residents can be made only after the securities have "come to rest" within the state or territory. Rule 147 retains these concepts, but provides more objective standards for determining when a person is considered a resident within a state for purposes of the rule and when securities have come to rest within a state.

The "Doing Business Within" Requirement

Because the primary purpose of the intrastate exemption was to allow an essentially local business to raise money within the state where the investors would be likely to be familiar with the business and with the management, the doing business requirement has traditionally been viewed strictly. First, not only should the business be located within the state, but the principal or predominant business must be carried on there. Second, substantially all of the proceeds of the offering must be put to use within the local area.

Rule 147 reinforces these requirements by providing specific percentage amounts of business that must be conducted within the state, and of proceeds from the offering that must be spent in connection with such business. In addition, the rule requires that the principal office of the issuer be within the state. * * *

[The text of Rule 147 is omitted.]

SMITH v. GROSS

United States Court of Appeals, Ninth Circuit, 1979.
604 F.2d 639.

Before CARTER and GOODWIN, CIRCUIT JUDGES, and WATERS, DISTRICT JUDGE.

PER CURIAM:

Gerald and Mary Smith appeal from the district court's judgment dismissing their action against the defendants. The Smiths brought suit against Gross, Gaddie, and the two corporate defendants for violation of the federal securities laws. The district court dismissed the suit without prejudice for lack of subject matter jurisdiction on the ground that there was no security involved in the transactions between the parties. * * *

We reverse. The transaction between the parties involved an investment contract.[25]

FACTS

The following statement of facts is taken from the Smiths' amended complaint and Gerald Smith's affidavit. Seller Gross, in a promotional newsletter, solicited buyer-investors to raise earthworms in order to help Gross reach his quotas of selling earthworms to fishermen. In the newsletter, buyers were promised that the seller's growing instructions would enable buyers to have a profitable farm, that the time involved would be similar to raising a garden, that the earthworms double in quantity every sixty days, and that the seller would buy back all bait size worms produced by buyers at $2.25 per pound. After responding to the newsletter, the Smiths were told by Gross that very little work was required, that success was guaranteed by the agreement to repurchase the Smiths' production, and that Gross needed the Smiths' help in the common enterprise of supplying worms for the bait industry. The Smiths alleged that they would not have purchased the worms without Gross's promise to repurchase the Smiths' production at $2.25 per pound. The Smiths were assured that they need not be worried about the market for worms because Gross would handle the marketing.

The Smiths alleged that, contrary to Gross's representations, worms multiply at a maximum of eight rather than 64 times per year, and that they could achieve the promised profits only if the multiplication rate was as fast as represented and Gross purchased the Smiths' production at $2.25 per pound. They also alleged that $2.25 is greater than the true market price and that Gross could pay that price only by selling the worms to new worm farmers at inflated prices. The price at

---

25. [By the Editor] See generally the definition of "security" in § 2(1), p. 341 supra. If the interest sold to the plaintiffs is an "investment contract," the defendants have sold a security, and since that security was not registered under the Securities Act of 1933, the plaintiffs have the statutory right to rescind the transaction under § 12.

which Gross sold the worms to worm farmers was ten times in excess of the true market value. There is little market for worms in the Phoenix area. * * *

INVESTMENT CONTRACT

The Smiths contend that the transactions between the parties involved an investment contract type of security. In SEC v. W.J. Howey Co., 328 U.S. 293, 301, 66 S.Ct. 1100, 1104, 90 L.Ed. 1244 (1946), the Supreme Court set out the conditions for an investment contract: "[t]he test is whether the scheme involves [1] an investment of money [2] in a common enterprise [3] with profits to come solely from the efforts of others." This court in SEC v. Glenn W. Turner Enterprises, Inc., 474 F.2d 476, 482 (9th Cir.), cert. denied, 414 U.S. 821, 94 S.Ct. 117, 38 L.Ed.2d 53 (1973), held that despite the Supreme Court's use of the word "solely", the third element of the *Howey* test is "whether the efforts made by those other than the investor are the undeniably significant ones, those essential managerial efforts which affect the failure or success of the enterprise." The *Turner* court defined a common enterprise as "one in which the fortunes of the investor are interwoven with and dependent upon the efforts and success of those seeking the investment or of third parties." Id. at 482 n. 7.

We find this case virtually identical with Miller v. Central Chinchilla Group, Inc., 494 F.2d 414 (8th Cir.1974). In *Miller* the defendants entered into contracts under which they sold chinchillas to the plaintiffs with the promise to repurchase the offspring. The plaintiffs were told that it was simple to breed chinchillas according to the defendants' instructions and that the venture would be highly profitable. The plaintiffs alleged that the chinchillas were difficult to raise and had a high mortality rate, and that the defendants could return the promised profits only if they repurchased the offspring and sold them to other prospective chinchilla raisers at an inflated price.

The *Miller* court focused on two features in holding that there was an investment contract: (1) the defendants persuaded the plaintiffs to invest by representing that the efforts required of them would be very minimal; and (2) that if the plaintiffs diligently exerted themselves, they still would not gain the promised profits because those profits could be achieved only if the defendants secured additional investors at the inflated prices. 494 F.2d at 417. Both of these features are present in the instant case. We find *Miller* to be persuasive and consistent with *Turner*.

The defendants argue that *Miller* is distinguishable on the ground that there the contract prohibited buyers from reselling to anyone other than the sellers; whereas here the buyers were free to resell to anyone they wanted to. The defendants contend that this distinguishing feature shows that the agreement was not a common enterprise.

The defendants' argument is without merit. There was a common enterprise as required by *Turner*. The Smiths alleged that, although they were free under the terms of the contract to sell their production anywhere they wished, they could have received the promised profits only if the defendants repurchased above the market price, and that the defendants could have repurchased above the market price only if the defendants secured additional investors at inflated prices. Thus, the fortune of the Smiths was interwoven with and dependent upon the efforts and success of the defendants.

We also find that here, as in *Miller,* the third element of an investment contract set forth in *Turner*—that the efforts of those other than the investor are the undeniably significant ones—was present here. The *Miller* court noted that the plaintiffs there had been assured by the sellers that the effort needed to raise chinchillas was minimal. The significant effort necessary for success in the endeavor was that of the seller in procuring new investors who would purchase the chinchillas at inflated prices. Here, the Smiths alleged that they were promised that the effort necessary to raise worms was minimal and they alleged that they could not receive the promised income unless the defendants purchased their harvest.

We find the analysis in *Miller* persuasive and hold that the Smiths alleged facts that, if true, were sufficient to establish an investment contract.

The defendants contend that the agreement between the parties was analogous to a franchise agreement. Franchise agreements are not securities. See, e.g., Bitter v. Hoby's International, Inc., 498 F.2d 183 (9th Cir.1974). This argument is not persuasive. The franchise cases are distinguishable. In *Bitter* this court focused on the fact that a franchisee independently determines his own success. Here, according to the Smiths' allegations, the only market in the Phoenix area for their production was the guaranteed right to resell to the sellers, and, thus, the Smiths were not solely responsible for their own success. We also note that the ultimate buyers in *Bitter* were the consuming public and not as here the offering party.

The facts as alleged in the Smiths' amended complaint and affidavit establish that an investment contract existed. * * * The judgment of the district court is reversed.

Notes

(1) Faded Fliers, Wall Street Journal, p. g22, December 2, 1988, col 1:

[T]he worm-farm idea, * * * reached its full flowering in the 1970s. The lowly earthworm, said its promoters, was a gold mine. It was desperately needed as an ingredient in dog food and shampoo, and countless numbers would be employed in waste disposal. The promoters sold worms to the investors—charging, in some cases, $800 for a batch of the critters that could have been bought elsewhere for $25. The worms would quietly and effortlessly multiply (they don't make a fuss and don't eat much), and the promoters would buy back the expanded population.

Again, the promoters were nowhere to be found when buy-back time rolled around. It seems no one was crying out for shampoo earthworms, dog-food earthworms, or waste disposal earthworms.

(2) The legal approach taken in this case permits a large number of ingenious investment schemes to be attacked successfully under the securities laws. Many of these investments are at best marginal and at worst fraudulent, though some entirely legitimate ones become ensnared in the broad definition of "security."

(3) The leading case is unquestionably SEC v. W.J. Howey Co., cited in the court's opinion. Basically, this case involved the sale of plots of land planted in citrus; purchases were often made in narrow strips of land arranged so that an acre consisted of a single row of 48 trees. The cultivation, harvesting, and marketing of the crop were largely centrally provided through service contracts with the seller of the land; the seller was also heavily involved in citrus production on adjoining land. The Supreme Court held that this arrangement constituted a "security" and thereby established the legal principle applied in the principal case.

(4) The broad definition of "security" set forth in this line of cases seems necessary in order to protect investors in marginal nontraditional schemes. Consider, however, a person who is thinking about the purchase of all the outstanding shares of common stock of a closely held corporation; such a person is clearly purchasing control of the business and will probably run it personally in order to make a profit. Fundamentally, the purchaser is buying assets, or control of assets, and not making a passive investment. Are shares of a closely held corporation in a control transaction a "security" under the *Howey* test applied in Smith v. Gross? This issue split the courts of appeal in the late 1970s and early 1980s, but in Landreth Timber Co. v. Landreth, 471 U.S. 681, 105 S.Ct. 2297, 85 L.Ed.2d 692 (1985), the Supreme Court rejected the so-called "sale of business doctrine" and held that the sale of all or a majority of the shares of a closely held corporation constituted the sale of a "security" subject to the federal securities acts. The principal argument of the court was a literal one based on the language of section 2(1). This holding makes available the protections of sections 12(2) and 17(a) to all sales of closely held shares (assuming that the facilities of interstate commerce are used).

G. ISSUANCE OF SHARES BY A GOING CONCERN: PREEMPTIVE RIGHTS AND DILUTION

STOKES v. CONTINENTAL TRUST CO. OF CITY OF NEW YORK

Court of Appeals of New York, 1906.
186 N.Y. 285, 78 N.E. 1090.

This action was brought by a stockholder to compel his corporation to issue to him at par such a proportion of an increase made in its capital stock as the number of shares held by him before such increase bore to the number of all the shares originally issued, and in case such additional shares could not be delivered to him for his damages in the premises. The defendant is a domestic banking corporation in the city of New York, organized in 1890, with a capital stock of $500,000, consisting of 5,000 shares of the par value of $100 each. The plaintiff was one of the original stockholders, and still owns all the stock issued to him at the date of organization, together with enough more acquired since to make 221 shares in all. On the 29th of January, 1902, the defendant had a surplus of $1,048,450.94, which made the book value of the stock at that time $309.69 per share. On the 2d of January, 1902, Blair & Co., a strong and influential firm of private bankers in the city of New York, made the following proposition to the defendant: "If your stockholders at the special meeting to be called for January 29th, 1902, vote to increase your capital stock from $500,000 to $1,000,000 you may deliver the additional stock to us as soon as issued at $450 per share ($100 par value) for ourselves and our associates, it being understood that we may nominate ten of the 21 trustees to be elected at the adjourned annual meeting of stockholders." The directors of the defendant promptly met and duly authorized a special meeting of the stockholders to be called to meet on January 29, 1902, for the purpose of voting upon the proposed increase of stock and the acceptance of the offer to purchase the same. Upon due notice a meeting of the stockholders was held accordingly, more than a majority attending either in person or by proxy. A resolution to increase the stock was adopted by the vote of 4,197 shares, all that were cast. Thereupon the plaintiff demanded from the defendant the right to subscribe for 221 shares of the new stock at par, and offered to pay immediately for the same, which demand was refused. A resolution directing a sale to Blair & Co. at $450 a share was then adopted by a vote of 3,596 shares to 241. The plaintiff voted for the first resolution, but against the last, and before the adoption of the latter he protested against the proposed sale of his proportionate share of the stock, and again demanded the right to subscribe and pay for the same, but the demand was refused. On the 30th day of January, 1902, the stock was increased, and on the same day was sold to Blair & Co. at the price named, although the plaintiff formerly renewed his demand for 221 shares of the new stock at par, and tendered payment therefor, but it was refused upon the ground that the stock had already been issued to Blair & Co. owing in part to the offer of Blair & Co. which had become known to the public, the market price of the stock had increased from $450 a share in September, 1901, to $550 in January, 1902, and at the time of the trial, in April, 1904, it was worth $700 per share. Prior to the special meeting of the stockholders, by authority of the board of directors, a circular letter was sent to each stockholder, including the plaintiff, giving notice of the proposition made by Blair & Co. and recommending that it be accepted. Thereupon the plaintiff notified the defendant that he wished to subscribe for his proportionate share of the new stock, if issued, and at no time did he waive his right to subscribe for the same.

Before the special meeting, he had not been definitely notified by the defendant that he could not receive his proportionate part of the increase, but was informed that his proposition would "be taken under consideration." After finding these facts in substance, the trial court found, as conclusions of law, that the plaintiff had the right to subscribe for such proportion of the increase, as his holdings bore to all the stock before the increase was made; that the stockholders, directors, and officers of the defendant had no power to deprive him of that right, and that he was entitled to recover the difference between the market value of 221 shares on the 30th of January, 1902, and the par value thereof, or the sum of $99,450, together with interest from said date. The judgment entered accordingly was reversed by the Appellate Division, and the plaintiff appealed to this court, giving the usual stipulation for judgment absolute in case the order of reversal should be affirmed.

VANN, J. (after stating the facts). * * * Thus the question presented for decision is whether according to the facts found the plaintiff had the legal right to subscribe for and take the same number of shares of the new stock that he held of the old? The subject is not regulated by statute, and the question presented has never been directly passed upon by this court, and only to a limited extent has it been considered by courts in this state. * * *

If the right claimed by the plaintiff was a right of property belonging to him as a stockholder, he could not be deprived of it by the joint action of the other stockholders, and of all the directors and officers of the corporation. What is the nature of the right acquired by a stockholder through the ownership of shares of stock? What rights can he assert against the will of a majority of the stockholders, and all the officers and directors? While he does not own and cannot dispose of any specific property of the corporation, yet he and his associates own the corporation itself, its charter, franchises, and all rights conferred thereby, including the right to increase the stock. He has an inherent right to his proportionate share of any dividend declared, or of any surplus arising upon dissolution, and he can prevent waste or misappropriation of the property of the corporation by those in control. Finally, he has the right to vote for directors and upon all propositions subject by law to the control of the stockholders, and this is his supreme right and main protection. Stockholders have no direct voice in transacting the corporate business, but through their right to vote they can select those to whom the law intrusts the power of management and control. A corporation is somewhat like a partnership, if one were possible, conducted wholly by agents where the copartners have power to appoint the agents, but are not responsible for their acts. The power to manage its affairs resides in the directors, who are its agents, but the power to elect directors resides in the stockholders. This right to vote for directors, and upon propositions to increase the stock or mortgage the assets, is about all the power the stockholder has. So long as the management is honest, within the corporate powers, and involves no waste, the stockholders cannot interfere, even if the administration is feeble and unsatisfactory, but must correct such evils through their power to elect other directors. Hence, the power of the individual stockholder to vote in proportion to the number of his shares is vital, and cannot be cut off or curtailed by the action of all the other stockholders, even with the co-operation of the directors and officers.

In the case before us the new stock came into existence through the exercise of a right belonging wholly to the stockholders. As the right to increase the stock belonged to them, the stock when increased belonged to them also, as it was issued for money and not for property or for some purpose other than the sale thereof for money. By the increase of stock the voting power of the plaintiff was reduced one-half, and while he consented to the increase he did not consent to the disposition of the new stock by a sale thereof to Blair & Co. at less than its market value, nor by sale to any person in any way except by an allotment to the stockholders. * * * The plaintiff had power, before the increase of stock, to vote on 221 shares of stock, out of a total of 5,000, at any meeting held by the stockholders for any purpose. By the action of the majority, taken against his will and protest, he now has only one-half the voting power that he had before, because the number of shares has been doubled while he still owns but 221. This touches him as a stockholder in such a way as to deprive him of a right of property. Blair & Co. acquired virtual control, while he and the other stockholders lost it. We are not discussing equities, but legal rights, for this is an action at law, and the plaintiff was deprived of a strictly legal right. If the result gives him an advantage over other stockholders, it is because he stood upon his legal rights, while they did not. The question is what were his legal rights, not what his profit may be under the sale to Blair & Co., but what it might have been if the new stock had been issued to him in proportion to his holding of the old. The other stockholders could give their property to Blair & Co., but they could not give his. * * *

We are thus led to lay down the rule that a stockholder has an inherent right to a proportionate share of new stock issued for money only and not to purchase property for the purposes of the corporation or to effect a consolidation, and while he can waive that right, he cannot be deprived of it without his consent except when the stock is issued at a fixed price not less than par, and he is given the right to take at that price in proportion to his holding, or in some other equitable way that will enable him to protect his interest by acting on his own judgment and using his own resources. This rule is just to all and tends to prevent the tyranny of majorities which needs restraint, as well as virtual attempts to blackmail by small minorities which should be prevented. * * *

[The court concluded that the plaintiff's damages should have been measured by the difference between the $450 sale price and the $540 market value of the shares rather than the difference between par value and market value of the shares.]

The order appealed from should be reversed and the judgment of the trial court modified by reducing the damages from the sum of $99,450, with interest from January 30, 1902, to the sum of $22,100, with interest from that date, and by striking out the extra allowance of costs, and as thus modified the judgment of the trial court is affirmed, without costs in this court or in the Appellate Division to either party.

HAIGHT, J. (dissenting). I agree that the rule that we should adopt is that a stockholder in a corporation has an inherent right to purchase a proportionate share of new stock issued for money only, and not to purchase property necessary for the purposes of the corporation or to effect a consolidation. While he can waive that right he cannot be deprived of it without his consent, except by sale at a fixed price at or above par, in which he may buy at that price in proportion to his holding or in some other equitable way that will enable him to protect his interest by acting on his own judgment and using his own resources. I, however, differ with Judge VANN as to his conclusions as to the rights of the plaintiff herein. Under the findings of the trial court the plaintiff demanded that his share of the new stock should be issued to him at par, or $100 per share, instead of $450 per share, the price offered by Blair & Co. and the price fixed at the stockholders' meeting at which the new stock was authorized to be sold. * * * There is no finding of fact or evidence in the record showing that he was ever ready or willing to pay $450 per share for the stock. * * * What, then, was the legal effect of the plaintiff's demand and tender? To my mind it was simply an attempt to make something out of his associates, to get for $100 per share the stock which Blair & Co. had offered to purchase for $450 per share; and that it was the equivalent of a refusal to pay $450 per share, and its effect is to waive his right to procure the stock by paying that amount. * * * But this is not all. It appears that prior to the offer of Blair & Co. the stock of the company had never been sold above $450 per share; that thereafter the stock rapidly advanced until the day of the completion of the sale on the 30th of January, when its market value was $550 per share; but this, under the stipulation of facts, was caused by the rumor and subsequent announcement and consummation of the proposition for the increase of the stock and the sale of such increase to Blair & Co. and their associates. It is now proposed to give the plaintiff as damages such increase in the market value of the stock, even though such value was based upon the understanding that Blair & Co. were to become stockholders in the corporation, which the acceptance of plaintiff's offer would have prevented. This, to my mind, should not be done. I, therefore, favor an affirmance.

CULLEN, C.J., and WERNER and HISCOCK, JJ., concur with VANN, J.; WILLARD BARLETT, J., concurs with HAIGHT, J.; O'BRIEN, J., absent.

Notes

(1) The common law preemptive right discussed in *Stokes* is now embodied in state statutes, of which there is considerable diversity. See RMBCA, § 6.30, which provides standard terms on an elective basis to codify many aspects of the preemptive right.

(2) It is now generally accepted that the preemptive right is not an inherent aspect of the ownership of shares but a right that may be granted or withheld by the articles of incorporation. The RMBCA adopts an "opt in" clause: under § 6.30(a), no preemptive right exists unless provision for it is expressly made. As a result, a "plain vanilla" corporation whose articles of incorporation contain the statutory minima will not have preemptive rights. Would not the converse (i.e. that a corporation has preemptive rights unless expressly denied in the articles of incorporation) be preferable? Many state statutes adopt an "opt out" rather than an "opt in" provision. Consider also the Historical Comment to § 6.30, 1 Model Bus.Corp.Act Ann. (3d Ed.), 453–54:

> The 1950 Model Act followed the basic approach of the post–1930 state statutes. Section 24 made preemptive rights optional but adopted an "opt out" approach by providing that the preemptive rights of shareholders "to acquire additional or treasury shares" may be limited or denied by provision in the articles. In 1953, the word "unissued" was substituted for "additional" to clearly include originally authorized as well as subsequently authorized shares.

> In 1955 the Model Act was amended by adding an "[alternative] section 24," that provided an "opt in" rather than "opt out" approach: under the alternative section, no preemptive rights existed unless a specific affirmative provision granting these rights was included in the articles. This alternative provision was based on revisions of the preemptive rights statutes adopted by several states during this period. In the 1969 Model Act, the "[alternative] section 24," containing the "opt in" provision, was renumbered section 26 while the previous section 24 was retitled "section 26A. Shareholders Preemptive Rights [Alternative]." Thus, the alternative approach of the 1950 Model Act was retained but the preference was reversed with the "opt in" provision becoming the standard section. This change in preference reflected increased skepticism as to the value of preemptive rights coupled with increased recognition of the problems they created for many corporations. On the other hand, the Committee was unwilling to ignore the long history of preemptive rights and eliminate the "opt out" provision entirely from the statute. The decision in the 1984 Model Act to adopt an "opt in" approach is thus consistent with the long term trend in the development of this Model Act provision.

> * * *

(3) The Official Comment to RMBCA § 6.30 states that the section "is primarily designed to protect voting power within the corporation from dilution." Was that the purpose of preemptive rights envisioned by the court in *Stokes?* The Official Comment adds, however, that preemptive

rights also "may serve in part the function of protecting the equity participation of shareholders."

(4) If a corporation elects preemptive rights, should that right extend to shares issued as compensation to directors or officers? See RMBCA § 6.30(b)(3)(i) and (ii). Does not that tend to frustrate the purpose of preemptive rights whenever one shareholder is an officer of the corporation and others are not? Why should shares "sold otherwise than for money" [RMBCA § 6.30(b)(iii)] not be subject to preemptive rights? What is the justification for the exception in RMBCA § 6.30(b)(iii) for shares issued within six months of the formation of the corporation? What about shares that are offered preemptively, but not purchased? May they be sold entirely free of such rights in the future? See RMBCA § 6.30(b)(6).

(5) Preemptive rights may create problems in corporations with multiple classes of shares. Consider RMBCA § 6.30(b)(4) and (5). The Official Comment states that creation of (a) a class of nonvoting common shares, or (b) a class of preferential shares with general voting rights, in particular "may give rise to possible conflict between the protection of voting interests and equity participation." Why is that?

KATZOWITZ v. SIDLER

Court of Appeals of New York, 1969.
24 N.Y.2d 512, 301 N.Y.S.2d 470, 249 N.E.2d 359.

KEATING, JUDGE.

Isador Katzowitz is a director and stockholder of a close corporation. Two other persons, Jacob Sidler and Max Lasker, own the remaining securities and, with Katzowitz, comprise Sulburn Holding Corp.'s board of directors. Sulburn was organized in 1955 to supply propane gas to three other corporations controlled by these men. Sulburn's certificate of incorporation authorized it to issue 1,000 shares of no par value stock for which the incorporators established a $100 selling price. Katzowitz, Sidler and Lasker each invested $500 and received five shares of the corporation's stock.

The three men had been jointly engaged in several corporate ventures for more than 25 years. In this period they had always been equal partners and received identical compensation from the corporations they controlled. Though all the corporations controlled by these three men prospered, disenchantment with their inter-personal relationship flared into the open in 1956. At this time, Sidler and Lasker joined forces to oust Katzowitz from any role in managing the corporations. * * *

Before the issue could be tried, the three men entered into a stipulation in 1959 whereby Katzowitz withdrew from active participation in the day-to-day operations of the business. The agreement provided that he would remain on the boards of all the corporations, and each board would be limited to three members composed of the three stockholders or their designees. Katzowitz was to receive the same compensation and other fringe benefits which the controlled corporations paid Lasker and Sidler. The stipulation also provided that Katzowitz, Sidler and Lasker were "equal stockholders and each of said parties now owns the same number of shares of stock in each of the defendant corporations and that such shares of stock shall continue to be in full force and effect and unaffected by this stipulation, except as hereby otherwise expressly provided." The stipulation contained no other provision affecting equal stock interests.

The business relationship established by the stipulation was fully complied with. Sidler and Lasker, however, were still interested in disassociating themselves from Katzowitz * * *

In December of 1961 Sulburn was indebted to each stockholder to the extent of $2,500 for fees and commissions earned up until September, 1961. Instead of paying this debt, Sidler and Lasker wanted Sulburn to loan the money to another corporation which all three men controlled. Sidler and Lasker called a meeting of the board of directors to propose that additional securities be offered at $100 per share to substitute for the money owed to the directors. The notice of meeting for October 30, 1961 had on its agenda "a proposition that the corporation issue common stock of its unissued common capital stock, *the total par value which shall equal the total sum of the fees and commissions now owing by the corporation to its * * * directors*". (Emphasis added.) Katzowitz made it quite clear at the meeting that he would not invest any additional funds in Sulburn in order for it to make a loan to this other corporation. The only resolution passed at the meeting was that the corporation would pay the sum of $2,500 to each director.

With full knowledge that Katzowitz expected to be paid his fees and commissions and that he did not want to participate in any new stock issuance, the other two directors called a special meeting of the board on December 1, 1961. The only item on the agenda for this special meeting was the issuance of 75 shares of the corporation's common stock at $100 per share. The offer was to be made to stockholders in "accordance with their respective preemptive rights for the purpose of acquiring additional working capital". The amount to be raised was the exact amount owed by the corporation to its shareholders. The offering price for the securities was 1/18 the book value of the stock. Only Sidler and Lasker attended the special board meeting. They approved the issuance of the 75 shares.

Notice was mailed to each stockholder that they had the right to purchase 25 shares of the corporation's stock at $100 a share. The offer was to expire on December 27, 1961. Failure to act by that date was stated to constitute a waiver. At about the same time Katzowitz received the notice, he received a check for $2,500 from the corporation for his fees and commissions. Katzowitz did not exercise his option to buy the additional shares. Sidler and Lasker purchased their full complement, 25 shares each. This purchase by Sidler and Lasker caused an immediate dilution of the book value of the outstanding securities.

On August 25, 1962 the principal asset of Sulburn, a tractor trailer truck, was destroyed. On August 31, 1962 the directors unanimously voted to dissolve the corporation. Upon dissolution, Sidler and Lasker each received $18,885.52 but Katzowitz only received $3,147.59.

The plaintiff instituted a declaratory judgment action to establish his right to the proportional interest in the assets of Sulburn in liquidation less the $5,000 which Sidler and Lasker used to purchase their shares in December, 1961.

Special Term (Westchester County) found the book value of the corporation's securities on the day the stock was offered at $100 to be worth $1,800. The court also found that "the individual defendants * * * decided that in lieu of taking that sum in cash [the commissions and fees due the stockholders], they preferred to add to their investment by having the corporate defendant make available and offer each stockholder an additional twenty-five shares of unissued stock." The court reasoned that Katzowitz waived his right to purchase the stock or object to its sale to Lasker and Sidler by failing to exercise his preemptive right and found his protest at the time of dissolution untimely.

On the substantive legal issues and findings of fact, the Appellate Division [two Justices dissenting, 29 App.Div.2d 955, 289 N.Y.S.2d 324] was in agreement with Special Term. The majority agreed that the book value of the corporation's stock at the time of the stock offering was $1,800. The Appellate Division reasoned, however, that showing a disparity between book value and offering price was insufficient without also showing fraud or overreaching. Disparity in price by itself was not enough to prove fraud. The Appellate Division also found that the plaintiff had waived his right to object to his recovery in dissolution by failing to either exercise his pre-emptive rights or take steps to prevent the sale of the stock.

The concept of pre-emptive rights was fashioned by the judiciary to safeguard two distinct interests of stockholders—the right to protection against dilution of their equity in the corporation and protection against dilution of their proportionate voting control. (Ballantine, Corporations [rev. ed., 1946], § 209.) After early decisions (Gray v. Portland Bank, 3 Mass. 364; Stokes v. Continental Trust Co., 186 N.Y. 285, 78 N.E. 1090, 12 L.R.A., N.S., 969), legislation fixed the right enunciated with respect to proportionate voting but left to the judiciary the role of protecting existing shareholders from the dilution of their equity (e.g., Stock Corporation Law, § 39, now Business Corporation Law, Consol.Laws, c. 4, § 622; see Drinker, The Preemptive Right of Shareholders to Subscribe to New Shares, 43 Harv.L.Rev. 586; Frey, Shareholders' Pre-emptive Rights, 38 Yale L.J. 563).

It is clear that directors of a corporation have no discretion in the choice of those to whom the earnings and assets of the corporation should be distributed. Directors, being fiduciaries of the corporation, must, in issuing new stock, treat existing shareholders fairly. Though there is very little statutory control over the price which a corporation must receive for new shares the power to determine price must be exercised for the benefit of the corporation and in the interest of all the stockholders.

Issuing stock for less than fair value can injure existing shareholders by diluting their interest in the corporation's surplus, in current and future earnings and in the assets upon liquidation. Normally, a stockholder is protected from the loss of his equity from dilution, even though the stock is being offered at less than fair value, because the shareholder receives rights which he may either exercise or sell. If he exercises, he has protected his interest and, if not, he can sell the rights, thereby compensating himself for the dilution of his remaining shares in the equity of the corporation.[26]

When new shares are issued, however, at prices far below fair value in a close corporation or a corporation with only a limited market for its shares, existing stockholders, who do not want to invest or do not have the capacity to invest additional funds, can have their equity interest in the corporation diluted to the vanishing point.

The protection afforded by stock rights is illusory in close corporations. Even if a buyer could be found for the rights, they would have to be sold at an inadequate price because of the nature of a close corporation. Outsiders are normally discouraged from acquiring minority interests after a close corporation has been organized. Certainly a stockholder in a close corporation is at a total loss to safeguard his equity from dilution if no rights are offered and he does not want to invest additional funds.

Though it is difficult to determine fair value for a corporation's securities and courts are therefore reluctant to get into the thicket, when the issuing price is shown to be markedly below book value in a close corporation and when the remaining shareholder-directors benefit from the issuance, a case for judicial relief has been established. In that instance, the corporation's directors must show that the issuing price falls within some range which can be justified on the basis of valid business reasons. If no such showing is made by the directors, there is no reason for the judiciary to abdicate its function to a majority of the board or stockholders who have not seen fit to come forward and justify the propriety of diverting property from the corporation and allow the issuance of securities to become an oppressive device permitting the dilution of the equity of dissident stockholders.

The defendant directors here make no claim that the price set was a fair one. No business justification is offered to sustain it. Admittedly, the stock was sold at less than book value. The defendants simply

---

26. [By the Court] There is little justification for issuing stock far below its fair value. The only reason for issuing stock below fair value exists in publicly held corporations where the problem of floating new issues through subscription is concerned. The reason advanced in this situation is that it insures the success of the issue or that it has the same psychological effect as a dividend.

contend that, as long as all stockholders were given an equal opportunity to purchase additional shares, no stockholder can complain simply because the offering dilutes his interest in the corporation.

The defendants' argument is fallacious.

The corollary of a stockholder's right to maintain his proportionate equity in a corporation by purchasing additional shares is the right not to purchase additional shares without being confronted with dilution of his existing equity if no valid business justification exists for the dilution.

A stockholder's right not to purchase is seriously undermined if the stock offered is worth substantially more than the offering price. Any purchase at this price dilutes his interest and impairs the value of his original holding. "A corporation is not permitted to sell its stock for a legally inadequate price at least where there is objection. Plaintiff has a right to insist upon compliance with the law whether or not he cares to exercise his option. He cannot block a sale for a fair price merely because he disagrees with the wisdom of the plan but he can insist that the sale price be fixed in accordance with legal requirements." (Bennett v. Breuil Petroleum Corp., [34 Del.Ch. 6, 14–15, 99 A.2d 236, 241.]) Judicial review in this area is limited to whether under all the circumstances, including the disparity between issuing price of the stock and its true value, the nature of the corporation, the business necessity for establishing an offering price at a certain amount to facilitate raising new capital, and the ability of stockholders to sell rights, the additional offering of securities should be condemned because the directors in establishing the sale price did not fix it with reference to financial considerations with respect to the ready disposition of securities.

Here the obvious disparity in selling price and book value was calculated to force the dissident stockholder into investing additional sums. No valid business justification was advanced for the disparity in price, and the only beneficiaries of the disparity were the two director-stockholders who were eager to have additional capital in the business.

It is no answer to Katzowitz' action that he was also given a chance to purchase additional shares at this bargain rate. The price was not so much a bargain as it was a tactic, conscious or unconscious on the part of the directors, to place Katzowitz in a compromising situation. The price was so fixed to make the failure to invest costly. However, Katzowitz at the time might not have been aware of the dilution because no notice of the effect of the issuance of the new shares on the already outstanding shares was disclosed. In addition, since the stipulation entitled Katzowitz to the same compensation as Sidler and Lasker, the disparity in equity interest caused by their purchase of additional securities in 1961 did not affect stockholder income from Sulburn and, therefore, Katzowitz possibly was not aware of the effect of the stock issuance on his interest in the corporation until dissolution.

No reason exists at this time to permit Sidler and Lasker to benefit from their course of conduct. Katzowitz' delay in commencing the action did not prejudice the defendants. By permitting the defendants to recover their additional investment in Sulburn before the remaining assets of Sulburn are distributed to the stockholders upon dissolution, all the stockholders will be treated equitably. Katzowitz, therefore, should receive his aliquot share of the assets of Sulburn less the amount invested by Sidler and Lasker for their purchase of stock on December 27, 1961.

Accordingly, the order of the Appellate Division should be reversed, with costs, and judgment granted in favor of the plaintiff against the individual defendants.

BURKE, SCILEPPI, BERGAN, BREITEL and JASEN, JJ., concur with KEATING, J.

FULD, C.J., dissents and votes to affirm on the opinion at the Appellate Division.

Notes

(1) What is the source of the principle that the court applied to hold improper the issuance of additional shares? If Katzowitz' preemptive rights were fully honored, as they appear to have been, why should he be permitted to complain about the dilution which he could have avoided simply by exercising that right?

(2) The transaction involved in *Katzowitz* is a type of "freeze out." A similar type of freeze-out occurs when inside shareholders pay for their additional shares by cancelling debts owed to them by the corporation (representing, in effect, capital that they have already invested in the business) while outside shareholders are put to the painful choice of investing fresh capital (which, of course, they may not have) over which they lose effective control or see their proportionate interest decline drastically. In Hyman v. Velsicol Corp., 342 Ill.App. 489, 97 N.E.2d 122 (1951), for example, an outside shareholder was given the choice of investing an additional $136,000 in order to stay even or watching his proportional interest decline from 20 per cent to a fraction of one per cent. What did the shareholder do? He sued, of course, but lost when the Court concluded that the plan "was not an abuse of discretion" and not "fraudulently oppressive." As in *Katzowitz*, the shareholder's preemptive right was fully protected and shares were issued at par value, arguably below "true value." However, there was a business justification for the transaction since the majority shareholders were cancelling outstanding indebtedness owed to them. Also, the plaintiff was a former employee who was interested in a competing business.

(3) Some freeze out cases have been brought under the theory that the plan constitutes a violation of fiduciary duties, discussed in a later chapter. See generally Kessler, Elimination of Minority Interests by Cash Merger: Two Recent Cases, 30 Bus.Law. 699 (1975). Recent cases have also sometimes adopted the view that transactions literally complying with statutory requirements may be set aside if they do not meet a standard of "entire fairness" since they involve conflict of interest transactions. See Weinberger v. UOP, Inc., p. 792 infra; see also Alpert v. 28 Williams St. Corp.,

63 N.Y.2d 557, 483 N.Y.S.2d 667, 473 N.E.2d 19 (1984). The modern trend seems clearly to be running in the direction of imposing a fiduciary duty on dilutive transactions such as those involved in *Katzowitz.* In the words of the Mississippi Supreme Court, "[t]he traditional view that shareholders have no fiduciary duty to each other, and transactions constituting 'freeze outs' or 'squeeze outs' generally cannot be attacked as a breach of duty of loyalty or good faith to each other, is outmoded." Fought v. Morris, 543 So. 2d 167, 169 (Miss.1989). In the light of this trend, it is doubtful that older cases such as Hyman v. Velsicol [note (2) above] would be decided the same way if they arose today. See generally O'Neal, Oppression of Minority Shareholders: Protecting Minority Rights, 35 Cleve.St.L.Rev. 121 (1987).

H. DISTRIBUTIONS BY A CLOSELY HELD CORPORATION

GOTTFRIED v. GOTTFRIED

Supreme Court of New York, 1947.
73 N.Y.S.2d 692.

CORCORAN, JUSTICE.

This action was brought in the early part of 1945 by minority stockholders of Gottfried Baking Corporation (hereinafter called "Gottfried"), to compel the Board of Directors of that corporation to declare dividends on its common stock. The defendants are Gottfried itself, its directors, and Hanscom Baking Corporation (hereinafter called "Hanscom"), a wholly owned subsidiary of Gottfried. Gottfried is a closely held family corporation. All of its stockholders, with minor exceptions, are children of the founder of the business, Elias Gottfried, and their respective spouses.

Both corporations are engaged in the manufacture and sale of bakery products; Gottfried for distribution at wholesale, and Hanscom for distribution at retail in its own stores. Each corporation functions separately, in the manufacture and sale of its respective products.

At the end of 1946 the outstanding capitalization of Gottfried consisted of 4500 shares of "A" stock, without nominal or par value, and 20,862 shares of common stock without par value. The "A" stock is entitled to dividends of $8 per share before any dividends may be paid upon the common stock, as well as a further participation in earnings. At the end of 1944, immediately before this action was commenced, Gottfried also had outstanding preferred stock in the face amount of $79,000, and Hanscom had outstanding $86,000 face amount of preferred stock. The plaintiffs in the aggregate owned approximately 38% of each of these classes of securities. The individual defendants owned approximately 62 per cent.

From 1931 until 1945 no dividends had been paid upon the common stock, although dividends had been paid regularly upon the outstanding preferred stock and intermittently upon the "A" stock. There seems to be no question with respect to the policy of the Board of Directors in not declaring dividends prior to 1944. An analysis of the financial statements of the corporation shows a net working capital deficit at the end of 1941, in which year a consolidated loss of $109,816 had been incurred. Moreover, until the end of 1943 the earned surplus was relatively small in relation to the volume of business done and the growing requirements of the business.

Although the action was brought in the early part of 1945 to compel the declaration of dividends upon the common stock, dividends actually were declared and paid upon said stock in 1945, and subsequently. The purpose of the action now, therefore, is to compel the payment of dividends upon the common stock in such amount as under all the circumstances is fair and adequate.

The action is predicated upon the claim that the policy of the Board of Directors with respect to the declaration of dividends is animated by considerations other than the best welfare of the corporations or their stockholders. The plaintiffs claim that bitter animosity on the part of the directors, who own the controlling stock, against the plaintiff minority stockholders, as well as a desire to coerce the latter into selling their stock to the majority interests at a grossly inadequate price, and the avoidance of heavy personal income taxes upon any dividends that might be declared, have been the motivating factors that have dominated the defendants. Plaintiffs, contend, moreover, that the defendants by excessive salaries, bonuses and corporate loans to themselves or some of them, have eliminated the immediate need of dividends in so far as they were concerned, while at the same time a starvation dividend policy with respect to the minority stockholders—not on the payroll—operates designedly to compel the plaintiffs to sacrifice their stock by sale to the defendants.

There is no essential dispute as to the principles of law involved. If an adequate corporate surplus is available for the purpose, directors may not withhold the declaration of dividends in bad faith. But the mere existence of an adequate corporate surplus is not sufficient to invoke court action to compel such a dividend. There must also be bad faith on the part of the directors.

There are no infallible distinguishing ear-marks of bad faith. The following facts are relevant to the issue of bad faith and are admissible in evidence: Intense hostility of the controlling faction against the minority; exclusion of the minority from employment by the corporation; high salaries, or bonuses or corporate loans made to the officers in control; the fact that the majority group may be subject to high personal income taxes if substantial dividends are paid; the existence of a desire by the controlling directors to acquire the minority stock interests as cheaply as possible. But if they are not motivating causes they do not constitute "bad faith" as a matter of law.

The essential test of bad faith is to determine whether the policy of the directors is dictated by their personal interests rather than the corporate welfare. Directors are fiduciaries. Their cestui que trust are the corporation and the stockholders as a body. Circumstances such as those above mentioned and any other significant factors, appraised in the light of the financial condition and requirements of the corporation, will determine the conclusion as to whether the directors have or have not been animated by personal, as distinct from corporate, considerations.

The court is not concerned with the direction which the exercise of the judgment of the Board of Directors may take, provided only that such exercise of judgment be made in good faith. It is axiomatic that the court will not substitute its judgment for that of the Board of Directors.

It must be conceded that closely held corporations are easily subject to abuse on the part of dominant stockholders, particularly in the direction of action designed to compel minority stockholders to sell their stock at a sacrifice. But close corporation or not, the court will not tolerate directorate action designed to achieve that or any other wrongful purpose. Even in the absence of bad faith, however, the impact of dissension and hostility among stockholders falls usually with heavier force in a closely held corporation. In many such cases, a large part of a stockholder's assets may be tied up in the corporation. It is frequently contemplated by the parties, moreover, that the respective stockholders receive their major livelihood in the form of salaries resulting from employment by the corporation. If such employment be terminated, the hardship suffered by the minority stockholder or stockholders may be very heavy. Nevertheless, such situations do not in themselves form a ground for the interposition of a court of equity.

There is no doubt that in the present case bitter dissension and personal hostility have existed for a long time between the individual plaintiffs and defendants. The plaintiffs Charles Gottfried and Harold Gottfried have both been discontinued from the corporate payrolls.

It is true too that several of the defendants have in recent years received as compensation substantial sums. * * *

The evidence also discloses that substantial advances or loans have been made from time to time to several of the defendants, part of which still remain outstanding. Advances and loans of this character in varying amounts likewise had been made for many years to stockholders and directors. Without passing upon the propriety or legality of these transactions, the evidence does not sustain an inference that they were made with a view to the dividend policy of the corporation. They were incurred, in large part, long before any controversy arose with respect to dividends, nor is the aggregate amount thereof of sufficient magnitude to affect in a material way the capacity of Gottfried to pay dividends.

Plaintiff Charles Gottfried testified that Benjamin Gottfried, one of the defendants, told him that he and the other minority stockholders would never get any dividends because the majority could freeze them out and that the majority had other ways than declaring dividends of getting money out of the companies. Benjamin Gottfried denied that he had ever made such statements. There is no evidence, moreover, that such statements were made by any of the other defendants. The court does not believe that this disputed testimony carries much weight upon the question of a concerted policy on the part of the directors to refrain from declaring dividends for the purpose of "freezing out" the plaintiffs.

Nor does the evidence with respect to the financial condition of the corporation and its business requirements sustain the plaintiffs' claims. * * * The evidence discloses that * * * expenditures [actually made in 1945] * * * included the retirement of the then outstanding preferred stocks of Gottfried and Hanscom in the sum of $165,000. Since all the parties held these preferred stocks in the same ratio as they held Gottfried "A" stock and common stock, each of the stockholders, including the plaintiffs, participated proportionately in the benefits of such retirement. After said retirement their respective pro rata interests in Gottfried were precisely the same as before these distributions were made. From this point of view the plaintiffs were in at least as good a position as a result of this preferred stock retirement as though dividends had been paid upon the common stock in the sum of $165,000, which is almost equivalent to the entire net earnings for the year 1944. It is noteworthy in this connection, moreover, that the retirement of the preferred stock was urged by both Charles and Harold Gottfried, two of the plaintiffs, at the annual meeting of the stockholders of Gottfried held on December 5, 1944. Harold went so far as to request that funds be borrowed from a bank in order to effect such retirement. These stockholders certainly cannot complain because a sum almost equivalent to the prior year's entire net income was defrayed, in accordance with their own request, in the form of retirement of preferred stock rather than by payment of dividends on the common stock.

Other major items of expenditure in 1945, * * * were payments of dividends on Gottfried preferred stock in the sum of $5,031, dividends on Hanscom preferred stock in the sum of $5,597, and dividends on the "A" stock of $36,000. In all of these payments of dividends on stock prior to the common stock the plaintiffs were pro rata beneficiaries. In 1945 there were also payments upon outstanding mortgages in the sum of $133,626. Reduction of mortgage indebtedness seems to have been a standard policy of Gottfried when its financial condition permitted it. Payments for sites for new plants and properties deemed necessary for the corporations' operations aggregated more than $214,000.

In addition to the above-mentioned expenditures * * * Gottfried in 1945 paid $31,532 in dividends on the common stock. It may be, of course, that the payment of these dividends was stimulated by the commencement of this suit. The fact remains that they were paid.

* * *

The ratio of dividends paid in 1945 to the earnings of the immediately preceding year was 44.87%.

Under these circumstances, it may not be said that the directorate policy regarding common stock dividends at the time the suit was brought was unduly conservative. It certainly does not appear to have been inspired by bad faith. * * *

The complaint is dismissed and judgment directed for the defendants. Settle judgment.

DODGE v. FORD MOTOR CO.

Supreme Court of Michigan, 1919.
204 Mich. 459, 170 N.W. 668.

Ostrander, C.J.

[Editor: Plaintiffs are minority shareholders in the Ford Motor Company. At the time, Henry Ford, President of the Company, owned 58 per cent of the outstanding capital stock.] * * *

When plaintiffs made their complaint and demand for further dividends, the Ford Motor Company had concluded its most prosperous year of business. The demand for its cars at the price of the preceding year continued. It could make and could market in the year beginning August 1, 1916, more than 500,000 cars. Sales of parts and repairs would necessarily increase. The cost of materials was likely to advance, and perhaps the price of labor; but it reasonably might have expected a profit for the year of upwards of $60,000,000. It had assets of more than $132,000,000, a surplus of almost $112,000,000, and its cash on hand and municipal bonds were nearly $54,000,000. Its total liabilities, including capital stock, was a little over $20,000,000. It had declared no special dividend during the business year except the October, 1915, dividend. It had been the practice, under similar circumstances, to declare larger dividends. Considering only these facts, a refusal to declare and pay further dividends appears to be not an exercise of discretion on the part of the directors, but an arbitrary refusal to do what the circumstances required to be done. These facts and others call upon the directors to justify their action, or failure or refusal to act. In justification, the defendants have offered testimony tending to prove, and which does prove, the following facts: It had been the policy of the corporation for a considerable time to annually reduce the selling price of cars, while keeping up, or improving, their quality. As early as in June, 1915, a general plan for the expansion of the productive capacity of the concern by a practical duplication of its plant had been talked over by the executive officers and directors and agreed upon; not all of the details having been settled, and no formal action of directors having been taken. The erection of a smelter was considered, and engineering and other data in connection therewith secured. In consequence, it was determined not to reduce the selling price of cars for the year beginning August 1, 1915, but to maintain the price and to accumulate a large surplus to pay for the proposed expansion of plant and equipment, and perhaps to build a plant for smelting ore. It is hoped, by Mr. Ford, that eventually, 1,000,000 cars will be annually produced. The contemplated changes will permit the increased output.

The plan, as affecting the profits of the business for the year beginning August 1, 1916, and thereafter, calls for a reduction in the selling price of the cars. It is true that this price might be at any time increased, but the plan called for the reduction in price of $80 a car. The capacity of the plant, without the additions thereto voted to be made (without a part of them at least), would produce more than 600,000 cars annually. This number, and more, could have been sold for $440 instead of $360, a difference in the return for capital, labor, and materials employed of at least $48,000,000. In short, the plan does not call for and is not intended to produce immediately a more profitable business, but a less profitable one; not only less profitable than formerly, but less profitable than it is admitted it might be made. The apparent immediate effect will be to diminish the value of shares and the returns to shareholders.

It is the contention of plaintiffs that the apparent effect of the plan is intended to be the continued and continuing effect of it, and that it is deliberately proposed, not of record and not by official corporate declaration, but nevertheless proposed, to continue the corporation henceforth as a semi-eleemosynary institution and not as a business institution. In support of this contention, they point to the attitude and to the expressions of Mr. Henry Ford.

Mr. Henry Ford is the dominant force in the business of the Ford Motor Company. No plan of operations could be adopted unless he consented, and no board of directors can be elected whom he does not favor. One of the directors of the company has no stock. One share was assigned to him to qualify him for the position, but it is not claimed that he owns it. A business, one of the largest in the world, and one of the most profitable, has been built up. It employs many men, at good pay.

"My ambition," said Mr. Ford, "is to employ still more men, to spread the benefits of this industrial system to the greatest possible number, to help them build up their lives and their homes. To do this we are putting the greatest share of our profits back in the business."

> "With regard to dividends, the company paid sixty per cent. on its capitalization of two million dollars, or $1,200,000, leaving $58,000,000 to reinvest for the growth of the company. This is Mr. Ford's policy at present, and it is understood that the other stockholders cheerfully accede to this plan."

He had made up his mind in the summer of 1916 that no dividends other than the regular dividends should be paid, "for the present."

> "Q. For how long? Had you fixed in your mind anytime in the future, when you were going to pay—A. No.

"Q. That was indefinite in the future? A. That was indefinite; yes, sir."

The record, and especially the testimony of Mr. Ford, convinces that he has to some extent the attitude towards shareholders of one who has dispensed and distributed to them large gains and that they should be content to take what he chooses to give. His testimony creates the impression, also, that he thinks the Ford Motor Company has made too much money, has had too large profits, and that, although large profits might be still earned, a sharing of them with the public, by reducing the price of the output of the company, ought to be undertaken. We have no doubt that certain sentiments, philanthropic and altruistic, creditable to Mr. Ford, had large influence in determining the policy to be pursued by the Ford Motor Company—the policy which has been herein referred to.

* * * There should be no confusion (of which there is evidence) of the duties which Mr. Ford conceives that he and the stockholders owe to the general public and the duties which in law he and his codirectors owe to protesting, minority stockholders. A business corporation is organized and carried on primarily for the profit of the stockholders. The powers of the directors are to be employed for that end. The discretion of directors is to be exercised in the choice of means to attain that end, and does not extend to a change in the end itself, to the reduction of profits, or to the nondistribution of profits among stockholders in order to devote them to other purposes.

There is committed to the discretion of directors, a discretion to be exercised in good faith, the infinite details of business, including the wages which shall be paid to employés, the number of hours they shall work, the conditions under which labor shall be carried on, and the price for which products shall be offered to the public.

It is said by appellants that the motives of the board members are not material and will not be inquired into by the court so long as their acts are within their lawful powers. As we have pointed out, and the proposition does not require argument to sustain it, it is not within the lawful powers of a board of directors to shape and conduct the affairs of a corporation for the merely incidental benefit of shareholders and for the primary purpose of benefiting others, and no one will contend that, if the avowed purpose of the defendant directors was to sacrifice the interests of shareholders, it would not be the duty of the courts to interfere.

We are not, however, persuaded that we should interfere with the proposed expansion of the business of the Ford Motor Company. In view of the fact that the selling price of products may be increased at any time, the ultimate results of the larger business cannot be certainly estimated. The judges are not business experts. It is recognized that plans must often be made for a long future, for expected competition, for a continuing as well as an immediately profitable venture. The experience of the Ford Motor Company is evidence of capable management of its affairs. It may be noticed incidentally, that it took from the public the money required for the execution of its plan, and that the very considerable salaries paid to Mr. Ford and to certain executive officers and employés were not diminished. We are not satisfied that the alleged motives of the directors, in so far as they are reflected in the conduct of the business, menace the interests of shareholders. It is enough to say, perhaps, that the court of equity is at all times open to complaining shareholders having a just grievance.

Assuming the general plan and policy of expansion and the details of it to have been sufficiently, formally, approved at the October and November, 1917, meetings of directors, and assuming further that the plan and policy and the details agreed upon were for the best ultimate interest of the company and therefore of its shareholders, what does it amount to in justification of a refusal to declare and pay a special dividend or dividends? The Ford Motor Company was able to estimate with nicety its income and profit. It could sell more cars than it could make. Having ascertained what it would cost to produce a car and to sell it, the profit upon each car depended upon the selling price. That being fixed, the yearly income and profit was determinable, and, within slight variations, was certain. * * *

Defendants say, and it is true, that a considerable cash balance must be at all times carried by such a concern. But, as has been stated, there was a large daily, weekly, monthly, receipt of cash. The output was practically continuous and was continuously, and within a few days, turned into cash. Moreover, the contemplated expenditures were not to be immediately made. The large sum appropriated for the smelter plant was payable over a considerable period of time. So that, without going further, it would appear that, accepting and approving the plan of the directors, it was their duty to distribute on or near the 1st of August, 1916, a very large sum of money to stockholders.

In reaching this conclusion, we do not ignore, but recognize, the validity of the proposition that plaintiffs have from the beginning profited by, if they have not lately, officially, participated in, the general policy of expansion pursued by this corporation. We do not lose sight of the fact that it had been, upon an occasion, agreeable to the plaintiffs to increase the capital stock to $100,000,000 by a stock dividend of $98,000,000. These things go only to answer other contentions now made by plaintiffs, and do not and cannot operate to estop them to demand proper dividends upon the stock they own. It is obvious that an annual dividend of 60 per cent, upon $2,000,000 or $1,200,000, is the equivalent of a very small dividend upon $100,000,000, or more.

The decree of the court below fixing and determining the specific amount to be distributed to stockholders is affirmed. * * *

STEERE, FELLOWS, STONE, and BROOKE, JJ., concurred with Os-TRANDER, J.

MOORE, J. ∗ ∗ ∗ I do not agree with all that is said by [JUSTICE OSTRANDER] in his discussion of the question of dividends. I do agree with him in his conclusion that the accumulation of so large a surplus establishes the fact that there has been an arbitrary refusal to distribute funds that ought to have been distributed to the stockholders as dividends. I therefore agree with the conclusion reached by him upon that phase of the case.

BIRD, C.J., and KUHN, J., concurred with MOORE, J.

Notes

(1) Before the Tax Reform Act of 1986, the federal income tax rates applicable to corporations and individuals encouraged corporations to accumulate earnings and never pay dividends if that could be avoided. Accumulated earnings might be distributed indirectly in the form of salaries, rent or interest to shareholders, the provision of fringe benefits (all of which hopefully might be deducted by the corporation as business expenses), or by the grant of loans to shareholders. Earnings that could not be so distributed might be retained by the corporation indefinitely with the hope that the shareholders might at some time "bail out" by selling the stock or liquidating the corporation at favorable capital gains tax rates. Of course, a policy of indirect distributions and no formal dividends had serious consequences for minority shareholders who were not employed by the corporation or who were hostile to the controlling shareholders. They did not share in the indirect distributions in proportion to their shareholdings, and, indeed, might not share in them at all. While doubtless in many instances these adverse consequences to minority shareholders were consistent with the selfish long term interests of the controlling shareholders, they were also a natural consequence of the federal income tax structure.

(2) Before the 1986 Tax Act rates went into effect, the S corporation election did not mitigate the natural "no dividend" policy encouraged by the tax laws. Profitable corporations simply did not elect S corporation treatment since individual rates were generally higher than corporate rates on the same income. Thus, during most of this century, there was a strong tax inducement for corporations to adopt a "no dividend" policy.

(3) Congress viewed corporations that accumulated earnings and did not pay dividends as a serious tax avoidance device. It sought to compel the payment of dividends by such corporations by imposing a special tax on earnings accumulated by a corporation "formed or availed of for the purpose of avoiding the income tax with respect to its shareholders ∗ ∗ ∗ by permitting earnings and profits to accumulate instead of being divided or distributed." Internal Revenue Code § 532(a). The tax imposed by § 531 is in addition to the normal income tax applicable to corporations and is 27½ per cent of the accumulated taxable income in excess of $100,000, and 38½ per cent of the accumulation in excess of $100,000. However, there is a substantial floor below which earnings may be accumulated free of concern about this tax, and in any event, its application was never automatic but depends on a finding that the corporation was "availed of" for tax avoidance purposes.

(4) The penalty tax on unreasonable accumulations of earnings and profits is difficult to administer because liability for this tax depends on the purpose of the underlying accumulations. Section 533(a) creates a presumption that tax avoidance is the motive where "earnings and profits * * * are permitted to accumulate beyond the reasonable needs of the business," but that simply moves the inquiry down one level to what are the reasonably anticipated needs of the business. Not surprisingly, managers have often found plausible or fanciful justifications for specific accumulations that have sometimes been rejected by suspicious revenue agents and judges. Certainly, the combination of large accumulations and evidence of excessive salaries or loans to shareholders or favored relatives is particularly dangerous and often leads to the imposition of the section 531 tax. See e.g. Bahan Textile Machinery Co. v. United States, 453 F.2d 1100 (4th Cir. 1972).

(5) Many corporations have been persuaded to pay a dividend only after a revenue agent raised the question about the possible applicability of the unreasonable accumulation tax to the corporation. Thus, the effect of this tax undoubtedly has been greater than the number of successfully litigated cases would indicate.

(6) Assume that a corporation has made prudent investments in the past that have greatly appreciated in value. In determining whether the corporation has unreasonably accumulated income, should readily marketable securities be valued at cost (as shown on the corporate books) or current market value? See Ivan Allen Co. v. United States, 422 U.S. 617, 95 S.Ct. 2501, 45 L.Ed.2d 435 (1975), holding that they must be entered at market value. There was a vigorous dissent by three Justices.

(7) The penalty tax imposed by section 531 has become less important as a result of the broadened availability of the S corporation election and revisions in tax rates under the 1986 Tax Reform Act. In a corporation that is not eligible for the S corporation election, and where "zeroing out" is impractical, accumulation of earnings is still more attractive than paying dividends that are subject to double taxation. Hence, it is theoretically possible that the section 531 tax may be imposed even after the 1986 Tax Reform Act. The retention of the section 531 tax may arguably be justified on the theory that when a corporation does not qualify for subchapter S, it and its shareholders must continue to live in a two-tier tax world in which corporate and individual taxes are payable on corporate earnings. Arguably, therefore, it should be required to distribute excess earnings to shareholders.

HERBERT G. HATT

28 T.C.M. 1194 (1969).

FEATHERSTON, JUDGE: * * *

FINDINGS OF FACT

Hatt was a legal resident of Evansville, Indiana, at the time his petition was filed. * * *

Johann is a corporation organized under the laws of the State of Indiana. At the time its petition was filed its principal place of business was Evansville, Indiana. Johann filed corporation income tax returns for the calendar years 1955 and 1957 through 1961 with the district director of internal revenue, Indianapolis, Indiana. During the years in issue Johann operated a funeral home and embalming business.

Hatt was born July 9, 1932. He finished grade school, attended high school for four or five months, and then entered the Army in 1952, being discharged therefrom in August or September 1954. Prior to his military service he had held numerous jobs, such as delivering newspapers, picking up and delivering laundry and dry cleaning, and working as a helper for a lathe operator. Upon his discharge from the Army he worked in California for a short time as a taxicab driver and as a salesman in a jewelry store. Thereafter, in late 1954, he returned to Indianapolis, Indiana, where he had resided as a child, and started working for Household Sewing Machine Company as a salesman.

In the fall of 1955 Hatt opened a place of business known as the "Select Sewing Center," an individual proprietorship located in Evansville, Indiana, which engaged in the business of selling sewing machines. The business consisted primarily of contacting customers in their homes after they had answered advertisements.

Prior to 1957 Hatt became acquainted with Dorothy Echols (hereinafter Dorothy), the president and majority stockholder of Johann. They were married on March 2, 1957, at which time Hatt was approximately 25 years of age and she was about 43. Pursuant to an antenuptial agreement she then transferred to him 130 shares, a majority, of the stock of Johann, and he became the president and general manager of the corporation. * * *

ISSUE 2.   REASONABLENESS OF SALARY PAID TO HATT

Upon marrying Dorothy in March 1957 Hatt became president of Johann. Prior to that time he had had no formal experience or training in the funeral home business, and was not, nor did he ever become, a licensed funeral director or embalmer. However, he had gained some sales experience while operating the Select Sewing Center. In his capacity as the president of Johann, a position he continued to hold to the date of this trial, he served as its chief executive officer with the responsibility and authority of making decisions relating to the following: All expenditures of funds; purchases of capital equipment (including a hearse and two ambulances); renovation and maintenance of the corporation's principal place of business and its related facilities; promotional and advertising activities; manufacture of caskets and vaults; selection and supervision of personnel; financial arrangements with the families of decedents; efforts to collect delinquent accounts; and other similar matters.

The prevailing salary of managers of funeral homes in the Evansville area during the years in controversy was $175 to $200 per week, depending upon tenure, duties, and other factors. Johann's income tax returns reflect that Dorothy received a salary of $15,576.94 in 1955 and $21,424 in 1956 when she served as its president. She was the principal stockholder of the corporation during those years.

For the years 1958 through 1962 Johann's board of directors authorized salaries and bonuses for Hatt in the total amounts of $20,800, $15,300, $16,500, $16,500, and $5,200, respectively. However the full amounts of these salaries and bonuses were not paid, due to the fact that the corporation was short of cash.

Respondent determined that $9,100 per annum was reasonable compensation for the services performed by Hatt, allowed Johann deductions in that amount, and disallowed as excessive, deductions claimed by Johann for Hatt's compensation to the extent of $7,638.49 in 1958, $2,256.14 in 1959, and $7,945.95 in 1960. * * *

ISSUE 3. EXPENSES FOR (A) BOAT, (B) AIRPLANES, [AND] (C) FREDA
HATT'S SALARY * * *

(a) In December 1957 Hatt sold Johann a Chris–Craft boat for $6,500. The words "Johann Funeral Home" were painted on the boat. Johann claimed deductions for the years 1958 through 1962 for expenses incurred in the operation of this boat. Respondent disallowed one-half of the claimed deductions, and determined that the disallowed amounts constituted constructive dividends to Hatt from Johann, as follows:

1958	1959	1960	1961	1962
$413.62	$233.23	$286.68	$118.28	$163.10

The deficiency notice also disallowed a deduction claimed by Johann for boat expenses for 1957 in the amount of $359.27.

(b) In December 1957 Johann purchased for $2,250 a Stinson aircraft, which was subsequently destroyed by fire. A Bonanza airplane was purchased in 1959 for $6,000, of which $4,000 was paid by Hatt individually and $2,000 was paid by Johann. Neither of these airplanes was ever used in Johann's business. Johann claimed deductions for airplane expenses in the following amounts, which respondent disallowed and determined to be taxable to Hatt as constructive dividends:

1958	1959	1960	1961	1962
$465.67	$2,034.45	$1,475.60	$1,979.75	$151.65

Hatt took flying lessons at or about the time he became president of Johann and obtained a pilot's license.

(c) One of Johann's employees was Freda Hatt (hereinafter Freda), Hatt's mother. During the period Freda lived in Evansville, Indiana, she resided in Hatt's apartment located on the premises of the corporation. Freda's primary duty was to provide cosmetic and hairdressing services for female corpses prepared for burial by Johann; outside beauticians charged $5 to $10 per corpse for these services, and Johann handled 90 to 100 female corpses each year. In addition Freda served as an attendant, answered the telephone, received and arranged flowers sent to the funeral home, did cleaning work, fixed meals for employees, and performed other duties. Johann claimed deductions for the salary paid to Freda. Respondent determined that $40 per week was reasonable compensation for her services, allowed Johann deductions in that amount, and disallowed the remaining sums of $285, $25, and $1,250 as excessive compensation to Freda for the years 1958, 1961, and 1962, respectively. Respondent further determined that these amounts were constructive dividends to Hatt.   *   *   *

OPINION   *   *   *

ISSUE 2.   REASONABLENESS OF SALARY PAID TO HATT

Section 162(a)(1) limits deductions for salaries and other compensation of employees to a "reasonable allowance." The determination of what is a reasonable salary depends upon the facts of the particular case, e.g., the nature, extent, and scope of the employee's duties, his qualifications and prior earning capacity, the prevailing rates of compensation for similar work, the volume of business handled by the employee, the net earnings of the employer from such business, and all the other factors which enter into the determination of the amount of an employee's wages.

Petitioner's own expert witness testified that the prevailing salary for a funeral home manager in the Evansville area during the years in controversy was $175 to $200 per week. Respondent's allowance of a deduction of $9,100 per year (i.e., $175 per week) is, therefore, within the salary range prevailing in the area for work similar to that performed by Hatt. We do not think the evidence justifies a higher allowance.

Hatt's youth (25 years of age when he became president of Johann in 1957), lack of formal business training, failure to obtain a license either as an embalmer or a funeral director, and complete lack of experience in the funeral business prior to 1957, and the statutory strictures on participation in a funeral business by non-licensed individuals, would necessarily place him at the lower end of the prevailing salary scale. Moreover, the practical results of Hatt's management, in terms of steadily decreasing sales and net earnings, summarized in our findings, confirm this evaluation. While Hatt suggested in his testimony that Johann's financial adversities were explained in part by unfavorable publicity which resulted from the stormy marital relationship between himself and Dorothy, eventually culminating in a divorce, the personal qualities of an employee, particularly in a business like this one, are not without significance in determining his value to his employer. Finally, we do not think the amount of salary paid to

Johann's president prior to Hatt's ascendancy to that position is a guide to his value to the corporation.

ISSUE 3.   EXPENSES FOR (A) BOAT, (B) AIRPLANES, [AND] (C) FREDA HATT'S SALARY * * *

(a) Respondent allowed Johann deductions, as promotional expenses, of one-half of the cost of operating a Chris–Craft boat on which the legend "Johann Funeral Home" was painted, and disallowed the remainder. On this record we think the allowance is generous. There was no showing that the use of the boat aided Johann's business. Hatt's uncorroborated testimony that he used the boat to build goodwill by providing rides for orphans and senior citizens is not convincing. The personal use of the boat constitutes a constructive dividend to Hatt.

(b) Johann seeks to justify the expense of operating the two airplanes through testimony that they were acquired in an effort to build an air ambulance service. We do not find this explanation convincing. The fact is that neither of the airplanes was ever used for this purpose, and there is no evidence to show that any considered judgment was ever made as to the feasibility of establishing a profitable air ambulance service. Hatt was evasive when asked whether any of his competitors provided such a service. While he testified that the airplanes were never airworthy enough for his personal use, we note that he had qualified as a pilot and, among invoices introduced into evidence, we find numerous bills for aviation gasoline bought on numerous occasions in various cities.

Johann has failed to show that the airplane expenses were "ordinary and necessary" within the meaning of § 162(a). On this record we must conclude that the airplanes were maintained for Hatt's personal use and convenience, and, consequently, the disputed expenses are not deductible by Johann and are constructive dividends to him.

(c) Respondent's allowance of deductions of $40 per week for payments to Hatt's mother, Freda Hatt, necessarily involves a determination that she performed services for Johann. The evidence confirms this determination. The sums disallowed in excess of $40 per week— $285 in 1958, $25 in 1961, and $1,250 in 1962—are not so substantial as to suggest that corporate earnings were being diverted to her, through the device of her salary, for Hatt's benefit or the benefit of any other shareholder. A fair evaluation of the testimony as to her services establishes, we believe, that Johann's salary payments to her were reasonable in relation to the services which she rendered, and are deductible in full. * * *

Notes

(1) *Herbert G. Hatt* was affirmed per curiam on the authority of the Tax Court's decision. Hatt v. Commissioner, 457 F.2d 499 (7th Cir.1972). The Court stated that "Judge Featherston entered meticulous findings of

fact on all issues and rendered a well considered opinion in which we fully concur * * *."

(2) Tax controversies over issues such as those involved in the principal case were very common before the Tax Reform Act of 1986. They continue to arise in C corporations since there is a tax advantage in adopting a no-dividend policy and "zeroing out" the corporate income. Such controversies are less likely to arise in S corporations, though they still may arise in such corporations for non-tax reasons, e.g. if the shareholders active in the business seek to minimize the income allocable to inactive or less active shareholders.

(3) Could a minority shareholder use the decision by the tax authorities and the courts as the basis of a derivative suit to require Hatt to restore the excessive amounts to the corporation? What about a direct suit against the corporation to compel the payment of a dividend to a minority shareholder in an amount sufficient to equalize the dividends per share?

WILDERMAN v. WILDERMAN

Court of Chancery of Delaware, 1974.
315 A.2d 610.

Marvel, Vice Chancellor:

Eleanor M. Wilderman, the plaintiff in this action, sues in her own right and in her capacity as a stockholder with an interest in one-half of the issued and outstanding stock of the defendant Marble Craft Company, Inc. She primarily seeks a ruling to the effect that the defendant Joseph M. Wilderman (the president of the corporate defendant and her former husband) for the fiscal years ending March 31, from 1971 through 1973, caused excessive and unauthorized payments to be made to himself out of earnings of the corporate defendant and that such payments, made in the form of unearned and unauthorized salary and bonuses, must accordingly be returned to the treasury of Marble Craft Company.

Plaintiff asks that upon the Court ordered return of such excessive payments to the corporate treasury that they be treated as corporate profits and required to be distributed as dividends, thereby opening the way to plaintiff to share in the net corporate profits as a stockholder with a 50% equity in her corporation. Plaintiff also asks that appropriate adjustments be made in the corporate defendant's pension plan so as to reflect the return to the corporate treasury of amounts found to be excessive compensation received by the defendant for the fiscal years in question. Also sought is an injunction against disbursement by the individual defendant of moneys from corporate funds or the transfer by such defendant of corporate assets without the approval of the board of directors of the corporation. Finally, plaintiff seeks an order directing the continuance of the business of the corporate defendant under a custodian as provided for under the provisions of 8 Del.C. § 226.

Marble Craft is engaged in the business of installing ceramic tile and marble facings in residences and commercial buildings, such business having been organized by the individual parties to this action some fifteen years ago, being originally operated from the family home. Defendant's initial knowledge of the tile business was gained while working briefly for his father-in-law prior to going into business with his former wife, and there is no doubt but that defendant has been the major force in the business of the corporate defendant inasmuch as he has done most of the estimating, supervising and business getting for the corporation, working up to sixty hours or more per week on corporate business. Plaintiff, on the other hand, has been primarily a bookkeeper for the business, although there is no doubt but that plaintiff is fully versed in the tile business, her father having started such a business in 1929. Significantly, in the beginning of the enterprise the parties' respective compensation was not entirely disparate, as it is now, defendant having initially drawn $125 a week compared to plaintiff's $75.

The business proved successful as a family venture, and in 1961 it was incorporated under the name of Marble Craft Company, Inc., its authorized capital shares consisting of one hundred shares of stock being issued to plaintiff and defendant as joint tenants in exchange for the assets of the business. By-laws providing for the election of two directors were adopted, and the parties, as the duly elected directors, thereupon chose themselves to fill the designated corporate offices, defendant being elected president and the plaintiff vice president, secretary, and treasurer.

The controversy here involved primarily centers around the amount of compensation which defendant has caused to be paid to himself for the fiscal years 1971, 1972 and 1973, compensation which had its origin in a policy [27] designed to avoid corporate taxation by paying out the net corporate profits of Marble Craft Company in the form of executive compensation before the end of each taxable year, thus avoiding double taxation. Accordingly, dividends attributable to corporate profits have never been formally paid until ordered by the Court in the course of this litigation. Such policy of avoiding dividend payments initially worked to the advantage of both parties and their two children, the financial advantage to plaintiff in the plan having been virtually destroyed by the parties' separation and divorce. Thus, following the breakup of the home, plaintiff was largely excluded from the benefits enuring to defendant as a result of the large amounts he proceeded to pay himself. Asserting his authority as the chief executive officer of the corporate defendant, defendant caused the amount of compensation to be paid to him to be increased from $25,000 in 1963 to $60,000 in 1970, the last year for which salary payments to defendant

27. [By the Court] This policy, however, encountered the opposition of the Internal Revenue Service which reduced the deduction allowable to Marble Craft for salary paid to defendant from $30,000 to $20,000 for 1965, from $30,000 to $25,000 for 1966, and from $60,000 to $40,000 for 1970. Presumably the effect of this action was twofold (1) the amount of disallowance was taxed as income to the corporation, and (2) the amount of disallowance less the tax due thereon became a de facto dividend.

are not questioned, such salary having concededly been authorized by corporate resolution. Next, despite the pendency of this action defendant paid himself a bonus of $71,738.71 in addition to a flat salary of $20,800 for the fiscal year 1971, the salary being based on an authorized draw of $400 per week, this being the first year after marital differences arose in which defendant could not point to at least tacit corporate authorization as to the full amount of his compensation. For the fiscal year 1972 defendant paid himself total compensation of $35,000, a year in which corporate profits were substantially lower than those of the previous year due to a building trades strike, and for the fiscal year ending March 31, 1973, defendant caused payment to himself of total compensation in the amount of $86,893.40. During this same period plaintiff received the annual sum of $7,800 for her services to the corporation.

On June 26, 1972, in an effort to work out some accommodation between the parties, a custodian was appointed by order of this Court as provided for by 8 Del.C. § 226(a)(2). However, the deadlock between the parties persisted, and on March 29, 1973, the defendant having caused the sum of $86,893.40 [28] to be paid to himself as compensation for such fiscal year, an order was entered, on the recommendation of the custodian, which stipulated that such payment was without prejudice to the right to contest defendant's compensation in excess of his authorized salary of $20,800. Also authorized and paid on the custodian's recommendation was a dividend of $20,000 to be divided equally between plaintiff and defendant.

The authority to compensate corporate officers is normally vested in the board of directors, 8 Del.C. § 122(5), and the compensating of corporate officers is usually a matter of contract.

Next, while defendant's authorized compensation for the fiscal year 1970 was concededly $60,000, his readoption of a formula basis for arriving at his compensation in the years following was clearly unauthorized, thus defendant's use of the previous formula method of calculating his compensation for the fiscal years 1971, 1972 and 1973 must be reexamined. I conclude that plaintiff's March 29th, 1971 letter concerning defendant's compensation, when read in the light of the filing of this action on April 7, 1971, clearly constituted an adequate expression of plaintiff's intention to rescind the 1970 resolution concerning defendant's compensation and hence served to revoke board authorization for the continuing payment to him of compensation on the basis recognized for 1970.

By early April 1971 the management of Marble Craft was clearly deadlocked with its owner-managers in complete disagreement as to the amount of compensation to be paid the defendant, the payment of anything above a $400 weekly salary being opposed by plaintiff. There-

---

28. [By the Court] Based on an authorized salary of $35,000 per annum plus 15% of gross receipts in excess of $300,000 a formula which was operative through the fiscal year 1970.

fore, the only amount agreed upon by the board and hence the only authorized payment to Mr. Wilderman for the fiscal years 1971, 1972 and 1973 would appear to have been at the rate of $20,800 per year, or $400 per week, and that additional compensation received by him for the years in question must find its authorization in the theory of quantum meruit.

Turning from the issue of corporate authorization of defendant's salary to the issue of the reasonableness of the compensation paid Mr. Wilderman, plaintiff contends that the compensation paid to defendant for the years in question was unreasonable, plaintiff arguing that although courts are hesitant to inquire into the reasonableness of executive compensation when it is fixed by a disinterested board, the standard for fixing executive compensation is obviously more strict when it is fixed by the recipient himself. And where, as in the case at bar, the recipient's vote as a director was necessary to the fixing of the amount of his compensation, then the burden of showing the reasonableness of such compensation clearly falls upon its recipient. This is so, of course, because of the fiduciary position which directors hold towards their corporation and its stockholders.

As to the facts to be considered in reaching a determination of the question as to whether or not defendant has met the burden he must carry there is little authority in Delaware. In Hall v. Isaacs, [37 Del. Ch. 530, 146 A.2d 602, aff'd in part, 39 Del.Ch. 244, 163 A.2d 288,] the Court was of the view that evidence of what other executives similarly situated received was relevant, and in Meiselman v. Eberstadt, [39 Del. Ch. 563, 170 A.2d 72] the ability of the executive was considered. Other factors which have been judicially recognized elsewhere are whether or not the Internal Revenue Service has allowed the corporation to deduct the amount of salary alleged to be unreasonable. Other relevant factors are whether the salary bears a reasonable relation to the success of the corporation, the amount previously received as salary, whether increases in salary are geared to increases in the value of services rendered, and the amount of the challenged salary compared to other salaries paid by the employer. See 2 Washington and Rothschild, Compensating the Corporate Executive, 848–873 (3rd Ed.1962). Dr. Seligman, an expert, testified that on the basis of a financial analysis of Marble Craft and its present earnings that reasonable compensation for defendant would range between $25,000 and $35,000. It also appears that the Internal Revenue Service proposes to permit Marble Craft a deduction of $52,000 for defendant's 1971 compensation of $92,538.

On the present record I am not convinced that defendant has discharged his burden as to the reasonableness of amounts he has drawn for all of the years in question. He has, first of all, failed to produce substantial evidence as to what other executives in the local tile business earn. Next, in light of the gross earnings of the corporate defendant and the facts concerning work of Marble Craft at Longwood Gardens there is some doubt as to whether or not defendant's work has been as truly essential and productive as he contends. Furthermore, defendant's compensation was caused by his own fiat to rise rapidly from $30,000 in 1966 to over $90,000 for 1971, although the earnings of Marble Craft rose only from about $380,000 in 1966 to approximately $680,000 for 1971.

I conclude from a consideration of all of the facts and circumstances surrounding defendant's services to his corporation, including the fact that the total number of employees of the business is about twenty, that compensation for defendant in excess of the compensation suggested by the financial analyst who testified at trial would be reasonable but that such compensation should be within the limits considered appropriate by the Internal Revenue Service. Such compensation should also constitute a reasonable increase over defendant's average salary of some $30,000 for the period 1963 through 1966 when the profits of Marble Craft were about half its 1971 earnings.

Thus, while for the fiscal years 1971, 1972 and 1973 Mr. Wilderman was technically entitled to be compensated for his services in the amount of only $20,800, I am of the opinion that in light of the nature of defendant's services to the corporation, which appear to have been important to its success, that he is entitled to compensation in the amount of $45,000 for the fiscal year 1971 and the same amount for fiscal 1973. Defendant's compensation of $35,000 for the fiscal year ending 1972 will be left undisturbed. Accordingly, he will be ordered to return $47,538 in excess compensation to the corporate treasury for fiscal 1971 and $41,893.40 for fiscal 1973, both amounts with interest.

Additionally, because payments to the Marble Craft pension fund have been tied to defendant's compensation for the years in question, defendant will be directed to repay to the defendant Marble Craft excessive payments to such fund in the same ratio as the refunds of his excessive compensation.

As to what should be appropriate dividends payable out of the reconstructed net profits of the company after the adjustments here directed to be made is, I believe, a matter for the board of directors in the first instance and in the event of deadlock for the custodian. I also decline to fix plaintiff's salary because such was not raised in the pleadings or at trial and for the reason given for declining to set a future dividend rate. * * *

An appropriate order may be submitted on notice.

Notes

In Mann–Paller Foundation v. Econometric Research, 644 F.Supp. 92 (D.D.C.1986), the majority shareholder of the defendant received compensation in the amount of $347,745 in 1985; the minority shareholder received nothing since no dividend was declared. The minority shareholder sued to recover $191,369.10 on the theory that the compensation to the majority shareholder constituted a "de facto dividend" that had not been paid in proportion to shareholdings. The court granted summary judgment for the defendants: the suit failed as a claim to compel the payment of a dividend since it did not allege "that the withholding of [a dividend] is explicable only on the theory of an oppressive or fraudulent abuse of discretion" (Id., at 98); the suit also failed as a claim alleging improper compensation to a shareholder-employee since such a suit must be brought in the name of and for the benefit of the corporation (a derivative suit) rather than directly on behalf of a minority shareholder. Compare Murphy v. Country House, Inc., 349 N.W.2d 289 (Minn.App.1984).

DONAHUE v. RODD ELECTROTYPE CO.

Supreme Judicial Court of Massachusetts, 1975.
367 Mass. 578, 328 N.E.2d 505.

Before TAURO, C.J., and REARDON, QUIRICO, BRAUCHER, KAPLAN and WILKINS, JJ.

TAURO, CHIEF JUSTICE.

The plaintiff, Euphemia Donahue, a minority stockholder in the Rodd Electrotype Company of New England, Inc. (Rodd Electrotype), a Massachusetts corporation, brings this suit against the directors of Rodd Electrotype, Charles H. Rodd, Frederick I. Rodd and Mr. Harold E. Magnuson, against Harry C. Rodd, a former director, officer, and controlling stockholder of Rodd Electrotype and against Rodd Electrotype (hereinafter called defendants). The plaintiff seeks to rescind Rodd Electrotype's purchase of Harry Rodd's shares in Rodd Electrotype and to compel Harry Rodd "to repay to the corporation the purchase price of said shares, $36,000, together with interest from the date of purchase." The plaintiff alleges that the defendants caused the corporation to purchase the shares in violation of their fiduciary duty to her, a minority stockholder of Rodd Electrotype.

The trial judge, after hearing oral testimony, dismissed the plaintiff's bill on the merits. He found that the purchase was without prejudice to the plaintiff and implicitly found that the transaction had been carried out in good faith and with inherent fairness. The Appeals Court affirmed with costs. Donahue v. Rodd Electrotype Co. of New England, Inc., 307 N.E.2d 8 (1974). * * *

The evidence may be summarized as follows: In 1935, the defendant, Harry C. Rodd, began his employment with Rodd Electrotype, then styled the Royal Electrotype Company of New England, Inc. (Royal of New England). At that time, the company was a wholly-owned subsidiary of a Pennsylvania corporation, the Royal Electrotype Company (Royal Electrotype). Mr. Rodd's advancement within the company was rapid. The following year he was elected a director, and, in 1946, he succeeded to the position of general manager and treasurer.

In 1936, the plaintiff's husband, Joseph Donahue (now deceased), was hired by Royal of New England as a "finisher" of electrotype plates. His duties were confined to operational matters within the plant. Although he ultimately achieved the positions of plant superintendent (1946) and corporate vice president (1955), Donahue never participated in the "management" aspect of the business.

In the years preceding 1955, the parent company, Royal Electrotype, made available to Harry Rodd and Joseph Donahue shares of the common stock in its subsidiary, Royal of New England. Harry Rodd took advantage of the opportunities offered to him and acquired 200 shares for $20 a share. Joseph Donahue, at the suggestion of Harry Rodd, who hoped to interest Donahue in the business, eventually obtained fifty shares in two twenty-five share lots priced at $20 a share. The parent company at all times retained 725 of the 1,000 outstanding shares. One Lawrence W. Kelley owned the remaining twenty-five shares.

In June of 1955, Royal of New England purchased all 725 of its shares owned by its parent company. The total price amounted to $135,000. Royal of New England remitted $75,000 of this total in cash and executed five promissory notes of $12,000 each, due in each of the succeeding five years. Lawrence W. Kelley's twenty-five shares were also purchased at this time for $1,000. A substantial portion of Royal of New England's cash expenditures was loaned to the company by Harry Rodd, who mortgaged his house to obtain some of the necessary funds.

The stock purchases left Harry Rodd in control of Royal of New England. Early in 1955, before the purchases, he had assumed the presidency of the company. His 200 shares gave him a dominant eighty per cent interest. Joseph Donahue, at this time, was the only minority stockholder.

Subsequent events reflected Harry Rodd's dominant influence. In June, 1960, more than a year after the last obligation to Royal Electrotype had been discharged, the company was renamed the Rodd Electrotype Company of New England, Inc. In 1962, Charles H. Rodd, Harry Rodd's son (a defendant here), who had long been a company employee working in the plant, became corporate vice president. In 1963, he joined his father on the board of directors. In 1964, another son, Frederick I. Rodd (also a defendant), replaced Joseph Donahue as plant superintendent. By 1965, Harry Rodd had evidently decided to reduce his participation in corporate management. That year Charles Rodd succeeded him as president and general manager of Rodd Electrotype.

From 1959 to 1967, Harry Rodd pursued what may fairly be termed a gift program by which he distributed the majority of his shares equally among his two sons and his daughter, Phyllis E. Mason. Each child received thirty-nine shares. Two shares were returned to the corporate treasury in 1966.

We come now to the events of 1970 which form the grounds for the plaintiff's complaint. In May of 1970, Harry Rodd was seventy-seven years old. The record indicates that for some time he had not enjoyed the best of health and that he had undergone a number of operations.

His sons wished him to retire. Mr. Rodd was not averse to this suggestion. However, he insisted that some financial arrangements be made with respect to his remaining eighty-one shares of stock. A number of conferences ensued. Harry Rodd and Charles Rodd (representing the company) negotiated terms of purchase for forty-five shares which, Charles Rodd testified, would reflect the book value and liquidating value of the shares.

A special board meeting convened on July 13, 1970. As the first order of business, Harry Rodd resigned his directorship of Rodd Electrotype. The remaining incumbent directors, Charles Rodd and Mr. Harold E. Magnuson (clerk of the company and a defendant and defense attorney in the instant suit), elected Frederick Rodd to replace his father. The three directors then authorized Rodd Electrotype's president (Charles Rodd) to execute an agreement between Harry Rodd and the company in which the company would purchase forty-five shares for $800 a share ($36,000).

The stock purchase agreement was formalized between the parties on July 13, 1970. Two days later, a sale pursuant to the July 13 agreement was consummated. At approximately the same time, Harry Rodd resigned his last corporate office, that of treasurer.

Harry Rodd completed divestiture of his Rodd Electrotype stock in the following year. * * * Thus, in March, 1971, the shareholdings in Rodd Electrotype were apportioned as follows: Charles Rodd, Frederick Rodd and Phyllis Mason each held fifty-one shares; the Donahues [29] held fifty shares.

A special meeting of the stockholders of the company was held on March 30, 1971. At the meeting, Charles Rodd, company president and general manager, reported the tentative results of an audit conducted by the company auditors and reported generally on the company events of the year. For the first time, the Donahues learned that the corporation had purchased Harry Rodd's shares. According to the minutes of the meeting, following Charles Rodd's report, the Donahues raised questions about the purchase. They then voted against a resolution, ultimately adopted by the remaining stockholders, to approve Charles Rodd's report. * * *

A few weeks after the meeting, the Donahues, acting through their attorney, offered their shares to the corporation on the same terms given to Harry Rodd. Mr. Harold E. Magnuson replied by letter that the corporation would not purchase the shares and was not in a financial position to do so.[30] This suit followed.

---

29. [By the Court] Joseph Donahue gave his wife, the plaintiff, joint ownership of his fifty shares in 1962. In 1968, they transferred five shares to their son, Dr. Robert Donahue. On Joseph Donahue's death, the plaintiff became outright owner of the forty-five share block. This was the ownership pattern which obtained in March, 1971.

30. [By the Court] Between 1965 and 1969, the company offered to purchase the Donahue shares for amounts between $2,000 and $10,000 ($40 to $200 a share). The Donahues rejected these offers.

In her argument before this court, the plaintiff has characterized the corporate purchase of Harry Rodd's shares as an unlawful distribution of corporate assets to controlling stockholders. She urges that the distribution constitutes a breach of the fiduciary duty owed by the Rodds, as controlling stockholders, to her, a minority stockholder in the enterprise, because the Rodds failed to accord her an equal opportunity to sell her shares to the corporation. The defendants reply that the stock purchase was within the powers of the corporation and met the requirements of good faith and inherent fairness imposed on a fiduciary in his dealings with the corporation. They assert that there is no right to equal opportunity in corporate stock purchases for the corporate treasury. For the reasons hereinafter noted, we agree with the plaintiff and reverse the decree of the Superior Court. However, we limit the applicability of our holding to "close corporations" * * *. Whether the holding should apply to other corporations is left for decision in another case, on a proper record. * * *

A. *Close Corporations.* In previous opinions, we have alluded to the distinctive nature of the close corporation, but have never defined precisely what is meant by a close corporation. There is no single, generally accepted definition. Some commentators emphasize an "integration of ownership and management" (Note, Statutory Assistance for Closely Held Corporations, 71 Harv.L.Rev. 1498 [1958]), in which the stockholders occupy most management positions. Others focus on the number of stockholders and the nature of the market for the stock. In this view, close corporations have few stockholders; there is little market for corporate stock. * * * We accept aspects of both definitions. We deem a close corporation to be typified by: (1) a small number of stockholders; (2) no ready market for the corporate stock; and (3) substantial majority stockholder participation in the management, direction and operations of the corporation.

As thus defined, the close corporation bears striking resemblance to a partnership. Commentators and courts have noted that the close corporation is often little more than an "incorporated" or "chartered" partnership. Ripin v. United States Woven Label Co., 205 N.Y. 442, 447, 98 N.E. 855, 856 (1912) ("little more (though not quite the same as) than chartered partnerships"). The stockholders "clothe" their partnership "with the benefits peculiar to a corporation, limited liability, perpetuity and the like." In the Matter of Surchin v. Approved Bus. Mach. Co., Inc., 55 Misc.2d 888, 889, 286 N.Y.S.2d 580, 581 (Sup.Ct. 1967). In essence, though, the enterprise remains one in which ownership is limited to the original parties or transferees of their stock to whom the other stockholders have agreed,[31] in which ownership and

---

31. [By the Court] The original owners commonly impose restrictions on transfers of stock designed to prevent outsiders who are unacceptable to the other stockholders from acquiring an interest in the close corporation. These restrictions often take the form of agreements among the stockholders and the corporation or by-laws which give the corporation or the other stockholders a right of "first refusal" when any stockholder desires to sell his shares. In a partnership, of course, a partner cannot transfer his interest in the partnership so as to give his assignee a right to partici-

management are in the same hands, and in which the owners are quite dependent on one another for the success of the enterprise. Many close corporations are "really partnerships, between two or three people who contribute their capital, skills, experience and labor." Kruger v. Gerth, 16 N.Y.2d 802, 805, 263 N.Y.S.2d 1, 3, 210 N.E.2d 355, 356 (1965) (Desmond, C.J., dissenting). Just as in a partnership, the relationship among the stockholders must be one of trust, confidence and absolute loyalty if the enterprise is to succeed. Close corporations with substantial assets and with more numerous stockholders are no different from smaller close corporations in this regard. All participants rely on the fidelity and abilities of those stockholders who hold office. Disloyalty and self-seeking conduct on the part of any stockholder will engender bickering, corporate stalemates, and, perhaps, efforts to achieve dissolution.

In Helms v. Duckworth, 101 U.S.App.D.C. 390, 249 F.2d 482 (1957), the United States Court of Appeals for the District of Columbia Circuit had before it a stockholders' agreement providing for the purchase of the shares of a deceased stockholder by the surviving stockholder in a small "two-man" close corporation. The court held the surviving stockholder to a duty "to deal fairly, honestly, and openly with * * * [his] fellow stockholders." Id. at 487. Judge Burger, now Chief Justice Burger, writing for the court, emphasized the resemblance of the two-man close corporation to a partnership: "In an intimate business venture such as this, stockholders of a close corporation occupy a position similar to that of joint adventurers and partners. While courts have sometimes declared stockholders 'do not bear toward each other that same relation of trust and confidence which prevails in partnerships,' this view ignores the practical realities of the organization and functioning of a small 'two-man' corporation organized to carry on a small business enterprise in which the stockholders, directors, and managers are the same persons" (footnotes omitted). Id. at 486.

Although the corporate form provides * * * advantages for the stockholders (limited liability, perpetuity, and so forth), it also supplies an opportunity for the majority stockholders to oppress or disadvantage minority stockholders. The minority is vulnerable to a variety of oppressive devices, termed "freeze-outs," which the majority may employ. See, generally, Note, Freezing Out Minority Shareholders, 74 Harv.L.Rev. 1630 (1961). An authoritative study of such "freeze-outs" enumerates some of the possibilities: "The squeezers [those who employ the freeze-out techniques] may refuse to declare dividends; they may drain off the corporation's earnings in the form of exorbitant salaries and bonuses to the majority shareholder-officers and perhaps to their relatives, or in the form of high rent by the corporation for property leased from majority shareholders * * *; they may deprive minority shareholders of corporate offices and of employment by the company;

pate in the management or business affairs of the continuing partnership without the agreement of the other partners. G.L. c.

108A, § 27. See Hazen v. Warwick, 256 Mass. 302, 308, 152 N.E. 342 (1926).

they may cause the corporation to sell its assets at an inadequate price to the majority shareholders * * *." F.H. O'Neal and J. Derwin, Expulsion or Oppression of Business Associates, 42 (1961). In particular, the power of the board of directors, controlled by the majority, to declare or withhold dividends and to deny the minority employment is easily converted to a device to disadvantage minority stockholders.

The minority can, of course, initiate suit against the majority and their directors. Self-serving conduct by directors is proscribed by the director's fiduciary obligation to the corporation. However, in practice, the plaintiff will find difficulty in challenging dividend or employment policies. Such policies are considered to be within the judgment of the directors. This court has said: "The courts prefer not to interfere * * * with the sound financial management of the corporation by its directors, but declare as a general rule that the declaration of dividends rests within the sound discretion of the directors, refusing to interfere with their determination unless a plain abuse of discretion is made to appear." Crocker v. Waltham Watch Co., 315 Mass. 397, 402, 53 N.E.2d 230, 233 (1944). Judicial reluctance to interfere combines with the difficulty of proof when the standard is "plain abuse of discretion" or bad faith, to limit the possibilities for relief. Although contractual provisions in an "agreement of association and articles of organization" or in by-laws have justified decrees in this jurisdiction ordering dividend declarations, generally, plaintiffs who seek judicial assistance against corporate dividend or employment policies [32] do not prevail. [Citations from numerous jurisdictions omitted]

Thus, when these types of "freeze-outs" are attempted by the majority stockholders, the minority stockholders, cut off from all corporation-related revenues, must either suffer their losses or seek a buyer for their shares. Many minority stockholders will be unwilling or unable to wait for an alteration in majority policy. Typically, the minority stockholder in a close corporation has a substantial percentage of his personal assets invested in the corporation. Galler v. Galler, 32 Ill.2d 16, 27, 203 N.E.2d 577 (1965). The stockholder may have anticipated that his salary from his position with the corporation would be his livelihood. Thus, he cannot afford to wait passively. He must liquidate his investment in the close corporation in order to reinvest the funds in income-producing enterprises.

At this point, the true plight of the minority stockholder in a close corporation becomes manifest. He cannot easily reclaim his capital. In a large public corporation, the oppressed or dissident minority stockholder could sell his stock in order to extricate some of his

---

32. [By the Court] Attacks on allegedly excessive salaries voted for officers and directors fare better in the courts. See Stratis v. Andreson, 254 Mass. 536, 150 N.E. 832 (1926); Sagalyn v. Meekins, Packard & Wheat, Inc., 290 Mass. 434, 195 N.E. 769 (1935). What is "reasonable compensation" is a question of fact. Black v. Parker Mfg. Co., 329 Mass. 105, 116, 106 N.E.2d 544 (1952). The proof which establishes an excess over such "reasonable compensation" appears easier than the proof which would establish bad faith or plain abuse of discretion.

invested capital. By definition, this market is not available for shares in the close corporation. In a partnership, a partner who feels abused by his fellow partners may cause dissolution by his "express will * * * at any time" ([UPA] § 31[1][b] and [2]) and recover his share of partnership assets and accumulated profits.[33] [UPA] § 38. If dissolution results in a breach of the partnership articles, the culpable partner will be liable in damages. [UPA] § 38(2)(a) II. By contrast, the stockholder in the close corporation or "incorporated partnership" may achieve dissolution and recovery of his share of the enterprise assets only by compliance with the rigorous terms of the applicable chapter of the General Laws. Rizzuto v. Onset Cafe, Inc., 330 Mass. 595, 597–598, 116 N.E.2d 249 (1953). "The dissolution of a corporation which is a creature of the Legislature is primarily a legislative function, and the only authority courts have to deal with this subject is the power conferred upon them by the Legislature." Leventhal v. Atlantic Fin. Corp., 316 Mass. 194, 205, 55 N.E.2d 20, 26 (1944). To secure dissolution of the ordinary close corporation subject to G.L. c. 156B, the stockholder, in the absence of corporate deadlock, must own at least fifty per cent of the shares or have the advantage of a favorable provision in the articles of organization. The minority stockholder, by definition lacking fifty per cent of the corporate shares, can never "authorize" the corporation to file a petition for dissolution under G.L. c. 156B, § 99(a), by his own vote. He will seldom have at his disposal the requisite favorable provision in the articles of organization.

Thus, in a close corporation, the minority stockholders may be trapped in a disadvantageous situation. No outsider would knowingly assume the position of the disadvantaged minority. The outsider would have the same difficulties. To cut losses, the minority stockholder may be compelled to deal with the majority. This is the capstone of the majority plan. Majority "freeze-out" schemes which withhold dividends are designed to compel the minority to relinquish stock at inadequate prices. When the minority stockholder agrees to sell out at less than fair value, the majority has won.

Because of the fundamental resemblance of the close corporation to the partnership, the trust and confidence which are essential to this scale and manner of enterprise, and the inherent danger to minority interests in the close corporation, we hold that stockholders [34] in the close corporation owe one another substantially the same fiduciary duty in the operation of the enterprise [35] that partners owe to one another.

---

33. [By the Court] The partnership agreement may control the amount and timing of distribution in a way which is disadvantageous to the retiring partner.

34. [By the Court] We do not limit our holding to majority stockholders. In the close corporation, the minority may do equal damage through unscrupulous and improper "sharp dealings" with an unsuspecting majority. See Helms v. Duck-worth, 101 U.S.App.D.C. 390, 249 F.2d 482 (1957).

35. [By the Court] We stress that the strict fiduciary duty which we apply to stockholders in a close corporation in this opinion governs *only* their actions relative to the operations of the enterprise and the effects of that operation on the rights and investments of other stockholders. We express no opinion as to the standard of duty

In our previous decisions, we have defined the standard of duty owed by partners to one another as the "utmost good faith and loyalty." Cardullo v. Landau, 329 Mass. 5, 8, 105 N.E.2d 843 (1952). Stockholders in close corporations must discharge their management and stockholder responsibilities in conformity with this strict good faith standard. They may not act out of avarice, expediency or self-interest in derogation of their duty of loyalty to the other stockholders and to the corporation.

We contrast this strict good faith standard with the somewhat less stringent standard of fiduciary duty to which directors and stockholders [36] of all corporations must adhere in the discharge of their corporate responsibilities. Corporate directors are held to a good faith and inherent fairness standard of conduct (Winchell v. Plywood Corp., 324 Mass. 171, 177, 85 N.E.2d 313 [1949]) and are not "permitted to serve two masters whose interests are antagonistic." Spiegel v. Beacon Participations, Inc., 297 Mass. 398, 411, 8 N.E.2d 895, 904 (1937). "Their paramount duty is to the corporation, and their personal pecuniary interests are subordinate to that duty." Durfee v. Durfee & Canning, Inc., 323 Mass. 187, 196, 80 N.E.2d 522, 527 (1948).

The more rigorous duty of partners and participants in a joint adventure, here extended to stockholders in a close corporation, was described by then Chief Judge Cardozo of the New York Court of Appeals in Meinhard v. Salmon, 249 N.Y. 458, 164 N.E. 545 (1928): "Joint adventurers, like copartners, owe to one another, while the enterprise continues, the duty of the finest loyalty. Many forms of conduct permissible in a workaday world for those acting at arm's length, are forbidden to those bound by fiduciary ties. * * * Not honesty alone, but the punctilio of an honor the most sensitive, is then the standard of behavior." Id. at 463–464, 164 N.E. at 546.

Application of this strict standard of duty to stockholders in close corporations is a natural outgrowth of the prior case law. In a number of cases involving close corporations, we have held stockholders participating in management to a standard of fiduciary duty more exacting than the traditional good faith and inherent fairness standard because of the trust and confidence reposed in them by the other stockholders.

* * *

[W]e have imposed a duty of loyalty more exacting than that duty owed by a director to his corporation (Spiegel v. Beacon Participations, Inc., 297 Mass. 398, 410–411, 8 N.E.2d 895 [1937]) or by a majority stockholder to the minority in a public corporation [37] because of facts particular to the close corporation in the cases. In the instant case, we

applicable to transactions in the shares of the close corporation when the corporation is not a party to the transaction. Cf. Andrews, The Stockholder's Right to Equal Opportunity in the Sale of Shares, 78 Harv.L.Rev. 505 (1965).

36. [By the Court] The rule set out in many jurisdictions is: "The majority has

the right to control; but when it does so, it occupies a fiduciary relation toward the minority, as much so as the corporation itself or its officers and directors." Southern Pac. Co. v. Bogert, 250 U.S. 483, 487–488, 39 S.Ct. 533, 535, 64 L.Ed. 1099 (1919).

37. [By the Court] See n. 34, supra.

extend this strict duty of loyalty to all stockholders in close corporations. The circumstances which justified findings of relationships of trust and confidence in these particular cases exist universally in modified form in all close corporations. See Kruger v. Gerth, 16 N.Y.2d 802, 806, 263 N.Y.S.2d 1, 210 N.E.2d 355 (1965) (Fuld, J., dissenting). Statements in other cases which suggest that stockholders of a corporation do not stand in a relationship of trust and confidence to one another will not be followed in the close corporation context.

B. *Equal Opportunity in a Close Corporation.* Under settled Massachusetts law, a domestic corporation, unless forbidden by statute, has the power to purchase its own shares. Dupee v. Boston Water Power Co., 114 Mass. 37, 43 (1873). * * * When the corporation reacquiring its own stock is a close corporation, the purchase is subject to the additional requirement, in the light of our holding in this opinion, that the stockholders, who, as directors or controlling stockholders, caused the corporation to enter into the stock purchase agreement, must have acted with the utmost good faith and loyalty to the other stockholders.

To meet this test, if the stockholder whose shares were purchased was a member of the controlling group, the controlling stockholders must cause the corporation to offer each stockholder an equal opportunity to sell a ratable number of his shares to the corporation at an identical price.[38] Purchase by the corporation confers substantial benefits on the members of the controlling group whose shares were purchased. These benefits are not available to the minority stockholders if the corporation does not also offer them an opportunity to sell their shares. The controlling group may not, consistent with its strict duty to the minority, utilize its control of the corporation to obtain special advantages and disproportionate benefit from its share ownership. Cf. Brudney and Chirelstein, Fair Shares in Corporate Mergers and Takeovers, 88 Harv.L.Rev. 297, 334 (1974).

The benefits conferred by the purchase are twofold: (1) provision of a market for shares; (2) access to corporate assets for personal use. By definition, there is no ready market for shares of a close corporation. The purchase creates a market for shares which previously had been unmarketable. It transforms a previously illiquid investment into a liquid one. If the close corporation purchases shares only from a member of the controlling group, the controlling stockholder can convert his shares into cash at a time when none of the other stockholders can. Consistent with its strict fiduciary duty, the controlling group may not utilize its control of the corporation to establish an exclusive market in previously unmarketable shares from which the minority stockholders are excluded. See Jones v. H.F. Ahmanson & Co., 1 Cal.3d 93, 115, 81 Cal.Rptr. 592, 460 P.2d 464 (1969).

38. [By the Court] Of course, a close corporation may purchase shares from one stockholder without offering the others an equal opportunity if all other stockholders give advance consent to the stock purchase arrangements through acceptance of an appropriate provision in the articles of organization, the corporate by-laws or a stockholder's agreement. Similarly, all other stockholders may ratify the purchase.

The purchase also distributes corporate assets to the stockholder whose shares were purchased. Unless an equal opportunity is given to all stockholders, the purchase of shares from a member of the controlling group operates as a *preferential* distribution of assets. In exchange for his shares, he receives a percentage of the contributed capital and accumulated profits of the enterprise. The funds he so receives are available for his personal use. The other stockholders benefit from no such access to corporate property and cannot withdraw their shares of the corporate profits and capital in this manner unless the controlling group acquiesces. Although the purchase price for the controlling stockholder's shares may seem fair to the corporation and other stockholders under the tests established in the prior case law, the controlling stockholder whose stock has been purchased has still received a relative advantage over his fellow stockholders, inconsistent with his strict fiduciary duty—an opportunity to turn corporate funds to personal use.

The rule of equal opportunity in stock purchases by close corporations provides equal access to these benefits for all stockholders. We hold that, in any case in which the controlling stockholders have exercised their power over the corporation to deny the minority such equal opportunity, the minority shall be entitled to appropriate relief.[39] To the extent that language in Spiegel v. Beacon Participations, Inc., 297 Mass. 398, 431, 8 N.E.2d 895 (1937), and other cases suggests that there is no requirement of equal opportunity for minority stockholders when a close corporation purchases shares from a controlling stockholder, it is not to be followed.

C. *Application of the Law to this Case.* We turn now to the application of the learning set forth above to the facts of the instant case.

The strict standard of duty is plainly applicable to the stockholders in Rodd Electrotype. Rodd Electrotype is a close corporation. Members of the Rodd and Donahue families are the sole owners of the corporation's stock. In actual numbers, the corporation, immediately prior to the corporate purchase of Harry Rodd's shares, had six stockholders. The shares have not been traded, and no market for them seems to exist. Harry Rodd, Charles Rodd, Frederick Rodd, William G. Mason (Phyllis Mason's husband), and the plaintiff's husband all

---

39. [By the Court] Under the Massachusetts law, "[n]o stockholder shall have any pre-emptive right to acquire stock of the corporation except to the extent provided in the articles of organization or in a by-law adopted by and subject to amendment only by the stockholders." G.L. c. 156B, § 20. We do not here suggest that such preemptive rights are required by the strict fiduciary duty applicable to the stockholders of close corporations. However, to the extent that a controlling stockholder or other stockholder, in violation of his fiduciary duty, causes the corporation to issue stock in order to expand his holdings or to dilute holdings of other stockholders, the other stockholders will have a right to relief in court. Even under the traditional standard of duty applicable to corporate directors and stockholders generally, this court has looked favorably upon stockholder challenges to stock issues which, in violation of a fiduciary duty, served personal interests of other stockholder/directors and did not serve the corporate interest. See, e.g., Elliott v. Baker, 194 Mass. 518, 80 N.E. 450 (1907).

worked for the corporation. The Rodds have retained the paramount management positions.

Through their control of these management positions and of the majority of the Rodd Electrotype stock, the Rodds effectively controlled the corporation. In testing the stock purchase from Harry Rodd against the applicable strict fiduciary standard, we treat the Rodd family as a single controlling group. We reject the defendants' contention that the Rodd family cannot be treated as a unit for this purpose. From the evidence, it is clear that the Rodd family was a close-knit one with strong community of interest. Harry Rodd had hired his sons to work in the family business, Rodd Electrotype. As he aged, he transferred portions of his stock holdings to his children. Charles Rodd and Frederick Rodd were given positions of responsibility in the business as he withdrew from active management. In these circumstances, it is realistic to assume that appreciation, gratitude, and filial devotion would prevent the younger Rodds from opposing a plan which would provide funds for their father's retirement.

Moreover, a strong motive of interest requires that the Rodds be considered a controlling group. When Charles Rodd and Frederick Rodd were called on to represent the corporation in its dealings with their father, they must have known that further advancement within the corporation and benefits would follow their father's retirement and the purchase of his stock. * * *

On its face, then, the purchase of Harry Rodd's shares by the corporation is a breach of the duty which the controlling stockholders, the Rodds, owed to the minority stockholders, the plaintiff and her son. The purchase distributed a portion of the corporate assets to Harry Rodd, a member of the controlling group, in exchange for his shares. The plaintiff and her son were not offered an equal opportunity to sell their shares to the corporation. In fact, their efforts to obtain an equal opportunity were rebuffed by the corporate representative. As the trial judge found, they did not, in any manner, ratify the transaction with Harry Rodd.

Because of the foregoing, we hold that the plaintiff is entitled to relief. Two forms of suitable relief are set out hereinafter. The judge below is to enter an appropriate judgment. The judgment may require Harry Rodd to remit $36,000 with interest at the legal rate from July 15, 1970, to Rodd Electrotype in exchange for forty-five shares of Rodd Electrotype treasury stock. * * * In the alternative, the judgment may require Rodd Electrotype to purchase all of the plaintiff's shares for $36,000 without interest. In the circumstances of this case, we view this as the equal opportunity which the plaintiff should have received. Harry Rodd's retention of thirty-six shares, which were to be sold and given to his children within a year of the Rodd Electrotype purchase, cannot disguise the fact that the corporation acquired one hundred per cent of that portion of his holdings (forty-five shares) which he did not intend his children to own. The plaintiff is entitled to have one hundred per cent of her forty-five shares similarly purchased.[40] * * * The case is remanded to the Superior Court for entry of judgment in conformity with this opinion.

So ordered.

WILKINS, JUSTICE (concurring).

I agree with much of what the Chief Justice says in support of granting relief to the plaintiff. However, I do not join in any implication * * * that the rule concerning a close corporation's purchase of a controlling stockholder's shares applies to all operations of the corporation as they affect minority stockholders. That broader issue, which is apt to arise in connection with salaries and dividend policy, is not involved in this case. The analogy to partnerships may not be a complete one.

Notes

(1) Even though the principal case talks about freezeouts, the actual transaction successfully attacked in the case involves an arguably unfair redemption of shares rather than a freezeout. Other courts have followed *Donahue* in this respect and have set aside a partial redemption of the majority's shares to the exclusion of the minority, e.g. Tillis v. United Parts, Inc., 395 So.2d 618 (Fla.App.1981), or the redemption of a third person's shares in order to assure the retention of control by one faction, Comolli v. Comolli, 241 Ga. 471, 246 S.E.2d 278 (1978). The broad language of *Donahue* about the fiduciary duties of majority shareholders has also been cited approvingly by courts in a substantial number of states. See, e.g. 68th Street Apts., Inc. v. Lauricella, 142 N.J.Super. 546, 362 A.2d 78 (1976); Knaebel v. Heiner, 663 P.2d 551 (Alaska 1983); Russell v. First York Savings Co., 218 Neb. 112, 352 N.W.2d 871 (1984). Estate of Schroer v. Stamco Supply, Inc., 19 Ohio App.3d 34, 482 N.E.2d 975 (1984); Forinash v. Daugherty, 697 S.W.2d 294 (Mo.App.1985); Balvik v. Sylvester, 411 N.W. 2d 383 (N.D.1987); Sundberg v. Abbott, 423 N.W.2d 686 (Minn.App.1988); Estate of Meller v. Adolf Meller Co., 554 A.2d 648 (R.I.1989).

(2) As might be expected, the broad language in *Donahue* has been often cited in Massachusetts cases, and clearly has influenced the development of legal principles in that state on a variety of different issues. Between 1975 and 1989, the Massachusetts appellate courts decided some fifteen cases in which the *Donahue* principles were sought to be applied. For example, in Smith v. Atlantic Properties, Inc., 12 Mass.App.Ct. 201, 422 N.E.2d 798 (1981), the court imposed liability on a minority shareholder for the claimed misuse of a veto power to prevent the payment of all dividends. In Hallahan v. Haltom Corp., 7 Mass.App.Ct. 68, 385 N.E.2d 1033 (1979), the court ordered shares secretly acquired by an equal co-owner of shares in an effort to shift the balance of control be returned to the seller at cost. And in Wilkes v. Springside Nursing Home, Inc., 370 Mass. 842, 353 N.E.2d

40. [By the Court] If there has been a significant change in corporate circumstances since this case was argued, this is a matter which can be brought to the attention of the court below and may be considered by the judge in granting appropriate relief in the form of a judgment.

657 (1976), the court ordered the reinstatement of a minority shareholder
to the corporate payroll after he had been fired in connection with an
attempted freezeout. However, the Massachusetts Supreme Court in its
opinion in *Wilkes* retreated to some extent from the language of *Donahue*.
The court stated:

> * * * We are concerned that untempered application of the
> strict good faith standard enunciated in *Donahue* to cases such as the
> one before us will result in the imposition of limitations on legitimate
> action by the controlling group in a close corporation which will
> unduly hamper its effectiveness in managing the corporation in the
> best interests of all concerned. The majority, concededly, have certain
> rights to what has been termed "selfish ownership" in the corporation
> which should be balanced against the concept of their fiduciary obliga-
> tion to the minority.

> Therefore, when minority stockholders in a close corporation bring
> suit against the majority alleging a breach of the strict good faith duty
> owed to them by the majority, we must carefully analyze the action
> taken by the controlling stockholders in the individual case. It must
> be asked whether the controlling group can demonstrate a legitimate
> business purpose for its action. In asking this question, we acknowl-
> edge the fact that the controlling group in a close corporation must
> have some room to maneuver in establishing the business policy of the
> corporation. It must have a large measure of discretion, for example,
> in declaring or withholding dividends, deciding whether to merge or
> consolidate, establishing the salaries of corporate officers, dismissing
> directors with or without cause, and hiring and firing corporate em-
> ployees.

> When an asserted business purpose for their action is advanced by
> the majority, however, we think it is open to minority stockholders to
> demonstrate that the same legitimate objective could have been
> achieved through an alternative course of action less harmful to the
> minority's interest. If called on to settle a dispute, our courts must
> weigh the legitimate business purpose, if any, against the practicability
> of a less harmful alternative.

> Applying this approach to the instant case it is apparent that the
> majority stockholders in Springside have not shown a legitimate busi-
> ness purpose for severing Wilkes from the payroll of the corporation or
> for refusing to reelect him as a salaried officer and director. * * *
> There was no showing of misconduct on Wilkes's part as a director,
> officer or employee of the corporation which would lead us to approve
> the majority action as a legitimate response to the disruptive nature of
> an undesirable individual bent on injuring or destroying the corpora-
> tion. On the contrary, it appears that Wilkes had always accomplished
> his assigned share of the duties competently, and that he had never
> indicated an unwillingness to continue to do so.

353 N.E.2d at 663–64. The court returned to the same theme in Zimmerman v. Bogoff, 402 Mass. 650, 524 N.E.2d 849 (1988), where it said, "the
Donahue remedy is not intended to place a strait jacket on legitimate
corporate activity. Where the alleged wrongdoer can demonstrate a legiti-

mate business purpose for his action, no liability will result unless the wronged shareholder succeeds in showing that the proffered legitimate objective could have been achieved through a less harmful, reasonably practicable, alternative mode of action." 524 N.E.2d at 853.

On the other hand, in Goode v. Ryan, 397 Mass. 85, 489 N.E.2d 1001 (1986), the court held that *Donahue* did not permit the estate of a minority shareholder to insist that its shares be repurchased by the corporation to simplify the settlement of the estate in the absence of a contractual obligation by the corporation to repurchase the shares. The difficulty of resale, the court said, "is merely one of the risks of ownership of stock in a close corporation," and "[i]t is not the proper function of this court to reallocate the risks inherent in the ownership of corporate stock in the absence of corporate or majority shareholder misconduct." 489 N.E.2d at 1005. Similarly, a *Donahue* argument was rejected in a suit to compel the price in a contract to sell shares to be increased so as to more closely reflect current market value or to permit the sellers in such a contract to disaffirm their contract. Evangelista v. Holland, 27 Mass.App.Ct. 244, 537 N.E.2d 589 (1989).

(3) In Toner v. Baltimore Envelope Co., 304 Md. 256, 498 A.2d 642 (1985), the court declined to adopt "a per se equal opportunity rule" in the case of a selective redemption of shares in a closely held corporation. The court commented that, while controlling shareholders and directors "can violate their duty in the context of causing a selective corporate repurchase of its shares," that conclusion "should be based on all the relevant facts." 498 A.2d at 650. The court viewed *Donahue, Comolli,* and *Tillis* as creating a "per se" rule, and stated that it preferred the approach taken by the Supreme Judicial Court of Massachusetts in *Wilkes*.

(4) Leader v. Hycor, Inc., 395 Mass. 215, 479 N.E.2d 173 (1985), involved a "reverse stock split" at the ratio of one new share for each 4,000 old shares, with fractional shares to be purchased for cash at a specified amount per share. After the reverse stock split, all of the minority shareholders owned less than a full share and thus were "cashed out." Is there anything wrong with that if the price is fair?

R. HAMILTON, FUNDAMENTALS OF MODERN BUSINESS

Pp. 366–368 (1989).

An important type of distributive transaction is the purchase by the corporation of its own stock. Superficially, a purchase of stock by the corporation may not be thought of as involving a distribution at all. It appears to be the purchase of an asset rather than the making of a distribution. That analysis, however, confuses transactions in which the corporation repurchases its own stock and transactions in which it purchases stock issued by another corporation. The former is a distribution, the latter is an investment.

When a corporation buys back its own stock, it does not receive anything of value in the hands of the corporation. The remaining shareholders continue to own 100 percent of the corporate assets (now reduced by the amount of the payment used to reacquire the shares). A corporation cannot treat stock in itself that it has purchased as an asset any more than it can treat its authorized but unissued stock as an asset. One cannot own 10 percent of oneself and have one's total worth be 110 percent of the value of one's assets. This point is so fundamental that it may be well to reread the last few sentences. Stock issued by another corporation is entirely different. That does not create the same circularity problem. Shares of corporation B have value based on the assets owned by corporation B; if shares of corporation B are purchased by corporation A they are an asset in the hands of corporation A.

The fact that a repurchase of shares constitutes a distribution can be most easily appreciated by considering a proportionate repurchase of stock by the corporation from each shareholder. Assume that three persons each own 100 shares of stock in a corporation, its entire outstanding stock. The shareholders decide that each of them will sell 10 shares back to the corporation for $100 per share, or a total of $1,000 each. When the transaction is completed, each shareholder continues to own one-third of the corporation (now represented by 90 shares rather than 100 shares), the corporation is $3,000 poorer and the shareholders are each $1,000 richer. Clearly there has been a distribution even though the transaction was cast in the form of a repurchase of stock rather than a direct distribution.

Under most state statutes, the 300 shares reacquired by the corporation in the previous example are called treasury shares and may be held by the corporation in a sort of twilight zone until they are either retired permanently or resold to someone else in the future. Treasury shares are not an asset even though they are salable and may be sold at some later time. Exactly the same thing can be said of every share of authorized but unissued stock. Assume that the corporation in the above example decides to resell the treasury shares to X (a non-shareholder) for $3,000. The interests of each of the three original shareholders have been diluted: There are now four shareholders owning shares in the ratio 90–90–90–30. The corporation could have paid the original shareholders a cash dividend of $1,000 each and then sold 33 shares of authorized but unissued stock to X for $3,000 with exactly the same economic result. (In this variation, the shares are owned 100–100–100–33 rather than 90–90–90–30; the percentage ownership interest, however, is as a practical matter, identical.)

The difference between treasury shares and shares issued by other corporations is reflected in the accounting treatment of transactions in shares. When corporation A buys shares in corporation B, the transaction is reflected solely on the left hand side of the balance sheet: The journal entry shows a reduction of cash and an increase in an asset account "investments in other corporations." However, when a corporation buys its own shares, the reduction of cash on the left hand side of the balance sheet is offset by a reduction in one or more right hand shareholders' equity accounts. The precise account to be debited may vary depending on the status of the accounts themselves; the important point is that the transaction is reflected by adjustments to the right hand shareholders' equity accounts. A straight cash dividend is treated for accounting purposes in the same way: A reduction of the cash account on the left hand side of the balance sheet is offset by a reduction in retained earnings or similar account on the left hand side of the balance sheet.

A repurchase of shares by the corporation is a distribution even if the corporation purchases only shares owned by one shareholder rather than proportionately from each shareholder. Such a transaction is a disproportionate distribution (i.e., one not shared proportionately by all shareholders). The corporation has made a distribution to a single shareholder equal to the purchase price it paid for the shares. This transaction is not all bad from the standpoint of the other shareholders, however, since it simultaneously increases their percentage interest in the corporation. For example, if the corporation with three shareholders in the above example repurchased all 100 shares owned by shareholder A for $10,000, the interests of shareholders B and C in the corporation are each increased from 33.3 percent to 50 percent. The assets of the corporation are reduced by the $10,000 purchase price paid to shareholder A to eliminate his or her interest in the corporation.

Distributions in the form of repurchases of shares are very common in real life. In closely held corporations, the elimination of one shareholder's interest in a corporation is almost routinely effected by a repurchase of shares by the corporation. Such a transaction permits the use of corporate rather than personal assets, has favorable tax consequences, and does not affect the relative interests of the remaining shareholders.

Notes

(1) Consider the situation where one shareholder in a closely held corporation wishes to leave the enterprise, and the other shareholders are willing or committed to purchasing his or her shares. The price may be established either by negotiation or by prior agreement. How should the transaction be structured? Should the remaining shareholders each purchase their proportional number of shares? Should the corporation purchase the departing shares? Does it make any economic difference which way the transaction is structured?

(a) One can readily envision practical problems in a proportional purchase transaction. Some of the shareholders may not have readily available liquid assets to make the purchase. Some may be unwilling to increase their investment in the business with funds that were set aside for personal or family purposes. Unless the schedule of purchases is strictly adhered to, the proportional interests of the remaining shareholders will be affected; in some instances even a modest change in percentage ownership will dramatically affect a carefully balanced sharing of control. While these problems usually can be solved, perhaps by arranging for the corporation to loan funds to the reluctant shareholder, the alternative solution seems neater and cleaner: simply have the corporation purchase and retire the shares of the departing shareholder.

(b) A redemption of shares by the corporation also provides tax benefits. From the standpoint of the departing shareholder, there is no difference: a redemption of shares is treated as a sale or exchange of the shares giving rise to taxable income equal to the difference between the redemption price of the shares and the shareholder's basis.[41] But what about the tax position of the other shareholders if the corporation is a C corporation with earnings and profits? If the corporation distributed the redemption price to the other shareholders in order for them to purchase the shares, there would clearly have been a taxable dividend. Could not the IRS argue that the redemption itself is essentially equivalent to a dividend to the remaining shareholders? Consult Rands, Closely Held Corporations: Federal Tax Consequences of Stock Transfer Restrictions, 7 J.Corp.Law 449, 456–457 (1982):

> Over the years the IRS has argued repeatedly that certain redemptions are constructive dividends to non-redeemed shareholders.
>
> * * *
>
> The vortex of the controversy is the disproportionate redemption. A disproportionate redemption necessarily causes an increase in the percentage of stock owned by some shareholders. For a simple illustration, suppose a corporation with net assets worth $2,000 has two 50 percent shareholders. The corporation redeems all of the stock of one of them. Before the redemption the non-redeemed shareholder owns 50 percent of the stock. After the redemption he owns 100 percent of the stock. The constructive dividend argument is facially attractive for two reasons: first, the corporation is spending funds to confer a benefit on the non-redeemed shareholder—an increase in his percentage of stock ownership; and second, there is no benefit to the corporation, which has no legal interest in the identity of its shareholders.
>
> A fault in this syllogism is that for many redemptions, the increase in the percentage of stock ownership is offset by a corresponding decrease in the assets owned by the corporation. The non-redeemed shareholder may now own 100 percent of the stock, but the corporation probably distributed 50 percent of its net assets to redeem the other shareholder's stock. Before the redemption, the non-redeemed shareholder owned 50 percent of a corporation with $2,000 worth of assets. Now he owns 100 percent of a corporation with $1,000 worth of assets. The book value of his stock is $1,000 before and after the redemption.
>
> In not every redemption is the increase in the percentage of stock ownership fully offset by a decrease in the value of the corporation's

---

41. [By the Editor] "Basis" is a tax term generally meaning the cost of or the amount invested in, the asset being sold. Exceptions to the statement in the text exist. For example, if the sale is "essentially equivalent to a dividend," the redemption is treated as a dividend giving rise to ordinary income rather than as a sale or exchange giving rise to a capital gain or loss. With the elimination of the special tax treatment for capital gains the classification as ordinary income or capital gain or loss has declined in importance, though it continues to have some tax consequences, particularly if the sale or exchange yields a loss rather than a gain.

assets. Suppose that the redemption price is less than the book value of the redeemed stock. Assuming the value of the stock is equal to its book value, the non-redeemed shareholder clearly reaps an economic benefit from the redemption. Not only does the percentage of his stock ownership increase, so does the book value of his stock. In the example above, the book value of the non-redeemed shareholder's stock was $1,000 before the redemption. If the corporation paid only $400 to redeem the stock of the withdrawing stockholder the redemption would result in an increase in the book value of non-redeemed shareholder's stock to $1,600.

Such were the facts in *Holsey v. Commissioner*.[42] The increase in the percentage of stock ownership was not fully offset by a decrease in the value of assets owned by the corporation, because the redemption price was less than the book value of the stock redeemed. The IRS convinced the Tax Court that the redemption was for the "personal benefit" of the non-redeemed shareholder and redemption proceeds were constructively received by him. Thus, the net effect of the transaction was the equivalent of a dividend to him. On appeal the government's Tax Court victory was reversed by the Third Circuit, where the non-redeemed shareholder deftly raised a fatal defect in the government's position. While the non-redeemed shareholder received a benefit from the redemption, the benefit was merely an increase in the value of the stock already held by him. Since the Supreme Court in *Eisner v. Macomber*[43] decided that mere appreciation in the value of property is not taxable income within the meaning of the sixteenth amendment, the non-redeemed shareholder in *Holsey* could not be taxed on the increased value of his stock until he disposed of it.[44]

Accepting the *Holsey* rationale, the IRS at last conceded that the mere enhancement in value of the non-redeemed shareholder's stock does not constitute a constructive dividend to him.[45]

The remaining problem area, one which lawyers can avoid, is the transfer restriction which requires the non-redeemed shareholder to purchase the stock of the retiring shareholder. If the corporation redeems the stock, its payment discharges a personal obligation of the non-redeemed shareholder and is a constructive dividend to him.[46] Constructive dividend treatment is not surprising, there is no reason to distinguish the redemption from other corporate payments to discharge a shareholder's personal obligation. What is surprising is the leniency accorded the non-redeemed shareholder by the tax law. He receives a

42. [By the Author] 258 F.2d 865 (3d Cir.1958), reversing, 28 T.C. 962 (1957).

43. [By the Author] 252 U.S. 189, 40 S.Ct. 189, 64 L.Ed. 521 (1920).

44. [By the Author] 258 F.2d at 868.

45. [By the Author] The IRS said it would follow *Holsey* and "will not treat the purchase by a corporation of one shareholder's stock as a dividend to the remaining shareholders merely because their percentage interests in the corporation are increased." Rev.Rul. 614, 1958–2 C.B. 920. This concession is significant. The threat of constructive dividend treatment for every disproportionate redemption would have undermined the usefulness of buy-sell restrictions.

46. [By the Author] See, e.g., Sullivan v. United States, 363 F.2d 724, 729 (8th Cir. 1966) cert. denied 387 U.S. 905, 87 S.Ct. 1683, 18 L.Ed.2d 622 (1967); Rev.Rul. 608, 1969–2 C.B. 43.

constructive dividend only if he is subject to an "existing primary and unconditional obligation" to make the payment himself. * * *

Redemption of shares thus provides a device by which C corporations' earnings and profits may be utilized for the benefit of shareholders without incurring the double taxation applicable to dividends. There is generally no analogous benefit for a corporation that has elected S corporation treatment.

(2) As noted earlier, redemptions of shares are treated by corporation statutes as distributions subject to the legal restraints on dividends and distributions described in the following section. A redemption in violation of these restrictions probably may be enjoined. See e.g. Neimark v. Mel Kramer Sales, Inc., 102 Wis.2d 282, 306 N.W.2d 278 (App.1981). What should be done if the shareholders wish to have the corporation redeem the shares but the corporation fails to meet fully these tests for the legality of the redemption?

(3) A very common feature of disproportionate redemption transactions is that the corporation may pay only a portion of the purchase price in cash when the transaction is closed, the balance being represented by promissory notes payable over an extended period of time. The deferred purchase price may simply reflect the reality that the corporation lacks liquid assets sufficient to acquire the redeemed shares entirely for cash at the closing. The future payments may be made out of subsequent earnings or cash flow, thereby in effect making payment of the purchase price in part contingent on the future success of the business. A deferred sale may also reflect further tax planning within a C corporation, since future earnings may in effect be diverted for the benefit of shareholders without incurring the double taxation on dividends.

I. LEGAL RESTRICTIONS ON DISTRIBUTIONS

The statutes of virtually every state today establish tests for the legality of distributions, principally dividends and corporate redemptions of shares, that build on traditional accounting concepts for corporate capital. It is fair to state that the problems involved in determining the legality of dividends and redemptions, particularly under pre-RMBCA statutes, are among the most complex and confusing in the entire field of corporate law. The provisions of the RMBCA discussed below go a long way toward rationalizing these restrictions. It is probable that most states will ultimately revise their statutes in this area, but the older statutes will continue to be applicable in some states for many years to come. The balance of this note is designed to give a somewhat impressionistic understanding of these older dividend statutes and the RMBCA.

(1) "Earned Surplus" Dividend Statutes

The pre–1979 Model Act established the general tests for the legality of a dividend as (1) the availability of "earned surplus" out of which the dividend may be paid, and (2) a solvency test to be applied immediately after giving effect to the dividend. (See MBCA (1969) § 45.) A large number of states followed the Model Act in this regard. The definition of "earned surplus" in MBCA (1969) § 2(1), apparently contemplated the aggregation of income from all profit-and-loss statements going back to the time the corporation was organized. This approach created practical and theoretical problems that are well described in Hackney, The Financial Provisions of the Model Business Corporation Act, 70 Harv.L.Rev. 1357, 1368–1369 (1957): *

> Even for a new corporation, the air of simplicity about a statutory rule allowing dividends only out of the undistributed balance of all corporate income is misleading. Actually, the correct computation of income for any one year is not only incredibly difficult but is so far from an exact science—which of course it does not purport to be—that it is meaningless to attempt to say precisely in dollars what any corporation's income actually is. The determination of income requires allocations of receipts, expenses, and losses to fiscal periods, such allocations being sometimes based on fact but sometimes estimated, or conventional, or based on assumptions as to future events which may prove invalid. Accounting principles are not fundamental truths, capable of scientific proof, but are derived from experience and reason; proved utility is the criterion. Rapidly changing accounting principles show that accounting income is not a fixed concept but one subject to both differences of opinion and variations from year to year. One "sophisticated accountant" has been quoted as defining income as "anything which good accounting practice accepts as income."

> Nor is it clear what is meant by the Model Act definition's repetitive terms, "net profits," "income," and "gains and losses." Paragraphs 28–34 of Accounting Terminology Bulletin No. 1 indicate that while these terms have had varying meanings in the past there is an increasing tendency to regard the terms "income" and "profit and loss" as coextensive. There is no indication of how the term "gains" might differ in meaning from "profits" or from "income," nor why the word "earnings" is left out of the definition, nor why the word "net" must precede "profits" but not "income," "gains," or "losses." * * *.

The earned surplus statutes raise two additional questions that are answered in various ways in specific state statutes: (i) May a corporation eliminate deficits in earned surplus by transferring amounts from capital surplus or some other surplus account to earned surplus? See MBCA (1969) § 2(1), which inferentially permits such transfers. Such a transaction is usually called a "quasi-reorganization," and is not permitted under the statutes of some states. (ii) May a corporation with a negative earned surplus from earlier years pay a dividend out of current earnings, or must it first apply current earnings to eliminate past deficits? The pre–1979 Model Act contained an alternative § 45(a), which allowed dividends from current earnings; such divi-

* Copyright © 1957 by the Harvard Law Review Association.

dends, usually known as "nimble dividends," are permitted in many but not all states.

(2) "Impairment of Capital" Dividend Statutes

Many non-Model Act statutes establish a test for determining the legality of dividends that appears to be based on a balance sheet rather than income statement analysis. The Delaware statute, for example, permits a corporation to pay dividends only "out of its surplus," Del. Gen.Corp.Law § 170, and defines "surplus" to include everything in excess of the aggregate par values of the issued shares plus whatever else the corporation has elected to add to its capital account. New York also applies a "surplus" test but adds the requirement that "the net assets of the corporation remaining after such declaration, payment or distribution shall at least equal the amount of its stated capital * * *" N.Y.—McKinney's Bus.Corp.Law § 510. Other statutes talk in terms of not "impairing capital" or of prohibiting dividends "except from surplus, or from the net profits arising from the business." This last clause in particular seems to clearly contemplate the payment of dividends out of sources other than earnings (because of the use of the disjunctive "or"), but all of these impairment of capital statutes were construed to permit such distributions. For example, Randall v. Bailey, 288 N.Y. 280, 43 N.E.2d 43 (1942), arising under an earlier version of the New York statute, involved, among other issues, an attempt by a corporation to create surplus by writing up the value of appreciated assets on its books. The court permitted the corporation to increase its dividend-paying capacity by such a book-keeping entry. Presumably, such a "reevaluation surplus" is "surplus" under such statutes and payments out of it would not "impair capital." Could an argument be made that reevaluation surplus might be "earned surplus" as a "gain" under the definition of "earned surplus" in MBCA (1969) § 2(1)? Randall v. Bailey also involved an asset of "good will" that apparently was added to the balance sheet as a balancing entry in an earlier corporate acquisition. This entry, of course, did not represent any specific property. In applying the balance sheet tests of "surplus" for determining when a dividend can be paid, shouldn't only "real" assets be counted? The court permitted recognition of the asset of good will under the circumstances, but the lower court commented that "[d]irectors obviously cannot create assets by fiat." 23 N.Y.S.2d 173, 177 (1940).

Cases such as Randall v. Bailey raise a basic question: To what extent should the legality of dividends be determined on the basis of accounting conventions or principles? For example, from an accounting standpoint, write-ups of assets to reflect market appreciation are generally frowned on if not flatly prohibited. Should such principles (which are subject to change from time to time and probably do not command universal respect) be relevant in deciding whether a corporation may legally pay a dividend out of "reevaluation surplus"? These statutes rely on accounting concepts in establishing limitations on distributions; on the other hand, it seems odd to make the legality of dividends depend on the shifting sands of accounting "rules" or conventions. Further, since much of the litigation relating to the legality of dividends arose in the context of creditors seeking to surcharge directors for declaring unlawful dividends, transactions such as involved in Randall v. Bailey also raise the question whether directors can rely on the books of the corporation as presented to them by corporate officers or could rely on the advice of attorneys or accountants for the corporation as to the availability of funds for the payment of dividends. In this connection see RMBCA §§ 6.40(d), 8.33.

(3) Distributions of Capital under "Earned Surplus" Statutes

To complicate matters even further, the old Model Act (in its pre–1979 form) freely permitted distributions out of "capital surplus" with the proper authorization. See MBCA (1969) § 46. Not all Model Act states did so, however; some included no provisions at all for distributions out of capital or other surplus, or permitted distributions out of capital or other surplus only for narrow purposes, or hedged distributions out of such surplus with substantive or procedural requirements. Some states adopted the phrase "partial liquidation" for such distributions to emphasize that they were not distributions of earnings but distributions of part of the capital of the corporation. Many statutes also imposed special limitations on capital surplus that was created by the reduction of stated capital (e.g. by amending the articles to reduce the par value of outstanding shares or cancelling previously outstanding shares)—defined as "reduction surplus" in some states.

Statutes based on the old Model Act that permit distributions of capital with little or no restriction probably lead to rules of distribution not very different from the rules applicable in states such as New York or Delaware. However, the language of each statute has to be examined carefully and certainly confusion or uncertainty existed in many states.

Notes

(1) How should these legal capital restrictions be applied to a transaction in which the corporation repurchases shares on a deferred payment basis? Should the restrictions be applied only at the time of the closing of the transaction when the shares are returned to the corporation or should they be applied consecutively to each payment when made? As a practical matter, it is quite possible for a corporation to have adequate earned surplus at the time of the original closing, but that earned surplus may be dissipated through operating losses before the payments are to be made. Similarly, it is possible that a corporation may meet the solvency test at the time of the original repurchase but not at the time later payments come due. The limited case law on this issue tended in the direction of applying both standards to each payment, though that makes little sense at least in the case of earned surplus limitations. Consult Herwitz, Installment Repurchase of Stock: Surplus Limitations, 79 Harv.L.Rev. 303 (1965). For a case rejecting this conclusion, but based on the precise language of a

state corporation statute, see Williams v. Nevelow, 513 S.W.2d 535 (Tex. 1974). The RMBCA accepts this conclusion. Is that the proper answer?

(2) Reacquisitions of shares on a deferred payment basis also raise a second question: should a former shareholder who holds promissory notes of the corporation for part of the purchase price for shares be treated on a parity with general trade creditors, or should his or her claim be subordinated? A leading case subordinating this debt is Robinson v. Wangemann, 75 F.2d 756 (5th Cir.1935). The RMBCA squarely addresses this question in RMBCA § 6.40(e)(1) and (f) and places such a creditor on a parity with general trade creditors. Is that the proper answer?

(4) The Revised Model Business Corporation Act

Section 6.40 of the Revised Model Business Corporation Act sweeps away most of the complex issues and problems under earlier statutes. One of the major issues faced by the revisers of the Model Act was whether the validity of distributions should be measured solely by an insolvency test, or whether both an insolvency test and a balance sheet test should be retained. If a balance sheet test is retained, consideration of the underlying accounting principles is necessary if the test is to have any substance at all. The decision to retain a balance sheet test was based on several considerations: the historical reliance on balance sheet tests in state statutes, protection for senior securities interests provided by section 6.40(c)(2), and the desire for specific tests, so far as practical, in evaluating the lawfulness of distributions. There was some sentiment for the incorporation of "generally accepted accounting principles" into the section, at least as a "safe harbor" for directors approving a distribution, but the final compromise on this issue now appears in section 6.40(d). The decision not to include a reference to GAAP in the statute was based partially on concern that the content of GAAP principles varied over time. Is there anything wrong with a state statute incorporating by reference a changing body of principles controlled by other persons?

The Official Comment to section 6.40 explains the operation of the tests for distributions in some detail:

Equity Insolvency Test

As noted above, older statutes prohibited payments of dividends if the corporation was, or as a result of the payment would be, insolvent in the equity sense. This test is retained, appearing in section 6.40(c)(1).

In most cases involving a corporation operating as a going concern in the normal course, information generally available will make it quite apparent that no particular inquiry concerning the equity insolvency test is needed. While neither a balance sheet nor an income statement can be conclusive as to this test, the existence of significant shareholders' equity and normal operating conditions are of themselves a strong indication that no issue should arise under that test. Indeed, in the case of a corporation having regularly audited financial statements, the absence of any qualification in the most recent auditor's opinion as to the corporation's status as a "going concern," coupled with a lack of subsequent adverse events, would normally be decisive.

It is only when circumstances indicate that the corporation is encountering difficulties or is in an uncertain position concerning its liquidity and operations that the board of directors or, more commonly, the officers or others upon whom they may place reliance under section 8.30(b), may need to address the issue. Because of the overall judgment required in evaluating the equity insolvency test, no one or more "bright line" tests can be employed. However, in determining whether the equity insolvency test has been met, certain judgments or assumptions as to the future course of the corporation's business are customarily justified, absent clear evidence to the contrary. These include the likelihood that (a) based on existing and contemplated demand for the corporation's products or services, it will be able to generate funds over a period of time sufficient to satisfy its existing and reasonably anticipated obligations as they mature, and (b) indebtedness which matures in the near-term will be refinanced where, on the basis of the corporation's financial condition and future prospects and the general availability of credit to businesses similarly situated, it is reasonable to assume that such refinancing may be accomplished. To the extent that the corporation may be subject to asserted or unasserted contingent liabilities, reasonable judgments as to the likelihood, amount, and time of any recovery against the corporation, after giving consideration to the extent to which the corporation is insured or otherwise protected against loss, may be utilized. There may be occasions when it would be useful to consider a cash flow analysis, based on a business forecast and budget, covering a sufficient period of time to permit a conclusion that known obligations of the corporation can reasonably be expected to be satisfied over the period of time that they will mature.

In exercising their judgment, the directors are entitled to rely, under section 8.30(b) as noted above, on information, opinions, reports, and statements prepared by others. Ordinarily, they should not be expected to become involved in the details of the various analyses or market or economic projections that may be relevant. Judgments must of necessity be made on the basis of information in the hands of the directors when a distribution is authorized. They should not, of course, be held responsible as a matter of hindsight for unforeseen developments. This is particularly true with respect to assumptions as to the ability of the corporation's business to repay long-term obligations which do not mature for several years, since the primary focus of the directors' decision to make a distribution should normally be on the corporation's prospects and obligations in the shorter term, unless special factors concerning the corporation's prospects require the taking of a longer term perspective. * * *

Balance Sheet Test

Section 6.40(c)(2) requires that, after giving effect to any distribution, the corporation's assets equal or exceed its liabilities plus (with some exceptions) the dissolution preferences of senior equity securities.

Section 6.40(d) authorizes asset and liability determinations to be made for this purpose on the basis of either (1) financial statements prepared on the basis of accounting practices and principles that are reasonable in the circumstances or (2) a fair valuation or other method that is reasonable in the circumstances. The determination of a corporation's assets and liabilities and the choice of the permissible basis on which to do so are left to the judgment of its board of directors. In making a judgment under section 6.40(d), the board may rely under section 8.30(b) upon opinions, reports, or statements, including financial statements and other financial data prepared or presented by public accountants or others.

Section 6.40 does not utilize particular accounting terminology of a technical nature or specify particular accounting concepts. In making determinations under this section, the board of directors may make judgments about accounting matters, giving full effect to its right to rely upon professional or expert opinion.

In a corporation with subsidiaries, the board of directors may rely on unconsolidated statements prepared on the basis of the equity method of accounting (see American Institute of Certified Public Accountants, APB Opinion No. 18 (1971)) as to the corporation's investee corporations, including corporate joint ventures and subsidiaries, although other evidence would be relevant in the total determination.

Generally accepted accounting principles

The board of directors should in all circumstances be entitled to rely upon reasonably current financial statements prepared on the basis of generally accepted accounting principles in determining whether or not the balance sheet test of section 6.40(c)(2) has been met, unless the board is then aware that it would be unreasonable to rely on the financial statements because of newly-discovered or subsequently arising facts or circumstances. But section 6.40 does not mandate the use of generally accepted accounting principles; it only requires the use of accounting practices and principles that are reasonable in the circumstances. While publicly-owned corporations subject to registration under the Securities Exchange Act of 1934 must, and many other corporations in fact do, utilize financial statements prepared on the basis of generally accepted accounting principles, a great number of smaller or closely-held corporations do not. Some of these corporations maintain records solely on a tax accounting basis and their financial statements are of necessity prepared on that basis. Others prepare financial statements that substantially reflect generally accepted accounting principles but may depart from them in some respects (e.g., footnote disclosure). These facts of corporate life indicate that a statutory standard of reasonableness, rather than stipulating generally accepted accounting principles as the normative standard, is appropriate in order to achieve a reasonable degree of flexibility and to accommodate the needs of the many different types of business corporations which might be subject to these provisions, including in particular closely-held corporations. Accordingly, the revised Model Business Corporation Act contemplates that generally acceptable accounting principles are always "reasonable in the circumstances" and that other accounting principles may be perfectly acceptable, under a general standard of reasonableness, even if they do not involve the "fair value" or "current value" concepts that are also contemplated by section 6.40(d).

Other principles

Section 6.40(d) specifically permits determinations to be made under section 6.40(c)(2) on the basis of a fair valuation or other method that is reasonable in the circumstances. Thus the statute authorizes departures from historical cost accounting and sanctions the use of appraisal and current value methods to determine the amount available for distribution. No particular method of valuation is prescribed in the statute, since different methods may have validity depending upon the circumstances, including the type of enterprise and the purpose for which the determination is made. For example, it is inappropriate in most cases to apply a "quick-sale liquidation" method to value an enterprise, particularly with respect to the payment of normal dividends. On the other hand, a "quick-sale liquidation" valuation method might be appropriate in certain circumstances for an enterprise in the course of reducing its asset or business base by a material degree. In most cases, a fair valuation method or a going-concern basis would be appropriate if it is believed that the enterprise will continue as a going concern.

Ordinarily a corporation should not selectively revalue assets. It should consider the value of all of its material assets, whether or not reflected in the financial statements (e.g., a valuable executory contract). Likewise, all of a corporation's material obligations should be considered and revalued to the extent appropriate and possible. In any event, section 6.40(d) calls for the application under section 6.40(c)(2) of a method of determining the aggregate amount of assets and liabilities that is reasonable in the circumstances.

Section 6.40(d) also refers to some "other method that is reasonable in the circumstances." This phrase is intended to comprehend within section 6.40(c)(2) the wide variety of possibilities that might not be considered to fall under a "fair valuation" or "current value" method but might be reasonable in the circumstances of a particular case.

Preferential Dissolution Rights and the Balance Sheet Test

Section 6.40(c)(2) provides that a distribution may not be made unless the total assets of the corporation exceed its liabilities plus the amount that would be needed to satisfy any shareholder's superior preferential rights upon dissolution if the corporation were to be dissolved at the time of the distribution. This requirement in effect treats preferential dissolution rights of shares for distribution purposes as if they were liabilities for the sole purpose of determining the amount available for distributions, and carries forward analogous treatment of shares having preferential dissolution rights from earlier versions of the Model Act. * * *

Application to Reacquisition of Shares

The application of the equity insolvency and balance sheet tests to distributions that involve the purchase, redemption, or other acquisition of the corporation's shares creates unique problems; section 6.40 provides a specific rule for the resolution of these problems as described below.

Time of measurement

Section 6.40(c)(1) provides that the time for measuring the effect of a distribution under section 6.40(c), if shares of the corporation are reacquired, is the earlier of (i) the payment date, or (ii) the date the shareholder ceased to be a shareholder with respect to the shares, except as provided in section 6.40(g).

When tests are applied to redemption-related debt

In an acquisition of its shares, a corporation may transfer property or incur debt to the former holder of the shares. The case law on the status of this debt is conflicting. However, share repurchase agreements involving payment for shares over a period of time are of special importance in closely-held corporate enterprises. Section 6.40(e) provides a clear rule for this situation: the legality of the distribution must be measured at the time of the issuance of incurrence of the debt, not at a later date when the debt is actually paid, except as provided in section 6.40(g). Of course, this does not preclude a later challenge of a payment on account of redemption-related debt by a bankruptcy trustee on the ground that it constitutes a preferential payment to a creditor.

Priority of debt distributed directly or incurred in connection with a reacquisition of shares

Section 6.40(f) provides that indebtedness created to acquire the corporation's shares or issued as a distribution is on a parity with the indebtedness of the corporation to its general, unsecured creditors, except to the extent subordinated by agreement. General creditors are better off in these situations than they would have been if cash or other property had been paid out for the shares or distributed (which is proper under the statute), and no worse off than if cash had been paid or distributed and then lent back to the corporation, making the shareholders (or former shareholders) creditors. The parity created by section 6.40(f) is logically consistent with the rule established by section 6.40(e) that these transactions should be judged at the time of the issuance of the debt.

Treatment of certain indebtedness

Section 6.40(g) provides that indebtedness need not be taken into account as a liability in determining whether the tests of section 6.40(c) have been met if the terms of the indebtedness provide that payments of principal or interest can be made only if and to the extent that payment of a distribution could then be made under section 6.40. This has the effect of making the holder of the indebtedness junior to all other creditors but senior to the holders of all classes of shares, not only during the time the corporation is operating but also upon dissolution and liquidation. It should be noted that the creation of such indebtedness, and the related limitations on payments of principal and interest, may create tax problems or raise other legal questions.

Although section 6.40(g) is applicable to all indebtedness meeting its tests, regardless of the circumstances of its issuance, it is anticipated that it will be applicable most frequently to permit the reacquisition of shares of the corporation at a time when the deferred purchase price exceeds the net worth of the corporation. This type of reacquisition will often be necessary in the case of businesses in early stages of development or service businesses whose value derives principally from existing or prospective net income or cash flow rather than from net asset value. In such situations, it is anticipated that net worth will grow over time from operations so that when payments in respect of the indebtedness are to be made the two insolvency tests will be satisfied. In the meantime, the fact that the indebtedness is outstanding will not prevent distributions that could be made under subsection (c) if the indebtedness were not counted in making the determination.

Chapter Eight

MANAGEMENT AND CONTROL OF THE CLOSELY HELD CORPORATION

A. THE TRADITIONAL ROLES OF SHAREHOLDERS AND DIRECTORS

McQUADE v. STONEHAM

Court of Appeals of New York, 1934.
263 N.Y. 323, 189 N.E. 234.

POUND, CHIEF JUDGE.

The action is brought to compel specific performance of an agreement between the parties, entered into to secure the control of National Exhibition Company, also called the Baseball Club (New York Nationals or "Giants"). This was one of Stoneham's enterprises which used the New York polo grounds for its home games. McGraw was manager of the Giants. McQuade was at the time the contract was entered into a city magistrate. He resigned December 8, 1930.

Defendant Stoneham became the owner of 1,306 shares, or a majority of the stock of National Exhibition Company. Plaintiff and defendant McGraw each purchased 70 shares of his stock. Plaintiff paid Stoneham $50,338.10 for the stock he purchased. As a part of the transaction, the agreement in question was entered into. It was dated May 21, 1919. Some of its pertinent provisions are

"VIII. The parties hereto will use their best endeavors for the purpose of continuing as directors of said Company and as officers thereof the following:

"Directors:

"Charles A. Stoneham,

"John J. McGraw,

"Francis X. McQuade

421

"—with the right to the party of the first part [Stoneham] to name all additional directors as he sees fit:

"Officers:

"Charles A. Stoneham, President,

"John J. McGraw, Vice President,

"Francis X. McQuade, Treasurer.

"IX. No salaries are to be paid to any of the above officers or directors, except as follows:

"President $45,000
"Vice–President 7,500
"Treasurer 7,500

"X. There shall be no change in said salaries, no change in the amount of capital, or the number of shares, no change or amendment of the by-laws of the corporation or any matters regarding the policy of the business of the corporation or any matters which may in anywise affect, endanger or interfere with the rights of minority stockholders, excepting upon the mutual and unanimous consent of all of the parties hereto. * * *

"XIV. This agreement shall continue and remain in force so long as the parties or any of them or the representative of any, own the stock referred to in this agreement, to wit, the party of the first part, 1,166 shares, the party of the second part 70 shares and the party of the third part 70 shares, except as may otherwise appear by this agreement. * * *"

In pursuance of this contract Stoneham became president and McGraw vice president of the corporation. McQuade became treasurer. In June, 1925, his salary was increased to $10,000 a year. He continued to act until May 2, 1928, when Leo J. Bondy was elected to succeed him. The board of directors consisted of seven men. The four outside of the parties hereto were selected by Stoneham and he had complete control over them. At the meeting of May 2, 1928, Stoneham and McGraw refrained from voting, McQuade voted for himself, and the other four voted for Bondy. Defendants did not keep their agreement with McQuade to use their best efforts to continue him as treasurer. On the contrary, he was dropped with their entire acquiescence. At the next stockholders' meeting he was dropped as a director although they might have elected him.

The courts below have refused to order the reinstatement of McQuade, but have given him damages for wrongful discharge, with a right to sue for future damages.

The cause for dropping McQuade was due to the falling out of friends. McQuade and Stoneham had disagreed. The trial court has found in substance that their numerous quarrels and disputes did not affect the orderly and efficient administration of the business of the corporation; that plaintiff was removed because he had antagonized the dominant Stoneham by persisting in challenging his power over the corporate treasury and for no misconduct on his part. The court also finds that plaintiff was removed by Stoneham for protecting the corporation and its minority stockholders. We will assume that Stoneham put him out when he might have retained him, merely in order to get rid of him.

Defendants say that the contract in suit was void because the directors held their office charged with the duty to act for the corporation according to their best judgment and that any contract which compels a director to vote to keep any particular person in office and at a stated salary is illegal. Directors are the exclusive executive representatives of the corporation, charged with administration of its internal affairs and the management and use of its assets. They manage the business of the corporation. (General Corporation Law, Consol. Laws, c. 23, § 27.) "An agreement to continue a man as president is dependent upon his continued loyalty to the interests of the corporation." Fells v. Katz, 256 N.Y. 67, 72, 175 N.E. 516, 517. So much is undisputed.

Plaintiff contends that the converse of this proposition is true and that an agreement among directors to continue a man as an officer of a corporation is not to be broken so long as such officer is loyal to the interests of the corporation and that, as plaintiff has been found loyal to the corporation, the agreement of defendants is enforceable.

Although it has been held that an agreement among stockholders whereby it is attempted to divest the directors of their power to discharge an unfaithful employee of the corporation is illegal as against public policy (Fells v. Katz, supra), it must be equally true that the stockholders may not, by agreement among themselves, control the directors in the exercise of the judgment vested in them by virtue of their office to elect officers and fix salaries. Their motives may not be questioned so long as their acts are legal. The bad faith or the improper motives of the parties does not change the rule. Manson v. Curtis, 223 N.Y. 313, 324, 119 N.E. 559, Ann.Cas.1918E, 247. Directors may not by agreements entered into as stockholders abrogate their independent judgment. Creed v. Copps, 103 Vt. 164, 152 A. 369, 71 A.L.R. 1287, annotated.

Stockholders may, of course, combine to elect directors. That rule is well settled. As Holmes, C.J., pointedly said (Brightman v. Bates, 175 Mass. 105, 111, 55 N.E. 809, 811): "If stockholders want to make their power felt, they must unite. There is no reason why a majority should not agree to keep together." The power to unite is, however, limited to the election of directors and is not extended to contracts whereby limitations are placed on the power of directors to manage the business of the corporation by the selection of agents at defined salaries.

The minority shareholders whose interest McQuade says he has been punished for protecting, are not, aside from himself, complaining about his discharge. He is not acting for the corporation or for them in this action. It is impossible to see how the corporation has been injured by the substitution of Bondy as treasurer in place of McQuade. As McQuade represents himself in this action and seeks redress for his own wrongs, "we prefer to listen to [the corporation and the minority stockholders] before any decision as to their wrongs." Faulds v. Yates, 57 Ill. 416, 417, 11 Am.Rep. 24.

It is urged that we should pay heed to the morals and manners of the market place to sustain this agreement and that we should hold that its violation gives rise to a cause of action for damages rather than base our decision on any outworn notions of public policy. Public policy is a dangerous guide in determining the validity of a contract and courts should not interfere lightly with the freedom of competent parties to make their own contracts. We do not close our eyes to the fact that such agreements, tacitly or openly arrived at, are not uncommon, especially in close corporations where the stockholders are doing business for convenience under a corporate organization. We know that majority stockholders, united in voting trusts, effectively manage the business of a corporation by choosing trustworthy directors to reflect their policies in the corporate management. Nor are we unmindful that McQuade has, so the court has found, been shabbily treated as a purchaser of stock from Stoneham. We have said: "A trustee is held to something stricter than the morals of the market place" (Meinhard v. Salmon, 249 N.Y. 458, 464, 164 N.E. 545, 546, 62 A.L.R. 1), but Stoneham and McGraw were not trustees for McQuade as an individual. Their duty was to the corporation and its stockholders, to be exercised according to their unrestricted lawful judgment. They were under no legal obligation to deal righteously with McQuade if it was against public policy to do so.

The courts do not enforce mere moral obligations, nor legal ones either, unless someone seeks to establish rights which may be waived by custom and for convenience. We are constrained by authority to hold that a contract is illegal and void so far as it precludes the board of directors, at the risk of incurring legal liability, from changing officers, salaries, or policies, or retaining individuals in office, except by consent of the contracting parties. On the whole, such a holding is probably preferable to one which would open the courts to pass on the motives of directors in the lawful exercise of their trust. * * *

[As an alternative ground for its decision, the Court held that the contract also violated public policy in light of a New York criminal statute that prohibited a city magistrate from engaging "in any other business or profession" and required him to "devote his whole time and capacity * * * to the duties of his office."]

The judgment of the Appellate Division and that of the Trial Term should be reversed and the complaint dismissed, with costs in all courts.

CRANE, KELLOGG, O'BRIEN, and HUBBS, JJ., concur with POUND, C.J.

LEHMAN, J., concurs in result in opinion in which CROUCH, J., concurs. [This concurring opinion is omitted.]

Notes

(1) Model Bus.Corp.Act Ann. (3d Ed.), 784–85:

Business corporations in common law jurisdictions have long followed the tradition of a representative form of governance by the election of a board of directors by the shareholders, voting by interest and not per capita. The board has traditionally been charged with the duty and responsibility of managing the business and affairs of the corporation, determining corporate policies, and selecting the officers and agents who carry on the detailed administration of the business. In large, publicly held corporations, the role of directors has been increasingly seen as involving oversight and review rather than actual management.

Legal writers have developed various theories as to the status of directors and the source of their powers: (1) the agency theory (all powers reside in the shareholders who have delegated certain powers to the directors as their agents); (2) the concession theory (the powers of directors are derived from the state, which authorizes them to perform certain functions, so that this power does not flow from the shareholders); (3) the Platonic guardian theory (the board is an aristocracy or group of overseers created by statutory enactment); and (4) the sui generis theory (directors are not agents; they are fiduciaries whose duties run to the corporation but their relationship with the corporation is sui generis since they are not trustees). Of these various theories, the first has been generally rejected, and probably most commentators today would agree that the fourth most accurately describes the modern role of directors.

(2) Two subsequent cases have largely defined the scope of the principle originally set forth in Manson v. Curtis and articulated in the principal case:

(a) In Clark v. Dodge, 269 N.Y. 410, 199 N.E. 641 (1936), Clark owned 25 per cent and Dodge owned 75 per cent of the stock of each of two corporations. Clark and Dodge entered into a written agreement under seal in which it was agreed that Clark would continue to manage the business and in that connection would disclose a secret formula to Dodge's son that was necessary for the successful operation of the business. In return, Dodge agreed that he would vote his stock and also vote as director so that (i) Clark would be retained as general manager (so long as he should be "faithful, efficient and competent"), (ii) Clark would receive one-fourth of the net income either by way of salary or dividends, and (iii) that no unreasonable salary would be paid to reduce the net income so as to materially affect Clark's profits. The agreement also provided that Clark would be retained as a director, and that Clark agreed to bequeath his stock—assuming no issue survived him—to Dodge's wife and children. After a falling out, Clark sought specific performance of the agreement, which was granted despite the provisions restricting Dodge's discretion as a director:

The only question which need be discussed is whether the contract is illegal as against public policy within the decision in McQuade v. Stoneham, 263 N.Y. 323, 189 N.E. 234, upon the authority of which the complaint was dismissed by the Appellate Division.

"The business of a corporation shall be managed by its board of directors." General Corporation Law (Consol.Laws, c. 23) § 27. That is the statutory norm. Are we committed by the McQuade Case to the doctrine that there may be no variation, however slight or innocuous, from that norm, where salaries or policies or the retention of individuals in office are concerned? There is ample authority supporting that doctrine. E.g., West v. Camden, 135 U.S. 507, 10 S.Ct. 838, 34 L.Ed. 254; Jackson v. Hooper, 76 N.J.Eq. 592, 75 A. 568, 27 L.R.A. (N.S.) 658. But cf. Salomon v. Salomon & Co. [1897] A.C. 22, 44, and something may be said for it, since it furnishes a simple, if arbitrary, test. Apart from its practical administrative convenience, the reasons upon which it is said to rest are more or less nebulous. Public policy, the intention of the Legislature, detriment to the corporation, are phrases which in this connection mean little. Possible harm to bona fide purchasers of stock or to creditors or to stockholding minorities have more substance; but such harms are absent in many instances. If the enforcement of a particular contract damages nobody—not even in any perceptible degree, the public—one sees no reason for holding it illegal, even though it impinges slightly upon the broad provision of section 27. Damage suffered or threatened is a logical and practical test, and has come to be the one generally adopted by the courts. See 28 Columbia Law Review 366, 372. Where the directors are the sole stockholders, there seems to be no objection to enforcing an agreement among them to vote for certain people as officers. There is no direct decision to that effect in this court, yet there are strong indications that such a rule has long been recognized. The opinion in Manson v. Curtis, 223 N.Y. 313, 325, 119 N.E. 559, 562, Ann.Cas. 1918E, 247, closed its discussion by saying: "The rule that all the stockholders by their universal consent may do as they choose with the corporate concerns and assets, provided the interests of creditors are not affected, because they are the complete owners of the corporation, cannot be invoked here." That was because all the stockholders were not parties to the agreement there in question. So, where the public was not affected, "the parties in interest, might, by their original agreement of incorporation, limit their respective rights and powers," even where there was a conflicting statutory standard. Ripin v. United States Woven Label Co., 205 N.Y. 442, 448, 98 N.E. 855, 857. "Such corporations were little more (though not quite the same as) than chartered partnerships." (Id., 205 N.Y. 442, 447, 98 N.E. 855, 856.) In Lorillard v. Clyde, 86 N.Y. 384, and again in Drucklieb v. Sam H. Harris, 209 N.Y. 211, 102 N.E. 599, where the questioned agreements were entered into by all the stockholders of small corporations about to be organized, the fact that the agreements conflicted to some extent with the statutory duty of the directors to manage the corporate affairs was thought not to render the agreements illegal as against public policy, though it was said they might not be binding upon the directors of the corporation when organized.

Cf. Lehman, J., dissenting opinion in the McQuade Case. The rule recognized in Manson v. Curtis, and quoted above, was thus stated by Blackmar, J., in Kassel v. Empire Tinware Co., 178 App.Div. 176, 180, 164 N.Y.S. 1033, 1035: "As the parties to the action are the complete owners of the corporation, there is no reason why the exercise of the power and discretion of the directors cannot be controlled by valid agreement between themselves, provided that the interests of creditors are not affected." * * *

Except for the broad dicta in the McQuade opinion, we think there can be no doubt that the agreement here in question was legal and that the complaint states a cause of action. There was no attempt to sterilize the board of directors, as in the Manson and McQuade Cases. The only restrictions on Dodge were (a) that as a stockholder he should vote for Clark as a director—a perfectly legal contract; (b) that as director he should continue Clark as general manager so long as he proved faithful, efficient, and competent—an agreement which could harm nobody; (c) that Clark should always receive as salary or dividends one-fourth of the "net income." For the purposes of this motion, it is only just to construe that phrase as meaning whatever was left for distribution after the directors had in good faith set aside whatever they deemed wise; (d) that no salaries to other officers should be paid, unreasonable in amount or incommensurate with services rendered—a beneficial and not a harmful agreement.

If there was any invasion of the powers of the directorate under that agreement, it is so slight as to be negligible; and certainly there is no damage suffered by or threatened to anybody. The broad statements in the McQuade opinion, applicable to the facts there, should be confined to those facts.

(b) In Long Park, Inc. v. Trenton–New Brunswick Theatres Co., 297 N.Y. 174, 77 N.E.2d 633 (1948), all the shareholders of the Theatre Company entered into an agreement giving one shareholder "full authority and power to supervise and direct the operation and management" of certain theatres. Such shareholder could be removed as manager only by arbitration among the shareholders. The court stated:

By virtue of these provisions the management of all theatres leased or operated by Trenton or any subsidiary is vested in Keith, without approval of the directors, and this management may not be changed by the directors but only as provided in section 4 above quoted. The directors may neither select nor discharge the manager, to whom the supervision and direction of the management and operation of the theatres is delegated with full authority and power. Thus the powers of the directors over the management of its theatres, the principal business of the corporation, were completely sterilized. Such restrictions and limitations upon the powers of the directors are clearly in violation of section 27 of the General Corporation Law of this State and the New Jersey statute. * * *

We think these restrictions and limitations went far beyond the agreement in Clark v. Dodge, 269 N.Y. 410, 199 N.E. 641. We are not confronted with a slight impingement or innocuous variance from the statutory norm, but rather with the deprivation of all the powers of the board insofar as the selection and supervision of the management of the corporation's theatres, including the manner and policy of their operation, are concerned. * * *

77 N.E.2d at 634–635.

(3) Precisely what is the status of the rule of the McQuade case following these two decisions?

(4) A number of possible consequences flow from the common law concept of the independent role of the board of directors. For example—

(a) If the majority shareholder demands that the board enter into a specific transaction on behalf of the corporation, must the directors comply? The common law answer was a clear "no." See Automatic Self–Cleansing Filter Syndicate Co., Ltd. v. Cunninghame, Court of Appeal of England [1906] 2 Ch. 34.

(b) Should a majority shareholder be permitted to remove directors simply because they refuse to do as they agreed to do or as the shareholder wishes? See RMBCA § 8.08 which reverses the common law rule.

(c) Are long term management contracts entered into by the corporation with a person who is not a director enforceable? Does it make any difference if the delegation is total or partial? For five years or twenty-five? Compare Sherman & Ellis, Inc. v. Indiana Mut. Cas. Co., 41 F.2d 588 (7th Cir.1930) with Jones v. Williams, 139 Mo. 1, 39 S.W. 486 (1897).

(d) What about delegation of managerial authority to a committee of the board of directors? See RMBCA § 8.25.

(e) What about one board binding a later board, e.g. by a 99 year lease? What about a two-year employment contract with the president of the corporation? Should it make any difference that by-laws of corporations usually state that the president shall be elected annually? Or should the relevance of that depend on whether the directors have authority to amend by-laws? See Realty Acceptance Corp. v. Montgomery, 51 F.2d 636 (3d Cir. 1930), affirmed on other grounds 284 U.S. 547, 52 S.Ct. 215, 76 L.Ed. 476 (1932); Pioneer Specialties, Inc. v. Nelson, 161 Tex. 244, 339 S.W.2d 199 (1960). See RMBCA § 10.20. What about inferences that may be drawn from RMBCA § 8.43(b)?

GALLER v. GALLER

Supreme Court of Illinois, 1964.
32 Ill.2d 16, 203 N.E.2d 577.

UNDERWOOD, JUSTICE.

Plaintiff, Emma Galler, sued in equity for an accounting and for specific performance of an agreement made in July, 1955, between plaintiff and her husband, of one part, and defendants, Isadore A. Galler and his wife, Rose, of the other. Defendants appealed from a decree of the superior court of Cook County granting the relief prayed. The First District Appellate Court reversed the decree and denied specific performance, affirming in part the order for an accounting, and modifying the order awarding master's fees. (45 Ill.App.2d 452, 196

N.E.2d 5.) That decision is appealed here on a certificate of importance.

There is no substantial dispute as to the facts in this case. From 1919 to 1924, Benjamin and Isadore Galler, brothers, were equal partners in the Galler Drug Company, a wholesale drug concern. In 1924 the business was incorporated under the Illinois Business Corporation Act, each owning one half of the outstanding 220 shares of stock. In 1945 each contracted to sell 6 shares to an employee, Rosenberg, at a price of $10,500 for each block of 6 shares, payable within 10 years. They guaranteed to repurchase the shares if Rosenberg's employment were terminated, and further agreed that if they sold their shares, Rosenberg would receive the same price per share as that paid for the brothers' shares. Rosenberg was still indebted for the 12 shares in July, 1955, and continued to make payments on account even after Benjamin Galler died in 1957 and after the institution of this action by Emma Galler in 1959. Rosenberg was not involved in this litigation either as a party or as a witness, and in July of 1961, prior to the time that the master in chancery hearings were concluded, defendants Isadore and Rose Galler purchased the 12 shares from Rosenberg. A supplemental complaint was filed by the plaintiff, Emma Galler, asserting an equitable right to have 6 of the 12 shares transferred to her and offering to pay the defendants one half of the amount that the defendants paid Rosenberg. The parties have stipulated that pending disposition of the instant case, these shares will not be voted or transferred. For approximately one year prior to the entry of the decree by the chancellor in July of 1962, there were no outstanding minority shareholder interests.

In March, 1954, Benjamin and Isadore, on the advice of their accountant, decided to enter into an agreement for the financial protection of their immediate families and to assure their families, after the death of either brother, equal control of the corporation. In June, 1954, while the agreement was in the process of preparation by an attorney-associate of the accountant, Benjamin suffered a heart attack. Although he resumed his business duties some months later, he was again stricken in February, 1955, and thereafter was unable to return to work. During his brother's illness, Isadore asked the accountant to have the shareholders' agreement put in final form in order to protect Benjamin's wife, and this was done by another attorney employed in the accountant's office. On a Saturday night in July, 1955, the accountant brought the agreement to Benjamin's home, and 6 copies of it were executed there by the two brothers and their wives. The accountant then collected all signed copies of the agreement and informed the parties that he was taking them for safe keeping. Between the execution of the agreement in July, 1955, and Benjamin's death in December, 1957, the agreement was not modified. Benjamin suffered a stroke late in July, 1955, and on August 2, 1955, Isadore and the accountant and a notary public brought to Benjamin for signature two powers of attorney which were retained by the accountant after Benjamin executed them with Isadore as a witness. The plaintiff did not read the powers and she never had them. One of the powers authorized the transfer of Benjamin's bank account to Emma and the other power enabled Emma to vote Benjamin's 104 shares. Because of the state of Benjamin's health, nothing further was said to him by any of the parties concerning the agreement. It appears from the evidence that some months after the agreement was signed, the defendants Isadore and Rose Galler and their son, the defendant, Aaron Galler sought to have the agreements destroyed. The evidence is undisputed that defendants had decided prior to Benjamin's death they would not honor the agreement, but never disclosed their intention to plaintiff or her husband.

On July 21, 1956, Benjamin executed an instrument creating a trust naming his wife as trustee. The trust covered, among other things, the 104 shares of Galler Drug Company stock and the stock certificates were endorsed by Benjamin and delivered to Emma. When Emma presented the certificates to defendants for transfer into her name as trustee, they sought to have Emma abandon the 1955 agreement or enter into some kind of a noninterference agreement as a price for the transfer of the shares. Finally, in September, 1956, after Emma had refused to abandon the shareholders' agreement, she did agree to permit defendant Aaron to become president for one year and agreed that she would not interfere with the business during that year. The stock was then reissued in her name as trustee. During the year 1957 while Benjamin was still alive, Emma tried many times to arrange a meeting with Isadore to discuss business matters but he refused to see her.

Shortly after Benjamin's death, Emma went to the office and demanded the terms of the 1955 agreement be carried out. Isadore told her that anything she had to say could be said to Aaron, who then told her that his father would not abide by the agreement. He offered a modification of the agreement by proposing the salary continuation payment but without her becoming a director. When Emma refused to modify the agreement and sought enforcement of its terms, defendants refused and this suit followed.

During the last few years of Benjamin's life both brothers drew an annual salary of $42,000. Aaron, whose salary was $15,000 as manager of the warehouse prior to September, 1956, has since the time that Emma agreed to his acting as president drawn an annual salary of $20,000. In 1957, 1958, and 1959 a $40,000 annual dividend was paid. Plaintiff has received her proportionate share of the dividend.

The July, 1955, agreement in question here, entered into between Benjamin, Emma, Isadore and Rose, recites that Benjamin and Isadore each own 47½% of the issued and outstanding shares of the Galler Drug Company, an Illinois corporation, and that Benjamin and Isadore desired to provide income for the support and maintenance of their immediate families. No reference is made to the shares then being purchased by Rosenberg. The essential features of the contested portions of the agreement are substantially as set forth in the opinion of the Appellate Court: (2) that the bylaws of the corporation will be amended to provide for a board of four directors; that the necessary quorum shall be three directors; and that no directors' meeting shall be held without giving ten days notice to all directors. (3) The shareholders will cast their votes for the above named persons (Isadore, Rose, Benjamin and Emma) as directors at said special meeting and at any other meeting held for the purpose of electing directors. (4, 5) In the event of the death of either brother his wife shall have the right to nominate a director in place of the decedent. (6) Certain annual dividends will be declared by the corporation. The dividend shall be $50,000 payable out of the accumulated earned surplus in excess of $500,000. If 50% of the annual net profits after taxes exceeds the minimum $50,000, then the directors shall have discretion to declare a dividend up to 50% of the annual net profits. If the net profits are less than $50,000, nevertheless the minimum $50,000 annual dividend shall be declared, providing the $500,000 surplus is maintained. Earned surplus is defined. (9) The certificates evidencing the said shares of Benjamin Galler and Isadore Galler shall bear a legend that the shares are subject to the terms of this agreement. (10) A salary continuation agreement shall be entered into by the corporation which shall authorize the corporation upon the death of Benjamin Galler or Isadore Galler, or both, to pay a sum equal to twice the salary of such officer, payable monthly over a five-year period. Said sum shall be paid to the widow during her widowhood, but should be paid to such widow's children if the widow remarries within the five-year period. (11, 12) The parties to this agreement further agree and hereby grant to the corporation the authority to purchase, in the event of the death of either Benjamin or Isadore, so much of the stock of Galler Drug Company held by the estate as is necessary to provide sufficient funds to pay the federal estate tax, the Illinois inheritance tax and other administrative expenses of the estate. If as a result of such purchase from the estate of the decedent the amount of dividends to be received by the heirs is reduced, the parties shall nevertheless vote for directors so as to give the estate and heirs the same representation as before (2 directors out of 4, even though they own less stock), and also that the corporation pay an additional benefit payment equal to the diminution of the dividends. In the event either Benjamin or Isadore decides to sell his shares he is required to offer them first to the remaining shareholders and then to the corporation at book value, according each six months to accept the offer.

The Appellate Court found the 1955 agreement void because "the undue duration, stated purpose and substantial disregard of the provisions of the Corporation Act outweigh any considerations which might call for divisibility" and held that "the public policy of this state demands voiding this entire agreement".

While the conduct of defendants towards plaintiff was clearly inequitable, the basically controlling factor is the absence of an objecting minority interest, together with the absence of public detriment. * * * [Discussion of Illinois cases omitted.]

The power to invalidate the agreements on the grounds of public policy is so far reaching and so easily abused that it should be called into action to set aside or annul the solemn engagement of parties dealing on equal terms only in cases where the corrupt or dangerous tendency clearly and unequivocally appears upon the face of the agreement itself or is the necessary inference from the matters which are expressed, and the only apparent exception to this general rule is to be found in those cases where the agreement, though fair and unobjectionable on its face, is a part of a corrupt scheme and is made to disguise the real nature of the transaction. * * *

At this juncture it should be emphasized that we deal here with a so-called close corporation. Various attempts at definition of the close corporation have been made. For a collection of those most frequently proffered, see O'Neal, Close Corporations, § 1.02 (1958). For our purposes, a close corporation is one in which the stock is held in a few hands, or in a few families, and wherein it is not at all, or only rarely, dealt in by buying or selling. Moreover, it should be recognized that shareholder agreements similar to that in question here are often, as a practical consideration, quite necessary for the protection of those financially interested in the close corporation. While the shareholder of a public-issue corporation may readily sell his shares on the open market should management fail to use, in his opinion, sound business judgment, his counterpart of the close corporation often has a large total of his entire capital invested in the business and has no ready market for his shares should he desire to sell. He feels, understandably, that he is more than a mere investor and that his voice should be heard concerning all corporate activity. Without a shareholder agreement, specifically enforceable by the courts, insuring him a modicum of control, a large minority shareholder might find himself at the mercy of an oppressive or unknowledgeable majority. Moreover, as in the case at bar, the shareholders of a close corporation are often also the directors and officers thereof. With substantial shareholding interests abiding in each member of the board of directors, it is often quite impossible to secure, as in the large public-issue corporation, independent board judgment free from personal motivations concerning corporate policy. For these and other reasons too voluminous to enumerate here, often the only sound basis for protection is afforded by a lengthy, detailed shareholder agreement securing the rights and obligations of all concerned. For a discussion of these and other considerations, see Note, "A Plea for Separate Statutory Treatment of the Close Corporation", 33 N.Y.U.L.Rev. 700 (1958).

As the preceding review of the applicable decisions of this court points out, there has been a definite, albeit inarticulate, trend toward eventual judicial treatment of the close corporation as *sui generis*. Several shareholder-director agreements that have technically "violated" the letter of the Business Corporation Act have nevertheless been upheld in the light of the existing practical circumstances, i.e., no apparent public injury, the absence of a complaining minority interest, and no apparent prejudice to creditors. However, we have thus far not attempted to limit these decisions as applicable only to close corporations and have seemingly implied that general considerations regarding judicial supervision of all corporate behavior apply.

The practical result of this series of cases, while liberally giving legal efficacy to particular agreements in special circumstances notwithstanding literal "violations" of statutory corporate law, has been to inject much doubt and uncertainty into the thinking of the bench and corporate bar of Illinois concerning shareholder agreements. See e.g., Cary, "How Illinois Corporations May Enjoy Partnership Advantages: Planning for the Closely Held Firm," 48 N.W.U.L.Rev. 427; Note, "The Validity of Stockholders' Voting Agreements in Illinois," 3 U.Chi.L.Rev. 640.

It is therefore necessary, we feel, to discuss the instant case with the problems peculiar to the close corporation particularly in mind.

It would admittedly facilitate judicial supervision of corporate behavior if a strict adherence to the provisions of the Business Corporation Act were required in all cases without regard to the practical exigencies peculiar to the close corporation. West v. Camden, 135 U.S. 507, 10 S.Ct. 838, 34 L.Ed. 254. However, courts have long ago quite realistically, we feel, relaxed their attitudes concerning statutory compliance when dealing with close corporate behavior, permitting "slight deviations" from corporate "norms" in order to give legal efficacy to common business practice. See e.g., Clark v. Dodge, 269 N.Y. 410, 199 N.E. 641; Benintendi v. Kenton Hotel, 294 N.Y. 112, 60 N.E.2d 829, 159 A.L.R. 280 (dissenting opinion subsequently legislatively approved). This attitude is illustrated by the following language in Clark v. Dodge: "Public policy, the intention of the Legislature, detriment to the corporation, are phrases which in this connection [the court was discussing a shareholder-director agreement whereby the directors pledged themselves to vote for certain people as officers of the corporation] mean little. Possible harm to bona fide purchasers of stock or to creditors or to stockholding minorities have more substance; but such harms are absent in many instances. If the enforcement of a particular contract damages nobody—not even, in any perceptible degree, the public—one sees no reason for holding it illegal, even though it impinges slightly upon the broad provisions of [the relevant statute providing that the business of a corporation shall be managed by its board of directors]. Damage suffered or threatened is a logical and practical test, and has come to be the one generally adopted by the courts. See 28 Columbia Law Review 366, 372." Clark v. Dodge, 199 N.E. 641, 642.

Again, "As the parties to the action are the complete owners of the corporation, there is no reason why the exercise of the power and discretion of the directors cannot be controlled by valid agreement between themselves, provided that the interests of creditors are not affected." Clark v. Dodge, 199 N.E. 641, 643, quoting from Kassel v. Empire Tinware Co., 178 App.Div. 176, 180, 164 N.Y.S. 1033, 1035.

Numerous helpful textual statements and law review articles dealing with the judicial treatment of the close corporation have been pointed out by counsel. One article concludes with the following: "New needs compel fresh formulation of corporate 'norms'. There is no reason why mature men should not be able to adapt the statutory form to the structure they want, so long as they do not endanger other stockholders, creditors, or the public, or violate a clearly mandatory provision of the corporation laws. In a typical close corporation the stockholders' agreement is usually the result of careful deliberation among all initial investors. In the large public-issue corporation, on the other hand, the 'agreement' represented by the corporate charter is not consciously agreed to by the investors; they have no voice in its formulation, and very few ever read the certificate of incorporation. Preservation of the corporate norms may there be necessary for the protection of the public investors." Hornstein, "Stockholders' Agreements in the Closely Held Corporation", 59 Yale L.Journal, 1040, 1056.

This court has recognized, albeit *sub silentio,* the significant conceptual differences between the close corporation and its public-issue counterpart in, among other cases, Kantzler v. Bensinger, 214 Ill. 589, 73 N.E. 874, where an agreement quite similar to the one under attack here was upheld. Where, as in *Kantzler* and here, no complaining minority interest appears, no fraud or apparent injury to the public or creditors is present, and no clearly prohibitory statutory language is violated, we can see no valid reason for precluding the parties from reaching any arrangements concerning the management of the corporation which are agreeable to all.

Perhaps, as has been vociferously advanced, a separate comprehensive statutory scheme governing the close corporation would best serve here. See Note "A Plea for Separate Statutory Treatment of the Close Corporation", 33 N.Y.U.L.Rev. 700. Some states have enacted legislation dealing specifically with the close corporation.

At any rate, however, the courts can no longer fail to expressly distinguish between the close and public-issue corporation when confronted with problems relating to either. What we do here is to illuminate this problem—before the bench, corporate bar, and the legislature, in the context of a particular fact situation. To do less would be to shirk our responsibility, to do more would, perhaps be to invade the province of the legislative branch.

We now, in the light of the foregoing, turn to specific provisions of the 1955 agreement.

The Appellate Court correctly found many of the contractual provisions free from serious objection, and we need not prolong this opinion with a discussion of them here. That court did, however, find difficulties in the stated purpose of the agreement as it relates to its duration, the election of certain persons to specific offices for a number of years, the requirement for the mandatory declaration of stated dividends (which the Appellate Court held invalid), and the salary continuation agreement.

Since the question as to the duration of the agreement is a principal source of controversy, we shall consider it first. The parties provided no specific termination date, and while the agreement concludes with a paragraph that its terms "shall be binding upon and shall inure to the benefits of" the legal representatives, heirs and assigns of the parties, this clause is, we believe, intended to be operative only as long as one of the parties is living. It further provides that it shall be so construed as to carry out its purposes, and we believe these must be determined from a consideration of the agreement as a whole. Thus viewed, a fair construction is that its purposes were accomplished at the death of the survivor of the parties. While these life spans are not precisely ascertainable, and the Appellate Court noted Emma Galler's life expectancy at her husband's death was 26.9 years, we are aware of no statutory or public policy provision against stockholder's agreements which would invalidate this agreement on that ground. * * *

The clause that provides for the election of certain persons to specified offices for a period of years likewise does not require invalidation. In Kantzler v. Bensinger, 214 Ill. 589, 73 N.E. 874, this court upheld an agreement entered into by all the stockholders providing that certain parties would be elected to the offices of the corporation for a fixed period. In Faulds v. Yates, 57 Ill. 416, we upheld a similar agreement among the majority stockholders of a corporation, notwithstanding the existence of a minority which was not before the court complaining thereof.

We turn next to a consideration of the effect of the stated purpose of the agreement upon its validity. The pertinent provision is: "The said Benjamin A. Galler and Isadore A. Galler desire to provide income for the support and maintenance of their immediate families." Obviously, there is no evil inherent in a contract entered into for the reason that the persons originating the terms desired to so arrange their property as to provide post-death support for those dependent upon them. Nor does the fact that the subject property is corporate stock alter the situation so long as there exists no detriment to minority stock interests, creditors or other public injury. It is, however, contended by defendants that the methods provided by the agreement for implementation of the stated purpose are, as a whole, violative of the Business Corporation Act to such an extent as to render it void *in toto*.

The terms of the dividend agreement require a minimum annual dividend of $50,000, but this duty is limited by the subsequent provision that it shall be operative only so long as an earned surplus of $500,000 is maintained. It may be noted that in 1958, the year prior to commencement of this litigation, the corporation's net earnings after taxes amounted to $202,759 while its earned surplus was $1,543,270, and this was increased in 1958 to $1,680,079 while earnings were $172,964. The minimum earned surplus requirement is designed for the protection of the corporation and its creditors, and we take no exception to the contractual dividend requirements as thus restricted.

The salary continuation agreement is a common feature, in one form or another, of corporate executive employment. It requires that the widow should receive a total benefit, payable monthly over a five-year period, aggregating twice the amount paid her deceased husband in one year. This requirement was likewise limited for the protection of the corporation by being contingent upon the payments being income tax-deductible by the corporation. The charge made in those cases which have considered the validity of payments to the widow of an officer and shareholder in a corporation is that a gift of its property by a noncharitable corporation is in violation of the rights of its shareholders and *ultra vires*. Since there are no shareholders here other than the parties to the contract, this objection is not here applicable, and its effect, as limited, upon the corporation is not so prejudicial as to require its invalidation.

Having concluded that the agreement, under the circumstances here present, is not vulnerable to the attack made on it, we must consider the accounting feature of this action. The trial court allowed the relief prayed, an action we deem proper except as to the master's fees which were modified by the Appellate Court. Since no question is here raised regarding them, we affirm the action of that court in this respect. The questions as to salary which the Appellate Court correctly held were improperly increased became ones of fact to be determined by the trial court.

We hold defendants must account for all monies received by them from the corporation since September 25, 1956, in excess of that theretofore authorized.

Accordingly, the judgment of the Appellate Court is reversed except insofar as it relates to fees, and is, as to them affirmed. The cause is remanded to the circuit court of Cook County with directions to proceed in accordance herewith.

Affirmed in part and reversed in part, and remanded with directions.

Notes

(1) All was not sweetness and light in the Galler family in the years following the rendition of this progressive decision. See Galler v. Galler, 69 Ill.App.2d 397, 217 N.E.2d 111 (1966), dismissing an appeal from an order directing that a meeting of shareholders be held and that designated persons be elected directors; Galler v. Galler, 95 Ill.App.2d 340, 238 N.E.2d 274 (1968), affirming an order establishing salaries for 1966 and later years; and Galler v. Galler, 21 Ill.App.3d 811, 316 N.E.2d 114 (1974), affirming orders that Isadore Galler repay the corporation $266,666, plus interest, and that Aaron Galler repay the corporation $41,666 plus interest for

excessive salaries paid during the period 1957 through 1966. This order was itself affirmed by the Supreme Court of Illinois in an opinion that reviews the prior litigation. Galler v. Galler, 61 Ill.2d 464, 336 N.E.2d 886 (1975).

(2) Before 1983, the Illinois Business Corporation Act stated that the power to amend by-laws is "vested in the board of directors unless reserved to the shareholders by the articles of incorporation." Ill.Bus.Corp.Act § 25 (1954). [Compare the language of RMBCA § 10.20.] In Somers v. AAA Temporary Services, Inc., 5 Ill.App.3d 931, 284 N.E.2d 462 (1972) two shareholders owning all the stock of the corporation sought to amend the by-laws to reduce the number of directors from three to two and to appoint themselves as the two directors. They acted, however, as shareholders, not as directors and there was no reservation of the power to amend by-laws by the shareholders in the corporation's articles. The Court rejected an argument that *Galler* permitted a shareholder's agreement to amend the by-laws to be enforced despite the statutory language. [The plaintiff was the third director, a non-shareholder.] The Court said:

> * * * The principal thrust of the *Galler* decision is that, in the context of a particular fact situation, there is no reason for preventing those in control of a close corporation from reaching any agreements concerning the management of the corporation which are agreeable to all, though such agreements are not within the letter of the Business Corporation Act.

It is important to note, however, that the Supreme Court in *Galler* imposed limitations on the operation and use of this general rule for close corporations. First, the Court indicated that such agreements should be permitted only where no fraud or apparent injury would be worked upon the public, minority interests or creditors. Then, more directly in point to the instant case, the Court went on to caution that shareholder agreements which violate statutory language are not permitted. The Court said in its opinion:

> There is no reason why mature men should not be able to adapt the statutory form to the structure they want, so long as they do not endanger other stockholders, creditors, or the public, *or violate a clearly mandatory provision of the corporation laws.* (Emphasis added.)

The *Galler* Court did not say that the Illinois Business Corporation Act may be disregarded in the case of a close corporation. Slight deviations from corporate norms may be permitted. However, action by the shareholders which is in direct contravention of the statute cannot be allowed. Appellant's contention that there is no conceivable way in which *Galler* can be distinguished from the instant case must, therefore, be rejected. The language of Section 25 of the Business Corporation Act is clearly mandatory regarding the amendment of the corporate by-laws. Accordingly, it is obvious to us that the holding in the *Galler* case gives no sanction to appellants to disregard the clear and unambiguous language of that section of the Act. * * *

284 N.E.2d at 464–465. Is this not an unduly restrictive reading of *Galler*? Does it seek to return Illinois to the test of Clark v. Dodge?

(3) Section 2.25 of the Illinois Business Corporation Act of 1983 provides:

> **2.25 By–Laws.** Unless the power to make, alter, amend or repeal the by-laws is reserved to the shareholders by the articles of incorporation, the by-laws of the corporation may be made, altered, amended or repealed by the shareholders or the board of directors, but no by-law adopted by the shareholders may be altered, amended or repealed by the board of directors if the by-laws so provide. The by-laws may contain any provisions for the regulation and management of the affairs of the corporation not inconsistent with law or the articles of incorporation.

Would this statute change the result in *Somers?*

ZION v. KURTZ

Court of Appeals of New York, 1980.
50 N.Y.2d 92, 428 N.Y.S.2d 199, 405 N.E.2d 681.

MEYER, JUDGE.

On these appeals we conclude that when all of the stockholders of a Delaware corporation agree that, except as specified in their agreement, no "business or activities" of the corporation shall be conducted without the consent of a minority stockholder, the agreement is, as between the original parties to it, enforceable even though all formal steps required by the statute have not been taken. We hold further that the agreement made by the parties to this action was violated when the corporation entered into two agreements without the minority stockholder's consent. ＊ ＊ ＊

[Editor: Kurtz formed a Delaware corporation, Lombard–Wall Group, Inc. ("Group"). Group acquired all the stock of Lombard–Wall Incorporated ("L–W"), in a complex transaction in which Zion made available property and assets to be used as security for a loan to finance the acquisition. As part of the transaction, Zion acquired all the Class A stock of Group while Kurtz continued to own all of the Class B stock. Zion and Kurtz also executed a shareholder's agreement, which provided in section 3.01(a) that without the consent of the holders of the Class A stock, Group would not "engage in any business or activities of any kind, directly or indirectly, whether through any Subsidiary or by way of a loan, guarantee or otherwise, other than the acquisition and ownership of the stock of L–W as contemplated by this Agreement ＊ ＊ ＊." The articles of incorporation of Group did not refer to any veto power in the holders of the Class A stock. Group's board of directors approved two agreements over the objection of Zion. Zion then brought suit to cancel the two agreements as violating the shareholder's consent agreement.]

I

The stockholders' agreement expressly provided that it should be "governed by and construed and enforced in accordance with the laws of the State of Delaware as to matters governed by the General Corporation Law of that State", and that is the generally accepted choice-of-law rule with respect to such "internal affairs" as the relationship between shareholders and directors (cf. Greenspun v. Lindley, 36 N.Y.2d 473, 478, 369 N.Y.S.2d 123, 330 N.E.2d 79; see Restatement, Conflict of Laws 2d, § 302, Comment *g*). Subdivision (a) of section 141 of the General Corporation Law of Delaware provides that the business and affairs of a corporation organized under that law "shall be managed by a board of directors, except as may be otherwise provided in this chapter or in its certificate of incorporation." Included in the chapter referred to are provisions relating to close corporations,[1] which explicitly state that a written agreement between the holders of a majority of such a corporation's stock "is not invalid, as between the parties to the agreement, on the ground that it so relates to the conduct of the business and affairs of the corporation as to restrict or interfere with the discretion or powers of the board of directors" (§ 350) or "on the ground that it is an attempt by the parties to the agreement or by the stockholders of the corporation to treat the corporation as if it were a partnership" (§ 354), and further provides that "The certificate of incorporation of a close corporation may provide that the business of the corporation shall be managed by the stockholders of the corporation rather than the board of directors" and that such a provision may be inserted in the certificate by amendment if "all holders of record of all of the outstanding stock" so authorize (§ 351).

Clear from those provisions is the fact that the public policy of Delaware does not proscribe a provision such as that contained in the shareholders' agreement here in issue even though it takes all management functions away from the directors. Folk, in his work on the Delaware Corporation Law, states concerning section 350 that "Although some decisions outside Delaware have sustained 'reasonable' restrictions upon director discretion contained in stockholder agreements, the theory of § 350 is to declare unequivocally, as a matter of public policy, that stockholder agreements of this character are not invalid" (at p. 518), that section 351 "recognizes a special subclass of close corporations which operate by direct stockholder management" (at p. 520), and with respect to section 354 that it "should be liberally construed to authorize all sorts of internal agreements and arrangements which are not affirmatively improper or, more particularly, injurious to third parties" (at p. 526).

1. [By the Editor] Section 342(a) of the General Corporation Law of Delaware defines a "close corporation" as a corporation whose certificate of incorporation provides that:

(1) All of the corporation's issued stock of all classes, exclusive of treasury shares, shall be represented by certificates and shall be held of record by not more than a specified number of persons, not exceeding 30; and

(2) All of the issued stock of all classes shall be subject to one or more of the restrictions on transfer permitted by § 202 of this title; and

(3) The corporation shall make no offering of any of its stock of any class which would constitute a "public offering" within the meaning of the United States Securities Act of 1933, as it may be amended from time to time.

Defendants argue, however, that Group was not incorporated as a close corporation and the stockholders' agreement provision was never incorporated in its certificate. The answer is that any Delaware corporation can elect to become a close corporation by filing an appropriate certificate of amendment (Del.General Corporation Law, § 344) and by such amendment approved by the holders of all of its outstanding stock may include in its certificate provisions restricting directors' authority (ibid., § 351). Here, not only did defendant Kurtz agree in paragraph 8.05(b) of the stockholders' agreement to "without further consideration, do, execute and deliver, or cause to be done, executed and delivered, all such further acts, things and instruments as may be reasonably required more effectively to evidence and give effect to the provisions and the intent and purposes of this Agreement", but also as part of the transaction by which the * * * guarantee was made and Zion became a Group stockholder, defendant Kurtz, while he was still the sole stockholder and sole director of Group, executed a consent to the various parts of the transaction under which he was "authorized and empowered to execute and deliver, or cause to be executed and delivered, all such other and further instruments and documents and take, or cause to be taken, all such other and further action as he may deem necessary, appropriate or desirable to implement and give effect to the Stockholders Agreement and the transactions provided for therein." Since there are no intervening rights of third persons, the agreement requires nothing that is not permitted by statute, and all of the stockholders of the corporation assented to it, the certificate of incorporation may be ordered reformed, by requiring Kurtz to file the appropriate amendments, or more directly he may be held estopped to rely upon the absence of those amendments from the corporate charter (see Delaney, The Corporate Director: Can His Hands Be Tied In Advance, 50 Col.L.Rev. 52, 66).[2]

The result thus reached accords with the weight of authority which textwriter F. Hodge O'Neal tells us sustains agreements made by all shareholders dealing with matters normally within the province of the directors (1 Close Corporations § 5.24, p. 83), even though the shareholders could have, but had not, provided similarly by charter or by-law provision sanctioned by statute (ibid., § 5.19, pp. 73–74). Moreover, though we have not yet had occasion to construe subdivision (b) of section 620 of the Business Corporation Law,[3] which did not become

2. [By the Court] The fallacy of the dissent is that it converts a shield into a sword. The notice devices on which the concept of the dissent turns are wholly unnecessary to protect the original parties, who may be presumed to have known what they agreed to. To protect an original party who has not been hurt (indeed, has expressly agreed to the limitation he is being protected against and affirmatively covenanted to see to it that all necessary steps to validate the agreement were tak-

en) because a third party without notice could have been hurt had he been involved can only be characterized as a perversion of the liberal legislative purpose demonstrated by the Delaware statutes quoted in the text above.

3. [By the Court] That provision reads: "(b) A provision in the certificate of incorporation otherwise prohibited by law because it improperly restricts the board in its management of the business of the cor-

effective until September 1, 1963, it is worthy of note that in adopting that provision the Legislature had before it the Revisers' Comment that: "Paragraph (b) expands the ruling in Clark v. Dodge, 269 N.Y. 410, 199 N.E. 637 [641] (1936), and, to the extent therein provided, overrules Long Park, Inc. v. Trenton–New Brunswick Theatres Co., 297 N.Y. 174, 77 N.E.2d 633 (1948); Manson v. Curtis, 223 N.Y. 313, 119 N.E. 559 (1919) and McQuade v. Stoneham, 263 N.Y. 323, 189 N.E. 234 (1934)." Thus it is clear that no New York public policy stands in the way of our application of the Delaware statute and decisional law above referred to (cf. Kessler, Shareholder–Managed Close Corporation Under the New York Business Corporation Law, 43 Fordham L.Rev. 197; Hoffman, New Horizons For The Close Corporation in New York Under Its New Business Corporation Law, 28 Brooklyn L.Rev. 1, 9–10).

II

Defendants' arguments against summary judgment for plaintiffs on the first cause of action center on the use in section 3.01 of the word "engage", which they suggest involves continuity of action rather than a single act, the presence of other proscriptions that would be unnecessary if section 3.01(a) by itself gave Zion an absolute veto over corporate action, and the purpose of the guarantee. * * *

The difficulty with limiting the provision to multiple action is that though in many contexts "engage" does denote more than a single transaction (Black's Law Dictionary [4th ed.], p. 622),[4] its meaning is necessarily governed by the context in which it is used. Defendants' argument ignores the fact that the parties agreed, as indicated by what they wrote, that without Zion's consent Group would not engage in "*any* business or activities of *any* kind, *directly or indirectly, whether through any Subsidiary* or by way of a loan, guarantee *or otherwise*" (emphasis supplied). As we have held in Randall v. Bailey, 288 N.Y. 280, 285, 43 N.E.2d 43, the word "any" means "all" or "every" and imports no limitation. It is difficult to imagine (short, as the old chestnut puts it, of adding in the opening clause of section 3.01 after "Corporation" the word "positively") a more comprehensive proscription than one against "any business or activities of any kind, directly or indirectly". * * *

For the foregoing reasons the order of the Appellate Division should be modified, as above indicated.

poration, or improperly transfers to one or more shareholders or to one or more persons or corporations to be selected by him or them, all or any part of such management otherwise within the authority of the board under this chapter, shall nevertheless be valid: (1) If all the incorporators or holders of record of all outstanding shares, whether or not having voting power, have authorized such provision in the certificate of incorporation or an amendment thereof; and (2) If, subsequent to the adoption of such provision, shares are transferred or issued only to persons who had knowledge or notice thereof or consented in writing to such provision."

4. [By the Court] But note that Black's Fifth Edition (at p. 474) drops that part of the definition which states that more than a single transaction is denoted by "engage".

GABRIELLI, JUDGE (dissenting in part).

* * * I conclude that the agreement requiring plaintiff's consent was invalid under well-established public policies. * * * [It was] an illegal attempt by shareholders to deprive the board of directors of its inherent authority to exercise its discretion in managing the affairs of the corporation. * * * I would [, therefore,] reverse the determination of the Appellate Division with respect to plaintiff's * * * cause of action and hold that plaintiff cannot maintain a suit based upon defendants' failure to obtain his consent prior to executing the disputed * * * agreements.

It is beyond dispute that shareholder agreements such as the one relied upon by plaintiff in this case are, as a general rule, void as against public policy. Section 3.01 of the agreement, as interpreted both by plaintiff and by a majority of this court, would have precluded the board of directors of Group from taking any action on behalf of the corporation without first obtaining plaintiff's consent. This contractual provision, if enforced, would effectively shift the authority to manage every aspect of corporate affairs from the board to plaintiff, a minority shareholder who has no fiduciary obligations with respect to either the corporation or its other shareholders. As such, the provision represents a blatant effort to "sterilize" the board of directors in contravention of the statutory and decisional law of both Delaware and New York.

Under the statutes of Delaware, the State in which Group was incorporated, the authority to manage the affairs of a corporation is vested solely in its board of directors (Del.General Corporation Law, § 141, subd. [a]). The same is true under the applicable New York statutes (Business Corporation Law, § 701). Significantly, in both States, the courts have declined to give effect to agreements which purport to vary the statutory rule by transferring effective control of the corporation to a third party other than the board of directors (see Abercrombie v. Davies, 35 Del.Ch. 599, 604–611, 123 A.2d 893, rev'd on other grounds 36 Del.Ch. 371, 130 A.2d 338; Long Park, Inc. v. Trenton–New Brunswick Theatres Co., 297 N.Y. 174, 178–179, 77 N.E.2d 633; McQuade v. Stoneham, 263 N.Y. 323, 189 N.E. 234; Manson v. Curtis, 223 N.Y. 313, 323, 119 N.E. 559; see, generally, Delaney, The Corporate Director: Can His Hands Be Tied in Advance, 50 Col.L.Rev. 52, 54–57). The common-law rule in Delaware was aptly stated in Abercrombie v. Davies, 35 Del.Ch. at p. 611, 123 A.2d at p. 899, supra: "So long as the corporate form is used as presently provided by our statutes this Court cannot give legal sanction to agreements which have the effect of removing from directors in a very substantial way their duty to use their own best judgment on management matters".

True, the common-law rule has been modified somewhat in recent years to account for the business needs of the so-called "close corporation". The courts of our State, for example, have been willing to enforce shareholder agreements where the incursion on the board's authority was insubstantial (Clark v. Dodge, 269 N.Y. 410, 199 N.E. 641) or where the illegal provisions were severable from the otherwise legal provisions which the shareholder sought to enforce (Triggs v. Triggs, 46 N.Y.2d 305, 413 N.Y.S.2d 325, 385 N.E.2d 1254). Neither the courts of our State nor the courts of Delaware, however, have gone so far as to hold that an agreement among shareholders such as the agreement in this case, which purported to "sterilize" the board of directors by completely depriving it of its discretionary authority, can be regarded as legal and enforceable. To the contrary, the common-law rule applicable to both closely and publicly held corporations continues to treat agreements to deprive the board of directors of substantial authority as contrary to public policy.

Indeed, there heretofore has been little need for the courts to modify the general common-law rule against "sterilizing" boards of directors to accommodate the needs of closely held corporations. This is because the Legislatures of many States, including New York and Delaware, have enacted laws which enable the shareholders of closely held corporations to restrict the powers of the board of directors if they comply with certain statutory prerequisites (Del.General Corporation Law, §§ 350, 351; Business Corporation Law, § 620, subd. [b]). The majority apparently construes these statutes as indications that the public policies of the enacting States no longer proscribe the type of agreement at issue here in cases involving closely held corporations. Hence, the majority concludes that there is no bar to the enforcement of the shareholder agreement in this case, even though the statutory requirements for close corporations were not fulfilled. I cannot agree.

Under Delaware law, as the majority notes, the shareholders of a close corporation are free to enter into private, binding agreements among themselves to restrict the powers of their board of directors (Del. General Corporation Law, § 350). The same appears to be true under the present New York statutes (Business Corporation Law, § 620, subd. [b]). Both the Delaware and the New York statutory schemes, however, contemplate that such variations from the corporate norm will be recorded on the face of the certificate of incorporation (Del.General Corporation Law, § 351; Business Corporation Law, § 620, subd. [b]). New York additionally requires that the existence of a substantial restriction on the powers of the board "shall be noted conspicuously on the face or back of every certificate for shares issued by [the] corporation" (Business Corporation Law, § 620, subd. [g]). Significantly, in both Delaware and New York, a provision in the certificate of incorporation restricting the discretion of the board has the effect of shifting liability for any mismanagement from the directors to the managing shareholders (Del.General Corporation Law, § 351, subds. [2]-[3]; Business Corporation Law, § 620, subd. [f]).

In my view, these statutory provisions are not merely directory, but rather are evidence of a clear legislative intention to permit deviations from the statutory norms for corporations only under controlled conditions. In enacting these statutes, which are tailored for "close corporations", the Legislatures of Delaware and New York were apparently attempting to accommodate the needs of those who wished to take advantage of the limited liability inherent in the corporate format, but who also wished to retain the internal management structure of a partnership (see, generally, 1 O'Neal, Close Corporations, § 5.02). At the same time, however, the Legislatures were obviously mindful of the danger to the public that exists whenever shareholders privately agree among themselves to shift control of corporate management from independent directors to the shareholders, who are not necessarily bound by the fiduciary obligations imposed upon the board. In order to protect potential purchasers of shares and perhaps even potential creditors of the corporation, the Legislatures of Delaware and New York imposed specific strictures upon incorporated businesses managed by shareholders, the most significant of which is the requirement that restrictions on the statutory powers of the board of directors be evidenced in the certificate of incorporation. This requirement is an essential component of the statutory scheme because it ensures that potential purchasers of an interest in the corporation will have at least record notice that the corporation is being managed in an unorthodox fashion. Absent an appropriate notice provision in the certificate, there can be no assurance that an unsuspecting purchaser, not privy to the private shareholder agreement, will not be drawn into an investment that he might otherwise choose to avoid.

Since I regard the statutory requirements discussed above as essentially prophylactic in nature, I cannot subscribe to the notion that the agreement in this case should be enforced merely because there has been no showing that the interests of innocent third parties have actually been impaired. As is apparent from the design of the relevant statutes, the public policies of our own State as well as those of the State of Delaware remain opposed to shareholder agreements to "sterilize" the board of directors unless notice of the agreement is provided in the certificate of incorporation. Where such notice is provided, the public policy objections to the agreement are effectively eliminated and there is no further reason to preclude enforcement (see Lehrman v. Cohen, 43 Del.Ch. 222, 235, 222 A.2d 800). On the other hand, where, as here, the shareholders have entered into a private agreement to "sterilize" the board of directors and have failed to comply with the simple statutory prerequisites for "close corporations", the agreement must be deemed void and unenforceable in light of the inherent potential for fraud against the public. Indeed, since it is this very potential for public harm which renders these agreements unlawful, the mere fortuity that no one was actually harmed, if that be the case, cannot be the controlling factor in determining whether the agreement is legally enforceable. For the same reason, the illegality in the instant agreement cannot be cured retroactively, as the majority suggests, by requiring defendants to file the appropriate amendments to the certificate of incorporation. And, of course, it is elementary that a party to an agreement cannot be estopped from asserting its invalidity when the agreement is prohibited by law or is contrary to public policy (e.g., Brick v. Campbell, 122 N.Y. 337, 25 N.E. 493).

By its holding today, the majority has, in effect, rendered inoperative both the language and the underlying purpose of the relevant Delaware and New York statutes governing "close corporations". According to the majority's reasoning, the only requirements for upholding an otherwise unlawful shareholder agreement which concededly deprives the directors of all discretionary authority are that all of the shareholders concur in the agreement and that no "intervening rights of third persons" exist at the time enforcement of the agreement is sought. The statutes in question also recognize these factors as conditions precedent to the enforcement of shareholder agreements to "sterilize" a corporate board of directors. But the laws of both jurisdictions go further, requiring in each case that the "close corporation" give notice of its unorthodox management structure through its filed certificate of incorporation. The obvious purpose of such a requirement is to prevent harm to the public before it occurs. If, as the majority's holding suggests, this requirement of notice to the public through the certificate of incorporation is without legal effect unless and until a third party's interests have actually been impaired, then the prophylactic purposes of the statutes governing "close corporations" would effectively be defeated. It is this aspect of the majority's ruling that I find most difficult to accept.

For all of the foregoing reasons, I must respectfully dissent and cast my vote to modify the order of the Appellate Division by directing dismissal of plaintiff's first cause of action.

JASEN, JONES and FUCHSBERG, JJ., concur with MEYER, J,

GABRIELLI, J, dissents in part and votes to modify in a separate opinion in which COOKE, C.J., and WACHTLER, J., concur.

Notes

(1) The statutory provisions of Delaware and New York discussed in the principal case are part of special statutory treatments of closely held corporations. More than a dozen states have adopted similar statutes since 1965. While the provisions of these integrated "close corporation" statutes vary from state to state, they are all "opt in" statutes—usually by a simple statement in the articles of incorporation that the corporation is (or elects to be) a statutory close corporation. The options available to an electing close corporation generally include (1) the elimination of the board of directors entirely so that the shareholders may conduct the business directly, and (2) the validation without limitation of restrictions on the discretion of directors that appear in the articles of incorporation. Other provisions of these statutes are discussed at various points in this chapter. Cases dealing with the legal effect of such provisions include Walton Motor Sales, Inc. v. Ross, 736 F.2d 1449 (11th Cir.1984) [applying the Georgia statute authorizing shareholders' agreements restricting the discretion of

directors over "fiscal and credit" policy] and Graczykowski v. Ramppen, 101 A.D.2d 978, 477 N.Y.S.2d 454 (1984) ["managing shareholders" in Delaware corporation that has dispensed with board of directors have the inspection and other rights of directors as well as shareholders].

(2) If the result in *Zion* is correct, what is left of the *McQuade* principle in states with close corporation statutes? What is the status of a shareholders' agreement restricting the discretion of directors that is entered into by less than all of the shareholders?

(3) Adler v. Svingos, 80 A.D.2d 764, 436 N.Y.S.2d 719 (1981) applied the *Zion* holding to a two-shareholder corporation formed under the New York Business Corporation Law.

(4) A Model Statutory Close Corporation Supplement ("MCCS") accompanies the RMBCA. This Supplement was "developed for states that determine that it is advisable to enact an integrated statute dealing with the problems of closely held corporations." 4 Model Bus.Corp.Ann. (3d Ed.) 1805. However, it "is not part of the [RMBCA], and the decision whether to enact this Supplement should be considered independently of the enactment of the Model Act." Election to come under this Supplement is available to corporations with less than 50 shareholders. Among the options available under this Supplement are provisions authorizing the corporation to dispense with a board of directors (MCCS § 21) and authorizing shareholders to enter into agreements that restrict the discretion of directors (MCCS § 20). Consider RMBCA § 8.01(c), a provision that is not limited to electing close corporations. Why should this option be available to non-electing corporations with less than 50 shareholders? If a close corporation is to adopt non-traditional forms of governance, should not it be required expressly to elect close corporation status? Consider also § 8.01(b). Does not the last phrase of this section in effect allow all non-electing corporations to eliminate the McQuade principle simply by putting the clause in the articles of incorporation?

MATTER OF AUER v. DRESSEL

Court of Appeals of New York, 1954.
306 N.Y. 427, 118 N.E.2d 590.

DESMOND, JUDGE.

This article 78 of the Civil Practice Act proceeding was brought by class A stockholders of appellant R. Hoe & Co., Inc., for an order in the nature of mandamus to compel the president of Hoe to comply with a positive duty imposed on him by the corporation's by-laws. Section 2 of article I of those by-laws says that "It shall be the duty of President to call a special meeting whenever requested in writing so to do, by stockholders owning a majority of the capital stock entitled to vote at such meeting". On October 16, 1953, petitioners submitted to the president written requests for a special meeting of class A stockholders, which writings were signed in the names of the holders of record of slightly more than 55% of the class A stock. The president failed to call the meeting and, after waiting a week, the petitioners brought the present proceeding. The answer of the corporation and its president was not forthcoming until October 28, 1953, and it contained, in response to the petition's allegation that the demand was by more than a majority of class A stockholders, only a denial that the corporation and the president had any knowledge or information sufficient to form a belief as to the stockholding of those who had signed the requests. Since the president, when he filed that answer, had had before him for at least ten days the signed requests themselves, his denial that he had any information sufficient for a belief as to the adequacy of the number of signatures was obviously perfunctory and raised no issue whatever. There was no discretion in this corporate officer as to whether or not to call a meeting when a demand therefor was put before him by owners of the required number of shares. The important right of stockholders to have such meetings called will be of little practical value if corporate management can ignore the requests, force the stockholders to commence legal proceedings, and then, by purely formal denials, put the stockholders to lengthy and expensive litigation, to establish facts as to stockholdings which are peculiarly within the knowledge of the corporate officers. In such a situation, Special Term did the correct thing in disposing of the matter summarily, as commanded by section 1295 of the Civil Practice Act.

The petition was opposed on the further alleged ground that none of the four purposes for which petitioners wished the meeting called was a proper one for such a class A stockholders' meeting. Those four stated purposes were these: (A) to vote, upon a resolution indorsing the administration of petitioner Joseph L. Auer, who had been removed as president by the directors, and demanding that he be reinstated as such president; (B) voting upon a proposal to amend the charter and by-laws to provide that vacancies on the board of directors, arising from the removal of a director by stockholders or by resignation of a director against whom charges have been preferred, may be filled, for the unexpired term, by the stockholders only of the class theretofore represented by the director so removed or so resigned; (C) voting upon a proposal that the stockholders hear certain charges preferred, in the requests, against four of the directors, determine whether the conduct of such directors or any of them was inimical to the corporation and, if so, to vote upon their removal and vote for the election of their successors; and (D) voting upon a proposal to amend the by-laws so as to provide that half of the total number of directors in office and, in any event, not less than one-third of the whole authorized number of directors constitute a quorum of the directors.

The Hoe certificate of incorporation provides for eleven directors, of whom the class A stockholders, more than a majority of whom join in this petition, elect nine and the common stockholders elect two. The obvious purpose of the meeting here sought to be called (aside from the indorsement and reinstatement of former president Auer) is to hear charges against four of the class A directors, to remove them if the charges be proven, to amend the by-laws so that the successor directors be elected by the class A stockholders, and further to amend the by-laws so that an effective quorum of directors will be made up of no fewer than half of the directors in office and no fewer than one third of the whole authorized number of directors. No reason appears why the class A stockholders should not be allowed to vote on any or all of those proposals.

The stockholders, by expressing their approval of Mr. Auer's conduct as president and their demand that he be put back in that office, will not be able, directly, to effect that change in officers, but there is nothing invalid in their so expressing themselves and thus putting on notice the directors who will stand for election at the annual meeting. As to purpose (B), that is, amending the charter and by-laws to authorize the stockholders to fill vacancies as to class A directors who have been removed on charges or who have resigned, it seems to be settled law that the stockholders who are empowered to elect directors have the inherent power to remove them for cause, In re Koch, 257 N.Y. 318, 321, 322, 178 N.E. 545, 546. Of course, as the Koch case points out, there must be the service of specific charges, adequate notice and full opportunity of meeting the accusations, but there is no present showing of any lack of any of those in this instance. Since these particular stockholders have the right to elect nine directors and to remove them on proven charges, it is not inappropriate that they should use their further power to amend the by-laws to elect the successors of such directors as shall be removed after hearing, or who shall resign pending hearing. Quite pertinent at this point is Rogers v. Hill, 289 U.S. 582, 589, 53 S.Ct. 731, 734, 77 L.Ed. 1385, which made light of an argument that stockholders, by giving power to the directors to make by-laws, had lost their own power to make them; quoting a New Jersey case, In re Griffing Iron Co., 63 N.J.L. 168, 41 A. 931, the United States Supreme Court said: " 'It would be preposterous to leave the real owners of the corporate property at the mercy of their agents, and the law has not done so' ". Such a change in the by-laws, dealing with class A directors only, has no effect on the voting rights of the common stockholders, which rights have to do with the selection of the remaining two directors only. True, the certificate of incorporation authorizes the board of directors to remove any director on charges, but we do not consider that provision as an abdication by the stockholders of their own traditional, inherent power to remove their own directors. Rather, it provides an additional method. Were that not so, the stockholders might find themselves without effective remedy in a case where a majority of the directors were accused of wrongdoing and, obviously, would be unwilling to remove themselves from office.

We fail to see, in the proposal to allow class A stockholders to fill vacancies as to class A directors, any impairment or any violation of paragraph (h) of article Third of the certificate of incorporation, which says that class A stock has exclusive voting rights with respect to all matters "other than the election of directors." That negative language should not be taken to mean that class A stockholders, who have an absolute right to elect nine of these eleven directors, cannot amend their by-laws to guarantee a similar right, in the class A stockholders and to the exclusion of common stockholders, to fill vacancies in the class A group of directors.

There is urged upon us the impracticability and unfairness of constituting the numerous stockholders a tribunal to hear charges made by themselves, and the incongruity of letting the stockholders hear and pass on those charges by proxy. Such questions are really not before us at all on this appeal. The charges here are not, on their face, frivolous or inconsequential, and all that we are holding as to the charges is that a meeting may be held to deal with them. Any director illegally removed can have his remedy in the courts.

The order should be affirmed, with costs, and the Special Term directed forthwith to make an order in the same form as the Appellate Division order with appropriate changes of dates.

VAN VOORHIS, JUDGE (dissenting).

* * * An examination of the request for a special meeting by these stockholders indicates that none of the proposals could be voted upon legally at the projected meeting. The purposes of the meeting are listed as A, B, C and D. Purpose A is described as "Voting upon a resolution endorsing the administration of Joseph L. Auer, as President of the corporation, and demanding his immediate reinstatement as President." For the stockholders to vote on this proposition would be an idle gesture, since it is provided by section 27 of the General Corporation Law, Consol.Laws, c. 23, that "The business of a corporation shall be managed by its board of directors". The directors of Hoe have been elected by the stockholders for stated terms which have not expired, and it is their function and not that of the stockholders to appoint the officers of the corporation, Stock Corporation Law, Consol. Laws, c. 59, § 60.

Purpose B of the special meeting is to vote upon a proposal to amend the certificate and the by-laws so as to provide "that vacancies on the Board of Directors arising from the removal of a director by stockholders or by resignation of a director against whom charges have been preferred may be filled, for the unexpired term, only by the stockholders of the class theretofore represented by the director so removed." This proposal is interwoven with the next one (C), which is about to be discussed, which is to remove four directors from office before the expiration of their terms in order to alter the control of the corporation. Proposal B must be read in the context that the certificate of incorporation provides for eleven directors, of whom the class A stockholders elect nine and the common stockholders two. So long as any class A shares are outstanding, the voting rights with respect to all matters "other than the election of directors" are vested exclusively in the holders of class A stock, with one exception now irrelevant. This means that the common stockholders are entitled to participate directly in the election of two directors, who, in turn, are authorized by the certificate to vote to fill vacancies occurring among the directors elected by the class A shareholders. This proposed amendment would deprive the directors elected by the common stockholders of the power to participate in filling the vacancies which petitioners hope to create among the class A directors, four of whom they seek to remove by proposal C which is about to be discussed. Such an alteration would impair the existing right of the common stockholders to participate in filling vacancies upon the board of directors and could not be legally adopted at this meeting demanded by petitioners from which the common stockholders are excluded. The effect would be to reclassify voting powers of the common stockholders within the meaning of subdivision 3 of section 35 of the Stock Corporation Law, which is something that section 51 prohibits without the vote of "the holders of all shares of any class or classes that will be adversely affected", and this is ordained even "regardless of any provision to the contrary in the certificate of incorporation".

Purpose C of the special meeting is to vote "upon a proposal that the Stockholders (1) hear the charges preferred against Harry K. Barr, William L. Canady, Neil P. Cullom and Edwin L. Munzert, and their answers thereto; (2) determine whether such conduct on their part or on the part of any of them was inimical to the best interest of R. Hoe & Co., Inc., and if so (3) vote upon the removal of said persons or any of them as directors of R. Hoe & Co., Inc., for such conduct, and (4) vote for the election of directors to fill any vacancies on the Board of Directors which the Stockholders may be authorized to fill." By means of this proposal, it is sought to change the control of the corporation and to accomplish what A could not achieve, viz., remove the existing president and reappoint Mr. Joseph L. Auer as president of the corporation. Neither the language nor the policy of the corporation law subjects directors to recall by the stockholders before their terms of office have expired, merely for the reason that the stockholders wish to change the policy of the corporation. In People ex rel. Manice v. Powell, 201 N.Y. 194, 201, 94 N.E. 634, 637, this court said that "It would be somewhat startling to the business world if we definitely announced that the directors of a corporation were mere employeés and that the stockholders of the corporation have the power to convene from time to time and remove at will any or all of the directors, although their respective terms of office have not expired." Fraud or breach of fiduciary duty must be shown, Matter of Koch, 257 N.Y. 318, 178 N.E. 545. In that event, directors may be removed from office before expiration of term by an action brought under subdivision 4 of section 60 of the General Corporation Law. In addition to such procedure, paragraph Fourteenth of the certificate of incorporation states: "Any director of the corporation may at any time be removed for cause as such director by resolution adopted by a majority of the whole number of directors then in office, provided that such director, prior to his removal, shall have received a copy of the charges against him and shall have had an opportunity to be heard thereon by the board. The By-Laws may provide the manner of presentation of the charges and of the hearing thereon."

Petitioners have instituted this proceeding on the theory that although no power is conferred upon the stockholders by the certificate or the by-laws to remove directors before the expiration of their terms, with or without cause, power to do so for cause is inherent in them as the body authorized to elect the directors, citing Matter of Koch, 257 N.Y. 318, 178 N.E. 545, supra. Petitioners have argued that the grant of this power to the board of directors to remove some of their number for cause after trial, does not eliminate what is asserted to be the inherent right of the stockholders to do likewise. No cases are cited in support of the latter proposition. * * * Such cases as have been cited in support of a power in the stockholders to remove directors for cause are clear in holding that such action can be taken only subject to the rule that "specific charges must be served, adequate notice must be given, and full opportunity of meeting the accusations must be afforded." Matter of Koch, 257 N.Y. 318, 322, 178 N.E. 545, 546, supra.

Although the demand by these petitioners for a special meeting contains no specification of charges against these four directors, the proxy statement, circulated by their protective committee, does describe certain charges. No point appears to be made of the circumstance that they are not contained in the demand for the meeting. Nevertheless, although this proxy statement enumerates these charges and announces that a resolution will be introduced at the special meeting to hear them, to determine whether sufficient cause exists for the removal of said persons as directors, and, if so, to remove them and to fill the resulting vacancies, the stockholders thus solicited are requested to sign proxies running to persons nominated by petitioners' protective committee. Inasmuch as this committee, with which petitioners are affiliated, has already charged in the most forceful terms that at least one of these directors has been guilty of misconduct and that "his *clique* of directors have removed Joseph L. Auer as President," it is reasonable to assume that the case of the accused directors has already been prejudged by those who will vote the proxies alleged to represent 255,658 shares of class A stock, and that the 1,200 shareholders who are claimed to have signed proxies have (whether they know it or not) voted, in effect, to remove these directors before they have been tried. The consequence is that these directors are to be adjudged guilty of fraud or breach of faith in absentia by shareholders who have neither heard nor ever will hear the evidence against them or in their behalf. Such a procedure does not conform to the requirements of Matter of Koch, supra, nor the other authorities which have been cited, and is far removed from "a law which hears before it condemns, which proceeds upon inquiry, and renders judgment only after trial." Brief by Daniel Webster in Trustees of Dartmouth Coll. v. Woodward, 4 Wheat. [U.S.] 518, 581, 4 L.Ed. 629. The charges against these directors enumerated in the proxy statement are described as having been preferred by one John Kadel and are to the effect that these four accused directors supported a resolution on July 2, 1953, that severance pay of $50,000 be granted to Mr. Auer "upon condition that he resign and that he sign an agreement not to participate, with any stockholders group or otherwise, in any action against any of the directors or officers of the Company." This money was not in fact paid to Auer. The charge based thereon against these directors is that there was a breach of trust in offering to pay $50,000 of the corporation's money in consideration of a covenant by Auer not to participate (as the minutes of the directors' meeting of July 2, 1953, actually read) in "any hostile action against the company, its officers and directors." It is not clear how this constituted actionable misconduct in view of the circumstance that none of this money actually was paid, and that there was no showing in this record any misconduct on the part of these four directors which might have furnished a basis for a stockholders' derivative action by Auer against these directors. It is not so plain that these directors should be subjected to trial by stockholders, acting through proxies who are evidently prepared to oust them with or without cause, that a mandamus order should, in any event, be issued to compel the calling of a special meeting for that purpose. The other charges, viz., that Mr. Cullom was paid $300 a month as rental for office space in his suite at 63 Wall Street, and that he engaged one of his personal friends and clients in connection with appraisal proceedings involving the common stock of the company for which the friend was paid $5,000 are not supplemented by further facts indicating that such conduct was hostile to the interest of the corporation.

It is not for the courts to determine which of these warring factions is pursuing the wiser policy for the corporation. If these petitioners consider that the stockholders made a mistake in the election of the present directors, they should not be permitted to correct it by recalling them before the expiration of their terms on charges of fraud or breach of fiduciary duty without a full and fair trial, which, if not conducted in court under section 60 of the General Corporation Law, is required to be held before the remaining directors under paragraph Fourteenth of the certificate of incorporation. The difficulty inherent in conducting such a trial by proxy may well have been the reason on account of which the incorporators delegated that function to the board of directors under paragraph Fourteenth of the certificate of incorporation. If it were to develop (the papers before the court do not contain evidence of such a fact) that enough of the other directors would be disqualified so that it would be impossible to obtain a quorum for the purpose, it may well be doubted that these directors could be tried before so large a number of stockholders sitting in person (if it were possible to assemble them in one place) or that they could sit in judgment by proxy. In ancient Athens evidence is said to have been heard and judgment pronounced in court by as many as 500 jurors known as dicasts, but in this instance, if petitioners be correct in their figures, there are 1,200 class A stockholders who have signed requests or proxies, and these are alleged to hold only somewhat more than half of the outstanding shares. Since it would be impossible for so large a number to conduct a trial in person, they could only do so by proxy. Voting by proxy is the accepted procedure to express the will of large numbers of stockholders on questions of corporate policy within their province to determine, and it would be suitable in this instance if the certificate of incorporation had reserved to stockholders the power to recall directors without cause before expiration of term, as in Abberger v. Kulp, 156 Misc. 210, 281 N.Y.S. 373, but it is altogether unsuited to the performance of duties which partake of the nature of the judicial function, involving, as this would need to do if the accused directors are to be removed before the expiration of their terms, a decision after trial that they have been guilty of faithlessness or fraud. Section 60 of the General Corporation Law is always available for that purpose if the occasion requires.

The final proposal to be voted on at this special meeting (D) relates simply to an amendment to the by-laws so as to provide that a quorum shall consist of not less than one half of the number of directors holding office and in no event less than one third of the authorized number of directors. Section 8 of article II of the by-laws already provides that one half of the total number of directors shall constitute a quorum; the modification that a quorum shall in no event be less than one third of the authorized number of directors whom petitioners seek to eliminate.

Inasmuch as we consider that for the foregoing reasons none of the business for which the special meeting is proposed to be called could legally be transacted, this proceeding should be dismissed. It is not necessary to analyze whether under other circumstances an order would lie in the nature of an alternative rather than a peremptory mandamus.

The petition should be dismissed, with costs in all courts.

LEWIS, C.J., and DYE, FULD and FROESSEL, JJ., concur with DESMOND, J.

VAN VOORHIS, J., dissents in opinion in which CONWAY, J., concurs.

B. SHAREHOLDERS

SALGO v. MATTHEWS

Court of Civil Appeals of Texas, 1974.
497 S.W.2d 620, writ ref'd n.r.e.

GUITTARD, JUSTICE.

This equitable proceeding involves a proxy contest for control of General Electrodynamics Corporation, a Texas corporation. Stockholders Joe W. Matthews and Paul Thorp, representing the faction opposed to current management, sought the aid of the district court in requiring the president, as chairman of the stockholders' meeting, and the election inspector appointed by him, to accept certain disputed proxies, count the votes of the stockholders cast under these proxies, and declare that the candidates supported by plaintiffs had been elected directors of the corporation. We hold that the court erred in granting injunctive relief, both temporary and final, in absence of any showing that plaintiffs could not have obtained adequate relief by the statutory remedy of quo warranto after the completion of the election.

FACTS

The facts are substantially without dispute. * * *

Before the special stockholders' meeting, proxies had been solicited on behalf of management for a slate of candidates for the board of directors, consisting of the president, defendant Francis Salgo, and four others, and also by an opposing faction for a slate composed of plaintiff Joe Matthews and four others. The meeting was convened on the afternoon of November 8, 1972. Defendant Salgo, acting as chairman of the meeting, appointed defendant Julian Meer, an attorney, as election inspector. Plaintiffs have never denied his authority to act in that capacity, although they question the extent of his authority. The chairman opened the polls and plaintiffs tendered their proxies and ballots to the inspector for examination and tabulation. Before the tabulation was complete a motion was made and carried to adjourn the meeting, but the court found this adjournment to be only a temporary recess. After the recess was called, examination and tabulation of the proxies continued for several hours until discontinued by agreement and was resumed the following morning, November 9. In the course of this process, plaintiffs presented to defendant Meer four proxy documents purporting to have been executed in plaintiffs' favor on behalf of Pioneer Casualty Company, the registered owner of 29,934 shares of stock. Beneficial title to these shares had been transferred to Don Shepherd, who was in bankruptcy, and two of the proxy documents were signed, "Pioneer Casualty Company By Don Shepherd." Plaintiffs also presented to the inspector an order of the 126th District Court of Travis County, Texas, directing Tom I. McFarling as receiver of Pioneer Casualty Company to give Shepherd a proxy to vote these shares by giving his proxy to plaintiffs Matthews and Thorp, and plaintiffs also presented a proxy document signed by the receiver in accordance with this order. Defendant Meer refused to accept any of these proxies, and their validity is the principal matter in controversy. Defendant Meer also refused to accept two telegraphic proxies aggregating 5,000 shares from stockholders Candis and Wrobliske when plaintiff Thorp presented them to him on the afternoon of November 9. * * *

The cause came on for trial before the court without a jury on December 4, and on December 26 the court issued a final decree ordering defendant Salgo to reconvene the stockholders' meeting before the court on January 15, 1973, for the sole purpose of declaring plaintiff Matthews and the other nonmanagement candidates elected as directors of the corporation and for the purpose of entertaining a motion to adjourn the meeting sine die. The decree recites findings, later repeated in the court's formal findings of fact, to the effect that the disputed proxies of Pioneer, Candis and Wrobliske were duly executed and timely presented to the election inspector, that he should have accepted them, and that when so accepted and the votes under them counted, the result of the voting was to elect plaintiff Matthews and the other candidates of the nonmanagement slate as directors of the corporation. The court further found that the mathematical accuracy of the count and tabulation of proxies by defendant Meer as election inspector was conceded by all parties. According to that tabulation, if the votes of the Pioneer Casualty Company shares and also of the Candis and Wrobliske shares were voted in favor of the nonmanagement candidates, they were elected, but if either the Pioneer votes or the Candis and Wrobliske votes were rejected, then defendant Salgo and the pro-management candidates were elected.

The court's findings also show that in conformity with the final decree, defendant Salgo did on the morning of January 15, 1973, reconvene the meeting in open court and did formally announce the results of the election as ordered by the court, and that the meeting was then adjourned sine die. * * *

DISCRETION OF ELECTION INSPECTOR

Since plaintiffs have not shown that they would suffer irreparable injury if left to their remedy by quo warranto, the relief granted cannot be justified on the ground that defendant Meer exceeded his authority as election inspector in refusing to accept the Pioneer Casualty Company proxies and count the votes cast under them. Moreover, we hold that the inspector was not subject to judicial control in the performance of his duties because he had discretionary authority to make a preliminary determination of the validity of the proxies for the purpose of tabulating them, counting the votes, and certifying the result, although the correctness of his decision was subject to review after the election by proceeding in quo warranto.

Plaintiffs' contention that the function of an election inspector is purely ministerial rather than judicial has support in opinions from several jurisdictions, but most of the statements to this effect must be taken in context to mean that the decision of the inspector is not binding on the court in subsequent litigation to review the election. Other courts have recognized that election inspectors have a measure of discretion and have refused to disturb their findings even after the election if made fairly, honestly and in good faith. Since the authority of the election inspector here is not defined by statute or bylaw, we have no basis to hold that his decision concerning validity of the disputed proxies cannot be judicially reviewed after the election. However, we do hold that he has discretionary authority to decide such matters for the purpose of making an initial determination of the result of the election. Consequently his exercise of that discretion cannot be controlled by mandamus or mandatory injunction under the established rule that such relief is not available to control the action of an officer in the exercise of discretion or judgment.

Recognition of such discretionary authority on the part of the inspector best serves the interest of stockholders in prompt resolution of proxy contests. The function of the inspector is to determine the result of the election accurately and declare the result promptly so that the affairs of the corporation may go forward, and in performing that function he must make some sort of decision on whatever problems may arise, including validity of proxies tendered to him. That function ought not to be interrupted while opposing factions litigate. If he errs, the losing party may resort to the courts after the election to determine whether the result was properly declared.

The importance of such discretion is demonstrated by the problem presented to the inspector in this case. The facts determining validity of the disputed proxies were complex, the law was uncertain, and the lawyers representing the two factions were in sharp disagreement. The inspector, himself a lawyer, was required to exercise judgment, and apparently he exercised that judgment by refusing to recognize the disputed proxies. In the orderly course of the corporation's affairs he should have been permitted to complete his duties and declare the result of the election before the court attempted to review his decision. Consequently, we hold that the court erred in granting extraordinary mandatory relief.

VALIDITY OF DISPUTED PROXIES

Our holding that an election inspector has discretionary authority to determine the validity of disputed proxies for the purpose of declaring the result of the election should not be interpreted as meaning that he may go beyond the corporate records in determining the identity of stockholders entitled to vote. Defendants argue that the trial court's findings establish that beneficial ownership of the 29,934 shares registered in the name of Pioneer Casualty Company was not in Pioneer's receiver or in Don Shepherd, to whom these shares had been transferred, but was vested in Shepherd's bankruptcy trustee, and, consequently, that neither the receiver nor Shepherd had the right to vote. We assume that Shepherd's trustee was the beneficial owner, but, as against the corporation and its officers, beneficial ownership does not carry with it the right to vote without having the shares transferred on the books. A bylaw of General Electrodynamics Corporation provides that stock is transferable only on its books. This bylaw indicates the strong interest of the corporation and its stockholders in determining stock ownership quickly by reference to the corporate records. If beneficial title is in dispute, that dispute cannot properly be decided by the election inspector, and neither should the losing faction be able to go into court to invalidate the election on the ground that the ownership of certain shares was not correctly shown by the corporate records. For even greater reason the election should not be interrupted or suspended while complicated questions of title to stock are litigated to final judgment.

The rule that under such a bylaw, eligibility to vote at corporate elections is determined by the corporate records rather than by the ultimate judicial decision of beneficial title of disputed shares is well sustained by authority. In re Giant Portland Cement Co., 26 Del.Ch. 32, 21 A.2d 697 (Ch.1941). This rule is in accordance with Tex.Bus. Corp.Act Ann. art. 2.27(A) (1956), V.A.T.S., which provides, "The original stock transfer books shall be prima-facie evidence as to who are the shareholders entitled * * * to vote at any meeting of shareholders." According to E. Aranow & H. Einhorn, supra at 386, although such a statute uses the term "prima-facie," it has the effect of making stock records conclusive on the inspector. The term "prima-facie" avoids any implication that the stock record is conclusive in a suit concerning title to the stock.

The binding effect of the stock record on corporate officers does not leave a beneficial owner without remedy. He may be presumed to know that the record owner can vote the stock. The beneficial owner can protect his interest by requiring a transfer on the books or by demanding a proxy from the record owner, and if voluntary compliance is not forthcoming, relief is available by injunction or mandamus. In the present case Shepherd's trustee, the beneficial owner, made no effort to vote the shares. He sought no proxy from the receiver or the receivership court. In these circumstances neither the corporate officers nor any of the other stockholders were in a position to assert that only the trustee had the right to vote.

The question presented to the inspector was, who was entitled to act for the record owner? The shares were registered in the name of Pioneer Casualty Company, which was in receivership and had no officers to act for it. The only person entitled to act for Pioneer was its receiver under orders of the 126th district court of Travis County. The receiver, acting under such an order, gave a proxy to Shepherd to act for Pioneer, with instructions to give a further proxy to plaintiffs Matthews and Thorp, and Shepherd, acting for Pioneer in accordance with the proxy to him, gave a proxy to plaintiffs. This transaction was essentially the same as if the receiver, acting under the court's order, had given the proxy directly to plaintiffs. The recitation in the order that Shepherd was the beneficial owner is of no consequence, since the beneficial owner, whether Shepherd or his trustee, had no right under the bylaws to vote the shares as against General Electrodynamics Corporation and its officers. * * * Since the stockholder of record was Pioneer Casualty Company, and the receiver was authorized by court order to act for Pioneer, the inspector's proper course was to accept the stock record as determining that the right to vote was in Pioneer Casualty Company, and to accept the proxies given by the receiver to Shepherd and by him to plaintiffs as valid.

Defendants argue that if the inspector was authorized to go behind the stock book and recognize the voting rights of the receiver for Pioneer Casualty Company, he was authorized to go further and determine the beneficial ownership of the stock for the purpose of the election. We do not agree. The inspector was bound by the stock book to consider Pioneer Casualty Company the legal owner for the purpose of the election, but he was required to determine who could act for the record owner, just as if someone had challenged the authority of a person purporting to act as an officer of a corporate stockholder. Since Pioneer was in receivership, the inspector could consider that fact and should have treated the receiver as the authorized representative of the record owner. It is quite another matter to say that the inspector should have inquired into beneficial ownership of the stock and recognized the right of Shepherd or his trustee in bankruptcy to vote the shares. * * *

Reversed and rendered.

Notes

(1) The principal case is noted at 52 Tex.L.Rev. 1433 (1974). It appears that the lower court's order, reversed in the principal case, led to a shift in control of the corporation to the "nonmanagement" faction pending the appeal. Salgo subsequently discovered that it was not easy to return to the previous status. See Salgo v. Hoffman, 515 S.W.2d 756 (Tex.Civ.App.— Dallas 1974, no writ); Salgo v. Hoffman, 521 S.W.2d 922 (Tex.Civ.App.— Dallas 1975, no writ). Hoffman, incidentally, is the trial judge that originally heard the case and whose order was reversed in the principal case.

(2) Underlying the holding in the principal case is the basic concept that shares are always issued in the name of a specific person. See RMBCA §§ 6.25(b)(2), 7.07(a). That person is usually referred to as the "record holder" and may or may not be the beneficial owner. As discussed subsequently, certificates of publicly held corporations are often issued in the name of a broker ("street name") or nominee in order to facilitate transfer. Indeed, in modern securities practice, there may be one or more additional layers of intermediaries between the record owner and the beneficial owner of publicly traded shares.

(3) The mechanics of establishing the date on which shareholders entitled to vote will be determined is set forth in RMBCA § 7.07. See also, id. § 7.20.

(4) Action by shareholders at a meeting requires the existence of a quorum and the approval by the requisite number of votes at a meeting at which a quorum is present. See RMBCA §§ 7.25(a), 7.25(c), 7.26, 7.27, 7.28(a). These are often viewed as mundane, technical matters, but there are a number of substantive issues that may arise. For example,

(a) May a disgruntled faction of shareholders withdraw from a meeting in order to "break" a quorum? See RMBCA § 7.25(b).

(b) Why should there be a different rule for determining the election of directors [RMBCA § 7.28(a)] than for approval or disapproval of other matters [RMBCA § 7.25(c)]?

(c) What is all the statutory language about "voting groups" about, anyway? See e.g. RMBCA §§ 1.40(26), 8.04, 10.04.

(d) Earlier versions of the Model Act provided that the affirmative vote "of the majority of the shares represented" at a meeting at which a quorum was present was necessary to take action by shareholders. MBCA (1969) § 32. Does RMBCA § 7.25(c) adopt a different test? What about shares that are present at the meeting but abstain [e.g. by casting blank ballots or by not casting ballots at all]? The Official Comment to § 7.25 offers this illustration:

> [I]f a corporation has 1,000 shares of a single class outstanding, all entitled to cast one vote each, a quorum consists of 501 shares; if 600 shares are represented and the vote on a proposed action is 280 in favor, 225 opposed, and 95 abstaining, the action is not approved [under the 1969 Model Act] since fewer than a majority of the 600 shares voted in favor of the action. This is anomalous since if the shares abstaining had not been present at the meeting at all a quorum would have been present and the action would have been approved. Under § 7.25(c) the action would not be defeated by the 95 abstaining votes.

Cumulative vs. Straight Voting. The workings of these two methods of voting to elect directors can be most simply described by an illustration. Let us assume a corporation with two shareholders, A with 18 shares, and B with 82 shares. Further, let us assume that there are five directors and each shareholder nominates five candidates. Directors run "at large" rather than for specific places; hence the five persons receiving the most votes are elected. If only straight voting is permitted, A may cast 18 votes for each of five candidates, and B may cast 82 votes for each of five candidates. The result, of course, is that all five of B's candidates are elected. If cumulative voting is permitted the number of total votes that each shareholder may cast is first computed and each shareholder is permitted to distribute these votes as he sees fit over one or more candidates. In the example above, A is entitled to cast a total of 90 votes (18×5) and B is entitled to cast 410 votes (82×5). If A casts all 90 votes for A_1, A_1 is ensured of election because B cannot divide 410 votes among five candidates in such a way as to give each candidate more than 90 votes and preclude A_1's election. Obviously, the effect of cumulative voting is that it increases minority participation on the board of directors. In straight voting, the shareholder with 51 per cent of the vote elects the entire board; in cumulative voting, a relatively small faction (18 per cent in the above example) may obtain representation on the board. Whether this is good or bad depends on one's point of view.[5]

5. [By the Editor] Numerous arguments for and against cumulative voting have been made. Arguments in favor of such voting include: (1) it is democratic in that persons with large (but minority) holdings should have a voice in the conduct of the corporation; (2) it is desirable to have as many viewpoints as possible represented on the Board of Directors; and (3) the presence of a minority director may discourage conflicts of interest by management since discovery is considerably more likely. Arguments in opposition include: (1) the introduction of a partisan on the Board is inconsistent with the notion that the Board should represent all interests in

One undesirable aspect of cumulative voting is that it tends to be a little tricky. If a shareholder casts votes in an irrational or inefficient way, he may not get the directorships his position entitles him to; when voting cumulatively it is relatively easy to make a mistake in spreading votes around. The most graphic illustration of this are the cases where a majority shareholder votes in such a way that he elects only a minority of the directors.[6] This is most likely to occur when one shareholder votes "straight" and another cumulates. For example, if A has 60 shares and B only 40, with five directors to be elected, B may nevertheless elect a majority of the Board if A votes "straight", and B knows that A is doing so. The result might look like this:

A_1–60, A_2–60, A_3–60, A_4–60, A_5–60; B_1–67, B_2–66, B_3–65, B_4–1, B_5–1.[7]

This is daring of B because he is spreading his vote over three persons when he can be sure only of electing two. If B decides to do this, and A knows that B will try to elect three persons, then A, by properly cumulating his votes, can elect four directors, in effect "stealing" one of B's.[8]

The following formula is useful in determining the number of shares needed to elect one director:

$$\frac{S}{D + 1} + 1.$$

where S equals the total number of shares voting, and D equals the number of directors to be elected.[9] The analogous formula to elect n directors is:

$$\frac{nS}{D + 1} + 1.$$

the corporation; (2) a partisan director may cause disharmony which reduces the efficiency of the board; (3) a partisan director may criticize management unreasonably so as to make it less willing to take risky (but desirable) action; (4) a partisan director may leak confidential information; and (5) in practice cumulative voting is usually used to further narrow partisan goals, particularly to give an insurgent group a toehold in the corporation in an effort to obtain control. See generally Williams, Cumulative Voting, 33:3 Harv.Bus. Rev. 108, 111 (1955).

6. [By the Editor] There are at least six such cases, while in several others the majority shareholder saved himself from disaster by recasting his votes on a cumulative basis before the results of the election were announced.

7. [By the Editor] The theory of B is not to create tie votes among his own candidates. If he does so, and the tie candidates come in fifth and sixth in an election for five directorships, the tie may be broken by a new election for only the fifth seat; A may be able to vote his shares in the new election for his own candidate, thereby causing B to lose a seat. Of

course, in the above hypothetical, B might distribute his votes over only three candidates without creating a tie.

8. [By the Editor] The results of such an election might be as follows: A_1–73, A_2–74, A_3–75, A_4–76, A_5–2, B_1–67, B_2–66, B_3–65, B_4–1, B_5–1.

9. [By the Editor] A minor modification may sometimes be necessary. The first portion of the formula, $\frac{S}{D + 1}$ establishes the maximum number of shares voted for a single person which are *insufficient* to elect that person as a director. Any share, or fraction thereof, in excess of that amount will be sufficient to elect a director. The formula in the text ignores fractional shares which sometimes may lead to a one share-error. For example, where there are 100 shares voting and five directors to be elected, the first portion of the formula is $\frac{100}{5 + 1}$, or $\frac{100}{6}$. In this example, 16 shares will not elect a director, but 17 shares will, since the first part of the formula yields 16⅔. The formula in the text yields an answer of 17⅔.

Notes

(1) In Stancil v. Bruce Stancil Refrigeration, Inc., 81 N.C.App. 567, 344 S.E.2d 789 (1986), all the shares of stock of a North Carolina corporation were owned by two brothers: Bruce Stancil (12,500 shares) and Howard Stancil (12,500 shares). North Carolina requires cumulative voting by statute for corporations with less than 2,000 shareholders and provides that directors are elected by a "plurality of the votes cast." N.C.G.S. § 55–67(c). Before the election in question, the board of directors consisted of Bruce Stancil, Eva Stancil, Bruce's wife, and Howard Stancil. At the shareholders' meeting, each brother was represented by counsel. Bruce, "without a majority vote or consent, asserted his 'right' to act as chairman of the meeting and in fact conducted the proceedings at the meeting, acting with and upon the advice and consultation of his attorney, Wiley L. Lane, Jr." 344 S.E.2d at 790. Howard announced that he planned to vote cumulatively in conformity with the North Carolina statutes but Bruce did not acknowledge this statement (or grant the recess the North Carolina statute provides for after such an announcement is made). Bruce nominated himself, his wife, Eva, and one Sarah Barnes. Howard nominated himself, his wife, Clara, and one Henry Babb. The trial court's findings and conclusions describe what happened then:

15. The Respondent, Bruce Stancil, cast his votes for his nominees for director as follows:

Bruce Stancil	12,500 Votes
Sarah Barnes	12,500 Votes
Eva Stancil	12,500 Votes

The Petitioner, Howard K. Stancil, cast his votes for his nominees for director as follows:

Howard K. Stancil	18,750 Votes
Clara Stancil	18,750 Votes
Henry Babb	0 Votes

16. The Respondent, Bruce Stancil, after casting 12,500 votes for each of his three nominees (totaling 37,500 votes as allowed by law), purported to cast an additional 18,750 votes against Howard Stancil and 18,750 votes against Clara Stancil.

17. There is no provision in the North Carolina Business Corporation Act providing for the casting of shareholder votes against a nominee for director, and the purported "votes" cast by the Respondent, Bruce Stancil, subsequent to the casting of his affirmative votes totaling 37,500 for his three nominees, were void and of no lawful effect.

18. Bruce Stancil, Sarah Barnes and Eva Stancil, all being Respondents herein and recipients of 12,500 votes each, failed, as to each of them, to receive a plurality of the votes cast, as required by G.S. 55–67(c), and were not lawfully elected as directors of the Respondent corporation.

344 S.E.2d at 791.

The appellate court affirmed the trial court's conclusion as to the result of the election. Do you agree with this conclusion? Does the board of directors now consist of Howard and Clara with one vacancy? What about the possible application of a statute similar to RMBCA § 8.05(e)? If a vacancy exists, can Bruce demand another meeting and at that meeting elect himself to fill that vacancy? Is there any way, at following annual meetings, he can get the situation back to where it was before the election, that is, where he and his wife filled two of the three positions on the board?

(2) If you had been Wiley L. Lane, Jr., what should you have done to preserve your client's apparently dominant position on the board of directors?

HUMPHRYS v. WINOUS CO.

Supreme Court of Ohio, 1956.
165 Ohio St. 45, 133 N.E.2d 780.

BELL, JUSTICE.

It can not be disclaimed that by reason of the stock distribution of this particular corporation a classification of the three directors into three classes containing one director each effectively divests the minority shareholders of a measure of control they formerly exercised over the corporation by electing one member of the board through the expedient of cumulative voting.

The issue herein, however, is not whether a particular result was accomplished but whether, under the statutes, such a result can legally be accomplished.

Section 1701.64, Revised Code, provides, in part, as follows:

"The articles or the code of regulations may provide for the term of office of all of the directors or, if classified upon the basis of the expiration of the terms of office of the directors, of each class thereof, provided that no term shall be fixed for a period of more than three years from the date of their election and until the election of their successors."

Section 1701.58, Revised Code, after providing that any shareholder may, upon giving 24 hours notice of his desire to do so, cumulate such voting power as he possesses and give one candidate as many votes as the number of directors multiplied by the number of his votes equals, then provides that "such right to vote cumulatively shall not be restricted or qualified by the articles or the code of regulations."

The Court of Appeals sustained the contention of appellees and held that, since Section 1701.58, Revised Code, was specific in character, it constituted a limitation upon the applicability of Section 1701.64, Revised Code, and that, since the classification by appellants, attempted under the authority of Section 1701.64, Revised Code, did restrict the right to vote cumulatively as specifically guaranteed by Section 1701.58, Revised Code, such classification was invalid. * * *

In enacting Section 1701.58, Revised Code, did the General Assembly intend, as urged by appellants, to guarantee only that the *right* to vote cumulatively shall not be restricted or qualified? Or did it intend to guarantee that the effectiveness of cumulative voting to ensure minority representation on the board of directors shall not be restricted or qualified? * * *

It is interesting to note that, as early as 1893, the organized bar of Ohio began to interest itself in the rights of minority shareholders. In an address before the annual meeting of the Ohio State Bar Association held at Put–in–Bay in July 1893, John H. Doyle, then president of the association, said:

"* * * While there is a unanimity of purpose and an accord of thought amongst [sic] the shareholders, the corporation moves smoothly, and its directors represent and carry out the wishes of such shareholders.

"But that is not always the case, and under the present law, as it has been interpreted by the Supreme Court, a bare majority can absolutely exclude the minority from all voice in its management. To illustrate:

"In a corporation represented by 100 shares of capital stock, the owners of 51 shares could manage the corporation without the voice of the remaining 49 shares being heard, and the one odd share would be the available power; the 51 shares might be made very valuable, while the 49 could be rendered valueless, and the odd share or the balance of power receive an immense value. These suggestions will show that any statute providing for minority representation in corporations would not lead to 'absurd or improbable results,' but would be marked with wisdom and a fair regard for the rights of the parties.

"The old story, so often told, of a prominent Eastern newspaper-man's reply to the question of what the shares in his company were worth, is very apt:

"'There are 51 shares,' said he, 'that are worth $250,000. There are 49 shares that are not worth a ——.'

"I think the law should be so amended as to allow the 49 shares to elect two out of the five directors or three out of seven, as the case may be.

"In other words, that the shareholders be allowed to cumulate their votes on one or more directors, as they see fit, so that all interests may be fairly represented, without destroying the right of the majority to control.

"It would result in increased confidence in the management of such concerns, prevent the freezing-out process so often resorted to, and very often prevent fraud and corruption in the management of private corporations."

At the annual meeting of the bar association on July 20, 1897, the Committee on Judicial Administration and Legal Reform submitted the following as a part of its report to the association:

"The annual address of Judge Doyle to this association in 1893 recommended the amendment of the law respecting the management of private corporations so as to secure a representation in that management to minority stockholders, in proportion to the amount of stock held by them. * * *

"Your committee is of the opinion that our laws need amendment * * *. The minority of stockholders are entitled to such opportunity of knowledge of its business and the conduct thereof as would enable them to form judgment concerning the same, and are entitled also to have such judgment and their advice expressed in the body charged with the duty of such management. This privilege, secured by law, would be effective in preventing oppressive abuse of power by the majority of stockholders, exercised for illegitimate, selfish, and fraudulent ends. We are of the opinion that the law should be so modified as to secure these rights to a minority stockholder. * * * "

If we may assume that the General Assembly was motivated by the recommendation of the bar association, it is obvious that it intended to assure minority representation on a corporate board of directors by permitting cumulative voting.

The provision for classification of directors appears for the first time in Ohio as * * * part of the General Corporation Act, effective June 9, 1927, 112 Ohio Laws, p. 32. * * *

Strangely enough, however, prior to 1955, there were only two cases which discussed the effect of classification of directors on cumulative voting. In Pittsburgh Steel Co. v. Walker (Court of Common Pleas, Allegheny County, Pennsylvania, 1944), three judges said there was doubt as to the constitutionality of the staggered system, but did not pass directly on the question. In Heeps v. Byers Co. (Court of Common Pleas, Allegheny County, Pennsylvania, 1950), one judge denied a preliminary injunction against the holding of a staggered-voting election on constitutional and other grounds. The Supreme Court of Pennsylvania, in affirming the judgment of the lower court, merely denied any right to question the granting of preliminary injunctions. Cohen v. A.M. Byers Co., 363 Pa. 618, 70 A.2d 837.

But on February 1, 1955, the Circuit Court of Cook County, Illinois, decided the case of Wolfson v. Avery. The action grew out of the much-publicized battle between Sewell Avery and Louis E. Wolfson for control of the board of directors of Montgomery Ward & Company. The Wolfson group sought a declaratory judgment that a bylaw of Montgomery Ward providing for the annual election of only one-third of the nine members of the board of directors is in violation of Section 3, Article XI of the Illinois Constitution, S.H.A., which among other things, provides for cumulative voting. Since the bylaw is specifically authorized by Section 35 of the Illinois Business Corporation Act, Illinois Revised Statutes 1953, Chapter 32, paragraph 157.35, the complaint also sought to have that portion of the statute declared unconstitutional. The Circuit Court granted the plaintiff's motion for judgment on the pleadings, declaring Section 35 of the Business Corporation Act unconstitutional.

The trial judge in the Wolfson case adopted the theory that the Constitution requires that a minority shareholder be given the right— by cumulative voting—to exercise his "maximum voting strength proportionate to his share holding." He rejected the argument that the constitutional provision merely gives minority shareholders an opportunity to have some representation on the board of directors, whether proportionate or not. 23 Law Week, 2393.

The Supreme Court of Illinois, 6 Ill.2d 78, 126 N.E.2d 701, 711, after reviewing at some length the proceedings of the constitutional convention and the publications which interpreted the constitutional provision which was ratified on July 2, 1870, concluded that "Section 35 of the Business Corporation Act, in authorizing the classification of directors, is inconsistent with the constitutional right of a stockholder to cumulate his shares through multiplying them by the 'number of directors,' and cannot be sustained."

The Illinois court, in disposing of the defendant's reliance upon the fact that a law authorizing classification was passed by the first Illinois Legislature, and that this Legislature included 13 members who had served on the Constitutional Convention, said that "that is a fact to be given some weight, but it is by no means controlling (cf. Marbury v. Madison, 1 Cranch. 137, 2 L.Ed. 60) and in this case it must yield to the evidence supplied by the constitutional debates and the contemporary accounts in the press."

The only other reported case discussing the conflict between classification and cumulative voting is the report of the decision of the Court of Appeals in the present case. See 125 N.E.2d 204. As distinguished from a conflict between a constitutional provision and a statutory provision as in the Wolfson case, we have here a conflict between two statutory provisions. * * *

That cumulative voting is generally accepted is evidenced by the facts that mandatory cumulative voting provisions are found in the Constitutions of 13 states and in the statutes of eight others, and that permissive cumulative voting is authorized in 18 states. Cumulative voting is provided for in Section 31 of the Model Business Corporation Act, drawn by the American Bar Association, and in Section 28 of the Model Business Corporation Act, proposed by the Commissioners on Uniform State Laws. Despite the seemingly obvious conflict between classification of directors and cumulative voting, provisions for staggered elections are made in approximately 33 states. See Williams, Cumulative Voting for Directors (1951), 7; Cumulative Voting and Classification of Directors, St. John's Law Review, 83, 86.

The problem will never arise in three jurisdictions because annual election of all directors is required by statute. See Section 22, Title 10, Alabama Code; Sections 805, 2201, California Corporation Code; Section 44–109, Wyoming Compiled Statutes.

Obviously, a provision in the articles or code of regulations to the effect that a shareholder may not vote cumulatively would restrict the right given by statute and would therefore be invalid in Ohio. Similarly a provision that a shareholder could vote cumulatively only if he held a certain percentage of the corporate stock would be invalid. But the same result might easily be accomplished without running afoul of the prohibition of Section 1701.58, Revised Code.

And majority shareholders have in many instances succeeded in curtailing or eliminating cumulative voting through a number of devices. In states where the right to vote cumulatively is permissive rather than mandatory, the charters of certain corporations have been amended to replace cumulative voting with straight voting. Cumulative voting may also be circumvented by removing minority-elected directors without cause. A third method employed to prevent effective use of cumulative voting is that of reducing the number of directors.

For example, suppose in a corporation having a board of nine members a minority shareholder, by cumulating his voting power, is able to elect one member of the board. But suppose, also, at the next meeting, the code of regulations is amended to reduce the directorate from nine to seven, as permitted under Section 1701.68, Revised Code. The minority shareholder, although not deprived of his *right* to vote cumulatively, has been deprived of representation on the board just as effectively as if he had not had the right. Similar examples could be given, depending on the number of shares held by the minority and the number of directors to be elected. Can it be said that the legislative intent in enacting Section 1701.58, Revised Code, was to limit Section 1701.64, Revised Code, and not limit Section 1701.68, Revised Code, and other sections of the corporation act? We do not think so.

If effect is to be given to both enactments of the General Assembly, the guaranty provided in Section 1701.58, Revised Code, must be construed as one granting a *right* that may not be restricted or qualified rather than one *ensuring* minority representation on the board of directors.

To hold otherwise would require a complete annihilation of the provision for classification because any classification would necessarily be a restriction or qualification on the effectiveness of cumulative voting, and no corporation could ever avail itself of the privilege of classification. We do not believe the General Assembly intended any such result.

Both the Ohio State Bar Association and the General Assembly recognized that, under the law of Ohio as it existed in January 1954, the action taken here by the corporation could have been accomplished. Consequently, the bar association recommended a change in the corporation law of Ohio to the effect that any class of directors could contain not less than two directors. In commenting on the proposed change, the Corporation Law Committee of the association said: "A new provision is that the number of directors in a given class shall be not less than two. This is for the purpose of meeting the objection that has been raised to the effect that under the present law the majority shareholders may fix the number of directors at three, each director to be in a separate class so that at each annual meeting only one director is to be elected. This device would prevent the minority, even though holding 49 per cent of the shares, from electing a single director."

Subsequently, Section 1701.57, Revised Code, was enacted, supplanting former Section 1701.64, Revised Code, to require that each class of directors must consist of not less than three directors each. 126 Ohio Laws, H70, effective October 11, 1955. Thus did the General Assembly obviate the possibility of a recurrence of the action taken by The Winous Company.

It can not be gainsaid that the action taken here effectively eliminated the minority shareholders from exercising any control over the corporation. But we are of the opinion that the throwing of an aura of uncertainty and confusion around the statutory provision for classification of directors is not required by the construction of the statutory provision for cumulative voting. We hold, therefore, that Section 1701.58, Revised Code, guarantees to minority shareholders only the right of cumulative voting and does not necessarily guarantee the effectiveness of the exercise of that right to elect minority representation on the board of directors. * * *

The judgment of the Court of Appeals is reversed and the judgment of the Court of Common Pleas is modified and, as modified, is affirmed.

Judgment reversed.

MATTHIAS, STEWART and TAFT, JJ., concur.

WEYGANDT, C.J., and HART, J., dissent.

WEYGANDT, CHIEF JUSTICE, dissents on the ground of the cogent reasoning of the Court of Appeals that "the right of a shareholder in an Ohio corporation to cumulate his vote has been provided by statute in this state for more than fifty years. The legislature in adopting the revision of the statute dealing with corporate organization in 1927, showed clearly that it intended to strengthen the cumulative voting provision by adding to existing law the provision that a corporation cannot restrict cumulative voting by its articles or code of regulations. And when in the same act the legislature, for the first time provides that there may be classification of directors when provided for by its code of regulations, it could not have been intended that the exercise of such right could be so used as to nullify the right of cumulative voting. When the minimum number of three directors is provided for, and their terms of office are for three years, one to be elected each year, the right to cumulative voting is, in such case, *completely nullified*"—an utterly futile result hardly contemplated by the emphatic language of the General Assembly in its attempt to *strengthen* the right. (Italics supplied.)

Notes

(1) Consider RMBCA §§ 7.28(b), (c), (d), 8.04. Under the RMBCA, cumulative voting, like preemptive rights, is an "opt in" election to be chosen by an appropriate provision in the articles of incorporation. A large number of states have an "opt out" election, and, several states still make cumulative voting mandatory on all corporations either by state constitutional provision or by statute. The number of states with mandatory cumulative voting, however, is declining. For example, in 1990 California, long the bastion of mandatory cumulative voting, made that manner of voting permissive for corporations with shares listed on a public exchange or with more than 800 shareholders of record. Cal.Gen.Corp.Law § 301.5. If a corporation has opted to grant cumulative voting under the Revised Model Act, may it thereafter amend the articles of incorporation by less than unanimous vote to delete that requirement? See RMBCA § 10.01. What rights does a minority shareholder have who objects to such an amendment? See RMBCA § 13.02(a)(4)(iv).

(2) As a practical matter, how valuable is the protection afforded by cumulative voting? In a state where cumulative voting is permissive, would you provide for such voting in the typical small, closely held corporation with, say, three or four shareholders? What if one of them has an absolute majority of shares? What about a publicly held corporation with thousands of shareholders? At the 1980 annual meeting of Exxon, a shareholder proposed that Exxon permit cumulative voting. This proposal was vigorously opposed by management on the ground that a director "elected by the cumulative votes of a particular group of shareholders might be inclined to act on the business of the corporation in accordance with the special interests of that particular group, as distinguished from the interests of shareholders as a whole." The proposal received the affirmative vote of less than 3.5 per cent of the total cast. Similar proposals have been made by small shareholders in a number of other publicly held corporations, with essentially the same result.

(3) What devices are available to minimize the impact of cumulative voting where that voting is mandatory? What about creating classes of directors consisting of one director each, such as involved in the Winous Co. case? See RMBCA § 8.06. Even a decision to classify the board of directors in a permissible way may be attacked as a breach of fiduciary duty in some circumstances if made without business justification and in the midst of a proxy campaign to elect one director. Coalition to Advocate Public Util. Responsibility, Inc. v. Engels, 364 F.Supp. 1202 (D.Minn.1973). What about removal of a director elected by minority votes? See RMBCA §§ 8.08, 8.09. What about "freezing out" the minority director by denying that director access to information, refusing to appoint him or her to any committees, and then holding "unofficial meetings" and "ramming through * * * decisions with little discussion"? It is reported that these tactics were used by a public corporation, Bunker Ramo, Inc. against a director elected by a dissident group. Wall Street Journal (March 31, 1980), p. 10, col. 2.

(4) What is the purpose of notice requirements of RMBCA § 7.28(d)?

(5) Is there any real value in the permissible staggering of the board of directors (RMBCA § 8.06)? Is its use to minimize the impact of mandatory cumulative voting a positive value? What about its use as a defensive tactic by public held corporations against unwanted cash tender offers? This has become a popular antitakeover device when combined with a limitation against removal of directors without cause. Such a board creates an obstacle to a prompt takeover by an outside group that purchases more than one-half of the outstanding shares since it will not be able to replace a majority of the board for two years.

RINGLING BROS.–BARNUM & BAILEY COMBINED SHOWS v. RINGLING

Supreme Court of Delaware, 1947.
29 Del.Ch. 610, 53 A.2d 441.

PEARSON, JUDGE.

The Court of Chancery was called upon to review an attempted election of directors at the 1946 annual stockholders meeting of the corporate defendant. The pivotal questions concern an agreement between two of the three present stockholders, and particularly the effect of this agreement with relation to the exercise of voting rights by these two stockholders. At the time of the meeting, the corporation had outstanding 1000 shares of capital stock held as follows: 315 by petitioner Edith Conway Ringling; 315 by defendant Aubrey B. Ringling Haley (individually or as executrix and legatee of a deceased husband); and 370 by defendant John Ringling North. The purpose of the meeting was to elect the entire board of seven directors. The shares could be voted cumulatively. Mrs. Ringling asserts that by virtue of the operation of an agreement between her and Mrs. Haley, the latter was bound to vote her shares for an adjournment of the meeting, or in the alternative, for a certain slate of directors. Mrs. Haley contends that she was not so bound for reason that the agreement was invalid, or at least revocable.

The two ladies entered into the agreement in 1941. It makes like provisions concerning stock of the corporate defendant and of another corporation, but in this case, we are concerned solely with the agreement as it affects the voting of stock of the corporate defendant. The agreement recites that each party was the owner "subject only to possible claims of creditors of the estates of Charles Ringling and Richard Ringling, respectively" (deceased husbands of the parties), of 300 shares of the capital stock of the defendant corporation; that in 1938 these shares had been deposited under a voting trust agreement which would terminate in 1947, or earlier, upon the elimination of certain liability of the corporation; that each party also owned 15 shares individually; that the parties had "entered into an agreement in April 1934 providing for joint action by them in matters affecting their ownership of stock and interest in" the corporate defendant; that the parties desired "to continue to act jointly in all matters relating to their stock ownership or interest in" the corporate defendant (and the other corporation). The agreement then provides as follows:

"Now, Therefore, in consideration of the mutual covenants and agreements hereinafter contained the parties hereto agree as follows:

"1. Neither party will sell any shares of stock or any voting trust certificates in either of said corporations to any other person whosoever, without first making a written offer to the other party hereto of all of the shares or voting trust certificates proposed to be sold, for the same price and upon the same terms and conditions as in such proposed sale, and allowing such other party a time of not less than 180 days from the date of such written offer within which to accept same.

"2. In exercising any voting rights to which either party may be entitled by virtue of ownership of stock or voting trust certificates held by them in either of said corporation, each party will consult and confer with the other and the parties will act jointly in exercising such voting rights in accordance with such agreement as they may reach with respect to any matter calling for the exercise of such voting rights.

"3. In the event the parties fail to agree with respect to any matter covered by paragraph 2 above, the question in disagreement shall be submitted for arbitration to Karl D. Loos, of Washington, D.C. as arbitrator and his decision thereon shall be binding upon the parties hereto. Such arbitration shall be exercised to the end of assuring for the respective corporations good management and such participation therein by the members of the Ringling family as the experience, capacity and ability of each may warrant. The parties may at any time by written agreement designate any other individual to act as arbitrator in lieu of said Loos.

"4. Each of the parties hereto will enter into and execute such voting trust agreement or agreements and such other instruments as, from time to time they may deem advisable and as they may be advised by counsel are appropriate to effectuate the purposes and objects of this agreement.

"5. This agreement shall be in effect from the date hereof and shall continue in effect for a period of ten years unless sooner terminated by mutual agreement in writing by the parties hereto.

"6. The agreement of April 1934 is hereby terminated.

"7. This agreement shall be binding upon and inure to the benefit of the heirs, executors, administrators and assigns of the parties hereto respectively."

The Mr. Loos mentioned in the agreement is an attorney and has represented both parties since 1937, and, before and after the voting trust was terminated in late 1942, advised them with respect to the exercise of their voting rights. At the annual meetings in 1943 and the two following years, the parties voted their shares in accordance with mutual understandings arrived at as a result of discussions. In each of these years, they elected five of the seven directors. Mrs. Ringling and

Mrs. Haley each had sufficient votes, independently of the other, to elect two of the seven directors. By both voting for an additional candidate, they could be sure of his election regardless of how Mr. North, the remaining stockholder, might vote.[10]

Some weeks before the 1946 meeting, they discussed with Mr. Loos the matter of voting for directors. They were in accord that Mrs. Ringling should cast sufficient votes to elect herself and her son; and that Mrs. Haley should elect herself and her husband; but they did not agree upon a fifth director. The day before the meeting, the discussions were continued, Mrs. Haley being represented by her husband since she could not be present because of illness. In a conversation with Mr. Loos, Mr. Haley indicated that he would make a motion for an adjournment of the meeting for sixty days, in order to give the ladies additional time to come to an agreement about their voting. On the morning of the meeting, however, he stated that because of something Mrs. Ringling had done, he would not consent to a postponement. Mrs. Ringling then made a demand upon Mr. Loos to act under the third paragraph of the agreement "to arbitrate the disagreement" between her and Mrs. Haley in connection with the manner in which the stock of the two ladies should be voted. At the opening of the meeting, Mr. Loos read the written demand and stated that he determined and directed that the stock of both ladies be voted for an adjournment of sixty days. Mrs. Ringling then made a motion for adjournment and voted for it. Mr. Haley, as proxy for his wife, and Mr. North voted against the motion. Mrs. Ringling (herself or through her attorney, it is immaterial which,) objected to the voting of Mrs. Haley's stock in any manner other than in accordance with Mr. Loos' direction. The chairman ruled that the stock could not be voted contrary to such direction, and declared the motion for adjournment had carried. Nevertheless, the meeting proceeded to the election of directors. Mrs. Ringling stated that she would continue in the meeting "but without prejudice to her position with respect to the voting of the stock and the fact that adjournment had not been taken." Mr. Loos directed Mrs. Ringling to cast her votes.

882 for Mrs. Ringling,

882 for her son, Robert, and

441 for a Mr. Dunn, who had been a member of the board for several years. She complied. Mr. Loos directed that Mrs. Haley's votes be cast

10. [By the Court] Each lady was entitled to cast 2205 votes (since each had the cumulative voting rights of 315 shares, and there were 7 vacancies in the directorate). The sum of the votes of both is 4410, which is sufficient to allow 882 votes for each of 5 persons. Mr. North, holding 370 shares, was entitled to cast 2590 votes, which obviously cannot be divided so as to give to more than two candidates as many as 882 votes each. It will be observed that in order for Mrs. Ringling and Mrs. Haley to be sure to elect five directors (regardless of how Mr. North might vote) they must act together in the sense that their combined votes must be divided among five different candidates and at least one of the five must be voted for by both Mrs. Ringling and Mrs. Haley.

882 for Mrs. Haley,

882 for Mr. Haley, and

441 for Mr. Dunn.

Instead of complying, Mr. Haley attempted to vote his wife's shares

1103 for Mrs. Haley, and

1102 for Mr. Haley.

Mr. North voted his shares

864 for a Mr. Woods,

863 for a Mr. Griffin, and

863 for Mr. North.

The chairman ruled that the five candidates proposed by Mr. Loos, together with Messrs. Woods and North, were elected. The Haley–North group disputed this ruling insofar as it declared the election of Mr. Dunn; and insisted that Mr. Griffin, instead, had been elected. A directors' meeting followed in which Mrs. Ringling participated after stating that she would do so "without prejudice to her position that the stockholders' meeting had been adjourned and that the directors' meeting was not properly held." Mr. Dunn and Mr. Griffin, although each was challenged by an opposing faction, attempted to join in voting as directors for different slates of officers. Soon after the meeting, Mrs. Ringling instituted this proceeding.

The Vice Chancellor determined that the agreement to vote in accordance with the direction of Mr. Loos was valid as a "stock pooling agreement" with lawful objects and purposes, and that it was not in violation of any public policy of this state. He held that where the arbitrator acts under the agreement and one party refuses to comply with his direction, "the Agreement constitutes the willing party * * * an implied agent possessing the irrevocable proxy of the recalcitrant party for the purpose of casting the particular vote". It was ordered that a new election be held before a master, with the direction that the master should recognize and give effect to the agreement if its terms were properly invoked.

Before taking up defendants' objections to the agreement, let us analyze particularly what it attempts to provide with respect to voting, including what functions and powers it attempts to repose in Mr. Loos, the "arbitrator". The agreement recites that the parties desired "to continue to act jointly in all matters relating to their stock ownership or interest in" the corporation. The parties agreed to consult and confer with each other in exercising their voting rights and to act jointly—that is, concertedly; unitedly; towards unified courses of action—in accordance with such agreement as they might reach. Thus, so long as the parties agree for whom or for what their shares shall be voted, the agreement provides no function for the arbitrator. His role is limited to situations where the parties fail to agree upon a course of action. In such cases, the agreement directs that "the question in disagreement shall be submitted for arbitration" to Mr. Loos "as arbitrator and his decision thereon shall be binding upon the parties". These provisions are designed to operate in aid of what appears to be a primary purpose of the parties, "to act jointly" in exercising their voting rights, by providing a means for fixing a course of action whenever they themselves might reach a stalemate.

Should the agreement be interpreted as attempting to empower the arbitrator to carry his directions into effect? Certainly there is no express delegation or grant of power to do so, either by authorizing him to vote the shares or to compel either party to vote them in accordance with his directions. The agreement expresses no other function of the arbitrator than that of deciding questions in disagreement which prevent the effectuation of the purpose "to act jointly". The power to enforce a decision does not seem a necessary or usual incident of such a function. Mr. Loos is not a party to the agreement. It does not contemplate the transfer of any shares or interest in shares to him, or that he should undertake any duties which the parties might compel him to perform. They provided that they might designate any other individual to act instead of Mr. Loos. The agreement does not attempt to make the arbitrator a trustee of an express trust. What the arbitrator is to do is for the benefit of the parties, not for his own benefit. Whether the parties accept or reject his decision is no concern of his, so far as the agreement or the surrounding circumstances reveal. We think the parties sought to bind each other, but to be bound only to each other, and not to empower the arbitrator to enforce decisions he might make.

From this conclusion, it follows necessarily that no decision of the arbitrator could ever be enforced if both parties to the agreement were unwilling that it be enforced, for the obvious reason that there would be no one to enforce it. Under the agreement, something more is required after the arbitrator has given his decision in order that it should become compulsory: at least one of the parties must determine that such decision shall be carried into effect. Thus, any "control" of the voting of the shares, which is reposed in the arbitrator, is substantially limited in action under the agreement in that it is subject to the overriding power of the parties themselves.

The agreement does not describe the undertaking of each party with respect to a decision of the arbitrator other than to provide that it "shall be binding upon the parties". It seems to us that this language, considered with relation to its context and the situations to which it is applicable, means that each party promised the other to exercise her own voting rights in accordance with the arbitrator's decision. The agreement is silent about any exercise of the voting rights of one party by the other. The language with reference to situations where the parties arrive at an understanding as to voting plainly suggests "action" by each, and "exercising" voting rights by each, rather than by one for the other. There is no intimation that this method should be different where the arbitrator's decision is to be carried into effect. Assuming that a power in each party to exercise the voting rights of the other might be a relatively more effective or convenient means of enforcing a decision of the arbitrator than would be available without the power, this would not justify implying a delegation of the power in the absence of some indication that the parties bargained for that means. The method of voting actually employed by the parties tends to show that they did not construe the agreement as creating powers to vote each other's shares; for at meetings prior to 1946 each party apparently exercised her own voting rights, and at the 1946 meeting, Mrs. Ringling, who wished to enforce the agreement, did not attempt to cast a ballot in exercise of any voting rights of Mrs. Haley. We do not find enough in the agreement or in the circumstances to justify a construction that either party was empowered to exercise voting rights of the other.

Having examined what the parties sought to provide by the agreement, we come now to defendants' contention that the voting provisions are illegal and revocable. They say that the courts of this state have definitely established the doctrine "that there can be no agreement, or any device whatsoever, by which the voting power of stock of a Delaware corporation may be irrevocably separated from the ownership of the stock, except by an agreement which complies with Section 18" of the Corporation Law, Rev.Code 1935, § 2050, and except by a proxy coupled with an interest. They rely on Perry v. Missouri–Kansas P.L. Co., 22 Del.Ch. 33, 191 A. 823; In re Public Industrials Corporation, 19 Del.Ch. 398, reported as In re Chilson, 168 A. 82; Aldridge v. Franco Wyoming Oil Co., 24 Del.Ch. 126, 7 A.2d 753, affirmed in 24 Del.Ch. 349, 14 A.2d 380; Belle Isle Corporation v. Corcoran, Del.Sup., 49 A.2d 1; and contend that the doctrine is derived from Section 18 itself, Rev. Code of Del.1935, § 2050. The statute reads, in part, as follows:

> "Sec. 18. Voting Trusts: * * *—One or more stockholders may by agreement in writing deposit capital stock of an original issue with or transfer capital stock to any person or persons, or corporation or corporations authorized to act as trustee, for the purpose of vesting in said person or persons, corporation or corporations, who may be designated Voting Trustee or Voting Trustees, the right to vote thereon for any period of time determined by such agreement, not exceeding ten years, upon the terms and conditions stated in such agreement. Such agreement may contain any other lawful provisions not inconsistent with said purpose. * * * Said Voting Trustees may vote upon the stock so issued or transferred during the period in such agreement specified; stock standing in the names of such Voting Trustees may be voted either in person or by proxy, and in voting said stock, such Voting Trustees shall incur no responsibility as stockholder, trustee or otherwise, except for their own individual malfeasance." [11]

11. [By the Court] Omitted portions of the section provide requirements for the filing of a copy of the agreement in the principal Delaware office of the corporation for the issuance of certificates of stock to the voting trustees, for the voting of

In our view, neither the cases nor the statute sustain the rule for which the defendants contend. Their sweeping formulation would impugn well-recognized means by which a shareholder may effectively confer his voting rights upon others while retaining various other rights. For example, defendants' rule would apparently not permit holders of voting stock to confer upon stockholders of another class, by the device of an amendment of the certificate of incorporation, the exclusive right to vote during periods when dividends are not paid on stock of the latter class. The broad prohibitory meaning which defendants find in Section 18 seems inconsistent with their concession that proxies coupled with an interest may be irrevocable, for the statute contains nothing about such proxies. The statute authorizes, among other things, the deposit or transfer of stock in trust for a specified purpose, namely, "vesting" in the transferee "the right to vote thereon" for a limited period; and prescribes numerous requirements in this connection. Accordingly, it seems reasonable to infer that to establish the relationship and accomplish the purpose which the statute authorizes, its requirements must be complied with. But the statute does not purport to deal with agreements whereby shareholders attempt to bind each other as to how they shall vote their shares. Various forms of such pooling agreements, as they are sometimes called, have been held valid and have been distinguished from voting trusts. We think the particular agreement before us does not violate Section 18 or constitute an attempted evasion of its requirements, and is not illegal for any other reason. Generally speaking, a shareholder may exercise wide liberality of judgment in the matter of voting, and it is not objectionable, that his motives may be for personal profit, or determined by whims or caprice, so long as he violates no duty owed his fellow shareholders. Heil v. Standard G. & E. Co., 17 Del.Ch. 214, 151 A. 303. The ownership of voting stock imposes no legal duty to vote at all. A group of shareholders may, without impropriety, vote their respective shares so as to obtain advantages of concerted action. They may lawfully contract with each other to vote in the future in such way as they, or a majority of their group, from time to time determine. (See authorities listed above.) Reasonable provisions for cases of failure of the group to reach a determination because of an even division in their ranks seem unobjectionable. The provision here for submission to the arbitrator is plainly designed as a deadlock-breaking measure, and the arbitrator's decision cannot be enforced unless at least one of the parties (entitled to cast one-half of their combined votes) is willing that it be enforced. We find the provision reasonable. It does not appear that the agreement enables the parties to take any unlawful advantage of the outside shareholder, or of any other person. It offends no rule of law or public policy of this state of which we are aware.

Legal consideration for the promises of each party is supplied by the mutual promises of the other party. The undertaking to vote in

stock where there is more than one voting trustee, and for the extension of the agreement for additional periods, not exceeding ten years each.

accordance with the arbitrator's decision is a valid contract. The good faith of the arbitrator's action has not been challenged and, indeed, the record indicates that no such challenge could be supported. Accordingly, the failure of Mrs. Haley to exercise her voting rights in accordance with his decision was a breach of her contract. It is no extenuation of the breach that her votes were cast for two of the three candidates directed by the arbitrator. His directions to her were part of a single plan or course of action for the voting of the shares of both parties to the agreement, calculated to utilize an advantage of joint action by them which would bring about the election of an additional director. The actual voting of Mrs. Haley's shares frustrates that plan to such an extent that it should not be treated as a partial performance of her contract.

Throughout their argument, defendants make much of the fact that all votes cast at the meeting were by the registered shareholders. The Court of Chancery may, in a review of an election, reject votes of a registered shareholder where his voting of them is found to be in violation of rights of another person. Compare: In re Giant Portland Cement Co., Del.Ch., 21 A.2d 697. It seems to us that upon the application of Mrs. Ringling, the injured party, the votes representing Mrs. Haley's shares should not be counted. Since no infirmity in Mr. North's voting has been demonstrated, his right to recognition of what he did at the meeting should be considered in granting any relief to Mrs. Ringling; for her rights arose under a contract to which Mr. North was not a party. With this in mind, we have concluded that the election should not be declared invalid, but that effect should be given to a rejection of the votes representing Mrs. Haley's shares. No other relief seems appropriate in this proceeding. Mr. North's vote against the motion for adjournment was sufficient to defeat it. With respect to the election of directors, the return of the inspectors should be corrected to show a rejection of Mrs. Haley's votes, and to declare the election of the six persons for whom Mr. North and Mrs. Ringling voted.

This leaves one vacancy in the directorate. The question of what to do about such a vacancy was not considered by the court below and has not been argued here. For this reason, and because an election of directors at the 1947 annual meeting (which presumably will be held in the near future) may make a determination of the question unimportant, we shall not decide it on this appeal. If a decision of the point appears important to the parties, any of them may apply to raise it in the Court of Chancery, after the mandate of this court is received there.

An order should be entered, directing a modification of the order of the Court of Chancery in accordance with this opinion.

Notes

(1) Does the remedy adopted by the court uphold the purpose of the agreement? What is the net effect of depriving Mrs. Haley of the right to vote?

(2) Is the decision upholding the Agreement consistent with the court's action in McQuade v. Stoneham, p. 421, supra?

(3) The Chancellor held that "the Agreement constitutes the willing party to the Agreement an implied agent possessing the irrevocable proxy of the recalcitrant party for the purpose of casting the particular vote." Do you see any practical problem this might create?

(4) Consider RMBCA § 7.31. The Official Comment states that section 7.31(b) "avoids the result reached in the Ringling case." Does it?

McKINNEY'S N.Y.BUS.CORP.LAW

§ 609. Proxies—

(a) Every shareholder entitled to vote at a meeting of shareholders or to express consent or dissent without a meeting may authorize another person or persons to act for him by proxy.

(b) Every proxy must be signed by the shareholder or his attorney-in-fact. No proxy shall be valid after the expiration of eleven months from the date thereof unless otherwise provided in the proxy. Every proxy shall be revocable at the pleasure of the shareholder executing it, except as otherwise provided in this section.

(c) The authority of the holder of a proxy to act shall not be revoked by the incompetence or death of the shareholder who executed the proxy unless, before the authority is exercised, written notice of an adjudication of such incompetence or of such death is received by the corporate officer responsible for maintaining the list of shareholders.

(d) Except when other provision shall have been made by written agreement between the parties, the record holder of shares which he holds as pledgee or otherwise as security or which belong to another, shall issue to the pledgor or to such owner of such shares, upon demand therefor and payment of necessary expenses thereof, a proxy to vote or take other action thereon.

(e) A shareholder shall not sell his vote or issue a proxy to vote to any person for any sum of money or anything of value, except as authorized in this section and section 620 (Agreements as to voting; provision in certificate of incorporation as to control of directors).

(f) A proxy which is entitled "irrevocable proxy" and which states that it is irrevocable, is irrevocable when it is held by any of the following or a nominee of any of the following:

(1) A pledgee;

(2) A person who has purchased or agreed to purchase the shares;

(3) A creditor or creditors of the corporation who extend or continue credit to the corporation in consideration of the proxy if the proxy states that it was given in consideration of such extension or continuation of credit, the amount thereof, and the name of the person extending or continuing credit;

(4) A person who has contracted to perform services as an officer of the corporation, if a proxy is required by the contract of employment, if the proxy states that it was given in consideration of such contract of employment, the name of the employee and the period of employment contracted for;

(5) A person designated by or under an agreement under paragraph (a) of section 620.

(g) Notwithstanding a provision in a proxy, stating that it is irrevocable, the proxy becomes revocable after the pledge is redeemed or the debt of the corporation is paid, or the period of employment provided for in the contract of employment has terminated, or the agreement under paragraph (a) of section 620 has terminated; and in a case provided for in subparagraphs (f)(3) or (4), becomes revocable three years after the date of the proxy or at the end of the period, if any, specified therein, whichever period is less, unless the period of irrevocability is renewed from time to time by the execution of a new irrevocable proxy as provided in this section. This paragraph does not affect the duration of a proxy under paragraph (b).

(h) A proxy may be revoked, notwithstanding a provision making it irrevocable, by a purchaser of shares without knowledge of the existence of the provision unless the existence of the proxy and its irrevocability is noted conspicuously on the face or back of the certificate representing such shares.

N.Y. § 620. Agreements as to Voting; Provision in Certificate of Incorporation as to Control of Directors

(a) An agreement between two or more shareholders, if in writing and signed by the parties thereto, may provide that in exercising any voting rights, the shares held by them shall be voted as therein provided, or as they may agree, or as determined in accordance with a procedure agreed upon by them. * * *

Notes

(1) A proxy, like other grants of authority to an agent, is usually revocable whether or not it is stated to be irrevocable. Several situations exist, however, where the common law courts felt it necessary to recognize irrevocable proxies. These situations were usually analyzed as those involving a "proxy coupled with an interest," a notion roughly analogous to a "power coupled with an interest" in the law of agency. The leading case is Hunt v. Rousmanier's Adm'rs, 21 U.S. (8 Wheat.) 174, 5 L.Ed. 589 (1823). Of course, the phrase "proxy coupled with an interest" does not help to decide anything, and at common law the whole area was one of confusion. See Thomas, Irrevocable Proxies, 43 Tex.L.Rev. 733 (1965). In New York, the vagueness of this test is eliminated by § 609(f), which covers the most common kinds of "interests" that a proxy may be "coupled" with, thereby becoming irrevocable. Do you see any underlying principle or theory by which these types of interests were selected? Do you see any risk or

danger in compiling such a list and making it exclusive? Compare the language of RMBCA § 7.22(d) with section 609 of the New York statute in this regard.

(2) Consider § 609(e) of the New York statute, a provision which has no analogue in the RMBCA. Does this mean that all sales of votes are per se invalid no matter what the circumstances? In Schreiber v. Carney, 447 A.2d 17 (Del.Ch.1982) the court was faced with a situation where a major shareholder committed itself to withdraw its opposition to a merger in exchange for a favorable loan from a participant in the merger. There was full disclosure of the arrangement to the independent shareholders, who overwhelmingly approved the proposed transaction. The court stated:

> It is clear that the loan constituted vote-buying as that term has been defined by the courts. Vote-buying, despite its negative connotation, is simply a voting agreement supported by consideration personal to the stockholder, whereby the stockholder divorces his discretionary voting power and votes as directed by the offeror. The record clearly indicates that Texas International purchased or "removed" the obstacle of Jet Capital's opposition. Indeed, this is tacitly conceded by the defendants. However, defendants contend that the analysis of the transaction should not end here because the legality of vote-buying depends on whether its object or purpose is to defraud or in some manner disenfranchise the other stockholders. Defendants contend that because the loan did not defraud or disfranchise any group of shareholders, but rather enfranchised the other shareholders by giving them a determinative vote in the proposed merger, it is not illegal *per se.* Defendants, in effect, contend that vote-buying is not void *per se* because the end justified the means. * * *

> The present case presents a peculiar factual setting in that the proposed vote-buying consideration was conditional upon the approval of a majority of the disinterested stockholders after a full disclosure to them of all pertinent facts and was purportedly for the best interests of all Texas International stockholders. It is therefore necessary to do more than merely consider the fact that Jet Capital saw fit to vote for the transaction after a loan was made to it by Texas International. As stated in Oceanic Exploration Co. v. Grynberg, Del.Supr., 428 A.2d 1 (1981), a case involving an analogous situation, to do otherwise would be tantamount to "[d]eciding the case on * * * an abstraction divorced from the facts of the case and the intent of the law." 428 A.2d 5. * * *

> There are essentially two principles which appear in [the traditional vote-buying] cases. The first is that vote-buying is illegal *per se* if its object or purpose is to defraud or disenfranchise the other stockholders. A fraudulent purpose is as defined at common law, as a deceit which operates prejudicially upon the property rights of another.

> The second principle which appears in these old cases is that vote-buying is illegal *per se* as a matter of public policy, the reason being that each stockholder should be entitled to rely upon the independent judgment of his fellow stockholders. Thus, the underlying basis for this latter principle is again fraud but as viewed from a sense of duty

owed by all stockholders to one another. The apparent rationale is that by requiring each stockholder to exercise his individual judgment as to all matters presented, "[t]he security of the small stockholders is found in the natural disposition of each stockholder to promote the best interests of all, in order to promote his individual interests." Cone v. Russell, 48 N.J.Eq. 208, 21 A. 847, 849 (1891). In essence, while self interest motivates a stockholder's vote, theoretically, it is also advancing the interests of the other stockholders. Thus, any agreement entered into for personal gain, whereby a stockholder separates his voting right from his property right was considered a fraud upon this community of interests. * * *

An automatic application of this rationale to the facts in the present case, however, would be to ignore an essential element of the transaction. The agreement in question was entered into primarily to further the interests of Texas International's other shareholders. Indeed, the shareholders, after reviewing a detailed proxy statement, voted overwhelmingly in favor of the loan agreement. Thus, the underlying rationale for the argument that vote-buying is illegal *per se,* as a matter of public policy, ceases to exist when measured against the undisputed reason for the transaction.

Moreover, the rationale that vote-buying is, as a matter of public policy, illegal *per se* is founded upon considerations of policy which are now outmoded as a necessary result of an evolving corporate environment. According to 5 Fletcher *Cyclopedia Corporation* (Perm.Ed.) § 2066:

> "The theory that each stockholder is entitled to the personal judgment of each other stockholder expressed in his vote, and that any agreement among stockholders frustrating it was invalid, is obsolete because it is both impracticable and impossible of application to modern corporations with many widely scattered stockholders, and the courts have gradually abandoned it." * * *

This is not to say, however, that vote-buying accomplished for some laudable purpose is automatically free from challenge. Because vote-buying is so easily susceptible of abuse it must be viewed as a voidable transaction subject to a test for intrinsic fairness.

447 A.2d at 23–26. The court refused to grant summary judgment invalidating the transaction on the ground that it constituted vote-buying.

(3) Del.Gen.Corp.Law § 228 permits action by shareholders without a meeting if a consent in writing, setting forth the action taken "shall be signed by the holders of outstanding stock having not less than the minimum number of votes that would be necessary to authorize or take such action at a meeting at which all shares entitled to vote thereon were present and voted." Contrast RMBCA § 7.04. The Delaware statute allows decisions by majority action to be effected in publicly held corporations without holding a meeting. In a publicly held corporation, unanimity as a practical matter is of course impossible to attain; as a result the RMBCA provision can only be used by corporations with relatively few shareholders. Not so § 228 of the Delaware statute. Indeed, the power of shareholders to act by majority consent without a meeting is a potentially

fearsome weapon in the hands of aggressors in contested take-over bids. Through this device, an aggressor who is able to obtain a majority of the outstanding voting shares may act immediately to replace the board of directors, oust incumbent management, amend bylaws, and defuse anti-takeover defenses. As noted by the Delaware Supreme Court, the "broad use [of § 228] in takeover battles, which we now observe, was not contemplated" in 1967 when this section was added to the Delaware General Corporation Law. Allen v. Prime Computer, Inc., 540 A.2d 417, 419 (Del. 1988). But is not such a provision simply basic shareholder democracy in action? If a majority of the shareholders desire to do X, why should they have to wait until a meeting to do so? Is there an advantage in having a discussion at a meeting as a prerequisite to action? On the other hand, how realistic is that argument when the corporation is publicly held and virtually all consents are signed long before the meeting?

(4) Once the powerful force of the majority consent provision was recognized, corporations quickly attempted to defuse that aggressive weapon. In Datapoint Corp. v. Plaza Securities Co., 496 A.2d 1031 (Del.1985), the Delaware Supreme Court held that a corporation could not impose procedural restrictions on § 228 by bylaw [12] that significantly delayed the effective date of an action taken by majority consent under that section. The court nevertheless recognized that consummation of shareholder action by consent might be deferred "until a ministerial-type review has been performed." 496 A.2d at 1036. In Allen v. Prime Computer, supra, the court held that a mandatory 20 day delay, ostensibly to enable the corporation to determine whether the consents were lawfully obtained, was more than "ministerial-type" review and was invalid.

(5) Section 213(b) of the Delaware General Corporation Law provides that the "record date for determining shareholders entitled to express consent to corporate action in writing without a meeting * * * shall be the first day on which a signed written consent is delivered to the corporation." Why is this provision necessary? What if notice that consents are being solicited is received by the corporation but no actual written consent has been received; may the board of directors establish a record date for that purpose, say, 45 days later? See Empire of Carolina, Inc. v. Deltona Corp., 514 A.2d 1091 (Del.1985).

(6) Should consents be subject to the same rules of revocability as an ordinary proxy? Or should consents be deemed to be "self executing" so that once a majority has executed consents, the corporation has irrevocably acted? Or should they be analogized to voting agreements which are not revocable because they constitute contracts? In Calumet Indus., Inc. v. MacClure, 464 F.Supp. 19 (N.D.Ill.1978) the court accepted the proxy analogy, a view that was also accepted in dictum in Allen v. Prime Computer, Inc., supra, at 420. See also Pabst Brewing Co. v. Jacobs, 549 F.Supp. 1068 (D.Del.1982). Accepting that result, how long should a consent remain effective? In 1987, the Delaware legislature amended § 228 by adding a new subsection (c) that requires all consents to be dated

12. [By the Editor] Section 228 permits the articles of incorporation to limit or qualify the effect of that section. Such an amendment, however, requires action by the shareholders while the bylaw amendment effected in *Datapoint* was implemented by the directors acting alone.

and provides that consents are effective only if they are dated within sixty days after the earliest dated consent is delivered to the corporation.

BROWN v. McLANAHAN

United States Court of Appeals, Fourth Circuit, 1945.
148 F.2d 703.

Before PARKER, SOPER, and DOBIE, CIRCUIT JUDGES.

DOBIE, CIRCUIT JUDGE.

This appeal from an order granting a motion to dismiss, involves the equitable rights attaching to certain voting trust certificates representing shares of preferred stock of the Baltimore Transit Company (hereinafter called the Company).

The appellant, Dorothy K. Brown (hereinafter referred to as plaintiff), as the holder of voting trust certificates representing 500 shares of the preferred stock of the Company, brought a class action against the voting trustees, the directors of the Company, the Company itself, the indenture trustee for the holders of the Company's debentures, and the debenture holders as a class (herein collectively referred to as defendants), seeking to set aside as unlawful an amendment of the Company's charter which purports to vest voting rights in the debenture holders. On oral argument before this Court, it was stated that the holders of 45,000 shares of preferred stock have indicated their approval of this suit.

The securities involved in this litigation were issued under a plan of reorganization of the United Railways and Electric Company of Baltimore, and The Maryland Electric Railways Company and Subsidiary Companies, under Section 77B of the Bankruptcy Act, 11 U.S.C.A. § 207. The plan was approved by the United States District Court for the District of Maryland. In re United Railways & Electric Co. of Baltimore's Reorganization, 11 F.Supp. 717.

That part of the reorganization plan relevant to the question before us may be briefly summarized.

The plan provided for the issuance of three types of securities. Debentures in the amount of $22,083,381 and 233,427 shares of preferred stock were issued to the holders of all first lien bonds on the basis of $500 principal amount of debentures, and five shares of preferred stock, par value $100 per share for each $1,000 principal amount of the bonds; 169,112 shares of new common stock, without par value, were issued to the old common stockholders and to unsecured creditors.

Under the plan of reorganization, voting rights were vested exclusively in the preferred and common stock. Each share of preferred entitled the holder to one vote on all corporate matters (except that the power to elect one director was exclusively vested in the common stock) and further, so long as any six months' installment of dividends on the preferred remained in arrears, the holders of the preferred stock held the *exclusive right* to vote for the election of all but one director. Three shares of common stock entitled the holder to one vote.

The plan also provided for the establishment of a voting trust of all the preferred and common stock of the reorganized company for a period of ten years, the maximum period permitted by Maryland law. In accordance with this provision, all the stock was issued to eight voting trustees under a voting trust agreement which was to terminate on July 1, 1945. The trustees in turn issued voting trust certificates to those entitled to distribution under the plan. Under the plan, the voting rights were to revert, on termination of the trust, to the certificate holders in proportion to the number of shares represented.

No dividends have ever been paid on the preferred stock, and pursuant to the charter provision, at all times since dividends have been in arrears, the exclusive right to elect all but one director has been vested in the preferred stock.

The eight voting trustees are also a majority of the directors of the Company, elected as such by their own vote as trustees. On June 21, 1944, *without notice of any kind to the certificate holders,* the directors passed a resolution recommending, and the voting trustees as stockholders voted to adopt, an amendment to the Company's charter.

Article VII of the Voting Trust Agreement, by authority of which the trustees purportedly acted, provides in part as follows:

"(1) Until the termination of the trusts of this instrument the entire right to vote upon or with respect to all shares of Preferred and/or Common Stock deposited, or at any time held hereunder, and the right to otherwise authorize, approve or oppose on behalf of said shares of stock any corporate action of The Baltimore Transit Company shall be vested exclusively in said Trustees; without limiting the generality or scope of the foregoing provisions such rights shall include the right to vote or act with respect to any amendment of the certificate of incorporation of the Company, the increase, reduction, classification, reclassification of its capital stock, change in the par value, preference and restrictions and qualifications of all shares, the creation of any debts or liens, any amendment to the By-Laws, the election or removal of directors, the acceptance of stock in payment of dividends as well as every other right of an absolute owner of said shares, * * *"

Briefly, the amendment effected several changes in voting rights. It eliminated the arrearage clause which had provided for exclusive voting rights in the preferred stock. It also granted voting rights to the holders of debentures, one vote for each $100 principal amount of the debentures, thus creating approximately 221,000 new votes eligible to be cast in all corporate matters. And, further, as of the date of termination of the voting trust agreement on July 1, 1945, the common stockholders would be deprived of their exclusive right to elect one director.

These facts are all substantially set forth in plaintiff's complaint. The complaint alleges, and for purposes of the motion to dismiss these allegations must be accepted as true, that the creation of 221,000 new votes in the debentures will dilute the voting power of the stock; that the amendment will deprive the voting trust certificate holders of their right to control the management of the Company, and the election of its directors after the expiration of the voting trust; that these voting trustees are holders of substantial amounts of debentures, either in their own right, or as officers of various banks.

Plaintiff contends that the action of the voting trustees in adopting the amendment was a breach of the fiduciary duty owed to the certificate holders and seeks fourfold relief that: (1) The amendment of June 21, 1944, be declared null and void; (2) the voting trustees be removed; (3) the voting trust be terminated; and (4) damages be allowed in the alternative.

The crux of the complaint is that the voting trustees, faced with the fact that the voting trust would shortly expire and that they would no longer be able to control the corporation, proceeded to amend its charter so that they would be able to hold on to the control by giving voting rights to the debentures (thereby enhancing the value of these debentures) which were largely owned or controlled by them or by corporations in which they were interested and to take away from the preferred stock the power of control which resided in it when dividends were in arrears. * * *

Plaintiff contends that such action on the part of the trustees was invalid for three reasons: (1) Because it was beyond the powers vested in the trustees to diminish the voting power, which they held in trust for the holders of preferred stock as well as for other stockholders and debenture holders, so that upon the termination of the trust they would not be able to return it to those from whom they had received it in the same condition in which it was received; (2) because it was an abuse of trust to use the voting power which the trustees held in trust for the benefit of preferred stockholders as well as of the debenture holders to the advantage of the latter and the detriment of the former; and (3) that it was an abuse of trust to use the voting power for their own benefit and the benefit of corporations in which they were interested and to the detriment of preferred stockholders who were beneficiaries of the trust. We think the action of the trustees was invalid for all three reasons. As to the third reason, it could well be that the evidence at the trial may show the facts to be different from the facts as alleged. There seems to be no dispute as to the facts to which the first and second reasons apply.

As to the first and second reasons, we think it perfectly clear that it was not intended by the voting trust agreement to vest the trustees with power either to impair the voting power of the preferred stock which they held in trust or to use the power for the benefit of the debenture holders and to the detriment of the holders of preferred stock. It is true that the power to amend the charter for proper purposes was conferred upon them; but at the time of the creation of

the voting trust it was not permissible under the law to vest voting power in the debenture holders. An amendment of the law made it legal to do this; but it could not have been intended at the time of the creation of the voting trust that the trustees should exercise the voting power in a way which the law did not then recognize and which would result in taking from the holders of stock a part of the very power which they had conferred upon the trustees to be held in trust for their benefit. It is elementary that a trustee may not exercise powers granted in a way that is detrimental to the cestuis que trustent; nor may one who is trustee for different classes favor one class at the expense of another. Such an exercise of power is in derogation of the trust and may not be upheld, even though the thing done be within the scope of powers granted to the trustees in general terms. It is well settled that the depositaries of the power to vote stock are trustees in the equitable sense, Henry L. Doherty & Co. v. Rice, C.C., 186 F. 204, 214, and a voting trust is a trust in the accepted equitable view.
* * *

Defendants strongly urge that the real beneficiaries here and now are the debenture holders and not the certificate holders. Such cases as Mackin v. Nicollet Hotel, 8 Cir., 25 F.2d 783, and Clark v. Foster, 98 Wash. 241, 167 P. 908, are cited for the proposition that it is the existence of a voting trust, in many cases restricting the powers of the stockholder, that attracts lending by bondholders. Assuming the correctness of this contention, we still find no such situation here. This plan of reorganization was an attempt to salvage utility companies sinking in the quagmire of bankruptcy. These debenture holders accepted, in lieu of their old obligations, two kinds of property, ownership of the company and a creditor's lien. Ownership control, for purposes of judicious management, was placed in the hands of trustees. When the debenture holders sold their ultimate rights to stock ownership with its attendant control of the Company's affairs, they retained only their creditor's lien. We are not at liberty here to distort the established rules of property and to find that by some process of corporate alchemy the legal ownership of the Company has been transmuted into evidence of debt.

The sale of the voting trust certificates by the original holders vested all equitable rights in their transferees and we cannot say that one might sell the equitable rights in preferred stock to a bona fide purchaser, and subsequently by indirection, impair or destroy the inherent equitable property in those certificates, to the benefit of the original seller. Meinhard v. Salmon, 249 N.Y. 458, 464, 164 N.E. 545, 62 A.L.R. 1. * * *

We are of the opinion, and so hold, that the action taken by these trustees was beyond the limit of their authority. The motion to dismiss should therefore have been denied.

The judgment of the District Court will be reversed and the cause remanded for further proceedings in accordance with the views herein expressed. The amendment to the charter of June 21, 1944 should be declared void, but what further relief should be granted upon the complaint is a matter resting in the sound discretion of the District Court.

Reversed and remanded.

Notes

(1) Consider RMBCA § 7.30.

(2) Brown v. McLanahan involves the use of a voting trust in a newly reorganized corporation where the old debenture holders and others in control of the reorganized corporation presumably have no prior management experience. Could a pooling agreement have worked in that situation? What other situations dictate the use of a voting trust rather than the more informal pooling agreement?

(a) A voting trust may be used, of course, as a control device. For example, the oldest child of the sole shareholder of a business who has recently died leaving several heirs may wish to try to run the business for a period of time free of sibling rivalry or criticism. The other children may be willing to give such a person an opportunity to try, and may place their shares in a voting trust for a temporary period. Of course, the sole shareholder before his death may create a voting trust in order to effectuate exactly the same purpose.

(b) Creditors may insist that controlling shares be placed in a voting trust as a condition to the extension of credit. The most spectacular illustration of this was the voting trust in which creditors of Trans World Airlines required Howard Hughes to place his 75 per cent of TWA stock as a condition to making loans of over $80 million to finance the purchase of jumbo jets. After the trust was created, Hughes had no voice in TWA management, and that corporation brought suit against Hughes Tool Company and Hughes individually for damages under the antitrust laws for conduct occurring prior to the voting trust. Who was the *cestui* of that voting trust under Brown v. McLanahan? Hughes later agreed to sell the shares of TWA in the voting trust, and this sale took place when TWA was near its historic high in price. Mr. Hughes received a check for $546,549,771 from this sale. See McDonald, Howard Hughes's Biggest Surprise, Fortune, July 1, 1966 at 119–120. Despite the sale, the antitrust suit continued its tortured path. Major stopping points include Trans World Airlines, Inc. v. Hughes, 332 F.2d 602 (2d Cir.1964), certiorari dismissed as improvidently granted 380 U.S. 248, 85 S.Ct. 934, 13 L.Ed.2d 817 (1965), upholding the entry of a default judgment for the refusal of Hughes Tool Co. to submit to discovery and, particularly, the refusal of Howard Hughes to submit to a deposition, and Trans World Airlines, Inc. v. Hughes, 449 F.2d 51 (2d Cir.1971) affirming the entry of a judgment for $137,611,435.95 and the ultimate reversal of the case by the United States Supreme Court on a ground that had been repeatedly argued but never accepted during approximately 10 years of litigation. Hughes Tool Co. v. Trans World Airlines, Inc., 409 U.S. 363, 93 S.Ct. 647, 34 L.Ed.2d 577 (1973), rehearing denied 410 U.S. 975, 93 S.Ct. 1435, 35 L.Ed.2d 707 (1973).

(c) Regulatory agencies may insist that voting control of a regulated corporation be placed in a voting trust as a condition for permitting private parties to acquire the regulated corporation, or, more commonly, the parent corporation of a regulated corporation when the corporation is a relatively small portion of the parent's business. For example, section 5 of the Interstate Commerce Act, 49 U.S.C.A. § 11343(a), provides that certain acquisitions of common carriers may only be carried out with the approval and authorization of the ICC. In 1979, the ICC adopted "Guidelines for the Proper Use of Voting Trusts" which provide:

> In order to avoid an unlawful control violation, the independent voting trust should be established before a controlling block of voting securities is purchased. * * *

> The trust should remain in effect until certain events, specified in the trust occur. For example, the trust might remain in effect until (1) all the deposited stock is sold to a person not affiliated with the settlor or (2) the trustee receives [an ICC] decision authorizing the settlor to acquire control of the carrier or authorizing the release of the securities for any reason.

49 C.F.R. §§ 1013.1(a), 1013.2(b). The establishment of a trust pursuant to these guidelines permits the transaction to proceed immediately even though ICC approval that may take several months has not been obtained. For a recent use of the voting trust in this connection, see Chicago West Pullman Corporation and Chicago West Pullman Transportation Corporation, 1989 ICC Lexis 41 (1989). The Federal Communications Commission follows a somewhat similar practice with respect to transfers of holders of radio or television licenses. Some state insurance commissions permit transfers of control of regulated insurance companies if the shares are placed in an irrevocable voting trust with acceptable trustees.

(3) The early attitude of courts to voting trusts was unfavorable, and mistrust may still continue to some extent in some states. The Securities and Exchange Commission has historically opposed the use of voting trusts, and the New York Stock Exchange refuses to list voting stock where there exists "a voting trust, irrevocable proxy, or any similar arrangement to which the company or any of its officers or directors is a party, either directly or indirectly." Compare the comment of Mr. Justice Douglas (in a non-judicial context) that a voting trust is "little more than a vehicle for corporate kidnapping." W. Douglas, Democracy and Finance, p. 43 (1940). On the other hand, there has been some recognition that a voting trust should be viewed as simply another control mechanism that may in certain situations be the subject of abuse but generally is no more subject to criticism than other control devices. This perspective is most clearly set forth in Oceanic Exploration Co. v. Grynberg, 428 A.2d 1, 7–8 (Del.1981):

> It is important to recognize that there has been a significant change from the days of our original 1925 statute. Voting trusts were viewed with "disfavor" or "looked upon with indulgence" by the courts. Other contractual arrangements interfering with stock ownership, such as irrevocable proxies, were viewed with suspicion. The desire for flexibility in modern society has altered such restrictive thinking. The trend of liberalization was markedly apparent in the 1967 changes to

our own § 218. Voting or other agreements and irrevocable proxies
were given favorable treatment and restrictive judicial interpretations
as to the absolute voiding of voting trusts for terms beyond the
statutory limit were changed by statute. The trend was not to extend
the voting trust restrictions beyond the class of trust being regulated
and beyond the reasons for statutory regulation.

LEHRMAN v. COHEN

Supreme Court of Delaware, 1966.
43 Del.Ch. 222, 222 A.2d 800.

HERRMANN, JUSTICE.

The primary problem presented on this appeal involves the applicability of the Delaware Voting Trust Statute. Other questions involve
the legality of stock having voting power but no dividend or liquidation
rights except repayment of par value, and an alleged unlawful delegation of directorial duties and powers.

These are the material facts:

Giant Food Inc. (hereinafter the "Company") was incorporated in
Delaware in 1935 by the defendant N.M. Cohen and Samuel Lehrman,
deceased father of the plaintiff Jacob Lehrman. From its inception, the
Company was controlled by the Cohen and Lehrman families, each of
which owned equal quantities of the voting stock, designated Class AC
(held by the Cohen family) and Class AL (held by the Lehrman family)
common stock. The two classes of stock have cumulative voting rights
and each is entitled to elect two members of the Company's four-
member board of directors.

Over the years, as may have been expected, there were differences
of opinion between the Cohen and Lehrman families as to operating
policies of the Company. Samuel Lehrman died in 1949; each of his
children inherited part of his stock in the Company; but a dispute
arose among the children regarding an *inter vivos* gift of certain shares
made to the plaintiff by his father shortly before his death. To
eliminate the Lehrman family dispute and its possible disruption of the
affairs of the Company, an arrangement was made which settled the
dispute and permitted the plaintiff to acquire all of the outstanding
Class AL stock, thereby vesting in him voting power equal to that held
by the Cohen family. The arrangement involved repurchase by the
Company of the stock held by the plaintiff's brothers and sister, their
relinquishment of any claim to the stock gift, and an equalizing
surrender of certain stock by the Cohens to the Company for retirement. An essential part of the arrangement, upon the insistence of the
Cohens, was the establishment of a fifth directorship to obviate the risk
of deadlock which would have continued if the equal division of voting
power between AL and AC stock were continued.

To implement the arrangement, on December 31, 1949, the Company's certificate of incorporation was amended, *inter alia,* to create a
third class of voting stock, designated Class AD common stock, entitled

to elect the fifth director. Article Fourth of the amendment to the certificate of incorporation provided for the issuance of one share of Class AD stock, having a par value of $10. and the following rights and powers:

> "The holder of Class AD common stock shall be entitled to all of the rights and privileges pertaining to common stock without any limitations, prohibitions, restrictions or qualifications except that the holder of said Class AD stock shall not be entitled to receive any dividends declared and paid by the corporation, shall not be entitled to share in the distribution of assets of the corporation upon liquidation or dissolution either partial or final, except to the extent of the par value of said Class AD common stock, and in the election of Directors shall have the right to vote for and elect one of the five Directors hereinafter provided for.

> "The corporation shall have the right, at any time, to redeem and call in the Class AD stock by paying to the holder thereof the par value of said stock, provided however, that such redemption or call shall be authorized and directored by the affirmative vote of four of the five Directors hereinafter provided for." [13]

By resolution of the board of directors, the share of Class AD stock was issued forthwith to the defendant Joseph B. Danzansky, who had served as counsel to the Company since 1944. All corporate action regarding the creation and the issuance of the Class AD stock was accomplished by the unanimous vote of the AC and AL stockholders and of the board of directors. In April 1950, pursuant to the arrangement, Danzansky voted his share of AD stock to elect himself as the Company's fifth director; and he served as such until the institution of this action in 1964. During that entire period, the AC and AL stock have been voted to elect two directors each. From 1950 through 1964, Danzansky regularly attended board meetings, raised and discussed general items of business, and voted on all issues as they came before the board. He was not obliged to break any deadlock among the directors prior to October 1, 1964 because no such deadlock arose before that date.

Beginning in December 1959, 200,000 shares of non-voting common stock of the Company were sold in a public issue for over $3,000,000. Each prospectus published in connection with the public issue contained the following statement:

---

13. [By the Court] Article Fourth of the amendment also co-related the Class AL and the Class AC common stock as follows:

"The holders of Class AL common stock shall be entitled to all of the rights and privileges pertaining to common stock without any limitations, prohibitions, restrictions, or qualifications except that the holder or holders of said Class AL common stock, in the election of Directors, shall have the right to vote for and elect two of the five Directors hereinafter provided for.

"The holders of Class AC common stock shall be entitled to all of the rights and privileges pertaining to common stock without any limitations, prohibitions, restrictions, or qualifications except that the holder or holders of said Class AC common stock, in the election of Directors, shall have the right to vote for and elect two of the five Directors hereinafter provided for."

"Common Stock AD is not a participating stock, and the only purpose for the provision and issuance of such stock is to prevent a deadlock in case the Directors elected by the Common Stock AC and the Directors elected by the Common Stock AL cannot reach an agreement."

Similarly, a letter on behalf of the Company to the Commissioner of Internal Revenue, dated July 15, 1959, contained the following statement:

"As can be seen from the enclosed certified copy of the stock provisions of the certificate of Incorporation, as amended, the Class AD common stock is not a participating stock, the only purpose for the provision and issuance of such a stock being to prevent a deadlock in case the AC and AL Directors cannot reach an agreement."

From the outset and until October 1, 1964, the defendant N.M. Cohen was president of the Company. On that date, a resolution was adopted at the Company's annual stockholders' meeting to give Danzansky a fifteen year executive employment contract at an annual salary of $67,600, and options for 25,000 shares of the non-voting common stock of the Company. The AC and AD stock were voted in favor and the AL stock was voted against the resolution. At a directors meeting held the same day, Danzansky was elected president of the Company by a 3–2 vote, the two AL directors voting in opposition. On December 11, 1964, Danzansky resigned as director and voted his share of AD stock to elect as the fifth director Millard F. West, Jr., a former AL director and investment banker whose firm was one of the underwriters of the public issue of the Company's stock. The newly constituted board ratified the election of Danzansky as president; and, on January 27, 1965, after the commencement of this action and after a review and report by a committee consisting of the new AD director and one AL director, Danzansky's employment contract was approved and adopted with certain modifications.

The plaintiff brought this action on December 11, 1964, basing it upon two claims: The First Claim charges that the creation, issuance, and voting of the one share of Class AD stock resulted in an arrangement illegal under the law of this State for the reasons hereinafter set forth. The Second Claim, addressed to the events of October 1, 1964, charges that the election of Danzansky as president of the Company and his employment contract violated the terms of the 1959 deadlock-breaking arrangement, as made between the holders of the AC and AL stock, and constituted breaches of contract and fiduciary duty. The plaintiff and the defendants filed cross-motions for summary judgment as to the First Claim. The Court of Chancery, after considering the contentions now before us and discussed infra, granted summary judgment in favor of the defendants and denied the plaintiff's motion for summary judgment. The plaintiff appeals.

I.

The plaintiff's primary contention is that the Class AD stock arrangement is, in substance and effect, a voting trust; that, as such, it is illegal because not limited to a ten year period as required by the Voting Trust Statute. The defendants deny that the AD stock arrangement constitutes a disguised voting trust; but they concede that if it is, the arrangement is illegal for violation of the Statute. Thus, issue is clearly joined on the point.

The criteria of a voting trust under our decisions have been summarized by this Court in Abercrombie v. Davies, 36 Del.Ch. 371, 130 A.2d 338 (1957). The tests there set forth, accepted by both sides of this cause as being applicable,[14] are as follows: (1) the voting rights of the stock are separated from the other attributes of ownership; (2) the voting rights granted are intended to be irrevocable for a definite period of time; and (3) the principal purpose [15] of the grant of voting rights is to acquire voting control of the corporation.

Adopting and applying these tests, the plaintiff says, as to the first element, that the AD arrangement provides for a divorcement of voting rights from beneficial ownership of the AC and AL stock; that the creation and issuance of the share of AD stock is tantamount to a pooling by the AC and AL stockholders of a portion of their voting stock and giving it to a trustee, in the person of the AD stockholder, to vote for the election of the fifth director; that after the creation of the AD stock, the AC and AL stockholders each hold but 40% of the voting power, and the AD stockholder holds the controlling balance of 20%; that the AD stock has no property rights except the right to a return of the $10. paid as the par value; and that, therefore, there has been a transfer of the voting rights devoid of any participating property rights. So runs the argument of the plaintiff in support of his contention that the first of the *Abercrombie* criteria for a voting trust is met.

The contention is unacceptable. The AD arrangement did not separate the voting rights of the AC or the AL stock from the other attributes of ownership of those classes of stock. Each AC and AL stockholder retains complete control over the voting of his stock; each can vote his stock directly; no AL or AC stockholder is divested of his right to vote his stock as he sees fit; no AL or AC stock can be voted against the shareholder's wishes; and the AL and AC stock continue to elect two directors each.

The AD stock arrangement, as we view it, became a part of the capitalization of the Company. The fact that there is but a single share, or that the par value is nominal, is of no legal significance; the

14. [By the Court] While the tests and criteria set forth in the *Abercrombie* case prevail, its facts are entirely different. There, several stockholders, each representing a minority interest, agreed to place their stock in escrow for a period of ten years, in exchange for stock receipts, for the purpose of acquiring voting control of the corporation. Agents were appointed and, by irrevocable proxies, the agents were given joint and several voting rights and sole power of decision; no stockholder retained the right to vote his own stock. On those facts, an attempt having been thus made to separate the vote from the stock, this Court held that the stockholders had created a voting trust subject to the controls and limitations of § 218.

15. [By the Court] It is noteworthy, in this connection, that in Abercrombie, this Court distinguished between purpose and motive, stating that it considered only purpose to be material (130 A.2d 338, 341).

one share and the $10. par value might have been multiplied many times over, with the same consequence. It is true that the creation of the separate class of AD stock may have diluted the voting *power* which had previously existed in the AC and AL stock—the usual consequence when additional voting stock is created—but the creation of the new class did not divest and separate the voting *rights* which remain vested in each AC and AL shareholder, together with the other attributes of the ownership of that stock. The fallacy of the plaintiff's position lies in his premise that since the voting power of the AC and AL stock was reduced by the creation of the AD stock, the percentage of reduction became the *res* of a voting trust. In any recapitalization involving the creation of additional voting stock, the voting power of the previously existing stock is diminished; but a voting trust is not necessarily the result.

Since the holders of the Class AC and Class AL stock of the Company did not separate the voting rights from the other attributes of ownership of those classes when they created the Class AD stock, the first *Abercrombie* test of a voting trust is not met.

This conclusion disposes of the second and third *Abercrombie* tests, i.e., that the voting rights granted are irrevocable for a definite period of time, and that the principal object of the grant of voting rights is voting control of the corporation. Having held that the AC and AL stockholders have not divested themselves of their voting rights, although they may have diluted their voting powers, we do not reach the remaining *Abercrombie* tests, both of which assume the divestiture of voting rights.

In the final analysis, the essence of the question raised by the plaintiff in this connection is this: Is the substance and purpose of the AD stock arrangement sufficiently close to the substance and purpose of § 218 to warrant its being subjected to the restrictions and conditions imposed by that Statute? The answer is negative not only for the reasons above stated, but also because § 218 regulates trusts and pooling agreements amounting to trusts, not other and different types of arrangements and undertakings possible among stockholders. Compare Ringling Bros.–Barnum & Bailey Combined Shows Inc. v. Ringling, 29 Del.Ch. 610, 53 A.2d 441 (1947); Abercrombie v. Davies, supra. The AD stock arrangement is neither a trust nor a pooling agreement.

We hold, therefore, that the Class AD stock arrangement is not controlled by the Voting Trust Statute.

II.

The plaintiff's second point is that even if the Class AD stock arrangement is not a voting trust in substance and effect, the AD stock is illegal, nevertheless, because the creation of a class of stock having voting rights only, and lacking any substantial participating proprietary interest in the corporation, violates the public policy of this State as declared in § 218.

The fallacy of this argument is twofold: First, it is more accurate to say that what the law has disfavored, and what the public policy underlying the Voting Trust Statute means to control, is the separation of the vote from the stock—not from the stock ownership. Clearly, the AD stock arrangement is not violative of that public policy. Secondly, there is nothing in § 218, either expressed or implied, which requires that all stock of a Delaware corporation must have both voting rights and proprietary interests. Indeed, public policy to the contrary seems clearly expressed by 8 Del.C. § 151(a) which authorizes, in very broad terms, such voting powers and participating rights as may be stated in the certificate of incorporation. Non-voting stock is specifically authorized by § 151(a); and in the light thereof, consistency does not permit the conclusion, urged by the plaintiff, that the present public policy of this State condemns the separation of voting rights from beneficial stock ownership.

We conclude that the plaintiff's contention in this regard cannot withstand the force and effect of § 151(a). In our view, that Statute permits the creation of stock having voting rights only, as well as stock having property rights only. The voting powers and the participating rights of the Class AD stock being specified in the Company's certificate of incorporation, we are of the opinion that the Class AD stock is legal by virtue of § 151(a). * * *

We are told that if the AD stock arrangement is allowed thus to stand, our Voting Trust Statute will become a "dead letter" because it will be possible to evade and circumvent its purpose simply by issuing a class of non-participating voting stock, as was done here. We have three negative reactions to this argument:

First, it presupposes a divestiture of the voting rights of the AC and AL stock—an untenable supposition as has been stated. Secondly, it fails to take into account the main purpose of a Voting Trust Statute: to avoid secret, uncontrolled combinations of stockholders formed to acquire voting control of the corporation to the possible detriment of non-participating shareholders. It may not be said that the AD stock arrangement contravenes that purpose. Finally on this point, if we misconceive the legislative intent, and if the AD stock arrangement in this case reveals a loophole in § 218 which should be plugged, it is for the General Assembly to accomplish—not for us to attempt by interstitial judicial legislation.

III.

The plaintiff advances yet another reason for invalidating the AD stock. The essence of this argument is that the only function of that class of stock is to break directorial deadlocks; that the issuance of the AD stock is merely a technical device to permit that result; that, as such, it is illegal because it permits the AC and AL directors of the Company to delegate their statutory duties to the AD director as an arbitrator.

We see nothing inherently wrong or contrary to the public policy of this State, as plaintiff seems to suggest, about a device, otherwise lawful, designed by the stockholders of a corporation to break deadlocks of directors. The plaintiff says in this connection, that if public policy sanctioned such device, our General Corporation Law would provide for it. The fallacy of this argument lies in the assumption that legislative silence is a dependable indicator of public policy. We know of no reason, either under our statutes or our decisions, which would prevent the stockholders of a Delaware corporation from protecting themselves and their corporation, by a plan otherwise lawful, against the paralyzing and often fatal consequences of a stalemate in the directorate of the corporation. We hold, therefore, that the AD stock arrangement had a proper purpose.

As to the means adopted for the accomplishment of that purpose, we find the AD stock arrangement valid by virtue of § 141(a) of the Delaware Corporation Law which provides:

> "The business of every corporation organized under the provisions of this chapter shall be managed by a board of directors, except as hereinafter or in its certificate of incorporation otherwise provided."

The AD stock arrangement was created by the unanimous action of the stockholders of the Company by amendment to the certificate of incorporation. The stockholders thereby provided how the business of the corporation is to be managed, as is their privilege and right under § 141(a). It was this stockholder action which delegated to the AD director whatever powers and duties he possesses; they were not delegated to him by his fellow directors, either out of their own powers and duties, or otherwise.

It is settled, of course, as a general principle, that directors may not delegate their duty to manage the corporate enterprise. But there is no conflict with that principle where, as here, the delegation of duty, if any, is made not by the directors but by stockholder action under § 141(a), via the certificate of incorporation.

In our judgment, therefore, the AD stock arrangement is not invalid on the ground that it permits the AC and AL directors of the Company to delegate their statutory duties to the AD director.

On this point, the plaintiff relies mainly upon the Chancery Court decision in Abercrombie v. Davies, 35 Del.Ch. 599, 611, 123 A.2d 893 (1956). There, in considering an agreement requiring all eight directors to submit a disputed question to an arbitrator if seven were unable to agree, the Chancery Court stated that legal sanction may not be accorded to an agreement, at least when made by less than all the stockholders, which takes from the board of directors the power of determining substantial management policy. The plaintiff's reliance is misplaced, because, *inter alia*, the *Abercrombie* arrangement was not created by the certificate of incorporation, within the authority of § 141(a). The plaintiff also relies in this connection upon Field v. Carlisle Corp., 31 Del.Ch. 227, 68 A.2d 817 (1949) and Adams v. Clearance Corp., 35 Del.Ch. 459, 121 A.2d 302 (1956). The *Field* case is not in point because it involved delegation of authority by the directors themselves, rather than, as here, by the stockholders speaking through the certificate of incorporation. The *Adams* case is of no aid to the plaintiff's position because there, too, the certificate of incorporation was not involved in the delegation of directorial duties asserted. Finally, the plaintiff relies upon Sterling Industries, Inc. v. Ball Bearing Pen Corp., 298 N.Y. 483, 84 N.E.2d 790, 10 A.L.R.2d 694 (1949) and 7 White, New York Corporations, ¶ 8.18 (1953). The New York authorities, uncontrolled by § 141(a), are inapposite. * * *

Our conclusions upon these questions make it unnecessary to discuss the defendants' contentions that the plaintiff's action is barred by the principles of estoppel, laches, acquiescence and ratification.

Finding no error in the judgment below, it is affirmed.

Notes

(1) In accord is Stroh v. Blackhawk Holding Corp., 48 Ill.2d 471, 272 N.E.2d 1 (1971), where a corporation, before selling Class A shares to the public at $4.00 per share, created 500,000 shares of voting Class B stock which had no right to dividends and no rights on dissolution. These shares, constituting 28.78 per cent of the voting stock, were sold to the promoters for ¼ cent per share. The Court upheld the validity of the Class B shares over the dissent of Justice Schaefer, who accused the majority of stating "that the ownership incidents of ownership may be eliminated. What remains, then, is a disembodied right to manage the assets of a corporation, divorced from any financial interest in those assets except such as may accrue from the power to manage them. In my opinion, what is left after the economic rights 'are removed and eliminated' is not a share of corporate stock under the law of Illinois." 272 N.E.2d at 8.

(2) Another case supporting the general conclusion in Lehrman v. Cohen is Providence and Worcester Co. v. Baker, 378 A.2d 121 (Del.1977). The corporation's certificate of incorporation provided that a shareholder was entitled to (i) one vote per share for each share he owned up to fifty shares and (ii) one vote for every twenty shares he owned in excess of fifty, but (iii) no shareholder might vote more than one fourth of all the outstanding shares. The Court upheld this voting arrangement under the Delaware statute. These voting restrictions, it should be noted, did not limit the power of persons to cast large numbers of votes by proxy but rather limited the voting power of individual owners of shares. Would this voting arrangement be upheld under the last sentence of RMBCA § 6.01(a)?

(3) Is not the decision in the principal case correct since it is not possible to draw a line between the permissible and the impermissible?

LING AND CO. v. TRINITY SAV. AND LOAN ASS'N

Supreme Court of Texas, 1972.
482 S.W.2d 841.

REAVLEY, JUSTICE.

Trinity Savings and Loan Association sued Bruce W. Bowman for the balance owed on a promissory note and also to foreclose on a certificate for 1500 shares of Class A Common Stock in Ling & Company, Inc. pledged by Bowman to secure payment of the note. Ling & Company was made a party to the suit by Trinity Savings and Loan because of Ling & Company's insistence that the transfer of its stock was subject to restrictions that were unfulfilled. Bowman did not appear and has not appealed from the judgment against him. The trial court entered summary judgment in favor of Trinity Savings and Loan, against the contentions of Ling & Company, foreclosing the security interest in the stock and ordering it sold. The court of civil appeals affirmed. 470 S.W.2d 441. We reverse the judgments and remand the case to the trial court.

The objection to the foreclosure and public sale of this stock is based upon restrictions imposed upon the transfer of the stock by the articles of incorporation of Ling & Company. It is conceded that no offer of sale has been made to the other holders of this class of stock and that the approval of the pledge of the stock has not been obtained from the New York Stock Exchange. It is the position of Trinity Savings and Loan that all of the restrictions upon the transfer of any interest in this stock are invalid and of no effect. This has been the holding of the courts below.

The face and back of the stock certificate are reproduced and attached to this opinion.

The restrictions appear in Article Four of the Ling & Company articles of incorporation, as amended and filed with the Secretary of State in 1968. Section D requires the holder to obtain written approval of the New York Stock Exchange prior to the sale or encumbrance of the stock if, at the time, Ling & Company is a member corporation of the Exchange. Then Section E(4) prevents the sale of the stock without first affording the corporation the opportunity to buy and, if it fails to purchase, giving that opportunity to all holders of the same class of stock. The method of computation of the price, based upon the corporate books, is provided in this section of the articles.

The court of civil appeals struck down the restrictions for three reasons: the lack of conspicuous notice thereof on the stock certificate, the unreasonableness of the restrictions, and statutory prohibition against an option in favor of other stockholders whenever they number more than twenty. These objections will be examined in that order.

CONSPICUOUSNESS

The Texas Business Corporation Act as amended in 1957, V.A.T.S. Bus.Corp.Act, art. 2.22, subd. A, provides that a corporation may impose restrictions on the transfer of its stock if they are "expressly set forth in the articles of incorporation * * * and * * * copied at length or in summary form on the face or so copied on the back and referred to on the face of each certificate * * *" Article 2.19, subd. F, enacted by the Legislature at the same time, permits the incorporation by reference on the face or back of the certificate of the provision of the articles of incorporation which restricts the transfer of the stock. The court of civil appeals objected to the general reference to the articles of incorporation and the failure to print the full conditions imposed upon the transfer of the shares. However, reference is made on the face of the certificate to the restrictions described on the reverse side; the notice on the reverse side refers to the particular article of the articles of incorporation as restricting the transfer or encumbrance and requiring "the holder hereof to grant options to purchase the shares represented hereby first to the Corporation and then pro rata to the other holders of the Class A Common Stock * * *" We hold that the content of the certificate complies with the requirements of the Texas Business Corporation Act.

There remains the requirement of the Texas [Uniform Commercial] Code that the restriction or reference thereto on the certificate must be conspicuous. Sec. [8–204] requires that a restriction on transferability be "noted conspicuously on the security." Sec. [1–201(10)] defines "conspicuous" and makes the determination a question of law for the court to decide. It is provided that a conspicuous term is so written as to be noticed by a reasonable person. Examples of conspicuous matter are given there as a "printed heading in capitals * * * [or] larger or other contrasting type or color." This means that something must appear on the face of the certificate to attract the attention of a reasonable person when he looks at it. 1 Anderson, Uniform Commercial Code 87 (2nd ed. 1970). The line of print on the face of the Ling & Company certificate does not stand out and cannot be considered conspicuous.

Our holding that the restriction is not noted conspicuously on the certificate does not entitle Trinity Savings and Loan to a summary judgment under this record. Sec. [8–204] provides that the restriction is effective against a person with actual knowledge of it. The record does not establish conclusively that Trinity Savings and Loan lacked knowledge of the restriction on January 28, 1969, the date the record indicates when Bowman executed an assignment of this stock to Trinity Savings and Loan.

REASONABLENESS

Art. 2.22, subd. A of the Texas Business Corporation Act provides that a corporation may impose restrictions on disposition of its stock if the restrictions "do not unreasonably restrain or prohibit transferability." The court of civil appeals has held that the restrictions on the transferability of this stock are unreasonable for two reasons: because of the required approval of the New York Stock Exchange and because of successive options to purchase given the corporation and the other holders of the same class of stock.

Ling & Company in its brief states that it was a brokerage house member of the New York Stock Exchange at an earlier time and that Rule 315 of the Exchange required approval of any sale or pledge of the stock. Under these circumstances we must disagree with the court of civil appeals holding that this provision of article 4D of the articles of incorporation is "arbitrary, capricious, and unreasonable." Nothing appears in the summary judgment proof on this matter, and the mere provision in the article is no cause for vitiating the restrictions as a matter of law.

It was also held by the intermediate court that it is unreasonable to require a shareholder to notify all other record holders of Class A Common Stock of his intent to sell and to give the other holders a ten day option to buy. The record does not reveal the number of holders of this class of stock; we only know that there are more than twenty. We find nothing unusual or oppressive in these first option provisions. See 2 O'Neal, Close Corporations, § 7.13 (1971). Conceivably the number of stockholders might be so great as to make the burden too heavy upon the stockholder who wishes to sell and, at the same time, dispel any justification for contending that there exists a reasonable corporate purpose in restricting the ownership. But there is no showing of that nature in this summary judgment record.

STATUTORY LIMIT ON OPTIONEES

Art. 2.22, subd. B of the Texas Business Corporation Act provides that, in addition to other reasonable restrictions, any of the following restrictions may be imposed upon the transfer of corporate shares:

(1) Restrictions reasonably defining pre-emptive or prior rights of the corporation or its shareholders of record, to purchase any of its shares offered for transfer.

(2) Restrictions reasonably defining rights and obligations of the holders of shares of any class, in connection with buy-and-sell agreements binding on all holders of shares of that class, so long as there are no more than twenty (20) holders of record of such class.

(3) Restrictions reasonably defining rights of the corporation or of any other person or persons, granted as an option or options or refusal or refusals on any shares.

The court of civil appeals regarded subsection (2) as being applicable to the stock restriction in this case. Since it was stipulated that there were more than twenty holders of record of Class A stock, it has been held that the restriction fails for this reason. We disagree. Subsection (2) is not applicable to the Ling & Company restriction. It seems that a "buy and sell agreement" usually refers to a contract between shareholders rather than a restriction imposed by the corporation. In any event, there is no obligation to purchase this stock placed upon anyone, and these restrictions can only be considered as options and not "buy and sell agreements." 2 O'Neal, Close Corporations, § 7.10 (1971); Fletcher Cyc. Corp. § 5461.1 (1971).

The summary judgment proof does not justify the holding that restrictions on the transfer of this stock were ineffective as to Trinity Savings and Loan Association. The judgment below is reversed and the cause is remanded to the trial court.

DANIEL, J., concurs in result.

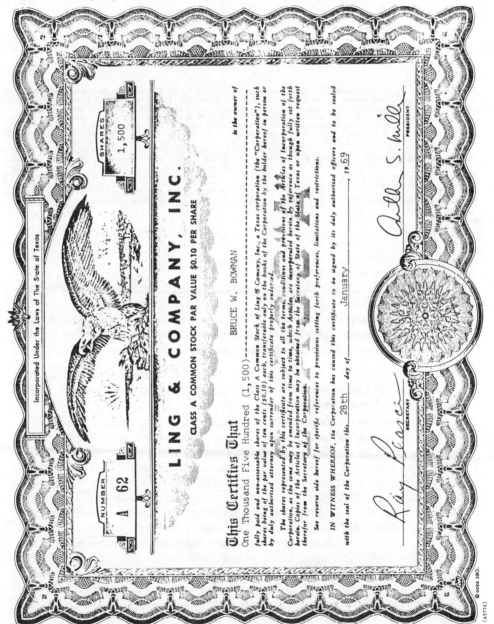

For Value Received,_____ hereby sell, assign and transfer unto_____ Shares of the Capital Stock represented by the within Certificate, and do hereby irrevocably constitute and appoint_____ Attorney to transfer the said Stock on the books of the within named Corporation with full power of substitution in the premises Dated_____ 19

In presence of

NOTICE THE SIGNATURE OF THIS ASSIGNMENT MUST CORRESPOND WITH THE NAME AS WRITTEN UPON THE FACE OF THE CERTIFICATE, IN EVERY PARTICULAR WITHOUT ALTERATION OR ENLARGEMENT OR ANY CHANGE WHATEVER

NOTICE: The shares represented by this certificate are subject to all the terms, conditions and provisions of the Articles of Incorporation of the Corporation, as the same may be amended from time to time, which Articles are incorporated herein by reference as though fully set forth herein. Copies of the Articles of Incorporation may be obtained from the Secretary of State of the State of Texas or upon written request therefor from the Secretary of the Corporation. Reference is specifically made to the provisions of Article Four of the Articles of Incorporation which set forth the designations, preferences, limitations and relative rights of the shares of each class of capital stock authorized to be issued, which deny pre-emptive rights, prohibit cumulative voting, restrict the transfer, sale, assignment, pledge, hypothecation or encumbrance of any of the shares represented hereby under certain conditions, and which under certain conditions require the holder hereof to grant options to purchase the shares represented hereby first to the Corporation and then pro rata to the other holders of the Class A Common Stock, all as set forth in said Article Four. Reference is also specifically made to the provisions of Article Nine which vests the power to adopt, alter, amend or repeal the by-laws in the Board of Directors except to the extent such power may be modified or divested by action of shareholders representing a majority of the holders of the Class A Common Stock.

[A5775]

Notes

(1) Consider RMBCA §§ 6.27, 1.40(3). It will be noted that, unlike the Texas statute involved in *Ling,* there is no statutory limit on the number of offerees in buy-sell agreements. The Texas statute in this regard was atypical and the statute was amended to eliminate the restriction on the number of offerees after the decision in the principal case.

(2) Share transfer restrictions essentially constitute contractual obligations that limit the power of owners to freely transfer their shares. There are several different justifications for imposing share transfer restrictions, and the type of restriction imposed may depend on the objective. Consider RMBCA § 6.27(c). What kinds of "status" is referred to in subsection (c) (1)? The Official Comment refers to election of close corporation status under an integrated close corporation statute, subchapter S, and "entitlement to a program or eligibility for a privilege administered by governmental agencies or securities exchanges." Presumably, the share transfer restriction involved in *Ling* was of the latter type, designed to allow the New York Stock Exchange to police ownership interests in member firms. RMBCA § 6.27(c)(3) also refers to "other reasonable purpose[s]". What might they be? The most likely relate to closely held corporations, designed to enable the owners to remain close, i.e. to select the persons with whom they will be associated in business, and to permit withdrawing participants to liquidate their investments on some reasonable basis. See the Waldbaum excerpt that follows (page 501, infra).

(3) A variety of possible share transfer restrictions are described in RMBCA § 6.27(d). In closely held corporations, the two most common types of restrictions are buy-sell agreements [see subsection (d)(1)] and option agreements [see subsection (d)(2)]. Obviously, an option does not guarantee the shareholder a specified price, whereas a buy-sell agreement does. The restrictions described in subsections (d)(3) and (d)(4) are potentially more onerous since they may prohibit all transfers to anyone at any price; it will be noted that they are valid only if the prohibition "is not manifestly unreasonable." Does it follow that (d)(1) and (d)(2) restrictions are valid even if they are "manifestly unreasonable"?

(4) Some share transfer restrictions in closely held corporations are phrased as rights of first refusal, giving the corporation or the shareholders an opportunity to meet the best price the shareholder has been able to obtain from outsiders. Do you think that this kind of restraint might "chill" the interest of outsiders in making offers for shares?

(5) Fender v. Prescott, 101 A.D.2d 418, 476 N.Y.S.2d 128 (1984) involved a buy-sell agreement under which "either party could offer to buy out the other, and thereupon, the offeree had the option to elect to be either the purchaser or the seller in accordance with the terms of the offer." 476 N.Y.S.2d at 130. Is there any reason not to enforce this type of restraint?

(6) The traditional view is that share transfer restrictions constitute a restraint on alienation, and therefore are strictly construed. This attitude is changing. One recent case, for example, has described this attitude as "anachronistic." Bruns v. Rennebohm Drug Stores, Inc., 151 Wis.2d 88, 442 N.W.2d 591, 596 (App.1989). Nevertheless, because of this historic approach, it is important to specify clearly and unambiguously the essential attributes of the restrictions. In a close corporation, this should include whether the purchase is optional or mandatory, the persons who may or must purchase the shares and the sequence in which they may purchase, the manner in which the price is to be determined, the time periods during which persons may decide whether or not to purchase (if an option), and the events (e.g. proposed sale, death, bankruptcy, family gift, etc.) which are to be covered by the restriction. It has been held, for example, that a restriction against sales "to the public" does not prohibit a sale to another shareholder, or that a prohibition against an "officer-stockholder" does not cover a corporation owned by an officer-stockholder.

WALDBAUM, BUY–SELL AGREEMENTS
The Practical Accountant, May/June 1972, at pp. 17–25.

One of the legal characteristics of a corporation is that it has perpetual existence. Yet, the death or withdrawal of a share-holder-officer in a small corporation is often followed by the demise of the business. *In many cases, this termination is due to the lack of an effective and fair buy-sell agreement.*

Take a fairly common situation: Tom, Dick and Harry are equal shareholders of a small corporation. They have no buy-sell agreement. But they do have a common interest in taking substantial risks and plowing as much of the earnings back into the business as they can afford in order to build for the future.

Tom dies and the interests of Tom's family become almost immediately antagonistic to those of Dick and Harry. While Dick and Harry still remain interested in the growth of the corporation, Tom's family needs security and a return from the business.

Almost without exception, closely held corporations do not pay dividends. So, unless Tom's family can provide some services to the corporation and thereby get on the payroll, the prospects for their receiving any return from Tom's shares are very poor indeed. Even if there were no unfavorable tax consequences, the surviving shareholders would be disinclined to pay dividends. The funds could be better used for corporate growth and a payout might require a reduction of their salaries.

The problem of what are fair salaries and what is a fair return on invested capital is a thorny one. It is a problem not likely to be satisfactorily solved by Tom's widow and the surviving shareholders.

Tom's widow, as a minority shareholder, now finds herself the proud owner of shares of stock from which she receives no return.

Would Tom's widow be in a secure position if she had inherited a controlling interest? Not necessarily. This fact offers no assurance that the business will continue, for Dick and Harry may well be unwilling to continue under such circumstances. Worse yet, they may well be capable of starting a competing business on their own.

If the corporation had elected Subchapter S treatment, then Dick and Harry may be justifiably concerned that the election will be terminated. If any of the transferees of Tom's shares refuse to consent to the election, or if Tom's shares are transferred to several beneficiaries so that the number of shareholders is increased to more than [thirty-five], or if one of the transferees is a corporation, trust, partnership, or non-resident alien, then the Subchapter S status will be lost.

Frequently the only solution is for Tom's estate to sell his shares to the surviving shareholders. But there is an obvious conflict of interest between the survivors and Tom's family in establishing the price to be paid for the shares.

What are the magic ingredients in buy-sell agreements which solve these problems? There are two: First, bargaining positions are usually equal since none of the shareholders knows whether he will be on the buying end or the selling end of the agreement. Secondly, once there is an agreement everybody knows where he stands and can plan accordingly.

Finding a Fair Price. The key to any buy-sell agreement is, of course, the fairness of the price to be paid to the deceased shareholder's estate for his shares. Usually this price is determined in one of four ways:

(1) Use book value of the shares as of the date of death or the end of the preceding accounting period. The desirability of this method depends upon the extent market value corresponds to book value.

(2) Use a fixed price set out in the agreement, arrived at between the shareholders. This method works only if it is periodically reviewed and updated.

(3) Have the price fixed by appraisal after death. Two difficulties with this method are *uncertainty* and *delay*.

(4) Use a self-adjusting formula. There is no end to the formulas which can be used. * * *

If the buy-sell agreement was arrived at through arm's-length negotiations, then, according to Rev.Rul. 54–77, in the absence of other circumstances, the agreed price will be accepted as the fair market value at date of death.

Two Basic Agreements. There are two basic types of buy-sell agreements and there are substantial differences between them.

The first type is a cross-purchase agreement between the shareholders. Each shareholder agrees to personally purchase his proportionate share of the stock of the other shareholders in the event of their death, and binds his estate to sell the shares he owns to the surviving shareholders in proportion to their respective holdings. The capitalization of the corporation remains unchanged.

The second type is a stock-redemption agreement. The corporation becomes a party to the agreement as well as the shareholders. The corporation would agree to redeem or purchase the shares of the first shareholder to die, and each of the two shareholders would bind his estate to sell or tender for redemption the shares he owns. Upon the death of the first shareholder, the corporation buys his shares using corporate funds.

Both types of buy-sell agreements fix the price to be paid for the shares and specify the terms for payment. In addition to the two basic types of agreements, there are hybrid agreements which consist of both a cross-purchase agreement and a redemption agreement. For instance, if a corporation has two shareholders, each owning 100 shares of stock, there could be cross-purchase agreement with respect to 50 shares of stock and a stock-redemption agreement with respect to the remaining 50 shares.

In community property states buy-sell agreements always include the wife's community interest. Therefore, the wives of all the shareholders should be signatories to the agreement.

Which type of agreement is used usually depends upon where the money is. Where neither the corporation nor the shareholders have sufficient funds, the agreements are usually funded by insurance.

Whichever type of agreement is used, it should set forth the method of payment and the interest which will accrue on any deferred portion of the purchase price. As security for such deferred portion, a pledge of all the shares of the corporation, including those being purchased, may be required.

Cross-purchase agreements are deceptively simple. However, they have several practical disadvantages and are sometimes difficult to fund by insurance.

Their obvious disadvantage is that the shares of a deceased shareholder must be paid for with after-tax dollars of the surviving shareholders. Another disadvantage is that the obligation to purchase usually falls most heavily upon the shareholders least able to bear it.

Also although cross-purchase agreements are reasonably satisfactory where there are only a few shareholders, they become increasingly cumbersome as the number of shareholders increase. Consequently, many cross-purchase agreements are drafted to terminate upon the first death. * * *

In *stock-redemption agreements* the corporation itself buys back the deceased shareholder's shares using corporate funds. In some instances, the corporation may hold the shares as treasury stock rather than cancelling them. For practical purposes, however, the results are the same.

[T]he stock-redemption agreement has several advantages. The most obvious is that corporate earnings and profits are being used for the benefit of shareholders without the usual dividend or tax cost result. Such agreements are also easier to handle where there are a number of shareholders.

However, there are some practical problems even in a simple unfunded redemption agreement.

One is whether the corporation will have sufficient surplus, as required by the laws of most states, to redeem the shares tendered by the estate of a deceased shareholder.

If not, there are several possible solutions: (1) the stockholders could agree to a change in the corporate capitalization so as to create the required surplus; (2) the shareholder could agree to contribute sufficient additional capital to allow redemptions; (3) the shareholders could agree to purchase such shares as the corporation is unable to redeem.

A more common problem is that the corporation cannot spare the necessary funds and still continue to operate efficiently.

One solution is for the corporation to fund its obligations by the purchase of insurance. Or, the corporation could distribute some of its assets, such as real estate, to the estate of the deceased shareholder and then lease them back. A third arrangement is to provide for the payments to the estate of the deceased shareholder to be spread over a period of years in the hope that the required funds can be provided out of future earnings. * * *

Notes

(1) The Prudential Life Insurance Company has prepared a set of sample forms for "Model Business Insurance Agreements" that it distributes free to attorneys. The Foreward states:

> We deem it a Privilege to address these prefatory remarks to our friends in the legal profession, for whom this booklet is primarily intended. There is a growing awareness on the part of attorneys of the serious financial problems created by the untimely death of a successful businessman. Prudence demands that proper measures on sound legal advise be taken to formulate a plan that will effectively prevent disastrous economic results and provide for orderly disposition of business interests at death. In many cases, a carefully drawn Buy-and-Sell Agreement will prove to be an essential element of such a plan. Given a Buy-and-Sell Agreement it is apparent that life insurance is the ideal method of funding it.

(2) Consider the restrictions on corporate repurchases of stock set forth in RMBCA § 6.40, discussed in Chapter Seven, Section I, supra. Might they permit a corporation to refuse to redeem shares pursuant to a buy-sell agreement? If so, a carefully prepared estate plan may go awry. Is there any way to avoid these restrictions? Should the other shareholders be asked to bind themselves in advance to cause the corporation to meet the requirements of § 6.40 if possible? Should they be asked to guarantee the performance of the buy-sell agreement by the corporation? If so, how should such provisions be phrased? Would such an obligation have unfavorable tax consequences?

(3) Consider also the possible impact of the special penalty tax on unreasonable accumulations of surplus also discussed in Chapter Seven, Section H. If a corporation enters into a buy-sell agreement, may it accumulate its earnings to meet its obligations under that agreement without fear of running afoul of that tax? Can IRS argue that an accumulation for this purpose is for the needs of the shareholders rather than the needs of the corporation? Consult Herwitz, Stock Redemptions and the Accumulated Earnings Tax, 74 Harv.L.Rev. 866 (1961).

(4) Many close corporation situations continue to arise in which no buy/sell agreement exists despite the obvious advantages of such agreements. Should the legislature create a mandatory buy-out obligation in an integrated close corporation statute? In other words, what about including provisions in a close corporation statute analogous to the provisions of the Uniform Partnership Act that permit the estate of a deceased partner to have the value of the interest of the estate ascertained and paid to it? (See pages 84–88 supra.) A few states have experimented with such provisions but they seem more controversial than in the partnership setting. How should the price be set? A liquidation or book value may be inappropriate since minority shareholders usually cannot compel a dissolution; since there is no market for the shares, a statute will presumably have to provide a judicially determined fair price with the attendant costs and uncertainties. A judicial determination of fair price may lead to a price that is quite a bit higher than the maximum price the corporation might have been

willing to pay for the shares on a voluntary basis or a price quite a bit lower than the shareholder would have accepted voluntarily. Is it reasonable to impose a mandatory buy-out obligation on a small business? If so, the threat of invoking a mandatory buy-out remedy at an unconvenient time may carry considerable weight. Might that not be one reason the corporate form, with its greater permanence, was originally chosen?

If it is decided to create a "mandatory" buy-out remedy, should a corporation be able to "opt out" of the provision? In § 14 of the Model Close Corporation Supplement, a buy-out provision is included but only on an "opt in" basis with the result that it is likely to have only limited usefulness. 3 M.B.C.A.Ann. 1822, 1823 (1985). This provision was adopted only after considerable debate about the need to balance the interests of the disadvantaged shareholder with the interests of the continuing enterprise.

C. DIRECTORS

BALDWIN v. CANFIELD

Supreme Court of Minnesota, 1879.
26 Minn. 43, 1 N.W. 261.

[Editor: A corporation, The Minneapolis Agricultural and Mechanical Association, owned valuable real estate. All the shares of stock were owned by William S. King. In late 1872, King borrowed $10,000 from Baldwin, the cashier of the State National Bank. The loan was secured by a pledge of the stock of the Association, and King stated to Baldwin that the stock represented the land. In August 1873, King entered into a contract with Canfield to sell the real estate owned by the Association for $65,000 in bonds issued by the Northern Pacific Railroad Corporation. Originally King agreed to convey the real estate personally, but Canfield learned that it was held by the Association, and King agreed that he would have the Association convey the real estate to Canfield, and in addition would redeem the pledged shares and deliver them to Canfield.

King caused the directors of the Association to execute a deed as described by the Court below and delivered it to Canfield. Canfield delivered the bonds to King but "through inadvertence" did not demand a delivery of the stock. King did not redeem the pledged shares but converted the bonds to his own use.]

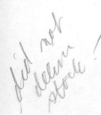

BERRY, J.

* * * After the agreement of August 14, 1873, between King and Canfield, King, in pursuance thereof and in order to carry it out, caused a deed to be executed by the several persons heretofore named as the directors of said association. This deed, which is in form one of bargain and sale without covenants, purports to be a conveyance of the fair ground property by the Minneapolis Agricultural and Mechanical Association to Thomas H. Canfield, and is signed as follows, viz.:

"The Minneapolis Agricultural and Mechanical Association

[Seal]

"By R.J. Mendenhall, Thomas Lowry, W.D. Washburn, C.G. Goodrich, G.F. Stevens, Wm. S. King, Levi Butler, W.W. Eastman, W.P. Westfall, Dorilus Morrison, Geo. A. Brackett, directors of said corporation."

The execution of this deed was never authorized or directed at or by any meeting of said directors of said association, nor was any resolution ever passed by said board of directors in reference to the execution of said deed by said last-named parties, or any of them, or authorizing the seal of said corporation to be attached to any such deed, or authorizing the sale or conveyance of said property in any way to said Canfield. The deed was executed by the parties above named separately and at different times, wherever they happened to be, at the request of King or his attorney, for the purpose of enabling King to convey said property to Canfield. The deed was executed by Stevens at Utica, in the state of New York, by Morrison and Brackett in the city of New York, and by the other signers thereof in Hennepin county.

* * *

This action was brought by Baldwin and the State National Bank of Minneapolis, as plaintiffs, against the Minneapolis Agricultural and Mechanical Association, and King and Canfield, as defendants. Canfield appeared and answered. Neither of the other defendants was served with process or appeared in the action. * * *

The fourth conclusion is called in question by the counsel for defendant Canfield, but we have no doubt of its correctness. As we have already seen, the court below finds that, by its articles of incorporation, the government of the Minneapolis Agricultural and Mechanical Association, and the management of its affairs, was vested in the board of directors. The legal effect of this was to invest the directors with such government and management *as a board,* and not otherwise. This is in accordance with the general rule that the governing body of a corporation, as such, are agents of the corporation only as a board, and not individually. Hence it follows that they have no authority to act, save when assembled at a board meeting. The separate action, individually, of the persons composing such governing body, is not the action of the constituted body of men clothed with corporate powers. In Vermont a somewhat different rule is allowed, as in the Bank of Middlebury v. Rutland & Washington R. Co., 30 Vt. 159. In that case, and perhaps others in that state, it is held that directors may bind their corporation by acting separately, if this is their usual practice in transacting the corporate business. But we think that the general rule before mentioned is the more rational one, and it is supported by the great weight of authority. From the application of this rule to the facts of this case, it follows that the fourth conclusion of law, viz., that the deed purporting to be made by the association was not the act and deed of such association, and therefore did not convey the title to the premises in question to Canfield, is correct. The directors took no action as a board with reference to the sale of the premises or the execution of any deed thereof. So far as in any way binding the corporation is concerned, their action in executing the deed was a nullity. They could not bind it by their separate and individual action. Hence it follows that the so-called deed is not only ineffectual as a conveyance of real property, but equally so as a contract to convey.

[An order cancelling Canfield's deed as a cloud upon the title of the real estate was affirmed.]

MICKSHAW v. COCA COLA BOTTLING CO.

Superior Court of Pennsylvania, 1950.
166 Pa.Super. 148, 70 A.2d 467.

DITHRICH, JUDGE.

This is an action in assumpsit brought to recover the difference in pay between what plaintiff received for his military service in World War II and what he would have received had he continued to work for defendant.

On October 1, 1940, the following article appeared in the Sharon Herald:

"Coca–Cola Firm to Pay All Draftees

"The Coca–Cola Bottling Co., Inc. of Sharon to-day took a place among the outstanding patriotic firms of the Shenango Valley.

"William Feinberg, Manager, announced that any employee called to the colors through the conscription law will not lose a cent in wages. The company is prepared to pay the difference between the government wages and the amount the employee received before he went to camp.

"Feinberg said this ruling will protect every man employed by the company and the 'pay while away' plan will be continued as long as the man is in service.

"The announcement, made to employees today, gives them a more optimistic view on the approaching draft. If called, they will be able to leave with knowledge that dependents will continue to receive customary income as long as they are away."

Plaintiff testified that Feinberg, manager and secretary of the defendant, showed the article to him and two of the three other employees liable to be conscripted, stating " * * * that he was going to take care of us when he went into the service, that he would pay the difference between what we made at the Coca Cola Company and what the government paid us."

Plaintiff continued in defendant's employ for two years. Then in October 1942, having received notice to report for his Selective Service physical examination, he enlisted in the Coast Guard and served with that branch some 37 months. He returned from the service and resumed working for defendant in December 1945. In May 1947 he left the employ of defendant, and in September of that year first made demand for payment for those years during which he was in service. He said the reason for the delay was that since he had returned to the employ of defendant he was afraid that demand for the difference in pay during his absence in the service would imperil his job. His claim was for $3,588. Upon trial the jury awarded him $1,000. From the denial of motions for a new trial and for judgment n.o.v. defendant appeals. * * *

The remaining three questions are answered in the following excerpts from the opinion of President Judge Rowley, which we adopt:

" 'If the statement was made, did William Feinberg have the authority to bind the Coca Cola Bottling Company, a corporation?" * * *

"The control of the business of a private corporation is vested in its board of directors. There were three directors of the defendant corporation, William Feinberg, Myer Ackerman, and his father, Samuel Ackerman.

"Director Feinberg testified that he authorized the publication which stated that announcement of the proposal had been made to the employees that day. Director Myer Ackerman testified that he knew of the published announcement on the day it appeared. Upon direct examination, Myer Ackerman was asked

" 'Q. Did the directors take any action, approving the payment, making up the difference between what employees of your company would receive, if they were drafted, and what they would have received if they had remained in your employ? A. It was not discussed until after we saw it in the paper.

" 'Q. Did you have anything to do with putting in the paper that particular article? A. I didn't object to it.'

"It therefore appears that the directors of the corporation did discuss the proposal; that director Feinberg authorized the proposal, and director Myer Ackerman acquiesced in it.

"Feinberg, secretary and director, Myer Ackerman, vice-president and director, Arnold Hyman, assistant manager and all the employees, Mickshaw, Zoldan, Rossi and Gray, knew of the published proposal on or about the date of its appearance. It would not be a violent assumption to infer that the third director, Samuel Ackerman, then president of the company, also knew of it. However that may be, Feinberg and Myer Ackerman constituted a majority of the board and we think that their conduct was a sufficient ratification of the proposal.

"It would be grossly unjust to require a claimant against a corporation to prove his case by formal corporate records. It is well known that corporations which include few stockholders do not often act with as much formality as larger companies. This is especially so where the members of the board, actually and directly, personally conduct the business. * * *

"Plaintiff's suit is based upon an oral proposal alleged to have been made to him by Feinberg. The substance of the proposal was embodied in the newspaper item published at the direction of Feinberg. This publication was, tacitly at least, approved by Myer Ackerman. There was no disavowal by Samuel Ackerman, the third director, or by the corporation, of Feinberg's authority to make the published proposal. If the circumstances warranted the inference that the corporation, by previous authorization, or by subsequent ratification, or by acquiescence with knowledge of the facts, approved Feinberg's published offer, we think it may be assumed that he could bind his company by an oral proposal of substantially the same terms to the same persons.

"It was undisputed that the proposal was published, that the publication was directed by Feinberg; that Myer Ackerman approved it; and that Samuel Ackerman did not disavow it; that no officer of the company had disavowed it to the date of trial. * * *

"It seems to us that the trial revolved about two points: first whether Feinberg could bind the corporation without a resolution of the board of directors, and second, whether Feinberg made the proposal as claimed by plaintiff. The first question was answered by the Court, the second by the jury. * * * *"

HURLEY v. ORNSTEEN

Supreme Judicial Court of Massachusetts, 1942.
311 Mass. 477, 42 N.E.2d 273.

DOLAN, JUSTICE.

This is an action of contract, brought by the trustee in bankruptcy of Feldman & Company, Inc., to recover a balance alleged to be due from the defendant on account of various transactions concerning the purchase and sale of securities. The defendant's answer contained a general denial, a plea of payment, and a plea of accord and satisfaction. The judge found for the plaintiff, and the case comes before us upon the defendant's exceptions to the judge's refusal to grant certain of his requests for rulings. No findings of fact were made by the judge.

There was evidence that the bankrupt, a Massachusetts corporation authorized to carry on a stock brokerage and investment business, was originally organized under the name of Feldman, Rothstein & Company, Inc. In 1934 its name was changed to Feldman & Company, Inc., the present name of the company.

The management and control of the company's business were in the board of directors, the agreement of association providing that "The Board of Directors shall have the entire control and management of the corporation, its property and business." The original members of the board of directors of the corporation were Albert Feldman, Richard Feldman and Soloman Rothstein. On April 6, 1934, when it was voted to change the name of the corporation, its officers were described in the articles of amendment as a president and treasurer and three directors, Albert Feldman being named as president, treasurer and a director, and Richard Feldman being named as clerk and a director. They were also described as a majority of the directors.

The defendant opened an account with the corporation and as a result of transactions concerning the purchase and sale of securities between July 31, 1933, and December 19, 1933, there was a balance due from him to the corporation of $1,561.60. The defendant testified that Richard Feldman was the only representative of Feldman & Company, Inc., with whom he ever had any transactions; that in general he did his business with him, opened his account with him, made financial arrangements with him, and dealt with him with reference to whether he would have to furnish collateral security and, if so, the amount thereof. The corporation held as collateral for the payment of the balance due from the defendant six hundred shares of stock owned by him.

The defendant introduced in evidence a carbon copy of a letter written to him dated September 10, 1934, which read as follows: "Your account at the present time, based on present markets, is so far under water that against the balance due us of about $1460.00 there is a present market value of about $775.00. It is my understanding that you are in no position to provide additional collateral and if it is agreeable to you, I will wipe this account off the books and send you a receipted bill. This would involve a loss to us about $675.00. If you think this procedure is fair, please advise. Sincerely." The defendant testified that the original letter was signed by Albert Feldman; that upon its receipt he talked with Richard Feldman and told him about the letter; that Richard told him that the corporation would take whatever collateral the defendant had deposited with it and would "wipe off the account on that basis"; that he told Richard "to dispose of it in whatever way he had to, to settle the account"; that the latter stated that "whatever securities the corporation had on hand it would accept in payment for whatever [was] owed the corporation and would sell said securities"; and that he told Richard Feldman "to go ahead and do so." There is nothing in the record to show who the third director of the corporation was at that time.

At the close of the evidence the defendant requested the judge to rule: "1. The evidence establishes that there was an accord and satisfaction between the plaintiff's bankrupt and the defendant. 2. The evidence warrants the finding that there was an accord and satisfaction between the plaintiff's bankrupt and the defendant. 4. Upon all the evidence, Richard Feldman had authority to enter into an accord and satisfaction with the defendant." The judge denied these requests subject to the defendant's exceptions and found for the plaintiff in the sum of $926.10. * * *

The second request, however, was for a ruling that the evidence was sufficient to warrant a finding of an accord and satisfaction. If such a finding was supportable on the evidence, the defendant was entitled to the ruling requested or to a statement by the judge of findings of fact sufficient to show that it had become irrelevant.

We are of opinion, however, that it cannot be said properly that the evidence would support a finding in the present case of an accord and satisfaction that was binding upon the corporation. It is true as argued by the defendant that the corporation through its board of directors had authority to compromise claims in its favor or against it under the terms of the agreement of association whereby "the entire control and management of the corporation, its property and business" was confided to the directors. See G.L. (Ter.Ed.) c. 156, § 25. It is also true that where a majority of a board of directors of a corporation participate in the doing of a corporate act within their powers and the other directors have knowledge of and adopt it by acquiescence or otherwise the corporation is bound by their action, and this without a formal meeting and vote of the board, but this does not mean that a majority may bind the corporation by an act required to be performed by the directors where the other members of the board have no knowledge of the transaction at the time it is entered into, and do not subsequently adopt it either expressly or impliedly, except in some rare and unusual circumstances not shown to have been present in the case at bar.

In the present case there is nothing to show that the third director of the corporation had any knowledge of the alleged accord and satisfaction between Albert Feldman and Richard Feldman and the defendant. Although Albert Feldman was president and treasurer as well as a director of the corporation, and Richard Feldman was clerk and a director of the corporation, their respective offices as president and treasurer and as clerk, of themselves, did not confer upon them any power to bind the corporation outside of a "comparatively narrow circle of functions specially pertaining to their offices."

The evidence in the present case would warrant a finding that Richard Feldman had apparent or ostensible authority to deal with the defendant in the matter of the purchase and sale of securities and to determine whether he would have to furnish collateral security and, if so, the amount thereof, since an implied delegation of authority to an agent may arise from a course of conduct showing that a principal has repeatedly acquiesced therein and adopted acts of the same kind. The apparent scope of an agent's authority is limited, however, to that which falls within the general class of acts done by him over a considerable period of time. And in the case before us there was no evidence that either Albert or Richard Feldman or both had at any time prior to the alleged accord and satisfaction entered into any compromise of claims in favor of or against the corporation, or of any course of conduct on their part tending to show any implied or ostensible authority from the board to compromise claims. "It is settled that an agent or officer of a corporation has not ordinarily authority to cancel or release a contract of his principal which is in force."

There is nothing, moreover, to show any knowledge of or ratification by acquiescence or otherwise of the alleged accord and satisfaction by the third member of the board of directors. No book entries disclosing the transaction or the application of the collateral to its alleged consummation appear in the record, whatever would be the effect of such entries, in the light of the other evidence, had they been shown to have existed.

In these circumstances we cannot say rightly that a finding of an accord and satisfaction that was binding upon the corporation was supportable upon the evidence. It follows that there was no error in the denial of the defendant's second requested ruling.

Exceptions overruled.

Notes

(1) Consider particularly RMBCA § 8.21. To what extent does this section supplant various common law doctrines such as ratification, estoppel, acquiescence, and unjust enrichment that might lead a court to hold a corporation bound on an obligation even though it was not formally approved by the board of directors acting at a meeting?

(2) Since a majority of the board acting at a meeting can bind the corporation, why should not a majority acting informally pursuant to RMBCA § 8.21 also bind the corporation? Some states authorize a majority of shareholders to act informally without a meeting (see p. 480 supra). Why not directors as well?

(3) The various mechanics and requirements for directors and directors meetings are set forth in RMBCA §§ 8.20–8.25.

D. OFFICERS

BLACK v. HARRISON HOME CO.
Supreme Court of California, 1909.
155 Cal. 121, 99 P. 494.

ANGELLOTTI, J. This action is one originally brought by plaintiffs to compel specific performance of an alleged contract for the sale by defendant corporation to plaintiffs of lots 1 and 2 in block J of the Morris Vineyard tract, in the city of Los Angeles. The interveners sought specific performance of another alleged contract for the sale by said defendant to them of the same property. The trial court found that defendant corporation never entered into either of said contracts, and gave judgment for defendant against both plaintiffs and interveners. Plaintiffs appeal from such judgment and from an order denying their motion for a new trial. Interveners appeal only from the order denying their motion for a new trial.

The evidence is practically without conflict. Defendant corporation was organized by C.G. Harrison in the year 1889, its purposes, as stated in the articles of incorporation, being generally to acquire by gift, purchase, and otherwise, real and personal property, to manage the same, and to sell and dispose of the same. Its original assets consisted entirely of the community property conveyed to it by C.G. Harrison and his wife, Sarah J. Harrison. Its stock was divided into 1,000 shares of the par value of $100 each, and this stock was subscribed for and issued as follows: C.G. Harrison, 1 share; Sarah J. Harrison, 499 shares; Olive M. Harrison, a daughter, 498 shares; Lewis G. Harrison, a son, 1 share; F.H. Pieper, a brother-in-law of Mr. Harrison, 1 share. At the first meeting of the directors, being the above-named persons, C.G. Harrison was elected president, Mrs. Harrison vice president, and Olive M. Harrison secretary and treasurer. The by-laws of the corporation made it the duty of the president to sign all contracts which had first been approved by the directors, authorized him to draw checks of the corporation on banks where the funds thereof were deposited, and gave him direction of the affairs of the corporation, subject to the advice of the directors. It further provided that, in the event of his inability to act, the vice president should take his place and perform his duties. At the first meeting of the board of directors, held in September, 1899, the following resolution was adopted: "Resolved that the president and secretary of the Harrison Home Company be and the same are hereby authorized, empowered and directed to sell, contract to sell, mortgage, lease and convey any and all property of said corporation, on such terms as they may deem best and advisable, and the said president and secretary are hereby authorized, empowered and directed to execute all deeds, mortgages, releases, leases or other instruments necessary to carry into effect the sales, mortgages, leases as otherwise herein provided." At the second meeting, held in November, 1899, a resolution was adopted authorizing the president and secretary to purchase, receive, and accept such property as the president or secretary deemed advisable, and authorizing the president and secretary to exchange property of the corporation for other property, and to execute the necessary papers. The minutes of the board of directors show that meetings of that body were frequently had up to December 27, 1902. At these meetings reports were received from the president, C.G. Harrison, and "accepted" by the directors, showing the business transacted, including sales of many parcels of the property of the corporation; but there is nothing therein, or in any other evidence submitted, tending to show that any contract of sale or conveyance was ever executed by the president alone, or in any other manner than as authorized by the resolution relative thereto, viz., by the president and secretary jointly. No meeting of the stockholders was held after the first meeting until July 5, 1905, and no meeting of the directors from December 27, 1902, until July 11, 1905. No new officers of the corporation were elected until July, 1905.

C.G. Harrison died intestate September 7, 1904, and no administration had been commenced in the matter of his estate at the time of the transactions in question or the time of the trial of this case. Until his death he acted as president of the corporation, but it does not appear that the course of business in regard to the transfer of real estate owned by the corporation ever differed from the method prescribed by the resolution hereinbefore set forth. From the time of his death Mrs. Harrison acted as president, as she was entitled to do under the by-laws; but the very few conveyances of real estate made prior to the transaction in question were executed by her and the secretary jointly, and no departure from the prior course of business in that regard is shown. She signed checks alone as her husband had previously done, but that was expressly authorized by the by-laws. The funds of the corporation were drawn upon in many instances for the private use of the widow, daughter, and son; but we do not regard that as material in determining the question before us. On May 31, 1905, Olive M. Harrison, the secretary, died. It was stipulated by the parties that she died intestate, never having been married and being without issue. She was then a woman of about 35 years of age. She died the owner of the 498 shares issued to her at the time of the formation of the corporation. No administration in the matter of her estate had been commenced at the time of the trial of this action. There is nothing to show that she did not leave debts which must be paid out of her estate, sufficient in amount to entirely exhaust it.

Within 15 days after the death of Olive M. Harrison, namely, on June 15, 1905, the writing which serves as the basis of plaintiffs' claim was executed by Mrs. Harrison, purporting to bind the defendant corporation by her, as president. It read as follows: "Los Angeles, Cal., June 15, 1905. I hereby authorize Henry R. Higgins as exclusive agent to sell lots 1 and 2, in block J. Morris Vineyard tract, * * * at any time within fifteen days from this date, to net me the sum of (12,000) twelve thousand dollars cash. Said Higgins must get his commission and pay for his services over and above said sum of $12,000 such sum as he adds to $12,000. I agree to convey or cause to be conveyed said property by deed, free and clear of all incumbrance on the payment to me of said sum of $12,000 net cash. I also agree to furnish the purchaser a complete certificate of title to said premises. Harrison Home Company. Sarah J. Harrison, Pres. Witness: Hugh W. Harrison. In Duplicate." * * * On June 28, 1905, Mrs. Harrison, by a letter written by her attorney and approved by her, notified the Title Insurance & Trust Company that she declined to do anything further under either of the alleged contracts, "on account of misunderstanding and seeming misrepresentations" by which they were obtained, and also "by reason of the fact that Mrs. Harrison has not the requisite authority to enter into such a contract or to fulfill it on behalf of the Harrison Home Company." This refusal was duly communicated to the parties, and this action followed.

It is an elementary principle of corporation law that the president of a corporation has no power, merely because he is president, to bind the corporation by contract. The management of the affairs of a corporation is ordinarily in the hands of its board of directors, and the president has only such power as has been given him by the by-laws and by the board of directors, and such other power as may arise from his having assumed and exercised the power in the past with the apparent consent and acquiescence of the corporation. The general rule in this regard is stated in 2 Cook on Corporations § 716, as follows: "The president of a corporation has no power to buy, sell, or contract for the corporation, nor to control its property, funds, or management. This is a rule which prevails everywhere, excepting possibly in the state of Illinois. * * * It is true that the board of directors may expressly authorize the president to contract; or his authority to contract may arise from his having assumed and exercised that power in the past; or the corporation may ratify his contract or accept the benefits of it, and thereby be bound. But the general rule is that the president cannot act or contract for the corporation any more than any other one director." It is clear that the president of defendant corporation was never expressly authorized by by-laws or resolution of the board of directors to execute on behalf of the corporation a contract for the sale of real estate. So far as the by-laws are concerned, his power in regard to contracts for the sale of real estate was to sign such contracts as had first been approved by the directors, and the provision that he should have direction of the affairs of the corporation, subject to the advice of the directors, did not limit the effect of the prior provision so far as such contracts were concerned. The resolution of the board of directors authorized such contracts only when jointly executed by the president and secretary. The president's want of express authority to make either of these contracts on behalf of the corporation is thus affirmatively made to appear. It is also clear that the power to execute a binding contract of sale of real estate owned by the corporation could not be implied from the mere fact that he was the principal executive officer of the corporation invested with general direction of its affairs. It was not within the apparent scope of the business intrusted to him that he should have any such power.

The principal claim of plaintiffs and interveners is that defendant corporation is estopped to deny the binding effect of the acts of Mrs. Harrison. In the discussion of this branch of the case, much is made by appellants of the asserted fact that Mrs. Harrison is the owner of all the stock of the defendant corporation and is really the only person interested therein, and that she is here using the corporation simply to protect herself against her contract for the conveyance of what is practically her own property. If we assume that her ownership of all the stock would be a material factor, the trouble with appellants' position is that the record does not warrant the conclusion that the stock is so owned. Olive M. Harrison, the daughter, upon the record before us, must be held to have been the absolute owner, at the time of her death, only two weeks before the transactions in question, of 498 shares, practically one-half of the entire stock of the corporation. Giving the utmost force to the stipulation of the parties as to her dying intestate, never having been married and without issue, the property left by her is subject to administration and the payment of her debts, and Mrs. Harrison will have only what is left after administration. It cannot be assumed that Olive M. Harrison did not leave creditors, or that it will not be necessary to sell in due course of administration all or some portion of her stock to pay debts and expenses of the administration. Under these circumstances, Mrs. Harrison did not have absolute control of such stock at the time of the transactions in question, or at any time prior to the trial of this action, and cannot be held to have been such an owner thereof that her acts could affect the stock owned by her daughter at the time of her death.

There is nothing in the record warranting the assumption of learned counsel for plaintiffs and interveners that prior to the transaction in question the president of defendant corporation had ever assumed and exercised any power to bind the corporation by his own contract for the disposition of its real estate. So far as appears, the course of business of the corporation in relation to sales of real property had always been in strict accord with the method prescribed by the by-laws and the resolution of the board of directors, and the transactions in question were the first instances of any different course. The conveyances introduced in evidence were all executed by the president and secretary jointly, and, for aught that appears here, contracts for sale had been similarly executed. The minutes of the corporation do not show anything inconsistent with this view. We have not therefore a case where the corporation can be held estopped from denying the power of the president by a course of dealing on the part of that officer acquiesced in by the corporation through its board of directors. The authorities cited by counsel in support of the well-settled rule that a corporation may be so estopped cannot be held applicable. * * * The cases we have referred to are examples of the general line of cases relied on by appellants. They simply affirm what are well-settled rules, viz., that a corporation will be bound so far as third persons are concerned by the acts of its agent which are within the apparent scope of his authority, and that the authority of an officer to make certain contracts on behalf of the corporation may arise as to third persons from his having assumed and exercised that authority in the past with the acquiescence of the corporation, and that a corporation may ratify and render binding a contract entered into by one of its officers in excess of his authority. None of these rules has, in our judgment, any application upon the record before us.

There was no acceptance by defendant of any benefit of either of these transactions, and consequently no estoppel on that ground. * * *

The judgment and orders denying a new trial are affirmed.

Notes

(1) The comments in the principal case about the relative roles of the board of directors and the president of a corporation are not only representative of early judicial thinking but also seem firmly grounded on the

language in many corporation statutes. Compare RMBCA §§ 8.01, 8.41, last paragraph.

(2) Most corporation statutes specify that every corporation must have designated officers, usually a president, one or more vice presidents, a secretary, and a treasurer. Earlier versions of the Model Business Corporation Act also specified these officers, but the revised Model Act generally does not. Compare RMBCA § 8.40(a); see, however, §§ 8.40(c), 1.40(20). Why not require designated officers? The Official Comment suggests that "[e]xperience has shown * * * that little purpose is served by a statutory requirement that there be certain officers, and statutory requirements may sometimes create problems of implied or apparent authority or confusion with nonstatutory offices the corporation desires to create."

(3) Presumably, the chief executive officer of a small corporation, no matter what his or her formal title, will be required to take a number of actions on his or her own authority. For example, who is to hire secretaries, order needed equipment and supplies and the like? Where does one go to find the basis of authority? Consider Appendix 3, infra, art. IV, § 5 and art. V, § 1. Where else might one go? What should be the dividing line between the proper and the improper, i.e. between things the operating officer can do on his own and the things that should be approved by the board of directors?

LEE v. JENKINS BROS.

United States Court of Appeals, Second Circuit, 1959.
268 F.2d 357.

MEDINA, CIRCUIT JUDGE. * * *

[Editor: In 1919, the Crane Company agreed to sell its Bridgeport, Connecticut, plant to a New Jersey Corporation, Jenkins Brothers. Jenkins Brothers felt it needed to employ competent personnel, and sought to employ Lee, the business manager of Crane Company. Yardley, the President of Jenkins Brothers and a substantial stockholder, met with Lee at a hotel on June 1, 1920, and sought to entice him to join Jenkins Brothers. Also present was a vice president and his wife, though at the time of the trial in October 1957 only Lee was alive to describe the conversation.]

First, Lee testified:

"As far as the pension that I had earned with Crane Company he said the company [Jenkins Brothers] would pay that pension (and) if they didn't or, if anything came up, he would assume the liability himself, he would guarantee payment of the pension; and in consideration of that promise I agreed to go to work for Jenkins Bros. on June 1, 1920."

"The amount of the pension referred to by Mr. Yardley was a maximum of $1500 a year and that would be paid me when I reached the age of 60 years; regardless of what happened in the meantime, if I were with the company or not, I would be given a credit for those 13 years of service with the maximum pension of $1500."

Later Lee put it this way:

> "Mr. Farnham Yardley said that Jenkins would assume the obligation for my credit pension record with Crane Company and, if anything happened and they did not pay it, he would guarantee it himself."

> "Mr. Yardley's words were 'regardless of what happens, you will get that pension if you join our company.'"

Finally, Lee summarized his position:

> "My claim is that the company through the chairman of the board of directors and the president, promised me credit for my 13 years of service with Crane Company, regardless of what happened I would receive a pension at the age of 60, not to exceed $1,500 a year. If I was discharged in 1921 or 1922 or left I would still get that pension. That is what I am asking for."

This agreement was never reduced to writing.

Lee's prospects with Jenkins turned out to be just about as bright as he had hoped. He subsequently became vice president and general manager in charge of manufacturing and a director of the company. At that time he was receiving a salary of $25,000 from Jenkins, $8,000 more from an affiliate, plus an annual 10 per cent bonus. In 1945, however, after 25 years with Jenkins, Lee was discharged at the age of 55 * * *.

In the discussion which follows we assume *arguendo*, that there was evidence sufficient to support a finding that Yardley orally agreed on behalf of the corporation that Lee would be paid at the age of 60 a pension not to exceed $1500, and that Yardley's words "regardless of what happens" were, as Lee contends, to be interpreted as meaning that Lee would receive this pension even if he were not working for Jenkins at the time the pension became payable. Jenkins asserts that Yardley had no authority to bind it to such an "extraordinary" contract, express, implied, or apparent and the trial court so found. There is nothing in the proofs submitted by Lee to warrant any finding of actual authority in Yardley. The Certificate of Incorporation and By-Laws of Jenkins are not in evidence nor was any course of conduct shown as between the corporation and Yardley. Accordingly, on the phase of the case now under discussion, we are dealing only with apparent authority. See 2 Fletcher, Cyclopedia Corporations, Section 449 (Perm.Ed.1954). * * *

The ascertainment of the Connecticut law on this critical question of Yardley's apparent authority is a far from simple task. The Connecticut cases have not yet quite come to grips with the question. Hence, it is necessary to consult the "general" law on the subject, on the assumption that, if a general rule can be found, Connecticut would follow it. * * *

Our question on this phase of the case then boils itself down to the following: can it be said as a matter of law that Yardley as president, chairman of the board, substantial stockholder and trustee and son-in-law of the estate of the major stockholder, had no power in the presence of the company's most interested vice president to secure for a "reasonable" length of time badly needed key personnel by promising an experienced local executive a life pension to commence in 30 years at the age of 60, even if Lee were not then working for the corporation, when the maximum liability to Jenkins under such a pension was $1500 per year.

A survey of the law on the authority of corporate officers does not reveal a completely consistent pattern. For the most part the courts perhaps have taken a rather restrictive view on the extent of powers of corporate officials, but the dissatisfaction with such an approach has been manifested in a variety of exceptions such as ratification, estoppel, and promissory estoppel. For the most part also there has been limited discussion of the problem of apparent authority, perhaps on the assumption that if authority could not be implied from a continuing course of action between the corporation and the officer, it could not have been apparent to third parties either.

Such an assumption is ill-founded. The circumstances and facts known to exist between officer and corporation, from which actual authority may be implied, may be entirely different from those circumstances known to exist as between the third party and the corporation. The two concepts are separate and distinct even though the state of the proofs in a given case may cause considerable overlap.

The rule most widely cited is that the president only has authority to bind his company by acts arising in the usual and regular course of business but not for contracts of an "extraordinary" nature. The substance of such a rule lies in the content of the term "extraordinary" which is subject to a broad range of interpretation.

The growth and development of this rule occurred during the late nineteenth and early twentieth centuries when the potentialities of the corporate form of enterprise were just being realized. As the corporation became a more common vehicle for the conduct of business it became increasingly evident that many corporations, particularly small closely held ones, did not normally function in the formal ritualistic manner hitherto envisaged. While the boards of directors still nominally controlled corporate affairs, in reality officers and managers frequently ran the business with little, if any, board supervision. The natural consequence of such a development was that third parties commonly relied on the authority of such officials in almost all the multifarious transactions in which corporations engaged. The pace of modern business life was too swift to insist on the approval by the board of directors of every transaction that was in any way "unusual."

The judicial recognition given to these developments has varied considerably. Whether termed "apparent authority" or an "estoppel" to deny authority, many courts have noted the injustice caused by the practice of permitting corporations to act commonly through their executives and then allowing them to disclaim an agreement as beyond the authority of the contracting officer, when the contract no longer suited its convenience. Other courts, however, continued to cling to the past with little attempt to discuss the unconscionable results obtained or the doctrine of apparent authority. Such restrictive views have been generally condemned by the commentators.

The summary of holdings pro and con in general on the subject of what are and what are not "extraordinary" agreements is inconclusive at best, as shown by the authorities collected in the footnote. But the pattern becomes more distinct when we turn to the more limited area of employment contracts.

It is generally settled that the president as part of the regular course of business has authority to hire and discharge employees and fix their compensation. In so doing he may agree to hire them for a specific number of years if the term selected is deemed reasonable. But employment contracts for life or on a "permanent" basis are generally regarded as "extraordinary" and beyond the authority of any corporate executive if the only consideration for the promise is the employee's promise to work for that period. Jenkins would have us analogize the pension agreement involved herein to these generally condemned lifetime employment contracts because it extends over a long period of time, is of indefinite duration, and involves an indefinite liability on the part of the corporation.

It is not surprising that lifetime employment contracts have met with substantial hostility in the courts, for these contracts are often oral, uncorroborated, vague in important details and highly improbable. Accordingly, the courts have erected a veritable array of obstacles to their enforcement. They have been construed as terminable at will, too indefinite to enforce, *ultra vires*, lacking in mutuality or consideration, abandoned or breached by subsequent acts, and the supporting evidence deemed insufficient to go to the jury, as well as made without proper authority.

However, at times such contracts have been enforced where the circumstances tended to support the plausibility of plaintiff's testimony. Thus when the plaintiff was injured in the course of employment and he agreed to settle his claim of negligence against the company for a lifetime job, authority has been generally found and the barrage of other objections adequately disposed of. And where additional consideration was given such as quitting other employment, giving up a competing business, or where the services were "peculiarly necessary" to the corporation, the courts have divided on the enforceability of the contract.

What makes the point now under discussion particularly interesting is the failure of the courts denying authority to make lifetime contracts to evolve any guiding principle. More often than not we find a mere statement that the contract is "extraordinary" with a citation of cases which say the same thing, without giving reasons. And even in some of the leading cases the question of apparent authority is not even mentioned. All this is a not uncommon indication that the law in a particular area is in a state of evolution, and there seems every reason to believe that the law affecting numerous features of employer-employee relationship, is far from static.

Where reasons have been given to support the conclusion that lifetime employments are "extraordinary," and hence made without authority, a scrutiny of these reasons may be helpful for their bearing on the analogous field of pension agreements. It is said that: they unduly restrict the power of the shareholders and future boards of directors on questions of managerial policy; they subject the corporation to an inordinately substantial amount of liability; they run for long and indefinite periods of time. Of these reasons the only one applicable to pension agreements is that they run for long and indefinite periods of time. There the likeness stops. Future director or shareholder control is in no way impeded; the amount of liability is not disproportionate; the agreement was not only not unreasonable but beneficial and necessary to the corporation; and pension contracts are commonly used fringe benefits in employment contracts. Moreover, unlike the case with life employment contracts, courts have often gone out of their way to find pension promises binding and definite even when labeled gratuitous by the employer. The consideration given to the employee involved is not at all dependent on profits or sales, nor does it involve some other variable suggesting director discretion.

In this case Lee was hired at a starting salary of $4,000 per year plus a contemplated pension of $1500 per year in thirty years. Had Lee been hired at a starting salary of $10,000 per year the cost to the corporation over the long run would have been substantially greater, yet no one could plausibly contend that such an employment contract was beyond Yardley's authority.

The cases on executive authority to make pension agreements are few. In West v. Hunt Foods, Inc., 1951, 101 Cal.App.2d 597, 225 P.2d 978, the most recent case on the subject, a nonsuit was reversed on the theory that the jury might have decided in plaintiff's favor either upon the basis of authority in the president and vice-president to make the promise of a pension or on the basis of a promissory estoppel. In Langer v. Superior Steel Corp., 1935, 318 Pa. 490, 178 A. 490, authority was found lacking in the president, who acted in direct violation of a directors' resolution, to promise a pension for life in return for past services. His apparent authority was not discussed. In Plowman v. Indian Refining Co., D.C.E.D.Ill.1937, 20 F.Supp. 1, the vice president was found to lack authority gratuitously to promise 18 employees life pensions at half wages. In Rennie v. Mutual Life Ins. Co., 1 Cir., 1910, 176 F. 202, plaintiff orally was promised in 1886 by the defendant's president that if plaintiff would go to Australia to act as general manager and "if, on the termination of his employment as said general manager, the plaintiff had not succeeded in building up a satisfactory renewal commission account, the defendant would pay to him annually for the remainder of his life an amount sufficient to support him." The case seems distinguishable on its facts and in the setting of 1886 would not seem particularly helpful today.

Apparent authority is essentially a question of fact. It depends not only on the nature of the contract involved, but the officer negotiating it, the corporation's usual manner of conducting business, the size of the corporation and the number of its stockholders, the circumstances that give rise to the contract, the reasonableness of the contract, the amounts involved, and who the contracting third party is, to list a few but not all of the relevant factors. In certain instances a given contract may be so important to the welfare of the corporation that outsiders would naturally suppose that only the board of directors (or even the shareholders) could properly handle it. It is in this light that the "ordinary course of business" rule should be given its content. Beyond such "extraordinary" acts, whether or not apparent authority exists is simply a matter of fact.

Accordingly, we hold that, assuming there was sufficient proof of the making of the pension agreement, Connecticut, in the particular circumstances of this case, would probably take the view that reasonable men could differ on the subject of whether or not Yardley had apparent authority to make the contract, and that the trial court erred in deciding the question as a matter of law. We do not think Connecticut would adopt any hard and fast rule against apparent authority to make pension agreements generally, on the theory that they were in the same category as lifetime employment contracts. * * *

Notes

Consider RMBCA § 8.01(b). Does this grant of authority to directors have a negative implication with respect to the actual or apparent authority of corporate officers? Assume that all corporate powers are being exercised "under the direction of" (rather than "by") the board of directors, as is almost always the case in large, publicly held corporations. Should that give the senior officers of the corporation greater authority than a senior executive with the same title might have in a corporation where corporate powers are being exercised "by" the board? Consider American Law Institute, Principles of Corporate Governance: Analysis and Recommendations, Tent.Draft No. 2, Reporter's Note, 63–65 (1984) *:

In general, questions concerning the authority of senior executives are normally special issues of agency law, and, as in agency law, the major relevant concepts are those of actual and apparent authority.

* * *

The law on the apparent authority of executives other than the president is relatively sparse (except for special rules relating to the corporation's secretary). In contrast, there are a number of cases concerning the apparent authority of a president by virtue of his position. While the rules on this issue have varied in the past, the accepted modern rule is that (unless restricted by a corporate standard which the third person has reason to know) the president has apparent authority by virtue of his position to take actions in the ordinary course of business, but not extraordinary actions. * * *

Until recently, the courts have often tended to be somewhat restrictive in determining the apparent authority of a president, perhaps influenced by statutory language that the business of the corporation shall be managed by the board. Some of the recent cases tend to interpret the president's apparent authority in a more expansive manner, perhaps influenced by the growing realization that in practice the management of the business of the corporation is normally conducted by or under the supervision of its executives. * * * But see, e.g., Lucey v. Hero Int'l Corp., 361 Mass. 569, 281 N.E.2d 266 (1972); Nelms v. A & A Liquor Stores, Inc., 445 S.W.2d 256 (Tex.Civ.App.1969). There are also indications that this more expansive approach is also being applied to the apparent authority of other senior executives. See American Anchor & Chain Corp. v. United States, 331 F.2d 860 (Ct.Cl. 1964); Monteleone v. Southern California Vending Corp., 264 Cal.App. 2d 798 (1968). Section 3.01 [similar to RMBCA § 8.01(b)] does not directly alter the basic rules in this area, but it should reinforce the judicial tendency to give the authority of senior executives an expansive interpretation in cases involving third persons—a tendency built on a sound understanding of the normal expectations of third persons dealing with such executives.

IN RE DRIVE–IN DEVELOPMENT CORP.

United States Court of Appeals, Seventh Circuit, 1966.
371 F.2d 215.

SWYGERT, CIRCUIT JUDGE.

The principal question in this appeal relates to the circumstances which may bind a corporation to a guaranty of the obligations of a related corporation when it is contended that the corporate officer who executed the guaranty had no authority to do so. The facts giving rise to the question underlie a claim filed by the National Boulevard Bank of Chicago in an arrangement proceeding under chapter XI of the Bankruptcy Act, 11 U.S.C.A. §§ 701–799, in which the Drive In Development Corporation was the debtor. National Boulevard's claim was disallowed by the referee, whose decision was confirmed by the district court.

Drive In was one of four subsidiary companies controlled by Tastee Freez Industries, Inc., a holding company that conducted no business of its own. * * *

[Editor: The officers of Drive In executed a guarantee of payment to induce National Boulevard Bank to make a loan to Drive In's parent corporation. The guarantee was executed by one Maranz on behalf of Drive In as "Chairman" and one Dick attested to its execution as secretary. National Boulevard requested a copy of the authorizing resolution of the board of directors of Drive In. A copy, certified by Dick with the corporate seal affixed was duly delivered. No such resolution, however, was contained in Drive In's corporate minute book, and the directors' testimony was uncertain whether any such resolution had ever been considered or approved at a directors meeting. National Boulevard advanced substantial sums under the guaranty.]

Turning to the merits of the objections to National Boulevard's claim, the referee found that Drive In's minute book did not show that a resolution authorizing Maranz to sign the guaranty was adopted by the directors and that Dick could not recall a specific directors' meeting at which such a resolution was approved. From these findings, the referee concluded that Maranz, who signed the guaranty on behalf of Drive In, had no authority, "either actual or implied or apparent," to bind Drive In. This conclusion was erroneous. Drive In was estopped to deny Maranz' express authority to sign the guaranty because of the certified copy of a resolution of Drive In's board of directors purporting to grant such authority furnished to the bank by Dick, whether or not such a resolution was in fact formally adopted. Dick was the secretary of the corporation. Generally, it is the duty of the secretary to keep the corporate records and to make proper entries of the actions and resolutions of the directors. Therefore it was within the authority of Dick to certify that a resolution such as challenged here was adopted. Statements made by an officer or agent in the course of a transaction in which the corporation is engaged and which are within the scope of his authority are binding upon the corporation. Consequently Drive In was estopped to deny the representation made by Dick in the certificate forwarded to National Boulevard, in the absence of actual or constructive knowledge on the part of the bank that the representation was untrue.

In McMan Oil & Gas Co. v. Hurley, 24 F.2d 776 (5th Cir.1928), resolutions of an executive committee and a board of directors authorizing the conveyance of an interest in oil lands were challenged as not having been adopted by majority vote. The court, however, found sufficient authority for the execution of the conveyance, stating:

> The resolutions, both of the executive committee and of the board of directors, purport to have been adopted by majority votes. It is conclusively presumed that they were so adopted by reason of the certificates to that effect issued by the secretary and delivered to appellant by the general attorney of the [corporation]. A corporation is estopped to deny the representations of its officers and agents made within the scope of their authority. Id., at 778. * * *

The objectors argue that since William Schneider, a vice president of National Boulevard, requested Dick to furnish the certified copy of a resolution granting authority to execute the guaranty, and since Hugh Driscoll, another vice president of National Boulevard, was also a director of Tastee Freez and was familiar with the organization of the subsidiaries, the bank was somehow in a position to know that no resolution had in fact been adopted by Drive In's board of directors. These facts, however, fall far short of proving such knowledge on the part of National Boulevard.

Looking at this case realistically, it is apparent that Drive In was one of a number of subsidiary corporations in a complex dominated by Maranz. Drive In was part of an integrated business enterprise, and whatever benefited one part of the enterprise benefited all. Although the objectors do not contend that Drive In's guaranty was ultra vires,[16] they argue that a guaranty by one corporation of the obligation of another not shown to be in furtherance of the first corporation's business is an extraordinary and unusual contract, and that in such a situation unusual powers of corporate officers are not to be lightly inferred. Although intercorporate contracts of guaranty do not usually occur in the regular course of commercial business, here the interrelationship of Tastee Freez and its subsidiaries presented a situation in which the guaranty was not so unusual as would ordinarily obtain. Furthermore, the realities of modern corporate business practices do not contemplate that those who deal with officers or agents acting for a corporation should be required to go behind the representations of those who have authority to speak for the corporation and who verify the authority of those who presume to act for the corporation. * * *

The order of the district court confirming the referee's order is reversed in part and affirmed in part.

Notes

What if the third person should know that the directors could not have possibly adopted the resolution being certified to by the secretary on the date specified? In Keystone Leasing Corp. v. Peoples Protective Life Ins. Co., 514 F.Supp. 841 (E.D.N.Y.1981) the court refused to grant the third person the benefit of the estoppel principle set forth in *In re Drive–In* where the third person "must have been aware" that the transaction had not been authorized by the board of directors. See also American Union Financial Corp. v. University Nat'l Bank of Peoria, 44 Ill.App.3d 566, 3 Ill. Dec. 248, 358 N.E.2d 646 (1976).

16. [By the Court] The objectors concede that the only question here is an agency question, that if Maranz had authority to act for Drive In in executing the guaranty, Drive In could not assert lack of power as a defense in light of Ill.Rev.Stat. ch. 32, § 157.8 (1965), which reads in part:

No act of a corporation * * * shall be invalid by reason of the fact that the corporation was without capacity or power to do such act * * *.

E. DISSENSION, DEADLOCK AND OPPRESSION

GEARING v. KELLY

Court of Appeals of New York, 1962.
11 N.Y.2d 201, 227 N.Y.S.2d 897, 182 N.E.2d 391.

PER CURIAM.

Appellants, who own 50% of the stock of the Radium Chemical Company, Inc., seek, within the provisions of section 25 of the General Corporation Law, Consol.Laws, c. 23, to set aside the election of a director.

In a proceeding under that section, the court sits as a court of equity which may order a new election "as justice may require". We have concluded, as did the majority of the Appellate Division, that appellants have failed to show that justice requires a new election, in that they may not now complain of an irregularity which they themselves have caused.

Mrs. Meacham stayed away from the meeting of March 6, 1961 for the sole purpose of preventing a quorum from assembling, and intended, in that manner, to paralyze the board. There can be no doubt, and indeed it is not even suggested, that she lacked notice or in any manner found it temporarily inconvenient to present herself at that particular time and place. It is certain, then, that Mrs. Meacham's absence from the noticed meeting of the board was intentional and deliberate. Much is said by appellants about a desire to protect their equal ownership of stock through equal representation on the board. It is, however, clear that such balance was voluntarily surrendered in 1955. Whether this was done in reliance on representations of Kelly, Sr., as alleged in the plenary suit, is properly a matter for that litigation, rather than the summary type of action here.

The relief sought by appellants, the ordering of a new election, would, furthermore, be of no avail to them, for Mrs. Meacham would then be required, as evidence of her good faith, to attend. Such a futile act will not be ordered.

The identity of interests of the appellants is readily apparent. Mrs. Gearing has fully indorsed and supported all of the demands and actions of her daughter, and has associated herself with the refusal to attend the directors' meeting. A court of equity need not permit Mrs. Gearing to attack actions of the board of directors which were marred through conduct of the director whom she has actively encouraged. To do so would allow a director to refuse to attend meetings, knowing that thereafter an associated stockholder could frustrate corporate action until all of their joint demands were met.

The failure of Mrs. Meacham to attend the directors' meeting, under the present circumstances, bars appellants from invoking an exercise of the equitable powers lodged in the courts under the statute.

The order appealed from should be affirmed, with costs.

FROESSEL, JUDGE (dissenting).

The by-laws of Radium Chemical Company, Inc., provided for a board of four directors, a majority of whom "shall constitute a quorum for the transaction of business". Prior to 1955 the board consisted of appellant Meacham, who had succeeded her father (appellant Gearing's late husband), respondent Kelly, Sr., and Margaret E. Lee. In 1955 Kelly, Jr., was elected to the then vacant directorship. The board continued thus until Margaret Lee offered her resignation in 1961 and, on March 6 of that year, at a meeting of the board of directors at which she and the two Kellys were present, her resignation was accepted. Thereupon the two Kellys elected Julian Hemphill, a son-in-law of Kelly, Sr., to replace Margaret Lee.

I agree with Justice Eager, who dissented in the Appellate Division, that two members of the board were insufficient to constitute a quorum in this case for the purpose of electing the new director. It necessarily follows that the election of Julian Hemphill is not merely irregular, as the majority hold, but is wholly void and must be set aside.

Section 25 of the General Corporation Law grants to the court two alternatives in a case such as this: (1) to confirm the election, or (2) to order a new election as justice may require (Matter of Faehndrich, 2 N.Y.2d 468, 474, 161 N.Y.S.2d 99, 104, 141 N.E.2d 597, 600). As we held in the case just cited, the clause "as justice may require" does not enlarge the court's power nor authorize it to grant different relief from that specified in the statute. There is no basis whatever here for the application of the doctrine of estoppel, and in no event could it reasonably be applied to the nondirector, appellant Gearing, a substantial stockholder in this corporation. The purported election is, therefore, a nullity.

This is a mere contest for control, and the court should not assist either side, each of which holds an equal interest in the corporation, particularly where, as here, petitioners were willing that director Meacham attend meetings for the purpose of transacting all the necessary business of the board, but were unwilling that she attend a meeting, the purpose of which was to strip them of every vestige of control. Appellant Meacham had surrendered nothing in 1955 when she permitted Kelly, Jr., to become a director as well as his father, for Margaret Lee was then a third director.

The statute mandates a new election and that should be ordered. It is no answer to say that the results will probably be the same. If the parties are deadlocked, whether as directors or stockholders, and choose to remain that way, they have other remedies, and I see no reason why we should help one side or the other by disregarding a by-law that follows the statute (General Corporation Law, § 27), particularly when it results in giving the Kellys complete control of the corporation.

I would, therefore, reverse the order appealed from, and modify the order of Special Term by ordering a special election and affirming it in all other respects.

DESMOND, C.J., and FULD, VAN VOORHIS, BURKE and FOSTER, JJ., concur in Per Curiam opinion.

FROESSEL, J., dissents in an opinion in which DYE, J., concurs.

Notes

(1) Many state statutes relating to the filling of vacancies on the board of directors are based on section 38 of the 1969 Model Business Corporation Act, which provides "any vacancy occurring in the board of directors may be filled by the affirmative vote of a majority of the remaining directors though less than a quorum of the board of directors." MBCA (1969 Ed.) § 38, first sentence. If this statute had been in effect in New York at the time Gearing v. Kelly arose, would the Kellys need the presence of Mrs. Meacham in order to elect Hemphill? What does the clause "though less than a quorum" in section 38 modify? Compare RMBCA § 8.10(a)(3). Does the language of that section resolve all possible ambiguity?

(2) Consider also the possible application of RMBCA § 8.05(e) to the facts of this case. Judge Eager, dissenting in the court below, commented:

> It is obvious that the assembling of a quorum of the directors for the purpose of the filling of the vacancy in the board would tend to perpetuate in the Kelly family the control of this corporation. The vacancy would be filled by a Kelly nominee. Thereupon, the Kelly family with their fifty per cent stock holdings could deadlock the vote at future stockholders' meetings and effectively block an election of new or other directors by stockholders. Thus, their controlled board would continue in office. All this would tend to relegate the petitioners to the status of mere minority stockholders and defeat their rights as holders of fifty per cent of the stock. This would give the Kelly family an undue and unconscionable advantage and thus, clearly, estoppel as a doctrine applicable for the promotion of justice, should not be applied here.

Gearing v. Kelly, 15 A.D.2d 219, 222–223, 222 N.Y.S.2d 474, 478 (1961). Is he correct or does it depend on the manner in which directors are to be elected? Compare, for example, the election strategies that should have been followed in the *Stancil* case (page 461) where an odd number of directors was being elected by cumulative voting in a corporation also owned equally by two factions.

IN RE RADOM & NEIDORFF, INC.

Court of Appeals of New York, 1954.
307 N.Y. 1, 119 N.E.2d 563.

DESMOND, JUDGE.

Radom & Neidorff, Inc., the proposed dissolution of which is before us here, is a domestic corporation which has for many years, conducted, with great success, the business of lithographing or printing musical compositions. For some thirty years prior to February 18, 1950, Henry Neidorff, now deceased, husband of respondent Anna Neidorff, and David Radom, brother-in-law of Neidorff and brother of Mrs. Neidorff, were the sole stockholders, each holding eighty shares. Henry Neidorff's will made his wife his executrix and bequeathed her the stock, so that, ever since his death, petitioner-appellant David Radom and Anna Neidorff, brother and sister, have been the sole and equal stockholders. Although brother and sister, they were unfriendly before Neidorff's death and their estrangement continues. On July 17, 1950, five months after Neidorff's death, Radom brought this proceeding, praying that the corporation be dissolved under section 103 of the General Corporation Law, Consol.Laws, c. 23, the applicable part of which is as follows:

"§ 103. *Petition in Case of Deadlock*

"Unless otherwise provided in the certificate of incorporation, if a corporation has an even number of directors who are equally divided respecting the management of its affairs, or if the votes of its stockholders are so divided that they cannot elect a board of directors, the holders of one-half of the stock entitled to vote at an election of directors may present a verified petition for dissolution of the corporation as prescribed in this article."

That statute, like others in article 9 of the General Corporation Law, describes the situations in which dissolution may be petitioned for, but, as we shall show later, it does not mandate the granting of the relief in every such case.

The petition here stated to the court that the corporation is solvent and its operations successful, but that, since Henry Neidorff's death, his widow (respondent here) has refused to co-operate with petitioner as president, and that she refuses to sign his salary checks, leaving him without salary, although he has the sole burden of running the business. It was alleged, too, that, because of "unresolved disagreements" between petitioner and respondent, election of any directors, at a stockholders' meeting held for that purpose in June, 1950, had proved impossible. A schedule attached to the petition showed corporate assets consisting of machinery and supplies worth about $9,500, cash about $82,000, and no indebtedness except about $17,000 owed to petitioner (plus his salary claim). Mrs. Neidorff's answering papers alleged that, while her husband was alive, the two owners had each drawn about $25,000 per year from the corporation, that, shortly after her husband's death, petitioner had asked her to allow him alone to sign all checks, which request she refused, that he had then offered her $75,000 for her stock, and, on her rejection thereof, had threatened to have the corporation dissolved and to buy it in at a low price or, if she should be the purchaser, that he would start a competing business. She further alleged that she has not, since her husband's death, interfered with Radom's conduct of the business and has signed all corporate checks sent her by him except checks for his own salary which, she says, she declined to sign because of a stockholder's derivative suit brought by her against Radom, and still pending, charging him with enriching himself at this corporation's expense.

Because of other litigation now concluded, see matter of Radom's Estate, 305 N.Y. 679, 112 N.E.2d 768, to which Mrs. Neidorff was not a party, but which had to do with a contest as to the ownership of the Radom stock, respondent's answering papers in this dissolution proceeding were not filed until three years after the petition was entered. From the answering papers it appears, without dispute, that for those three years, the corporation's profits before taxes had totaled about $242,000, or an annual average of about $71,000, on a gross annual business of about $250,000, and that the corporation had, in 1953, about $300,000 on deposit in banks. There are many other accusations and counteraccusations in these wordy papers, but the only material facts are undisputed: first, that these two equal stockholders dislike and distrust each other; second, that, despite the feuding and backbiting, there is no stalemate or impasse as to corporate policies; third, that the corporation is not sick but flourishing; fourth, that dissolution is not necessary for the corporation or for either stockholders; and, fifth, that petitioner, though he is in an uncomfortable and disagreeable situation for which he may or may not be at fault, has no grievance cognizable by a court except as to the nonpayment of his salary, hardly a ground for dissolving the corporation.

Special Term held that these papers showed a basic and irreconcilable conflict between the two stockholders requiring dissolution, for the protection of both of them, if the petition's allegations should be proven. An order for a reference was, accordingly, made, but respondent appealed therefrom, and no hearings were held by the Referee. The Appellate Division reversed the order and dismissed the petition, pointing out, among other things, that not only have the corporation's activities not been paralyzed but that its profits have increased and its assets trebled during the pendency of this proceeding, that the failure of petitioner to receive his salary did not frustrate the corporate business and was remediable by means other than dissolution. The dismissal of the proceeding was "without prejudice, however, to the bringing of another proceeding should deadlock in fact arise in the selection of a board of directors, at a meeting of stockholders to be duly called, or if other deadlock should occur threatening impairment or in fact impairing the economic operations of the corporation." 282 App. Div. 854, 124 N.Y.S.2d 424, 425. Petitioner then appealed to this court.

It is worthy of passing mention, at least, that respondent has, in her papers, formally offered, and repeated the offer on the argument of the appeal before us, "to have the third director named by the American Arbitration Association, any Bar Association or any recognized and respected public body."

Clearly, the dismissal of this petition was within the discretion of the Appellate Division. General Corporation Law, § 106. There is no absolute right to dissolution under such circumstances. Even when majority stockholders file a petition because of internal corporate conflicts, the order is granted only when the competing interests "are so discordant as to prevent efficient management" and the "object of its corporate existence cannot be attained." Hitch v. Hawley, 132 N.Y. 212, 221, 30 N.E. 401, 404. The prime inquiry is, always, as to necessity for dissolution, that is, whether judicially-imposed death "will be beneficial to the stockholders or members and not injurious to the public," General Corporation Law, § 117; Hitch v. Hawley, supra. * * * Taking everything in the petition as true, this was not such a case, and so there was no need for a reference, or for the taking of proof, under sections 106 and 113 of the General Corporation Law.

The order should be affirmed, with costs.

FULD, JUDGE (dissenting).

Section 103 of the General Corporation Law, insofar as here relevant, permits a petition for dissolution of a corporation by the holders of one half of the shares of stock entitled to vote for directors "if the votes of its stockholders are so divided that they cannot elect a board of directors". That is the precise situation in the case before us, for the petition explicitly recites that petitioner Radom and respondent Neidorff "are hopelessly deadlocked with respect to the management and operation of the corporation" and that serious disputes have developed between them with the result that "the votes of the two stockholders are so divided that they cannot elect a Board of Directors." * * *

For upwards of thirty years, petitioner Radom and Henry Neidorff, respondent's husband, shared equally in the ownership and management of Radom & Neidorff, Inc. Through all that time, their relationship was harmonious as well as profitable. Neidorff died in 1950, at which time respondent, through inheritance, acquired her present 50% stock interest in the business. Since then, all has been discord and conflict. The parties, brother and sister, are at complete loggerheads; they have been unable to elect a board of directors; dividends have neither been declared nor distributed, although the corporation has earned profits; debts of the corporation have gone unpaid, although the corporation is solvent; petitioner, who since Neidorff's death has been the sole manager of the business, has not received a penny of his salary—amounting to $25,000 a year—because respondent has refused to sign any corporate check to his order. More, petitioner's business judgment and integrity, never before questioned, have been directly attacked in the stockholder's derivative suit, instituted by respondent, charging that he has falsified the corporation's records, converted its assets and otherwise enriched himself at its expense. Negotiations looking to the purchase by one stockholder of the other's interest were begun—in an effort to end the impasse—but they, too, have failed.

In very truth, as petitioner states in his papers, "a corporation of this type, with only two stockholders in it cannot continue to operate with incessant litigation and feuding between the two stockholders, and with differences as fundamental and wholly irreconcilable as are those of Mrs. Neidorff and myself. * * * settlement of these differences cannot be effected, while continuance on the present basis is impossible, so that there is no alternative to judicial dissolution." Indeed, petitioner avers, in view of the unceasing discord and the fact that he has had to work without salary and advance his own money to the corporation, he does not, whether or not dissolution be granted, "propose to continue to labor in and operate this business."

It is, then, undisputed and indisputable that the stockholders are not able to elect a board of directors. In addition, it is manifest, on the facts alleged, that the Supreme Court could find that the stockholders are hopelessly deadlocked vis-à-vis the management of the corporation; that the corporation cannot long continue to function effectively or profitably under such condition; that petitioner's resignation as president and manager—which he contemplates—will be highly detrimental to the interests of both corporation and stockholders and cannot help but result in substantial loss; and that petitioner is not responsible for the deadlock that exists. In such circumstances, the requisite statutory hearing may well establish that dissolution is indispensable, the only remedy available. As the high court of New Jersey recently declared in applying to somewhat comparable facts a statute similar to section 103 of our General Corporation Law, Matter of Collins–Doan Co., 3 N.J. 382, 396, 70 A.2d 159, 166, 13 A.L.R.2d 1250, "In the case at hand, *there is a want of that community of interest essential to corporate operation.* Dissolution will serve the interests of the shareholders as well as public policy. * * * And, if the statutory authority be deemed discretionary in essence, there is no ground for withholding its affirmative exercise here, *for there is no alternative corrective remedy.* * * * The dissension is such as to defeat the end for which the corporation was organized." (Emphasis supplied.)

Here, too, the asserted dissension, the court could find, permits of no real or effective remedy but a section 103 dissolution. And that is confirmed by a consideration of the alternatives seemingly open to petitioner. He could remain as president and manager of the corporation, without compensation, completely at odds with his embittered sister—certainly neither a natural nor a satisfying way in which to conduct a business. Or he could carry out his present plan to quit the enterprise—and thereby risk a loss, to corporation and stockholders, far greater than that involved in terminating the business. Or he could, without quitting, set up a competing enterprise—and thereby expose himself to suit for breach of fiduciary duty to the corporation. Cf. Duane Jones Co. v. Burke, 306 N.Y. 172, 117 N.E.2d 237. It is difficult to believe that the legislature could have intended to put one in petitioner's position to such a choice. Reason plainly indicates, and the law allows, the reasonable course of orderly dissolution pursuant to section 103.

Respondent, however, suggests that, in view of the fact that petitioner is managing the business profitably, he should continue to do so, defendant against the stockholder's suit which she brought attacking his honor and integrity and himself start an action for the compensation denied him for more than three years. But, it seems self-evident, more and further litigation would only aggravate, not cure, the underlying deadlock of which petitioner complains. And, if he were to bring the suggested suit for salary due him, the question arises, whom should he sue, and who is to defend? The mere proposal that petitioner embark on a series of actions against the corporation, of which he is president and half owner, indicates the extent of the present impasse, as well as the futility of perpetuating it. The same is true of the other alternative suggested by respondent, namely, that the third of the three directors, required by section 5 of the Stock Corporation Law, Consol. Laws, c. 59, be appointed by an impartial party. The deadlock of which petitioner complains is between the stockholders, not the directors, and when stockholders are deadlocked, section 103 calls for dissolution, not arbitration. Beyond that, and even if the offer to elect an impartial director were relevant, it would still be necessary to inquire when it was made and under what circumstances. It does not justify, alone or in conjunction with the other facts, a summary dismissal of the proceeding without a hearing.

Although respondent relies on the fact that the corporation is now solvent and operating at a profit, it is manifest that, if petitioner carries out his plan to resign as president and quits the business, there may be irreparable loss, not alone to him and respondent, as the owners of the corporation, but also to the corporation's creditors. Quite apart from that, however, the sole issue under section 103 is whether there is a deadlock as to the management of the corporation, not whether business is being conducted at a profit or loss. Whether the petition should or should not be entertained surely cannot be made to turn on proof that the corporation is on the verge of ruin or insolvency.

Insolvency may be a predicate for dissolution, but not under section 103. By virtue of other provisions of Article 9 of the General Corporation Law—sections 101 and 102—directors and stockholders may seek dissolution, when the corporation is insolvent, in order to prevent further loss to the owners and creditors. Section 103, however—which bears the title, *"Petition in case of deadlock"*—was designed to serve a far different purpose. As amended in 1944, upon the recommendation of the Law Revision Commission, that section provides for dissolution "if the votes of its stockholders are so divided that they cannot elect a board of directors." Nothing in the statute itself or in its legislative history suggests that a "Petition in case of deadlock" must wait until the corporation's profits have dried up and financial reverses set in. Had the commission or the legislature intended to incorporate such a qualification into section 103, it could readily have done so. The only test envisaged by the commission, however, was that which the legislature enacted, and a court may not import any other. * * *

The order of the Appellate Division should be reversed and that at Special Term affirmed.

CONWAY, DYE and VAN VOORHIS, JJ., concur with DESMOND, J.

FULD, J., dissents in opinion in which LEWIS, C.J., and FROESSEL, J., concur.

Notes

(1) See RMBCA § 14.30(2), a statute that is typical of many state involuntary dissolution statutes. The Official Comment to this section makes it clear that the use of the word "may" in the preambular material preserves the court's discretion (applied in *Radom*) "as to whether dissolution is appropriate even though grounds exist under the specific circumstances." Why shouldn't the remedy of involuntary dissolution be generally available to minority shareholders in closely held corporations to the same extent that remedy is available to partners in a general partnership?

(2) Compare RMBCA §§ 14.01, 14.02, 14.20. Might a dissatisfied shareholder in a closely held corporation be able to use these alternative dissolution provisions to avoid the limitations of § 14.30(2)?

(3) For an interesting evaluation of the dynamics of the interaction between Mrs. Neidorff and her brother, see Chayes, Madame Wagner and the Close Corporation, 73 Harv.L.Rev. 1532, 1545–7 (1960).

(4) In In re Hedberg–Freidheim & Co., 233 Minn. 534, 535–7, 47 N.W.2d 424, 426–7 (1951), the Court was faced with a request for involuntary dissolution under the following circumstances:

> The allegations of the petition * * * show that since the year 1935 there has been continuous dissension, which has become more pronounced in recent years, between the two families with respect to the operation of the business of the corporation. * * *

> Fred Hedberg has been in charge of production for the corporation, and Charles Freidheim has had charge of collections, credits, financial details, the supervision and construction of new buildings, purchasing of equipment, and arranging for the possible expansion and further development of the business. However, for the last two or three years Hedberg has practically taken over the operation of the corporation's business without consultation with the other directors.

> Since 1947, Hedberg has refused to speak to or converse with Freidheim in connection with the business and affairs of the corporation except at formal meetings of its board of directors and sharehold-

ers. In order for Freidheim to communicate with Hedberg, Freidheim has been compelled to send messages to Hedberg through Hedberg's son. Recently, Hedberg caused a partition to be built in the office of the corporation between their respective desks so as to remove himself from personal contact with Freidheim. He has openly expressed himself to the corporation's employes of his bitterness toward Freidheim to such an extent that the employes have become fearful and dissatisfied. Suggestions made by Freidheim with respect to operation of the business, business policies, bonuses to employes, and various public relations are always vetoed by Hedberg without regard to the consideration of the merits thereof. Differences exist between them on a number of basic questions of corporate policy and management. They need not be enumerated here. It is sufficient to state that because of the lack of cooperation, exchange of ideas, and refusal on Hedberg's part to permit proposals made by Freidheim to be put into effect, even those relating to the departments of the business over which Freidheim is supposed to have charge, a stalemate has been reached, * * *

The Court ordered dissolution even though the business of the corporation had prospered in the past.

DAVIS v. SHEERIN

Court of Appeals of Texas, 1988.
754 S.W.2d 375, error denied.

Before EVANS, C.J., and SAM BASS and DUNN, JJ.

OPINION

DUNN, JUSTICE.

This is an appeal from portions of a trial court's judgment, in which James L. Sheerin ("appellee") was declared to own a 45% share in a corporation * * *. The major challenges are against an ordered buy-out of appellee's stock in the corporation * * *. William H. Davis ("appellant") is the owner of the remaining 55% interest in * * * [the corporation].

In May of 1985, appellee brought suit individually in his own right, and as a shareholder on behalf of W.H. Davis Co., Inc., a Texas corporation ("the corporation"), against William H. Davis and Catherine L. Davis ("appellants") based on allegations of appellants' oppressive conduct toward appellee as a minority shareholder, and their breaches of fiduciary duties owed to appellee and the corporation. * * *

In 1955, William Davis and appellee incorporated a business, initially started by William Davis, in which appellant Davis owned 55% and appellee owned 45% of the corporation's stock. Appellants and appellee all served as directors and officers, with William Davis serving as president and running the day-to-day operations of the business. Appellee, unlike appellants, was not employed by the corporation. In

1960, appellee and appellant William Davis formed a partnership for the purpose of acquiring real estate.

The precipitating cause of appellee's lawsuit in 1985 was appellants' denial of appellee's right to inspect the corporate books, unless appellee produced his stock certificate. Appellants claimed that appellee had made a gift to them, in the late 1960's, of his 45% interest.

* * *

Following a six-week trial to a jury, the trial court, in addition to declaring that appellee owned a 45% interest in the corporation, * * * ordered a "buy-out" by appellants of appellee's 45% of the stock in the corporation for $550,000, the fair value determined by the jury * * *.

In points of error one through seven, appellants challenge the court's order that they buy-out appellee's 45% interest in the corporation. Appellants' basic argument is two fold: (1) the remedy of a "buy-out" is not available to a minority shareholder under Texas law, and (2) if such a remedy were available, the facts of this case are not appropriate for, nor do the jury's findings support, the application of this remedy based on the court's determination of oppressive conduct.

The Texas Business Corporation Act does not expressly provide for the remedy of a "buy-out" for an aggrieved minority shareholder. Tex. Bus.Corp.Act. art. 7.05 (Vernon 1980) does provide for the appointment of a receiver, with the eventual possibility of liquidation, for aggrieved shareholders who can establish the existence of one of five situations, including illegal, oppressive, or fraudulent conduct by those in control.

Nor do we find any Texas cases where the particular remedy of a "buy-out" has been ordered, unless provided for in a contract between the parties. But courts of other jurisdictions have recognized a "buy-out" as an appropriate remedy, even in the absence of express statutory or contractual authority. *See Alaska Plastics, Inc. v. Coppock,* 621 P.2d 270 (Alaska 1980); *Sauer v. Moffitt,* 363 N.W.2d 269 (Iowa Ct.App.1984); *McCauley v. Tom McCauley & Son, Inc.,* 104 N.M. 523, 724 P.2d 232 (Ct. App.1986) (granting the option of liquidation or "buy-out"); *In re Wiedy's Furniture Clearance Center Co.,* 108 A.D.2d 81, 487 N.Y.S.2d 901 (1985); *Delaney v. Georgia–Pacific Corp.,* 278 Or. 305, 564 P.2d 277 (1977). Alaska, Iowa, New Mexico, New York, and Oregon all have statutes that provide for liquidation as the remedy for oppressive acts, and, in the above cited cases, the courts allowed a "buy-out" as a less harsh remedy. Other states' statutes specifically provide for a "buy-out," either as a remedy for an aggrieved minority shareholder, * * * [citing the statutes of five states], or as an option available to a majority shareholder to avoid a liquidation order, * * * [citing the statutes of two states].

Both parties rely on *Patton v. Nicholas,* 154 Tex. 385, 279 S.W.2d 848 (1955), to support their respective arguments in favor of or against a court's authority in Texas to order a "buy-out." In that case, the court reversed an order of liquidation in a suit brought by an aggrieved minority shareholder, although it found that liquidation might be an appropriate remedy in some instances. * * * [A discussion of earlier Texas law is omitted.]

We conclude that Texas courts, under their general equity power, may decree a "buy-out" in an appropriate case where less harsh remedies are inadequate to protect the rights of the parties.

Having decided that a "buy-out" is an available remedy under the court's general equity powers, we must decide whether it was appropriate in this case. The trial court's judgment reflects that its "buy-out" order was based on the jury's finding of conspiracy to deprive appellee of his stock, on the evidence and arguments, and on its conclusion that appellants acted oppressively against appellee and would continue to do so. * * *

Oppressive conduct is the most common violation for which a "buy-out" was found to be an appropriate remedy in other jurisdictions. Courts take an especially broad view of the application of oppressive conduct to a closely-held corporation, where oppression may more easily be found. *Skierka v. Skierka Bros. Inc.,* 629 P.2d 214 (Mont.1981). An ordered "buy-out" of stock at its fair value is an especially appropriate remedy in a closely-held corporation, where the oppressive acts of the majority are an attempt to "squeeze out" the minority, who do not have a ready market for the corporation's shares, but are at the mercy of the majority.

The Texas Business Corporation Act, which provides a cause of action based on oppressive conduct, does not define oppressive conduct. *See* art. 7.05. Nor do we find any Texas decision providing a definition. We therefore turn again to decisions of other jurisdictions to consider what constitutes oppressive conduct.

Oppressive conduct has been described as an expansive term that is used to cover a multitude of situations dealing with improper conduct, and a narrow definition would be inappropriate. *McCauley,* 724 P.2d at 236. Courts may determine, according to the facts of the particular case, whether the acts complained of serve to frustrate the legitimate expectations of minority shareholders, or whether the acts are of such severity as to warrant the requested relief.

The New York court in *Wiedy's* held that oppression should be deemed to arise only when the majority's conduct substantially defeats the expectations that objectively viewed were both reasonable under the circumstances and were central to the minority shareholder's decision to join the venture. *Wiedy's,* 487 N.Y.2d at 903.

Courts in states with statutes containing situations establishing causes of action for minority shareholders, similar to those allowed in the Texas statute, have held that oppressive conduct is an independent ground for relief not requiring a showing of fraud, illegality, mismanagement, wasting of assets, nor deadlock, the other grounds available for shareholders, though these factors are frequently present. *Fix v.*

Fix Material Co., Inc., 538 S.W.2d 351, 358 (Mo.Ct.App.1976) (citing *Gidwitz v. Lanzit Corrugated Box Co.,* 20 Ill.2d 208, 170 N.E.2d 131, 135[1] (1960)).

While noting that general definitions are of little value for application in a specific case, the Oregon supreme court in *Baker* cited the most quoted definitions of oppressive conduct as:

> 'burdensome, harsh and wrongful conduct,' 'a lack of probity and fair dealing in the affairs of a company to the prejudice of some of its members,' or 'a visible departure from the standards of fair dealing, and a violation of fair play on which every shareholder who entrusts his money to a company is entitled to rely.'

Baker, 507 P.2d at 393.   *   *   *

Even though there were findings of the absence of some of the typical "squeeze out" techniques used in closely held corporations, e.g., no malicious suppression of dividends or excessive salaries, we find that conspiring to deprive one of his ownership of stock in a corporation, especially when the corporate records clearly indicate such ownership, is more oppressive than either of those techniques. Appellant's conduct not only would substantially defeat any reasonable expectations appellee may have had, as required by the New York Court in *Wiedy's,* but would totally extinguish any such expectations.   *   *   *

We therefore hold that the jury's finding of conspiracy to deprive appellee of his interest in the corporation, together with the acts of willful breach of a fiduciary duty as found by the jury, and the undisputed evidence indicating that appellee would be denied any future voice in the corporation, are sufficient to support the trial court's conclusion of oppressive conduct and the likelihood that it would continue in the future.

Under the analysis set out by the *Patton* court in its determination of whether liquidation was appropriate, we must determine whether lesser remedies than a "buy-out" could adequately protect appellee's interests. In *Patton,* the court found sufficient evidence to support only the malicious suppression of dividends claim, and thus concluded that a mandatory injunction to pay reasonable dividends then and in the future was adequate, with the additional protection of the court retaining jurisdiction.

In this case, the award of damages and certain injunctions might be sufficient to remedy the willful breaches of fiduciary duty found by the jury, i.e., informal dividends to appellants by making contributions to the profit sharing plan and waste of corporate funds for legal fees. However, based on appellants' conduct denying appellee any interest or voice in the corporation, we find that these remedies are inadequate to protect appellee's interest and his rights in the corporation.

Appellants' oppressive conduct, along with their attempts to purchase appellee's stock, are indications of their desire to gain total control of the corporation. That is exactly what a "buy-out" will achieve. We disagree with appellants' suggestion that a "buy-out" is a more drastic remedy than liquidation. *See Stefano v. Coppock,* 705 P.2d 443, 446 (Alaska 1985). This is especially true in light of the fact that appellants do not challenge the jury's finding of $550,000 as the fair value of appellee's stock, which is the amount set by the trial court for the "buy-out." * * *

Based on the facts of this case, we find that a "buy-out" was an appropriate remedy, and that the trial court did not abuse its discretion.

Points of error one through seven are overruled.

Notes

(1) In this opinion the court states that a mandatory buyout remedy is most often invoked in cases involving "oppressive conduct." Would it also be an appropriate remedy for cases of "deadlock" such as Gearing v. Kelly? Radom v. Neidorff? Or do these cases also involve "oppression"?

(2) Other recent cases agree that a court may order a buyout even where the statute, like RMBCA § 14.30(2), only refers to dissolution as the appropriate remedy. See e.g. Balvik v. Sylvester, 411 N.W.2d 383 (N.D.1987). These cases, however, may not be as radical as they first appear. Consider Haynsworth, The Effectiveness of Involuntary Dissolution Suits as a Remedy for Close Corporation Dissension, 35 Clev.St.L.Rev. 25, 50–55 (1987):

What results actually occur in close corporation involuntary dissolution suits? One way to answer this question is to examine existing published opinions. For the purposes of this article, the opinions published in 1984 and 1985 in which involuntary dissolution was one of the major causes of action were analyzed. These two years were chosen simply because they were the two most recent years for which decisions were available. Given the number and variety of cases during 1984 and 1985, it is doubtful that increasing the number of years in the sample would have yielded any significantly different or additional conclusions.

The 1984 and 1985 involuntary dissolution cases present an interesting statistical profile. There were a total of forty-seven cases that qualified for the sample. Forty-five of the cases came from twenty different states * * *.

Ten of the cases in the sample involved technical legal issues in which no decision on the type of relief, if any, had been made at the time the opinion was issued. * * *

Of the remaining thirty-seven cases, a buy-out was the most frequent relief ordered by the court or elected by the defendants. This result occurred in twenty of the decisions (fifty-four percent). Dissolution was ordered in ten of the cases (twenty-seven percent). In four of the cases (eleven percent), no substantial relief was granted to the plaintiff on the merits. Finally, in the three other cases (eight percent) relief other than either dissolution or a buy-out was the exclusive remedy ordered; and in eleven of the dissolution and buy-out cases (thirty percent of the total and thirty-seven percent of the dissolution and buy-out cases), additional relief was also granted. This additional relief included compensatory damages, punitive damages, an accounting, cancellation of issued stock, partial liquidation and other innovative orders * * *.

That a court-supervised buy-out was the predominant form of ultimate relief and that a buy-out occurred twice as frequently as a court-ordered liquidation is not surprising. A buy-out, assuming fair value is received for the shares, gives the plaintiff a cash-out right that he or she would not otherwise have, and in many cases, this is undoubtedly the principal motivation behind the lawsuit. Getting rid of a dissatisfied shareholder permanently is also advantageous to the corporation and remaining shareholders. Moreover, * * * judges have consistently stated that dissolution should be ordered only as a last resort when no alternative remedy is feasible; and the dissolution cases in the sample used in this article illustrate that in this instance, judges are practicing what they preach.

What is somewhat surprising is the number of cases in which a court-supervised buy-out is the result of the involuntary dissolution suit. In a previous study of the fifty-four involuntary dissolution opinions decided between 1960–1976 conducted by Professors J.A.C. Hetherington and Michael P. Dooley of the University of Virginia,[17] a court-ordered or court supervised buy-out was involved in only three of the cases, whereas dissolution was ordered in sixteen of the twenty-seven cases in which some affirmative relief was granted.

Two reasons probably account for the rather dramatic change in the mix between dissolution and buy-out cases in the two samples. First, a number of states have in recent years enacted statutes that allow the defendants to exercise a statutory buy-out right to purchase the shares of the plaintiff, thereby terminating the involuntary dissolution cause of action. This statutory buy-out right was exercised in eight of the twenty buy-out cases in the 1984–1985 opinions. Six of these were from New York, which enacted this type of statute in 1979. Second, courts in recent years seem to be increasingly willing to order a buy-out. Perhaps this in turn reflects a greater willingness of courts to consider options other than dissolution or dismissal. Of the involuntary dissolution cases analyzed by Professor Hetherington and Dooley, no affirmative relief was granted in twenty-seven cases, and in eighteen of those cases, dissolution was either denied, or the complaint was dismissed. Only four of the thirty-seven decisions on the merits in 1984 and 1985, however, resulted in no substantial relief being granted.

Professors Hetherington and Dooley not only analyzed the judicial opinions issued between 1960 and the end of 1976, but they also followed up on each case to determine the ultimate outcome. Interestingly, out of all the cases, including those for which relief had been

---

17. [By the Author] Hetherington & Dooley, Illiquidity And Exploitation: A Proposed Statutory Solution to the Re-

maining Close Corporation Problem, 63 Va. L.Rev. 1 (1976) [hereinafter Hetherington & Dooley].

denied, fifty-four percent actually ended up with one side buying out the other. This is exactly the same percentage as the buy-out cases in the 1984–1985 decisions. This parallelism suggests that recent decisions more accurately mirror the results ultimately negotiated by the parties than the decisions rendered a decade or more ago.

(3) The statutes of several jurisdictions recognize that a range of remedies, including a buyout, may be an appropriate judicial response to problems of deadlock or oppression. The Close Corporation Supplement to the Revised Model Business Corporation Act, § 41, for example, lists, in addition to a mandatory buyout (§ 42) and dissolution (§ 43), the following:

> (a) If the court finds that one or more of the grounds for relief described in section 40(a) exist, it may order one or more of the following types of relief:
>
> > (1) the performance, prohibition, alteration, or setting aside of any action of the corporation or of its shareholders, directors, or officers of or any other party to the proceeding;
> >
> > (2) the cancellation or alteration of any provision in the corporation's articles of incorporation or bylaws;
> >
> > (3) the removal from office of any director or officer;
> >
> > (4) the appointment of any individual as a director or officer;
> >
> > (5) an accounting with respect to any matter in dispute;
> >
> > (6) the appointment of a custodian to manage the business and affairs of the corporation;
> >
> > (7) the appointment of a provisional director (who has all the rights, powers, and duties of a duly elected director) to serve for the term and under the conditions prescribed by the court;
> >
> > (8) the payment of dividends;
> >
> > (9) the award of damages to any aggrieved party.

(4) As indicated in the Haynsworth excerpt and in the principal case, an increasing number of state statutes also expressly recognize a mandatory buyout as an available remedy. In considering these statutes, one should distinguish between statutes applicable to corporations generally and those applicable only to corporations that have elected special close corporation treatment, though decisions such as Zion v. Kurtz (p. 438 supra) and the principal case probably make that distinction less important than might first appear.

(5) The word "oppressive" does not carry "an essential inference of imminent disaster; it can contemplate a continued course of conduct." Gidwitz v. Lanzit Corrugated Box Co., 20 Ill.2d 208, 214, 170 N.E.2d 131, 135 (1960). The same court stated that "oppressive" is not synonymous with "illegal" or "fraudulent" and its application does not necessarily involve a finding of mismanagement or misapplication of assets. Other courts have referred to general concepts of "a lack of probity and fair dealing" or departure from standards of "fair play." White v. Perkins, 213 Va. 129, 134, 189 S.E.2d 315, 319–320 (1972). Exadaktilos v. Cinnaminson Realty Co., 167 N.J.Super. 141, 154–6, 400 A.2d 554, 561–2 (1979) involved § 14A:12–7(1)(c) of the New Jersey statute authorizing, in the case of a

corporation with less than 25 shareholders, the appointment of a custodian if the persons in control of the corporation "have acted oppressively or unfairly toward one or more minority shareholders in their capacities as shareholders, directors, officers or employees." The Court stated:

> To implement the intent of the Legislature, a method must be developed whereby it can be decided when a particular course of corporate conduct has resulted in the oppression of a minority shareholder.

> The special circumstances, arrangements and personal relationships that frequently underly the formation of close corporations generate certain expectations among the shareholders concerning their respective roles in corporate affairs, including management and earnings. These expectations preclude the drawing of any conclusions about the impact of a particular course of corporate conduct on a shareholder without taking into consideration the role that he is expected to play. Accordingly, a court must determine initially the understanding of the parties in this regard. Armed with this information, the court can then decide whether the controlling shareholders have acted in a fashion that is contrary to this understanding or in the language of the statute, "have acted oppressively * * * toward one or more minority shareholders."

> The expectations of the parties in the instant suit with regard to their participation in corporate affairs are not established by any agreement; they must be gleaned from the evidence presented. Here, the corporation is close and small and operates a single restaurant. Three of its shareholders had lengthy experience in the restaurant business prior to the corporation's formation. Although the corporation operates, technically, with one director who is not the largest stockholder, its business decisions actually have been made informally by these three shareholders. Except for its organizational meeting, no director or shareholder meetings have been held since the corporation's inception in 1972. Plaintiff, the fourth shareholder, had no restaurant experience at the time he received his stock as a gift from his father-in-law. By giving him the stock, Skordas sought to provide him with an opportunity to learn the restaurant business and eventually take part in its management.

> There is some indication that plaintiff's opportunity was extended over the objections of the other two shareholders and it is clear that they never welcomed him as a fellow participant in the enterprise. The evidence shows that plaintiff failed to get along with employees, causing the loss of key personnel, that he quit on more than one occasion, without reason or notice, and that he was not compatible with the other principals. Plaintiff's discharge from employment with the corporation, therefore, was because of his unsatisfactory performance.

> The circumstances under which the parties' expectations in these areas were disappointed do not establish oppressive action toward plaintiff by the controlling shareholders. The promise of employment was honored, the opportunity being lost to plaintiff through no fault of defendants. The parties' expectation that plaintiff would at some time

participate in management was likewise thwarted by plaintiff's failure to satisfy the condition precedent to participation, i.e., that he learn the business.

SHELL, ARBITRATION AND CORPORATE GOVERNANCE
67 No.Car.L.Rev. 517, 528–531 (1989).*

Although commentators have questioned the utility of arbitration in the close corporation setting,[18] investors in close corporations have included arbitration clauses in negotiated shareholder agreements for many decades.[19] Repeated legislative and judicial reforms have been needed, however, to establish arbitration as a legitimate means of dispute resolution in the close corporation context. A brief history of the legal development of corporate arbitration in the state of New York is illustrative of the hurdles that close corporation shareholders have had to overcome. * * *

Prior to 1920 neither New York nor the United States had a statute regulating the use of arbitration. Hence, common-law rules regarding arbitration provided the only guidelines for its use. Under common-law arbitration rules, agreements to arbitrate future disputes were deemed against public policy because they "ousted the jurisdiction of the courts." Even agreements to arbitrate existing disputes were revocable at any time prior to the rendering of an arbitration award. Thus, corporate arbitration in these early days was used successfully only when the shareholders agreed to submit their existing dispute to

---

18. [By the Author] Some commentators have said that arbitration is effective only for resolving "discrete, nonrecurring disagreements" and that it "cannot restore consensus." Hetherington & Dooley, [Illiquidity and the Close Corporation Problem, 63 Va.L.Rev. 1,] at 37. Although there is truth in this assertion, case law reveals instances in which arbitration has been used more than once to resolve disputes in a single close corporation. *See, e.g., In re* Denihan, 119 A.D.2d 144, 506 N.Y.S.2d 39 (1986) (describing family corporation that had been involved in a total of six arbitrations over a 15–year period), *aff'd,* 69 N.Y.2d 725, 504 N.E.2d 694, 572 N.Y.S.2d 367 (1987); *cf. In re* Darman, 105 A.D.2d 1028, 483 N.Y.S.2d 469 (1984) (describing the successful use of arbitrators to draft a comprehensive buy-sell agreement to govern ongoing relationship among parties). Other commentators have counseled that arbitration poses risks for close corporation shareholders because arbitrators may substitute their business judgment for that of

the managing shareholder or, worse still, may render a compromise award "that is unsatisfactory to both sides." Haynsworth, [The Effectiveness of Involuntary Dissolution Suits as a Remedy for Close Corporation Dissension, 35 Clev.St.L.Rev. 25,] at 29.

19. [By the Author] *See, e.g., In re* Carl, 263 A.D. 887, 32 N.Y.S.2d 410 (1942); Lumsden v. Lumsden Bros. & Taylor Inc., 242 A.D. 852, 275 N.Y.S. 221 (1934). Typically, close-corporation arbitration clauses are found in shareholder agreements entered into at the formation stage of the enterprise but not, curiously, in corporate charters. Research reveals no American cases involving an arbitration provision found solely in the charter of a close corporation. However, commentators have for years recommended that arbitration clauses be placed in both shareholder agreements and the articles of incorporation of new close corporations. *See, e.g.,* Hornstein, *Stockholders' Agreements in the Closely Held Corporation,* 59 Yale L.J. 1040, 1054 (1950). It seems likely therefore that some corporate charters have contained such provisions.

the arbitral forum and no party changed his mind prior to the moment when the arbitrators made their award.

Even after the passage in 1920 of New York's landmark arbitration statute, which mandated judicial enforcement of agreements to arbitrate future disputes, the New York Court of Appeals frustrated attempts by shareholders to bypass the courts. In *In re Fletcher* [20] the court held that an agreement among close corporation shareholders for arbitrators to determine the transfer price of closely held shares was not enforceable under the New York statute because valuations and appraisals were not "controversies" subject to statutory arbitration. The New York legislature overruled *Fletcher* in 1952 by amending its arbitration statute to cover "questions arising out of valuations, appraisals or other controversies which may be collateral, incidental, precedent or subsequent to or independent of any issue between the parties." [21]

Similarly, the New York courts were reluctant to approve the use of arbitration for control and management disputes within close corporations because such controversies were "nonjusticiable" matters that could not be heard in a court. [22] Once again the New York legislature amended the arbitration statute to make such disputes arbitrable "without regard to the justiciable character of the controversy." [23]

A third obstacle to the enforcement of arbitration agreements arose from the rigid statutory requirement that corporate affairs be managed solely by a board of directors. Courts have refused to permit shareholders to use governance structures, including arbitration, more tailored to

---

20. [By the Author] 237 N.Y. 440, 143 N.E. 248 (1924).

21. [By the Author] Act of Apr. 15, 1952, ch. 757, 1952 N.Y.Laws 1632 (amending Civil Practice Act, ch. 925 § 1448, 1920 N.Y.Laws 486 (replaced by N.Y.Civ.Prac.L. & R. § 7501 (McKinney 1981))); *see* O'Neal, *Resolving Disputes in Closely Held Corporations: Intra–Institutional Arbitration*, 67 Harv.L.Rev. 786, 796–97 (1954). The present New York arbitration statute omits this language because it was felt that the broad language of N.Y.Civ.Prac.L. & R. § 7501 clearly encompassed valuation and appraisal questions.

22. [By the Author] *See In re* Burkin, 1 N.Y.2d 570, 136 N.E.2d 862, 154 N.Y.S.2d 898 (1956). In *Burkin* the New York Court of Appeals held that a broad arbitration agreement between shareholders of a close corporation did not cover a dispute over removal of a shareholder-director because New York did not recognize a private right of action to remove a corporate director, and the state arbitration statute suggested that controversies were arbitrable only if they "might be the subject of an action." *Id.* at 571, 136 N.E.2d at 864, 154 N.Y.S.2d

at 900 ∗ ∗ ∗; *see also In re* Ades, 12 Misc.2d 913, 914, 177 N.Y.S.2d 582, 584 (1958) (motion to compel arbitration to remove director denied since only attorney general has right to remove director); *In re* Scuderi, 265 A.D. 1054, 1054, 39 N.Y.S.2d 422, 423 (1943) (refusing to permit arbitration regarding the validity of the election of a member of the board because the election "was governed by the by-laws of the corporation," not the shareholders' agreement).

23. [By the Author] N.Y.Civ.Prac.L. & R. § 7501 (McKinney 1980 & Supp.1988). There is evidence that this change to the New York arbitration statute was in process before the *Burkin* decision was handed down and was responsive to a general sense that the restrictive language in the statute served no justifiable purpose. In the famous case of Ringling Brothers, Barnum & Bailey Combined Shows, Inc. v. Ringling, 29 Del.Ch. 610, 53 A.2d 441 (1947), the Delaware court exhibited a reluctance to give full effect to an arbitration agreement between close corporation shareholders regarding the election, rather than the removal, of directors. ∗ ∗ ∗

their individual needs on the ground that such structures "sterilize the board." [24] * * *

A fourth close corporation arbitration problem that has vexed the New York courts is whether shareholder derivative claims may be arbitrated. A number of early New York cases suggested that arbitration of derivative suits violated public policy.[25] Other cases found a more technical means of avoiding arbitration by focusing on the fact that the corporation, on whose behalf the derivative claim is brought, was not a party to the shareholder arbitration agreement.[26]

Legal commentators quickly devised a means of solving the technical problem: have the corporation sign the arbitration agreement. As to the public policy argument, recent cases have refused to draw a distinction between close corporations and their shareholders and have thus permitted derivative suits to be arbitrated.[27] These courts have found that derivative claims of managerial waste and misappropriation are, realistically, disputes among the shareholders, not between the

24. [By the Author] 297 N.Y. 174, 77 N.E.2d 633 (1948). The New York courts have exhibited confusion on the question of when an arbitration agreement sterilizes the board. In one early case involving the removal of a shareholder as an officer and director of a close corporation, a New York court refused to enforce an arbitration agreement on the grounds that "the duty of the board of directors to manage the affairs of the corporation in accordance with their best judgment would be wholly abrogated in all cases" if arbitration prevailed. *In re* Allied Fruit & Extract Co., 243 A.D. 52, 56, 276 N.Y.S. 153, 157 (1934). Less than 10 years later, however, another New York court held on nearly identical facts that the removal of a shareholder as an officer and employee of a close corporation was properly subject to arbitration under a shareholder agreement. Martocci v. Martocci, 2 Misc.2d 330, 42 N.Y.S.2d 222, *aff'd*, 266 A.D. 840, 43 N.Y.S.2d 279 (1944). Other New York cases have approved arbitration involving a variety of management issues without regard to the sterilization issue. *See, e.g., In re* Lane, 50 N.Y.2d 864, 407 N.E.2d 1337, 430 N.Y.S.2d 41 (1980) (compensation and employment dispute); *In re* Glekel, 30 N.Y.2d 93, 281 N.E.2d 171 (1972) (agreement regarding registration of shares for a public offering); *In re* Groval Knitted Fabrics, Inc., 72 Misc. 2d 513, 339 N.Y.S.2d 58 (1971) (dispute over termination of salary and "freeze out" of minority shareholder), *aff'd*, 31 N.Y.2d 796, 291 N.E.2d 395, 339 N.Y.S.2d 117 (1972); Crandall v. Master–Eagle Photoengraving Corp., 27 Misc.2d 475, 211 N.Y.S. 2d 535 (1960) (claim of excessive compensation being paid to manager-shareholders),

aff'd, 13 A.D.2d 726, 217 N.Y.S.2d 469 (1961).

25. [By the Author] *See, e.g.,* Pfeiffer v. Berke, 4 Misc.2d 918, 920, 121 N.Y.S.2d 774, 777 (1953) ("An agreement to arbitrate the issues arising in a shareholder's derivative suit [is] unenforcible [sic] as against public policy."); *Application of* Diamond, 80 N.Y.S.2d 465, 467 (1948), ("The issues involved in the stockholder's derivative action are not referable to arbitration under the contract, and . . . [even if they were], they would be unenforceable as against public policy. . . ."), *aff'd*, 274 A.D. 762, 79 N.Y.S.2d 924 (1948); Lumsden v. Lumsden Bros. & Taylor, Inc., 242 A.D. 852, 275 N.Y.S. 221, 222 (1934) ("It does not appear how there could be an agreement to arbitrate a controversy of this nature made in advance. . . ."). *But see In re* Carl, 263 A.D. 887, 32 N.Y.S.2d 410 (1942) (enforcing arbitration's agreement on petition by defendant in derivative action).

26. [By the Author] *See* Hotcaveg v. Lightman, 27 Misc.2d 573, 574, 211 N.Y.S. 2d 533, 534 (1960); *Diamond*, 80 N.Y.S.2d at 466–67. Corporate arbitration clauses are frequently contained in shareholders' agreements to which the corporations are not parties. Thus, there is no written agreement to arbitrate binding the corporation.

27. [By the Author] Siegal v. Ribak, 43 Misc.2d 7, 13, 249 N.Y.S.2d 903, 909 (1964) ("From a logical and practical viewpoint, the conclusion is irresistible that in a close corporation a dispute concerning acts of waste is a matter involving stockholders *inter se*. To say that the corporate entity is the real party is to disregard reality.")

corporation and the alleged wrongdoer. The public policy of litigating derivative claims has therefore now given way to the policy of encouraging arbitration.[28]

A final problem involving the arbitration of close corporation disputes concerns dissolution. Early New York cases refused to enforce arbitration when the stockholder resisting arbitration sought to petition for dissolution of the corporation.[29] Subsequent decisions, however, have made clear that arbitration can be compelled even in the face of a petition for dissolution [30] and, indeed, that arbitrators have broad authority to order both dissolution and buyouts as remedies in arbitration.[31]

In summary, after nearly seventy years of legal evolution, arbitration is now utilized in New York as a close corporation remedy for virtually every kind of corporate dispute. Indeed, detailed case administration statistics compiled by the American Arbitration Association reveal that between 1984 and August 1988 the AAA received over one thousand claims and counterclaims worth over $118,000,000 under its case administration category dealing with close corporation disputes. These claims include disputes regarding stock valuation and appraisal, allegations of breach of contract, mismanagement, misrepresentation, wrongful discharge, and breach of fiduciary duty.

The few exceptions to the present pro-arbitration policy that may remain in New York or elsewhere are now subject to a new challenge. As noted earlier, the Supreme Court has recently reinterpreted the FAA [Federal Arbitration Act, 9 U.S.C. § 1, et seq.] as preempting attempts by the states to preclude access to the arbitral forum.[32] When parties can convince a court that their close corporation dispute involves interstate commerce,[33] they may be able to bypass even express

---

28. [By the Author] *Id.* ("On broad principles of practicality, the courts should encourage arbitration to dispose of the problems created by disputes within close corporations. Arbitration avoids the delay inherent in litigation and weeds out from our courts the very type of time consuming dispute that we have in the instant case.").

* * *

29. [By the Author] *In re* Cohen, 183 Misc. 1034, 1035, 52 N.Y.S.2d 671, 671 (1944) ("The disputes between these parties . . . may be decided by arbitration, but arbitration cannot compel a stockholder holding [50%] of the stock to desist from seeking its dissolution. No stockholder is required to continue in a state of constant legal warfare with the remaining [50%] interest."), *aff'd*, 269 A.D. 663, 53 N.Y.S.2d 467 (1945).

30. [By the Author] *See In re* Levy, 79 A.D.2d 684, 434 N.Y.S.2d 39 (1980).

31. [By the Author] *In re* Denihan, 119 A.D.2d 144, 506 N.Y.S.2d 39 (1986) (order-

ing arbitration of dissolution dispute), *aff'd*, 69 N.Y.2d 725, 504 N.E.2d 694, 512 N.Y.S.2d 367 (1987).

32. [By the Editor] Southland Corp. v. Keating, 465 U.S. 1, 104 S.Ct. 852, 79 L.Ed. 2d 1 (1984).

33. [By the Author] Many close corporations involve wholly intrastate commerce. Thus, state arbitration law would be the correct source of rules for interpreting arbitration agreements involving such entities. But when equity funds have been raised from out-of-state residents, when the corporation transacts business across state lines, or where the dispute at issue involves the use of interstate mails, telephones, or other means of communication, it is arguable that the arbitration provision is in a contract that involves interstate commerce and that the FAA should apply. *See* West Point–Pepperell, Inc. v. Multi–Line Indus., 231 Ga. 329, 201 S.E.2d 452 (1973). It could also be argued that an arbitration clause, viewed as a governance

statutory restrictions on arbitration, such as the New York requirement that an arbitration clause appear in the charter.[34] Not only do
FAA standards facilitate enforcement of arbitration clauses, federal law
also supports confirmation of corporate arbitration awards involving
attorneys' fees, punitive and multiple damages, and other extraordinary relief that might be prohibited under state law.

Notes

(1) The present New York statute, McKinney's Civ.Prac.Law § 7501,
provides that "a written agreement to submit any controversy thereafter
arising * * * is enforceable without regard to the justiciable character of
the controversy."

(2) The integrated close corporation statutes of a number of states
build off of the arbitration concept. Del.Gen.Corp.Law, § 353 is typical:

§ 353. Appointment of a Provisional Director in Certain Cases

(a) Notwithstanding any contrary provision of the certificate of
incorporation or the by-laws or agreement of the stockholders, the
Court of Chancery may appoint a provisional director for a close
corporation if the directors are so divided respecting the management
of the corporation's business and affairs that the votes required for
action by the board of directors cannot be obtained with the consequence that the business and affairs of the corporation can no longer
be conducted to the advantage of the stockholders generally.

(b) An application for relief under this section must be filed (1) by
at least one-half of the number of directors then in office, (2) by the
holders of at least one-third of all stock then entitled to elect directors,
or, (3) if there be more than one class of stock then entitled to elect one
or more directors, by the holders of two-thirds of the stock of any such
class; but the certificate of incorporation of a close corporation may
provide that a lesser proportion of the directors or of the stockholders
or of a class of stockholders may apply for relief under this section.

(c) A provisional director shall be an impartial person who is
neither a stockholder nor a creditor of the corporation or of any
subsidiary or affiliate of the corporation, and whose further qualifications, if any, may be determined by the Court of Chancery. A provisional director is not a receiver of the corporation and does not have
the title and powers of a custodian or receiver appointed under sections
226 and 291 of this title. A provisional director shall have all the
rights and powers of a duly elected director of the corporation, includ-

device, should be interpreted according to
the corporate and arbitration laws of the
state in which the entity is incorporated
[under the] "internal affairs doctrine".
* * * The internal affairs doctrine, however, is a choice of law rule distinguishing
among sources of *state* law. The question
of which arbitration statute to apply, by
contrast, is an issue of federalism, involving the supremacy of federal over state law

in matters involving congressional statutes
that regulate interstate commerce. Thus,
so long as the close corporation affects interstate commerce, the FAA should apply
to the enforcement of any arbitration provision and the confirmation of any award.

34. [By the Author] N.Y.Bus.Corp.Law
§ 620(b) (McKinney 1986).

ing the right to notice of and to vote at meetings of directors, until such time as he shall be removed by order of the Court of Chancery or by the holders of a majority of all shares then entitled to vote to elect directors or by the holders of two-thirds of the shares of that class of voting shares which filed the application for appointment of a provisional director. His compensation shall be determined by agreement between him and the corporation subject to approval of the Court of Chancery, which may fix his compensation in the absence of agreement or in the event of disagreement between the provisional director and the corporation.

(d) Even though the requirements of subsection (b) of this section relating to the number of directors or stockholders who may petition for appointment of a provisional director are not satisfied, the Court of Chancery may nevertheless appoint a provisional director if permitted by subsection (b) of section 352 of this title.

Is a "provisional director" different from an "arbitrator"? A "custodian"? Del.Gen.Corp.Law, § 226 authorizes the court to appoint a "custodian" for a corporation that is deadlocked in the election of directors or is suffering or threatened with irreparable injury; the authority of a custodian "is to continue the business of the corporation and not to liquidate its affairs and distribute its assets * * *." Del.Gen.Corp.Law, § 226(b). A "receiver", on the other hand, is directed "to take charge of [the corporation's] assets, estate, effects, business and affairs, and to collect the outstanding debts, claims, and property due and belonging to the corporation * * *." Del.Gen.Corp.Law, § 291.

(4) Under the Delaware statute, a corporation electing close corporation status does not have the option of electing out of section 353. Should it? Similarly, a Delaware corporation not electing close corporation status is not eligible for the appointment of a provisional director, though a custodian may be appointed. Giuricich v. Emtrol Corp., 449 A.2d 232 (Del. 1982). Why shouldn't the provisional director remedy be available to all deadlocked corporations?

KRUGER v. GERTH

Court of Appeals of New York, 1965.
16 N.Y.2d 802, 263 N.Y.S.2d 1, 210 N.E.2d 355.

Appeal from Supreme Court, Appellate Division, Second Department, 22 A.D.2d 916, 255 N.Y.S.2d 498.

Minority stockholders of corporation brought action against the corporation and two of the corporation's three directors to compel the two directors to dissolve the corporation, and to enjoin, as waste, the payment by the corporation of certain bonuses to one of the directors and two employees of the corporation, and to recover such bonus payments as had been made.

The Supreme Court, Special Term, Nassau County, Daniel G. Albert, J., entered a judgment directing the two directors to take all steps and procedures provided by Article 10 of the Business Corporation

Law to cause the corporation to be dissolved, and the two directors appealed.

The Supreme Court, Appellate Division, Second Department, entered an order on December 21, 1964 which reversed, on the law and the facts, the judgment of the Special Term and dismissed the cause of action for dissolution of the corporation.

The Appellate Division reversed findings of fact of the Special Term and found, as facts, that director Arthur Gerth owned 53% of the common stock of the corporation and one-half of its preferred stock, and that his brother, director Harry Gerth, owned 1% of its common stock, and that the minority stockholders owned the remainder of the preferred and common stock, which they had acquired under will of deceased testator, and that in 1950 the deceased testator and director Arthur Gerth were both employed by the corporation and received equal salaries of $6,000 but in that year the testator became ill and retired from active participation in the corporate business, though he continued to receive a salary from the corporation until his death, and that in 1951 the salary of director Arthur Gerth was increased to $7,500 and that he began to take bonuses, and that in the years 1958, 1959, and 1960 his salary was $9,000, and $9,374.94 for 1961, and that his bonus for each of those four years was $5,827.20, $7,153.20, $6,480, and $6,120, and that net worth of corporation during those years was more than $100,000 and its annual sales ranged from about $245,000 to about $275,000, and its annual net profit was less than $2,000 before provision for income taxes.

The Appellate Division held that dissolution of the corporation was not justified on ground that amount of bonuses received by director Arthur Gerth so reduced net profit of corporation as to leave an insufficient amount to provide a fair return to minority stockholders on their stock.

The minority stockholders appealed to the Court of Appeals.

Order affirmed, without costs, upon the majority opinion at the Appellate Division.

Dye, Van Voorhis, Sclleppi and Bergan, JJ., concur.

Desmond, C.J., and Fuld, J., dissent in the following opinions in each of which Burke, J., concurs.

Desmond, Chief Judge (dissenting).

The majority opinion of the Appellate Division proceeds on the mistaken assumption that the plaintiffs are demanding dissolution of this two-man corporation solely because the defendant majority stockholder is taking for himself a bonus and salary in such amounts as to reduce the net corporate profit below the amount necessary to provide dividends to plaintiffs on their common stock. That is an understatement of the grounds for liquidation urged by plaintiffs and accepted as fact in the Special Term opinion. The undisputed fact is that this corporation in recent years has had net profits of only about 1 or 2%

annually on the value of its assets; that there is (as testified by the majority stockholder) no prospect of the corporation ever making enough profit to pay any dividend to its common stockholders; that plaintiffs' 46% of the common stock is, therefore, both unprofitable and unsalable; and that the corporation does not and cannot serve any purpose beyond paying a salary to defendant Arthur A. Gerth. The main point is not that Gerth's salary plus bonus is exorbitant but that the corporation is being kept alive solely to pay that salary plus bonus. Since there is no likelihood of any appreciation of the assets or of any future growth or increment, liquidation is the only means whereby all the stockholders as stockholders can get something out of the corporation. It is obvious that if Mr. Gerth should die or become incapacitated so as to be unable to earn his salary, no stockholder, minority or majority, would vote to keep the corporation in business in order to pay Mr. Gerth's successor a salary. As to the equities, the plaintiffs are the executors of the deceased 46% common stockholder and the latter's widow who is the income beneficiary under his will has no prospect of collecting any income.

That a minority stockholder may sue for dissolution when the directors and majority stockholders have breached their fiduciary duties to the minority is settled by Leibert v. Clapp, 13 N.Y.2d 313, 247 N.Y.S.2d 102, 196 N.E.2d 540. The authorities cited and approved by us in the Leibert opinion (particularly Gaines v. Adler, 15 A.D.2d 743, 223 N.Y.S.2d 1011, and the case cited therein; Drob v. National Mem. Park, 28 Del.Ch. 254, 270, 271, 41 A.2d 589; Hornstein, A Remedy for Corporate Abuse, 40 Col.L.Rev., at p. 220 et seq.) require a court of equity to intervene and grant relief in such a case as this. The modern and just rule as explained in the cited Columbia Law Review article is that a court of equity should wind up the affairs even of a solvent going corporation when gross mismanagement of fraudulent or inequitable conduct causes real danger of imminent loss to stockholders which danger cannot be prevented except by liquidation, and where the circumstances have created a real exigency and liquidation will serve a beneficial purpose to all stockholders.

Such small corporations, being really partnerships between two or three people who contribute their capital, skills, experience and labor should be treated by a court of equity as partnerships in many respects. A large corporation or one that has some prospect of becoming large is really an institution separate and distinct from its owners serving a separate purpose in our society by providing employment, accumulating capital for proper purposes and adding to community wealth and community service. Even if such a large or growing corporation is temporarily operating at a loss there may be quite reasonable expectations that its position will improve. Not so with the two-man corporation which owns no valuable trade secrets, market advantages or growth probabilities but simply continues to exist as the form in which two individuals pool their efforts. When one of those two dies and everything indicates that the corporation can never do more than pay a salary to the survivor, the reason for corporate existence is gone and the court of equity should make a dissolution decree fashioned to fit the facts and providing for an appropriate form of dissolution and sale of the assets whether to the survivor or by public auction or otherwise as may appear just.

The Appellate Division order should be reversed, with costs to abide the event, and the action remitted to the Supreme Court for further proceedings not inconsistent with this opinion.

FULD, JUDGE (dissenting).

Although I agree with the Chief Judge that there should be a reversal, I do not find it necessary, in reaching such a result, to rely on Leibert v. Clapp, 13 N.Y.2d 313, 247 N.Y.S.2d 102, 196 N.E.2d 540.

The enterprise before us is a "close corporation" in the strictest sense, that is, one in which, regardless of the distribution of the shareholdings, "management and ownership are substantially identical." (Israels, The Close Corporation and the Law, 33 Cornell L.Q. 488.) In such a case, it seems almost self-evident, the fiduciary obligation of the majority to the minority extends considerably beyond what would be its reach in the context of a larger or less closely held enterprise. Here the relationship between the shareholders is very much akin to that which exists between partners or joint venturers.

Each case must, of course, be determined upon its own facts but there is no inherent reason why a court of equity cannot treat the participants in a genuine close corporation, insofar as their relationship *inter sese* is concerned, as they regard themselves—as partners or joint venturers.[35] On this analysis, they become not only entitled to the benefits of the relationship but equally subject to its burdens, including the power of a court of equity to dissolve the venture and, in so doing, to impose terms. Thus, it is my opinion, particularly in view of the increasing trend to legislative and judicial recognition of the distinctive character of the genuine close corporation,[36] that the analogy of the relationship between the participants themselves—wholly apart from that of their corporate creature to the world at large—to an informal joint venture with the shares of the corporation as its asset is apposite and useful. (See Conway, The New York Fiduciary Concept in Incorporated Partnerships and Joint Ventures, 30 Fordham L.Rev. 297).

The concept of joint venture is not a rigid one; "it does not require," one thoughtful writer on the subject has noted, "an explicit agreement applying the label 'joint venture' to the activity or series of activities in question; and * * * the closest analogy is to a partner-

---

35. [By the Judge] Although I recognize that this view runs counter to decisions in this court (see Weisman v. Awnair Corp. of America, 3 N.Y.2d 444, 449, 165 N.Y.S.2d 745, 749, 144 N.E.2d 415, 417), it reflects a growing trend throughout the country (see, e.g., De Boy v. Harris, 207 Md. 212, 113 A.2d 903) and is likewise the view expressed in Judge Desmond's dissent in the Weisman case.

36. [By the Judge] See, e.g., Business Corporation Law, Consol.Laws, c. 4, §§ 616, 620, 709, 1002, by which the Legislature has greatly enlarged the power and freedom of shareholders to contract with respect to internal corporate government.

ship at will." (Israels, The Sacred Cow of Corporate Existence, 19 U. of Chi.L.Rev. 778, 792.) As the same writer went on to say, "[f]rom that analogy flows the power of the Chancellor to dissolve and liquidate as in a partnership * * * in any manner calculated to produce a fair result." Although the court would be empowered to direct that the stock (the asset of the venture) be voted for dissolution, such an extreme step may not be necessary to accomplish a fair result. For example, a practical solution might be found in a procedure under which either interest may purchase the shareholdings of the other, at an appraised value found by the court and upon terms set by it. Flexibility of remedy, tailored to all the facts and circumstances of the case, including the good faith of the parties on both sides, their conflicting interests and motivations, if any, is the key. (Cf. Partnership Law, Consol.Laws, c. 39, § 69, pursuant to which a court in partnership accounting may penalize partner for inequitable conduct.)

I would reverse the order appealed from and remand the case to Special Term for further proceedings.

Notes

(1) Does the conduct involved in this case fall into the category of "oppressive conduct"? Is there a "deadlock"?

(2) Despite the force of Justice Fuld's reasoning, there appears to be little or no modern support for the notion of "dissolution on demand" (in the absence of oppression or deadlock) in a close corporation, such as exists in a partnership, though, of course, such a right could be created by an appropriately drafted agreement. How might such an agreement be drafted? Might the draftsman rely on a voting trust? A pooling agreement? An irrevocable proxy? A simple contractual document that does not designate what voting device is to be employed to assure a minority of its right to compel dissolution? Perhaps the closest statutory provision to "dissolution on demand" is § 33 of the Model Close Corporation Supplement to the Revised Business Corporation Act:

> (a) The articles of incorporation of a statutory close corporation may authorize one or more shareholders, or the holders of a specified number or percentage of shares of any class or series, to dissolve the corporation at will or upon the occurrence of a specified event or contingency. The shareholder or shareholders exercising this authority must give written notice of the intent to dissolve to all the other shareholders. Thirty-one days after the effective date of the notice, the corporation shall begin to wind up and liquidate its business and affairs and file articles of dissolution * * *.

F. INTEGRATED CLOSE CORPORATION STATUTES

The apparent need for special statutory provisions to accommodate closely held corporations has been discussed for many years in law review articles and judicial opinions and, as indicated in the foregoing materials, such statutes have been adopted in varying forms in a number of states. Two of the most influential judicial opinions in this regard are Galler v. Galler, p. 428, supra, and Krueger v. Gerth, p. 549, supra. The first complete close corporation statute was enacted by Florida in 1963; this statute was repealed in 1975, but most of its major provisions were incorporated into the general corporation statute. About a dozen other states have since enacted similar provisions, most of them in the last 1960s or 1970s.

These statutes are "integrated" in the sense that they apply a number of special statutory provisions to eligible corporations that voluntarily elect to come within the terms. Prior materials in this chapter, beginning with Zion v. Kurtz, p. 438 supra, describe a number of innovative provisions that appear in these statutes. A few states have not adopted "integrated" close corporation statutes but have included provisions in their general corporation statute applicable to all corporations with less than a specified number of shareholders or to corporations that have never had a public offering of shares; these special statutes are in a sense "close corporation" statutes as well. See, for example, RMBCA §§ 8.01(c), 1.42, 10.21, 10.22. (The Official Comments to these last two sections state explicitly that they are designed primarily for closely held corporations.)

Provisions in integrated close corporation statutes vary widely. Earlier parts of this chapter dealt with provisions authorizing the corporation to dispense with a board of directors and permit the shareholders to manage the business of a corporation directly, and provisions relating to improving remedies for deadlock and dissension. Other provisions included in many integrated close corporation statutes are special provisions to encourage the use of share transfer restrictions and to simplify further the internal structure of the corporations. The Model Close Corporation Supplement, for example, sets forth an optional standard-form share transfer restriction that is automatically applicable to close corporation shares but may be modified as the corporation deems appropriate. It also contains provisions authorizing a corporation to dispense with bylaws, annual meetings, and any requirement that a document be executed by more than one person on behalf of the corporation.

Consider § 24 of the Model Close Corporation Supplement:

The failure of a statutory close corporation to observe the usual corporate formalities or requirements relating to the exercise of its corporate powers or management of its business and affairs is not a ground for imposing personal liability on the shareholders for liabilities of the corporation.

At what potential problem is this section directed?

The standards for the type of corporation that may elect close corporation status also vary from state to state. Most statutes impose a numerical limit on the number of shareholders and may also require that the corporation not have made a registered public offering of shares. A natural question that arises from these statutory definitions of a close corporation is what happens when the corporation has grown so that it now exceeds the statutory maxima. The Model Close Corporation Supplement, like the statutes of several states, does not attempt to cause a revocation of the election in these circumstances, but permits the corporation to continue to function as a statutory close corporation on the assumption that the close corporation provisions will ultimately prove to be unwieldy for a larger corporation. Other statutes, however, provide for such a corporation to reform itself to meet the requirements of an ordinary business corporation.

Notes

(1) Most of the legal commentary discussing the growth of close corporation statutes development has been either purely reportorial or uncritically enthusiastic. For a critical examination (and perhaps an unnecessarily negative analysis) see Karjala, A Second Look at Special Close Corporation Legislation, 58 Tex.L.Rev. 1207 (1980); Karjala, An Analysis of Close Corporation Legislation in the United States, 21 Ariz.St.L.J. 663 (1989). Several observations may be made about this phenomenon:

(a) It is based on little or no empirical examination of the need for such legislation. Provisions included in such legislation appear to be based on intuitive views as to what a close corporation probably needs; of course, as close corporation statutes have proliferated, the major source for provisions becomes provisions already enacted in other states.

Do you believe that empirical investigation is necessary at all in an area such as this? After all, the surge of close corporation legislation is largely based on the problems developed in actual litigation in a few cases and on the views of influential judges in such cases. Should not that be enough?

(b) Professor Karjala comments that attorneys in Arizona and California appear to take advantage of the close corporation options in only a minute fraction of the corporations that are eligible to do so. 58 Tex.L.Rev. 1207, 1266 n. 236. Attorneys knowledgeable with filings in Delaware and Texas believe that in those states also advantage is rarely taken of the close corporation options. Indeed, a study of a sample of 1,033 Texas filings showed that close corporation status was elected in only 37 instances (3.71%). Blunk, Analyzing Texas Articles of Incorporation: Is the Statutory Close Corporation Format Viable? 34 Sw.L.J. 941 (1980). Since this study, however, the Texas statute was considerably simplified and it is therefore likely that its use has increased somewhat since Blunk's study. To the extent such data are reliable and indicative of practices in other states, two conclusions might be drawn: (a) close corporation statutes may not be really needed, or (b) attorneys are very cautious about trying new and untested devices.

(2) Statutes in some states created problems because they were enacted hastily without full and careful consideration. The original Florida statute, for example, created significant difficulties. Consult Dickson, The

Florida Close Corporation Act: An Experiment that Failed, 21 U.Miami L.Rev. 842 (1967).

(3) As indicated in the foregoing materials, the response of most modern courts to close corporation problems has been sympathetic and innovative. In a few instances, however, the judicial response under these statutes has been literalistic, leading to results that appear to be at odds with the underlying purpose of the legislation. Perhaps the most egregious illustration is Blount v. Taft, 295 N.C. 472, 246 S.E.2d 763 (1978). North Carolina has enacted a shareholder's agreement provision similar to section 350 of the Delaware Code. (Quoted in Zion v. Kurtz, p. 438, supra). In *Blount,* the shares of a closely held corporation were divided among three family blocks—41 per cent, 41 per cent, and 18 per cent. One of the three groups became concerned about nepotism in employment by the corporation. When new bylaws were being developed, a member of that group recommended that an executive committee be created consisting of one member of each faction and that the committee be invested with the following power:

> "The Executive Committee shall have the exclusive authority to employ all persons who shall work for the corporation and that the employment of each individual shall be only after the unanimous consent of the committee and after interview." (Section 7)

This provision was unanimously adopted by the shareholders and included in the bylaws. Thereafter, however, internal disagreements became sharper, and three years later, the board of directors voted to amend the bylaws, eliminating the unanimous provision for employment. This amendment was strongly objected to by the director representing one faction. Section 4 of the bylaws was a general section authorizing bylaws to be amended by the directors even though originally enacted by the shareholders. The Court held that since the unanimous consent provision in Section 7 appeared only in the bylaws, it was itself subject to amendment under section 4 by majority vote of the directors and was not protected by the statutory provision relating to shareholders agreements:

> G.S. 55–73(b) permits shareholders to embody their agreement "In the charter or the bylaws or in any side agreement in writing signed by all the parties thereto." Had Section 7 been a "side agreement" signed by all the shareholders, and not been made a part of the bylaws, it is plausible to argue that absent an internal provision governing its amendment it could be amended only by unanimous consent of all the stockholders. * * * Had Section 4 been omitted from the bylaws, the directors would have been precluded from amending Section 7 since it is a bylaw adopted by the shareholders. G.S. 55–16(a)(1).
> * * *
>
> * * * Here Section 7 and Section 4 were unanimously incorporated into the bylaws at the same time. There being no internal provision in Section 7 or elsewhere in the bylaws prohibiting its amendment except by unanimous consent of the shareholders, we conclude that the parties intended Section 7 to be subject to amendment by the directors or shareholders according to the procedures applicable to the other bylaws. In any event, that is the agreement

they made. We hold, therefore, that if a shareholders' agreement is made a part of the charter or bylaws it will be subject to amendment as provided therein or, in the absence of an internal provision governing amendments, as provided by the statutory norms.

Ordinarily the function of a shareholders' agreement is to avoid the consequences of majority rule or other statutory norms imposed by the corporate form. Since the purpose of these arrangements is to deviate from the structures which are generally regarded as the incidents of a corporation, it is not unreasonable to require that the degree of deviation intended be explicitly set out. Most commentators advise the draftsman of a shareholders' agreement to include a specific provision governing amendments. * * * Requiring the insertion of such an amendment provision works no undue hardship on the parties if all are agreed upon its inclusion.

Having concluded that the shareholders made Section 7 subject to the amendment power conferred upon the directors by Section 4, it will be enforced unless enforcement would contravene some principle of equity or public policy. Plaintiffs have not alleged that the acts of defendant constituted oppression or a breach of a fiduciary duty imposed by G.S. 55–32, G.S. 55–73(c), or the common law. * * *

This decision, of course, will expose plaintiffs as minority shareholders in a close corporation to a risk from which Section 7 for a while protected them. However, minority shareholders who would have protection greater than that afforded by Chapter 55 of the General Statutes and the judicial doctrines prohibiting breach of a fiduciary relationship must secure it themselves in the form of "a well drawn" shareholders' agreement. * * *

246 S.E.2d at 773–775. But compare Penley v. Penley, 314 N.C. 1, 332 S.E.2d 51 (1985).

Chapter Nine

CONTROL AND MANAGEMENT IN THE PUBLICLY HELD CORPORATION

A. "SOCIAL RESPONSIBILITY" OR THE LACK THEREOF

THE ROLE OF GIANT CORPORATIONS IN THE AMERICAN AND WORLD ECONOMIES: CORPORATE SECRECY: OVERVIEWS

Hearings before the Subcommittee on Monopoly of the Select Committee on Small Business, United States Senate, 92nd Cong. 1st Sess., November 9 and 12, 1971.

SENATOR NELSON.   *   *   *

The subject matter of these hearings—corporate giantism and corporate secrecy—is as broad and complex as world commerce itself. But the basic issue may be expressed in one word.

The word is power. The issue is power: economic, political, social, cultural power.

Power to decide what kind of jobs will be created and what kind will be terminated.

Power to determine whether new jobs that are made and old jobs that are wiped out will be located in New York, San Francisco, Hong Kong or Frankfurt.

Power strongly to influence, if not finally settle, whether Americans will travel about their cities in vehicles that are polluting, expensive, and dangerous or clean, cheap and safe.

Power to overload every sanitary landfill in the country by substituting throwaway bottles for returnable pop and beer bottles.

Power to determine—and here we come down to the very particular interest and jurisdiction of this committee and subcommittee—

whether small, independent entrepreneurs will or will not have opportunities left open to them to enter and strive and compete in particular lines of commerce.

It is now many years since small business was forced out of most types of manufacturing, including almost all those of major economic importance. Today, retailing and farming are being made, by giant corporations, increasingly precarious occupations for entrepreneurs who are not also millionaires. * * *

Corporate giantism is a shorthand way of describing an economic and social development that is still quite new in American and world history.

The corporation is a human invention to serve human, social needs. In theory, it is subservient both to the State that creates it and the market in which it competes. If the corporation does not fulfill its social obligations, under the theory, the State can amend or even revoke its charter. If it lapses in economic efficiency, its market competitors will force it to improve—or force it out.

For most of the approximately 2 million American corporations, this theory is also close to fact. But for a very few corporations—less than 1 percent of the total—the theory no longer seems to fit the facts. These few corporations have become much larger in economic size and power than either the States that chartered them or the markets in which they buy and sell.

Compare, for example, Standard Oil Co. (New Jersey) with the State that granted its charter and whose name the company bears (in parentheses). Jersey Standard had 1967 sales of almost $13.3 billion. The combined general revenues of the State and all local governments of the State of New Jersey that year were under $3 billion. * * *

R. BARBER, THE AMERICAN CORPORATION *
Pp. 19–20 (1970).

General Motors' yearly operating revenues exceed those of all but a dozen or so countries. Its sales receipts are greater than the *combined* general revenues of New York, New Jersey, Pennsylvania, Ohio, Delaware, and the six New England states. Its 1,300,000 stockholders are equal to the population of Washington, Baltimore, or Houston. GM employees number well over 700,000 and work in 127 plants in the United States and forty-five in countries spanning Europe, South Africa, North America, and Australasia. Their total cash wages are more than twice the personal income of Ireland. GM's Federal corporate tax payments approach $2 billion, or enough to pay for all Federal grants in fiscal year 1970 in the field of health research. The enormity of General Motors, seen from whatever angle, is stupefying, but it should

* From THE AMERICAN CORPORATION by Richard J. Barber. Copyright © 1970 by Richard J. Barber. Reprinted by permission of the publisher, E.P. Dutton, a division of New American Library.

not be thought of as unique. Some 175 other manufacturing, merchandising, and transportation companies now have annual sales of at least a billion dollars. * * *

To gain a better impression of the scale of the bigger U.S. companies one has to view them against a larger industrial backdrop. Looked at this way, we find that a mere 100 firms—less than a tenth of 1 percent of a total 300,000 firms—account for fully a third of the value added by manufacturing (sales less the cost of materials and services purchased), employ 25 percent of manufacturing employees (and make a third of all wages payments), make nearly 40 percent of new capital expenditures, and own about half of all assets used in manufacturing. What this means is that the presidents of a hundred companies—a group sufficiently small to be seated comfortably in the reading room of the Union League Club in Philadelphia—represent almost as much wealth and control as large a share of the nation's economic activity as the next largest 300,000 manufacturers—a group that would completely fill four Yankee Stadiums.

PLAYBOY INTERVIEW: MILTON FRIEDMAN *

Playboy Magazine, at p. 59, Feb., 1973.

PLAYBOY: Quite apart from emission standards and effluent taxes, shouldn't corporate officials take action to stop pollution out of a sense of social responsibility?

FRIEDMAN: I wouldn't buy stock in a company that hired that kind of leadership. A corporate executive's responsibility is to make as much money for the stockholders as possible, as long as he operates within the rules of the game. When an executive decides to take action for reasons of social responsibility, he is taking money from someone else—from the stockholders, in the form of lower dividends; from the employees, in the form of lower wages; or from the consumer, in the form of higher prices. The responsibility of a corporate executive is to fulfill the terms of his contract. If he can't do that in good conscience, then he should quit his job and find another way to do good. He has the right to promote what he regards as desirable moral objectives only with his own money. If, on the other hand, the executives of U.S. Steel undertake to reduce pollution in Gary for the purpose of making the town attractive to employees and thus lowering labor costs, then they are doing the stockholders' bidding. And everybody benefits: The stockholders get higher dividends; the customer gets cheaper steel; the workers get more in return for their labor. That's the beauty of free enterprise.

RODEWALD, THE CORPORATE SOCIAL RESPONSIBILITY DEBATE: UNANSWERED QUESTIONS ABOUT THE CONSEQUENCES OF MORAL REFORM

25 Am.Bus.L.J. 443, 444–447, 450–453, 455–456, 460–463 (1987).

Consider a hypothetical case that represents the kind of corporate decisionmaking problem that moral reformers believe requires a new conception of the moral responsibilities of corporate managers. In this case, the top management of "ACE Manufacturing Inc.," headquartered in "North City," a city in the northeastern United States, has to decide whether or not to relocate to the Sunbelt.[1]

For the purposes of our present discussion, assume that the managers of ACE have only two viable options: (1) they can decide to stay in North City and remodel ACE's present facilities, or (2) they can sell these facilities and build new ones on a new site in a semirural area of the Sunbelt. From the point of view of maximizing long-range corporate profits, moving to the Sunbelt is the better alternative. However, this option will likely have seriously harmful consequences for North City and many of ACE's present workers. ACE's departure would significantly damage North City's tax base. Moreover, this damage is likely to become devastating if ACE's move provides a signal to other corporations that it is time for them to get out also.

In addition, most of ACE's lower-level employees will be unable to make the move to the Sunbelt. Two-thirds of the skilled workers will lose their jobs and 25% of these will not find new ones. All the unskilled workers will lose their jobs and most of these will have to go on welfare. These displaced workers may lose even more than their jobs and economic security, however. They also face an increased risk of losing their homes, their families, their self-respect, and sometimes their physical health or even their lives.

Given these facts, what should the managers of ACE decide to do?

Initially, it might seem that so long as ACE will not go broke in North City, top management ought to decide to continue doing business there in order to avoid the harm that relocating would cause others. Simply by being individual "moral agents," the managers of ACE have "natural moral duties" to tell the truth and be honest, keep their promises, pay their debts, treat others fairly, do no harm, do good, help others in need, and benefit those who have benefited them in the past (the duty of gratitude). It seems that a strong argument can be built for claiming that it would be morally wrong for the managers of ACE to move to the Sunbelt solely on the premise that they have a natural

---

1. [By the Author] The essentials of this case description have been borrowed from a simulation exercise that AT&T has used in its management training programs: Relocation: A Corporate Decision (Del Mar, Ca.: Simile II, 1977).

moral duty not to impose on others the kind of suffering this move would cause just for the sake of some economic gain.[2]

This argument is invalid, however. Even if the premise is true, the conclusion does not necessarily follow. What persons morally ought to do in any particular case is not determined solely by their natural moral duties. Our natural moral duties are only "prima facie" duties which, while generally binding on conduct, can sometimes be overridden by other considerations that are morally superior in particular cases. * * *

THE TRADITIONAL VIEW: MANAGERS AS THE AGENTS OF CAPITAL

The traditional theory of the role of corporate managers in democratic capitalist societies holds that managers are supposed to be agents of the owners of capital. They are morally responsible for promoting the private economic interests of the stockholders and other investors who put up the capital without which a corporation would not exist or continue to function. Given that the primary function of private enterprise is to engage in economic production and exchange for a profit, and that maximizing corporate profits is in the interest of investors, then managers are obligated to try to maximize corporate profits.[3]

However, it is important to emphasize that this obligation is constrained by the legal and moral rules which govern competition in capitalist markets. Classical capitalist ideology logically entails a market morality that makes individuals and firms responsible for maximizing profits so long as they comply with the law, adhere to familiar moral standards of honesty, fidelity and fairness, and respect those individual moral rights that are presupposed by capitalist market arrangements. Milton Friedman evidently had these moral constraints in mind when he suggested that the sole social responsibility of corporate managers is to maximize profits so long as this is done within the "basic rules of society" embodied in "law" and "ethical custom." We can call this the *agent-of-capital* view of corporate responsibility.
* * *

Given the traditional agent-of-capital view of corporate responsibility, the managers of ACE are not morally obligated to stay in North City just because moving to the Sunbelt would impose significant hardships

---

2. [By the Author] One moral reformer seems to make appeal to the natural duties of gratitude and fairness, and the duty to keep implicit promises to justify the conclusion that in deciding whether or not to relocate, a company has a moral obligation to its employees and the local community to "(1) take into account the impact of the proposed move on employees and the community; (2) avoid the move if reasonably possible; (3) notify the affected parties as soon as possible if the decision is to make the move; and (4) take positive measures to ameliorate the [harmful] effects of the move." *See* Kavanagh, *Ethical Issues in Plant Relocation,* in ETHICAL THEORY AND BUSINESS 107 (T. Beauchamp & N. Bowie eds. 2d ed. 1983).

3. [By the Author] I leave aside questions about whether corporate managers should pursue the long-run maximization of profits and other market goals like growth or a particular market share as opposed to trying to maximize quarterly or annual profits.

on many of those who remain behind. What this view implies is that if moving to the Sunbelt will maximize ACE's long-run profits and violate no laws or requirements of market morality, then this is what the managers of ACE are morally obligated to do. Of course, it also follows that they should not lie to their workers or misrepresent their plans to relocate in order to forestall any falloff of productivity that is likely to follow once workers discover that they are going to lose their jobs.

* * *

From the traditional point of view, the suffering that ACE's move to the Sunbelt would impose on North City and many of its workers is an unintended side-effect of a sound business decision. The suffering is a "negative externality" of ACE's business activities much like pollution is sometimes a negative externality of production. In the traditional view, it is the function of government to protect noninvestors from these sorts of externalities. * * *

OBJECTIONS TO THE TRADITIONAL VIEW

Moral reformers point to a host of current environmental, social and economic problems as evidence that "business as usual" is no longer working adequately. They claim that adherence to the traditional view of corporate responsibility has produced increasing pollution, environmental degradation, toxic wastes, unreasonable depletion of nonrenewable resources, hazardous and unreliable products, unsafe, alienating and dehumanizing working conditions, and capital flight, as well as contributed to cycles of recession and inflation, unemployment, economic inequality, poverty, urban sprawl and inner city decay. * * * Reformers generally conclude that market forces, the law and traditional market morality can no longer be relied upon to ensure that the pursuit of corporate profits will not produce these kinds of undesirable consequences.

Christopher Stone provides an influential argument for this point of view. He assumes that there are some cases in which everyone would agree that corporate profits should be sacrificed for the sake of some competing social or moral value. However, he argues that the mistake the traditional view makes is to rely on government to ensure that corporate managers will do the right thing in these cases.[4]

* * *

THE MORAL REFORM VIEW: MANAGERS AS AGENTS OF SOCIETY

Moral reformers like Stone claim that we need to adopt a new conception of corporate social responsibility. They put forth what we may call *agent-of-society* views of corporate responsibility. On these views corporate managers should go beyond considerations of profits, legality and market morality and take into account all of the human, social and environmental consequences of their business decisions. They should pursue profits within the law and the requirements of

---

4. [By the Author] Stone, *Corporate Regulation: The Place of Social Responsi-* bility, in CORRIGIBLE CORPORATIONS & UNRULY LAW (B. Fisse & P. French eds. 1985).

market morality, but they should also try to do whatever they can to use the resources at their command in nonharmful and socially useful ways. * * *

Consider our relocation case again. In any agent-of-society view of corporate responsibility, the managers of ACE should give serious weight to all of the economic and noneconomic human costs that moving to the Sunbelt would likely impose upon their displaced workers and the citizens of North City. Take a narrow version that only requires managers to do no harm and to come to the aid of others in need when they can do so at a reasonable cost to their firms. Initially, this view seems to require that the managers of ACE should be prepared to stay in North City and make a reasonable sacrifice of profits in order to avoid these costs. However, if staying would be unreasonably costly to ACE, they should inform those who will be affected about their intentions to move as soon as reasonably possible. Moreover, they should be prepared to provide reasonable aid and compensation to North City and those workers who would lose their jobs in order to ameliorate their suffering during the transition between ACE's departure and the time when new industries take its place and its displaced workers find new jobs. In this way, ACE can internalize some of the costs of the negative externalities its move would produce.

However, management's moral responsibilities in this case are even more complicated. Given that workers in the Sunbelt need jobs and Sunbelt cities need new industries, ACE's failure to move might violate the obligation to come to their aid. Moreover, whether they stay and take the less profitable alternative or move and expend economic resources compensating North City and those workers who lose their jobs, the managers of ACE will have fewer resources available to expend on supplies, price cuts, higher wages, new jobs, new investments to fend off competition, dividends and the like. Thus, whatever they decide to do, they will impose financial costs on their stockholders, suppliers and customers, as well as their present and future workers.

Consequently, even in a narrow agent-of-society view, ACE's managers must attempt to estimate not only the costs that will be imposed upon their present workers and the citizens of North City if they decide to relocate, but also the harm that others will suffer if they do not. If it is reasonable to expect that relatively greater harm will be imposed by moving than by staying, then they would have to weigh the balance of harm against the rights of stockholders whose interests are served by moving. In light of all this, they would have to try to determine what would count as a reasonable sacrifice of profits to either avoid or ameliorate this harm.

Wider agent-of-society views only complicate matters further by expanding the range of nonmarket considerations that the managers of ACE would be morally required to take into account and the number of social and moral goals they ought to pursue. Take just one example: If it turns out that the work force they would end up with in the Sunbelt would be comprised of far fewer women and minorities, ACE's management might have to weigh the claims of justice that require working toward greater race and sex equality against the economic benefits of a more profitable ACE doing business in the Sunbelt.   *   *   *

WILL AGENT-OF-SOCIETY VIEWS WORK?

Consider the kinds of problems that agent-of-society views would require corporate managers to try to solve. For example, take the fundamental issue that has to be decided in our relocation case. Under an agent-of-society view, the managers of ACE have to decide how much of their economic resources they should divert from their most profitable uses to protecting persons from the unintended harmful consequences of these uses. What makes their decision difficult is that there is no alternative they can choose that will be in the best interests of everyone affected. Whatever they decide to do, they will benefit some persons and disadvantage others.

How should the managers of ACE settle this conflict of interests? To what principles should they appeal in allocating resources in cases like this one?   *   *   * [I]t seems unlikely that contemporary corporate managers will make the factual and moral judgments that reformers want them to make, given this list of considerations and given plausible assumptions about the nature of their situations, knowledge, interests, values, moral beliefs and the competitive pressures of their social role. For one thing, it seems that corporate managers are typically not in a good position to have access to sufficient information about the human, environmental, and social consequences of their business activities to make accurate social cost/benefit judgments of the sort that reformers want them to make.   *   *   *

Moreover, as a result of their background, training, life experiences and interests, it seems doubtful that many corporate managers will share the most important social and moral values and beliefs of moral reformers. Managers seem more likely than others to be risk-takers who value market activities and opportunities to work and compete to acquire relatively greater shares of economic power and wealth than others. They are likely to have conceptions of the good life that place greater value on the kinds of goods that markets produce than on the shared enjoyment of nonmarket, collective or public goods that unregulated market activities frequently threaten. In addition, they are more likely than reformers to be committed to the system of capitalist competition that has satisfied many of their important wants, and which provides the source of their motivation and standards of achievement and self-worth, and, ultimately, their economic, social and political power and prerogatives. Moreover, managers are likely to believe that because competitive markets provide neutral and impartial mechanisms for allocating the community's economic resources, the goals of maximizing the common good and social justice will be served best if they pursue traditional market goals and allow markets to function as freely as possible from external interferences.

Managers are also unlikely to hold the same views as moral reformers about individual moral rights, or about the requirements of justice when the rights of stockholders conflict with the needs of noninvestors or with the claims of the common good. Managers are less likely to believe that workers have a right to have their interests considered equally with the interests of stockholders. They are more likely than reformers to believe that the property rights of stockholders override the interests of noninvestors in all but those cases in which noninvestors are threatened with direct and serious harm. * * *

Finally, given the reality of competitive market pressures and the way in which corporate careers are made and broken, managers are likely to be under significant competitive pressures to maximize profits and achieve traditional market goals. In the absence of uniformly binding legal requirements to engage in socially beneficial activities, any individual manager or firm that decides to sacrifice profits in order to produce nonmarket social benefits risks being at a competitive disadvantage in relation to those who do not. Managers then will frequently tend to give greater weight to market considerations and to perceive the costs of such deviations to be greater than disinterested observers will.

Given the above, it is difficult to understand why reformers believe that corporations will produce better outcomes if managers take moral responsibility for using their economic power and resources in the ways that they believe will best promote the common good and social justice.

* * *

FISCHEL, THE CORPORATE GOVERNANCE MOVEMENT

35 Vand.L.Rev. 1259, 1268–1271 (1982).

It has become fashionable to argue that the pursuit of profit maximization by corporations is at variance with the public interest. Proponents of this argument, however, face the insuperable problem of defining what the public interest is, and when the pursuit of profit maximization should be sacrificed for these ends. As Harold Demsetz has remarked, centuries of philosophers and economists have tried and failed to provide any workable definition of "the fair price," "the just wage," or "fair competition," let alone what constitutes "the good society." [5] * * *

Although potential conflict exists between profit maximization and pursuit of other goals, far more consistency is present between the two than generally assumed. A successful business venture provides jobs to workers and goods and services that consumers want to buy. While

---

5. [By the Author] Demsetz, Social Responsibility in the Enterprise Economy, 10 Sw.U.L.Rev. 1, 1 (1978).

these benefits may not appear to be particularly dramatic, they should not be underestimated, as the tens of thousands of workers in distressed industries who have had to give back concessions previously won or have lost their jobs outright will readily attest. Much the same is true is other areas. Critics commonly assume, for example, that profit maximization is inconsistent with other goals such as providing safe working conditions or maintaining a clean environment. These other goals, however, are most likely to be sacrificed precisely in those times when firms are not profitable because of a perception that the costs they impose are too high. Substantial overlap exists, therefore, between the pursuit of profit maximization and other social goals.

Frequently this harmony of interests exists, but is difficult to perceive. Firms that close plants to move to different geographical areas commonly are accused, for example, of lacking a sense of responsibility to affected workers and the community as a whole. The difficulty with this argument is that it ignores the presumably greater benefits that will accrue to workers and the community in the new locale where the firm can operate more profitably. A firm that causes dislocations by moving a plant is behaving no more "unethically" than a firm that causes dislocations by, say, inventing a new technology that causes competitors to go out of business.

I do not mean to suggest that profit maximization will always lead to the socially optimal result. In those situations in which externalities are present—pollution is the most common example—a firm may impose costs on others without providing compensation. But even this situation is misunderstood. If a firm dumps pollutants in a stream, the firm imposes costs on the users of the stream that may exceed the benefits to the firm. It does not follow, however, that pollution is immoral behavior which should be halted. Consider the reciprocal case in which the firm does not pollute because of concern for users of the stream and instead relies on a more expensive method of disposing wastes. In this situation the users of the stream impose costs on the firm's investors, employees, and consumers that may exceed the benefits to users of the stream. Neither polluting nor failing to pollute is *a priori* the "ethically" or "morally" correct course of action. The difficulty is establishing a property right in the stream so that the ultimate result will duplicate what the parties would have bargained for had they been able to do so at no cost.[6] While this itself is a complicated task, it is necessary regardless of what corporate governance structure exists, or, for that matter, regardless of the type of society involved.[7] To view pollution as a question of corporate governance, therefore, only serves to obscure the relevant issues.

6. [By the Author] *See* Coase, *The Problem of Social Cost,* 3 J.L. & Econ. 1, 19–28 (1960).

7. [By the Author] As Michael Dooley has pointed out, Soviet plants pollute as much or more than those in America but produce goods and services in lesser numbers and of inferior quality. Dooley, *Controlling Giant Corporations: The Question of Legitimacy,* in Corporate Governance: Past and Future 28, 30 (H. Manne ed. 1982).

* * * Laws currently exist that restrict pollution, foreign payments, and anticompetitive behavior as well as other practices; when these laws are violated an argument could be made that a breakdown in accountability has occurred. But even here the situation is more complicated than may first appear. Because many laws can be violated inadvertently or by subordinates, the costs of preventing violations may far exceed the gains from avoiding violations. A firm may also find it advantageous to violate a law deliberately and pay the penalty for the same reason that an individual in some cases may prefer to breach a contract and pay damages. Because the gains from breach or violation presumably exceed the social costs (as reflected in the penalty), compliance with the statute or contract is undesirable from a personal as well as a social perspective. The optimal level of violations of law, therefore, is not zero. The remedy for those who believe that the level of violations is too high is to seek to increase the penalty to reflect the "real" social costs of the activity. Once again, however, the solution to the problem, assuming one exists, is in the political process, not in changing the governance of corporations.

AMERICAN LAW INSTITUTE, PRINCIPLES OF CORPORATE GOVERNANCE: ANALYSIS & RECOMMENDATIONS *

Tent. Draft No. 2, § 2.01 (1984).

§ 2.01 The Objective and Conduct of the Business Corporation

A business corporation should have as its objective the conduct of business activities with a view to enhancing corporate profit and shareholder gain, except that, whether or not corporate profit and shareholder gain are thereby enhanced, the corporation, in the conduct of its business

(a) is obliged, to the same extent as a natural person, to act within the boundaries set by law,

(b) may take into account ethical considerations that are reasonably regarded as appropriate to the responsible conduct of business, and

(c) may devote a reasonable amount of resources to public welfare, humanitarian, educational, and philanthropic purposes.

PENNSYLVANIA 1988 BUSINESS CORPORATION LAW § 1721

§ 1721 Board of Directors—

(b) Standard of care: * * * A director shall stand in a fiduciary relation to the corporation and shall perform his duties as a director, including his duties as a member of any committee of the board upon which he may serve, in good faith, in a manner he reasonably believes to be in the best interests of the corporation and with such care, including reasonable inquiry, skill and diligence, as a person of ordinary prudence would use under similar circumstances. * * *

(c) Consideration of factors.—In discharging the duties of their respective positions, the board of directors, committees of the board and individual directors may, in considering the best interests of the corporation, consider the effects of any action upon employees, upon suppliers and customers of the corporation and upon communities in which offices or other establishments of the corporation are located, and all other pertinent factors. The consideration of those factors shall not constitute a violation of subsection (b).

(d) Presumption.—Absent breach of fiduciary duty, lack of good faith or self-dealing, actions taken as a director or any failure to take any action shall be presumed to be in the best interests of the corporation.

HANKS, NON–STOCKHOLDER CONSTITUENCY STATUTES: AN IDEA WHOSE TIME SHOULD NEVER HAVE COME*

Insights, Vol. 3, No. 12, at 20 (December 1989).

One of the most remarkable but least remarked developments in corporation law in many years has been the enactment in at least 24 states of statutes permitting (and in one case requiring) the board of directors of any corporation chartered in the state to consider, in discharging its duties, groups other than the stockholders. This growing collection of statutes has come to be known as "non-stockholder constituency" or "other constituency" statutes.

The idea that directors should be able to consider groups other than stockholders apparently originated in charter amendments adopted by Control Data Corporation and various other corporations several years ago. These provisions expanded the factors that boards could weigh in considering takeover offers and other proposals concerning changes in corporate control. The interests of the social activists meshed nicely with others' concerns over unsolicited takeovers. Opponents of hostile takeovers apparently felt that by giving directors a wider range of factors upon which to base a rejection of a takeover offer, they would help protect the directors from liability and thus encourage them to resist takeover offers. Advocates of non-stockholder constituency statutes also claim that these statutes help to spread the wealth that would otherwise be enjoyed solely by stockholders, especially in takeover situations yielding substantial premiums.

* Insights: The Corporate & Securities Law Advisor. Copyright Prentice Hall Law & Business.

Perhaps the most surprising fact in the emergence of these statutes in so many states in only a few years is the almost total lack of any considered deliberation concerning this legislation. Typically, these statutes have been hustled through the state legislatures by business and bar groups determined to add as many weapons as possible to the anti-takeover arsenal. In fact, however, there is good reason for those concerned about the effects of hostile takeovers to be concerned with the impact of non-stockholder constituency statutes. Any benefit in increased latitude for board decision-making is more than offset by countervailing costs. * * *

LACK OF SUBSTANTIVE STANDARDS

Most states have developed, either through statute or case law, standards of conduct for directors. Section 8.30 of the Revised Model Business Corporation Act, for example, requires directors to perform their duties in good faith, in a manner reasonably believed to be in the best interest of the corporation and with the care of an ordinarily prudent person in a like position under similar circumstances. Nothing in the non-stockholder constituency statutes gives any indication as to how they are to intersect with standard-of-conduct statutes like Section 8.30. For example, a director seeking to act in the "best" interest of the corporation may wonder how he may give any consideration at all to non-stockholders in the absence of some related benefit to stockholders. As many directors of both publicly—and privately-held corporations know, it is difficult enough to determine the best interests of the corporation and its stockholders; it will be even more difficult for directors of corporations chartered in states with non-stockholder constituency statutes to determine the interests of other constituencies, much less weigh the often-competing claims of these groups. Indeed, non-stockholder constituency statutes introduce the possibility of an almost unlimited number of potential new competitors for the residual assets of the corporation and, therefore, for directors' attention.

A related question is whether the "interests" of the corporation and the common stockholders are co-extensive. If so, then even the permissive non-stockholder constituency statutes clash with statutes like Section 8.30 prescribing standards of conduct for directors; if not, then there may be no need for non-stockholder constituency statutes. Of course, there is no indication in these standards of conduct as to what these non-stockholder interests are, how they are to be measured or how conflicts between stockholder and non-stockholder interests should be resolved.

Even if it were possible to identify the nature and extent of non-stockholders constituencies' interests, none of the statutes offers any guidance as to how much weight should be given to the interests of one constituency versus another or the weight to be given to one claim of a constituency versus other possible claims of the same constituency. Proponents of these statutes have not articulated any standard for determining "how much" of the stockholders' wealth the directors should be permitted to allocate to other groups. Do they think, for example, that under a non-stockholder constituency statute a board could cause all of the stockholders' equity (or all of the premium in a takeover) to be paid out to the employees as a special bonus? It is evident that these statutes, especially those with open-ended language such as "any other factors the director considers pertinent," result in virtually standardless discretion. This absence of standards is likely to lead not only to greater uncertainty and unpredictability in the board-room but also to difficulty in judicial review.

LACK OF PROCEDURAL STANDARDS

None of the non-stockholder constituency statutes provides any standard for what "may consider" means. Should directors take non-stockholder constituencies into account if their interests: (a) promote stockholder interests; (b) are not inconsistent with stockholder interests; (c) conflict with stockholder interests? Does "may consider" mean the board may try to obtain benefits for a non-stockholder group but does not have to disapprove an entire transaction if the benefits are not obtained? Or may the board reject the entire transaction if it is unable to achieve some level of benefits for non-stockholder constituencies even though the transaction would have been in the stockholders' (best?) interest? * * *

STANDING

By permitting directors to consider other constituencies, these statutes may give those constituencies rights enforceable against the board. It would not be surprising for a court to hold that the board is obligated to consider the wisdom and propriety of exercising any power available to it. If the board actually decides to consider the interests of a non-stockholder group but does a poor job (*e.g.,* gathers only scanty information or deliberates only briefly), is it liable to that group for either equitable relief or money damages? * * *

DETERRENCE OF INVESTMENT

If the real purpose of non-stockholder constituency statutes—to permit directors to benefit non-stockholder groups in the absence of any related benefit to the stockholders—is ever fully understood, much less achieved, corporations will find it significantly more difficult to raise equity capital. Potential investors will be faced with the possibility that their return may be diverted by the board at any time without any benefit to the stockholders. Moreover, in the absence of any standards for the exercise of this right, investors will not be able to calculate the probability or magnitude of this risk. It is likely that even today most stockholders of corporations chartered in states with non-stockholder constituency statutes are unaware that their directors are permitted to divert stockholder wealth to other groups. Certainly, the existence of a non-stockholder constituency statute is an item that should be disclosed in connection with the offering of equity securities.

Finally, the corporation is not the only form of business organization in which the residual owners benefit from goods and services furnished by others. If the rationale of non-stockholder constituency statutes—that return on equity should be shared with all who help to produce it even if they have already been compensated in accordance with statutory or contractual rights—is sound, then why limit it to corporations? Why not extend it to partnerships, trusts, even sole proprietorships? * * *

In summary, these statutes revolutionize corporation law in the states where they have been enacted (generally with little or no consideration of their consequences) * * *. They are a bad idea whose time should never have come.

Notes

(1) There is voluminous literature on the "social responsibility" of corporations, much of it polemical in nature and none of it discussing the implications of the statutes described by Mr. Hanks. Much of this literature dates back to the 1960s and 1970s. For an interesting and thoughtful analysis of the early literature, see Manning, Thinking Straight about Corporate Law Reform, reprinted in D. De Mott, Corporations at the Crossroads: Governance and Reform (1980) ch. one. Mr. Manning classifies corporate reformers into ten different "species."

(2) Professor Donald Schwartz has suggested that "the present movement is the third serious effort at corporate reform during this century." Schwartz Federalism and Corporate Governance, 45 Ohio S.L.J. 545, 547 (1984). The first he identified as occurring in the early 1900s during the administration of Presidents Roosevelt and Taft when serious consideration was first given to federalizing the law of corporations. The second period occurred during the 1930s. Certainly a rather similar debate over the proper rule of the modern corporation took place during this second period. Professor E. Merrick Dodd argued that a business corporation was an economic institution that had a social service as well as a profit-making function. Dodd, For Whom Are Corporate Managers Trustees?, 45 Harv.L. Rev. 1145 (1932). Professor Adolf A. Berle responded that there were no enforceable standards for such a broad obligation, and that the otherwise unchecked powers of corporate management should best be controlled by limiting obligations to economic obligations to the shareholders as a class. Berle, For Whom Corporate Managers Are Trustees: A Note, 45 Harv.L. Rev. 1365 (1932). Subsequently Professor Berle conceded that corporate theory had developed along the lines suggested by Professor Dodd. A. Berle, The 20th Century Capitalist Revolution 169 (1954). For a general survey of this debate, see Weiner, The Berle–Dodd Dialogue on the Concept of the Corporation, 64 Colum.L.Rev. 1458 (1964). Do you think that Professor Berle's concession was premature?

B. SHAREHOLDERS

UNITED STATES TEMPORARY NATIONAL ECONOMIC COMMITTEE

[BUREAUCRACY AND TRUSTEESHIP IN LARGE CORPORATIONS]

Monograph No. 11, pp. 19–23 (1940).

THE SEPARATION OF OWNERSHIP AND CONTROL

Another result of industrial concentration and the diffusion of ownership is so important that it deserves special consideration. It is the separation of ownership from control. Theoretically, of course, the holders of a majority of the voting stock control a corporation. But "the assumption that the owners of common or voting stock control a company is for the most part a fiction so far as the large corporations listed on exchanges are concerned."

Three general types or sources of control may be differentiated: control by the holders of a majority of the voting stock, control by an active minority, and control by management. Control by means of a legal device, such as a holding company, may usually be resolved into one or the other of the last two types, especially when one considers the proportionate interest of the dominant group in the securities of the bottom company.

We have already seen how rarely an individual or a small group owns a majority of the stock of one of the giant corporations. * * *

Minority control is much more common than majority control among the large companies. It arises where a compact group owns a substantial but minority interest which constitutes a majority of the stock actually represented at stockholders' meetings, or to which the control group can attract a sufficient number of proxies from scattered holders to constitute a majority at such meetings. The latter rather than the former is the usual means of minority control. * * *

The most common form of control among the large corporations may be termed management control. When stockholding is sufficiently diffuse the position of management becomes almost impregnable.

Management does not need to own stock; the strategic advantages of its location are quite sufficient. A presumption of worth is in its favor and, more concretely, the proxy machinery is at its disposal. Management chooses the proxy committee and by making appointments from among the members of management assures its own continuance. The effectiveness of this machinery is too formidable for small stockholders to overcome. The Financial Editor of the Chicago Daily News, for example, describes the situation thus:

> Taking industry as a whole, the methods of using proxies gives the average stockholder [no] * * * chance to express an opinion * * *.

He can agree or keep still. The proxy which is sent out lets him vote for the management: if he objects he can come to the meeting and register a kick. When he gets there he will be in the minority.

The management usually enters the meeting with enough votes to carry any measure, regardless of those present.

Only the cataclysmic uprising of an indignant majority of the stockholders is sufficient to overthrow the management. And before such a crucial stage is reached even a not too astute management will usually have made concessions, sometimes of a quite minor nature, which are adequate to prevent the revolt. In business as in politics, taking the enemy into camp often works admirably in extending peace between groups.

The relatively helpless position of the dispersed stockholders makes it imperative that those in command of the large corporations consider the rights of these disfranchised citizens of the economic community. In other words, the dispersion of stock ownership requires, in the interests of justice, that the control group act not only in its own interests, but also as a trustee for the interests of those who are unable to make their demands effective. A 1928 statement by a subsequent chairman of Marshall Field and Company and chairman of the board of the American Management Association may be appropriately repeated. James O. McKinsey commented that the dispersion of stock ownership—

> has brought about the situation in which the board of directors acts in a fiduciary capacity. If they fully realize their responsibility, this naturally leads them to exercise closer supervision over the activities of the business than if they were not representing a large group who were not familiar with the activities of the business and who were not exercising any responsibility for the management of the business other than selecting the directors to represent them.

It must be recognized, on the other hand, that it is not easy for the control group to give consideration to the interests of the scattered stockholders. One important reason for this is that their interests may be divergent. The concern of management with high salaries may result in lower dividends to the stockholders than would otherwise be possible. Or again, since those in control of a corporation are the first to gain information which will have an effect upon the value of the stock, the insiders may be able to buy or sell in such a way as to make substantial profits at the expense of those who are induced to sell or of new stockholders who are induced to buy without having inside information.

J. LIVINGSTON, THE AMERICAN SHAREHOLDER *
Pp. 60–61, 66–67 (1958).

Here's a natural question: If a stockholder is not satisfied with a company's management, why should he start a proxy fight, why should he sue, why shouldn't he just sell his stock and be done with it?

Answer: That is what most stockholders do.

It is the easiest, cheapest, and, from many points of view, the most practical way to express stockholder dissatisfaction with a management, a company, or an industry.

The right to sell is a vote. And the stock market—Wall Street—is the polling booth. If the price of a stock goes up, it registers stockholder—investor—satisfaction. If it goes down, it registers dissatisfaction in the market place. * * *

This right to sell stock—to vote for or against a management in the market place—is different from a vote at a stockholders' meeting. When a stockholder votes against a slate of directors, he is exercising his right as a stockholder, as an owner. He hopes to change the management and improve the company. But a stockholder who sells says to hell with it. He is not going to reform the company. He is not an owner trying to increase the value of his property. He says, in effect, "Include me out." * * *

Thus, the market-place vote has power. It is a positive warning, a financial warning, to an incumbent management, of stockholder dissatisfaction. It lets the officers know that dissatisfaction has got beyond the discussion stage. The "big boys" are selling. So, the management might bestir itself—make changes—to strengthen the company's position. For that reason, selling stock is not an entirely empty gesture. True, the big investors do not fight for a change; they do not stay with the company that is retrogressing. But their leave-taking has an effect.

FISCHEL, EFFICIENT CAPITAL MARKET THEORY, THE MARKET FOR CORPORATE CONTROL, AND THE REGULATION OF CASH TENDER OFFERS
57 Tex.L.Rev. 1, 3–5, 8–9 (1978)

An efficient capital market [8] is one in which a trader cannot improve his overall chances of speculative gain by obtaining public

---

* From The American Stockholder by Livingston. Reprinted by permission of J.A. Livingston. Copyright © 1958 by J.A. Livingston. Reprinted by permission of J.B. Lippincott Company.

8. [By the Author] Two major implications of efficient capital market theory are that (1) security prices adjust rapidly and in an unbiased manner to any new information, and (2) price changes behave in a random manner. B. Lev, Financial Statement Analysis: A New Approach 212 (1974). If prices of securities did not adjust rapidly and without bias, investors could profit by trading during the time during which securities did not reflect all available information or during periods when the market either overcompensated or un-

information about the companies whose securities are in the market and evaluating that information intelligently in determining which stocks to buy and sell. Paradoxically, the efficiency of the market results from the competitive efforts of securities analysts and investors who strive to earn superior returns by identifying mispriced securities—securities that are either overvalued or undervalued. The goal of securities analysis is to discover information that suggests differences between current market prices and what these prices "should" be, the securities' intrinsic values. The securities analyst acts on this information by buying, selling, or recommending securities. The process ensures that market prices reflect all available information. * * * [I]n an efficient capital market in which a large number of buyers and sellers react through a market mechanism such as the New York Stock Exchange to cause market prices to reflect fully and instantly all available information about a company's securities, investors should not be able to "beat the market" systematically by identifying undervalued or overvalued securities. * * *

Efficient capital market theory implies that if a publicly traded company is poorly or less than optimally managed, the price of its securities will reflect this fact accurately and promptly. That a capital market is efficient, however, does not imply that there is a similarly efficient mechanism whereby control shifts from less capable managers to others who can manage corporate assets more profitably. The market for corporate control, so called by Henry Manne in his groundbreaking work on the subject,[9] must perform that function in our economic system.

Poor performance of a company's securities in the capital market is a common indication of poor management. The lower the market price

dercompensated for new information. Similarly, if security prices did not move randomly, investors could capitalize on systematic price movements to earn above average returns.

The empirical support for efficient capital market theory exists in three forms—weak, semi-strong, and strong. The weak form has focused on the significance of securities' past price movements. Repeated studies have demonstrated that historic patterns of past prices are of no value in predicting future price movements. The semi-strong form asserts that security prices reflect all publicly available information about that security. Empirical tests of the semi-strong form have tested the speed of adjustment of security prices to such events as stock splits, annual earnings announcements and large secondary offerings of common stock. These tests indicate a quick price adjustment process in which the information revealed by specific events is anticipated by the market. The strong form of efficient capital market theory is that even nonpublic information is quickly reflected in security prices. Tests of the strong form have proven inconclusive. Several studies of professionally managed mutual funds have concluded that these funds, despite huge expenditures to identify mispriced securities, were unable to consistently outperform the market. Other studies have found, however, that corporate insiders can profit by trading on inside information not available to other investors.

For a survey of the literature on the empirical support for efficient capital market theory, see Note, The Efficient Capital Market Hypothesis, Economic Theory and the Regulation of the Securities Industry, 29 Stan.L.Rev. 1031, 1041–54 (1977).

9. [By the Author] E.g., Manne, Cash Tender Offers for Shares—A Reply to Chairman Cohen, 1967 Duke L.J. 231; Manne, Mergers and the Market for Corporate Control, 73 J.Pol.Econ. 110 (1965).

of the securities compared to what it would be with better management, the more attractive the firm is to outsiders with the ability to take the firm over. The most common takeover device is the merger. This takeover device is not available, however, when incumbent management opposes the shift in control because merger statutes uniformly require approval by the directors of the two corporations. The two techniques that can be used to shift control when there is opposition are the direct purchase of shares and the proxy contest. * * *

One of the basic themes of corporation law is the significance for shareholders of the modern corporation's separation of ownership and control. In their famous work on this subject, Professors Berle and Means assumed that managers do not seek to maximize what is most important to shareholders—appreciation of the shareholders' underlying investment.

Berle and Means failed to recognize, however, that unity of ownership and control is not a necessary condition of efficient performance of a firm. If the owner of a wholly owned firm is its manager, he will make operating decisions that maximize his utility.[10] After the owner-manager sells equity in the firm to raise capital, however, his incentive to search out new profitable ventures diminishes because he now bears only a fraction of the losses resulting from less profitable investments.[11] The agency relationship between shareholders and managers inevitably calls into question the identity of the agent's decisions with decisions that would maximize the welfare of shareholders.[12]

Various market mechanisms exist, however, to minimize this divergence of interests between managers and shareholders. As Alchian has illustrated, an architect or builder does not share in its profits or losses (as only the owners do) absent contractual arrangement. Yet the architect or builder is vitally interested in the success of the building. The greater the profits generated by his efforts, the greater the demand for his services. Corporate managers are in precisely the same situation. While they do not directly share in the profits of an enterprise, successful performance increases the demand for their services as managers. Managers have a further incentive to maximize profit if their compensation is in some way linked to performance—stock options are a common example of this type of arrangement. Intensity of competition in the firm's product market also provides an incentive for managerial efficiency.

The market for corporate control and the threat of cash tender offers in particular are of great importance in creating incentives for

---

10. [By the Author] Jensen & Meckling, Theory of the Firm: Managerial Behavior: Agency Costs and Ownership Structure, 3 J.Fin.Econ. 305, 312 (1976).

11. [By the Author] Similarly, as the owner-manager's share of the equity falls and his fractional claim on the outcome falls, he will have greater incentives to

appropriate larger amounts of corporate resources in the form of perquisites. Id. at 313.

12. [By the Author] In addition to this inevitable residual loss, other costs of the agency relationship are monitoring expenditures by the principal and bonding expenditures by the agent. Id. at 308.

management to maximize the welfare of shareholders. Theoretically, shareholders may oust poor management on their own initiative, but the costs to individual shareholders of monitoring management performance and campaigning for its defeat in shareholder elections when performance is poor are prohibitive. On the other hand, inefficient performance by management is reflected in share price thus making the corporation a likely candidate for a takeover bid. Since a successful takeover bid often results in the displacement of current management, managers have a strong incentive to operate efficiently and keep share prices high.

R. BARBER, THE AMERICAN CORPORATION *
Pp. 54–55, 57–58 (1970).

Managerial control of the world's largest public enterprises is a crucial distinguishing characteristic of twentieth century capitalism, but that is hardly a recent discovery. What is new, a contribution of the postwar years, and particularly the last decade, is the shift from individual to institutional corporate shareownership. This is the era of the financial institution, not the personal investor. Increasingly, individuals are investing in U.S. industry indirectly, via mutual funds, pension funds, and bank-managed trusts. One in six adults now owns stock in a corporation listed on the New York Stock Exchange compared with only one in sixteen in 1952. That proportion, though, has not increased since 1962 for a very simple reason: currently individuals are selling more stock than they buy. In the years 1962 through 1969 their individual corporate stock declined in value by over $10 billion. While people have added greatly to their personal savings (up from an annual rate of $22 billion in 1962 to near $60 billion in 1969), it has not been through the direct purchase of corporate stock. Instead, in the last decade individuals have been indirectly enlarging their stake in American industry through institutional investments.

These institutions take many forms, but primarily they are the mutual funds, pension funds, and insurance companies—all with varying degrees of bank involvement. Collectively, these institutions own securities representing more than a third of the value of all listed stocks on the New York Stock Exchange. Their role makes them the major new force in the trading of stocks and bonds and establishes their preeminent position in the control of corporate America.

Notes

(1) The following data may give an appreciation of the size and extent of the holdings of institutional shareholders at the end of the 1980s:

(a) On June 7, 1989, Chairman David Ruder of the Securities and Exchange Commission, at a press conference, estimated that the current

* From THE AMERICAN CORPORA-   permission of the publisher, E.P. Dutton, a
TION by Richard J. Barber. Copyright ©   division of New American Library.
1970 by Richard J. Barber. Reprinted by

value of all common stocks traded on the New York Stock Exchange was approximately $2.6 trillion. Institutional investors owned approximately $1.2 trillion, or 45 per cent of the total value of all stocks traded on the NYSE. Chairman Ruder also estimated that there were "several hundred" institutional investors with portfolios in excess of $3 billion.

(b) Business Week's annual survey of the financial position of 900 publicly traded domestic corporations in 1989 estimated that institutional investors in 1988 on the average owned 50 per cent of the outstanding securities of the 900 corporations surveyed. The average number of institutional investors per corporation was 238. Institutional holdings varied from as low as 1 per cent for WLR Foods, a chicken and turkey processor, to over 80 per cent for a variety of better known companies, such as U.S. Shoe, Whirlpool, and Gibson Greeting Cards. Business Week Investment Outlook Scoreboard (Dec. 25, 1989) at 155 et seq.

(c) Conard, Beyond Managerialism: Investor Capitalism, 22 U.Mich.J. Law Ref. 117, 132–134 (1988):

> Institutional holdings are not, of course, equally distributed among enterprises, and the power of institutional investors depends in large part on the level of holdings and the number of holders in particular companies. For institutions to exert influence in any particular enterprise, it is necessary not only that the institutions hold a large proportion of the shares, but also that the number of institutions involved be small enough to facilitate collaboration among them. In order to find out how often these conditions coexist, an analysis was made of the holdings reported by 100 randomly chosen issuers of actively traded equities.[13]

> Institutional holdings in the 100 companies ranged from over 90 percent at the high end to a little more than 6 percent at the low end. Thirty of the 100 enterprises were owned by institutions to the extent of more than 60 percent. Sixty of the 100 were owned by institutions to the extent of 40 percent or more. * * *

> The number of institutions holding these proportions of equities is also important, because the ease of collaboration among institutions varies inversely with the number of institutions that must collaborate to attain a critical mass. For 66 of the 100 companies, the number of institutional investors was no more than 200. In eighty-four of the

---

13. [By the Author] The 100 companies were chosen from the 944 companies reported in Moody's Handbook of Common Stocks (Winter 1986–87 ed.) [hereinafter Moody's]. These companies were characterized by the publisher as companies whose stocks have "high investor interest," Moody's, supra, at 2; they were all listed on the New York Stock Exchange. The fact that they had high investor interest suggests that they may have had higher institutional participation than a random sample of all publicly traded equities would have. The institutional investors, whose holdings in the 944 issuers were reported by the Handbook, included about 1412 domestic and foreign investment companies, 1100 insurance companies, 250 national banks, 442 investment advisers, pension funds and other managers of $100 million or more, and 239 colleges. In view of the small size of the sample, and its possible bias, it should be regarded as suggestive, rather than definitive, of the potential influence of institutional investors on publicly held enterprises.

100, the number of institutional investors was no more than 400.[14]

* * *

The key to institutional power, however, is the concurrence of a high proportion of institutional ownership with a small number of institutional owners. When that happens, institutional investors can organize an influential block with relative ease. In one of the 100 companies in the sample, 80 percent of the shares were held by no more than 400 institutions. Of the 30 enterprises that were more than 60 percent owned by institutions, 12 had no more than 200 institutional holders, and 20 had no more than 400.

CONARD, BEYOND MANAGERIALISM: INVESTOR CAPITALISM

22 U.Mich.J.Law Ref. 117, 139, 144–148 (1988)

Whether institutional investors will exert their latent power to enhance the profitability of enterprises will depend, in large part, on the motivation of institutional managers. They are presumably no more and no less faithful than enterprise managers to their fiduciary duties. Like enterprise managers, institutional managers can be expected to maximize the financial returns of their funds, so long as the effort to do so contributes to their own rewards and job security. When their rewards are threatened and, even more, when their job security is imperiled, some of them are likely, like enterprise managers, to put their personal rewards and job security ahead of the interests of their constituents. * * *

According to a broad current of conventional wisdom, investors of all kinds are wise to forgo active participation in corporate governance, because they can protect their interests at less expense by selling their shares in enterprises that are inefficiently managed and switching their resources to better-managed companies. This principle of investor behavior has been called the "Wall Street rule." Its validity is said to be corroborated by the infrequency of investor opposition to management proposals and the even greater infrequency of investor nominations of directorial candidates to oppose the managers' nominations.

Although the Wall Street rule fits a typical individual investor, there are reasons to doubt that it fits a typical institutional investor in the 1980s. Selling out is a good alternative only for the holder of a small block of shares who gets the news before it is public or before others have time to act on it. The holding of a large fund or a large family of funds may be too large to liquidate without pushing down the price. * * *

14. [By the Author] Forty-three of the 100 enterprises had no more than 100 institutional investors, 89 had no more than 500, and none had more than 1000. The companies in the sample with more than 500 institutional holders were General Motors (920), Philip Morris (830), Citicorp (606), Ameritech (604), Union Pacific (581), Allied–Signal (547), Ford Motor (533), Aetna (528), Dun & Bradstreet (530), Raytheon (513), and Warner–Lambert (502).

Moreover, the costs that any one institution would incur in organizing joint action with other institutions are much less than the magnitude of the losses imposed upon funds, or of the gains denied them, by managers' antitakeover tactics. The size of institutions' holdings enables them to assemble an impressive block of votes by canvassing a few hundred alert and sophisticated institutional holders, rather than thousands of passive individuals.[15] * * *

The recent emergence of activism on the part of pension funds indicates that the Wall Street Rule is no longer a pervasive principle of conduct among institutional investors. As institutional holdings grow, the rule will become less and less tenable as a canon of investment behavior. * * *

The structure of institutional investment presents a peculiar obstacle to the participation of institutional managers in corporate governance. Although the community of funds might increase total returns by causing enterprise managers to accept tender offers rather than repel them by nonproductive expenditures, the effort required would cost time and money to the portfolio managers that would undertake it, while the benefits would be shared by all the other portfolios that hold shares in the same enterprise. The other managers would take a "free ride" on the efforts of the activists. Since the activists' funds would gain no more than the passive ones, but would incur expenses that the passive funds would escape, the activist managers would be likely to record lower returns than the passive ones.

The costs of activism may include not only the time of employees that is diverted from trading to rallying votes, but also a loss of access to opinions of enterprise managers who would be antagonized by the fund's activism, so that the fund would be disadvantaged in its trading. Although these costs may be incapable of separate measurement, they may diminish the activists' rate of return enough to divert business from activist funds to passive ones. * * *

Under these circumstances, one cannot be surprised to find that institutional investors generally neglect their chances to enhance their returns by supervising enterprise managers. What is surprising is that some institutions have become active in opposing managerial tactics. In 1986 and 1987, very large funds with highly diversified portfolios made the effort to organize shareholder voting on questions like poison pills. In the spring of 1987, shareholder proposals were made in more than 60 companies by large institutional shareholders, including the

---

15. [By the Author] Richard Schlefer, Investment Officer of College Retirement Equities Fund (CREF), offered the following cost-benefit analysis in an interview with the author on October 19, 1987. About one fourth of CREF's equity holdings of $30 billion, or $7.5 billion, are vulnerable to takeover bids. Surveys have shown that poison pills reduce the market values of shares by an average of one percent, which would amount to $75 million in CREF's holdings. CREF's anti-poison pill campaign in 1987 involved total costs in time and communications of less than $10,000—about one tenth of one percent of CREF's stake in the outcome of the campaign.

Public Employees and Teachers Funds of California, the Wisconsin Investment Board, and the College Retirement Equities Fund.

Various explanations for these funds' activism may be suggested. In the first place, managers of these funds may reasonably expect their constituencies of governmental employees and teachers to applaud their efforts to restrain managerial self-serving, without questioning the possible costs. Besides, their holdings may be large enough so that a very minor enhancement of their rate of return offsets the costs of activism. Finally, the managers of these broadly based pension funds are much less vulnerable than portfolio managers to the danger of losing accounts if their rates of return are a shade under those of competitors; the teachers and civil servants whom they serve usually have no opportunity to switch their savings from the pension fund designated by their employer to an independent fund that is recording higher returns.

Notes

(1) The principal kinds of institutional investors are (a) pension funds created by corporate employers, by states and cities for their employees, and by universities, churches, and foundations; (b) mutual funds (and other types of investment companies) that offer persons opportunities to invest in broad portfolios of securities; (c) insurance companies, both life and casualty; (d) foundations; (e) university and charitable endowments; (f) banks investing trust funds; (g) brokerage firms; and (h) a variety of investment vehicles for sophisticated investors, many in the form of limited partnerships. As indicated in the excerpts from Professor Conard's article, institutional investors almost always have fiduciary duties to persons other than the issuers of the portfolio securities in which they invest. For example, pension funds have a duty to the employees covered by the fund to maximize the funds available for retirement benefits. These duties to third parties are construed by most institutional investors as requiring that they strive to maximize the gain to the institutional investor even though the gain is on a short term basis. This short-horizon investment philosophy, when being applied by a relatively small number of shareholders which collectively may own more than 50 per cent of the outstanding securities issued by the largest domestic corporations has itself been a source of concern. Not all institutional investors, obviously, adopt a policy of short term maximization of gains.

(2) Implicit in Professor Conard's analysis of the beginning stirring of activism by institutional investors in the area of corporate governance are two underlying principles: (a) institutional investors generally vote shares as they think best without seeking to ascertain the wishes of the beneficiaries as to how shares should be voted (indeed, an investigation of beneficiary desires probably is impractical in most situations), and (b) the historical voting pattern of institutional investors has been consistent and unwavering support of positions recommended by management. The basic reason for this voting pattern is that institutional investors view their roles as investors in, not managers of, portfolio companies; when one purchases

shares in a company one is investing in its management as well as in its business and one should therefore adopt a policy of supporting management. The activism described by Professor Conard had its roots in the takeover area, where the interests of the institutional investor and the portfolio company management may diverge dramatically. Cash purchases of shares at premium prices over market play a critical role in most modern takeover attempts. The typical modern takeover attempt involves a public offer by an aggressor to purchase for cash all or most of the publicly held shares of the target corporation. The offer succeeds if enough shareholders tender their shares to the offeror; it fails if the offer is withdrawn by the offeror or not enough shareholders elect to sell. See generally Ch. 12, section B, infra. Since the premiums paid to shareholders on a successful takeover may be as much as 50 per cent over the market price of the target shares immediately before the offer was made, most institutional investors feel that they have no choice consistent with their fiduciary duties to third persons except to accept the offer. Management of the target corporation, on the other hand, may face ouster if the offer is successful; the managers therefore have a strong incentive to erect defenses against an offer, including so-called "poison pills." See generally Ch. 12, section C, infra. This is the setting in which conflict between the issuer of the investment shares and the institutional investors is most apparent and where the activism of institutional investors described by Professor Conard began.

(3) One should not assume, however, that institutional investors speak with a single voice on takeover attempts. The shareholder proposal that has generally received the greatest institutional investor support is a resolution calling on the issuer to revoke poison pill takeover defenses. While these proposals have had some spectacular successes—for example, in 1988, a 51.9 per cent favorable vote of shareholders of USAir Group and a 61.2 per cent favorable vote of shareholders of Santa Fe/Southern Pacific—such proposals have generally failed. In the aggregate, during the 1989 "proxy season" the support for these proposals constituted 27.9 per cent of the shares voting, up only slightly from the 26.4 per cent during the 1988 season. Wall Street Journal, July 25, 1989, p. c23, col 2. While this is an impressive showing, a significant number of institutional investors clearly voted in favor of management rather than with the petitioning institutional investors.

(4) Consider also Heard, Shareholder Activism, Pension Fund Proxy Campaigns Highlight 1989 Annual Meeting Season, Insights, June 1989, Vol 3, No. 6, 20 at 21 * :

> More significant than the voting results, however, was the number of companies that agreed to the actions requested. In exchange for withdrawal of a proposal sponsored by Cal PERS [the California Public Employees Retirement System], Great Northern Nekoosa agreed either to redeem its poison pill or to submit it for shareholder approval within three years. Dayton Hudson reached a similar understanding with

* Insights: The Corporate & Securities
Law Advisor. Copyright Prentice Hall
Law & Business.

CREF [College Retirement Equities Fund], and CREF withdrew its proposal. (Texaco submitted its poison pill to shareholders for their approval at the company's May 9 annual meeting. However, Texaco's action was not prompted by shareholder resolution, but rather by pressures from the Equity Security Holders Committee created during Texaco's Chapter 11 bankruptcy and subsequent reorganization.) Six companies—American Home Products, Continental, First Interstate Bancorp, J.C. Penney, TRW and Unocal—agreed to adopt confidential voting in exchange for withdrawal of secret ballot proposals.

The willingness of these companies to consider the merits of the shareholder proposals offers evidence that, even though activist institutions are still losing the votes, the shareholder campaigns of the past three years are beginning to have an effect. The willingness of both institutional activists and corporate management to discuss the issues, and their ability to reach compromise, suggests that constructive dialogue may be possible on a wide range of issues. * * *

One [new] approach is the establishment of shareholder advisory committees to advise companies on corporate governance issues and other significant matters. * * *

(5) In 1989, the California Public Employees' Retirement System proposed a significant revision of the SEC proxy system (discussed generally in section D below). The import of the proposed revisions is to improve the effectiveness of the voice of institutional investors voting as shareholders of publicly held corporations.

ROLE OF GIANT CORPORATIONS

HEARINGS BEFORE THE SUBCOMMITTEE ON MONOPOLY OF THE SELECT COMMITTEE ON SMALL BUSINESS

United States Senate, 92nd Cong., 2d Sess., Pt. 4, at 5322–24 (1972) (Correspondence of W.S. Mitchell, President, Safeway Stores, Inc.)

Safeway Stores, Inc., Top 30 Shareholders, Mar. 3, 1972

[Number of shares]

Kane & Co., Chase Manhattan Bank [16]	2,206,363
Cede & Co., NYSE	1,372,062
Merrill Lynch Pierce Fenner	646,752
Ince & Co., Morgan Guaranty Trust	594,224
Myers & Co., Windsor Fund	512,000
Cudd & Co., Chase Manhattan	305,828
King & Co., First National City Bank	259,326
Food & Co., Bank of California	233,000
Sigler & Co., Manu. Hanover Trust	202,225

16. [By the Editor] The registered holder of the shares in this list is the nominee whose name appears on the left (e.g., "Kane & Co."). The name of the institution was added by the person preparing the list for presentation to the Senate Subcommittee. Of course, in the records of Safeway Stores only the name of the nominee appears.

Egger & Co., Chase Manhattan Bank	188,664
Brown Brothers Harriman & Co.	182,229
Eddy & Co., Bankers Trust Co.	167,325
Finman & Co., Bankers Trust Co.	166,400
Sabat Co., Savings Banks Trust Co.	162,700
Salkeld & Co., Bankers Trust Co.	151,705
O'Neill & Co., Bank of New York	150,000
Lynn & Co., Morgan Guaranty Trust	125,000
Seafirst & Co., Seattle Nat. Bank	123,439
Ferro & Co., Nat. Shawmut Bank of Boston	114,100
Gmster & Co., Bank of America	93,000
Loeb Rhoades & Co.	80,919
Gunther & Co., Swiss Bank Corp.	74,138
Bid & Co., New England Merchants National Bank	72,000
Seatel & Co., Seattle First National Bank	70,000
Dicot & Co., Bank of America	65,000
Spinnaker & Co., State Street Bank and Trust	57,000
Nay & Co., Security Pacific National Bank	56,058
Safinsco	55,000
Trund & Co., United California Bank	54,500
Gavin & Co., Morgan Guaranty Trust	52,800
Total	8,593,757

Total outstanding shares, 25,620,931.

WHO OWNS US?

[From Safeway News, February–March 1972]
(By the Roving Reporter)

* * * Who owns Safeway? The fact is that nobody actually knows or can know. This is because a corporation is owned by the people who, at any given time, own its shares. It should be easy to figure out who they are except that many of the people or "institutions" who own shares own them in the name of a "nominee," and they don't necessarily own them for an extended period of time. Yesterday's ownership is not today's.

I once gave my wife a few shares of Safeway stock, for instance, as a present. She is now duly listed as an owner under her own name. She is a shareholder, recognized, as such. My daughter, on the other hand, owns some shares of a mutual fund which operates in the stock market on a "growth theory." From time to time her fund owns Safeway stock and proportionately, she does too. But she isn't listed as a Safeway shareholder because her interest is secondary or indirect. What with funds, trusts and other institutional holdings, no one can say at any given time who owns and profits from our Company. Certainly, all of us who work for it benefit in many ways, but only those who are direct owners (as my wife) or indirect (as my daughter) participate fully or partially in its good or ill fortunes.

By far the largest number of our shareholders are small investors. Out of almost 68,000 listed shareholders as of the end of last year, a little more than 34% owned fewer than 50 shares. (This isn't peanuts either; on December 31, 1971, 50 shares of Safeway stock was worth about $1,795.) A smaller number of shareholders (less than 10,000) were invested in Safeway at the rate of 50 to 99 shares. Taken together, while these two groups of stockholders represent around 48% of the total owners, they represent directly about 4% of our total ownership.

The foregoing may suggest that our major ownership must be highly concentrated and in the control of a few shareholders. In a sense this is true. It may shock you to know that at the end of last year only 114 shareholders owned about 48% of our company.

But before you jump up and down about the concentration of ownership in a "few" hands, you have to take a look at who these owners are. For the most part, each "owner" represents thousands of investors, such as my daughter's fund does. * * * Brokerage houses, on their own accounts and on those of thousands of their clients who don't want to be bothered with actual stock certificates (known as "street" accounts), are counted as single shareholders although their actual ownership is widely spread. * * *

This is only an indication, of course, of the breadth of our ownership. Standard and Poor's, a repository of information on the prices and movements of common shares on various exchange estimated in December of last year that 117 different institutions (insurance companies, pension funds, mutual funds, banks, trusts) held about 2,500,000 shares of our stock. At roughly the same time, Kidder Peabody (another brokerage house) estimated that over "100 institutions held 3,200,000 shares."

Safeway employees, while not yet large owners as a group, are also important individual participants in ownership. Indirectly, some participate as the result of funds invested under the Safeway Retirement Plan. Directly, about 4,000 of us are buying Safeway stock in our own names under the Employees' Stock Purchase Plan, * * *.

The few large institutional holders, representing their masses of individual investors and beneficiaries, appear on our rolls as single owners. The smaller investors also appear as single owners, but they are far more easily identified as the kind of people we all know. They are the retired couple on the corner lot; they are the young couple who put a small inheritance in trust for their new baby; they are the store manager in Kansas, the mailman who serves his store and the truck driver who brings his supplies. * * *

Notes

(1) Other material in this testimony indicates that Kane & Co. represents the employees' Profit Sharing Plan, and King & Co. and Food and Company represent the Safeway Retirement Plan.

(2) In 1986, Safeway Stores was acquired in a leveraged buyout by Kohlberg, Kravis, Roberts, for a purchase price of $4.25 billion, and ceased to be a listed publicly-held company.

FINAL REPORT OF THE SECURITIES AND EXCHANGE COMMISSION ON THE PRACTICE OF RECORDING THE OWNERSHIP OF SECURITIES IN THE RECORDS OF THE ISSUER IN OTHER THAN THE NAME OF THE BENEFICIAL OWNER OF SUCH SECURITIES *

A. BACKGROUND

The practice of registering securities in the records of issuers in other than the name of the beneficial owner is commonly referred to as "nominee" and "street" name registration. Nominee name registration refers to arrangements used by institutional investors (insurance companies and investment companies among others) and financial intermediaries (brokers, banks and trust companies) for the registration of securities held by them for their own account or for the account of their customers who are the beneficial owners of the securities.[17] Street name registration, a specialized type of nominee name registration, refers to the practice of a broker registering in its name, or in the name of its nominee, securities left with it by customers or held by it for its own account.

American institutions first began extensively to register securities in nominee name in the 1930's [18] in an effort to escape onerous transfer requirements placed on corporations and fiduciaries by issuers seeking to protect themselves from judicially imposed liability for improper transfers.[19] Customarily, issuers required the submission of all sup-

---

* (December 3, 1976) Pp. 1–6. This report is usually called "The Street Name Study."

17. [By the Commission] A nominee is, typically, a partnership formed exclusively to act as the recordholder of securities. Each of the nominee's general partners is an employee of the professional fiduciary or corporate institutional investor and legally is empowered to make transfers of nominee stock. As employees depart or assume other duties, they retire from the partnership, and new partners are admitted so that the partnership continues as a creature of the parent entity. Often, the partnership name is short, is derived from the name of a partner or former partner, and includes at the end "& Co.," the traditional indication of a partnership. The name may have no relation to the name of the fiduciary or institution for which the nominee acts.

18. [By the Commission] Brokers at that time employed street name registra-

tion primarily as a convenient method of holding securities pledged by customers in connection with margin transactions and as a means of avoiding transfer taxes.

19. [By the Commission] An issuer transferring record ownership of its securities was obligated to protect equitable, or beneficial, interests, as well as legal, or record, interests. If the character of a transfer made in breach of trust were discoverable on reasonable inquiry, failure to make that inquiry rendered the issuer liable to the beneficial owner. This doctrine was established in Lowry v. Commercial and Farmers' Bank, 15 F.Cas. 1040 (No. 8581) (C.C.Md.1848), which held that corporations were responsible for the propriety of transfers of their stock by fiduciaries. A corporation was: "* * * the custodian of the shares of stock, and clothed with power sufficient to protect the rights of everyone interested, from unauthorized transfers; it is a trust placed in the hands of the corporation for the protection of individual in-

porting documents [20] before transferring stock held by fiduciaries and required corporate investors to demonstrate the authority and incumbency of the individual officer or employee acting on their behalf. The use of the nominee as the registered holder of stock eliminated from the issuer's records any evidence of a fiduciary relationship and made the recordholder a non-corporate entity. Thus nominees could transfer securities without meeting the requirements placed on corporate or fiduciary shareholders.

Nominee registration still serves to facilitate transfers, but today it provides other important benefits to the securities industry as well. The widespread use of nominee registration, however, has collateral effects which may be disadvantageous. First, it makes communications between issuers and their shareowners more circuitous due to the interpositioning of intermediaries. Second, it tends to complicate regulation by masking beneficial owners of securities. Third, since the jurisdiction of certain sections of the Securities Exchange Act of 1934 (the "Act") is based upon a shareholder-of-record standard, the concentration of securities ownership in nominees may have the effect of inappropriately removing or excluding issuers from the jurisdiction of the Act.

Because of concern regarding these consequences, Congress, in June 1975, enacted Section 12(m) of the Act. Section 12(m) authorized and directed the Commission to undertake a study and investigation of the practice of recording the ownership of securities in the records of the issuer in other than the name of the beneficial owner of such securities and to determine (1) whether the practice is consistent with the purposes of the Act * * * and (2) whether steps can be taken to facilitate communications between issuers and the beneficial owners of their securities while at the same time retaining the benefits of such practice. * * *

D. SUMMARY OF CONCLUSIONS AND RECOMMENDATIONS

The Commission has concluded that the practice of registering securities in the records of the issuer in other than the name of the beneficial owner of such securities is consistent with the purposes of the Act * * * The practice benefits investors and the securities industry by facilitating the transfer of record ownership and the clearance and settlement of securities transactions. In addition, it is integral to the operation of securities depositories. At the same time, the widespread use of nominee and street name registration causes certain problems. The Commission has found, however, that established procedures have overcome many of these problems, and the Commission believes that

terests, and like every other trustee it is bound to execute the trust with proper diligence and care, and is responsible for any injury sustained by its negligence or misconduct." Id. at 1047.

20. [By the Commission] For example, a certified copy of the will, trust instrument, or court order of sale.

the problems which remain can be mitigated within the framework of the current system.

The Commission, therefore, recommends that no steps be taken which would discourage the use of nominee and street name registration or diminish the benefits which the practice provides. * * *

Notes

(1) The mechanics of the system by which information is supplied to beneficial owners and voting decisions by such owners are transmitted to corporations is described below. See pp. 630–640 infra.

(2) A unique problem is presented by the nominee Cede and Company, that is listed as being among the 30 largest shareholders in many corporations:

> Cede and Company was started in 1967 and became fully operational on February 24, 1969, as the nominee for the Stock Clearing Corporation, a wholly owned subsidiary of the New York Stock Exchange, which furnishes a central stock clearing service to numerous member brokerage firms. * * *

> For example, as reported by General Electric, the 2,822,602 shares listed under Cede and Company (the third largest holder of GE stock) represented holdings of 188 participants. Similarly, American Airlines reported that there were 144 members firms with shares in the Cede name, none of which separately would be among the top 30 stockholders. * * *

> It is perhaps not surprising, in view of this relationship between Cede and Company and member brokerage firms, that there has been some inconsistency in manner of reporting of Cede and Company's holdings. * * *

Disclosure of Corporate Ownership, Sen.Doc. 93–62 (93rd Cong. 2d Sess.), Pp. 131, 132 (1974).

(3) Beneficial owners of publicly traded securities today rarely hold record ownership to the securities. In the case of an owner who is an individual, the usual manner of ownership is by simple book entry in the records of the brokerage firm with which the individual deals. The brokerage firm, in turn, (assuming it is a participant in the central clearing service maintained by the Depository Trust Company) also does not hold record title to its customers' shares. Rather, the shares are held of record by Cede & Company and the brokerage firm's total holdings of those shares for all customers are reflected by a single book entry in DTC's records. If a customer of brokerage firm A sells shares to a customer of brokerage firm B, the closing of the transaction is reflected by a simple book entry in DTC's books. The process does not record individual transactions in DTC's books; rather all transactions in a specific stock by customers of firm A— both purchases and sales—are netted together each day and only a single entry, plus or minus, is made on DTC's books. The same is true for firm B and for all other member brokerage firms of DTC. If a customer of firm A buys 100 shares of stock while another customer of firm A sells 100 shares of the same stock on the same day, no entry at all is made on DTC's

books, though the records of the brokerage firm will, of course, reflect that a different customer now owns 100 shares. This system is undeniably efficient in a trading sense—it permits the trading of hundreds of millions of shares in a single day with a minimum of paper flow—but it has the consequence of interposing two intermediaries between the issuer and the beneficial owner.

(4) The customer who purchases securities may become a record owner by requesting the brokerage firm to obtain a certificate. Most customers, however, do not bother. Presumably the average customer is unaware that record title of the shares is in fact somewhere else in the name of Cede & Company. If the customer wishes to take some action with respect to the shares that must be taken by the record owner, the customer must notify the broker who in turn must notify Cede & Co. to take the requisite action. Dividends are handled in an analogous manner, with payments being directed first from the paying corporation to Cede and Company and then to the brokerage firm who reflects the distribution by increasing the cash balance of customers or by sending a check drawn by the brokerage firm to the customers who have requested that service.

(5) The development of the central clearing system has given rise to problems since state statutes continue to require action by record owners. The problems this system creates for the distribution of proxy statements and voting by shareholders are discussed in section D of this Chapter. Other examples of problems created by the superimposition of a book entry recordation system on a record ownership legal system, include Tabbi v. Pollution Control Industries, Inc., 508 A.2d 867 (Del.Ch.1986) [in order to perfect the right of appraisal following a merger, state law requires that a demand letter must be received from the record owner before the vote is taken on the merger (compare RMBCA § 13.21); "a demand filed by Cede & Co. on behalf of Shearson Lehman/American Express, Inc.) with respect to 44,500 shares held beneficially" was untimely even though Shearson had prepared the demand letter two days before the meeting and sent it by overnight courier to Cede & Company; for some reason it was delivered one day late and Cede & Company's demand letter to the issuer was received by the issuer one hour and five minutes after the polls were closed]; Enstar Corporation v. Senouf, 535 A.2d 1351 (Del.1987) [right to stock appraisal not validly perfected when demand for appraisal was made in the name of the beneficial owner and signed by an employee of the brokerage firm but not in the name of Cede & Company]; Carey v. Pennsylvania Enterprises, Inc., 876 F.2d 333 (3d Cir.1989) [a "dividend reinvestment plan" (DRIP) administered by a bank provided for a "pass through" of voting rights to beneficial owners; however, shares purchased through the DRIP were formally held of record by two nominees for the bank; the plan administrator failed to cause the nominees to give proxies to the beneficial owners or otherwise have the nominees vote as the beneficial owners directed; held, none of the votes of the DRIP shares may be counted even though votes by the beneficial holders of those shares had been solicited and tabulated precisely by the corporation as part of the process of voting of non-DRIP shares].

(6) See RMBCA § 7.23. The Official Comment suggests that a "corporation may limit or qualify the procedure as it deems appropriate," and

that "it is expected that experimentation with various devices under this section may reveal other areas which the corporation's plan should address." Do not the cases summarized in the previous note indicate that a system of voting of the type contemplated by this section should be made compulsory?

(7) An absolutely essential ingredient to the modern central clearing system for securities transactions is the Securities Investors Protection Corporation (SIPC), created by Congress in 1970. SIPC insures investors against loss caused by the insolvency of brokerage firms.

C. DIRECTORS

HAMILTON, RELIANCE AND LIABILITY STANDARDS FOR OUTSIDE DIRECTORS

24 Wake Forest L.Rev. 5, 9–12 (1989).

Modern boards of directors have practically nothing to do with the day-to-day business of the corporation. Publicly held corporations are immense economic entities. They may have hundreds of plants, tens or hundreds of thousands of employees, billions of dollars in sales, and hundreds of thousands of shareholders. They may have operations in foreign countries that rival in size their American operations. The internal organization of such large economic entities necessarily involves complex hierarchical structures in which successively higher levels of management are given increasingly broad discretion and responsibility. Indeed, starting at the lowest level of corporate management, such as shop foreman or a similar position, successive layers of broader responsibility can be traced up through several levels of management. By following this process through to its logical conclusion, the highest level reached still would be below the level of the board of directors.

Even this description does not adequately describe the complexity of the internal structure of many publicly held corporations. Many corporations today are so large and are involved in so many diverse lines of business that business decision-making is diversified and diffused. Several largely independent internal hierarchical structures may exist within the lower levels of the corporate bureaucracy, each culminating in a single person or, in rare instances, a small committee that has responsibility for one or more areas of operations.[21] A person may be "President of the Plastics Division" or "Head of the Chemicals Sector" of a large corporation with responsibility for the profitability of a multi-plant business with sales of billions of dollars per year and yet be several hierarchical levels below the highest management level within the corporation itself.

21. [By the Author] For example, Johnson & Johnson has 165 autonomous units world-wide. General Electric is considerably more centralized; it has "only" 14 key businesses along with four additional support businesses that report directly to corporate headquarters. Byrne & Baum, *The Limits of Power,* Bus.Wk., October 23, 1987, at 34 (special ed.).

Above these lower level internal hierarchies there is an "umbrella organization," the "corporate headquarters" or "home office" of the publicly held corporation, of which the board of directors loosely forms a part. The "Plastics Division" or "Chemical Sector" in this situation may be structured as a wholly owned subsidiary of the publicly held corporation, or it may be a department or division of the corporation with no separate legal structure. In either event, it may have its own "board of directors," consisting usually of management personnel drawn from the operating components and from corporate headquarters staff, to advise and assist its managers. It may function as a largely autonomous business having wide discretion over research, product development, advertising, sales policies, and other matters. These semi-autonomous businesses within a single corporate structure often are described as "profit centers."

There are centralized levels of bureaucracy in corporate headquarters above these profit centers that have general oversight of the management of each profit center. Corporate headquarters imposes constraints on autonomy by setting profit goals or objectives for each center that are expected to be met—or sought—each year in terms of net profit, return on invested capital, or other similar measures. The operating head of the profit center has the responsibility for meeting these goals and may lose his or her job if the goals are not met. In addition, corporate headquarters usually handles certain core functions for all branches of the business. These functions relate to the processes of evaluation of performance and control over funds, specifically auditing, legal services, management compensation policies, fringe benefits, and accounting. Others are handled centrally because of perceived efficiency. It is not uncommon, for example, for corporate headquarters to handle the investment of excess funds. Under such a system, each profit center is required to turn over all excess funds on a daily basis to headquarters for investment, with the profit center having the privilege of withdrawing funds as needed for operations. Typically, corporate headquarters also has the sole responsibility of raising capital and allocating it among the profit centers. These functions require centralized review and approval of proposed capital investments by profit centers to assure that the corporation divides its limited resources among competing proposals put forth by autonomous profit centers in order to maximize overall return. Despite these restraints by corporate headquarters, many profit centers are sufficiently discrete and independent that they may be sold off by the corporation or be spun off as entirely separate entities without major changes in operating procedures.

Corporate headquarters itself has a hierarchical structure. At the highest levels are a series of executive managers, usually organized on a functional rather than a product basis, who have ultimate authority over broad areas of corporate activities. They have titles, such as "chief legal officer," "chief operations officer," "chief financial officer," and "chief accounting officer," that bear no relationship to the traditional corporate officers of "President," "Secretary," or "Treasurer" referred to in older state corporation statutes. At the ultimate apex is an individual referred to almost universally as the chief executive officer (the "CEO")[22] who has responsibility for the enterprise as a whole. The CEO may have additional titles and roles, such as "President" or "Chairman of the Board of Directors," but many CEOs do not. The CEO has responsibility for the management team that directs the enterprise. If, for example, he loses confidence in the chief financial officer, the CEO must replace him and find a more satisfactory one. In theory, the CEO has power to call the shots in the corporate bureaucracy on narrow issues as well as broad ones, where and when he wishes. Of course, the CEO, as the head of a large bureaucratic organization, cannot hope to run details of the business operations; if he is to be effective, authority over details must be delegated to subordinates, and the CEO must concentrate on the broadest issues relating to the corporation.[23]

Because the CEO has ultimate responsibility for the success or failure of the business, he—and quite possibly he alone—will make the final decision on whether to embark upon a radical change in business strategy that may lead to the loss of his or her job if the change turns out to be disastrous. He may decide, for example, to close fifteen plants in order to redirect the primary emphasis of the corporation, or to develop a new product such as a state-of-the-art airplane or modern computer that will strain the economic resources of the entire entity and may well be unsuccessful; "betting the company" is the slang phrase that describes such fundamental and risky decisions. Such decisions may or may not be reviewed by the board of directors before they are implemented, but it is almost certain that if the CEO wishes to embark on such a course of action, the board of directors will acquiesce in that decision despite the reservations of many, or even all, members.[24]

22. [By the Author] Surveys of CEOs of publicly held corporations reveal that they are almost all white and male. Of the 1,000 CEO's in a recent survey by *Business Week*, only two were female; none were black. [Byrne & Baum, *The Limits of Power*, Bus.Wk., October 23, 1987, at 34 (special ed.).]

In unusual and very rare circumstances, the functions of the CEO may be divided among two or three persons who are expected to act collectively. Generally, these arrangements do not work out satisfactorily in practice, in part because of natural rivalries among the individuals involved, and in part because of the dilution of responsibility when several persons participate in ultimate and far-reaching decisions.

23. [By the Author] The effect of this delegation of details has been characterized as follows:

[P]ower—having great influence, force, and authority—is slipping through the chief executive's hands, and has been for some time. . . . Now a chief executive hardly ever "runs" anything. . . . Chief executives, many management gurus agree, are less powerful today than they were 10 or 15 years ago. The most significant reason is that their task is much bigger. It's one thing to manage a single operation well. It's another thing to decide that you're no longer in a certain business, to change, cut back, deal with foreign competition. The agenda has been greatly expanded. . . .

Id. at 33–34.

24. [By the Author] A vote on an issue of the nature described in the text is, in effect, a vote of confidence on the stewardship of the CEO. For example, the CEO of United Airlines in 1985 proposed that the

Where then does the board of directors fit in? It does not have a place in the clearly demarcated hierarchy that leads from shop foreman or steward to CEO. The board is also not part of a direct chain of command above the CEO, since many or most important business decisions do not come before the board at all. Rather, it is somewhere above the CEO, and floating off to one side. Its principal source of power is a cataclysmic one: If it loses confidence in the CEO, it can compel his resignation and the installation of a successor. Obviously, such a power is an extreme one with wide-reaching implications upon the management of the business and is used only rarely and in extreme circumstances. Furthermore, it is not exercised easily. Because of the manner of their selection and the nature of their working relationships with the CEO, directors tend to give the CEO the benefit of the doubt. Even a discussion among directors about the possibility of replacing the CEO is a serious matter fraught with danger and uncertainty.

H. LAND, BUILDING A MORE EFFECTIVE BOARD OF DIRECTORS

[An undated promotional brochure published in about 1972 by H.R. Land & Company, Management Consultants, Los Angeles, California.]

The corporate Board of Directors is a topic of increasing concern to Chief Executive Officers. Directors, now keenly aware of their legal liabilities, are pressing for greater participation in corporate affairs and new forms of compensation. In response to this greater interest on the part of their directors, a number of Chief Executives are rethinking the use of their boards and adopting new policies intended to strengthen the director/management relationship.

This report is designed to assist the Chief Executive Officer in dealing with his board. It is based upon independent interviews conducted by H.R. Land & Company with Chief Executives and Directors representing more than 60 corporations active in all segments of the economy. The survey sample purposely included small privately held firms and medium sized regionally traded companies as well as widely traded Fortune 500 corporations.

No attempt has been made to develop statistical tabulations of the findings. Rather, *the emphasis is on policies and techniques which could be of practical value to large numbers of Chief Executive Officers.* Because of the many types of corporations included in the study, not all of the ideas presented are suitable for use in any one firm. Our intent has been to present a number of ideas from which a Chief Executive

corporation branch out into related areas such as hotel management and car rental. He also proposed that the name of the corporation be changed to Allegis Corporation to reflect the broader area of operations. When this proposal was presented to the board of directors, a majority concluded that the proposed diversification was unwise and voted against the proposal. The CEO promptly resigned, as everyone understood that the vote was a vote of lack of confidence in the CEO's stewardship. *Id.* at 34. * * *

might select and adopt those which are appropriate for use in his own firm.

THE CEO DETERMINES THE BOARD'S EFFECTIVENESS

The Principal Determinant of the Effectiveness of a Board of Directors is the Chief Executive Officer. His personal convictions on what a board should be will do more to shape the role of his directors than any other single factor. In most instances we found the board to be a mirror image of the CEO's desires and intentions. Exceptions tended to occur only where the board was made up of individuals representing major equity interests or financial institutions who were not necessarily of the CEO's choosing.

The attitude of the CEO is critical; he creates the atmosphere—hopefully one of candor and frankness in which the directors feel their participation is of real value. The ideal CEO/director relationship is one of professional respect and admiration. Friendship is a part of the relationship, but it must remain a "business" friendship rather than a "personal" relationship if the directors' "check and balance" function is to remain intact. The most effective boards seem to share a philosophy in which both the CEO and each director consider themselves as donors and recipients in a mutually beneficial relationship.

Obviously the CEO's actions have a major impact on the board. What he does to select, attract, involve, motivate, compensate and protect his directors is the subject of the remainder of this booklet. Equally important are the personal touches—periodically inviting a director to lunch, remembering his individual likes and dislikes, being cognizant of his other business and personal obligations, letting him know you are thinking of him on special occasions. * * *

THE SELECTION OF DIRECTORS

A successful board is built one member at a time. Each selection is critical, for its impact will be felt not only on the company and its existing board, but also on the firm's ability to attract the caliber of directors it will need in the future.

The criteria for selecting a potential director are a function of the company's size, ownership, management, and objectives. Over time these factors change, necessitating directors of varying talents as the corporation grows and prospers. Our talks with CEO's and directors revealed eight criteria which were useful in the selection process regardless of the circumstances of the individual firm. Each potential candidate should be considered in light of the following questions:

- Does he have broad experience with general management problems?
- Is he a good listener who is not afraid to speak his mind?
- Does he have sufficient time available?
- Potentially how great is his interest?
- Is he free from a current or potential conflict of interest?

- Is he compatible with management and the other directors?
- Is his stature at least equal to that of the other directors?
- Does he have a unique contribution to make?

Suggestions for potential candidates seem to come most frequently from other board members, lawyers, management consultants, executive search firms, investment bankers, financial public relations firms and professional groups of which the CEO may be a member—such as the Young Presidents Organization. * * *

With the exception of very large corporations, most CEO's seem to prefer a relatively small board of 5 to 9 members. The philosophy seems to be to get fewer and better men; then work them hard and pay them well.

Age should not be a major factor in selection of a director—only productivity. The principal use an upper age limit serves is to allow the CEO to avoid facing the unpleasant task of asking a man off the board.

There is no easy way to ask a man to resign. The best technique is to make it clear from the start that an individual will be a director only as long as it is in the company's best interest. If his subsequent performance is then reviewed annually it will be obvious both to him and to the CEO when he is no longer a contributor.

How a Potential Director Views Board Membership

* * * In asking directors what motivated them to accept membership on individual boards the most frequent responses centered on (1) existing or potential *personal relationships* with management and the other directors, (2) the *experience and satisfaction* accompanying board membership, and (3) *status and prestige* attached to being a corporate director. Annual retainers and meeting fees were rarely cited as a reason for accepting, although the opportunity for a *capital gain* is obviously a strong motivating factor. In this regard, one professional director told us that he looks for companies whose stock is depressed, whose management has an equity position strong enough to provide him with a "fair" block of stock, and whose circumstances are such that outside help is clearly needed.

Getting Directors Involved

The Key to Making a Director Effective is to Involve Him Personally. A good way to establish the feeling of "our company" is with financial participation. Some publicly traded firms make attractive investment financing available for their directors; in a privately held business financial involvement can be achieved by allowing a director to buy in at book and, when he resigns, to sell at book. * * *

Notes

The author of the foregoing brochure presumably never dreamed that it would find its way into a law school casebook or a set of readings as to the role of directors in corporations. As a result its point of view is revealing in terms of traditional views about the role of directors and its unconscious bias with respect to women and minority groups. In theory, the shareholders elect directors who in turn appoint officers and agents. Is that the way the relationship is seen in the real world? Who selects whom? In theory, the board manages and management executes the policies set by the board. In Land's view, who determines whose roles?

A. GOLDBERG,[25] DEBATE ON OUTSIDE DIRECTORS *

New York Times, Oct. 29, 1972, Sec. 3, at p. 1.

The major problem in the corporate director system is the gap between what the law decrees to be the governing role of the corporate director and the reality of management control of the corporation.

Contrary to legal theory, the boards of directors of most of our larger companies do not in fact control and manage their companies, nor are they equipped to do so. Instead, the management hired by the board, presumably to execute decisions of the board, in fact generally decides the course of operations and periodically requests the board to confirm the determinations of the management.

Thus, the board is relegated to an advisory and legitimizing function that is substantially different from the role of policy maker and guardian of shareholder and public interest contemplated by the law of corporations.

At the very best, outside directors of almost all large corporate enterprises under the present system cannot acquire more than a smattering of knowledge about any large and far-flung company of which they are directors. As a result, outside directors often are even unable to ask discerning questions when presented with a complex management decision for approval at the board meetings.

This can result in the outside director not fulfilling his fiduciary responsibility to the shareholders. As one former Penn Central director frankly admitted: "I don't think anybody was aware that it was that close to collapse."

The implication of the Penn Central fiasco for the future of the current director system is that outside directors must ponder how best to reassert the managerial and policy-making functions of the board. A

25. [By The New York Times] Mr. Goldberg is a former Associate Justice of the Supreme Court and Ambassador to the United Nations. He is now engaged in a private legal practice.

On Oct. 18 Mr. Goldberg resigned as a director of Trans World Airlines following a dispute over the proper role of directors who come from outside the company's management. He had unsuccessfully tried to establish an independent committee of outside directors to review the actions and recommendations of management, arguing that outside directors should be allowed to meet independently and hire an autonomous staff of technical specialists to help them in making decisions.

Mr. Goldberg elaborated his views at the request of The New York Times.

board of directors not aware of recent legal and related developments is not fulfilling its legal and public responsibilities and is only asking for trouble.

Notes

(1) Mr. Goldberg suggested that the board establish a "committee of overseers" composed of outside directors with general responsibility for supervising company operations and making periodic reports to the board. Mr. Goldberg further suggested:

> To perform these duties adequately this committee would need authorization to hire a small staff of experts who would be responsible only to the board and would be totally independent of management control. In addition, the committee should also be empowered to engage the services of consultants of the highest competence.

> As the eyes and ears of the directors, these independent experts and their staff assistants and consultants would look into major policy questions and report to the committee and through them to the board as a whole before decisions are taken on management recommendations.

The suggestion that the board, or a committee of the board, be routinely given its own independent staff has been strongly opposed by persons within corporate management, and apparently has never been tested. The concerns usually expressed about such a proposal are that it would be divisive, that it would create a "we-against-they" attitude, and that it would not be conducive to the mutual trust required for the smooth functioning of the board and of the corporation. Do you agree? Are such costs justified by the need for an independent watchdog? How much oversight can one really expect from a "small" staff in a multibillion dollar corporation?

(2) With the perspective of nearly two decades, it is now clear that Mr. Goldberg put his finger on a central problem of corporate governance that has since troubled commentators, the Securities and Exchange Commission and members of Congress. At the time his article appeared, however, it sparked a few letters to the editor but little extended debate or interest.

(3) Following Watergate in 1974, it was revealed that a large number of publicly-held corporations had engaged in a significant amount of illegal or questionable conduct: paying bribes or "commissions" to high-placed officials in friendly countries, making illegal campaign contributions to American politicians, and the like. About four hundred corporations voluntarily admitted such conduct, including such well known names as Lockheed Aircraft Corporation, Gulf Oil Corporation, Northrop Corporation, and G.D. Searle and Company. A. Sommer, The Impact of the SEC on Corporate Governance, Reprinted in D. DeMott, Corporations at the Crossroads, Governance and Reform (1980), at 200. Some of this conduct might be explainable on the basis of the arguments, "it is not illegal over there" or "everyone does it." Some of the conduct, however, constituted clear and knowing violations of criminal law: for example, an officer of Northrop Corporation personally delivered a suitcase containing $50,000 in cash to

President Nixon as a campaign contribution, knowing that it came from corporate funds and was therefore illegal. A number of individuals and corporations pleaded guilty or nolo contendere to criminal charges based on similar conduct. In some instances, the SEC brought suit to compel changes in the governance of specific corporations, and in other instances negotiated plans for impartial investigations of responsibility for misconduct.

(4) Throughout these widespread disclosures it was apparent that many directors were unaware of the existence of illegal or inappropriate conduct within their own corporations. Indeed, in some instances it was also doubtful that top management knew of the illegal use of fairly large sums of money. The magnitude and volume of these disclosures prompted the most massive review of corporate governance since the 1930s, led to the development of a modern theory of corporate governance described below, and ultimately led to the American Law Institute's ongoing Corporate Governance Project.

(5) If directors do not manage, what do they do? A partial answer is provided by a 1971 study, M. Mace, Directors: Myth and Reality (1971). Professor Mace concludes that directors at regular meetings—particularly outside directors—perform only two basic functions:

(a) They provide advice and counsel to management. They may be a sounding board from which a variety of views on board or difficult questions may be obtained. The views of a director with expertise in an area such as law or finance may be given greater weight with respect to questions arising within his or her area of expertise. Nevertheless, Professor Mace concludes that "sometimes, but not too frequently" the views of outside directors will provoke reconsideration or modification, and that "occasionally, but only very rarely" does it lead to a reversal of a decision. Mace, The President and the Board of Directors, 50 Harv.Bus.Rev. 37 (March–April 1972).

(b) They provide discipline to management, who must appear before them and present information and defend business decisions. Even though the board almost never questions the management's conclusion, the mere fact that it exists requires an organization of thoughts and points of view and a careful review of work of subordinates. The mere fact that a difficult question *might* be asked ensures that the chief executive officer will prepare carefully for his appearance before the board. Of course, the extent to which the board effectively serves this function is probably impossible to quantify. Professor Mace's conclusions are based on interviews with a large number of persons familiar with the role of directors.

(6) Professor Mace also concludes that directors generally do *not*—

(a) Establish basic objectives, corporate strategies and broad policies of the company;

(b) Ask discerning questions at meetings; or

(c) Select the chief executive officer.

With respect to the selection of the operational management, Mace concludes that the controlling element in the naming of a new chief executive officer is usually the person presently holding that position.

(7) Professor Mace points out that in one type of situation the role of the board of directors is more than advisory. That is the crisis situation. When a 45 year old corporate president suddenly dies of a heart attack, the board must decide on a successor usually without the advice or guidance of the incumbent. Also the board sometimes may have to decide whether to replace the chief executive officer because of incompetence, criminal conduct or failure of performance. This delicate situation is particularly difficult for directors to handle:

When conditions in a company deteriorate because of what seems to be the incompetence of the president, and the outside directors become uneasily aware that some action needs to be taken by the board, three alternative courses were found to be employed.

(1) *Hire a management consultant.* Employing management consultants to recommend the taking of unpleasant management actions is not an uncommon approach to difficult and sensitive problem areas. Certainly one of these is the problem of a group of friendly outside board members trying to communicate to a company president that he is not doing a satisfactory job as chief executive officer. Periodic total management and organization audits by competent professional consultants are performed for very successful company managements who are aware that corporate success may be dulling their responses to change. Accordingly the suggestion by a group of outside directors that consultants be employed to review a company's operations is consistent with good management practice, and therefore not immediately offensive to the president. ＊ ＊ ＊

(2) *Resign from the board.* Resignation from the board was found to be the most common and typical response of a director who has concluded that the company's president is inadequate. ＊ ＊ ＊

(3) *Take action requesting the president to resign.* Occasionally a financial page of the press carries a brief story: "It was announced today by Mr. R.J. Jones, Chairman of the XYZ Company, that Mr. Paul Brown, president, resigned because of policy differences with the board." In companies where management and outside directors own little common stock, it is rare that outside directors take the drastic action outlined in the press release of asking the president to resign. If the president is involved in a personal scandal such as the commission of a major crime or in conflicts of interest from which he has profited personally at the company's expense, or if he is identified with bribery or some other generally unacceptable conduct, the resignation of the president is not uncommon. But when the president is *not* guilty of any of these transgressions, and his only shortcoming is the lack of capacity to manage the company effectively, then outside directors are most reluctant to ask for his resignation. ＊ ＊ ＊

Asking a president to resign is a traumatic experience under any circumstances. Loyalties, working relationships, and social relationships all get in the way of complete objectivity in appraising and concluding what is best for the company. Most outside directors try to avoid the high level of emotion that almost always attends a forced resignation. As indicated earlier, most outside directors resign to avoid the unpleasantness inevitably involved. And even some of those who choose not to resign, but to stay and participate in an eventual solution, tend to procrastinate and to defer the ultimate but necessary decision. They seem to keep hoping that things will somehow improve. This attitude was found particularly in outside directors who had professional financial or legal-service relationships with the company.

• In one case poor management by the president resulted in the steady decline of sales and profits in a once-profitable and distinguished midwestern company. There were seven outside board members on a board of sixteen, and although there was mounting evidence that the president was incapable of leading the enterprise, no action was initiated by the board members. Finally, after a succession of three loss years, a vice president of the principal lending bank, and not a director of the company, asked to meet with the board, and stated that unless a change was made, the bank loans would not be renewed. With this leverage from the bank, the outside directors made the decision to ask the president to resign—but, it should be noted, with considerable reluctance. * * *

• The president of another company recounted an experience of a fellow director. "A responsible board member on the board *can* be there when it counts. One of my closest friends, Dave Donald, a partner of an investment banking firm, was a director of the Paine Company. You remember the to-do in the press about this company a year ago. The Paine Company was going down hill rapidly. Bad performance was followed by unbelievably terrible performance. Poor Dave was staying awake nights wondering what to do. If the company went bankrupt, there would be mud on Dave's face. If he resigned, that would be backing away from a deal for which he felt some responsibility. So Dave decided that the only hope for the enterprise was to fire the president. Dave called a couple of other outside directors, and this small group, led by Dave, finally, after some time had passed, was able to get the president to resign. Then, as a search committee, they found an outsider to come in and pick up the pieces. For better or worse—we don't really know yet—a change was made in the presidency. But Dave took it upon himself to fulfill his personal understanding of his responsibilities as a director. It was a huge pain in the neck, but he did it. Here the system worked. Here a director was faced with a problem, and he did not back away. When a company gets to the brink of disaster because of lousy management, who can do anything about it except a director? The old president of Paine certainly was not going to fire himself."

M. Mace, Directors: Myth and Reality, pp. 32–33, 36–39 (1971).*

(8) Of course companies vary with regard to the location of power, particularly where there is a substantial block of stock in the hands of an individual. Such a person, if he or she serves on the board but is no longer connected with management may diminish the chief executive officer's power. Professor Mace also indicates that there are situations where

---

control lies in a person who is neither a director nor an officer. Such situations, of course, are more likely to occur in the small or medium-sized corporation than in the very large corporation.

(9) For somewhat different analyses of the functions of directors in the public corporation see Eisenberg, Legal Models of Management Structure in the Modern Corporation, 63 Calif.L.Rev. 375 (1975); Hamilton, Reliance and Liability Standards for Outside Directors, 24 Wake Forest L.Rev. 5, 12–15 (1989).

MANNING, THE BUSINESS JUDGMENT RULE AND THE DIRECTOR'S DUTY OF ATTENTION: TIME FOR REALITY *

39 Bus.Law 1477, 1481–1492 (August, 1984).

Practically all the current debate centers upon "outside" directors. In the real world, what do such directors—"good" directors—actually do in the discharge of their responsibilities? What is generally expected of them in the market place.[26]

TIME DEVOTED

The outside directors of a corporation are part-time people with respect to the amount of working time that is allocated to the affairs of the company. The most recent survey (1982) shows that the average director of a publicly held company devotes a total of about 123 hours per year to his board and committee work, including travel.[27] That averages less than 3 hours a week, or about 1.5 working days a month.

Directors of companies in crisis conditions often find themselves compelled to devote much greater amounts of time. Also, in some companies, special agreements (with or without special compensation) between the company and a particular director may obligate him to devote more time to his directorship than the rest of the members of the board. * * *

No human being can stay on top of all [the problems] in a major company on a one-and-a-half-day-a-month basis.

PACE AND DELIBERATION

Much of the routine housekeeping work of a board of directors does not demand or warrant significant deliberation. Some important matters that come to the board can be and are dealt with in a deliberate manner over several meetings. A few matters, like the choice of a new CEO from among several in-house candidates, can often be pondered and observed carefully over a period of years, but most significant

26. [By the Author] While an effort will be made here to keep in mind the great diversity of the nation's tens of thousands of corporations, most of our available data relates to larger companies, and the descriptions offered here may be correspondingly skewed.

27. [By the Author] Korn Ferry International Board of Directors, Tenth Annual Study, Feb. 1983, at 9.

matters cannot be dealt with in that way by a board. The pace of commercial events often demands quick response or even, as in take-over situations, almost instant response. Even issues that are fully recognized to be vitally important can often not be considered extensively by a board because its agenda is at the time crammed with other exigent items or with matters which, though less significant, are mandated as compulsory agenda items under applicable laws or regulations.

UNCERTAINTY AND RISK–TAKING

Businessmen make business decisions. They are not courts, able and willing to pursue a matter to the last argument in the search of the "right" answer. They are not researchers meticulously seeking truth. They are not scientists striving for ever more refined solutions in a field of narrow specialization. And when an issue comes to a board of directors, the process of discussion and decision is nothing like the lawyer's world of briefs and adversary argumentation. The decisions the businessman must make are fraught with risk, and he is quite accustomed to making these decisions in a hurry on the basis of hunch and manifestly sparse data. The businessman and the board of directors thrive or die in a sea of uncertainty. * * *

DIVERSITY OF DIRECTORS

CEOs understandably prefer other CEOs and corporate officers as directors because of their familiarity with the boardroom process and with the realities of business management,[28] but today, increasing numbers of outside directors are persons who fall into other categories. Academics and persons with political backgrounds are often members of the modern board, while the percentage of lawyers and bankers has declined. A changing society has brought more women and persons of minority ethnic background into the boardroom. Moreover, it is increasingly common to include on boards some persons who have specialized skills that are invaluable to the work of the board, such as the musician on the board of the record company or the physicist board member of Silicon Valley, Inc. These increasingly diverse members can and do contribute significantly to the total work product of the board, but, at the same time, these members of diverse nonbusiness backgrounds are often not knowledgeable about many matters that come up on the board's agenda. They are even less aware of many aspects of the normal business life of the enterprise that do not customarily rise to the level of board attention.

DECISIONAL PROCESS

To judge by their statements, many lawyers without personal boardroom experience have a total misconception of the decisional process as it actually functions in the boardroom. The lawyer's profes-

---

28. [By the Author] Korn Ferry International Board of Directors, Tenth Annual Study, Feb. 1983, at 5.

sional experience in courts, legislatures, and semi-political bodies tends to lead him to assume that all decisional process is inevitably made up of a series of discrete, separate issues presented one at a time, debated by both or all sides, and voted on. In fact boards of directors typically do not operate that way at all, except, perhaps, in conditions of internal warfare or mortal crisis. Actions are usually by consensus. If a significant sentiment of disagreement is sensed by the chairman, the matter is usually put over for later action, and sources of compromise and persuasion are pursued in the interim. Advice from individual directors is most often volunteered to, or solicited by, the CEO informally on a one-on-one basis, rather than pursued in group debate at a board meeting.

CHARACTER OF THE AGENDA

A transcript of a typical board meeting will reflect four kinds of items on the agenda. Fully three quarters of the board's time will be devoted to reports by the management and board committees, routine housekeeping resolutions passed unanimously with little or no discussion, and information responding to specific questions that had earlier been put to the management by directors about a wide range of topics sometimes accompanied by suggestions from the board members, usually procedural in character. Perhaps the remaining one quarter of the meeting time will be addressed to a decision, typically unanimous, on one or two specific different business items, such as the sale of a subsidiary or the establishment of a compensation plan. If, as is the average, a board meets eight times a year, the arithmetic would indicate that a full year of the board's work would contain only ten or fifteen discrete transactional decisions of the type that are generally assumed to make up the main work of the board, and of those discrete transactional matters, many will be neither very important nor controversial, such as a decision to terminate a long-standing banking relationship in favor of a new one that provides better service.

Contrariwise, some issues that have little economic significance may, because of their delicacy, consume great amounts of the board's time—such as the awkward matter of imposing mandatory retirement on the aging founder, builder, and principal owner of the company.

AGENDA–SETTING—INITIATIVES BY THE BOARD

Agenda-setting and the scope of board initiative together comprise the single most important, and least understood, aspect of the board's work life.

With the two very important exceptions noted below, the question of what the board will discuss and act on is typically determined by the management or by the corporation's automatic built-in secular equivalent of an ecclesiastical calendar, that is, shareholders' meeting date, fiscal year, cycle of audit committee meetings, and similar matters. The board can, and a good board will, from time to time suggest topics for exploration or discussion, or request the management to report in the near future on this or that matter of interest to the board. The board can press management to get on with a necessary undertaking or desired program, such as the establishment of a job classification system, and to report back to the board about the action taken. But the board itself has little capacity to generate significant proposals, other than generalized suggestions looking toward the establishment of procedures or systems. Almost all of what a board does is made up of matters that are brought to it; matters generated by the board itself are very rare. Typically, boards cannot take, and are not expected to take, initiatives.

There are two major exceptions to this generalization about agenda-setting. Both are of extreme importance, and both are fully understood by normal, healthily functioning boards and managements.

First, no board can deny the existence of a built-in paramount responsibility with regard to what may be called the organic or structural integrity of the company. This organic integrity is essentially made up of two elements. A company must have a *functioning management* in place and operating at all times. A board can itself see that this is done. And a company must have an *internal information system* in place that is generally suitable for an enterprise of the company's character to keep the management informed about what is going on and particularly to provide the accounting data on which to base financial statements. The board cannot design, install, operate, or monitor the operation of such systems; but the board can press for the installation and call for periodic assurances that they are in place. As to these two organic elements of the enterprise, the directors may not wait for the management to bring issues to their attention. The responsibility of the board in these two key regards is inherent and ongoing; it is up to the board to take the initiative to keep itself informed about them and to take such periodic action as its business judgment dictates.

Second, no director or group of directors may choose to ignore credible signals of serious trouble in the company. If a director is informed through a credible source that there is reason to believe that the chief financial officer is a compulsive gambler, the director must take an initiative; he may not sit back and wait for the management to bring the matter to the board's attention. There will usually be a wide range of possible actions which a director could reasonably take to pursue such a matter and thereby fulfill his obligation as a director; but he cannot simply do nothing. Execution of this responsibility of a director will be episodic and, typically, infrequent, but the responsibility itself is ongoing and present every day.

ACTIONS NOT TAKEN

All these realities of directional life add up to a deeper one. From among an infinite number of useful things that a board of directors *might* reasonably have done or looked into in a given time period, the number that will *not* have been done by the most qualified, best-run, and most diligent board in the world will always be far greater than the number that *were* done. If a corporate transaction goes sour, or a company fails, any plaintiff's lawyer of even the most modest talent and imagination will always be able to find a subject matter X as to which he can denounce its directors, declaiming: "Surely any reasonable prudent person in these circumstances would have explored subject X, but this board sat back, did nothing, and did not even inquire into it." That argument in hindsight will always sound plausible. It may appeal to some juries, or even some courts, inexperienced in the reality of business life. But it is most often just hokum and rhetoric.

No court confronted with this retrospective argument about directional delinquency should ever allow itself to forget the reality that at any given time the roster of possible candidates for a place on the agenda of the board is infinite and that agenda items are mutually exclusive, that is, hours spent on one agenda item are hours not spent on an infinity of other possible agenda items. The number of items considered will always be vastly exceeded by the number not considered. And the plaintiff's retrospective indictment, though apparently plausible, is in fact hollow, because it can be as easily designed to hurl against the best-performing board as against the worst.[29] * * *

HOMEWORK AND SCOPE OF INQUIRY

Assume that a particular item has in ordinary course come onto the board's agenda and that it is one of that limited number that specifically calls for affirmative decisional action. No one disputes that the board should look into the matter before acting, but in a particular situation, what does that mean? How much time should be devoted to the item (to the exclusion of others)? Is it enough for the directors to read the papers sent by the management? The appendices? A summary cover letter? With what degree of concentration? And what degree of comprehension by the individual director? Regardless of the topic's technical character, what of the director's specialized experience or absence of qualification in the subject? In what degree, if any, should the director carry out research going beyond the documentation provided to him by the company or draw on recollection of data (or rumors) acquired elsewhere? Should the director insist that he be provided an opinion of outside consultants in support of the information and recommendations made by the management?

One does not have to reflect very long about such questions to come to two realizations. The first is that there is no conceivable way to lay down *a priori* answers to such questions. The second is that the point made earlier about agenda-setting in general context has even greater application in the specific. At all times and in all circumstances, the

29. [By the Author] Indeed, the argument can be framed to be even more applicable to the best of boards than to the worst, by the contention that the outstanding board had to have been sloppy in not exploring subject X, since a board composed of such experienced men and women was bound to be more aware than an average board that subject X was a problem.

scope of investigation actually undertaken on a matter, whatever it is, will always be less than the possible scope and depth of investigation that could have been undertaken. In every instance of corporate misfortune, it will therefore be an easy cheap shot to fling at the director on the witness stand, "You mean you voted to proceed with this birdcage transaction without even consulting the definitive manual on birdcages put out by the U.S. Department of Commerce?" * * *

ATTENDANCE

* * * How important is attendance, taken alone? In the real world, the answer will depend on the decisional process actually utilized by the CEO and his board. If the CEO is in continuous consultation with his directors, and if decisions of substance are worked out through prior soundings so that the meeting is only a formality (a very common pattern), or if the CEO arranges the agenda so that big issues do not come up unless his key qualified directors are present to participate, then the whole issue of frequency of attendance may be peripheral at best. A judge who does not regularly show up in his courtroom can be safely concluded not to be doing his job and to be either ill or delinquent, but that image cannot be automatically transferred to the wholly different processes of boards of directors. In most circumstances it will be very hard for a plaintiff to demonstrate that a director's sporadic attendance was causally linked to later difficulties of the company.

RELIANCE

The Model Act and the ALI drafts are quite realistic in their recognition that directors may safely rely upon officers and employees of the corporation, accountants, engineers, lawyers, and other expert consultants who they have reason to believe are competent. Expert consultation inspired by a perceived need to know on the part of the board is obviously constructive and indispensable. An inoculation of expert outside opinion is also of help in preventing an epidemic of liability in the boardroom. The law has also become more realistic in recognizing that much of a board's work is, and must be, done in committee, and in according to the board the privilege of reliance upon the work product of its committees.

It is less widely understood, and not explicitly recognized in the law, that the dynamics of the boardroom are also deeply dependent upon a matrix of other reliances among individual officers and directors. Director X, at a meeting asks in respect of particular transaction A, "Will we have any trouble with our auditors if we do A?" Director Y, who is recognized by his colleagues to be the board's most knowledgeable member in matters of accounting (who may, or may not, be a member of the audit committee) says, "Don't worry, X, I don't think we'll have any problem there." Thereupon the conversation moves on to another topic, the group deferring in an informal way to the expertise and judgment of one of its members in whom it has confidence. (The same interchange could, of course, have involved the company's chief financial officer rather than Y.) Does this kind of interchange among businessmen comply with legally articulated standards like "duty to inquire," or "duty to inform itself"? If the answer is "no" (as at least some commentators would undoubtedly say), then the tension between the law and reality is in a crisis condition. To operate at all, any group decisional process must be built on a substrate of such interconnected informal delegation and deference. A board is free to ask any question, but a board that does not have confidence in and rejects the answer it receives is at a point of pathological collapse as a decisional apparatus.

A correlative of the board's reliance must be a special informal obligation on the part of the person or committee relied upon to do his or its homework well or to be willing to answer to a board member's question, "I do not know." The expectations of the rest of the board are that they will receive a specially informed opinion, and they are entitled to get it.

So, once again, the normal decisional process in the boardroom is quite different from the piece-by-piece, person-by-person, issue-by-issue, question-by-question, adversary interrogational and debate process which a lawyer or judge tends to perceive as the normal way to arrive at professional conclusions. (That is one of the major reasons why businessmen think lawyers make poor directors until they learn, if they learn, that corporate decision-making requires other ways of doing.)

DEPTH OF INQUIRY

The point about deference and reliance as an element of "inquiry" has another aspect with which the lawyer will more readily empathize because it matches part of his own working experience. Assuming that the director specifically undertakes to "inquire" into a matter, how deeply should he go? Wherever the questioning stops, it would always be possible to question still further, as every lawyer knows. * * *

JUDGMENT

Finally, we come to the matter of judgment itself. Assume, again, that a board is going through one of those episodes of discrete transactional decision which lawyers' discourse assumes to be normal but is in fact rare. Assume that questions have been asked and inquiry made to a satisfactory extent, whatever that may mean. Now, as perceived by the legal writing, the board weighs the matter and makes a judgment, and it is that judgment that is protected by the business judgment rule.

Boardroom reality is far different from this lawyer-oriented model, not only in the respects discussed earlier but usually in the character of "judgment" itself. The differences are fundamental and warrant comment. * * * Problems come in galaxies. Responsive actions are multiple aggregates. The actions taken are the result of dozens of different tradeoffs including, importantly, tradeoffs of different degrees of certainty and uncertainty and short-term payoffs in exchange for hoped-for long-term payoffs—and vice versa. No issue is free-standing, and no action taken can be evaluated as though it were an isolated thing. * * * As a result, seeking in retrospect to revisit and evaluate a single "judgment on an issue" by a board of directors will almost always be a distortion of reality, because no such free-standing single judgment ever happened. * * *

Second, * * * judgments of boards of directors are mainly in the nature of decisions whether to hurl a veto.

A chief executive who generally enjoys the confidence of his board will usually be able to carry any proposal he makes if he does his homework, prepares his supporting arguments, is backed up by his other officers, and—of key importance—personally throws his full weight behind the proposal. Courts and the public must understand that quite commonly a director will go along with a business proposal that he does not really like. He may well think, and will sometimes say aloud in the board meeting, "I do not like this proposal. It seems risky and I believe other uses for the same resources would be more promising. But I may be wrong; I respect the contrary views of my colleagues; and I have to accord great weight to the CEO's strong support for this project. *After all, he is the one who will have the primary responsibility for seeing to it that it works out successfully.* So I will not vote no." When that happens, everyone in the corporate world knows the meaning of the italicized words. The director is saying that he will go along this time, but the CEO is on notice that if he proves to be wrong and the project fails, he may well have lost that director's confidence.

To cite another illustration. Even if a director is strongly opposed to a project, he may still go along because the CEO is determined to proceed and, in the director's best judgment, the disruption that would be caused by firing the CEO at this time would be more injurious to the interests of the company and its shareholders than the negative risks of the project proposed. In such a case, the real business judgment the director makes is not to throw his javelin today. That kind of aggregative judgment is not, in the lawyer's sense, "on the merits" of the narrow particular issue at hand, but it is very much on the issue of the director's perception of the best interests of the company. How can a court later evaluate such a nonjudgment judgment?

Thus, the decisional process of a board of directors only occasionally involves a go or no-go issue at all; often involves a cost-benefit mix of tradeoffs on multiple issues, in search of the least bad result; and is continuously obscured by the weight given by directors to the injury that will likely be visited upon the interests of the company and shareholders if the board splinters or if it suddenly dumps its CEO. * * *

Companies * * * differ from each other markedly in personality and in operating style. Contemporary literature has hit upon the term "corporate culture" to refer to the evident fact that each company is a distinctive social organization with its own viewpoints, management style, attitudes, self-image, and ways of doing. Every board of directors also has its own personality and manner of working with the management. * * *

SPASMODIC INTENSITY OF ATTENTION

Not only is company A different from company B. An additional clearly observable phenomenon in the sociology of boardroom life is that the board of company A behaves differently at different times. The intensity and quantity of all forms of the board's attention rises and falls as the company passes through calm or stormy seas. When matters are going well, the board tends to settle into watchful but quiet routine, confident in the management's performance and willing to be led. If the wind begins to rise, the board will stir and come to life, ask many questions, occasionally exercise its veto, and perhaps oust the CEO. If the hurricane comes, the board members will typically respond energetically out of their sense of responsibility, pouring time, energy, study, attention, and initiative into the company's affairs, sometimes to the point of temporarily assuming full executive control. When the storm is weathered, perhaps with a new captain installed, the board will resume a less active but watchful mode. Thus, a degree of attention that would be normal in usual circumstances could be considered as insufficient when the going gets rough. * * *

CORPORATE DIRECTOR'S GUIDEBOOK

33 Bus.Law 1591, 1619–1627 (April 1978).*

A PROPOSED MODEL FOR THE BOARD OF DIRECTORS OF A PUBLICLY–OWNED CORPORATION

This section sets forth a structural model for the governance of a publicly-owned business corporation. * * * The structure suggested is one which the Committee on Corporate Laws believes is likely to produce an appropriate environment for the governance of publicly-owned corporations. At the same time, it is not so novel as to require radical change in the present governance structures and practices of most publicly-owned corporations.

* * * [T]he model should not be construed as a profile of current law and practices, is not intended as a fundamental statement for legislative action, and does not represent a definitive recommendation for board structure such that continuance or adoption of differing procedures would or should place in question compliance with legal norms or contemporary practices.

This section accepts the basic proposition, now codified in [section 8.01 of the Revised Model Business Corporation Act] that the directors of a corporation are not expected to participate in the day-to-day management of the corporation's operations. Normally, the initiative for development and implementation of basic corporate objectives and programs rests with management, and directors, as such, are expected to review and evaluate management proposals. On occasion, however, directors may initiate policy, calling upon management to take the lead in development and planning. * * *

If the board of directors is to function effectively in its role as reviewer of management initiatives and monitor of corporate performance, a significant number of its members should be able to provide independent judgment regarding the proposals under consideration. Accordingly, for the purpose of suggesting a board structure, directors are classified herein as "management directors" or "non-management directors." A director should be regarded as a management director if he devotes substantially full time and attention to the affairs of the corporation, one of its subsidiaries, or any other corporation controlling or controlled by the corporation. * * *

A director who formerly was an officer or employee of the corporation, but who no longer has staff or operating responsibilities by reason of retirement or otherwise, should nevertheless normally be regarded as a management director since he may often be called upon to review or otherwise act in connection with matters in which he was involved while in active management. * * *

Even though a director has not been active in the management of the corporation, he may have some relationship with the corporation or its management which could be viewed as interfering with the exercise of independent judgment. It is particularly important that the audit, compensation and nominating committees of the board, whose functions are discussed more fully below, be composed of non-management directors at least a majority of whom have no affiliation with the corporation or its management which might affect their independent judgment. Accordingly, for the purpose of suggesting a board structure, non-management directors are further classified as "affiliated non-management directors" and "unaffiliated non-management directors".

Examples of individuals who may be affiliated directors would be commercial bankers, investment bankers, attorneys [30], and others who supply services or goods to the corporation. One who has close familial ties to a member of key management may also be viewed as an affiliated director. Factors relevant in determining whether a director is to be regarded as an affiliated director would include the extent to which disclosure of any interest in transactions with the corporation has been required by the proxy rules under the Federal securities laws, the period of time during which the relationship has existed, the existence of any cross-affiliations through corporate directorships or otherwise, and the materiality of the relationship to the corporation or to the director or others with whom he is associated. The decision

---

30. [By the Committee] The question whether or not an attorney should serve on his client's board of directors is not addressed in this *Guidebook*.

whether or not an individual may be regarded as an unaffiliated non-management director must ultimately be based on the judgment of the board (which should be exercised in the first instance through its nominating committee) that the individual is free of any relationship which would interfere with the exercise of his independent judgment as a member of the board committee on which he is to serve. A director having no such economic or familial relationships is regarded as an unaffiliated non-management director. * * *

It is important to emphasize that the role of the director is to monitor, in an environment of loyal but independent oversight, the conduct of the business and affairs of the corporation in behalf of those who invest in the corporation. The director should not be perceived as, or perceive himself as, a representative of any other constituency, either private or public. Were the role of any director—whether management or non-management—to be otherwise, profound changes would be required in defining the director's rights and obligations in a variety of contexts.

It is also important to emphasize that the model for corporate governance here proposed is not intended to create tensions between management and non-management directors nor to alter the fundamental responsibility of management to conduct the business of the corporation. Although tensions can arise from time to time in any governance structure, it is intended that the model here proposed will permit management to function in a collaborative environment permitting board committee and full board oversight to be performed with independent judgment, but also with the recognition that management has the primary responsibility for initiating and implementing the corporation's objectives and policies. While independent judgment is an essential of the director's responsibility and attention is an essential of his duty, the emphasis in this *Guidebook* on "disinterested oversight" and "monitoring" contemplates their exercise in a framework of collaborative support to operating management of such nature as to stimulate the best exercise of their leadership qualities. * * *

No maximum limitation on the size of a board of directors is recommended. The corporation should have discretion to determine the optimum size necessary to accommodate several objectives: (a) the board should be sufficiently large to allow non-management directors to staff a minimum of three working board committees (the audit, compensation and nominating committees); (b) key members of senior management should serve on the board; and (c) the board should function effectively in terms of discussion and decision-making.

In approaching the question of appropriate board composition, it is useful to recognize that certain situations will arise in which it will be desirable to have decisions made by directors who have no personal interest in the subject matter under review; for example:

(a) *Selection of Key Management.* * * *

(b) *Approval of Transactions in Which Directors Have a Pecuniary Interest.* * * *

(c) *Review of Integrity of Financial Reporting and Internal Financial Controls of the Corporation.* * * *

(d) *Review of Situations Where an Individual Director or Officer May Be Subject to Sanction.* From time to time an officer or director may engage in conduct which is alleged to be damaging to the corporation or to society. * * * In cases involving a director, the response of the corporation in such circumstances and the extent to which the individual should be supported or subjected to sanction should be based on a review by directors who have no interest in the particular matter. In other cases, the matter would normally be resolved by management, with appropriate reporting to, and upon occasion review by, the board of directors. * * *

The foregoing illustrations suggest that, with regard to some matters, disinterested review may be required only infrequently (e.g., a proposed merger with an "affiliated" corporation) and might be dealt with by *ad hoc* arrangements. Disinterested review of other matters (e.g., management compensation, audit committee oversight, appraisal of management) will occur more frequently and require the continuing presence of a significant number of directors capable of exercising such a disinterested review function.

In view of the foregoing objectives, the question may then be asked—what portion of the board should be composed of management directors and what portion should be composed of non-management directors? Since it is believed desirable that the audit, compensation and nominating committees of the board be staffed by non-management directors, a significant number of the directors should be non-management directors. Conversely, it would not appear desirable to adopt the suggestion advanced by some that all directors should be non-management directors. Management directors possess expertise and knowledge essential to the work of a board. Furthermore, since one of the functions of the board is to evaluate and select key management successors, the non-management directors should have the opportunity to work closely with others in management who might succeed the chief executive officer. In many corporations, this evaluation process may best be carried out through frequent contact over a period of time at meetings of the board of directors and committees of the board. In addition, senior managers will unquestionably benefit from the experience of participating in board responsibilities involving policy-oriented guidance and direction.

A substantial number of large, publicly held business corporations have tended increasingly in recent years to structure their boards of directors so that a majority of the board is composed of non-management directors. While it is not believed necessary that this pattern be mandated for all corporations, it is highly recommended as a means of maintaining a board and committee environment conducive to effective exercise of independent judgment. * * *

It is believed desirable to have at least three working committees composed of non-management directors with functional responsibility in the most commonly recurring areas where disinterested oversight is needed—the nominating committee, the compensation committee, and the audit committee. Some question the need for total exclusion of management directors from these committees. However, it is believed that such exclusion will avoid possible inhibiting influences upon free and open discussion which might arise from potential personal interest or involvement in the matters under consideration. Furthermore, there is no compelling need for management directors to serve on these committees since their input can be effectively provided or obtained in a variety of ways that do not depend upon committee membership.

The executive committee and finance committee, which can play an important role in the effective functioning of the board of directors, are not here addressed for the reason that they typically do not deal with questions and issues calling for the disinterested oversight under consideration. * * *

(a) *The Nominating Committee.* The nominating committee is potentially the most significant channel for improved corporate governance, since over a period of time it can have a marked impact on the composition of the board of directors and the manner in which management succession is effected. This committee should have the responsibility for recommending to the full board of directors nominees to fill board vacancies. Shareholders should be advised of this nominating committee role and encouraged to submit their recommendations to the committee. This procedure will, it is believed, be a more effective and workable method of affording access to the nominating process to individual shareholders than a direct "right" of nominating in the corporation's proxy material.

The nominating committee should also have the responsibility for bringing to the full board recommendations for the membership of the committees of the board, and recommending to the full board a successor to the chief executive officer when a vacancy occurs through retirement or otherwise.

It is expected that the chief executive officer will work closely with the nominating committee in the formulation of its recommendations. However, it is desirable that the nominating committee be composed of directors who are completely disinterested and, accordingly, this committee should be composed exclusively of unaffiliated non-management directors.[31] Occasionally, these functions of the nominating committee are performed by the full board.

31. [By the Committee] A strong view is held by some that, in order to facilitate the fullest participation of the corporation's chief executive officer in the deliberations of the nominating committee, he should be a member of that committee.

(b) *The Compensation Committee.* The compensation committee should have the responsibility for approving (or recommending to the full board) the compensation arrangements for senior management of the corporation. This committee should also approve (or recommend to the full board) adoption of any compensation plans in which officers and directors of the corporation are eligible to participate, as well as the granting of stock options or other benefits under any such plans. The compensation committee should be composed of non-management directors, a majority of whom should be unaffiliated non-management directors, for the purpose of providing independent judgment as to the fairness of compensation arrangements for senior management as well as providing the recipients of compensation the protection afforded by such independent oversight.

(c) *The Audit Committee.*[32] In its capacity as the communication link between the board of directors as representative of stockholders, on the one hand, and the independent auditors, on the other hand, the audit committee should have prime responsibility for the discharge of at least the following four functions:

1. To recommend the particular persons or firm to be employed by the corporation as its independent auditors;

2. To consult with the persons so chosen to be the independent auditors with regard to the plan of audit;

3. To review, in consultation with the independent auditors, their report of audit, or proposed report of audit, and the accompanying management letter, if any; and

4. To consult with the independent auditors (periodically, as appropriate, out of the presence of management) with regard to the adequacy of internal controls and, if need be, to consult also with the internal auditors (since their product has a strong influence on the quality and integrity of the resulting independent audit).

The audit committee should be composed of non-management directors, a majority of whom are unaffiliated non-management directors.

* * *

The non-management directors should have access to the corporation's regular corporate counsel and to its independent auditors. For general inquiries, the non-management directors should also be provided from time to time with staff assistance from within the corporation as required. No regular outside staff should be made available to the

---

32. [By the Committee] The Board of Directors of The New York Stock Exchange, Inc. has approved a requirement, as a condition of continued listing after June 30, 1978, that every domestic listed company establish and maintain an audit committee composed of one or more directors who are independent of management and who are free of any relationship which, in the opinion of the board, would interfere with the exercise of independent judgment as a committee member. Under the new requirement, officers, employees and affiliates would not be qualified for audit committee membership, but a former officer may qualify if the board determines that he will exercise independent judgment and will materially assist in the function of the committee.

non-management directors on a continuing basis; however, in specific situations the non-management directors should be able to employ their own legal counsel, accountants or other experts, at the corporation's expense, to deal with specific problems of oversight.

Notes

(1) This Guidebook is the product of a group composed primarily of corporation attorneys many of whom regularly represent corporate management. As a result it has received considerable attention. The American Law Institute Corporate Governance Project has also proposed a similar committee structure for large publicly-held corporations.

(2) What do you think of the proposals of then Chairman Harold Williams of the Securities and Exchange Commission, made in a speech in January, 1978, that there should be only one management representative on the board, that that person should be the corporation's chief executive officer, and that he should be barred from also acting as chairman of the board? Wall Street Journal, Jan. 19, 1978, p. 4, col. 2.

(3) Surveys of corporate practice in publicly held corporations from several sources reveal that most such companies now have boards in which non-management directors constitute the majority. In 1982, for example, the Securities and Exchange Commission released a study of proxy material from a sample of 1200 reporting companies. This study showed that over 70 per cent of the reporting companies with more than $150 million of assets had, in 1981, boards of directors a majority of which consisted of independent directors, i.e. persons with no employment or significant financial relationship with the company. For smaller reporting companies, this figure dropped off somewhat: 34 per cent of companies with assets between $50 million and $150 million had majorities of their boards composed of independent directors while 32.6 per cent of reporting companies with less than $50 million fell within this category. Securities and Exchange Commission, Analysis of Results of 1981 Proxy Statement Disclosure Monitoring Program, SEC Rel. No. 34–18532, 47 Fed.Reg. 10792, 10797, Table 7 (1982).

A private survey by SpencerStuart Executive Search Consultants (a "headhunter" that recruits high level executives and directors) of 100 large publicly held corporations reveals that between 1984 and 1989 the ratio of outside directors to inside directors increased from 2/1 to 3/1. During this period, boards of directors became somewhat smaller with most of the attrition occurring in the number of inside directors. Other trends relate to compensation of outside directors: average total compensation was over $36,000, up significantly from earlier this decade; an increasing percentage of this compensation was being paid in the form of bargain stock purchases or options. A Good Director is Getting Harder to Find, Wall Street Journal, February 9, 1988, p. 29, col. 3; Corporate Boards Are Shrinking, New York Times, December 19, 1989, p. D3, col. 3.

(4) Historically, it has been very common for lawyers for a corporation to serve on its board of directors. This practice has been the subject of some concern both from an ethical standpoint and from possible effect on

the objectivity of the legal advice thereby obtained. A comparison of proxy statement filings with the Securities and Exchange Commission between 1979 and 1981 revealed a 25 per cent decline in the number of counsel/ directors during this period. Over forty-three per cent of the reporting companies, however, had at least one attorney on its board of directors in 1981. Analysis of Results of 1981 Proxy Statement Disclosure Monitoring Program, SEC Rel. No. 34–18532, 47 Fed.Reg. 10792, 10793 (1982). During the 1980s, the number of lawyers serving on boards of directors of their clients—or indeed on the board of directors of any public corporation— almost certainly continued to decline, though empirical data appears to be lacking. To some extent corporations find the lawyer/director less necessary: "The view of most chairmen I've worked with is that if he needs solid legal advice he can go buy it." Comments of Thomas J. Neff, president of SpencerStuart, quoted in A Good Director is Getting Harder to Find, supra. Another factor, however, is of increasing importance: the fear of personal liability or exposure to litigation for failing to fulfill the various duties and obligations of directors. Lawyers who are themselves in corporate practice and well aware of the law on the subject of director liabilities are particularly reluctant to serve.

(5) As indicated in the preceding readings, outside directors come from a variety of different backgrounds and there has been some conscious effort to diversify persons selected to serve as such directors. The major source of such directors, however, is clearly CEOs and retired CEOs from other corporations. For example, the GM board of directors in 1988 consisted of 12 outside directors and 5 inside directors; however, of the 12 outside directors, 9 were CEOs or former CEOs of other large publicly held corporations. Furthermore, the CEOs most in demand to serve on other boards are the successful ones. As stated by Mr. Neff, "One client I have wants the performance record of the company a person is from, no matter if he is a household name. If the company is not performing in terms of return on investment, he is automatically off the list." A Good Director is Getting Harder to Find, supra.

Is this reliance on CEOs from other corporations desirable? While CEOs of other corporations will, as Manning suggests, understand how modern boards of directors work, is there not also a risk that they will defer to incumbent management on the theory that is what they expect from their boards of directors? Should the "monitoring model" also create guidelines for balance within the group of outside directors?

(6) A number of suggestions have been made from time to time as to the composition of boards of directors. One often-stated suggestion is that the board should be "broadened" to include representatives of varied constituencies or "stakeholders." Perhaps the following persons or groups deserve representation:

(a) The general public.

(b) Customers.

(c) The Internal Revenue Service.

(d) The Department of Justice or Federal Trade Commission.

(e) Employees. [The Continental European board of directors does contain employee representatives, and there is experience with this suggestion in the United States. See Blue Collars in the Boardroom: Putting Business First, Business Week (Dec. 14, 1987) 126, listing "employee designated board members" in eight corporations, including Chrysler, three steel companies, Pan American Airlines, and Kaiser Aluminum.]

(f) Institutional investors. [See Two of Texaco's Institutional Holders to Seek a Role in Nominating Directors, Wall Street Journal (Aug. 17, 1988) 25, col. 1. Rather than having representatives of such investors select individual board members directly, the proposed pattern is the creation of a pool of independent director candidates from which management can select candidates for director.]

(g) Small shareholders.

(h) The mayor of the city in which the corporation's home office is located.

(i) The governor of the state in which that city is located.

(j) Minority groups.

What about the creation of a cadre of professional directors who devote their full time and activity to serving as directors on a limited number of boards? There has long existed an unorganized group of individuals who serve as professional directors as their principal or sole occupation. At current levels of directoral compensation, service on four or five boards would provide a comfortable income.

(7) With respect to constituency representation generally, consider the following comments of Professor Ben Enis, a professor of marketing at the University of Southern California, in a Letter to the Editor of the Wall Street Journal (July 25, 1989) at A19:

> This is a recipe for disaster. Directors would represent competing interest groups, e.g. those wanting short-term dividends, those advancing various political agendas * * *, those favoring increased investments in basic research, or whatever. These director blocs would cause stockholder meetings to resemble U.N. debates: lots of rhetorical, little action. The only ones to gain would be the activists (presumably not businesspeople) elected to such directorships, and lawyers (including perhaps those contemplating a career shift from public to private sector) who represent those activists in stockholder suits against management.

Professor Enis was responding to a suggestion that directors should be selected from slates of outside candidates that reflect categories of shareholders.

(8) Conference Panel Discussion: Federalism Issues in Corporate Governance, 45 Ohio S.L.J. 591, 591–595 (1984):

> Prof. Mofsky: * * * [L]et's take a look at a popular assumption that independent directors are better able to monitor and assure management success and honesty than is management itself. You have all heard, I am sure, many of the arguments that have been advanced to support this assumption. But maybe you haven't heard

some of the other arguments advanced for the other side of that proposition. Maybe it would be useful to take a look at them for a moment. Nick Wolfson and others have pointed out that senior managers have an incentive to monitor their colleagues of equal rank, and that even junior managers have an incentive to monitor more senior persons, since the success of both their peers and superiors will benefit their own reputation and their own future compensation.

On the other hand, if you look at independent directors, it would appear on the surface at least that they are in a far worse position than are senior managers to monitor employees of the firm. As part-timers, they will have less time to spend on monitoring activities. Additionally, independent directors, unlike managers, have no financial incentive to act quickly and decisively to correct management inefficiency since their compensation and the amount of it is not tied to the success of the firm. Generally speaking, they are paid on a flat fee basis. Indeed, one could draw a sketch of the world where one could expect independent directors to be less entrepreneurial minded than managers, more receptive than managers to the demands of public interest groups than to the interests of shareholders, and in the end less efficient than managers in disciplining inefficient employees.

Now, my point is not that inside directors are necessarily more desirable than independent ones. In fact, we know very little about the way boards of directors work. Rather, my point is that rational arguments exist on both sides of that question and that the answer depends upon empirical research. Since there is no proof that independent boards are better than ones dominated by insiders, it strikes me as highly inadvisable to impose a requirement for independent boards when we already have a rule that permits boards of such differing composition as may be particularly desirable and effective for a particular firm. * * * [O]ne could perform with respect to the desirability of independent audit, compensation, and nominating committees the same kind of analysis that I have suggested here today with regard to the question of independent boards. And for each of those issues, as well as for all the other issues at stake in the debate over corporate governance, I would draw the same conclusions. Namely, I conclude that we are dealing with empirical propositions for which plausible arguments can be made on both sides. Accordingly, in my view, the proponents of corporate reform have not proved their case. They have not proved the need for reform. Why change a system if there doesn't appear to be an awfully good reason to do it, especially when the present system has lasted so long and appears to have done so well? * * *

Prof. Eisenberg: * * * [T]here are many institutions that work in [the direction of accountability of managers for their performance] and all of them are important. [One of these] is the market for corporate control; another is the commodities market, with the attendant sanction of bankruptcy; and another is the market for corporate capital. Those markets are important constraints on inefficiency. Their importance is not to be minimized. Neither, however, is it to be maximized. A perfect market works perfectly. An imperfect market doesn't. All these markets are highly imperfect. * * *

Therefore, we need another, supplementary constraint on managerial inefficiency, * * *

[I]f you look at the corporate statutes of seventy-five years ago or so, I think that they in effect had an accountability scheme built into them. The accountability scheme was this: The board of directors would manage the corporation, and the shareholders would monitor the board of directors. Now, maybe that scheme reflected reality seventy-five or a hundred years ago, but it doesn't reflect reality now, because the management function has dropped one step in the corporate pyramid. The management function has dropped from the board to the executives. Correspondingly, the accountability function or the monitoring or oversight function needs to drop from the shareholders to the board. Yet to get a properly monitoring board, a board that we can count on to oust inefficient managers, I think it's fairly obvious that we need a board that is independent of the managers. * * *

[Y]ou cannot prove conclusively by empirical data that an independent board is more likely to oust inefficient management than a non-independent board. But that's the way life is when we are dealing with social phenomena. It is normally impossible to prove in a conclusive way that one legal rule will function better than another. * * * [T]he empirical evidence issue in the form in which it is presented by Jim is—maybe "red herring" is too strong—but it's really an argument against all law. * * *

(9) There have been at least two attempts to study the empirical question whether independent directors improve corporate performance. In a study commissioned by the Business Roundtable Professor MacAvoy concluded that independent persons on boards of directors had no discernable effect on compliance with law by corporations. MacAvoy, ALI Proposals for Increased Control of the Corporation by the Board of Directors: An Economic Analysis, in Statement of the Business Roundtable on the American Law Institute's Proposed "Principles of Corporate Governance and Structure: Restatement and Recommendations" (1983). In a second study, Baysinger and Butler concluded that the presence of a few independent directors appeared to improve corporate profit performance, but that the effect of the number of independent directors was subject to diminishing marginal increases—and indeed absolute declines in relative performance as their number increased. Baysinger and Butler concluded that the number of independent directors should not exceed 30 percent of the board for maximum effectiveness. Baysinger and Butler, Revolution Versus Evolution in Corporation Law: The ALI's Project and the Independent Director, 52 Geo.Wash.L.Rev. 557 (1984). For criticisms of the methodologies of these two studies, see Eisenberg, Conference Panel Discussion: Federalism Issues in Corporate Governance, 45 Ohio S.L.J. 591, 596–597; Eisenberg, New Modes of Discourse in the Corporate Law Literature, 52 Geo.Wash.L.Rev. 582, 598–603 (Baysinger and Butler), 603–608 (MacAvoy).

(10) Eighty-six percent of all reporting companies in the SEC survey described above in note (3) had audit committees in 1981; 72 percent had

compensation committees; 30.4 percent had nomination committees. For New York Stock Exchange listed companies, the percentages were significantly higher: 99 percent had audit committees, 90 percent had compensation committees, and 48 percent had nominating committees. All three of these committees were manned primarily by independent directors: of the audit committees, nearly 90 percent of the members were not employed by or had substantial ties to the company; of the compensation and nomination committees, between 70 and 80 percent of the members consisted of such directors. Again, in the smaller reporting companies, these numbers were significantly lower. Of course, the growth in the use of audit committees by New York Stock Exchange listed corporations is partially a result of the Exchange requirement of such committees referred to in note 32, page 615, supra. This requirement became effective on June 30, 1978. During the 1970s, the SEC also strongly urged the use of audit committees generally through a combination of proposed legislation, proposed regulation, and the imposition of such committees in specific cases by consent decree. However, the trend towards the wider use of such committees appears to be independent of governmental compulsion.

(11) Of course, the creation of a board primarily consisting of non-management directors, and the naming of such directors to a majority of the positions on key committees does not automatically guarantee the end of management domination of the board or of those committees. This point was graphically made in April, 1978, in connection with a struggle for control of Beatrice Foods which led to the reinstitution of an insider-dominated board and the rejection of the outside directors' nominee for chief executive officer. This and several other illustrations of the new board philosophy in action are discussed in an article entitled End of the Directors' Rubber Stamp: More Risk and Less Willingness to Say Yes, Bus. Week (September 10, 1979), at 72.

On the other hand, there are many anecdotal incidents that indicate that the independence of boards of directors have increased during the 1980s, fueled partially, at least, by concerns about lawsuits being filed against the outside directors in takeover situations. The flavor of these anecdotal stories are reflected in titles to news stories and articles during the 1980s: GM's Outside Directors Are Ending Their Passive Role, Wall Street Journal, August 17, 1988, p. 4, col. 1; Taking Charge: Corporate Directors Start to Flex Their Muscle, Business Week, July 3, 1989, at 66; Tales From the Boardroom: Some Boards are Showing A New Assertiveness . . . Some Are Starting to Look More Independent . . . But Others Seem Like Rubber Stamps, ibid.; Ted Turner Faces Showdown with Board; New Directors Pose Challenge to Autocracy, Wall Street Journal, December 29, 1987, p. 2, col. 2; Pan Am's New Chief: In the Cockpit—But Not Yet in Control: Plaskett Could Have a Hard Time Wresting Authority from the Board, Business Week (Feb. 8, 1988) 30.

D. PROXY REGULATION

1. SCOPE OF REGULATION

SECURITIES EXCHANGE ACT OF 1934
§§ 14(a), 12(a), 12(g)
15 U.S.C.A. §§ 78n, 78*l* (1981).

PROXIES

Section 14. (a) It shall be unlawful for any person, by the use of the mails or by any means or instrumentality of interstate commerce or of any facility of a national securities exchange or otherwise, in contravention of such rules and regulations as the Commission may prescribe as necessary or appropriate in the public interest or for the protection of investors, to solicit or to permit the use of his name to solicit any proxy or consent or authorization in respect of any security (other than an exempted security) registered pursuant to section 12 of this title.

REGISTRATION REQUIREMENTS FOR SECURITIES

Section 12. (a) It shall be unlawful for any member, broker, or dealer to effect any transaction in any security (other than an exempted security) on a national securities exchange unless a registration is effective as to such security for such exchange in accordance with the provisions of this title and the rules and regulations thereunder.
*   *   *

(g)(1) Every issuer which is engaged in interstate commerce, or in a business affecting interstate commerce, or whose securities are traded by use of the mails or any means or instrumentality of interstate commerce shall—

> (A) within one hundred and twenty days after the last day of its first fiscal year ended after the effective date of this subsection on which the issuer has total assets exceeding $1,000,000 and a class of equity security (other than an exempted security) held of record by seven hundred and fifty or more persons; and

> (B) within one hundred and twenty days after the last day of its first fiscal year ended after two years from the effective date of this subsection on which the issuer has total assets exceeding $1,000,000 and a class of equity security (other than an exempted security) held of record by five hundred or more but less than seven hundred and fifty persons,

register such security by filing with the Commission a registration statement *   *   *

(4) Registration of any class of security pursuant to this subsection shall be terminated ninety days, or such shorter period as the Commission may determine, after the issuer files a certification with the Commission that the number of holders of record of such class of security is reduced to less than three hundred persons. *   *   *

(5) For the purposes of this subsection the term "class" shall include all securities of an issuer which are of substantially similar character and the holders of which enjoy substantially similar rights and privileges. * * *

Notes

(1) The "effective date" referred to in § 12(g)(1) is July 1, 1964. Pub. Law 88–467, § 13(1), 78 Stat. 565.

(2) The SEC has adopted the following regulations under section 12(g):

§ 240.12g–1 Exemption from section 12(g).

An issuer shall be exempt from the requirement to register any class of equity securities pursuant to section 12(g)(1) if on the last day of its most recent fiscal year the issuer had total assets not exceeding $5 million * * *

§ 240.12g–4 Certifications of termination of registration under section 12(g).

(a) Termination of registration of a class of securities shall take effect 90 days * * * after the issuer certifies to the Commission * * * that:

(1) Such class of securities is held of record by: (i) Less than 300 persons; or (ii) by less than 500 persons, where the total assets of the issuer have not exceeded $5 million on the last day of each of the issuer's most recent three fiscal years. * * *

17 C.F.R. §§ 240.12g–1, 240.12g–4 (1989). The statutory provision, of course, requires registration of corporations with more than $1 million of assets if they meet the number of shareholders requirement. In 1982, the SEC increased the asset requirement from $1 million to $3 million primarily as an "inflation adjustment" to the original statutory criterion established in 1964. SEC Rel. No. 34–18647, 47 Fed.Reg. 17046 (1982). The increase from $3 million to $5 million was proposed in 1985 and promulgated in 1986. SEC Rel. 34–23406, 51 Fed.Reg. 25360 (1986). The justifications given for this subsequent increase were as follows:

First, it implements "one of the recommendations of the 1984 SEC Government–Business Forum on Small Business Capital Formation" which specifically proposed the increase in the threshold amount.

Second, the cost of compliance with Exchange Act continuous reporting requirements is relatively greater for small corporations than for larger ones; such compliance is particularly important for shares that are listed on public trading markets, but most corporations with less than $5 million of assets do not have securities that are publicly traded.

Third, the change makes the 1934 Exchange Act reporting requirements "somewhat parallel" to the exemptions under the 1933 Act that relate to public offerings of less than $5 million dollars.

The release estimates that about 700 issuers were likely to be affected by the increase in the asset requirement from $3 million to $5 million. SEC Rel. No. 34–22483, 50 Fed.Reg. 41162 (1985).

(3) Under section 12(g) and rules 12g–1 and 12g–4 how should the following problems be resolved:

(a) Company A sells securities under section 4(2) of the Securities Act of 1933 every year for three years. It eventually has total assets of $10 million and 450 shareholders. Does Company A have to register under section 12?

(b) Company B sells securities under section 4(2) every year for three years. Eventually it has total assets of $4.8 million and 700 shareholders. Does Company B have to register under section 12?

(c) Company C has been registered under section 12(g) for four years, and has consistently had $4.8 million in total assets and 450 shareholders. May its registration under section 12 be terminated?

(4) A corporation that is required to register a securities issue under section 12 is subject to a significant degree of regulation under various sections of the Securities Exchange Act of 1934 in addition to the regulation of proxy solicitations. Many of these sections are discussed below and in the following chapters. When considering federally imposed requirements under the 1934 Act it is important to ascertain whether the requirements are applicable only to corporations required to register under section 12, or whether they are more broadly applicable to all corporations using the mails or the facilities of interstate commerce.

(5) Registration of the publicly held securities of an issuer under section 12 of the 1934 Act should be distinguished from the registration of an issue for its public distribution under the 1933 Act described in Chapter 6. Registration under section 12 of the 1934 Act involves the submission of information about the issuer, its organization, its finances, its securities, and similar matters. There is also a requirement for the periodic revision of information; these periodic reports are colloquially referred to as 8–K and 10–K reports. Historically, registration of an issue under the 1933 Act for sale to the public was considered more onerous and difficult than supplying information for registration under section 12. The emphasis on full disclosure at the time an issue is sold publicly under the 1933 Act is partly an historical accident, and a more rational system would doubtless emphasize issuer registration and periodic full disclosure rather than full disclosure only when the issuer wishes to sell securities. In 1982 the SEC achieved essentially this result by regulation through its integrated disclosure program, SEC Rel. No. 33–6383, AS Rel. No. 306, 47 Fed.Reg. 11380 (1982). This program permits issuers that have been in the 1934 Exchange Act reporting program for at least three years to incorporate by reference information from the 1934 Act reports into a 1933 Act registration statement for a new issue of securities. If the corporation is "seasoned," with a market value of more than $150,000,000 of publicly held shares and an annual trading volume of more than 3,000,000 shares, no disclosure of the 1934 Act information is required in reliance on the "efficient market theory." If the corporation has been in the reporting program for three years but does not meet the requirements for a "seasoned company" it may

incorporate the 1934 Act information in its registration statement but must provide offerees with an annual report or the equivalent. If the corporation has not been in the 1934 Act reporting program for three years, a full scale 1933 Act registration is required. These three levels of 1933 Act disclosure are usually referred to by the number of the registration statement: S–1 is the registration statement for a full scale registration, S–2 is the registration statement for a company that has been in the 1934 Act reporting program for three years but is not a "seasoned company," while S–3 is the registration statement for a "seasoned company."

(6) Why should proxy regulation be a federal matter? As previously indicated (see p. 477, supra), the Revised Model Business Corporation Act and most state business corporation acts are essentially silent on proxy rules and requirements. Also, when most publicly held corporations solicit proxies, they in fact are soliciting shareholders in every state.

(7) Accepting the notion of federal regulation, is it nevertheless desirable for Congress to give an administrative agency, such as the Securities and Exchange Commission, such a totally blank check as section 14(a)? The conditions giving rise to this broad grant of power have been described as follows:

> At the time of the enactment of the Securities Exchange Act of 1934, the proxy had become a device for continuing management in corporate office and for ratifying its policies. The control of corporations by insiders had been perpetuated through the solicitation of proxies by management, which simply requested that stockholders execute and return proxies without disclosing the purposes for which the proxies were to be used.

> The legislative history of the Securities Exchange Act of 1934 indicates, however, that the Congress was concerned also with the abuse of proxies by seekers of corporate power. A congressional report (Sen.Rep. No. 1455, 73d Cong., 2d Sess., 77 (1934)) states that "the rules and regulations promulgated by the Commission will protect investors from promiscuous solicitation of their proxies, on the one hand by irresponsible outsiders seeking to wrest control of a corporation away from honest and conscientious corporate officials; and on the other hand by unscrupulous corporate officials seeking to retain control of the management by concealing or distorting facts."

Orrick, The Revised Proxy Rules of the Securities and Exchange Commission, 11 Bus.Law. (No. 3) 32–33 (April, 1956).*

STUDEBAKER CORP. v. GITTLIN

United States Court of Appeals, Second Circuit, 1966.
360 F.2d 692.

FRIENDLY, CIRCUIT JUDGE:

Richard Gittlin, a stockholder of Studebaker Corporation, a Michigan corporation, appeals from an order of the District Court for the

Southern District of New York, in an action brought against him by the corporation. The order enjoined the use of other stockholders' authorizations in a New York state court proceeding to obtain inspection of Studebaker's shareholders list, N.Y. Business Corporation Law, McKinney's Consol.Laws, c. 4, § 1315, save after compliance with the Proxy Rules of the Securities and Exchange Commission issued under § 14(a) of the Securities Exchange Act. * * *

Studebaker's resort to the district court was occasioned by the service upon it on March 21 of papers in a proceeding begun by Gittlin in the Supreme Court of New York to inspect the record of the company's shareholders. Gittlin's application to the New York court recited that he was the record owner of 5,000 shares of Studebaker stock and that he was acting on behalf of himself and on written authorization from 42 other shareholders owning in excess of 145,000 shares which constituted more than 5% of the company's stock; that he and his associates had been endeavoring to get the Studebaker management to agree to certain changes in its board of directors and had announced their intention to solicit proxies for the forthcoming annual meeting if the request was not met; and that when these talks had broken down, he had requested access to the stockholders list and had been refused.

Studebaker's affidavit and subsequent complaint allege that Gittlin obtained the authorization from the 42 other stockholders in violation of the Proxy Rules issued by the SEC under § 14(a) of the Securities Exchange Act. Specifically the company contends that Gittlin claimed to be holding the authorizations as early as March 14, and that at that time he had made no filing of proxy material with the SEC. * * *

The contention most heavily pressed is that § 14(a) of the Securities Exchange Act does not include authorizations for the limited purpose of qualifying under a state statute permitting the holders of a given percentage of shares to obtain inspection of a stockholders list. The statute is worded about as broadly as possible, forbidding any person "to solicit any proxy or consent or authorization" in respect of any security therein specified "in contravention of such rules and regulations as the Commission may prescribe as necessary or appropriate in the public interest or for the protection of investors"; the definitions in the Proxy Rules, 14a–1, exhaust the sweep of the power thus conferred. The assistant general counsel of the SEC, which responded to our request for its views with promptness and definitude, stated at the argument that the Commission believes § 14(a) should be construed, in all its literal breadth, to include authorizations to inspect stockholders lists, even in cases where obtaining the authorizations was not a step in a planned solicitation of proxies.[33]

33. [By the Court] The Commission states in a letter to the court:

"Section 14(a) of the Securities Exchange Act of 1934 and the Commission's rules thereunder apply to any proxy, consent, authorization and are not limited to proxies, consents, and authorizations in situations involving elections to office. There is no reason to suppose that Congress intended that the protec-

We need not go that far to uphold the order of the district court. In SEC v. Okin, 132 F.2d 784 (2d Cir.1943), this court ruled that a letter which did not request the giving of any authorization was subject to the Proxy Rules if it was part of "a continuous plan" intended to end in solicitation and to prepare the way for success. This was the avowed purpose of Gittlin's demand for inspection of the stockholders list and, necessarily, for his soliciting authorizations sufficient to aggregate the 5% of the stock required by § 1315 of New York's Business Corporation Law. Presumably the stockholders who gave authorizations were told something and, as Judge L. Hand said in *Okin*, "one need only spread the misinformation adequately before beginning to solicit, and the Commission would be powerless to protect shareholders." 132 F.2d at 786. Moreover, the very fact that a copy of the stockholders list is a valuable instrument to a person seeking to gain control, is a good reason for insuring that shareholders have full information before they aid its procurement. We see no reason why, in such a case, the words of the Act should be denied their literal meaning. * * *

This brings us to Gittlin's claim that Studebaker made no adequate showing of need for injunctive relief in failing to demonstrate "irreparable injury." Recitation of this term generally produces more dust than light. A plaintiff asking an injunction because of the defendant's violation of a statute is not required to show that otherwise rigor mortis will set in forthwith; all that "irreparable injury" means in this context is that unless an injunction is granted, the plaintiff will suffer harm which cannot be repaired. At least that is enough where, as here, the only consequence of an injunction is that the defendant must effect a compliance with the statute which he ought to have done before. To be sure, time is of the essence in proxy contests—at least the participants generally think it to be. But the district court could properly have considered that the public interest in enforcing the Proxy Rules outweighed any inconvenience to Gittlin in having to start again. In this aspect decision rested in the judge's sound discretion; we find no abuse.

Affirmed.

Notes

The question of what constitutes a "solicitation" has also arisen in other contexts, particularly in connection with proxy fights and other struggles for control discussed in Chapter 12. See e.g. Brown v. Chicago, Rock Island & Pac. R.R. Co., 328 F.2d 122 (7th Cir.1964) [an advertisement directed to "Rock Island Stockholders, Employees, Shippers, and Midwest Communities" is not a "solicitation"]. Conagra, Inc. v. Tyson Foods, Inc., 708 F.Supp. 257 (D.Neb.1989) [press release issued close to the time of a

tive provisions of the proxy rules should not reach other situations in which a stockholder is requested to permit another to act for him, whatever may be the purpose of the authorization."

The Proxy Rules [14a–2(b)], exempt solicitation otherwise than on behalf of management where the total number of persons solicited is not more than ten.

critical vote on a merger was designed to influence voting and therefore was a proxy solicitation].

2. PROXIES, PROXY STATEMENTS, AND ANNUAL REPORTS

The comprehensive federal proxy regulations provide the basic structure for whatever corporate democracy that exists in the modern public corporation. The import of these rather lengthy and detailed regulations is difficult to summarize. Further, the sequence in which they are set forth by the SEC is not very logical. It is simpler to discuss them by subject matter rather than numerically even though the result is skipping around the numbers. Portions of these regulations are discussed in this Chapter, and in Chapter 12, and together all the significant areas are covered. The mere listing of the principal areas should give an introductory notion of their scope:

(a) The regulations relating to the form of proxy, the proxy statement, and annual reports are discussed immediately below;

(b) The regulation prohibiting false and misleading statements in connection with proxies is discussed in subpart (3) of this section of this Chapter;

(c) The regulation requiring the inclusion of certain shareholder proposals in the proxy solicitation is discussed in subpart (4) of this section of this Chapter;

(d) The regulation requiring communications to be mailed to securities holders in certain circumstances is discussed in section E of this Chapter; and

(e) The regulations relating to proxy fights are discussed in Chapter 12.

Rule 14a–4 of the proxy regulations contains specific requirements as to the form of proxy documents. The purpose of this rule is to ensure that shareholders in fact have the option to vote to approve or disapprove issues submitted to them, and to vote for or against the directors proposed by the persons soliciting the proxy, usually management. Broad grants of discretionary power to the nominee are prohibited subject to certain exceptions; for example, generally a proxy may not confer power to vote for a person as a director unless he is named in the proxy statement as a nominee. However, a proxy may confer discretion to vote for a person not named to replace a bona fide nominee who is unable to serve or for good cause will not serve. Similarly, a proxy must be for a specified meeting, and undated or postdated proxies are prohibited (Rule 14a–10).

Rule 14a–3 requires that a proxy solicitation be accompanied by a proxy statement containing the information set forth in Schedule 14A, 17 C.F.R. § 240.14a–101 (1989). The type of information required depends of course on the type of issue to be presented to the shareholders for their vote; for example, the following item is substantially the full description of the disclosure requirements applicable to a proposal to act on a compensation plan for management:

Item 10. Compensation Plans. If action is to be taken with respect to any plan pursuant to which cash or non-cash compensation may be paid, furnish the following information:

(a) *All Plans.* (1) Describe briefly the material features of the plan being acted upon, identify each class of persons who will be eligible to participate therein, indicate the approximate number of persons in each such class and state the basis of such participation.

(2) State the benefits or amounts which will be received by or allocated to each of the following under the plan being acted upon, if such benefits or amounts are determinable: (i) Each person * * * specified in paragraph (a)(1)(i) of Item 402 of Regulation S–K; [34] (ii) all current executive officers as a group; (iii) all current directors who are not executive officers as a group; and (iv) all employees, including all current officers who are not executive officers, as a group. If such benefits or amounts are not determinable, state the benefits or amounts which would have been received by or allocated to each of the following for the last fiscal year if the plan had been in effect, if such benefits or amounts may be determined;

(3) Furnish the information called for by Item 402(b) of Regulation S–K [35] with respect to all compensation plans now in effect or in effect during the last three years * * *.

(4) If the plan to be acted upon can be amended, otherwise than by a vote of security holders, to increase the cost thereof to the registrant or to alter the allocation of the benefits as between

---

34. [By the Editor] Item 402(a)(1)(i) of Regulation S–K reads as follows:

(i) *Five executive officers.* Each of the registrant's five most highly compensated executive officers whose cash compensation required to be disclosed pursuant to this paragraph exceeds $60,000, naming each such person * * *.

35. [By the Editor] Item 402(b) of Regulation S–K reads as follows:

(b)(1) *Compensation pursuant to plans.* Describe briefly all plans, pursuant to which cash or non-cash compensation was paid or distributed during the last fiscal year, or is proposed to be paid or distributed in the future, to the named individuals and group specified in paragraph (a) of this section. * * * The description of each plan shall include the following * * *:

(i) A summary of how the plan operates and who is covered by the plan;

(ii) The criteria used to determine amounts payable, including any performance formula or measure;

(iii) The time periods over which the measurement of benefits will be determined;

(iv) Payment schedules;

(v) Any recent material amendments to the plan;

(vi) Amounts paid or distributed pursuant to the plan to the named individuals and the group during the last fiscal year less any amount relating to the same plan which previously has been disclosed as accrued pursuant to paragraph (b)(1)(vii) of this section or a predecessor provision; and

(vii) Amounts accrued pursuant to the plan for the accounts of the named individuals and group during the last fiscal year, the distribution or unconditional vesting of which are not subject to future events.

the groups specified in paragraph (a)(3), state the nature of the amendments which can be so made.

(b) *Specific Plans.* (1) With respect to any pension or retirement plan submitted for security holder action, state: (i) The approximate total amount necessary to fund the plan with respect to past services, the period over which such amount is to be paid and the estimated annual payments necessary to pay the total amount over such period; and (ii) the estimated annual payment to be made with respect to current services. * * *

(2) With respect to any specific grant of or any plan containing options, warrants or rights submitted for security holder action; (i) state: (A) The title and amount of securities called for or to be called for by such options, warrants or rights; (B) the prices, expiration dates and other material conditions upon which the options, warrants or rights may be exercised; (C) the consideration received or to be received by the registrant or subsidiary for the granting or extension of the options, warrants or rights; (D) the market value of the securities called for or to be called for by the options, warrants or rights as of the latest practicable date; and (E) in the case of options, the federal income tax consequences of the issuance and exercise of such options to the recipient and to the registrant; and (ii) state separately the amount of such options received or to be received by the following persons if such benefits or amounts are determinable: (A) Each person (stating name and position) specified in paragraph (a)(1)(i) of Item 402 * * * (B) all current executive officers as a group; (C) all current directors who are not executive officers as a group; (D) each nominee for election as a director; (E) each associate of any of such directors, executive officers or nominees; (F) each other person who received or is to receive 5 percent of such options, warrants or rights; and (G) All employees, including all current officers who are not executive officers, as a group.

Instructions * * *

2. If action is to be taken with respect to a material amendment or modification of an existing plan, the item shall be answered with respect to the plan as proposed to be amended or modified and shall indicate any material differences from the existing plan.

3. If the plan to be acted upon is set forth in a written document, three copies thereof shall be filed with the Commission at the time preliminary copies of the proxy statement and form of proxy are filed pursuant to paragraph (a) of Rule 14a–6.

4. Paragraphs (a)(3) and (b)(2)(ii) do not apply to warrants or rights to be issued to security holders as such on a pro rata basis.

5. The Commission should be informed, as supplemental information, when the proxy statement in preliminary form is filed, as to when the options, warrants or rights and the shares called for thereby will be registered under the Securities Act or, if such registration is not contemplated, the section of the Securities Act or rule of the Commission under which exemption from such registration is claimed and the facts relied upon to make the exemption available.

Schedule 14A, Item 10 [17 C.F.R. § 240.14a–101 (1989)]. The information in the proxy statement must be "clearly presented." Rule 14a–5. Furthermore, there is a procedure by which preliminary copies of soliciting material are submitted to the SEC. Rule 14a–6. Copies of the definitive documents must also be filed with the SEC when they are distributed to shareholders. See J.I. Case v. Borak, infra, for a description of the review of such materials provided by SEC staff.

Rule 14a–3 provides that if a solicitation is by management and relates to an annual meeting at which directors are to be elected, the solicitation must be accompanied or preceded by an *annual report* containing the financial information and other material described in the Rule. 17 C.F.R. § 240.14a–3(b) (1989). Many state incorporation statutes do not require the distribution of even such minimal information to shareholders; see, however, RMBCA §§ 16.20–16.23. The SEC has long recognized that the annual report is the most effective single means of communication between management and security holders. In part this was because annual reports are generally readable and avoid legalistic and technical terminology. In its integration of filings under the various securities acts, the SEC broadened somewhat the information required to be included in annual reports but added a postscript:

> The Commission is aware that increasing the amount of required disclosure in annual security holder reports involves a risk that readability may be impaired. Although it is difficult to predict with certainty what the effect may be, the Commission does not believe that the changes implemented today should or will have general adverse consequences. The Commission staff, however, will continue to monitor the situation and, if adverse effects do occur, the new disclosure requirements will be revisited promptly.

SEC Rel. No. 33–6231, 34–17114, 45 Fed.Reg. 63630, 63631 (1980).

Generally, it is difficult to give an accurate description of these disclosure documents. The following is an example of a routine proxy that meets SEC requirements. The notice of annual meeting and proxy statement that accompanied this routine proxy are set forth in Appendix Four, p. 1223 infra. It was not feasible to reproduce a sample annual report, but students who have never seen such a document should make an effort to do so.

PROXY   **AMERICAN EXPLORATION COMPANY**   PROXY

**PROXY SOLICITED ON BEHALF OF THE BOARD OF DIRECTORS
FOR THE ANNUAL MEETING OF STOCKHOLDERS TO BE HELD
THURSDAY, JUNE 9, 1988**

The undersigned hereby appoints J. Curtis Grindal and Russell P. Pennoyer, jointly and severally, proxies, with full power of substitution and with discretionary authority, to vote all shares of Common Stock which the undersigned is entitled to vote at the Annual Meeting of Stockholders of American Exploration Company ("American") to be held on Thursday, June 9, 1988, at The Drake Hotel, 440 Park Avenue at 56th Street, New York, New York at 9:30 a.m., New York time, or at any adjournment thereof, hereby revoking any proxy heretofore given.

1. ☐   FOR the election of Mark Andrews, Walter J. P. Curley, Phillip Frost, Peter G. Gerry, H. Phipps Hoffstot, III, John E. Justice, III, Mark Kavanagh, Peter P. Nitze, John B. Quay and Peter G. Schiff as directors except as indicated below; or

☐   WITHHOLD AUTHORITY to vote for all nominees in such election.

(INSTRUCTION: To withhold authority to vote for any individual nominee, write that nominee's name in the space provided below.)

2. APPROVAL OF THE APPOINTMENT OF ARTHUR ANDERSEN & CO. as independent public accountants of American for 1988.   [F2476]

☐   FOR   ☐   AGAINST   ☐   ABSTAIN

3. With discretionary authority as to such other matters as may properly come before the meeting.

THIS PROXY, WHEN PROPERLY EXECUTED, WILL BE VOTED IN THE MANNER DIRECTED HEREIN. IN THE ABSENCE OF SPECIFIC DIRECTIONS TO THE CONTRARY, THIS PROXY WILL BE VOTED FOR THE ELECTION AS DIRECTORS OF ALL OF THE FOREGOING NOMINEES AND IN FAVOR OF THE PROPOSAL TO APPROVE THE APPOINTMENT OF ARTHUR ANDERSEN & CO.

The undersigned hereby acknowledges receipt of the Notice of, and Proxy Statement for, the aforesaid Annual Meeting.

_____

(Signature)

Date _____, 1988

(When signing as attorney, administrator, executor, guardian, trustee or corporate officer, please add your title as such.)
[F2477]

Notes

Most publicly held corporations find it necessary to solicit proxies in order to ensure that a quorum will be present at the annual meeting. However, in some corporations one person, or a group of persons active in the management of the corporation, may own enough shares to constitute a quorum without the aid of proxies solicited from the public. Until 1964 such corporations could avoid the disclosure requirements of the proxy rules. However, in that year, Congress added Section 14(c) to require all corporations registered pursuant to Section 12 who do not solicit proxies to transmit to all holders of record "information substantially equivalent to the information which would be required to be transmitted if a solicitation were made."

———————

The value of the information and disclosure requirements of the proxy regulations presumably depends on the various documents getting into the hands of the beneficial owners of the shares who have power to vote them. The SEC first attacked this problem in 1965 by requiring issuers to deliver to banks, securities dealers, brokers or voting trustees, upon their request, sufficient copies of annual reports and other materials to provide beneficial owners with copies. However, many record owners did not in fact receive such material. One study in 1973, for example, revealed that of the 17 per cent of corporate stock then held in street name, as many as 68 per cent of the beneficial owners were not receiving annual reports. The Silence Imposed by Street Names, Bus. Week, December 8, 1973, at 40. In 1974, the SEC significantly revised the rules to improve the transmission of materials to beneficial owners; the rules of securities exchanges and the National Association of Securities Dealers were also amended to require brokers and dealers to obtain and forward such materials to beneficial owners in a timely manner. These rules now primarily appear in 17 C.F.R. §§ 240.14a–3, 240.14b–1, 240.14b–2, and to a lesser extent, 240.14c–7 (1989).

FINAL REPORT OF THE SECURITIES AND EXCHANGE COMMISSION ON THE PRACTICE OF RECORDING THE OWNERSHIP OF SECURITIES IN THE RECORDS OF THE ISSUER IN OTHER THAN THE NAME OF THE BENEFICIAL OWNER OF SUCH SECURITIES

(December 3, 1976), pages 6–7, 13–21.

The transmission of communications to shareowners who hold securities of record is a straightforward procedure. Typically, the issuer or its transfer agent prepares a list of recordholders and from this list generates mailing labels; the communication then is packaged, labeled, and distributed. The rules, procedures and practices governing issuer-shareowner communications have been developed not primarily to facilitate communication with shareholders of record, but rather to assure timely transmission of communications from issuers to unknown beneficial owners whose securities are held of record by intermediaries. It is the system for transmitting shareowner communications through intermediaries with which this section is concerned.

a. The Role of Banks

Although it is common practice to refer to the distribution of shareowner communications through intermediaries "such as brokers and banks," the Commission has found that banks do not participate as intermediaries in the distribution of materials to the extent generally assumed. * * *

b. The Role of Brokers

Between 900 and 1200 brokers are involved to some degree in transmitting issuer-shareowner communications. These brokers handle the vast percentage of the shareowner communications transmitted through intermediaries, but the range of their involvement and sophistication varies greatly. At one end of the spectrum is a highly automated broker which can print proxies, proxy statements and even annual reports in-house if an issuer fails to provide an adequate supply.

At the other end, the Study interviewed several small brokers who package and address materials manually.

c. Transmission of Proxy Materials and Solicitation of Proxies

(i) Transmission of Proxy Materials

Prior to the annual meeting of shareholders, the board of directors of an issuer establishes a record date for purposes of determining the shareholders entitled to notice of, or to vote at, the meeting. Under the law of most states, the record date must be not more than 50 nor less than ten days prior to the meeting of shareholders. Shortly before the record date, the issuer sends known intermediaries a "search letter" or "search card" inquiring as to the number of sets of proxy materials needed for transmission to shareowners.[36]

The typical search card consists of two parts. Half is a postcard addressed to the intermediary which provides information about the issuer's record date and meeting date and advises the intermediary of the materials to be supplied. The other half is a tear-off form addressed to the issuer which provides space for the intermediary to indicate the number of sets of materials which will be needed. The search card advises the broker of the number of pieces and the dimensions of the material to be mailed, provides the broker with the name and address of the proper person in the issuer's organization from whom materials should be ordered, and permits the broker to advise the issuer of the address to which materials are to be sent. Moreover, the distinctive blue color of the search card facilitates its processing in busy mail rooms during proxy season.[37]

Upon receipt of the return portion of the form, the issuer forwards materials, usually in bulk, to the intermediary. In addition to proxy materials, issuers may supply mailing envelopes, return envelopes and other stationery needs. The intermediary breaks down the materials into individual sets and may supplement the materials with various inserts relating to the customer's account with the intermediary.[38] The

---

36. [By the SEC] The procedure of sending search cards to known intermediaries is regulated by Rules 14a–3(d) and 14c–7 under the Act. Under the rules, an issuer must send an inquiry to any broker, bank or voting trustee which is known to hold of record shares of any class of an issuer's securities entitled to vote at a meeting of shareholders. Notes to Rules 14a–3(d) and 14c–7 require the issuer to make an appropriate inquiry of a depository as to the participants in such depository who may hold the issuer's securities on behalf of a beneficial owner. Thereafter, the issuer must send an inquiry to such participants. Frequently, the issuer also will send search cards to brokers and banks which it believes may have become intermediary holders of its stock since the last solicitation but do not appear as recordholders. This blind mailing of search cards is employed because, for example, brokers purchasing stock often leave it in the street name of another broker until the record date for a dividend. In an effort to reach all intermediaries, many issuers send far more search cards than are expected to be returned.

37. [By the SEC] This description is based on the procedures outlined in the Manual for Proxy Solicitation of Stock in Brokers' Names (1976), a manual of standardized procedures published as a joint report of the American Society of Corporate Secretaries, Inc., the Amex, the NASD, the NYSE, and the Securities Industry Association. * * *

38. [By the SEC] For example, many brokers include a letter which discusses

intermediary packages the materials, addresses the envelopes to the shareowners and distributes them. The shareowner is instructed to return the enclosed proxy card either directly to the issuer or to the intermediary depending on the intermediary's procedures for voting securities.

(ii) Solicitation of Proxies

(a) General

A shareowner cannot give a proxy with respect to securities held of record by an intermediary since the shareowner does not appear on the issuer's records as a shareholder entitled to vote. There are, basically, three procedures used to vote securities of non-record shareowners through an intermediary: (1) the intermediary advises the shareowner of the matters to be voted on and requests voting instructions which the intermediary carries out; (2) the intermediary signs a blank proxy card and forwards it to the shareowner who then votes and forwards the card to the issuer; or (3) the intermediary is given voting discretion by the shareowner and votes thereafter without consulting the shareowner.

(b) Voting by Banks

Banks have voting discretion with regard to most securities they hold in nominee name and generally exercise it. When they do not have voting discretion, fifteen percent of the responding banks send unsigned proxy cards to their customers and request voting instructions; 50 percent of the responding banks send signed but unvoted proxy cards to their customers and instruct them to return the proxy directly to the issuer; and the other responding banks use a combination of these procedures.

(c) Voting by Brokers

The rules of most national securities exchanges provide that under certain circumstances a broker may vote securities which it holds for a customer if the customer fails to give voting instructions. If the broker forwards proxy materials to the customer at least 15 days prior to the meeting, the broker may give a proxy during the ten days prior to the meeting on certain non-controversial matters if no voting instructions are received.[39] The rule further provides that the broker may give a proxy only if he has no knowledge of any contest as to the action to be taken at the meeting and if the action does not involve a merger or consolidation or any other matter which may "affect substantially the rights or privileges of such stock." Under the NYSE and Amex rules, a customer may still give voting instructions less than ten days before the

the broker's procedure for giving a proxy when the customer fails to indicate his voting preference.

directors. The rule is commonly referred to as the "ten-day rule."

39. [By the SEC] Most notably the appointment of auditors and the election of

meeting, in which case the broker must submit a revised proxy to the issuer if the customer's instructions countermand the first proxy.

If a broker intends to give a proxy pursuant to a ten-day rule, he encloses with the proxy materials sent to his customers a letter explaining generally the provisions of the ten-day rule and advising each customer that the broker will give a proxy for his shares under the ten-day rule if the customer does not provide voting instructions. As voting instructions are received, the broker tabulates the vote and, within ten days of the meeting, gives a proxy for his entire position. Shares unvoted by customers are voted for management.[40]

Brokers who do not vote pursuant to a ten-day rule generally sign a blank proxy and forward it to their customers. * * *

(e) Special Situations

A few issuers each year become involved in a proxy contest, have an item which requires a two-thirds vote or become the subject of a tender offer. In those instances, special procedures are used to distribute communications and, other than in the tender offer situation, to solicit proxies. Many issuers employ a proxy solicitation firm to handle these special situations.

Proxy solicitation firms provide a variety of services suited to the needs of the particular issuer. Typically, the proxy solicitation firm will speed distribution of materials by hand delivering them to intermediaries across the country and will obtain proxies by writing or telephoning intermediaries and individual customers. In addition, the firm may provide consulting services with regard to strategy in fighting the tender offer or proxy contest and may play a role in overseeing the preparation, design, and printing of materials.

(f) Reimbursement of Expenses

After distributing an issuer's materials to their customers, most brokers seek reimbursement from the issuer for their expenses. The amount of reimbursement sought is normally based upon guidelines established by the major securities exchanges and the NASD. Eight of the 13 distributing banks routinely seek reimbursement for expenses, while one bills only in certain cases. The other four distributing banks, as well as most of the other responding banks, refrain from seeking reimbursement. * * *

SUMMARY OF CONCLUSIONS AND RECOMMENDATIONS * * *

Empirical data demonstrate that the existing issuer-shareowner communications system is, on the whole, effective in transmitting materials to shareowners in a timely manner and in providing an effective mechanism for the solicitation of proxies. Moreover, most issuers perceive the system as meeting their needs, and all but a small percentage of shareowners, whether they hold stock directly or through

---

40. [By the SEC] All of the responding brokers who vote under the ten-day rule indicated that they always vote their position for management.

a broker or bank, are satisfied with the service they receive. Brokers and banks strongly favor retention of the current system.

While problems exist, they are not evidence of systemic weaknesses but result from failures by individual brokers and issuers. In general, legislative or regulatory action does not appear to be necessary to correct these problems. * * *

The Commission has concluded that none of the alternative approaches to shareowner communications presented in the Preliminary Report, at this time, could effect improvements in issuer-shareowner communications at an acceptable cost while preserving the advances made in recent years in the processing of securities transactions. * * *

———

Developments during the 1970s and 1980s—particularly the growth of the central clearing system for securities transactions in which at least two intermediaries are between the issuer and the beneficial owner—have placed increased strains on this distribution process.

In 1983, the SEC developed a more direct means of communication between registrants and their beneficial owners. 17 C.F.R. § 240.14b–1(a)(1)(c) (1989) sets forth the basic concept. It requires each broker/ dealer to:

> (1) Provide the registrant, upon the registrant's request, with the names, addresses and securities positions, compiled as of a date specified in the registrant's request which is no earlier than five business days after the date the registrant's request is received, of its customers who are beneficial owners of the registrant's securities and who have not objected to disclosure of such information; Provided, however, That if the broker or dealer has informed the registrant that a designated office(s) or department(s) is to receive such requests, receipt shall mean receipt by such designated office(s) or department(s); and (2) transmit the data specified in paragraph (c)(1) of this section to the registrant no later than five business days after the record date or other date specified by the registrant.

The implementation of this novel scheme of bypassing nominees and intermediaries was deferred until the end of 1985 to permit the interested parties to devise a system to assure the confidentiality of the information provided, to develop a workable system that would be of maximum benefit to registrants and not burdensome to brokers, and to provide an appropriate schedule of reimbursement. Essentially the same process was extended to banks and thrift institutions in 1985 by legislation known as the "Shareholders Communications Act of 1985," Pub.L. 99–222, enacted December 28, 1985. The regulations implementing this scheme are of considerable complexity since they are being superimposed upon a distribution system for documents that handles a very large volume of documents within relatively short time periods.

Notes

(1) The reaction of the brokerage community to the non-objecting beneficial owner (NOBO) approach has been strongly negative.

> [B]rokerage firms in particular, as well as many fiduciary institutions, strongly disfavor the adoption of procedures which will disclose the identity of underlying beneficial holders. They fear it creates a shopping list of clients on which their competitors may prey. In addition, institutional holders often wish that their positions remain confidential. While participation in direct registration is optional at the shareholder level, an institution may fear pressure toward directly registering its position if that opportunity becomes available. On the other hand, many beneficial owners may want to be directly, not indirectly, involved in the solicitation process and not have communications pass through an intermediary layer.

Doret, Crozier and Miller, Carey v. PEI: Voting Shortcuts Cut Short, Insights, vol. 3, no. 12 (December 1989), 3, 7.

(2) Consider the following detailed description of the present process and a proposed private, non-governmental solution:

> Corporate Secretaries of large and small companies alike generally agree that the proxy system, insofar as it pertains to beneficial as opposed to record shareholders, has become increasingly complex. It has become more difficult for publicly-owned companies to obtain voting instructions from their institutionally-held shares on a timely basis. Overall voting totals remain at or near previous levels, but there is a growing sense that the vote is somewhat hastily assembled at the last-minute and a fair number of voting instructions are not received until after the meetings have been held.

> Several factors have contributed to the strains on the existing proxy system. The chief factor is layered ownership patterns whereby voting instructions are relayed from the person with voting authority to one or more intermediary custodians, who pass them on to an independent service bureau which in turn passes them on to the issuer's tabulator. * * *

> While the system still works, it could be made to work significantly better. The flaws in the system, which primarily arise from the fact that the person with the actual voting authority is hidden from the tabulator by one or more intermediary layers, are as follows. First, the current system relies upon estimates rather than actual proxy searches. * * *

> Second, the need to pass voting instructions along a chain of intermediaries before they reach the tabulator creates the potential for clerical error. The concept of passing voting instructions between different entities is akin to that of a relay in which runners exchange a baton under the pressures of a race. Even Olympians occasionally drop the baton, and errors have occurred along the chain of intermediaries in reporting votes. * * *

Lateness is another nervous-making aspect of the proxy system. Companies frequently lack a quorum less than five business days prior to their shareholder meetings. When Corporate Secretaries or their solicitors seek to obtain the missing votes by calling the fund manager or person with voting authority, the caller is frequently told that the fund manager's voting instructions have already been passed to the fund manager's custodian bank who in turn should have passed them to the independent service bureau whose procedures call for them to tabulate the instructions before forwarding them to the issuer's solicitor or tabulator. Thus, there is much needless chasing of votes that have already been sent and the occasional re-sending of voting instructions that sometimes overtake the original, with the increased pressure on the tabulator to avoid double counting. * * *

A workable concept has been proposed whereby institutions, money managers, clients of second-tier banks and other non-record holders with voting rights could be linked directly to the issuers or their transfer agents. It is called the Direct Registration System (DRS) and has been developed by members of the Securities Transfer Association. Under the DRS concept, the names and addresses of the beneficial owner or entity with voting authority would be maintained by the DRS record keeper (generally the issuer's transfer agent). This would permit issuers to mail proxy material directly to the voter and permit the beneficial owner/voter to return its proxy card directly to the issuer's tabulator. Thus, DRS provides the same direct two-way communication and voting efficiencies that are enjoyed by record shareholders. At the same time, it permits the beneficial owner to maintain all the advantages of street name ownership, including the convenience of leaving certificates with a bank or broker (e.g. direct flow of dividends into money market accounts, ease of transfer, use of the stock as collateral for margin loans, etc.).

The key to the DRS concept is establishing an electronic interface between the DRS record keeper (generally the issuer's transfer agent) and the depositories (e.g. Depository Trust Company, Midwest Securities Trust Co., Philadep) so that all transactions by beneficial owners are communicated to the DRS record keepers. To accomplish this, the depositories need to assume the additional role of switching network between the clearing corporations, the depositories' member banks and brokers and the DRS record keepers.

Under the DRS concept, each time an institution or individual bought or sold 100 shares of XYZ Corp, the buying broker would confirm the trade and instruct the depository via the existing computer linkage between brokers and the depository (called the Participant Terminal System or PTS) to credit XYZ Corp to the broker's depository position maintained at XYZ Corp's transfer agent. At the same time, the instructions from the buying broker also would advise XYZ Corp's transfer agent via the PTS system to establish a subsidiary account for the 100 share position of its client, the purchaser. In this way, transfer agents could keep up-to-date name and address records of beneficial owners as they now keep for record holders. * * *

[One] issue to be decided involves confidentiality. Many institutions have asked that their voting instructions be kept from management, at least until after the shareholders meeting, lest management be in a position to exert pressure on them to vote according to managements' recommendations. In the view of these institutions, DRS could further erode confidentiality by providing management with direct access to their votes. The importance of confidentiality to institutions is evidenced by their active support of proposals to establish confidential balloting and tabulating procedures at a number of companies. While institutions may acknowledge the greater efficiencies of DRS, they may balk at accepting it until their concerns about confidentiality are addressed. To resolve this issue, DRS vote tabulators may have to graft confidentiality procedures onto the DRS system that isolate voting tabulations from management. The nature and scope of such procedures will have to be determined (i.e. whether they should permit management to know who has voted, but not how; whether they should be in place only in the case of routine, noncontested meetings, etc.).

Norman, Shareholder Communications: Direct Registration of Beneficial Shareholders, Insights, vol. 3, no. 6 (June 1989) 10, 10–12. Is the proposed DRS system different from that authorized by § 7.23 of the RMBCA? Would it be authorized by that section?

———

As the activism of institutional investors in corporate governance has increased, proposals for the improvement of the proxy solicitation and tabulation processes have been made. In 1989, the California Public Employees' Retirement System requested that the SEC conduct a complete review of the federal proxy rules. Koppes, Guest Editorial: Can the Proxy System Bring Shareholders and Management Together? Insights, December 1989, vol. 3 No. 12, at 2:*

[The] submission, which included 48 recommendations for change, is intended to promote system-wide improvements. Currently, the federal proxy rules represent the principal means by which outside shareholders of large, publicly traded companies communicate with management. This may not be optimal, but it is, for the moment, the best that we have, and it has lasted, with varying degrees of efficiency, for a good many years. Ownership of public companies is, however, changing dramatically as public policy has placed greater and greater emphasis on pension benefits and as the economics of the market place have presented increased benefits from collective share ownership. Given these changes, and given the importance of the proxy system to our corporate governance model, we believe it is imperative that the proxy system, which largely has evolved in the context of small, individual shareholders, be rethought to accommodate a corporate

* Insights: The Corporate & Securities Law Advisor. Copyright Prentice Hall Law & Business.

governance system in which institutional and large holders play an increasingly active and responsible role. * * *

Notes

The California Public Employee's Retirement System is a long term investor. Its portfolio turnover is among the lowest of the institutional investors. It is also among the largest shareholders of a substantial number of companies. Its views and concerns seem clearly to warrant the attention of both the SEC and publicly held corporations. Yet the response of management has been suspicious. A representative of the Business Roundtable has described these corporate governance initiatives as counterproductive and unrelated to economic performance. Other business spokesmen have urged institutions to focus on economic performance and to address their concerns to boards of directors rather than seeking to compel changes through the use of the proxy process. See generally Heard, Activist Institutions Focus on Governance and Performance, Insights, vol. 3, no. 12 (December 1989) 10, 13.

3. FALSE OR MISLEADING STATEMENTS IN CONNECTION WITH PROXY SOLICITATIONS

REGULATION 14A. SOLICITATION OF PROXIES

17 C.F.R. § 240.14a–9 (1989).

§ 240.14a–9 False or Misleading Statements

(a) No solicitation subject to this regulation shall be made by means of any proxy statement, form of proxy, notice of meeting or other communication, written or oral, containing any statement which, at the time and in the light of the circumstances under which it is made, is false or misleading with respect to any material fact, or which omits to state any material fact necessary in order to make the statements therein not false or misleading or necessary to correct any statement in any earlier communication with respect to the solicitation of a proxy for the same meeting or subject matter which has become false or misleading.

(b) The fact that a proxy statement, form of proxy or other soliciting material has been filed with or examined by the Commission shall not be deemed a finding by the Commission that such material is accurate or complete or not false or misleading, or that the Commission has passed upon the merits of or approved any statement contained therein or any matter to be acted upon by security holders. No representation contrary to the foregoing shall be made.

Note: The following are some examples of what, depending upon particular facts and circumstances, may be misleading within the meaning of this section.

(a) Predictions as to specific future market values.

(b) Material which directly or indirectly impugns character, integrity or personal reputation, or directly or indirectly makes charges concerning improper, illegal or immoral conduct or associations, without factual foundation.

(c) Failure to so identify a proxy statement, form of proxy and other soliciting material as to clearly distinguish it from the soliciting material of any other person or persons soliciting for the same meeting or subject matter.

(d) Claims made prior to a meeting regarding the results of a solicitation.

Notes

(1) Is this provision a restatement of common law principles or is it broader? Of course, with the broadening of section 12 in 1964, most publicly held corporations are subject to this rule. In a pre–1964 case, Bresnick v. Home Title Guar. Co., 175 F.Supp. 723 (S.D.N.Y.1959), the Court stated that the test at common law "is not compliance with the technical rules, but rather whether the proxy soliciting material was so tainted with fraud that an inequitable result was accomplished." 175 F.Supp., at 725.

(2) The note to Rule 14a–9 formerly included, as examples of potentially misleading statements, "predictions as to specific future market values, earnings, or dividends," and was changed to its present form in July, 1979. SEC Rel. No. 34–15944, 44 Fed.Reg. 38810 (1979). The pre–1979 note reflected the historical position of the SEC that full disclosure should be limited to "hard"—that is readily verifiable—historical data and that projections or predictions were "soft"—that is, unverifiable—and therefore inherently misleading. This position permitted easy administration by the SEC but was unrealistic: investors generally are interested in future predictions rather than past events, investors are certainly less able to make reliable predictions about the future from past data than knowledgeable management, and undue emphasis on historical data leads to long and unreadable prospectuses and proxy statements. Consult H. Kripke, The SEC and Corporate Disclosure: Regulation in Search of a Purpose (1979). The SEC decided to permit projections of financial data, discussion of management objectives and goals for future performance, and the assumptions underlying such statements, only after considerable soul searching and a study by an advisory committee, SEC Rel. No. 33–5993, 43 Fed.Reg. 53251 (1978). In 1979, the SEC adopted a "safe harbor" rule that provided that such statements would not be deemed false or misleading unless they were "made or reaffirmed without a reasonable basis or disclosed other than in good faith." 17 C.F.R. §§ 230.175; 240.3b–6 (1989). Item 10(b) of Regulation S–K encourages the use of "management's projections of future economic performance that have a reasonable basis and are presented in an appropriate format." 17 C.F.R. § 229.10(b) (1989). This regulation sets forth extensive guidelines for the use and presentation of projections.

(3) The SEC's change in position with respect to "soft" information described in the previous note has led to litigation over the question whether the failure to disclose such information might constitute a violation of Rule 14a–9 under certain circumstances. Before the change in SEC position, courts faced with this question uniformly relied on the SEC policy

to answer the question in the negative; since then, however, several courts of appeal have found Rule 14a–9 violations in some circumstances. See e.g. Flynn v. Bass Brothers Enterprises, Inc., 744 F.2d 978 (3d Cir.1984). Other courts have disagreed, though under different circumstances. See generally Symposium, Affirmative Disclosure Obligations Under the Securities Laws, 46 Maryland L.Rev. 907 (1987), and particularly articles in that symposium by Kerr, A Walk Through the Circuits: The Duty to Disclose Soft Information, id. at 1071, and Hiler, The SEC and the Courts' Approach to Disclosure of Earnings Projections, Asset Appraisals, and Other Soft Information: Old Problems, Changing Views, id., at 1114. The general problem of affirmative disclosure in the non-proxy context is discussed in Chapter 13, section B, p. 1001 infra.

J.I. CASE CO. v. BORAK
Supreme Court of the United States, 1964.
377 U.S. 426, 84 S.Ct. 1555, 12 L.Ed.2d 423.

MR. JUSTICE CLARK delivered the opinion of the Court.

This is a civil action brought by respondent, a stockholder of petitioner J.I. Case Company, charging deprivation of the preemptive rights of respondent and other shareholders by reason of a merger between Case and the American Tractor Corporation. It is alleged that the merger was effected through the circulation of a false and misleading proxy statement by those proposing the merger. The complaint was in two counts, the first based on diversity and claiming a breach of the directors' fiduciary duty to the stockholders. The second count alleged a violation of § 14(a) of the Securities Exchange Act of 1934 with reference to the proxy solicitation material. The trial court held that as to this count it had no power to redress the alleged violations of the Act but was limited solely to the granting of declaratory relief thereon under § 27 of the Act.[41] The court held Wis.Stat., 1961, § 180.405(4), which requires posting security for expenses in derivative actions,[42] applicable to both counts, except that portion of Count 2

41. [By the Court] Section 27 of the Act, provides in part: "The district courts of the United States, the Supreme Court of the District of Columbia, and the United States courts of any Territory or other place subject to the jurisdiction of the United States shall have exclusive jurisdiction of violations of this title or the rules and regulations thereunder, and of all suits in equity and actions at law brought to enforce any liability or duty created by this title or the rules and regulations thereunder. Any criminal proceeding may be brought in the district wherein any act or transaction constituting the violation occurred. Any suit or action to enforce any liability or duty created by this title or rules and regulations thereunder, or to enjoin any violation of such title or rules and regulations, may be brought in any such district or in the district wherein the defendant is found or is an inhabitant or transacts business, and process in such cases may be served in any other district of which the defendant is an inhabitant or wherever the defendant may be found."

42. [By the Editor] D. DeMott, Shareholder Derivative Actions: Law & Practice § 3.01 (1987) describes "security for expenses" statutes as follows:

Nineteen states have statutes permitting the corporation, and in some instances other defendants, to demand that the plaintiff in a derivative suit provide security for the expenses, including attorney fees, that may be incurred in the defense of the suit. The amount of security is determined by the court. With few exceptions, these statutes apply *only*

requesting declaratory relief. It ordered the respondent to furnish a bond in the amount of $75,000 thereunder and upon his failure to do so, dismissed the complaint, save that part of Count 2 seeking a declaratory judgment. On interlocutory appeal the Court of Appeals reversed on both counts, holding that the District Court had the power to grant remedial relief and that the Wisconsin statute was not applicable. 317 F.2d 838. We granted certiorari. 375 U.S. 901, 84 S.Ct. 195, 11 L.Ed.2d 143. We consider only the question of whether § 27 of the Act authorizes a federal cause of action for rescission or damages to a corporate stockholder with respect to a consummated merger which was authorized pursuant to the use of a proxy statement alleged to contain false and misleading statements violative of § 14(a) of the Act. This being the sole question raised by petitioners in their petition for certiorari, we will not consider other questions subsequently presented.

I.

Respondent, the owner of 2,000 shares of common stock of Case acquired prior to the merger, brought this suit based on diversity jurisdiction seeking to enjoin a proposed merger between Case and the American Tractor Corporation (ATC) on various grounds, including breach of the fiduciary duties of the Case directors, self-dealing among the management of Case and ATC and misrepresentations contained in the material circulated to obtain proxies. The injunction was denied and the merger was thereafter consummated. Subsequently successive amended complaints were filed and the case was heard on the aforesaid

to plaintiffs whose stockholdings fall beneath a percentage amount stated in the statute, typically five percent of a class of outstanding stock or $25,000 in market value. Defendants may have recourse to the security if they prevail in the litigation, although some statutes limit recourse to those cases which the court determines were brought without reasonable cause. * * *

Plaintiffs may be able to avoid the security requirements by purchasing more shares themselves or by seeking the intervention as plaintiffs of additional stockholders, so that the aggregate holdings of the plaintiffs and intervenors exceed the amount or percentage provided by the statute. The potential impact of security for expense statutes is also limited by the fact that Congress has never enacted a general security statute applicable to all derivative actions raising federal claims. * * *

The significance of security for expense statutes is that, in the cases to which they apply, the plaintiff confronts a substantial economic risk should the defendants prevail in the action. This risk is one that is not typically imposed on the plaintiff in the United States; the

"American" rule generally is that, with a few exceptions, both parties bear their own litigation expenses, including, most importantly, attorney fees, and that the court does not shift the prevailing party's attorney fees to the nonprevailing party at the termination of the litigation. When applicable, security for expense statutes obviously depart from this basic rule; further, the statutes, by permitting defendants to demand that security be posted well in advance of a final outcome to the litigation, may impose a greater economic risk on the plaintiff than would a rule which simply shifted the successful defendant's expenses to the plaintiff after the final resolution of the litigation. It was originally believed that these statutes would deter baseless derivative suits, or suits brought solely to extract a settlement through the "annoyance value" of the suit. The present trend appears to be away from reposing great confidence in the ability of security requirements to deter strike suits.

Reprinted with permission. Published by Callaghan & Co.

See also chapter 15, page 1135, infra.

two-count complaint. The claims pertinent to the asserted violation of the Securities Exchange Act were predicated on diversity jurisdiction as well as on § 27 of the Act. They alleged: that petitioners, or their predecessors, solicited or permitted their names to be used in the solicitation of proxies of Case stockholders for use at a special stockholders' meeting at which the proposed merger with ATC was to be voted upon; that the proxy solicitation material so circulated was false and misleading in violation of § 14(a) of the Act and Rule 14a–9 which the Commission had promulgated thereunder; that the merger was approved at the meeting by a small margin of votes and was thereafter consummated; that the merger would not have been approved but for the false and misleading statements in the proxy solicitation material; and that Case stockholders were damaged thereby. The respondent sought judgment holding the merger void and damages for himself and all other stockholders similarly situated, as well as such further relief "as equity shall require." The District Court ruled that the Wisconsin security for expenses statute did not apply to Count 2 since it arose under federal law. However, the court found that its jurisdiction was limited to declaratory relief in a private, as opposed to a government, suit alleging violation of § 14(a) of the Act. Since the additional equitable relief and damages prayed for by the respondent would, therefore, be available only under state law, it ruled those claims subject to the security for expenses statute. After setting the amount of security at $75,000 and upon the representation of counsel that the security would not be posted, the court dismissed the complaint, save that portion of Count 2 seeking a declaration that the proxy solicitation material was false and misleading and that the proxies and, hence, the merger were void.

II.

It appears clear that private parties have a right under § 27 to bring suit for violation of § 14(a) of the Act. Indeed, this section specifically grants the appropriate District Courts jurisdiction over "all suits in equity and actions at law brought to enforce any liability or duty created" under the Act. The petitioners make no concessions, however, emphasizing that Congress made no specific reference to a private right of action in § 14(a); that, in any event, the right would not extend to derivative suits and should be limited to prospective relief only. In addition, some of the petitioners argue that the merger can be dissolved only if it was fraudulent or non-beneficial, issues upon which the proxy material would not bear. But the causal relationship of the proxy material and the merger are questions of fact to be resolved at trial, not here. We therefore do not discuss this point further.

III.

While the respondent contends that his Count 2 claim is not a derivative one, we need not embrace that view, for we believe that a right of action exists as to both derivative and direct causes.

The purpose of § 14(a) is to prevent management or others from obtaining authorization for corporate action by means of deceptive or inadequate disclosure in proxy solicitation. The section stemmed from the congressional belief that "[f]air corporate suffrage is an important right that should attach to every equity security bought on a public exchange." H.R.Rep. No. 1383, 73d Cong., 2d Sess., 13. It was intended to "control the conditions under which proxies may be solicited with a view to preventing the recurrence of abuses which * * * [had] frustrated the free exercise of the voting rights of stockholders." Id., at 14. "Too often proxies are solicited without explanation to the stockholder of the real nature of the questions for which authority to cast his vote is sought." S.Rep. No. 792, 73d Cong., 2d Sess., 12. These broad remedial purposes are evidenced in the language of the section which makes it "unlawful for any person * * * to solicit or to permit the use of his name to solicit any proxy or consent or authorization in respect of any security * * * registered on any national securities exchange in contravention of such rules and regulations as the Commission may prescribe as necessary or appropriate in the public interest *or for the protection of investors.*" (Italics supplied.) While this language makes no specific reference to a private right of action, among its chief purposes is "the protection of investors," which certainly implies the availability of judicial relief where necessary to achieve that result.

The injury which a stockholder suffers from corporate action pursuant to a deceptive proxy solicitation ordinarily flows from the damage done the corporation, rather than from the damage inflicted directly upon the stockholder. The damage suffered results not from the deceit practiced on him alone but rather from the deceit practiced on the stockholders as a group. To hold that derivative actions are not within the sweep of the section would therefore be tantamount to a denial of private relief. Private enforcement of the proxy rules provides a necessary supplement to Commission action. As in antitrust treble damage litigation, the possibility of civil damages or injunctive relief serves as a most effective weapon in the enforcement of the proxy requirements. The Commission advises that it examines over 2,000 proxy statements annually and each of them must necessarily be expedited. Time does not permit an independent examination of the facts set out in the proxy material and this results in the Commission's acceptance of the representations contained therein at their face value, unless contrary to other material on file with it. Indeed, on the allegations of respondent's complaint, the proxy material failed to disclose alleged unlawful market manipulation of the stock of ATC, and this unlawful manipulation would not have been apparent to the Commission until after the merger.

We, therefore, believe that under the circumstances here it is the duty of the courts to be alert to provide such remedies as are necessary to make effective the congressional purpose. As was said in Sola Electric Co. v. Jefferson Electric Co., 317 U.S. 173, 176, 63 S.Ct. 172, 174, 87 L.Ed. 165 (1942):

"When a federal statute condemns an act as unlawful, the extent and nature of the legal consequences of the condemnation, though left by the statute to judicial determination, are nevertheless federal questions, the answers to which are to be derived from the statute and the federal policy which it has adopted."

It is for the federal courts "to adjust their remedies so as to grant the necessary relief" where federally secured rights are invaded. "And it is also well settled that where legal rights have been invaded, and a federal statute provides for a general right to sue for such invasion, federal courts may use any available remedy to make good the wrong done." Bell v. Hood, 327 U.S. 678, 684, 66 S.Ct. 773, 777, 90 L.Ed. 939 (1946). Section 27 grants the District Courts jurisdiction "of all suits in equity and actions at law brought to enforce any liability or duty created by this title * * *." In passing on almost identical language found in the Securities Act of 1933, the Court found the words entirely sufficient to fashion a remedy to rescind a fraudulent sale, secure restitution and even to enforce the right to restitution against a third party holding assets of the vendor. Deckert v. Independence Shares Corp., 311 U.S. 282, 61 S.Ct. 229, 85 L.Ed. 189 (1940). This significant language was used:

"The power to *enforce* implies the power to make effective the right of recovery afforded by the Act. And the power to make the right of recovery effective implies the power to utilize any of the procedures or actions normally available to the litigant according to the exigencies of the particular case." At 288 of 311 U.S., at 233 of 61 S.Ct.

Nor do we find merit in the contention that such remedies are limited to prospective relief. This was the position taken in Dann v. Studebaker–Packard Corp., 6 Cir., 288 F.2d 201, where it was held that the "preponderance of questions of state law which would have to be interpreted and applied in order to grant the relief sought. * * * is so great that the federal question involved * * * is really negligible in comparison." At 214. But we believe that the overriding federal law applicable here would, where the facts required, control the appropriateness of redress despite the provisions of state corporation law, for it "is not uncommon for federal courts to fashion federal law where federal rights are concerned." Textile Workers Union of America v. Lincoln Mills, 353 U.S. 448, 457, 77 S.Ct. 912, 918, 1 L.Ed.2d 972 (1957). In addition, the fact that questions of state law must be decided does not change the character of the right; it remains federal. As Chief Justice Marshall said in Osborn v. Bank of United States, 9 Wheat. 738, 6 L.Ed. 204 (1824):

"If this were sufficient to withdraw a case from the jurisdiction of the federal Courts, almost every case, although involving the construction of a law, would be withdrawn * * *." At 819–820 of 9 Wheat.

Moreover, if federal jurisdiction were limited to the granting of declaratory relief, victims of deceptive proxy statements would be obliged to go into state courts for remedial relief. And if the law of the State happened to attach no responsibility to the use of misleading proxy statements, the whole purpose of the section might be frustrated. Furthermore, the hurdles that the victim might face (such as separate suits, as contemplated by Dann v. Studebaker–Packard Corp., supra, security for expenses statutes, bringing in all parties necessary for complete relief, etc.) might well prove insuperable to effective relief.

IV.

Our finding that federal courts have the power to grant all necessary remedial relief is not to be construed as any indication of what we believe to be the necessary and appropriate relief in this case. We are concerned here only with a determination that federal jurisdiction for this purpose does exist. Whatever remedy is necessary must await the trial on the merits.

The other contentions of the petitioners are denied.

Affirmed.

Notes

(1) The significant issue in the Borak case, discussed by the Court rather summarily, was whether a private cause of action existed for violations of rule 14a–9. During the 1970s the United States Supreme Court has faced similar issues in several cases which have the overall effect of sharply limiting the availability of private remedies under the securities acts and other federal statutes. While the Borak case has not been overruled, the Court has not followed the rather free-wheeling approach of Mr. Justice Clark towards this question. Indeed, in two cases the reasoning of *Borak* itself was sharply questioned:

(a) Mr. Justice Rehnquist in the opinion for the Court in Touche Ross & Co. v. Redington, 442 U.S. 560, 99 S.Ct. 2479, 2489–2490, 61 L.Ed.2d 82 (1979) [holding that a private right of action does not exist under the record keeping requirements of § 17 of the Securities Exchange Act of 1934]:

In *Borak,* the Court found in § 14(a) of the 1934 Act, an implied cause of action for damages in favor of shareholders for losses resulting from deceptive proxy solicitations in violation of § 14(a). SIPC and the Trustee emphasize language in *Borak* that discusses the remedial purposes of the 1934 Act and § 27 of the Act, which, *inter alia,* grants to federal district courts the exclusive jurisdiction of violations of the Act and suits to enforce any liability or duty created by the Act or the rules and regulations thereunder. * * * The reliance of SIPC and the Trustee on § 27 is misplaced. Section 27 grants jurisdiction to the federal courts and provides for venue and service of process. It creates no cause of action of its own force and effect; it imposes no liabilities. The source of plaintiffs' rights must be found, if at all, in the substantive provisions of the 1934 Act which they seek to enforce, not in the jurisdictional provision. The Court in *Borak* found a private cause of action implicit in § 14(a). We do not now question the actual holding of that case, but we decline to read the opinion so broadly that virtually every provision of the securities acts gives rise to an implied private cause of action.

The invocation of the "remedial purposes" of the 1934 Act is similarly unavailing. Only last Term, we emphasized that generalized references to the "remedial purposes" of the 1934 Act will not justify reading a provision "more broadly than its language and the statutory scheme reasonably permit." SEC v. Sloan, 436 U.S. 103, 116, 98 S.Ct. 1702, 1711, 56 L.Ed.2d 148 (1978). Certainly, the mere fact that § 17(a) was designed to provide protection for brokers' customers does not require the implication of a private damage action in their behalf. To the extent our analysis in today's decision differs from that of the Court in *Borak,* it suffices to say that in a series of cases since *Borak* we have adhered to a stricter standard for the implication of private causes of action, and we follow that stricter standard today. The ultimate question is one of congressional intent, not one of whether this Court thinks that it can improve upon the statutory scheme that Congress enacted into law.

(b) Mr. Justice Powell dissenting in Cannon v. University of Chicago, 441 U.S. 677, 99 S.Ct. 1946, 1977–1978, 60 L.Ed.2d 560 (1979) [arguing that no private cause of action should exist under Title IX of the Education Amendments of 1972]:

A break in this pattern occurred in J.I. Case Co. v. Borak. There the Court held that a private party could maintain a cause of action under § 14(a) of the Securities Exchange Act of 1934, in spite of Congress' express creation of an administrative mechanism for enforcing that statute. I find this decision both unprecedented and incomprehensible as a matter of public policy. The decision's rationale, which lies ultimately in the judgment that "[p]rivate enforcement of the proxy rules provides a necessary supplement to Commission action," ignores the fact that Congress, in determining the degree of regulation to be imposed on companies covered by the Securities Exchange Act, already had decided that private enforcement was unnecessary. More significant for present purposes, however, is the fact that *Borak,* rather than signaling the start of a trend in this Court, constitutes a singular and, I believe, aberrant interpretation of a federal regulatory statute.

Since *Borak,* this Court has upheld the implication of private causes of actions derived from federal statutes in only three extremely limited sets of circumstances. * * *

(2) For a useful discussion of the modern law of implied remedies under federal statutes, see Ashford, Implied Causes of Action Under Federal Laws: Calling the Court Back to *Borak,* 79 Nw.U.L.Rev. 227 (1984).

(3) The private cause of action recognized in the principal case was materially strengthened by the Supreme Court's decision in Mills v. Electric Auto–Lite Co., 396 U.S. 375, 90 S.Ct. 616, 24 L.Ed.2d 593 (1970). This case involved a proxy statement relating to a proposed merger where the misstatement did not go to the value of the transaction itself but to the manner of its approval. The proxy statement had prominently disclosed that Electric Autolite's board of directors had recommended approval of the

merger but did not disclose that Autolite's board had in fact been selected by the other party to the merger, Merganthaler Linotype Company, which had owned or controlled about 54 per cent of Autolite's shares for several years. Would the failure to disclose this additional information have influenced the decisions of shareholders as to whether or not to vote in favor of the merger? The principal issue before the Supreme Court, however, was not whether the statements made in the proxy statement were materially misleading but rather, assuming that they were, what standard of causation should exist between the materially misleading statement and the transaction in order to set forth a claim under Rule 14a–9. Mr. Justice Harlan's opinion set forth a rule that could easily be applied:

> [T]he Court of Appeals for the Seventh Circuit * * * affirmed the District Court's conclusion that the proxy statement was materially deficient, but reversed on the question of causation. The court acknowledged that, if an injunction had been sought a sufficient time before the stockholders' meeting, "corrective measures would have been appropriate." 403 F.2d 429, 435 (1968). However, since this suit was brought too late for preventive action, the courts had to determine "whether the misleading statement and omission caused the submission of sufficient proxies," as a prerequisite to a determination of liability under the Act. If the respondents could show, "by a preponderance of probabilities, that the merger would have received a sufficient vote even if the proxy statement had not been misleading in the respect found," petitioners would be entitled to no relief of any kind. Id., at 436.

> The Court of Appeals acknowledged that this test corresponds to the common-law fraud test of whether the injured party relied on the misrepresentation. However, rightly concluding that "[r]eliance by thousands of individuals, as here, can scarcely be inquired into" (id., at 436 n. 10), the court ruled that the issue was to be determined by proof of the fairness of the terms of the merger. If respondents could show that the merger had merit and was fair to the minority shareholders, the trial court would be justified in concluding that a sufficient number of shareholders would have approved the merger had there been no deficiency in the proxy statement. In that case respondents would be entitled to a judgment in their favor. * * *

> The decision below, by permitting all liability to be foreclosed on the basis of a finding that the merger was fair, would allow the stockholders to be bypassed, at least where the only legal challenge to the merger is a suit for retrospective relief after the meeting has been held. A judicial appraisal of the merger's merits could be substituted for the actual and informed vote of the stockholders. The result would be to insulate from private redress an entire category of proxy violations—those relating to matters other than the terms of the merger. Even outrageous misrepresentations in a proxy solicitation, if they did not relate to the terms of the transaction, would give rise to no cause of action under § 14(a). Particularly if carried over to enforcement actions by the Securities and Exchange Commission itself, such a result

would subvert the congressional purpose of ensuring full and fair disclosure to shareholders.

Further, recognition of the fairness of the merger as a complete defense would confront small shareholders with an additional obstacle to making a successful challenge to a proposal recommended through a defective proxy statement. The risk that they would be unable to rebut the corporation's evidence of the fairness of the proposal, and thus to establish their cause of action, would be bound to discourage such shareholders from the private enforcement of the proxy rules that "provides a necessary supplement to Commission action." J.I. Case Co. v. Borak, 377 U.S., at 432, 84 S.Ct. at 1560.[43] * * *

Where the misstatement or omission in a proxy statement has been shown to be "material," as it was found to be here, that determination itself indubitably embodies a conclusion that the defect was of such a character that it might have been considered important by a reasonable shareholder who was in the process of deciding how to vote.[44] This requirement that the defect have a significant *propensity* to affect the voting process is found in the express terms of Rule 14a–9, and it adequately serves the purpose of ensuring that a cause of action cannot be established by proof of a defect so trivial, or so unrelated to the transaction for which approval is sought, that correction of the defect or imposition of liability would not further the interests protected by § 14(a).

There is no need to supplement this requirement, as did the Court of Appeals, with a requirement of proof of whether the defect actually had a decisive effect on the voting. Where there has been a finding of

---

43. [By the Court] The Court of Appeals' ruling that "causation" may be negated by proof of the fairness of the merger also rests on a dubious behavioral assumption. There is no justification for presuming that the shareholders of every corporation are willing to accept any and every fair merger offer put before them; yet such a presumption is implicit in the opinion of the Court of Appeals. That court gave no indication of what evidence petitioners might adduce, once respondents had established that the merger proposal was equitable, in order to show that the shareholders would nevertheless have rejected it if the solicitation had not been misleading. Proof of actual reliance by thousands of individuals would, as the court acknowledged, not be feasible, see R. Jennings & H. Marsh, Securities Regulation, Cases and Materials 1001 (2d ed. 1968); and reliance on the *nondisclosure* of a fact is a particularly difficult matter to define or prove, see 3 L. Loss, Securities Regulation 1766 (2d ed. 1961). In practice, therefore, the objective fairness of the proposal would seemingly be determinative of liability. But, in view of the many other factors that might lead shareholders to prefer their current

position to that of owners of a larger, combined enterprise, it is pure conjecture to assume that the fairness of the proposal will always be determinative of their vote.

44. [By the Court] In this case, where the misleading aspect of the solicitation involved failure to reveal a serious conflict of interest on the part of the directors, the Court of Appeals concluded that the crucial question in determining materiality was "whether the minority shareholders were sufficiently alerted to the board's relationship to their adversary to be on their guard." 403 F.2d, at 434. An adequate disclosure of this relationship would have warned the stockholders to give more careful scrutiny to the terms of the merger than they might to one recommended by an entirely disinterested board. Thus, the failure to make such a disclosure was found to be a material defect "as a matter of law," thwarting the informed decision at which the statute aims, regardless of whether the terms of the merger were such that a reasonable stockholder would have approved the transaction after more careful analysis.

materiality, a shareholder has made a sufficient showing of causal relationship between the violation and the injury for which he seeks redress if, as here, he proves that the proxy solicitation itself, rather than the particular defect in the solicitation materials, was an essential link in the accomplishment of the transaction. This objective test will avoid the impracticalities of determining how many votes were affected, and, by resolving doubts in favor of those the statute is designed to protect, will effectuate the congressional policy of ensuring that the shareholders are able to make an informed choice when they are consulted on corporate transactions.

90 S.Ct., at 619–622.

(4) Why didn't the plaintiffs in *Mills* seek a temporary restraining order? Not having done so, and the merger having been completed, what remedy can the court provide? Mr. Justice Harlan also considered this question:

> Our conclusion that petitioners have established their case by showing that proxies necessary to approval of the merger were obtained by means of a materially misleading solicitation implies nothing about the form of relief to which they may be entitled. We held in *Borak* that upon finding a violation the courts were "to be alert to provide such remedies as are necessary to make effective the congressional purpose," noting specifically that such remedies are not to be limited to prospective relief. 377 U.S., at 433, 434, 84 S.Ct. at 1560. In devising retrospective relief for violation of the proxy rules, the federal courts should consider the same factors that would govern the relief granted for any similar illegality or fraud. One important factor may be the fairness of the terms of the merger. Possible forms of relief will include setting aside the merger or granting other equitable relief, but, as the Court of Appeals below noted, nothing in the statutory policy "requires the court to unscramble a corporate transaction merely because a violation occurred." 403 F.2d, at 436. In selecting a remedy the lower courts should exercise " 'the sound discretion which guides the determinations of courts of equity,' " keeping in mind the role of equity as "the instrument for nice adjustment and reconciliation between the public interest and private needs as well as between competing private claims." Hecht Co. v. Bowles, 321 U.S. 321, 329–330, 64 S.Ct. 587, 591–592, 88 L.Ed. 754 (1944), quoting from Meredith v. Winter Haven, 320 U.S. 228, 235, 64 S.Ct. 7, 11, 88 L.Ed. 9 (1943).
>
> * * *
>
> Monetary relief will, of course, also be a possibility. Where the defect in the proxy solicitation relates to the specific terms of the merger, the district court might appropriately order an accounting to ensure that the shareholders receive the value that was represented as coming to them. On the other hand, where, as here, the misleading aspect of the solicitation did not relate to terms of the merger, monetary relief might be afforded to the shareholders only if the merger resulted in a reduction of the earnings or earnings potential of their holdings. In short, damages should be recoverable only to the extent that they can be shown. If commingling of the assets and

operations of the merged companies makes it impossible to establish direct injury from the merger, relief might be predicated on a determination of the fairness of the terms of the merger at the time it was approved. These questions, of course, are for decision in the first instance by the District Court on remand, and our singling out of some of the possibilities is not intended to exclude others.

90 S.Ct., at 622–624. Are damages really an appropriate remedy for a violation such as that involved in *Mills*?

(5) In Gould v. American–Hawaiian S.S. Co., 535 F.2d 761 (3d Cir.1976) certain "favored shareholders" in a merger received different interests than the public shareholders generally. The Court concluded that the proxy materials inadequately disclosed the difference in treatment, inaccurately characterized the reasons for the difference, and eliminated any opportunity for an informed evaluation of the premium. Is this an appropriate case for monetary damages? The Court concluded that it was, and the plaintiffs ultimately recovered, either by settlement or by judgment, more than $5,000,000. Awards in this range raise two questions: who should be liable, and what standard of conduct should give rise to liability? Assume that a director knows that the proxy statement is misleading. If he or she permits it to be used, does the director become liable for the full damage suffered by the public shareholders? What if the director does not read it carefully and as a result negligently permits its use? Do the less guilty defendants have a claim over against the more guilty ones?

(6) In *Mills*, Mr. Justice Harlan also concluded that the minority shareholders' attorneys should be entitled to an interim award of attorneys' fees from Autolite (actually from Merganthaler, its successor, since the merger had been completed) on the basis of a partial summary judgment on the issue of liability:

> Although the question of relief must await further proceedings in the District Court, our conclusion that petitioners have established their cause of action indicates that the Court of Appeals should have affirmed the partial summary judgment on the issue of liability. The result would have been not only that respondents, rather than petitioners, would have borne the costs of the appeal, but also, we think, that petitioners would have been entitled to an interim award of litigation expenses and reasonable attorneys' fees. We agree with the position taken by petitioners, and by the United States as *amicus*, that petitioners, who have established a violation of the securities laws by their corporation and its officials, should be reimbursed by the corporation or its survivor for the costs of establishing the violation.

> The absence of express statutory authorization for an award of attorneys' fees in a suit under § 14(a) does not preclude such an award in cases of this type. * * *

> While the general American rule is that attorneys' fees are not ordinarily recoverable as costs, both the courts and Congress have developed exceptions to this rule for situations in which overriding considerations indicate the need for such a recovery. A primary judge-created exception has been to award expenses where a plaintiff has successfully maintained a suit, usually on behalf of a class, that

benefits a group of others in the same manner as himself. To allow the others to obtain full benefit from the plaintiff's efforts without contributing equally to the litigation expenses would be to enrich the others unjustly at the plaintiff's expense. This suit presents such a situation. The dissemination of misleading proxy solicitations was a "deceit practiced on the stockholders as a group," J.I. Case Co. v. Borak, 377 U.S., at 432, 84 S.Ct., at 1560, and the expenses of petitioners' lawsuit have been incurred for the benefit of the corporation and the other shareholders.

The fact that this suit has not yet produced, and may never produce, a monetary recovery from which the fees could be paid does not preclude an award based on this rationale. * * *

In many suits under § 14(a), particularly where the violation does not relate to the terms of the transaction for which proxies are solicited, it may be impossible to assign monetary value to the benefit. Nevertheless, the stress placed by Congress on the importance of fair and informed corporate suffrage leads to the conclusion that, in vindicating the statutory policy, petitioners have rendered a substantial service to the corporation and its shareholders. Whether petitioners are successful in showing a need for significant relief may be a factor in determining whether a further award should later be made. But regardless of the relief granted, private stockholders' actions of this sort "involve corporate therapeutics," and furnish a benefit to all shareholders by providing an important means of enforcement of the proxy statute. To award attorneys' fees in such a suit to a plaintiff who has succeeded in establishing a cause of action is not to saddle the unsuccessful party with the expenses but to impose them on the class that has benefited from them and that would have had to pay them had it brought the suit.

396 U.S., at 389–397, 90 S.Ct., at 624–628. This last holding was too much for Mr. Justice Black, who commented that he did not agree with the holding "that stockholders who hire lawyers to prosecute their claims in such a case can recover attorneys' fees in the absence of a valid contractual agreement so providing or an explicit statute creating such a right of recovery." He added, "the courts are interpreters, not creators, of legal rights to recover and if there is a need for recovery of attorneys' fees to effectuate the policies of the Act here involved, that need should in my judgment be met by Congress, not by this Court." 396 U.S. at 397, 90 S.Ct. at 628. The leading post-Mills case involving the shifting of attorneys' fees is Alyeska Pipeline Serv. Co. v. Wilderness Soc'y, 421 U.S. 240, 95 S.Ct. 1612, 44 L.Ed.2d 141 (1975), where the Court held that it was improper to award attorneys' fees to several environmental organizations on the theory that they were acting as "private attorney general". *Mills* was cited as an example of the "historic power of equity to permit the trustee of a fund or property, or a party preserving or recovering a fund for the benefit of others in addition to himself, to recover his costs, including his attorneys' fees, from the fund or property itself or directly from the other parties enjoying the benefit." 421 U.S. at 257–58, 95 S.Ct. at 1621–22. The dissent argued that *Mills* and other cases simply cannot be reconciled with the

majority's argument.   Does *Alyeska* significantly limit the recovery of attorneys' fees for proxy violations?

(7) Both the causation holding and the interim award of attorneys' fees in *Mills* undoubtedly encouraged the development of entrepreneurial litigation by plaintiffs' attorneys in the securities area.   Mr. Justice Black's dissent in *Mills* apparently assumed that the individual shareholders who served as plaintiffs in this litigation determined who their lawyers should be.   The reality, however, is often far different.   Consult Coffee, Understanding the Plaintiff's Attorney: The Implications of Economic Theory for Private Enforcement of Law Through Class and Derivative Actions, 86 Colum.L.Rev. 669, 677–679, 681–684 (1986): *

> In theory, a fundamental premise of American legal ethics is that clients, not their attorneys, should define litigation objectives.   Yet, in the context of class and derivative actions, it is well understood that the actual client generally has only a nominal stake in the outcome of the litigation.   Empirical studies have shown this, and courts, when dissatisfied with the performance of plaintiff's attorneys, are prone to emphasize that the plaintiff's attorney has no "true" identifiable client. Despite these grumblings, our legal system has long accepted, if somewhat uneasily, the concept of the plaintiff's attorney as an entrepreneur who performs the socially useful function of deterring undesirable conduct.   This acceptance is manifested in a variety of ways: by permitting the attorney to advance the expenses of the litigation and receive reimbursement only if successful; by sometimes permitting the attorney to settle a class or derivative action over the objections of the actual client who is serving as representative of the class; and by allowing the use of fee formulas that view "the lawyer as a calculating entrepreneur regulated by calculating judges."   Thus, although our law publicly expresses homage to individual clients, it privately recognizes their limited relevance in this context.

> Although this legal structure is largely unparalleled in other common law systems, it has its obvious advantages.   First, it enables clients who are dispersed or have suffered relatively small injuries to receive legal representation without incurring the substantial transaction costs of coordination.   Absent such a system, a classic "free rider" problem would arise because litigation is a form of "public good" in which the benefits of an action accrue to persons who are not required to bear their share of the action's costs.   * *   * Second, because the attorney as private enforcer looks to the court, not the client, to award him a fee if successful, the attorney can find the legal violation first and the client second.   In principle, this system should encourage the attorney to invest in search costs and seek out violations of the law that are profitable for him to challenge, rather than wait passively for an aggrieved client to arrive at his door.   Thus, the attorney becomes a "bounty hunter"—or, less pejoratively, an independent monitoring

force—motivated to prosecute legal violations still unknown to prospective clients. * * *

What happens when client control is so weak as to make the attorney virtually an independent entrepreneur? In some areas of contemporary litigation, the pattern is typically one of the lawyer finding the client, rather than vice versa. A principal characteristic of these areas is that plaintiff's attorneys typically have low search costs. That is, plaintiff's attorneys can discover the existence of potentially meritorious legal claims at low cost to themselves. * * *

For example, a dramatic market decline in a corporation's stock value may lead the plaintiff's attorney to infer the existence of previously undisclosed and material adverse information. The plaintiff's attorney will thus be motivated to search for a securities law violation. The mass tort, such as an airplane crash or a toxic disaster, provides another obvious example. Similarly, a publicized takeover attempt may lead to a "greenmail" transaction, the adoption of a "poison pill," or some other defensive measure by the board of directors of a target corporation, thereby indicating the potential for a derivative suit.

Empirical evidence suggests that such dramatic, highly visible events underlie most securities class actions and derivative suits. * * *

Once the plaintiff's attorney has decided to bring suit, identifying and securing a nominal client is often only a necessary procedural step that seldom poses a substantial barrier for the experienced professional. In the securities and derivative suit areas, there are well-known individuals who possess broad (but thin) securities portfolios and have served as the lead plaintiff in numerous previous class actions.[45] Formerly, some plaintiff's law firms even invested their own firm's profit-sharing plan broadly in the stocks of numerous corporations in order to have an in-house plaintiff at hand.[46] Although the payment of a forwarding fee is generally forbidden by legal ethics, there is reason

45. [By the Author] A near legendary example is a Mr. Harry Lewis, who by his own account in sworn depositions has served as the named plaintiff in "several hundred" filed cases and at least 52 reported corporate and securities law decisions in federal courts. See Branson, The American Law Institute Principles of Corporate Governance and the Derivative Action: A View from the Other Side, 2 n. 9 (1985) (unpublished manuscript) (upcoming in Wash & Lee L.Rev.) What motivates such a client? Some suspect there are secret fee-splitting arrangements in such cases, but it is also possible that professional plaintiffs simply enjoy litigation and can engage in it relatively costlessly.

46. [By the Author] See, e.g., Lowenschuss v. Kane, 520 F.2d 255, 259 n. 2 (2d Cir.1975) (plaintiff was attorney whose firm's pension plan invested in takeover target). In fact, any "cooperative" pension or profit-sharing plan can provide the plaintiff's attorney with a client that can obtain standing to sue many companies in the stock market. Recent interpretations of legal ethics have indicated that a law firm cannot represent itself or its affiliates. See Kramer v. Scientific Control Corp., [1975–1976 Transfer Binder] Fed.Sec.L. Rep. (CCH) ¶ 95,530 (3d Cir.1976); cf. Lorber v. Beebe, 407 F.Supp. 279, 293 (S.D. N.Y.1975) (partner of attorney-class representative disqualified from serving as counsel for the class). There is no apparent basis for distinguishing between the disqualification of a lawyer's spouse and other affiliates, such as a controlled corporation or a trust. Frequently, however, one plaintiff's attorney will serve as a client for another. See, e.g., Weiss v. Temporary Inv. Fund, Inc., 692 F.2d 928 (3d Cir.1982) (Mr. Melvyn Weiss is a well-known securities plaintiff's attorney.).

to believe in some fields that nonspecialist attorneys often direct a client who has legal standing to a plaintiff's attorney in return for such a fee (or for a nominal role in the case that will entitle the nonspecialist attorney to a share of any court awarded attorney's fees). * * *

As a normative matter, such a description of the attorney-client relationship may seem offensive to those accustomed to viewing the relationship as a fiduciary one. Yet for analytical purposes, one better understands the behavior of the plaintiff's attorney in class and derivative actions if one views him not as an agent, but more as an entrepreneur who regards a litigation as a risky asset that requires continuing investment decisions. Furthermore, a purely fiduciary perspective is misleading because it assumes that the client's preferences with respect to when an action should be settled are exogenously determined, when, in fact, they are largely influenced by the fee award formula adopted by the court. * * *

Professor Coffee has written a series of thoughtful articles on the problems of entrepreneurial litigation and private attorneys general, the latest of which is Coffee, The Regulation of Entrepreneurial Litigation: Balancing Fairness and Efficiency in the Large Class Action, 54 U.Chi.L.Rev. 877 (1987).

(8) In Mills v. Electric Auto–Lite Co., 552 F.2d 1239 (7th Cir.1977) cert. denied, 434 U.S. 922, 98 S.Ct. 398, 54 L.Ed.2d 279, the Court reversed the lower court's award of damages of $1,233,918.35, plus interest, and, concluding that the merger terms were fair, held that the plaintiffs should recover nothing. The Court further held that plaintiffs were not entitled to compensation for fees and expenses incurred after their initial victory in the United States Supreme Court, citing *Alyeska.*

TSC INDUSTRIES, INC. v. NORTHWAY, INC.

Supreme Court of the United States, 1976.
426 U.S. 438, 96 S.Ct. 2126, 48 L.Ed.2d 757.

MR. JUSTICE MARSHALL delivered the opinion of the Court.

The proxy rules promulgated by the Securities and Exchange Commission under the Securities Exchange Act of 1934 bar the use of proxy statements that are false or misleading with respect to the presentation or omission of material facts. We are called upon to consider the definition of a material fact under those rules, and the appropriateness of resolving the question of materiality by summary judgment in this case.

I

The dispute in this case centers on the acquisition of petitioner TSC Industries, Inc., by petitioner National Industries, Inc. In February 1969 National acquired 34% of TSC's voting securities by purchase from Charles E. Schmidt and his family. Schmidt, who had been TSC's founder and principal shareholder, promptly resigned along with his son from TSC's board of directors. Thereafter, five National nominees were placed on TSC's board; and Stanley R. Yarmuth, National's president and chief executive officer, became chairman of the TSC board, and Charles F. Simonelli, National's executive vice president, became chairman of the TSC executive committee. On October 16, 1969, the TSC board, with the attending National nominees abstaining, approved a proposal to liquidate and sell all of TSC's assets to National. The proposal in substance provided for the exchange of TSC common and Series 1 preferred stock for National Series B preferred stock and warrants.[47] On November 12, 1969, TSC and National issued a joint proxy statement to their shareholders, recommending approval of the proposal. The proxy solicitation was successful, TSC was placed in liquidation and dissolution, and the exchange of shares was effected.

This is an action brought by respondent Northway, a TSC shareholder, against TSC and National, claiming that their joint proxy statement was incomplete and materially misleading in violation of § 14(a) of the Securities Exchange Act of 1934, and Rules 14a–3 and 14a–9, promulgated thereunder. The basis of Northway's claim under Rule 14a–3 is that TSC and National failed to state in the proxy statement that the transfer of the Schmidt interests in TSC to National had given National control of TSC. The Rule 14a–9 claim, insofar as it concerns us, is that TSC and National omitted from the proxy statement material facts relating to the degree of National's control over TSC and the favorability of the terms of the proposal to TSC shareholders.

Northway filed its complaint in the United States District Court for the Northern District of Illinois on December 4, 1969, the day before the shareholder meeting on the proposed transaction, but while it requested injunctive relief it never so moved. In 1972 Northway amended its complaint to seek money damages, restitution, and other equitable relief. Shortly thereafter, Northway moved for summary judgment on the issue of TSC's and National's liability. The District Court denied the motion, but granted leave to appeal pursuant to 28 U.S.C.A. § 1292(b). The Court of Appeals for the Seventh Circuit agreed with the District Court that there existed a genuine issue of fact as to whether National's acquisition of the Schmidt interests in TSC had resulted in a change of control, and that summary judgment was therefore inappropriate on the Rule 14a–3 claim. But the Court of Appeals reversed the District Court's denial of summary judgment to Northway on its Rule 14a–9 claims, holding that certain omissions of fact were material as a matter of law. 512 F.2d 324 (1975).

We granted certiorari because the standard applied by the Court of Appeals in resolving the question of materiality appeared to conflict with the standard applied by other Courts of Appeals. 423 U.S. 820, 96

---

47. [By the Court] Each share of TSC common stock brought .5 share of National Series B preferred stock and 1½ National warrants. Each share of TSC Series 1 preferred stock brought .6 share of National Series B preferred stock and one National warrant. National Series B preferred stock is convertible into .75 share of National common stock. A National warrant entitles the holder to purchase one share of National common stock at a fixed price until October 1978.

S.Ct. 33, 46 L.Ed.2d 37 (1975). We now hold that the Court of Appeals erred in ordering that partial summary judgment be granted to Northway.

II

A

As we have noted on more than one occasion, § 14(a) of the Securities Exchange Act "was intended to promote 'the free exercise of the voting rights of stockholders' by ensuring that proxies would be solicited with 'explanation to the stockholder of the real nature of the questions for which authority to cast his vote is sought.' " Mills v. Electric Auto–Lite Co., 396 U.S. 375, 381, 90 S.Ct. 616, 620, 24 L.Ed.2d 593 (1970). See also J.I. Case Co. v. Borak, 377 U.S. 426, 431, 84 S.Ct. 1555, 1559, 12 L.Ed.2d 423 (1964). In Borak, the Court held that § 14(a)'s broad remedial purposes required recognition under § 27 of the Securities Exchange Act, of an implied private right of action for violations of the provision. And in Mills, we attempted to clarify to some extent the elements of a private cause of action for violation of § 14(a). In a suit challenging the sufficiency under § 14(a) and Rule 14a–9 of a proxy statement soliciting votes in favor of a merger, we held that there was no need to demonstrate that the alleged defect in the proxy statement actually had a decisive effect on the voting. So long as the misstatement or omission was material, the causal relation between violation and injury is sufficiently established, we concluded, if "the proxy solicitation itself * * * was an essential link in the accomplishment of the transaction." 396 U.S., at 385, 90 S.Ct., at 622. After Mills, then, the content given to the notion of materiality assumes heightened significance.[48]

B

The question of materiality, it is universally agreed, is an objective one, involving the significance of an omitted or misrepresented fact to a reasonable investor. Variations in the formulation of a general test of materiality occur in the articulation of just how significant a fact must be or, put another way, how certain it must be that the fact would affect a reasonable investor's judgment.

The Court of Appeals in this case concluded that material facts include "all facts which a reasonable shareholder *might* consider important." 512 F.2d, at 330 (emphasis added). This formulation of the test of materiality has been explicitly rejected by at least two courts as setting too low a threshold for the imposition of liability under Rule 14a–9. Gerstle v. Gamble–Skogmo, Inc., 478 F.2d 1281, 1301–1302 (C.A.2 1973); Smallwood v. Pearl Brewing Co., 489 F.2d 579, 603–604

---

48. [By the Court] Our cases have not considered, and we have no occasion in this case to consider, what showing of culpability is required to establish the liability under § 14(a) of a corporation issuing a materially misleading proxy statement, or of a person involved in the preparation of a materially misleading proxy statement. See Ernst & Ernst v. Hochfelder, 425 U.S. 185, 209 n. 28, 96 S.Ct. 1375, 1388, 47 L.Ed. 2d 668 (1976).

(C.A.5 1974). In these cases, panels of the Second and Fifth Circuits opted for the conventional tort test of materiality—whether a reasonable man *would* attach importance to the fact misrepresented or omitted in determining his course of action. See Restatement (Second) of Torts § 538(2)(a) (Tent.Draft No. 10, Apr. 20, 1964). See also American Law Institute, Federal Securities Code § 256(a) (Tent.Draft No. 2, 1973). Gerstle v. Gamble–Skogmo, supra, at 1302, also approved the following standard, which had been formulated with reference to statements issued in a contested election: "whether, taking a properly realistic view, there is a substantial likelihood that the misstatement or omission may have led a stockholder to grant a proxy to the solicitor or to withhold one from the other side, whereas in the absence of this he would have taken a contrary course." * * *

C

In formulating a standard of materiality under Rule 14a–9, we are guided, of course, by the recognition in *Borak* and *Mills* of the Rule's broad remedial purpose. That purpose is not merely to ensure by judicial means that the transaction, when judged by its real terms, is fair and otherwise adequate, but to ensure disclosures by corporate management in order to enable the shareholders to make an informed choice. As an abstract proposition, the most desirable role for a court in a suit of this sort, coming after the consummation of the proposed transaction, would perhaps be to determine whether in fact the proposal would have been favored by the shareholders and consummated in the absence of any misstatement or omission. But as we recognized in *Mills*, supra, at 382 n. 5, 90 S.Ct., at 620, such matters are not subject to determination with certainty. Doubts as to the critical nature of information misstated or omitted will be commonplace. And particularly in view of the prophylactic purpose of the Rule and the fact that the content of the proxy statement is within management's control, it is appropriate that these doubts be resolved in favor of those the statute is designed to protect.

We are aware, however, that the disclosure policy embodied in the proxy regulations is not without limit. Some information is of such dubious significance that insistence on its disclosure may accomplish more harm than good. The potential liability for a Rule 14a–9 violation can be great indeed, and if the standard of materiality is unnecessarily low, not only may the corporation and its management be subjected to liability for insignificant omissions or misstatements, but also management's fear of exposing itself to substantial liability may cause it simply to bury the shareholders in an avalanche of trivial information—a result that is hardly conducive to informed decision-making. Precisely these dangers are presented, we think, by the definition of a material fact adopted by the Court of Appeals in this case—a fact which a reasonable shareholder *might* consider important. We agree with Judge Friendly, speaking for the Court of Appeals in

Gerstle, that the "might" formulation is "too suggestive of mere possibility, however unlikely." 478 F.2d, at 1302.

The general standard of materiality that we think best comports with the policies of Rule 14a–9 is as follows: An omitted fact is material if there is a substantial likelihood that a reasonable shareholder would consider it important in deciding how to vote. This standard is fully consistent with *Mills* general description of materiality as a requirement that "the defect have a significant *propensity* to affect the voting process." It does not require proof of a substantial likelihood that disclosure of the omitted fact would have caused the reasonable investor to change his vote. What the standard does contemplate is a showing of a substantial likelihood that, under all the circumstances, the omitted fact would have assumed actual significance in the deliberations of the reasonable shareholder. Put another way, there must be a substantial likelihood that the disclosure of the omitted fact would have been viewed by the reasonable investor as having significantly altered the "total mix" of information made available.[49]

D

The issue of materiality may be characterized as a mixed question of law and fact, involving as it does the application of a legal standard to a particular set of facts. In considering whether summary judgment on the issue is appropriate, we must bear in mind that the underlying objective facts, which will often be free from dispute, are merely the starting point for the ultimate determination of materiality. The determination requires delicate assessments of the inferences a "reasonable shareholder" would draw from a given set of facts and the significance of those inferences to him, and these assessments are peculiarly ones for the trier of fact. Only if the established omissions are "so obviously important to an investor, that reasonable minds cannot differ on the question of materiality" is the ultimate issue of materiality appropriately resolved "as a matter of law" by summary judgment. * * *

[In Part III of its opinion the Court conducts a careful reexamination of the facts and concludes that none of the claimed omissions were material.]

IV

In summary, none of the omissions claimed to have been in violation of Rule 14a–9 were, so far as the record reveals, materially misleading as a matter of law, and Northway was not entitled to partial

---

49. [By the Court] In defining materiality under Rule 14a–9, we are, of course, giving content to a rule promulgated by the SEC pursuant to broad statutory authority to promote "the public interest" and "the protection of investors." Cf. Ernst & Ernst v. Hochfelder, 425 U.S., at 212–214, 96 S.Ct., at 1390–1391. Under these circumstances, the SEC's view of the proper balance between the need to insure adequate disclosure and the need to avoid the adverse consequences of setting too low a threshold for civil liability is entitled to consideration. The standard we adopt is supported by the SEC.

summary judgment. The judgment of the Court of Appeals is reversed, and the case is remanded for further proceedings consistent with this opinion.

It is so ordered.

MR. JUSTICE STEVENS took no part in the consideration or decision of this case.

Notes

(1) What are the implications of this decision for the interim recovery of plaintiffs' fees and expenses under *Mills?*

(2) Shidler v. All American Life & Financial Corp., 775 F.2d 917 (8th Cir.1985) involved a proxy statement for a merger that included a statement that under Iowa law the transaction required the approval of two-thirds of all classes of shares, common and preferred, voting together in a single election. This statement turned out to be incorrect since the Iowa Supreme Court later concluded that Iowa law required a two-thirds vote of each class of shares, voting separately. Shidler v. All American Life & Financial Corp., 298 N.W.2d 318 (Iowa 1980). This result, however, could hardly have been predicted with certainty since the issue was a novel one under Iowa law. In holding that no claim for relief under rule 14a–9 was stated, the court concluded that rule 14a–9 did not impose strict liability, and that the lower court's conclusion that the corporation and its directors were not negligent in including the incorrect statement was not "clearly erroneous." The court held, however, that a claim might be stated under Iowa law for damages for conversion or breach of contract. Consult also Nelson v. All American Life & Financial Corp., 889 F.2d 141 (8th Cir. 1989).

4. SHAREHOLDER PROPOSALS

REGULATION 14A. SOLICITATION OF PROXIES

17 C.F.R. § 240.14a–8 (1989).

§ 240.14a–8 Proposals of security holders.

(a) If any security holder of a registrant notifies the registrant of his intention to present a proposal for action at a forthcoming meeting of the registrant's security holders, the registrant shall set forth the proposal in its proxy statement and identify it in its form of proxy and provide means by which security holders can make the specification required by Rule 14a–(b).[50] Notwithstanding the foregoing, the registrant shall not be required to include the proposal in its proxy statement or form of proxy unless the security holder (hereinafter, the

---

50. [By the Editor] The provision referred to reads as follows:

(b)(1) Means shall be provided in the form of proxy whereby the person solicited is afforded an opportunity to specify by boxes a choice between approval or disapproval of, or abstention with respect to, each matter or group of related matters referred to therein as intended to be acted upon, other than elections to office. A proxy may confer discretionary authority with respect to matters as to which a choice is not specified by the security holder provided that the form of proxy states in bold-face type how it is intended to vote the shares represented by the proxy in each such case.

"proponent") has complied with the requirements of this paragraph and paragraphs (b) and (c) of this section:

(1) *Eligibility.* At the time he submits the proposal, the proponent shall be a record or beneficial owner of at least 1% or $1000 in market value of securities entitled to be voted on the proposal at the meeting and have held such securities for at least one year, and he shall continue to own such securities through the date on which the meeting is held. * * * In the event the registrant includes the proponent's proposal in its proxy soliciting material for the meeting and the proponent fails to comply with the requirement that he continuously hold such securities through the meeting date, the registrant shall not be required to include any proposals submitted by the proponent in its proxy material for any meeting held in the following two calendar years.

(2) *Notice and Attendance at the Meeting.* At the time he submits a proposal, a proponent shall provide the registrant in writing with his name, address, the number of the registrant's voting securities that he holds of record or beneficially, the dates upon which he acquired such securities, and documentary support for a claim of beneficial ownership. A proposal may be presented at the meeting either by the proponent or his representative who is qualified under state law to present the proposal on the proponent's behalf at the meeting. In the event that the proponent or his representative fails, without good cause, to present the proposal for action at the meeting, the registrant shall not be required to include any proposals submitted by the proponent in its proxy soliciting material for any meeting held in the following two calendar years.

(3) *Timeliness.* The proponent shall submit his proposal sufficiently far in advance of the meeting so that it is received by the issuer within the following time periods: * * *

(4) *Number of Proposals.* The proponent may submit no more than one proposal and an accompanying supporting statement for inclusion in the registrant's proxy materials for a meeting of security holders. If the proponent submits more than one proposal, or if he fails to comply with the 500 word limit mentioned in paragraph (b)(1) of this section, he shall be provided the opportunity to reduce the items submitted by him to the limits required by this rule, within 14 calendar days of notification of such limitations by the registrant.

(b)(1) *Supporting Statement.* The registrant, at the request of the proponent, shall include in its proxy statement a statement of the proponent in support of the proposal, which statement shall not include the name and address of the proponent. A proposal and its supporting statement in the aggregate shall not exceed 500 words. The supporting statement shall be furnished to the registrant at the time that the proposal is furnished, and the registrant shall not be responsible for such statement and the proposal to which it relates.

(2) *Identification of Proponent.* The proxy statement shall also include either the name and address of the proponent and the number of shares of the voting security held by the proponent or a statement that such information will be furnished by the registrant to any person, orally or in writing as requested, promptly upon the receipt of any oral or written request therefor.

(c) The registrant may omit a proposal and any statement in support thereof from its proxy statement and form of proxy under any of the following circumstances:

(1) If the proposal is, under the laws of the registrant's domicile, not a proper subject for action by security holders.

NOTE. Whether a proposal is a proper subject for action by security holders will depend on the applicable state law. Under certain states' laws, a proposal that mandates certain action by the registrant's board of directors may not be a proper subject matter for shareholder action, while a proposal recommending or requesting such action of the board may be proper under such state laws.

(2) If the proposal, if implemented, would require the registrant to violate any state law or Federal law of the United States, or any law of any foreign jurisdiction to which the registrant is subject, except that this provision shall not apply with respect to any foreign law compliance with which would be violative of any state law or Federal law of the United States;

(3) If the proposal or the supporting statement is contrary to any of the Commission's proxy rules and regulations, including Rule 14a–9 * * *;

(4) If the proposal relates to the redress of a personal claim or grievance against the registrant or any other person, or if it is designed to result in a benefit to the proponent or to further a personal interest, which benefit or interest is not shared with the other security holders at large;

(5) If the proposal relates to operations which account for less than 5 percent of the registrant's total assets at the end of its most recent fiscal year, and for less than 5 percent of its net earnings and gross sales for its most recent fiscal year, and is not otherwise significantly related to the registrant's business;

(6) If the proposal deals with a matter beyond the registrant's power to effectuate;

(7) If the proposal deals with a matter relating to the conduct of the ordinary business operations of the registrant;

(8) If the proposal relates to an election to office;

(9) If the proposal is counter to a proposal to be submitted by the registrant at the meeting;

(10) If the proposal has been rendered moot;

(11) If the proposal is substantially duplicative of a proposal previously submitted to the registrant by another proponent, which proposal will be included in the registrant's proxy material for the meeting;

(12) If the proposal deals with substantially the same subject matter as a prior proposal submitted to security holders in the registrant's proxy statement and form of proxy relating to any annual or special meeting of security holders held within the preceding five calendar years, it may be omitted from the registrant's proxy materials relating to any meeting of security holders held within three calendar years after the latest such previous submission: *Provided, That*

(i) If the proposal was submitted at only one meeting during such preceding period, it received less than three percent of the total number of votes cast in regard thereto; or

(ii) If the proposal was submitted at only two meetings during such preceding period, it received at the time of its second submission less than six percent of the total number of votes cast in regard thereto; or

(iii) If the prior proposal was submitted at three or more meetings during such preceding period, it received at the time of its latest submission less than 10 percent of the total number of votes cast in regard thereto; or

(13) If the proposal relates to specific amounts of cash or stock dividends.

(d) Whenever the registrant asserts, for any reason, that a proposal and any statement in support thereof received from a proponent may properly be omitted from its proxy statement and form of proxy, it shall file with the Commission * * * the following items:

(1) the proposal;

(2) any statement in support thereof as received from the proponent;

(3) a statement of the reasons why the registrant deems such omission to be proper in the particular case; and

(4) where such reasons are based on matters of law, a supporting opinion of counsel. The registrant shall at the same time, if it has not already done so notify the proponent of its intention to omit the proposal from its proxy statement and form of proxy and shall forward to him a copy of the statement of reasons why the registrant deems the omission of the proposal to be proper and a copy of such supporting opinion of counsel.

(e) If the registrant intends to include in the proxy statement a statement in opposition to a proposal received from a proponent, it shall * * * promptly forward to the proponent a copy of the statement in opposition to the proposal. In the event the proponent believes that the statement in opposition contains materially false or misleading statements within the meaning of Rule 14a-9 and the proponent wishes to bring this matter to the attention of the Commission, the proponent promptly should provide the staff with a letter setting forth the reasons for this view and at the same time promptly provide the registrant with a copy of his letter.

RAUCHMAN v. MOBIL CORPORATION
United States Court of Appeals, Sixth Circuit, 1984.
739 F.2d 205.

Before ENGEL and KEITH, CIRCUIT JUDGES, and WEICK, SENIOR CIRCUIT JUDGE.

ENGEL, CIRCUIT JUDGE.

The principal issue in this appeal is whether defendant Mobil Corporation properly refused to include in its proxy statement a proposal which would amend Mobil's bylaws to prevent a citizen of an OPEC country from sitting on Mobil's board of directors. The plaintiff's claim is premised upon the existence of an implied private cause of action under section 14(a) of the Securities Exchange Act, and upon rule 14a–8 promulgated thereunder. Rauchman asserts that Mobil was required to include the proposal in the corporation's proxy statement for the 1982 annual meeting.

I.

The plaintiff, Irvin Rauchman, owns sixty-four voting shares of Mobil stock. In 1981, pursuant to Securities Exchange Commission (SEC or Commission) rule 14a–8(a), Rauchman submitted a proposed amendment to Mobil's bylaws for inclusion in Mobil's proxy statement for the company's 1982 annual meeting.

The proposal read as follows:

Proposal: It is resolved that the bylaws of the Corporation are amended to read as follows: Citizens of countries belonging to OPEC are not qualified for election to, or membership on, the Corporation's Board of Directors.

Supporting Statement: On October 31, 1980, Mobil's directors appointed a Saudi Arabian citizen to its Board of Directors. This individual reportedly has ties to members of the present Saudi Arabian government. Saudi Arabia, of course, makes harmful political use of its oil supply. Mobil, by appointing a Saudi Arabian to its Board of Directors, is, in effect, also approving of Saudi Arabia's activities.

Other corporations successfully transact business with OPEC countries without appointing citizens of those countries to their boards. Other means are available to obtain a working relationship with OPEC. Mobil has erred by associating with a country that has, for example, provided an abundance of cash and weapons to the Palestine Liberation Organization. A provision in Mobil's bylaws excluding citizens of OPEC countries from its Board of Directors will be a step in the right direction.

The[r]e are qualified American citizens who can contribute to the continued success of Mobil. It is unnecessary for Mobil to prostitute itself to the power of OPEC and become a silent partner to OPEC's destructive activities.

Evidently, Mr. Rauchman's concern with the presence of an OPEC citizen on the Mobil board was caused by the appointment to the board of Suliman S. Olayan, a Saudi Arabian citizen.

After receiving Rauchman's proposal, Mobil wrote to the SEC staff requesting that the staff recommend to the Commission that no action be taken if Mobil did not include Rauchman's proposal in the proxy statement. Mobil maintained in its letter to the SEC that under rule 14a–8(c)(8), which allows a company to exclude a proposal if it relates to an election to office of the company's board of directors, the proposal need not be included. Mobil took this position because Olayan was eligible for reelection at Mobil's 1982 annual meeting. The SEC staff responded with a letter indicating that it would not recommend any enforcement action to the Commission if Mobil omitted the proposal. In its letter the staff noted that

> [t]here appears to be some basis for your opinion that the proposal may be omitted from the Company's proxy material under Rule 14a–8(c)(8), since it relates to the election to office of the Company's Board of Directors. In the staff's view, the proposal and supporting statement call into question the qualifications of Mr. Olayan for reelection and thus the proposal may be deemed an effort to oppose management's solicitation on behalf of the reelection of this person. Under the circumstances, this Division will not recommend any enforcement action to the Commission if the Company omits the proposal from its proxy material.

Following the staff's determination, Rauchman brought suit in the United States District Court for the Southern District of Ohio to force Mobil to include the proposal in the Company's proxy statement. The district court assumed that Rauchman had a private right of action under section 14(a) of the Securities Exchange Act and rule 14a–8 promulgated thereunder. The court then found that Mobil properly excluded Rauchman's proposal from its proxy statement because the proposal related to an election to office. The court found that the proposal was related to the reelection of Olayan to Mobil's board of directors because, had the proposal been adopted, Mr. Olayan would have been ineligible to sit on Mobil's board. Thus, the court concluded: "Rauchman's proposal * * * is clearly intended to render Mr. Olayan ineligible to serve as a Mobil director." Based on these findings the district court granted Mobil's motion for summary judgment.

II.

We observe initially that we have substantial reservations concerning the existence of an implied private cause of action based upon a violation of rule 14a–8. We are especially uncertain in light of recent Supreme Court decisions limiting the availability of private causes of action generally. See Universities Research Ass'n v. Coutu, 450 U.S. 754, 101 S.Ct. 1451 (1981); Transamerica Mortgage Advisers, Inc. v.

Lewis, 444 U.S. 11, 100 S.Ct. 242 (1979); Touche Ross & Co. v. Redington, 442 U.S. 560, 99 S.Ct. 2479 (1979). Furthermore, rule 14a–8 seems unrelated to prohibiting the inclusion of misleading or dishonest information in proxy statements, which is the primary object of the statute. See, e.g., J.I. Case Co. v. Borak, 377 U.S. 426, 431, 84 S.Ct. 1555, 1559 (1964) (The purpose of § 14(a) is to prevent management or others from obtaining authorization for corporate action by means of deceptive or inadequate disclosure in proxy solicitation.) Rather, the rule is aimed at accomplishing what would appear to us to be "at best a subsidiary purpose of the federal legislation." Santa Fe Industries v. Green, 430 U.S. 462, 478, 97 S.Ct. 1292, 1303 (1977) (quoting Cort v. Ash, 422 U.S. 66, 80, 95 S.Ct. 2080, 2089 (1975)).

Nonetheless, in *Borak,* the Supreme Court found an implied cause of action in section 14(a). Although *Borak* involved rule 14a–9, the Supreme Court, in a unanimous decision, did not premise its finding of a private cause of action upon the purpose of the rule. Rather, the Court focused on the authority conferred by Congress in enacting section 14(a):

> It appears clear that private parties have a right under § 27 to bring suit for violation of § 14(a) of the Act. Indeed, this section specifically grants the appropriate District Courts jurisdiction over "all suits in equity and actions at law brought to enforce any liability or duty created" under the Act.

377 U.S. at 430–31. We note also that at least two other recent decisions by the Supreme Court have recognized an implied right of action under § 14(a). TSC Industries, Inc. v. Northway, Inc., 426 U.S. 438, 96 S.Ct. 2126 (1976); Mills v. Electric Auto–Lite Co., 396 U.S. 375, 90 S.Ct. 616 (1970). We therefore assume for the purposes of this decision that an implied private cause of action exists under section 14(a), even when it is premised upon an alleged violation of rule 14a–8 rather than 14a–9.

III.

Turning therefore to the merits of the appeal, we conclude that the district judge did not err in granting Mobil's motion for summary judgment. It was undisputed that Suliman S. Olayan, a Saudi Arabian citizen, was running for reelection to Mobil's board of directors. The election of Olayan to the board would have been forbidden by the proposed bylaw amendment, since the amendment would have made him ineligible to sit on the board. Paragraph one of the proposed comment submitted by Rauchman unmistakably and expressly referred to Olayan, although not by name. In our view, this circumstance sufficiently supports the trial judge's holding that the proposal relates to an election to office and, under the rules of the Commission, was not required to be included.

It is suggested on appeal that the proposal would have only an incidental impact upon Olayan's reelection. We disagree. As the district court noted, "Mobile [sic] stockholders could not vote for Rauchman's proposal and at the same time ratify the nomination of

Mr. Olayan." By forcing the shareholders to choose between ratifying the proposal and reelecting Olayan, Rauchman's proposal could clearly be viewed as an "effort to oppose management's solicitation on behalf of" Olayan's reelection. It is a form of electioneering which Mobil was not required to include in its proxy statement.

Plaintiff suggests in his brief that if we conclude that Mr. Olayan's presence on the Mobil board of directors invalidates Rauchman's "otherwise proper proposal," the remedy would be to insert a "grandfather clause" rendering the bylaw inapplicable to Olayan. We are not aware that this suggestion was ever made to the district court or to Mobil until this appeal. We are not disposed to act on that suggestion at this late date and at this level.

Mobil argued that the proposed bylaw would transgress the laws of the state of Mobil's incorporation (Delaware) and of the state of its principal place of business (New York). Mobil also argued that Rauchman's proposal conflicts with the executive agreement of November 7, 1983, 48 Stat. 1826, between the United States and Saudi Arabia. In view of our decision that the proposal relates to an election to office, it is unnecessary for us to consider Mobil's contention that the proposal could be excluded under rule 14a–8(c)(2) which permits a company to omit any proposal which, if implemented, would "require the issuer to violate any state law or federal law of the United States."

We believe that Mobil was fully within its rights in declining to submit the proposed proxy material, at least in the form proposed by Mr. Rauchman. Affirmed.

Notes

(1) Recent institutional investor activism in shareholder governance matters has utilized extensively the shareholder proposal mechanism. In the 1988 and 1989 "proxy seasons," for example, institutional investors submitted proposals to some 40 corporations dealing with the following issues:

(a) Adoption of secret ballot procedures for shareholder voting;

(b) Adoption of cumulative voting procedures for election to the board of directors;

(c) Rotation of the location of annual meetings; and

(d) Action with respect to "poison pill" defenses implemented without shareholder approval—repeal, redemption of the poison pill stock, or a requirement that the plan be submitted to shareholders for a vote.

The effectiveness of this effort is described in Heard, Shareholder Activism: Pension Fund Proxy Campaigns Highlight 1989 Annual Meeting Season, Insights, vol. 3, no. 6, (June 1989) 20, 20–21: *

> The proposals that came to a vote [in 1989] received impressive levels of support. Support for the poison pill proposals exceeded 40 percent of the shares voted at several companies, and at one company,

* Insights: The Corporate & Securities Law Advisor. Copyright Prentice Hall Law & Business.

Consolidated Freightways, 52 percent of the shares voted on the question were voted in favor of a proposal to submit the company's poison pill to shareholders for approval. Confidential voting proposals received somewhat lower levels of support; even so, support for some of these proposals exceeded 30 percent of the shares voted.

More significant than the voting results, however, was the number of companies that agreed to the actions requested. In exchange for withdrawal of a proposal sponsored by Cal PERS, Great Northern Nekoosa agreed either to redeem its poison pill or to submit it for shareholder approval within three years. Dayton Hudson reached a similar understanding with CREF, and CREF withdrew its proposal. * * * Six companies—American Home Products, Continental, First Interstate Bancorp, J.C. Penney, TRW and Unocal—agreed to adopt confidential voting in exchange for withdrawal of secret ballot proposals.

The willingness of these companies to consider the merits of the shareholder proposals offers evidence that, even though activist institutions are still losing the votes, the shareholder campaigns of the past three years are beginning to have an effect. The willingness of both institutional activists and corporate management to discuss the issues, and their ability to reach compromise, suggests that constructive dialogue may be possible on a wide range of issues.

(2) Of course, institutional investor proxy activity may not be limited to shareholder proposals. There have been a few instances in which such investors have actually conducted proxy solicitations, including compliance with SEC proxy regulations. In a few instances also, institutional investors have announced that they intend to vote against management nominees for directors. See Heard, Corporate Accountability: Activist Institutions Focus on Fundamentals of Governance and Performance, Insights, vol. 3, no. 12 (Dec.1989), 10, 11: *

Large institutions also are prepared in 1990 to oppose, and actively solicit against, management proposals. The success that several institutions had in blocking the adoption of a package of antitakeover measures at Honeywell in 1989, mounting an active countersolicitation with the assistance of a proxy solicitor, has convinced some institutions that they can in fact defeat management proposals that are harmful to shareholder interests.

Finally, a number of institutions have adopted policies for 1990 that call for voting against director nominees in a variety of circumstances. One major fund, the New York State Common Retirement Fund (NYS Fund), has already begun to vote against board nominees at companies that do not have a majority of outside directors. Another fund, the Pennsylvania Public School Employees' Retirement System, has indicated that it is prepared to vote against director nominees, and perhaps actively solicit against their election, if it believes the directors

* Insights: The Corporate & Securities
Law Advisor. Copyright Prentice Hall
Law & Business.

to be unqualified, or if it determines that the directors have failed to properly monitor compliance with legal and ethical norms.

(3) A second major use of shareholder proposals deals with issues of political or public concern. In 1968 an organization called the Medical Committee for Human Rights requested Dow Chemical Company to include the following "resolution" in its proxy statement:

> "RESOLVED, that the shareholders of the Dow Chemical Company request the Board of Directors, in accordance with the laws of the State of Delaware, and the Composite Certificate of Incorporation of the Dow Chemical Company, to adopt a resolution setting forth an amendment to the Composite Certificate of Incorporation of the Dow Chemical Company that napalm shall not be sold to any buyer unless that buyer gives reasonable assurance that the substance will not be used on or against human beings."

The letter concluded with the following statement:

> Finally, we wish to note that our objections to the sale of this product [are] primarily based on the concerns for human life inherent in our organization's credo. However, we are further informed by our investment advisers that this product is also bad for our company's business as it is being used in the Vietnamese War. It is now clear from company statements and press reports that it is increasingly hard to recruit the highly intelligent, well-motivated, young college men so important for company growth. There is, as well, an adverse impact on our global business, which our advisers indicate, suffers as a result of the public reaction to this product.

Should a political proposal of this type be includible under rule 14a–8? This proposal led to the leading early decision under rule 14a–8, Medical Committee for Human Rights v. SEC, 432 F.2d 659 (D.C.Cir.1970), vacated as moot 404 U.S. 403, 92 S.Ct. 577, 30 L.Ed.2d 560 (1972). The court did not hold that this proposal was includible, but strongly intimated that it was, and that rule 14a–8 was an important mechanism for shareholder democracy and control of management:

> The management of Dow Chemical Company is repeatedly quoted in sources which include the company's own publications as proclaiming that the decision to continue manufacturing and marketing napalm was made not *because* of business considerations, but *in spite of* them; that management in essence decided to pursue a course of activity which generated little profit for the shareholders and actively impaired the company's public relations and recruitment activities because management considered this action morally and politically desirable. The proper political and social role of modern corporations is, of course, a matter of philosophical argument extending far beyond the scope of our present concern; the substantive wisdom or propriety of particular corporate political decisions is also completely irrelevant to the resolution of the present controversy. What *is* of immediate concern, however, is the question of whether the corporate proxy rules can be employed as a shield to isolate such managerial decisions from shareholder control. After all, it must be remembered that "[t]he control of great corporations by a very few persons was the abuse at which

Congress struck in enacting Section 14(a)." SEC v. Transamerica Corp., * * * 163 F.2d at 518. We think that there is a clear and compelling distinction between management's legitimate need for freedom to apply its expertise in matters of day-to-day business judgment, and management's patently illegitimate claim of power to treat modern corporations with their vast resources as personal satrapies implementing personal political or moral predilections. It could scarcely be argued that management is more qualified or more entitled to make these kinds of decisions than the shareholders who are the true beneficial owners of the corporation; and it seems equally implausible that an application of the proxy rules which permitted such a result could be harmonized with the philosophy of corporate democracy which Congress embodies in section 14(a) of the Securities Exchange Act of 1934.

432 F.2d at 681. The Supreme Court appeal, incidentally became moot after the corporation voluntarily submitted the Medical Committee proposal to its shareholders, where it received the support of less than 3 per cent of the shares voting on the issue.

(4) Since *Medical Committee,* rule 14a–8 has been widely used by certain groups to further their own political or social causes. A number of companies, for example have been asked to include resolutions on highly politicized subjects, including:

(a) Reports to the shareholders of the corporations' specific policies regarding the Arab boycott of firms trading with Israel.

(b) Policies with respect to operations and loans in South Africa, and to a lesser extent in South American countries such as Chile.

(c) Requesting moratoriums on construction or operation of nuclear power plants.

(d) Sales of infant formula in "Third World" countries.

(e) Animal testing.

(5) What about a proposal that an importer of various food products make a study of the methods by which its French supplier of paté de foie gras forcefeeds its geese to determine whether these methods cause undue pain or suffering to these animals? See Lovenheim v. Iroquois Brands, Ltd., 618 F.Supp. 554 (D.D.C.1985). Would it make any difference under rule 14a–8 if the defendant's sale of paté produced only $79,000 of its annual gross revenues of about $141,000,000?

(6) General Motors Proxy Statement for annual meeting of May 20, 1988, at ii:

Occasionally, inquiries have been made as to why the Board of Directors opposes these proposals [by shareholders] in the Proxy Statement. The Board of Directors does not disagree with all stockholder proposals submitted to the Corporation. When the Board finds that a stockholder proposal is consistent with the best interests of the Corporation and the stockholders, it normally can be implemented without need for a stockholder vote. The Corporation, over the years, has adopted a number of stockholder proposals and other suggestions. Thus, the stockholder proposals that appear in the Proxy Statement are those with which the Board of Directors disagrees and believes it must oppose in fulfilling its obligations to represent and safeguard the best interest of stockholders as a whole.

(7) SEC Rel. No. 34–19135, 47 Fed.Reg. 47420, 47424 (1982), states that in 1976, the American Telephone & Telegraph Company estimated that the cost of including five proposals in its proxy statement was $22,450 per proposal. AT & T estimated that its cost of handling eleven additional proposals that were excluded from the proxy statement was $3,740 per proposal.

(8) Liebeler, A Proposal to Rescind the Shareholder Proposal Rule, 18 Ga.L.Rev. 425 (1984), and Dent, SEC Rule 14a–8: A Study in Regulatory Failure, 30 N.Y.L.Sch.L.Rev. 1 (1985), both argue that rule 14a–8 is undesirable from a policy standpoint, that its cost greatly exceeds its benefits, and that the rule is probably invalid. Professor Dent comments that rule 14a–8 guarantees that, "for a price of no more than $1,000, * * * a shareholder will receive not only securities presumably valued at the price paid, but also many thousands of dollars worth of publicity for his pet peeves." Id., at 32. Both of these articles were written before the full dimensions of institutional activism in this area became apparent. See also Ryan, Rule 14a–8, Institutional Shareholder Proposals and Corporate Democracy, 23 Ga.L.Rev. 97 (1988).

E. INSPECTION OF SHAREHOLDERS LISTS, BOOKS AND RECORDS UNDER STATE LAW

Assume that you are a shareholder in a corporation and you desire to communicate with the other shareholders. How do you find out who they are? Or, assume that you are a shareholder in a closely held corporation and that you wish to examine the books and records of the corporation to determine how much your stock is worth. Will the corporation permit you to do so?

Consider RMBCA §§ 7.20, 16.01(e), 16.02(a), 16.02(b), 16.22. Under which section or sections would you proceed? Consider also the position of management when it receives a request to inspect shareholders lists or books and records. Isn't it clear that all such requests will be viewed with great suspicion, since in most cases such requests come from unfriendly sources? Indeed, obtaining a list of shareholders is often the first step in a proxy fight or takeover attempt. What, if anything, can the shareholder do about it if a corporate officer flatly refuses to provide a shareholders list even though the shareholder's request seems to comply squarely with the statute? What can the shareholder do if the corporation produces a list of 26,000 names (many of them nominees), but refuses a request to reproduce the list and make the copy available, and further refuses a request to permit the shareholder to remove the list so that he can arrange to have it photocopied?

Consider also the problems of shareholder inspection of financial or business records from the standpoint of the corporation. What should management do if the requesting shareholder owns only a few shares and management has learned that he is employed by a competitor? By a customer or supplier? By a mail order company which solicits heavily through the mails?

Problems such as these were considered in the drafting of chapter 16 of the Revised Model Business Corporation Act. Do you think that the compromises struck in this chapter give appropriate weight to the various interests and concerns described above?

STATE EX REL. PILLSBURY v. HONEYWELL, INC.

Supreme Court of Minnesota, 1971.
291 Minn. 322, 191 N.W.2d 406.

KELLY, JUSTICE.

Petitioner appeals from an order and judgment of the district court denying all relief prayed for in a petition for writs of mandamus to compel respondent, Honeywell, Inc. (Honeywell) to produce its original shareholder ledger, current shareholder ledger, and all corporate records dealing with weapons and munitions manufacture. We must affirm.

The issues raised by petitioner are as follows: (1) Whether Minnesota or Delaware law determines the right of a shareholder to inspect respondent's corporate books and records; (2) whether petitioner, who bought shares in respondent corporation for the purpose of changing its policy of manufacturing war munitions, had a proper purpose germane to a shareholder's interest; * * *

Petitioner attended a meeting on July 3, 1969, of a group involved in what was known as the "Honeywell Project." Participants in the project believed that American involvement in Vietnam was wrong, that a substantial portion of Honeywell's production consisted of munitions used in that war, and that Honeywell should stop this production of munitions. Petitioner had long opposed the Vietnam war, but it was at the July 3rd meeting that he first learned of Honeywell's involvement. He was shocked at the knowledge that Honeywell had a large government contract to produce anti-personnel fragmentation bombs. Upset because of knowledge that such bombs were produced in his own community by a company which he had known and respected, petitioner determined to stop Honeywell's munitions production.

On July 14, 1969, petitioner ordered his fiscal agent to purchase 100 shares of Honeywell. He admits that the sole purpose of the purchase was to give himself a voice in Honeywell's affairs so he could persuade Honeywell to cease producing munitions. Apparently not aware of that purpose, petitioner's agent registered the stock in the name of a Pillsbury family nominee—Quad & Co. Upon discovering the nature of the registration, petitioner bought one share of Honeywell in his own name on August 11, 1969. In his deposition testimony petitioner made clear the reason for his purchase of Honeywell's shares:

> "Q * * * [D]o I understand that you requested Mr. Lacey to buy these 100 shares of Honeywell in order to follow up on the desire you had to bring to Honeywell management and to stockholders these theses that you have told us about here today?
>
> "A Yes. That was my motivation."

The "theses" referred to are petitioner's beliefs concerning the propriety of producing munitions for the Vietnam war.

During July 1969, *subsequent* to the July 3, 1969, meeting and after he had ordered his agent to purchase the 100 shares of Honeywell stock, petitioner inquired into a trust which had been formed for his benefit by his grandmother. The purpose of the inquiry was to discover whether shares of Honeywell were included in the trust. It was then, *for the first time,* that petitioner discovered that he had a contingent beneficial interest under the terms of the trust in 242 shares of Honeywell.

Prior to the instigation of this suit, petitioner submitted two formal demands to Honeywell requesting that it produce its original shareholder ledger, current shareholder ledger, and all corporate records dealing with weapons and munitions manufacture. Honeywell refused.

On November 24, 1969, a petition was filed for writs of mandamus ordering Honeywell to produce the above mentioned records. In response, Honeywell answered the petition and served a notice of deposition on petitioner, who moved that the answer be stricken as procedurally premature and that an order be issued to limit the deposition. After a hearing, the trial court denied the motion, and the deposition was taken on December 15, 1969.

In the deposition petitioner outlined his beliefs concerning the Vietnam war and his purpose for his involvement with Honeywell. He expressed his desire to communicate with other shareholders in the hope of altering Honeywell's board of directors and thereby changing its policy. To this end, he testified, business records are necessary to insure accuracy.

A hearing was held on January 8, 1970, during which Honeywell introduced the deposition, conceded all material facts stated therein, and argued that petitioner was not entitled to any relief as a matter of law. Petitioner asked that alternative writs of mandamus issue for all the relief requested in his petition. On April 8, 1970, the trial court dismissed the petition, holding that the relief requested was for an improper and indefinite purpose. Petitioner contends in this appeal that the dismissal was in error.

1. Honeywell is a Delaware corporation doing business in Minnesota. Both petitioner and Honeywell spent considerable effort in arguing whether Delaware or Minnesota law applies. The trial court, applying Delaware law, determined that the outcome of the case rested

upon whether or not petitioner has a proper purpose germane to his interest as a shareholder. Del.Code Ann. tit. 8, § 220 (Supp.1968). This test is derived from the common law and is applicable in Minnesota. Minn.St. c. 300, upon which petitioner relies, applies only to firms incorporated under that chapter. We need not rule on whether the lower court applied the right state law since the test used was correct.

Under the Delaware statute the shareholder must prove a proper purpose to inspect corporate records other than shareholder lists. This facet of the law did not affect the trial court's findings of fact. The case was decided solely on the pleadings and the deposition of petitioner, the court determining from them that petitioner was not entitled to relief as a matter of law. Thus, problems of burden of proof did not confront the trial court and this issue was not even raised in this court.

2. The trial court ordered judgment for Honeywell, ruling that petitioner had not demonstrated a proper purpose germane to his interest as a stockholder. Petitioner contends that a stockholder who disagrees with management has an absolute right to inspect corporate records for purposes of soliciting proxies. He would have this court rule that such solicitation is per se a "proper purpose." Honeywell argues that a "proper purpose" contemplates concern with investment return. We agree with Honeywell.

This court has had several occasions to rule on the propriety of shareholders' demands for inspection of corporate books and records. Minn.St. 300.32, not applicable here, has been held to be declaratory of the common-law principle that a stockholder is entitled to inspection for a proper purpose germane to his business interests. While inspection will not be permitted for purposes of curiosity, speculation, or vexation, adverseness to management and a desire to gain control of the corporation for economic benefit does not indicate an improper purpose.

Several courts agree with petitioner's contention that a mere desire to communicate with other shareholders is, per se, a proper purpose. This would seem to confer an almost absolute right to inspection. We believe that a better rule would allow inspections only if the shareholder has a proper purpose for such communication. This rule was applied in McMahon v. Dispatch Printing Co., 101 N.J.L. 470, 129 A. 425 (1925), where inspection was denied because the shareholder's objective was to discredit politically the president of the company, who was also the New Jersey secretary of state.

The act of inspecting a corporation's shareholder ledger and business records must be viewed in its proper perspective. In terms of the corporate norm, inspection is merely the act of the concerned owner checking on what is in part his property. In the context of the large firm, inspection can be more akin to a weapon in corporate warfare. The effectiveness of the weapon is considerable:

> "Considering the huge size of many modern corporations and the necessarily complicated nature of their bookkeeping, it is plain that to

permit their thousands of stockholders to roam at will through their records would render impossible not only any attempt to keep their records efficiently, but the proper carrying on of their businesses." Cooke v. Outland, 265 N.C. 601, 611, 144 S.E.2d 835, 842 (1965).

Because the power to inspect may be the power to destroy, it is important that only those with a bona fide interest in the corporation enjoy that power.

That one must have proper standing to demand inspection has been recognized by statutes in several jurisdictions. Courts have also balked at compelling inspection by a shareholder holding an insignificant amount of stock in the corporation.

Petitioner's standing as a shareholder is quite tenuous. He only owns one share in his own name, bought for the purposes of this suit. He had previously ordered his agent to buy 100 shares, but there is no showing of investment intent. While his agent had a cash balance in the $400,000 portfolio, petitioner made no attempt to determine whether Honeywell was a good investment or whether more profitable shares would have to be sold to finance the Honeywell purchase. Furthermore, petitioner's agent had the power to sell the Honeywell shares without his consent. Petitioner also had a contingent beneficial interest in 242 shares. Courts are split on the question of whether an equitable interest entitles one to inspection. Indicative of petitioner's concern regarding his equitable holdings is the fact that he was unaware of them until he had decided to bring this suit.

Petitioner had utterly no interest in the affairs of Honeywell before he learned of Honeywell's production of fragmentation bombs. Immediately after obtaining this knowledge, he purchased stock in Honeywell for the sole purpose of asserting ownership privileges in an effort to force Honeywell to cease such production. We agree with the court in Chas. A. Day & Co. v. Booth, 123 Maine 443, 447, 123 A. 557, 558 (1924) that "where it is shown that such stockholding is only colorable, or solely for the purpose of maintaining proceedings of this kind, [we] fail to see how the petitioner can be said to be a 'person interested,' entitled as of right to inspect * * *." But for his opposition to Honeywell's policy, petitioner probably would not have bought Honeywell stock, would not be interested in Honeywell's profits and would not desire to communicate with Honeywell's shareholders. His avowed purpose in buying Honeywell stock was to place himself in a position to try to impress his opinions favoring a reordering of priorities upon Honeywell management and its other shareholders. Such a motivation can hardly be deemed a proper purpose germane to his economic interest as a shareholder.[51]

51. [By the Court] We do not question petitioner's good faith incident to his political and social philosophy; nor did the trial court. In a well-prepared memorandum, the lower court stated: "By enumerating the foregoing this Court does not mean to belittle or to be derisive of Petitioner's motivations and intentions because this Court cannot but draw the conclusion that the Petitioner is sincere in his political and social philosophy, but this Court does not feel that this is a proper forum for the

3. The fact that petitioner alleged a proper purpose in his petition will not necessarily compel a right to inspection. "A mere statement in a petition alleging a proper purpose is not sufficient. The facts in each case may be examined." Sawers v. American Phenolic Corp., 404 Ill. 440, 449, 89 N.E.2d 374, 379 (1949). Neither is inspection mandated by the recitation of proper purpose in petitioner's testimony. Conversely, a company cannot defeat inspection by merely alleging an improper purpose. From the deposition, the trial court concluded that petitioner had already formed strong opinions on the immorality and the social and economic wastefulness of war long before he bought stock in Honeywell. His sole motivation was to change Honeywell's course of business because that course was incompatible with his political views. If unsuccessful, petitioner indicated that he would sell the Honeywell stock.

We do not mean to imply that a shareholder with a bona fide investment interest could not bring this suit if motivated by concern with the long- or short-term economic effects on Honeywell resulting from the production of war munitions. Similarly, this suit might be appropriate when a shareholder has a bona fide concern about the adverse effects of abstention from profitable war contracts on his investment in Honeywell.

In the instant case, however, the trial court, in effect, has found from all the facts that petitioner was not interested in even the long-term well-being of Honeywell or the enhancement of the value of his shares. His sole purpose was to persuade the company to adopt his social and political concerns, irrespective of any economic benefit to himself or Honeywell. This purpose on the part of one buying into the corporation does not entitle the petitioner to inspect Honeywell's books and records.[52]

---

advancement of these political-social views by way of direct contact with the stockholders of Honeywell Company or any other company. If the courts were to grant these rights on the basis of the foregoing, anyone who has a political-social philosophy which differs with that of a company in which he becomes a shareholder can secure a writ and any company can be faced with a rash and multitude of these types of actions which are not bona fide efforts to engage in a proxy fight for the purpose of taking over the company or electing directors, which the courts have recognized as being perfectly legitimate and acceptable."

52. [By the Court] Petitioner cites Medical Committee for Human Rights v. S.E.C., 139 App.D.C. 226, 432 F.2d 659 (1970), for the proposition that economic benefit and community service may, in the motives of a shareholder, blend together. We have ruled that petitioner does not meet this test because he had no investment motiva-

tion for his inspection demands. The Medical Committee case did not reach the merits, the court ruling only that S.E.C. actions concerning the inclusion of proxy statements are reviewable. It is interesting to note, however, that the case presents an analogous factual situation. Shareholders sought to solicit proxies to stop the Dow Chemical Company's manufacture of napalm on grounds that management had "decided to pursue a course of activity which generated little profit * * * and actively impaired the company's public relations and recruitment activities because *management considered this action morally and politically desirable.*" 139 App.D.C. 249, 432 F.2d 681. (Italics supplied.) The court, in dictum, expressed its disapproval of Dow's claim that it could use its power to impose management's personal political and moral prejudices. It would be even more anomalous if an outsider with no economic concern for the corporation could

4. Petitioner argues that he wishes to inspect the stockholder ledger in order that he may correspond with other shareholders with the hope of electing to the board one or more directors who represent his particular viewpoint. On p. 30 of his brief he states that this purpose alone compels inspection:

> " * * * [T]his Court has said that a stockholder's motives or 'good faith' are not a test of his right of inspection, except as 'bad faith' actually manifests some recognized 'improper purpose'—such as vexation of the corporation, or purely destructive plans, or *nothing specific, just pure idle curiosity,* or necessarily illegal ends, or *nothing germane to his interests.* State ex rel. G.M. Gustafson Co. v. Crookston Trust Co. [222 Minn. 17, 22 N.W.2d 911 (1946)] * * *." (Italics supplied.)

While a plan to elect one or more directors is specific and the election of directors normally would be a proper purpose, here the purpose was not germane to petitioner's or Honeywell's economic interest. Instead, the plan was designed to further petitioner's political and social beliefs. Since the requisite propriety of purpose germane to his or Honeywell's economic interest is not present, the allegation that petitioner seeks to elect a new board of directors is insufficient to compel inspection.

* * *

The order of the trial court denying the writ of mandamus is affirmed.

Notes

(1) As can readily be surmised, the rule that shareholders may inspect books, records, and shareholders lists only for "proper" purposes has given rise to a considerable amount of litigation, much of it summarized in the *Pillsbury* opinion. If communication with other shareholders is a proper purpose to obtain a list of shareholders, should not the plaintiff always win since he or she can always make such an allegation? Was not Mr. Pillsbury's problem that he was (a) too forthright and (b) careless? If valuing the worth of closely held shares is a proper purpose to examine the financial records of a corporation, should not the plaintiff also always win in attempts to examine such records of a closely held corporation?

(2) In some instances a dissident shareholder may also be a director of the corporation. This regularly occurs, for example, in closely held corporations in which cumulative voting is mandatory. Does a director have inspection rights greater than those of a shareholder? See Pilat v. Broach Systems, Inc., 108 N.J.Super. 88, 93–98, 260 A.2d 13, 16–18 (1969):

> The cases, however, distinguish between the right of a shareholder and those of a director of a corporation. * * * Some hold that a director may be denied the right to examine the corporate records where it is shown that he has a hostile or improper motive. * * *

attempt to adapt Honeywell's policies to his own social convictions.

Other jurisdictions, however, have held a director's right of inspection to be unqualified. In the New York case of Davis v. Keilsohn Offset Co., 273 App.Div. 695, 79 N.Y.S.2d 540 (App.Div.1948), it was held that:

"The petitioner, as a director of the corporation, has an absolute right to [inspection]. All that he need show is that he is a director of the company; that he has demanded permission to examine and that his demand has been refused. It is the duty of the petitioner to keep himself informed of the business of the corporation. To perform this duty intelligently he has the unqualified right to inspect its books and records. It is of no consequence that petitioner may be hostile to the corporation. His object in seeking the examination is immaterial. His right of inspection is not dependent upon his being able to satisfy other officers of the corporation that his motives are adequate." [79 N.Y.S. 2d at 541]

Even if this court were to follow the reasoning of the first-mentioned jurisdictions, there is no showing of plaintiff's hostile intent so as to preclude him from inspection. Nevertheless, this court must follow the New Jersey decisions and it is therefore held that a director has an absolute, unqualified right to inspect the corporate books and records of account, irrespective of motive, and that in the instant case plaintiff is entitled to such inspection either with or without an attorney or accountant, as soon as conveniently possible. * * *

(3) American Law Institute, Principles of Corporate Governance: Analysis and Recommendations (Tent.Draft No. 2, 1984) § 3.08 (later renumbered § 8.04): *

(a) Every director should have the right, within the limits of § 3.08(b), to inspect and copy all books, records, and documents of every kind, and to inspect the physical properties, of the corporation and of its subsidiaries, domestic or foreign, at any reasonable time, in person or by an attorney or other agent.

(b)(1) A judicial order to enforce such right should be granted unless it is proved that the information to be obtained by exercise of the right is not reasonably related to the performance of directorial functions and duties, or that the director or his agent is likely to use the information in a manner that would violate his fiduciary obligation to the corporation and that such use would not be effectively prevented by a judicial order prohibiting him from using the information in that manner. * * *

(3) Such an order may contain provisions protecting the corporation from undue burden or expense, and prohibiting the director from using the information in a manner that would violate his fiduciary obligation to the corporation. * * *

This section was tentatively approved by the American Law Institute at its annual meeting in 1985. A motion from the floor to make absolute and

* Copyright 1984 by The American Law Institute. Reprinted with the permission of The American Law Institute.

unqualified the right of inspection by directors was defeated by a substantial vote.

REGULATION 14A. SOLICITATION OF PROXIES

17 C.F.R. § 240.14a–7 (1989).

§ 240.14a–7 Mailing Communications for Security Holders

If the registrant has made or intends to make any solicitation subject to this regulation, the registrant shall perform such of the following acts as may be duly requested in writing with respect to the same subject matter or meeting by any security holder who is entitled to vote on such matter or to vote at such meeting and who shall defray the reasonable expenses to be incurred by the registrant in the performance of the act or acts requested.

(a) The registrant shall mail or otherwise furnish to such security holder the following information as promptly as practicable after the receipt of such request:

(1) A statement of the approximate number of holders of record of any class of securities, any of the holders of which have been or are to be solicited on behalf of the registrant, or any group of such holders which the security holder shall designate.

(2) If the registrant has made or intends to make, through bankers, brokers or other persons any solicitation of the beneficial owners of securities of any class, a statement of the approximate number of such beneficial owners, or any group of such owners which the security holder shall designate.

(3) An estimate of the cost of mailing a specified proxy statement, form of proxy or other communication to such holders, including insofar as known or reasonably available, the estimated handling and mailing costs of the bankers, brokers or other persons specified in paragraph (a)(2) of this section.

(b)(1) Copies of any proxy statement, form of proxy or other communication furnished by the security holder shall be mailed by the registrant to such of the holders of record specified in paragraph (a)(1) of this section as the security holder shall designate. The registrant shall also mail to each banker, broker, or other person specified in paragraph (a)(2) of this section a sufficient number of copies of such proxy statement, form of proxy or other communication as will enable the banker, broker, or other person to furnish a copy thereof to each beneficial owner solicited or to be solicited through him.

(2) Any such material which is furnished by the security holder shall be mailed with reasonable promptness by the registrant after receipt of a tender of the material to be mailed, of envelopes or other containers therefor and of postage or payment for postage.

(3) The registrant shall not be responsible for such proxy statement, form of proxy or other communication.

(c) In lieu of performing the acts specified in paragraphs (a) and (b) of this section, the registrant may at its option, furnish promptly to such security holder a reasonably current list of the names and addresses of such of the holders of record specified in paragraph (a)(1) of this section as the security holder shall designate, and a list of the names and addresses of such of the bankers, brokers or other persons specified in paragraph (a)(2) of this section as the security holder shall designate together with a statement of the approximate number of beneficial owners solicited or to be solicited through each such banker, broker or other person and a schedule of the handling and mailing costs of each such banker, broker or other person if such schedule has been supplied to the management of the registrant. The foregoing information shall be furnished promptly upon the request of the security holder or at daily or other reasonable intervals as it becomes available to the registrant.

Notes

(1) This rule, like all the SEC proxy rules, of course, is applicable only to corporations with securities registered under section 12 of the Securities Exchange Act of 1934.

(2) Would you recommend that an issuer receiving a request under this rule follow the procedure set forth in paragraph (c) or in paragraphs (a) and (b)?

(3) Does this rule add significantly to the rights of a shareholder seeking to communicate with the other shareholders?

Chapter Ten

DUTY OF CARE AND THE
BUSINESS JUDGMENT RULE

LITWIN v. ALLEN

Supreme Court of New York, 1940.
25 N.Y.S.2d 667.

SHIENTAG, JUSTICE.

[Editor: This was a derivative suit brought on behalf of persons owning 36 shares of the stock of Guaranty Trust Company ("Trust Company") out of 900,000 outstanding against the directors of Guaranty Trust, members of the banking firm of J.P. Morgan & Co., and directors of a subsidiary of the Trust Company called Guaranty Company of New York ("Guaranty Company."). The complaint sought to impose liability on the defendants for losses incurred as a result of four transactions. The Court concluded that no liability existed for three of the transactions. The portions of the opinion set forth below relate to the Justice's general discussion and the fourth transaction on which liability was imposed. The sequence of the paragraphs set forth below has been rearranged.] * * *

II.

THE MISSOURI PACIFIC BOND TRANSACTION

This transaction involves the participation by the Trust Company or Guaranty Company or both, to the extent of $3,000,000, in a purchase of Missouri Pacific convertible debentures on October 16, 1930, through the firm of J.P. Morgan & Co. at par, with an option to the seller, Alleghany Corporation to repurchase them at the same price at any time within six months.

In the fall of 1930, the question of putting Alleghany Corporation in funds to the extent of $10,500,000 was first broached. Alleghany had purchased certain terminal properties in Kansas City and St. Joseph, Missouri, and the balance of the purchase price, amounting to slightly in excess of $10,000,000 and interest, had to be paid by October

16. Alleghany needed money to make this payment. Because of the borrowing limitation in Alleghany's charter (which limitation had been reached or exceeded in October 1930) Alleghany was unable to borrow the money. To overcome this borrowing limitation and solely to enable Alleghany to consummate the purchase of the terminal properties, discussions were commenced concerning the means whereby the necessary money could be raised. It is important that this circumstance be constantly kept in mind, in order that the purpose and pattern of the transaction as it did take place be fully understood.

Not being able to make a loan, the way that Alleghany could raise the necessary funds was by sale of some of the securities that it held. Among them was a large block of about $23,500,000 of Missouri Pacific convertible 5½% debentures. These were unsecured and subordinate to other Missouri Pacific bond issues. They were convertible into common stock at the rate of ten shares for each $1,000 bond. In 1929, Guaranty Company had participated to the extent of $1,500,000 in the underwriting of these bonds at 97½. At one time in 1929 the bonds had sold as high as 124 and had never gone below par except in November 1929 when they sold at 97. Between October 1 and October 10, 1930 Missouri Pacific common stock had dropped from 53 to 44. There was a decline in the bonds from 113 in April 1930 to 107 on October 1, 1930, and thereafter a decline of about two more points to 105½ by the date of the consummation of the transaction we are considering on October 16, 1930.

The Van Sweringens suggested that $10,000,000 of these bonds be sold to J.P. Morgan & Co. for cash at par, the latter to give an option to Alleghany to buy them back within six months for the price paid. If the transaction were carried through on that basis, namely, a sale by Alleghany with an option to them to repurchase at the same price, the same purpose would be accomplished, for Alleghany at any rate, as if a loan had been made.

The defendants testified that they were informed that the Van Sweringens insisted upon the option to repurchase within six months in order that there might be no possibility of their loss of control of Missouri Pacific through Alleghany, since these bonds were convertible and the privilege to do so might be exercised by third parties in the event of a distribution of these bonds in the market; this, despite the fact that the common stock of Missouri Pacific was then quoted in the neighborhood of 44, while the conversion price was 100.

The fact is that the only purpose served by the option was to make the transaction conform as closely as possible to a loan without the usual incidents of a loan transaction. * * *

At or shortly before the time that the Trust Company made its written commitment to J.P. Morgan & Co. to participate in the bond purchase, the Guaranty Company committed itself to the Trust Company to take up the bonds from the Trust Company at the end of the six-months' period, on April 16, 1931, for the same price that the Trust

Company paid, that is, par and interest, if Alleghany failed to exercise its option to repurchase. * * *

The decline in the market continued. On October 23, 1930, when the Executive Committee of the Trust Company approved the transaction the Missouri Pacific bonds were at 103⅞. On November 5, 1930, when the Board of Directors of the Trust Company gave its approval, the bonds sold for 102⅞, and on November 18, 1930, when the board of the Guaranty Company approved its commitment, the bonds had dropped to 98⅝. At the end of the six months' period, on April 16, 1931, the bonds sold at 86 high and 81 low (the quotations being for the week ending April 18), and Guaranty Company took them over from the Trust Company at par and accrued interest and carried them on its books as an investment. * * *

[T]he main transactions attacked in this case * * * took place in October, 1930. There had been a crash in the stock market in October, 1929. In April, 1930, there was an upswing in the market. Shortly thereafter there began a slow but steady decline until October, 1930, when there was another severe break. The real significance of what was taking place was, generally speaking, missed at the time, but is plain in retrospect. Forces were at work which for the most part were unforeseeable. Men who were judging conditions in October, 1930, by what had been the course and the experience of past panics thought that the bottom had been reached and that the worst of the depression was over; that any change would be for the better and that recovery might reasonably be envisaged for the near future. Experience turned out to be fallacious and judgment proved to be erroneous; but that did not become apparent until some time in 1931. In order to judge the transactions complained of, therefore, we must not only hold an inquest on the past but, what is much more difficult, we must attempt to take ourselves back to the time when the events here questioned occurred and try to put ourselves in the position of those who engaged in them. * * *

There is no evidence in this case of any improper influence or domination of the directors or officers of the Trust Company or of the Guaranty Company by J.P. Morgan & Co. When J.P. Morgan & Co. were advised by Shriver that there would be a participation in the purchase to the extent of $5,000,000 the latter was told that such a commitment would be accepted only to the extent of $3,000,000 because the First National Bank of New York would be given a similar amount while Morgan & Co. themselves would participate to the extent of the balance amounting to $4,500,000. Moreover, there is no evidence to indicate that any of the defendants' officers or directors acted in bad faith or profited or attempted to profit or gain personally by reason of any phase of this transaction. * * *

I shall now proceed to consider generally the rules to be applied in determining the liability of directors. It has sometimes been said that directors are trustees. If this means that directors in the performance of their duties stand in a fiduciary relationship to the company, that statement is essentially correct. Bosworth v. Allen, 168 N.Y. 157, 61 N.E. 163, 55 L.R.A. 751, 85 Am.St.Rep. 667. "The directors are bound by all those rules of conscientious fairness, morality, and honesty in purpose which the law imposes as the guides for those who are under the fiduciary obligations and responsibilities. They are held, in official action, to the extreme measure of candor, unselfishness, and good faith. Those principles are rigid, essential, and salutary." Kavanaugh v. Kavanaugh Knitting Co., 226 N.Y. 185, 193, 123 N.E. 148, 151.

It is clear that a director owes loyalty and allegiance to the company—a loyalty that is undivided and an allegiance that is influenced in action by no consideration other than the welfare of the corporation. Any adverse interest of a director will be subjected to a scrutiny rigid and uncompromising. He may not profit at the expense of his corporation and in conflict with its rights; he may not for personal gain divert unto himself the opportunities which in equity and fairness belong to his corporation. He is required to use his independent judgment. In the discharge of his duties a director must, of course, act honestly and in good faith, but that is not enough. He must also exercise some degree of skill and prudence and diligence.

In a leading case the Court of Appeals, in referring to the duties of directors, said: "They should know of and give direction to the general affairs of the institution and its business policy, and have a general knowledge of the manner in which the business is conducted, the character of the investments, and the employment of the resources. No custom or practice can make a directorship a mere position of honor void of responsibility, or cause a name to become a substitute for care and attention. The personnel of a directorate may give confidence and attract custom; it must also afford protection." Kavanaugh v. Commonwealth Trust Co., 223 N.Y. 103, 106, 119 N.E. 237, 238.

In other words, directors are liable for negligence in the performance of their duties. Not being insurers, directors are not liable for errors of judgment or for mistakes while acting with reasonable skill and prudence. It has been said that a director is required to conduct the business of the corporation with the same degree of fidelity and care as an ordinarily prudent man would exercise in the management of his own affairs of like magnitude and importance. General rules, however, are not altogether helpful. In the last analysis, whether or not a director has discharged his duty, whether or not he has been negligent, depends upon the facts and circumstances of a particular case, the kind of corporation involved, its size and financial resources, the magnitude of the transaction, and the immediacy of the problem presented. A director is called upon "to bestow the care and skill" which the situation demands. New York Cent. Railroad Company v. Lockwood, 17 Wall. 357, 382, 383, 21 L.Ed. 627.

Undoubtedly, a director of a bank is held to stricter accountability than the director of an ordinary business corporation. A director of a bank is entrusted with the funds of depositors, and the stockholders look to him for protection from the imposition of personal liability. Gause v. Commonwealth Trust Co., 196 N.Y. 134, 153–155, 89 N.E. 476, 24 L.R.A., N.S., 967. But clairvoyance is not required even of a bank director. The law recognizes that the most conservative director is not infallible, and that he will make mistakes, but if he uses that degree of care ordinarily exercised by prudent bankers he will be absolved from liability although his opinion may turn out to have been mistaken and his judgment faulty.

Finally, in order to determine whether transactions approved by a director subject him to liability for negligence, we must "look at the facts as they exist at the time of their occurrence, not aided or enlightened by those which subsequently take place". Purdy v. Lynch, 145 N.Y. 462, 475, 40 N.E. 232, 236. "A wisdom developed after an event, and having it and its consequences as a source, is a standard no man should be judged by." Costello v. Costello, 209 N.Y. 252, 262, 103 N.E. 148, 152.   *   *   *

Although * * * there is no case precisely in point, it would seem that if it is against public policy for a bank, anxious to dispose of some of its securities, to agree to buy them back at the same price, it is even more so where a bank purchases securities and gives the seller the option to buy them back at the same price, thereby incurring the entire risk of loss with no possibility of gain other than the interest derived from the securities during the period that the bank holds them. Here, if the market price of the securities should rise, the holder of the repurchase option would exercise it in order to recover his securities from the bank at the lower price at which he sold them to the bank. If the market price should fall, the seller holding the option will not exercise it and the bank will sustain the loss. Thus, any benefit of a sharp rise in the price of the securities is assured the seller and any risk of heavy loss is inevitably assumed by the bank. If such an option agreement as is here involved were sustained, it would force the bank to set aside for six months whatever securities it had purchased. A bank certainly could not free itself from this obligation by engaging in a "short sale". In other words, while a resale option would force a bank to freeze an amount of cash equal to the selling price of the securities sold by it, a repurchase option would force a bank to freeze the securities themselves for the period of the option. In both situations the true financial condition of the bank could not be determined wholly from its books. It would depend upon the fluctuations of the market. In both cases there is a contingent liability which the balance sheet does not show.   *   *   *

Directors are not in the position of trustees of an express trust who, regardless of good faith, are personally liable for losses arising from an infraction of their trust deed. Matter of Smith, 279 N.Y. 479, 489, 18 N.E.2d 666; see Fletcher Cyc. Corp., Perm.Ed., § 847. If liability is to be imposed on these directors it should rest on a more solid foundation.

I find liability in this transaction because the entire arrangement was so improvident, so risky, so unusual and unnecessary as to be contrary to fundamental conceptions of prudent banking practice. A bank director when appointed or elected takes oath that he will, so far as the duty devolves on him "diligently and honestly administer the affairs of the bank or trust company." Banking Law, § 117. The oath merely adds solemnity to the obligation which the law itself imposes. Honesty alone does not suffice; the honesty of the directors in this case is unquestioned. But there must be more than honesty—there must be diligence, and that means care and prudence, as well. This transaction, it has been said, was unusual; it was unique, yet there is nothing in the record to indicate that the advice of counsel was sought. It is not surprising that a precedent cannot be found dealing with such a situation.

What sound reason is there for a bank, desiring to make an investment, short term or otherwise, to buy securities under an arrangement whereby any appreciation will inure to the benefit of the seller and any loss will be borne by the bank? The five and one-half point differential is no answer. It does not meet the fundamental objection that whatever loss there is would have to be borne by the Bank and whatever gain would go to the customer. There is more here than a question of business judgment as to which men might well differ. The directors plainly failed in this instance to bestow the care which the situation demanded. Unless we are to do away entirely with the doctrine that directors of a bank are liable for negligence in administering its affairs liability should be imposed in connection with this transaction.

The same result would be reached if we adopted the defendants' version of this transaction, namely, that it was initially a purchase by the Guaranty Company, with an option to the Alleghany Corporation to rebuy at the same price, and that the transaction was financed by the Bank, so that the immediate interest that the Bank had in it was a short term 5½% investment. * * *

Whichever way we look at this transaction, therefore, it was so improvident, so dangerous, so unusual and so contrary to ordinary prudent banking practice as to subject the directors who approved it to liability in a derivative stockholders' action.

Having determined that the transaction in litigation is such as to impose liability upon the participating defendants, the next question is what part of the loss can be attributed to the improper transaction? The defendants argue that if the option agreement was ultra vires, the Bank was free to sell the bonds at any time because it was not under any enforceable legal obligation to resell them to the Alleghany Corporation. Therefore defendants assert that no liability attaches since there is no direct causal connection between the option and the loss. Moreover, it was suggested by one of the witnesses that what he called a "forward sale" of a corresponding block of bonds might have been made for protection, if there had been any thought of possible loss. That would hardly have been the kind of transaction for the Trust Company or its wholly owned subsidiary to have made. Be that as it may, it is clear that the defendants never considered selling the bonds during the six months option period, but instead, they held them because of and in reliance on the repurchase option. If this were not so, how can the Guaranty Company's agreement to take over the bonds from the Trust Company at the end of six months if Alleghany failed to exercise its option, be explained? The Company in fact did take over the bonds from the Bank in April 1931, in accordance with this agreement. The defendants cannot now say that the Bank's holding of the bonds for six months had no relation to the repurchase option and the Company's agreement with the Bank. Clearly, whatever loss was occasioned during this six months period is directly attributable to the option agreement, and the participating defendants are liable therefor.

The real issue as to damages is whether the directors should be liable for the total loss suffered when the bonds were ultimately sold, approximately an 81% loss, or only for that portion of the loss which accrued within the six months option period, making allowance for a period thereafter during which defendants could make reasonable and diligent efforts to sell the bonds. The record discloses that none of the bonds were sold until October 8, 1931, about six months after the Alleghany option had expired, and that they were not completely disposed of until December 28, 1937. The Missouri Pacific Railroad went into receivership in April, 1933, and between August 2 and September 25, 1933, $126,000 more of the bonds were purchased by the Company in an attempt to reduce the loss. A total loss was sustained on the bonds of approximately $2,250,000.

I believe that as to the decline of the bonds after April 16, 1931, there is no causal connection with the option which had expired on that date. A director is not liable for loss or damage other than what was proximately caused by his own acts or omissions in breach of his duty. The portion of the present transaction which is tainted with improvidence and negligence is the repurchase option. Once the option had expired, there was nothing to prevent the directors of the Company, which had taken over the bonds in accordance with its agreement, from selling them. Any loss on the bonds which was incurred after the option had expired on April 16, 1931, was occasioned as a result of the directors' independent business judgment in holding them thereafter. The further loss should not be laid at the door of the improper but already expired repurchase option.

Therefore, defendants are only liable for the loss attributable to the improper repurchase option itself, and this option ceased to be the motivating cause of the loss within a reasonable time after April 16, 1931. The price of the bonds for the week ending April 18, 1931, was 86 high and 81 low and closing. The matter will be referred to a Referee for assessment of damages to determine what price could have been obtained for these bonds if defendants had proceeded to sell them after April 16, 1931.

DEFENDANTS CHARGED WITH LIABILITY

The next question to consider is: Against what defendants has liability been established?

1. All of the directors who were present and voted at the meetings of the Executive Committee of the Trust Company on October 23, 1930, and the meeting of the Board of Directors of the Trust Company on November 5, 1930, are liable.

After the transaction was consummated by the officers on October 16, 1930, it was submitted to the Executive Committee meeting of the Trust Company for approval. The report to that committee, which was approved, merely recited an investment in the Missouri Pacific bonds, with the notation "Repurchase Agreement". Mr. Potter testified that "in accordance with my universal custom, when reporting these loans to the executive committee, that I did so report this option agreement with respect to the Van Sweringen's repurchase option". When asked if it was his distinct recollection that the committee was so informed, he replied: "That is my belief". He further testified that he did not believe he had withheld the information from the directors.

In the absence of contrary evidence, Potter's testimony must be accepted, although he used the term "belief" instead of "recollection". Furthermore, the Executive Committee knew of the option agreement at the October 27th meeting because each member had received a memorandum prepared by Shriver in which the option was specifically mentioned. None expressed any surprise at the information in this memorandum.

On November 5, 1930, the Board of Directors of the Trust Company approved the action of the Executive Committee meeting of October 23rd. Mr. Conway, who attended that meeting, was asked whether the directors were advised of the full details of the transaction and answered: "I believe they were advised." Here again, in the absence of contrary evidence, we must accept Conway's testimony. Had the contrary been the fact it would have been a simple matter for defendants to call a witness so to testify.

Therefore, all of the defendants who were members of the Executive Committee and of the Board of the Trust Company, and who voted approval at the meetings referred to, had knowledge of the transaction and having ratified it are liable therefor. Kavanaugh v. Commonwealth Trust Co., 223 N.Y. 103, 112, 119 N.E. 237. Furthermore, ratification by directors of a transaction already consummated by the officers or by themselves acting as officers imposes liability upon the directors, since the ratification is equivalent to prior acquiescence. Fletcher, Cyc.Corp., Perm.Ed., § 782, and cases there collected. Ratification of the officer's acts was essential in order completely to bind the Bank and the Company, and in any case such ratification vitiated a possible later rescission on the ground that it was not authorized by the directors.

2. Mr. Swan is liable even though he did not actually vote on the transaction as a director. His active participation and acquiescence are sufficient.

3. The defendants Kimball, Shriver and Stephenson while not directors are liable as officers who actively participated in the transaction.

4. No director of the Guaranty Company, as such, except Walker, is liable. He admittedly knew of the transaction, but there is nothing in the record to show that the repurchase option was brought to the attention of the directors at the meeting of the Executive Committee or of the Board of Directors of Guaranty Company. * * *

SHLENSKY v. WRIGLEY

Appellate Court of Illinois, 1968.
95 Ill.App.2d 173, 237 N.E.2d 776.

SULLIVAN, JUSTICE.

This is an appeal from a dismissal of plaintiff's amended complaint on motion of the defendants. The action was a stockholders' derivative suit against the directors for negligence and mismanagement. The corporation was also made a defendant. Plaintiff sought damages and an order that defendants cause the installation of lights in Wrigley Field and the scheduling of night baseball games.

Plaintiff is a minority stockholder of defendant corporation, Chicago National League Ball Club (Inc.), a Delaware corporation with its principal place of business in Chicago, Illinois. Defendant corporation owns and operates the major league professional baseball team known as the Chicago Cubs. The corporation also engages in the operation of Wrigley Field, the Cubs' home park, the concessionaire sales during Cubs' home games, television and radio broadcasts of Cubs' home games, the leasing of the field for football games and other events and receives its share, as visiting team, of admission moneys from games played in other National League stadia. The individual defendants are directors of the Cubs and have served for varying periods of years. Defendant Philip K. Wrigley is also president of the corporation and owner of approximately 80% of the stock therein.

Plaintiff alleges that since night baseball was first played in 1935 nineteen of the twenty major league teams have scheduled night games. In 1966, out of a total of 1620 games in the major leagues, 932 were played at night. Plaintiff alleges that every member of the major leagues, other than the Cubs, scheduled substantially all of its home games in 1966 at night, exclusive of opening days, Saturdays, Sundays, holidays and days prohibited by league rules. Allegedly this has been done for the specific purpose of maximizing attendance and thereby maximizing revenue and income.

The Cubs, in the years 1961–65, sustained operating losses from its direct baseball operations. Plaintiff attributes those losses to inadequate attendance at Cubs' home games. He concludes that if the directors continue to refuse to install lights at Wrigley Field and schedule night baseball games, the Cubs will continue to sustain comparable losses and its financial condition will continue to deteriorate.

Plaintiff alleges that, except for the year 1963, attendance at Cubs' home games has been substantially below that at their road games, many of which were played at night.

Plaintiff compares attendance at Cubs' games with that of the Chicago White Sox, an American League club, whose weekday games were generally played at night. The weekend attendance figures for the two teams was similar; however, the White Sox week-night games drew many more patrons than did the Cubs' weekday games.

Plaintiff alleges that the funds for the installation of lights can be readily obtained through financing and the cost of installation would be far more than offset and recaptured by increased revenues and incomes resulting from the increased attendance.

Plaintiff further alleges that defendant Wrigley has refused to install lights, not because of interest in the welfare of the corporation but because of his personal opinions "that baseball is a 'daytime sport' and that the installation of lights and night baseball games will have a deteriorating effect upon the surrounding neighborhood." It is alleged that he has admitted that he is not interested in whether the Cubs would benefit financially from such action because of his concern for the neighborhood, and that he would be willing for the team to play night games if a new stadium were built in Chicago.

Plaintiff alleges that the other defendant directors, with full knowledge of the foregoing matters, have acquiesced in the policy laid down by Wrigley and have permitted him to dominate the board of directors in matters involving the installation of lights and scheduling of night games, even though they knew he was not motivated by a good faith concern as to the best interests of defendant corporation, but solely by his personal views set forth above. It is charged that the directors are acting for a reason or reasons contrary and wholly unrelated to the business interests of the corporation; that such arbitrary and capricious acts constitute mismanagement and waste of corporate assets, and that the directors have been negligent in failing to exercise reasonable care and prudence in the management of the corporate affairs.

The question on appeal is whether plaintiff's amended complaint states a cause of action. It is plaintiff's position that fraud, illegality and conflict of interest are not the only bases for a stockholder's derivative action against the directors. Contrariwise, defendants argue that the courts will not step in and interfere with honest business judgment of the directors unless there is a showing of fraud, illegality or conflict of interest.

The cases in this area are numerous and each differs from the others on a factual basis. However, the courts have pronounced certain ground rules which appear in all cases and which are then applied to the given factual situation. The court in Wheeler v. Pullman Iron and Steel Company, 143 Ill. 197, 207, 32 N.E. 420, 423, said:

"It is, however, fundamental in the law of corporations, that the majority of its stockholders shall control the policy of the corporation, and regulate and govern the lawful exercise of its franchise and business. * * * Every one purchasing or subscribing for stock in a corporation impliedly agrees that he will be bound by the acts and proceedings done or sanctioned by a majority of the shareholders, or by the agents of the corporation duly chosen by such majority, within the scope of the powers conferred by the charter, and courts of equity will not undertake to control the policy or business methods of a corporation, although it may be seen that a wiser policy might be adopted and the business more successful if other methods were pursued. The majority of shares of its stock, or the agents by the holders thereof lawfully chosen, must be permitted to control the business of the corporation in their discretion, when not in violation of its charter or some public law, or corruptly and fraudulently subversive of the rights and interests of the corporation or of a shareholder."

The standards set in Delaware are also clearly stated in the cases. In Davis v. Louisville Gas & Electric Co., 16 Del.Ch. 157, 142 A. 654, a minority shareholder sought to have the directors enjoined from amending the certificate of incorporation. The court said on page 659:

"We have then a conflict in view between the responsible managers of a corporation and an overwhelming majority of its stockholders on the one hand and a dissenting minority on the other—a conflict touching matters of business policy, such as has occasioned innumerable applications to courts to intervene and determine which of the two conflicting views should prevail. The response which courts make to such applications is that it is not their function to resolve for corporations questions of policy and business management. The directors are chosen to pass upon such questions and their judgment *unless shown to be tainted with fraud* is accepted as final. The judgment of the directors of corporations enjoys the benefit of a presumption that it was formed in good faith and was designed to promote the best interests of the corporation they serve." (Emphasis supplied) * * *

Plaintiff argues that the allegations of his amended complaint are sufficient to set forth a cause of action under the principles set out in Dodge v. Ford Motor Co., 204 Mich. 459, 170 N.W. 668. In that case plaintiff, owner of about 10% of the outstanding stock, brought suit against the directors seeking payment of additional dividends and the enjoining of further business expansion. In ruling on the request for dividends the court indicated that the motives of Ford in keeping so much money in the corporation for expansion and security were to benefit the public generally and spread the profits out by means of more jobs, etc. The court felt that these were not only far from related to the good of the stockholders, but amounted to a change in the ends of the corporation and that this was not a purpose contemplated or allowed by the corporate charter. The court relied on language found in Hunter v. Roberts, Thorp & Co., 83 Mich. 63, 47 N.W. 131, 134, wherein it was said:

> "Courts of equity will not interfere in the management of the directors unless it is clearly made to appear that they are guilty of fraud or misappropriation of the corporate funds, or refuse to declare a dividend when the corporation has a surplus of net profits which it can, without detriment to its business, divide among its stockholders, and when a refusal to do so would amount to such an abuse of discretion as would constitute a fraud or breach of that good faith which they are bound to exercise toward the stockholders."

From the authority relied upon in that case it is clear that the court felt that there must be fraud or a breach of that good faith which directors are bound to exercise toward the stockholders in order to justify the courts entering into the internal affairs of corporations. This is made clear when the court refused to interfere with the directors' decision to expand the business. The following appears on page 684 of 170 N.W.:

> "We are not, however, persuaded that we should interfere with the proposed expansion of the business of the Ford Motor Company. In view of the fact that the selling price of products may be increased at any time, the ultimate results of the larger business cannot be certainly estimated. *The judges are not business experts.* It is recognized that plans must often be made for a long future, for expected competition, for a continuing as well as an immediately profitable venture. * * * We are not satisfied that the alleged motives of the directors, in so far as they are reflected in the conduct of business, menace the interests of the shareholders." (Emphasis supplied)

Plaintiff in the instant case argues that the directors are acting for reasons unrelated to the financial interest and welfare of the Cubs. However, we are not satisfied that the motives assigned to Philip K. Wrigley, and through him to the other directors, are contrary to the best interests of the corporation and the stockholders. For example, it appears to us that the effect on the surrounding neighborhood might well be considered by a director who was considering the patrons who would or would not attend the games if the park were in a poor neighborhood. Furthermore, the long run interest of the corporation in its property value at Wrigley Field might demand all efforts to keep the neighborhood from deteriorating. By these thoughts we do not mean to say that we have decided that the decision of the directors was a correct one. That is beyond our jurisdiction and ability. We are merely saying that the decision is one properly before directors and the motives alleged in the amended complaint showed no fraud, illegality or conflict of interest in their making of that decision.

While all the courts do not insist that one or more of the three elements must be present for a stockholder's derivative action to lie, nevertheless we feel that unless the conduct of the defendants at least borders on one of the elements, the courts should not interfere. The trial court in the instant case acted properly in dismissing plaintiff's amended complaint.

We feel that plaintiff's amended complaint was also defective in failing to allege damage to the corporation.   *   *   *

There is no allegation that the night games played by the other nineteen teams enhanced their financial position or that the profits, if any, of those teams were directly related to the number of night games scheduled. There is an allegation that the installation of lights and scheduling of night games in Wrigley Field would have resulted in large amounts of additional revenues and incomes from increased attendance and related sources of income. Further, the cost of installation of lights, funds for which are allegedly readily available by financing, would be more than offset and recaptured by increased revenues. However, no allegation is made that there will be a net benefit to the corporation from such action, considering all increased costs.

Plaintiff claims that the losses of defendant corporation are due to poor attendance at home games. However, it appears from the amended complaint, taken as a whole, that factors other than attendance affect the net earnings or losses. For example, in 1962, attendance at home and road games decreased appreciably as compared with 1961, and yet the loss from direct baseball operation and of the whole corporation was considerably less.

The record shows that plaintiff did not feel he could allege that the increased revenues would be sufficient to cure the corporate deficit. The only cost plaintiff was at all concerned with was that of installation of lights. No mention was made of operation and maintenance of the lights or other possible increases in operating costs of night games and we cannot speculate as to what other factors might influence the increase or decrease of profits if the Cubs were to play night home games.   *   *   *

Finally, we do not agree with plaintiff's contention that failure to follow the example of the other major league clubs in scheduling night games constituted negligence. Plaintiff made no allegation that these teams' night schedules were profitable or that the purpose for which night baseball had been undertaken was fulfilled. Furthermore, it cannot be said that directors, even those of corporations that are losing money, must follow the lead of the other corporations in the field. Directors are elected for their business capabilities and judgment and the courts cannot require them to forego their judgment because of the decisions of directors of other companies. Courts may not decide these questions in the absence of a clear showing of dereliction of duty on the part of the specific directors and mere failure to "follow the crowd" is not such a dereliction.

For the foregoing reasons the order of dismissal entered by the trial court is affirmed.

Affirmed.

Notes

(1) Justice Shientag comments in *Litwin* that a higher standard of care is required of bank directors than of general business corporations. Is that suggested distinction justifiable?

(a) Most of the early cases in which directoral liability was imposed do involve bank directors. A good example is Bates v. Dresser, 251 U.S. 524, 40 S.Ct. 247, 64 L.Ed. 388 (1920). In this case, a bank president who was also a director was held liable for the amount stolen by one Coleman, a young bookkeeper at the bank. Mr. Justice Holmes explains:

> The position of the president is different. Practically he was the master of the situation. He was daily at the bank for hours, he had the deposit ledger in his hands at times and might have had it at any time. He had had hints and warnings in addition to those that we have mentioned, warnings that should not be magnified unduly, but still that taken with the auditor's report of 1903, the unexplained shortages, the suggestion of the teller, Cutting, in 1905, and the final seeming rapid decline in deposits, would have induced scrutiny but for an invincible repose upon the *status quo*. In 1908 one Fillmore learned that a package containing $150 left with the bank for safe keeping was not to be found, told Dresser of the loss, wrote to him that he could but conclude that the package had been destroyed or removed by someone connected with the bank, and in later conversation said that it was evident that there was a thief in the bank. He added that he would advise the president to look after Coleman, that he believed he was living at a pretty fast pace, and that he had pretty good authority for thinking that he was supporting a woman. In the same year or the year before, Coleman, whose pay was never more than twelve dollars a week, set up an automobile, as was known to Dresser and commented on unfavorably, to him. There was also some evidence of notice to Dresser that Coleman was dealing in copper stocks. In 1909 came the great and inadequately explained seeming shrinkage in the deposits. No doubt plausible explanations of his conduct came from Coleman and the notice as to speculations may have been slight, but taking the whole story of the relations of the parties, we are not ready to say that the two courts below erred in finding that Dresser had been put upon his guard. However little the warnings may have pointed to the specific facts, had they been accepted they would have led to an examination of the depositors' ledger, a discovery of past and a prevention of future thefts.

251 U.S. at 530–531, 40 S.Ct. at 249–250. The other directors were held not liable, since they reasonably relied on bank examinations and the president. The thefts in this case were reasonably well hidden.

(b) At least one case has held that under California law the standard for directors of financial institutions is the same as for directors of business corporations generally, namely "that degree of care that men of common prudence take of their own concerns." McDonnell v. American Leduc Petroleums, Ltd., 491 F.2d 380, 383 (2d Cir.1974).

(c) Bishop, Sitting Ducks and Decoy Ducks: New Trends in the Indemnification of Corporate Directors and Officers, 77 Yale L.J. 1078, 1099 (1968): *

> The search for cases in which directors of industrial corporations have been held liable in derivative suits for negligence uncomplicated by self-dealing is a search for a very small number of needles in a very large haystack. Few are the cases in which the stockholders do not allege conflict of interest, still fewer those among them which achieve even such partial success as denial of the defendants' motion to dismiss the complaint. Still, it cannot be denied that there is a small number of relatively recent cases which do seem to lend a modicum of substance to the fears of directors of industrial or mercantile corporations that they may be stuck for what they like to call "mere" or "honest" negligence. My own collection, based on extensive (although not exhaustive) investigation, includes four such specimens. * * *

However, Professor Bishop adds that none of these cases carry "real conviction," and that therefore there is in fact "little precedent for liability even for the kind of Merovingian supineness for which directors were held liable in the old bank cases." 77 Yale L.J., at 1100, 1101.

(2) In Francis v. United Jersey Bank, 87 N.J. 15, 432 A.2d 814 (1981), the sons of the founder of a corporation, an "insurance reinsurance" business, siphoned large sums of money from the corporation in the form of "shareholder loans" and other improper payments to family members. These distributions were reflected on the financial statements of the corporation as "shareholders loans." As a result of these transactions, the corporation became insolvent and the bankruptcy trustee brought suit against the widow of the founder for more than $10,000,000, representing funds transferred unlawfully from the firm to the family members while she was a director of the company. The court described the conduct of the defendant as follows:

> Mrs. Pritchard was not active in the business of Pritchard & Baird and knew virtually nothing of its corporate affairs. She briefly visited the corporate offices in Morristown on only one occasion, and she never read or obtained the annual financial statements. She was unfamiliar with the rudiments of reinsurance and made no effort to assure that the policies and practices of the corporation, particularly pertaining to the withdrawal of funds, complied with industry custom or relevant law. Although her husband had warned her that Charles, Jr. would "take the shirt off my back," Mrs. Pritchard did not pay any attention to her duties as a director or to the affairs of the corporation.

> After her husband died in December 1973, Mrs. Pritchard became incapacitated and was bedridden for a six-month period. She became listless at this time and started to drink rather heavily. Her physical

* Reprinted by permission of the Yale Law Journal Company and Fred B. Rothman & Company from the Yale Law Journal, Vol. 77, p. 1099.

condition deteriorated, and in 1978 she died. The trial court rejected testimony seeking to exonerate her because she "was old, was grief-stricken at the loss of her husband, sometimes consumed too much alcohol and was psychologically overborne by her sons." 162 N.J. Super. at 371, 392 A.2d 1233. That court found that she was competent to act and that the reason Mrs. Pritchard never knew what her sons "were doing was because she never made the slightest effort to discharge any of her responsibilities as a director of Pritchard & Baird." 162 N.J.Super. at 372, 392 A.2d 1233.

432 A.2d, at 819–820. The court stated that "directors are under a continuing obligation to keep informed about the activities of the corporation," that "while directors are not required to audit corporate books, they should maintain familiarity with the financial status of the corporation by a regular review of financial statements," and that "a director is not an ornament, but an essential component of corporate governance, * * * [and] cannot protect himself behind a paper shield bearing the motto, 'dummy director'." 432 A.2d at 822, 823. A judgment against the estate of the director was affirmed:

As a director of a substantial reinsurance brokerage corporation, she should have known that it received annually millions of dollars of loss and premium funds which it held in trust for ceding and reinsurance companies. Mrs. Pritchard should have obtained and read the annual statements of financial condition of Pritchard & Baird. Although she had a right to rely upon financial statements prepared in accordance with N.J.S.A. 14A:6–14, such reliance would not excuse her conduct. The reason is that those statements disclosed on their face the misappropriation of trust funds.

From those statements, she should have realized that, as of January 31, 1970, her sons were withdrawing substantial trust funds under the guise of "Shareholders' Loans." The financial statements for each fiscal year commencing with that of January 31, 1970, disclosed that the working capital deficits and the "loans" were escalating in tandem. Detecting a misappropriation of funds would not have required special expertise or extraordinary diligence; a cursory reading of the financial statements would have revealed the pillage. Thus, if Mrs. Pritchard had read the financial statements, she would have known that her sons were converting trust funds. When financial statements demonstrate that insiders are bleeding a corporation to death, a director should notice and try to stanch the flow of blood.

In summary, Mrs. Pritchard was charged with the obligation of basic knowledge and supervision of the business of Pritchard & Baird. Under the circumstances, this obligation included reading and understanding financial statements, and making reasonable attempts at detection and prevention of the illegal conduct of other officers and directors. She had a duty to protect the clients of Pritchard & Baird against policies and practices that would result in the misappropriation of money they had entrusted to the corporation. She breached that duty. * * *

Nonetheless, the negligence of Mrs. Pritchard does not result in liability unless it is a proximate cause of the loss.   *   *   *

Within Pritchard & Baird, several factors contributed to the loss of the funds: commingling of corporate and client monies, conversion of funds by Charles, Jr. and William and dereliction of her duties by Mrs. Pritchard. The wrongdoing of her sons, although the immediate cause of the loss, should not excuse Mrs. Pritchard from her negligence which also was a substantial factor contributing to the loss. Her sons knew that she, the only other director, was not reviewing their conduct; they spawned their fraud in the backwater of her neglect. Her neglect of duty contributed to the climate of corruption; her failure to act contributed to the continuation of that corruption. Consequently, her conduct was a substantial factor contributing to the loss.

Analysis of proximate cause is especially difficult in a corporate context where the allegation is that nonfeasance of a director is a proximate cause of damage to a third party. Where a case involves nonfeasance, no one can say "with absolute certainty what would have occurred if the defendant had acted otherwise." [W. Prosser, Law of Torts,] § 41 [(4th Ed.1971)] at 242. Nonetheless, where it is reasonable to conclude that the failure to act would produce a particular result and that result has followed, causation may be inferred. Ibid. We conclude that even if Mrs. Pritchard's mere objection had not stopped the depredations of her sons, her consultation with an attorney and the threat of suit would have deterred them. That conclusion flows as a matter of common sense and logic from the record. Whether in other situations a director has a duty to do more than protest and resign is best left to case-by-case determinations. In this case, we are satisfied that there was a duty to do more than object and resign. Consequently, we find that Mrs. Pritchard's negligence was a proximate cause of the misappropriations.

(3) Consider RMBCA § 8.30(a). This is obviously traditional language of "due care." Is it appropriate language to define the duty of due care in connection with duties of directors? One can usefully talk about "the care an ordinarily prudent person in a like position would exercise under similar circumstances" in a variety of ordinary-life situations, such as driving an automobile, felling trees, and the like. One can also conclude that Mrs. Pritchard's behavior did not constitute "due care" under the circumstances. But does the same standard have meaning in the more rarified world of directors of large publicly held corporations, acting in the melieu described by Manning (p. 602, supra)? Do the "similar circumstances" involve persons acting on other boards of directors? Is the "ordinarily prudent person" an "average Joe" in the United States, with an average IQ and whose formal education ended at high school?

Section 8.30(a) was taken directly from MBCA (1969 Ed.) § 35, added in 1974, after an extended discussion. This language is a distillate of the language adopted in several states, including New York and New Jersey. The Official Comment to § 8.30(a) expands somewhat on the meaning of these words:

Several of the phrases chosen to define the general standard of care in section 8.30(a) deserve specific mention:

(1) The reference to "ordinarily prudent person" embodies long traditions of the common law, in contrast to suggested standards that might call for some undefined degree of expertise, like "ordinarily prudent businessman." The phrase recognizes the need for innovation, essential to profit orientation, and focuses on the basic director attributes of common sense, practical wisdom, and informed judgment.

(2) The phrase "in a like position" recognizes that the "care" under consideration is that which would be used by the "ordinarily prudent person" if he were a director of the particular corporation.

(3) The combined phrase "in a like position * * * under similar circumstances" is intended to recognize that (a) the nature and extent of responsibilities will vary, depending upon such factors as the size, complexity, urgency, and location of activities carried on by the particular corporation, (b) decisions must be made on the basis of the information known to the directors without the benefit of hindsight, and (c) the special background, qualifications, and management responsibilities of a particular director may be relevant in evaluating his compliance with the standard of care. Even though the quoted phrase takes into account the special background, qualifications and management responsibilities of a particular director, it does not excuse a director lacking business experience or particular expertise from exercising the common sense, practical wisdom, and informed judgment of an "ordinarily prudent person."

(4) Consider Hansen, The ALI Corporate Governance Project: Of the Duty of Due Care and the Business Judgment Rule, 41 Bus.Law. 1237, 1238–42, 1247 (1986):*

[T]he Model Business Corporation Act, adopted by a number of states, contains an important section on directors' duties that, while supportable by dicta, does not reflect case holdings. * * *

The foundation stone of the American law of corporate governance is currently enunciated in the holdings (not the dicta) of the leading corporate law states: there must be a minimum of interference by the courts in internal corporate affairs. Except in the egregious case of bad judgment or when there is evidence of bad faith, courts have made no attempt to second-guess directors on the substantive soundness of decisions reached. The courts have assiduously sought to keep hands off the powerful yet delicate mechanism of corporate wealth production at the core of our economic well-being. * * *

The applicable duty as applied by the courts to a director's decision is intimately linked to, and limited by, the "business judgment rule," a doctrine limiting the liability of a director in the good faith pursuit of one's duties. Under that rule, as long as a director acts in good faith and with due care in the process sense, the director will not be found liable even though the decision itself was not that of the "ordinarily prudent person." The process due care test will be met if the director takes appropriate steps to become informed. Thus, the description of the duty in section 4.01(a) [of the ALI Corporate Governance Project] as "the care that an ordinarily prudent person would reasonably be expected to exercise in a like position and under similar circumstances" is misleading.

To focus the problem, can it be argued seriously that the director's decisions are to be judged against the standard of section 4.01(a)? If it can be established that the director's decision was not the decision of "an ordinarily prudent person . . . in a like position . . . under similar circumstances," will that director be liable for failure to use "due care"? The answer is obviously no, since the cases are legion, holding that under the business judgment rule a director's conduct is not to be so measured. *Cramer v. General Telephone & Electronics Corp.*, for example, states the appropriate principle of law: "Absent bad faith or some other corrupt motive, directors are normally not liable to the corporation for mistakes of judgment. . . ." [1] * * *

A careful reading of the cases illustrates the substantial difference between applying the due care test in tort law and the standard actually employed by the courts in reaching decisions under corporate law. In tort law, the due care standard is results oriented; that is, whether or not the acts of the director measure up to the behavior of the so-called reasonable person under the same or similar circumstances, in effect the test of section 4.01(a).

In contrast, under corporate law, the standard of due care is met if two tests are satisfied: (i) due care must be used in "ascertaining relevant facts and law before making the decision," and (ii) the decision must be made after reasonable deliberation. * * * Thus, the due care standard in corporate law is applied to the decision-making process and not to its result. Even though a decision made or a result reached is not that of the hypothetical ordinarily prudent person, no liability will attach as long as the decision-making process meets the standard. * * *

The one possible exception to applying the standard of due care to process, rather than to content or result, concerns egregious conduct. In a few outrageous cases, the objective reasonableness of a particular business judgment may be important. Thus, if the court finds the judgment itself "grossly unsound," "a gross abuse of discretion," one which would have been reached by "no person of sound ordinary business judgment," "so unwise or unreasonable as to fall outside the permissible bounds of the directors' sound discretion," or "an abuse of discretion," and "egregious," the directors will not meet the standards of the business judgment rule. * * * In the non-decision-making context, or when the director is not exercising business judgment, an

1. [By the Author] 582 F.2d 259, 274 (3d Cir.1978).

ordinarily prudent person due care formulation is closer to reality. Absent the affirmative exercise of business judgment, the business judgment rule and the necessary limitations it imposes on the duty of care do not apply.

Even in a non-decision-making context, however, the required due care standard would appear to be less stringent than that which "an ordinarily prudent person would reasonably be expected to exercise in a like position under similar circumstances." While it is true that this so-called traditional language appears in the cases, a careful examination of the facts of the cases and the holdings based thereon yields a different result. Using such an analysis, it would appear that directors have been found liable only in the non-decision-making context upon obvious and prolonged failure to exercise oversight or supervision.

A typical case is *Francis v. United Jersey Bank.*   *   *   *

(5) Does Hansen's analysis explain Litwin v. Allen? Shlensky v. Wrigley? Francis v. United Jersey Bank?

(6) All modern authorities recognize that the "business judgment rule" summarized briefly by Hansen (and the subject of the following principal case) is a major qualification to the sparse language of due care in § 8.30 of the RMBCA and the nearly equivalent language of § 4.01(a) of the Corporate Governance Project. Accepting this, shouldn't the text of § 8.30 give at least some minimal legislative recognition to the existence of such a major qualification? The Official Comment to § 8.30 explains:

In determining whether to impose liability, the courts recognize that boards of directors and corporate managers continuously make decisions that involve the balancing of risks and benefits for the enterprise. Although some decisions turn out to be unwise or the result of a mistake of judgment, it is unreasonable to reexamine these decisions with the benefit of hindsight. Therefore, a director is not liable for injury or damage caused by his decision, no matter how unwise or mistaken it may turn out to be, if in performing his duties he met the requirements of section 8.30.

Even before statutory formulations of directors' duty of care, courts sometimes invoked the business judgment rule in determining whether to impose liability in a particular case. In doing so, courts have sometimes used language similar to the standards set forth in section 8.30(a). The elements of the business judgment rule and the circumstances for its application are continuing to be developed by the courts. In view of that continuing judicial development, section 8.30 does not try to codify the business judgment rule or to delineate the differences, if any, between that rule and the standards of director conduct set forth in this section. That is a task left to the courts and possibly to later revisions of this Model Act.

This somewhat ambiguous formulation of very basic concepts about directoral liability was a compromise position taken by the Committee on Corporate Laws only after extended and extremely time-consuming efforts to codify the business judgment rule within the context of § 8.30; these efforts did not lead to anything nearly approaching consensus. The compromise set forth above was informally capsulated by one committee member who commented in effect, "we are saying that there is a business judgment rule, that we know what it is and when it should be applied, but we can't define it."

(7) The American Law Institute did not have the same problem of definition or articulation. American Law Institute, Principles of Corporate Governance: Analysis and Recommendations (Tent.Draft No. 4), § 4.01 (1985):*

(a) A director or officer has a duty to his corporation to perform his functions in good faith, in a manner that he reasonably believes to be in the best interests of the corporation, and with the care that an ordinarily prudent person would reasonably be expected to exercise in a like position and under similar circumstances.

(1) This duty includes the obligation to make, or cause to be made, such inquiry as the director or officer reasonably believes to be appropriate under the circumstances.

(2) In performing any of his functions (including his oversight functions), a director or officer is entitled to rely on materials and persons in accordance with §§ 4.02–.03.

(b) Except as otherwise provided by statute or by a standard of the corporation and subject to the board's ultimate responsibility for oversight, in performing its functions (including oversight functions), the board may delegate, formally or informally by course of conduct, any function (including the function of identifying matters requiring the attention of the board) to committees of the board or to directors, officers, employees, experts, or other persons; a director may rely on such committees and persons in fulfilling his duty under this Section with respect to any delegated function if his reliance is in accordance with §§ 4.02–.03

(c) A director or officer who makes a business judgment in good faith fulfills his duty under this Section if:

(1) he is not interested in the subject of his business judgment;

(2) he is informed with respect to the subject of his business judgment to the extent he reasonably believes to be appropriate under the circumstances; and

(3) he rationally believes that his business judgment is in the best interests of the corporation.

This provision was tentatively approved at the May, 1985 Institute plenary session, after a heated debate largely centered around the phrase "rationally believes."

(8) There is voluminous literature on the duty of care and the business judgment rule. Particularly helpful are the series of articles in two "Institutes on Dynamics of Corporate Control, reprinted in the *Business Lawyer:* 39 Bus.Law. 1461–1559 (1984); 40 Bus.Law. 1373–1455 (1985), that

contain references to most of the earlier literature. For discussions that are helpful in understanding the problems faced by the Committee on Corporate Laws in drafting article 8.30, see Veasey and Manning, Codified Standard—Safe Harbor or Uncharted Reef? 35 Bus.Law. 919 (1980); Arsht and Hinsey, Codified Standard—Same Harbor but Charted Channel: A Response, 35 Bus.Law. 947 (1980).

SMITH v. VAN GORKOM

Supreme Court of Delaware, 1985.
488 A.2d 858.

Before HERRMANN, C.J., and MCNEILLY, HORSEY, MOORE and CHRISTIE, JJ., constituting the Court en banc.

HORSEY, JUSTICE (for the majority):

This appeal from the Court of Chancery involves a class action brought by shareholders of the defendant Trans Union Corporation ("Trans Union" or "the Company"), originally seeking rescission of a cash-out merger of Trans Union into the defendant New T Company ("New T"), a wholly-owned subsidiary of the defendant, Marmon Group, Inc. ("Marmon"). Alternate relief in the form of damages is sought against the defendant members of the Board of Directors of Trans Union * * *.

Following trial, the former Chancellor granted judgment for the defendant directors by unreported letter opinion dated July 6, 1982. Judgment was based on two findings: (1) that the Board of Directors had acted in an informed manner so as to be entitled to protection of the business judgment rule in approving the cash-out merger; and (2) that the shareholder vote approving the merger should not be set aside because the stockholders had been "fairly informed" by the Board of Directors before voting thereon. The plaintiffs appeal.

Speaking for the majority of the Court, we conclude that both rulings of the Court of Chancery are clearly erroneous. Therefore, we reverse and direct that judgment be entered in favor of the plaintiffs and against the defendant directors for the fair value of the plaintiffs' stockholdings in Trans Union, in accordance with Weinberger v. UOP, Inc., Del.Supr., 457 A.2d 701 (1983).[2]

We hold: (1) that the Board's decision, reached September 20, 1980, to approve the proposed cash-out merger was not the product of an informed business judgment; (2) that the Board's subsequent efforts to amend the Merger Agreement and take other curative action were ineffectual, both legally and factually; and (3) that the Board did not deal with complete candor with the stockholders by failing to disclose all material facts, which they knew or should have known, before securing the stockholders' approval of the merger.

2. [By the Court] It has been stipulated that plaintiffs sue on behalf of a class consisting of 10,537 shareholders (out of a total of 12,844) and that the class owned 12,734,404 out of 13,357,758 shares of Trans Union outstanding.

I.

The nature of this case requires a detailed factual statement. The following facts are essentially uncontradicted:

–A–

Trans Union was a publicly-traded, diversified holding company, the principal earnings of which were generated by its railcar leasing business. During the period here involved, the Company had a cash flow of hundreds of millions of dollars annually. However, the Company had difficulty in generating sufficient taxable income to offset increasingly large investment tax credits (ITCs). Accelerated depreciation deductions had decreased available taxable income against which to offset accumulating ITCs. The Company took these deductions, despite their effect on usable ITCs, because the rental price in the railcar leasing market had already impounded the purported tax savings.

In the late 1970's, together with other capital-intensive firms, Trans Union lobbied in Congress to have ITCs refundable in cash to firms which could not fully utilize the credit. During the summer of 1980, defendant Jerome W. Van Gorkom, Trans Union's Chairman and Chief Executive Officer, testified and lobbied in Congress for refundability of ITCs and against further accelerated depreciation. By the end of August, Van Gorkom was convinced that Congress would neither accept the refundability concept nor curtail further accelerated depreciation.

Beginning in the late 1960's, and continuing through the 1970's, Trans Union pursued a program of acquiring small companies in order to increase available taxable income. In July 1980, Trans Union Management prepared the annual revision of the Company's Five Year Forecast. This report was presented to the Board of Directors at its July, 1980 meeting. The report projected an annual income growth of about 20%. The report also concluded that Trans Union would have about $195 million in spare cash between 1980 and 1985, "with the surplus growing rapidly from 1982 onward." The report referred to the ITC situation as a "nagging problem" and, given that problem, the leasing company "would still appear to be constrained to a tax breakeven." The report then listed four alternative uses of the projected 1982–1985 equity surplus: (1) stock repurchase; (2) dividend increases; (3) a major acquisition program; and (4) combinations of the above. The sale of Trans Union was not among the alternatives. The report emphasized that, despite the overall surplus, the operation of the Company would consume all available equity for the next several years, and concluded: "As a result, we have sufficient time to fully develop our course of action."

–B–

On August 27, 1980, Van Gorkom met with Senior Management of Trans Union. Van Gorkom reported on his lobbying efforts in Washington and his desire to find a solution to the tax credit problem more permanent than a continued program of acquisitions. Various alternatives were suggested and discussed preliminarily, including the sale of Trans Union to a company with a large amount of taxable income.

Donald Romans, Chief Financial Officer of Trans Union, stated that his department had done a "very brief bit of work on the possibility of a leveraged buy-out." This work had been prompted by a media article which Romans had seen regarding a leveraged buy-out by management. The work consisted of a "preliminary study" of the cash which could be generated by the Company if it participated in a leveraged buy-out. As Romans stated, this analysis "was very first and rough cut at seeing whether a cash flow would support what might be considered a high price for this type of transaction."

On September 5, at another Senior Management meeting which Van Gorkom attended, Romans again brought up the idea of a leveraged buy-out as a "possible strategic alternative" to the Company's acquisition program. Romans and Bruce S. Chelberg, President and Chief Operating Officer of Trans Union, had been working on the matter in preparation for the meeting. According to Romans: They did not "come up" with a price for the Company. They merely "ran the numbers" at $50 a share and at $60 a share with the "rough form" of their cash figures at the time. Their "figures indicated that $50 would be very easy to do but $60 would be very difficult to do under those figures." This work did not purport to establish a fair price for either the Company or 100% of the stock. It was intended to determine the cash flow needed to service the debt that would "probably" be incurred in a leveraged buyout, based on "rough calculations" without "any benefit of experts to identify what the limits were to that, and so forth." These computations were not considered extensive and no conclusion was reached.

At this meeting, Van Gorkom stated that he would be willing to take $55 per share for his own 75,000 shares. He vetoed the suggestion of a leveraged buy-out by Management, however, as involving a potential conflict of interest for Management. Van Gorkom, a certified public accountant and lawyer, had been an officer of Trans Union for 24 years, its Chief Executive Officer for more than 17 years, and Chairman of its Board for 2 years. It is noteworthy in this connection that he was then approaching 65 years of age and mandatory retirement.

For several days following the September 5 meeting, Van Gorkom pondered the idea of a sale. He had participated in many acquisitions as a manager and director of Trans Union and as a director of other companies. He was familiar with acquisition procedures, valuation methods, and negotiations; and he privately considered the pros and cons of whether Trans Union should seek a privately or publicly-held purchaser.

Van Gorkom decided to meet with Jay A. Pritzker, a well-known corporate takeover specialist and a social acquaintance. However, rather than approaching Pritzker simply to determine his interest in acquiring Trans Union, Van Gorkom assembled a proposed per share price for sale of the Company and a financing structure by which to accomplish the sale. Van Gorkom did so without consulting either his Board or any members of Senior Management except one: Carl Peterson, Trans Union's Controller. Telling Peterson that he wanted no other person on his staff to know what he was doing, but without telling him why, Van Gorkom directed Peterson to calculate the feasibility of a leveraged buy-out at an assumed price per share of $55. Apart from the Company's historic stock market price,[3] and Van Gorkom's long association with Trans Union, the record is devoid of any competent evidence that $55 represented the per share intrinsic value of the Company.

Having thus chosen the $55 figure, based solely on the availability of a leveraged buy-out, Van Gorkom multiplied the price per share by the number of shares outstanding to reach a total value of the Company of $690 million. Van Gorkom told Peterson to use this $690 million figure and to assume a $200 million equity contribution by the buyer. Based on these assumptions, Van Gorkom directed Peterson to determine whether the debt portion of the purchase price could be paid off in five years or less if financed by Trans Union's cash flow as projected in the Five Year Forecast, and by the sale of certain weaker divisions identified in a study done for Trans Union by the Boston Consulting Group ("BCG study"). Peterson reported that, of the purchase price, approximately $50–80 million would remain outstanding after five years. Van Gorkom was disappointed, but decided to meet with Pritzker nevertheless.

Van Gorkom arranged a meeting with Pritzker at the latter's home on Saturday, September 13, 1980. Van Gorkom prefaced his presentation by stating to Pritzker: "Now as far as you are concerned, I can, I think, show how you can pay a substantial premium over the present stock price and pay off most of the loan in the first five years. * * * If you could pay $55 for this Company, here is a way in which I think it can be financed."

Van Gorkom then reviewed with Pritzker his calculations based upon his proposed price of $55 per share. Although Pritzker mentioned $50 as a more attractive figure, no other price was mentioned. However, Van Gorkom stated that to be sure that $55 was the best price obtainable, Trans Union should be free to accept any better offer. Pritzker demurred, stating that his organization would serve as a "stalking horse" for an "auction contest" only if Trans Union would

---

3. [By the Court] The common stock of Trans Union was traded on the New York Stock Exchange. Over the five year period from 1975 through 1979, Trans Union's stock had traded within a range of a high of $39½ and a low of $24¼. Its high and low range for 1980 through September 19 (the last trading day before announcement of the merger) was $38¼–$29½.

permit Pritzker to buy 1,750,000 shares of Trans Union stock at market price which Pritzker could then sell to any higher bidder. After further discussion on this point, Pritzker told Van Gorkom that he would give him a more definite reaction soon.

On Monday, September 15, Pritzker advised Van Gorkom that he was interested in the $55 cash-out merger proposal and requested more information on Trans Union. Van Gorkom agreed to meet privately with Pritzker, accompanied by Peterson, Chelberg, and Michael Carpenter, Trans Union's consultant from the Boston Consulting Group. The meetings took place on September 16 and 17. Van Gorkom was "astounded that events were moving with such amazing rapidity."

On Thursday, September 18, Van Gorkom met again with Pritzker. At that time, Van Gorkom knew that Pritzker intended to make a cash-out merger offer at Van Gorkom's proposed $55 per share. Pritzker instructed his attorney, a merger and acquisition specialist, to begin drafting merger documents. There was no further discussion of the $55 price. However, the number of shares of Trans Union's treasury stock to be offered to Pritzker was negotiated down to one million shares; the price was set at $38—75 cents above the per share price at the close of the market on September 19. At this point, Pritzker insisted that the Trans Union Board act on his merger proposal within the next three days, stating to Van Gorkom: "We have to have a decision by no later than Sunday [evening, September 21] before the opening of the English stock exchange on Monday morning." Pritzker's lawyer was then instructed to draft the merger documents, to be reviewed by Van Gorkom's lawyer, "sometimes with discussion and sometimes not, in the haste to get it finished."

On Friday, September 19, Van Gorkom, Chelberg, and Pritzker consulted with Trans Union's lead bank regarding the financing of Pritzker's purchase of Trans Union. The bank indicated that it could form a syndicate of banks that would finance the transaction. On the same day, Van Gorkom retained James Brennan, Esquire, to advise Trans Union on the legal aspects of the merger. Van Gorkom did not consult with William Browder, a Vice–President and director of Trans Union and former head of its legal department, or with William Moore, then the head of Trans Union's legal staff.

On Friday, September 19, Van Gorkom called a special meeting of the Trans Union Board for noon the following day. He also called a meeting of the Company's Senior Management to convene at 11:00 a.m., prior to the meeting of the Board. No one, except Chelberg and Peterson, was told the purpose of the meetings. Van Gorkom did not invite Trans Union's investment banker, Salomon Brothers or its Chicago-based partner, to attend.

Of those present at the Senior Management meeting on September 20, only Chelberg and Peterson had prior knowledge of Pritzker's offer. Van Gorkom disclosed the offer and described its terms, but he furnished no copies of the proposed Merger Agreement. Romans announced that his department had done a second study which showed that, for a leveraged buy-out, the price range for Trans Union stock was between $55 and $65 per share. Van Gorkom neither saw the study nor asked Romans to make it available for the Board meeting.

Senior Management's reaction to the Pritzker proposal was completely negative. No member of Management, except Chelberg and Peterson, supported the proposal. Romans objected to the price as being too low;[4] he was critical of the timing and suggested that consideration should be given to the adverse tax consequences of an all-cash deal for low-basis shareholders; and he took the position that the agreement to sell Pritzker one million newly-issued shares at market price would inhibit other offers, as would the prohibitions against soliciting bids and furnishing inside information to other bidders. Romans argued that the Pritzker proposal was a "lock up" and amounted to "an agreed merger as opposed to an offer." Nevertheless, Van Gorkom proceeded to the Board meeting as scheduled without further delay.

Ten directors served on the Trans Union Board, five inside (defendants Bonser, O'Boyle, Browder, Chelberg, and Van Gorkom) and five outside (defendants Wallis, Johnson, Lanterman, Morgan and Reneker). All directors were present at the meeting, except O'Boyle who was ill. Of the outside directors, four were corporate chief executive officers and one was the former Dean of the University of Chicago Business School. None was an investment banker or trained financial analyst. All members of the Board were well informed about the Company and its operations as a going concern. They were familiar with the current financial condition of the Company, as well as operating and earnings projections reported in the recent Five Year Forecast. The Board generally received regular and detailed reports and was kept abreast of the accumulated investment tax credit and accelerated depreciation problem.

Van Gorkom began the Special Meeting of the Board with a twenty-minute oral presentation. Copies of the proposed Merger Agreement were delivered too late for study before or during the meeting.[5] He reviewed the Company's ITC and depreciation problems and the efforts theretofore made to solve them. He discussed his initial meeting with Pritzker and his motivation in arranging that meeting. Van Gorkom did not disclose to the Board, however, the methodology

---

4. [By the Court] Van Gorkom asked Romans to express his opinion as to the $55 price. Romans stated that he "thought the price was too low in relation to what he could derive for the company in a cash sale, particularly one which enabled us to realize the values of certain subsidiaries and independent entities."

5. [By the Court] The record is not clear as to the terms of the Merger Agreement. The Agreement, as originally presented to the Board on September 20, was never produced by defendants despite demands by the plaintiffs. Nor is it clear that the directors were given an opportunity to study the Merger Agreement before voting on it. All that can be said is that Brennan had the Agreement before him during the meeting.

by which he alone had arrived at the $55 figure, or the fact that he first proposed the $55 price in his negotiations with Pritzker.

Van Gorkom outlined the terms of the Pritzker offer as follows: Pritzker would pay $55 in cash for all outstanding shares of Trans Union stock upon completion of which Trans Union would be merged into New T Company, a subsidiary wholly-owned by Pritzker and formed to implement the merger; for a period of 90 days, Trans Union could receive, but could not actively solicit, competing offers; the offer had to be acted on by the next evening, Sunday, September 21; Trans Union could only furnish to competing bidders published information, and not proprietary information; the offer was subject to Pritzker obtaining the necessary financing by October 10, 1980; if the financing contingency were met or waived by Pritzker, Trans Union was required to sell to Pritzker one million newly-issued shares of Trans Union at $38 per share.

Van Gorkom took the position that putting Trans Union "up for auction" through a 90-day market test would validate a decision by the Board that $55 was a fair price. He told the Board that the "free market will have an opportunity to judge whether $55 is a fair price." Van Gorkom framed the decision before the Board not as whether $55 per share was the highest price that could be obtained, but as whether the $55 price was a fair price that the stockholders should be given the opportunity to accept or reject.[6]

Attorney Brennan advised the members of the Board that they might be sued if they failed to accept the offer and that a fairness opinion was not required as a matter of law.

Romans attended the meeting as chief financial officer of the Company. He told the Board that he had not been involved in the negotiations with Pritzker and knew nothing about the merger proposal until the morning of the meeting; that his studies did not indicate either a fair price for the stock or a valuation of the Company; that he did not see his role as directly addressing the fairness issue; and that he and his people "were trying to search for ways to justify a price in connection with such a [leveraged buy-out] transaction, rather than to say what the shares are worth." Romans testified:

> I told the Board that the study ran the numbers at 50 and 60, and then the subsequent study at 55 and 65, and that was not the same thing as saying that I have a valuation of the company at X dollars. But it was a way—a first step towards reaching that conclusion.

Romans told the Board that, in his opinion, $55 was "in the range of a fair price," but "at the beginning of the range."

Chelberg, Trans Union's President, supported Van Gorkom's presentation and representations. He testified that he "participated to make sure that the Board members collectively were clear on the

6. [By the Court] In Van Gorkom's words: The "real decision" is whether to "let the stockholders decide it" which is "all you are being asked to decide today."

details of the agreement or offer from Pritzker;" that he "participated in the discussion with Mr. Brennan, inquiring of him about the necessity for valuation opinions in spite of the way in which this particular offer was couched;" and that he was otherwise actively involved in supporting the positions being taken by Van Gorkom before the Board about "the necessity to act immediately on this offer," and about "the adequacy of the $55 and the question of how that would be tested."

The Board meeting of September 20 lasted about two hours. Based solely upon Van Gorkom's oral presentation, Chelberg's supporting representations, Romans' oral statement, Brennan's legal advice, and their knowledge of the market history of the Company's stock,[7] the directors approved the proposed Merger Agreement. However, the Board later claimed to have attached two conditions to its acceptance: (1) that Trans Union reserved the right to accept any better offer that was made during the market test period; and (2) that Trans Union could share its proprietary information with any other potential bidders. While the Board now claims to have reserved the right to accept any better offer received after the announcement of the Pritzker agreement (even though the minutes of the meeting do not reflect this), it is undisputed that the Board did not reserve the right to actively solicit alternate offers.

The Merger Agreement was executed by Van Gorkom during the evening of September 20 at a formal social event that he hosted for the opening of the Chicago Lyric Opera. Neither he nor any other director read the agreement prior to its signing and delivery to Pritzker.

* * *

On Monday, September 22, the Company issued a press release announcing that Trans Union had entered into a "definitive" Merger Agreement with an affiliate of the Marmon Group, Inc., a Pritzker holding company. Within 10 days of the public announcement, dissent among Senior Management over the merger had become widespread. Faced with threatened resignations of key officers, Van Gorkom met with Pritzker who agreed to several modifications of the Agreement. Pritzker was willing to do so provided that Van Gorkom could persuade the dissidents to remain on the Company payroll for at least six months after consummation of the merger.

Van Gorkom reconvened the Board on October 8 and secured the directors' approval of the proposed amendments—sight unseen. The Board also authorized the employment of Salomon Brothers, its investment banker, to solicit other offers for Trans Union during the proposed "market test" period.

---

7. [By the Court] The Trial Court stated the premium relationship of the $55 price to the market history of the Company's stock as follows:

* * * the merger price offered to the stockholders of Trans Union represented a premium of 62% over the average of the high and low prices at which Trans Union stock had traded in 1980, a premium of 48% over the last closing price, and a premium of 39% over the highest price at which the stock of Trans Union had traded any time during the prior six years.

The next day, October 9, Trans Union issued a press release announcing: (1) that Pritzker had obtained "the financing commitments necessary to consummate" the merger with Trans Union; (2) that Pritzker had acquired one million shares of Trans Union common stock at $38 per share; (3) that Trans Union was now permitted to actively seek other offers and had retained Salomon Brothers for that purpose; and (4) that if a more favorable offer were not received before February 1, 1981, Trans Union's shareholders would thereafter meet to vote on the Pritzker proposal.

It was not until the following day, October 10, that the actual amendments to the Merger Agreement were prepared by Pritzker and delivered to Van Gorkom for execution. As will be seen, the amendments were considerably at variance with Van Gorkom's representations of the amendments to the Board on October 8; and the amendments placed serious constraints on Trans Union's ability to negotiate a better deal and withdraw from the Pritzker agreement. Nevertheless, Van Gorkom proceeded to execute what became the October 10 amendments to the Merger Agreement without conferring further with the Board members and apparently without comprehending the actual implications of the amendments.   *   *   *

Salomon Brothers' efforts over a three-month period from October 21 to January 21 produced only one serious suitor for Trans Union—General Electric Credit Corporation ("GE Credit"), a subsidiary of the General Electric Company. However, GE Credit was unwilling to make an offer for Trans Union unless Trans Union first rescinded its Merger Agreement with Pritzker. When Pritzker refused, GE Credit terminated further discussions with Trans Union in early January.

In the meantime, in early December, the investment firm of Kohlberg, Kravis, Roberts & Co. ("KKR"), the only other concern to make a firm offer for Trans Union, withdrew its offer under circumstances hereinafter detailed.   *   *   *

[A later portion of the opinion gives the following additional information about the KKR and G.E. Credit overtures:]

The KKR proposal was the first and only offer received subsequent to the Pritzker Merger Agreement. The offer resulted primarily from the efforts of Romans and other senior officers to propose an alternative to Pritzker's acquisition of Trans Union. In late September, Romans' group contacted KKR about the possibility of a leveraged buy-out by all members of Management, except Van Gorkom. By early October, Henry R. Kravis of KKR gave Romans written notice of KKR's "interest in making an offer to purchase 100%" of Trans Union's common stock.

Thereafter, and until early December, Romans' group worked with KKR to develop a proposal. It did so with Van Gorkom's knowledge and apparently grudging consent. On December 2, Kravis and Romans hand-delivered to Van Gorkom a formal letter-offer to purchase all of Trans Union's assets and to assume all of its liabilities for an aggregate cash consideration equivalent to $60 per share. The offer was contingent upon completing equity and bank financing of $650 million, which Kravis represented as 80% complete. The KKR letter made reference to discussions with major banks regarding the loan portion of the buyout cost and stated that KKR was "confident that commitments for the bank financing * * * can be obtained within two or three weeks." The purchasing group was to include certain named key members of Trans Union's Senior Management, excluding Van Gorkom, and a major Canadian company. Kravis stated that they were willing to enter into a "definitive agreement" under terms and conditions "substantially the same" as those contained in Trans Union's agreement with Pritzker. The offer was addressed to Trans Union's Board of Directors and a meeting with the Board, scheduled for that afternoon, was requested.

Van Gorkom's reaction to the KKR proposal was completely negative; he did not view the offer as being firm because of its financing condition. It was pointed out, to no avail, that Pritzker's offer had not only been similarly conditioned, but accepted on an expedited basis. Van Gorkom refused Kravis' request that Trans Union issue a press release announcing KKR's offer, on the ground that it might "chill" any other offer.[8] Romans and Kravis left with the understanding that their proposal would be presented to Trans Union's Board that afternoon.

Within a matter of hours and shortly before the scheduled Board meeting, Kravis withdrew his letter-offer. He gave as his reason a sudden decision by the Chief Officer of Trans Union's rail car leasing operation to withdraw from the KKR purchasing group. Van Gorkom had spoken to that officer about his participation in the KKR proposal immediately after his meeting with Romans and Kravis. However, Van Gorkom denied any responsibility for the officer's change of mind.

At the Board meeting later that afternoon, Van Gorkom did not inform the directors of the KKR proposal because he considered it "dead." Van Gorkom did not contact KKR again until January 20, when faced with the realities of this lawsuit, he then attempted to reopen negotiations. KKR declined due to the imminence of the February 10 stockholder meeting.

GE Credit Corporation's interest in Trans Union did not develop until November; and it made no written proposal until mid-January. Even then, its proposal was not in the form of an offer. Had there been time to do so, GE Credit was prepared to offer between $2 and $5 per share above the $55 per share price which Pritzker offered. But GE Credit needed an additional 60 to 90 days; and it was unwilling to make a formal offer without a concession from Pritzker extending the

8. [By the Court] This was inconsistent with Van Gorkom's espousal of the September 22 press release following Trans Union's acceptance of Pritzker's proposal. Van Gorkom had then justified a press release as encouraging rather than chilling later offers.

February 10 "deadline" for Trans Union's stockholder meeting. As previously stated, Pritzker refused to grant such extension; and on January 21, GE Credit terminated further negotiations with Trans Union. Its stated reasons, among others, were its "unwillingness to become involved in a bidding contest with Pritzker in the absence of the willingness of [the Pritzker interests] to terminate the proposed $55 cash merger." * * *

On December 19, this litigation was commenced and, within four weeks, the plaintiffs had deposed eight of the ten directors of Trans Union, including Van Gorkom, Chelberg and Romans, its Chief Financial Officer. On January 21, Management's Proxy Statement for the February 10 shareholder meeting was mailed to Trans Union's stockholders. On January 26, Trans Union's Board met and, after a lengthy meeting, voted to proceed with the Pritzker merger. The Board also approved for mailing, "on or about January 27," a Supplement to its Proxy Statement. The Supplement purportedly set forth all information relevant to the Pritzker Merger Agreement, which had not been divulged in the first Proxy Statement. * * *

On February 10, the stockholders of Trans Union approved the Pritzker merger proposal. Of the outstanding shares, 69.9% were voted in favor of the merger; 7.25% were voted against the merger; and 22.85% were not voted.

II.

We turn to the issue of the application of the business judgment rule to the September 20 meeting of the Board.

The Court of Chancery concluded from the evidence that the Board of Directors' approval of the Pritzker merger proposal fell within the protection of the business judgment rule. The Court found that the Board had given sufficient time and attention to the transaction, since the directors had considered the Pritzker proposal on three different occasions, on September 20, and on October 8, 1980 and finally on January 26, 1981. On that basis, the Court reasoned that the Board had acquired, over the four-month period, sufficient information to reach an informed business judgment on the cash-out merger proposal. The Court ruled:

> * * * that given the market value of Trans Union's stock, the business acumen of the members of the board of Trans Union, the substantial premium over market offered by the Pritzkers and the ultimate effect on the merger price provided by the prospect of other bids for the stock in question, that the board of directors of Trans Union did not act recklessly or improvidently in determining on a course of action which they believed to be in the best interest of the stockholders of Trans Union.

The Court of Chancery made but one finding; i.e., that the Board's conduct over the entire period from September 20 through January 26, 1981 was not reckless or improvident, but informed. This ultimate conclusion was premised upon three subordinate findings, one explicit and two implied. The Court's explicit finding was that Trans Union's Board was "free to turn down the Pritzker proposal" not only on September 20 but also on October 8, 1980 and on January 26, 1981. The Court's implied, subordinate findings were: (1) that no legally binding agreement was reached by the parties until January 26; and (2) that if a higher offer were to be forthcoming, the market test would have produced it, and Trans Union would have been contractually free to accept such higher offer. However, the Court offered no factual basis or legal support for any of these findings; and the record compels contrary conclusions. * * *

[W]e conclude that the Court's ultimate finding that the Board's conduct was not "reckless or imprudent" is contrary to the record and not the product of a logical and deductive reasoning process.

The plaintiffs contend that the Court of Chancery erred as a matter of law by exonerating the defendant directors under the business judgment rule without first determining whether the rule's threshold condition of "due care and prudence" was satisfied. The plaintiffs assert that the Trial Court found the defendant directors to have reached an informed business judgment on the basis of "extraneous considerations and events that occurred after September 20, 1980." The defendants deny that the Trial Court committed legal error in relying upon post-September 20, 1980 events and the directors' later acquired knowledge. The defendants further submit that their decision to accept $55 per share was informed because: (1) they were "highly qualified;" (2) they were "well-informed;" and (3) they deliberated over the "proposal" not once but three times. On essentially this evidence and under our standard of review, the defendants assert that affirmance is required. We must disagree.

Under Delaware law, the business judgment rule is the offspring of the fundamental principle, codified in 8 Del.C. § 141(a), that the business and affairs of a Delaware corporation are managed by or under its board of directors. Pogostin v. Rice, Del.Supr., 480 A.2d 619, 624 (1984); Aronson v. Lewis, Del.Supr., 473 A.2d 805, 811 (1984); Zapata Corp. v. Maldonado, Del.Supr., 430 A.2d 779, 782 (1981). In carrying out their managerial roles, directors are charged with an unyielding fiduciary duty to the corporation and its shareholders. Loft, Inc. v. Guth, Del. Ch., 2 A.2d 225 (1938), aff'd, Del.Supr., 5 A.2d 503 (1939). The business judgment rule exists to protect and promote the full and free exercise of the managerial power granted to Delaware directors. Zapata Corp. v. Maldonado, supra at 782. The rule itself "is a presumption that in making a business decision, the directors of a corporation acted on an informed basis, in good faith and in the honest belief that the action taken was in the best interests of the company." Aronson, supra at 812. Thus, the party attacking a board decision as uninformed must rebut the presumption that its business judgment was an informed one.

The determination of whether a business judgment is an informed one turns on whether the directors have informed themselves "prior to making a business decision, of all material information reasonably available to them."

Under the business judgment rule there is no protection for directors who have made "an unintelligent or unadvised judgment." Mitchell v. Highland–Western Glass, Del.Ch., 167 A. 831, 833 (1933). A director's duty to inform himself in preparation for a decision derives from the fiduciary capacity in which he serves the corporation and its stockholders. Lutz v. Boas, Del.Ch., 171 A.2d 381 (1961). Since a director is vested with the responsibility for the management of the affairs of the corporation, he must execute that duty with the recognition that he acts on behalf of others. Such obligation does not tolerate faithlessness or self-dealing. But fulfillment of the fiduciary function requires more than the mere absence of bad faith or fraud. Representation of the financial interests of others imposes on a director an affirmative duty to protect those interests and to proceed with a critical eye in assessing information of the type and under the circumstances present here.

Thus, a director's duty to exercise an informed business judgment is in the nature of a duty of care, as distinguished from a duty of loyalty. Here, there were no allegations of fraud, bad faith, or self-dealing, or proof thereof. Hence, it is presumed that the directors reached their business judgment in good faith, Allaun v. Consolidated Oil Co., Del.Ch., 147 A. 257 (1929), and considerations of motive are irrelevant to the issue before us.

The standard of care applicable to a director's duty of care has also been recently restated by this Court. In Aronson, supra, we stated:

> While the Delaware cases use a variety of terms to describe the applicable standard of care, our analysis satisfies us that under the business judgment rule director liability is predicated upon concepts of gross negligence. (footnote omitted)

473 A.2d at 812.

We again confirm that view. We think the concept of gross negligence is also the proper standard for determining whether a business judgment reached by a board of directors was an informed one.[9]

In the specific context of a proposed merger of domestic corporations, a director has a duty under 8 Del.C. 251(b)[10] along with his fellow

---

9. [By the Court] Compare Mitchell v. Highland–Western Glass, supra, where the Court posed the question as whether the board acted "so far without information that they can be said to have passed an unintelligent and unadvised judgment." 167 A. at 833. Compare also Gimbel v. Signal Companies, Inc., 316 A.2d 599, aff'd per curiam Del.Supr., 316 A.2d 619 (1974), where the Chancellor, after expressly reiterating the Highland–Western Glass standard, framed the question, "Or to put the question in its legal context, did the Signal directors act without the bounds of reason and recklessly in approving the price offer of Burmah?" Id.

10. [By the Court] 8 Del.C. § 251(b) provides in pertinent part:

(b) The board of directors of each corporation which desires to merge or consolidate *shall adopt a resolution approv-*

directors, to act in an informed and deliberate manner in determining whether to approve an agreement of merger before submitting the proposal to the stockholders. Certainly in the merger context, a director may not abdicate that duty by leaving to the shareholders alone the decision to approve or disapprove the agreement. See Beard v. Elster, Del.Supr., 160 A.2d 731, 737 (1960). Only an agreement of merger satisfying the requirements of 8 Del.C. § 251(b) may be submitted to the shareholders under § 251(c).

It is against those standards that the conduct of the directors of Trans Union must be tested, as a matter of law and as a matter of fact, regarding their exercise of an informed business judgment in voting to approve the Pritzker merger proposal.

III.

The defendants argue that the determination of whether their decision to accept $55 per share for Trans Union represented an informed business judgment requires consideration, not only of that which they knew and learned on September 20, but also of that which they subsequently learned and did over the following four-month period before the shareholders met to vote on the proposal in February, 1981. The defendants thereby seek to reduce the significance of their action on September 20 and to widen the time frame for determining whether their decision to accept the Pritzker proposal was an informed one. Thus, the defendants contend that what the directors did and learned subsequent to September 20 and through January 26, 1981, was properly taken into account by the Trial Court in determining whether the Board's judgment was an informed one. We disagree with this post hoc approach.

The issue of whether the directors reached an informed decision to "sell" the Company on September 20, 1980 must be determined only upon the basis of the information then reasonably available to the directors and relevant to their decision to accept the Pritzker merger proposal. This is not to say that the directors were precluded from altering their original plan of action, had they done so in an informed manner. What we do say is that the question of whether the directors reached an informed business judgment in agreeing to sell the Company, pursuant to the terms of the September 20 Agreement presents, in

---

ing an agreement of merger or consolidation. The agreement shall state: (1) the terms and conditions of the merger or consolidation; (2) the mode of carrying the same into effect; (3) such amendments or changes in the certificate of incorporation of the surviving corporation as are desired to be effected by the merger or consolidation, or, if no such amendments or changes are desired, a statement that the certificate of incorporation of one of the constituent corporations shall be the certificate of incorporation of the surviving or resulting corporation; (4) the manner of con-

verting the shares of each of the constituent corporations * * * and (5) such other details or provisions as are deemed desirable. * * * The agreement so adopted shall be executed in accordance with section 103 of this title. Any of the terms of the agreement of merger or consolidation may be made dependent upon facts ascertainable outside of such agreement, provided that the manner in which such facts shall operate upon the terms of the agreement is clearly and expressly set forth in the agreement of merger or consolidation. (underlining added for emphasis)

reality, two questions: (A) whether the directors reached an informed business judgment on September 20, 1980; and (B) if they did not, whether the directors' actions taken subsequent to September 20 were adequate to cure any infirmity in their action taken on September 20. We first consider the directors' September 20 action in terms of their reaching an informed business judgment.

-A-

On the record before us, we must conclude that the Board of Directors did not reach an informed business judgment on September 20, 1980 in voting to "sell" the Company for $55 per share pursuant to the Pritzker cash-out merger proposal. Our reasons, in summary, are as follows:

The directors (1) did not adequately inform themselves as to Van Gorkom's role in forcing the "sale" of the Company and in establishing the per share purchase price; (2) were uninformed as to the intrinsic value of the Company; and (3) given these circumstances, at a minimum, were grossly negligent in approving the "sale" of the Company upon two hours' consideration, without prior notice, and without the exigency of a crisis or emergency.

As has been noted, the Board based its September 20 decision to approve the cash-out merger primarily on Van Gorkom's representations. None of the directors, other than Van Gorkom and Chelberg, had any prior knowledge that the purpose of the meeting was to propose a cash-out merger of Trans Union. No members of Senior Management were present, other than Chelberg, Romans and Peterson; and the latter two had only learned of the proposed sale an hour earlier. Both general counsel Moore and former general counsel Browder attended the meeting, but were equally uninformed as to the purpose of the meeting and the documents to be acted upon.

Without any documents before them concerning the proposed transaction, the members of the Board were required to rely entirely upon Van Gorkom's 20-minute oral presentation of the proposal. No written summary of the terms of the merger was presented; the directors were given no documentation to support the adequacy of $55 price per share for sale of the Company; and the Board had before it nothing more than Van Gorkom's statement of his understanding of the substance of an agreement which he admittedly had never read, nor which any member of the Board had ever seen. * * *

The defendants rely on the following factors to sustain the Trial Court's finding that the Board's decision was an informed one: (1) the magnitude of the premium or spread between the $55 Pritzker offering price and Trans Union's current market price of $38 per share; (2) the amendment of the Agreement as submitted on September 20 to permit the Board to accept any better offer during the "market test" period; (3) the collective experience and expertise of the Board's "inside" and "outside" directors; and (4) their reliance on Brennan's legal advice that the directors might be sued if they rejected the Pritzker proposal. We discuss each of these grounds *seriatim:*

(1)

A substantial premium may provide one reason to recommend a merger, but in the absence of other sound valuation information, the fact of a premium alone does not provide an adequate basis upon which to assess the fairness of an offering price. Here, the judgment reached as to the adequacy of the premium was based on a comparison between the historically depressed Trans Union market price and the amount of the Pritzker offer. Using market price as a basis for concluding that the premium adequately reflected the true value of the Company was a clearly faulty, indeed fallacious, premise, as the defendants' own evidence demonstrates. * * *

The parties do not dispute that a publicly-traded stock price is solely a measure of the value of a minority position and, thus, market price represents only the value of a single share. Nevertheless, on September 20, the Board assessed the adequacy of the premium over market, offered by Pritzker, solely by comparing it with Trans Union's current and historical stock price.

Indeed, as of September 20, the Board had no other information on which to base a determination of the intrinsic value of Trans Union as a going concern. As of September 20, the Board had made no evaluation of the Company designed to value the entire enterprise, nor had the Board ever previously considered selling the Company or consenting to a buy-out merger. Thus, the adequacy of a premium is indeterminate unless it is assessed in terms of other competent and sound valuation information that reflects the value of the particular business.

Despite the foregoing facts and circumstances, there was no call by the Board, either on September 20 or thereafter, for any valuation study or documentation of the $55 price per share as a measure of the fair value of the Company in a cash-out context. It is undisputed that the major asset of Trans Union was its cash flow. Yet, at no time did the Board call for a valuation study taking into account that highly significant element of the Company's assets.

We do not imply that an outside valuation study is essential to support an informed business judgment; nor do we state that fairness opinions by independent investment bankers are required as a matter of law. Often insiders familiar with the business of a going concern are in a better position than are outsiders to gather relevant information; and under appropriate circumstances, such directors may be fully protected in relying in good faith upon the valuation reports of their management. See 8 Del.C. § 141(e).

Here, the record establishes that the Board did not request its Chief Financial Officer, Romans, to make any valuation study or review of the proposal to determine the adequacy of $55 per share for sale of the Company. On the record before us: The Board rested on Romans' elicited response that the $55 figure was within a "fair price range" within the context of a leveraged buy-out. No director sought any further information from Romans. No director asked him why he put $55 at the bottom of his range. No director asked Romans for any details as to his study, the reason why it had been undertaken or its depth. No director asked to see the study; and no director asked Romans whether Trans Union's finance department could do a fairness study within the remaining 36–hour period available under the Pritzker offer.

Had the Board, or any member, made an inquiry of Romans, he presumably would have responded as he testified: that his calculations were rough and preliminary; and, that the study was not designed to determine the fair value of the Company, but rather to assess the feasibility of a leveraged buy-out financed by the Company's projected cash flow, making certain assumptions as to the purchaser's borrowing needs. Romans would have presumably also informed the Board of his view, and the widespread view of Senior Management, that the timing of the offer was wrong and the offer inadequate.

The record also establishes that the Board accepted without scrutiny Van Gorkom's representation as to the fairness of the $55 price per share for sale of the Company—a subject that the Board had never previously considered. The Board thereby failed to discover that Van Gorkom had suggested the $55 price to Pritzker and, most crucially, that Van Gorkom had arrived at the $55 figure based on calculations designed solely to determine the feasibility of a leveraged buy-out.[11] No questions were raised either as to the tax implications of a cash-out merger or how the price for the one million share option granted Pritzker was calculated.

We do not say that the Board of Directors was not entitled to give some credence to Van Gorkom's representation that $55 was an adequate or fair price. Under § 141(e), the directors were entitled to rely upon their chairman's opinion of value and adequacy, provided that such opinion was reached on a sound basis. Here, the issue is whether the directors informed themselves as to all information that was reasonably available to them. Had they done so, they would have learned of the source and derivation of the $55 price and could not reasonably have relied thereupon in good faith.

11. [By the Court] As of September 20 the directors did not know: that Van Gorkom had arrived at the $55 figure alone, and subjectively, as the figure to be used by Controller Peterson in creating a feasible structure for a leveraged buy-out by a prospective purchaser; that Van Gorkom had not sought advice, information or assistance from either inside or outside Trans Union directors as to the value of the Company as an entity or the fair price per share for 100% of its stock; that Van Gorkom had not consulted with the Company's investment bankers or other financial analysts; that Van Gorkom had not consulted with or confided in any officer or director of the Company except Chelberg; and that Van Gorkom had deliberately chosen to ignore the advice and opinion of the members of his Senior Management group regarding the adequacy of the $55 price.

None of the directors, Management or outside, were investment bankers or financial analysts. Yet the Board did not consider recessing the meeting until a later hour that day (or requesting an extension of Pritzker's Sunday evening deadline) to give it time to elicit more information as to the sufficiency of the offer, either from inside Management (in particular Romans) or from Trans Union's own investment banker, Salomon Brothers, whose Chicago specialist in merger and acquisitions was known to the Board and familiar with Trans Union's affairs.

Thus, the record compels the conclusion that on September 20 the Board lacked valuation information adequate to reach an informed business judgment as to the fairness of $55 per share for sale of the Company.   * * *

(2)

[The court concludes in this portion of the opinion that there was not a "post-September 20 market test" of the $55 price sufficient to confirm the reasonableness of the board's decision.]

(3)

The directors' unfounded reliance on both the premium and the market test as the basis for accepting the Pritzker proposal undermines the defendants' remaining contention that the Board's collective experience and sophistication was a sufficient basis for finding that it reached its September 20 decision with informed, reasonable deliberation.[12] Compare Gimbel v. Signal Companies, Inc., Del.Ch., 316 A.2d 599 (1974), aff'd per curiam, Del.Supr., 316 A.2d 619 (1974). There, the Court of Chancery preliminary enjoined a board's sale of stock of its wholly-owned subsidiary for an alleged grossly inadequate price. It did so based on a finding that the business judgment rule had been pierced for failure of management to give its board "the opportunity to make a reasonable and reasoned decision." 316 A.2d at 615. The Court there reached this result notwithstanding the board's sophistication and experience; the company's need of immediate cash; and the board's need to act promptly due to the impact of an energy crisis on the value of the underlying assets being sold—all of its subsidiary's oil and gas interests. The Court found those factors denoting competence to be outweighed by evidence of gross negligence; that management in effect sprang the deal on the board by negotiating the asset sale without

12. [By the Court] Trans Union's five "inside" directors had backgrounds in law and accounting, 116 years of collective employment by the Company and 68 years of combined experience on its Board. Trans Union's five "outside" directors included four chief executives of major corporations and an economist who was a former dean of a major school of business and chancellor of a university. The "outside" directors had 78 years of combined experience as chief executive officers of major corpora- tions and 50 years of cumulative experience as directors of Trans Union. Thus, defendants argue that the Board was eminently qualified to reach an informed judgment on the proposed "sale" of Trans Union notwithstanding their lack of any advance notice of the proposal, the shortness of their deliberation, and their determination not to consult with their investment banker or to obtain a fairness opinion.

informing the board; that the buyer intended to "force a quick decision" by the board; that the board meeting was called on only one-and-a-half days' notice; that its outside directors were not notified of the meeting's purpose; that during a meeting spanning "a couple of hours" a sale of assets worth $480 million was approved; and that the Board failed to obtain a *current* appraisal of its oil and gas interests. The analogy of *Signal* to the case at bar is significant.

(4)

Part of the defense is based on a claim that the directors relied on legal advice rendered at the September 20 meeting by James Brennan, Esquire, who was present at Van Gorkom's request. Unfortunately, Brennan did not appear and testify at trial even though his firm participated in the defense of this action. There is no contemporaneous evidence of the advice given by Brennan on September 20, only the later deposition and trial testimony of certain directors as to their recollections or understanding of what was said at the meeting. Since counsel did not testify, and the advice attributed to Brennan is hearsay received by the Trial Court over the plaintiffs' objections, we consider it only in the context of the directors' present claims. In fairness to counsel, we make no findings that the advice attributed to him was in fact given. We focus solely on the efficacy of the defendants' claims, made months and years later, in an effort to extricate themselves from liability.

Several defendants testified that Brennan advised them that Delaware law did not require a fairness opinion or an outside valuation of the Company before the Board could act on the Pritzker proposal. If given, the advice was correct. However, that did not end the matter. Unless the directors had before them adequate information regarding the intrinsic value of the Company, upon which a proper exercise of business judgment could be made, mere advice of this type is meaningless; and, given this record of the defendants' failures, it constitutes no defense here.[13] * * *

We conclude that Trans Union's Board was grossly negligent in that it failed to act with informed reasonable deliberation in agreeing to the Pritzker merger proposal on September 20; and we further conclude that the Trial Court erred as a matter of law in failing to address that question before determining whether the directors' later conduct was sufficient to cure its initial error.

A second claim is that counsel advised the Board it would be subject to lawsuits if it rejected the $55 per share offer. It is, of course, a fact of corporate life that today when faced with difficult or sensitive issues, directors often are subject to suit, irrespective of the decisions

---

13. [By the Court] Nonetheless, we are satisfied that in an appropriate factual context a proper exercise of business judgment may include, as one of its aspects, reasonable reliance upon the advice of counsel. This is wholly outside the statutory protections of 8 Del.C. § 141(e) involving reliance upon reports of officers, certain experts and books and records of the company.

they make. However, counsel's mere acknowledgement of this circumstance cannot be rationally translated into a justification for a board permitting itself to be stampeded into a patently unadvised act. While suit might result from the rejection of a merger or tender offer, Delaware law makes clear that a board acting within the ambit of the business judgment rule faces no ultimate liability. Pogostin v. Rice, supra. Thus, we cannot conclude that the mere threat of litigation, acknowledged by counsel, constitutes either legal advice or any valid basis upon which to pursue an uninformed course.

Since we conclude that Brennan's purported advice is of no consequence to the defense of this case, it is unnecessary for us to invoke the adverse inferences which may be attributable to one failing to appear at trial and testify. * * *

[In Part B of Section III of its opinion, the court considers the board's post-September 20 conduct and concludes that its actions on October 9, 1980 and January 26, 1981 did not cure the failures committed earlier.]

IV.

Whether the directors of Trans Union should be treated as one or individually in terms of invoking the protection of the business judgment rule and the applicability of 8 Del.C. § 141(c) are questions which were not originally addressed by the parties in their briefing of this case. This resulted in a supplemental briefing and a second rehearing en banc on two basic questions: (a) whether one or more of the directors were deprived of the protection of the business judgment rule by evidence of an absence of good faith; and (b) whether one or more of the outside directors were entitled to invoke the protection of 8 Del.C. § 141(e) by evidence of a reasonable, good faith reliance on "reports," including legal advice, rendered the Board by certain inside directors and the Board's special counsel, Brennan.

The parties' response, including reargument, has led the majority of the Court to conclude: (1) that since all of the defendant directors, outside as well as inside, take a unified position, we are required to treat all of the directors as one as to whether they are entitled to the protection of the business judgment rule; and (2) that considerations of good faith, including the presumption that the directors acted in good faith, are irrelevant in determining the threshold issue of whether the directors as a Board exercised an informed business judgment. For the same reason, we must reject defense counsel's *ad hominem* argument for affirmance: that reversal may result in a multi-million dollar class award against the defendants for having made an allegedly uninformed business judgment in a transaction not involving any personal gain, self-dealing or claim of bad faith.[14]

14. [By the Editor] In the petition for rehearing that was ultimately denied in this case, the Court quotes the beginning of the oral argument made by counsel for the individual defendants as follows:

In their brief, the defendants similarly mistake the business judgment rule's application to this case by erroneously invoking presumptions of good faith and "wide discretion":

> This is a case in which plaintiff challenged the exercise of business judgment by an independent Board of Directors. There were no allegations and no proof of fraud, bad faith, or self-dealing by the directors. * * *

> The business judgment rule, which was properly applied by the Chancellor, allows directors wide discretion in the matter of valuation and affords room for honest differences of opinion. In order to prevail, plaintiffs had the heavy burden of proving that the merger price was so grossly inadequate as to display itself as a badge of fraud. That is a burden which plaintiffs have not met.

However, plaintiffs have not claimed, nor did the Trial Court decide, that $55 was a grossly inadequate price per share for sale of the Company. That being so, the presumption that a board's judgment as to adequacy of price represents an honest exercise of business judgment (absent proof that the sale price was grossly inadequate) is irrelevant to the threshold question of whether an informed judgment was reached.

V.

The defendants ultimately rely on the stockholder vote of February 10 for exoneration. The defendants contend that the stockholders' "overwhelming" vote approving the Pritzker Merger Agreement had the legal effect of curing any failure of the Board to reach an informed business judgment in its approval of the merger.

The parties tacitly agree that a discovered failure of the Board to reach an informed business judgment in approving the merger constitutes a voidable, rather than a void, act. Hence, the merger can be sustained, notwithstanding the infirmity of the Board's action, if its approval by majority vote of the shareholders is found to have been based on an informed electorate. Cf. Michelson v. Duncan, Del.Supr., 407 A.2d 211 (1979), aff'g in part and rev'g in part, Del.Ch., 386 A.2d 1144 (1978). The disagreement between the parties arises over: (1) the Board's burden of disclosing to the shareholders all relevant and material information; and (2) the sufficiency of the evidence as to whether the Board satisfied that burden. * * *

[The court concluded that the shareholders were not fully informed of all material and "germane" facts when the transaction was approved on February 10, 1981.]

COUNSEL: I'll make the argument on behalf of the nine individual defendants against whom the plaintiffs seek more than $100,000,000 in damages. That is the ultimate issue in this case, whether or not nine honest, experienced businessmen should be subject to damages in a case where—

At this point counsel was interrupted by the Court with a question and never returned to the beginning point.

We hold, therefore, that the Trial Court committed reversible error in applying the business judgment rule in favor of the director defendants in this case.

On remand, the Court of Chancery shall conduct an evidentiary hearing to determine the fair value of the shares represented by the plaintiffs' class, based on the intrinsic value of Trans Union on September 20, 1980. Such valuation shall be made in accordance with Weinberger v. UOP, Inc., supra. Thereafter, an award of damages may be entered to the extent that the fair value of Trans Union exceeds $55 per share. * * *

REVERSED and REMANDED for proceedings consistent herewith.

McNEILLY, JUSTICE, dissenting:

The majority opinion reads like an advocate's closing address to a hostile jury. And I say that not lightly. Throughout the opinion great emphasis is directed only to the negative, with nothing more than lip service granted the positive aspects of this case. In my opinion Chancellor Marvel (retired) should have been affirmed. The Chancellor's opinion was the product of well reasoned conclusions, based upon a sound deductive process, clearly supported by the evidence and entitled to deference in this appeal. Because of my diametrical opposition to all evidentiary conclusions of the majority, I respectfully dissent.

It would serve no useful purpose, particularly at this late date, for me to dissent at great length. I restrain myself from doing so, but feel compelled to at least point out what I consider to be the most glaring deficiencies in the majority opinion. The majority has spoken and has effectively said that Trans Union's Directors have been the victims of a "fast shuffle" by Van Gorkom and Pritzker. That is the beginning of the majority's comedy of errors. The first and most important error made is the majority's assessment of the directors' knowledge of the affairs of Trans Union and their combined ability to act in this situation under the protection of the business judgment rule.

Trans Union's Board of Directors consisted of ten men, five of whom were "inside" directors and five of whom were "outside" directors. The "inside" directors were Van Gorkom, Chelberg, Bonser, William B. Browder, Senior Vice–President–Law, and Thomas P. O'Boyle, Senior Vice–President–Administration. At the time the merger was proposed the inside five directors had collectively been employed by the Company for 116 years and had 68 years of combined experience as directors. The "outside" directors were A.W. Wallis, William B. Johnson, Joseph B. Lanterman, Graham J. Morgan and Robert W. Reneker. With the exception of Wallis, these were all chief executive officers of Chicago based corporations that were at least as large as Trans Union. The five "outside" directors had 78 years of combined experience as chief executive officers, and 53 years cumulative service as Trans Union directors.

The inside directors wear their badge of expertise in the corporate affairs of Trans Union on their sleeves. But what about the outsiders? Dr. Wallis is or was an economist and math statistician, a professor of economics at Yale University, dean of the graduate school of business at the University of Chicago, and Chancellor of the University of Rochester. Dr. Wallis had been on the Board of Trans Union since 1962. He also was on the Board of Bausch & Lomb, Kodak, Metropolitan Life Insurance Company, Standard Oil and others.

William B. Johnson is a University of Pennsylvania law graduate, President of Railway Express until 1966, Chairman and Chief Executive of I.C. Industries Holding Company, and member of Trans Union's Board since 1968.

Joseph Lanterman, a Certified Public Accountant, is or was President and Chief Executive of American Steel, on the Board of International Harvester, Peoples Energy, Illinois Bell Telephone, Harris Bank and Trust Company, Kemper Insurance Company and a director of Trans Union for four years.

Graham Morgan is a chemist, was Chairman and Chief Executive Officer of U.S. Gypsum, and in the 17 and 18 years prior to the Trans Union transaction had been involved in 31 or 32 corporate takeovers.

Robert Reneker attended University of Chicago and Harvard Business Schools. He was President and Chief Executive of Swift and Company, director of Trans Union since 1971, and member of the Boards of seven other corporations including U.S. Gypsum and the Chicago Tribune.

Directors of this caliber are not ordinarily taken in by a "fast shuffle". I submit they were not taken into this multi-million dollar corporate transaction without being fully informed and aware of the state of the art as it pertained to the entire corporate panorama of Trans Union. True, even directors such as these, with their business acumen, interest and expertise, can go astray. I do not believe that to be the case here. These men knew Trans Union like the back of their hands and were more than well qualified to make on the spot informed business judgments concerning the affairs of Trans Union including a 100% sale of the corporation. Lest we forget, the corporate world of then and now operates on what is so aptly referred to as "the fast track". These men were at the time an integral part of that world, all professional business men, not intellectual figureheads.

The majority of this Court holds that the Board's decision, reached on September 20, 1980, to approve the merger was not the product of an *informed* business judgment, that the Board's subsequent efforts to amend the Merger Agreement and take other curative action were *legally and factually* ineffectual, and that the Board did *not deal with complete candor* with the stockholders by failing to disclose all material facts, which they knew or should have known, before securing the stockholders' approval of the merger. I disagree. * * *

Notes

(1) Why did the defendants' lawyers in *Van Gorkom* adopt a "one for all and all for one" approach? Assuming there was negligence is it not clear that some of the directors might have had a defense that would not have been available to Van Gorkom himself and possibly other inside directors?

(2) Following the Delaware Supreme Court opinion in *Van Gorkom*, the case was settled with the approval of the Delaware Chancery Court. The settlement involved the payment by the defendants of $23,500,000, $10,000,000 of which was provided through the defendants' directors' and officers' (D&O) liability insurance policy. The plaintiffs' attorneys are reputed to have received $18 million of this recovery and the shareholders $5.5 million. Some time after the sale of Trans Union, Van Gorkom was appointed Undersecretary for Management in the Department of State. Secretary of State Schultz was reported to have selected Van Gorkom personally because he wanted a "trusted confidant" in that position. So far as Trans Union itself is concerned, the Pritzker buyout was apparently not as successful as Pritzker had expected. These miscellaneous facts are taken from Fleischer, Hazard and Klipper, Board Games (1988), Chapter 1.

(3) The response of the corporate bar to *Van Gorkom* was one of shocked incredulity. "The Delaware Supreme Court * * * exploded a bomb. Stated minimally, the Court * * * pierced the Business Judgment Rule and imposed liability on independent (even eminent) outside directors of Trans Union Corporation * * * because (roughly) the Court thought they had not been careful enough, and had not enquired enough, before deciding to accept and recommend to Transunion's shareholders a cash-out merger at a per share price that was less than the 'intrinsic value' of the shares. * * * The corporate bar generally views the decision as atrocious and predicts the most dire consequences as directors come to realize how exposed they have become." B. Manning, in an unpublished newsletter for his clients. Professor Richard Buxbaum, in a CLE newsletter for California Bar subscribers, headlined his analysis of the case "Summer Lightning Out of Delaware."

(4) Herzel and Katz, Smith v. Van Gorkom: The Business of Judging Business Judgment, 41 Bus.Law. 1187, 1188–1191 (1986):*

> To most (including the authors) the court's decision seems misguided and Trans Union's actions entirely proper. Van Gorkom was a seasoned chief executive officer and substantial stockholder. He was well placed and motivated to strike a good deal, even when acting by himself. The other directors were also experienced and sophisticated. There was no reason why they shouldn't have been able to recognize and approve a good deal at the drop of a hat. Investment bankers are expensive and surely not indispensable. When a good offer is in hand, they may well be superfluous. Merger documents are written by lawyers for lawyers, and typically no one else scrutinizes them. Admittedly, the board was a bit slapdash in its compliance with corporate

---

formalities—did Van Gorkom really have to sign at a social affair for the opera? But that's not a breach of the duty of care. * * *

The other effect of *Smith v. Van Gorkom* will be greater formalism on the part of the board, as it goes about the business of cultivating an aura of care, diligence, thoroughness, and circumspection. (As one director put it: "Prudence and diligence are no longer assumed but require a certain amount of posturing.")

Such formalism has a lot of costs. Most obviously, it will mean more reliance on and more fees for lawyers, investment bankers, accountants, management consultants, and economists, and who knows, maybe sociologists, statisticians, psychologists, demographers, and population geneticists. In short, experts of every stripe, whose advice might shed some light on some aspect of the board's decision. After all, every decision has untold consequences and ramifications.

(5) Hamilton, Reliance and Liability Standards for Outside Directors, 24 Wake Forest L.Rev. 5, 28–9 (1989):

Whether the result reached by the Delaware Supreme Court in *Van Gorkom* was correct or incorrect, the immediate consequences of the decision on the business community were deeply disturbing. Many outside directors began to reassess their willingness to serve as directors at all, and isolated instances of resignations were reported.[15] The number of lawyers serving on boards of directors of their clients declined. Even some inside directors began to have qualms about the desirability of their service on the board of directors of the company that employed them. The prestige and financial rewards of serving on boards of directors of publicly held corporations had to be weighed against the remote risk of a crushing liability being imposed on the board members. Many potential outside directors, in particular, decided that this risk outweighed the benefits. It became considerably more difficult to find desirable persons who were willing to become outside directors. On another level, general counsels made recommendations to boards of directors that they hire expensive financial advisers, commission extensive studies, and otherwise improve the paper record of their decisional process in order to reduce the risk of liability in situations similar to *Van Gorkom*. It was a widely held belief that the cost of this exercise exceeded the benefits to the decisional process.

---

15. [By the Author] See Baum & Byrne, *The Job Nobody Wants*, Bus. Wk., Sept. 8, 1986, at 56 (reporting ten instances of mass resignations of outside directors). The decision in *Van Gorkom* was handed down during a "liability insurance crisis" in the United States. During this period insurance companies writing liability insurance in a variety of areas were reducing their exposure by reducing coverage limits, increasing premiums, and declining entirely to insure specific risks. Directors' and officers' liability insurance was involved in this process, and some of the activities described in the text may have been the consequence of the difficulties some companies were experiencing in obtaining or maintaining acceptable levels of liability insurance for their directors. See Lewin, *Director Insurance Drying Up*, N.Y. Times, March 7, 1986, at D1, col. 3 ("[b]ecause of increased litigation, large court awards and a rapidly shrinking pool of available insurance, many companies can no longer find, or afford, insurance for their directors and officers"). Anecdotal evidence indicates that this crisis has eased and that the availability of such insurance has improved in the last couple of years. See Glaberson, *Liability Rates Flattening Out as Crisis Eases*, N.Y. Times, Feb. 9, 1987, at A1, col. 5 ("companies that could not buy [insurance] coverage at any price are [now] finding it").

(6) In an article entitled Risky Business: Companies are Finding it Difficult Now to Obtain Liability Insurance for Their Directors, Wall Street Journal, p. 1, col. 6 (July 10, 1985), Walter B. Wriston, a member of the board of directors of nine corporations and the former chief executive officer of a major bank, is reported as stating, "I don't know of anybody who would join a board without D & O insurance." Such insurance is usually augmented by a corporate policy of indemnifying directors against costs of litigation to the maximum extent permissible under public policy. Indemnification and insurance are discussed in Chapter 14. It seems clear that the availability of D & O insurance was limited during the period of the middle 1980s. For a speculative assessment of the causes, see Romano, What Went Wrong with Directors' and Officers' Liability Insurance, 14 Del. J.Corp.L. 1 (1989). Arguably, the decision in *Van Gorkom* contributed to this drying up of insurance; Professor Romano, however, comments:

> The court [in *Van Gorkom*] further indicated that if specific procedures had been followed, such as obtaining an investment banker's fairness opinion, there would have been no liability. Given * * * standard business practice, the opinion is not a scandalous harbinger of increased exposure. Quite to the contrary, the decision arguably lowered the standard of conduct by defining breaches of the duty of care in terms of "gross" rather than "ordinary" negligence.

14 Del.J.Corp.L., at 24. Of course, the sheer magnitude of the potential liability in cases like *Van Gorkom* makes it difficult to satisfy any risk adverse potential director that the insurance being provided, no matter how large, is adequate.

(7) In evaluating the conduct of directors, should a distinction be drawn between "outside" directors and those who are employees and officers of the corporation? What about between directors who reside in the city in which the principal offices of the corporation are located and those who reside at distant points?

(8) Should it not be an absolute defense that a director sought the advice of counsel for the corporation and acted only after receiving an informal opinion that the conduct was lawful? Consider RMBCA § 8.30. Compare Tillman v. Wheaton–Haven Recreation Ass'n, Inc., 517 F.2d 1141 (4th Cir.1975), where directors of a non-profit corporation were held personally liable under 42 U.S.C.A. § 1983 for unlawfully discriminating against black plaintiffs despite the fact that they had been assured by counsel that the exclusion of blacks from the neighborhood swimming pool association was lawful. The Court stated:

> The flaw in the directors' argument is their failure to place the defense of due diligence in its proper context. Due diligence is a defense for corporate directors who are charged with failing to exercise reasonable care. Its genesis is the law of negligence. None of the cases on which the directors rely applies the doctrine to an intentionally tortious act against a third person. An analysis of the cases cited as supporting the directors exposes the fallacy of their position.

517 F.2d at 1144. Judge Boreman dissented, arguing that at the time the discrimination took place it was not possible to know whether or not the conduct was legal, and that "[t]o hold the directors to a standard of legal

acumen greater than that possessed by the federal judiciary would be unconscionable." Id., at 1151.

DEL. GEN. CORP. LAW
§ 102(b)(7).

§ 102 CONTENTS OF CERTIFICATE OF INCORPORATION * * *

(b) In addition to the matters required to be set forth in the certificate of incorporation by subsection (a) of this section, the certificate of incorporation may also contain any or all of the following matters: * * *

(7) A provision eliminating or limiting the personal liability of a director to the corporation or its stockholders for monetary damages for breach of fiduciary duty as a director, provided that such provision shall not eliminate or limit the liability of a director (i) for any breach of the director's duty of loyalty to the corporation or its stockholders, (ii) for acts or omissions not in good faith or which involve intentional misconduct or a knowing violation of law, (iii) under section 174 of this Title,[16] or (iv) for any transaction from which the director derived an improper personal benefit. No such provision shall eliminate or limit the liability of a director for any act or omission occurring prior to the date when such provision becomes effective. * * *

HANKS, RECENT STATE LEGISLATION ON DIRECTOR AND OFFICER LIABILITY LIMITATION AND INDEMNIFICATION*
43 Bus.Law. 1207, 1209–1213, 1216–1217, 1219–1220, 1231–1235 (1988).

The first state to respond to the developments of the mid–1980s was Indiana, in April 1986, followed by Delaware in June. Since then, forty other states have adopted some form of legislation designed to reduce the risk of directors' personal liability for money damages. * * *

CHARTER OPTION STATUTES

The most popular form of director liability statute has been the so-called "charter option" statute, first enacted by Delaware, effective July 1, 1986. Since then, charter option statutes have been adopted by thirty other states. * * * [The Delaware statute] authorizes restricting liability for money damages, but not expanding it as, for example, making directors liable for simple negligence.

The statutory language also means that, while the stockholders may decide for themselves whether to eliminate or limit the liability of directors, they may not delegate this power to the directors. * * *

---

16. [By the Editor] Section 174 refers to the liability of directors for unlawful dividends and stock repurchases or redemptions.

ed with the permission of the American Bar Association and its Section of Corporation, Banking and Business Law.

In the two years since the Delaware statute became effective, stockholders of hundreds—probably thousands—of American corporations have approved, generally by substantial majorities, liability-limitation charter amendments. Many charter amendments simply repeat the language of the statute, including its exceptions. Other amendments provide for elimination of liability to the maximum extent permitted by law from time to time. * * *

The potentially most troublesome of the Delaware exceptions is the one for breach of the duty of loyalty. The phrase "duty of loyalty" appears nowhere else in the Delaware General Corporation Law or, so far as is known, anywhere else in the corporation statute of any other state that has adopted this exception in a charter option statute. Even Delaware lawyers concede that the Delaware courts are unclear as to the parameters of the duty of loyalty. The Delaware Supreme Court itself has had difficulty in distinguishing the duty of care from the duty of loyalty. The fact that one of the other exceptions to the Delaware statute is for "improper personal benefit" suggests that breach of the duty of loyalty means something more than just self-dealing. Moreover, case law development of the duty of loyalty in Delaware has been based in substantial part on the duties of trustees under trust law. Delaware trust law includes concepts (e.g., the "exclusive benefit" rule) not necessarily appropriate to corporate directors and officers. Finally, many states have adopted a statutory standard of conduct for directors patterned after section 8.30(a) of the Revised Model Business Corporation Act, * * * Prohibiting liability limitation in language different from a statutory standard of care may lead to confusion in interpretation.

It will not be surprising, therefore, if stockholders of Delaware corporations that have adopted exculpatory charter provisions begin alleging violations of the duty of loyalty for acts or omissions that until now would have supported a claim for breach of the duty of care. * * *

The improper personal benefit exception could also be exploited, especially because it is not limited to the actual receipt of money, property, or services and therefore might be interpreted to include less easily measurable considerations, such as business goodwill, personal friendship, or social ingratiation. In voting against a takeover proposal, for example, a director might be charged with having received an improper personal benefit in the form of continued tenure on the board. * * *

Perhaps because Delaware was the first state to adopt a charter option statute and because changes in Delaware's corporate statute always attract attention, many corporations have reincorporated to Delaware. Meanwhile, hundreds of other corporations already incorporated in Delaware have amended or proposed amending their charters in order to add exculpatory provisions.

SELF–EXECUTING STATUTES

The most radical legislative approach to director liability is direct alteration of the standard of liability necessary to recover money damages from directors. This self-executing approach was pioneered by Indiana and subsequently adopted by [four other states]. Under the new Indiana Business Corporation Law, a director is liable only if he has breached or failed to perform his duties in compliance with the statutory standard of care *and* "the breach or failure to perform constitutes willful misconduct or recklessness." This limitation on liability applies to suits by third parties as well as by stockholders and includes both money damages and equitable relief. Moreover, the statute does not provide for an Indiana corporation to opt out of this provision even if its stockholders so desire. * * *

CAP ON MONEY DAMAGES

Virginia combines the charter option and self-executing approaches. It (i) limits the damages that may be assessed against an officer or director in a suit by or in the right of the corporation or by the stockholders directly to the greater of (a) $100,000 or (b) "the amount of cash compensation received by the officer or director from the corporation during the twelve months immediately preceding the act or omission for which liability was imposed" but (ii) permits the stockholders to reduce or eliminate (but not increase) this limit to the "monetary amount specified" in either a charter or by-law provision. Thus, if the shareholders take no action to amend the charter or by-laws, the liability of a director or officer of a Virginia corporation will be limited to the greater of $100,000 or his cash compensation over the year preceding the act or omission giving rise to the liability. * * *

The Virginia statute also provides:

> The liability of an officer or director shall not be limited . . . if the officer or director engaged in willful misconduct or a knowing violation of the criminal law or of any federal or state securities law, including, without limitation, any claim of unlawful insider trading or manipulation of the market for any security. * * *

RISK ALLOCATION

The principal public policy issue in director and officer liability legislation is the allocation of the economic cost of the directors' exculpated conduct. Under every director liability statute * * * liability is (under the self-executing statutes) or may be (under the charter option statutes) limited for at least simple negligence and gross negligence. * * *

Charter option statutes simply permit the stockholders to decide for themselves whether to assume this risk or to leave it with the directors. By contrast, the other director liability statutes enacted to date are direct or indirect determinations by the legislatures to shift the risk from the directors to the stockholders. * * * Generally, the legislatures that have enacted these statutes have done so with very little discussion of the benefits and costs of shifting from the directors to the stockholders the costs of the directors' misconduct. Most of these statutes have been enacted in the context of sharply increased premiums for D & O insurance (or its unavailability at any price) and the consequent loss or prospective loss of outside directors. The lobbying and editorial comments surrounding many of these statutes have often been accompanied by emphasis on economic development, including comparisons with statutes in other (especially neighboring) states. Little attention has been paid to the issue of whether limiting the liability of directors and officers is wise in the absence of an insurance "crisis" or after it recedes. * * *

Supporters of legislated (as opposed to stockholder-determined) exculpation for directors would probably * * * claim that it is more in society's interests to encourage competent, qualified individuals to serve as directors than to provide for recovery of the occasional loss to corporations caused by directors' acts or omissions. Indeed, good directors are probably less likely to cause injury to the corporation. As Judge Learned Hand declared: "The law ought not make trusteeship so hazardous that responsible individuals . . . will shy away from it."[17] Certainly, it is well within the power of state legislatures, not to mention the stockholders themselves, to make this choice. * * *

Notes

(1) Mr. Hanks' final conclusion is that:

> One policy behind the self-executing, no opt-out approach apparently is that there should be a uniform standard of liability for directors of all corporations. Moreover, it is arguable that corporations, particularly privately held corporations, that are unaware of the possibilities for limiting director liability should not be penalized simply because they have failed, possibly through their ignorance of this statute, to obtain the approval of the stockholders. * * *
>
> In the end, sounder policy reasons permit the stockholders to decide whether to limit the liability of their directors, at least as to suits by the corporation or the stockholders. After all, it is the stockholders' money at stake. As long as the right of the stockholders to exculpate their directors is limited to liability to the corporation or to the stockholders themselves (in either derivative or direct suits), the state's regulatory interests should be minimal.

43 Bus.Law., at 1236.

(2) Has litigation involving directoral action and the duty of care dried up as a result of the enactment of these limitation of liability statutes? Everyone following the flow of litigation, particularly in the takeover area from which Smith v. Van Gorkom arose, recognizes that litigation arising out of individual takeover disputes continues to arise, more as a function of the number of attempted takeovers than the applicability of limitation of liability statutes. There is, however, much less retrospective litigation seeking to hold the directors personally liable for consummated transactions; rather, the validity of directoral conduct is tested in suits brought to

---

17. [By the Author] Dabney v. Chase Nat'l Bank, 196 F.2d 668, 675 (2d Cir.1952).

enjoin defensive tactics or cash tender offers. Such litigation, of course, is unaffected by Del.G.C.L. § 102(b)(7) (since it does not impose personal liability on directors). Suits to enjoin directoral conduct appear to be brought even in situations where it is likely that a suit to surcharge directors would not be foreclosed by section 102(b)(7).

GALL v. EXXON CORP.

United States District Court, S.D. New York, 1976.
418 F.Supp. 508.

ROBERT L. CARTER, DISTRICT JUDGE.

Defendants have moved, pursuant to Rule 56, F.R.Civ.P., for summary judgment dismissing plaintiff's complaint on the grounds that the Special Committee on Litigation ("Special Committee"), acting as the Board of Directors of Exxon Corporation ("Exxon"), has determined in the good faith exercise of its sound business judgment that it is contrary to the interests of Exxon to institute suit on the basis of any matters raised in plaintiff's complaint. Defendants' motion is hereby denied without prejudice to its renewal after plaintiff has conducted relevant discovery.

I

FACTS

Plaintiff's complaint arises out of the alleged payment by Exxon Corporation of some $59 million in corporate funds as bribes or political payments, which were improperly contributed to Italian political parties and others during the period 1963–1974, in order to secure special political favors as well as other allegedly illegal commitments.

Plaintiff sues derivatively on behalf of Exxon and its shareholders. Her complaint is in four counts. Count I charges that the individual defendants filed or caused to be filed with the SEC financial statements or other reports which were false and misleading in that they failed to disclose the allegedly illegal political contributions, in violation of Section 13(a) of the Securities Act of 1934 and Rule 13a–1 promulgated thereunder. Count II charges that the individual defendants used the mails and other instrumentalities of interstate commerce in order to file or cause to be filed false and misleading proxy statements, and solicited proxies from Exxon shareholders pursuant to such false statements in violation of Section 14(a) of the Securities Exchange Act of 1934 and Rule 14a–9 promulgated thereunder, in that such statements omitted reference to the allegedly illegal political contributions. Count III charges the individual defendants with waste, spoliation and misuse of corporate assets. Count IV charges the individual defendants with breach of their fiduciary duties to Exxon.

The complaint demands that the individual defendants be held jointly and severally liable for damages, including loss of goodwill, allegedly suffered by Exxon. It further demands, among other things, the commencement of an investigation through independent auditors in conjunction with plaintiff's counsel, the immediate election of four new members of the Board of Directors proposed by plaintiff and, within 12 months, the election of a new Chairman of the Board and President, and reconstituting the composition of the membership of the Board of Directors and Executive Committee, such that at least 55% of the Board and the Executive Committee be made up of independent outside directors.

II

On September 24, 1975, Exxon's Board of Directors unanimously resolved, pursuant to Article III, Section 1, of Exxon's By–Laws to establish a Special Committee on Litigation, composed of Exxon directors Jack F. Bennett, Richard P. Dobson and Edward G. Harness,[18] and refer to the Special Committee for the determination of Exxon's action the matters raised in this and several other pending actions relating to the Italian expenditures. * * *

On January 23, 1976, after an investigation of approximately four months, including interviews with over 100 witnesses, the Special Committee issued the "Determination and Report of the Special Committee on Litigation" ("Report"), an 82–page document summarizing the Committee's findings and recommendations. The facts as uncovered by the Special Committee may be briefly summarized as follows.
* * *

[Editor: The Committee report described a pattern of secret payments made for various purposes between 1963 and 1972 and political contributions to Italian political parties during the same period. The secret payments, totalling about 39 million dollars, were made through secret bank accounts not reflected on the books of Exxon's Italian subsidiary, Esso Italiana. The political contributions, totalling about 20 million dollars, were channeled through newspaper and public relations firms connected with Italian political parties; these payments were reflected by fictitious invoices purportedly for services rendered.

Several of the Exxon directors named as defendants in this suit were aware of the existence of at least the political payments in Italy prior to their termination in 1972. Some of the defendants had simply been advised of the existence of the payments; others, in positions of responsibility within corporate management urged that the contributions be phased out as promptly as possible. Some of the defendant-directors were also aware of the payments made through the secret bank accounts, but apparently the knowledge of these payments was more limited than the knowledge about the political contributions.]

18. [By the Court] * * * According to the affidavits submitted, each of the members of the Special Committee has confirmed that he has not been in any way connected or involved with the matters relating to the Italian expenditures referred to in this action or in the other related actions and none has been named as a defendant in any of the pending actions. Indeed, none of the members of the Committee was elected to the Exxon Board until long after the Italian expenditures complained of were terminated and Exxon had taken steps to ensure that such expenditures would not be resumed.

III

After careful review, analysis and investigation, and with the advice and concurrence of Special Counsel,[19] the Special Committee unanimously determined on January 23, 1976, that it would be contrary to the interests of Exxon and its shareholders for Exxon, or anyone on its behalf, to institute or maintain a legal action against any present or former Exxon director or officer.[20] The Committee further resolved to direct and authorize the proper officers of Exxon and its General Counsel to oppose and seek dismissal of all shareholder derivative actions relating to payments made by or on behalf of Esso Italiana S.p. A., which had been filed against any present or former Exxon director or officer.

IV

DISCUSSION

There is no question that the rights sought to be vindicated in this lawsuit are those of Exxon and not those of the plaintiff suing derivatively on the corporation's behalf. Since it is the interests of the corporation which are at stake, it is the responsibility of the directors of the corporation to determine, in the first instance, whether an action should be brought on the corporation's behalf. It follows that the decision of corporate directors whether or not to assert a cause of action held by the corporation rests within the sound business judgment of the management. See, e.g., United Copper Securities Co. v. Amalgamated Copper Co., 244 U.S. 261, 263–4, 37 S.Ct. 509, 61 L.Ed. 1119 (1917).

This principle, which has come to be known as the business judgment rule, was articulated by Mr. Justice Brandeis speaking for a unanimous Court in United Copper Securities Co. v. Amalgamated Copper Co., supra, 244 U.S. at 263–64, 37 S.Ct. at 510. In that case the directors of a corporation chose not to bring an antitrust action against a third party. Mr. Justice Brandeis said:

> "Whether or not a corporation shall seek to enforce in the courts a cause of action for damages is, like other business questions, ordinarily a matter of internal management, and is left to the discretion of the directors, in the absence of instruction by vote of the stockholders. Courts interfere seldom to control such discretion intra vires the corporation, except where the directors are guilty of misconduct equivalent to a breach of trust, or where they stand in a dual relation which prevents an unprejudiced exercise of judgment. * * *

It is clear that absent allegations of fraud, collusion, self-interest, dishonesty or other misconduct of a breach of trust nature, and absent

19. [By the Court] At its second meeting on October 29, 1975, the Special Committee appointed Justice Joseph Weintraub, former Chief Justice of the New Jersey Supreme Court, as its Special Counsel.

20. [By the Court] Among the factors cited by the Special Committee in reaching its decision were the unfavorable prospects for success of the litigation, the cost of conducting the litigation, interruption of corporate business affairs and the undermining of personnel morale.

allegations that the business judgment exercised was grossly unsound, the court should not at the instigation of a single shareholder interfere with the judgment of the corporate officers.

The question remains as to the requisite showing of good faith on the part of the corporate directors sufficient to warrant a dismissal based on the business judgment rule defense. ＊　＊　＊

In this regard, plaintiff challenges the independence of the Special Committee's judgment, arguing that the decision of the Special Committee was, in effect, a decision by those accused of the wrongdoing or by a body under the control of those accused of the wrongdoing. Thus, plaintiff contends that it was the decision of the full Board of Directors themselves to uphold and follow the determination of the Special Committee, and not the Committee's determination, which governs the present posture taken by Exxon in this suit. ＊　＊　＊

This argument clearly misses the mark. The focus of the business judgment rule inquiry is on those who actually wield the decision-making authority, not on those who might have possessed such authority at different times and under different circumstances. In no sense was the decision of the Special Committee not to sue merely an advisory one. Indeed, in carrying out its investigation and in reaching its conclusions, the Special Committee exercised the full powers of the Board.

Plaintiff next argues that the challenged political payments were illegal and that such illegality removes this case from the operation of the business judgment rule. ＊　＊　＊

[However,] even assuming that the political payments in Italy were illegal where made, the business judgment rule is nonetheless applicable. The decision not to bring suit with regard to past conduct which may have been illegal is not itself a violation of law and does not result in the continuation of the alleged violation of law.[21] Rather, it is a decision by the directors of the corporation that pursuit of a cause of action based on acts already consummated is not in the best interest of the corporation. Such a determination, like any other business decision, must be made by the corporate directors in the exercise of their sound business judgment. The conclusive effect of such a judgment cannot be affected by the allegedly illegal nature of the initial action which purportedly gives rise to the cause of action. Cf. Miller v. American Telephone & Telegraph Co., 507 F.2d 759 (3d Cir.1974).[22]

21. [By the Court] Put another way, the decision by the Special Committee not to sue does not constitute the ratification of an illegal act. The question of the good faith exercise of sound business judgment is entirely separate from the question of ratification.

22. [By the Court] In *Miller,* stockholders of AT & T brought a derivative action against the corporation and various of its directors based on the failure of AT & T to collect a debt owed to it by the Democratic National Committee. Failure to collect the debt was alleged to have involved a breach of defendant directors' duty to exercise diligence in conducting the affairs of the corporation to have violated 47 U.S. C.A. § 202(a) by affording a preference in collection procedures to the Democratic National Committee, and to constitute a "contribution" to the DNC in violation of 18 U.S.C.A. § 610. The District Court dis-

Moreover, this conclusion is all the more appropriate in view of the fact that there is not a scintilla of evidence on the record before me that the political payments in issue here were illegal either under the laws of the United States or of Italy. On the contrary, the Special Committee on the basis of its intensive investigation, and with the concurrence of its Special Counsel, determined that there was no basis for concluding that the Italian payments were in any way illegal.

In recent months, the legality and morality of foreign political contributions, bribes and other payments by American corporations has been widely debated. The issue before me for decision, however, is not whether the payments made by Esso Italiana to Italian political parties and other unauthorized payments were proper or improper. Were the court to frame the issue in this way, it would necessarily involve itself in the business decisions of every corporation, and be required to mediate between the judgment of the directors and the judgment of the shareholders with regard to particular corporate actions. As Mr. Justice Brandeis said in his concurring opinion in Ashwander v. Tennessee Valley Authority, 297 U.S. [288,] at 343, 56 S.Ct. [466,] at 481, "[i]f a stockholder could compel the officers to enforce every legal right, courts instead of chosen officers, would be the arbiters of the corporation's fate." Rather, the issue is whether the Special Committee, acting as Exxon's Board of Directors and in the sound exercise of their business judgment, may determine that a suit against any present or former director or officer would be contrary to the best interests of the corporation.

Again, to quote Mr. Justice Brandeis,

> "Mere belief that corporate action, taken or contemplated, is illegal gives the stockholder no greater right to interfere than is possessed by any other citizen. Stockholders are not guardians of the public. The function of guarding the public against the acts deemed illegal rests with the public officials." Ashwander v. Tennessee Valley Authority, supra, 297 U.S. at 343, 56 S.Ct. at 481.

Nor can this court ask, as did Juvenal, "Sed quis custodiet ipsos custodes." [23]

missed the action based on the business judgment rule, 364 F.Supp. 648 (E.D.Pa. 1973), and the Third Circuit reversed. The Court noted that had plaintiffs' complaint alleged only a failure to pursue a corporate claim, application of the business judgment rule would support the district court's ruling that a shareholder could not attack the decision of the directors. The Court went on to note, however, that where the decision not to collect the debt owed to the corporation was *itself* alleged to be an illegal act, a different rule would apply. Since the Court found that issues had been raised as to whether the defendant direc-

tors had breached 18 U.S.C.A. § 610 as plaintiffs had charged, it concluded that plaintiffs' complaint stated a claim upon which relief could be granted sufficient to withstand a motion to dismiss. In the instant case, the decision by the Special Committee not to sue based on the prior acts of the defendant directors is not *itself* an illegal act or the perpetuation of an illegal act.

23. [By the Court] "But who is to guard the guards themselves?" VI Juvenal, *Satires*, 1.347.

V

Plaintiff also calls into question the disinterestedness and bona fides of the Special Committee, suggesting that the members of the Special Committee may have been personally involved in the transactions in question, or, at the least, interested in the alleged wrongdoing "in a way calculated to impair their exercise of business judgment on behalf of the corporation." Klotz v. Consolidated Edison of New York, Inc., supra, 386 F.Supp. at 581.[24]

With the foregoing in mind, I am constrained to conclude that it is premature at this stage of the lawsuit to grant summary judgment. Plaintiff must be given an opportunity to test the bona fides and independence of the Special Committee through discovery and, if necessary, at a plenary hearing. Issues of intent, motivation, and good faith are particularly inappropriate for summary disposition.

Accordingly, defendants' motion for summary judgment is hereby denied without prejudice to its renewal after plaintiff has conducted relevant discovery. * * *

Notes

(1) *Gall* involved a decision by presumably independent directors not to pursue a derivative suit brought against other directors. In invoking the business judgment rule, Judge Carter relied on *United Copper Securities Co.*, a case involving a decision by directors not to sue an unrelated third party. Are these situations really comparable?

(2) The device adopted by Exxon to seek dismissal of the Gall suit has been widely embraced by boards of directors since 1976, in an effort to obtain dismissal of derivative suits they do not desire to have pursued. This device in effect transmutes a discussion of the merits of the plaintiffs' suit into a discussion of the *bona fides* of the business judgment of the board (or, as in *Gall*, a special committee of the board) to discontinue inconvenient litigation. What about the argument that plaintiffs should be entitled to a hearing on their complaints and that the *Gall* approach may permit wrongful conduct to go unpunished? Is this problem really as simple as that? Should not directors who are really independent and disinterested be able to determine what litigation should be pursued?

(3) The development of the independent litigation committee has produced a torrent of law review commentary. Consider the policy arguments in the following excerpts:

24. [By the Court] * * * At a hearing held on February 27, 1976, plaintiff, for the first time, questioned the independence and bona fides of the members of the Special Committee. Subsequently, on March 2, 1976, plaintiff submitted to the court a statement * * * challenging defendants' assertion that the resolution of the Special Committee was made in the independent, disinterested and good faith exercise of their business judgment. Rule 56, F.R.Civ. P., requires that the moving party demonstrate, on the basis of admissible evidence adduced from persons with personal knowledge of the facts, that "there is no genuine issue as to any material fact." Where this initial showing is not made, summary judgment will be denied, even though the party opposing the motion has submitted no probative evidence to support its position or to establish that there is a genuine issue for trial.

(a) Cox, Searching for the Corporation's Voice in Derivative Suit Litigation: A Critique of *Zapata* and the ALI Project, 1982 Duke L.J. 959, 960–961 (1982):

> As a starting point, * * * [I assume,] that the corporation has a legitimate interest in raising at any stage in the litigation its concern that a derivative suit does it more harm than good. A derivative suit against managers or directors may ultimately lead to charges against the corporation for the defendant's litigation costs, the corporation's own litigation costs incident to its participation as a nominal defendant, and the more indefinite costs associated with any litigation, such as loss of morale, deflection of employee time, and injury to the corporate reputation. Even if the defendant's fault is conceded, the recoverable amount after deduction of the attorney's fees of the plaintiff may be insufficient to cover the costs of the suit; if the complaint is less well-founded, the cost-benefit ratio is even higher.
>
> The derivative suit plaintiff is self-selected; without election or appointment he presents himself as spokesman for the corporate interest. Because the plaintiff usually has no significant financial interest in the corporation, the possibly harmful economic effects of prosecuting the suit cannot be expected to guide his decision to litigate.

(b) Comment, The Propriety of Judicial Deference to Corporate Boards of Directors, 96 Harv.L.Rev. 1894, 1896–1897, 1905–1908 (1983): *

> The corporate board is a group, and as such it is likely to exhibit certain behavioral tendencies identified by researchers in the field of social psychology known as group dynamics. * * *
>
> [A]ny constructive influence that the board's collective decision-making might have on solutions to particular problems is likely to be outweighed by the destructive effect, known as "conformity" or "groupthink," that group dynamics demonstrably and inevitably produce. This conformity may simply be outward: individuals may publicly agree with the group's judgment while privately believing that judgment to be incorrect. Yet the group may well also shape the individual's inward view of the correct judgment: the individual may rely on the group's perceptions and evaluations in assessing the alternatives and reaching a conclusion.
>
> The occurrence of either outward or inward conformity in a boardroom would lead one to doubt the meaningfulness of board approval. In fact, both outward and inward conformity are likely: as will be shown, boards of directors are characterized by the sorts of factors that, social psychologists assert, increase the degree of conformity within a group. * * *
>
> When it is the board that decides to seek dismissal or not to sue, the implications of group dynamics clearly make questionable a legal rule according the decision any weight in the disposition of the motion to dismiss. * * * [T]he directors will be aware that a vote to proceed with the suit could greatly harm management, with whom the

* Copyright © 1983 by the Harvard Law
Review Association.

directors must associate both professionally and socially and to whom the directors owe their prestigious positions. In an ongoing, cohesive group like a board, these factors will encourage at least outward conformity. The directors are thus apt to vote as management would obviously want them to: they will routinely decide to seek dismissal. Judicial deference to the board's decision amounts to deference to the challenged decision by management and hence seriously impairs the shareholders' ability to protect their interests.

When the decision not to pursue the suit is made by a specially appointed, disinterested committee, the argument that approval by board members ought to be legally irrelevant might seem less persuasive. * * * Management defendants are absent when the committee reviews the facts and reaches its decision about the suit; moreover, the committee often consists of new directors appointed for the primary purpose of staffing the committee. The committee is therefore not subject to pressure arising from preexisting ties with board members and managers. Nevertheless, the committee members know that they will continue to associate—both professionally and socially—with the defendant directors after they make their determination about the suit. In addition, newly appointed directors probably feel a considerable affinity with those who appointed them. Thus, the pressures on the committee members to conform their judgment to the wishes of management defendants may not be significantly less weighty than the pressures on the board. Like a decision by the board, a decision by a special committee is essentially made by challenged management and ought to be of no legal consequence.

For an even stronger statement that directors have a "structural bias" in favor of dismissing all derivative litigation, see Cox and Munsinger, Bias in the Boardroom: Psychological Foundations and Legal Implications of Corporation Cohesion, 48 Law & Contem.Prob. 83 (1985). Many corporate lawyers reject the underlying premise of this argument, which is also not accepted by some commentators familiar with the underlying social science research. See Haft, Business Decisions by the New Board: Behavioral Science and Corporate Law, 80 Mich.L.Rev. 1 (1981).

(4) Several pre-1981 cases accept apparently without reservation the reasoning set forth in *Gall*. Auerbach v. Bennett, 47 N.Y.2d 619, 419 N.Y.S.2d 920, 393 N.E.2d 994 (1979) [New York law definitively construed by the New York Court of Appeals]; Abbey v. Control Data Corp., 603 F.2d 724 (8th Cir.1979) [Delaware law]; Lewis v. Anderson, 615 F.2d 778 (9th Cir.1979) [California law]. Burks v. Lasker, 441 U.S. 471, 99 S.Ct. 1831, 60 L.Ed.2d 404 (1979), involved the dismissal of a suit against a registered investment company; the major issue was whether state or federal law (represented by the Investment Company Act of 1940) controlled. The court held that state law controlled, but in passing commented that "[t]here may well be situations in which the independent directors could reasonably believe that the best interests of the shareholders call for a decision not to sue * * * " and that in certain cases "it would certainly be consistent with the Act to allow the independent directors to terminate a suit, even though not frivolous." 441 U.S. at 483–485, 99 S.Ct. at 1841. A concurring

opinion referred to "this generally accepted principle" and stated that a decision not to sue a wrongdoer "is no different" from other collective directoral decisions. Galef v. Alexander, 615 F.2d 51 (2d Cir.1980) on the other hand, held the business judgment rule approach of *Gall* inapplicable to suits based on section 14(a) of the Securities Exchange Act of 1934. The court argued that the goal of section 14(a) is "that communications from management be accurate and complete as to all material facts," and the achievement of that goal "would quite clearly be frustrated if a director who was made a defendant in a derivative action for providing inadequate information in connection with a proxy solicitation were permitted to cause the dismissal of that action simply on the basis of his judgment that its pursuit was not in the best interests of the corporation." 615 F.2d at 63.

(5) One practical question involving the procedure followed in *Gall* is how independent must the "litigation committees" be? If you were attorney for a plaintiff faced with the prospect of a Gall-type defense, would you not name all the directors as defendants in every case? Could a director without direct involvement in a transaction be sufficiently independent to satisfy the *Gall* principle, if named a nominal defendant? Finally, what about bringing a derivative suit claiming that a decision by an independent committee was itself a violation of fiduciary duty; even if the prospects for such a suit are slim, could it be used to disqualify directors from serving on the "litigation committee?"

ZAPATA CORP. v. MALDONADO
Supreme Court of Delaware, 1981.
430 A.2d 779.

[Editor: The Delaware Chancery Court described the underlying controversy involved in this case as follows:

"The relevant facts, construed most favorably to Maldonado, show that in 1970 Zapata's board of directors adopted a stock option plan under which certain of Zapata's officers and directors were granted options to purchase Zapata common stock at $12.15 per share. The plan provided for the exercise of the options in five separate installments, the last of which was to occur on July 14, 1974. In 1971 this plan was ratified by Zapata's stockholders. As the date for the exercise of the final options grew near, however, Zapata was planning a tender offer for 2,300,000 of its own shares. Announcement of the tender offer was expected to be made just prior to July 14, 1974, and it was predicted that the effect of the announcement would be to increase the then market price of Zapata stock from $18–$19 per share to near the tender offer price of $25 per share.

"Zapata's directors, most of whom were optionees under the 1970 plan, were aware that the optionees would incur substantial additional federal income tax liability if the options were exercised after the date of the tender offer announcement and that this additional liability could be avoided if the options were exercised prior to the announcement. This was so because the amount of capital gain for federal income tax purposes to the optionees would have been an amount equal to the difference between the $12.15 option price and the price on the date of the exercise of the option: $18–$19 if the options were exercised prior to the tender offer announcement, or nearly $25 if the options were exercised immediately after the announcement.

"In order to reduce the amount of federal income tax liability the optionees would incur in exercising their options, Zapata's directors accelerated the date on which the options could be exercised to July 2, 1974. On that day the optionees exercised their options and the directors requested the New York Stock Exchange to suspend trading in Zapata shares pending 'an important announcement'. On July 8, 1974 Zapata announced the tender offer. The market price of Zapata stock promptly rose to $24.50." 413 A.2d 1251, 1254–5.]

Before DUFFY, QUILLEN and HORSEY, JJ.

QUILLEN, JUSTICE:

This is an interlocutory appeal from an order entered on April 9, 1980, by the Court of Chancery denying appellant-defendant Zapata Corporation's (Zapata) alternative motions to dismiss the complaint or for summary judgment. The issue to be addressed has reached this Court by way of a rather convoluted path.

In June, 1975, William Maldonado, a stockholder of Zapata, instituted a derivative action in the Court of Chancery on behalf of Zapata against ten officers and/or directors of Zapata, alleging, essentially, breaches of fiduciary duty. Maldonado did not first demand that the board bring this action, stating instead such demand's futility because all directors were named as defendants and allegedly participated in the acts specified.[25] * * *

By June, 1979, four of the defendant-directors were no longer on the board, and the remaining directors appointed two new outside directors to the board. The board then created an "Independent Investigation Committee" (Committee), composed solely of the two new directors, to investigate Maldonado's actions, as well as a similar derivative action then pending in Texas, and to determine whether the corporation should continue any or all of the litigation. The Committee's determination was stated to be "final, * * * not * * * subject to review by the Board of Directors and * * * in all respects * * * binding upon the Corporation."

Following an investigation, the Committee concluded, in September, 1979, that each action should "be dismissed forthwith as their continued maintenance is inimical to the Company's best interests * * *." Consequently, Zapata moved for dismissal or summary judgment * * *.

On March 18, 1980, the Court of Chancery, in a reported opinion, the basis for the order of April 9, 1980, denied Zapata's motions, holding that Delaware law does not sanction this means of dismissal.

---

25. [By the Court] Court of Chancery Rule 23.1 states in part: "The complaint shall also allege with particularity the efforts, if any, made by the plaintiff to obtain the action he desires from the directors or comparable authority and the reasons for his failure to obtain the action or for not making the effort."

More specifically, it held that the "business judgment" rule is not a grant of authority to dismiss derivative actions and that a stockholder has an individual right to maintain derivative actions in certain instances. Maldonado v. Flynn, Del.Ch., 413 A.2d 1251 (1980). * * * We limit our review in this interlocutory appeal to whether the Committee has the power to cause the present action to be dismissed.

We begin with an examination of the carefully considered opinion of the Vice Chancellor which states, in part, that the "business judgment" rule does not confer power "to a corporate board of directors to terminate a derivative suit", 413 A.2d at 1257. His conclusion is particularly pertinent because several federal courts, applying Delaware law, have held that the business judgment rule enables boards (or their committees) to terminate derivative suits * * *.

As the term is most commonly used, and given the disposition below, we can understand the Vice Chancellor's comment that "the business judgment rule is irrelevant to the question of whether the Committee has the authority to compel the dismissal of this suit". 413 A.2d at 1257. Corporations, existing because of legislative grace, possess authority as granted by the legislature. Directors of Delaware corporations derive their managerial decision making power, which encompasses decisions whether to initiate, or refrain from entering, litigation,[26] from 8 Del.C. § 141(a).[27] This statute is the fount of directorial powers. The "business judgment" rule is a judicial creation that presumes propriety, under certain circumstances, in a board's decision.[28] Viewed defensively, it does not create authority. In this sense the "business judgment" rule is not relevant in corporate decision making until after a decision is made. It is generally used as a defense to an attack on the decision's soundness. The board's managerial decision making power, however, comes from § 141(a). The judicial creation and legislative grant are related because the "business judgment" rule evolved to give recognition and deference to directors' business expertise when exercising their managerial power under § 141(a).

In the case before us, although the corporation's decision to move to dismiss or for summary judgment was, literally, a decision resulting from an exercise of the directors' (as delegated to the Committee) business judgment, the question of "business judgment", in a defensive sense, would not become relevant until and unless the decision to seek termination of the derivative lawsuit was attacked as improper. This

26. [By the Court] See Dent, The Power of Directors to Terminate Shareholder Litigation: The Death of the Derivative Suit? 75 Nw.U.L.Rev. 96, 98 & n. 14 (1980); Comment, The Demand and Standing Requirements in Stockholder Derivative Actions, 44 U.Chi.L.Rev. 168, 192 & nn. 153–54 (1976) (herein Stockholder Derivative Actions).

27. [By the Court] 8 Del.C. § 141(a) states:

"The business and affairs of every corporation organized under this chapter shall be managed by or under the direction of a board of directors.

28. [By the Court] See Arsht, The Business Judgment Rule Revisited, 8 Hofstra L.Rev. 93, 97, 130–33 (1979).

question was not reached by the Vice Chancellor because he determined that the stockholder had an individual right to maintain this derivative action.

Thus, the focus in this case is on the power to speak for the corporation as to whether the lawsuit should be continued or terminated. As we see it, this issue in the current appellate posture of this case has three aspects: the conclusions of the Court below concerning the continuing right of a stockholder to maintain a derivative action; the corporate power under Delaware law of an authorized board committee to cause dismissal of litigation instituted for the benefit of the corporation; and the role of the Court of Chancery in resolving conflicts between the stockholder and the committee.

Accordingly, we turn first to the Court of Chancery's conclusions concerning the right of a plaintiff stockholder in a derivative action. We find that its determination that a stockholder, once demand is made and refused, possesses an independent, individual right to continue a derivative suit for breaches of fiduciary duty over objection by the corporation, as an absolute rule, is erroneous. * * * McKee v. Rogers, Del.Ch. 156 A. 191 (1931), stated "as a general rule" that "a stockholder cannot be permitted * * * to invade the discretionary field committed to the judgment of the directors and sue in the corporation's behalf when the managing body refuses. This rule is a well settled one." 156 A. at 193.

The *McKee* rule, of course, should not be read so broadly that the board's refusal will be determinative in every instance. Board members, owing a well-established fiduciary duty to the corporation, will not be allowed to cause a derivative suit to be dismissed when it would be a breach of their fiduciary duty. Generally disputes pertaining to control of the suit arise in two contexts.

Consistent with the purpose of requiring a demand, a board decision to cause a derivative suit to be dismissed as detrimental to the company, after demand has been made and refused, will be respected unless it was wrongful.[29] See, e.g., United Copper Securities Co. v. Amalgamated Copper Co., 244 U.S. 261, 263–64, 37 S.Ct. 509, 510, 61 L.Ed. 1119, 1124 (1917). A claim of a wrongful decision not to sue is thus the first exception and the first context of dispute. Absent a wrongful refusal, the stockholder in such a situation simply lacks legal managerial power.

29. [By the Court] In other words, when stockholders, after making demand and having their suit rejected, attack the board's decision as improper, the board's decision falls under the "business judgment" rule and will be respected if the requirements of the rule are met. See Dent, supra note 24, 75 Nw.U.L.Rev. at 100–01 & nn. 24–25. That situation should be distinguished from the instant case, where demand was not made, and the power of the board to seek a dismissal, due to disqualification, presents a threshold issue. For examples of what has been held to be a wrongful decision not to sue, see Stockholder Derivative Actions, supra note 24, 44 U.Chi.L.Rev. at 193–98. We recognize that the two contexts can overlap in practice.

But it cannot be implied that, absent a wrongful board refusal, a stockholder can never have an individual right to initiate an action. For, as is stated in *McKee,* a "well settled" exception exists to the general rule.

> "[A] stockholder may sue in equity in his derivative right to assert a cause of action in behalf of the corporation, *without prior demand* upon the directors to sue, when it is apparent that a demand would be futile, that the officers are under an influence that sterilizes discretion and could not be proper persons to conduct the litigation."

156 A. at 193 (emphasis added). This exception, the second context for dispute, is consistent with the Court of Chancery's statement below, that "[t]he stockholders' individual right to bring the action does not ripen, however, * * * unless he can show a demand to be futile."

These comments in *McKee* and in the opinion below make obvious sense. A demand, when required and refused (if not wrongful), terminates a stockholder's legal ability to initiate a derivative action.[30] But where demand is properly excused, the stockholder does possess the ability to initiate the action on his corporation's behalf.

These conclusions, however, do not determine the question before us. Rather, they merely bring us to the question to be decided. It is here that we part company with the Court below. Derivative suits enforce corporate rights and any recovery obtained goes to the corporation. "The right of a stockholder to file a bill to litigate corporate rights is, therefore, solely for the purpose of preventing injustice where it is apparent that material corporate rights would not otherwise be protected." We see no inherent reason why the "two phases" of a derivative suit, the stockholder's suit to compel the corporation to sue and the corporation's suit should automatically result in the placement in the hands of the litigating stockholder sole control of the corporate right throughout the litigation. To the contrary, it seems to us that such an inflexible rule would recognize the interest of one person or group to the exclusion of all others within the corporate entity. Thus, we reject the view of the Vice Chancellor as to the first aspect of the issue on appeal.

The question to be decided becomes: When, if at all, should an authorized board committee be permitted to cause litigation, properly initiated by a derivative stockholder in his own right, to be dismissed? As noted above, a board has the power to choose not to pursue litigation when demand is made upon it, so long as the decision is not wrongful. If the board determines that a suit would be detrimental to the company, the board's determination prevails. Even when demand is excusable, circumstances may arise when continuation of the litigation would not be in the corporation's best interests. Our inquiry is whether, under such circumstances, there is a permissible procedure under

---

30. [By the Court] Even in this situation it may take litigation to determine the stockholder's lack of power, i.e., standing.

§ 141(a) by which a corporation can rid itself of detrimental litigation. If there is not, a single stockholder in an extreme case might control the destiny of the entire corporation. This concern was bluntly expressed by the Ninth Circuit in Lewis v. Anderson, 9th Cir., 615 F.2d 778, 783 (1979), cert. denied, ___ U.S. ___, 101 S.Ct. 206, 66 L.Ed.2d 89 (1980): "To allow one shareholder to incapacitate an entire board of directors merely by leveling charges against them gives too much leverage to dissident shareholders." But, when examining the means, including the committee mechanism examined in this case, potentials for abuse must be recognized. This takes us to the second and third aspects of the issue on appeal.

Before we pass to equitable considerations as to the mechanism at issue here, it must be clear that an independent committee possesses the corporate power to seek the termination of a derivative suit. Section 141(c) allows a board to delegate all of its authority to a committee. Accordingly, a committee with properly delegated authority would have the power to move for dismissal or summary judgment if the entire board did.

Even though demand was not made in this case and the initial decision of whether to litigate was not placed before the board, Zapata's board, it seems to us, retained all of its corporate power concerning litigation decisions. If Maldonado had made demand on the board in this case, it could have refused to bring suit. Maldonado could then have asserted that the decision not to sue was wrongful and, if correct, would have been allowed to maintain the suit. The board, however, never would have lost its statutory managerial authority. The demand requirement itself evidences that the managerial power is retained by the board. When a derivative plaintiff is allowed to bring suit after a wrongful refusal, the board's authority to choose whether to pursue the litigation is not challenged although its conclusion—reached through the exercise of that authority—is not respected since it is wrongful. Similarly, Rule 23.1, by excusing demand in certain instances, does not strip the board of its corporate power. It merely saves the plaintiff the expense and delay of making a futile demand resulting in a probable tainted exercise of that authority in a refusal by the board or in giving control of litigation to the opposing side. But the board entity remains empowered under § 141(a) to make decisions regarding corporate litigation. The problem is one of member disqualification, not the absence of power in the board.

The corporate power inquiry then focuses on whether the board, tainted by the self-interest of a majority of its members, can legally delegate its authority to a committee of two disinterested directors. We find our statute clearly requires an affirmative answer to this question. As has been noted, under an express provision of the statute, § 141(c), a committee can exercise all of the authority of the board to the extent provided in the resolution of the board. Moreover, at [least] by analogy to our statutory section on interested directors, 8 Del.C. § 141, it seems clear that the Delaware statute is designed to permit disinterested directors to act for the board.[31]

We do not think that the interest taint of the board majority is per se a legal bar to the delegation of the board's power to an independent committee composed of disinterested board members. The committee can properly act for the corporation to move to dismiss derivative litigation that is believed to be detrimental to the corporation's best interest.

Our focus now switches to the Court of Chancery which is faced with a stockholder assertion that a derivative suit, properly instituted, should continue for the benefit of the corporation and a corporate assertion, properly made by a board committee acting with board authority, that the same derivative suit should be dismissed as inimical to the best interests of the corporation.

At the risk of stating the obvious, the problem is relatively simple. If, on the one hand, corporations can consistently wrest bona fide derivative actions away from well-meaning derivative plaintiffs through the use of the committee mechanism, the derivative suit will lose much, if not all, of its generally-recognized effectiveness as an intra-corporate means of policing boards of directors. If, on the other hand, corporations are unable to rid themselves of meritless or harmful litigation and strike suits, the derivative action, created to benefit the corporation, will produce the opposite, unintended result. * * * It thus appears desirable to us to find a balancing point where bona fide stockholder power to bring corporate causes of action cannot be unfairly trampled on by the board of directors, but the corporation can rid itself of detrimental litigation.

---

31. [By the Court] 8 Del.C. § 144 states:

"§ 144. Interested directors; quorum.

(a) No contract or transaction between a corporation and 1 or more of its directors or officers, or between a corporation and any other corporation, partnership, association, or other organization in which 1 or more of its directors or officers are directors or officers, or have a financial interest, shall be void or voidable solely for this reason, or solely because the director or officer is present at or participates in the meeting of the board or committee which authorizes the contract or transaction, or solely because his or their votes are counted for such purpose, if:

(1) The material facts as to his relationship or interest and as to the contract or transaction are disclosed or are known to the board of directors or the committee, and the board or committee in good faith authorizes the contract or transaction by the affirmative votes of a majority of the disinterested directors, even though the disinterested directors be less than a quorum; or

(2) The material facts as to his relationship or interest and as to the contract or transaction are disclosed or are known to the shareholders entitled to vote thereon, and the contract or transaction is specifically approved in good faith by vote of the shareholders; or

(3) The contract or transaction is fair to the corporation as of the time it is authorized, approved or ratified, by the board of directors, a committee, or the shareholders.

(b) Common or interested directors may be counted in determining the presence of a quorum at a meeting of the board of directors or of a committee which authorizes the contract or transaction."

As we noted, the question has been treated by other courts as one of the "business judgment" of the board committee. If a "committee, composed of independent and disinterested directors, conducted a proper review of the matters before it, considered a variety of factors and reached, in good faith, a business judgment that [the] action was not in the best interest of [the corporation]", the action must be dismissed. The issues become solely independence, good faith, and reasonable investigation. The ultimate conclusion of the committee, under that view, is not subject to judicial review.

We are not satisfied, however, that acceptance of the "business judgment" rationale at this stage of derivative litigation is a proper balancing point. While we admit an analogy with a normal case respecting board judgment, it seems to us that there is sufficient risk in the realities of a situation like the one presented in this case to justify caution beyond adherence to the theory of business judgment.

The context here is a suit against directors where demand on the board is excused. We think some tribute must be paid to the fact that the lawsuit was properly initiated. It is not a board refusal case. Moreover, this complaint was filed in June of 1975 and, while the parties undoubtedly would take differing views on the degree of litigation activity, we have to be concerned about the creation of an "Independent Investigation Committee" four years later, after the election of two new outside directors. Situations could develop where such motions could be filed after years of vigorous litigation for reasons unconnected with the merits of the lawsuit.

Moreover, notwithstanding our conviction that Delaware law entrusts the corporate power to a properly authorized committee, we must be mindful that directors are passing judgment on fellow directors in the same corporation and fellow directors, in this instance, who designated them to serve both as directors and committee members. The question naturally arises whether a "there but for the grace of God go I" empathy might not play a role. And the further question arises whether inquiry as to independence, good faith and reasonable investigation is sufficient safeguard against abuse, perhaps subconscious abuse.

There is another line of exploration besides the factual context of this litigation which we find helpful. The nature of this motion finds no ready pigeonhole, as perhaps illustrated by its being set forth in the alternative. It is perhaps best considered as a hybrid summary judgment motion for dismissal because the stockholder plaintiff's standing to maintain the suit has been lost. But it does not fit neatly into a category described in Rule 12(b) of the Court of Chancery Rules nor does it correspond directly with Rule 56 since the question of genuine issues of fact on the merits of the stockholder's claim are not reached.

*   *   *

Whether the Court of Chancery will be persuaded by the exercise of a committee power resulting in a summary motion for dismissal of a derivative action, where a demand has not been initially made, should rest, in our judgment, in the independent discretion of the Court of Chancery. We thus steer a middle course between those cases which yield to the independent business judgment of a board committee and this case as determined below which would yield to unbridled plaintiff stockholder control. In pursuit of the course, we recognize that "[t]he final substantive judgment whether a particular lawsuit should be maintained requires a balance of many factors—ethical, commercial, promotional, public relations, employee relations, fiscal as well as legal." But we are content that such factors are not "beyond the judicial reach" of the Court of Chancery which regularly and competently deals with fiduciary relationships, disposition of trust property, approval of settlements and scores of similar problems. We recognize the danger of judicial overreaching but the alternatives seem to us to be outweighed by the fresh view of a judicial outsider. Moreover, if we failed to balance all the interests involved, we would in the name of practicality and judicial economy foreclose a judicial decision on the merits. At this point, we are not convinced that is necessary or desirable.

After an objective and thorough investigation of a derivative suit, an independent committee may cause its corporation to file a pretrial motion to dismiss in the Court of Chancery. The basis of the motion is the best interests of the corporation, as determined by the committee. The motion should include a thorough written record of the investigation and its findings and recommendations. Under appropriate Court supervision, akin to proceedings on summary judgment, each side should have an opportunity to make a record on the motion. As to the limited issues presented by the motion noted below, the moving party should be prepared to meet the normal burden under Rule 56 that there is no genuine issue as to any material fact and that the moving party is entitled to dismiss as a matter of law.[32] The Court should apply a two-step test to the motion.

First, the Court should inquire into the independence and good faith of the committee and the bases supporting its conclusions. Limited discovery may be ordered to facilitate such inquiries. The corporation should have the burden of proving independence, good faith and a reasonable investigation, rather than presuming independence, good faith and reasonableness.[33] If the Court determines either that the

32. [By the Court] We do not foreclose a discretionary trial of factual issues but that issue is not presented in this appeal. See Lewis v. Anderson, supra, 615 F.2d at 780. Nor do we foreclose the possibility that other motions may proceed or be joined with such a pretrial summary judgment motion to dismiss, e.g., a partial motion for summary judgment on the merits.

33. [By the Court] Compare Auerbach v. Bennett, 47 N.Y.2d 619, 419 N.Y.S.2d

920, 928–29, 393 N.E.2d 994 (1979). Our approach here is analogous to and consistent with the Delaware approach to "interested director" transactions, where the directors, once the transaction is attacked, have the burden of establishing its "intrinsic fairness" to a court's careful scrutiny. See, e.g., Sterling v. Mayflower Hotel Corp., Del.Supr., 93 A.2d 107 (1952).

committee is not independent or has not shown reasonable bases for its conclusions, or, if the Court is not satisfied for other reasons relating to the process, including but not limited to the good faith of the committee, the Court shall deny the corporation's motion. If, however, the Court is satisfied under Rule 56 standards that the committee was independent and showed reasonable bases for good faith findings and recommendations, the Court may proceed, in its discretion, to the next step.

The second step provides, we believe, the essential key in striking the balance between legitimate corporate claims as expressed in a derivative stockholder suit and a corporation's best interests as expressed by an independent investigating committee. The Court should determine, applying its own independent business judgment, whether the motion should be granted.[34] This means, of course, that instances could arise where a committee can establish its independence and sound bases for its good faith decisions and still have the corporation's motion denied. The second step is intended to thwart instances where corporate actions meet the criteria of step one, but the result does not appear to satisfy its spirit, or where corporate actions would simply prematurely terminate a stockholder grievance deserving of further consideration in the corporation's interest. The Court of Chancery of course must carefully consider and weigh how compelling the corporate interest in dismissal is when faced with a non-frivolous lawsuit. The Court of Chancery should, when appropriate, give special consideration to matters of law and public policy in addition to the corporation's best interests.

If the Court's independent business judgment is satisfied, the Court may proceed to grant the motion, subject, of course, to any equitable terms or conditions the Court finds necessary or desirable.

The interlocutory order of the Court of Chancery is reversed and the cause is remanded for further proceedings consistent with this opinion.

Notes

(1) Following this decision, several courts refused to grant decisions by litigation committees the finality that appeared to be required under pre-Zapata decisions. Among these cases are Joy v. North, 692 F.2d 880 (2d Cir.1982), cert. denied sub nom. Citytrust v. Joy, 460 U.S. 1051, 103 S.Ct. 1498 (1983) [nominally decided under Connecticut law]; Hasan v. CleveTrust Realty Investors, 729 F.2d 372 (6th Cir.1984) [no presumption of regularity or good faith to support litigation committee decision]; In Matter of Continental Illinois Securities Litigation, 732 F.2d 1302 (7th Cir. 1984). While there were dissents in some of these cases, the majority opinions reflect skepticism about the wisdom of uncritical acceptance of the

---

34. [By the Court] This step shares some of the same spirit and philosophy of the statement by the Vice Chancellor: "Under our system of law, courts and not litigants should decide the merits of litigation." 413 A.2d at 1263.

principle that plaintiffs attacking a corporate transaction should be remitted only to an attack on the independence and good faith of a litigation committee.

(2) Basically accepting the "structural bias" argument, the court in Miller v. Register & Tribune Syndicate, Inc., 336 N.W.2d 709 (Iowa 1983), held that the board of directors was unable to delegate the power to bind the corporation to an independent litigation committee if the board of directors was itself unable to act because a majority was interested in the transaction; the court suggested that a committee might be appointed by judicial order in this situation.

ARONSON v. LEWIS
Supreme Court of Delaware, 1984.
473 A.2d 805.

Before MCNEILLY, MOORE and CHRISTIE, JJ.

MOORE, JUSTICE:

In the wake of Zapata Corp. v. Maldonado, Del.Supr., 430 A.2d 779 (1981), this Court left a crucial issue unanswered: when is a stockholder's demand upon a board of directors, to redress an alleged wrong to the corporation, excused as futile prior to the filing of a derivative suit? We granted this interlocutory appeal to the defendants, Meyers Parking System, Inc. (Meyers), a Delaware corporation, and its directors, to review the Court of Chancery's denial of their motion to dismiss this action, pursuant to Chancery Rule 23.1, for the plaintiff's failure to make such a demand or otherwise demonstrate its futility. The Vice Chancellor ruled that plaintiff's allegations raised a "reasonable inference" that the directors' action was unprotected by the business judgment rule. Thus, the board could not have impartially considered and acted upon the demand. See Lewis v. Aronson, Del.Ch., 466 A.2d 375, 381 (1983).

We cannot agree with this formulation of the concept of demand futility. In our view demand can only be excused where facts are alleged with particularity which create a reasonable doubt that the directors' action was entitled to the protections of the business judgment rule. Because the plaintiff failed to make a demand, and to allege facts with particularity indicating that such demand would be futile, we reverse the Court of Chancery and remand with instructions that plaintiff be granted leave to amend the complaint.

I.

The issues of demand futility rest upon the allegations of the complaint. The plaintiff, Harry Lewis, is a stockholder of Meyers. The defendants are Meyers and its ten directors, some of whom are also company officers.

In 1979, Prudential Building Maintenance Corp. (Prudential) spun off its shares of Meyers to Prudential's stockholders. Prior thereto Meyers was a wholly owned subsidiary of Prudential. Meyers provides parking lot facilities and related services throughout the country. Its stock is actively traded over-the-counter.

This suit challenges certain transactions between Meyers and one of its directors, Leo Fink, who owns 47% of its outstanding stock. Plaintiff claims that these transactions were approved only because Fink personally selected each director and officer of Meyers.[35]

Prior to January 1, 1981, Fink had an employment agreement with Prudential which provided that upon retirement he was to become a consultant to that company for ten years. This provision became operable when Fink retired in April 1980. Thereafter, Meyers agreed with Prudential to share Fink's consulting services and reimburse Prudential for 25% of the fees paid Fink. Under this arrangement Meyers paid Prudential $48,332 in 1980 and $45,832 in 1981.

On January 1, 1981, the defendants approved an employment agreement between Meyers and Fink for a five year term with provision for automatic renewal each year thereafter, indefinitely. Meyers agreed to pay Fink $150,000 per year, plus a bonus of 5% of its pre-tax profits over $2,400,000. Fink could terminate the contract at any time, but Meyers could do so only upon six months' notice. At termination, Fink was to become a consultant to Meyers and be paid $150,000 per year for the first three years, $125,000 for the next three years, and $100,000 thereafter for life. Death benefits were also included. Fink agreed to devote his best efforts and substantially his entire business time to advancing Meyers' interests. The agreement also provided that Fink's compensation was not to be affected by any inability to perform services on Meyers' behalf. Fink was 75 years old when his employment agreement with Meyers was approved by the directors. There is no claim that he was, or is, in poor health.

Additionally, the Meyers board approved and made interest-free loans to Fink totalling $225,000. These loans were unpaid and outstanding as of August 1982 when the complaint was filed. At oral argument defendants' counsel represented that these loans had been repaid in full.

The complaint charges that these transactions had "no valid business purpose", and were a "waste of corporate assets" because the amounts to be paid are "grossly excessive", that Fink performs "no or little services", and because of his "advanced age" cannot be "expected to perform any such services". The plaintiff also charges that the existence of the Prudential consulting agreement with Fink prevents him from providing his "best efforts" on Meyers' behalf. Finally, it is alleged that the loans to Fink were in reality "additional compensation" without any "consideration" or "benefit" to Meyers.

The complaint alleged that no demand had been made on the Meyers board because:

35. [By the Court] The Court of Chancery stated that Fink had been chief executive officer of Prudential prior to the spin-off and thereafter became chairman of Meyers' board.

"13. ∗ ∗ ∗ such attempt would be futile for the following reasons:

"(a) All of the directors in office are named as defendants herein and they have participated in, expressly approved and/or acquiesced in, and are personally liable for, the wrongs complained of herein.

"(b) Defendant Fink, having selected each director, controls and dominates every member of the Board and every officer of Meyers.

"(c) Institution of this action by present directors would require the defendant-directors to sue themselves, thereby placing the conduct of this action in hostile hands and preventing its effective prosecution."

The relief sought included the cancellation of the Meyers–Fink employment contract and an accounting by the directors, including Fink, for all damage sustained by Meyers and for all profits derived by the directors and Fink. ∗ ∗ ∗

IV.

A.

A cardinal precept of the General Corporation Law of the State of Delaware is that directors, rather than shareholders, manage the business and affairs of the corporation. 8 Del.C. § 141(a). ∗ ∗ ∗ The existence and exercise of this power carries with it certain fundamental fiduciary obligations to the corporation and its shareholders.[36] Loft, Inc. v. Guth, Del.Ch., 2 A.2d 225 (1938), aff'd, Del.Supr., 5 A.2d 503 (1939). Moreover, a stockholder is not powerless to challenge director action which results in harm to the corporation. The machinery of corporate democracy and the derivative suit are potent tools to redress the conduct of a torpid or unfaithful management. The derivative action developed in equity to enable shareholders to sue in the corporation's name where those in control of the company refused to assert a claim belonging to it. The nature of the action is two-fold. First, it is the equivalent of a suit by the shareholders to compel the corporation to sue. Second, it is a suit by the corporation, asserted by the shareholders on its behalf, against those liable to it.

---

36. [By the Court] The broad question of structuring the modern corporation in order to satisfy the twin objectives of managerial freedom of action and responsibility to shareholders has been extensively debated by commentators. See, e.g., Fischel, The Corporate Governance Movement, 35 Vand.L.Rev. 1259 (1982); Dickstein, Corporate Governance and the Shareholders' Derivative Action: Rules and Remedies for Implementing the Monitoring Model, 3 Cardozo L.Rev. 627 (1982); Haft, Business Decisions by the New Board: Behavioral Science and Corporate Law, 80 Mich.L.Rev. 1 (1981); Dent, The Revolution in Corporate Governance, The Monitoring Board, and The Director's Duty of Care, 61 B.U.L.Rev. 623 (1981); Moore, Corporate Officer & Director Liability: Is Corporate Behavior Beyond the Control of Our Legal System? 16 Capital U.L.Rev. 69 (1980); Jones, Corporate Governance: Who Controls the Large Corporation? 30 Hastings L.J. 1261 (1979); Small, The Evolving Role of the Director in Corporate Governance, 30 Hastings L.J. 1353 (1979).

By its very nature the derivative action impinges on the managerial freedom of directors.[37] Hence, the demand requirement of Chancery Rule 23.1 exists at the threshold, first to ensure that a stockholder exhausts his intracorporate remedies, and then to provide a safeguard against strike suits. Thus, by promoting this form of alternate dispute resolution, rather than immediate recourse to litigation, the demand requirement is a recognition of the fundamental precept that directors manage the business and affairs of corporations.

In our view the entire question of demand futility is inextricably bound to issues of business judgment and the standards of that doctrine's applicability. The business judgment rule is an acknowledgment of the managerial prerogatives of Delaware directors under Section 141(a). See Zapata Corp. v. Maldonado, 430 A.2d at 782. It is a presumption that in making a business decision the directors of a corporation acted on an informed basis, in good faith and in the honest belief that the action taken was in the best interests of the company. Kaplan v. Centex Corp., Del.Ch., 284 A.2d 119, 124 (1971); Robinson v. Pittsburgh Oil Refinery Corp., Del.Ch., 126 A. 46 (1924). Absent an abuse of discretion, that judgment will be respected by the courts. The burden is on the party challenging the decision to establish facts rebutting the presumption. See Puma v. Marriott, Del.Ch., 283 A.2d 693, 695 (1971).

The function of the business judgment rule is of paramount significance in the context of a derivative action. It comes into play in several ways—in addressing a demand, in the determination of demand futility, in efforts by independent disinterested directors to dismiss the action as inimical to the corporation's best interests, and generally, as a defense to the merits of the suit. However, in each of these circumstances there are certain common principles governing the application and operation of the rule.

First, its protections can only be claimed by disinterested directors whose conduct otherwise meets the tests of business judgment. From the standpoint of interest, this means that directors can neither appear on both sides of a transaction nor expect to derive any personal financial benefit from it in the sense of self-dealing, as opposed to a benefit which devolves upon the corporation or all stockholders general-

---

37. [By the Court] Like the broader question of corporate governance, the derivative suit, its value, and the methods employed by corporate boards to deal with it have received much attention by commentators. See, e.g., Brown, Shareholder Derivative Litigation and the Special Litigation Committee, 43 U.Pitt.L.Rev. 601 (1982); Coffee and Schwartz, The Survival of the Derivative Suit: An Evaluation and a Proposal for Legislative Reform, 81 Colum.L.Rev. 261 (1981); Shnell, A Procedural Treatment of Derivative Suit Dismissals by Minority Directors, 69 Calif.L.Rev. 885 (1981); Dent, The Power of Directors to Terminate Shareholder Litigation: The Death of the Derivative Suit? 75 N.W.U.L. Rev. 96 (1980); Jones, An Empirical Examination of the Incidence of Shareholder Derivative and Class Action Lawsuits, 1971–1978, 60 B.U.L.Rev. 306 (1980); Comment, The Demand and Standing Requirements in Stockholder Derivative Actions, 44 U.Chi.L.Rev. 168 (1976); Dykstra, The Revival of the Derivative Suit, 116 U.Pa.L. Rev. 74 (1967); Note, Demand on Directors and Shareholders as a Prerequisite to a Derivative Suit, 73 Harv.L.Rev. 729 (1960).

ly. Sinclair Oil Corp. v. Levien, Del.Supr., 280 A.2d 717, 720 (1971); Cheff v. Mathes, Del.Supr., 199 A.2d 548, 554 (1964). See also 8 Del.C. § 144. Thus, if such director interest is present, and the transaction is not approved by a majority consisting of the disinterested directors, then the business judgment rule has no application whatever in determining demand futility.

Second, to invoke the rule's protection directors have a duty to inform themselves, prior to making a business decision, of all material information reasonably available to them. Having become so informed, they must then act with requisite care in the discharge of their duties. While the Delaware cases use a variety of terms to describe the applicable standard of care, our analysis satisfies us that under the business judgment rule director liability is predicated upon concepts of gross negligence.[38] See Veasey & Manning, Codified Standard—Safe Harbor or Uncharted Reef? 35 Bus.Law. 919, 928 (1980).

However, it should be noted that the business judgment rule operates only in the context of director action. Technically speaking, it has no role where directors have either abdicated their functions, or absent a conscious decision, failed to act.[39] But it also follows that under applicable principles, a conscious decision to refrain from acting may nonetheless be a valid exercise of business judgment and enjoy the protections of the rule.

The gap in our law, which we address today, arises from this Court's decision in *Zapata Corp. v. Maldonado.* There, the Court defined the limits of a board's managerial power granted by Section 141(a) and restricted application of the business judgment rule in a factual context similar to this action. Zapata Corp. v. Maldonado, 430 A.2d at 782–86, rev'g, Maldonado v. Flynn, Del.Ch., 413 A.2d 1251 (1980).

By way of background, this Court's review in *Zapata* was limited to whether an independent investigation committee of disinterested direc-

---

38. [By the Court] While the Delaware cases have not been precise in articulating the standard by which the exercise of business judgment is governed, a long line of Delaware cases holds that director liability is predicated on a standard which is less exacting than simple negligence. Sinclair Oil Corp. v. Levien, Del.Supr., 280 A.2d 717, 722 (1971), rev'g, Del.Ch., 261 A.2d 911 (1969) ("fraud or gross overreaching"); Getty Oil Co. v. Skelly Oil Co., Del.Supr., 267 A.2d 883, 887 (1970), rev'g, Del.Ch., 255 A.2d 717 (1969) ("gross and palpable overreaching"); Warshaw v. Calhoun, Del. Supr., 221 A.2d 487, 492–93 (1966) ("bad faith * * * or a gross abuse of discretion"); Moskowitz v. Bantrell, Del.Supr., 190 A.2d 749, 750 (1963) ("fraud or gross abuse of discretion"); Penn Mart Realty Co. v. Becker, Del.Ch., 298 A.2d 349, 351 (1972) ("directors may breach their fiducia-

ry duty * * * by being grossly negligent"); Kors v. Carey, Del.Ch., 158 A.2d 136, 140 (1960) ("fraud, misconduct or abuse of discretion"); Allaun v. Consolidated Oil Co., Del.Ch., 147 A. 257, 261 (1929) ("reckless indifference to or a deliberate disregard of the stockholders").

39. [By the Court] Although questions of director liability in such cases have been adjudicated upon concepts of business judgment, they do not in actuality present issues of business judgment. See Graham v. Allis–Chalmers Manufacturing Co., Del. Supr., 188 A.2d 125 (1963); Kelly v. Bell, Del.Ch., 254 A.2d 62 (1969), aff'd, Del.Supr., 266 A.2d 878 (1970); Lutz v. Boas, Del.Ch., 171 A.2d 381 (1961). See also Arsht, Fiduciary Responsibilities of Directors, Officers & Key Employees, 4 Del.J.Corp.L. 652, 659 (1979).

tors had the *power* to cause the derivative action to be dismissed. Preliminarily, it was noted in *Zapata* that "[d]irectors of Delaware corporations derive their managerial decision making power, which encompasses decisions whether to initiate, or refrain from entering, litigation, from 8 Del.C. § 141(a)". In that context, this Court observed that the business judgment rule has no relevance to corporate decision making until *after a decision has been made*. In *Zapata,* we stated that a shareholder does not possess an independent individual right to continue a derivative action. Moreover, where demand on a board has been made and refused, we apply the business judgment rule in reviewing the board's refusal to act pursuant to a stockholder's demand. Unless the business judgment rule does not protect the refusal to sue, the shareholder lacks the legal managerial power to continue the derivative action, since that power is terminated by the refusal. We also concluded that where demand is excused a shareholder possesses the ability to initiate a derivative action, but the right to prosecute it may be terminated upon the exercise of applicable standards of business judgment. The thrust of *Zapata* is that in either the demand-refused or the demand-excused case, the board still retains its Section 141(a) managerial authority to make decisions regarding corporate litigation. Moreover, the board may delegate its managerial authority to a committee of independent disinterested directors. See 8 Del.C. § 141(c). Thus, even in a demand-excused case, a board has the power to appoint a committee of one or more independent disinterested directors to determine whether the derivative action should be pursued or dismissal sought. Under *Zapata,* the Court of Chancery, in passing on a committee's motion to dismiss a derivative action in a demand excused case, must apply a two-step test. First, the court must inquire into the independence and good faith of the committee and review the reasonableness and good faith of the committee's investigation. Second, the court must apply its own independent business judgment to decide whether the motion to dismiss should be granted.

After *Zapata* numerous derivative suits were filed without prior demand upon boards of directors. The complaints in such actions all alleged that demand was excused because of board interest, approval or acquiescence in the wrongdoing. In any event, the *Zapata* demand-excused/demand-refused bifurcation, has left a crucial issue unanswered: when is demand futile and, therefore, excused? * * *

The trial court correctly recognized that demand futility is inextricably bound to issues of business judgment, but stated the test to be based on allegations of fact, which, if true, "show that there is a reasonable inference" the business judgment rule is not applicable for purposes of a pre-suit demand.

The problem with this formulation is the concept of reasonable inferences to be drawn against a board of directors based on allegations in a complaint. As is clear from this case, and the conclusory allegations upon which the Vice Chancellor relied, demand futility becomes virtually automatic under such a test. Bearing in mind the presumptions with which director action is cloaked, we believe that the matter must be approached in a more balanced way.

Our view is that in determining demand futility the Court of Chancery in the proper exercise of its discretion must decide whether, under the particularized facts alleged, a reasonable doubt is created that: (1) the directors are disinterested and independent and (2) the challenged transaction was otherwise the product of a valid exercise of business judgment. Hence, the Court of Chancery must make two inquiries, one into the independence and disinterestedness of the directors and the other into the substantive nature of the challenged transaction and the board's approval thereof. As to the latter inquiry the court does not assume that the transaction is a wrong to the corporation requiring corrective steps by the board. Rather, the alleged wrong is substantively reviewed against the factual background alleged in the complaint. As to the former inquiry, directorial independence and disinterestedness, the court reviews the factual allegations to decide whether they raise a reasonable doubt, as a threshold matter, that the protections of the business judgment rule are available to the board. Certainly, if this is an "interested" director transaction, such that the business judgment rule is inapplicable to the board majority approving the transaction, then the inquiry ceases. In that event futility of demand has been established by any objective or subjective standard.[40] See, e.g., Bergstein v. Texas Internat'l Co., Del.Ch., 453 A.2d 467, 471 (1982) (because five of nine directors approved stock appreciation rights plan likely to benefit them, board was interested for demand purposes and demand held futile). This includes situations involving self-dealing directors. See Sinclair Oil Corp. v. Levien, Del. Supr., 280 A.2d 717 (1971).

However, the mere threat of personal liability for approving a questioned transaction, standing alone, is insufficient to challenge either the independence or disinterestedness of directors, although in rare cases a transaction may be so egregious on its face that board approval cannot meet the test of business judgment, and a substantial likelihood of director liability therefore exists. See Gimbel v. Signal Cos., Inc., Del.Ch., 316 A.2d 599, aff'd, Del.Supr., 316 A.2d 619 (1974). In sum the entire review is factual in nature. The Court of Chancery in the exercise of its sound discretion must be satisfied that a plaintiff has alleged facts with particularity which, taken as true, support a reasonable doubt that the chal-

---

40. [By the Court] We recognize that drawing the line at a majority of the board may be an arguably arbitrary dividing point. Critics will charge that we are ignoring the structural bias common to corporate boards throughout America, as well as the other unseen socialization processes cutting against independent discussion and decisionmaking in the boardroom. The difficulty with structural bias in a demand futile case is simply one of establishing it in the complaint for purposes of Rule 23.1. We are satisfied that discretionary review by the Court of Chancery of complaints alleging specific facts pointing to bias on a particular board will be sufficient for determining demand futility.

lenged transaction was the product of a valid exercise of business judgment. Only in that context is demand excused.

B.

Having outlined the legal framework within which these issues are to be determined, we consider plaintiff's claims of futility here: Fink's domination and control of the directors, board approval of the Fink–Meyers employment agreement, and board hostility to the plaintiff's derivative action due to the directors' status as defendants.

Plaintiff's claim that Fink dominates and controls the Meyers' board is based on: (1) Fink's 47% ownership of Meyers' outstanding stock, and (2) that he "personally selected" each Meyers director. Plaintiff also alleges that mere approval of the employment agreement illustrates Fink's domination and control of the board. In addition, plaintiff argued on appeal that 47% stock ownership, though less than a majority, constituted control given the large number of shares outstanding, 1,245,745.

Such contentions do not support any claim under Delaware law that these directors lack independence. In Kaplan v. Centex Corp., Del. Ch., 284 A.2d 119 (1971), the Court of Chancery stated that "[s]tock ownership alone, at least when it amounts to less than a majority, is not sufficient proof of domination or control". Id. at 123. Moreover, in the demand context even proof of majority ownership of a company does not strip the directors of the presumptions of independence, and that their acts have been taken in good faith and in the best interests of the corporation. There must be coupled with the allegation of control such facts as would demonstrate that through personal or other relationships the directors are beholden to the controlling person. See Mayer v. Adams, Del.Ch., 167 A.2d 729, 732, aff'd, Del.Supr., 174 A.2d 313 (1961). To date the principal decisions dealing with the issue of control or domination arose only after a full trial on the merits. Thus, they are distinguishable in the demand context unless similar particularized facts are alleged to meet the test of Chancery Rule 23.1.

The requirement of director independence inheres in the conception and rationale of the business judgment rule. The presumption of propriety that flows from an exercise of business judgment is based in part on this unyielding precept. Independence means that a director's decision is based on the corporate merits of the subject before the board rather than extraneous considerations or influences. While directors may confer, debate, and resolve their differences through compromise, or by reasonable reliance upon the expertise of their colleagues and other qualified persons, the end result, nonetheless, must be that each director has brought his or her own informed business judgment to bear with specificity upon the corporate merits of the issues without regard for or succumbing to influences which convert an otherwise valid business decision into a faithless act.

Thus, it is not enough to charge that a director was nominated by or elected at the behest of those controlling the outcome of a corporate election. That is the usual way a person becomes a corporate director. It is the care, attention and sense of individual responsibility to the performance of one's duties, not the method of election, that generally touches on independence.

We conclude that in the demand-futile context a plaintiff charging domination and control of one or more directors must allege particularized facts manifesting "a direction of corporate conduct in such a way as to comport with the wishes or interests of the corporation (or persons) doing the controlling". Kaplan, 284 A.2d at 123. The shorthand shibboleth of "dominated and controlled directors" is insufficient. In recognizing that *Kaplan* was decided after trial and full discovery, we stress that the plaintiff need only allege specific facts; he need not plead evidence. * * *

Here, plaintiff has not alleged any facts sufficient to support a claim of control. The personal-selection-of-directors allegation stands alone, unsupported. At best it is a conclusion devoid of factual support. The causal link between Fink's control and approval of the employment agreement is alluded to, but nowhere specified. The director's approval, alone, does not establish control, even in the face of Fink's 47% stock ownership. See Kaplan v. Centex Corp., 284 A.2d at 122, 123. The claim that Fink is unlikely to perform any services under the agreement, because of his age, and his conflicting consultant work with Prudential, adds nothing to the control claim. Therefore, we cannot conclude that the complaint factually particularizes any circumstances of control and domination to overcome the presumption of board independence, and thus render the demand futile.

C.

Turning to the board's approval of the Meyers–Fink employment agreement, plaintiff's argument is simple: all of the Meyers directors are named defendants, because they approved the wasteful agreement; if plaintiff prevails on the merits all the directors will be jointly and severally liable; therefore, the directors' interests in avoiding personal liability automatically and absolutely disqualifies them from passing on a shareholder's demand.

Such allegations are conclusory at best. * * * The complaint does not allege particularized facts indicating that the agreement is a waste of corporate assets. Indeed, the complaint as now drafted may not even state a cause of action, given the directors' broad corporate power to fix the compensation of officers.

In essence, the plaintiff alleged a lack of consideration flowing from Fink to Meyers, since the employment agreement provided that compensation was not contingent on Fink's ability to perform any services. The bare assertion that Fink performed "little or no services" was plaintiff's conclusion based solely on Fink's age and the existence of the

Fink–Prudential employment agreement. As for Meyers' loans to Fink, beyond the bare allegation that they were made, the complaint does not allege facts indicating the wastefulness of such arrangements. Again, the mere existence of such loans, given the broad corporate powers conferred by Delaware law, does not even state a claim.[41]

In sustaining plaintiff's claim of demand futility the trial court relied on Fidanque v. American Maracaibo Co., Del.Ch., 92 A.2d 311, 321 (1952), which held that a contract providing for payment of consulting fees to a retired president/director was a waste of corporate assets. In *Fidanque*, the court found after trial that the contract and payments were in reality compensation for past services. This was based upon facts not present here: the former president/director was a 70 year old stroke victim, neither the agreement nor the record spelled out his consulting duties at all, the consulting salary equalled the individual's salary when he was president and general manager of the corporation, and the contract was silent as to continued employment in the event that the retired president/director again became incapacitated and unable to perform his duties. Contrasting the facts of *Fidanque* with the complaint here, it is apparent that plaintiff has not alleged facts sufficient to render demand futile on a charge of corporate waste, and thus create a reasonable doubt that the board's action is protected by the business judgment rule.

D.

Plaintiff's final argument is the incantation that demand is excused because the directors otherwise would have to sue themselves, thereby placing the conduct of the litigation in hostile hands and preventing its effective prosecution. This bootstrap argument has been made to and dismissed by other courts. See, e.g., Lewis v. Graves, 701 F.2d 245, 248–49 (2d Cir.1983). Its acceptance would effectively abrogate Rule 23.1 and weaken the managerial power of directors. Unless facts are alleged with particularity to overcome the presumptions of independence and a proper exercise of business judgment, in which case the directors could not be expected to sue themselves, a bare claim of this sort raises no legally cognizable issue under Delaware corporate law.

V.

In sum, we conclude that the plaintiff has failed to allege facts with particularity indicating that the Meyers directors were tainted by interest, lacked independence, or took action contrary to Meyers' best interests in order to create a reasonable doubt as to the applicability of the business judgment rule. Only in the presence of such a reasonable doubt may a demand be deemed futile. Hence, we reverse the Court of Chancery's denial of the motion to dismiss, and remand with instructions that plaintiff be granted leave to amend his complaint to bring it

---

41. [By the Court] Plaintiff's allegation ignores 8 Del.C. § 143 which expressly authorizes interest-free loans to "any officer or employee of the corporation * * *

whenever, in the judgment of the directors, such loan * * * may reasonably be expected to benefit the corporation." 8 Del. C. § 143.

into compliance with Rule 23.1 based on the principles we have announced today. * * *

Reversed and Remanded.

Notes

(1) Block and Prussin, Termination of Derivative Suits Against Directors on Business Judgment Grounds: From Zapata to Aronson, 39 Bus.Law. 1503, 1505–1506 (Aug. 1984): *

> In *Zapata* the court held that the two-step test is to apply only in "demand-excused" cases, that is, cases where the shareholder was not required to make a demand upon the directors prior to commencing suit. In cases where demand is required and is refused, under *Zapata* the two-step test does not apply, and the directors' decision not to bring an action will be respected so long as it satisfies the standards of the business judgment rule.
>
> *Aronson* makes it clear that demand will almost always be required unless a majority of the Board is so directly self-interested in the challenged transaction that there is serious doubt that the business judgment rule would protect that transaction. Self-interest, for these purposes, is defined in terms of direct financial interest in the challenged transaction: the fact that a majority of directors voted to approve the transaction—and are therefore named as defendants in the action—does *not* constitute the requisite self-interest and will not excuse demand. After *Aronson* there should be relatively few demand-excused cases, and therefore relatively few cases where the *Zapata* two-step test will be applied. Thus, in run-of-the-mill cases the test actually applied will be the same under Delaware and New York law, the business judgment rule.

(2) In Alford v. Shaw, 318 N.C. 289, 349 S.E.2d 41 (1986), the North Carolina Supreme Court uncritically adopted the *Gall* approach in a case involving charges of fraud and self-dealing by a majority of the board of directors; defendant directors participated in the selection of new directors to serve as the special litigation committee. See DeMott, The Corporate Fox and the Shareholders' Henhouse: Reflections on Alford v. Shaw, 65 N.C.L.Rev. 569 (1987). The North Carolina court then granted a petition for rehearing, and significantly modified—indeed, virtually rejected the underlying premises of—its earlier opinion. 320 N.C. 465, 358 S.E.2d 323 (1987). Relying largely on section 55–55 of the North Carolina statutes [similar to § 7.45 of the RMBCA] the Court stated:

> To make the required assessment under section 55–55, the court must of necessity evaluate the adequacy of materials prepared by the corporation which support the corporation's decision to settle or dismiss a derivative suit along with the plaintiff's forecast of evidence. If it appears likely that plaintiff could prevail on the merits, but that the amount of the recovery would not be sufficient to outweigh the detriment to the corporation, the court could still allow discontinuance, dismissal, compromise, or settlement.

Although the recommendation of the special litigation committee is not binding on the court, in making this determination the court may choose to rely on such recommendation. To rely blindly on the report of a corporation-appointed committee which assembled such materials on behalf of the corporation is to abdicate the judicial duty to consider the interests of shareholders imposed by the statute. This abdication is particularly inappropriate in a case such as this one, where shareholders allege serious breaches of fiduciary duties owed to them by the directors controlling the corporation.

Section 55–55(c) is a broadening of the *Zapata* approach. * * *

The *Zapata* Court limited its two-step judicial inquiry to cases in which demand upon the corporation was futile and therefore excused. However, we find no justification for such limitation in our statutes. The language of section 55–55(c) is inclusive and draws no distinctions between demand-excused and other types of cases. *Cf.* ALI Principles of Corporate Governance: Analysis and Recommendations § 7.08 & Reporter's Notes 2 & 4 at 135–139 (Council Draft No. 6, Oct. 10, 1986) (issue of demand of minimal importance in determining scope of review; demand-excused/demand-required distinction not determinative). Thus, court approval is required for disposition of *all* derivative suits, even where the directors are not charged with fraud or self-dealing, or where the plaintiff and the board agree to discontinue, dismiss, compromise, or settle the lawsuit.

358 S.E.2d at 327. Consult Cox, Heroes in the Law: Alford v. Shaw, 66 N.C.L.Rev. 565 (1988).

(3) Grobow v. Perot, 539 A.2d 180 (Del.1988) involved a derivative complaint challenging the transaction in which H. Ross Perot's interest in General Motors was reacquired by the company, and Perot resigned as a director. The Chancery Court dismissed the complaint, since no demand had been made and the plaintiffs' complaint failed to allege particularized facts "sufficient to sustain 'a judicial finding' either of director interest or lack of director independence, or whether the directors exercised proper business judgment in approving the challenged transaction—placing the transaction between the protection of the business judgment rule." 539 A.2d at 183. The Delaware Supreme Court held that the "judicial finding" standard was erroneous but the Court nevertheless affirmed on the ground that even under the more relaxed standard the complaint did not allege facts sufficient to establish demand futility. The Court stated:

[W]e find the Vice Chancellor's use of a "judicial finding" criterion for judging a derivative claim for demand excusal to be erroneous, but not reversible error. First, the Court's "judicial finding" criterion would impose a more stringent standard for demand futility than is warranted under *Aronson*. The test for demand futility should be whether the well-pleaded facts of the particular complaint support a reasonable doubt of business judgment protection, not whether the facts support a judicial finding that the directors' actions are not protected by the business judgment rule. See Aronson, 473 A.2d at 815.

Second, given the highly factual nature of the inquiry presented to the Trial Court by a Rule 23.1 defense, we conclude that it would be neither practicable nor wise to attempt to formulate a criterion of general application for determining reasonable doubt. The facts necessary to support a finding of reasonable doubt either of director disinterest or independence, or whether proper business judgment was exercised in the transaction will vary with each case. Reasonable doubt must be decided by the trial court on a case-by-case basis employing an objective analysis. Were we to adopt a standard criterion for resolving a motion to dismiss based on Rule 23.1, the test for demand excusal would, in all likelihood, become rote and inelastic.

Finally, since a Rule 23.1 motion normally precedes rather than follows discovery, a plaintiff may be able in one case and without formal discovery to plead facts sufficient to raise a reasonable doubt of business judgment protection, but be unable in another case without such discovery to plead facts sufficient to support a judicial finding of the lack of business judgment protection. On the other hand, if a derivative complaint alleges facts which would support a judicial finding of a lack of business judgment protection, then such facts would more than satisfy *Aronson*'s reasonable doubt standard.

Therefore, we decline to approve the use of a "judicial finding" standard as the minimum criterion below which presuit demand will not be excused. We think it sufficient simply to say that the Court of Chancery must weigh the presumption of the business judgment rule that attaches to a board of directors' decision against the well-pleaded facts alleged in a plaintiff's demand-futility complaint. In that respect, the suggestion in the Trial Court's Opinion that a transaction is first analyzed from the standpoint of fairness is erroneous. Fairness becomes an issue only if the presumption of the business judgment rule is defeated. *Aronson,* 473 A.2d at 812–817. * * *

539 A.2d at 186–187.

(4) Easterbrook, Circuit Justice, concurring in Starrels v. First Nat. Bank of Chicago, 870 F.2d 1168, 1172–1176 (7th Cir.1989):

This case illustrates, * * * the difficulty courts have had with the rule of *Aronson* —which in *Grobow* led the Supreme Court of Delaware to dress down the Chancellor for misunderstanding the rule. Perhaps a federal judge may be forgiven the temerity of suggesting to members of the state bench that the problem lies not in the Chancellor's appreciation of *Aronson* but in the approach taken by that case. This is a subject of mutual interest, not only because *Aronson* governs proceedings directly in diversity cases but also because federal courts apply their own demand rules when claims are based wholly on federal law, and in the latter they must decide whether to absorb into the body of federal law the rule stated by *Aronson.*

Why must shareholders demand that corporations act before filing suit? The rule could reflect a hope that the dispute will go away without litigation, that the board of directors will "do something" (or persuade the putative plaintiff that suit is pointless). Demand then initiates a form of alternative dispute resolution, much like mediation. Steps to control the volume of litigation are welcome, and courts give this as a justification for the demand rule. It is not, however, a powerful one, because on balance the rule creates more litigation than it prevents. It is difficult to identify cases in which the board's response to a demand satisfied the shareholder and thus prevented litigation; even if the board acts the shareholder may believe the board did too little. It is easy to point to hundreds of cases, including this one, in which the demand requirement was itself the centerpiece of the litigation.

An approach uncertain in scope and discretionary in operation— that is, any rule except one invariably requiring or excusing demand— promotes litigation. When the stakes are high (as they frequently are in cases of this character), even a small disagreement between the parties about the application of a legal rule makes it difficult to resolve disagreements peaceably. It will be especially hard to resolve disputes out of court when, as in Delaware, making a demand affects the merits. A demand may be understood to concede that the board of directors possesses the discretion not to pursue the claim—and to block the investor's pursuit of it too. See Zapata Corp. v. Maldonado, 430 A.2d 779 (Del.1981). The case reports overflow with decisions concerning the demand requirement, and under *Aronson*'s approach litigation to determine whether a demand should have been made entails questions closely associated with "the merits". As a way to curtail litigation, the demand rule is a flop.[42]

The persuasive rationale for the demand requirement is that it allows directors to make a business decision about a business question: whether to invest the time and resources of the corporation in litigation. Firms must make operational decisions; if these misfire, they must decide what to do next. Each decision must be made with the interests of the corporation at heart. Whether to fire a negligent employee, or to extend another chance, is no less a "business decision" than the choice to hire him initially or approve his strategy. So too the decision to file a lawsuit or choose something simpler—discharge, demotion, dressing-down, ratification—in the wake of questionable conduct. Even doing nothing is justified when the resources of top managers required to act exceed the injury to the firm; when "something must be done", acts short of litigation could have net benefits exceeding those of litigation. If the directors run the show, then they must control litigation (versus other remedies) to the same extent as they make the initial business decision. They may conclude that internal remedies such as discharge or a reduction in compensation are more cost-effective for the firm. A lawsuit that seems to have good prospects and a positive value (net of attorneys' fees) still may be an unwise business decision because of the value of managerial time that would have to be invested, time unavailable to pursue the principal business of the corporation. Similarly, a lawsuit that appears to have a negative net value may be useful to the firm if it deters future misconduct.

Choosing between litigation and some other response may be difficult, depending on information unavailable to courts and a sense of the situation in which business executives are trained. Managers who make such judgment calls poorly ultimately give way to superior executives; no such mechanism "selects out" judges who try to make business decisions. In the long run firms are better off when business decisions are made by business specialists, even granting the inevitable

---

42. [By the Judge] Even without the link between demand and the board's ability to squelch the suit, there is a steady flow of litigation about the demand requirement. Why this should occur is something of a mystery. * * *

errors. If principles such as the "business judgment rule" preserve room for managers to err in making an operational decision, so too they preserve room to err in deciding what remedies to pursue.

This rationale need not, however, imply universal demand. If courts would not respect the directors' decision not to file suit, then demand would be an empty formality. Perhaps the directors are interested in the transaction, so that they have a financial stake in the transaction and bear the burden of establishing its propriety. In such duty-of-loyalty cases courts frequently say that demand would be "futile". Or perhaps all of the directors are so ensnarled in the transaction that even when only the duty of care is at stake, their judgment could not be respected. Again demand would be an empty gesture. Delaware attempts to identify these cases and excuse demand in them.[43]

Aronson surveys these justifications and limits. The court observes that a decision not to sue is a business judgment. * * * Yet the rule of law devised in *Aronson* does not track the court's own remarks. * * *

A final oddment in the *Aronson* approach. Rule 23.1 and its parallel in Delaware practice require the court to determine at the pleading stage whether demand was necessary. This requires courts to adjudicate the merits on the pleadings, for a decision that the business judgment rule shelters the challenged conduct *is* "the merits" in derivative litigation, and under *Aronson* also shows that demand was necessary. It is a bobtailed adjudication, without evidence. If facts suggesting (at the one-in-ten level) that the business judgment rule will not prevent recovery have come to light, the investor may plead them and litigate further, setting the stage for still another decision about the scope of the business judgment rule. If facts of this character would come to light only with discovery, then demand is necessary and plaintiff may not litigate at all—for in Delaware a demand-required case is one the board may elect to prevent or dismiss under *Zapata*. The amount of information in the public domain is unrelated to the ability of the board to make a business judgment concerning litigation, is unrelated indeed to any function of the demand requirement. Why should the board acquire the power to dismiss under *Zapata* just because the plaintiff needs discovery and so cannot make the required showing "with particularity" in the complaint? *Aronson* and its successors do not discuss the point.

A rule of universal demand, as the American Law Institute has proposed, would avoid these difficulties. If Delaware thinks it wise to

43. [By the Judge] Whether the game is worth the candle is a different question. Difficulties in sorting cases into demand-required and demand-excused bins might justify a universal requirement, with the understanding that requiring demand does not always give the corporation authority to block litigation. There is much to recommend the American Law Institute's proposal to require universal demand and decouple that requirement from doctrines concerning the board's ability to prevent or dismiss derivative litigation. Principles of Corporate Governance: Analysis and Recommendations §§ 7.03, 7.08, and commentary at 64–71 (Tent. Draft No. 8, 1988). (Section 7.03(b) of Tentative Draft No. 8 would excuse demand when "irreparable injury to the corporation would otherwise result", but the Institute voted to require the shareholder to serve demand even after commencing a suit in advance of demand in reliance on feared "irreparable injury".)

distinguish demand-required and demand-excused cases, then a rule requiring demand unless the board is so wrapped up in the transaction that it cannot be relied on to make a business decision about the wisdom of litigation would do nicely. It would reflect the functions of having a demand rule in the first place. A rule excusing demand when there is a serious question about the status of the "challenged transaction" does not respond to the reasons for thinking demand useful, and one wonders whether it might be better to have no demand requirement at all than to excuse demand when the board might want to sue and compel demand when the board could not responsibly litigate.

(4) For a staunch and relentless defense of the Delaware approach, see Dooley and Veasey, The Role of the Board in Derivative Litigation, 44 Bus. Law. 503 (1989). Every suggestion of even superficial judicial review of the merits of a litigation committee decision in the "demand required" context is systematically referred to by the authors as "judicially intrusive" review.

(5) In addition to the American Law Institute Corporate Governance Project proposals, summarized briefly in Judge Easterbrook's concurrence in *Starrels,* the Committee on Corporate Laws has developed a statutory solution to the litigation committee issue. See RMBCA §§ 7.42, 7.44 (adopted in December, 1989). The Official Comment to § 7.42 explains the new demand requirement:

> Section 7.42 requires a written demand on the corporation in all cases. The demand must be made at least 90 days before commencement of suit unless irreparable injury to the corporation would result. This approach has been adopted for two reasons. First, even though no director may be independent, the demand will give the board of directors the opportunity to reexamine the act complained of in the light of a potential lawsuit and take corrective action. Secondly, the provision eliminates the time and expense of the litigants and the court involved in litigating the question whether demand is required. It is believed that requiring a demand in all cases does not impose an onerous burden since a relatively short waiting period of 90 days is provided and this period may be shortened if irreparable injury to the corporation would result by waiting for the expiration of the 90 day period. Moreover, the cases in which demand is excused are relatively rare. Many plaintiffs' counsel as a matter of practice make a demand in all cases rather than litigate the issue whether demand is excused.

> * * *

> There is no obligation on the part of the corporation to respond to the demand. However, if the corporation, after receiving the demand, decides to institute litigation or, after a derivative proceeding has commenced, decides to assume control of the litigation, the shareholder's right to commence or control the proceeding ends unless it can be shown that the corporation will not adequately pursue the matter. As stated in *Lewis v. Graves,* 701 F.2d 245, 247–48 (2d Cir. 1983):

>> The [demand] rule is intended "to give the derivative corporation itself the opportunity to take over a suit which was brought on its behalf in the first place, and thus to allow the directors the chance to occupy their normal status as conductors of the corporation's affairs." Permitting corporations to assume control over share-

holder derivative suits also has numerous practical advantages. Corporate management may be in a better position to pursue alternative remedies, resolving grievances without burdensome and expensive litigation. Deference to directors' judgments may also result in the termination of meritless actions brought solely for their settlement or harassment value. Moreover, where litigation is appropriate, the derivative corporation will often be in a better position to bring or assume the suit because of superior financial resources and knowledge of the challenged transactions. [Citations omitted.]

The critical section dealing with the finality of committee and/or board of directors determinations is § 7.44. In discussing the standard to be applied in evaluating these determinations, the Official Comment elaborates upon the language of § 7.44(a):

Section 7.44(a) requires that the determination be made by the appropriate persons in good faith after conducting a reasonable inquiry upon which their conclusions are based. The word "inquiry" rather than "investigation" has been used to make it clear that the scope of the inquiry will depend upon the issues raised and the knowledge of the group making the determination with respect to the issues. In some cases, the issues may be so simple or the knowledge of the group so extensive that little additional inquiry is required. In other cases, the group may need to engage counsel and other professionals to make an investigation and assist the group in its evaluation of the issues.

The phrase "in good faith" modifies both the determination and the inquiry. The test, which is also included in sections 8.30 (general standards of conduct for directors) and 8.51 (authority to indemnify), is a subjective one, meaning "honestly or in an honest manner." "The Corporate Director's Guidebook," 33 Bus.Law. 1595, 1601 (1978). As stated in *Abella v. Universal Leaf Tobacco Co.,* 546 F.Supp. 795, 800 (E.D.Va.1982), "the inquiry intended by this phrase goes to the spirit and sincerity with which the investigation was conducted, rather than the reasonableness of its procedures or basis for conclusions."

The phrase "upon which its conclusions are based" requires that the inquiry and the conclusions follow logically. This provision authorizes the court to examine the determination to ensure that it has some support in the findings of the inquiry. * * * This phrase does not require the persons making the determination to prepare a written report that sets forth their determination and the bases therefor, since circumstances will vary as to the need for such a report. There may, however, be many instances where good corporate practice will commend such a procedure.

Section 7.44 is not intended to modify the general standards of conduct for directors set forth in section 8.30 of the Model Act, but rather to make those standards somewhat more explicit in the derivative proceeding context.

Is this proposed solution a reasonable accommodation between the interests of the plaintiff shareholders and the corporation? Does it return the law to *Auerbach?*

Chapter Eleven

DUTY OF LOYALTY AND CONFLICT OF INTEREST

A. SELF DEALING

MARCIANO v. NAKASH

Supreme Court of Delaware, 1987.
535 A.2d 400.

Before HORSEY, MOORE and WALSH, JJ.

WALSH, JUSTICE.

This is an appeal from a decision of the Court of Chancery which validated a claim in liquidation of Gasoline, Ltd. ("Gasoline"), a Delaware corporation, placed in custodial status pursuant to 8 *Del.C.* § 226 by reason of a deadlock among its board of directors. Fifty percent of Gasoline is owned by Ari, Joe, and Ralph Nakash (the "Nakashes") and fifty percent by Georges, Maurice, Armand and Paul Marciano (the "Marcianos"). The Vice Chancellor ruled that $2.5 million in loans made by the Nakashes faction to Gasoline were valid and enforceable debts of the corporation, notwithstanding their origin in self-dealing transactions. The Marcianos argue that the disputed debt is voidable as a matter of law but, in any event, the Nakashes failed to meet their burden of establishing full fairness. We conclude that the Vice Chancellor applied the proper standard for review of self-dealing transactions and the finding of full fairness is supported by the record. Accordingly, we affirm. * * *

The parties agree that the loans made by the Nakashes to Gasoline were interested transactions. The Nakashes as officers of Gasoline executed the various documents which supported the loans and at the same time guaranteed those loans extended through their wholly owned entities. It is also not disputed that, given the control deadlock, the questioned transactions did not receive majority approval of Gasoline's directors or shareholders. The Marcianos argue that the loan transaction is voidable at the option of the corporation notwithstanding its fairness or the good faith of its participants. A review of this contention, rejected by the Court of Chancery, requires analysis of the concept of director self-dealing under Delaware law.

It is a long-established principle of Delaware corporate law that the fiduciary relationship between directors and the corporation imposes fundamental limitations on the extent to which a director may benefit from dealings with the corporation he serves. *Guth v. Loft, Inc.*, Del. Supr., 5 A.2d 503 (1939). Thus, the "voting [for] and taking" of compensation may be deemed "constructively fraudulent" in the absence of shareholder ratification, or statutory or bylaw authorization. *Cahall v. Lofland,* Del.Ch., 114 A. 224, 232 (1921). Perhaps the strongest condemnation of interested director conduct appears in *Potter v. Sanitary Co. of America,* Del.Ch., 194 A. 87 (1937), a decision which the Marcianos advance as definitive of the rule of per se voidability. In *Potter* the Court of Chancery characterized transactions between corporations having common directors and officers "constructively fraudulent," absent shareholder ratification.

Support can also be found for the per se rule of voidability in this Court's decision in *Kerbs v. California Eastern Airways Inc.,* Del.Supr., 90 A.2d 652 (1952). The *Kerbs* court, in considering the validity of a profit sharing plan, ruled that the self-interest of the directors who voted on the plan caused the transaction to be voidable. The court concluded that the profit sharing plan was voidable based on the common law rule that the vote of an interested director will not be counted in determining whether the challenged action received the affirmative vote of a majority of the board of directors. *Id.* at 658 (*citing Bovay v. H.M. Byllesby & Co.,* Del.Supr., 38 A.2d 808 (1944)).

The principle of per se voidability for interested transactions, which is sometimes characterized as the common law rule, was significantly ameliorated by the 1967 enactment of Section 144 of the Delaware General Corporation Law.[1] The Marcianos argue that section 144(a) provides the only basis for immunizing self-interested transac-

---

1. [By the Court] Section 144 of Title 8 *Del.C.* now provides:

(a) No contract or transaction between a corporation and 1 or more of its directors or officers, or between a corporation and any other corporation, partnership, association, or other organization in which 1 or more of its directors or officers, are directors or officers, or have a financial interest, shall be void or voidable solely for this reason, or solely because the director or officer is present at or participates in the meeting of the board or committee which authorizes the contract or transaction, or solely because his or their votes are counted for such purpose, if:

(1) The material facts as to his relationship or interest and as to the contract or transaction are disclosed or are known to the board of directors or the committee, and the board or committee in good faith authorizes the contract or transaction by the affirmative votes of a majority of the disinterested directors, even though the disinterested directors be less than a quorum; or

(2) The material facts as to his relationship or interest and as to the contract or transaction are disclosed or are known to the shareholders entitled to vote thereon, and the contract or transaction is specifically approved in good faith by vote of the shareholders; or

(3) The contract or transaction is fair as to the corporation as of the time it is authorized, approved or ratified, by the board of directors, a committee or the shareholders.

tions and since none of the statute's component tests are satisfied the stricture of the common law per se rule applies. The Vice Chancellor agreed that the disputed loans did not withstand a section 144(a) analysis but ruled that the common law rule did not invalidate transactions determined to be intrinsically fair. We agree that section 144(a) does not provide the only validation standard for interested transactions.

It overstates the common law rule to conclude that relationship, alone, is the controlling factor in interested transactions. Although the application of the per se voidability rule in early Delaware cases resulted in the invalidation of interested transactions, the result was not dictated simply by a tainted relationship. Thus in *Potter,* the Court, while adopting the rule of voidability, emphasized that interested transactions should be subject to close scrutiny. Where the undisputed evidence tended to show that the transaction would advance the personal interests of the directors at the expense of stockholders, the stockholders, upon discovery, are entitled to disavow the transaction.

Further, the court examined the motives of the defendant directors and the effect the transaction had on the corporation and its shareholders.

In other Delaware cases, decided before the enactment of section 144, interested director transactions were deemed voidable only after an examination of the fairness of a particular transaction *vis-a-vis* the nonparticipating shareholders and a determination of whether the disputed conduct received the approval of a noninterested majority of directors or shareholders. *Keenan v. Eshleman,* Del.Supr., 2 A.2d 904, 908 (1938); *Blish v. Thompson Automatic Arms Corp.,* Del.Supr., 64 A.2d 581, 602 (1948). The latter test is now crystallized in the ratification criteria of section 144(a), although the nonquorum restriction of *Kerbs* has been superceded by the language of subparagraph (b) of section 144.

The Marcianos view compliance with section 144 as the sole basis for avoiding the per se rule of voidability. The Court of Chancery rejected this contention and we agree that it is not consonant with Delaware corporate law. This Court in *Fliegler v. Lawrence,* Del.Supr., 361 A.2d 218 (1976), a post-section 144 decision, refused to view section 144 as either completely preemptive of the common law duty of director fidelity or as constituting a grant of broad immunity. As we stated in *Fliegler:* "It merely removes an 'interested director' cloud when its terms are met and provides against invalidation of an agreement 'solely' because such a director or officer is involved." *Id.* at 222. In *Fliegler* this Court applied a two-tiered analysis: application of section 144 coupled with an intrinsic fairness test.

(b) Common or interested directors may be counted in determining the presence of a quorum at a meeting of the board of directors or of a committee which authorizes the contract or transaction.

If section 144 validation of interested director transactions is not deemed exclusive, as *Fliegler* clearly holds, the continued viability of the intrinsic fairness test is mandated not only by fact situations, such as here present, where shareholder deadlock prevents ratification but also where shareholder control by interested directors precludes independent review. Indeed, if an independent committee of the board, contemplated by section 144(a)(1) is unavailable, the sole forum for demonstrating intrinsic fairness may be a judicial one. In such situations the intrinsic fairness test furnishes the substantive standard against which the evidential burden of the interested directors is applied. * * *

This case illustrates the limitation inherent in viewing section 144 as the touchstone for testing interested director transactions. Because of the shareholder deadlock, even if the Nakashes had attempted to invoke section 144, it was realistically unavailable. The ratification process contemplated by section 144 presupposes the functioning of corporate constituencies capable of providing assents. Just as the statute cannot "sanction unfairness" neither can it invalidate fairness if, upon judicial review, the transaction withstands close scrutiny of its intrinsic elements.[2]

[The Court held that the Chancellor's decision that the terms of the loan met the "intrinsic fairness standard" was supported by the record and was the product of a logical deductive process.]

We hold, therefore, that the Court of Chancery properly applied the intrinsic fairness test in determining the validity of the interested director transactions and its finding of full fairness is clearly supported by the record. Accordingly, the decision is Affirmed.

Notes

(1) Consider the general problem of a director who enters into a business transaction with the corporation—for example, the purchase of property from or the sale of property to the corporation. Such transactions can take many forms but they have one element in common. There is an obvious risk that the transaction will be skewed in favor of the director and as a result will be harmful to the corporation. Such a risk, of course, is increased if the interested director owns sufficient shares so that he or she can name or remove a majority of the directors. What position should the law take with respect to such transactions? As described in the principal case, the position taken during the last part of the nineteenth century was

---

2. [By the Court] Although in this case none of the curative steps afforded under section 144(a) were available because of the director-shareholder deadlock, a non-disclosing director seeking to remove the cloud of interestedness would appear to have the same burden under section 144(a) (3), as under prior case law, of proving the intrinsic fairness of a questioned transaction which had been approved or ratified by the directors or shareholders. Folk,

The Delaware General Corp. Law: A Commentary and Analysis, 86 (1972). On the other hand, approval by fully-informed disinterested directors under section 144(a)(1), or disinterested stockholders under section 144(a)(2), permits invocation of the business judgment rule and limits judicial review to issues of gift or waste with the burden of proof upon the party attacking the transaction.

that all such transactions were voidable at the instance of the corporation or its shareholders without regard to the fairness or unfairness of the transaction. This absolute position now appears to be totally rejected, in part because it is clear that many such transactions are beneficial to the corporation and were entered into by the director to assist rather than to harm the corporation. The problem is what tests should be applied to sort out the harmful from the harmless. Several possible tests have received some degree of modern judicial approval in the absence of statute:

(a) Such a transaction is voidable if it is not approved or ratified by a disinterested majority of the directors or by the shareholders;

(b) Such a transaction is *not* voidable if the interested director can show that the transaction is fair to the corporation;

(c) Such a transaction is voidable if the plaintiff shows that the transaction is unfair to the corporation;

(d) Such a transaction is voidable if the plaintiff shows that the transaction constitutes fraud, waste, or serious overreaching;

(e) Such a transaction is *not* voidable if it has been approved or ratified by a disinterested majority of the directors, and no further inquiry need be made into its fairness;

(f) Such a transaction is *not* voidable if it has been approved or ratified by a majority of the shareholders and no further inquiry need be made into its fairness;

(g) Such a transaction is always voidable if the vote of the interested director is necessary to approve the transaction or his presence is necessary to form a quorum;

(h) Such a transaction is always voidable if the interested director participates in the decision-making process, urging approval of the transaction, but does not vote.

Thought will reveal that these alternatives are not exclusive, since some relate to the *procedures* by which the transaction was approved while others (particularly (b), (c), and (d)) relate to the *substance*—the effect of the transaction on the corporation—and it is possible to combine them. For example, one might establish a rule that such a transaction is voidable if it is unfair (alternative (c)) or constitutes waste (alternative (d)) but the majority of the shareholders may ratify the transaction (alternative (f)). Would such a rule be desirable? Or, one might establish the rule that a transaction that is voidable under alternative (a) may be made not voidable if the director can establish fairness (alternative (b)). Would that rule be desirable? Of course, at the extreme, there probably is no reason to consider setting aside a transaction approved by *all* the shareholders, no matter how damaging to the corporation, though one can imagine situations involving injury to creditors or senior interests.

To the extent the procedures followed in approving a transaction are determinative, difficult issues arise relating to who has the burden of proof, the identification of what types of interest should disqualify a person from being "disinterested," and what degree of participation by an "interested" director or shareholder should be viewed as tainting the outcome. Many of these issues are now addressed specifically by statute.

(2) While many transactions between directors and their corporation have been held to be valid in the absence of a controlling statute, considerable confusion exists in the case law as to the circumstances which may validate such transactions. If one examines the results of the cases (as contrasted with statements in the opinions), the following comments accurately reflect most of the numerous decisions:

(a) If the court feels the transaction to be fair to the corporation, it will be upheld;

(b) If the court feels that the transaction involves fraud, undue overreaching or waste of corporate assets (e.g. a director using corporate assets for personal purposes without paying for them), the transaction will be set aside; and

(c) If the court feels that the transaction does not involve fraud, undue overreaching or waste of corporate assets, but is not convinced that the transaction is fair, the transaction will be upheld only where the interested director can convincingly show that the transaction was approved (or ratified) by a truly disinterested majority of the board of directors without participation by the interested director or by a majority of the shareholders, after full disclosure of all relevant facts.

(3) Statutes similar to § 144 of the Delaware General Corporation Law (quoted by the court in n. 1) are of relatively recent origin and long postdate the judicial development of the common law principles discussed above. Today, over thirty states have statutes similar to § 144 dealing with conflict of interest transactions. Most of these statutes were enacted after 1975.

(4) Consider carefully the suggestion by the Delaware Supreme Court in n. 2 that where "fully informed, disinterested directors" or "disinterested stockholders" approve a conflict of interest transaction under § 144, the business judgment rule may be invoked to limit judicial review to "issues of gift or waste." Is that consistent with the language of § 144? Is it a desirable limitation on directoral or shareholder review of conflict of interest transactions? Under § 144, may a shareholder who is involved in the conflict of interest transaction vote as a shareholder to ratify the transaction? It seems clear that such a shareholder would not be a "disinterested stockholder" within the court's dictum in n. 2.

(5) As originally promulgated, § 8.31 of the RMBCA [set forth in a footnote in the statutory supplement] closely followed the structure of these conflict-of-interest statutes. Section 8.31 differed from § 144 of the Delaware statute in part because it stated expressly that the fairness (or "intrinsic fairness") of a conflict of interest transaction validated that transaction even in the absence of any directoral or shareholder action. Thus, under § 8.31, fairness appeared to be an alternative to directoral or shareholder approval as a basis for validating a conflict of interest transaction. Like § 144, moreover, the Official Comment to § 8.31 stated that the purpose of § 8.31 was to eliminate the "automatic rule of voidability" of the early case law, and § 8.31 "does not mean that all transactions that meet one or more of the tests set forth in § 8.31(a) are automatically valid." Section 8.31 has been included in the codifications of several recent state corporation statutes.

(6) In December, 1988, the Committee on Corporate Laws approved a new treatment of conflict of interest transactions, now codified as §§ 8.60 through 8.63 of the RMBCA.   Section 8.31 of the RMBCA has been withdrawn.   The new subchapter F, as it is usually called, is a much more ambitious undertaking than § 144 of the Delaware statute or § 8.31. Subchapter F is structured similarly to § 8.31: a conflict of interest transaction is not voidable by the corporation if (a) it has been approved by disinterested directors or shareholders, or (b) the interested director establishes the fairness of the transaction.   Unlike § 8.31, however, subchapter F is designed to create a series of "bright line" principles that increase predictability and enhance practical administrability.   Does the conflict of interest area lend itself to "bright line" treatment?

(a) Subchapter F deals only with "transactions" between a director and the corporation.   It does not deal with issues such as whether an opportunity is or is not a corporate opportunity, or non-transactional policy decisions, e.g., whether the corporation should establish a divisional headquarters in the director's home town, or whether a director may compete directly with the corporation in its business.   Whatever rules are applicable to judge the validity and propriety of such transactions are unaffected by Subchapter F.

(b) One important "bright line" is that the definition of "conflicting interest" in § 8.60(1) is exclusive—an interest of a director is a conflicting interest *if and only if* it meets the requirements of this definition.   As an example of an interest of a director that may influence his or her decision but does not constitute a statutory "conflicting interest" the Official Comment uses this hypothetical: if D (a director of X Co.) is a major creditor of Y Co., and the issue is some transaction between X Co. and Y Co., D's creditor interest in Y Co. may possibly influence D's vote as a director of X Co. on a contemplated transaction between X Co. and Y Co.   D's creditor interest in Y Co., however, does not create a "conflicting interest" when D votes as a director of X Co. on the transaction, since D's creditor interest in Y Co. does not fit any subcategory of the definition of "conflicting interest" in § 8.60(1)(ii) or of "related person" in § 8.60(3).

(c) The definition of "director's conflicting interest transaction" in § 8.60(2) is similarly preclusive: it not only designates the exclusive area within which the rules of subchapter F are to be applied under § 8.61(b) but also prohibits a court from applying conflict of interest provisions to circumstances that lie outside that definition.   This preclusive effect is described by the following two illustrations drawn from the Official Comment:

(i) "If a plaintiff charges that a director had a conflict of interest with respect to a transaction of the corporation because the other party was his cousin, the answer of the court should be: 'No.   A cousin, as such and without more, is not included in section 8.60(3) as a related person—and under section 8.61(a), I have no authority to reach out further.' "

(ii) "If a plaintiff contends that the director had a conflict of interest in a corporate transaction because the other party is president of the golf club the director wants desperately to join, the court should respond: 'No.   The only director's conflicting interest on the basis of which I can set aside a corporate transaction or impose other sanctions is a financial interest as defined in section 8.60.' "

(d) Section 8.62(d) creates a new defined term, "qualified director," to describe the directors who may vote to approve a director's conflicting interest transaction and thus "sanitize" the transaction. See § 8.61(b). Such approval, it should be noted, means that the transaction "may not be enjoined, set aside, or give rise to an award of damages or other sanctions, in a proceeding by a shareholder" because of the director's interest in the transaction.

(7) Would it be desirable to provide for at least some degree of judicial oversight of all conflict of interest transactions? If so, isn't Subchapter F a well meaning but flawed exercise?

(8) Abstractly, self dealing transactions have two attributes that make a substantial degree of judicial oversight desirable: (1) they are voluntary transactions on the part of the self dealing director and (2) they provide an opportunity for direct pecuniary enrichment at the expense of the corporation by the self dealing director. Indeed, almost all recent commentary on directors' duties recognize that breaches of the duty of loyalty raise serious problems that merit continuing judicial scrutiny. For example, in Scott, Corporation Law and the American Law Institute Corporate Governance Project, 35 Stan.L.Rev. 927 (1983), the author urged (long before the Trans Union case) that liability for violations of the duty of care should be entirely eliminated but that judicial vigilance over violations of the duty of loyalty should be vigorously encouraged. Does Subchapter F go against the grain of this analysis by withdrawing (or appearing to withdraw) all judicial scrutiny from conflict of interest cases, relying instead on the vote of "qualified directors" to protect the corporation and minority shareholders against overreaching transactions?

(9) Most modern self-dealing cases involve small, closely held corporations, and in most of these cases, the self dealing individual is a significant shareholder in the corporation. How useful is subchapter F in this context since most such corporations probably will not have "qualified directors" to review the transaction?

(10) The Official Comment to § 8.61(b) also includes the following commentary:

> Clause (1) of subsection (b) * * * [is] subject to one critically important predicate condition. The condition—an obvious one—is that the board's action must comply with the care, best interest, and good faith criteria prescribed in section 8.30(a) for all directors' actions. If the directors who voted for the conflicting interest transaction were qualified directors under subchapter F, but approved the transaction merely as an accommodation to the director with the conflicting interest, going through the motions of board action without complying with the requirements of section 8.30(a), the action of the board would not be given effect for purposes of section 8.61(b)(1).

> Board action on a director's conflicting interest transaction provides a context in which the function of the 'best interests of the corporation' language in section 8.30(a) is brought into clear focus.

Consider, for example, a situation in which it is established that the board of a manufacturing corporation approved a cash loan to a director where the duration, security, and interest terms of the loan were at prevailing commercial rates, but (i) the loan was not made in the course of the corporation's ordinary business and (ii) the loan required a commitment of limited working capital that would otherwise have been used in furtherance of the corporation's business activities. Such a loan transaction would not be afforded safe-harbor protection by section 8.62(b)(1) since the board did not comply with the requirement in section 8.30(a) that the board's action be, in its reasonable judgment, in the best interests of the corporation—that is that the action will, as the board judges the circumstances at hand, yield favorable results (or reduce detrimental results) as judged from the perspective of furthering the corporation's business activities.

If a determination is made that the terms of a director's conflicting interest transaction, judged according to the circumstances at the time of commitment, were manifestly unfavorable to the corporation, that determination would be relevant to an allegation that the director's action was not taken in good faith and therefore did not comply with section 8.30(a).

Isn't this an invitation for courts to examine the terms of the transaction to determine whether the terms are "manifestly unfavorable" and therefore constitute evidence that the approval was an "accommodation" rather than a "business judgment?" If a court should review a transaction to determine whether terms are "manifestly unfavorable," as a basis for deciding whether an appropriate business judgment was made by the qualified directors, why shouldn't it review the transaction directly for unfairness? Why should it have to go through the circumlocution of finding that the transaction was "manifestly unfavorable" and then concluding that § 8.30 was not complied with? If this standard of review was intended, should the quoted statements from the commentary have been included in the text of § 8.61 since they are, in effect, a major qualification upon a statute that on its face is unqualified?

(11) Most state statutes contain a provision restricting or prohibiting loans to employees or directors. For example, the 1960 Model Act provided:

No loans shall be made by a corporation to its officers or directors, and no loans shall be made by a corporation secured by its shares. 1 Mod. Bus.Corp.Act Ann. (1960 Ed.) § 42.

For a description of the background of such legislation and a plea for its retention, see Barnard, Corporate Loans to Directors and Officers: Every Business Now a Bank, 1988 Wisc.L.Rev. 237. Why should loans to a director be any different from any other self-dealing transaction? Why should loans by a corporation "secured by its shares" be subject to a special prohibition?

Section 8.32 of the RMBCA was based on these loan restriction statutes, though it liberalized the rules with respect to director loans to the point that only an unusual loan might fall subject to its prohibitions. However, when Subchapter F was adopted, the Committee on Corporate

Laws also withdrew § 8.32 in its entirety without discussing the justification for doing so. Of course, the hypothetical situation described in the Official Comment to Subchapter F (See note (10)) itself involves a corporate loan to a director.

HELLER v. BOYLAN
Supreme Court of New York, 1941.
29 N.Y.S.2d 653.

[Editor: Only the portions of this opinion dealing with the incentive compensation plan are included.]

COLLINS, JUSTICE.

In this derivative action 7 out of a total of 62,000 stockholders—holding under 1,000 out of a total of 5,074,076 shares—of the American Tobacco Company, seek recovery for the corporation from the Company's directors for alleged improper payments to certain of the Company's officers.

The suit derives from an incentive compensation by-law of the Company, known as Article XII, virtually unanimously adopted by the stockholders in March, 1912. Thereunder 10 per cent of the annual profits over the earnings of the corresponding properties in 1910 are to be distributed, 2½ per cent to the president and 1½ per cent to each of the five vice-presidents "in addition to the fixed salary of each of said officers."

The profits, and consequently the bonuses, undulated with the years; but at all times they were quite lush. By virtue of this by-law, the officers have received from and including 1929 to and including 1939—in addition to $3,784,999.69 in salaries—bonuses aggregating $11,672,920.27, or total compensation during that eleven-year period of $15,457,919.69. The president alone, George W. Hill, Sr., received $592,370 in 1929; $1,010,508 in 1930; $1,051,570 in 1931; $825,537.49 in 1932. The other payments to him during such period were obese, the thinnest being $137,042.65, in 1938, and the average around $400,000. The other officers likewise received handsome compensation though not as huge.

The plaintiffs maintain that these large bonus payments bore no relation to the value of the services for which they were given, that, consequently, they were in reality a gift in part, and that the majority stockholders committed waste and spoliation in thus giving away corporate property against the protest of the minority. Rogers v. Hill, 289 U.S. 582, 590–592, 53 S.Ct. 731, 77 L.Ed. 1385, 88 A.L.R. 744.

The validity of the by-law is not challenged. Indeed, its legality has been sustained. Rogers v. Hill, supra. Nor do plaintiffs impugn the principle of incentive compensation. Rather, they regard it "a legitimate means of accomplishing a desired result," and do not question "that the extra effort, spurred by the promise of extra compensation, may have been an important factor in the prosperity of the

Company." That the Company has been singularly prosperous is indubitable. Its growth has been prodigious, its record for earnings is an enviable one, the management has been extraordinarily efficient, and the stockholders, as well as the officers, have been the beneficiaries of this immensely capable organization. The Company has made money even in direful times. Its capital investment is $265,000,000. It produces more than 200,000,000 cigarettes a day. In 1939 the Company's sales amounted to $262,416,000, its most popular brand—"Lucky Strike"—yielding $218,542,749. The Company is one of the world's giant industrial enterprises. Its activities are farflung, if not worldwide. Nevertheless, charge the plaintiffs, the payments to the officers have become "so large as in substance and effect to amount to spoliation or waste of corporate property." Rogers v. Hill, supra.

This is not the first time some of these payments have been attacked. An earlier assault was made by another stockholder, Richard Reid Rogers, and from that litigation stems several of the issues involved in the present suit. It is the principle evoked by the Rogers case which mainly supplies the pattern for this one. * * *

[In] Rogers v. Hill, 289 U.S. 582, 53 S.Ct. 731, 735, 77 L.Ed. 1385, 88 A.L.R. 744, Butler, J., for the unanimous Court, enunciated the principle * * * thus:

"It follows from what has been shown that when adopted the by-law was valid. But plaintiff alleges that the measure of compensation fixed by it is not now equitable or fair. And he prays that the court fix and determine the fair and reasonable compensation of the individual defendants, respectively, for each of the years in question. The allegations of the complaint are not sufficient to permit consideration by the court of the validity or reasonableness of any of the payments on account of fixed salaries or of special credits or of the allotments of stock therein mentioned. Indeed, plaintiff alleges that other proceedings have been instituted for the restoration of special credits, and his suits to invalidate the stock allotments were recently considered here. Rogers v. Guaranty Trust Co., 288 U.S. 123, 53 S.Ct. 295, 77 L.Ed. 652 [89 A.L.R. 720]. The only payments that plaintiff by this suit seeks to have restored to the company are the payments made to the individual defendants under the by-law.

"We come to consider whether these amounts are subject to examination and revision in the District Court. As the amounts payable depend upon the gains of the business, the specified percentages are not per se unreasonable. The by-law was adopted in 1912 by an almost unanimous vote of the shares represented at the annual meeting and presumably the stockholders supporting the measure acted in good faith and according to their best judgment. The tabular statement in the margin shows the payments to individual defendants under the by-law. Plaintiff does not complain of any made prior to 1921. Regard is to be had to the enormous increase of the company's profits in recent years. The 2½ per cent. yielded President Hill $447,870.30 in 1929 and $842,507.72 in 1930. The 1½ per cent. yielded to each of the vice presidents, Neiley and Riggio, $115,141.86 in 1929 and $409,495.25 in 1930 and for these years payments under the by-law were in addition to the cash credits and fixed salaries shown in the statement.

"While the amounts produced by the application of the prescribed percentages give rise to no inference of actual or constructive fraud, the payments under the by-law have by reason of increase of profits become so large as to warrant investigation in equity in the interest of the company. Much weight is to be given to the action of the stockholders, and the by-law is supported by the presumption of regularity and continuity. But the rule prescribed by it cannot, against the protest of a shareholder, be used to justify payments of sums as salaries so large as in substance and effect to amount to spoliation or waste of corporate property. The dissenting opinion of Judge Swan indicates the applicable rule: 'If a bonus payment has no relation to the value of services for which it is given, it is in reality a gift in part, and the majority stockholders have no power to give away corporate property against the protest of the minority.' 60 F.2d 109, 113. The facts alleged by plaintiff are sufficient to require that the District Court, upon a consideration of all the relevant facts brought forward by the parties, determine whether and to what extent payments to the individual defendants under the by-laws constitute misuse and waste of the money of the corporation [citing cases]."

Following Rogers' victory in the Supreme Court, and before the "investigation in equity" was launched, negotiations for adjustment were started. These eventuated in a settlement, from which the Company benefited—at the time of the settlement in July, 1933—by $6,200,000 and a further saving of about $2,250,000 by March, 1940. Many more millions were saved—inasmuch as the settlement reduced the bonus base and the employee's stock subscription plan was revised. In addition, Rogers was paid a fee of $525,000, the net being $263,000, and the income tax thereon exhausting the remaining $262,000. Thus ended the Rogers campaign.

But the echoes therefrom persisted. Seven stockholders, including three of the plaintiffs in this action (Heller, Wile and Mandelkor), and represented by most of the attorneys who appear for the plaintiffs here, assailed the settlement and sought to have it cancelled on the ground that the huge fee to Rogers was in the nature of a bribe. * * *

THE PERPLEXITIES OF THE CASE

Quite obviously, this case carries a number of perplexities. A few of them will be noted:

1. The general reluctance of the Courts to interfere with the internal management of a corporation. Pragmatism by the Courts—interference or meddling with free and lawful enterprise honestly conducted—is repugnant to our concept of government. Of course the hesitancy is overcome if fraud or bad faith or over-reaching appears—if the fiduciaries have been faithless to their trust.

2. Though this is a derivative stockholders' action, only 7 out of 62,000 stockholders have joined the onslaught; these 7 holding less than 1,000 out of a total of 5,074,076 shares of the Company. This factor, though significant, bears only on the equities; it is by no means decisive. Tyranny over the minority by the majority is abhorrent and will not be tolerated. The majority cannot, save by due legal process, make that which is illegal, legal, nor can it confiscate the company's assets or dispense them as unearned bounties. Majority rule does not license subjugation or immunize spoliation. The possession of power does not authorize or excuse its abuse. Power is not a franchise to do wrong. The majority cannot any more than the minority violate the law with impunity.

3. This case differs from most stockholders suits in that in those cases it is the conduct of directors which forms the basis of the complaint, whereas here not only is the by-law a creature of the stockholders, but on at least two other occasions, one in April, 1933, and again in April, 1940, the stockholders, by almost unanimous vote, ratified many of the payments involved in this suit. To be sure, "the majority stockholders have no power to give away corporate property against the protest of the minority." Rogers v. Hill, supra [60 F. 114].

4. The fact that the by-law has been in existence since 1912 and has been held valid.

5. The embarrassment which some of the defendants might experience in refunding even a part of what they received, especially since taxes were paid thereon.

6. The language of finality contained in paragraph 4 of the by-law.[3]

7. The paucity of apposite precedents.

Let it be emphasized, however, that the above are alluded to only as difficulties; they enter into the equities, but do not constitute a bar.

*   *   *

Now, even a high-bracketer would deem [the stipends involved in this case] munificent. To the person of moderate income they would be princely—perhaps as something unattainable; to the wage-earner ekeing out an existence, they would be fabulous, and the unemployed might regard them as fantastic, if not criminal. To others they would seem immoral, inexcusably unequal, and an indictment of our economic system. The opinion of Judge Swan has been unfairly paraphrased as announcing that "no man can be worth $1,000,000 a year". But see

---

3. [By the Editor] Section 4 reads as follows:

"Section 4. The declaration of the Treasurer as to the amount of net profits for the year and the sum due anyone hereunder shall be binding and conclusive on all parties, and no one claiming hereunder shall have the right to question the said declaration, or to any examination of the books or accounts of the Company, and nothing herein contained shall give any incumbent of any office any right to claim to continue therein, or any other right except as herein specifically expressed."

George T. Washington, of the Cornell Law School, The Corporation Executive's living wage, Harvard Law Review, March, 1941, Vol. LIV. 759. Many economists advocate a ceiling for compensation.

At the stockholders meeting on April 3, 1941, a holder of 80 shares of common stock—who thought the compensation grandiose—offered a resolution to restrict the president's bonus to a maximum of $100,000 and to impose other limitations. But the resolution was defeated by 2,193,418 votes to 74,571. Harvard Law Review, supra 747.

Let it be boldly marked that the particular business before this Court is not the revamping of the social or economic order—*justiciable* disputes confront it. * * *

Here, the plaintiffs proffered no testimony whatever in support of their charge of waste. The figures, they reason, speak for themselves, and the defendants must justify them. The figures do speak, but just what do they say as a matter of equity? They are immense, staggeringly so. Even so, is that enough to compel the substitution of the Court's judgment for that of the stockholders? Larger compensation has been judicially approved. * * *

Assuming, arguendo, that the compensation should be revised, what yardstick is to be employed? Who or what is to supply the measuring-rod? The conscience of equity? Equity is but another name for human being temporarily judicially robed. He is not omnipotent or omniscient. Can equity be so arrogant as to hold that it knows more about managing this corporation than its stockholders?

Yes, the Court possesses the *power* to prune these payments, but openness forces the confession that the pruning would be synthetic and artificial rather than analytic or scientific. Whether or not it would be fair and just, is highly dubious. Yet, merely because the problem is perplexing is no reason for eschewing it. It is not timidity, however, which perturbs me. It is finding a rational or just gauge for revising these figures were I inclined to do so. No blueprints are furnished. The elements to be weighed are incalculable; the imponderables, manifold. To act out of whimsy or caprice or arbitrariness would be more than inexact—it would be the precise antithesis of justice; it would be a farce.

If comparisons are to be made, with whose compensation are they to be made—executives? Those connected with the motion picture industry? Radio artists? Justices of the Supreme Court of the United States? The President of the United States? Manifestly, the material at hand is not of adequate plasticity for fashioning into a pattern or standard. Many instances of positive underpayment will come to mind, just as instances of apparent rank overpayment abound. Haplessly, intrinsic worth is not always the criterion. A classic might perhaps produce trifling compensation for its author, whereas a popular novel might yield a titanic fortune. Merit is not always commensurately rewarded, whilst mediocrity sometimes unjustly brings incredibly lavish returns. Nothing is so divergent and contentious and inexplicable as values.

Courts are ill-equipped to solve or even to grapple with these entangled economic problems. Indeed, their solution is not within the juridical province. Courts are concerned that corporations be honestly and fairly operated by its directors, with the observance of the formal requirements of the law; but what is reasonable compensation for its officers is primarily for the stockholders. This does not mean that fiduciaries are to commit waste, or misuse or abuse trust property, with impunity. A just cause will find the Courts at guard and implemented to grant redress. But the stockholder must project a less amorphous plaint than is here presented.

On this branch of the case, I find for the defendants. Yet it does not follow that I affirmatively approve these huge payments. It means that I cannot by any reliable standard find them to be waste or spoliation; it means that I find no valid ground for disapproving what the great majority of stockholders have approved. In the circumstances, if a ceiling for these bonuses is to be erected, the stockholders who built and are responsible for the present structure must be the architects. Finally, it is not amiss to accent the antiseptic policy stressed by Judge Liebell in Winkelman et al. v. General Motors Corporation, D.C.S.D.N.Y. decided August 14, 1940, 39 F.Supp. 826, that: "The duty of the director executives participating in the bonus seems plain—they should be the first to consider unselfishly whether under all the circumstances their bonus allowances are fair and reasonable".

Notes

(1) Why is there reluctance to set aside "huge," "staggering," "munificent," or "quite lush" payments of salary to corporate officers? You may recall that in another class of cases, the courts review the reasonableness of salary payments routinely. See page 383, supra. Are the issues in the taxation cases really analogous to the problem of the principal case?

(2) Is the problem in *Heller* one of "self dealing"? Of course, essentially the same tests are applicable whether or not the officer receiving the salary is also a director. On salary matters, do review and approval by the disinterested directors, or more commonly, by a "compensation committee" consisting of outside directors, afford sufficient protection against excessive payments? What are the guidelines for determining what is excessive and what is not? At least some outside review is common today, at least for the compensation of the chief executive officer.

(3) Issues with respect to compensation of corporate executives often revolve around the federal income tax laws. Pension plans, stock plans, fringe benefits, expense accounts and other devices have the impact of providing tax-free benefits or allowing the tax-free accumulation of income. Nevertheless, because of changes in the tax laws during the 1980's, tax-oriented compensation has declined in importance and greater emphasis is

placed on straight salary and bonus payments and stock option or stock purchase plans that have no special tax breaks but tend to provide compensation tied to the success of the enterprise.

(4) In 1988, the average pay of the CEOs of the largest 1,000 publicly held corporations was $760,000 per year, exclusive of long term compensation. The largest single CEO salary plus bonus was $11.4 million for the CEO of Reebok; Sotheby's CEO received $7.7 million and Disney's CEO $7.5 million. Twenty-five CEOs made at least $2 million and another 218 made at least $1 million. A Portrait of the Boss, Business Week, October 20, 1989, 23, 25. While these compensation levels may seem extremely high, they are roughly comparable with compensation levels for popular professional athletes, entertainers, and TV "anchor persons." They are considerably higher than the salaries of high level Governmental officials with roughly comparable (or greater) responsibilities. Of course, to the "average American" with an income of less than $20,000 per year, even the salary of a brand new associate at a large New York City law firm must seem princely. The amount of compensation does not appear to be directly related either to the size of the business or its long-term profitability. Accidents of history, the supply and demand for corporate executives in specific lines of business, and industry tradition all go to determine salary patterns for individual corporations.

(5) Popular compensation devices include stock option plans, stock purchase plans, compensation or bonus plans that are tied to stock prices or corporate performance, and non-tax-qualified retirement plans. These devices may have differing tax and economic impact on both the employer and the employee, including whether the compensation is deductible by the employer, whether it is taxable as ordinary income or capital gain to the employee, whether it causes a cash drain on the employer, and whether the compensation is a charge against the employer's earnings or may be accounted for as a charge directly to surplus.

(a) A *stock option* is an agreement by which the executive is granted an option to purchase a specified number of shares for a limited time, usually several years, at a fixed price. If the market price of the stock rises, the option may be profitably exercised, though the effect is to dilute to a small extent the interest of other shareholders. Stock options may be the only way a "sick" corporation may hire away an executive from an established company. The tax treatment of options has careened widely over the years, with options called "restricted stock options" or "qualified stock options" formerly providing significant tax advantages, but then being repealed or made inapplicable to future grants of options on the ground that they permit excessive tax avoidance. On the other hand, "old" options of these types may continue to provide substantial long term compensation today since the option price may have been set years ago when stock prices were much lower and the favorable tax treatment of the gain may continue to be applicable to outstanding options at the time of repeal.

(b) A *restricted stock plan* involves the issuance of shares to an executive subject to substantial restrictions on transfer or substantial risks of forfeiture which affect its value and which provide incentive to remain with the corporation.

(c) A *phantom stock plan* does not involve the issuance of shares. Rather the executive is credited with "units" on the books of the corporation. The value of a "unit" is equal to the market value of a share of the corporation's stock when the "unit" is created, and is increased by the amount of dividends paid on a share of stock plus the increase in value of a share as of a date specified by the participant. Units may be paid on death or retirement, or with the consent of a committee if the participant voluntarily terminates his employment. The plan permits deferral of some income which is based on the market performance of the corporation's stock but no particular tax advantage. See Lieberman v. Koppers Co., 38 Del.Ch. 239, 149 A.2d 756 (1959), affirmed sub nom. Liberman v. Becker, 38 Del.Ch. 540, 155 A.2d 596 (1959).

(d) *Stock appreciation rights* (SARs) are bonus payments to executives computed on the basis of the growth in value of a predetermined number of hypothetical shares computable and payable at a time partially within the control of the recipient. SARs obviously provide benefits similar to stock options or phantom stock plans. *Performance unit payments* (PUPs) are bonus payments set on a predetermined formula for achieving long-term company goals, (e.g., a 10 per cent compound earnings growth per year over five years). Why are phantom stock plans, SARs, PUPs, and similar arrangements so attractive?

(6) Non-qualified retirement plans for executives are usually not funded; the only assurance that nonqualified benefits will actually be forthcoming in the future is the employer's unsecured promise to pay the benefits. Unfunded plans include many deferred compensation arrangements, severance compensation agreements, and retiree life and medical insurance plans. For many executives today unfunded plans represent the majority of the aggregate benefits promised to them. It is increasingly accepted that no corporation is too large to be taken over by some other corporation, or so successful as to be immune from all risk of insolvency. As a result, highly compensated employees may be uneasy about the reliability of unsecured promises; they demand some additional assurance or security that the promised benefits will actually be forthcoming. Such assurance is usually provided in the form of "rabbi trusts" or "secular trusts," or by the purchase of commercial insurance or annuity contracts. A "rabbi trust" is a revocable trust created with a bank or trust company as trustee that by its terms becomes irrevocable if a change in control occurs; the assets of such a trust become available to the corporation's creditors in the event of insolvency but the employee is assured of benefits in the absence of that unlikely event. A "secular trust" is similar to a rabbi trust except that in addition to protection against changes in control, the assets of the trust are unavailable to the creditors of the corporation in the event of insolvency. In a secular trust the employee is taxed on contributions to the trust in the year made; in a rabbi trust (if properly created) the employee is not taxed until the year in which specific benefits are paid or made available to the employee, obviously a desirable tax attribute from the standpoint of the

employee. See generally Barry, Securing Non–Qualified Benefits for Corporate Executives, Insights, Vol. 3, No. 11 (Nov.1989) 3.

(7) Consider Fischel, The "Race to the Bottom" Revisited: Reflections on Recent Developments in Delaware's Corporation Law, 76 Nw.U.L.Rev. 913, 918–919 (1982): *

> * * * In any agency relationship—such as the relationship between shareholders and managers—the interests of the agent will diverge from those of the principal. The agent will have incentives to consume excess leisure or otherwise act in ways inconsistent with maximizing the wealth of the principal. * * *

> [V]arious market forces exist to minimize the amount of agency costs. Managers, like other individuals, have strong incentives to maximize the market value of their services. Since the managerial labor market must use performance of the firm to evaluate a manager's ability, each manager has a stake not only in his own performance, but also in the performance of the other managers, both above and below him. Managers therefore monitor each other's performance to determine relative contributions to the success of the firm.

> Other market mechanisms exist to minimize the divergence of managers' interests from those of the shareholders. Various compensation packages such as stock option plans, which cause managers to share the risk bearing function with shareholders, provide managers with an incentive to maximize shareholders' wealth and keep stock prices high. * * *

SINCLAIR OIL CORP. v. LEVIEN
Supreme Court of Delaware, 1971.
280 A.2d 717.

WOLCOTT, CHIEF JUSTICE.

This is an appeal by the defendant, Sinclair Oil Corporation (hereafter Sinclair), from an order of the Court of Chancery, 261 A.2d 911 in a derivative action requiring Sinclair to account for damages sustained by its subsidiary, Sinclair Venezuelan Oil Company (hereafter Sinven), organized by Sinclair for the purpose of operating in Venezuela, as a result of dividends paid by Sinven, the denial to Sinven of industrial development, and a breach of contract between Sinclair's wholly-owned subsidiary, Sinclair International Oil Company, and Sinven.

Sinclair, operating primarily as a holding company, is in the business of exploring for oil and of producing and marketing crude oil and oil products. At all times relevant to this litigation, it owned about 97% of Sinven's stock. The plaintiff owns about 3000 of 120,000 publicly held shares of Sinven. Sinven, incorporated in 1922, has been engaged in petroleum operations primarily in Venezuela and since 1959 has operated exclusively in Venezuela.

* Reprinted by special permission of the Northwestern University Law Review, © by Northwestern University School of Law, Vol. 76, No. 6.

Sinclair nominates all members of Sinven's board of directors. The Chancellor found as a fact that the directors were not independent of Sinclair. Almost without exception, they were officers, directors, or employees of corporations in the Sinclair complex. By reason of Sinclair's domination, it is clear that Sinclair owed Sinven a fiduciary duty. Sinclair concedes this.

The Chancellor held that because of Sinclair's fiduciary duty and its control over Sinven, its relationship with Sinven must meet the test of intrinsic fairness. The standard of intrinsic fairness involves both a high degree of fairness and a shift in the burden of proof. Under this standard the burden is on Sinclair to prove, subject to careful judicial scrutiny, that its transactions with Sinven were objectively fair. Guth v. Loft, Inc., 23 Del.Ch. 255, 5 A.2d 503 (1939).

Sinclair argues that the transactions between it and Sinven should be tested, not by the test of intrinsic fairness with the accompanying shift of the burden of proof, but by the business judgment rule under which a court will not interfere with the judgment of a board of directors unless there is a showing of gross and palpable overreaching. Meyerson v. El Paso Natural Gas Co., 246 A.2d 789 (Del.Ch.1967). A board of directors enjoys a presumption of sound business judgment, and its decisions will not be disturbed if they can be attributed to any rational business purpose. A court under such circumstances will not substitute its own notions of what is or is not sound business judgment.

We think, however, that Sinclair's argument in this respect is misconceived. When the situation involves a parent and a subsidiary, with the parent controlling the transaction and fixing the terms, the test of intrinsic fairness, with its resulting shifting of the burden of proof, is applied. The basic situation for the application of the rule is the one in which the parent has received a benefit to the exclusion and at the expense of the subsidiary.

Recently, this court dealt with the question of fairness in parent-subsidiary dealings in Getty Oil Co. v. Skelly Oil Co., [267 A.2d 833 (Del. Sup.) 1970]. In that case, both parent and subsidiary were in the business of refining and marketing crude oil and crude oil products. The Oil Import Board ruled that the subsidiary, because it was controlled by the parent, was no longer entitled to a separate allocation of imported crude oil. The subsidiary then contended that it had a right to share the quota of crude oil allotted to the parent. We ruled that the business judgment standard should be applied to determine this contention. Although the subsidiary suffered a loss through the administration of the oil import quotas, the parent gained nothing. The parent's quota was derived solely from its own past use. The past use of the subsidiary did not cause an increase in the parent's quota. Nor did the parent usurp a quota of the subsidiary. Since the parent received nothing from the subsidiary to the exclusion of the minority stockholders of the subsidiary, there was no self-dealing. Therefore, the business judgment standard was properly applied.

A parent does indeed owe a fiduciary duty to its subsidiary when there are parent-subsidiary dealings. However, this alone will not evoke the intrinsic fairness standard. This standard will be applied only when the fiduciary duty is accompanied by self-dealing—the situation when a parent is on both sides of a transaction with its subsidiary. Self-dealing occurs when the parent, by virtue of its domination of the subsidiary, causes the subsidiary to act in such a way that the parent receives something from the subsidiary to the exclusion of, and detriment to, the minority stockholders of the subsidiary.

We turn now to the facts. The plaintiff argues that, from 1960 through 1966, Sinclair caused Sinven to pay out such excessive dividends that the industrial development of Sinven was effectively prevented, and it became in reality a corporation in dissolution.

From 1960 through 1966, Sinven paid out $108,000,000 in dividends ($38,000,000 in excess of Sinven's earnings during the same period). The Chancellor held that Sinclair caused these dividends to be paid during a period when it had a need for large amounts of cash. Although the dividends paid exceeded earnings, the plaintiff concedes that the payments were made in compliance with 8 Del.C. § 170, authorizing payment of dividends out of surplus or net profits. However, the plaintiff attacks these dividends on the ground that they resulted from an improper motive—Sinclair's need for cash. The Chancellor, applying the intrinsic fairness standard, held that Sinclair did not sustain its burden of proving that these dividends were intrinsically fair to the minority stockholders of Sinven.

Since it is admitted that the dividends were paid in strict compliance with 8 Del.C. § 170, the alleged excessiveness of the payments alone would not state a cause of action. Nevertheless, compliance with the applicable statute may not, under all circumstances, justify all dividend payments. If a plaintiff can meet his burden of proving that a dividend cannot be grounded on any reasonable business objective, then the courts can and will interfere with the board's decision to pay the dividend.

Sinclair contends that it is improper to apply the intrinsic fairness standard to dividend payments even when the board which voted for the dividends is completely dominated. In support of this contention, Sinclair relies heavily on American District Telegraph Co. [ADT] v. Grinnell Corp., (N.Y.Sup.Ct.1969) aff'd. 33 A.D.2d 769, 306 N.Y.S.2d 209 (1969). Plaintiffs were minority stockholders of ADT, a subsidiary of Grinnell. The plaintiffs alleged that Grinnell, realizing that it would soon have to sell its ADT stock because of a pending anti-trust action, caused ADT to pay excessive dividends. Because the dividend payments conformed with applicable statutory law, and the plaintiffs could not prove an abuse of discretion, the court ruled that the complaint did not state a cause of action. Other decisions seem to support Sinclair's contention. In Metropolitan Casualty Ins. Co. v. First State Bank of Temple, 54 S.W.2d 358 (Tex.Civ.App.1932), rev'd. on other grounds, 79

S.W.2d 835 (Sup.Ct.1935), the court held that a majority of interested directors does not void a declaration of dividends because all directors, by necessity, are interested in and benefited by a dividend declaration.

We do not accept the argument that the intrinsic fairness test can never be applied to a dividend declaration by a dominated board, although a dividend declaration by a dominated board will not inevitably demand the application of the intrinsic fairness standard. Moskowitz v. Bantrell, 41 Del.Ch. 177, 190 A.2d 749 (Del.Supr.1963). If such a dividend is in essence self-dealing by the parent, then the intrinsic fairness standard is the proper standard. For example, suppose a parent dominates a subsidiary and its board of directors. The subsidiary has outstanding two classes of stock, X and Y. Class X is owned by the parent and Class Y is owned by minority stockholders of the subsidiary. If the subsidiary, at the direction of the parent, declares a dividend on its Class X stock only, this might well be self-dealing by the parent. It would be receiving something from the subsidiary to the exclusion of and detrimental to its minority stockholders. This self-dealing, coupled with the parent's fiduciary duty, would make intrinsic fairness the proper standard by which to evaluate the dividend payments.

Consequently it must be determined whether the dividend payments by Sinven were, in essence, self-dealing by Sinclair. The dividends resulted in great sums of money being transferred from Sinven to Sinclair. However, a proportionate share of this money was received by the minority shareholders of Sinven. Sinclair received nothing from Sinven to the exclusion of its minority stockholders. As such, these dividends were not self-dealing. We hold therefore that the Chancellor erred in applying the intrinsic fairness test as to these dividend payments. The business judgment standard should have been applied.

We conclude that the facts demonstrate that the dividend payments complied with the business judgment standard and with 8 Del.C. § 170. The motives for causing the declaration of dividends are immaterial unless the plaintiff can show that the dividend payments resulted from improper motives and amounted to waste. The plaintiff contends only that the dividend payments drained Sinven of cash to such an extent that it was prevented from expanding.

The plaintiff proved no business opportunities which came to Sinven independently and which Sinclair either took to itself or denied to Sinven. As a matter of fact, with two minor exceptions which resulted in losses, all of Sinven's operations have been conducted in Venezuela, and Sinclair had a policy of exploiting its oil properties located in different countries by subsidiaries located in the particular countries.

From 1960 to 1966 Sinclair purchased or developed oil fields in Alaska, Canada, Paraguay, and other places around the world. The plaintiff contends that these were all opportunities which could have been taken by Sinven. The Chancellor concluded that Sinclair had not proved that its denial of expansion opportunities to Sinven was intrinsically fair. He based this conclusion on the following findings of fact. Sinclair made no real effort to expand Sinven. The excessive dividends paid by Sinven resulted in so great a cash drain as to effectively deny to Sinven any ability to expand. During this same period Sinclair actively pursued a company-wide policy of developing through its subsidiaries new sources of revenue, but Sinven was not permitted to participate and was confined in its activities to Venezuela.

However, the plaintiff could point to no opportunities which came to Sinven. Therefore, Sinclair usurped no business opportunity belonging to Sinven. Since Sinclair received nothing from Sinven to the exclusion of and detriment to Sinven's minority stockholders, there was no self-dealing. Therefore, business judgment is the proper standard by which to evaluate Sinclair's expansion policies.

Since there is no proof of self-dealing on the part of Sinclair, it follows that the expansion policy of Sinclair and the methods used to achieve the desired result must, as far as Sinclair's treatment of Sinven is concerned, be tested by the standards of the business judgment rule. Accordingly, Sinclair's decision, absent fraud or gross overreaching, to achieve expansion through the medium of its subsidiaries, other than Sinven, must be upheld.

Even if Sinclair was wrong in developing these opportunities as it did, the question arises, with which subsidiaries should these opportunities have been shared? No evidence indicates a unique need or ability of Sinven to develop these opportunities. The decision of which subsidiaries would be used to implement Sinclair's expansion policy was one of business judgment with which a court will not interfere absent a showing of gross and palpable overreaching. No such showing has been made here.

Next, Sinclair argues that the Chancellor committed error when he held it liable to Sinven for breach of contract.

In 1961 Sinclair created Sinclair International Oil Company (hereafter International), a wholly owned subsidiary used for the purpose of coordinating all of Sinclair's foreign operations. All crude purchases by Sinclair were made thereafter through International.

On September 28, 1961, Sinclair caused Sinven to contract with International whereby Sinven agreed to sell all of its crude oil and refined products to International at specified prices. The contract provided for minimum and maximum quantities and prices. The plaintiff contends that Sinclair caused this contract to be breached in two respects. Although the contract called for payment on receipt, International's payments lagged as much as 30 days after receipt. Also, the contract required International to purchase at least a fixed minimum amount of crude and refined products from Sinven. International did not comply with this requirement.

Clearly, Sinclair's act of contracting with its dominated subsidiary was self-dealing. Under the contract Sinclair received the products produced by Sinven, and of course the minority shareholders of Sinven were not able to share in the receipt of these products. If the contract was breached, then Sinclair received these products to the detriment of Sinven's minority shareholders. We agree with the Chancellor's finding that the contract was breached by Sinclair, both as to the time of payments and the amounts purchased.

Although a parent need not bind itself by a contract with its dominated subsidiary, Sinclair chose to operate in this manner. As Sinclair has received the benefits of this contract, so must it comply with the contractual duties.

Under the intrinsic fairness standard, Sinclair must prove that its causing Sinven not to enforce the contract was intrinsically fair to the minority shareholders of Sinven. Sinclair has failed to meet this burden. Late payments were clearly breaches for which Sinven should have sought and received adequate damages. As to the quantities purchased, Sinclair argues that it purchased all the products produced by Sinven. This, however, does not satisfy the standard of intrinsic fairness. Sinclair has failed to prove that Sinven could not possibly have produced or some way have obtained the contract minimums. As such, Sinclair must account on this claim.

Finally, Sinclair argues that the Chancellor committed error in refusing to allow it a credit or setoff of all benefits provided by it to Sinven with respect to all the alleged damages. The Chancellor held that setoff should be allowed on specific transactions, e.g., benefits to Sinven under the contract with International, but denied an overall setoff against all damages claimed. We agree with the Chancellor, although the point may well be moot in view of our holding that Sinclair is not required to account for the alleged excessiveness of the dividend payments.

We will therefore reverse that part of the Chancellor's order that requires Sinclair to account to Sinven for damages sustained as a result of dividends paid between 1960 and 1966, and by reason of the denial to Sinven of expansion during that period. We will affirm the remaining portion of that order and remand the cause for further proceedings.

Notes

(1) Serious problems can arise in a number of areas whenever there are minority shareholders in a corporate subsidiary. For example, the Internal Revenue Code permits a corporation to file a "consolidated return" with subsidiaries that are at least 80 per cent owned. The effect of consolidation is that a single return is filed covering the income or loss of all the corporations as a group, and the result may be that a valuable tax loss owned by a subsidiary may be utilized to offset income of the parent or of other subsidiaries within the group. What, if anything, can the courts do about such problems? See e.g. Case v. New York Central R.R. Co., 15

N.Y.2d 150, 256 N.Y.S.2d 607, 204 N.E.2d 643 (1965); Meyerson v. El Paso Natural Gas Co., 246 A.2d 789 (Del.Ch.1967); Alliegro v. Pan American Bank, 136 So.2d 656 (Fla.Dist.Ct.App.1962).

(2) Given such problems, does it help to include a clause in the subsidiary's articles of incorporation that attempts to validate all transactions between subsidiary and parent, and in effect warns shareholders that such transactions may take place? While such a clause will not provide total protection, it may be given some effect by shifting the burden of proving unfairness or "exonerating" the arrangement from "adverse inferences." See Spiegel v. Beacon Participations, Inc., 297 Mass. 398, 417, 8 N.E.2d 895, 907 (1937). Such clauses also usually cover transactions between corporations with common directors (interlocking directors) but with no ownership of securities of one corporation by the other.

(3) Problems such as those involved in the principal case can be avoided by the elimination of the minority shareholders. How can this be done? A buy-out? What if the minority is unwilling to sell at a reasonable price? Could Sinclair create a wholly owned subsidiary, "X Corporation," transfer its holdings of Sinven to it, and then merge Sinven into X Corporation, requiring the minority shareholders to accept cash rather than X Corporation stock? Compare RMBCA §§ 11.01(b)(3), 11.03(b), 11.04. What protection does the minority have? See RMBCA § 13.02(a) and, generally, ch. 13. Should there be any judicial review of the motives of the controlling shareholders proposing such mergers?

WEINBERGER v. UOP, INC.

Supreme Court of Delaware, 1983.
457 A.2d 701.

Before HERRMANN, C.J., McNEILLY, QUILLEN, HORSEY and MOORE, JJ., constituting the Court en Banc.

MOORE, JUSTICE:

This post-trial appeal was reheard en banc from a decision of the Court of Chancery. It was brought by the class action plaintiff below, a former shareholder of UOP, Inc., who challenged the elimination of UOP's minority shareholders by a cash-out merger between UOP and its majority owner, The Signal Companies, Inc. * * * [T]he defendants in this action were Signal, UOP, [and] certain officers and directors of those companies * * *. The present Chancellor held that the terms of the merger were fair to the plaintiff and the other minority shareholders of UOP. Accordingly, he entered judgment in favor of the defendants.

Numerous points were raised by the parties, but we address only the following questions presented by the trial court's opinion:

(1) The plaintiff's duty to plead sufficient facts demonstrating the unfairness of the challenged merger;

(2) The burden of proof upon the parties where the merger has been approved by the purportedly informed vote of a majority of the minority shareholders;

(3) The fairness of the merger in terms of adequacy of the defendants' disclosures to the minority shareholders;

(4) The fairness of the merger in terms of adequacy of the price paid for the minority shares and the remedy appropriate to that issue; and

(5) The continued force and effect of Singer v. Magnavox Co., Del. Supr., 380 A.2d 969, 980 (1977), and its progeny.   *   *   *

I.

The facts found by the trial court, pertinent to the issues before us, are supported by the record, and we draw from them as set out in the Chancellor's opinion.

Signal is a diversified, technically based company operating through various subsidiaries. Its stock is publicly traded on the New York, Philadelphia and Pacific Stock Exchanges. UOP, formerly known as Universal Oil Products Company, was a diversified industrial company engaged in various lines of business, including petroleum and petrochemical services and related products, construction, fabricated metal products, transportation equipment products, chemicals and plastics, and other products and services including land development, lumber products and waste disposal. Its stock was publicly held and listed on the New York Stock Exchange.

In 1974 Signal sold one of its wholly-owned subsidiaries for $420,000,000 in cash. See Gimbel v. Signal Companies, Inc., Del.Ch., 316 A.2d 599, aff'd, Del.Supr., 316 A.2d 619 (1974). While looking to invest this cash surplus, Signal became interested in UOP as a possible acquisition. Friendly negotiations ensued, and Signal proposed to acquire a controlling interest in UOP at a price of $19 per share. UOP's representatives sought $25 per share. In the arm's length bargaining that followed, an understanding was reached whereby Signal agreed to purchase from UOP 1,500,000 shares of UOP's authorized but unissued stock at $21 per share.

This purchase was contingent upon Signal making a successful cash tender offer for 4,300,000 publicly held shares of UOP, also at a price of $21 per share. This combined method of acquisition permitted Signal to acquire 5,800,000 shares of stock, representing 50.5% of UOP's outstanding shares. The UOP board of directors advised the company's shareholders that it had no objection to Signal's tender offer at that price. Immediately before the announcement of the tender offer, UOP's common stock had been trading on the New York Stock Exchange at a fraction under $14 per share.

The negotiations between Signal and UOP occurred during April 1975, and the resulting tender offer was greatly oversubscribed. However, Signal limited its total purchase of the tendered shares so that, when coupled with the stock bought from UOP, it had achieved its goal of becoming a 50.5% shareholder of UOP.

Although UOP's board consisted of thirteen directors, Signal nominated and elected only six. Of these, five were either directors or employees of Signal. The sixth, a partner in the banking firm of Lazard Freres & Co., had been one of Signal's representatives in the negotiations and bargaining with UOP concerning the tender offer and purchase price of the UOP shares.

However, the president and chief executive officer of UOP retired during 1975, and Signal caused him to be replaced by James V. Crawford, a long-time employee and senior executive vice president of one of Signal's wholly-owned subsidiaries. Crawford succeeded his predecessor on UOP's board of directors and also was made a director of Signal.

By the end of 1977 Signal basically was unsuccessful in finding other suitable investment candidates for its excess cash, and by February 1978 considered that it had no other realistic acquisitions available to it on a friendly basis. Once again its attention turned to UOP.

The trial court found that at the instigation of certain Signal management personnel, including William W. Walkup, its board chairman, and Forrest N. Shumway, its president, a feasibility study was made concerning the possible acquisition of the balance of UOP's outstanding shares. This study was performed by two Signal officers, Charles S. Arledge, vice president (director of planning), and Andrew J. Chitiea, senior vice president (chief financial officer). Messrs. Walkup, Shumway, Arledge and Chitiea were all directors of UOP in addition to their membership on the Signal board.

Arledge and Chitiea concluded that it would be a good investment for Signal to acquire the remaining 49.5% of UOP shares at any price up to $24 each. Their report was discussed between Walkup and Shumway who, along with Arledge, Chitiea and Brewster L. Arms, internal counsel for Signal, constituted Signal's senior management. In particular, they talked about the proper price to be paid if the acquisition was pursued, purportedly keeping in mind that as UOP's majority shareholder, Signal owed a fiduciary responsibility to both its own stockholders as well as to UOP's minority. It was ultimately agreed that a meeting of Signal's executive committee would be called to propose that Signal acquire the remaining outstanding stock of UOP through a cash-out merger in the range of $20 to $21 per share.

The executive committee meeting was set for February 28, 1978. As a courtesy, UOP's president, Crawford, was invited to attend, although he was not a member of Signal's executive committee. On his arrival, and prior to the meeting, Crawford was asked to meet privately with Walkup and Shumway. He was then told of Signal's plan to acquire full ownership of UOP and was asked for his reaction to the proposed price range of $20 to $21 per share. Crawford said he thought such a price would be "generous", and that it was certainly one which should be submitted to UOP's minority shareholders for their ultimate consideration. He stated, however, that Signal's 100% ownership could cause internal problems at UOP. He believed that employees would have to be given some assurance of their future place in a fully-owned Signal subsidiary. Otherwise, he feared the departure of essential personnel. Also, many of UOP's key employees had stock option incentive programs which would be wiped out by a merger. Crawford therefore urged that some adjustment would have to be made, such as providing a comparable incentive in Signal's shares, if after the merger he was to maintain his quality of personnel and efficiency at UOP.

Thus, Crawford voiced no objection to the $20 to $21 price range, nor did he suggest that Signal should consider paying more than $21 per share for the minority interests. Later, at the executive committee meeting the same factors were discussed, with Crawford repeating the position he earlier took with Walkup and Shumway. Also considered was the 1975 tender offer and the fact that it had been greatly oversubscribed at $21 per share. For many reasons, Signal's management concluded that the acquisition of UOP's minority shares provided the solution to a number of its business problems.

Thus, it was the consensus that a price of $20 to $21 per share would be fair to both Signal and the minority shareholders of UOP. Signal's executive committee authorized its management "to negotiate" with UOP "for a cash acquisition of the minority ownership in UOP, Inc., with the intention of presenting a proposal to [Signal's] board of directors * * * on March 6, 1978". Immediately after this February 28, 1978 meeting, Signal issued a press release stating:

> "The Signal Companies, Inc. and UOP, Inc. are conducting negotiations for the acquisition for cash by Signal of the 49.5 per cent of UOP which it does not presently own, announced Forrest N. Shumway, president and chief executive officer of Signal, and James V. Crawford, UOP president.

> Price and other terms of the proposed transaction have not yet been finalized and would be subject to approval of the boards of directors of Signal and UOP, scheduled to meet early next week, the stockholders of UOP and certain federal agencies."

The announcement also referred to the fact that the closing price of UOP's common stock on that day was $14.50 per share.

Two days later, on March 2, 1978, Signal issued a second press release stating that its management would recommend a price in the range of $20 to $21 per share for UOP's 49.5% minority interest. This announcement referred to Signal's earlier statement that "negotiations" were being conducted for the acquisition of the minority shares.

Between Tuesday, February 28, 1978 and Monday, March 6, 1978, a total of four business days, Crawford spoke by telephone with all of UOP's non-Signal, i.e., outside, directors. Also during that period, Crawford retained Lehman Brothers to render a fairness opinion as to the price offered the minority for its stock. He gave two reasons for this choice. First, the time schedule between the announcement and the board meetings was short (by then only three business days) and since Lehman Brothers had been acting as UOP's investment banker for many years, Crawford felt that it would be in the best position to respond on such brief notice. Second, James W. Glanville, a long-time director of UOP and a partner in Lehman Brothers, had acted as a financial advisor to UOP for many years. Crawford believed that Glanville's familiarity with UOP, as a member of its board, would also be of assistance in enabling Lehman Brothers to render a fairness opinion within the existing time constraints.

Crawford telephoned Glanville, who gave his assurance that Lehman Brothers had no conflicts that would prevent it from accepting the task. Glanville's immediate personal reaction was that a price of $20 to $21 would certainly be fair, since it represented almost a 50% premium over UOP's market price. Glanville sought a $250,000 fee for Lehman Brothers' services, but Crawford thought this too much. After further discussions Glanville finally agreed that Lehman Brothers would render its fairness opinion for $150,000.

During this period Crawford also had several telephone contacts with Signal officials. In only one of them, however, was the price of the shares discussed. In a conversation with Walkup, Crawford advised that as a result of his communications with UOP's non-Signal directors, it was his feeling that the price would have to be the top of the proposed range, or $21 per share, if the approval of UOP's outside directors was to be obtained. But again, he did not seek any price higher than $21.

Glanville assembled a three-man Lehman Brothers team to do the work on the fairness opinion. These persons examined relevant documents and information concerning UOP, including its annual reports and its Securities and Exchange Commission filings from 1973 through 1976, as well as its audited financial statements for 1977, its interim reports to shareholders, and its recent and historical market prices and trading volumes. In addition, on Friday, March 3, 1978, two members of the Lehman Brothers team flew to UOP's headquarters in Des Plaines, Illinois, to perform a "due diligence" visit, during the course of which they interviewed Crawford as well as UOP's general counsel, its chief financial officer, and other key executives and personnel.

As a result, the Lehman Brothers team concluded that "the price of either $20 or $21 would be a fair price for the remaining shares of UOP". They telephoned this impression to Glanville, who was spending the weekend in Vermont.

On Monday morning, March 6, 1978, Glanville and the senior member of the Lehman Brothers team flew to Des Plaines to attend the scheduled UOP directors meeting. Glanville looked over the assembled information during the flight. The two had with them the draft of a "fairness opinion letter" in which the price had been left blank. Either during or immediately prior to the directors' meeting, the two-page "fairness opinion letter" was typed in final form and the price of $21 per share was inserted.

On March 6, 1978, both the Signal and UOP boards were convened to consider the proposed merger. Telephone communications were maintained between the two meetings. Walkup, Signal's board chairman, and also a UOP director, attended UOP's meeting with Crawford in order to present Signal's position and answer any questions that UOP's non-Signal directors might have. Arledge and Chitiea, along with Signal's other designees on UOP's board, participated by conference telephone. All of UOP's outside directors attended the meeting either in person or by conference telephone.

First, Signal's board unanimously adopted a resolution authorizing Signal to propose to UOP a cash merger of $21 per share as outlined in a certain merger agreement and other supporting documents. This proposal required that the merger be approved by a majority of UOP's outstanding minority shares voting at the stockholders meeting at which the merger would be considered, and that the minority shares voting in favor of the merger, when coupled with Signal's 50.5% interest would have to comprise at least two-thirds of all UOP shares. Otherwise the proposed merger would be deemed disapproved.

UOP's board then considered the proposal. Copies of the agreement were delivered to the directors in attendance, and other copies had been forwarded earlier to the directors participating by telephone. They also had before them UOP financial data for 1974–1977, UOP's most recent financial statements, market price information, and budget projections for 1978. In addition they had Lehman Brothers' hurriedly prepared fairness opinion letter finding the price of $21 to be fair. Glanville, the Lehman Brothers partner, and UOP director, commented on the information that had gone into preparation of the letter.

Signal also suggests that the Arledge–Chitiea feasibility study, indicating that a price of up to $24 per share would be a "good investment" for Signal, was discussed at the UOP directors' meeting. The Chancellor made no such finding, and our independent review of the record, detailed infra, satisfies us by a preponderance of the evidence that there was no discussion of this document at UOP's board meeting. Furthermore, it is clear beyond peradventure that nothing in that report was ever disclosed to UOP's minority shareholders prior to their approval of the merger.

After consideration of Signal's proposal, Walkup and Crawford left the meeting to permit a free and uninhibited exchange between UOP's non-Signal directors. Upon their return a resolution to accept Signal's offer was then proposed and adopted. While Signal's men on UOP's board participated in various aspects of the meeting, they abstained from voting. However, the minutes show that each of them "if voting would have voted yes".

On March 7, 1978, UOP sent a letter to its shareholders advising them of the action taken by UOP's board with respect to Signal's offer. This document pointed out, among other things, that on February 28,

1978 "both companies had announced negotiations were being conducted".

Despite the swift board action of the two companies, the merger was not submitted to UOP's shareholders until their annual meeting on May 26, 1978. In the notice of that meeting and proxy statement sent to shareholders in May, UOP's management and board urged that the merger be approved. The proxy statement also advised:

> "The price was determined after *discussions* between James V. Crawford, a director of Signal and Chief Executive Officer of UOP, and officers of Signal which took place during meetings on February 28, 1978, and in the course of several subsequent telephone conversations." (Emphasis added.)

In the original draft of the proxy statement the word "negotiations" had been used rather than "discussions". However, when the Securities and Exchange Commission sought details of the "negotiations" as part of its review of these materials, the term was deleted and the word "discussions" was substituted. The proxy statement indicated that the vote of UOP's board in approving the merger had been unanimous. It also advised the shareholders that Lehman Brothers had given its opinion that the merger price of $21 per share was fair to UOP's minority. However, it did not disclose the hurried method by which this conclusion was reached.

As of the record date of UOP's annual meeting, there were 11,488,302 shares of UOP common stock outstanding, 5,688,302 of which were owned by the minority. At the meeting only 56%, or 3,208,652, of the minority shares were voted. Of these, 2,953,812, or 51.9% of the total minority, voted for the merger, and 254,840 voted against it. When Signal's stock was added to the minority shares voting in favor, a total of 76.2% of UOP's outstanding shares approved the merger while only 2.2% opposed it.

By its terms the merger became effective on May 26, 1978, and each share of UOP's stock held by the minority was automatically converted into a right to receive $21 cash.

II.

A.

A primary issue mandating reversal is the preparation by two UOP directors, Arledge and Chitiea, of their feasibility study for the exclusive use and benefit of Signal. This document was of obvious significance to both Signal and UOP. Using UOP data, it described the advantages to Signal of ousting the minority at a price range of $21–$24 per share. Mr. Arledge, one of the authors, outlined the benefits to Signal: [4]

---

4. [By the Court] The parentheses indicate certain handwritten comments of Mr. Arledge.

Purpose of the Merger

(1) Provides an outstanding investment opportunity for Signal—(Better than any recent acquisition we have seen).

(2) Increases Signal's earnings.

(3) Facilitates the flow of resources between Signal and its subsidiaries—(Big factor—works both ways).

(4) Provides cost savings potential for Signal and UOP.

(5) Improves the percentage of Signal's 'operating earnings' as opposed to 'holding company earnings'.

(6) Simplifies the understanding of Signal.

(7) Facilitates technological exchange among Signal's subsidiaries.

(8) Eliminates potential conflicts of interest.

Having written those words, solely for the use of Signal, it is clear from the record that neither Arledge nor Chitiea shared this report with their fellow directors of UOP. We are satisfied that no one else did either. This conduct hardly meets the fiduciary standards applicable to such a transaction. * * *

The Arledge–Chitiea report speaks for itself in supporting the Chancellor's finding that a price of up to $24 was a "good investment" for Signal. It shows that a return on the investment at $21 would be 15.7% versus 15.5% at $24 per share. This was a difference of only two-tenths of one percent, while it meant over $17,000,000 to the minority. Under such circumstances, paying UOP's minority shareholders $24 would have had relatively little long-term effect on Signal, and the Chancellor's findings concerning the benefit to Signal, even at a price of $24, were obviously correct.

Certainly, this was a matter of material significance to UOP and its shareholders. Since the study was prepared by two UOP directors, using UOP information for the exclusive benefit of Signal, and nothing whatever was done to disclose it to the outside UOP directors or the minority shareholders, a question of breach of fiduciary duty arises. This problem occurs because there were common Signal–UOP directors participating, at least to some extent, in the UOP board's decision making processes without full disclosure of the conflicts they faced.[5]

5. [By the Court] Although perfection is not possible, or expected, the result here could have been entirely different if UOP had appointed an independent negotiating committee of its outside directors to deal with Signal at arm's length. See, e.g., Harriman v. E.I. Du Pont de Nemours & Co., 411 F.Supp. 133 (D.Del.1975). Since fairness in this context can be equated to conduct by a theoretical, wholly independent, board of directors acting upon the matter before them, it is unfortunate that this course apparently was neither considered nor pursued. Johnston v. Greene, Del. Supr., 121 A.2d 919, 925 (1956). Particularly in a parent-subsidiary context, a showing that the action taken was as though each of the contending parties had in fact exerted its bargaining power against the other at arm's length is strong evidence that the transaction meets the test of fairness. Getty Oil Co. v. Skelly Oil Co., Del.Supr., 267 A.2d 883, 886 (1970).

B.

In assessing this situation, the Court of Chancery was required to:

"examine what information defendants had and to measure it against what they gave to the minority stockholders, in a context in which 'complete candor' is required. In other words, the limited function of the Court was to determine whether defendants had disclosed all information in their possession germane to the transaction in issue. And by 'germane' we mean, for present purposes, information such as a reasonable shareholder would consider important in deciding whether to sell or retain stock.

* * * Completeness, not adequacy, is both the norm and the mandate under present circumstances."

Lynch v. Vickers Energy Corp., Del.Supr., 383 A.2d 278, 281 (1977) (*Lynch I*). This is merely stating in another way the long-existing principle of Delaware law that these Signal designated directors on UOP's board still owed UOP and its shareholders an uncompromising duty of loyalty. The classic language of Guth v. Loft, Inc., Del.Supr., 5 A.2d 503, 510 (1939), requires no embellishment:

"A public policy, existing through the years, and derived from a profound knowledge of human characteristics and motives, has established a rule that demands of a corporate officer or director, peremptorily and inexorably, the most scrupulous observance of his duty, not only affirmatively to protect the interests of the corporation committed to his charge, but also to refrain from doing anything that would work injury to the corporation, or to deprive it of profit or advantage which his skill and ability might properly bring to it, or to enable it to make in the reasonable and lawful exercise of its powers. The rule that requires an undivided and unselfish loyalty to the corporation demands that there shall be no conflict between duty and self-interest."

Given the absence of any attempt to structure this transaction on an arm's length basis, Signal cannot escape the effects of the conflicts it faced, particularly when its designees on UOP's board did not totally abstain from participation in the matter. There is no "safe harbor" for such divided loyalties in Delaware. When directors of a Delaware corporation are on both sides of a transaction, they are required to demonstrate their utmost good faith and the most scrupulous inherent fairness of the bargain. Gottlieb v. Heyden Chemical Corp., Del.Supr., 91 A.2d 57, 57–58 (1952). The requirement of fairness is unflinching in its demand that where one stands on both sides of a transaction, he has the burden of establishing its entire fairness, sufficient to pass the test of careful scrutiny by the courts. Sterling v. Mayflower Hotel Corp., Del.Super., 93 A.2d 107, 110 (1952).

There is no dilution of this obligation where one holds dual or multiple directorships, as in a parent-subsidiary context. Levien v. Sinclair Oil Corp., Del.Ch., 261 A.2d 911, 915 (1969). Thus, individuals who act in a dual capacity as directors of two corporations, one of whom is parent and the other subsidiary, owe the same duty of good management to both corporations, and in the absence of an independent negotiating structure (see note 3, supra), or the directors' total abstention from any participation in the matter, this duty is to be exercised in light of what is best for both companies. Warshaw v. Calhoun, Del. Supr., 221 A.2d 487, 492 (1966). The record demonstrates that Signal has not met this obligation.

C.

The concept of fairness has two basic aspects: fair dealing and fair price. The former embraces questions of when the transaction was timed, how it was initiated, structured, negotiated, disclosed to the directors, and how the approvals of the directors and the stockholders were obtained. The latter aspect of fairness relates to the economic and financial considerations of the proposed merger, including all relevant factors: assets, market value, earnings, future prospects, and any other elements that affect the intrinsic or inherent value of a company's stock. Moore, The "Interested" Director or Officer Transaction, 4 Del.J.Corp.L. 674, 676 (1979). See Tri–Continental Corp. v. Battye, Del.Supr., 74 A.2d 71, 72 (1950); 8 Del.C. § 262(h). However, the test for fairness is not a bifurcated one as between fair dealing and price. All aspects of the issue must be examined as a whole since the question is one of entire fairness. However, in a non-fraudulent transaction we recognize that price may be the preponderant consideration outweighing other features of the merger. Here, we address the two basic aspects of fairness separately because we find reversible error as to both.

D.

Part of fair dealing is the obvious duty of candor required by *Lynch I,* supra. Moreover, one possessing superior knowledge may not mislead any stockholder by use of corporate information to which the latter is not privy. Lank v. Steiner, Del.Supr., 224 A.2d 242, 244 (1966). Delaware has long imposed this duty even upon persons who are not corporate officers or directors, but who nonetheless are privy to matters of interest or significance to their company. Brophy v. Cities Service Co., Del.Ch., 70 A.2d 5, 7 (1949). With the well-established Delaware law on the subject, and the Court of Chancery's findings of fact here, it is inevitable that the obvious conflicts posed by Arledge and Chitiea's preparation of their "feasibility study", derived from UOP information, for the sole use and benefit of Signal, cannot pass muster.

The Arledge–Chitiea report is but one aspect of the element of fair dealing. How did this merger evolve? It is clear that it was entirely initiated by Signal. The serious time constraints under which the principals acted were all set by Signal. It had not found a suitable outlet for its excess cash and considered UOP a desirable investment, particularly since it was now in a position to acquire the whole company for itself. For whatever reasons, and they were only Signal's, the entire transaction was presented to and approved by UOP's board within four business days. Standing alone, this is not necessarily indicative of any lack of fairness by a majority shareholder. It was what occurred, or more properly, what did not occur, during this brief period that makes the time constraints imposed by Signal relevant to the issue of fairness.

The structure of the transaction, again, was Signal's doing. So far as negotiations were concerned, it is clear that they were modest at best. Crawford, Signal's man at UOP, never really talked price with Signal, except to accede to its management's statements on the subject, and to convey to Signal the UOP outside directors' view that as between the $20–$21 range under consideration, it would have to be $21. The latter is not a surprising outcome, but hardly arm's length negotiations. Only the protection of benefits for UOP's key employees and the issue of Lehman Brothers' fee approached any concept of bargaining.

As we have noted, the matter of disclosure to the UOP directors was wholly flawed by the conflicts of interest raised by the Arledge–Chitiea report. All of those conflicts were resolved by Signal in its own favor without divulging any aspect of them to UOP.

This cannot but undermine a conclusion that this merger meets any reasonable test of fairness. The outside UOP directors lacked one material piece of information generated by two of their colleagues, but shared only with Signal. True, the UOP board had the Lehman Brothers' fairness opinion, but that firm has been blamed by the plaintiff for the hurried task it performed, when more properly the responsibility for this lies with Signal. There was no disclosure of the circumstances surrounding the rather cursory preparation of the Lehman Brothers' fairness opinion. Instead, the impression was given UOP's minority that a careful study had been made, when in fact speed was the hallmark, and Mr. Glanville, Lehman's partner in charge of the matter, and also a UOP director, having spent the weekend in Vermont, brought a draft of the "fairness opinion letter" to the UOP directors' meeting on March 6, 1978 with the price left blank. We can only conclude from the record that the rush imposed on Lehman Brothers by Signal's timetable contributed to the difficulties under which this investment banking firm attempted to perform its responsibilities. Yet, none of this was disclosed to UOP's minority.

Finally, the minority stockholders were denied the critical information that Signal considered a price of $24 to be a good investment. Since this would have meant over $17,000,000 more to the minority, we cannot conclude that the shareholder vote was an informed one. Under the circumstances, an approval by a majority of the minority was meaningless. Lynch I, 383 A.2d at 279, 281.

Given these particulars and the Delaware law on the subject, the record does not establish that this transaction satisfies any reasonable concept of fair dealing, and the Chancellor's findings in that regard must be reversed.

E.

Turning to the matter of price, plaintiff also challenges its fairness. His evidence was that on the date the merger was approved the stock was worth at least $26 per share. In support, he offered the testimony of a chartered investment analyst who used two basic approaches to valuation: a comparative analysis of the premium paid over market in ten other tender offer-merger combinations, and a discounted cash flow analysis.

In this breach of fiduciary duty case, the Chancellor perceived that the approach to valuation was the same as that in an appraisal proceeding. Consistent with precedent, he rejected plaintiff's method of proof and accepted defendants' evidence of value as being in accord with practice under prior case law. This means that the so-called "Delaware block" or weighted average method was employed wherein the elements of value, i.e., assets, market price, earnings, etc., were assigned a particular weight and the resulting amounts added to determine the value per share. This procedure has been in use for decades. See In re General Realty & Utilities Corp., Del.Ch., 52 A.2d 6, 14–15 (1947). However, to the extent it excludes other generally accepted techniques used in the financial community and the courts, it is now clearly outmoded. It is time we recognize this in appraisal and other stock valuation proceedings and bring our law current on the subject.

While the Chancellor rejected plaintiff's discounted cash flow method of valuing UOP's stock, as not corresponding with "either logic or the existing law," it is significant that this was essentially the focus, i.e., earnings potential of UOP, of Messrs. Arledge and Chitiea in their evaluation of the merger. Accordingly, the standard "Delaware block" or weighted average method of valuation, formerly employed in appraisal and other stock valuation cases, shall no longer exclusively control such proceedings. We believe that a more liberal approach must include proof of value by any techniques or methods which are generally considered acceptable in the financial community and otherwise admissible in court, subject only to our interpretation of 8 Del.C. § 262(h), infra. This will obviate the very structured and mechanistic procedure that has heretofore governed such matters. See Jacques Coe & Co. v. Minneapolis–Moline Co., Del.Ch., 75 A.2d 244, 247 (1950); Tri–Continental Corp. v. Battye, Del.Ch., 66 A.2d 910, 917–18 (1949).

Fair price obviously requires consideration of all relevant factors involving the value of a company. * * *

Although the Chancellor received the plaintiff's evidence, his opinion indicates that the use of it was precluded because of past Delaware practice. While we do not suggest a monetary result one way or the other, we do think the plaintiff's evidence should be part of the factual mix and weighed as such. Until the $21 price is measured on remand by the valuation standards mandated by Delaware law, there can be no finding at the present stage of these proceedings that the price is fair.

Given the lack of any candid disclosure of the material facts surrounding establishment of the $21 price, the majority of the minority vote, approving the merger, is meaningless.

The plaintiff has not sought an appraisal, but rescissory damages of the type contemplated by *Lynch v. Vickers Energy Corp.*, Del.Supr., 429 A.2d 497, 505–06 (1981) (*Lynch II*). In view of the approach to valuation that we announce today, we see no basis in our law for *Lynch II*'s exclusive monetary formula for relief. On remand the plaintiff will be permitted to test the fairness of the $21 price by the standards we herein establish, in conformity with the principle applicable to an appraisal—that fair value be determined by taking "into account all relevant factors" [see 8 Del.C. § 262(h), supra]. In our view this includes the elements of rescissory damages if the Chancellor considers them susceptible of proof and a remedy appropriate to all the issues of fairness before him. To the extent that Lynch II, 429 A.2d at 505–06, purports to limit the Chancellor's discretion to a single remedial formula for monetary damages in a cash-out merger, it is overruled.

While a plaintiff's monetary remedy ordinarily should be confined to the more liberalized appraisal proceeding herein established, we do not intend any limitation on the historic powers of the Chancellor to grant such other relief as the facts of a particular case may dictate. The appraisal remedy we approve may not be adequate in certain cases, particularly where fraud, misrepresentation, self-dealing, deliberate waste of corporate assets, or gross and palpable overreaching are involved. Cole v. National Cash Credit Association, Del.Ch., 156 A. 183, 187 (1931). Under such circumstances, the Chancellor's powers are complete to fashion any form of equitable and monetary relief as may be appropriate, including rescissory damages. Since it is apparent that this long completed transaction is too involved to undo, and in view of the Chancellor's discretion, the award, if any, should be in the form of monetary damages based upon entire fairness standards, i.e., fair dealing and fair price.

Obviously, there are other litigants, like the plaintiff, who abjured an appraisal and whose rights to challenge the element of fair value must be preserved.[6] Accordingly, the quasi-appraisal remedy we grant the plaintiff here will apply only to: (1) this case; (2) any case now pending on appeal to this Court; (3) any case now pending in the Court of Chancery which has not yet been appealed but which may be eligible for direct appeal to this Court; (4) any case challenging a cash-out merger, the effective date of which is on or before February 1, 1983; and (5) any proposed merger to be presented at a shareholders' meeting, the notification of which is mailed to the stockholders on or before February 23, 1983. Thereafter, the provisions of 8 Del.C. § 262, as herein construed, respecting the scope of an appraisal and the means for perfecting the same, shall govern the financial remedy available to

6. [By the Court] Under 8 Del.C. § 262(a), (d) & (e), a stockholder is required to act within certain time periods to perfect the right to an appraisal.

minority shareholders in a cash-out merger. Thus, we return to the well established principles of Stauffer v. Standard Brands, Inc., Del. Supr., 187 A.2d 78 (1962) and David J. Greene & Co. v. Schenley Industries, Inc., Del.Ch., 281 A.2d 30 (1971), mandating a stockholder's recourse to the basic remedy of an appraisal.

III.

Finally, we address the matter of business purpose. The defendants contend that the purpose of this merger was not a proper subject of inquiry by the trial court. The plaintiff says that no valid purpose existed—the entire transaction was a mere subterfuge designed to eliminate the minority. The Chancellor ruled otherwise, but in so doing he clearly circumscribed the thrust and effect of *Singer*. This has led to the thoroughly sound observation that the business purpose test "may be * * * virtually interpreted out of existence, as it was in *Weinberger* ".

The requirement of a business purpose is new to our law of mergers and was a departure from prior case law. In view of the fairness test which has long been applicable to parent-subsidiary mergers, Sterling v. Mayflower Hotel Corp., Del.Supr., 93 A.2d 107, 109–10 (1952), the expanded appraisal remedy now available to shareholders, and the broad discretion of the Chancellor to fashion such relief as the facts of a given case may dictate, we do not believe that any additional meaningful protection is afforded minority shareholders by the business purpose requirement of the trilogy of *Singer, Tanzer* [v. International General Industries, Inc., 379 A.2d 1121 (Del.1977)], [Roland International Corp. v.] *Najjar* [407 A.2d 1032 (Del.1979)], and their progeny. Accordingly, such requirement shall no longer be of any force or effect.

The judgment of the Court of Chancery, finding both the circumstances of the merger and the price paid the minority shareholders to be fair, is reversed. The matter is remanded for further proceedings consistent herewith. Upon remand the plaintiff's post-trial motion to enlarge the class should be granted. * * *

Reversed and Remanded.

Notes

(1) Do you understand the full implications of a "cash out" merger? It permits a parent corporation owning more than fifty per cent of the stock of a subsidiary corporation to compel the minority shareholders of the subsidiary to accept cash for their shares in an amount set by the parent, subject, however, to the appraisal rights provided in Chapter 13 of the RMBCA. In the modern law of corporations it is important to recognize that a "merger" is not limited to the intuitive notion of two independent corporations agreeing to fuse together with shareholders of both corporations having a continuing interest in the fused enterprise.

(2) Singer v. Magnavox, 380 A.2d 969 (Del.1977), overruled by the principal case, applied a double test to "cash out" mergers: the transaction

must meet a test of "entire fairness" and there must be a "business purpose" other than a purpose of eliminating the minority shareholders. Actual experience in Delaware with the "business purpose" test revealed that it apparently did not help to separate abusive transactions from proper ones. In Tanzer v. International Gen. Indus., Inc., 379 A.2d 1121 (Del.1977), for example, the court held that the parent corporation's actions should be measured by reference to its status and interest as a shareholder, including its own corporate concerns, and that a purpose "to facilitate long term debt financing" of the parent was a proper business purpose. Not all courts, however, have accepted the conclusion of *Weinberger* that no business purpose is required if the transaction is fair and if the minority shareholders are fairly dealt with. In Alpert v. 28 Williams St. Corp. 63 N.Y.2d 557, 483 N.Y.S.2d 667, 473 N.E.2d 19 (1984), for example, the New York Court of Appeals stated that in addition to fair dealing and fair price, the directors must justify the variant treatment between the majority and the minority by showing some business purpose for the transaction:

> In the context of a freeze-out merger, variant treatment of the minority shareholders—i.e., causing their removal—will be justified when related to the advancement of a general corporate interest. The benefit need not be great, but it must be for the corporation. For example, if the sole purpose of the merger is reduction of the number of profit sharers—in contrast to increasing the corporation's capital or profits, or improving its management structure—there will exist no "independent corporate interest". All of these purposes ultimately seek to increase the individual wealth of the remaining shareholders. What distinguishes a proper corporate purpose from an improper one is that, with the former, removal of the minority shareholders furthers the objective of conferring some general gain upon the corporation. Only then will the fiduciary duty of good and prudent management of the corporation serve to override the concurrent duty to treat all shareholders fairly. We further note that a finding that there was an independent corporate purpose for the action taken by the majority will not be defeated merely by the fact that the corporate objective could have been accomplished in another way, or by the fact that the action chosen was not the best way to achieve the bona fide business objective.

> In sum, in entertaining an equitable action to review a freeze-out merger, a court should view the transaction as a whole to determine whether it was tainted with fraud, illegality, or self-dealing, whether the minority shareholders were dealt with fairly, and whether there exists any independent corporate purpose for the merger.

473 N.E.2d, at 28. See also Coggins v. New England Patriots Football Club, 397 Mass. 525, 492 N.E.2d 1112, 1117 (1986), where the court said that "[u]nlike the Delaware court * * * we believe the 'business purpose' test is an additional useful means under our statute and caselaw for examining a transaction in which a controlling stockholder eliminates the minority interest in a corporation."

(3) Why isn't the appraisal remedy an acceptable solution for all "cash out" merger problems? If the minority shareholder is dissatisfied with the

amount offered by the corporation, a right to obtain the "fair value" of the shares as judicially determined seems reasonable. What can be wrong with that? While this remedy has superficial plausibility, in most states today it is not an attractive remedy since it often does not lead in fact to an adequate payment to dissenting shareholders. There are at least four problems with this remedy: (1) the shareholders must litigate with the corporation as to the fair value issue; the corporation usually has extensive resources and intimate knowledge of where the skeletons are while the shareholder does not; (2) the shareholder receives nothing until the litigation establishing fair value, including appeals, is exhausted; as a result he or she may receive nothing for five years or so (while a person accepting the transaction receives immediate payment), and an ultimate award of statutory interest is not likely to be viewed as adequate compensation for the loss of the use of the proceeds for a long period; (3) the shareholder must bear his or her own litigation expenses, which may be substantial, particularly if asset valuations are involved; and (4) the method of valuation routinely used in most states, the "Delaware block" approach discussed in *Weinberger,* may not yield a valuation that is realistic. These inadequacies, in part, were of course recognized in the court's opinion in *Weinberger;* they are also addressed in part in Chapter 13 of the RMBCA, which attempts to give the dissenter some immediate payment before the appraisal suit is filed. Nevertheless, the limitations and inadequacies of the traditional appraisal remedy are sometimes apparently not fully appreciated. See, for example, Mr. Justice Stevens concurring in Santa Fe Indus., Inc. v. Green, p. 976, infra. For an examination of the appraisal remedy which arguably understates the problems of this traditional remedy and overstates the reliability of market values in "thinly traded" markets, see Seligman, Reappraising the Appraisal Remedy, 52 Geo.Wash.L.Rev. 829 (1984).

(4) Because of the large number of publicly held corporations incorporated in Delaware and the high level of merger activity during the 1980's, the Delaware courts have had numerous opportunities to apply the *Weinberger* principles. This outpouring of post-*Weinberger* litigation has influenced developments in other states. Many courts find attractive the flexibility and open-endedness of the *Weinberger* tests of intrinsic fairness both in procedure and price.

(5) It has become customary in post-*Weinberger* cash out transactions to structure the procedure so that independent directors of the subsidiary negotiate the terms of the transaction with representatives of the parent. The merger documents also condition approval of the transaction upon an affirmative vote of a majority of the minority shareholders. One consequence is that it has become standard practice to place outside persons on the board of directors of subsidiaries that have publicly held minority shares. The leading post-*Weinberger* case discussing these procedural requirements is Rosenblatt v. Getty Oil Co., 493 A.2d 929 (Del.1985), where the negotiation over price seems clearly to have been at arms length. The Delaware courts, however, have not hesitated to enjoin cash out transactions when there was not full disclosure [e.g., Joseph v. Shell Oil Co., 482 A.2d 335 (Del.Ch.1984) holding affirmed in connected case, Selfe v. Joseph, 501 A.2d 409 (Del.1985)], manipulation of the transaction to minimize the

financial rights of minority shareholders, Rabkin v. Philip A. Hunt Chemical Corp., 498 A.2d 1099 (Del.1985), or the use of unfair or abusive tactics [Sealy Mattress Co. of N.J. v. Sealy, Inc., 532 A.2d 1324, 1335 (Del.Ch. 1987)]. In the Sealy case the court stated:

> Indeed, if one were setting out to write a textbook study on how one might violate as many fiduciary precepts as possible in the course of a single merger transaction, this case would be a good model.

In these cases, "recissory damages" may also be available if the transaction in question has been consummated and cannot readily be unwound.

B. CORPORATE OPPORTUNITY

MILLER v. MILLER
Supreme Court of Minnesota, 1974.
301 Minn. 207, 222 N.W.2d 71.

ROGOSHESKE, JUSTICE.

This is a shareholder's derivative action brought by Oscar M. Miller, a minority shareholder, for the benefit of Miller Waste Mills, Inc., (hereafter Miller Waste) to recover assets and profits of the other named defendant corporations. Those corporations (hereafter called defendant corporations) are owned and controlled by defendants Rudolph W. Miller and Benjamin A. Miller, who, while in active management of Miller Waste, established defendant corporations, and who, it is alleged, wrongfully diverted corporate opportunities properly belonging to Miller Waste to defendant corporations. Following a lengthy trial by the court sitting without a jury and the denial of post-trial motions, judgment was entered dismissing plaintiff's complaint, and he appeals. Based upon the facts as found by the trial court and application of the corporate opportunity doctrine as we interpret it, we hold that defendants Rudolph W. and Benjamin A. Miller did not wrongfully appropriate to defendant corporations or to themselves any corporate opportunities belonging to Miller Waste. Accordingly, we affirm the decision of the trial court.

The parties agree that the determinative facts as found by the trial court relevant to the main issue presented for review are not in substantial dispute. * * * Plaintiff and defendants Rudolph and Benjamin Miller are the sons of Joseph and Jennie Miller. In the 1890's, Joseph Miller established a general scrap business in Winona for dealing in metals, hides, paper, rags, and like reclaimable materials. His wife, Jennie, and their family of four sons and four daughters, including plaintiff and defendants Rudolph and Benjamin, all worked in his business at times. In 1923, Joseph purchased a "waste puller" machine to enter the waste business. The business thereafter consisted essentially of buying rags and waste threads and other textile materials from brokers and textile mills for the manufacture and sale of "packing waste" and "wiping waste." By use of the machine, these materials were processed by shredding, cutting, cording, and blending them into manufactured products known as "packing waste" and "wiping waste." Packing waste was sold to railroads for use, after saturation with oil, for packing journal boxes of freight cars to lubricate the cars' journals or axles. Wiping waste was used by railroads and other heavy industries for wiping engines and other machinery. The company also cut, trimmed, laundered, and sold rags to industries for wiping cloths.

The business was incorporated in 1927 as Miller Waste Mills, Inc., "to manufacture waste and wiping cloth" of all kinds and "to do such other business as may be incidental to or reasonably necessary to effectuate such manufacturing business." * * * Since its inception and in accordance with its charter, the corporation's primary business remained the buying, processing, and high-volume production of thread waste in bulk for journal box packing and for wiping, both of which types are typically shipped in bales weighing from 200 to 600 pounds.

* * *

Due to the demand for packing and wiping waste during the war years 1940 to 1943, Miller Waste flourished. It enjoyed gross sales of up to $2,000,000 and had increasing profits, reputable credit, and a stable capital structure. However, in order to secure government contracts for processed waste during World War II, the corporation was compelled to contract for delivery of packaged waste destined for governmental use in small 5- to 7-pound packages. Since the mill was structured for high-volume mass production of bulky, baled waste by unskilled millworkers, the corporation's efforts to meet this requirement were unsuccessful. Its attempts to satisfy its governmental commitments caused disruption of its mass production operations, frequent rejections of its small packages, and increasing financial losses. To solve the problem of the unavailability in Winona of a subcontractor for this small packaging part of the business, Rudolph, Benjamin, and their wives organized a partnership named Unit Manufacturing Company in 1943, and the small packaging business was then transferred to it. Also transferred from the corporation was the business of packaging wiper cloths and two small sideline businesses involving the manufacture of floor mops and an oxygen and acetylene tank business acquired by the corporation in 1940 when it purchased (and later liquidated) Joseph's scrap business to facilitate his retirement. The creation of Unit Manufacturing Company, its purpose, and its expanding operations were known to and observed and approved by at least Jennie. She and Joseph lived but a few blocks from Unit's plant, located on property adjacent to the original waste mill properties.[7] Under the

7. [By the Court] The trial court found formal corporate ratification of these transfers in these words: " * * * At the adjourned annual meeting of the stockholders of Miller Waste Mills, Inc., held on January 29, 1945, all stockholders were present in person including Jennie and Joseph Miller, although the latter left the meeting shortly after the opening thereof. The question of the formation of Unit Manufacturing Company was brought up by the defendants Rudolph Miller and Benjamin Miller, and a full and complete history of that company was given to the Shareholders. The stockholders, Joseph Miller being absent, ratified the formation of Unit

active management of the wives of Rudolph and Benjamin, and with advice from Rudolph and Benjamin, Unit's initial operations consisted of purchasing waste from Miller Waste, processing it, on an assembly line operated by women, into 5–pound packages, baling the packages in 50– to 60–pound bales, and selling the bales to Miller Waste at a profit to Unit equal to the premium paid by the government to Miller Waste on its contract for small package waste. Unit also packaged wiper cloth, a business which consisted of processing, trimming, laundering, cutting to size, and packaging 20– to 50–pound cartons of wiping cloth, which were then sold to machine shops, industrial plants, and garages. As a result of these transfers and the interrelationship, both Miller Waste and Unit Manufacturing Company earned substantial profits.

Unit Manufacturing Company gradually expanded and began manufacturing "filter element socks" and later "filter element cartridges." The "filter socks" were cut and sewn from new cloth, filled with waste, incorporated into metal-cased filter cartridges supplied by another manufacturer, and sold for use as oil filters in diesel engines and other large machines. Later the entire "filter element cartridges" were manufactured by Unit. At the time Unit began manufacturing these products, Miller Waste had no facilities to manufacture the "filter socks" and, much less, the sophisticated metal-cased "filter element cartridges." All waste used by Unit was purchased from Miller Waste "at a profit to the latter equal to or higher than any profit earned from sales to unrelated customers," and a captive market for the waste mill was thereby established. In 1954, the partnership business of Unit was transferred to defendant Filter Supply Corporation, which had been incorporated by Rudolph and Benjamin in 1951.

From 1940, to 1946, Rudolph continued the development of the patented felpax lubricator [8] under his separate business known as Miller–Felpax Company. This lubricator, which used no waste, utilized a laminated, virgin wool, felt wick and was designed for use in diesel locomotives. It was first marketed successfully after World War II when a commercially feasible version was developed by Robert Harkenrider while an employee of Miller–Felpax Company, incorporated in 1947 as defendant Miller–Felpax Corporation and wholly owned by Rudolph and his family. About 1950, utilizing principles of capillarity inherent in the felt wick lubricator, Harkenrider developed and patented, with Rudolph, the Miller lubricator. This lubricator was designed to replace the ordinary waste used in freight car journals. An

---

Manufacturing Company and the diversion to it of the wiper business, the small packaging business and the acetylene business. Furthermore, the stockholders present (representing all but three shares owned by Joseph Miller who had left the meeting) ratified and authorized the participation by the defendants Rudolph Miller and Benjamin Miller in Unit Manufacturing Company, and further provided that Miller Waste Mills, Inc. should not be involved in the affairs of the partnership except in the capacity of customers or suppliers, and that all transactions between the two companies should be carried out 'at arms' length.' "

8. [By the Editor] An omitted portion of this opinion indicates that Rudolph was the inventor of this device and had been working on its perfection since 1932 as an independent business.

essential component is a "blanket" of waste threads which, by use of a needling machine also designed by Harkenrider, were "needled to pressed cloth containing favorable capillary qualities." The source of the waste thread needed was Miller Waste, which sold bulk waste to defendant Filter Supply Corporation at a profit. This corporation, consonant with its manufacture of the "filter socks" for use in the "filter element cartridges," also manufactured the "blanket" used in the Miller lubricator. Filter Supply Corporation then sold the lubricator blanket to defendant Miller Lubricator Company, incorporated by Rudolph and Benjamin in 1953 for the purpose of manufacturing and selling the completed Miller lubricator. The trial court found that "[n]o personnel of Miller Waste Mills, Inc. had the technical ability to design and manufacture such lubricators nor did [it] have proper machinery or equipment to do so." For a period of about 4 years, this lubricator, approved by the American Association of Railroads from 1953 to 1959, enjoyed great commercial acceptance despite some 15 competing devices on the market, and at one time it was installed on almost 60 percent of all railroad freight cars in the United States. Although the Miller lubricator was in direct competition with Miller Waste's business of selling packing waste, Filter Supply Corporation's need for thread waste made its purchases a captive market of Miller Waste, replacing its declining sales of packing waste to railroads. During 1956 to 1959, Miller Waste sold more thread waste than it had previously sold to railroads for freight car journals. The trial court found:

> " * * * Had this 'captive market' not been available Miller Waste Mills, Inc. would have lost its journal 'waste' packing business to other more modern types of railroad car lubricating devices."

Following the suggestion of a friend of Benjamin, and a subsequent discussion between Rudolph, Benjamin, and their mother, Jennie, a decision to enter the plastic business was made, and Rudolph and Benjamin formed and financed defendant Fiberite Corporation in 1948 and defendant Melamine Plastics Corporation in 1952. The purpose of Fiberite Corporation, on whose board of directors Jennie served until about 1956, was to develop and manufacture thermo-setting "high impact phenolic molding compounds" to specifications furnished by molders of plastic products such as gears, housings, bearings, and electrical components. Fiberite Corporation did not become a profitable business until October 1950, when a new manager was able to acquire proper equipment and technical personnel and establish proper production quality controls. Melamine Plastics Corporation manufactured similar plastic compounds with a melamine resin base for use in manufacturing dinnerware for the Armed Services. A principal ingredient of both plastic compounds is cotton "cuttings" which serve as a filler or "reinforcing agent." After experiments proved waste threads to be unsatisfactory as a filler, Miller Waste developed sources of supply for the cotton "cuttings" and purchased, warehoused, and sold them to the Fiberite and Melamine corporations at a profit to Miller

Waste. The development and manufacture of both plastic compounds required the skill and supervision of trained chemists. Miller Waste had no "facilities, equipment, capacity, or technical knowledge" to engage in such businesses. * * *

Since the formation and expansion of these related businesses controlled by Rudolph and Benjamin, Miller Waste has also sold and leased real estate to the businesses and has furnished maintenance, labor, and accounting services to them. Although not negotiated at arm's length, the rentals have been higher than equivalent rentals in the Winona area and the sales of products and services by Miller–Waste to defendant corporations were made at prices equal to or higher than those to nonrelated customers. This resulted in "greater profits" to Miller Waste. All sales of real estate between the related corporations were made only after independent appraisals by the American Appraisal Association. Although at the end of the decade 1950–1960, Miller Waste's initial business of manufacturing and selling "wiping and packing waste" to railroads and other industries had declined, the net income of the corporation "was greater than in any year of the history of the company since its inception except for the Korean war year of 1950."

A corporate resolution of February 1943 charged Rudolph and Benjamin "to exert their best efforts" on behalf of Miller Waste, which they did. They were not required by contract or otherwise to devote their time exclusively to the corporation. Contrary to plaintiff's claim at trial, their compensation was neither "excessive nor unreasonable" in view of the corporation's success as compared to its competitors. Out of approximately 40 "waste mills" in the United States in the 1940's, at the time of trial in 1971 there were only four or five surviving, and Miller Waste "handle[d] more waste products of cotton mills and thread waste than all others combined, and [was then] the most successful waste mill in the United States."

Contrary to plaintiff's further assertion at trial, each of the defendant corporations was financed by Rudolph and Benjamin with "their own monies" and neither officer financed any of them by overdrafts on their accounts, by the handling of intercompany accounts, or by exploiting any "resources" of Miller Waste "other than their own energy, resourcefulness, and business acumen and judgment."

During the times when Rudolph and Benjamin formed and operated defendants Filter Supply Corporation, Miller Lubricator Company, Fiberite Corporation, and Melamine Plastic Corporation, each one's purpose and business were made known to all who were then officers and shareholders of Miller Waste, and particularly their mother, Jennie, was kept informed of the "status of accounts" between Miller Waste, her sons, and defendant corporation. There was no "concealment" from the [Miller Waste shareholders], including plaintiff, and financial statements were available to them for the "asking."

In dismissing plaintiff's complaint, the trial court found that none of the businesses of defendant corporations was a corporate opportunity of Miller Waste except the small packaging business of waste and wiper cloth and the manufacture of mops and the welding business, transferred to defendant Unit Manufacturing Company and later, defendant Filter Supply Company, and in addition, the manufacture of "filter element socks" by the latter. However, the court determined that no wrongful diversion was made since the transfers were made or the opportunities seized in good faith and duly ratified by the then officers and shareholders of the waste mill. * * *

The principal issue raised by plaintiff, and the one on which our disposition of this appeal rests, concerns the proper standards to be applied in determining whether defendants Rudolph and Benjamin Miller appropriated to themselves business opportunities properly belonging to Miller Waste. Even though the various opportunities were developed by defendant corporations, all were owned and controlled by Rudolph and Benjamin. Thus, we approach the issue in the same way as if the opportunities were appropriated by the defendants personally.[9]

Having conceded on oral argument, as plaintiff must, that the court's factual findings and the inference drawn therefrom which bear on this issue have ample evidentiary support, he vigorously argues that the trial court, constrained by our decision in Diedrick v. Helm, 217 Minn. 483, 14 N.W.2d 913, 153 A.L.R. 649 (1944), limited the holding of the landmark case of Guth v. Loft, Inc., 23 Del.Ch. 255, 5 A.2d 503 (1939), and thereby applied an unduly restrictive "line of business" test or standard in determining that defendants were not liable for any diversion of corporate opportunities, and that application of proper standards requires reversal.

At the outset we acknowledge the well-recognized, common-law principle that one entrusted with the active management of a corporation, such as an officer or director, occupies a fiduciary relationship to the corporation and may not exploit his position as an "insider" by appropriating to himself a business opportunity properly belonging to the corporation. If such a business opportunity is usurped for personal gain, it is equally well recognized that the opportunity and any property or profit acquired becomes subject to a constructive trust for the benefit of the corporation. Guth v. Loft, Inc. supra. This principle, usually referred to as the doctrine of corporate opportunity, is derived essentially from fundamental rules of agency concerning the duty of

---

9. [By the Court] Were defendant corporations not closely held, perhaps at least one of the opportunities, the manufacture of the Miller lubricator, could arguably be found to be more closely associated with the "line of business" of Miller–Felpax Corporation than with Miller Waste. In such cases, it is suggested that the question of which corporation has a prior claim to the opportunity be resolved before reaching the question of the liability of a corporate fiduciary managing two corporations in delivering to one corporation in preference to the other an opportunity which may be found to be in the "line of business" of both. Note, 74 Harv.L.Rev. 765, 771.

utmost good faith and loyalty owed by a fiduciary to his principal [10] and also from the law of constructive trusts embodying equitable principles of unjust enrichment.

Although the rule prohibiting usurpation of corporate opportunities is easy to state, difficulties arise in its application.   The main problem confronting courts concerns the proper test or standards to apply in determining whether a business opportunity properly belongs to the corporation.   Guth v. Loft, Inc., supra cited by virtually all jurisdictions confronted with the problem, adopted the following standards (23 Del.Ch. 271, 5 A.2d 510):

> "It is true that when a business opportunity comes to a corporate officer or director in his individual capacity rather than in his official capacity, and the opportunity is one which, because of the nature of the enterprise, is not essential to his corporation, and is one in which it has no interest or expectancy, the officer or director is entitled to treat the opportunity as his own, and the corporation has no interest in it, if of course the officer or director has not wrongfully embarked the corporation's resources therein. * * *

> "On the other hand, it is equally true that, if there is presented to a corporate officer or director a business opportunity which the corporation is financially able to undertake, is, from its nature, in the line of the corporation's business and is of practical advantage to it, is one in which the corporation has an interest or a reasonable expectancy, and, by embracing the opportunity, the self-interest of the officer or director will be brought into conflict with that of his corporation, the law will not permit him to seize the opportunity for himself."

While this court has dealt with the problem and has acknowledged the general principles embodied in the doctrine of corporate opportunity, the necessity of adopting a specific formula for determining when a business opportunity properly belongs to the corporation has not previously been directly presented.   Diedrick v. Helm, supra.   In Diedrick, our leading case, we cited the principles and standards set forth in Guth and also in Solimine v. Hollander, 128 N.J.Eq. 228, 16 A.2d 203 (1940), but expressly deemed it unnecessary to formulate "an all-inclusive definition of what constitutes a 'corporate opportunity'" for the decision in that case.   217 Minn. 493, 14 N.W.2d 919, 153 A.L.R. 658.   Even though the Diedrick case is cited as adopting what might be called the five-pronged Solimine test for determining the existence of corporate opportunities,[11] we interpret the court's opinion as relying mainly upon the "line of business" test enunciated in Guth.

---

10. [By the Court] Cf. Minn.St. 301.31: "Officers and directors shall discharge the duties of their respective positions in good faith, and with that diligence and care which ordinarily prudent men would exercise under similar circumstances in like positions."

11. [By the Court] According to Solimine v. Hollander, 128 N.J.Eq. 228,

246, 16 A.2d 203, 215 (1940), a business opportunity is not a corporate one "(a) wherever the fundamental fact of good faith is determined in favor of the director or officer charged with usurping the corporate opportunity, *or* (b) where the company is unable to avail itself of the opportunity, *or* (c) where availing itself of the opportunity is not *essential* to the company's busi-

Apart from our prior treatment of the problem, other jurisdictions have also experienced difficulties in applying proper standards. We have searched the case law and commentary in vain for an all-inclusive or "critical" test or standard by which a wrongful appropriation can be determined and are persuaded that the doctrine is not capable of precise definition. Rather, it appears that courts have opened or closed the business opportunity door to corporate managers upon the facts and circumstances of each case and by application of one or more of three variant but often overlapping tests or standards: (1) The "interest or expectancy" test, which precludes acquisition by corporate officers of the property of a business opportunity in which the corporation has a "beachhead" in the sense of a legal or equitable interest or expectancy growing out of a preexisting right or relationship; [12] (2) the "line of business" test, which characterizes an opportunity as corporate whenever a managing officer becomes involved in an activity intimately or closely associated with the existing or prospective activities of the corporation; and (3) the "fairness" test, which determines the existence of a corporate opportunity by applying ethical standards of what is fair and equitable under the circumstances.

The Guth case, most often cited as establishing the "line of business" test—more flexible in scope than the restrictive "interest or expectancy" test of earlier decisions—also recognized the practical fairness approach which has been employed in more recent decisions (23 Del.Ch. 279, 5 A.2d 514):

" * * * [T]he appellants say that the expression, 'in the line' of a business, is a phrase so elastic as to furnish no basis for a useful inference. The phrase is not within the field of precise definition, nor is it one that can be bounded by a set formula. *It has a flexible meaning, which is to be applied reasonably and sensibly to the facts and circumstances of the particular case. Where a corporation is engaged in a certain business, and an opportunity is presented to it embracing an activity as to which it has fundamental knowledge, practical experience and ability to pursue, which, logically and naturally, is adaptable to its business having regard for its financial position, and is one that is consonant with its reasonable needs and aspirations for expansion, it may be properly said that the opportunity is in the line of the corporation's business.*" (Italics supplied.)

ness, *or* (d) where the accused fiduciary does not exploit the opportunity by the employment of his company's resources, *or* (e) where by embracing the opportunity personally the director or officer is not brought into direct competition with his company and its business." Note that each of the above considerations is mutually exclusive and that the presence of any one consideration precludes the finding of a usurpation of a corporate opportunity.

12. [By the Court] For example, a corporation which possesses a lease on certain property or operates under a patent license is deemed to have an "interest" or "expectancy" in such property or license as to preclude the appropriation of such interests by the corporate fiduciaries. See, Feuer, Personal Liabilities of Corporate Officers and Directors, p. 79; Burg v. Horn, 380 F.2d 897 (2 Cir.1967); Slaughter, The Corporate Opportunity Doctrine, 18 Sw. L.J. 96.

In Durfee v. Durfee & Canning, 323 Mass. 187, 199, 80 N.E.2d 522, 529 (1948), the court, which placed strong emphasis on factors of fairness, rejected the "interest or expectancy" test and declared:

> We do not concur in the argument of counsel for the defendant to the effect that the test is whether the corporation has an existing interest or an expectancy thereof in the property involved, being of the opinion that *the true basis of the governing doctrine rests fundamentally on the unfairness in the particular circumstances of a director, whose relation to the corporation is fiduciary, "taking advantage of an opportunity [for his personal profit] when the interest of the corporation justly calls for protection. This calls for the application of ethical standards of what is fair and equitable * * * [in] particular sets of facts."* Ballantine on Corporations (Rev. ed. 1946) 204–205. (Italics supplied.)

In an effort hopefully to ameliorate the often-expressed criticism that the doctrine is vague and subjects today's corporate management to the danger of unpredictable liability, we believe a more helpful approach is to combine the "line of business" test with the "fairness" test and to adopt criteria involving a two-step process for determining the ultimate question of when liability for a wrongful appropriation of a corporate opportunity should be imposed. The threshold question to be answered is whether a business opportunity presented is also a "corporate" opportunity, i.e., whether the business opportunity is of sufficient importance and is so closely related to the existing or prospective activity of the corporation as to warrant judicial sanctions against its personal acquisition by a managing officer or director of the corporation. This question, necessarily one of fact, can best be resolved, we believe, by resort to a flexible application of the "line of business" test set forth in Guth v. Loft, Inc., supra. The inquiry of the factfinder should be directed to all facts and circumstances relevant to the question, the most significant being: Whether the business opportunity presented is one in which the complaining corporation has an interest or an expectancy growing out of an existing contractual right; the relationship of the opportunity to the corporation's business purposes and current activities—whether essential, necessary, or merely desirable to its reasonable needs and aspirations—; whether, within or without its corporate powers, the opportunity embraces areas adaptable to its business and into which the corporation might easily, naturally, or logically expand; the competitive nature of the opportunity—whether prospectively harmful or unfair—; whether the corporation, by reason of insolvency or lack of resources, has the financial ability to acquire the opportunity; and whether the opportunity includes activities as to which the corporation has fundamental knowledge, practical experience, facilities, equipment, personnel, and the ability to pursue. The fact that the opportunity is not within the scope of the corporation's powers, while a factor to be considered, should not be determinative, especially where the corporate fiduciary dominates the board of directors or is the majority shareholder.

If the facts are undisputed that the business opportunity presented bears no logical or reasonable relation to the existing or prospective business activities of the corporation or that it lacks either the financial or fundamental practical or technical ability to pursue it, then such opportunity would have to be found to be noncorporate as a matter of law. If the facts are disputed or reasonable minds functioning judicially could disagree as to whether the opportunity is closely associated with the existing or prospective activities of the corporation or its financial or technical ability to pursue it, the question is one of fact with the burden of proof resting upon the party attacking the acquisition.

Absent any evidence of fraud or a breach of fiduciary duty, if it is determined that a business opportunity is not a corporate opportunity, the corporate officer should not be held liable for its acquisition. If, however, the opportunity is found to be a corporate one, liability should not be imposed upon the acquiring officer if the evidence establishes that his acquisition did not violate his fiduciary duties of loyalty, good faith, and fair dealing toward the corporation. Thus the second step in the two-step process leading to the determination of the ultimate question of liability involves close scrutiny of the equitable considerations existing prior to, at the time of, and following the officer's acquisition. Resolution will necessarily depend upon a consideration of all the facts and circumstances of each case considered in the light of those factors which control the decision that the opportunity was in fact a corporate opportunity. Significant factors which should be considered are the nature of the officer's relationship to the management and control of the corporation; whether the opportunity was presented to him in his official or individual capacity; his prior disclosure of the opportunity to the board of directors or shareholders and their response; whether or not he used or exploited corporate facilities, assets, or personnel in acquiring the opportunity; whether his acquisition harmed or benefited the corporation; and all other facts and circumstances bearing on the officer's good faith and whether he exercised the diligence, devotion, care, and fairness toward the corporation which ordinarily prudent men would exercise under similar circumstances in like positions.

We are not to be understood, by adopting this two-step process, as suggesting that a finding of bad faith is essential to impose liability upon the acquiring officer. Nor, conversely, that good faith alone, apart from the officer's fiduciary duty requiring loyalty and fair dealing toward the corporation, will absolve him from liability. And it must be acknowledged, in adopting corporate opportunity doctrine expanded beyond the narrow preexisting property interest or expectancy standard, that there can be cases where the officer's personal seizure of an opportunity so clearly essential to the continuance of a corporation or so intimately related to its activities as to amount to a direct interference with its existing activities would negate any attempt by the officer to prove his good faith, loyalty, and fair dealing.

The burden of proof on the questions of good faith, fair dealing, and loyalty of the officer to the corporation should rest upon the officer who appropriated the business opportunity for his own advantage. Such a burden necessarily lies with the acquiring officer because a fiduciary with a conflict of interest should be required to justify his actions and because of the practical reality that the facts with regard to such questions are more apt to be within his knowledge.

Applying our interpretation of the doctrine of corporate opportunity to this case, we have no difficulty in affirming the trial court's determination that defendants Rudolph and Benjamin did not wrongfully appropriate to defendant corporations or to themselves any corporate opportunity properly belonging to Miller Waste. The question of whether the businesses of Melamine Plastics Corporation, Fiberite Corporation, Miller Lubricator Company, Miller–Felpax Corporation, and the business of manufacturing the "filter element cartridges" by Filter Supply Corporation, were in the line of business of Miller Waste is a disputed question of fact and clearly the trial court's findings that each was not have ample evidentiary support. Similarly, the findings that defendants Rudolph and Benjamin diverted from Miller Waste corporate opportunities transferred to Unit and Filter Supply are sustained by the evidence and are, in our view, consistent with the proper application of the standards to be applied in determining the question of whether a business opportunity presented to a corporate fiduciary is a corporate opportunity.

Apart from the trial court's findings with respect to ratification, nonliability of defendants Rudolph and Benjamin and defendant Filter Supply Corporation is justified by findings of the trial court that the transfer to Unit Manufacturing Company of the mop manufacturing and welding business which Miller Waste had acquired to facilitate Joseph's retirement was not significant to the business of Miller Waste; that the transfers and appropriations of the small packaging businesses and the manufacture and sale of the "filter element socks," found diverted, benefited and did not harm the corporation; that no corporate assets or facilities were used or exploited; that such diversions were made in good faith without concealment from the contingent beneficiaries and after full disclosure to and with the acquiescence, if not the approval, of all the then officers and shareholders of Miller Waste.

It may be observed that inferences from the facts as found by the court (disregarding the finding of consent to develop the patented lubricator) arguably would have justified the trial court's finding that the business of defendant Miller–Felpax Corporation and Miller Lubricating Company were in the line of business of Miller Waste, and thus a corporate opportunity of the waste mill.

Liability for such diversion would not be warranted however because, under the facts as found, the conclusion by the court that Rudolph and Benjamin discharged their fiduciary duties of good faith, loyalty, and fair dealing is compelling. In addition to the court's findings justifying the diversions found as summarized above, the unrefuted testimony at trial establishes that Rudolph and Benjamin, devoting their best efforts, worked exceedingly long hours at the waste mill; developed new lines of business for it, such as the sale of cotton "cuttings" and the division of plastic trading; loaned Miller Waste money when it needed financial assistance; and transacted all intercorporate activities at a profit to Miller Waste. No corporate assets were used in establishing any of defendant corporations, their activities were fully disclosed, and most important, Miller Waste was supplied with a captive market which has sustained the corporation and made it the "number one waste mill in the United States."

We must conclude therefore, based upon the record, that defendant brothers, by embracing business opportunities and as a result advancing their own self-interest, were not unfair, did not act in bad faith, and did not violate their duty of loyalty to Miller Waste. Accordingly, plaintiff's complaint was properly dismissed.

Affirmed.

Sheran, C.J., and Yetka and Scott, JJ., not having been members of this court at the time of the argument and submission, took no part in the consideration or decision of this case.

Notes

Brudney and Clark, A New Look at Corporate Opportunities, 94 Harv. L.Rev. 997, 998, n. 2 (1981): *

> The vast bulk of the case law asks whether the project appropriated is a corporate opportunity, and upon concluding that it is, holds that the defendant is at fault for taking it. In recent years, however, a few decisions have adopted a different linguistic convention: they separate the question whether a "corporate opportunity" is involved from that whether, if there is, it may nevertheless be appropriated. See, e.g., Miller v. Miller, 301 Minn. 207, 222 N.W.2d 71 (1974). * * *

> The new mode of speech both reflects and creates confusion in the thinking of those who use it. In the *Miller* case, for example, the court offers no convincing reason for its two-step analysis: the factors discussed in the second step seem just as relevant to determining whether the opportunity should be classified as a "corporate" one as those applied in the first step. The new methodology in fact adds only a new layer of confusion to an already murky area of law, without forwarding the analysis in any significant fashion.

* Copyright © 1981 by the Harvard Law Review Association.

KLINICKI v. LUNDGREN

Supreme Court of Oregon, 1985.
298 Or. 662, 695 P.2d 906.

JONES, JUSTICE.

The factual and legal background of this complicated litigation was succinctly set forth by Chief Judge Joseph in the Court of Appeals opinion as follows:

"In January, 1977, plaintiff Klinicki conceived the idea of engaging in the air transportation business in Berlin, West Germany. He discussed the idea with his friend, defendant Lundgren. At that time, both men were furloughed Pan American pilots stationed in West Germany. They decided to enter the air transportation business, planning to begin operations with an air taxi service and later to expand into other service, such as regularly scheduled flights or charter flights. In April, 1977, they incorporated Berlinair, Inc., as a closely held Oregon corporation. Plaintiff was a vice-president and a director. Lundgren was the corporation's president and a director. Each man owned 33 percent of the company stock. Lelco, Inc., a corporation owned by Lundgren and members of his family, owned 33 percent of the stock. The corporation's attorney owned the remaining one percent of the stock. Berlinair obtained the necessary governmental licenses, purchased an aircraft and in November, 1977, began passenger service.

"As president, Lundgren was responsible, in part, for developing and promoting Berlinair's transportation business. Plaintiff was in charge of operations and maintenance. In November, 1977, plaintiff and Lundgren, as representatives of Berlinair, met with representatives of the Berliner Flug Ring (BFR), a consortium of Berlin travel agents that contracts for charter flights to take sallow German tourists to sunnier climes. The BFR contract was considered a lucrative business opportunity by those familiar with the air transportation business, and plaintiff and defendant had contemplated pursuing the contract when they formed Berlinair. After the initial meeting, all subsequent contacts with BFR were made by Lundgren or other Berlinair employes acting under his directions.

"During the early stages of negotiations, Lundgren believed that Berlinair could not obtain the contract because BFR was then satisfied with its carrier. In early June, 1978, however, Lundgren learned that there was a good chance that the BFR contract might be available. He informed a BFR representative that he would make a proposal on behalf of a new company. On July 7, 1978, he incorporated Air Berlin Charter Company (ABC) and was its sole owner. On August 20, 1978, ABC presented BFR with a contract proposal, and after a series of discussions it was awarded the contract on September 1, 1978. Lundgren effectively concealed from plaintiff his negotiations with BFR and his diversion of the BFR contract to ABC, even though he used Berlinair working time, staff, money and facilities.

"Plaintiff, as a minority stockholder in Berlinair, brought a derivative action against ABC for usurping a corporate opportunity of Berlinair. He also brought an individual claim against Lundgren for compensatory and punitive damages based on breach of fiduciary duty.

"The trial court found that ABC, acting through Lundgren, had wrongfully diverted the BFR contract, which was a corporate opportunity of Berlinair. The court imposed a constructive trust on ABC in favor of Berlinair, ordered an accounting by ABC and enjoined ABC from transferring its assets. The trial court also found that Lundgren, as an officer and director of Berlinair, had breached his fiduciary duties of good faith, fair dealing and full disclosure owed to plaintiff individually and to Berlinair." * * *

ABC appealed to the Court of Appeals contending that it did not usurp a corporate opportunity of Berlinair * * *. The Court of Appeals affirmed the trial court. * * *

ABC petitions for review to this court contending that the concealment and diversion of the BFR contract was not a usurpation of a corporate opportunity, because Berlinair did not have the financial ability to undertake that contract. ABC argues that proof of financial ability is a necessary part of a corporate opportunity case and that plaintiff had the burden of proof on that issue and did not carry that burden.

There is no dispute that the corporate opportunity doctrine precludes corporate fiduciaries from diverting to themselves business opportunities in which the corporation has an expectancy, property interest or right, or which in fairness should otherwise belong to the corporation. The doctrine follows from a corporate fiduciary's duty of undivided loyalty to the corporation. ABC agrees that, unless Berlinair's financial inability to undertake the contract makes a difference, the BFR contract was a corporate opportunity of Berlinair.

We first address the issue, resolved by the Court of Appeals in Berlinair's favor, of the relevance of a corporation's financial ability to undertake a business opportunity to proving a diversion of corporate opportunity claim. This is an issue of first impression in Oregon.

The Court of Appeals held that a corporation's financial ability to undertake a business opportunity is not a factor in determining the existence of a corporate opportunity unless the defendant demonstrates that the corporation is technically or de facto insolvent. Without defining these terms, the Court of Appeals specifically placed the burden of proof as to this issue on the fiduciary by saying: "To avoid liability for usurping a corporate opportunity on the basis that the corporation was insolvent, the fiduciary must prove insolvency." 67 Or.App. at 165, 678 P.2d at 1254. The Court of Appeals then concluded "that ABC usurped a corporate opportunity belonging to Berlinair when, acting through Lundgren, the BFR contract was diverted" because nothing in Lundgren's testimony or otherwise in the record suggested that Berlinair was insolvent or was no longer a viable corporate entity. 67 Or.App. at 166, 678 P.2d at 1254. Accordingly, the Court of Appeals held that the constructive trust, injunction, duty to account and other relief granted by the trial court against ABC were appropriate remedies. * * *

Before proceeding further our initial task must be to define what is meant by "corporate opportunity," and to determine when, if ever, a corporate fiduciary may take personal advantage of such an opportunity. Our resolution of this case will be limited to announcing a rule to be applied when allegations of usurpation of a corporate opportunity are made against a director of a close corporation. The determination of a rule to apply to similar situations arising between a director and a publicly held corporation presents problems and concepts which may not necessarily require us to apply an identical rule in that similar but distinguishable context.

As we mentioned at the outset, this issue is a matter of first impression in this state. While courts universally stress the high standard of fiduciary duty owed by directors and officers to their corporation, there are distinct schools of thought on the circumstances in which business opportunities may be taken for personal advantage. One group of jurisdictions severely restricts the corporate official's freedom to take advantage of opportunities by saying that the ability to undertake the opportunity is irrelevant and usurpation is essentially prohibited; other jurisdictions use a test which gives relatively wide latitude to the corporate official on the theory that financial ability to undertake a corporate opportunity is a prerequisite to the existence of a corporate opportunity.

A rigid rule was applied in Irving Trust Co. v. Deutsch, 73 F.2d 121 (2nd Cir.1934). In that case a syndicate made up of directors of Acoustic Products Co. purchased for themselves from another corporation the rights to manufacture under certain radio patents which were concededly essential to Acoustic. They justified this on the ground that Acoustic was not financially able to purchase the patents on which the defendants later made very substantial profits. The court refused to inquire whether the conclusion of financial inability was justified. Referring to the facts which raised a question whether Acoustic actually did lack the funds or credit necessary to make the acquisition, the court said:

> " * * * Nevertheless, they [the facts in the case concerning whether Acoustic lacked funds to carry out the contract] tend to show the wisdom of a rigid rule forbidding directors of a solvent corporation to take over for their own profit a corporate contract on the plea of the corporation's financial inability to perform. If the directors are uncertain whether the corporation can make the necessary outlays, they need not embark it upon the venture; if they do, they may not substitute themselves for the corporation any place along the line and divert possible benefits into their own pockets. * * *" 73 F.2d at 124. * * *

Representing a more relaxed view of a corporate official's responsibility, in Guth v. Loft, Inc., 23 Del.Ch. 255, 272–73, 5 A.2d 503, 511 (1939), the Supreme Court of Delaware [described a corporate opportunity as] * * * "a business opportunity *which the corporation is financially able to undertake * * *.*" (Emphasis added.)

The language in *Guth* implies that financial ability to undertake a corporate opportunity is not only relevant, but perhaps a condition precedent to the existence of a corporate opportunity. But the language in *Guth* was dictum because that famous case, involving the creation of the Pepsi–Cola enterprise, did not involve the issue of financial ability to undertake the opportunity. * * *

On the other end of the legal spectrum from Irving Trust Co. v. Deutsch, supra, are two Minnesota cases: Miller v. Miller, 301 Minn. 207, 222 N.W.2d 71, 77 A.L.R.3d 941 (1974), and A.C. Petters v. St. Cloud Enterprises, Inc., 301 Minn. 261, 222 N.W.2d 83 (1974). In *Miller,* the Minnesota Supreme Court stated a two-step test to be applied in corporate opportunity cases. The first step, the "line of business" part of the test, was described as follows:

> "* * * The inquiry of the factfinder should be directed to all facts and circumstances relevant to the question, the most significant being: Whether the business opportunity presented is one in which the complaining corporation has an interest or an expectancy growing out of an existing contractual right; the relationship of the opportunity to the corporation's business purposes and current activities—whether essential, necessary, or merely desirable to its reasonable needs and aspirations—; whether within or without its corporate powers, the opportunity embraces areas adaptable to its business and into which the corporation might easily, naturally, or logically expand; the competitive nature of the opportunity—whether prospectively harmful or unfair—; *whether the corporation, by reason of insolvency or lack of resources, has the financial ability to acquire the opportunity;* and whether the opportunity includes activities as to which the corporation has a fundamental knowledge, practical experience, facilities, equipment, personnel, and the ability to pursue." * * * 301 Minn. at 224–25, 222 N.W.2d at 81 (emphasis added).

In other words, the court found that financial ability is a prerequisite to establishing a corporate opportunity. The court went on to hold that, where the facts were in dispute, the burden of proof on the financial issue rests upon the "party attacking the acquisition". * * *

Counsel for defendant, relying on *Miller,* contends there is no corporate opportunity if there is no capacity to take advantage of the corporate opportunity. We reject this argument. By the same token, we reject plaintiff's contention, relying on *Irving Trust,* that financial ability is totally irrelevant in an unlawful taking of a corporate opportunity. * * *

On April 13, 1984, the American Law Institute published its "Tentative Draft No. 3" concerning "Principles of Corporate Governance: Analysis and Recommendations." The draft, of course, does not represent the position of the ALI, but it does contain definitions and rules which we find helpful in resolving the main issue in this case. Section 5.12 of the draft, which contains the proposed general rule and definition, reads as follows:

"(a) *General Rule:*

"A director or principal senior executive may not take a corporate opportunity for himself or an associate unless:

(1) The corporate opportunity has first been offered to the corporation, and disclosure has been made to the corporate decisionmaker of all material facts known to the director or principal senior executive concerning his conflict of interest and the corporate opportunity (unless the corporate decisionmaker is otherwise aware of such material facts); and

(2) The corporate opportunity has been rejected by the corporation in a manner that meets one of the following standards:

(A) In the case of a rejection of a corporate opportunity that was authorized by disinterested directors following such disclosure, the directors who authorized the rejection acted in a manner that meets the standards of the business judgment rule set forth in § 4.01(d);

(B) In the case of a rejection that was authorized or ratified by disinterested shareholders following such disclosure, the rejection was not equivalent to a waste of corporate assets; and

(C) In the case of a rejection that was not authorized or ratified in the manner contemplated in § 5.12(a)(2)(A) or (B) or permitted by the terms of a [validly adopted] standard of the corporation * * *, the taking of the opportunity was fair to the corporation.

"(b) *Definition of a Corporate Opportunity:*

"A corporate opportunity means any opportunity to engage in a business activity (including acquisition or use of any contract right or other tangible or intangible property) that:

(1) In the case of a principal senior executive or any director, is an opportunity that is communicated or otherwise made available to him either:

(A) in connection with the performance of his obligations as a principal senior executive or director or under circumstances that should reasonably lead him to believe that the person offering the opportunity expects him to offer it to the corporation, or

(B) through the use of corporate information or property, if the resulting opportunity is one that the principal senior executive or director should reasonably be expected to believe would be of interest to the corporation; or

(2) In the case of a principal senior executive or a director who is a full-time employee of the corporation, is an opportunity that he knows or reasonably should know is closely related to the

business in which the corporation is engaged or may reasonably be expected to engage. (Bracketed section references omitted.)

Section 5.12 presents an approach very similar to that suggested by Chief Judge Joseph in the Court of Appeals decision rendered in this case. Section 5.12 generally would require an opportunity that could be advantageous to the corporation to be offered to the corporation by a director or principal senior executive before he takes it for himself. Section 5.12 declines to adopt the rigid rule expressed in Irving Trust Co. v. Deutsch, supra, which precludes a person subject to the duty of loyalty from pursuing a rejected opportunity. The proposed rule permits a director or principal senior executive to deal with his corporation so long as he deals fairly with full disclosure and bears the burden of proving fairness unless the corporate opportunity was rejected by disinterested directors or shareholders.

The comment to Section 5.12(a) reads:

"Section 5.12(a) sets forth the general rule requiring a director or principal senior executive to first offer an opportunity to the corporation before taking it for himself. If the opportunity is not offered to the corporation, the director or principal senior executive will have violated § 5.12(a).

"Section 5.12(a) contemplates that a corporate opportunity will be promptly offered to the corporation, and that the corporation will promptly accept or reject the opportunity. Failure to accept the opportunity promptly will be considered tantamount to a rejection. * * *"

and that

"* * * Rejection in the context of § 5.12(a)(2) may be based on one or more of a number of factors, such as lack of interest of the corporation in the opportunity, *its financial inability to acquire the opportunity,* legal restrictions on its ability to accept the opportunity, or unwillingness of a third party to deal with the corporation. * * *" (Emphasis added.)

The comment to Section 5.12(b) reads:

"Section 5.12(b) defines a corporate opportunity broadly as including any proposed acquisition of contract rights or other tangible or intangible property which falls into one of the categories set forth in §§ 5.12(b)(1) or 5.12(b)(2). * * *"

Whether the rejection was fair or not includes consideration of whether the corporation was financially or otherwise incapacitated from undertaking the corporate opportunity. We agree with the proposed ALI Principles of Corporate Governance, supra, as to the following rules for application in close corporation corporate opportunity cases.[13]

13. We have approved other ALI Tentative Drafts. See, Troutman v. Erlandson, 287 Or. 187, 598 P.2d 1211 (1979).

Where a director or principal senior executive of a close corporation wishes to take personal advantage of a "corporate opportunity," as defined by the proposed rule, the director or principal senior executive must comply strictly with the following procedure:

(1) the director or principal senior executive must promptly offer the opportunity and disclose all material facts known regarding the opportunity to the disinterested directors or, if there is no disinterested director, to the disinterested shareholders. If the director or principal senior executive learns of other material facts after such disclosure, the director or principal senior executive must disclose these additional facts in a like manner before personally taking the opportunity.

(2) The director or principal senior executive may take advantage of the corporate opportunity only after full disclosure and only if the opportunity is rejected by a majority of the disinterested directors or, if there are no disinterested directors, by a majority of the disinterested shareholders. If, after full disclosure, the disinterested directors or shareholders unreasonably fail to reject the offer,[14] the interested director or principal senior executive may proceed to take the opportunity if he can prove the taking was otherwise "fair" to the corporation. Full disclosure to the appropriate corporate body is, however, an absolute condition precedent to the validity of any forthcoming rejection as well as to the availability to the director or principal senior executive of the defense of fairness.

(3) An appropriation of a corporate opportunity may be ratified by rejection of the opportunity by a majority of disinterested directors or a majority of disinterested shareholders, after full disclosure subject to the same rules as set out above for prior offer, disclosure and rejection. Where a director or principal senior executive of a close corporation appropriates a corporate opportunity without first fully disclosing the opportunity and offering it to the corporation, absent ratification, that director or principal senior executive holds the opportunity in trust for the corporation.

Applying these rules to the facts in this case, we conclude:

(1) Lundgren, as director and principal executive officer of Berlinair, owed a fiduciary duty to Berlinair.

(2) The BFR contract was a "corporate opportunity" of Berlinair.

(3) Lundgren formed ABC for the purpose of usurping the opportunity presented to Berlinair by the BFR contract.

(4) Lundgren did not offer Berlinair the BFR contract.

---

14. [By the Court] A valid acceptance of the offer by the disinterested directors or shareholders would bar the fiduciary from appropriating the opportunity. An acceptance of the offer by the disinterested directors which failed to meet the standards of the business judgment rule, or an acceptance by the disinterested shareholders which was the equivalent of a waste of corporate assets would have the same effect as an unreasonable failure to reject. The corporate fiduciary could appropriate the opportunity only upon a showing that the taking was fair to the corporation. See ALI, Principles of Corporate Governance and Structure § 5.12(a)(2) (Tent.Draft No. 3 1984).

(5) Lundgren did not attempt to obtain the consent of Berlinair to his taking of the BFR corporate opportunity.

(6) Lundgren did not fully disclose to Berlinair his intent to appropriate the opportunity for himself and ABC.

(7) Berlinair never rejected the opportunity presented by the BFR contract.

(8) Berlinair never ratified the appropriation of the BFR contract.

(9) Lundgren, acting for ABC, misappropriated the BFR contract.

Because of the above, the defendant may not now contend that Berlinair did not have the financial ability to successfully pursue the BFR contract. As stated in proposed Section 5.12(c) of the Principles of Corporate Governance, supra, "If the challenging party satisfies the burden of proving that a corporate opportunity was taken without being offered to the corporation, the challenging party will prevail."

* * *

The Court of Appeals is affirmed.

Notes

For discussions of the corporate opportunity doctrine, see Chew, Competing Interests in the Corporate Opportunity Doctrine, 67 N.C.L.Rev. 435 (1989); Comment, The Corporate Opportunity Doctrine and Outside Business Interests, 56 U.Chi.L.Rev. 827 (1989).

C. IMPARTIALITY

ZAHN v. TRANSAMERICA CORP.
United States Court of Appeals, Third Circuit, 1947.
162 F.2d 36.

BIGGS, CIRCUIT JUDGE.

Zahn, a holder of Class A common stock of Axton–Fisher Tobacco Company, a corporation of Kentucky, sued Transamerica Corporation, a Delaware company, on his own behalf and on behalf of all stockholders similarly situated, in the District Court of the United States for the District of Delaware. His complaint as amended asserts that Transamerica caused Axton–Fisher to redeem its Class A stock at $80.80 per share on July 1, 1943, instead of permitting the Class A stockholders to participate in the assets on the liquidation of their company in June, 1944. He alleges in brief that if the Class A stockholders had been allowed to participate in the assets on liquidation of Axton–Fisher and had received their respective shares of the assets, he and the other Class A stockholders would have received $240 per share instead of $80.80. Zahn takes the position that he has two separate causes of action, one based on the Class A shares which were not turned back to the company for redemption; another based on the shares which were redeemed.[15] He prayed the court below to direct Transamerica to pay over to the shareholders who had not surrendered their stock the liquidation value and to pay over to those shareholders who had surrendered their stock the liquidation value less $80.80. Transamerica filed a motion to dismiss. The court below granted the motion holding that Zahn had failed to state a cause of action. See 63 F.Supp. 243. He appealed.

The facts follow as appear from the pleadings, which recite provisions of Axton–Fisher's charter. Prior to April 30, 1943, Axton–Fisher had authorized and outstanding three classes of stock, designated respectively as preferred stock, Class A stock and Class B stock. Each share of preferred stock had a par value of $100 and was entitled to cumulative dividends at the rate of $6 per annum and possessed a liquidation value of $105 plus accrued dividends. The Class A stock, specifically described in the charter as a "common" stock, was entitled to an annual cumulative dividend of $3.20 per share. The Class B stock was next entitled to receive an annual dividend of $1.60 per share. If further funds were made available by action of the board of directors by way of dividends, the Class A stock and the Class B stock were entitled to share equally therein. Upon liquidation of the company and the payment of the sums required by the preferred stock, the Class A stock was entitled to share with the Class B stock in the distribution of the remaining assets, but the Class A stock was entitled to receive twice as much per share as the Class B stock.[16]

Each share of Class A stock was convertible at the option of the shareholder into one share of Class B stock. All or any of the shares of Class A stock were callable by the corporation at any quarterly dividend date upon sixty days' notice to the shareholders, at $60 per share with accrued dividends.[17] The voting rights were vested in the Class B

15. [By the Court] The plaintiff was originally the holder of 235 shares of Class A stock purchased on four occasions between July 23 and August 10, 1943, inclusive. Between August 2 and August 20, 1943, the plaintiff surrendered for redemption 215 shares and retained 20 shares.

16. [By the Court] The charter provides as follows:

"In the event of the dissolution, liquidation, merger or consolidation of the corporation, or sale of substantially all its assets, whether voluntary or involuntary, there shall be paid to the holders of the preferred stock then outstanding $105 per share, together with all unpaid accrued dividends thereon, before any sum shall be paid to or any assets distributed among the holders of the Class A common stock and/or the holders of the Class B common stock. After such payment to the holders of the preferred stock, and all unpaid accrued dividends on the Class A common stock shall have been paid, then all remaining assets and funds of the corporation shall be divided among and paid to the holders of the Class A common stock and to the holders of the Class B common stock in the ratio of 2 to 1; that is to say, there shall be paid upon each share of Class A common stock twice the amount paid upon each share of Class B common stock, in any such event."

17. [By the Court] The charter provides as follows:

"The whole or any part of the Class A common stock of the corporation, at the option of the Board of Directors, may be redeemed on any quarterly dividend payment date by paying therefor in cash Sixty dollars ($60.00) per share and all unpaid and accrued dividends thereon at the date fixed for such redemption, upon sending by mail to the registered holders of the Class A common stock at least

stock but if there were four successive defaults in the payment of quarterly dividends, the class or classes of stock as to which such defaults occurred gained voting rights equal share for share with the Class B stock. By reason of this provision the Class A stock had possessed equal voting rights with the Class B stock since on or about January 1, 1937.

On or about May 16, 1941, Transamerica purchased 80,160 shares of Axton–Fisher's Class B common stock. This was about 71.5% of the outstanding Class B stock and about 46.7% of the total voting stocks of Axton–Fisher. By August 15, 1942, Transamerica owned 5,332 shares of Class A stock and 82,610 shares of Class B stock. By March 31, 1943, the amount of Class A stock of Axton–Fisher owned by Transamerica had grown to 30,168 shares or about 66⅔% of the total amount of this stock outstanding, and the amount of Class B stock owned by Transamerica had increased to 90,768 shares or about 80% of the total outstanding. Additional shares of Class B stock were acquired by Transamerica after April 30, 1943, and Transamerica converted the Class A stock owned by it into Class B stock so that on or about the end of May, 1944 Transamerica owned virtually all of the outstanding Class B stock of Axton–Fisher. Since May 16, 1941, Transamerica had control of and had dominated the management, directorate, financial policies, business and affairs of Axton–Fisher. Since the date last stated Transamerica had elected a majority of the board of directors of Axton–Fisher. These individuals are in large part officers or agents of Transamerica.

In the fall of 1942 and in the spring of 1943 Axton–Fisher possessed as its principal asset leaf tobacco which had cost it about $6,361,981. This asset was carried on Axton–Fisher's books in that amount. The value of leaf tobacco had risen sharply and, to quote the words of the complaint, "unbeknown to the public holders of * * * Class A common stock of Axton–Fisher, but known to Transamerica, the market value of * * * [the] tobacco had, in March and April of 1943, attained the huge sum of about $20,000,000."

The complaint then alleges the gist of the plaintiff's grievance, viz., that Transamerica, knowing of the great value of the tobacco which Axton–Fisher possessed, conceived a plan to appropriate the value of the tobacco to itself by redeeming the Class A stock at the price of $60 a share plus accrued dividends, the redemption being made to appear as if "incident to the continuance of the business of Axton–Fisher as a going concern," and thereafter, the redemption of the Class A stock being completed, to liquidate Axton–Fisher; that this would result, after the disbursal of the sum required to be paid to the preferred stock,

sixty (60) days' notice of the exercise of such option. If at any time the Board of Directors shall determine to redeem less than the whole amount of Class A common stock then outstanding, the particular stock to be so redeemed shall be determined in such manner as the Board of Directors shall prescribe; provided, however, that no holder of Class A common stock shall be preferred over any other holder of such stock."

in Transamerica gaining for itself most of the value of the warehouse tobacco. The complaint further alleges that in pursuit of this plan Transamerica, by a resolution of the Board of Directors of Axton–Fisher on April 30, 1943, called the Class A stock at $60 and, selling a large part of the tobacco to Phillip–Morris Company, Ltd., Inc., together with substantially all of the other assets of Axton–Fisher, thereafter liquidated Axton–Fisher, paid off the preferred stock and pocketed the balance of the proceeds of the sale. Warehouse receipts representing the remainder of the tobacco were distributed to the Class B stockholders. * * *

[The Court concludes that the law of Kentucky determines the scope of duties of the directors of Axton–Fisher, and quotes extensively from Taylor v. Axton–Fisher Tobacco Co., 295 Ky. 226, 173 S.W.2d 377, (1943) (a case involving another facet of the transaction in question) and other cases from Kentucky and other jurisdictions involving the fiduciary duties of directors.]

It is appropriate to emphasize at this point that the right to call the Class A stock for redemption was confided by the charter of Axton–Fisher to the directors and not to the stockholders of that corporation. We must also re-emphasize the statement * * * that there is a radical difference when a stockholder is voting strictly as a stockholder and when voting as a director; that when voting as a stockholder he may have the legal right to vote with a view of his own benefits and to represent himself only; but that when he votes as a director he represents all the stockholders in the capacity of a trustee for them and cannot use his office as a director for his personal benefit at the expense of the stockholders.

Two theories are presented on one of which the case at bar must be decided: One, vigorously asserted by Transamerica and based on its interpretation of the decision in the Taylor case, is that the board of directors of Axton–Fisher, whether or not dominated by Transamerica, the principal Class B stockholder, at any time and for any purpose, might call the Class A stock for redemption; the other, asserted with equal vigor by Zahn, is that the board of directors of Axton–Fisher as fiduciaries were not entitled to favor Transamerica, the Class B stockholder, by employing the redemption provisions of the charter for its benefit.

We must of course treat the decision of the Court of Appeals of Kentucky in the Taylor case as evidence of what is the law of Kentucky. The Court took the position on that record that the directors at any time might call the Class A stock for redemption and that the redemption provision of the charter was written as much for the benefit of the Class B stock as for the Class A stock. It is argued by Transamerica very persuasively that what the Court of Appeals of Kentucky held was that when the Class A stock received its allocation of $60 a share plus accrued dividends it received its full due and that the directors had the right at any time to eliminate Class A stock from the corporate setup for the benefit of the Class B stock. It does not appear from the opinion of the Court of Appeals of Kentucky whether or not the subsequent liquidation of Axton–Fisher was brought to the attention of the Court. * * *

The difficulty in accepting Transamerica's contentions in the case at bar is that the directors of Axton–Fisher, if the allegations of the complaint be accepted as true, were the instruments of Transamerica, were directors voting in favor of their special interest, that of Transamerica, could not and did not exercise an independent judgment in calling the Class A stock, but made the call for the purpose of profiting their true principal, Transamerica. In short a puppet-puppeteer relationship existed between the directors of Axton–Fisher and Transamerica.

The act of the board of directors in calling the Class A stock, an act which could have been legally consummated by a disinterested board of directors, was here effected at the direction of the principal Class B stockholder in order to profit it. Such a call is voidable in equity at the instance of a stockholder injured thereby. It must be pointed out that under the allegations of the complaint there was no reason for the redemption of the Class A stock to be followed by the liquidation of Axton–Fisher except to enable the Class B stock to profit at the expense of the Class A stock. As has been hereinbefore stated the function of the call was confided to the board of directors by the charter and was not vested by the charter in the stockholders of any class. It was the intention of the framers of Axton–Fisher's charter to require the board of directors to act disinterestedly if that body called the Class A stock, and to make the call with a due regard for its fiduciary obligations. If the allegations of the complaint be proved, it follows that the directors of Axton–Fisher, the instruments of Transamerica, have been derelict in that duty. Liability which flows from the dereliction must be imposed upon Transamerica which, under the allegations of the complaint, constituted the board of Axton–Fisher and controlled it. * * *

As has been stated the plaintiff has endeavored to set up a "First Cause of Action" and a "Second Cause of Action" in his complaint. The first cause of action is based upon his ownership of shares of Class A stock not surrendered by him to Axton–Fisher for redemption and is asserted not only on his own behalf but also on behalf of other Class A stockholders retaining their stock. The second cause of action is asserted by him on his own behalf and on behalf of other Class A stockholders in respect to the value of the stock which was surrendered for redemption. The two alleged separate causes of action, however, are in reality one. In our opinion, if the allegations of the complaint be proved, Zahn may maintain his cause of action to recover from Transamerica the value of the stock retained by him as that shall be represented by its aliquot share of the proceeds of Axton–Fisher on dissolution. It is also our opinion that he may maintain a cause of action to recover the difference between the amount received by him for the shares already surrendered and the amount which he would have received on liquidation of Axton–Fisher if he had not surrendered his stock. * * *

The judgment will be reversed.

SPEED v. TRANSAMERICA CORP.

United States Court of Appeals, Third Circuit, 1956.
235 F.2d 369.

Maris, Circuit Judge. * * *

In the Zahn and Friedman actions the district court found that Transamerica had exercised its position as controlling stockholder to cause the board of directors of Axton–Fisher to call the Class A stock for redemption and that although Transamerica at that time knew that the board was doing so on the assumption that it was for the purpose of improving the capital structure of the company as a going concern, the real purpose of Transamerica in causing the call to be made was by liquidation, merger, consolidation or sale of Axton–Fisher's assets to gain for itself the appreciation in the value of those assets. Accordingly the district court held Transamerica accountable to the Class A stockholders, both those who had redeemed their stock pursuant to the call and those who had not done so. * * * The court found that a disinterested board of directors of Axton–Fisher would undoubtedly have exercised its powers to call the Class A stock before liquidation, disclosing the intention to liquidate together with full information as to the appreciated value of Axton–Fisher's tobacco inventory, and that the Class A stockholders would thereupon have exercised their privilege to convert their stock, share for share, into Class B stock and would thus have participated equally with the Class B stockholders in the proceeds of the liquidation. Applying this rule in the Friedman and Zahn cases, after deducting the sum of $80.80 per share received by the Class A stockholders or set aside for them on the redemption call of April 30, 1943, the court found those stockholders entitled to $21.02 per share. Judgments were entered in favor of the stockholders * * * Speed v. Transamerica Corporation, D.C.1955, 135 F.Supp. 176. All the parties have appealed. Transamerica appeals from the judgments, categorically denying any liability. The Class A stockholders appeal from the judgments insofar as the liquidation proceeds were to be shared equally with the Class B stockholders. * * *

The Court of Appeals of Kentucky has held that the Axton–Fisher Class A stock, although designated as a common stock was in the nature of a junior preferred stock, and that the provision of the charter for the redemption of the Class A stock was a continuing option allowed to the holders of the Class B common stock which the board of directors could exercise in their favor. This construction of the Axton–Fisher charter by the highest court of the state of its incorporation was, of course, binding on the district court. We agree with the district court that the provisions of the Axton–Fisher charter with respect to liquidation must be read realistically with the provisions for redemption of the Class A stock and its conversion into Class B stock. When so read it becomes apparent that a disinterested board of directors discharging its responsibility to the Class B stockholders in case of liquidation would call the Class A stock for redemption at $60 per share if it appeared that the distribution in liquidation to that stock would exceed that figure on a two-to-one basis. Since the board would have the right to do this and the Class B stockholders would be entitled to such action, the failure to do so would be an arbitrary act which would confer a windfall to which they were not entitled under the charter upon the Class A stockholders at the direct expense of the holders of the Class B stock. The district court was therefore quite right in determining that the damages to be awarded to the Class A stockholders should be measured by what they would have received if they had converted their shares into Class B stock prior to the liquidation. The subject was very fully discussed by Chief Judge Leahy in his opinion upon the question of damages. D.C., 135 F.Supp. 176, 180–185. Finding ourselves in accord with what is there said we need only add that our prior decision in the Zahn case does not stand in the way since this particular question was not then in focus. * * *

Notes

(1) Considering the manner in which damages were ultimately computed, what precisely was the duty that was breached in this case?

(2) Where convertible securities are called, the general practice of corporations is to give notice and precise information as to which course is most desirable for shareholders under the circumstances. *Zahn* is atypical in this respect. Van Gemert v. Boeing Co., 520 F.2d 1373, cert. denied 423 U.S. 947, 96 S.Ct. 364, 46 L.Ed.2d 282 (1975), also held inadequate a notice of redemption. The facts of this case were summarized as follows in a subsequent Supreme Court decision affirming the allowance of plaintiffs' counsel fees:

> In March 1966, The Boeing Company called for the redemption of certain convertible debentures. Boeing announced the call through newspaper notices and mailings to investors who had registered their debentures. The notices, given in accordance with the indenture agreement, recited that each $100 amount of principal could be redeemed for $103.25 or converted into two shares of the Company's common stock. They set March 29 as the deadline for the exercise of conversion rights. Two shares of the Company's common stock on that date were worth $316.25. When the deadline expired, the holders of debentures with a face value of $1,544,300 had not answered the call. These investors were left with the right to redeem their debentures for slightly more than face value.

Boeing Co. v. Van Gemert, 444 U.S. 472, 474, 100 S.Ct. 745, 747, 62 L.Ed.2d 676 (1980). Boeing literally complied with the notice requirements of the indenture and the requirements of the New York Stock Exchange. But this was not enough:

> The duty of reasonable notice arises out of the contract between Boeing and the debenture holders, pursuant to which Boeing was exercising its right to redeem the debentures. An issuer of debentures has a duty to give adequate notice either on the face of the debentures, Abramson v. Burroughs Corp., (S.D.N.Y.1972) (Lumbard, C.J., sitting by designation), or in some other way, of the notice to be provided in the event the company decides to redeem the debentures. Absent such advice as to the specific notice agreed upon by the issuer and the trustee for the debenture holders, the debenture holders' reasonable expectations as to notice should be protected.

> For less sophisticated investors * * * putting the notice provisions only in the 113–page Indenture Agreement was effectively no notice at all. It was not reasonable for Boeing to expect these investors to send off for, and then to read understandingly, the 113–page Indenture Agreement referred to in both the prospectus and the debentures themselves in order to find out what notice would be provided in the event of redemption.

> Boeing could very easily have run more than two advertisements in a single paper prior to the eleventh hour (March 28), at which time it issued its belated news release and advertised for the third time in the Wall Street Journal and for the first time in the New York Times. Moreover, in the same period that the debentures were in the process of being redeemed, Boeing was preparing for its annual meeting (to be held April 24). Proxy materials were being prepared throughout March and were finally mailed sometime between March 24 and March 30. Management could readily have arranged the redemption dates and the proxy mailing so that notice of the redemption dates could have been included in the envelope with the proxy materials. Thus at no extra cost except that of printing brief notices, at least all Boeing shareholders would have received mail notice, and presumably a significant number of the plaintiff class owned Boeing common stock, as well as debentures, in 1966. Had Boeing attempted such mail notice, or mail notice to original subscribers, and also given further newspaper publicity either by appropriate news releases or advertising earlier in the redemption period, we would have a different case and reasonable and sufficient notice might well be found.

Van Gemert v. Boeing Co., 520 F.2d 1373, at 1383–1384 (2d Cir.1975). "[A]lmost all" of the newspaper notices actually published "were in fine print, buried in the multitude of information and data published about the financial markets and scarcely of a kind to attract the eye of the average lay investor or debenture holder." Id. at 1379. For an essentially inconsistent decision, see Meckel v. Continental Resources Co., 758 F.2d 811 (2d Cir. 1985).

Chapter Twelve

STRUGGLES FOR CONTROL

A. PROXY FIGHTS

A proxy contest is a struggle for control of a public corporation in which most of the high cards are usually held by management.[1] In a traditional proxy contest, a non-management group (usually referred to as "insurgents") competes with management in an effort to obtain sufficient proxies to elect a majority of the board of directors and thereby obtain control. Management has several advantages in such a fight: (1) it has the current list of shareholders, while the insurgents may have to go to court to get it; (2) within a broad range, management may finance its solicitation from the assets of the corporation, while the insurgents must finance their campaign from outside sources; and (3) shareholders may have a pro-management bias, since those who are dissatisfied presumably have sold their shares previously. However, despite these disadvantages, proxy fights do occur with some regularity.

In a traditional proxy fight, an insurgent group, desiring to contest management control, usually first purchases a block of shares in the open market before openly announcing its intentions. It must then obtain a list of the shareholders in order to conduct a political campaign to persuade shareholders to cast proxies in its favor. Specialized proxy contest firms are available to assist either management or the insurgents in the campaign. Large shareholders may be courted individually; with the modern growth of institutional investors, support from this segment of the financial community is usually essential if a bid for control is to have a chance of succeeding. The process can be expensive.

Traditional proxy fights are usually not viewed as feasible in the very large corporation with hundreds of thousands of shareholders, since the cost of solicitation is prohibitive. This may not be as true today as it was twenty years ago, because of the growth of institutional

1. See generally Aranow and Einhorn, Proxy Contests for Corporate Control (2d Ed.1968).

ownership and the tendency of institutional investors to concentrate their holdings in the largest publicly held corporations.

ROSENFELD v. FAIRCHILD ENGINE AND AIRPLANE CORP.

Court of Appeals of New York, 1955.
309 N.Y. 168, 128 N.E.2d 291.

FROESSEL, JUDGE.

In a stockholder's derivative action brought by plaintiff, an attorney, who owns 25 out of the company's over 2,300,000 shares, he seeks to compel the return of $261,522, paid out of the corporate treasury to reimburse both sides in a proxy contest for their expenses. The Appellate Division, 284 App.Div. 201, 132 N.Y.S.2d 273, has unanimously affirmed a judgment of an Official Referee, Sup., 116 N.Y.S.2d 840, dismissing plaintiff's complaint on the merits, and we agree. * * *

Of the amount in controversy $106,000 was spent out of corporate funds by the old board of directors while still in office in defense of their position in said contest; $28,000 were paid to the old board by the new board after the change of management following the proxy contest, to compensate the former directors for such of the remaining expenses of their unsuccessful defense as the new board found was fair and reasonable; payment of $127,000, representing reimbursement of expenses to members of the prevailing group, was expressly ratified by a 16 to 1 majority vote of the stockholders.

The essential facts are not in dispute, and, since the determinations below are amply supported by the evidence, we are bound by the findings affirmed by the Appellate Division. The Appellate Division found that the difference between plaintiff's group and the old board "went deep into the policies of the company," and that among these Ward's contract was one of the "main points of contention". The Official Referee found that the controversy "was based on an understandable difference in policy between the two groups, at the very bottom of which was the Ward employment contract" [116 N.Y.S.2d 844].

By way of contrast with the findings here, in Lawyers' Advertising Co. v. Consolidated Ry., Lighting & Refrigerating Co., 187 N.Y. 395, at page 399, 80 N.E. 199, at page 200, which was an action to recover for the cost of publishing newspaper notices not authorized by the board of directors, it was expressly found that the proxy contest there involved was "by one faction in its contest with another for the control of the corporation * * * a contest for the perpetuation of their offices and control." We there said by way of *dicta* that under *such* circumstances the publication of certain notices on behalf of the management faction was not a corporate expenditure which the directors had the power to authorize.

Other jurisdictions and our own lower courts have held that management may look to the corporate treasury for the reasonable expenses of soliciting proxies to defend its position in a bona fide policy contest. * * *

It should be noted that plaintiff does not argue that the aforementioned sums were fraudulently extracted from the corporation; indeed, his counsel conceded that "the charges were fair and reasonable", but denied "they were legal charges which may be reimbursed for". This is therefore not a case where a stockholder challenges specific items, which, on examination, the trial court may find unwarranted, excessive or otherwise improper. Had plaintiff made such objections here, the trial court would have been required to examine the items challenged.

If directors of a corporation may not in good faith incur reasonable and proper expenses in soliciting proxies in these days of giant corporations with vast numbers of stockholders, the corporate business might be seriously interfered with because of stockholder indifference and the difficulty of procuring a quorum, where there is no contest. In the event of a proxy contest, if the directors may not freely answer the challenges of outside groups and in good faith defend their actions with respect to corporate policy for the information of the stockholders, they and the corporation may be at the mercy of persons seeking to wrest control for their own purposes, so long as such persons have ample funds to conduct a proxy contest. The test is clear. When the directors act in good faith in a contest over policy, they have the right to incur reasonable and proper expenses for solicitation of proxies and in defense of their corporate policies, and are not obliged to sit idly by. The courts are entirely competent to pass upon their bona fides in any given case, as well as the nature of their expenditures when duly challenged.

It is also our view that the members of the so-called new group could be reimbursed by the corporation for their expenditures in this contest by affirmative vote of the stockholders. With regard to these ultimately successful contestants, as the Appellate Division below has noted, there was, of course, "no duty * * * to set forth the facts, with corresponding obligation of the corporation to pay for such expense." However, where a majority of the stockholders chose—in this case by a vote of 16 to 1—to reimburse the successful contestants for achieving the very end sought and voted for by them as owners of the corporation, we see no reason to deny the effect of their ratification nor to hold the corporate body powerless to determine how its own moneys shall be spent.

The rule then which we adopt is simply this: In a contest over policy, as compared to a purely personal power contest, corporate directors have the right to make reasonable and proper expenditures, subject to the scrutiny of the courts when duly challenged, from the corporate treasury for the purpose of persuading the stockholders of the correctness of their position and soliciting their support for policies which the directors believe, in all good faith, are in the best interests of the corporation. The stockholders, moreover, have the right to reimburse successful contestants for the reasonable and bona fide expenses incurred by them in any such policy contest, subject to like court scrutiny. That is not to say, however, that corporate directors can, under any circumstances, disport themselves in a proxy contest with the corporation's moneys to an unlimited extent. Where it is established that such moneys have been spent for personal power, individual gain or private advantage, and not in the belief that such expenditures are in the best interests of the stockholders and the corporation, or where the fairness and reasonableness of the amounts allegedly expended are duly and successfully challenged, the courts will not hesitate to disallow them.

The judgment of the Appellate Division should be affirmed, without costs.

DESMOND, JUDGE (concurring).

We granted leave to appeal in an effort to pass, and in the expectation of passing, on this question, highly important in modern-day corporation law: is it lawful for a corporation, on consent of a majority of its stockholders, to pay, out of its funds, the expenses of a "proxy fight", incurred by competing candidates for election as directors? Now that the appeal has been argued, I doubt that the question is presented by this record. The defendants served were Allis who was on the old board but was re-elected to the new board, McComas and Wilson, defeated members of the old board, and Fairchild, leader of the victorious group and largest stockholder in the corporation. The expenses of the old board, or management group, in the proxy fight, were about $134,000, and those of the victorious Fairchild group amounted to about $127,500. In the end, the corporation paid both those sums, and it is for the reimbursement thereof, to the corporation, that this stockholder's derivative action is brought. Of the proxy fight expenses of the management slate, about $106,000 was paid out on authorization of the old board while the old directors were still in office. The balance of those charges, as well as the whole of the expenses of the new and successful, Fairchild group, was paid by the corporation after the new directors had taken over and after a majority of stockholders had approved such expenditures. The election had been fought out on a number of issues, chief of which concerned a contract which Ward (a defendant not served), who was a director and the principal executive officer of the company, had obtained from the corporation, covering compensation for, and other conditions of, his own services. Each side, in the campaign for proxies, charged the other with seeking to perpetuate, or grasp, control of the corporation. The Fairchild group won the election by a stock vote of about two-to-one, and obtained, at the next annual stockholders' meeting and by a much larger vote, authorization to make the payments above described.

Plaintiff asserts that it was illegal for the directors (unless by unanimous consent of stockholders) to expend corporate moneys in the proxy contest beyond the amounts necessary to give to stockholders bare notice of the meeting and of the matters to be voted on thereat. Defendants say that the proxy contest revolved around disputes over corporate policies and that it was, accordingly, proper not only to assess against the corporation the expense of serving formal notices and of routine proxy solicitation, but to go further and spend corporate moneys, on behalf of each group, thoroughly to inform the stockholders. The reason why that important question is, perhaps, not directly before us in this lawsuit is because, as the Appellate Division properly held, [284 App.Div. 201, 132 N.Y.S.2d 280] plaintiff failed "to urge liability as to specific expenditures". The cost of giving routinely necessary notice is, of course, chargeable to the corporation. It is just as clear, we think, that payment by a corporation of the expense of "proceedings by one faction in its contest with another for the control of the corporation" is ultra vires, and unlawful. Lawyers' Advertising Co. v. Consolidated Ry., Lighting & Refrigerating Co., 187 N.Y. 395, 399, 80 N.E. 199, 200. Approval by directors or by a majority stock vote could not validate such gratuitous expenditures. Some of the payments attacked in this suit were, on their face, for lawful purposes and apparently reasonable in amount but, as to others, the record simply does not contain evidentiary bases for a determination as to either lawfulness or reasonableness. Surely, the burden was on plaintiff to go forward to some extent with such particularization and proof. It failed to do so, and so failed to make out a prima facie case.

We are, therefore, reaching the same result as did the Appellate Division but on only one of the grounds listed by that court, that is, failure of proof. We think it not inappropriate, however, to state our general views on the question of law principally argued by the parties, that is, as to the validity of corporate payments for proxy solicitations and similar activities in addition to giving notice of the meeting, and of the questions to be voted on. For an answer to that problem we could not do better than quote from this court's opinion in the Lawyers' Advertising Co. case, 187 N.Y. 395, 399, 80 N.E. 199, 200, supra: "The remaining notices were not legally authorized and were not legitimately incidental to the meeting or necessary for the protection of the stockholders. They rather were proceedings by one faction in its contest with another for the control of the corporation, and the expense thereof, as such, is not properly chargeable to the latter. This is so apparent as to the last two notices that nothing need be said in reference to them; but a few words may be said in regard to the first one, calling for proxies. It is to be noted that this is not the case of an ordinary circular letter sent out with and requesting the execution of proxies. The custom has become common upon the part of corporations to mail proxies to their respective stockholders, often accompanied by a brief circular of directions, and such custom when accompanied by no unreasonable expenditure, is not without merit in so far as it encourages voting by stockholders, through making it convenient and ready at hand. The notice in question, however, was not published until after

proxies had been sent out. It simply amounted to an urgent solicitation that these proxies should be executed and returned for use by one
faction in its contest, and we think there is no authority for imposing
the expense of its publication upon the company. * * * it would be
altogether too dangerous a rule to permit directors in control of a
corporation and engaged in a contest for the perpetuation of their
offices and control, to impose upon the corporation the unusual expense
of publishing advertisements or, by analogy, of dispatching special
messengers for the purpose of procuring proxies in their behalf."

A final comment: since expenditures which do not meet that test of
propriety are intrinsically unlawful, it could not be any answer to such
a claim as plaintiff makes here that the stockholder vote which purported to authorize them was heavy or that the change in management
turned out to be beneficial to the corporation.

The judgment should be affirmed, without costs.

VAN VOORHIS, JUDGE (dissenting).

* * * The Appellate Division held that stockholder authorization
or ratification was not necessary to reasonable expenditures by the
management group, the purpose of which was to inform the stockholders concerning the affairs of the corporation, and that, although these
incumbents spent or incurred obligations of $133,966 (the previous
expenses of annual meetings of this corporation ranging between $7,000
and $28,000), plaintiff must fail for having omitted to distinguish item
by item between which of these expenditures were warranted and
which ones were not; and the Appellate Division held that the insurgents also should be reimbursed, but subject to the qualification that
"The expenses of those who were seeking to displace the management
should not be reimbursed by the corporation except upon approval by
the stockholders." It was held that the stockholders had approved.

No resolution was passed by the stockholders approving payment to
the management group. It has been recognized that not all of the
$133,966 in obligations paid or incurred by the management group was
designed merely for information of stockholders. This outlay included
payment for all of the activities of a strenuous campaign to persuade
and cajole in a hard-fought contest for control of this corporation. It
included, for example, expenses for entertainment, chartered airplanes
and limousines, public relations counsel and proxy solicitors. However
legitimate such measures may be on behalf of stockholders themselves
in such a controversy, most of them do not pertain to a corporate
function but are part of the familiar apparatus of aggressive factions in
corporate contests. * * * [The Judge here quotes from Lawyers'
Advertising Co. v. Consolidated Ry., Lighting & Refrigerating Co., 187
N.Y. 395, 399, 80 N.E. 199, 201.]

The Appellate Division acknowledged in the instant case that "It is
obvious that the management group here incurred a substantial
amount of needless expense which was charged to the corporation," but
this conclusion should have led to a direction that those defendants who

were incumbent directors should be required to come forward with an explanation of their expenditures under the familiar rule that where it has been established that directors have expended corporate money for their own purposes, the burden of going forward with evidence of the propriety and reasonableness of specific items rests upon the directors. The complaint should not have been dismissed as against incumbent directors due to failure of plaintiff to segregate the specific expenditures which are *ultra vires,* but, once plaintiff had proved facts from which an inference of impropriety might be drawn, the duty of making an explanation was laid upon the directors to explain and justify their conduct.

The second ground assigned by the Appellate Division for dismissing the complaint against incumbent directors is stockholder ratification of reimbursement to the insurgent group. Whatever effect or lack of it this resolution had upon expenditures by the insurgent group, clearly the stockholders who voted to pay the insurgents entertained no intention of reimbursing the management group for their expenditures. The insurgent group succeeded as a result of arousing the indignation of these very stockholders against the management group; nothing in the resolution to pay the expenses of the insurgent group purported to authorize or ratify payment of the campaign expenses of their adversaries, and certainly no inference should be drawn that the stockholders who voted to pay the insurgents intended that the incumbent group should also be paid. Upon the contrary, they were removing the incumbents from control mainly for the reason that they were charged with having mulcted the corporation by a long-term salary and pension contract to one of their number, J. Carlton Ward, Jr. If these stockholders had been presented with a resolution to pay the expenses of that group, it would almost certainly have been voted down. The stockholders should not be deemed to have authorized or ratified reimbursement of the incumbents. * * *

Regarding the $127,556 paid by the new management to the insurgent group for their campaign expenditures, the question immediately arises whether that was for a corporate purpose. The Appellate Division has recognized that upon no theory could such expenditures be reimbursed except by approval of the stockholders and, as has been said, it is the insurgents' expenditures alone to which the stockholders' resolution of ratification was addressed. If *unanimous* stockholder approval had been obtained and no rights of creditors or of the public intervened, it would make no practical difference whether the purpose were *ultra vires*—i.e., not a corporate purpose. Upon the other hand, an act which is *ultra vires* cannot be ratified merely by a majority of the stockholders of a corporation. * * *

[W]ith the exception of an English decision, Peel v. London & North Western Ry. Co., [1907] 1 Ch. 5, all of the appellate court cases which have been cited, and Steinberg v. Adams, [90 F.Supp. 604 (S.D. N.Y.1950)] were decided under the law of the State of Delaware. The

Delaware law contains more latitude than in New York State * * *. We are called upon to decide whether to abandon the rule as previously established in this State and adopt the less strict doctrine of the State of Delaware.

The Delaware cases which are cited consist of Hall v. Trans–Lux Daylight Picture Screen Corp., 20 Del.Ch. 78, 171 A. 226; Empire Southern Gas Co. v. Gray, 29 Del.Ch. 95, 46 A.2d 741, and the Federal cases applying Delaware law, Hand v. Missouri–Kansas Pipe Line Co., D.C., 54 F.Supp. 649, and Steinberg v. Adams, supra. * * * The case most frequently cited and principally relied upon from among these Delaware decisions is Hall v. Trans–Lux Daylight Picture Screen Corp., supra. There the English case was followed of Peel v. London & North Western Ry. Co., supra, which distinguished between expenses merely for the purpose of maintaining control, and contests over policy questions of the corporation. In the Hall case the issues concerned a proposed merger, and a proposed sale of stock of a subsidiary corporation. These were held to be policy questions, and payment of the management campaign expenses was upheld.

In our view, the impracticability of such a distinction is illustrated by the statement in the Hall case, supra, 20 Del.Ch. at page 85, 171 A. at page 229, that "It is impossible in many cases of intracorporate contests over directors, to sever questions of policy from those of persons". This circumstance is stressed in Judge Rifkind's opinion in the Steinberg case, supra, 90 F.Supp. at page 608: "The simple fact, of course, is that generally policy and personnel do not exist in separate compartments. A change in personnel is sometimes indispensable to a change of policy. A new board may be the symbol of the shift in policy as well as the means of obtaining it."

That may be all very well, but the upshot of this reasoning is that inasmuch as it is generally impossible to distinguish whether "policy" or "personnel" is the dominant factor, any averments must be accepted at their face value that questions of policy are dominant. Nowhere do these opinions mention that the converse is equally true and more pervasive, that neither the "ins" nor the "outs" ever say that they have no program to offer to the shareholders, but just want to acquire or to retain control, as the case may be. In common experience, this distinction is unreal. * * * As in political contests, aspirations for control are invariably presented under the guise of policy or principle. * * *

CONWAY, C.J., and BURKE, J., concur with FROESSEL, J.; DESMOND, J., concurs in part in a separate opinion; VAN VOORHIS, J., dissents in an opinion in which DYE and FULD, JJ., concur.

Judgment affirmed.

Notes

(1) Consider carefully the division of the Justices in *Rosenfeld* and the positions taken by them. What position is the Court going to take in the

next case when the plaintiff argues that specific expenses are improper? Rather surprisingly, there has not been "the next case", though the language of Judge Froessel has been quoted favorably in a few cases.

(2) As indicated in the dissenting opinion, Delaware has clearly adopted the "policy-personality" distinction, despite the difficulties pointed out in the application of the distinction. Is not the Delaware position really that "anything goes" in charging expenses to the corporation? See also Levin v. Metro–Goldwyn–Mayer, Inc., 264 F.Supp. 797 (S.D.N.Y.1967), applying Delaware law and not referring to *Rosenfeld*.

(3) It has been suggested that reimbursement should be permitted *un*successful insurgents since they may perform a socially useful function. Latcham and Emerson Proxy Contest Expenses and Shareholder Democracy, 4 Western Res.L.Rev. 5 (1952). What is the socially useful function? What kinds of restrictions and limitations need be built into such a plan to prevent its abuse by publicity seekers, cranks, corporate "raiders" and the like? Not surprisingly, there appears to be no instance where management has voluntarily made a payment to unsuccessful insurgents.

––––––––

The Securities and Exchange Commission has promulgated special regulations applicable to proxy contests in corporations subject to section 14. 17 C.F.R. § 240.14a–11 (1989). These regulations require "participants" other than management in a proxy contest to file specified information with the SEC and the securities exchanges at least five days before a solicitation begins. "Participant" is defined so as to include anyone who contributes more than $500 for the purpose of financing the contest. The information that must be disclosed relates to the identity and background of the participants, their interests in securities of the corporation, when they were acquired, financing arrangements, participation in other proxy contests, and understandings with respect to future employment with the corporation. The solicitation of majority consents is also subject to these third party proxy solicitation rules, as is a solicitation by an institutional investor to more than ten other institutional investors to sit in concert on a matter relating to shareholder voting.

The general philosophy of these contested proxy regulations is well expressed by Judge Clark of the Second Circuit:

> Appellants' fundamental complaint appears to be that stockholder disputes should be viewed in the eyes of the law just as are political contests, with each side free to hurl charges with comparative unrestraint, the assumption being that the opposing side is then at liberty to refute and thus effectively deflate the "campaign oratory" of its adversary. Such, however, was not the policy of Congress as enacted in the Securities Exchange Act. There Congress has clearly entrusted to the Commission the duty of protecting the investing public against misleading statements made in the course of a struggle for corporate control.

Securities and Exchange Commission v. May, 229 F.2d 123, 124 (2d Cir. 1956).

The number of proxy fights subject to SEC jurisdiction historically has been rather small. For example, only thirty-seven companies were involved in proxy contests for the election of directors in fiscal 1977. Control was involved in twenty-six instances; in eight of these management retained control, three were settled by negotiation, five were won by nonmanagement factions, and ten were pending at the end of the year. In eleven instances representation, not control, was sought; management retained all places on the board in six contests and opposition candidates won places on the board in five cases. 1977 S.E.C. Annual Report, at 107. Similar data is not available for more recent years.

B. TENDER OFFERS AND OTHER TAKEOVER TECHNIQUES

The growth of takeover techniques other than the classic proxy fight has been perhaps the most spectacular development in corporate and securities law since World War II. These techniques have been in part the product of a fundamental economic development: the growth of very large pools of capital which made purchase-type takeovers of publicly-held corporations feasible. In part, this growth may be traced to favorable federal income tax laws for corporations that permit many large and profitable corporations to pay little or no tax. In part, it may be traced to the growth of institutional investors. During the 1980s the development of a market for "junk bonds" allowed relatively small companies and even a few individuals to tap these pools to raise hundreds of millions or billions of dollars of capital to purchase publicly held corporations. [A "junk bond" is simply a debt instrument that is not of ordinary investment quality; carrying a high rate of return the expectation of a purchaser of a "junk bond" is that the assets and cash flow of the acquired corporation will be used to satisfy these bonds.] The social and economic justifications for such massive transactions, and the defenses interposed by target companies, has been one of the most controversial areas of modern corporation law, giving rise to an immense literature.

An appropriate starting point is a brief description of the classic cash tender offer as it was developed in the late 1960s, before meaningful governmental regulation was imposed on such offers and before large pools of capital had developed.

Essentially, a cash tender offer is a public invitation to the shareholders of the target corporation to tender their shares to the aggressor for purchase for cash. As developed during the 1960s, the offering price was set usually 15–20 per cent in excess of the then current market price. The aggressor sought enough shares to ensure working control of the target corporation, though sometimes the aggressor was seeking a higher percentage of, or all of, the outstanding shares. The aggressor usually made a public offer or invitation for tenders of shares under which it was not obligated to purchase any shares unless the required amount was tendered; if an excess was tendered the aggressor could, at its option, purchase the excess shares or purchase the required amount only on a pro rata or first-come/first-serve basis. The tender offer was usually made by an advertisement in the financial press, and copies were often mailed to all shareholders as well. The offer also usually provided a generous commission to brokers who persuaded customers to tender shares.

These takeover techniques developed in lieu of the classic proxy fight because the probability of success in proxy fights was perceived to be low. Initially, the probability of success of a tender offer appeared to be greater than a proxy fight in part because of the element of surprise. During this period, it was not uncommon for management of target companies to learn of the offer only when the Wall Street Journal blossomed with full page ads announcing the precise details of the offer. Offers often remained open for a brief period so that little time was available to incumbent management to respond and shareholders were panicked into tendering quickly lest they lose out on the offer entirely. Also, in a cash tender offer, the individual shareholder's decision tended to be an investment-type of decision rather than a choice between competing factions for control. The shareholder thought in terms of "I paid X for this stock, I am now offered Y. Should I sell?" Or, "Yesterday this stock was at $50; I am now offered $65. Should I sell?" On the other hand, in a proxy contest, the shareholder's choice was pretty clearly a choice between competing factions for the right to run the corporation in which he would have a continuing interest.

When a cash tender offer was made the open market price for the shares usually increased dramatically. (Whether it equaled or exceeded the tender offer price depended on a variety of factors, including the probability that a competing offer at a higher price might be made, whether the offer was likely to be over-subscribed, whether it was on a first-come/first-served basis, and so forth.) Persons owning shares thus had the choice of selling their shares in the open market, retaining them, or tendering them. Most shares sold on the open market ultimately were tendered. A group of speculators, known as arbitragers, or risk arbitragers, purchased shares in the open market at prices below the tender offer price in order to tender them and profit by the difference between the two prices. In some tender offers, the volume of transactions effected by arbitragers appeared to have been very substantial—involving 25 per cent or more of the tendered shares.

This classic picture of the tender offer was significantly modified by the 1969 enactment of the "Williams Act," which technically was an amendment to sections 13 and 14 of the Securities Exchange Act of 1934 and not an independent statutory enactment. The Williams Act combined full disclosure obligations with a set of "rules of fair play" in tender offers. For example, the Act required tender offers to remain open for at least 20 days and required that oversubscribed offers be taken up on a prorated rather than a "first come-first served" basis. Because of the economic pressures in the takeover area, however, considerable ingenuity has led to the development of a number of devices to avoid or minimize the impact of these rules of fair play. These devices, in turn have often been followed by decisions by the SEC to promulgate regulations designed to modify or eliminate the devices in question, by enactment of state statutes to limit some tactics by aggressors, and, most importantly, by innovative defensive tactics. The overall result of these developments has been the creation of a regulatory scheme for tender offers of increasing, and sometimes bewildering, complexity.

In an earlier era, an important variation of the cash tender offer was the public exchange offer where the aggressor offered to exchange a package of its own securities for the shares of the target. The package usually consisted of both debt and equity interests, and often included highly speculative warrants or options to acquire further equity interests in the aggressor. Such interests sometimes were referred to derogatorily as "funny money." Arbitragers were also active in public exchange offers, buying the target corporation's shares and at the same time selling short or on "when issued" basis the package of the aggressor's securities. While shareholders of the target corporation who accepted the aggressor's offer received securities rather than cash, the availability of a public market for the aggressor's securities permitted target shareholders to liquidate their positions promptly after the exchange was completed, though not always at the value claimed by the aggressor for the original package. In any event, cash tender offers and public exchange offers could be utilized by different aggressors seeking control of a single target corporation. For example, in the fight for Armour & Co. in the late 1960s, a cash tender offer by Greyhound Lines, Inc. was met with a public exchange offer by General Host Corporation.

In a broad sense, public exchange offers can be viewed as a type of financing device by aggressors. An aggressor might sell its own securities to create a pool of capital in order to make offers to shareholders of a target corporation to buy shares for cash. Alternatively, the aggressor might offer its own securities directly to the target shareholders in a public exchange offer, eliminating the cash-raising step and making the target shareholders the source of capital for the takeover.

Important changes in takeover practices occurred during the 1970s and 1980s. The underlying development that spurred these changes was the growth of huge pools of capital that could be readily tapped by aggressors in order to make all-cash offers for either working control or for all of the shares of increasingly large corporations. Furthermore, the providers of capital began to look to the cash flow of the target as the source of profit on takeovers.

During the late 1980s, both the size and number of transactions increased dramatically. The previously little known securities firm of Drexel Burnham Lambert Inc., and the investment firm of Kohlberg Kravis Roberts & Co. became highly visible major players with access to billions of dollars that were available for the purchase of large publicly owned corporations. Multi-billion dollar all-cash transactions became commonplace. The largest takeover transaction ever attempted—the leveraged buyout of RJR–Nabisco, Inc. by the KKR firm for $24.8 billion at the end of 1988—may reflect either the harbinger of even larger transactions in the future or the high point of a movement.

These developments during the 1970s and 1980s were themselves shaped by increased sophistication in defensive tactics—the world of poison pills, lockups, and sales of crown jewels—and the enactment by states of control share acquisition statutes. However, the modern leveraged buyout appears to be the logical outcome of the creation of huge pools of capital available for investment in takeover bids.

During the 1980s there were numerous contested proxy or consent solicitation campaigns in connection with purchase-type takeover attempts. There are several explanations for the increase in the use of proxy fights as an adjunct or auxiliary to the cash tender offer phenomenon. In some instances, the target was simply too big for the aggressor to finance the purchase of a majority of the shares. The aggressor may have financial resources to acquire only fifteen or twenty per cent of the outstanding equity; the aggressor may then launch a short term proxy fight in an effort to attract sufficient additional proxies to oust incumbent management without purchasing an outright majority of the voting stock or, at least, mount a viable proxy fight threat to encourage the target to negotiate. A well known example of this strategy was Carl Icahn's proxy fight against the incumbent management of Texaco, Inc. in 1986. In other instances, takeover defenses proved to be impregnable against an outside cash tender offer, and the aggressor attempted an end run by launching a proxy fight or consent solicitation in order to compel the removal of the defenses. See Why the Proxy Fight is Back, Business Week, March 7, 1988, at 32; Whose Company Is It Anyway? Proxy Fights are Spreading as Shareholders Seek More Power, Business Week, April 25, 1988, at 60. In yet another type of case, proxy fights or majority consent solicitations were launched in an effort to persuade a target corporation to enter into a recapitalization or financial restructuring that involved a large extraordinary distribution to shareholders. Such a proxy fight or consent solicitation was likely to succeed since it proposed a transaction that was financially attractive to shareholders generally as well as the aggressor in particular.

R. HAMILTON, FUNDAMENTALS OF MODERN BUSINESS *

Pp. 394, 396–7 (1989).

* * * [M]ost successful aggressors ultimately desire to acquire 100 percent of the outstanding shares of the target. However, it is not possible, as a practical matter, ever to acquire 100 percent of the shares of a publicly held corporation by a tender offer. Even in an irresistibly attractive tender offer for all shares, a few shareholders always fail to tender by reason of inadvertence or inattention, and there always are a few small shareholders who hold out and refuse to accept an offer at any price. A follow-up transaction to eliminate the remaining public shareholders is an essential step in all tender offers where 100 percent ownership is desired. These follow-up transactions by themselves are called *back-end* or *mop-up transactions.* Technically, they are statutory mergers. A back-end transaction is not necessary if the aggressor is willing to accept the status of a majority shareholder in a publicly held corporation with minority shareholders.

In a public cash tender offer the aggressor may make the back-end transaction an affirmative weapon. The aggressor may make a partial tender offer, seeking to acquire a controlling interest less than all of the target's outstanding shares, and at the same time announce, as part of its takeover strategy, the terms of the back-end merger that will eliminate all of the remaining outstanding shares if the original partial offer is successful. Such an offer is known as a *two-tier offer.* The terms of the back-end part of the two-tier offer, moreover, may be less attractive than the terms of the original cash tender offer, thereby encouraging (or coercing) all shareholders to tender promptly to avoid the less attractive terms of the follow-up transaction. Such an offer is known as a *front-end loaded offer* * * *.

HAMILTON, CORPORATE MERGERS AND ACQUISITIONS

The Guide to American Law Yearbook
1990, 66, 72–75.

Most acquisition transactions since 1985 have involved all-cash purchases of the stock of the target corporation. * * * Even transactions involving little-known companies routinely involve all-cash transactions of hundreds of millions of dollars. The amounts involved in these transactions are so large as to have been almost unimaginable in a private transaction just two decades ago. An important question is that of where all the money is coming from.

In one sense, the answer is very simple: Most of the capital that goes into modern takeover attempts is borrowed. Borrowed money is what makes the modern takeover world go round; if that source of

* Reprinted with permission of Little, Brown & Company.

funding disappeared, the present takeover movement would stop instantly. It is true that aggressors such as Conoco and Texaco have immense operations of their own and can accumulate large amounts of cash, but even companies of that size cannot readily finance a multibillion dollar takeover entirely from internal sources. It is not uncommon for more speculative purchasers to borrow virtually all of the capital needed to purchase a going company.

Loans from commercial banks are the source of most of the borrowed capital in large takeover bids, but other sources of high-risk financing also exist. During the 1980s, a market for high-risk, below-investment-grade debt instruments or "bonds," usually called "junk bonds," was largely created by Drexel Burnham Lambert, Inc. This market has grown to the point that it is able to absorb several billion dollars of high-risk debt to finance specific takeover bids. Many institutional investors are active in this market because junk bonds pay interest at rates considerably higher than can be obtained from the less risky "investment-grade" bonds.

In addition, a major source of equity capital has been created by takeover firms such as KKR, which has attracted takeover funds from sophisticated investors, including many institutional investors. The proposed financing by KKR of its purchase of RJR Nabisco illustrates the operation of these modern financing sources. KKR needed $20.1 billion in cash to purchase RJR. (The remaining $4.8 billion was represented by the debt securities being issued to tendering RJR shareholders.) KKR raised the $20.1 billion from the following sources:

1. Bank loans were obtained from a large consortium of domestic and foreign (largely Japanese) banks—$13.3 billion.

2. Five billion dollars in "bridge financing" was provided by the brokerage houses of Drexel Burnham Lambert, Inc. ($3.5 billion) and Merrill Lynch & Company ($1.5 billion). This bridge financing was to be refinanced within a year by the sale of junk bonds to investors.

3. KKR limited partners put up $1.5 billion in equity capital. KKR itself put up only $15 million, or 1 percent of the entire risk capital and a tiny fraction of the total purchase price. Altogether, KKR raised $25.7 billion to cover the purchase price and expenses but invested only about $15 million of its own capital in order to acquire the nation's nineteenth largest commercial enterprise!

Why do banks and others agree to make such large loans to fund buyouts? For one thing, the return is good—interest rates on both takeover-directed bank loans and junk bonds are well above those available from other alternative investments. For another thing, fees for making loan commitments are earned whether or not the sale actually occurs. In the RJR Nabisco transaction, Merrill Lynch & Company and Drexel Burnham Lambert, Inc., received fees of about $200 million for their commitment to invest $5 billion, while the banks received a somewhat larger amount in commitment fees for making their much larger commitments. These fees are earned and paid when the commitment is made and are not dependent on the success of the bid.

Yet when all is said and done, commitment fees and high interest rates alone do not explain the attractiveness of these loans. One does not make money even from large loan commitment fees and high interest rates if the loans are so risky that they are unlikely to be repaid. These transactions are attractive because the risks are not as great as they first appear. An essential attribute of the ability of KKR and other takeover firms to raise immense amounts of capital is that these loans are in effect secured by the assets and cash flow of the target corporation itself. Such transactions are called "leveraged buyouts" or "bootstrap transactions." Approximately one-half of the recent takeover transactions were of this type. The banks were willing to lend more than $13 billion to KKR to purchase RJR Nabisco common stock because they were assured that, if the transaction succeeded, the assets and cash flow of RJR Nabisco would be used to pay the interest on and secure the repayment of the loans and junk bonds used to finance the purchase.

Of course, RJR Nabisco already had some indebtedness on its books. The new debt was simply added onto this existing debt and it is expected to repay the entire amount. Needless to say, Nabisco's existing creditors were not happy at these new obligations being assumed by RJR Nabisco. Since the proceeds of the new loans were used to pay shareholders, they did not benefit RJR Nabisco, and loans owed to existing creditors now were less secure and considerably more risky. But there was not very much they could do about the transaction.

After a leveraged buyout, the target may find that its total debt obligations greatly exceed its ability to repay them if business is continued as usual. Such a corporation may find it necessary to make Herculean efforts to reduce costs and increase cash flow. It may be compelled to sell portions of its business to third parties in order to liquidate at least a portion of the new indebtedness and permit the corporation to remain solvent. Transactions in which such later sales of components of the original business are contemplated at the time of the offer are called "bust-up transactions" or "bust-up acquisitions." Improvements in earnings and cash flow may also be achieved from the savings inherent in not being a reporting publicly-held corporation, from the immense tax deductions arising from the interest payments on its debt, from the elimination of dividends, and from economic improvements to the target's business. Indeed, the disciplinary effect of the increase in debt has been cited by some observers as a major benefit arising from leveraged transactions since it encourages increased efficiency and control of costs.

Many established businesses that have been acquired in leveraged buyouts have proven that they are able to carry large increases of indebtedness during periods of high economic activity. However, the recent spate of multibillion dollar leveraged buyouts, bust-up transactions, and junk bond financing—because of the immense sums of money involved—has caused concern among regulatory agencies, legislators, and the general public. The principal concern that has been expressed about the growth of such leveraged transactions generally is whether most of these debt-burdened businesses can survive when there is an economic downturn. Since there was no significant downturn during the 1980s, no one really knows the answer to this question. A secondary concern that has sometimes been expressed is whether the large investments by commercial banks and institutional investors in leveraged buyout loans and investments may harm the public's confidence in the nation's financial institutions during an economic downturn. If such a downturn occurs, the future of the spectacular mergers and acquisitions examined here will be in grave doubt.

Notes

(1) Consider Jensen, Eclipse of the Public Corporation, 67 Harv.Bus. Rev., No. 5 (Sept.–Oct.1989) 61, 61–64 *:

> The publicly held corporation, the main engine of economic progress in the United States for a century, has outlived its usefulness in many sectors of the economy and is being eclipsed. New organizations are emerging in its place—organizations that are corporate in form but have no public shareholders and are not listed or traded on organized exchanges. These organizations use public and private debt, rather than public equity, as their major source of capital. Their primary owners are not households but large institutions and entrepreneurs that designate agents to manage and monitor on their behalf and bind those agents with large equity interests and contracts governing the use and distribution of cash.
>
> Takeovers, corporate breakups, divisional spin-offs, leveraged buyouts, and going-private transactions are the most visible manifestations of a massive organizational change in the economy. These transactions have inspired criticism, even outrage, among many business leaders and government officials, who have called for regulatory and legislative restrictions. The backlash is understandable. Change is threatening; in this case, the threat is aimed at the senior executives of many of our largest companies.
>
> Despite the protests, this organizational innovation should be encouraged. By resolving the central weakness of the public corporation—the conflict between owners and managers over the control and use of corporate resources—these new organizations are making remarkable gains in operating efficiency, employee productivity, and shareholder value. Over the long term, they will enhance U.S. economic performance relative to our most formidable international competitor, Japan, whose companies are moving in the opposite direction. The governance and financial structures of Japan's public companies

increasingly resemble U.S. companies of the mid–1960s and early 1970s—an era of gross corporate waste and mismanagement that triggered the organizational transformation now under way in the United States. * * *

Developments as striking as the restructuring of our financial markets and major industries reflect underlying economic forces more fundamental and powerful than financial manipulation, management greed, reckless speculation, and the other colorful epithets used by defenders of the corporate status quo. The forces behind the decline of the public corporation differ from industry to industry. But its decline is real, enduring, and highly productive. It is not merely a function of the tax deductibility of interest. Nor does it reflect a transitory LBO phase through which companies pass before investment bankers and managers cash out by taking them public again. Nor, finally, is it premised on a systematic fleecing of shareholders and bondholders by managers and other insiders with superior information about the true value of corporate assets.

Jensen's revolutionary view of the modern scene is more fully described in M. Jensen, Organizational Change and the Market for Corporate Control (1990).

(2) As this note is written early in 1990, it is impossible to predict whether Jensen's vision of a "new order" is accurate.

COFFEE, REGULATING THE MARKET FOR CORPORATE CONTROL, A CRITICAL ASSESSMENT OF THE TENDER OFFER'S ROLE IN CORPORATE GOVERNANCE *

84 Colum.L.Rev. 1145, 1162–1173 (1984).

Those who have sought to explain the phenomenon of the hostile takeover have usually begun with its most striking fact: bidders have been willing to pay extraordinarily high premiums (sometimes over 100%) for the stock of target corporations,[2] even though the securities so solicited were presumably efficiently priced because they were typically traded on major stock exchanges. Why are such lucrative premiums paid? Most of the explanations can be grouped under one of the following four headings:

1. *The Disciplinary Hypothesis.* Viewed through the lens supplied by the "market for corporate control" thesis, the role of the tender offer

---

2. [By the Author] Professor Bradley has computed the average premium in a successful tender offer (based on market price two months prior to the offer's announcement) to be 49%. See Bradley, Interfirm Tender Offers and the Market for Corporate Control, 53 J.Bus. 545 (1980). A later study by Professors Jarrell and Bradley estimated that the average cash tender premium had risen to "about 73%" in the wake of state takeover statutes; this percentage was computed based on the target's share price 40 days prior to the offer. See Jarrell and Bradley, The Economic Effects of Federal and State Regulations of Cash Tender Offers, 23 J.Law & Econ. 371, 373 (1980).

is to replace inefficient management. The bidder, it is argued, pays a premium over the market price because it believes that the target's assets have not been optimally utilized and that under superior management they would earn a higher return, thereby justifying the tender offer premium. In this light, the higher the premium, the greater the degree of mismanagement that the bidder must perceive. So viewed, the hostile tender offer appears a benign and socially desirable phenomenon, which benefits both the bidder and the target's stockholders, who simply divide among themselves the value that the incumbent management's inefficiency denied them. * * *

2. *The Synergy Hypothesis.* An alternative explanation of the hostile takeover views the takeover premium as justified not by the suboptimal performance of the target, but rather as the result of the target's having a unique value to the bidder that is in excess of its value to the market generally. Put simply, the value of the combined enterprise is expected to be greater than the sum of its separate parts as independent companies. Such "synergistic gains" may be the result of a variety of factors that are independent of the inefficient management thesis: unique product complementarity between the two companies, specialized resources possessed by the target, economies of scale, cost reductions, lowered borrowing costs, or the capital market's response to the combined enterprise. * * * [This hypothesis] is subject to two important objections. First, studies of postacquisition experiences of acquiring companies have typically found that the expected synergy seldom materializes in the form of higher profits. Second, this theory gives little attention to the disciplinary or deterrent impact of hostile takeovers. These flaws do not invalidate the theory, but do suggest that it is only a partial explanation.

3. *The Empire Building Hypothesis.* A more skeptical explanation for high takeover premiums begins from the obvious possibility that the bidder simply may have overpaid. Those who take a "behavioral" view of the modern corporation have long argued that firms tend to maximize size, not profits. Management may pursue size maximization, even when it is not in the interests of shareholders, for any of a variety of reasons: (1) greater size tends to correspond with higher compensation for management; (2) increased size implies greater security from a takeover or other control contest; (3) enhanced prestige and psychic income are associated with increased size and national visibility; (4) greater size often translates into oligopolistic market power; or, finally, (5) expansion offers opportunities for advancement to the executive staff of the bidding firm. Under this "empire building" thesis, the high premiums paid in tender offers are less an indication of the potential latent in the target's assets than of an overly optimistic assessment by the bidder of its own capabilities as a manager. From this perspective, the takeover process may result not in greater efficiency, but only in a net transfer of wealth from the bidder's shareholders to those of the target. Much empirical data suggest that these wealth transfers occur frequently, but it is considerably more difficult to argue

that they predominate.[3] Nonetheless, the Empire Building Hypothesis suggests that the most important conflict of interests in corporate control contests may be on the bidder's side of the transaction— between the interests of the bidder's management and those of its own shareholders. In any case, as a model which explains takeover activity, the Empire Building Hypothesis focuses singlemindedly on only one variable (the effect on the bidder) and therefore cannot be taken as more than a partial explanation.

4. *The Exploitation Hypothesis.* Gain to the bidder in a takeover can come either through the creation of new value or through the transfer of existing value from other investors. Recent commentators have suggested that such wealth transfers may result from the target shareholders being trapped in a classic "prisoner's dilemma" in which they are faced with a choice between an unsatisfactory current price offered by the bidder and a potentially even lower price in the future.[4]

Two distinct scenarios have been suggested to explain how exploitation might occur. Professor Carney has pointed to the recent appearance of the two-tier bid, in which a high premium is paid in a partial bid for 51% of the target's stock, but then a takeout merger is eventually effected at a price below the pre-tender offer market price, with the result that the average price received amounts to a net loss for the target's shareholders. Actual transactions in which the bidder acquires the target at an average price below the pre-tender trading price remain exceedingly rare, however.

Another, more popular form of the exploitation thesis argues that bidders overreach target shareholders by exploiting temporary depressions in the target's stock price in order to seize control of the target in a bargain purchase. A variation on this same theme views the recent high rate of takeover activity as the product of systematic undervaluation on the part of the stock market * * *.

---

3. [By the Author] It is undisputed that in some cases bidder-shareholders have experienced dramatic declines in stock values in response to a takeover bid. * * * Nonetheless, after averaging the results of several studies, one survey has found bidders to average a gain in stock price of 3.8% (after adjustment for general market movement). This average figure is open to question on a variety of methodological grounds, both because it does not include extensive postacquisition experience and because alternate methodological approaches have been developed, which call into question much of the data so averaged. Based on this different approach to the computation of the gains, [one] study found that acquirers suffer significant losses in mergers.

4. [By the Author] Prisoner's dilemmas arise when the affected shareholders are unable to communicate or coordinate their actions to resist a tender offer. In the case of the two-tier takeover, the inability of shareholders to coordinate their actions and resist the initial partial tender offer at an attractive premium leaves them vulnerable to the second stage merger at a price below market. Rational investors, had they been able to coordinate, might have rejected the tender offer.

KRAAKMAN, TAKING DISCOUNTS SERIOUSLY: THE IMPLICATIONS OF "DISCOUNTED" SHARE PRICES AS AN ACQUISITION MOTIVE *

88 Colum.L.Rev. 891, 891–3 (1988).

Assume that the Acme Oil Company has 100,000 shares of stock trading at $10 per share, no debt, and a proven oil well as its only asset; how much should an identical firm pay to acquire Acme's oil well? Businessmen might fail the quiz, but finance students would probably answer: "Not more than $1,000,000 ($10 × 100,000), excluding synergy gains or tax savings."

This answer echoes a common presumption in the finance literature that informed securities prices credibly estimate the underlying value of corporate assets. Firms whose share prices fall below the market value of their assets—for example, many closed-investment funds, holding companies, or natural resource firms—are frequently tagged as anomalies on this view.[5] But these "anomalous" firms happen to be the only firms whose asset values are readily visible. Here, then, is the rub: The direct evidence, as far as it goes, is more consistent with the conjecture that securities prices *often* "discount"—or underprice—expected cash flows from corporate assets than with the standard presumption that share prices fully value these assets. If discounts are widespread, however, they have significant consequences for many areas of corporate behavior, including, above all, acquisition behavior and the takeover market.

As the Acme hypothetical suggests, the presumption that share prices fully value corporate assets carries a basic implication for acquisition premia. If share prices already reflect the value of targets' assets, then takeover premia, which now average over 50% of prebid share prices, must reflect something else of value that bidders bring to acquisitions: for example, better management or synergy gains. An astute acquirer would never pay $1,500,000 for Acme's shares unless it could earn at least $500,000, on a present value basis, more than what Acme already expects to earn. By contrast, on the view that share prices may discount asset values, takeover premia have an alternative source in the *existing* value of targets' assets. Acme's acquirer might pay $1,500,000 simply because Acme's oil well was reliably appraised at, say, $1,700,000. In this case, the "premium" received by Acme's shareholders might be more accurately described as a recaptured discount.

The discount claim conforms to an intuition, deeply rooted in corporate law and business practice, that share prices often diverge

5. [By the Author] * * * Of course, discrepancies between share prices and asset values would always be anomalies in a theoretical world of perfect capital and asset markets, no matter how pervasive they were in actual markets.

from asset values.[6] I will argue that this intuition is credible for important classes of acquisitions. Nevertheless, the discount claim is an incomplete account of acquisition gains absent an explanation of how share discounts might arise. Here, at least two familiar but divergent hypotheses are possible. One—the "misinvestment" hypothesis—holds that investors rationally expect managers of target firms to misinvest the future returns on corporate assets, and discount the value of these assets accordingly. The second hypothesis—the "market" hypothesis—asserts that share prices themselves may be noisy or skewed. On this view, market prices simply fail to reflect informed estimates of likely cash flows generated by target firms. Both discount hypotheses predict similar acquisition behavior and carry similar implications for other corporate behavior, including the influence of financial policy on share prices. Nevertheless, the distinction between these hypotheses is crucial, since the choice of a discount hypothesis will govern the regulatory implications of the discount claim. * * *

Three possibilities might occur to an observer who first learned that acquirers routinely pay large premia over share price for the assets of target firms: (1) acquirers may be discovering more valuable uses for target assets; (2) share prices may "underprice" these assets; or, finally, (3) acquirers may simply be paying too much. These same possibilities point to a useful typology of current explanations of acquisition gains. A broad class of "traditional" gains hypotheses assumes that acquirers can create or claim new value to pay for acquisition premia. These explanations accord with the assumption that informed share prices fully reflect asset values. They include all ways in which acquirers might expect to increase the net cash flows of targets, for example, by improving management or redeploying assets. A second class of "discount" hypotheses asserts that while acquirers' bid prices reflect real private gains, these gains result because share prices discount the underlying value of target assets. Finally, a third and more troubling class of "overbidding" hypotheses questions whether bid prices and takeover premia reflect real opportunities for acquisition gains at all. Under these theories, managers of acquiring firms may misperceive or misvalue targets out of "hubris," or they may pursue distinctly managerial interests such as corporate growth at great cost to shareholder interests.

---

6. [By the Author] See, e.g., Smith v. Van Gorkom, 488 A.2d 858, 875–76 (Del. 1985) (large premium, or spread between offer price and market price, may still undervalue corporate assets). A basic feature of the share contract is a redemption or appraisal right, triggered by fundamental corporate changes, against the going-concern value of the firms. See, e.g., Rosenblatt v. Getty Oil Co., 493 A.2d 929, 930 (Del.1985).

COFFEE, THE UNCERTAIN CASE FOR TAKEOVER REFORM: AN ESSAY ON STOCKHOLDERS, STAKEHOLDERS AND BUST–UPS

1988 Wisc.L.Rev. 435, 443–51.

This is an argumentative essay, longer on speculation than substantiation. * * * Modern institutional economics views the corporation as a "nexus of contracts"—a complex institutional mechanism, which is designed, at least in part, to uphold (and thus permit reliance upon) "implicit contracts" reached between the shareholders and other "stakeholders" in the corporation (e.g., managers, creditors, employees and possibly certain suppliers). The nature of these implicit contracts—that is, what is exchanged—can be variously defined. * * *

For present purposes, the differences among these "implicit contract" theories are of secondary importance, because in common all recognize the possibility that shareholders could opportunistically breach the implicit contract. In so doing, shareholder wealth is increased, but social wealth is not. On a more abstract level, the implicit contracting perspective produces an important paradigm shift, because it moves the focus of the debate away from the law's usual concern with reducing "agency costs" to protecting the interests of stakeholders who are arguably exposed to opportunistic behavior by shareholders. In effect, the participants in the corporate web of contracts who are mere "agents" from the perspective of a traditional "principal/agent" analysis become independent actors who are vulnerable to exploitation from an "implicit contracting" perspective. * * *

The implicit contract perspective leads directly to a recognition that shareholder wealth and social wealth do not necessarily coincide. This may seem an unexciting conclusion, except for the fact that it has not been seriously considered by financial economists. Yet, in theory, the gains accruing to shareholders in takeovers could simply be wealth transfers from other stakeholders in the corporation (for example, creditors, managers, etc.). Indeed, the social loss could easily exceed the private gain. Such an example has been forcefully posed by Professors Summers and Shleifer, who focus on the ripple effect when plants are closed in a small, one-company town (e.g., Bartlesville, Oklahoma, or Findley, Ohio—the bases of Phillips Petroleum and Marathon Oil, respectively).[7] Not only do employees lose salary, but the fixed investments of local suppliers and indeed the local infrastructure are jeopardized. Moreover, other firms are also affected because they may thereafter find it more difficult to induce other suppliers to make fixed investments or to encourage their employees to invest in "firm-specific" human capital. Finally, even if there is no net social loss, any wealth transfer here is probably in an anti-egalitarian direc-

7. [By the Author] See A. Shleifer & C. Summers, Hostile Takeovers as Breaches of Trust 4–7, 17–20 (National Bureau of Economic Research Working Paper on The Economic Effects of Mergers and Acquisitions, Feb. 1987).

tion, because employees are losing as shareholders gain. If we assume that money has a decreasing marginal utility—that the poor value one additional dollar more than the rich—then such transfers have negative social utility, even if there is no net financial loss. * * *

The claim that takeover gains are accounted for by the losses of other stakeholders remains unproven. No clear pattern is evident with respect to creditors,[8] and managerial losses are difficult to estimate. Conversely, * * * the scale of recent takeover gains (roughly $167 billion according to one recent study) cannot be plausibly explained simply on the basis of cost savings to shareholders from opportunistic breaches of implicit contracts. This becomes clearer if we consider takeovers on the micro level. Today, the average takeover premium is around 40 to 50 percent. One cannot generally explain a rational bidder paying $1.5 billion for a target whose prior aggregate stock market value was $1 billion, simply in terms of the cost savings that managerial layoffs are likely to effect. Indeed, for such a takeover to be rational on this basis, given both the risks and the notoriously high transaction costs, the bidder would have to expect to realize cost savings considerably greater than this $500 million premium in order for it to earn a reasonable profit. Although the total losses to third parties, such as local communities and suppliers, may conceivably approach this level, these losses do not necessarily make the bidder better off; the bidder is not one dollar richer because local store owners will sell less when the local plant closes. Moreover, there will be social gains elsewhere where new plants are opened and new suppliers hired, although this may occur abroad and thus not offset national social wealth loss. Given this asymmetry between private gains and social losses, social losses cannot by themselves explain the bidder's motivation.

Notes

Carley, Battle Tactics: Carl Icahn's Strategies in his Quest for TWA Are a Model for Raiders, Wall St.J., June 20, 1985, at 1, col. 6: *

NEW YORK—In a half-deserted bar at the Waldorf–Astoria Hotel last month, Carl Icahn leaned across a table toward C.E. Meyer, the president of Trans World Airlines. Mr. Icahn had been trying to take over TWA, and Mr. Meyer had been stoutly resisting.

After a series of verbal thrusts about the best interests of stockholders, the conversation turned bitter. As Mr. Icahn described it in a federal court deposition in New York City later last month, the talk went like this:

---

8. [By the Author] One recent survey estimates that bondholders have lost as much as $530 million in 1986 as the result of mergers, acquisitions and recapitalizations. See IRRC, Bondholders Fight Back Against Takeover Losses, 4 Corp. Governance Bull. 156 (Sept./Oct. 1987). Financial economists have, however, generally found no net losses. Id. at 157.

* Reprinted by permission of the Wall Street Journal, © Dow Jones & Company, Inc. (1985). All Rights Reserved.

"He [Mr. Meyer] said, 'All you want is a fast buck. That's all you have ever done in any of these [corporate raids], go for a fast buck.'"

"I said, if we are psychoanalyzing each other, why don't you admit * * * what you really care about is your job, and you are afraid I am going to take it away from you."

Then, according to Mr. Icahn, "We just sort of looked at each other."

Is not this exchange a realistic explanation of the motivations that really drive the takeover movement?

RONDEAU v. MOSINEE PAPER CORP.

Supreme Court of the United States, 1975.
422 U.S. 49, 95 S.Ct. 2069, 45 L.Ed.2d 12.

MR. CHIEF JUSTICE BURGER delivered the opinion of the Court.

We granted certiorari in this case to determine whether a showing of irreparable harm is necessary for a private litigant to obtain injunctive relief in a suit under § 13(d) of the Williams Act. The Court of Appeals held that it was not. We reverse.

I

Respondent Mosinee Paper Corporation is a Wisconsin company engaged in the manufacture and sale of paper, paper products, and plastics. Its principal place of business is located in Mosinee, Wisconsin, and its only class of equity security is common stock which is registered under § 12 of the Securities Exchange Act of 1934. At all times relevant to this litigation there were slightly more than 800,000 shares of such stock outstanding.

In April 1971 petitioner Francis A. Rondeau, a Mosinee businessman, began making large purchases of respondent's common stock in the over-the-counter market. Some of the purchases were in his own name; others were in the name of businesses and a foundation known to be controlled by him. By May 17, 1971, petitioner had acquired 40,413 shares of respondent's stock, which constituted more than 5% of those outstanding. He was therefore required to comply with the disclosure provisions of the Williams Act,[9] by filing a Schedule 13D

---

9. [By the Court] The Williams Act, which amended the Securities Exchange Act of 1934, provides in relevant part:

* * *

"[13](d)(1) Any person who, after acquiring directly or indirectly the beneficial ownership of any equity security of a class which is registered pursuant to section 12 of this title * * * is directly or indirectly the beneficial owner of more than 5 per centum of such class shall, within ten days after such acquisition, send to the issuer of the security at its principal executive office, by registered or certified mail, send to each exchange where the security is traded, and file with the Commission, a statement containing such of the following information, and such additional information, as the Commission may by rules and regulations prescribe as necessary or appropriate in the public interest or for the protection of investors—

"(A) the background and identity of all persons by whom or on whose behalf the purchases have been or are to be effected;

"(B) the source and amount of the funds or other consideration used or to

with respondent and the Securities and Exchange Commission within 10 days. That form would have disclosed, among other things, the number of shares beneficially owned by petitioner, the source of the funds used to purchase them, and petitioner's purpose in making the purchases.

Petitioner did not file a Schedule 13D but continued to purchase substantial blocks of respondent's stock; by July 30, 1971, he had acquired more than 60,000 shares. On that date the chairman of respondent's board of directors informed him by letter that his activity had "given rise to numerous rumors" and "seems to have created some problems under the Federal Securities Laws * * *" Upon receiving the letter petitioner immediately stopped placing orders for respondent's stock and consulted his attorney. On August 25, 1971, he filed a Schedule 13D which, in addition to the other required disclosures, described the "Purpose of Transaction" as follows:

> "Francis A. Rondeau determined during early part of 1971 that the common stock of Issuer [respondent] was undervalued in the over-the-counter market and represented a good investment vehicle for future income and appreciation. Francis A. Rondeau and his associates presently propose to seek to acquire additional common stock of the Issuer in order to obtain effective control of the Issuer, but such investments as originally determined were and are not necessarily made with this objective in mind. Consideration is currently being given to making a public cash tender offer to the shareholders of the Issuer at a price which will reflect current quoted prices for such stock with some premium added."

be used in making the purchases, and if any part of the purchase price or proposed purchase price is represented or is to be represented by funds or other consideration borrowed or otherwise obtained for the purpose of acquiring, holding, or trading such security, a description of the transaction and the names of the parties thereto, except that where a source of funds is a loan made in the ordinary course of business by a bank, as defined in section 3(a)(6) of this title, if the person filing such statement so requests, the name of the bank shall not be made available to the public;

"(C) if the purpose of the purchasers or prospective purchasers is to acquire control of the business of the issuer of the securities, any plans or proposals which such persons may have to liquidate such issuer, to sell its assets to or merge it with any other persons, or to make any other major change in its business or corporate structure;

"(D) the number of shares of such security which are beneficially owned, and

the number of shares concerning which there is a right to acquire, directly or indirectly, by (i) such person, and (ii) by each associate of such person, giving the name and address of each such associate; and

"(E) information as to any contracts, arrangements, or understandings with any person with respect to any securities of the issuer, including but not limited to transfer of any of the securities, joint ventures, loan or option arrangements, puts or calls, guaranties of loans, guaranties against loss or guaranties of profits, division of losses or profits, or the giving or withholding of proxies, naming the persons with whom such contracts, arrangements, or understandings have been entered into, and giving the details thereof."

The Commission requires the purpose of the transaction to be disclosed in every Schedule 13D, regardless of an intention to acquire control and make major changes in its structure. See 17 CFR § 240.13d-1-101 (1974).

Petitioner also stated that, in the event that he did obtain control of respondent, he would consider making changes in management "in an effort to provide a Board of Directors which is more representative of all of the shareholders, particularly those outside of present management * * * *" One month later petitioner amended the form to reflect more accurately the allocation of shares between himself and his companies.

On August 27 respondent sent a letter to its shareholders informing them of the disclosures in petitioner's Schedule 13D.[10] The letter stated that by his "tardy filing" petitioner had "withheld the information to which you [the shareholders] were entitled for more than two months, in violation of federal law." In addition, while agreeing that "recent market prices have not reflected the real value of your Mosinee stock," respondent's management could "see little in Mr. Rondeau's background that would qualify him to offer any meaningful guidance to a Company in the highly technical and competitive paper industry."

Six days later respondent initiated this suit in the United States District Court for the Western District of Wisconsin. Its complaint named petitioner, his companies, and two banks which had financed some of petitioner's purchases as defendants and alleged that they were engaged in a scheme to defraud respondent and its shareholders in violation of the securities laws. It alleged further that shareholders who had "sold shares without the information which defendants were required to disclose lacked information material to their decision to sell or hold," and that respondent "was unable to communicate such information to its shareholders, and to take such actions as their interest required." Respondent prayed for an injunction prohibiting petitioner and his codefendants from voting or pledging their stock and from acquiring additional shares, requiring them to divest themselves of stock which they already owned, and for damages. A motion for a preliminary injunction was filed with the complaint but later withdrawn.

After three months of pretrial proceedings petitioner moved for summary judgment. He readily conceded that he had violated the Williams Act, but contended that the violation was due to a lack of familiarity with the securities laws and that neither respondent nor its shareholders had been harmed. The District Court agreed. It found no material issues of fact to exist regarding petitioner's lack of willfulness in failing to timely file a Schedule 13D, concluding that he discovered his obligation to do so on July 30, 1971, and that there was no basis in the record for disputing his claim that he first considered the possibility of obtaining control of respondent some time after that date. The District Court therefore held that petitioner and his codefendants "did

---

10. [By the Court] Respondent simultaneously issued a press release containing the same information. Almost immediately the price of its stock jumped to $19–21 per share. A few days later it dropped back to the prevailing price of $12.50–$14.00 per share, where it remained.

not engage in intentional covert, and conspiratorial conduct in failing to timely file the 13D Schedule." [11]

Similarly, although accepting respondent's contention that its management and shareholders suffered anxiety as a result of petitioner's activities and that this anxiety was exacerbated by his failure to disclose his intentions until August 1971, the District Court concluded that similar anxiety "could be expected to accompany any change in management," and was "a predictable consequence of shareholder democracy." It fell far short of the irreparable harm necessary to support an injunction and no other harm was revealed by the record; as amended, petitioner's Schedule 13D disclosed all of the information to which respondent was entitled, and he had not proceeded with a tender offer. Moreover, in the view of the District Court even if a showing of irreparable harm were not required in all cases under the securities laws, petitioner's lack of bad faith and the absence of damage to respondent made this "a particularly inappropriate occasion to fashion equitable relief * * *" Thus, although petitioner had committed a technical violation of the Williams Act, the District Court held that respondent was entitled to no relief and entered summary judgment against it.

The Court of Appeals reversed with one judge dissenting. The majority stated that it was "giving effect" to the District Court's findings regarding the circumstances of petitioner's violation of the Williams Act, but concluded that those findings showed harm to respondent because "it was delayed in its efforts to make any necessary response to" petitioner's potential to take control of the company. In any event, the majority was of the view that respondent "need not show irreparable harm as a prerequisite to obtaining permanent injunctive relief in view of the fact that as issuer of the securities it is in the best position to assure that the filing requirements of the Williams Act are being timely and fully complied with and to obtain speedy and forceful remedial action when necessary." 7 Cir., 500 F.2d 1011, 1016–1017. The Court of Appeals remanded the case to the District Court with instructions that it enjoin petitioner and his codefendants from further violations of the Williams Act and from voting the shares purchased between the due date of the Schedule 13D and the date of its filing for a period of five years. It considered "such an injunctive decree appropriate to neutralize [petitioner's] violation of the Act and to deny him the benefit of his wrongdoing." 500 F.2d at 1017.

We granted certiorari to resolve an apparent conflict among the courts of appeals and because of the importance of the question presented to private actions under the Federal Securities Laws. We disagree with the Court of Appeals' conclusion that the traditional standards for

---

11. [By the Court] The District Court also concluded that respondent's management was not unaware of petitioner's activities with respect to its stock. It found that by July 1971, there was considerable "street talk" among brokers, bankers, and businessmen regarding his purchases and that the chairman of respondent's board had been monitoring them.

extraordinary equitable relief do not apply in these circumstances, and reverse.

II

As in the District Court and the Court of Appeals, it is conceded here that petitioner's delay in filing the Schedule 13D constituted a violation of the Williams Act. The narrow issue before us is whether this record supports the grant of injunctive relief, a remedy whose basis "in the federal courts has always been irreparable harm and inadequacy of legal remedies." Beacon Theatres, Inc. v. Westover, 359 U.S. 500, 506–507, 79 S.Ct. 948, 954, 3 L.Ed.2d 988 (1959).

The Court of Appeals' conclusion that respondent suffered "harm" sufficient to require sterilization of petitioner's stock need not long detain us. The purpose of the Williams Act is to insure that public shareholders who are confronted by a cash tender offer for their stock will not be required to respond without adequate information regarding the qualifications and intentions of the offering party.[12] By requiring disclosure of information to the target corporation as well as the Securities and Exchange Commission, Congress intended to do no more than give incumbent management an opportunity to express and explain its position. The Congress expressly disclaimed an intention to provide a weapon for management to discourage takeover bids or prevent large accumulations of stock which would create the potential for such attempts. Indeed, the Act's draftsmen commented upon the "extreme care" which was taken "to avoid tipping the balance of regulation either in favor of management or in favor of the person making the takeover bid." S.Rep. No. 550, 90th Cong., 1st Sess., 3 (1967); H.R.Rep. No. 1711, 90th Cong., 2d Sess., p. 4 (1968)

The short of the matter is that none of the evils to which the Williams Act was directed has occurred or is threatened in this case. Petitioner has not attempted to obtain control of respondent, either by a cash tender offer or any other device. Moreover, he has now filed a proper Schedule 13D, and there has been no suggestion that he will fail to comply with the Act's requirement of reporting any material changes in the information contained therein.[13] On this record there is no

---

12. [By the Court] The Senate Report describes the dilemma facing such a shareholder as follows:

"He has many alternatives. He can tender all of his shares immediately and hope they all are purchased. However, if the offer is for less than all the outstanding shares, perhaps only a part of them will be taken. In these instances, he will remain a shareholder in the company, under a new management which he has helped to install without knowing whether it will be good or bad for the company.

"The shareholder, as another alternative, may wait to see if a better offer develops but if he tenders late, he runs the risk that none of his shares will be taken. He may also sell his shares in the market and hope for the best. Without knowledge of who the bidder is and what he plans to do, the shareholder cannot reach an informed decision." S.Rep. No. 550, 90th Cong., 1st Sess., p. 2 (1967).

However, the Report also recognized "that takeover bids should not be discouraged because they serve a useful purpose in providing a check on entrenched but inefficient management." Id., at 3.

13. [By the Court] Because this case involves only the availability of injunctive

likelihood that respondent's shareholders will be disadvantaged should petitioner make a tender offer, or that respondent will be unable to adequately place its case before them should a contest for control develop. Thus, the usual basis for injunctive relief, "that there exists some cognizable danger of recurrent violation," is not present here. United States v. W.T. Grant Co., 345 U.S. 629, 633, 73 S.Ct. 894, 898, 97 L.Ed. 1303 (1953).

Nor are we impressed by respondent's argument that an injunction is necessary to protect the interests of its shareholders who either sold their stock to petitioner at predisclosure prices or would not have invested had they known that a takeover bid was imminent. As observed, the principal object of the Williams Act is to solve the dilemma of shareholders desiring to respond to a cash tender offer, and it is not at all clear that the type of "harm" identified by respondent is redressable under its provisions. In any event, those persons who allegedly sold at an unfairly depressed price have an adequate remedy by way of an action for damages, thus negating the basis for equitable relief. Similarly, the fact that the second group of shareholders for whom respondent expresses concern have retained the benefits of their stock and the lack of an imminent contest for control make the possibility of damage to them remote at best.

We turn, therefore, to the Court of Appeals' conclusion that respondent's claim was not to be judged according to traditional equitable principles, and that the bare fact that petitioner violated the Williams Act justified entry of an injunction against him. This position would seem to be foreclosed by Hecht Co. v. Bowles, 321 U.S. 321, 64 S.Ct. 587, 88 L.Ed. 754 (1944). * * *

Respondent urges, however, that the "public interest" must be taken into account in considering its claim for relief and relies upon the Court of Appeals' conclusion that it is entitled to an injunction because it "is in the best position" to insure that the Williams Act is complied with by purchasers of its stock. This argument misconceives, we think, the nature of the litigation. Although neither the availability of a private suit under the Williams Act nor respondent's standing to bring it has been questioned here, this cause of action is not expressly authorized by the statute or its legislative history. Rather, respondent is asserting a so-called implied private right of action established by cases such as J.I. Case Co. v. Borak, 377 U.S. 426, 84 S.Ct. 1555, 12 L.Ed. 2d 423 (1964). Of course, we have not hesitated to recognize the power of federal courts to fashion private remedies for securities laws violations when to do so is consistent with the legislative scheme and necessary for the protection of investors as a supplement to enforcement by the Securities and Exchange Commission. * * * However,

relief to remedy a § 13(d) violation following compliance with the reporting requirements, it does not require us to decide whether or under what circumstances a corporation could obtain a decree enjoining a shareholder who is currently in violation of § 13(d) from acquiring further shares, exercising voting rights, or launching a takeover bid, pending compliance with the reporting requirements.

it by no means follows that the plaintiff in such an action is relieved of the burden of establishing the traditional prerequisites of relief. Indeed, our cases hold that quite the contrary is true. * * *

Accordingly, the judgment of the Court of Appeals is reversed and the case is remanded to it with directions to reinstate the judgment of the District Court.

Reversed and remanded with directions.

MR. JUSTICE MARSHALL dissents.

MR. JUSTICE BRENNAN with whom MR. JUSTICE DOUGLAS joins, dissenting.

I dissent. Judge Pell, dissenting below, correctly in my view, read the decision of the Court of Appeals to construe the Williams Act, as I also construe it, to authorize injunctive relief upon the application of the management interests "irrespective of motivation, irrespective of irreparable harm to the corporation, and irrespective of whether the purchases were detrimental to investors in the company's stock. The violation timewise is * * * all that is needed to trigger this result." 500 F.2d 1011, 1018 (CA 7 1974). In other words, the Williams Act is a prophylactic measure conceived by Congress as necessary to effect the congressional objective "that investors and management be notified at the earliest possible moment of the potential for a shift in corporate control." 500 F.2d, at 1016. The violation itself establishes the actionable harm and no showing of other harm is necessary to secure injunctive relief. Today's holding completely undermines the congressional purpose to preclude inquiry into the results of the violation.

Notes

(1) Do you believe that the disclosure requirement of section 13(d) provides a significant regulatory constraint on tender or exchange offers?

(2) Do you agree with Mr. Justice Brennan's comment that the majority's holding "completely undermines the congressional purpose to preclude inquiry into the results of the violation"? It is perhaps unnecessary to point out that Rondeau did have on file the appropriate Schedule 13D when all this litigation was taking place.

(3) Section 13(d)(3) is a potentially troublesome provision that reads as follows: "[w]hen two or more persons act as a partnership, limited partnership, syndicate, or other group for the purpose of acquiring, holding, or disposing of securities of an issuer, such syndicate or group shall be deemed a 'person' for the purposes of [Section 13(d)]." Assume that five shareholders who each own more than one per cent of the stock of an issuer agree to pool their shares in an effort to seize control, but they do not buy additional shares. Does the mere formation of the group trigger an obligation to file? Compare GAF Corp. v. Milstein, 453 F.2d 709 (2d Cir.1971) with Bath Industries, Inc. v. Blot, 427 F.2d 97 (7th Cir.1970); Wellman v. Dickinson, 475 F.Supp. 783 (S.D.N.Y.1979), affirmed 682 F.2d 355 (2d Cir.1982), cert. denied 460 U.S. 1069, 103 S.Ct. 1522, 75 L.Ed.2d 946 (1983).

PIPER v. CHRIS–CRAFT INDUSTRIES, INC.

Supreme Court of the United States, 1977.
430 U.S. 1, 97 S.Ct. 926, 51 L.Ed.2d 124.

MR. CHIEF JUSTICE BURGER delivered the opinion of the Court.

We granted certiorari in these cases to consider, among other issues, whether an unsuccessful tender offeror in a contest for control of a corporation has an implied cause of action for damages under § 14(e) of the Securities Exchange Act of 1934, as amended by the Williams Act of 1968 [14] * * *.

I

BACKGROUND

The factual background of this complex contest for control, including the protracted litigation culminating in the case now before us, is essential to a full understanding of the contending parties' claims.

The three petitions present questions of first impression, arising out of a "sophisticated and hard fought contest" for control of Piper Aircraft Corporation, a Pennsylvania-based manufacturer of light aircraft. Piper's management consisted principally of members of the Piper family, who owned 31% of Piper's outstanding stock. Chris–Craft Industries, Inc. a diversified manufacturer of recreational products, attempted to secure voting control of Piper through cash and exchange tender offers for Piper common stock. Chris–Craft's takeover attempt failed, and Bangor Punta Corporation, with the support of the Piper family, obtained control of Piper in September 1969. Chris–Craft brought suit under § 14(e) of the Securities Exchange Act of 1934 and Rule 10b–6, alleging that Bangor Punta achieved control of the target corporation as a result of violations of the federal securities laws by the Piper family, Bangor Punta, and Bangor Punta's underwriter, First Boston Corporation, who together had successfully repelled Chris–Craft's takeover attempt.

The struggle for control of Piper began in December 1968. At that time, Chris–Craft began making cash purchases of Piper common stock. By January 22, 1969, Chris–Craft had acquired 203,700 shares, or approximately 13% of Piper's 1,644,790 outstanding shares. On the next day, following unsuccessful preliminary overtures to Piper by Chris–Craft's president, Herbert Siegel, Chris–Craft publicly announced

---

14. [By the Editor] Section 14(e) provides:

"(e) It shall be unlawful for any person to make any untrue statement of a material fact or omit to state any material fact necessary in order to make the statements made, in the light of the circumstances under which they are made, not misleading, or to engage in any fraudulent, deceptive, or manipulative acts or practices, in connection with any tender offer or request or invitation for tenders, or any solicitation of security holders in opposition to or in favor of any such offer, request, or invitation. The Commission shall, for the purposes of this subsection, by rules and regulations define, and prescribe means reasonably designed to prevent, such acts and practices as are fraudulent, deceptive, or manipulative."

a cash tender offer for up to 300,000 Piper shares [15] at $65 per share, which was approximately $12 above the then current market price. Responding promptly to Chris–Craft's bid, Piper's management met on the same day with the company's investment banker, First Boston, and other advisers. On January 24, the Piper family decided to oppose Chris–Craft's tender offer. As part of its resistance to Chris–Craft's takeover campaign, Piper management sent several letters to the company's stockholders between January 25–27, arguing against acceptance of Chris–Craft's offer. On January 27, a letter to shareholders from W.T. Piper, Jr., president of the company, stated that the Piper Board "has carefully studied this offer and is convinced that it is inadequate and not in the best interests of Piper's shareholders."

In addition to communicating with shareholders, Piper entered into an agreement with Grumman Aircraft Corporation on January 29, whereby Grumman agreed to purchase 300,000 authorized but unissued Piper shares at $65 per share. The agreement increased the amount of stock necessary for Chris–Craft to secure control and thus rendered Piper less vulnerable to Chris–Craft's attack. A Piper press release and letter to shareholders announced the Grumman transaction but failed to state either that Grumman had a "put" or option to sell the shares back to Piper at cost, plus interest, or that Piper was required to maintain the proceeds of the transaction in a separate fund free from liens.

Despite Piper's opposition, Chris–Craft succeeded in acquiring 304,606 shares by the time its cash tender offer expired on February 3. To obtain the additional 17% of Piper stock needed for control, Chris–Craft decided to make an exchange offer of Chris–Craft securities for Piper stock. Although Chris–Craft filed a registration statement and preliminary prospectus with the SEC in late February 1969, the exchange offer did not go into effect until May 15, 1969.

In the meantime, Chris–Craft made cash purchases of Piper stock on the open market until Mr. Siegel, the company's president, was expressly warned by SEC officials that such purchases, when made during the pendency of an exchange offer, violated SEC Rule 10b–6. At Mr. Siegel's direction, Chris–Craft immediately complied with the SEC's directive and canceled all outstanding orders for purchases of Piper stock.

While Chris–Craft's exchange offer was in registration, Piper in March 1969 terminated the agreement with Grumman and entered into negotiations with Bangor Punta. Bangor had initially been contacted by First Boston about the possibility of a Piper takeover in the wake of Chris–Craft's initial cash tender offer in January. With Grumman out of the picture, the Piper family agreed on May 8, 1969, to exchange their 31% stockholdings in Piper for Bangor Punta securities. Bangor also agreed to use its best efforts to achieve control of Piper by means of

15. [By the Court] The cash tender offer indicated that Chris–Craft reserved the right to purchase shares in excess of the 300,000 specified amount.

an exchange offer of Bangor securities for Piper common stock. A press release issued the same day announced the terms of the agreement, including a provision that the forthcoming exchange offer would involve Bangor securities to be valued, in the judgment of First Boston, "at not less than $80 per Piper share."[16]

While awaiting the effective date of its exchange offer, Bangor in mid–May 1969 purchased 120,200 shares of Piper stock in privately negotiated, off-exchange transactions from three large institutional investors. All three purchases were made after the SEC's issuance of a release on May 5 announcing proposed Rule 10b–13, a provision which, upon becoming effective in November 1969, would expressly prohibit a tender offeror from making purchases of the target company's stock during the pendency of an exchange offer. The SEC release stated that the proposed rule was "in effect, a codification of existing interpretations under Rule 10b–6," the provision invoked by SEC officials against Mr. Siegel of Chris–Craft a month earlier. Bangor officials, although aware of the release at the time of the three off-exchange purchases, made no attempt to secure an exemption for the transactions from the SEC, as provided by Rule 10b–6(f). The Commission, however, took no action concerning these purchases as it had with respect to Chris–Craft's open market transactions.

With these three block purchases, amounting to 7% of Piper stock, Bangor Punta in mid–May took the lead in the takeover contest. The contest then centered upon the competing exchange offers. Chris–Craft's first exchange offer, which began in mid–May 1969, failed to produce tenders of the specified minimum number of Piper shares (80,000). Meanwhile, Bangor Punta's exchange offer, which had been announced on May 8, became effective on July 18. The registration materials which Bangor filed with the SEC in connection with the exchange offer included financial statements, reviewed by First Boston, representing that one of Bangor's subsidiaries, the Bangor and Aroostock Railroad (BAR), had a value of $18.4 million. This valuation was based upon a 1965 appraisal by investment bankers after a proposed sale of the BAR failed to materialize. The financial statements did not indicate that Bangor was considering the sale of BAR or that an offer to purchase the railroad for $5 million had been received.[17]

In the final phase of the see-saw of competing offers Chris–Craft modified the terms of its previously unsuccessful exchange offer to make it more attractive. The revised offer succeeded in attracting 112,089 additional Piper shares, while Bangor's exchange offer, which

16. [By the Court] Less than three weeks later, the SEC brought an action in Federal District Court charging that the Bangor press release violated "gun-jumping" provisions and Rule 135, by stating a specific dollar valuation for unregistered securities. Without admitting any of the allegations, Bangor and Piper consented to a permanent injunction against similar releases before the effective date of Bangor's registration statement.

17. [By the Court] Shortly after the contest for control was completed, Bangor entered into an agreement to sell BAR for $5 million, thereby resulting in a $13.8 million book loss.

terminated on July 29, resulted in the tendering of 110,802 shares. By August 4, 1969, at the conclusion of both offers, Bangor Punta owned a total of 44.5%, while Chris–Craft owned 40.6% of Piper stock. The remainder of Piper stock, 14.9%, remained in the hands of the public.

After completion of their respective exchange offers, both companies renewed market purchases of Piper stock,[18] but Chris–Craft, after purchasing 29,200 shares for cash in mid–August, withdrew from competition.[19] Bangor Punta continued making cash purchases until September 5, by which time it had acquired a majority interest in Piper. The final tally in the nine-month takeover battle showed that Bangor Punta held over 50% and Chris–Craft held 42% of Piper stock.

II

Before either side had achieved control, the contest moved from the marketplace to the courts. Then began more than seven years of complex litigation growing out of the contest for control of Piper Aircraft.

[Editor: This litigation involved hearings and opinions at the district court level on (1) a request for a preliminary injunction, 303 F.Supp. 191 (S.D.N.Y.1969), (2) a request by the SEC for an injunction against Bangor Punta, 331 F.Supp. 1154 (S.D.N.Y.1971), (3) the issue of defendants' liability for damages for violation of the Williams Act, 337 F.Supp. 1128 (S.D.N.Y.1971), and (4) finally, the amount of damages, 384 F.Supp. 507 (S.D.N.Y.1974). The Court of Appeals for the Second Circuit affirmed the denial of the preliminary injunction *en banc*, 426 F.2d 589 (CA2 1970) and reversed the trial judge's dismissal of Chris Craft's suit on the question of liability, 480 F.2d 341 (CA2 1973), cert. denied 414 U.S. 910, holding that § 14(e) had been violated by Piper's description of the Chris–Craft offer, by the failure to disclose the "put" provision in the Grumman agreement, and by the BAR omission in the description of Bangor Punta. Finally, after remand and an award of damages by the District Court of $1,673,988, the Court of Appeals modified the judgment on its own motion to increase it to $25,793,365, and prejudgment interest from $600,000 to about $10,000,000. This judgment is the one under review by the Supreme Court. Throughout this protracted litigation, all lower court judges either concluded or assumed that Chris–Craft had a private cause of action for violations of § 14(e) of the Williams Act.]

18. [By the Court] Since the respective distributions of securities pursuant to the exchange offers had been completed at this point, the legality of these market purchases was unchallenged.

19. [By the Court] The reason for Chris–Craft's withdrawal from the contest is a matter in dispute. According to one view, espoused by Judge Mansfield at one stage in the ensuing litigation, Chris–Craft had "'shot its bolt' in the financial sense by early February 1969. * * * It was in no position to purchase for cash any appreciable amount of Piper shares over and above the 304,606 tendered in response to its initial cash offer." 480 F.2d 341, 402 (CA2 1973).

III

THE WILLIAMS ACT

We turn first to an examination of the Williams Act, which was adopted in 1968 in response to the growing use of cash tender offers as a means for achieving corporate takeovers.[20] Prior to the 1960's, corporate takeover attempts had typically involved either proxy solicitations, regulated under § 14 of the Securities Exchange Act or exchange offers of securities, subject to the registration requirements of the 1933 Act. The proliferation of cash tender offers, in which publicized requests are made and intensive campaigns conducted for tenders of shares of stock at a fixed price, removed a substantial number of corporate control contests from the reach of existing disclosure requirements of the federal securities laws.

To remedy this gap in federal regulation, Senator Harrison Williams introduced a bill in October 1965 to subject tender offerors to advance disclosure requirements. The original proposal, S. 2732, evolved over the next two years in response to positions expressed by the SEC and other interested parties from private industry and the New York Stock Exchange. 113 Cong.Rec. 854 (Jan. 18, 1967) (remarks of Sen. Williams). As subsequently enacted, the legislation requires takeover bidders to file a statement with the Commission indicating, among other things, the "background and identity" of the offeror, the source and amount of funds or other consideration to be used in making the purchases, the extent of the offeror's holdings in the target corporation, and the offeror's plans with respect to the target corporation's business or corporate structure.

In addition to disclosure requirements, which protect all target shareholders, the Williams Act provides other benefits for target shareholders who elect to tender their stock. First, stockholders who accept the tender offer are given the right to withdraw their shares during the first seven days of the tender offer and at any time after 60 days from the commencement of the offer. Second, where the tender offer is for less than all outstanding shares and more than the requested number of shares are tendered, the Act requires that the tendered securities be taken up pro rata by the offeror during the first 10 days of the offer.[21] This provision, according to Senator Williams, was specifically designed to reduce pressures on target shareholders to deposit their shares

---

20. [By the Court] The proliferation of cash tender offers as devices for securing corporate control is analyzed in detail in Hayes and Taussig, Tactics of Cash Takeover Bids, 45 Harv.L.Bus.Rev. 135 (1967). See also E. Aranow and H. Einhorn, Developments in Tender Offers for Corporate Control 2–10 (1973).

21. [By the Court] The SEC had proposed that the pro rata requirement be applied throughout the duration of the of-

fer. Hearings on S. 510 before the Subcommittee on Securities of the Senate Committee on Banking and Currency, 90th Cong., 1st Sess., 200 (1967). This openended proposal came under substantial criticism in the legislative hearings, and Congress finally enacted a 10–day limitation on the pro rata acceptance requirement. The 10–day period was identical to the practice followed by the New York Stock Exchange.

hastily when the takeover bidder makes its tender offer on a first-come, first-served basis. 113 Cong.Rec. 856 (Jan. 18, 1967). Finally, the Act provides that if, during the course of the offer, the amount paid for the target shares is increased, all tendering shareholders are to receive the additional consideration, even if they tendered their stock before the price increase was announced.

Besides requiring disclosure and providing specific benefits for tendering shareholders, the Williams Act also contains a broad antifraud prohibition, which is the basis of Chris–Craft's claim. Section 14(e) of the Act * * * was expressly directed at the conduct of a broad range of persons, including those engaged in making or opposing tender offers or otherwise seeking to influence the decision of investors or the outcome of the tender offer.

The threshold issue in these cases is whether tender offerors such as Chris–Craft, whose activities are regulated by the Williams Act, have a cause of action for damages against other regulated parties under the statute on a claim that antifraud violations by other parties have frustrated the bidder's efforts to obtain control of the target corporation. Without reading such a cause of action into the Act, none of the other issues need be reached.

IV

Our analysis begins, of course, with the statute itself. Section 14(e), like § 10(b), makes no provision whatever for a private cause of action, such as those explicitly provided in other sections of the 1933 and 1934 Acts. E.g., §§ 11, 12, 15 of the 1933 Act; §§ 9, 16, 18, 20 of the 1934 Act. This Court has nonetheless held that in some circumstances a private cause of action can be implied with respect to the 1934 Act's antifraud provisions, even though the relevant provisions are silent as to remedies. J.I. Case Co. v. Borak, 377 U.S. 426, 84 S.Ct. 1555, 12 L.Ed.2d 423 (1964) (§ 14(a)); Superintendent of Ins. v. Bankers Life & Cas. Co., 404 U.S. 6, 13 n. 9, 92 S.Ct. 165, 169, 30 L.Ed.2d 128 (1971) (§ 10b).

The reasoning of these holdings is that, where congressional purposes are likely to be undermined absent private enforcement, private remedies may be implied in favor of the particular class intended to be protected by the statute. For example, in J.I. Case Co. v. Borak, supra, recognizing an implied right of action in favor of a shareholder complaining of a misleading proxy solicitation, the Court concluded as to such a shareholder's right:

> "While [§ 14(a)] makes no specific reference to a private right of action, among its chief purposes is *'the protection of investors,'* which certainly implies the availability of judicial relief *where necessary to achieve that result.*" 377 U.S., at 432, 84 S.Ct., at 1560. (Emphasis supplied.)

Indeed, the Court in *Borak* carefully noted that because of practical limitations upon the SEC's enforcement capabilities, "[p]rivate enforce-

ment provides *a necessary supplement to Commission action*." Ibid.
(Emphasis added.) Similarly, the Court's opinion in Blue Chip Stamps
v. Manor Drug Stores, 421 U.S. 723, 730 (1975), in reaffirming the
availability of a private right of action under § 10(b), specifically
alluded to the language in *Borak* concerning the *necessity* for supplemental private remedies without which congressional protection of
shareholders would be defeated. See also Rondeau v. Mosinee Paper
Corp., 422 U.S. 49, 62, 95 S.Ct. 2069, 2078, 45 L.Ed.2d 12 (1975).

Against this background we must consider whether § 14(e), which
is entirely silent as to private remedies, permits this Court to read into
the statute a damages remedy for unsuccessful tender offerors. To
resolve that question we turn to the legislative history to discern the
congressional purpose underlying the specific statutory prohibition in
§ 14(e). Once we identify the legislative purpose, we must then determine whether the creation by judicial interpretation of the implied
cause of action asserted by Chris–Craft is necessary to effectuate
Congress' goals.

A

Reliance on legislative history in divining the intent of Congress is,
as has often been observed, a step to be taken cautiously. Department
of Air Force v. Rose, 425 U.S. 352, 388–389, 96 S.Ct. 1592, 1611–1612, 48
L.Ed.2d 11 (1976) (Blackmun, J., dissenting); Scripps–Howard Radio v.
FCC, 316 U.S. 4, 11, 62 S.Ct. 875, 880, 86 L.Ed. 1229 (1942). In this case
both sides press legislative history on the Court not so much to explain
the meaning of the language of a statute as to explain the absence of
any express provision for a private cause of action for damages. As Mr.
Justice Frankfurter reminded us, "We must be wary against interpolat-
ing our notions of policy in the interstices of legislative provisions."
Scripps–Howard Radio v. FCC, 316 U.S., at 11, 62 S.Ct. at 880. With
that *caveat,* we turn to the legislative history of the Williams Act.
* * *

[The Court here quotes extensively from the legislative history
italicizing single words or phrases which refer to the purpose of protecting investors or shareholders.]

In the face of this legislative history, the Court of Appeals understandably did not rely upon the legislative materials to support an
implied cause of action for damages in favor of Chris–Craft. In this
Court, however, Chris–Craft and the SEC contend that Congress clearly
intended to protect tender offerors as part of a "pervasive scheme of
federal regulation of tender offers." In support of their reading of the
legislative history, they emphasize, first, that in enacting the legislation
Congress was intent upon establishing a policy of even-handedness in
takeover regulation. Congress was particularly anxious, Chris–Craft
argues, "to avoid tipping the balance of regulation * * *."

Congress was indeed committed to a policy of neutrality in contests
for control, but its policy of even-handedness does not go either to the

purpose of the legislation or to whether a private cause of action is implicit in the statute. Neutrality is, rather, but one characteristic of legislation directed toward a different purpose—the protection of investors. Indeed, the statements concerning the need for Congress to maintain a neutral posture in takeover attempts are contained in the section of the Senate Report entitled, "Protection of Investors." Taken in their totality, these statements confirm that what Congress had in mind was the protection of shareholders, the "pawn[s] in a form of industrial warfare." The Senate Report expressed the purpose as "placing investors on an equal footing with the takeover bidder," Senate Report, at 4, without favoring either the tender offeror or existing management. This express policy of neutrality scarcely suggests an intent to confer highly important, new rights upon the class of participants whose activities prompted the legislation in the first instance. * * *

Besides the policy of even-handedness, Chris–Craft emphasizes that the matter of implied private causes of action was raised in written submissions to the Senate Subcommittee. Specifically, Chris–Craft points to the written statements of Professors Israels and Painter, who made reference to J.I. Case v. Borak, supra. Chris–Craft contends, therefore, that Congress was aware that private actions were implicit in § 14(e).

But this conclusion places more freight on the passing reference to *Borak* than can reasonably be carried. Even accepting the value of written statements received without comment by the committee and without cross-examination, the statements do not refer to implied private actions by *offeror-bidders*. * * *

More important, these statements referred to a case in which the remedy was afforded to shareholders—the *direct* and *intended* beneficiaries of the legislation. In *Borak*, the Court emphasized that § 14(a), the proxy provision, was adopted expressly for "the protection of investors," 377 U.S., at 432, 84 S.Ct., at 1559, the very class of persons there seeking relief. The Court found no difficulty in identifying the legislative objective and concluding that remedies should be available if necessary "to make effective the congressional purposes." Id., at 433. *Borak* did not involve, and the statements in the legislative history relied upon by Chris–Craft do not implicate, the interests of parties such as offeror-bidders who are outside the scope of the concerns articulated in the evolution of this legislation.[22] * * *

The legislative history thus shows that the sole purpose of the Williams Act was the protection of investors who are confronted with a

22. [By the Court] In this connection, Chris–Craft emphasizes Congress' intent to treat tender offers in the same way as proxy solicitations, since both are devices for seeking corporate control. This argument, however, does not support the proposition that Chris–Craft should have a cause of action for damages, since this Court had not then held, nor has it since, that defeated insurgents in a proxy fight, suing in a capacity other than that of a shareholder, have a cause of action for damages. There is no occasion to resolve that question in this case.

tender offer. As we stated in Rondeau v. Mosinee Paper Corp., 422 U.S., at 58, 95 S.Ct., at 2075: "[t]he purpose of the Williams Act is to insure that public shareholders who are confronted by a cash tender offer for their stock will not be required to respond without adequate information. * * *" We find no hint in the legislative history, on which respondent so heavily relies, that Congress contemplated a private cause of action for damages by one of several contending offerors against a successful bidder or by a losing contender against the target corporation. * * *

C

What we have said thus far suggests that, unlike J.I. Case v. Borak, supra, judicially creating a damages action in favor of Chris–Craft is unnecessary to ensure the fulfillment of Congress' purposes in adopting the Williams Act. Even though the SEC operates in this context under the same practical restraints recognized by the Court in Borak, institutional limitations alone do not lead to the conclusion that any party interested in a tender offer should have a cause of action for damages against a competing bidder.[23] First, as Judge Friendly observed in Electronic Specialty Co. v. International Controls Corp., 409 F.2d 937, 947 (CA2 1969), in corporate control contests the stage of preliminary injunctive relief, rather than post-contest lawsuits, "is the time when relief can best be given." Furthermore, awarding damages to parties other than the protected class of shareholders has only a remote, if any, bearing upon implementing the congressional policy of protecting shareholders who must decide whether to tender or retain their stock.[24] Indeed, as we suggested earlier, a damages award of this nature may well be inconsistent with the interests of many members of the protected class and of only indirect value to shareholders who accepted the exchange offer of the defeated takeover contestant.

23. [By the Court] The dissent suggests that the SEC's "intimate involvement in the passage of the Act entitle[s] its views to respect." We note, first, that the present position of the SEC is not consistent with the testimony of the SEC Chairman in the legislative evolution of § 14(e). Even if the agency spoke with a consistent voice, however, its presumed "expertise" in the securities-law field is of limited value when the narrow legal issue is one peculiarly reserved for judicial resolution, namely whether a cause of action should be implied by judicial interpretation in favor of a particular class of litigants. Indeed, in our prior cases relating to implied causes of action, the Court has understandably not invoked the "administrative deference" rule, even when the SEC supported the result reached in the particular case. J.I. Case v. Borak, supra; Superintendent of Insurance v. Bankers Life & Cas. Co. That rule is more appropriately applicable in instances where, unlike here, an agency has rendered binding, consistent, official interpretations of its statute over a long period of time.

24. [By the Court] Our holding is a limited one. Whether shareholders-offerees, the class protected by § 14(e), have an implied cause of action under § 14(e) is not before us, and we intimate no view on the matter. Nor is the target corporation's standing to sue in issue in this case. We hold only that a tender offeror, suing in its capacity as a takeover bidder, does not have standing to sue for damages under § 14(e).

Our precise holding disposes of many observations made in dissent. Thus, the argument with respect to the "exclusion" from standing for "persons most interested in effective enforcement" is simply unwarranted in light of today's narrow holding.

We therefore conclude that Chris–Craft, as a defeated tender offeror, has no implied cause of action for damages under § 14(e). * * *

VI

* * * [T]he Court of Appeals also ordered the District Court to enjoin Bangor Punta from voting the illegally acquired Piper shares for a period of five years. In compliance with that directive, Judge Pollack on remand entered an injunction to remain in effect for a period of five years from November 25, 1974, the date on which judgment was entered. On appeal, the Court of Appeals affirmed that portion of the District Court's order.

We hold that, under the circumstances presented here, this injunction should not have been granted. As we previously indicated, Chris–Craft prior to the trial on liability expressly waived any claim to injunctive relief. The case was tried in the District Court, without a jury, exclusively as a suit for damages. Under these circumstances, our holding that Chris–Craft does not have a cause of action for damages under § 14(e) or Rule 10b–6 renders that injunction inappropriate, premised as it was upon the impermissible award of damages. The inappropriateness of the injunction is particularly acute in this litigation, where the order was entered almost four years after the contest for control had ended and where no regard was given to the interests of the protected class of shareholders-offerees, many of whom would be at least indirectly disadvantaged by the award.

Accordingly, the judgment of the Court of Appeals is

Reversed.

MR. JUSTICE BLACKMUN, concurring in the judgment.

I concur in the judgment. For the reasons set out in Mr. Justice Stevens' dissenting opinion, I am willing to begin with the premise that respondent Chris–Craft had "standing" in the sense that it possessed an implied right to sue under § 14(e) of the Securities Exchange Act of 1934. Unlike the dissenters, however, I do not conclude, from this, that the Court of Appeals' judgment as to liability is to be affirmed. Since I am of the opinion that respondent failed to prove that petitioners' violations of the securities laws caused its injury, I agree with the Court that the judgment below should be reversed. * * *

MR. JUSTICE STEVENS, with whom MR. JUSTICE BRENNAN joins, dissenting.

The Williams Act was passed for the protection of investors. The threshold question in this case is whether the holder of a large block of stock who is seeking to retain or to acquire control of a corporation is one of the investors the statute was intended to protect.

The critical issue can be framed by concentrating on the exchange offers in July 1969. The conclusion that Bangor Punta's offer violated § 14(e) is established by prior proceedings and is not now open for review. When that violation occurred, Chris–Craft owned 556,206 shares of Piper stock and was attempting to acquire sufficient addition-al shares to constitute control. As a result of Bangor Punta's viola-tions, Chris–Craft claims that it was injured in two ways: the value of its investment in Piper stock was impaired, and it lost the opportunity to purchase enough additional shares to control Piper. The Court holds that Chris–Craft has no "standing" to recover damages for either injury no matter how flagrant Bangor Punta's violation may have been, no matter how direct the causal connection between that violation and Chris–Craft's injury, and no matter how serious the injury. I disagree with this holding.

No one seriously questions the premise that Congress implicitly created a private right of action when it enacted § 14(e) in 1968.[25] Also beyond serious question is the proposition that the members of the class which Congress was especially interested in protecting may invoke that private remedy and, further, that the shareholders of a target corpora-tion are members of that class. The Court nevertheless holds that Chris–Craft may not recover because the protected class does not include tender-offerors even though they may also be shareholders; and, at least implicitly, that to the extent Chris–Craft was injured in its status as a shareholder, its injury is not of a kind that the statute was intended to avoid. I am persuaded that both holdings are erroneous.

I

* * * Section 14(e) was patterned after § 14(a), which regulates proxy contests. It is clear that a shareholder may recover in a suit under § 14(a) even though he was not himself deceived by the misrepre-sentation.[26] I do not understand why § 14(e) should receive any nar-

25. [By the Justice] Although original-ly one might have argued that the private remedies created by the Securities Acts are limited to those expressly described in the legislation itself, history has foreclosed any such argument today. The statutes origi-nally enacted in 1933 and 1934 have been amended so often with full congressional awareness of the judicial interpretation of Rule 10b–5 as implicitly creating a private remedy, that we must now assume that Congress intended to create rights for the specific beneficiaries of the legislation as well as duties to be policed by the SEC. This case therefore does not present the same kind of issue discussed in Cort v. Ash, 422 U.S. 66, 95 S.Ct. 2080, 45 L.Ed.2d 26, namely, *whether* the statute created an implied private remedy. Rather, the ques-tion presented here is *who* may invoke that remedy. Nevertheless, it is noteworthy that none of the factors identified in the *Cort* opinion militates against implying a private cause of action in favor of Chris–Craft. Indeed, it is beyond dispute that here, as in J.I. Case Co. v. Borak, 377 U.S. 426, 431–433, 84 S.Ct. 1555, 1559–1560, 12

L.Ed.2d 423, the asserted private remedy would unquestionably aid the "primary goal" of the statute.

26. [By the Justice] In Mills v. Electric Auto–Lite, 396 U.S. 375, 90 S.Ct. 616, 24 L.Ed.2d 593 (1970), minority shareholders brought suit to set aside a merger on the ground that a proxy solicitation had been misleading. The suit was brought before the merger; obviously the plaintiffs were then aware of the misrepresentation, and in fact they voted against the merger which was consummated despite their votes. This Court held that the minority shareholders were entitled to some relief, and while not specifying that relief, noted that "[m]onetary relief will, of course, also, be a possibility." 396 U.S., at 388, 90 S.Ct., at 623. If the defect in the proxy solicita-tion related to a term of the merger, an accounting could be ordered so that the shareholders would "receive the value that was represented as coming to them"; oth-erwise, monetary relief would be available "if the merger resulted in a reduction of

rower construction.[27] At the very least, the Court should allow all shareholders injured by a violation of § 14(e) to assert a damage claim against the wrongdoer. Neither the extraordinary size of Chris–Craft's investment in Piper stock, nor the fact that the stock had been owned for only a few months, should deprive Chris–Craft of the right to assert a remedy available to the other members of the shareholder class which § 14(e) was plainly designed to protect.

II

Even if we disregard Chris–Craft's stock ownership in Piper and focus only on its status as a tender-offeror, it remains clear to me that its legal rights were invaded by the defendants' violation of § 14(e). This conclusion is compelled by (a) a fair evaluation of the legislative purpose in the light of the rationale of J.I. Case Co. v. Borak, 377 U.S. 426, 84 S.Ct. 1555, 12 L.Ed.2d 423; and (b) respect for the opinions of the Securities and Exchange Commission and the numerous federal judges who have recognized that § 14(e) is little more than a restatement of Rule 10b–5 unless it has broadened the class of potential litigants who may challenge defective cash tender offers to include rival contestants for control as well as shareholders. * * *

Notes

(1) The majority opinion describes its holding as "a limited one" and "narrow" (see n. 24). Do you agree?

(2) Who now has standing under § 14(e)? In part because of the opacity of the *Chris–Craft* opinion, the state of the law with respect to private suits under section 14(e) is less than satisfactory. Suits by competing *offerors* for damages appear to be completely foreclosed by *Chris–Craft;* some courts, however, have permitted offerors to sue for equitable relief to compel correction of misleading statements. The leading case to this effect is Mobil Corp. v. Marathon Oil Co., 669 F.2d 366 (6th Cir.1981). The correctness of this result has been questioned, see e.g. Astronics Corp. v. Protective Closures, Inc., 561 F.Supp. 329 (W.D.N.Y.1983), but usually an offeror is also a shareholder of the target and should be able to sue on that basis. Macfadden Holdings, Inc. v. J.B. Acquisition Corp., 802 F.2d 62 (2d Cir.1986). Recent cases have also sometimes allowed the *issuer* to bring suits to enjoin violations of section 14(e) on a *jus tertii* theory on behalf of shareholders. See Polaroid Corp. v. Disney, 862 F.2d 987 (3d Cir.1988); City Capital Associates v. Interco, Inc., 860 F.2d 60 (3d Cir.1988); Florida Commercial Banks v. Culverhouse, 772 F.2d 1513 (11th Cir.1985). Again,

---

the earnings or earnings potential of their holdings." Id., at 388–389. * * *

27. [By the Justice] The tender offer is just one species of solicitation that either an incumbent or an outside group may use in a contest for control of a corporation. Power to direct the destiny of the corporation may be obtained by acquiring proxies for a majority of the shares, by acquiring the shares themselves, or more typically by a combination of proxies and actual purchases. Section 14 broadly prohibits fraudulent solicitations, not merely to protect the individual shareholder from casting a misguided vote or from making an ill-advised sale, but more importantly to protect the corporate entity as a whole from the consequences of a vital decision procured by fraud.

however, there are dissenting voices. Gateway Industries, Inc. v. Agency Rent-A-Car Inc., 495 F.Supp. 92 (N.D.Ill.1980). It seems clear that shareholders of the target themselves have standing since they are the specific beneficiaries of the disclosure requirements of the Williams Act. E.g. Plaine v. McCabe, 797 F.2d 713 (9th Cir.1986). Indeed one suspects that if courts close off section 14(e) suits by competing offerors and issuers, one would find more shareholders intervening or suing on their own, perhaps with financial assistance from competing offerors and issuers. There appears to be no case in which money damages have been awarded under section 14(e) for failure to comply with disclosure requirements.

(3) Schreiber v. Burlington Northern, Inc., 472 U.S. 1, 105 S.Ct. 2458, 86 L.Ed.2d 1 (1985), involved a suit by a shareholder of El Paso Gas Company who had tendered shares to Burlington pursuant to a hostile bid for El Paso. Thereafter Burlington and El Paso worked out a settlement by which the original tender offer was withdrawn and a new offer for significantly fewer shares was made. As a result persons tendering under the second offer had substantially fewer shares purchased under the SEC proration rules than they would have under the first offer. Plaintiff argued that the substitution of tender offers was "manipulative" and a violation of section 14(e). The Supreme Court held, relying on Santa Fe Industries, Inc. v. Green, p. 969 infra, that section 14(e) only covers "manipulative" acts that involve misrepresentation or nondisclosure and no cause of action was stated since the transactions in question were fully disclosed.

(4) People who are specialists in any area develop their own slang references to the phenomena they deal with every day. Persons who specialize in tender and exchange offers—attorneys representing either targets or aggressors, financial advisers, brokers, proxy solicitation firm employees, and others—are no exception. Consider the following:

(a) "Saturday Night Special"—a pre-Williams Act surprise tender offer which expires in one week. Designed to capitalize on panic and haste, such an offer may be made Friday afternoon to take advantage of the fact that markets and most offices are closed on Saturday and Sunday.

(b) "Bear Hug"—a takeover attempt that consists of a proposal made to the directors. The proposal may be for a merger or for a cash tender or exchange offer not opposed by management. Though the approach may be friendly, there is a veiled or explicit threat that if the target chooses not to negotiate, an unfriendly offer may result.

(c) "White knight"—a friendly suitor, e.g. Bangor Punta or Grumman.

(d) "Gray knight"—a bidder not solicited by a target who opportunistically tries to take advantage of the resistance of the target.

(e) "Smoking gun"—a mistake by the aggressor that may be used by the target to gain additional time.

(f) "Show stopper"—a smoking gun that is so serious that the entire takeover attempt must be cancelled.

(g) "Arbs"—arbitragers. Arbs are natural allies of aggressors. Arbs may purchase shares in advance of a takeover attempt that involves a bear hug and then vote or urge the directors to accept the proposal.

(h) "Shark repellent"—originally the state tender offer statutes described below; more generally amendments to articles of incorporation or other defensive preparation in advance of a tender offer to make tender offers more difficult.

(i) "Porcupine provisions"—defensive provisions in articles of incorporation or bylaws designed to make unwanted takeover attempts impossible or impractical without the consent of the target's management. Porcupine provisions are also discussed below.

(j) "Lockup"—the setting aside of securities for purchase by friendly interests in order to defeat or make more difficult a takeover attempt. An option giving friendly interests the right to buy a "crown jewel" at a favorable price is also referred to as a "lockup."

(k) "Golden parachutes"—lucrative employment and fringe benefit contracts given to top management in target corporations. The purposes of such contracts in part may be to assure the continued loyalty of management in stressful situations, and in part to increase the cost of a successful takeover by increasing the costs chargeable to the target corporation after it is taken over.

(l) "Pac-man defense"—a counter tender offer by the target for the aggressor's shares as a device to fend off an unwanted takeover attempt.

(m) "Scorched earth defense"—the strategy of entering into commitments to dispose of the target's most desirable assets on condition that the takeover succeeds. The object is to deprive a successful aggressor of the assets he is seeking, thereby deterring unwanted takeovers.

(n) "Crown Jewel"—the most prized asset of a corporation, i.e. that which makes it an attractive takeover target. A defensive tactic against a hostile tender offer may be to sell this asset to another party, thereby removing the assets that the unfriendly bidder was hoping to acquire and encouraging it to cease its offer without purchasing any shares of the subject company.

(o) "Poison pill"—a class of securities of the target company convertible upon consummation of any merger or similar transaction into more valuable rights or interests; poison pills apply only to transactions not approved by the target's board of directors.

(p) "Greenmail"—the purchase of a substantial block of the subject company's securities by an unfriendly suitor with the primary purpose of coercing the subject company into repurchasing the block at a premium over the amount paid by the suitor. In 1987, Congress enacted a special 50 percent non-deductible "anti-greenmail" excise tax. Some state statutes also attempt to make greenmail unprofitable.

(q) "Bust up" or "break up" takeovers—takeovers with the stated intention of breaking up the target and selling component parts. Bust up takeovers assume that the sum of the parts may sometimes be greater than the value of the whole.

(r) "Lollypop"—an offer to all shareholders except the aggressor to repurchase for cash or debt a portion of each shareholder's holding. [A "lollypop" tastes good to all the shareholders except the hostile bidder.]

(s) Bridge loans—Financing provided by investment bankers usually from their own resources that is viewed as temporary and to be refinanced at a later date, usually by the issuance of junk bonds.

(t) Junk—Junk bonds or other securities that are below investment grade and used by aggressors as a substitute for cash.

(u) LBO—A leveraged buyout.

(v) MBO—An LBO instituted by management or one in which management is a major participant.

(w) Mezzanine financing—A type of bridge loan.

(x) Standstill agreement—A contract between a former aggressor and a target in which the aggressor agrees not to acquire additional shares of the target for a specified period without the consent of the target's management.

(5) In December, 1977, Chris–Craft sold its interest in Piper to Bangor Punta for $40 million in cash and a one year promissory note for $9.8 million.

CTS CORPORATION v. DYNAMICS CORP. OF AMERICA

Supreme Court of the United States, 1987.
481 U.S. 69, 107 S.Ct. 1637, 95 L.Ed.2d 67.

JUSTICE POWELL delivered the opinion of the Court.

This case presents the questions whether the Control Share Acquisitions Chapter of the Indiana Business Corporation Law, Ind.Code § 23–1–42–1 *et seq.* (Supp.1986), is preempted by the Williams Act or violates the Commerce Clause of the Federal Constitution, Art. I, § 8, cl. 3.

I

A

On March 4, 1986, the Governor of Indiana signed a revised Indiana Business Corporation Law, Ind.Code § 23–1–17–1 *et seq.* (Supp. 1986). That law included the Control Share Acquisitions Chapter (Indiana Act or Act). Beginning on August 1, 1987, the Act will apply to any corporation incorporated in Indiana, § 23–1–17–3(a), unless the corporation amends its articles or incorporation or bylaws to opt out of the Act, § 23–1–42–5. Before that date, any Indiana corporation can opt into the Act by resolution of its board of directors. § 23–1–17–3(b). The Act applies only to "issuing public corporations." The term "corporation" includes only businesses incorporated in Indiana. See § 23–1–20–5. An "issuing public corporation" is defined as:

"a corporation that has:

"(1) one hundred (100) or more shareholders;

"(2) its principal place of business, its principal office, or substantial assets within Indiana; and

"(3) either:

"(A) more than ten percent (10%) of its shareholders resident in Indiana;

"(B) more than ten percent (10%) of its shares owned by Indiana residents; or

"(C) ten thousand (10,000) shareholders resident in Indiana." § 23–1–42–4(a).[28]

The Act focuses on the acquisition of "control shares" in an issuing public corporation. Under the Act, an entity acquires "control shares" whenever it acquires shares that, but for the operation of the Act, would bring its voting power in the corporation to or above any of three thresholds: 20%, 33⅓%, or 50%. § 23–1–42–1. An entity that acquires control shares does not necessarily acquire voting rights. Rather, it gains those rights only "to the extent granted by resolution approved by the shareholders of the issuing public corporation." § 23–1–42–9(a). Section 23–1–42–9(b) requires a majority vote of all disinterested[29] shareholders holding each class of stock for passage of such a resolution. The practical effect of this requirement is to condition acquisition of control of a corporation on approval of a majority of the pre-existing disinterested shareholders.

The shareholders decide whether to confer rights on the control shares at the next regularly scheduled meeting of the shareholders, or at a specially scheduled meeting. The acquiror can require management of the corporation to hold such a special meeting within 50 days if

---

28. [By the Court] These thresholds are much higher than the 5% threshold acquisition requirement that brings a tender offer under the coverage of the Williams Act.

29. [By the Court] "Interested shares" are shares with respect to which the acquiror, an officer, or an inside director of the corporation "may exercise or direct the exercise of the voting power of the corporation in the election of directors." § 23–1–42–3. If the record date passes before the acquiror purchases shares pursuant to the tender offer, the purchased shares will not be "interested shares" within the meaning of the Act; although the acquiror may own the shares on the date of the meeting, it will not "exercise . . . the voting power" of the shares.

As a practical matter, the record date usually will pass before shares change hands. Under Securities and Exchange Commission (SEC) regulations, the shares cannot be purchased until 20 business days after the offer commences. 17 CFR § 240.14e–1(a) (1986). If the acquiror seeks an early resolution of the issue—as most acquirors will—the meeting required by the Act must be held no more than 50 calendar days after the offer commences, about three weeks after the earliest date on which the shares could be purchased. See § 23–1–42–7. The Act requires management to give notice of the meeting "as promptly as reasonably practicable . . . to all shareholders of record as of the record date set for the meeting." § 23–1–42–8(a). It seems likely that management of the target corporation would violate this obligation if it delayed setting the record date and sending notice until after 20 business days had passed. Thus, we assume that the record date usually will be set before the date on which federal law first permits purchase of the shares.

it files an "acquiring person statement," [30] requests the meeting, and agrees to pay the expenses of the meeting. See § 23–1–42–7. If the shareholders do not vote to restore voting rights to the shares, the corporation may redeem the control shares from the acquiror at fair market value, but it is not required to do so. § 23–1–42–10(b). Similarly, if the acquiror does not file an acquiring person statement with the corporation, the corporation may, if its bylaws or articles of incorporation so provide, redeem the shares at any time after 60 days after the acquiror's last acquisition. § 23–1–42–10(a).

B

On March 10, 1986, appellee Dynamics Corporation of America (Dynamics) owned 9.6% of the common stock of appellant CTS Corporation, an Indiana corporation. On that day, six days after the Act went into effect, Dynamics announced a tender offer for another million shares in CTS; purchase of those shares would have brought Dynamics' ownership interest in CTS to 27.5%. Also on March 10, Dynamics filed suit in the United States District Court for the Northern District of Illinois, alleging that CTS had violated the federal securities laws in a number of respects no longer relevant to these proceedings. On March 27, the board of directors of CTS, an Indiana corporation, elected to be governed by the provisions of the Act, see § 23–1–17–3.

Four days later, on March 31, Dynamics moved for leave to amend its complaint to allege that the Act is pre-empted by the Williams Act, and violates the Commerce Clause, Art. I, § 8, cl. 3. Dynamics sought a temporary restraining order, a preliminary injunction, and declaratory relief against CTS' use of the Act. On April 9, the District Court ruled that the Williams Act pre-empts the Indiana Act and granted Dynamics' motion for declaratory relief. 637 F.Supp. 389 (N.D.Ill.1986). Relying on Justice White's plurality opinion in *Edgar v. MITE Corp.*, 457 U.S. 624, 102 S.Ct. 2629, 73 L.Ed.2d 269 (1982), the court concluded that the Act "wholly frustrates the purpose and objective of Congress in striking a balance between the investor, management, and the takeover bidder in takeover contests." 637 F.Supp., at 399. A week later, on April 17, the District Court issued an opinion accepting Dynamics' claim that the Act violates the Commerce Clause. This holding rested on the court's conclusion that "the substantial interference with interstate commerce created by the [Act] outweighs the articulated local benefits so as to create an impermissible indirect burden on interstate commerce." *Id.*, at 406. The District Court certified its decisions on the Williams Act and Commerce Clause claims as final under Federal Rule of Civil Procedure 54(b). Ibid.

CTS appealed the District Court's holdings on these claims to the Court of Appeals for the Seventh Circuit. Because of the imminence of CTS' annual meeting, the Court of Appeals consolidated and expedited

---

30. [By the Court] An "acquiring person statement" is an information statement describing, *inter alia*, the identity of the acquiring person and the terms and extent of the proposed acquisition. See § 23–1–42–6.

the two appeals. On April 23rd—23 days after Dynamics first contested application of the Act in the District Court—the Court of Appeals issued an order affirming the judgment of the District Court. The opinion followed on May 28. 794 F.2d 250 (C.A.7 1986).

After disposing of a variety of questions not relevant to this appeal, the Court of Appeals examined Dynamics' claim that the Williams Act pre-empts the Indiana Act. The court looked first to the plurality opinion in *Edgar v. MITE Corp., supra,* in which three Justices found that the Williams Act pre-empts state statutes that upset the balance between target management and a tender offeror. The court noted that some commentators had disputed this view of the Williams Act, concluding instead that the Williams Act was "an anti-takeover statute, expressing a view, however benighted, that hostile takeovers are bad." 794 F.2d, at 262. It also noted:

> "[I]t is a big leap from saying that the Williams Act does not itself exhibit much hostility to tender offers to saying that it implicitly forbids states to adopt more hostile regulations. . . . But whatever doubts of the Williams' Act preemptive intent we might entertain as an original matter are stilled by the weight of precedent." *Ibid.*

Once the court had decided to apply the analysis of the *MITE* plurality, it found the case straightforward:

> "Very few tender offers could run the gauntlet that Indiana has set up. In any event, if the Williams Act is to be taken as a congressional determination that a month (roughly) is enough time to force a tender offer to be kept open, 50 days is too much; and 50 days is the minimum under the Indiana act if the target corporation so chooses." *Id.,* at 263.

The court next addressed Dynamic's Commerce Clause challenge to the Act. Applying the balancing test articulated in *Pike v. Bruce Church, Inc.,* 397 U.S. 137, 90 S.Ct. 844, 25 L.Ed.2d 174 (1970), the court found the Act unconstitutional:

> "Unlike a state's blue sky law the Indiana statute is calculated to impede transactions between residents of other states. For the sake of trivial or even negative benefits to its residents Indiana is depriving nonresidents of the valued opportunity to accept tender offers from other nonresidents.

> ". . . Even if a corporation's tangible assets are immovable, the efficiency with which they are employed and the proportions in which the earnings they generate are divided between management and shareholders depends on the market for corporate control—an interstate, indeed international, market that the State of Indiana is not authorized to opt out of, as in effect it has done in this statute." 794 F.2d, at 264.

Finally, the court addressed the "internal affairs" doctrine, a "principle of conflict of laws . . . designed to make sure that the law of only one state shall govern the internal affairs of a corporation or other association." *Ibid.* It stated:

"We may assume without having to decide that Indiana has a broad latitude in regulating those affairs, even when the consequence may be to make it harder to take over an Indiana corporation. . . . But in this case the effect on the interstate market in securities and corporate control is direct, intended, and substantial. . . . [T]hat the mode of regulation involves jiggering with voting rights cannot take it outside the scope of judicial review under the commerce clause." *Ibid.*

Accordingly, the court affirmed the judgment of the District Court.

Both Indiana and CTS filed jurisdictional statements. We noted probable jurisdiction and now reverse. * * *

II

The first question in these cases is whether the Williams Act pre-empts the Indiana Act. As we have stated frequently, absent an explicit indication by Congress of an intent to pre-empt state law, a state statute is pre-empted only

" 'where compliance with both federal and state regulations is a physical impossibility. . .,' *Florida Lime & Avocado Growers, Inc. v. Paul,* 373 U.S. 132, 142–143 (83 S.Ct. 1210, 1217, 10 L.Ed.2d 248) (1963), or where the state 'law stands as an obstacle to the accomplishment and execution of the full purposes and objectives of Congress.' *Hines v. Davidowitz,* 312 U.S. 52, 67 (61 S.Ct. 399, 404, 85 L.Ed. 581) (1941). . . ." *Ray v. Atlantic Richfield Co.,* 435 U.S. 151, 158, 98 S.Ct. 988, 994, 55 L.Ed.2d 179 (1978).

Because it is entirely possible for entities to comply with both the Williams Act and the Indiana Act, the state statute can be pre-empted only if it frustrates the purposes of the federal law.

A

Our discussion begins with a brief summary of the structure and purposes of the Williams Act. Congress passed the Williams Act in 1968 in response to the increasing number of hostile tender offers. Before its passage, these transactions were not covered by the disclosure requirements of the federal securities laws. See *Piper v. Chris-Craft Industries, Inc.,* 430 U.S. 1, 22, 97 S.Ct. 926, 939–940, 51 L.Ed.2d 124 (1977). The Williams Act, backed by regulations of the SEC, imposes requirements in two basic areas. First, it requires the offeror to file a statement disclosing information about the offer, including: the offeror's background and identity; the source and amount of the funds to be used in making the purchase; the purpose of the purchase, including any plans to liquidate the company or make major changes in its corporate structure; and the extent of the offeror's holdings in the target company.

Second, the Williams Act, and the regulations that accompany it, establish procedural rules to govern tender offers. For example, stockholders who tender their shares may withdraw them during the first 15 business days of the tender offer and, if the offeror has not purchased their shares, any time after 60 days from commencement of the offer.

The offer must remain open for at least 20 business days. If more shares are tendered than the offeror sought to purchase, purchases must be made on a pro rata basis from each tendering shareholder. Finally, the offeror must pay the same price for all purchases; if the offering price is increased before the end of the offer, those who already have tendered must receive the benefit of the increased price.

B

The Indiana Act differs in major respects from the Illinois statute that the Court considered in *Edgar v. MITE Corp.*, 457 U.S. 624, 102 S.Ct. 2629, 73 L.Ed.2d 269 (1982). After reviewing the legislative history of the Williams Act, Justice White, joined by Chief Justice Burger and Justice Blackmun (the plurality), concluded that the Williams Act struck a careful balance between the interests of offerors and target companies, and that any state statute that "upset" this balance was pre-empted. *Id.*, at 632–634, 102 S.Ct., at 2635–2636.

The plurality then identified three offending features of the Illinois statute. Justice White's opinion first noted that the Illinois statute provided for a 20–day precommencement period. During this time, management could disseminate its views on the upcoming offer to shareholders, but offerors could not publish their offers. The plurality found that this provision gave management "a powerful tool to combat tender offers." *Id.*, at 635, 102 S.Ct., at 2637. This contrasted dramatically with the Williams Act; Congress had deleted express precommencement notice provisions from the Williams Act. According to the plurality, Congress had determined that the potentially adverse consequences of such a provision on shareholders should be avoided. Thus, the plurality concluded that the Illinois provision "frustrate[d] the objectives of the Williams Act." *Ibid.* The second criticized feature of the Illinois statute was a provision for a hearing on a tender offer that, because it set no deadline, allowed management " 'to stymie indefinitely a takeover,' " *id.*, at 637, 102 S.Ct., at 2638. * * * The plurality noted that " 'delay can seriously impede a tender offer,' " 457 U.S., at 637, 102 S.Ct., at 2638 (quoting *Great Western United Corp. v. Kidwell*, 577 F.2d 1256, 1277 (CA5 1978) (Wisdom, J.)), and that "Congress anticipated that investors and the takeover offeror would be free to go forward without unreasonable delay," 457 U.S., at 639, 102 S.Ct., at 2639. Accordingly, the plurality concluded that this provision conflicted with the Williams Act. The third troublesome feature of the Illinois statute was its requirement that the fairness of tender offers would be reviewed by the Illinois Secretary of State. Noting that "Congress intended for investors to be free to make their own decisions," the plurality concluded that " '[t]he state thus offers investor protection at the expense of investor autonomy—an approach quite in conflict with that adopted by Congress.' " *Id.*, at 639–640, 102 S.Ct., at 2639 (quoting *MITE Corp. v. Dixon, supra*, at 494).

C

As the plurality opinion in *MITE* did not represent the views of a majority of the Court, we are not bound by its reasoning. We need not question that reasoning, however, because we believe the Indiana Act passes muster even under the broad interpretation of the Williams Act articulated by Justice White in *MITE*. As is apparent from our summary of its reasoning, the overriding concern of the *MITE* plurality was that the Illinois statute considered in that case operated to favor management against offerors, to the detriment of shareholders. By contrast, the statute now before the Court protects the independent shareholder against both of the contending parties. Thus, the Act furthers a basic purpose of the Williams Act, " 'plac[ing] investors on an equal footing with the takeover bidder,' " *Piper v. Chris–Craft Industries,* 430 U.S., at 30, 97 S.Ct., at 943 (quoting the Senate Report accompanying the Williams Act, S.Rep. No. 550, 90th Cong., 1st Sess., 4 (1967)).[31]

The Indiana Act operates on the assumption, implicit in the Williams Act, that independent shareholders faced with tender offers often are at a disadvantage. By allowing such shareholders to vote as a group, the Act protects them from the coercive aspects of some tender offers. If, for example, shareholders believe that a successful tender offer will be followed by a purchase of nontendering shares at a depressed price, individual shareholders may tender their shares—even if they doubt the tender offer is in the corporation's best interest—to protect themselves from being forced to sell their shares at a depressed price. As the SEC explains: "The alternative of not accepting the tender offer is virtual assurance that, if the offer is successful, the shares will have to be sold in the lower priced, second step." Two–Tier Tender Offer Pricing and Non–Tender Offer Purchase Programs, SEC Exchange Act Rel. No. 21079 (June 21, 1984) (hereinafter SEC Release No. 21079). See Lowenstein, Pruning Deadwood in Hostile Takeovers: A Proposal for Legislation, 83 Colum.L.Rev. 249, 307–309 (1983). In such a situation under the Indiana Act, the shareholders as a group, acting in the corporation's best interest, could reject the offer, although individual shareholders might be inclined to accept it. The desire of the Indiana Legislature to protect shareholders of Indiana corporations

---

31. [By the Court] Dynamics finds evidence of an intent to favor management in several features of the Act. * * *

The Act * * * imposes some added expenses on the offeror, requiring it, *inter alia,* to pay the costs of special shareholder meetings to vote on the transfer of voting rights, see § 23–1–42–7(a). In our view, the expenses of such a meeting fairly are charged to the offeror. A corporation pays the costs of annual meetings that it holds to discuss its affairs. If an offeror—who has no official position with the corporation—desires a special meeting solely to discuss the voting rights of the offeror, it is not unreasonable to have the offeror pay for the meeting.

Of course, by regulating tender offers, the Act makes them more expensive and thus deters them somewhat, but this type of reasonable regulation does not alter the balance between management and offeror in any significant way. The principal result of the Act is to grant shareholders the power to deliberate collectively about the merits of tender offers. This result is fully in accord with the purposes of the Williams Act.

from this type of coercive offer does not conflict with the Williams Act. Rather, it furthers the federal policy of investor protection.

In implementing its goal, the Indiana Act avoids the problems the plurality discussed in *MITE*. Unlike the *MITE* statute, the Indiana Act does not give either management or the offeror an advantage in communicating with the shareholders about the impending offer. The Act also does not impose an indefinite delay on tender offers. Nothing in the Act prohibits an offeror from consummating an offer on the 20th business day, the earliest day permitted under applicable federal regulations. Nor does the Act allow the state government to interpose its views of fairness between willing buyers and sellers of shares of the target company. Rather, the Act allows *shareholders* to evaluate the fairness of the offer collectively.

D

The Court of Appeals based its finding of pre-emption on its view that the practical effect of the Indiana Act is to delay consummation of tender offers until 50 days after the commencement of the offer. 794 F.2d, at 263. As did the Court of Appeals, Dynamics reasons that no rational offeror will purchase shares until it gains assurance that those shares will carry voting rights. Because it is possible that voting rights will not be conferred until a shareholder meeting 50 days after commencement of the offer, Dynamics concludes that the Act imposes a 50–day delay. This, it argues, conflicts with the shorter 20–business–day period established by the SEC as the minimum period for which a tender offer may be held open. We find the alleged conflict illusory.

* * *

Finally, we note that the Williams Act would pre-empt a variety of state corporate laws of hitherto unquestioned validity if it were construed to pre-empt any state statute that may limit or delay the free exercise of power after a successful tender offer. State corporate laws commonly permit corporations to stagger the terms of their directors. See Model Business Corp. Act § 37 (1969 draft) in 3 Model Business Corp. Act Ann. (2d ed. 1971) (hereinafter MBCA); American Bar Foundation, Revised Model Business Corp. Act § 8.06 (1984 draft) (1985) (hereinafter RMBCA).[32] By staggering the terms of directors, and thus having annual elections for only one class of directors each year, corporations may delay the time when a successful offeror gains control of the board of directors. Similarly, state corporation laws commonly provide for cumulative voting. See MBCA § 33, par. 4; RMBCA § 7.28. By enabling minority shareholders to assure themselves of representation in each class of directors, cumulative voting provisions can delay further the ability of offerors to gain untrammeled authority over the affairs of the target corporation. See Hochman & Folger, Deflecting

---

32. [By the Court] Every State except Arkansas and California allows classification of directors to stagger their terms of office. See 2 Model Business Corp. Act Ann. § 8.06, p. 830 (3d ed., Supp.1986).

Takeovers: Charter and By–Law Techniques, 34 Bus.Law. 537, 538–539 (1979).

In our view, the possibility that the Indiana Act will delay some tender offers is insufficient to require a conclusion that the Williams Act pre-empts the Act. The longstanding prevalence of state regulation in this area suggests that, if Congress had intended to pre-empt all state laws that delay the acquisition of voting control following a tender offer, it would have said so explicitly. The regulatory conditions that the Act places on tender offers are consistent with the text and the purposes of the Williams Act. Accordingly, we hold that the Williams Act does not pre-empt the Indiana Act.

III

As an alternative basis for its decision, the Court of Appeals held that the Act violates the Commerce Clause of the Federal Constitution. We now address this holding. * * * [The Court concludes that the Indiana Act does not discriminate against interstate commerce nor does it adversely affect interstate commerce by subjecting activities to inconsistent regulations.]

C

The Court of Appeals did not find the Act unconstitutional for either of these threshold reasons. Rather, its decision rested on its view of the Act's potential to hinder tender offers. We think the Court of Appeals failed to appreciate the significance for Commerce Clause analysis of the fact that state regulation of corporate governance is regulation of entities whose very existence and attributes are a product of state law. As Chief Justice Marshall explained:

> "A corporation is an artificial being, invisible, intangible, and existing only in contemplation of law. Being the mere creature of law, it possesses only those properties which the charter of its creation confers upon it, either expressly, or as incidental to its very existence. These are such as are supposed best calculated to effect the object for which it was created." *Trustees of Dartmouth College v. Woodward,* 4 Wheat. 518, 636, 4 L.Ed. 518 (1819).

Every State in this country has enacted laws regulating corporate governance. By prohibiting certain transactions, and regulating others, such laws necessarily affect certain aspects of interstate commerce. This necessarily is true with respect to corporations with shareholders in States other than the State of incorporation. Large corporations that are listed on national exchanges, or even regional exchanges, will have shareholders in many States and shares that are traded frequently. The markets that facilitate this national and international participation in ownership of corporations are essential for providing capital not only for new enterprises but also for established companies that need to expand their businesses. This beneficial free market system depends at its core upon the fact that a corporation— except in the rarest situations—is organized under, and governed by, the law of a single jurisdiction, traditionally the corporate law of the State of its incorporation.

These regulatory laws may affect directly a variety of corporate transactions. Mergers are a typical example. In view of the substantial effect that a merger may have on the shareholders' interests in a corporation, many States require supermajority votes to approve mergers. See, *e.g.*, MBCA § 73 (requiring approval of a merger by a majority of all shares, rather than simply a majority of votes cast); RMBCA § 11.03 (same). By requiring a greater vote for mergers than is required for other transactions, these laws make it more difficult for corporations to merge. State laws also may provide for "dissenters' rights" under which minority shareholders who disagree with corporate decisions to take particular actions are entitled to sell their shares to the corporation at fair market value. See, *e.g.*, MBCA §§ 80, 81; RMBCA § 13.02. By requiring the corporation to purchase the shares of dissenting shareholders, these laws may inhibit a corporation from engaging in the specified transactions.[33]

It thus is an accepted part of the business landscape in this country for States to create corporations, to prescribe their powers, and to define the rights that are acquired by purchasing their shares. A State has an interest in promoting stable relationships among parties involved in the corporations it charters, as well as in ensuring that investors in such corporations have an effective voice in corporate affairs.

There can be no doubt that the Act reflects these concerns. The primary purpose of the Act is to protect the shareholders of Indiana corporations. It does this by affording shareholders, when a takeover offer is made, an opportunity to decide collectively whether the resulting change in voting control of the corporation, as they perceive it, would be desirable. A change of management may have important effects on the shareholders' interests; it is well within the State's role

---

33. [By the Court] Numerous other common regulations may affect both nonresident and resident shareholders of a corporation. Specified votes may be required for the sale of all of the corporation's assets. See MBCA § 79; RMBCA § 12.02. The election of directors may be staggered over a period of years to prevent abrupt changes in management. See MBCA § 37; RMBCA § 8.06. Various classes of stock may be created with differences in voting rights as to dividends and on liquidation. See MBCA § 15; RMBCA § 6.01(c). Provisions may be made for cumulative voting. See MBCA § 33, par. 4; RMBCA § 7.28. Corporations may adopt restrictions on payment of dividends to ensure that specified ratios of assets to liabilities are maintained for the benefit of the holders of corporate bonds or notes. See MBCA § 45 (noting that a corporation's articles of incorporation can restrict payment of dividends); RMBCA § 6.40 (same). Where the shares of a corporation are held in States other than that of incorporation, actions taken pursuant to these and similar provisions of state law will affect all shareholders alike wherever they reside or are domiciled.

Nor is it unusual for partnership law to restrict certain transactions. For example, a purchaser of a partnership interest generally can gain a right to control the business only with the consent of other owners. See Uniform Partnership Act § 27, Revised Uniform Limited Partnership Act §§ 702, 704. These provisions—in force in the great majority of the States—bear a striking resemblance to the Act at issue in this case.

as overseer of corporate governance to offer this opportunity. The autonomy provided by allowing shareholders collectively to determine whether the takeover is advantageous to their interests may be especially beneficial where a hostile tender offer may coerce shareholders into tendering their shares.

Appellee Dynamics responds to this concern by arguing that the prospect of coercive tender offers is illusory, and that tender offers generally should be favored because they reallocate corporate assets into the hands of management who can use them most effectively.[34] See generally Easterbrook & Fischel, The Proper Role of a Target's Management in Responding to a Tender Offer, 94 Harv.L.Rev. 1161 (1981). * * * Indiana's concern with tender offers is not groundless. Indeed, the potentially coercive aspects of tender offers have been recognized by the SEC, see SEC Release No. 21079, and by a number of scholarly commentators, see, *e.g.,* Bradley & Rosenzweig, Defensive Stock Repurchases, 99 Harv.L.Rev. 1377, 1412–1413 (1986). * * * The Constitution does not require the States to subscribe to any particular economic theory. We are not inclined "to second-guess the empirical judgments of lawmakers concerning the utility of legislation," *Kassel v. Consolidated Freightways Corp.,* 450 U.S., at 679, 101 S.Ct., at 1321 (Brennan, J., concurring in judgment). In our view, the possibility of coercion in some takeover bids offers additional justification for Indiana's decision to promote the autonomy of independent shareholders.

Dynamics argues in any event that the State has " 'no legitimate interest in protecting the nonresident shareholders.' " Dynamics relies heavily on the statement by the *MITE* Court that "[i]nsofar as the . . . law burdens out-of-state transactions, there is nothing to be weighed in the balance to sustain the law." 457 U.S., at 644, 102 S.Ct., at 2641. But that comment was made in reference to an Illinois law that applied as well to out-of-state corporations as to in-state corporations. We agree that Indiana has no interest in protecting nonresident shareholders *of nonresident corporations.* But this Act applies only to corporations incorporated in Indiana. We reject the contention that Indiana has no interest in providing for the shareholders of its corporations the voting autonomy granted by the Act. Indiana has a substantial interest in preventing the corporate form from becoming a shield for unfair business dealing. Moreover, unlike the Illinois statute invalidated in *MITE,* the Indiana Act applies only to corporations that have a substantial number of shareholders in Indiana. See Ind.Code § 23–1–

---

34. [By the Court] It is appropriate to note when discussing the merits and demerits of tender offers that generalizations usually require qualification. No one doubts that some successful tender offers will provide more effective management or other benefits such as needed diversification. But there is no reason to *assume* that the type of conglomerate corporation that may result from repetitive takeovers necessarily will result in more effective management or otherwise be beneficial to shareholders. The divergent views in the literature—and even now being debated in the Congress—reflect the reality that the type and utility of tender offers vary widely. Of course, in many situations the offer to shareholders is simply a cash price substantially higher than the market price prior to the offer.

42–4(a)(3) (Supp.1986). Thus, every application of the Indiana Act will affect a substantial number of Indiana residents, whom Indiana indisputably has an interest in protecting.

D

Dynamics' argument that the Act is unconstitutional ultimately rests on its contention that the Act will limit the number of successful tender offers. There is little evidence that this will occur. But even if true, this result would not substantially affect our Commerce Clause analysis. We reiterate that this Act does not prohibit any entity—resident or nonresident—from offering to purchase, or from purchasing, shares in Indiana corporations, or from attempting thereby to gain control. It only provides regulatory procedures designed for the better protection of the corporations' shareholders. We have rejected the "notion that the Commerce Clause protects the particular structure or methods of operation in a . . . market." *Exxon Corp. v. Governor of Maryland,* 437 U.S., at 127, 98 S.Ct., at 2215. The very commodity that is traded in the securities market is one whose characteristics are defined by state law. Similarly, the very commodity that is traded in the "market for corporate control"—the corporation—is one that owes its existence and attributes to state law. Indiana need not define these commodities as other States do; it need only provide that residents and nonresidents have equal access to them. This Indiana has done. Accordingly, even if the Act should decrease the number of successful tender offers for Indiana corporations, this would not offend the Commerce Clause.

IV

On its face, the Indiana Control Share Acquisitions Chapter evenhandedly determines the voting rights of shares of Indiana corporations. The Act does not conflict with the provisions or purposes of the Williams Act. To the limited extent that the Act affects interstate commerce, this is justified by the State's interests in defining the attributes of shares in its corporations and in protecting shareholders. Congress has never questioned the need for state regulation of these matters. Nor do we think such regulation offends the Constitution. Accordingly, we reverse the judgment of the Court of Appeals.

It is so ordered.

JUSTICE SCALIA, concurring in part and concurring in the judgment.

* * * [H]aving found * * * that the Indiana Control Share Acquisitions Chapter neither "discriminates against interstate commerce," nor "create[s] an impermissible risk of inconsistent regulation by different States," I would conclude without further analysis that it is not invalid under the dormant Commerce Clause. * * * Whether the control shares statute "protects shareholders of Indiana corporations," or protects incumbent management seems to me a highly debatable question, but it is extraordinary to think that the constitutionality of the Act should depend on the answer. Nothing in the Constitution says

that the protection of entrenched management is any less important a "putative local benefit" than the protection of entrenched shareholders, and I do not know what qualifies us to make that judgment—or the related judgment as to how effective the present statute is in achieving one or the other objective—or the ultimate (and most ineffable) judgment as to whether, given importance-level x, and effectiveness-level y, the worth of the statute is "outweighed" by impact-on-commerce z.

* * *

I also agree with the Court that the Indiana control shares Act is not pre-empted by the Williams Act, but I reach that conclusion without entering into the debate over the purposes of the two statutes. The Williams Act is governed by the antipre-emption provision of the Securities Exchange Act of 1934, 15 U.S.C. § 78bb(a), which provides that nothing it contains "shall affect the jurisdiction of the securities commission (or any agency or officer performing like functions) of any State over any security or any person insofar as it does not conflict with the provisions of this chapter or the rules and regulations thereunder." Unless it serves no function, that language forecloses pre-emption on the basis of conflicting "purpose" as opposed to conflicting "provision." Even if it does not have literal application to the present case (because, perhaps, the Indiana agency responsible for securities matters has no enforcement responsibility with regard to this legislation), it nonetheless refutes the proposition that Congress meant the Williams Act to displace *all* state laws with conflicting purpose. And if any are to survive, surely the States' corporation codes are among them. It would be peculiar to hold that Indiana could have pursued the purpose at issue here through its blue-sky laws, but cannot pursue it through the State's even more sacrosanct authority over the structure of domestic corporations. Prescribing voting rights for the governance of state-chartered companies is a traditional state function with which the Federal Congress has never, to my knowledge, intentionally interfered. I would require far more evidence than is available here to find implicit pre-emption of that function by a federal statute whose provisions concededly do not conflict with the state law.

I do not share the Court's apparent high estimation of the beneficence of the state statute at issue here. But a law can be both economic folly and constitutional. The Indiana Control Share Acquisitions Chapter is at least the latter. I therefore concur in the judgment of the Court.

JUSTICE WHITE, with whom JUSTICE BLACKMUN and JUSTICE STEVENS join as to Part II, dissenting.

The majority today upholds Indiana's Control Share Acquisitions Chapter, a statute which will predictably foreclose completely some tender offers for stock in Indiana corporations. I disagree with the conclusion that the Chapter is neither pre-empted by the Williams Act nor in conflict with the Commerce Clause. The Chapter undermines the policy of the Williams Act by effectively preventing minority shareholders, in some circumstances, from acting in their own best interests by selling their stock. In addition, the Chapter will substantially burden the interstate market in corporate ownership, particularly if other States follow Indiana's lead as many already have done. The Chapter, therefore, directly inhibits interstate commerce, the very economic consequences the Commerce Clause was intended to prevent. The opinion of the Court of Appeals is far more persuasive than that of the majority today, and the judgment of that court should be affirmed.

it inhibits interstate commerce

* * *

Given the impact of the Control Share Acquisitions Chapter, it is clear that Indiana is directly regulating the purchase and sale of shares of stock in interstate commerce. Appellant CTS' stock is traded on the New York Stock Exchange, and people from all over the country buy and sell CTS' shares daily. Yet, under Indiana's scheme, any prospective purchaser will be effectively precluded from purchasing CTS' shares if the purchaser crosses one of the Chapter's threshold ownership levels and a majority of CTS' shareholders refuse to give the purchaser voting rights. This Court should not countenance such a restraint on interstate trade. * * *

Notes

(1) Prior to the decision in the principal case, and based largely on language in the plurality opinion in *MITE,* a number of academic scholars of the Chicago "law and economics school" argued that an interstate market for corporate control existed that states were powerless to regulate. Under this approach state statutes regulating tender offers seemed clearly unconstitutional and even traditional state corporation law provisions might be invalidated if they unreasonably restricted or interfered with the market for corporate control. This type of argument was basically accepted by Judge Posner in the opinion reversed by the Supreme Court in the principal case. The "market for corporate control" idea was clearly appealing to economists but was troublesome to many lawyers because it seemed to be a "slippery slope" that could federalize much of the state law of corporations to the extent applied to publicly held corporations. The CTS opinion is of major importance in the corporate area because of its dicta about the relative rules of federal and state law in this area.

(2) Langevoort, The Supreme Court and the Politics of Corporate Takeovers: A Comment on CTS Corp. v. Dynamics Corp. of America, 101 Harv.L.Rev. 96, 106–108 (1987): *

> The Indiana law of corporations presumably applies to all corporations chartered there. The Control Shares Acquisition statute, by contrast, applies only to Indiana corporations with (1) their principal place of business, principal office, or substantial assets in Indiana, and (2) a certain concentration of shareholders in Indiana. If the legislature was genuinely concerned with protecting *shareholders*—the predicate for the statute's commerce clause validity—why would it deny its

* Copyright © (1987) by the Harvard Law Review Association.

"protection" to the shareholders of Indiana corporations just because the principal activities and assets of the firm happen to be in Ohio or New York?

From this, one is drawn to the conclusion that Indiana's real interest was in protecting *local businesses* from the rigors of the interstate market for corporate control and that the state was using the claim of shareholder protection largely as a means to that end, hoping that the Act would indeed have a chilling effect. This observation, coupled with the implausibility of the shareholder protection rationale in the first place, strongly suggests that the Indiana statute only creates the illusion of true corporation law. Such a subterfuge is not surprising; the history of tender offer regulation (state and federal) is one of using shareholder protection as a justification for regulation that is really motivated by other objections to hostile bids, notwithstanding the intuitively compelling point that, financially, shareholders are substantial net gainers from the takeover phenomenon.

* * *

The Court's reluctance to question the state's motive may have stemmed from its inability to formulate a workable test to identify legislative motive in the corporate context. The variety of motivations underlying a statute makes it nearly impossible to isolate accurately the impact of protectionist sentiment. To force the courts to determine actual motivation would set them adrift in a lawmaking process characterized by immense special interest pressure, minimal direct voice for shareholder interests, and, perhaps most powerfully, competition among states to retain jurisdiction over local corporations and to attract new ones—any one of which may by itself explain legislation like Indiana's.

(3) Romano, The Future of Hostile Takeovers: Legislation and Public Opinion, 57 Cincinnati Law Review 457, 461–3 (1988):

Although more than twenty states enacted second generation statutes in the years between the *MITE* and *CTS* decisions, legislators and lobbyists were often reluctant to promote legislation for fear of constitutional infirmities. The most frequently adopted version of a second generation statute was therefore one with limited regulatory scope. After the *CTS* decision, however, the pace and scope of legislation changed: fourteen new statutes were adopted within approximately six months. More important, several of the new statutes strengthened less restrictive second generation statutes by using Indiana as a model, and many test *CTS*'s limits by mandating constraints on bidders that go further than the Indiana statute.

The political history of second generation takeover statutes is similar across the states. The statutes are typically enacted rapidly, with virtually unanimous support and little public notice, let alone discussion. They are frequently pushed through the legislature at the behest of a major local corporation that is the target of a hostile bid or apprehensive that it will become a target.[35] This phenomenon is

---

35. [By the Author] There are at least a dozen examples among second generation statutes: Connecticut for Aetna; Florida for Harcourt Brace Jovanovich (hostile bid

consistent with the positive correlation between the enactment of state statutes and tender offer activity, for as the overall number of takeovers increases, the probability that any one state will be the home of a target, and hence discover the need for a takeover law, may increase.

* * *

The statutes are not, however, as some might intuit, promoted by a broad coalition of business, labor, and community leaders who fear that a firm's takeover will have a detrimental effect on the local economy. While some legislators may be concerned about such an effect, labor and community groups are not at the forefront in the attack on takeovers. In fact, the organization most actively involved in promoting the legislation besides corporate management and business groups, in nearly all states, is the local bar association. * * * There is no doubt that the corporate bar's interest can differ from that of managers and shareholders. For example, corporate lawyers profit from takeover litigation, and a statute that prevented all hostile takeovers would, presumably, also eliminate the lawsuits. A factor mitigating the incentive for maintaining some modicum of takeover activity is that a merged firm typically retains the acquiror's legal counsel. Because the acquiror and, correspondingly, its counsel are quite often out-of-state entities, the local bar's interest will be similar to that of incumbent management, in seeking to block takeovers. As we can conjecture plausible, diverse incentives for corporate lawyers independent of their clients' interests, we cannot identify *a priori* what motivates their behavior. * * *

by Robert Maxwell); Massachusetts for Gillette (hostile bid by Revlon Group); North Carolina for Burlington Industries (hostile bid by Dominion Textile and Asher Edelman); Kentucky for Ashland Oil (hostile bid by the Belzberg brothers); Pennsylvania for Scott Paper (hostile stockholder Brascan Ltd. trying to increase stake); Ohio for Goodyear Tire & Rubber (hostile bid by Sir Oliver Goldsmith); Ohio for Federated Department Stores (hostile bid by Campeau Corp., statute regulating foreign bidders); Arizona for Greyhound; Minnesota for Dayton Hudson (hostile bid by Dart Group); Wisconsin for G. Heileman Brewing Co. (hostile bid by Bond Holdings); Washington for Weyerhauser; Indiana for Arvin Industries (hostile bid by the Belzbergs), AMOCO also promoted bill; Illinois for an unidentified corporation, see

McKenna & Bitner, The "Fair Price Amendment" in the Illinois Business Corporation Act, 67 Chicago Bar Rec., 64, 74 n. 59 (1986) ("one prominent Illinois Corporation" promoted statute); Maine for an unidentified corporation, see Maine Legislative Record—House, June 3, 1985, at 918 (remarks of Rep. Stevens, referring to the "corporation that was the instigator" of the bill); Washington for Boeing (facing possible hostile bid by T. Boone Pickens, statute for foreign resident corporation); Missouri for TWA (hostile bid by Carl Icahn, statute for foreign resident corporation). In addition, one proposed statute was not enacted in large part because it was being pushed by a target of a hostile bid at the time: New York for CBS (hostile bid by Ted Turner).

VEASEY, FINKELSTEIN & SHAUGHNESSY, THE DELAWARE TAKEOVER LAW: SOME ISSUES, STRATEGIES AND COMPARISONS *

43 Bus.Law. 865, 866–73 (1988).

Some states have followed the Indiana model, while others adopted different approaches. For example, New York in 1986 and New Jersey in 1987 adopted statutes prohibiting an acquiror from accomplishing a second-step "business combination"—such as a merger—with the target for a period of five years. Concern was raised that states were trying to outdo each other in their attempts to regulate tender offers of corporations domiciled in other states (notably Delaware), thus leading to a worrisome balkanization of state tender offer statutes. In *TLX Acquisition Corp. v. Telex Corp.*, the federal district court sitting in Oklahoma held that an Oklahoma statute that purported to regulate the tender offer process and thus the internal affairs of a Delaware corporation was unconstitutional even though there were substantial contacts with Oklahoma.[36] * * *

The major question in that national puzzle was whether Delaware would adopt any legislation and, if so, how far it would go. Delaware, of course, is the principal architect and steward of a "national corporation law" since it is the domicile of over 180,000 corporations, many of which are major, national public corporations with no substantial operations in Delaware. Indeed, over half of the Fortune 500 companies are Delaware corporations. As at least one commentator has noted, Delaware has always been wary of antitakeover legislation for at least three reasons: doubts about constitutionality (at least pre–*CTS*); concerns over preemption; and the fact that such statutes simply don't fit comfortably into the mold of a state enabling statute governing internal corporate affairs.[37]

Nevertheless, there was an expectation following *CTS* that Delaware would do something, and it did. After a lengthy "on-again, off-again" process stretching from May 1987 through January 1988, the Delaware State Bar Association proposed a new takeover statute,[38]

---

36. [By the Authors] TLX Acquisition Corp. v. Telex Corp., 679 F.Supp. 1022 (W.D.Okla.1987).

37. [By the Authors] See Black, Why Delaware Is Wary of Anti–Takeover Law, Wall St.J., July 10, 1987, at 18, col. 3.

Although Delaware prides itself on being a leader in corporation law, it has always been wary of laws regulating tender offers. For one thing, such laws have never fit well in corporation statutes. For another, they don't work. Efforts to regulate tender offers at the federal level under the Williams Act have distorted the process. Since the Williams Act was enacted in 1968, the Securities and Exchange Commission (and the states, through such acts as the now-validated Indiana law) has played an endless game of catch up, adopting rules that seem to fix one problem only to give rise to another.

38. [By the Authors] The Delaware statute is the product of a lengthy study by the Corporation Law Section of the Delaware State Bar Association. In June 1987, following the *CTS* decision, the section studied and sought national comment on a

which was adopted in late January substantially in *haec verba* by the Delaware General Assembly. It became effective with the signature of Governor Castle on February 2, 1988. The statute is codified as new section 203 of the Delaware General Corporation Law. Section 203 is a modified "business combination" statute based on the concept, adopted in New York and New Jersey,[39] of regulating second-step transactions between acquirors and the corporation rather than regulating the initial acquisition of stock or voting rights.

With the enactment of section 203, Delaware became the twenty-eighth state to enact a post-*MITE* takeover statute. About half of these statutes were adopted in the wake of the Supreme Court opinion in *CTS*. California is the only major state (in terms of the number of incorporations) without a takeover law.

OPERATION OF SECTION 203

Section 203 is not an enabling (or "opt-in") provision * * * Rather, section 203 is an "opt-out" statute. It automatically applies (with certain exceptions) to every public corporation formed under the laws of Delaware unless (i) the corporation's original charter contains a provision opting out of the protection of the statute, or (ii) within ninety days of the effective date of the statute (February 2, 1988), the board of directors adopts a by-law opting out of the statute. In addition, the holders of a majority of shares entitled to vote can opt out by amending the certificate or the by-laws. Although such an amendment can be adopted at any time, it will not become effective for twelve months and will not apply to a business combination with a person who was an interested stockholder at or prior to the time of the amendment.

draft control share acquisition statute of the type upheld by the Supreme Court in that case. CTS Corp. v. Dynamics Corp. of America, 107 S.Ct. 1637 (1987). There were many uncertainties regarding the operation and effect of such legislation, including concern that it may, ironically, help put "in play" corporations which might not otherwise become takeover targets. Accordingly, the section determined that it would not be appropriate to propose such a statute for Delaware. Nevertheless, because of continued interest in takeover legislation, the council of the section began a new study in the late summer of 1987. An exposure draft of a "business combination statute" was released for public comment in November. Over 150 comment letters were received from corporations, lawyers, Commissioners of the Securities and Exchange Commission and the Federal Trade Commission, executives, institutional investors, academics, and many others. Some comments were based on broad policy grounds, some made narrower policy suggestions, and still others recommended drafting changes. During the bar association debate and the legislative process, some law firms represented specific clients and took positions as a firm. Richards, Layton & Finger [the firm in which the authors are partners] did not take a position as a firm and would not accept representation by a client to lobby for or against the bill. Each lawyer in the firm had the freedom to express his or her own personal view since the clients of the firm had divergent views. Some members of the firm fully supported the statute; others supported it with a few specific reservations (for example whether 85% should be 80% and whether the grandfather date should be the effective date); others opposed it on broad policy grounds. Governor Castle strongly supported the legislation, but he said that the issue is "neither black nor white, but gray."

39. [By the Authors] New York Bus. Corp.Law § 912 (McKinney 1986); N.J. Stat.Ann. § 14A:10A (West Supp.1987), *as amended by* 1988 N.J.Laws 380 (effective Jan. 8, 1988).

Assuming the statute is applicable and the corporation has not opted out, its operative effect can be briefly summarized as follows. If a person acquires fifteen percent or more of a corporation's voting stock (thereby becoming an "interested stockholder"), he may not engage in a wide range of transactions with the corporation, unless the board has approved the transaction or exempted the stockholder before he reaches the fifteen-percent threshold or unless one of two exceptions is satisfied: (i) Upon consummation of the transaction which resulted in such person becoming an interested stockholder, the interested stockholder owned at least eighty-five percent of the corporation's voting stock outstanding at the time the transaction commenced (excluding shares owned by officer-directors and shares owned by employee stock plans in which participants do not have the right to determine confidentially whether shares will be tendered in a tender or exchange offer); or (ii) after the acquiror becomes an interested stockholder, the business combination is approved by the board of directors and authorized by the affirmative vote (at an annual or special meeting, and not by written consent) of at least two-thirds of the outstanding voting stock excluding that owned by the interested stockholder. * * *

Notes

(1) Suits testing the constitutionality of section 203 have been unsuccessful. Black & Decker Corp. v. American Standard Inc., 679 F.Supp. 1183 (D.Del.1988); SWT Acquisition Corp. v. TW Services, Inc., 700 F.Supp. 1323 (D.Del.1988). However, Wisconsin has a business combination statute that is even more restrictive than Delaware's. Under this statute, no Wisconsin corporation having its headquarters, substantial operations, 10 per cent of its shares or 10 per cent of its shareholders in Wisconsin may enter into a "business combination" with an interested shareholder (defined as one with a ten per cent interest in the corporation) for a period of three years after the interested shareholder acquired his or her stock unless the board of directors has approved the business combination *before* the interested shareholder's acquisition of shares. In Amanda Acquisition Corp. v. Universal Foods Corp., 877 F.2d 496 (7th Cir.1989), cert. denied ___ U.S. ___, 110 S.Ct. 367, 107 L.Ed.2d 353 (1989), the court, per Easterbrook, C.J., upheld this statute despite the "almost hermetic separation of bidder and target for three years after the bidder obtains 10 per cent of the stock—unless the target's board consented before then. No matter how popular the offer, the ban applies: obtaining 85% (even 100%) of the stock held by non-management shareholders won't allow the bidder to engage in a business combination, as it would under Delaware law." 877 F.2d at 498. After expressing its distaste for the economics and policies that Wisconsin has apparently embraced, Judge Easterbrook concluded that the Wisconsin law is constitutional under *CTS:*

At the end of the day, however, it does not matter whether these countermeasures are "enough". The Commerce Clause does not demand that states leave bidders a "meaningful opportunity for success". * * * A state with the power to forbid mergers has the power to defer them for three years. Investors can turn to firms incorporated in states committed to the dominance of market forces, or they can turn on legislators who enact unwise laws. The Constitution has room for many economic policies. "[A] law can be both economic folly and constitutional." *CTS*, 481 U.S. at 96–97, 107 S.Ct. at 1653–54 (Scalia, J., concurring). Wisconsin's law may well be folly; we are confident that it is constitutional.

Id., at 508–509.

(2) Is the process followed by Delaware consistent with the criticism voiced by Professor Romano that states have adopted post-*CTS* statutes at the behest of individual companies and without consideration of all interests?

(3) In addition to control share acquisition statutes of the Indiana type and restrictions on "second step" transactions of the Delaware—New York—New Jersey type, other types of statutes exist. Most of these statutes were enacted during the interim period after *MITE* and before *CTS* when any state legislation in the takeover area was under a constitutional cloud. The most popular of these statutes are "fair price" and "super-majority voting" requirements for second step transactions with interested shareholders patterned after the Maryland statutes [Md.Corps. & Assn's.Code Ann. §§ 3–601—3–603] and adopted by about fifteen states. Other statutes provided for an appraisal-type "cash out" privilege for minority shareholders upon the acquisition of a specified percentage of the corporation's shares. See e.g., Pa.Bus.Corp.L. §§ 2542–2548 [acquisition of 20 percent or more of voting shares (subject to certain exceptions) triggers buy-out right].

C. DEFENSIVE TACTICS

Assuming that an all-cash takeover offer is made, does incumbent management have a duty to oppose it? To support it? To remain neutral and neither support nor oppose it? These questions raise fundamental issues about the role of shareholders and of management that are at the center of the modern debate over takeovers. If, as will normally be the case, the aggressor has the financial strength to carry out the contemplated offer, shareholders of the target corporation will almost certainly realize more for their shares if the offer succeeds than if it fails. If one accepts the basic proposition that the sole goal of management should be to maximize shareholder wealth, does it not follow that management certainly should not be permitted to actively oppose an offer, and that very probably it should further have an affirmative obligation either to support the offer or at least remain neutral with respect to it? One possible exception might be that management should oppose the offer to the limited extent of finding even more favorable offers from other sources.

The underlying justification for the twenty-odd state statutes that authorize consideration of non-shareholder constituencies (see Chapter 9, Section A, supra) is to free management from the chains of the apparently compelling theoretical argument that they have a duty to maximize the financial interests of the shareholders which means they should not try to block the takeover.

On the other hand, an all-cash takeover offer threatens incumbent management in a most fundamental way: Individuals face the loss of prestigious positions, seven-figure salaries, desirable "percs," lucrative fringe benefits, and the loss of power to control a large enterprise. It is not surprising that management usually feels it is a matter of the highest urgency to defeat such an offer at all costs. Defensive tactics that involve purely an effort to defeat the offer in order to preserve one's position are usually described by the term "entrenchment," and involve a breach of the duty of loyalty (since the tactics are not for a corporate purpose but to preserve the position of the managers). Open descriptions of one's motive to entrench and preserve one's position therefore are clear losers; other justifications to defeat the offer must be developed. Examples might include (1) the offered price is too low and does not reflect the "true" value of the corporate assets; (2) the offeror's reputation for sound fiscal management is not good; (3) the aggressor is assuming debt obligations which it probably cannot meet without using the target's assets, thereby injuring remaining common shareholders or senior security or debt holders, (4) it is simply in the best long run interests of the shareholders for the corporation to remain independent (the "just say no" defense); (5) management has already embarked on long range plans to improve the corporation's profits and stock price and the decision to pursue those plans is protected by the business judgment rule; (6) the proposed transaction would result in the violation of the antitrust laws or some other federal or state statute; or (7) the offer is a partial one and is structured in a way that makes it unfair to shareholders by "coercing" them to tender. Whether or not such arguments are persuasive or even plausible obviously depends on the facts of the particular takeover.

If one accepts the general explanation that takeovers occur primarily to weed out less efficient managers, the conclusion that management should be sharply restricted in the defensive tactics it may employ in order to let basic economic forces work is considerably strengthened.

The economic stakes in a takeover battle are so great that litigation to test the validity of any defenses employed by management is a virtual certainty. This litigation usually is in the form of suits for equitable relief based either on violations of the Williams Act or on breaches of the duty of care or loyalty by management. However, if management effectively defeats a tender offer, without providing an offsetting management buyout or leveraged recapitalization that replaces some or all of the lost value to shareholders, there will be a precipitous decline in the market price of the target stock and litigation may be brought on the theory that the directors should be held personally liable for the losses since they opposed the takeover not for the benefit of the corporation generally or its shareholders but to preserve their positions with the corporation. Litigation on this theory first foundered on the business judgment rule in its more permissive form. The leading case is Panter v. Marshall Field & Co., 646 F.2d 271 (7th Cir.1981), cert. denied 454 U.S. 1092, 102 S.Ct. 658, 70 L.Ed.2d 631 (1981), where Marshall Field successfully fended off an unwanted takeover bid from Carter Hawley Hale (CHH), a national retail chain that operated Nieman–Marcus and other stores. Marshall Field adopted and vigorously pursued a policy of independence; among other things, it adopted an expansion program that led to Marshall Field stores coming into direct competition with Nieman–Marcus in several markets. When CHH withdrew its bid in part because of the antitrust complications, the price of the Marshall Field common stock precipitously declined from about $34 per share to $19 per share. The court held that the business judgment rule and the presumption of good faith was applicable: "The plaintiffs also contend that the 'defensive acquisitions' of the five Liberty House stores and the Galleria were imprudent, and designed to make Field's less attractive as an acquisition, as well as to exacerbate any antitrust problems created by the CHH merger. It is precisely this sort of Monday-morning-quarterbacking that the business judgment rule was intended to prevent." 646 F.2d at 297.

This approach was too much for Judge Cudahy:

> Unfortunately, the majority here has moved one giant step closer to shredding whatever constraints still remain upon the ability of corporate directors to place self-interest before shareholder interest in resisting a hostile tender offer for control of the corporation. There is abundant evidence in this case to go to the jury on the state claims for breach of fiduciary duty. I emphatically disagree that the business judgment rule should clothe directors, battling blindly to fend off a threat to their control, with an almost irrebuttable presumption of sound business judgment, prevailing over everything but the elusive hobgoblins of fraud, bad faith or abuse of discretion. * * *

> Addressing first the state law claims of breach of fiduciary duty by the Board, the majority has adopted an approach which would virtually immunize a target company's board of directors against liability to shareholders, provided a sufficiently prestigious (and expensive) array of legal and financial talent were retained to furnish *post hoc* rationales for fixed and immutable policies of resistance to takeover. Relying on several recent decisions interpreting the Delaware business judgment rule, the majority fails to make the important distinction

>> between the activity of a corporation in managing a business enterprise and its function as a vehicle for collecting and using capital and distributing profits and losses. The former involves corporate functioning in competitive business affairs in which judicial interference may be undesirable. *The latter involves only the corporation-shareholder relationship, in which the courts may more justifiably intervene to insist on equitable behavior.*

Note, *Protection for Shareholder Interests in Recapitalizations of Publicly Held Companies*, 58 Colum.L.Rev. 1030, 1066 (1958) (emphasis supplied).

The theoretical justification for the "hands off" precept of the business judgment rule is that courts should be reluctant to review the acts of directors in situations where the expertise of the directors is likely to be greater than that of the courts. But, where the directors are afflicted with a conflict of interest, relative expertise is no longer crucial. Instead, the great danger becomes the channeling of the directors' expertise along the lines of their personal advantage—sometimes at the expense of the corporation and its stockholders. Here courts have no rational choice but to subject challenged conduct of directors and questioned corporate transactions to their own disinterested scrutiny. Of course, the self-protective bias of interested directors may be entirely devoid of corrupt motivation, but it may nonetheless constitute a serious threat to stockholder welfare. * * *

Directors of a New York Stock Exchange-listed company are, at the very least, "interested" in their own positions of power, prestige and prominence (and in their not inconsequential perquisites). They are "interested" in defending against outside attack the management which they have, in fact, installed or maintained in power—"their" management (to which, in many cases, they owe their directorships). And they are "interested" in maintaining the public reputation of their own leadership and stewardship against the claims of "raiders" who say that they can do better. Thus, regardless of their technical "independence," directors of a target corporation are in a very special position, where the slavish application of the majority's version of the good faith presumption is particularly disturbing.

Whether or not Panter v. Marshall Field involved a proper application of the business judgment rule may be debated. To some extent the decision may have been influenced by the threatened imposition of immense liabilities on outside directors who did not materially benefit from the transaction.[40]

Powerful defensive tactics have been developed that are directed squarely against the aggressor and its offer. These tactics are so effective that they have necessitated a modification of the almost-simplistic application of the business judgment rule of *Panter*. In *Unocal v. Mesa Petroleum Co.*, 493 A.2d 946 (Del.Supr.1985), for example, Mesa launched a takeover fight against Unocal, a major oil company. Mesa offered $54 per share for 64,000,000 shares, just enough to bring its ownership to 50 per cent. The bulk of the $3.4 billion purchase price was to be borrowed in the form of junk bonds. At the same time, Mesa announced that if it were successful in the tender offer it would thereafter purchase the balance of the Unocal stock it did

---

40. [By the Editor] This type of litigation against directors for damages is probably not precluded by Del.Gen.Corp.L. § 102(a)(7) [discussed at page 730, supra] because it involves an arguable breach of the duty of loyalty or the receipt of an improper, personal benefit. It may be barred by some statutes enacted after *Van Gorkom*.

not already own through a second-step merger in which the holders would receive "highly subordinated securities" (presumably subordinated to the borrowings needed to raise the initial $3.4 billion) with a value that the Delaware Supreme Court stated was "purportedly" also $54 per share.   Unocal's ultimate defense was an "exchange offer" that provided that if Mesa bought the 64,000,000 shares it sought, the remaining Unocal shareholders could exchange all of their remaining shares for debt securities worth $72 per share that would be senior to Mesa's junk bond financing.   The exchange offer expressly provided that Mesa and persons affiliated with Mesa were not eligible to participate in the offer.   The effect of the "Mesa exclusion"—the provision allowing Unocal to offer debt securities to all of its shareholders other than Mesa—devastated Mesa's financing.   If it completed its tender offer and obtained control of Unocal, the remaining Unocal shareholders would swap their shares for senior Unocal debt, and Mesa would end up owning virtually 100 per cent of a corporation that was awash in debt.   Indeed, this defense involves such strong medicine and is so devastatingly effective that it seems ill-matched with the very permissive business judgment rule.   The Delaware Supreme Court evolved a somewhat different principle for determining the validity of such draconian defensive tactics:

> In the board's exercise of corporate power to forestall a takeover bid our analysis begins with the basic principle that corporate directors have a fiduciary duty to act in the best interests of the corporation's stockholders.   Guth v. Loft, Inc., Del.Supr., 5 A.2d 503, 510 (1939).   As we have noted, their duty of care extends to protecting the corporation and its owners from perceived harm whether a threat originates from third parties or other shareholders.[41]   But such powers are not absolute.   A corporation does not have unbridled discretion to defeat any perceived threat by any Draconian means available.

> The restriction placed upon a selective stock repurchase is that the directors may not have acted solely or primarily out of a desire to perpetuate themselves in office.   See Cheff v. Mathes, 199 A.2d 548, 556 (1964).

> Of course, to this is added the further caveat that inequitable action may not be taken under the guise of law.   Schnell v. Chris–Craft Industries, Inc., Del.Supr., 285 A.2d 437, 439 (1971).[42]   The standard of proof established in Cheff v. Mathes * * * is designed to ensure that a defensive measure to thwart or impede a takeover is indeed motivated by a good faith concern for the welfare of the corporation and its stockholders, which in all circumstances must be free of any fraud or

---

41.   [By the Court].   It has been suggested that a board's response to a takeover threat should be a passive one.   Easterbrook & Fischel, 36 Bus.Law. at 1750.   However, that clearly is not the law of Delaware, and as the proponents of this rule of passivity readily concede, it has not been adopted either by courts or state legislatures.   Easterbrook & Fischel, supra, 94 Harv.L.Rev. at 1194.

42.   [By the Editor]   In *Schnell,* the Delaware courts enjoined a corporation from shifting its annual meeting date primarily in order to shorten the time period an insurgent had to solicit proxies in a proxy contest.

other misconduct. Cheff v. Mathes, 199 A.2d at 554–55. However, this does not end the inquiry.

A further aspect is the element of balance. If a defensive measure is to come within the ambit of the business judgment rule, it must be reasonable in relation to the threat posed. This entails an analysis by the directors of the nature of the takeover bid and its effect on the corporate enterprise. Examples of such concerns may include: inadequacy of the price offered, nature and timing of the offer, questions of illegality, the impact on "constituencies" other than shareholders (i.e., creditors, customers, employees, and perhaps even the community generally), the risk of nonconsummation, and the quality of securities being offered in the exchange. 40 Bus.Law. 1403 (1985) While not a controlling factor, it also seems to us that a board may reasonably consider the basic stockholder interests at stake, including those of short term speculators, whose actions may have fueled the coercive aspect of the offer at the expense of the long term investor.[43] Here, the threat posed was viewed by the Unocal board as a grossly inadequate two-tier coercive tender offer coupled with the threat of greenmail.

* * *

In adopting the selective exchange offer, the board stated that its objective was either to defeat the inadequate Mesa offer or, should the offer still succeed, provide the 49% of its stockholders, who would otherwise be forced to accept "junk bonds", with $72 worth of senior debt. We find that both purposes are valid.

However, such efforts would have been thwarted by Mesa's participation in the exchange offer. First, if Mesa could tender its shares, Unocal would effectively be subsidizing the former's continuing effort to buy Unocal stock at $54 per share. Second, Mesa could not, by definition, fit within the class of shareholders being protected from its own coercive and inadequate tender offer.

Thus, we are satisfied that the selective exchange offer is reasonably related to the threats posed. It is consistent with the principle that "the minority stockholder shall receive the substantial equivalent in value of what he had before." Sterling v. Mayflower Hotel Corp., Del. Supr., 93 A.2d 107, 114 (1952). This concept of fairness, while stated in the merger context, is also relevant in the area of tender offer law. Thus, the board's decision to offer what it determined to be the fair

---

43. [By the Court] There has been much debate respecting such stockholder interests. One rather impressive study indicates that the stock of over 50 percent of target companies, who resisted hostile takeovers, later traded at higher market prices than the rejected offer price, or were acquired after the tender offer was defeated by another company at a price higher than the offer price. See Lipton, 35 Bus. Law. at 106–109, 132–133. Moreover, an update by Kidder Peabody & Company of this study, involving the stock prices of target companies that have defeated hostile tender offers during the period from 1973 to 1982 demonstrates that in a majority of cases the target's shareholders benefited from the defeat. The stock of 81% of the targets studied has, since the tender offer, sold at prices higher than the tender offer price. When adjusted for the time value of money, the figure is 64%. The thesis being that this strongly supports application of the business judgment rule in response to takeover threats. There is, however, a rather vehement contrary view. See Easterbrook & Fischel, supra 36 Bus. Law. at 1739–1745.

value of the corporation to the 49% of its shareholders, who would otherwise be forced to accept highly subordinated "junk bonds", is reasonable and consistent with the directors' duty to ensure that the minority stockholders receive equal value for their shares.

Notes

(1) See generally Gilson and Kraakman, Delaware's Intermediate Standard for Defensive Tactics: Is There Substance To Proportionality Review? 44 Bus.Law. 247 (1989).

(2) Shortly after the Delaware Supreme Court's opinion in *Unocal,* the SEC adopted Rule 14d–10, 17 C.F.R. § 240.14d–10 (1989), 51 Fed.Reg. 25882 (1986), popularly known as the "All Holders Rule":

(a) No bidder shall make a tender offer unless:

(1) The tender offer is open to all security holders of the class of securities subject to the tender offer; and

(2) The consideration paid to any security holder pursuant to the tender offer is the highest consideration paid to any other security holder during such tender offer. * * *

(c) Paragraph (a)(2) of this section shall not prohibit the offer of more than one type of consideration in a tender offer, *Provided,* That:

(1) Security holders are afforded equal right to elect among each of the types of consideration offered; and

(2) The highest consideration of each type paid to any security holder is paid to any other security holder receiving that type of consideration. * * *

(e) This section shall not apply to any tender offer with respect to which the Commission, upon written request or upon its own motion, either unconditionally or on specified terms and conditions, determines that compliance with this section is not necessary or appropriate in the public interest or for the protection of investors.

In proposing this Rule, the SEC explained its purpose as follows:

A major aspect of the legislative effort to protect investors was to avoid favoring either management or the takeover bidder. In implementing this policy of neutrality, the Commission has administered the Williams Act in an even-handed fashion favoring neither side in a contest. Also implicit in these provisions, and necessary for the functioning of the Williams Act are the requirements that a bidder make a tender offer to all security holders of the class of securities which is the subject of the offer and that the offer made to all holders on the same terms.

The investor protection purposes of the Exchange Act would not be achieved without these requirements because tender offers could be extended to some security holders but not to others or to all security holders but on different terms. * * *

SEC Rel. No. 34–22198 (1985). The SEC also stated in its accompanying release that the all holders rule "codifies existing interpretations by the Commission's staff."

(3) In Polaroid Corp. v. Disney, 862 F.2d 987 (3d Cir.1988), the court upheld the all holders rule on the theory that it broadly related to disclosure. The court also held that disadvantaged shareholders had standing to enjoin violations of the all holders rule by a third party but that the issuer did not have standing to sue on its own behalf. The court noted, however, that the question was "a difficult one" and that since it was likely that disadvantaged shareholders would intervene if the issuer were not able to maintain a suit on their behalf, the issuer should be accorded standing on the theory of jus tertii, or the right to sue on behalf of a related third party.

(4) Does the all holders rule principle cover the private repurchase of shares at a premium, i.e., "greenmail"? Should it?

(5) From a relatively early time, courts have indicated that more or less brazen attempts to perpetuate incumbent management in office would not be countenanced. In Schnell v. Chris–Craft Industries, Inc., 285 A.2d 430 (Ch.1971), rev'd 285 A.2d 437 (Del.1971), discussed in *Unocal*, incumbent management was faced with a proxy fight. It exercised the power it possessed under Delaware law to change the date of the meeting from January 11, 1972 to December 8, 1971, thereby cutting down the period the insurgents had to obtain approval by the SEC of their proxy solicitation materials and to solicit proxies, and moved the meeting site to an "isolated town in up-state New York." The defendants attempted to justify these changes on the ground of "weather conditions in Cortland, New York, in January, as opposed to early December, * * * [and] the normal delays in delivery of notices to stockholders resulting from Christmas mails." 285 A.2d at 439. The lower court concluded that these arguments were basically pretexts. The Supreme Court of Delaware concluded that the record revealed "that management has attempted to utilize the corporate machinery and the Delaware Law for the purpose of obstructing the legitimate efforts of dissident shareholders in the exercise of their rights to undertake a proxy contest against management. These are inequitable purposes, contrary to established principles of corporate democracy * * * and may not be permitted to stand." 285 A.2d at 439. The court also responded to the argument that all actions taken by management were strictly in compliance with Delaware law by the rather tart observation that "inequitable action does not become permissible simply because it becomes legally possible." Id. at 439.

(6) Several cases have expanded upon the *Schnell* principle in the takeover context. Aprahamian v. HBO & Co., 531 A.2d 1204 (Del.Ch.1987) enjoined a change of the date of the annual meeting after directors learned that a dissident shareholder had successfully obtained a large number of proxies. Blasius Industries, Inc. v. Atlas Corp., 564 A.2d 651 (Del.Ch.1988) enjoined the addition of two new persons to a staggered board that had the effect of making impractical a transaction that was being proposed in a pending consent solicitation. In both of these cases, the enjoined actions would clearly have been protected by the business judgment rule in the

absence of pending shareholder action on the same subject and an intention to defeat the shareholder-initiated action.

———

Almost immediately following *Unocal* another major Delaware case involving defensive tactics arose. The dispute arose when Pantry Pride made a hostile tender offer for any and all shares of Revlon, Inc. for $47.50 per share. Viewing this price as inadequate, considering the value of Revlon's assets, and receiving information that Pantry Pride planned to break up and sell off Revlon component businesses, Revlon management instituted a series of defensive tactics, including an offer to purchase 10,000,000 of its own shares for notes and preferred stock that had "poison pill" type provisions (described in *Moran*, p. 915, infra). Pantry Pride then increased its offer in a series of steps, first to $50 per share, then to $53, and then to $56.25, contingent in each case on Pantry Pride waiving the poison pill features of the notes. Faced with this steady pressure, Revlon decided to seek possible alternative purchasers, a white knight. After some negotiations with Forstmann during which Forstmann was given access to financial information about Revlon that had been denied Pantry Pride, a leveraged buyout transaction was agreed upon by Forstmann and Revlon management at a price of $57.25 per share. A critical aspect of the Forstmann agreement was that Forstmann received "a lock-up option to purchase Revlon's Vision Care and National Health Laboratories divisions for $525 million, some $100–$175 million below the value ascribed to them by Lazard Freres, if another acquiror got 40% of Revlon's shares." Pantry Pride then raised its price to $58 per share contingent upon removal not only of the poison pill provisions but also the Forstmann "lock up." When Revlon management decided to go through with the Forstmann sale (apparently in large part because Forstmann promised to support the price of the notes issued earlier by Revlon to create poison pill protection), the decision moved into the Delaware courts. Revlon v. MacAndrews & Forbes Holdings, Inc., 506 A.2d 173 (Del. 1985). The Delaware Supreme Court first upheld Revlon's actions to fight off Pantry Pride's initial inadequate offers but then enunciated a new principle for the later portions of the contest:

> However, when Pantry Pride increased its offer to $50 per share, and then to $53, it became apparent to all that the break-up of the company was inevitable. The Revlon board's authorization permitting management to negotiate a merger or buyout with a third party was a recognition that the company was for sale. The duty of the board had thus changed from the preservation of Revlon as a corporate entity to the maximization of the company's value at a sale for the stockholders' benefit. This significantly altered the board's responsibilities under the *Unocal* standards. It no longer faced threats to corporate policy and effectiveness, or to the stockholders' interests, from a grossly inadequate bid. The whole question of defensive measures became moot. The directors' role changed from defenders of the corporate

bastion to auctioneers charged with getting the best price for the stockholders at a sale of the company. * * *

The original threat posed by Pantry Pride—the break-up of the company—had become a reality which even the directors embraced. Selective dealing to fend off a hostile but determined bidder was no longer a proper objective. Instead, obtaining the highest price for the benefit of the stockholders should have been the central theme guiding director action. Thus, the Revlon board could not make the requisite showing of good faith by preferring the noteholders and ignoring its duty of loyalty to the shareholders. The rights of the former already were fixed by contract. Wolfensohn v. Madison Fund, Inc., Del.Supr., 253 A.2d 72, 75 (1969); Harff v. Kerkorian, Del.Ch., 324 A.2d 215 (1974). The noteholders required no further protection, and when the Revlon board entered into an auction-ending lock-up agreement with Forstmann on the basis of impermissible considerations at the expense of the shareholders, the directors breached their primary duty of loyalty.

The Revlon board argued that it acted in good faith in protecting the noteholders because *Unocal* permits consideration of other corporate constituencies. Although such considerations may be permissible, there are fundamental limitations upon that prerogative. A board may have regard for various constituencies in discharging its responsibilities, provided there are rationally related benefits accruing to the stockholders. *Unocal,* 493 A.2d at 955. However, such concern for non-stockholder interests is inappropriate when an auction among active bidders is in progress, and the object no longer is to protect or maintain the corporate enterprise but to sell it to the highest bidder.
* * *

While Forstmann's $57.25 offer was objectively higher than Pantry Pride's $56.25 bid, the margin of superiority is less when the Forstmann price is adjusted for the time value of money. In reality, the Revlon board ended the auction in return for very little actual improvement in the final bid. The principal benefit went to the directors, who avoided personal liability to a class of creditors to whom the board owed no further duty under the circumstances. Thus, when a board ends an intense bidding contest on an insubstantial basis, and where a significant by-product of that action is to protect the directors against a perceived threat of personal liability for consequences stemming from the adoption of previous defensive measures, the action cannot withstand the enhanced scrutiny which *Unocal* requires of director conduct.
* * *

In conclusion, the Revlon board was confronted with a situation not uncommon in the current wave of corporate takeovers. A hostile and determined bidder sought the company at a price the board was convinced was inadequate. The initial defensive tactics worked to the benefit of the shareholders, and thus the board was able to sustain its *Unocal* burdens in justifying those measures. However, in granting an asset option lock-up to Forstmann, we must conclude that under all the circumstances the directors allowed considerations other than the maximization of shareholder profit to affect their judgment, and followed a course that ended the auction for Revlon, absent court intervention, to the ultimate detriment of its shareholders. No such defensive measure can be sustained when it represents a breach of the directors' fundamental duty of care. See Smith v. Van Gorkom, Del. Supr., 488 A.2d 858, 874 (1985). In that context the board's action is not entitled to the deference accorded it by the business judgment rule.

* * *

Notes

(1) The *Revlon* decision permits management to justify poison pills and other defensive tactics because they may lead to an auction and thereby produce a better price for shareholders than would a sale to the first serious bidder. See Oesterle, Target Managers as Negotiating Agents for Target Shareholders in Tender Offers: A Reply to the Passivity Thesis, 71 Cornell L.Rev. 53 (1985). For a recent example of this use of a poison pill, see CRTF Corp. v. Federated Department Stores, Inc., 683 F.Supp. 422 (S.D. N.Y.1988).

(2) The *Revlon* opinion raises basic questions. First, when is the duty to conduct an auction triggered? Second, how is an auction to be conducted to meet the standards set forth by Justice Moore? Third, when may the board of directors decide that it is concluded? Fourth, what should the board do if a single offer at an attractive price is unexpectedly received? In a sense, *Revlon* and *Unocal* are alternative sides of a coin since an effort to defeat an offer under *Unocal* may lead to a decision to sell the corporation, at which time the role of management shifts abruptly from a partisan to an impartial auctioneer.

(3) The relationship between *Revlon* and *Unocal* has been addressed by a series of post-*Revlon* decisions by the Delaware Supreme Court. Ivanhoe Partners v. Newmont Mining Corp., 535 A.2d 1334 (Del.1987) establishes the basic principle that the shift from *Unocal* to *Revlon* principles occurs when the sale of the business becomes "inevitable" though the facts of that case are unusual. The major opinion describing the duty of objectivity when conducting a *Revlon* auction is Mills Acquisition Co. v. Macmillan, Inc., 559 A.2d 1261 (Del.1989) (an unusually strongly worded opinion). In Paramount Communications Inc. v. Time, Inc., 571 A.2d 1140 (Del.1990) the Court upheld Chancellor Allen's conclusion that where Time had developed a long-term plan to acquire Warner Communications, Inc., management could pursue this goal even in the face of an intervening cash tender offer by Paramount. The Paramount offer almost certainly would have been irresistably attractive to Time shareholders if Time had been required to put the corporation up for sale at auction.

(4) In Cottle v. Storer Communications, Inc., 849 F.2d 570 (11th Cir. 1988), the court upheld under the business judgment rule a lockup granted to one bidder in a two-person bidding contest on the theory "auctions must end some time" and the management may decide when that time is, so long as the auction was conducted fairly and the successful bidder had in fact made the higher of the two bids. The directors in this case recognized that

they were proceeding under the *Revlon* principle and attempted to conduct a fair auction.

(5) The *Revlon* principle accepts the view that at some point the goal of the corporation is to maximize the return to shareholders. This principle, of course, is a matter of Delaware law, a state that has not broadened its statute to recognize the rights of other "constituencies." In a state that recognizes the right of directors to consider the effects of their decisions on debtholders, employees, and localities, should the auction principle of *Revlon* have any place? In this connection, consider Ind.Bus.Corp.L. § 23–1–35–1(f), (g) [amended by P.L. 227–1989, eff. 1–31–89]:

> (f) In enacting this article * * * [t]he general assembly intends to reaffirm certain of these corporate governance rules to ensure that the directors of Indiana corporations, in exercising their business judgment, are not required to approve a proposed corporate action if the directors in good faith determine, after considering and weighing as they deem appropriate the effects of such action on the corporation's constituents, that such action is not in the best interests of the corporation. In making such determination, directors are not required to consider the effects of a proposed corporate action on any particular corporate constituent group or interest as a dominant or controlling factor. * * * Certain judicial decisions in Delaware and other jurisdictions, which might otherwise be looked to for guidance in interpreting Indiana corporate law, including decisions relating to potential change of control transactions that impose a different or higher degree of scrutiny on actions taken by directors in response to a proposed acquisition of control of the corporation, are inconsistent with the proper application of the business judgment rule under this article.
>
> * * *
>
> (g) In taking or declining to take any action, or in making or declining to make any recommendation to the shareholders of the corporation with respect to any matter, a board of directors may, in its discretion, consider both the short term and long term best interests of the corporation, taking into account, and weighing as the directors deem appropriate, the effects thereof on the corporation's shareholders and the other corporate constituent groups and interests listed or described in subsection (d), as well as any other factors deemed pertinent by the directors under subsection (d). If a determination is made with respect to the foregoing with the approval of a majority of the disinterested directors of the board of directors, that determination shall conclusively be presumed to be valid unless it can be demonstrated that the determination was not made in good faith after reasonable investigation.

Is it clear under this section that *Revlon* has no application in Indiana?

PROXY STATEMENT SAFEWAY STORES, INC.

For 1980 Annual Meeting Held on May 20, 1980, Pages 14–16.

PROPOSAL 2—ADOPTION OF ANTI–TAKEOVER CHARTER AMENDMENTS

The proposed anti-takeover Charter amendments (Proposal 2) are:

1. Classification of the Board of Directors into 3 Classes, with Stockholder election of only 1 Class of Directors each year; and

2. Requiring approval by 75% of the holders of shares of the Company's Common Stock for any merger or disposition of substantially all of the Company's assets unless the proposal for such a transaction is approved by 80% of the Directors.

* * *

Reasons for Anti-takeover Charter Amendments. The primary purpose of the Board in adopting these measures and recommending their approval by the Stockholders is to discourage "hostile" or un-friendly attempts to take control of the Company. The Board recognizes the increase in frequency of attempts by one corporation or groups of investors to acquire control of another corporation through the acquisition of a substantial number of its shares followed by the absorption by merger or similar transaction of the corporation whose stock was acquired.

The Board is concerned that such an attempt could result in the Stockholders receiving less than the intrinsic investment value in their shares. It believes that these changes are in the best interests of the Stockholders in that they promote continuity of the Company's operations by providing a way to resist any surprise or unnegotiated takeover attempts and by discouraging such attempts.

The Board is not committed to oppose all tender offers which could affect control of the Company, but considers it a duty to the Stockholders to do what is possible to provide them with adequate opportunity to make an informed investment decision after receiving relevant information regarding an offer and other alternatives.

The Board of Directors is not aware of any pending or proposed takeover bid or tender offer, and there have been no preliminary contacts or negotiations with the Board on that subject. The Board has no present plans to propose any additional Charter amendments which would further restrict takeover bids or tender offers.

Caution to Stockholders. The proposed amendments will make it more difficult to remove the Board and Management for any reason. The proposed changes may deter takeover bids or tender offers which could be considered attractive by some or all of the Company's Stockholders. These consequences should be taken into account by Stockholders when considering the recommendation of the Board to vote for approval and adoption of the proposed Amendments.

Classification of Board of Directors. Proposed Article FIFTH of the Charter would divide the Board of Directors into three Classes. At the 1980 Annual Meeting, Directors of Class I would be elected for a term of one year, Directors of Class II for a term of two years, and Directors of Class III for a term of three years. All Directors would hold office until the election and qualification of their successors. At each Annual Meeting the successors to the Directors of the Class whose terms expire in that year would be elected to hold office for a term of three years from the date of their election, so that the term of office on one Class of Directors would expire in each year.

Directors could be removed during their term of office only "for cause" and any vacancy which occurs on the Board could be filled by a majority vote of the remaining Directors or by the Stockholders. A Director elected by the Board to fill a vacancy would serve until the next Annual Meeting of the Stockholders and until his or her successor is elected and qualifies; a Director elected by the Stockholders to fill a vacancy which results from the removal of a Director would serve for the balance of the term of the removed Director.

The purposes of the classification of the Board are to (i) discourage "unfriendly" takeover or tender offers designed to change control of the Company and to (ii) provide continuity and stability on the Board by retaining in office experienced Directors. As so amended, the Charter would require at least two Annual Meetings to change a majority of Directors. * * *

Supermajority Vote Requirement. Proposed Article SIXTH of the Charter would require approval by the holders of not less than 75% of the outstanding Common Stock to authorize, adopt or approve certain types of agreements or Charter amendments which could result in a change of control of the Company **unless** such agreements or amendments were approved by 80% of all of the Directors.

The types of agreements or amendments are (i) a merger or consolidation of the Company with or into another entity, (ii) a sale or liquidation or other disposition of substantially all of the Company's property, (iii) a reclassification of shares of stock of the Company which would be entitled to vote in elections of Directors, and (iv) an amendment of the Article of the Charter providing for a classified Board of Directors.

Maryland Law. The laws of Maryland, under which the Company was formed, authorize adoption of classified boards of directors. It requires that Charter amendments be approved by the affirmative vote of two-thirds of all votes entitled to be cast on the matter or, as permitted by Maryland law and as provided in the Company's present Charter, approval must be by a majority of the votes entitled to be cast. If Proposals 2 and 3 are adopted, the approval or repeal of a Charter amendment other than one of the types mentioned in the preceding paragraph would continue to require the affirmative vote of a majority in number of the votes to which the holders of all shares of the Common Stock are entitled.

The Board of Directors Recommends A Vote "For" Proposal 2.

Notes

(1) These proposals were approved by the shareholders of Safeway on May 20, 1980, with approximately 77 per cent of the shares voting approving, 14 per cent opposing, and 9 per cent abstaining. This was an unusually large opposition to a management-sponsored proposal. Despite these protections, Safeway disappeared in an LBO transaction in 1986.

(2) Consider RMBCA §§ 7.27, 10.21. Compare New York Bus.Corp. Law § 616(b), (c) which requires a two-thirds vote to adopt a supermajority amendment to the articles of incorporation and also requires a conspicuous reference to such a provision on each share certificate. Do you think that such provisions provide adequate protection to the shareholders or to the public against possible misuse of porcupine provisions?

(3) Other types of "porcupine provisions" that have had some degree of popularity in recent years include:

(a) A requirement that 80 per cent or more of the shareholders be required to approve certain transactions (e.g., mergers) between the corporation and persons that own more than 10 per cent of the corporate shares—e.g., Southwest Airlines.

(b) A requirement that a majority of the shares other than shares owned by a party to a proposed transaction approve the proposed transaction—e.g., Baldor Electric, Inc.

(c) A requirement that 95 per cent approval of certain transactions between the corporation and large shareholders be obtained unless the transaction meets certain precise price and other substantive terms set forth in the articles or bylaws—e.g., Anchor Hocking Corporation.

(d) A provision that allows minority shareholders to redeem their shares for cash from the corporation at a price set forth in the articles or bylaws for a limited period following any transaction in which a person acquires a majority of the outstanding shares or a majority shareholder increases his holdings—e.g., Rubbermaid Corporation.

(e) A provision creating special classes of preferred shares to be held by a limited number of holders, and requiring approval of that class of shares of certain classes of transactions—e.g., Outdoor Sports Industries, Inc.

(f) Fair price amendments to articles of incorporation that mandate that shareholders receive equivalent consideration (both in terms of amount and form) on both ends of a two-tiered bid.

(g) Antigreenmail provisions: amendments to articles of incorporation prohibiting the repurchase by the company of stock at a premium from a three percent or greater holder unless the repurchase is approved by a majority vote of the shareholders—e.g., International Minerals & Chemical Corporation.

(4) A corporation is of course totally takeover-proof only if a majority of its voting shares is held by a single person or entity. [It is often assumed

that the very large corporations such as IBM or Exxon are takeover-proof because of their size, but the validity of that assumption remains to be seen.]   Many family-owned corporations were once safely takeover-proof even though minority shares were widely held and traded on securities exchanges.   Because of deaths of founders, sales by heirs, and the natural desire of many family members to diversify the investment of their inherited wealth, these companies tend to become subject to takeovers over time as family ownership is dissipated.   In order to slow this process, many prominent corporations have issued supervoting stock (shares with multiple votes per share but a lower dividend) to family members to guarantee family control over the enterprise despite their now-minority position.   The supervoting stock is not itself transferable to third persons but may be converted at the request of the shareholder into the regular common stock that is traded on a national securities exchange.   Outside shareholders will presumably convert their supervoting common stock promptly into regular common stock to obtain the larger dividend and liquidity provided by the market, while the inside group will retain the higher voting, lower yielding supervoting stock.   Two well known corporations that have followed this strategy are the Washington Post Company and Dow Jones, Inc., the publisher of the *Wall Street Journal.*

(5) The potential of a defensive technique of "parking" supervoting stock in safe hands to guarantee voting control was not lost on managements fearing takeovers.   One major restraint on this technique was the longstanding rule of the New York Stock Exchange that threatened delisting of corporations that issued non-voting common shares, shares subject to a voting trust, or shares with "unusual voting provisions."   New York Stock Exchange Listed Company Manual, §§ 313.000 and 802.00.   However, with the growth of the over-the-counter market, particularly NASDAQ and the National Market, which had much more liberal listing requirements, the threat of delisting by the NYSE became less serious and a large number of publicly held corporations seriously considered the creation of supervoting stock as the ultimate antitakeover device.   The dispute over "one share one vote" however, was triggered not by a takeover proposal but by General Motor's plan to issue "H" and "E" shares to permit shareholders to invest in its Hughes Aircraft and EDS subsidiaries.   When the NYSE proposed to eliminate its prohibition in order to avoid having to delist General Motors, a lively controversy developed in both political and academic circles.   Ultimately the SEC acted to require uniform delisting requirements for disparate voting plans.   S.E.C. Red. 34–25891 (July 7 and 13, 1988), adopting Rule 19c–4, finally known as the "Shareholder Disenfranchisement Rule."   17 C.F.R. § 240.19c–4 (1989).   The SEC, however, "grandfathered" existing disparate voting rights structures, and also provided important exceptions for initial public offerings, for subsequent issues of lesser voting stock, and for a variety of other transactions.

MORAN v. HOUSEHOLD INTERNATIONAL, INC.

Supreme Court of Delaware, 1985.
500 A.2d 1346.

McNEILLY, JUSTICE.

This case presents to this Court for review the most recent defensive mechanism in the arsenal of corporate takeover weaponry—the Preferred Share Purchase Rights Plan ("Rights Plan" or "Plan"). The validity of this mechanism has attracted national attention. *Amici curiae* briefs have been filed in support of appellants by the Security and Exchange Commission ("SEC") [44] and the Investment Company Institute. An *amicus curiae* brief has been filed in support of appellees ("Household") by the United Food and Commercial Workers International Union.

In a detailed opinion, the Court of Chancery upheld the Rights Plan as a legitimate exercise of business judgment by Household. Moran v. Household International, Inc., Del.Ch., 490 A.2d 1059 (1985). We agree, and therefore, affirm the judgment below.

I

* * * A review of the basic facts is necessary for a complete understanding of the issues.

On August 14, 1984, the Board of Directors of Household International, Inc. adopted the Rights Plan by a fourteen to two vote. [45] The intricacies of the Rights Plan are contained in a 48–page document entitled "Rights Agreement". Basically, the Plan provides that Household common stockholders are entitled to the issuance of one Right per common share under certain triggering conditions. There are two triggering events that can activate the Rights. The first is the announcement of a tender offer for 30 percent of Household's shares ("30% trigger") and the second is the acquisition of 20 percent of Household's shares by any single entity or group ("20% trigger").

If an announcement of a tender offer for 30 percent of Household's shares is made, the Rights are issued and are immediately exercisable to purchase ¹⁄₁₀₀ share of new preferred stock for $100 and are redeemable by the Board for $.50 per Right. If 20 percent of Household's shares are acquired by anyone, the Rights are issued and become nonredeemable and are exercisable to purchase ¹⁄₁₀₀ of a share of preferred. If a Right is not exercised for preferred, and thereafter, a merger or

---

44. [By the Court] The SEC split 3–2 on whether to intervene in this case. The two dissenting Commissioners have publicly disagreed with the other three as to the merits of the Rights Plan. 17 Securities Regulation & Law Report 400; The Wall Street Journal, March 20, 1985, at 6.

45. [By the Court] Household's Board has ten outside directors and six who are members of management. Messrs. Moran (appellant) and Whitehead voted against the Plan. The record reflects that Whitehead voted against the Plan not on its substance but because he thought it was novel and would bring unwanted publicity to Household.

consolidation occurs, the Rights holder can exercise each Right to purchase $200 of the common stock of the tender offeror for $100. This "flip-over" provision of the Rights Plan is at the heart of this controversy.

Household is a diversified holding company with its principal subsidiaries engaged in financial services, transportation and merchandising. HFC, National Car Rental and Vons Grocery are three of its wholly-owned entities.

Household did not adopt its Rights Plan during a battle with a corporate raider, but as a preventive mechanism to ward off future advances. The Vice–Chancellor found that as early as February 1984, Household's management became concerned about the company's vulnerability as a takeover target and began considering amending its charter to render a takeover more difficult. After considering the matter, Household decided not to pursue a fair price amendment.

In the meantime, appellant Moran, one of Household's own Directors and also Chairman of the Dyson–Kissner–Moran Corporation, ("D–K–M") which is the largest single stockholder of Household, began discussions concerning a possible leveraged buy-out of Household by D–K–M. D–K–M's financial studies showed that Household's stock was significantly undervalued in relation to the company's break-up value. It is uncontradicted that Moran's suggestion of a leveraged buy-out never progressed beyond the discussion stage.

Concerned about Household's vulnerability to a raider in light of the current takeover climate, Household secured the services of Wachtell, Lipton, Rosen and Katz ("Watchell, Lipton") and Goldman, Sachs & Co. ("Goldman, Sachs") to formulate a takeover policy for recommendation to the Household Board at its August 14 meeting. After a July 31 meeting with a Household Board member and a pre-meeting distribution of material on the potential takeover problem and the proposed Rights Plan, the Board met on August 14, 1984.

Representatives of Wachtell, Lipton and Goldman, Sachs attended the August 14 meeting. The minutes reflect that Mr. Lipton explained to the Board that his recommendation of the Plan was based on his understanding that the Board was concerned about the increasing frequency of "bust-up" takeovers, the increasing takeover activity in the financial service industry, such as Leucadia's attempt to take over Arco, and the possible adverse effect this type of activity could have on employees and others concerned with and vital to the continuing successful operation of Household even in the absence of any actual bust-up takeover attempt. Against this factual background, the Plan was approved.

Thereafter, Moran and the company of which he is Chairman, D–K–M, filed this suit. On the eve of trial, Gretl Golter, the holder of 500 shares of Household, was permitted to intervene as an additional plaintiff. The trial was held, and the Court of Chancery ruled in favor of Household. Appellants now appeal from that ruling to this Court.

II

The primary issue here is the applicability of the business judgment rule as the standard by which the adoption of the Rights Plan should be reviewed. Much of this issue has been decided by our recent decision in Unocal Corp. v. Mesa Petroleum Co., Del.Supr., 493 A.2d 946 (1985). In *Unocal,* we applied the business judgment rule to analyze Unocal's discriminatory self-tender. We explained:

> When a board addresses a pending takeover bid it has an obligation to determine whether the offer is in the best interests of the corporation and its shareholders. In that respect a board's duty is no different from any other responsibility it shoulders, and its decisions should be no less entitled to the respect they otherwise would be accorded in the realm of business judgment.

Id. at 954 (citation and footnote omitted).

Other jurisdictions have also applied the business judgment rule to actions by which target companies have sought to forestall takeover activity they considered undesirable. See Gearhart Industries, Inc. v. Smith International, 5th Cir., 741 F.2d 707 (1984) (sale of discounted subordinate debentures containing springing warrants); Treco, Inc. v. Land of Lincoln Savings and Loan, 7th Cir., 749 F.2d 374 (1984) (amendment to by-laws); Panter v. Marshall Field, 7th Cir., 646 F.2d 271 (1981) (acquisitions to create antitrust problems); Johnson v. Trueblood, 3d Cir., 629 F.2d 287 (1980), cert. denied, 450 U.S. 999, 101 S.Ct. 1704, 68 L.Ed.2d 200 (1981) (refusal to tender); Crouse–Hinds Co. v. InterNorth, Inc., 2d Cir., 634 F.2d 690 (1980) (sale of stock to favored party); Treadway v. Care Corp., 2d Cir., 638 F.2d 357 (1980) (sale to White Knight), Enterra Corp. v. SGS Associates, E.D.Pa., 600 F.Supp. 678 (1985) (standstill agreement); Buffalo Forge Co. v. Ogden Corp., S.D.N.Y., 555 F.Supp. 892, aff'd, 717 F.2d 757 (2d Cir.), cert. denied, 464 U.S. 1018, 104 S.Ct. 550, 78 L.Ed.2d 724 (1983) (sale of treasury shares and grant of stock option to White Knight); Whittaker Corp. v. Edgar, N.D.Ill., 535 F.Supp. 933 (1982) (disposal of valuable assets); Martin Marietta Corp. v. Bendix Corp., D.Md., 549 F.Supp. 623 (1982) (Pac–Man defense).

This case is distinguishable from the ones cited, since here we have a defensive mechanism adopted to ward off possible future advances and not a mechanism adopted in reaction to a specific threat. This distinguishing factor does not result in the Directors losing the protection of the business judgment rule. To the contrary, pre-planning for the contingency of a hostile takeover might reduce the risk that, under the pressure of a takeover bid, management will fail to exercise reasonable judgment. Therefore, in reviewing a pre-planned defensive mechanism it seems even more appropriate to apply the business judgment rule. See Warner Communications v. Murdoch, D.Del., 581 F.Supp. 1482, 1491 (1984).

Of course, the business judgment rule can only sustain corporate decision making or transactions that are within the power or authority of the Board. Therefore, before the business judgment rule can be applied it must be determined whether the Directors were authorized to adopt the Rights Plan.

III

Appellants vehemently contend that the Board of Directors was unauthorized to adopt the Rights Plan. First, appellants contend that no provision of the Delaware General Corporation Law authorizes the issuance of such Rights. Secondly, appellants, along with the SEC, contend that the Board is unauthorized to usurp stockholders' rights to receive hostile tender offers. Third, appellants and the SEC also contend that the Board is unauthorized to fundamentally restrict stockholders' rights to conduct a proxy contest. We address each of these contentions in turn.

A.

While appellants contend that no provision of the Delaware General Corporation Law authorizes the Rights Plan, Household contends that the Rights Plan was issued pursuant to 8 *Del.C.* §§ 151(g) and 157. It explains that the Rights are authorized by § 157 [46] and the issue of preferred stock underlying the Rights is authorized by § 151.[47] Appellants respond by making several attacks upon the authority to issue the Rights pursuant to § 157.

Appellants begin by contending that § 157 cannot authorize the Rights Plan since § 157 has never served the purpose of authorizing a takeover defense. Appellants contend that § 157 is a corporate financing statute, and that nothing in its legislative history suggests a purpose that has anything to do with corporate control or a takeover defense. Appellants are unable to demonstrate that the legislature, in its adoption of § 157, meant to limit the applicability of § 157 to only the issuance of Rights for the purposes of corporate financing. Without such affirmative evidence, we decline to impose such a limitation upon

---

46. [By the Court] The power to issue rights to purchase shares is conferred by 8 *Del.C.* § 157 which provides in relevant part:

> Subject to any provisions in the certificate of incorporation, every corporation may create and issue, whether or not in connection with the issue and sale of any shares of stock or other securities of the corporation, rights or options entitling the holders thereof to purchase from the corporation any shares of its capital stock of any class or classes, such rights or options to be evidenced by or in such instrument or instruments as shall be approved by the board of directors.

47. [By the Court] 8 *Del.C.* § 151(g) provides in relevant part:

> When any corporation desires to issue any shares of stock of any class or of any series of any class of which the voting powers, designations, preferences and relative, participating, optional or other rights, if any, or the qualifications, limitations or restrictions thereof, if any, shall not have been set forth in the certificate of incorporation or in any amendment thereto but shall be provided for in a resolution or resolutions adopted by the board of directors pursuant to authority expressly vested in it by the provisions of the certificate of incorporation or any amendment thereto, a certificate setting forth a copy of such resolution or resolutions and the number of shares of stock of such class or series shall be executed, acknowledged, filed, recorded, and shall become effective, in accordance with § 103 of this title.

the section that the legislature has not. Compare Providence & Worchester Co. v. Baker, Del.Supr., 378 A.2d 121, 124 (1977) (refusal to read a bar to protective voting provisions into 8 *Del.C.* § 212(a)).

As we noted in *Unocal:*

> [O]ur corporate law is not static. It must grow and develop in response to, indeed in anticipation of, evolving concepts and needs. Merely because the General Corporation Law is silent as to a specific matter does not mean that it is prohibited.

493 A.2d at 957. See also Cheff v. Mathes, Del.Supr., 199 A.2d 548 (1964).

Secondly, appellants contend that § 157 does not authorize the issuance of sham rights such as the Rights Plan. They contend that the Rights were designed never to be exercised, and that the Plan has no economic value. In addition, they contend the preferred stock made subject to the Rights is also illusory, citing *Telvest, Inc. v. Olson,* Del. Ch., C.A. No. 5798, Brown, V.C. (March 8, 1979).

Appellants' sham contention fails in both regards. As to the Rights, they can and will be exercised upon the happening of a triggering mechanism, as we have observed during the current struggle of Sir James Goldsmith to take control of Crown Zellerbach. See Wall Street Journal, July 26, 1985, at 3, 12. As to the preferred shares, we agree with the Court of Chancery that they are distinguishable from sham securities invalidated in *Telvest,* supra. The Household preferred, issuable upon the happening of a triggering event, have superior dividend and liquidation rights.

Third, appellants contend that § 157 authorizes the issuance of Rights "entitling holders thereof to purchase from the corporation any shares of *its* capital stock of any class . . ." (emphasis added). Therefore, their contention continues, the plain language of the statute does not authorize Household to issue rights to purchase another's capital stock upon a merger or consolidation.

Household contends, *inter alia,* that the Rights Plan is analogous to "anti-destruction" or "anti-dilution" provisions which are customary features of a wide variety of corporate securities. While appellants seem to concede that "anti-destruction" provisions are valid under Delaware corporate law, they seek to distinguish the Rights Plan as not being incidental, as are most "anti-destruction" provisions, to a corporation's statutory power to finance itself. We find no merit to such a distinction. We have already rejected appellants' similar contention that § 157 could only be used for financing purposes. We also reject that distinction here.

"Anti-destruction" clauses generally ensure holders of certain securities of the protection of their right of conversion in the event of a merger by giving them the right to convert their securities into whatever securities are to replace the stock of their company. See Broad v. Rockwell International Corp., 5th Cir., 642 F.2d 929, 946, cert. denied,

454 U.S. 965, 102 S.Ct. 506, 70 L.Ed.2d 380 (1981). The fact that the rights here have as their purpose the prevention of coercive two-tier tender offers does not invalidate them.

Fourth, appellants contend that Household's reliance upon § 157 is contradictory to 8 *Del.C.* § 203.[48] Section 203 is a "notice" statute which generally requires that timely notice be given to a target of an offeror's intention to make a tender offer. Appellants contend that the lack of stronger regulation by the State indicates a legislative intent to reject anything which would impose an impediment to the tender offer process. Such a contention is a *non sequitur.* The desire to have little state regulation of tender offers cannot be said to also indicate a desire to have little private regulation. Furthermore, as we explain *infra,* we do not view the Rights Plan as much of an impediment on the tender offer process.

Fifth, appellants contend that if § 157 authorizes the Rights Plan it would be unconstitutional pursuant to the Commerce Clause and Supremacy Clause of the United States Constitution. * * * since it is an obstacle to the accomplishment of the policies underlying the Williams Act. Appellants put heavy emphasis upon the case of Edgar v. MITE Corp., 457 U.S. 624, 102 S.Ct. 2629, 73 L.Ed.2d 269 (1982), in which the United States Supreme Court held that the Illinois Business Takeover Act was unconstitutional, in that it unduly burdened interstate commerce in violation of the Commerce Clause. We do not read the analysis in *Edgar* as applicable to the actions of private parties. The fact that directors of a corporation act pursuant to a state statute provides an insufficient nexus to the state for there to be state action which may violate the Commerce Clause or Supremacy Clause. See

---

48. [By the Court] 8 *Del.C.* § 203 provides in relevant part:

"(a) No offeror shall make a tender offer unless:

"(1) Not less than 20 nor more than 60 days before the date the tender offer is to be made, the offeror shall deliver personally or by registered or certified mail to the corporation whose equity securities are to be subject to the tender offer, at its registered office in this State or at its principal place of business, a written statement of the offeror's intention to make the tender offer. * * *

"(2) The tender offer shall remain open for a period of at least 20 days after it is first made to the holders of the equity securities, during which period any stockholder may withdraw any of the equity securities tendered to the offeror, and any revised or amended tender offer which changes the amount or type of consideration offered or the number of equity securities for which the

offer is made shall remain open at least 10 days following the amendment; and

"(3) The offeror and any associate of the offeror will not purchase or pay for any tendered equity security for a period of at least 20 days after the tender offer is first made to the holders of the equity securities, and no such purchase or payment shall be made within 10 days after an amended or revised tender offer if the amendment or revision changes the amount or type of consideration offered or the number of equity securities for which the offer is made. If during the period the tender offer must remain open pursuant to this section, a greater number of equity securities is tendered than the offeror is bound or willing to purchase, the equity securities shall be purchased pro rata, as nearly as may be, according to the number of shares tendered during such period by each equity security holder."

Data Probe Acquisition Corp. v. Datatab, Inc., 2d Cir., 722 F.2d 1, 5 (1983).

Having concluded that sufficient authority for the Rights Plan exists in 8 *Del.C.* § 157, we note the inherent powers of the Board conferred by 8 *Del.C.* § 141(a), concerning the management of the corporation's "business and *affairs*" (emphasis added), also provides the Board additional authority upon which to enact the Rights Plan.

B.

Appellants contend that the Board is unauthorized to usurp stockholders' rights to receive tender offers by changing Household's fundamental structure. We conclude that the Rights Plan does not prevent stockholders from receiving tender offers, and that the change of Household's structure was less than that which results from the implementation of other defensive mechanisms upheld by various courts.

Appellants' contention that stockholders will lose their right to receive and accept tender offers seems to be premised upon an understanding of the Rights Plan which is illustrated by the SEC *amicus* brief which states: "The Chancery Court's decision seriously understates the impact of this plan. In fact, as we discuss below, the Rights Plan will deter not only two-tier offers, but virtually all hostile tender offers."

The fallacy of that contention is apparent when we look at the recent takeover of Crown Zellerbach, which has a similar Rights Plan, by Sir James Goldsmith. Wall Street Journal, July 26, 1985, at 3, 12. The evidence at trial also evidenced many methods around the Plan ranging from tendering with a condition that the Board redeem the Rights, tendering with a high minimum condition of shares and Rights, tendering and soliciting consents to remove the Board and redeem the Rights, to acquiring 50% of the shares and causing Household to self-tender for the Rights. One could also form a group of up to 19.9% and solicit proxies for consents to remove the Board and redeem the Rights. These are but a few of the methods by which Household can still be acquired by a hostile tender offer.

In addition, the Rights Plan is not absolute. When the Household Board of Directors is faced with a tender offer and a request to redeem the Rights, they will not be able to arbitrarily reject the offer. They will be held to the same fiduciary standards any other board of directors would be held to in deciding to adopt a defensive mechanism, the same standard as they were held to in originally approving the Rights Plan.

In addition, appellants contend that the deterence of tender offers will be accomplished by what they label "a fundamental transfer of power from the stockholders to the directors." They contend that this transfer of power, in itself, is unauthorized.

The Rights Plan will result in no more of a structural change than any other defensive mechanism adopted by a board of directors. The

Rights Plan does not destroy the assets of the corporation. The implementation of the Plan neither results in any outflow of money from the corporation nor impairs its financial flexibility. It does not dilute earnings per share and does not have any adverse tax consequences for the corporation or its stockholders. The Plan has not adversely affected the market price of Household's stock.

Comparing the Rights Plan with other defensive mechanisms, it does less harm to the value structure of the corporation than do the other mechanisms. Other mechanisms result in increased debt of the corporation. See Whittaker Corp. v. Edgar, supra (sale of "prize asset"), Cheff v. Mathes, supra, (paying greenmail to eliminate a threat), Unocal Corp. v. Mesa Petroleum Co., supra, (discriminatory self-tender).

There is little change in the governance structure as a result of the adoption of the Rights Plan. The Board does not now have unfettered discretion in refusing to redeem the Rights. The Board has no more discretion in refusing to redeem the Rights than it does in enacting any defensive mechanism.

The contention that the Rights Plan alters the structure more than do other defensive mechanisms because it is so effective as to make the corporation completely safe from hostile tender offers is likewise without merit. As explained above, there are numerous methods to successfully launch a hostile tender offer.

C.

Appellants' third contention is that the Board was unauthorized to fundamentally restrict stockholders' rights to conduct a proxy contest. Appellants contend that the "20% trigger" effectively prevents any stockholder from first acquiring 20% or more shares before conducting a proxy contest and further, it prevents stockholders from banding together into a group to solicit proxies if, collectively, they own 20% or more of the stock.[49] In addition, at trial, appellants contended that read literally, the Rights Agreement triggers the Rights upon the mere acquisition of the right to vote 20% or more of the shares through a proxy solicitation, and thereby precludes any proxy contest from being waged.[50]

Appellants seem to have conceded this last contention in light of Household's response that the receipt of a proxy does not make the recipient the "beneficial owner" of the shares involved which would trigger the Rights. In essence, the Rights Agreement provides that the Rights are triggered when someone becomes the "beneficial owner" of 20% or more of Household stock. Although a literal reading of the Rights Agreement definition of "beneficial owner" would seem to in-

49. [By the Court] Appellants explain that the acquisition of 20% of the shares trigger the Rights, making them non-redeemable, and thereby would prevent even a future friendly offer for the ten-year life of the Rights.

50. [By the Court] The SEC still contends that the mere acquisition of the right to vote 20% of the shares through a proxy solicitation triggers the rights. We do not interpret the Rights Agreement in that manner.

clude those shares which one has the right to vote, it has long been recognized that the relationship between grantor and recipient of a proxy is one of agency, and the agency is revocable by the grantor at any time. Henn, *Corporations* § 196, at 518. Therefore, the holder of a proxy is not the "beneficial owner" of the stock. As a result, the mere acquisition of the right to vote 20% of the shares does not trigger the Rights.

The issue, then, is whether the restriction upon individuals or groups from first acquiring 20% of shares before waging a proxy contest fundamentally restricts stockholders' right to conduct a proxy contest. Regarding this issue the Court of Chancery found:

> Thus, while the Rights Plan does deter the formation of proxy efforts of a certain magnitude, it does not limit the voting power of individual shares. On the evidence presented it is highly conjectural to assume that a particular effort to assert shareholder views in the election of directors or revisions of corporate policy will be frustrated by the proxy feature of the Plan. Household's witnesses, Troubh and Higgins described recent corporate takeover battles in which insurgents holding less than 10% stock ownership were able to secure corporate control through a proxy contest or the threat of one.

490 A.2d at 1080.

We conclude that there was sufficient evidence at trial to support the Vice–Chancellor's finding that the effect upon proxy contests will be minimal. Evidence at trial established that many proxy contests are won with an insurgent ownership of less than 20%, and that very large holdings are no guarantee of success. There was also testimony that the key variable in proxy contest success is the merit of an insurgent's issues, not the size of his holdings.

<h1 style="text-align:center">IV</h1>

Having concluded that the adoption of the Rights Plan was within the authority of the Directors, we now look to whether the Directors have met their burden under the business judgment rule.

The business judgment rule is a "presumption that in making a business decision the directors of a corporation acted on an informed basis, in good faith and in the honest belief that the action taken was in the best interests of the company." Aronson v. Lewis, Del.Supr., 473 A.2d 805, 812 (1984) (citations omitted). Notwithstanding, in *Unocal* we held that when the business judgment rule applies to adoption of a defensive mechanism, the initial burden will lie with the directors. The "directors must show that they had reasonable grounds for believing that a danger to corporate policy and effectiveness existed. . . . [T]hey satisfy that burden 'by showing good faith and reasonable investigation . . .'" *Unocal,* 493 A.2d at 955 (citing Cheff v. Mathes, 199 A.2d at 554–55). In addition, the directors must show that the defensive mechanism was "reasonable in relation to the threat posed." *Unocal,* 493 A.2d at 955. Moreover, that proof is materially enhanced, as we noted in *Unocal*, where, as here, a majority of the board favoring the proposal consisted of outside independent directors who have acted in accordance with the foregoing standards. *Unocal*, 493 A.2d at 955; *Aronson*, 473 A.2d at 815. Then, the burden shifts back to the plaintiffs who have the ultimate burden of persuasion to show a breach of the directors' fiduciary duties. *Unocal*, 493 A.2d at 958.

There are no allegations here of any bad faith on the part of the Directors' action in the adoption of the Rights Plan. There is no allegation that the Directors' action was taken for entrenchment purposes. Household has adequately demonstrated, as explained above, that the adoption of the Rights Plan was in reaction to what it perceived to be the threat in the market place of coercive two-tier tender offers. Appellants do contend, however, that the Board did not exercise informed business judgment in its adoption of the Plan. * * * Appellants contend the Delaware counsel did not express an opinion on the flip-over provision of the Rights, rather only that the Rights would constitute validly issued and outstanding rights to subscribe to the preferred stock of the company.

To determine whether a business judgment reached by a board of directors was an informed one, we determine whether the directors were grossly negligent. Smith v. Van Gorkom, Del.Supr., 488 A.2d 858, 873 (1985). Upon a review of this record, we conclude the Directors were not grossly negligent. The information supplied to the Board on August 14 provided the essentials of the Plan. The Directors were given beforehand a notebook which included a three-page summary of the Plan along with articles on the current takeover environment. The extended discussion between the Board and representatives of Wachtell, Lipton and Goldman, Sachs before approval of the Plan reflected a full and candid evaluation of the Plan. Moran's expression of his views at the meeting served to place before the Board a knowledgeable critique of the Plan. The factual happenings here are clearly distinguishable from the actions of the directors of Trans Union Corporation who displayed gross negligence in approving a cash-out merger.

In addition, to meet their burden, the Directors must show that the defensive mechanism was "reasonable in relation to the threat posed". The record reflects a concern on the part of the Directors over the increasing frequency in the financial services industry of "boot-strap" and "bust-up" takeovers. The Directors were also concerned that such takeovers may take the form of two-tier offers.[51] In addition, on August 14, the Household Board was aware of Moran's overture on behalf of D–K–M. In sum, the Directors reasonably believed Household was vulnerable to coercive acquisition techniques and adopted a reasonable defensive mechanism to protect itself.

---

51. [By the Court] We have discussed the coercive nature of two-tier tender offers in Unocal, 493 A.2d at 956, n. 12. We explained in *Unocal* that a discriminatory self-tender was reasonably related to the threat of two-tier tender offers and possible greenmail.

V

＊ ＊ ＊ While we conclude for present purposes that the Household Directors are protected by the business judgment rule, that does not end the matter. The ultimate response to an actual takeover bid must be judged by the Directors' actions at that time, and nothing we say here relieves them of their basic fundamental duties to the corporation and its stockholders. Smith v. Van Gorkom, 488 A.2d at 872–73. Their use of the Plan will be evaluated when and if the issue arises.

Affirmed.

Notes

(1) Richards, Brussard & Williams, Rights Plans Developments and Recent Litigation, The National Law Journal, May 23, 1988, pp. 28, 29: ＊

Since its first appearance in 1984, the stock purchase rights plan, often referred to as a "poison pill," has been adopted in varying forms by more than 500 corporations. The central thrust of most such plans has remained essentially the same—to induce would-be acquirers, by threat of unacceptable dilution, to negotiate with the board of directors to neutralize the pill through redemption of the rights, thus protecting the shareholders against unfair offers. The form and structure of the rights plans, on the other hand, has continued to evolve.

In its initial form, as upheld in Moran v. Household International Inc., ＊ ＊ ＊ the heart of the plan, designed to deal with the then-current phenomena of two-tier, front-end loaded tender offers and related techniques, was found in the "flip-over" provision. ＊ ＊ ＊

Early experience with the original form of rights plan—including among other things the experience of Crown Zellerbach Corp. when Sir James Goldsmith crossed the acquisition threshold under its rights plan—ultimately led to several refinements in the original provisions. ＊ ＊ ＊

Of greater significance was the development of the so-called flip-in provision, of both the self-dealing and stock ownership varieties. Although the original form of rights plan provided strong inducement to negotiate in advance with the board if an acquirer desired to effectuate a second-step transaction in the near term, it provided substantially less—or no—deterrence for an acquirer willing to wait out the duration of the plan following the initial acquisition of control.

The self-dealing, and later the stock ownership, flip-ins were devised to fill this gap and protect against potential takeover abuses not addressed by the flip-over, including creeping acquisitions and street sweeps. The self-dealing flip-in provision provides that if an acquirer, after having crossed the initial acquisition threshold, engages in any of a number of self-dealing transactions—modeled closely on the typical fair-price charter provisions—then the holders of the rights, excluding the acquirer, are entitled to purchase common stock of the target corporation at 50 percent of the market price.

Similarly, under the stock ownership flip-in, in the event that an acquirer becomes the owner of more than a specified percentage of the outstanding common stock—typically 25 percent to 40 percent, although more recently going as low as 10 percent—each holder of rights other than such acquirer is entitled to purchase common stock of the target corporation at a 50 percent discount. * * *

By the early summer of 1987, the typical rights plan had come to include a flip-over provision, a self-dealing flip-in provision and, more often than not, a stock ownership flip-in provision. This was and remains the typical form of rights plan usually adopted as a prospective defensive measure. * * *

(2) As indicated in the foregoing excerpt, the poison pill was originally designed expressly to combat two-tiered and partial tender offers. In part as a result of the success of the poison pill, these types of offers have virtually disappeared. Today the type of offer faced by most issuers is an all-cash offer for any-and-all shares using borrowed funds and junk bonds—in other words, a leveraged buyout. "Flip in" and "flip over" pills are also major impediments to such offers since they greatly increase in the cost of a takeover unless they are voluntarily withdrawn by the issuer's board of directors. In order to maximize the pressure on the issuer's board of directors to accept an all-cash offer, it has now become customary to (1) provide that tenders include poison pill rights as well as the underlying shares, or (2) make the offer itself conditional upon the issuer's board voluntarily redeeming the poison pill. It has also become customary to file suit against the issuer contemporaneously with the offer to enjoin the issuer from invoking the poison pill. The force of these strategies should not be underestimated given the Delaware Supreme Court's test of defensive tactics in *Unocal* and its emphasis on fiduciary principles in *Household Finance*. A good illustration of the pressures on the issuer's board of directors in this situation was the all-cash tender offer by Grand Metropolitan PLC for Pillsbury Co. in late 1988. Grand Met. originally offered $60 per share, later increased to $66 per share, or a total price of $5.75 billion. The stock previously had been trading at about $40 per share. Pillsbury refused to withdraw its poison pill even though more than 70 percent of its stock had been tendered into the Grand Met offer. This stubborn retention of a poison pill in the face of an all-cash offer found attractive by most Pillsbury shareholders seems difficult to justify under the test of *Unocal* that the action "be reasonable in relation to the threat imposed." Rather mercifully, the Delaware Chancery Court ordered the poison pill withdrawn and Pillsbury management capitulated.

(3) Lipton, Is This the End of Takeovers? [Memorandum distributed to clients of Wachtell, Lipton Rosen & Katz on October 28, 1988]:

The state takeover laws did not stop them. Litigation—antitrust and other—did not stop them. The reaction to the PacMan defense of Martin–Marietta against Bendix did not stop them. Shark repellants and poison pills did not stop them. The October 19, 1987 crash did not stop them. And jawboning by the Fed and the failure of the Federated Department Stores junk bond offering will not stop them.

Our Nation is blindly rushing to the precipice. As with tulip bulbs, South Sea bubbles, pyramid investment trusts, Florida land, REITs, LDC loans, Texas banks and all the other financial market frenzies of the past, the denouement will be a crash. We and our children will pay a gigantic price for allowing abusive takeover tactics and boot-strap, junk-bond takeovers. We are overleveraging American companies and forcing them to focus on short-term stock market results. Research, new product development and capital investment are no longer the keys to business success. To the contrary they have become the invitation to a junk-bond, bust-up party. While the rest of the industrialized world is investing for the future, we are squandering our assets in a speculative binge of junk bonds, financial futures, program trading, put and call options and the other games of today's financial market casinos. * * *

Curbing the abuses being perpetrated by institutional investors is not enough. As long as our tax laws favor junk bonds over equity, the pressure to overleverage will remain. We must remove the tax advantage that junk bonds enjoy.

At the moment, the courts are our only hope. The poison pill is an effective defense against abusive takeovers. The courts are now recognizing this. Hopefully, they will make it clear that a board of directors does not have to redeem a pill and either auction the company to the highest bidder or restructure by turning equity into debt. In other words, the courts should affirm that a board of directors, acting in good faith and on reasonable grounds, has the absolute right to reject any takeover bid. At other moments in our history, the courts have stepped in to solve social and economic problems that were beyond the Congress. What is necessary today is that they defer to the honest business judgment of boards of directors. While corporate raiders in league with institutional investors may shift from tender offers to proxy fights to force boards into auctions or restructuring, that shift will slow down the process, expose the role of the institutions and further the opportunity for legislation regulating the institutions.

(4) A survey by the Investor Responsibility Research Center of the 1,440 largest public corporations (representing some 93 per cent of the total capitalization of all companies listed on the NYSE, ASE, and NASDAQ) as of June, 1989, showed that—

(a) 616 companies (43 per cent) have poison pills;

(b) 781 companies (54 per cent) elect directors to staggered terms— classified boards;

(c) 455 companies (32 per cent) have adopted fair price charter amendments requiring all shareholders to be paid the same price;

(d) 241 companies (17 per cent) require a supermajority vote for proposed mergers;

(e) 106 companies (7.4 per cent) have dual class capitalization plans with different classes of voting shares not subject to SEC Rule 19c–4 (because that rule does not apply to dual capitalization plans in place before January 1, 1987);

(f) 266 companies (18.5 per cent) provide for cumulative voting;

(g) 324 companies (23 per cent) have adopted provisions limiting the power of shareholders to act by written consent without a shareholders' meeting;

(h) 301 companies (21 per cent) have adopted charter amendments limiting the power of shareholders to call special shareholders' meetings;

(i) 80 companies (5.6 per cent) have enacted charter amendments to discourage greenmail;

(j) 32 companies (2.2 per cent) have adopted secret shareholder ballot amendments; and

(k) 86 companies (6 per cent) have authorized boards to consider interests other than shareholders in evaluating merger proposals.

Many companies have adopted more than one of the above proposals. The above data does not take into account state statutes that may automatically make the above provisions applicable to corporations incorporated in specific states.

Chapter Thirteen

TRANSACTIONS IN SHARES BY DIRECTORS AND OTHERS

A. INTRODUCTION: THE APPROACH OF STATE COURTS

GOODWIN v. AGASSIZ

Supreme Judicial Court of Massachusetts, 1933.
283 Mass. 358, 186 N.E. 659.

RUGG, CHIEF JUSTICE.

A stockholder in a corporation seeks in this suit relief for losses suffered by him in selling shares of stock in Cliff Mining Company by way of accounting, rescission of sales, or redelivery of shares. * * *

The facts * * * are these: The defendants, in May, 1926, purchased through brokers on the Boston stock exchange seven hundred shares of stock of the Cliff Mining Company which up to that time the plaintiff had owned. Agassiz was president and director and MacNaughton a director and general manager of the company. They had certain knowledge, material as to the value of the stock, which the plaintiff did not have. The plaintiff contends that such purchase in all the circumstances without disclosure to him of that knowledge was a wrong against him. That knowledge was that an experienced geologist had formulated in writing in March, 1926, a theory as to the possible existence of copper deposits under conditions prevailing in the region where the property of the company was located. That region was known as the mineral belt in Northern Michigan, where are located mines of several copper mining companies. Another such company, of which the defendants were officers, had made extensive geological surveys of its lands. In consequence of recommendations resulting from that survey, exploration was started on property of the Cliff Mining Company in 1925. That exploration was ended in May, 1926, because completed unsuccessfully, and the equipment was removed. The defendants discussed the geologist's theory shortly after it was formulated. Both felt that the theory had value and should be tested, but they agreed that, before starting to test it, options should be obtained by another copper company of which they were officers on land adjacent to or nearby in the copper belt, that if the geologist's theory were known to the owners of such other land there might be difficulty in securing options, and that that theory should not be communicated to any one unless it became absolutely necessary. Thereafter, options were secured which, if taken up, would involve a large expenditure by the other company. The defendants both thought, also that, if there was any merit in the geologist's theory, the price of Cliff Mining Company stock in the market would go up. Its stock was quoted and bought and sold on the Boston Stock Exchange. Pursuant to agreement, they bought many shares of that stock through agents on joint account. The plaintiff first learned of the closing of exploratory operations on property of the Cliff Mining Company from an article in a paper on May 15, 1926, and immediately sold his shares of stock through brokers. It does not appear that the defendants were in any way responsible for the publication of that article. The plaintiff did not know that the purchase was made for the defendants and they did not know that his stock was being bought for them. There was no communication between them touching the subject. The plaintiff would not have sold his stock if he had known of the geologist's theory. The finding is express that the defendants were not guilty of fraud, that they committed no breach of duty owed by them to the Cliff Mining Company, and that that company was not harmed by the nondisclosure of the geologist's theory, or by their purchases of its stock, or by shutting down the exploratory operations.

The contention of the plaintiff is that the purchase of his stock in the company by the defendants without disclosing to him as a stockholder their knowledge of the geologist's theory, their belief that the theory was true, had value, the keeping secret the existence of the theory, discontinuance by the defendants of exploratory operations begun in 1925 on property of the Cliff Mining Company and their plan ultimately to test the value of the theory, constitute actionable wrong for which he as stockholder can recover.

The trial judge ruled that conditions may exist which would make it the duty of an officer of a corporation purchasing its stock from a stockholder to inform him as to knowledge possessed by the buyer and not by the seller, but found, on all the circumstances developed by the trial and set out at some length by him in his decision, that there was no fiduciary relation requiring such disclosure by the defendants to the plaintiff before buying his stock in the manner in which they did.

* * *

The directors of a commercial corporation stand in a relation of trust to the corporation and are bound to exercise the strictest good faith in respect to its property and business. The contention that directors also occupy the position of trustee toward individual stockholders in the corporation is plainly contrary to repeated decisions of this court and cannot be supported. In Smith v. Hurd, 12 Metc. 371, 384, 46 Am.Dec. 690, it was said by Chief Justice Shaw: "There is no legal privity, relation, or immediate connection, between the holders of shares in a bank, in their individual capacity, on the one side, and the directors of the bank on the other. The directors are not the bailees, the factors, agents or trustees of such individual stockholders." * * * In Blabon v. Hay, 269 Mass. 401, 407, 169 N.E. 268, 271, occurs this language with reference to sale of stock in a corporation by a stockholder to two of its directors: "The fact that the defendants were directors created no fiduciary relation between them and the plaintiff in the matter of the sale of his stock."

The principle thus established is supported by an imposing weight of authority in other jurisdictions. A rule holding that directors are trustees for individual stockholders with respect to their stock prevails in comparatively few states; but in view of our own adjudications it is not necessary to review decisions to that effect.

While the general principle is as stated, circumstances may exist requiring that transactions between a director and a stockholder as to stock in the corporation be set aside. The knowledge naturally in the possession of a director as to the condition of a corporation places upon him a peculiar obligation to observe every requirement of fair dealing when directly buying or selling its stock. Mere silence does not usually amount to a breach of duty, but parties may stand in such relation to each other that an equitable responsibility arises to communicate facts. Wellington v. Rugg, 243 Mass. 30, 35, 136 N.E. 831. Purchases and sales of stock dealt in on the stock exchange are commonly impersonal affairs. An honest director would be in a difficult situation if he could neither buy nor sell on the stock exchange shares of stock in his corporation without first seeking out the other actual ultimate party to the transaction and disclosing to him everything which a court or jury might later find that he then knew affecting the real or speculative value of such shares. Business of that nature is a matter to be governed by practical rules. Fiduciary obligations of directors ought not to be made so onerous that men of experience and ability will be deterred from accepting such office. Law in its sanctions is not coextensive with morality. It cannot undertake to put all parties to every contract on an equality as to knowledge, experience, skill and shrewdness. It cannot undertake to relieve against hard bargains made between competent parties without fraud. On the other hand, directors cannot rightly be allowed to indulge with impunity in practices which do violence to prevailing standards of upright business men. Therefore, where a director personally seeks a stockholder for the purpose of buying his shares without making disclosure of material facts within his peculiar knowledge and not within reach of the stockholder, the transaction will be closely scrutinized and relief may be granted in appropriate instances. Strong v. Repide, 213 U.S. 419, 29 S.Ct. 521, 53 L.Ed. 853 * * * See, also, Old Dominion Copper Mining & Smelting

Co. v. Bigelow, 203 Mass. 159, 194, 195, 89 N.E. 193, 40 L.R.A. (N.S.) 314. The applicable legal principles "have almost always been the fundamental ethical rules of right and wrong." Robinson v. Mollett, L.R. 7 H.L. 802, 817.

The precise question to be decided in the case at bar is whether on the facts found the defendants as directors had a right to buy stock of the plaintiff, a stockholder. Every element of actual fraud or misdoing by the defendants is negatived by the findings. Fraud cannot be presumed; it must be proved. Brown v. Little, Brown & Co., Inc., 269 Mass. 102, 117, 168 N.E. 521, 66 A.L.R. 1284. The facts found afford no ground for inferring fraud or conspiracy. The only knowledge possessed by the defendants not open to the plaintiff was the existence of a theory formulated in a thesis by a geologist as to the possible existence of copper deposits where certain geological conditions existed common to the property of the Cliff Mining Company and that of other mining companies in its neighborhood. This thesis did not express an opinion that copper deposits would be found at any particular spot or on property of any specified owner. Whether that theory was sound or fallacious, no one knew, and so far as appears has never been demonstrated. The defendants made no representations to anybody about the theory. No facts found placed upon them any obligation to disclose the theory. A few days after the thesis expounding the theory was brought to the attention of the defendants, the annual report by the directors of the Cliff Mining Company for the calendar year 1925, signed by Agassiz for the directors, was issued. It did not cover the time when the theory was formulated. The report described the status of the operations under the exploration which had been begun in 1925. At the annual meeting of the stockholders of the company held early in April, 1926, no reference was made to the theory. It was then at most a hope, possibly an expectation. It had not passed the nebulous stage. No disclosure was made of it. The Cliff Mining Company was not harmed by the nondisclosure. There would have been no advantage to it, so far as appears, from a disclosure. The disclosure would have been detrimental to the interests of another mining corporation in which the defendants were directors. In the circumstances there was no duty on the part of the defendants to set forth to the stockholders at the annual meeting their faith, aspirations and plans for the future. Events as they developed might render advisable radical changes in such views. Disclosure of the theory, if it ultimately was proved to be erroneous or without foundation in fact, might involve the defendants in litigation with those who might act on the hypothesis that it was correct. The stock of the Cliff Mining Company was bought and sold on the stock exchange. The identity of buyers and sellers of the stock in question in fact was not known to the parties and perhaps could not readily have been ascertained. The defendants caused the shares to be bought through brokers on the stock exchange. They said nothing to anybody as to the reasons actuating them. The plaintiff was no novice. He was a member of the Boston stock exchange and had kept a record of sales of Cliff Mining Company stock. He acted upon his own judgment in selling his stock. He made no inquiries of the defendants or of other officers of the company. The result is that the plaintiff cannot prevail.

Decree dismissing bill affirmed with costs.

Notes

(1) The managers of a corporation inevitably will know more about corporate affairs than outside shareholders or members of the public who may be interested in purchasing shares. There is an obvious temptation to utilize this superior knowledge to turn a personal profit. Where the transaction takes place through the facilities of an anonymous stock exchange, as in the principal case, the common law seems to have no doctrine that prohibits or regulates such transactions. Where, however, the managers deal personally with the shareholder or hide their identities by the use of intermediaries, concepts of fraud, misrepresentation and reliance may be applicable. This is well illustrated by two cases that are widely cited:

(a) In Strong v. Repide, referred to in the principal case, the majority shareholder was conducting negotiations to sell certain real estate owned by the corporation to the Philippine Government. A formal offer to purchase had been made, but the shareholder was holding out for more money. While negotiations were pending, he purchased the plaintiff's stock in the following manner:

> While this state of things existed, and before the final offer had been made by the governor, the defendant, although still holding out for a higher price for the lands, took steps, about the middle or latter part of September, 1903, to purchase the 800 shares of stock in his company owned by Mrs. Strong, which he knew were in the possession of F. Stuart Jones, as her agent. The defendant, having decided to obtain these shares, instead of seeing Jones, who had an office next door, employed one Kauffman, a connection of his by marriage, and Kauffman employed a Mr. Sloan, a broker, who had an office some distance away, to purchase the stock for him, and told Sloan that the stock was for a member of his wife's family. Sloan communicated with the husband of Mrs. Strong and asked if she desired to sell her stock. The husband referred him to Mr. Jones for consultation, who had the stock in his possession. Sloan did not know who wanted to buy the shares, nor did Jones when he was spoken to. Jones would not have sold at the price he did had he known it was the defendant who was purchasing, because, as he said, it would show increased value, as the defendant would not be likely to purchase more stock unless the price was going up. As the articles of incorporation, by subdivision 20, required a resolution of the general meeting of stockholders for the purpose of selling more than one hacienda, and as no such general meeting had been called at the time of the sale of the stock, Mr. Jones might well have supposed there was no immediate prospect of a sale of the lands being made, while at the same time defendant had knowledge of the probabilities thereof, which he had acquired by his conduct of

the negotiations for their sale, as agent of all the shareholders, and while acting specially for them and himself.

213 U.S. at 425, 29 S.Ct. at 523. The price for the purchased shares was approximately one tenth what they were worth three months later after the real estate was sold to the Government.

The Court concluded that the complaint stated a cause of action. Even if it were conceded that the ordinary relationship between director and shareholder was not of such a fiduciary nature as to require disclosure "of the general knowledge which [a director] may possess" regarding the value of shares, the Court stated, "yet there are cases where, by reason of the special facts, such duty exists." The "special facts" pointed to by the Court included the role of the defendant as director, principal shareholder and sole negotiator for the corporation with full power to accept or reject the Government's offer as well as the affirmative steps taken to conceal the identity of the defendant as the purchaser of the shares.

(b) In Hotchkiss v. Fischer, 136 Kan. 530, 16 P.2d 531 (1932), the plaintiff, a widow in need of funds, had inherited 2,300 shares of The Elmhurst Company. Shortly before the annual meeting of the Company she traveled from her home in Burr Oak, Kansas, to Topeka to talk with defendant, the President of the Company. Her plan was to retain the shares if a dividend were declared, but to sell them, at a sacrifice if necessary, if there was to be no dividend. She talked with the defendant on January 12 and 13, 1926. When asked whether a dividend would be declared, defendant replied that he could not inform plaintiff on that subject and would have no information until he conferred with directors coming from New York. He showed her financial statements, and stated that the Company was in sound financial position and had improved its position under his management, but painted a rather dark picture about specific matters. When asked what her stock was worth, he replied that he could supply information but what she thought the stock was worth "is a matter you have to determine yourself."

On January 15, 1926 the defendant purchased the plaintiff's shares for $1.25 per share; on January 16, 1926, he met with the New York directors and ascertained that they were in favor of paying a dividend. On January 18, 1926, the directors declared a dividend of $1 per share.

In the course of finding for plaintiff, the Court defined the duty of the defendant to the plaintiff in the following terms:

> It is commonly said that directors of a corporation are "trustees" for stockholders. Accuracy of nomenclature need not be discussed. Directors act in a fiduciary capacity in management of corporate affairs, and a director negotiating with a shareholder for purchase of shares acts in a relation of scrupulous trust and confidence. The court deems it proper to withhold application of its rule relating to purchase of trust property by trustees proper, to purchase by a director of corporate shares, but such transactions must be subjected to the closest scrutiny, and, unless conducted with the utmost fairness, the wronged shareholder may invoke proper remedy.

136 Kan. at 538, 16 P.2d at 535.

(2) Do you think that the courts in *Goodwin, Strong,* and *Hotchkiss,* are applying essentially the same test despite the variations in language? Subsequent case law treats the Kansas view as a "minority rule" and a rule of "strict accountability." See Blazer v. Black, 196 F.2d 139 (10th Cir.1952); Amen v. Black, 234 F.2d 12 (10th Cir.1956); Delano v. Kitch, 542 F.2d 550 (10th Cir.1976), cert. denied 456 U.S. 946, 102 S.Ct. 2012, 72 L.Ed.2d 468 (1982). On the other hand, the language of *Strong* that only "special facts" create a duty to disclose appears in a number of opinions.

(3) In the absence of affirmative misrepresentation or a combination of reliance and tight-lipped silence, as in *Hotchkiss,* is there any social, moral or economic policy that should limit transactions by managers in the shares of the corporations they manage? Assume, for example, that the managers learn of a serious, adverse development that will seriously depress the value of the shares. May they sell before the bad news is publicly announced? If they learn of good news, or if their efforts create good news, may they buy before the news is announced?

DIAMOND v. OREAMUNO
Court of Appeals of New York, 1969.
24 N.Y.2d 494, 301 N.Y.S.2d 78, 248 N.E.2d 910.

FULD, CHIEF JUDGE.

Upon this appeal from an order denying a motion to dismiss the complaint as insufficient on its face, the question presented—one of first impression in this court—is whether officers and directors may be held accountable to their corporation for gains realized by them from transactions in the company's stock as a result of their use of material inside information.

The complaint was filed by a shareholder of Management Assistance, Inc. (MAI) asserting a derivative action against a number of its officers and directors to compel an accounting for profits allegedly acquired as a result of a breach of fiduciary duty. It charges that two of the defendants—Oreamuno, chairman of the board of directors, and Gonzalez, its president—had used inside information, acquired by them solely by virtue of their positions, in order to reap large personal profits from the sale of MAI shares and that these profits rightfully belong to the corporation. Other officers and directors were joined as defendants on the ground that they acquiesced in or ratified the assertedly wrongful transactions.

MAI is in the business of financing computer installations through sale and lease back arrangements with various commercial and industrial users. Under its lease provisions, MAI was required to maintain and repair the computers but, at the time of this suit, it lacked the capacity to perform this function itself and was forced to engage the manufacturer of the computers, International Business Machines (IBM), to service the machines. As a result of a sharp increase by IBM of its charges for such service, MAI's expenses for August of 1966 rose considerably and its net earnings declined from $262,253 in July to

$66,233 in August, a decrease of about 75%. This information, although earlier known to the defendants, was not made public until October of 1966. Prior to the release of the information, however, Oreamuno and Gonzalez sold off a total of 56,500 shares of their MAI stock at the then current market price of $28 a share.

After the information concerning the drop in earnings was made available to the public, the value of a share of MAI stock immediately fell from the $28 realized by the defendants to $11. Thus, the plaintiff alleges, by taking advantage of their privileged position and their access to confidential information, Oreamuno and Gonzalez were able to realize $800,000 more for their securities than they would have had this inside information not been available to them. Stating that the defendants were "forbidden to use [such] information * * * for their own personal profit or gain", the plaintiff brought this derivative action seeking to have the defendants account to the corporation for this difference. A motion by the defendants to dismiss the complaint—pursuant to CPLR 3211 (subd. [a], par. 7)—for failure to state a cause of action was granted by the court at Special Term. The Appellate Division, with one dissent, modified Special Term's order by reinstating the complaint as to the defendants Oreamuno and Gonzalez. The appeal is before us on a certified question.

In reaching a decision in this case, we are, of course, passing only upon the sufficiency of the complaint and we necessarily accept the charges contained in that pleading as true.

It is well established, as a general proposition, that a person who acquires special knowledge or information by virtue of a confidential or fiduciary relationship with another is not free to exploit that knowledge or information for his own personal benefit but must account to his principal for any profits derived therefrom. This, in turn, is merely a corollary of the broader principal, inherent in the nature of the fiduciary relationship, that prohibits a trustee or agent from extracting secret profits from his position of trust.

In support of their claim that the complaint fails to state a cause of action, the defendants take the position that, although it is admittedly wrong for an officer or director to use his position to obtain trading profits for himself in the stock of his corporation, the action ascribed to them did not injure or damage MAI in any way. Accordingly, the defendants continue, the corporation should not be permitted to recover the proceeds. They acknowledge that, by virtue of the exclusive access which officers and directors have to inside information, they possess an unfair advantage over other shareholders and, particularly, the persons who had purchased the stock from them but, they contend, the corporation itself was unaffected and, for that reason, a derivative action is an inappropriate remedy.

It is true that the complaint before us does not contain any allegation of damages to the corporation but this has never been considered to be an essential requirement for a cause of action founded on a breach of fiduciary duty. This is because the function of such an action, unlike an ordinary tort or contract case, is not merely to compensate the plaintiff for wrongs committed by the defendant but, as this court declared many years ago (Dutton v. Willner, 52 N.Y. 312, 319), "to *prevent* them, by removing from agents and trustees all inducement to attempt dealing for their own benefit in matters which they have undertaken for others, or to which their agency or trust relates." (Emphasis supplied.)

Just as a trustee has no right to retain for himself the profits yielded by property placed in his possession but must account to his beneficiaries, a corporate fiduciary, who is entrusted with potentially valuable information, may not appropriate that asset for his own use even though, in so doing, he causes no injury to the corporation. The primary concern, in a case such as this, is not to determine whether the corporation has been damaged but to decide, as between the corporation and the defendants, who has a higher claim to the proceeds derived from the exploitation of the information. In our opinion, there can be no justification for permitting officers and directors, such as the defendants, to retain for themselves profits which, it is alleged, they derived solely from exploiting information gained by virtue of their inside position as corporate officials.

In addition, it is pertinent to observe that, despite the lack of any specific allegation of damage, it may well be inferred that the defendants' actions might have caused some harm to the enterprise. Although the corporation may have little concern with the day-to-day transactions in its shares, it has a great interest in maintaining a reputation of integrity, an image of probity, for its management and in insuring the continued public acceptance and marketability of its stock. When officers and directors abuse their position in order to gain personal profits, the effect may be to cast a cloud on the corporation's name, injure stockholder relations and undermine public regard for the corporation's securities. As Presiding Justice Botein aptly put it, in the course of his opinion for the Appellate Division, "[t]he prestige and good will of a corporation, so vital to its prosperity, may be undermined by the revelation that its chief officers had been making personal profits out of corporate events which they had not disclosed to the community of stockholders." (29 A.D.2d at p. 287, 287 N.Y.S.2d at p. 303.)

The defendants maintain that extending the prohibition against personal exploitation of a fiduciary relationship to officers and directors of a corporation will discourage such officials from maintaining a stake in the success of the corporate venture through share ownership, which, they urge, is an important incentive to proper performance of their duties. There is, however, a considerable difference between corporate officers who assume the same risks and obtain the same benefits as other shareholders and those who use their privileged position to gain special advantages not available to others. The sale of shares by the defendants for the reasons charged was not merely a wise investment decision which any prudent investor might have made. Rather, they were assertedly able in this case to profit solely because they had information which was not available to any one else—including the other shareholders whose interests they, as corporate fiduciaries, were bound to protect.

Although no appellate court in this State has had occasion to pass upon the precise question before us, the concept underlying the present cause of action is hardly a new one. (See, e.g., Securities Exchange Act of 1934 § 16[b] [15 U.S.C.A. § 78p(b)], Restatement, 2d, Agency, § 388, comment c.) Under Federal law (Securities Exchange Act of 1934, § 16[b]), for example, it is conclusively presumed that, when a director, officer or 10% shareholder buys and sells securities of his corporation within a six-month period, he is trading on inside information. The remedy which the Federal statute provides in that situation is precisely the same as that sought in the present case under State law, namely, an action brought by the corporation or on its behalf to recover all profits derived from the transactions.

In providing this remedy, Congress accomplished a dual purpose. It not only provided for an efficient and effective method of accomplishing its primary goal—the protection of the investing public from unfair treatment at the hands of corporate insiders—but extended to the corporation the right to secure for itself benefits derived by those insiders from their exploitation of their privileged position. The United States Court of Appeals for the Second Circuit has stated the policy behind section 16(b) in the following terms (Adler v. Klawans, 267 F.2d 840, 844):

> "The undoubted congressional intent in the enactment of § 16(b) was to discourage what was reasonably thought to be a widespread abuse of a fiduciary relationship—specifically to discourage if not prevent three classes of persons from making private and gainful use of information acquired by them by virtue of their official relationship to a corporation."

Although the provisions of section 16(b) may not apply to all cases of trading on inside information, it demonstrates that a derivative action can be an effective method for dealing with such abuses which may be used to accomplish a similar purpose in cases not specifically covered by the statute. In Brophy v. Cities Serv. Co. (31 Del.Ch. 241, 70 A.2d 5, supra), for example, the Chancery Court of Delaware allowed a similar remedy in a situation not covered by the Federal legislation. One of the defendants in that case was an employee who had acquired inside information that the corporate plaintiff was about to enter the market and purchase its own shares. On the basis of this confidential information, the employee, who was not an officer and, hence, not liable under Federal law, bought a large block of shares and, after the corporation's purchases had caused the price to rise, resold them at a profit. The court sustained the complaint in a derivative action brought for an accounting, stating that "[p]ublic policy will not permit an employee occupying a position of trust and confidence toward his employer to abuse that relation to his own profit, regardless of whether his employer suffers a loss" (31 Del.Ch., at p. 246, 70 A.2d, at p. 8). And a similar view has been expressed in the Restatement, 2d, Agency (§ 388, comment c):

> "c. *Use of confidential information.* An agent who acquires confidential information in the course of his employment or in violation of his duties has a duty * * * to account for any profits made by the use of such information, although this does not harm the principal. * * * So, if [a corporate officer] has 'inside' information that the corporation is about to purchase or sell securities, or to declare or to pass a dividend, profits made by him in stock transactions undertaken because of his knowledge are held in constructive trust for the principal."

In the present case, the defendants may be able to avoid liability to the corporation under section 16(b) of the Federal law since they had held the MAI shares for more than six months prior to the sales. Nevertheless, the alleged use of the inside information to dispose of their stock at a price considerably higher than its known value constituted the same sort of "abuse of a fiduciary relationship" as is condemned by the Federal law. Sitting as we are in this case as a court of equity, we should not hesitate to permit an action to prevent any unjust enrichment realized by the defendants from their allegedly wrongful act.

The defendants recognize that the conduct charged against them directly contravened the policy embodied in the Securities Exchange Act but, they maintain, the Federal legislation constitutes a comprehensive and carefully wrought plan for dealing with the abuse of inside information and that allowing a derivative action to be maintained under State law would interfere with the Federal scheme. Moreover, they urge, the existence of dual Federal and State remedies for the same act would create the possibility of double liability.

An examination of the Federal regulatory scheme refutes the contention that it was designed to establish any particular remedy as exclusive. In addition to the specific provisions of section 16(b), the Securities and Exchange Act contains a general anti-fraud provision in section 10(b) which, as implemented by rule 10b–5 [17 C.F.R. § 240.10b–5] under that section, renders it unlawful to engage in a variety of acts considered to be fraudulent. In interpreting this rule, the Securities and Exchange Commission and the Federal courts have extended the common-law definition of fraud to include not only affirmative misrepresentations, relied upon by the purchaser or seller, but also a failure to disclose material information which might have affected the transaction. (See, e.g., Securities & Exch. Comm. v. Texas Gulf Sulpher Co., 2 Cir., 401 F.2d 833, 847–848; Myzel v. Fields, 8 Cir., 386 F.2d 718, 733–735.)

Accepting the truth of the complaint's allegations, there is no question but that the defendants were guilty of withholding material information from the purchasers of the shares and, indeed, the defendants acknowledge that the facts asserted constitute a violation of rule 10b–5. The remedies which the Federal law provides for such violation, however, are rather limited. An action could be brought, in an exceptional case, by the SEC for injunctive relief. This, in fact, is what happened in the *Texas Gulf Sulphur* case (401 F.2d 833, supra). The purpose of such an action, however, would appear to be more to establish a principle than to provide a regular method of enforcement. A class action under the Federal rule might be a more effective remedy but the mechanics of such an action have, as far as we have been able to ascertain, not yet been worked out by the Federal courts and several questions relating thereto have never been resolved. These include the definition of the class entitled to bring such an action, the measure of damages, the administration of the fund which would be recovered and its distribution to the members of the class. Of course, any individual purchaser, who could prove an injury as a result of a rule 10b–5 violation can bring his own action for rescission but we have not been referred to a single case in which such an action has been successfully prosecuted where the public sale of securities is involved. The reason for this is that sales of securities, whether through a stock exchange or over-the-counter, are characteristically anonymous transactions, usually handled through brokers, and the matching of the ultimate buyer with the ultimate seller presents virtually insurmountable obstacles. Thus, unless a section 16(b) violation is also present, the Federal law does not yet provide a really effective remedy.

In view of the practical difficulties inherent in an action under the Federal law, the desirability of creating an effective common-law remedy is manifest. "Dishonest directors should not find absolution from retributive justice", Ballantine observed in his work on Corporations ([rev. ed., 1946], p. 216), "by concealing their identity from their victims under the mask of the stock exchange." There is ample room in a situation such as is here presented for a "private Attorney General" to come forward and enforce proper behavior on the part of corporate officials through the medium of the derivative action brought in the name of the corporation. Only by sanctioning such a cause of action will there be any effective method to prevent the type of abuse of corporate office complained of in this case.

There is nothing in the Federal law which indicates that it was intended to limit the power of the States to fashion additional remedies to effectuate similar purposes. Although the impact of Federal securities regulation has on occasion been said to have created a "Federal corporation law," in fact, its effect on the duties and obligations of directors and officers and their relation to the corporation and its shareholders is only occasional and peripheral. The primary source of the law in this area ever remains that of the State which created the corporation. Indeed, Congress expressly provided against any implication that it intended to pre-empt the field by declaring, in section 28(a) of the Securities Exchange Act of 1934 that "[t]he rights and remedies provided by this title shall be in addition to any and all other rights and remedies that may exist at law or in equity".

Nor should we be deterred, in formulating a State remedy, by the defendants' claim of possible double liability. Certainly, as already indicated, if the sales in question were publicly made, the likelihood that a suit will be brought by purchasers of the shares is quite remote. But, even if it were not, the mere possibility of such a suit is not a defense nor does it render the complaint insufficient. It is not unusual for an action to be brought to recover a fund which may be subject to a superior claim by a third party. If that be the situation, a defendant should not be permitted to retain the fund for his own use on the chance that such a party may eventually appear. A defendant's course, if he wishes to protect himself against double liability, is to interplead any and all possible claimants and bind them to the judgment.

In any event, though, no suggestion has been made either in brief or on oral argument that any purchaser has come forward with a claim against the defendants or even that anyone is in a position to advance such a claim.[1] As we have stated, the defendants' assertion that such a party may come forward at some future date is not a basis for permitting them to retain for their own benefit the fruits of their allegedly wrongful acts. For all that appears, the present derivative action is the only effective remedy now available against the abuse by these defendants of their privileged position. ＊ ＊ ＊

The order appealed from should be affirmed, with costs, and the question certified answered in the affirmative.

Notes

(1) Judgment as to the accuracy of the court's comments about the adequacy of the Federal remedy should be reserved until the materials relating to that remedy are considered.

(2) What is the relationship between the corporate right of recovery created by the principal case and the right of the persons purchasing the shares under rule 10b-5 or the "special facts" doctrine? The desirability of permitting a corporate recovery may depend on the ability to determine the identity of the persons who purchased Oreamuno's and Gonzalez's shares. But why should those persons, who by chance happened to purchase from two specific persons, be any better off than other purchasers who by chance purchased from other sellers? Is it not better to have *only* a corporate remedy in these circumstances?

Or perhaps the best solution is to make Oreamuno and Gonzalez liable to *all* persons who purchased MAI shares during the period before the

---

1. [By the Court] In the absence of any such appearance by adverse claimants, we need not now decide whether the corporation's recovery would be affected by any amounts which might have to be refunded by the defendant to the injured purchasers.

information became public. Such a liability, of course, could be staggering, far exceeding any profits made by the two insiders.

Even where shares are traded on an exchange, it is sometimes possible to ascertain who purchased or sold specific securities. The process is, at best, a difficult one, involving a matching of the exchange tape and clearinghouse reports. Where numerous transactions are made between the same broker-dealer in the same security, or where the market is extremely active, it may be impossible to reconstruct fully the market. See Securities and Exchange Commission, Report of Special Study of Securities Markets, H.R.Doc. No. 95, 88th Cong., 1st Sess., pt. 2, 355–356 (1963); A. Bromberg and L. Lowenfels, Securities Fraud and Commodities Fraud, § 7.1, n. 3 (1989). It is somewhat easier to reconstruct transactions in the over-the-counter market. Comment, Civil Liability under Section 10(b) and Rule 10b–5: A Suggestion for Replacing the Doctrine of Privity, 74 Yale L.J. 658, 662, n. 27 (1965).

(3) Under the doctrine of the principal case, when can Oreamuno and Gonzalez safely sell their stock? Do they have to "ride it all the way down"? When does a person know that point has been reached?

(4) In Schein v. Chasen, 478 F.2d 817 (2d Cir.1973), a diversity case arising under Florida law, the Second Circuit extended the *Diamond* principle to permit a corporation to recover profits made by persons who had inside information (supplied by the president of the corporation) but who were not themselves officers or directors of the corporation. The Court recognized that there was no applicable Florida precedent as to whether *Diamond* would be recognized, much less extended. It held, however, that there was a "common enterprise" and that the logic of the *Diamond* holding compelled its extension. Judge Kaufman dissented. The United States Supreme Court vacated the judgment and ordered the Court to reconsider Judge Kaufman's suggestion that the Court obtain a definitive statement as to Florida law by utilizing the Florida certified question statute. Lehman Bros. v. Schein, 416 U.S. 386, 94 S.Ct. 1741, 40 L.Ed.2d 215 (1974). The Florida Supreme Court stated firmly that it wanted nothing to do with this new-fangled securities jurisprudence:

> * * * [N]ot only will we not give the unprecedented expansive reading to *Diamond* sought by appellants but furthermore, we do not choose to adopt the innovative ruling of the New York Court of Appeals in *Diamond*. We adhere to previous precedent established by the courts in this state that actual damage to the corporation must be alleged in the complaint to substantiate a stockholders' derivative action.

Schein v. Chasen, 313 So.2d 739, 746 (Fla.1975). See also Freeman v. Decio, 584 F.2d 186, 196 (7th Cir.1978), where the Court concluded that the Supreme Court of Indiana "would most likely join the Florida Supreme Court in refusing to adopt the New York court's innovative ruling."

(5) In In re ORFA Securities Litigation, 654 F.Supp. 1449 (D.N.J.1987) and National Westminster Banccorp NJ v. Leone, 702 F.Supp. 1132 (D.N.J. 1988), two district judges concluded that New Jersey would probably recognize *Diamond*-type liability for insider trading on corporate informa-

tion. See Ash, State Regulation of Insider Trading—A Timely Resurgence? 49 Ohio St.L.J. 393 (1988).

(6) People v. Florentino, 116 Misc.2d 692, 456 N.Y.S.2d 638 (N.Y.City Crim.Ct.1982) involved the criminal prosecution of an attorney representing aggressors in takeovers who made trading profits by purchasing shares of target companies before the offer and selling them after the takeover was announced. The court held this conduct violated a New York statute prohibiting "any fraud, deception, concealment [or] suppression * * * where engaged in to induce or promote the * * * purchase * * * of any securities" and was punishable as a misdemeanor.

B. RULE 10b–5: THE BASIC FEDERAL ANTIFRAUD PROHIBITION

SECURITIES EXCHANGE ACT OF 1934
15 U.S.C.A. § 78; (1981).

Section 10. It shall be unlawful for any person, directly or indirectly, by the use of any means or instrumentality, of interstate commerce or of the mails, or of any facility of any national securities exchange—* * *

(b) To use or employ, in connection with the purchase or sale of any security registered on a national securities exchange or any security not so registered, any manipulative or deceptive device or contrivance in contravention of such rules and regulations as the Commission may prescribe as necessary or appropriate in the public interest or for the protection of investors.

RULE 10b–5: EMPLOYMENT OF MANIPULATIVE AND DECEPTIVE DEVICES
17 C.F.R. § 240.10b–5 (1989).

It shall be unlawful for any person, directly or indirectly, by the use of any means or instrumentality of interstate commerce, or of the mails or of any facility of any national securities exchange,

(a) to employ any device, scheme, or artifice to defraud,

(b) to make any untrue statement of a material fact or to omit to state a material fact necessary in order to make the statements made, in the light of the circumstances under which they were made, not misleading, or

(c) to engage in any act, practice, or course of business which operates or would operate as a fraud or deceit upon any person,

in connection with the purchase or sale of any security.

Notes

(1) Comments of Milton V. Freeman, Conference on Codification of the Federal Securities Laws, 22 Bus.Law. 793, 922 (April, 1967): *

* * * I think it would be appropriate for me now to make a brief statement of what actually happened when 10b–5 was adopted, where it would be written down and be available to everybody, not just the people who are willing to listen to me.

It was one day in the year 1943, I believe. I was sitting in my office in the S.E.C. building in Philadelphia and I received a call from Jim Treanor who was then the Director of the Trading and Exchange Division. He said, "I have just been on the telephone with Paul Rowen," who was then the S.E.C. Regional Administrator in Boston, "and he has told me about the president of some company in Boston who is going around buying up the stock of his company from his own shareholders at $4.00 a share, and he has been telling them that the company is doing very badly, whereas, in fact, the earnings are going to be quadrupled and will be $2.00 a share for this coming year. Is there anything we can do about it?" So he came upstairs and I called in my secretary and I looked at Section 10(b) and I looked at Section 17, and I put them together, and the only discussion we had there was where "in connection with the purchase or sale" should be, and we decided it should be at the end.

We called the Commission and we got on the calendar, and I don't remember whether we got there that morning or after lunch. We passed a piece of paper around to all the commissioners. All the commissioners read the rule and they tossed it on the table, indicating approval. Nobody said anything except Sumner Pike who said, "Well," he said, "we are against fraud, aren't we?" That is how it happened.

Louis [2] is absolutely right that I never thought that twenty-odd years later it would be the biggest thing that had ever happened. It was intended to give the Commission power to deal with this problem. It had no relation in the Commission's contemplation to private proceedings. * * *

(2) Despite this modest beginning, rule 10b–5 has had a spectacular and checkered history which neatly falls into two periods:

(a) Until approximately 1975 its scope grew steadily as it was applied to new types of transactions and potentially limiting doctrines were considered and usually rejected. During this period it seemed quite possible that rule 10b–5 would ultimately eclipse all more narrowly drawn federal antifraud statutory provisions, as well as the state-created law of fiduciary duties. The following paragraphs of this note describe the factors that led to this spectacular growth and created the potential that rule 10b–5 seemed

2. [By the Editor] The reference is to Professor Louis Loss of the Harvard Law School, author of the major treatise on Securities Regulations, and Chief Reporter for the proposed Federal Securities Code.

to possess for occupying the universe of regulation of securities transactions.

(b) Beginning in about 1975 rule 10b–5 was sharply narrowed and limited by three decisions by the United States Supreme Court. These decisions are considered immediately below. Despite the limiting doctrines established by these decisions, rule 10b–5 continues to be widely relied on, widely cited, and widely applied. Many precedents from the pre–1975 era continue to have at least some vitality; the effect of the Supreme Court decisions have not shifted attention away from rule 10b–5; rather they have confined it to a narrower area and opened new arguments about the boundaries of those areas.

(3) One other preliminary point should be made. Rule 10b–5 is widely viewed as being primarily directed against the problem of insider trading. Certainly this is a central problem addressed by rule 10b–5 but it is not the only one.

(4) In a broad sense, the early history of rule 10b–5 is a tribute to the ingenuity of federal judges and the flexibility of the American case law system. During this entire tumultuous period, the deceptively simple language of rule 10b–5 has remained the same. The first step—and in retrospect most certainly a significant one—was the holding by Judge Kirkpatrick in 1947 that rule 10b–5 could be the basis of a private suit to rescind a securities transaction. Kardon v. National Gypsum Co., 73 F.Supp. 798 (E.D.Pa.1947). The facts of this case, as set forth by Judge Kirkpatrick, were as follows:

> The plaintiffs, Morris and Eugene B. Kardon (father and son), and the defendants, Leon A. Slavin and William Slavin (brothers), owned all the capital stock of Western Board and Paper Co. and Michigan Paper Stock Co., its affiliate, each of the four holding one fourth. Western was engaged in manufacturing paper board and other paper products, having its plant located at Kalamazoo, and Michigan was a purchasing agent dealing chiefly in waste paper and similar materials for Western. All four were officers and together constituted the entire board of directors, the two Slavins and Eugene Kardon living in Kalamazoo and being actively engaged in operating the plant and Morris Kardon living in Philadelphia. All four were familiar with the plant, assets and business of the corporation.

> Prior to March 18, 1946, Leon Slavin had agreed for the corporation, by written instrument, considered by the parties to it to be binding, to sell to National Gypsum, the plant and equipment of Western for the sum of $1,500,000. * * * The agreement was signed by Leon Slavin in his capacity as Executive Vice President of Western.

> On March 18, 1946, the Slavins purchased all the stock of the Kardons in the two corporations, Western and Michigan, for $504,000. At that time the Kardons knew nothing whatever about the negotiations with National Gypsum, and the Slavins did not disclose any of the facts relating to them although admittedly, at the meeting at which the sale of the stock was consummated, Leon Slavin, in answer

to a preliminary question by the Kardons' attorney, whether he had made any agreement for the sale of the stock, answered No.[3]

Having acquired the plaintiffs' stock, the Slavins proceeded to consummate the transaction with National Gypsum. * * *

73 F.Supp. at 800. On the critical question whether rule 10b–5 might be used as the basis for a private cause of action in federal court, the judge simply stated that while the statute and rule "does not even provide in express terms for a remedy, * * * the existence of a remedy is implicit under general principles of the law." Id. at 802. Is this not a simple, garden variety fraud case of little national or federal interest? Why should such litigation be in the federal courts in the absence of diversity? Rather surprisingly, the limiting doctrines for rule 10b–5 later developed by the Supreme Court do not affect at all the availability of that rule for plaintiffs in *Kardon* type cases, and such cases may continue to be freely brought in federal courts under the federal cause of action provided by rule 10b–5. See e.g. Glick v. Campagna, 613 F.2d 31 (3d Cir.1980). Indeed, one possible doctrine that might deflect many of these garden variety of fraud cases back to state court—the so-called sale of business doctrine—was expressly rejected by the United States Supreme Court. See Landreth Timber Co. v. Landreth, 471 U.S. 681, 105 S.Ct. 2297, 85 L.Ed.2d 692 (1985), described at p. 362, supra.

(5) A variety of factors contributed to the original growth of rule 10b–5. The language of the rule was broad, flexible, and not hedged with qualifications or limiting doctrine. Further, much of the litigation under rule 10b–5 arose on motions to dismiss in which the allegations in the complaint were accepted as true for purposes of the motion. Judicial unwillingness to dispose of plausible allegations summarily on the pleadings, led to the development of precedents generally favorable to plaintiffs and such precedents in turn began to feed on themselves: liberal decisions under rule 10b–5 served as precedents for even broader developments. In many instances, complaints under rule 10b–5 described conduct that also arguably constituted breach of a state-created fiduciary duty. However, since there was usually little or no favorable case law in the state courts, plaintiffs naturally preferred the federal forum with its rule 10b–5 precedents and state law either atrophied or never had a chance to develop.

(6) The decisions of the United States Supreme Court relating to rule 10b–5 before 1975, while not numerous, undoubtedly contributed to this trend. The first case reaching the Supreme Court, Securities and Exchange Comm'n v. National Securities, Inc., 393 U.S. 453, 89 S.Ct. 564, 21 L.Ed.2d 668 (1969), well illustrates the initial attitude of the Court to this rule. The basic claim by the SEC in this case was that two insurance companies had been merged by the use of a proxy statement that contained false and misleading statements; section 14 did not apply because the case

---

3. [By the Court] At this point there is the only substantial dispute of fact in the case. I accept the plaintiffs' version to the effect that the question expressly mentioned the assets as well as the stock. However, it makes very little difference because even if the version given by the defendants is accepted it is perfectly clear that, in the light of the circumstances under which Leon Slavin's answer was made, he omitted to state a material fact necessary to make his answer not misleading, Rule X–10B–5(2).

arose before the 1964 amendments to section 12 of the Securities Exchange
Act of 1934. The Court, through Justice Marshall, stated:

> Although § 10(b) and rule 10b–5 may well be the most litigated
> provisions in the federal securities laws, this is the first time this Court
> has found it necessary to interpret them. We enter this virgin territo-
> ry cautiously. The questions presented are narrow ones. They arise
> in an area where glib generalizations and unthinking abstractions are
> major occupational hazards. Accordingly, in deciding this particular
> case, remembering what is not involved is as important as determining
> what is. With this in mind, we turn to respondents' particular conten-
> tions. * * *

> According to the amended complaint, Producers' shareholders
> were misled in various material respects prior to their approval of a
> merger. The deception furthered a scheme which resulted in their
> losing their status as shareholders in Producers and becoming share-
> holders in a new company. Moreover, by voting in favor of the merger,
> each approving shareholder individually lost any right under Arizona
> law to obtain an appraisal of his stock and payment for it in cash.
> Ariz.Rev.Stat.Ann. § 10–347 (1956). Whatever the terms "purchase"
> and "sale" may mean in other contexts, here an alleged deception has
> affected individual shareholders' decisions in a way not at all unlike
> that involved in a typical cash sale or share exchange. The broad
> antifraud purposes of the statute and the rule would clearly be fur-
> thered by their application to this type of situation. Therefore we
> conclude that Producers' shareholders "purchased" shares in the new
> company by exchanging them for their old stock. * * *

> Respondents' alternative argument that rule 10b–5 does not cover
> misrepresentations which occur in connection with proxy solicitations
> can be dismissed rather quickly. Section 14 of the 1934 Act, and the
> rules adopted pursuant to that section, set up a complex regulatory
> scheme covering proxy solicitations. * * * The two sections of the
> Act apply to different sets of situations. Section 10(b) applies to all
> proscribed conduct in connection with a purchase or sale of any
> security; § 14 applies to all proxy solicitations, whether or not in
> connection with a purchase or sale. The fact that there may well be
> some overlap is neither unusual nor unfortunate. * * *

393 U.S. at 463–468, 89 S.Ct. at 571–573. This rather free-wheeling
approach toward rule 10b–5 moved Mr. Justice Harlan, with whom Mr.
Justice Stewart joined, to dissent:

> * * * I am at a loss to understand why the Court finds it
> necessary to * * * construe Rule 10b–5 promulgated under § 10(b)
> of the Securities Exchange Act of 1934. The Court of Appeals did not
> reach this question * * *. The Government's petition for certiorari
> is similarly limited. * * * When the respondents' brief on the
> merits argued that Rule 10b–5 did not apply to the present case, the
> Solicitor General did not even attempt to present the Government's
> position on that score because he quite properly believed that "the
> question is not appropriately before this Court for decision."

Despite the fact that we have not heard the views of the Securities and Exchange Commission, the Court chooses this case as a vehicle to construe for the first time one of the most important and elusive provisions of the securities laws. Moreover, the decision has far-reaching radiations, despite the fact that the precise issue presented is a narrow one. Courts and commentators have long debated whether Rule 10b–5 should be read as a sweeping prohibition against fraud in the securities industry when this results in rendering nullities of the other antifraud provisions of more limited scope which can be found in the statute books. * * * Even those who take an extremely broad view of the scope of the Rule have recognized that it could well be argued that the courts should not rush in to apply § 10(b) to regulate proxy solicitations where Congress has refused to permit the Commission to intervene under § 14. * * * Nevertheless, the majority believes it can answer this question "rather quickly," without any real recognition of the basic principles which hang in the balance. * * *

I am unwilling to decide these fundamental matters without full-dress argument. Indeed, if the courts of appeals are not to be permitted to develop the law in this area on a case-by-case basis, I think it much wiser for us to consider the basic issues in a case which squarely raises them rather than in one which is of marginal importance.

393 U.S. at 468–70, 89 S.Ct. at 573–4. Two other Supreme Court decisions that reflect expansive readings of rule 10b–5 are Superintendent of Insurance of New York v. Bankers Life and Casualty Co., 404 U.S. 6, 92 S.Ct. 165, 30 L.Ed.2d 128 (1971) and Affiliated Ute Citizens of Utah v. United States, 406 U.S. 128, 92 S.Ct. 1456, 31 L.Ed.2d 741 (1972). In these opinions, the Supreme Court gave every indication of following the development of rule 10b–5 by the lower federal courts, particularly the Second Circuit, and no indication that a dramatic turn was about to occur. In many respects, *Superintendent of Insurance* decided in 1971, reflects the high point in the growth of rule 10b–5.

(7) In addition to this fertile soil (from the plaintiff's standpoint), procedural advantages also encouraged the use of rule 10b–5. Plaintiffs in securities cases favor the federal forum; suits under rule 10b–5 are the exclusive province of federal courts, while suits for breach of state-created duties must be brought in the state court (unless, of course, there is diversity of citizenship and the jurisdictional amount is exceeded). The federal forum was viewed as superior for several reasons: nationwide service of process under section 27 of the Securities Exchange Act of 1934, liberal venue provisions, and generous discovery rules. The doctrine of pendent jurisdiction permits a federal court to hear both the rule 10b–5 claim and the state claim in a single proceeding, while a state court cannot hear the rule 10b–5 claim. Further, the state security-for-expenses statutes for derivative suits are inapplicable to rule 10b–5 suits, and hence a plaintiff may avoid posting an expensive bond simply by framing his complaint under that rule. Finally, there may have been a belief that federal judges were more sympathetic to plaintiffs than state judges.

(8) Is there likely to be a problem meeting the jurisdictional requirements of rule 10b–5 and section 10(b)? What about the use of an *intra-*

state telephone? What about using a private mail system such as Federal Express or Airborne? What about computer networks or telefax? Section 3(a)(17) of the Securities Exchange Act of 1934, as amended in 1975, states that the term "interstate commerce" includes "intrastate use of (A) any facility of a national securities exchange or of a telephone or other interstate means of communication or (B) any other interstate instrumentality." 15 U.S.C.A. § 78c 3(A)(17). Does that solve all possible problems? What about hand-carrying cash or checks across a city? In an office elevator? What about a bank transmitting a check for collection?

BLUE CHIP STAMPS v. MANOR DRUG STORES
Supreme Court of the United States, 1975.
421 U.S. 723, 95 S.Ct. 1917, 44 L.Ed.2d 539.

MR. JUSTICE REHNQUIST delivered the opinion of the Court.

This case requires us to consider whether the offerees of a stock offering, made pursuant to an antitrust consent decree and registered under the Securities Act of 1933, (1933 Act), may maintain a private cause of action for money damages where they allege that the offeror has violated the provisions of Rule 10b–5 of the Securities and Exchange Commission, but where they have neither purchased nor sold any of the offered shares. See Birnbaum v. Newport Steel Corp., 193 F.2d 461 (CA2), cert. denied, 343 U.S. 956, 72 S.Ct. 1051, 96 L.Ed. 1356 (1952).

I

In 1963 the United States filed a civil antitrust action against Blue Chip Stamp Company ('Old Blue Chip'), a company in the business of providing trading stamps to retailers, and nine retailers who owned 90% of its shares. In 1967 the action was terminated by the entry of a consent decree. The decree contemplated a plan of reorganization whereby Old Blue Chip was to be merged into a newly formed corporation, Blue Chip Stamps 'New Blue Chip'. The holdings of the majority shareholders of Old Blue Chip were to be reduced, and New Blue Chip, one of the petitioners here, was required under the plan to offer a substantial number of its shares of common stock to retailers who had used the stamp service in the past but who were not shareholders in the old company. Under the terms of the plan, the offering to non-shareholder users was to be proportional to past stamp usage and the shares were to be offered in units consisting of common stock and debentures.

The reorganization plan was carried out, the offering was registered with the SEC as required by the 1933 Act, and a prospectus was distributed to all offerees as required by § 5 of that Act. Somewhat more than 50% of the offered units were actually purchased. In 1970, two years after the offering, respondent, a former user of the stamp service and therefore an offeree of the 1968 offering, filed this suit in the United States District Court for the Central District of California. Defendants below and petitioners here are Old and New Blue Chip, eight of the nine majority shareholders of Old Blue Chip, and the directors of New Blue Chip (collectively called 'Blue Chip').

Respondent's complaint alleged, *inter alia,* that the prospectus prepared and distributed by Blue Chip in connection with the offering was materially misleading in its overly pessimistic appraisal of Blue Chip's status and future prospects. It alleged that Blue Chip intentionally made the prospectus overly pessimistic in order to discourage respondent and other members of the allegedly large class whom it represents from accepting what was intended to be a bargain offer, so that the rejected shares might later be offered to the public at a higher price. The complaint alleged that class members because of and in reliance on the false and misleading prospectus failed to purchase the offered units. Respondent therefore sought on behalf of the alleged class some $21,400,000 in damages representing the lost opportunity to purchase the units; the right to purchase the previously rejected units at the 1968 price, and in addition, it sought some $25,000,000 in exemplary damages.

The only portion of the litigation thus initiated which is before us is whether respondent may base its action on Rule 10b–5 of the Securities and Exchange Commission without having either bought or sold the securities described in the allegedly misleading prospectus. * * *

II

During the early days of the New Deal, Congress enacted two landmark statutes regulating securities. The 1933 Act was described as an Act "to provide full and fair disclosure of the character of securities sold in interstate and foreign commerce and through the mails, and to prevent frauds in the sale thereof, and for other purposes." The Securities Exchange Act of 1934, was described as an Act "to provide for the regulation of securities exchanges and of over-the-counter markets operating in interstate and foreign commerce and through the mails, to prevent inequitable and unfair practices on such exchanges and markets, and for other purposes."

The various sections of the 1933 Act dealt at some length with the required contents of registration statements and prospectuses, and expressly provided for private civil causes of action. Section 11(a) gave a right of action by reason of a false registration statement to "any person acquiring" the security, and § 12 of that Act gave a right to sue the seller of a security who had engaged in proscribed practices with respect to prospectuses and communication to "the person purchasing such security from him."

The 1934 Act was divided into two titles. Title I was denominated "Regulation of Securities Exchanges," and Title II was denominated "Amendments to Securities Act of 1933." Section 10 of that Act makes it "unlawful for any person * * * (b) [t]o use or employ, in connection with the purchase or sale of any security registered on a national securities exchange or any security not so registered, any manipulative or deceptive device or contrivance in contravention of such rules and regulations as the Commission may prescribe as necessary or appropriate in the public interest or for the protection of investors." The "Commission" referred to [in] the section was the Securities and Exchange Commission created by § 4(a) of the 1934 Act. Section 29 of that Act provided that "[e]very contract made in violation of any provision of this chapter or of any rule or regulation thereunder" should be void.

In 1942, acting under the authority granted to it by § 10(b) of the 1934 Act, the Commission promulgated Rule 10b–5 * * * .

Section 10(b) of the 1934 Act does not by its terms provide an express civil remedy for its violation. Nor does the history of this provision provide any indication that Congress considered the problem of private suits under it at the time of its passage. Similarly there is no indication that the Commission in adopting Rule 10b–5 considered the question of private civil remedies under this provision.

Despite the contrast between the provisions of Rule 10b–5 and the numerous carefully drawn express civil remedies provided in the Acts of both 1933 and 1934, it was held in 1946 by the United States District Court for the Eastern District of Pennsylvania that there was an implied private right of action under the Rule. Kardon v. National Gypsum Co., 69 F.Supp. 512 (1946). This Court had no occasion to deal with the subject until 25 years later, and at that time we confirmed with virtually no discussion the overwhelming consensus of the district courts and courts of appeals that such a cause of action did exist. Superintendent of Insurance v. Bankers Life and Cas. Co., 404 U.S. 6, 13 n. 9, 92 S.Ct. 165, 169, 30 L.Ed.2d 128 (1971); Affiliated Ute Citizens v. United States, 406 U.S. 128, 150–154, 92 S.Ct. 1456, 1470–1472, 31 L.Ed.2d 741 (1972). Such a conclusion was, of course, entirely consistent with the Court's recognition in J.I. Case Co. v. Borak, 377 U.S. 426, 432, 84 S.Ct. 1555, 1561, 12 L.Ed.2d 423 (1964), that private enforcement of Commission rules may "[provide] a necessary supplement to Commission action."

Within a few years after the seminal *Kardon* decision the Court of Appeals for the Second Circuit concluded that the plaintiff class for purposes of a private damage action under § 10(b) and Rule 10b–5 was limited to actual purchasers and sellers of securities. Birnbaum v. Newport Steel Corp., *supra*.

The Court of Appeals in this case did not repudiate *Birnbaum;* indeed, another panel of that court (in an opinion by Judge Ely) had but a short time earlier affirmed the rule of that case. Mount Clemens Industries v. Bell, 464 F.2d 339 (CA9 1972). But in this case a majority of the Court of Appeals found that the facts warranted an exception to the *Birnbaum* rule. For the reasons hereinafter stated, we are of the opinion that *Birnbaum* was rightly decided, and that it bars respondent from maintaining this suit under Rule 10b–5.

III

The panel which decided *Birnbaum* consisted of Chief Judge Swan and Judges Learned Hand and Augustus Hand: the opinion was written by the latter. Since both § 10(b) and Rule 10b–5 proscribed only fraud "in connection with the purchase or sale" of securities, and since the history of § 10(b) revealed no congressional intention to extend a private civil remedy for money damages to other than defrauded purchasers or sellers of securities, in contrast to the express civil remedy provided by § 16(b) of the 1934 Act, the court concluded that the plaintiff class in a Rule 10b–5 action was limited to actual purchasers and sellers.

Just as this Court had no occasion to consider the validity of the *Kardon* holding that there was a private cause of action under Rule 10b–5 until 20–odd years later, nearly the same period of time has gone by between the *Birnbaum* decision and our consideration of the case now before us. As with *Kardon,* virtually all lower federal courts facing the issue in the hundreds of reported cases presenting this question over the past quarter century have reaffirmed *Birnbaum's* conclusion that the plaintiff class for purposes of § 10(b) and Rule 10b–5 private damage action is limited to purchasers and sellers of securities. See 6 L. Loss, Securities Regulation 3617 (1969). * * *

The longstanding acceptance by the courts, coupled with Congress' failure to reject *Birnbaum's* reasonable interpretation of the wording of § 10(b), wording which is directed towards injury suffered "in connection with the purchase or sale" of securities,[4] argues significantly in favor of acceptance of the *Birnbaum* rule by this Court. Blau v. Lehman, 368 U.S. 403, 413, 82 S.Ct. 451, 456, 7 L.Ed.2d 403 (1962).

Available evidence from the texts of the 1933 and 1934 Acts as to the congressional scheme in this regard, though not conclusive, supports the result reached by the *Birnbaum* court. * * *

The principal express nonderivative private civil remedies, created by Congress contemporaneously with the passage of § 10(b), for violations of various provisions of the 1933 and 1934 Acts are by their terms expressly limited to purchasers or sellers of securities. * * * It would indeed be anomalous to impute to Congress an intention to

---

4. [By the Court] Mr. Justice Blackmun, dissenting, finds support in the literal language of § 10(b) since he concludes that in his view "the word 'sale' ordinarily and naturally may be understood to mean, not only a single, individualized act transferring property from one party to another, but also the generalized event of public disposal of property through advertisement, auction, or some other market mechanism." But this ignores the fact that this carefully drawn statute itself defines the term "sale" for purposes of the Act and Congress expressly deleted from the Act's definition events such as offers and advertisements which may ultimately lead to a completed sale. Moreover, the extension of the word "sale" to include offers, is quite incompatible with Congress' separate definition and use of these terms in the 1933 and 1934 Acts. Beyond this, the wording of § 10(b), making fraud *in connection with the purchase or sale of a security* a violation of the Act, is surely badly strained when construed to provide a cause of action not to purchasers and sellers of securities, but to the world at large.

expand the plaintiff class for a judicially implied cause of action beyond the bounds it delineated for comparable express causes of action.[5]

Having said all this, we would by no means be understood as suggesting that we are able to divine from the language of § 10(b) the express "intent of Congress" as to the contours of a private cause of action under Rule 10b–5. When we deal with private actions under Rule 10b–5, we deal with a judicial oak which has grown from little more than a legislative acorn. Such growth may be quite consistent with the congressional enactment and with the role of the federal judiciary in interpreting it, see J.I. Case v. Borak, supra, but it would be disingenuous to suggest that either Congress in 1934 or the Securities and Exchange Commission in 1942 foreordained the present state of the law with respect to Rule 10b–5. It is therefore proper that we consider, in addition to the factors already discussed, what may be described as policy considerations when we come to flesh out the portions of the law with respect to which neither the congressional enactment nor the administrative regulations offer conclusive guidance.

Three principal classes of potential plaintiffs are presently barred by the *Birnbaum* rule. First are potential purchasers of shares, either in a new offering or on the Nation's post-distribution trading markets, who allege that they decided not to purchase because of an unduly gloomy representation or the omission of favorable material which made the issuer appear to be a less favorable investment vehicle than it actually was. Second are actual shareholders in the issuer who allege that they decided not to sell their shares because of an unduly rosy representation or a failure to disclose unfavorable material. Third are shareholders, creditors, and perhaps others related to an issuer who suffered loss in the value of their investment due to corporate or insider activities in connection with the purchase or sale of securities which violate Rule 10b–5. It has been held that shareholder members of the second and third of these classes may frequently be able to circumvent the *Birnbaum* limitation through bringing a derivative action on behalf of the corporate issuer if the latter is itself a purchaser or seller of securities. But the first of these classes, of which respondent is a member, can not claim the benefit of such a rule.

5. [By the Court] Mr. Justice Blackmun, dissenting, finds the *Birnbaum* rule incompatible with the purpose and history of § 10(b) and Rule 10b–5. But it is worthy of more than passing note that the history of Rule 10b–5 itself * * * strongly supports the purchaser-seller limitation. As the dissent notes, Rule 10b–5 was adopted in order to close "a loophole in the protections against fraud * * * by prohibiting individuals or companies from buying securities if they engage in fraud in their purchase." See SEC Release No. 3230 (May 21, 1942); remarks of Milton Freeman, Conference on Codification of the Federal Securities Laws, 22 Bus.Law. 793, 922 (1967). The modest aims and origins of the Rule as recounted by the dissent stand in stark contrast with its far ranging conclusion that a remedy exists under Rule 10b–5 whenever there is "a logical nexus between the alleged fraud and the purchase or sale of a security." On these facts, as we have indicated, extension of a Rule 10b–5 cause of action, far from closing an unforeseen loophole, would extend a private right of action for misrepresentations in a 1933 Act prospectus to those whom Congress excluded from the express civil remedies provided in the 1933 Act to cover such a violation.

A great majority of the many commentators on the issue before us have taken the view that the *Birnbaum* limitation on the plaintiff class in a Rule 10b–5 action for damages is an arbitrary restriction which unreasonably prevents some deserving plaintiffs from recovering damages which have in fact been caused by violations of Rule 10b–5. See, e.g., Lowenfels, The Demise of the *Birnbaum* Doctrine: A New Era for Rule 10b–5, 54 Va.L.Rev. 268 (1968). The Securities and Exchange Commission has filed an *amicus* brief in this case espousing that same view. We have no doubt that this is indeed a disadvantage of the *Birnbaum* rule,[6] and if it had no countervailing advantages it would be undesirable as a matter of policy, however much it might be supported by precedent and legislative history. But we are of the opinion that there are countervailing advantages to the *Birnbaum* rule, purely as a matter of policy, although those advantages are more difficult to articulate than is the disadvantage.

There has been widespread recognition that litigation under Rule 10b–5 presents a danger of vexatiousness different in degree and in kind from that which accompanies litigation in general. * * *

We believe that the concern expressed for the danger of vexatious litigation which could result from a widely expanded class of plaintiffs under Rule 10b–5 is founded in something more substantial than the common complaint of the many defendants who would prefer avoiding lawsuits entirely to either settling them or trying them. These concerns have two largely separate grounds.

The first of these concerns is that in the field of federal securities laws governing disclosure of information even a complaint which by objective standards may have very little chance of success at trial has a settlement value to the plaintiff out of any proportion to its prospect of success at trial so long as he may prevent the suit from being resolved against him by dismissal or summary judgment. The very pendency of the lawsuit may frustrate or delay normal business activity of the defendant which is totally unrelated to the lawsuit. * * *

The potential for possible abuse of the liberal discovery provisions of the Federal Rules of Civil Procedure may likewise exist in this type of case to a greater extent than they do in other litigation. The prospect of extensive deposition of the defendant's officers and associates and the concomitant opportunity for extensive discovery of business documents, is a common occurrence in this and similar types of litigation. To the extent that this process eventually produces relevant evidence which is useful in determining the merits of the claims asserted by the parties, it bears the imprimatur of the Federal Rules of

---

6. [By the Court] Obviously this disadvantage is attenuated to the extent that remedies are available to nonpurchasers and nonsellers under state law. Thus for example in *Birnbaum* itself, while the plaintiffs found themselves without federal remedies, the conduct alleged as the grava-men of the federal complaint later provided the basis for recovery in a cause of action based on state law. And in the immediate case, respondent has filed a state court class action held in abeyance pending the outcome of this suit.

Civil Procedure and of the many cases liberally interpreting them. But to the extent that it permits a plaintiff with a largely groundless claim to simply take up the time of a number of other people, with the right to do so representing an *in terrorem* increment of the settlement value, rather than a reasonably founded hope that the process will reveal relevant evidence, it is a social cost rather than a benefit. Yet to broadly expand the class of plaintiffs who may sue under Rule 10b–5 would appear to encourage the least appealing aspect of the use of the discovery rules.

Without the *Birnbaum* rule, an action under Rule 10b–5 will turn largely on which oral version of a series of occurrences the jury may decide to credit, and therefore no matter how improbable the allegations of the plaintiff, the case will be virtually impossible to dispose of prior to trial other than by settlement.   *   *   *

The *Birnbaum* rule, on the other hand, permits exclusion prior to trial of those plaintiffs who were not themselves purchasers or sellers of the stock in question. The fact of purchase of stock and the fact of sale of stock are generally matters which are verifiable by documentation, and do not depend upon oral recollection, so that failure to qualify under the *Birnbaum* rule is a matter that can normally be established by the defendant either on a motion to dismiss or on a motion for summary judgment.

Obviously there is no general legal principle that courts in fashioning substantive law should do so in a manner which makes it easier, rather than more difficult, for a defendant to obtain a summary judgment. But in this type of litigation, where the mere existence of an unresolved lawsuit has settlement value to the plaintiff not only because of the possibility that he may prevail on the merits, an entirely legitimate component of settlement value, but because of the threat of extensive discovery and disruption of normal business activities which may accompany a lawsuit which is groundless in any event, but cannot be proved so before trial, such a factor is not to be totally dismissed. The *Birnbaum* rule undoubtedly excludes plaintiffs who have in fact been damaged by violations of Rule 10b–5, and to that extent it is undesirable. But it also separates in a readily demonstrable manner the group of plaintiffs who actually purchased or actually sold, and whose version of the facts is therefore more likely to be believed by the trier of fact, from the vastly larger world of potential plaintiffs who might successfully allege a claim but could seldom succeed in proving it. And this fact is one of its advantages.

The second ground for fear of vexatious litigation is based on the concern that, given the generalized contours of liability, the abolition of the *Birnbaum* rule would throw open to the trier of fact many rather hazy issues of historical fact the proof of which depended almost entirely on oral testimony. We in no way disparage the worth and frequent high value of oral testimony when we say that dangers of its abuse appear to exist in this type of action to a peculiarly high degree.

The Securities and Exchange Commission, while opposing the adoption of the *Birnbaum* rule by this Court, states that it agrees with petitioners "that the effect, if any, of a deceptive practice on someone who has neither purchased nor sold securities may be more difficult to demonstrate than is the effect on a purchaser or seller." The brief also points out that frivolous suits can be brought whatever the rules of standing, and reminds us of this Court's recognition "in a different context" that "the expense and annoyance of litigation is 'part of the social burden of living under government.'" Petroleum Exploration, Inc. v. Public Service Comm'n, 304 U.S. 209, 222, 58 S.Ct. 834, 841, 82 L.Ed. 1294. The Commission suggests that in particular cases additional requirements of corroboration of testimony and more limited measure of damages would correct the dangers of an expanded class of plaintiffs.

But the very necessity, or at least the desirability, of fashioning unique rules of corroboration and damages as a correlative to the abolition of the *Birnbaum* rule suggests that the rule itself may have something to be said for it. * * *

In today's universe of transactions governed by the 1934 Act, privity of dealing or even personal contact between potential defendant and potential plaintiff is the exception and not the rule. The stock of issuers is listed on financial exchanges utilized by tens of millions of investors and corporate representations reach a potential audience, encompassing not only the diligent few who peruse filed corporate reports or the sizeable number of subscribers to financial journals, but the readership of the Nation's daily newspapers. Obviously neither the fact that issuers or other potential defendants under Rule 10b–5 reach a large number of potential investors, or the fact that they are required by law to make their disclosures conform to certain standards, should in any way absolve them from liability for misconduct which is proscribed by Rule 10b–5.

But in the absence of the *Birnbaum* rule, it would be sufficient for a plaintiff to prove that he had failed to purchase or sell stock by reason of a defendant's violation of Rule 10b–5. The manner in which the defendant's violation caused the plaintiff to fail to act could be as a result of the reading of a prospectus, as respondent claims here, but it could just as easily come as a result of a claimed reading of information contained in the financial pages of a local newspaper. Plaintiff's proof would not be that he purchased or sold stock, a fact which would be capable of documentary verification in most situations, but instead that he decided *not* to purchase or sell stock. Plaintiff's entire testimony could be dependent upon uncorroborated oral evidence of many of the crucial elements of his claim, and still be sufficient to go to the jury. The jury would not even have the benefit of weighing the plaintiff's version against the defendant's version, since the elements to which the plaintiff would testify would be in many cases totally unknown and unknowable to the defendant. The very real risk in permitting those in respondent's position to sue under Rule 10b–5 is that the door will be open to recovery of substantial damages on the part of one who offers only his own testimony to prove that he ever consulted a prospectus of the issuer, that he paid any attention to it, or that the representations contained in it damaged him.[7] The virtue of the *Birnbaum* rule, simply stated, in this situation, is that it limits the class of plaintiffs to those who have at least dealt in the security to which the prospectus, representation, or omission relates. And their dealing in the security, whether by way of purchase or sale, will generally be an objectively demonstrable fact in an area of the law otherwise very much dependent upon oral testimony. In the absence of the *Birnbaum* doctrine, by-standers to the securities marketing process could await developments on the sidelines without risk, claiming that inaccuracies in disclosure caused nonselling in a falling market and that unduly pessimistic predictions by the issuer followed by a rising market caused them to allow retrospectively golden opportunities to pass.

While much of the development of the law of deceit has been the elimination of artificial barriers to recovery on just claims, we are not the first court to express concern that the inexorable broadening of the class of plaintiff who may sue in this area of the law will ultimately result in more harm than good. In Ultramares Corp. v. Touche, 255 N.Y. 170, 174 N.E. 441 (1931), Chief Judge Cardozo observed with respect to "a liability in an indeterminate amount for an indeterminate time to an indeterminate class" that:

> "The hazards of a business conducted on these terms are so extreme as to enkindle doubt whether a flaw may not exist in the implication of a duty that exposes to these consequences." 174 N.E., at 444. * * *

We quite agree that if Congress had legislated the elements of a private cause of action for damages, the duty of the Judicial Branch would be to administer the law which Congress enacted; the Judiciary may not circumscribe a right which Congress has conferred because of any disagreement it might have with Congress about the wisdom of creating so expansive a liability. But as we have pointed out, we are not dealing here with any private right created by the express language

---

7. [By the Court] The SEC, recognizing the necessity for limitations on nonpurchaser, nonseller plaintiffs in the absence of the *Birnbaum* rule, suggests two such limitations to mitigate the practical adverse effects flowing from abolition of the rule. First it suggests requiring some corroborative evidence in addition to oral testimony tending to show that the investment decision of a plaintiff was affected by an omission or misrepresentation. Apparently ownership of stock or receipt of a prospectus or press release would be sufficient corroborative evidence in the view of the SEC to reach the jury. We do not believe that such a requirement would adequately respond to the concerns in part

underlying the *Birnbaum* rule. Ownership of stock or receipt of a prospectus says little about whether a plaintiff's investment decision was affected by a violation of Rule 10b–5 or whether a decision was even made. Second, the SEC would limit the vicarious liability of corporate issuers to nonpurchasers and nonsellers to situations where the corporate issuer has been unjustly enriched by a violation. We have no occasion to pass upon the compatibility of this limitation with § 20(a) of the 1934 Act. We do not believe that this proposed limitation is relevant to the concerns underlying in part the *Birnbaum* rule as we have expressed them. * * *

of § 10(b) or of Rule 10b–5. No language in either of those provisions speaks at all to the contours of a private cause of action for their violation. However flexibly we may construe the language of both provisions, nothing in such construction militates against the *Birnbaum* rule. We are dealing with a private cause of action which has been judicially found to exist, and which will have to be judicially delimited one way or another unless and until Congress addresses the question. Given the peculiar blend of legislative, administrative, and judicial history which now surrounds Rule 10b–5, we believe that practical factors to which we have adverted, and to which other courts have referred, are entitled to a good deal of weight.

Thus we conclude that what may be called considerations of policy, which we are free to weigh in deciding this case, are by no means entirely on one side of the scale. Taken together with the precedential support for the *Birnbaum* rule over a period of more than 20 years, and the consistency of that rule with what we can glean from the intent of Congress, they lead us to conclude that it is a sound rule and should be followed. * * *

[The Court concludes that an exception to the general *Birnbaum* principle should not be created for offerees of securities in the position of the plaintiffs.]

Reversed.

MR. JUSTICE POWELL, with whom MR. JUSTICE STEWART and MR. JUSTICE MARSHALL join, concurring.

Although I join the opinion of the Court, I write to emphasize the significance of the texts of the Acts of 1933 and 1934 and especially the language of § 10(b) and Rule 10b–5.

I

The starting point in every case involving construction of a statute is the language itself. The critical phrase in both the statute and the rule is "in connection with the *purchase* or *sale* of any security." (emphasis added). Section 3(a)(14) of the 1934 Act, provides that the term "sale" shall "include any contract to sell or otherwise dispose of" securities. There is no hint in any provision of the Act that the term "sale," as used in § 10(b), was intended—in addition to its long-established legal meaning—to include an "offer to sell." * * *

This case involves no "purchase or sale" of securities. Respondent was a mere offeree, which instituted this suit some two years after the shares were issued and after the market price had soared. Having "missed the market" on a stock, it is hardly in a unique position. * * *

MR. JUSTICE BLACKMUN'S dissent charges the Court with "a preternatural solicitousness for corporate well-being and a seeming callousness toward the investing public." [8]   Our task in this case is to construe a statute.   In my view, the answer is plainly compelled by the language as well as the legislative history of the 1933 and 1934 Acts.   * * *

MR. JUSTICE BLACKMUN, with whom MR. JUSTICE DOUGLAS and MR. JUSTICE BRENNAN join, dissenting.

Today the Court graves into stone *Birnbaum's* arbitrary principle of standing.   For this task the Court, unfortunately, chooses to utilize three blunt chisels: (1) reliance on the legislative history of the 1933 and 1934 Securities Acts, conceded as inconclusive in this particular context; (2) acceptance as precedent of two decades of lower court decisions following a doctrine, never before examined here, that was pronounced by a justifiably esteemed panel of that Court of Appeals regarded as the "Mother Court" in this area of the law, but under entirely different circumstances; and (3) resort to utter pragmaticality and a conjectural assertion of "policy considerations" deemed to arise in distinguishing the meritorious Rule 10b–5 suit from the meretricious one.   In so doing, the Court exhibits a preternatural solicitousness for corporate well-being and a seeming callousness toward the investing public quite out of keeping, it seems to me, with our own traditions and the intent of the securities laws.

The plaintiff's complaint—and that is all that is before us now—raises disturbing claims of fraud.   * * *

From a reading of the complaint in relation to the language of § 10(b) of the 1934 Act and of Rule 10b–5, it is manifest that plaintiff has alleged the use of a deceptive scheme "in connection with the purchase or sale of any security."   To my mind, the word "sale" ordinarily and naturally may be understood to mean, not only a single individualized act transferring property from one party to another, but also the generalized event of public disposal of property through advertisement, auction, or some other market mechanism.   Here, there is an obvious, indeed a court-ordered, "sale" of securities in the special offering of New Blue Chip shares and debentures to former users.   Yet the Court denies this plaintiff the right to maintain a suit under Rule 10b–5 because it does not fit into the mechanistic categories of either "purchaser" or "seller."   This, surely, is an anomaly, for the very purpose of the alleged scheme was to inhibit this plaintiff from ever acquiring the status of "purchaser."   Faced with this abnormal diver-

---

8. [By the Justice] The dissent also charges that we are callous toward the "investing public"—a term it does not define.   It would have been more accurate, perhaps to have spoken of the noninvesting public, because the Court's decision does not abandon the investing public.   The great majority of registered issues of securities are offered by established corporations that have shares outstanding and held by members of the investing public.   The types of suits that the dissent would

encourage could result in large damage claims, costly litigation, generous settlements to avoid such cost, and often—where the litigation runs its course—in large verdicts.   The shareholders of the defendant corporations—the "investing public"— would ultimately bear the burden of this litigation, including the fraudulent suits that would not be screened out by the dissent's bare requirement of a "logical nexus between the alleged fraud and the sale or purchase of a security."

gence from the usual pattern of securities frauds, the Court pays no heed to the unremedied wrong or to the portmanteau nature of § 10(b).

* * *

Instead of the artificiality of *Birnbaum,* the essential test of a valid Rule 10b–5 claim, it seems to me, must be the showing of a logical nexus between the alleged fraud and the sale or purchase of a security. It is inconceivable that Congress could have intended a broadranging antifraud provision, such as § 10(b), and, at the same time, have intended to impose, or be deemed to welcome, a mechanical overtone and requirement such as the *Birnbaum* doctrine. The facts of this case, if proved and accepted by the factfinder, surely are within the conduct that Congress intended to ban. Whether this particular plaintiff, or any plaintiff, will be able eventually to carry the burdens of proving fraud and of proving reliance and damage—that is, causality and injury—is a matter that should not be left to speculations of "policy" of the kind now advanced in this forum so far removed from witnesses and evidence.

Finally, I am uneasy about the type of precedent the present decision establishes. Policy considerations can be applied and utilized in like fashion in other situations. The acceptance of this decisional route in this case may well come back to haunt us elsewhere before long. I would decide the case to fulfill the broad purpose that the language of the statutes and the legislative history dictate, and I would avoid the Court's pragmatic solution resting upon a 20–odd–year–old, severely criticized doctrine enunciated for a factually distinct situation.

In short, I would abandon the *Birnbaum* doctrine as a rule of decision in favor of a more general test of nexus, just as the Seventh Circuit did in Eason v. General Motors Acceptance Corp., 490 F.2d 654, 661 (1973), cert. denied, 416 U.S. 960, 94 S.Ct. 1979, 40 L.Ed.2d 312 (1974). I would not worry about any imagined inability of our federal trial and appellate courts to control the flowering of the types of cases that the Court fears might result. Nor would I yet be disturbed about dire consequences that a basically pessimistic attitude foresees if the *Birnbaum* doctrine were allowed quietly to expire. Sensible standards of proof and of demonstrable damages would evolve and serve to protect the worthy and shut out the frivolous.

Notes

(1) In Birnbaum v. Newport Steel Corp., 193 F.2d 461 (2d Cir.1952), cert. denied 343 U.S. 956, 72 S.Ct. 1051, 96 L.Ed. 1356 (1952), the case which of course gave rise to the "Birnbaum doctrine" enshrined in the principal case, the court summarized its holding as follows:

> * * * [Section 10(b)] was directed solely at the type of misrepresentation or fraudulent practice usually associated with the sale or purchase of securities rather than at fraudulent mismanagement of corporate affairs, and * * * Rule 10b–5 extended protection only to the defrauded purchaser or seller.

193 F.2d, at 464. Is there not more than one possible test as to the coverage of section 10(b) and rule 10b–5 wrapped up in this language? Does *Blue Chip* validate all of these possible tests?

(2) One issue discussed in *Blue Chip:* whether rule 10b–5 might apply to transactions that fall within express liability provisions of other Federal securities laws, was definitively answered in Herman & MacLean v. Huddleston, 459 U.S. 375, 103 S.Ct. 683, 74 L.Ed.2d 548 (1983). The Court unanimously held that a cause of action may be maintained under rule 10b–5 for fraudulent misrepresentations and omissions in a 1933 Act prospectus even though that conduct might also be actionable under section 11 of the 1933 Act. The Court stated that the two sections covered different conduct and liability of different persons, and that "[i]t would be anomalous indeed if the special protection afforded to purchasers in a registered offering by the 1933 Act were deemed to deprive such purchasers of the protections against manipulation and deception that § 10(b) makes available to all persons who deal in securities." 459 U.S. at 382, 103 S.Ct. at 687. The Court also concluded that liability may be established under rule 10b–5 by "a preponderance of the evidence" rather than by "clear and convincing evidence," the standard of proof required in civil fraud actions at common law.

(3) Consider carefully the way Mr. Justice Rehnquist classified possible plaintiffs that are eliminated by the requirement of *Birnbaum.* Is his classification exclusive, or might there be other types of potential plaintiffs which might not be buyers or sellers?

(4) The Birnbaum principle involves a qualifying test for *plaintiffs* in rule 10b–5 suits. A *defendant* may readily violate rule 10b–5 even though it is not a purchaser or seller of securities, e.g. by influencing the market by a false press release or preparing a prospectus that contains false statements.

ERNST & ERNST v. HOCHFELDER

Supreme Court of the United States, 1976.
425 U.S. 185, 96 S.Ct. 1375, 47 L.Ed.2d 668.

MR. JUSTICE POWELL delivered the opinion of the Court.

The issue in this case is whether an action for civil damages may lie under § 10(b) of the Securities Exchange Act of 1934 (1934 Act), and Securities and Exchange Commission Rule 10b–5, in the absence of an allegation of intent to deceive, manipulate, or defraud on the part of the defendant.

I

Petitioner, Ernst & Ernst, is an accounting firm. From 1946 through 1967 it was retained by First Securities Company of Chicago (First Securities), a small brokerage firm and member of the Midwest Stock Exchange and of the National Association of Securities Dealers, to perform periodic audits of the firm's books and records. In connection with these audits Ernst & Ernst prepared for filing with the Securities and Exchange Commission (Commission) the annual reports required of First Securities under § 17(a) of the 1934 Act.[9]   It also prepared for First Securities responses to the financial questionnaires of the Midwest Stock Exchange (Exchange).

Respondents were customers of First Securities who invested in a fraudulent securities scheme perpetrated by Leston B. Nay, president of the firm and owner of 92% of its stock.   Nay induced the respondents to invest funds in "escrow" accounts that he represented would yield a high rate of return.   Respondents did so from 1942 through 1966, with the majority of the transactions occurring in the 1950's.   In fact, there were no escrow accounts as Nay converted respondents' funds to his own use immediately upon receipt.   These transactions were not in the customary form of dealings between First Securities and its customers. The respondents drew their personal checks payable to Nay or a designated bank for his account.   No such escrow accounts were reflected on the books and records of First Securities, and none was shown on its periodic accounting to respondents in connection with their other investments.   Nor were they included in First Securities' filings with the Commission or the Exchange.

This fraud came to light in 1968 when Nay committed suicide, leaving a note that described First Securities as bankrupt and the escrow accounts as "spurious."   Respondents subsequently filed this action for damages against Ernst & Ernst in the United States District Court for the Northern District of Illinois under § 10(b) of the 1934 Act. The complaint charged that Nay's escrow scheme violated § 10(b) and Commission Rule 10b–5,[10] and that Ernst & Ernst had "aided and abetted" Nay's violations by its "failure" to conduct proper audits of First Securities.   As revealed through discovery, respondents' cause of action rested on a theory of negligent nonfeasance.   The premise was that Ernst & Ernst had failed to utilize "appropriate auditing procedures" in its audits of First Securities, thereby failing to discover

9. [By the Court] Section 17(a) requires that securities brokers or dealers "make * * * and preserve * * * such accounts * * * books, and other records, and make such reports, as the Commission by its rules and regulations may prescribe as necessary or appropriate in the public interest or for the protection of investors." During the period relevant here, Commission Rule 17a–5, 17 CFR § 240.17a–5 (1975), required that First Securities file an annual report of its financial condition that included a certificate stating "clearly the opinion of the accountant with respect to the financial statement covered by the certificate and the accounting principles and practices reflected therein."   The rule required Ernst & Ernst to state in its certificate, *inter alia*, "whether the audit was made in accordance with generally accepted auditing standards applicable in the circumstances" and provided that nothing in the rule should "be construed to imply

authority for the omission of any procedure which independent accountants would ordinarily employ in the course of an audit for the purpose of expressing the opinions required" by the rule.

10. [By the Court] Immediately after Nay's suicide the Commission commenced receivership proceedings against First Securities.   In those proceedings all of the respondents except two asserted claims based on the fraudulent escrow accounts. These claims ultimately were allowed in SEC v. First Securities Co., 463 F.2d 981, 986 (CA7), cert. denied, 409 U.S. 880, 93 S.Ct. 85, 34 L.Ed.2d 134 (1972), where the court held that Nay's conduct violated § 10(b) and Rule 10b–5, and that First Securities was liable for Nay's fraud as an aider and abettor.   The question of Ernst & Ernst's liability was not considered in that case.

internal practices of the firm said to prevent an effective audit. The practice principally relied on was Nay's rule that only he could open mail addressed to him at First Securities or addressed to First Securities to his attention, even if it arrived in his absence. Respondents contended that if Ernst & Ernst had conducted a proper audit, it would have discovered this "mail rule." The existence of the rule then would have been disclosed in reports to the Exchange and to the Commission by Ernst & Ernst as an irregular procedure that prevented an effective audit. This would have led to an investigation of Nay that would have revealed the fraudulent scheme. Respondents specifically disclaimed the existence of fraud or intentional misconduct on the part of Ernst & Ernst.[11] * * *

The Court of Appeals for the Seventh Circuit * * * [held] that one who breaches a duty of inquiry and disclosure owed another is liable in damages for aiding and abetting a third party's violation of Rule 10b–5 if the fraud would have been discovered or prevented but for the breach. 503 F.2d 1100 (1974). The court reasoned that Ernst & Ernst had a common-law and statutory duty of inquiry into the adequacy of First Securities' internal control system because it had contracted to audit First Securities and to prepare for filing with the Commission the annual report of First Securities' financial condition required under § 17 of the 1934 Act and Rule 17a–5. The court further reasoned that respondents were beneficiaries of the statutory duty to inquire[12] and the related duty to disclose any material irregularities that were discovered. The court concluded that there were genuine issues of fact as to whether Ernst & Ernst's failure to discover and comment upon Nay's mail rule constituted a breach of its duties of inquiry and disclosure, and whether inquiry and disclosure would have led to the discovery or prevention of Nay's fraud.

We granted certiorari to resolve the question whether a private cause of action for damages will lie under § 10(b) and Rule 10b–5 in the absence of any allegation of "scienter"—intent to deceive, manipulate, or defraud.[13] 421 U.S. 909, 95 S.Ct. 1557, 43 L.Ed.2d 773 (1975). We conclude that it will not and therefore we reverse.

11. [By the Court] In their response to interrogatories in the District Court respondents conceded that they did "not accuse Ernst & Ernst of deliberate, intentional fraud," merely with "inexcusable negligence."

12. [By the Court] The court concluded that the duty of inquiry imposed on Ernst & Ernst under § 17(a) was "grounded on a concern for the protection of investors such as [respondents]," without reaching the question whether the statute imposed a "direct duty" to the respondents. 503 F.2d, at 1105. The court held that Ernst & Ernst owed no common-law duty of inquiry to respondents arising from its contract with First Securities since Ernst & Ernst did not specifically foresee that respondents' limited class might suffer from a negligent audit, compare Glanzer v. Shepard, 233 N.Y. 236, 135 N.E. 275 (1922), with Ultramares Corp. v. Touche, 255 N.Y. 170, 174 N.E. 441 (1931). Moreover, respondents conceded that they did not rely on the financial statements and reports prepared by Ernst & Ernst or on its certificate of opinion. 503 F.2d, at 1107.

13. [By the Court] Although the verbal formulations of the standard to be applied have varied, several Courts of Appeals have held in substance that negligence alone is sufficient for civil liability under § 10(b) and Rule 10b–5. See, e.g., White v. Abrams, 495 F.2d 724, 730 (CA9 1974)

II

Federal regulation of transactions in securities emerged as part of the aftermath of the market crash in 1929. The Securities Act of 1933 (1933 Act), as amended was designed to provide investors with full disclosure of material information concerning public offerings of securities in commerce, to protect investors against fraud and, through the imposition of specified civil liabilities, to promote ethical standards of honesty and fair dealing. The 1934 Act was intended principally to protect investors against manipulation of stock prices through regulation of transactions upon securities exchanges and in over-the-counter markets, and to impose regular reporting requirements on companies whose stock is listed on national securities exchanges. Although the Acts contain numerous carefully drawn express civil remedies and criminal penalties, Congress recognized that efficient regulation of securities trading could not be accomplished under a rigid statutory program. As part of the 1934 Act Congress created the Commission, which is provided with an arsenal of flexible enforcement powers. * * * [The Court quotes section 10(b) and Rule 10b–5].

Although § 10(b) does not by its terms create an express civil remedy for its violation, and there is no indication that Congress, or the Commission when adopting Rule 10b–5, contemplated such a remedy, the existence of a private cause of action for violations of the statute and the rule is now well established. Blue Chip Stamps v. Manor Drug Stores, 421 U.S. 723, 730, 95 S.Ct. 1917, 1922, 44 L.Ed.2d 539, 546 (1975); Affiliated Ute Citizens v. United States, 406 U.S. 128, 150–154, 92 S.Ct. 1456, 1470–1472, 31 L.Ed.2d 741, 759–761 (1972); Superintendent of Insurance v. Bankers Life and Cas. Co., 404 U.S. 6, 13 n. 9, 92 S.Ct. 165, 169, 30 L.Ed.2d 128, 134 (1971). During the 30–year period since a private cause of action was first implied under § 10(b) and Rule 10b–5, a substantial body of case law and commentary has developed as to its elements. Courts and commentators long have differed with regard to whether scienter is a necessary element of such a cause of

("flexible duty" standard); Myzel v. Fields, 386 F.2d 718, 735 (CA8 1967), cert. denied, 390 U.S. 951, 88 S.Ct. 1043, 19 L.Ed.2d 1143 (1968) (negligence sufficient); Kohler v. Kohler Co., 319 F.2d 634 (CA7 1963) (knowledge not required). Other courts of appeals have held that some type of scienter—i.e., intent to defraud, reckless disregard for the truth, or knowing use of some practice to defraud—is necessary in such an action. See, e.g., Clegg v. Conk, 507 F.2d 1351, 1361–1362 (CA10 1974), cert. denied, 422 U.S. 1007, 95 S.Ct. 2628, 45 L.Ed.2d 669 (1975) (an element of "scienter or conscious fault"); Lanza v. Drexel & Co., 479 F.2d 1277, 1306 (CA2 1973) ("willful or reckless disregard" of the truth). But few of the decisions announcing that some form of negligence suffices for civil liability under § 10(b) and Rule 10b–5 actually have involved only negligent conduct.

In this opinion the term "scienter" refers to a mental state embracing intent to deceive, manipulate, or defraud. In certain areas of the law recklessness is considered to be a form of intentional conduct for purposes of imposing liability for some act. We need not address here the question whether, in some circumstances, reckless behavior is sufficient for civil liability under § 10(b) and Rule 10b–5.

Since this case concerns an action for damages we also need not consider the question whether scienter is a necessary element in an action for injunctive relief under § 10(b) and Rule 10b–5.

action, or whether negligent conduct alone is sufficient. In addressing this question, we turn first to the language of § 10(b), for "[t]he starting point in every case involving construction of a statute is the language itself." Blue Chip Stamps, supra, at 756 (Powell, J., concurring).

A

Section 10(b) makes unlawful the use or employment of "any manipulative or deceptive device or contrivance" in contravention of Commission rules. The words "manipulative or deceptive" used in conjunction with "device or contrivance" strongly suggest that § 10(b) was intended to proscribe knowing or intentional misconduct. See SEC v. Texas Gulf Sulphur Co., 401 F.2d 833, 868 (CA2 1968) (Friendly, J., concurring), cert. denied *sub nom.* Coates v. SEC, 394 U.S. 976 (1969).

In its *amicus curiae* brief, however, the Commission contends that nothing in the language "manipulative or deceptive device or contrivance" limits its operation to knowing or intentional practices. In support of its view, the Commission cites the overall congressional purpose in the 1933 and 1934 Acts to protect investors against false and deceptive practices that might injure them. The Commission then reasons that since the "effect" upon investors of given conduct is the same regardless of whether the conduct is negligent or intentional, Congress must have intended to bar all such practices and not just those done knowingly or intentionally. The logic of this effect-oriented approach would impose liability for wholly faultless conduct where such conduct results in harm to investors, a result the Commission would be unlikely to support. But apart from where its logic might lead, the Commission would add a gloss to the operative language of the statute quite different from its commonly accepted meaning. The argument simply ignores the use of the words "manipulative," "device," and "contrivance"—terms that make unmistakable a congressional intent to proscribe a type of conduct quite different from negligence.[14] Use of the word "manipulative" is especially significant. It is and was virtually a term of art when used in connection with securities markets. It connotes intentional or willful conduct designed to deceive or defraud investors by controlling or artificially affecting the price of securities.[15]

* * * In view of the language of § 10(b), which so clearly connotes intentional misconduct, and mindful that the language of a

14. [By the Court] Webster's International Dictionary (2d ed. 1934) defines "device" as "[t]hat which is devised, or formed by design; a contrivance; an invention; project; scheme; often, a scheme to deceive; a stratagem; an artifice," and "contrivance" in pertinent part as "[a] thing contrived or used in contriving; a scheme, plan, or artifice." In turn, "contrive" in pertinent part is defined as "[t]o devise; to plan; to plot * * * [t]o fabricate * * * design; invent * * * to scheme * * *." The Commission also ig-

nores the use of the terms "[t]o use or employ," language that is supportive of the view that Congress did not intend § 10(b) to embrace negligent conduct.

15. [By the Court] Webster's International Dictionary, supra, defines "manipulate" as "to manage or treat artfully or fraudulently; as to *manipulate* accounts * * * 4. *Exchanges.* To force (prices) up or down, as by matched orders, wash sales, fictitious reports * * *; to rig."

statute controls when sufficiently clear in its context, further inquiry may be unnecessary. We turn now, nevertheless, to the legislative history of the 1934 Act to ascertain whether there is support for the meaning attributed to § 10(b) by the Commission and respondents.

B

* * * [After reviewing the scant legislative history and relying primarily on Mr. Corcoran's comment about preventing "cunning devices" the Court concludes:] The section was described rightly as a "catch all" clause to enable the Commission "to deal with new manipulative [or cunning] devices." It is difficult to believe that any lawyer, legislative draftsman, or legislator would use these words if the intent was to create liability for merely negligent acts or omissions. Neither the legislative history nor the briefs supporting respondents identify any usage or authority for construing "manipulative [or cunning] devices" to include negligence. * * *

D

We have addressed, to this point, primarily the language and history of § 10(b). The Commission contends, however, that subsections (b) and (c) of Rule 10b–5 are cast in language which—if standing alone—could encompass both intentional and negligent behavior. * * * Viewed in isolation the language of subsection (b), and arguably that of subsection (c), could be read as proscribing, respectively, any type of material misstatement or omission, and any course of conduct, that has the effect of defrauding investors, whether the wrongdoing was intentional or not.

We note first that such a reading cannot be harmonized with the administrative history of the rule, a history making clear that when the Commission adopted the rule it was intended to apply only to activities that involved scienter.[16] More importantly, Rule 10b–5 was adopted pursuant to authority granted the Commission under § 10(b). The

---

16. [By the Court] Apparently the rule was a hastily drafted response to a situation clearly involving intentional misconduct. * * * See Conference on Codification of the Federal Securities Laws, 22 Bus. Law. 793, 922 (1967) (remarks of Milton Freeman, one of the rule's co-drafters). * * * There is no indication in the administrative history of the Rule that any of the subsections was intended to proscribe conduct not involving scienter. Indeed the Commission's release issued contemporaneously with the rule explained:

"The Securities and Exchange Commission today announced the adoption of a rule prohibiting fraud by any person in connection with the purchase of securities. The previously existing rules against fraud in the purchase of securities applied only to brokers and dealers. The new rule closes a loophole in the protections against fraud administered by the Commission by prohibiting individuals or companies from buying securities if they engage in fraud in their purchase." SEC Release No. 3230 (May 21, 1942).

That same year, in its Annual Report, the Commission again stated that the purpose of the rule was to protect investors against "fraud":

"During the fiscal year the Commission adopted Rule X–10B–5 as an additional protection to investors. The new rule prohibits fraud by any person in connection with the purchase of securities, while the previously existing rules against fraud in the purchase of securities applied only to brokers and dealers." 1942 Annual Report of the Securities Exchange Commission 10.

rulemaking power granted to an administrative agency charged with the administration of a federal statute is not the power to make law. Rather, it is " 'the power to adopt regulations to carry into effect the will of Congress as expressed by the statute.' " Dixon v. United States, 381 U.S. 68, 74, 85 S.Ct. 1301, 1305, 14 L.Ed.2d 223, 228 (1965). Thus, despite the broad view of the Rule advanced by the Commission in this case, its scope cannot exceed the power granted the Commission by Congress under § 10(b). For the reasons stated above, we think the Commission's original interpretation of Rule 10b–5 was compelled by the language and history of § 10(b) and related sections of the Acts. When a statute speaks so specifically in terms of manipulation and deception, and of implementing devices and contrivances—the commonly understood terminology of intentional wrongdoing—and when its history reflects no more expansive intent, we are quite unwilling to extend the scope of the statute to negligent conduct.[17]

III

Recognizing that § 10(b) and Rule 10b–5 might be held to require proof of more than negligent nonfeasance by Ernst & Ernst as a precondition to the imposition of civil liability, respondents further contend that the case should be remanded for trial under whatever standard is adopted. Throughout the lengthy history of this case respondents have proceeded on a theory of liability premised on negligence, specifically disclaiming that Ernst & Ernst had engaged in fraud or intentional misconduct. In these circumstances, we think it inappropriate to remand the action for further proceedings.

The judgment of the Court of Appeals is Reversed.

Mr. Justice Stevens took no part in the consideration or decision of this case.

MR. JUSTICE BLACKMUN, with whom MR. JUSTICE BRENNAN joins, dissenting.

Once again—see Blue Chip Stamps v. Manor Drug Stores, 421 U.S. 723, 730, 95 S.Ct. 1917, 1922, 44 L.Ed.2d 539, 546 (1975)—the Court interprets § 10(b) of the Securities Exchange Act of 1934, * * * [and]

---

17. [By the Court] As we find the language and history of § 10(b) dispositive of the appropriate standard of liability, there is no occasion to examine the additional considerations of "policy," set forth by the parties, that may have influenced the lawmakers in their formulation of the statute. We do note that the standard urged by respondents would significantly broaden the class of plaintiffs who may seek to impose liability upon accountants and other experts who perform services or express opinions with respect to matters under the Acts. * * *

This case, on its facts, illustrates the extreme reach of the standard urged by respondents. As investors in transactions initiated by Nay, not First Securities, they were not foreseeable users of the financial statements prepared by Ernst & Ernst. Respondents conceded that they did not rely on either these financial statements or Ernst & Ernst's certificates of opinion. See n. 13, supra. The class of persons eligible to benefit from such a standard, though small in this case, could be numbered in the thousands in other cases. Acceptance of respondents' view would extend to new frontiers the "hazards" of rendering expert advice under the Acts, raising serious policy questions not yet addressed by Congress.

Rule 10b–5, restrictively and narrowly and thereby stultifies recovery for the victim. This time the Court does so by confining the statute and the Rule to situations where the defendant has "scienter," that is, the "intent to deceive, manipulate, or defraud." Sheer negligence, the Court says, is not within the reach of the statute and the Rule, and was not contemplated when the great reforms of 1933, 1934, and 1942 were effectuated by Congress and the Commission.

Perhaps the Court is right, but I doubt it. The Government and the Commission doubt it too, as is evidenced by the thrust of the brief filed by the Solicitor General on behalf of the Commission, as *amicus curiae*. The Court's opinion, to be sure, has a certain technical consistency about it. It seems to me, however, that an investor can be victimized just as much by negligent conduct as by positive deception, and that it is not logical to drive a wedge between the two, saying that Congress clearly intended the one but certainly not the other.

No one questions the fact that the respondents here were the victims of an intentional securities fraud practiced by Leston B. Nay. What is at issue, of course, is the petitioner accountant firm's involvement and that firm's responsibility under Rule 10b–5. * * *

The critical importance of the auditing accountant's role in insuring full disclosure cannot be overestimated. The SEC has emphasized that in certifying statements the accountant's duty "is to safeguard the public interest, not that of his client." In re Touche, Niven, Bailey & Smart, 37 S.E.C. 629, 670–671 (1957). "In our complex society the accountant's certificate and the lawyer's opinion can be instruments for inflicting pecuniary loss more potent than the chisel or the crowbar." United States v. Benjamin, 328 F.2d 854, 863 (CA2), cert. denied sub nom. Howard v. United States, 377 U.S. 953, 84 S.Ct. 1631, 12 L.Ed.2d 497 (1964). In this light, the initial inquiry into whether Ernst & Ernst's preparation and certification of the financial statements of First Securities Company of Chicago were negligent, because of the failure to perceive Nay's extraordinary mail rule, and in other alleged respects, and thus whether Rule 10b–5 was violated, should not be thwarted.

But the Court today decides that it is to be thwarted; and so once again it rests with Congress to rephrase and to re-enact, if investor victims, such as these, are ever to have relief under the federal securities laws that I thought had been enacted for their broad, needed, and deserving benefit.

Notes

(1) In footnote 13 (originally footnote 17 of his opinion), Mr. Justice Powell carefully reserves the question whether scienter should be required in SEC enforcement actions seeking injunctive relief. Despite the fact that the reasoning in his opinion would appear to dictate an affirmative answer, a number of lower courts concluded that scienter was not required in such suits; however, the issue was definitely resolved in Aaron v. Securities and Exchange Comm'n, 446 U.S. 680, 100 S.Ct. 1945, 64 L.Ed.2d 611 (1980)

where the Court firmly held that scienter was a critical ingredient of all rule 10b–5 cases. Mr. Justice Blackmun, with whom Justices Brennan and Marshall joined, dissented, disagreeing with the Court's "textual exegesis and its assessment of history, [and particularly its] failure to appreciate the structural interrelationship among equitable remedies in the 1933 and 1934 Acts." 446 U.S. at 713, 100 S.Ct. at 1964.

(2) In the same footnote, Mr. Justice Powell also carefully reserves the question whether "reckless disregard" might constitute "scienter." Virtually all lower courts addressing this issue since *Hochfelder* have concluded that a rule 10b–5 violation may be grounded on "recklessness" or "reckless disregard of the truth" and that knowing, intentional misconduct was not a necessary ingredient of establishing liability. See e.g., Keirnan v. Homeland, Inc., 611 F.2d 785 (9th Cir.1980), a case that is typical of many other decisions. Do you think that a sharp line may be maintained between "ordinary negligence" (for which no rule 10b–5 liability exists under *Hochfelder*) and "reckless conduct"?

(3) The decision in *Hochfelder* influenced the SEC's practices in charging violations of the securities laws in marginal cases. Whereas before *Hochfelder*, a violation of rule 10b–5 was sort of an omnibus charge appearing in every complaint, increasing attention is now paid toward other possible sections in the securities acts as forming the basis of a complaint.

SANTA FE INDUS., INC. v. GREEN

Supreme Court of the United States, 1977.
430 U.S. 462, 97 S.Ct. 1292, 51 L.Ed.2d 480.

MR. JUSTICE WHITE delivered the opinion of the Court.

The issue in this case involves the reach and coverage of § 10(b) of the Securities Exchange Act of 1934 and Rule 10b–5 thereunder in the context of a Delaware short-form merger transaction used by the majority stockholder of a corporation to eliminate the minority interest.

I

In 1936, petitioner Santa Fe Industries, Inc. (Santa Fe) acquired control of 60% of the stock of Kirby Lumber Corporation (Kirby), a Delaware corporation. Through a series of purchases over the succeeding years, Santa Fe increased its control of Kirby's stock to 95%; the purchase prices during the period 1968–1973 ranged from $65 to $92.50 per share.[18] In 1974, wishing to acquire 100% ownership of Kirby, Santa Fe availed itself of § 253 of the Delaware Corporation Law, known as the "short-form merger" statute. Section 253 permits a parent corporation owning at least 90% of the stock of a subsidiary to merge with that subsidiary, upon approval by the parent's board of directors, and to make payment in cash for the shares of the minority stockholders. The statute does not require the consent of, or advance notice to, the minority stockholders. However, notice of the merger

18. [By the Court] Santa Fe controlled Kirby through its wholly owned subsidiary, Santa Fe Natural Resources, Inc., which owned the Kirby stock.

must be given within 10 days after its effective date, and any stockholder who is dissatisfied with the terms of the merger may petition the Delaware Court of Chancery for a decree ordering the surviving corporation to pay him the fair value of his shares, as determined by a court-appointed appraiser subject to review by the court. Del.Code Ann., Tit. 8, §§ 253, 262 (1975 ed. and Supp.1976).

Santa Fe obtained independent appraisals of the physical assets of Kirby—land, timber, buildings, and machinery—and of Kirby's oil, gas, and mineral interests. These appraisals, together with other financial information, were submitted to Morgan, Stanley & Company (Morgan Stanley) an investment banking firm retained to appraise the fair market value of Kirby stock. Kirby's physical assets were appraised at $320 million (amounting to $640 for each of the 500,000 shares); Kirby's stock was valued by Morgan Stanley at $125 per share. Under the terms of the merger, minority stockholders were offered $150 per share.

The provisions of the short-form merger statute were fully complied with.[19] The minority stockholders of Kirby were notified the day after the merger became effective and were advised of their right to obtain an appraisal in Delaware court if dissatisfied with the offer of $150 per share. They also received an information statement containing, in addition to the relevant financial data about Kirby, the appraisals of the value of Kirby's assets and the Morgan Stanley appraisal concluding that the fair market value of the stock was $125 per share.

Respondents, minority stockholders of Kirby, objected to the terms of the merger, but did not pursue their appraisal remedy in the Delaware Court of Chancery. Instead, they brought this action in federal court on behalf of the corporation and other minority stockholders, seeking to set aside the merger or to recover what they claimed to be the fair value of their shares. The amended complaint asserted that, based on the fair market value of Kirby's physical assets as revealed by the appraisal included in the information statement sent to minority shareholders, Kirby's stock was worth at least $772 per share.[20] The complaint alleged further that the merger took place without prior notice to minority stockholders; that the purpose of the

19. [By the Court] The merger became effective on July 31, 1974, and was accomplished in the following way. A new corporation, Forest Products, Inc., was organized as a Delaware corporation. The Kirby stock, together with cash, was transferred from Santa Fe's wholly owned subsidiary (see n. 21, supra) to Forest Products in exchange for all of the Forest Products stock. The new corporation was then merged into Kirby, with Kirby as the surviving corporation. The cash transferred to Forest Products was used to make the purchase offer for the Kirby shares not owned by the Santa Fe subsidiary.

20. [By the Court] The figure of $772 per share was calculated as follows:

"The difference of $311,000,000 ($622 per share) between the fair market value of Kirby's land and timber, alone, as per the defendants' own appraisal thereof at $320,000,000 and the $9,000,000 book value of said land and timber, added to the $150 per share, yields a pro rata share of the value of the physical assets of Kirby of at least $772 per share. The value of the stock was at least the pro rata value of the physical assets."

merger was to appropriate the difference between the "conceded pro
rata value of the physical assets" and the offer of $150 per share—to
"freez[e] out the minority stockholders at a wholly inadequate price,"
and that Santa Fe, knowing the appraised value of the physical assets,
obtained a "fraudulent appraisal" of the stock from Morgan Stanley
and offered $25 above that appraisal "in order to lull the minority
stockholders into erroneously believing that [Santa Fe was] generous."
This course of conduct was alleged to be "a violation of Rule 10b–5
because defendants employed a 'device, scheme or artifice to defraud'
and engaged in an 'act, practice or course of business which operates or
would operate as a fraud or deceit upon any person, in connection with
the purchase or sale of any security.'"[21] Morgan Stanley assertedly
participated in the fraud as an accessory by submitting its appraisal of
$125 per share although knowing the appraised value of the physical
assets.

The District Court dismissed the complaint for failure to state a
claim upon which relief could be granted. 391 F.Supp. 849 (SDNY
1975). * * * A divided Court of Appeals for the Second Circuit
reversed. 533 F.2d 1283 (1976). * * * [Its] view was that, although
the Rule plainly reached material misrepresentations and nondisclo-
sures in connection with the purchase or sale of securities, neither
misrepresentation nor nondisclosure was a necessary element of a Rule
10b–5 action; the rule reached "breaches of fiduciary duty by a majority against minority shareholders without any charge of misrepresentation or lack of disclosure."[22] The court went on to hold that the
complaint, taken as a whole, stated a cause of action under the Rule:

> "We hold that a complaint alleges a claim under Rule 10b–5 when it
> charges, in connection with a Delaware short-form merger, that the
> majority has committed a breach of its fiduciary duty to deal fairly with
> minority shareholders by effecting the merger without any justifiable
> business purpose. The minority shareholders are given no prior notice of
> the merger, thus having no opportunity to apply for injunctive relief, and
> the proposed price to be paid is substantially lower than the appraised
> value reflected in the Information Statement." Id., at 1291.

We granted the petition for certiorari challenging this holding
because of the importance of the issue involved to the administration of

---

21. [By the Court] The complaint also
alleged a breach of fiduciary duty under
state law and asserted that the federal
court had both diversity and pendent jurisdiction over this claim. The District Court
found an absence of complete diversity of
citizenship between the plaintiffs and defendants because of the defendant Morgan
Stanley and refused to exercise pendent
jurisdiction because it held that the complaint failed to state a claim under the
federal securities laws.

22. [By the Court] Id., at 1287. The
court concluded its discussion thus:

"Whether full disclosure has been
made is not the crucial inquiry since it is
the merger and the undervaluation
which constituted the fraud, and not
whether or not the majority determines
to lay bare their real motives. If there is
no valid corporate purpose for the merger, then even the most brazen disclosure
of that fact to the minority shareholders
in no way mitigates the fraudulent conduct."

533 F.2d, at 1292.

the federal securities laws. 429 U.S. 814, 97 S.Ct. 54, 50 L.Ed.2d 74 (1976). We reverse.

II

* * * The court below construed the term "fraud" in Rule 10b–5 by adverting to the use of the term in several of this Court's decisions in contexts other than the 1934 Act and the related Securities Act of 1933.[23] The Court of Appeals' approach to the interpretation of Rule 10b–5 is inconsistent with that taken by the Court last Term in Ernst & Ernst v. Hochfelder, 425 U.S. 185, 96 S.Ct. 1375, 47 L.Ed.2d 668 (1976).

Ernst & Ernst makes clear that in deciding whether a complaint states a cause of action for "fraud" under rule 10b–5, "we turn first to the language of § 10(b), for '[t]he starting point in every case involving construction of a statute is the language itself.'" Id., at 197. In holding that a cause of action under rule 10b–5 does not lie for mere negligence, the Court began with the principle that "[a]scertainment of congressional intent with respect to the standard of liability created by a particular section of the [1933 and 1934] Acts must * * * rest primarily on the language of that section," 425 U.S., at 200, 96 S.Ct., at 1384, and then focused on the statutory language of § 10(b)—"[t]he words 'manipulative or deceptive' used in conjunction with 'device or contrivance.'" Id., at 197, 96 S.Ct., at 1383. The same language and the same principle apply to this case.

To the extent that the Court of Appeals would rely on the use of the term "fraud" in rule 10b–5 to bring within the ambit of the rule all breaches of fiduciary duty in connection with a securities transaction, its interpretation would, like the interpretation rejected by the Court in *Ernst & Ernst*, "add a gloss to the operative language of the statute quite different from its commonly accepted meaning." Id., at 199. But as the Court there held, the language of the statute must control the interpretation of the rule.[24] * * * Thus the claim of fraud and

---

23. [By the Court] The Court of Appeals quoted passages from Pepper v. Litton, 308 U.S. 295, 306, 311, 60 S.Ct. 238, 245, 247, 84 L.Ed. 281 (1939) (where this Court upheld the disallowance of a bankruptcy claim of a controlling stockholder who violated his fiduciary obligation to the other stockholders), and from 1 J. Story, Equity Jurisprudence § 187 (1835); the court also cited cases that quoted the passage from Mr. Justice Story's treatise— Moore v. Crawford, 130 U.S. 122, 128, 9 S.Ct. 447, 448, 32 L.Ed. 878 (1889) (a diversity suit to compel execution of a deed held in constructive trust), and SEC v. Capital Gains Research Bureau, 375 U.S. 180, 194, 84 S.Ct. 275, 284, 11 L.Ed.2d 237 (1963) (Investment Advisers Act of 1940 prohibits, as a "fraud or deceit upon any client," a registered investment adviser's failure to disclose to his clients his own financial interest in his recommendations). Al-

though *Capital Gains* involved a federal securities statute, the Court's references to fraud in the "equitable" sense of the term were premised on its recognition that Congress intended the Investment Advisers Act to establish federal fiduciary standards for investment advisers. See id., at 191–192, 194, 84 S.Ct., at 282–283, 284. Moreover, the fraud that the SEC sought to enjoin in *Capital Gains* was, in fact, a nondisclosure.

24. [By the Court] The case for adhering to the language of the statute is even stronger here than in *Ernst & Ernst*, where the interpretation of Rule 10b–5 rejected by the Court was strongly urged by the Commission. See also Piper v. Chris–Craft Industries, Inc., 430 U.S. 1, 97 S.Ct. 926, 51 L.Ed.2d 124 (1977), and Blue Chip Stamps v. Manor Drug Stores, 421 U.S. 723, 95 S.Ct. 1917, 44 L.Ed.2d 539 (1975) (rejecting

fiduciary breach in this complaint states a cause of action under any part of rule 10b–5 only if the conduct alleged can be fairly viewed as "manipulative or deceptive" within the meaning of the statute.

III

It is our judgment that the transaction, if carried out as alleged in the complaint, was neither deceptive nor manipulative and therefore did not violate either § 10(b) of the Act or rule 10b–5.

As we have indicated, the case comes to us on the premise that the complaint failed to allege a material misrepresentation or material failure to disclose. The finding of the District Court, undisturbed by the Court of Appeals, was that there was no "omission" or "misstatement" in the information statement accompanying the notice of merger. On the basis of the information provided, minority shareholders could either accept the price offered or reject it and seek an appraisal in the Delaware Court of Chancery. Their choice was fairly presented, and they were furnished with all relevant information on which to base their decision.[25]

We therefore find inapposite the cases relied upon by respondents and the court below, in which the breaches of fiduciary duty held violative of rule 10b–5 included some element of deception.[26] Those cases forcefully reflect the principle that "[§] 10(b) must be read flexibly, not technically and restrictively" and that the statute provides a cause of action for any plaintiff who "suffer[s] an injury as a result of deceptive practices touching its sale [or purchase] of securities. * * *" Superintendent of Insurance v. Bankers Life & Cas. Co., 404

interpretations of Rule 10b–5 urged by the SEC as *amicus curiae*). * * *

25. [By the Court] In addition to their principal argument that the complaint alleges a fraud under clauses (a) and (c) of Rule 10b–5, respondents also argue that the complaint alleges nondisclosure and misrepresentation in violation of clause (b) of the Rule. Their major contention in this respect is that the majority stockholder's failure to give the minority advance notice of the merger was a material nondisclosure, even though the Delaware short-form merger statute does not require such notice. But respondents do not indicate how they might have acted differently had they had prior notice of the merger. Indeed, they accept the conclusion of both courts below that under Delaware law they could not have enjoined the merger because an appraisal proceeding is their sole remedy in the Delaware courts for any alleged unfairness in the terms of the merger. Thus the failure to give advance notice was not a material nondisclosure within the meaning of the statute or the Rule. Cf. TSC Industries, Inc. v.

Northway, Inc., 426 U.S. 438, 96 S.Ct. 2126, 48 L.Ed.2d 757 (1976).

26. [By the Court] The decisions of this Court relied upon by respondents all involved deceptive conduct as part of the Rule 10b–5 violation alleged. Affiliated Ute Citizens v. United States, 406 U.S. 128, 92 S.Ct. 1456, 31 L.Ed.2d 741 (1972) (misstatements of material fact used by bank employees in position of market maker to acquire stock at less than fair value); Superintendent of Insurance v. Bankers Life & Cas. Co., 404 U.S. 6, 9, 92 S.Ct. 165, 167, 30 L.Ed.2d 128 (1971) ("seller [of bonds] was duped into believing that it, the seller, would receive the proceeds"). Cf. SEC v. Capital Gains Research Bureau, 375 U.S. 180, 84 S.Ct. 275, 11 L.Ed.2d 237 (1963) (injunction under Investment Advisers Act of 1940 to compel registered investment adviser to disclose to his clients his own financial interest in his recommendations).

We have been cited to a large number of cases in the Courts of Appeals, all of which involved an element of deception as part of the fiduciary misconduct held to violate Rule 10b–5. * * *

U.S. 6, 12–13, 92 S.Ct. 165, 169, 30 L.Ed.2d 128 (1971). But the cases do not support the proposition, adopted by the Court of Appeals below and urged by respondents here, that a breach of fiduciary duty by majority stockholders, without any deception, misrepresentation, or nondisclosure, violates the statute and the Rule.

It is also readily apparent that the conduct alleged in the complaint was not "manipulative" within the meaning of the statute. "Manipulation" is "virtually a term of art when used in connection with securities markets." Ernst & Ernst, 425 U.S., at 199, 96 S.Ct., at 1384. The term refers generally to practices, such as wash sales, matched orders, or rigged prices, that are intended to mislead investors by artificially affecting market activity. * * * Section 10(b)'s general prohibition of practices deemed by the SEC to be "manipulative"—in this technical sense of artificially affecting market activity in order to mislead investors—is fully consistent with the fundamental purpose of the 1934 Act "to substitute a philosophy of full disclosure for the philosophy of caveat emptor. * * *" Affiliated Ute Citizens v. United States, 406 U.S. 128, 151, 92 S.Ct. 1456, 1471, 31 L.Ed.2d 741 (1972). Indeed, nondisclosure is usually essential to the success of a manipulative scheme. No doubt Congress meant to prohibit the full range of ingenious devices that might be used to manipulate securities prices. But we do not think it would have chosen this "term of art" if it had meant to bring within the scope of § 10(b) instances of corporate mismanagement such as this, in which the essence of the complaint is that shareholders were treated unfairly by a fiduciary.

IV

The language of the statute is, we think, "sufficiently clear in its context" to be dispositive here, Ernst & Ernst, 425 U.S., at 201, 96 S.Ct., at 1385; but even if it were not, there are additional considerations that weigh heavily against permitting a cause of action under Rule 10b–5 for the breach of corporate fiduciary duty alleged in this complaint. Congress did not expressly provide a private cause of action for violations of § 10(b). Although we have recognized an implied cause of action under that section in some circumstances, Superintendent of Insurance v. Bankers Life & Cas. Co., supra, we have also recognized that a private cause of action under the antifraud provisions of the Securities Exchange Act should not be implied where it is "unnecessary to ensure the fulfillment of Congress' purposes" in adopting the Act. Piper v. Chris–Craft Industries, 430 U.S., at 41, 97 S.Ct., at 949 (1977). As we noted earlier, the Court repeatedly has described the "fundamental purpose" of the Act as implementing a "philosophy of full disclosure"; once full and fair disclosure has occurred, the fairness of the terms of the transaction is at most a tangential concern of the statute. As in Cort v. Ash, 422 U.S. 66, 78, 80, 95 S.Ct. 2080, 2087, 2090, 45 L.Ed. 2d 26 (1975), we are reluctant to recognize a cause of action here to serve what is "at best a subsidiary purpose" of the federal legislation.

A second factor in determining whether Congress intended to create a federal cause of action in these circumstances is "whether 'the cause of action [is] one traditionally relegated to state law. * * * '" Piper v. Chris–Craft Industries, Inc., 430 U.S., at 40, 97 S.Ct., at 949, quoting Cort v. Ash, 422 U.S., at 78, 95 S.Ct., at 2087. The Delaware Legislature has supplied minority shareholders with a cause of action in the Delaware Court of Chancery to recover the fair value of shares allegedly undervalued in a short-form merger. Of course, the existence of a particular state law remedy is not dispositive of the question whether Congress meant to provide a similar federal remedy, but as in *Cort* and *Piper,* we conclude that "it is entirely appropriate in this instance to relegate respondent and others in his situation to whatever remedy is created by state law." 422 U.S., at 84, 95 S.Ct., at 2091; 430 U.S., at 41, 97 S.Ct., at 949.

The reasoning behind a holding that the complaint in this case alleged fraud under Rule 10b–5 could not be easily contained. It is difficult to imagine how a court could distinguish, for purposes of Rule 10b–5 fraud, between a majority stockholder's use of a short-form merger to eliminate the minority at an unfair price and the use of some other device, such as a long-form merger, tender offer, or liquidation, to achieve the same result; or indeed how a court could distinguish the alleged abuses in these going private transactions from other types of fiduciary self-dealing involving transactions in securities. The result would be to bring within the Rule a wide variety of corporate conduct traditionally left to state regulation. In addition to posing a "danger of vexatious litigation which could result from a widely expanded class of plaintiffs under Rule 10b–5." Blue Chip Stamps v. Manor Drug Stores, 421 U.S., at 740, 95 S.Ct., at 1927 (1975), this extension of the federal securities laws would overlap and quite possibly interfere with state corporate law. Federal courts applying a "federal fiduciary principle" under Rule 10b–5 could be expected to depart from state fiduciary standards at least to the extent necessary to ensure uniformity within the federal system.[27] Absent a clear indication of congressional intent, we are reluctant to federalize the substantial portion of the law of corporations that deals with transactions in securities, particularly where established state policies of corporate regulation would be overridden. As the Court stated in Cort v. Ash, supra, "Corporations are creatures of state law, and investors commit their

---

27. [By the Court] For example, some States apparently require a "valid corporate purpose" for the elimination of the minority interest through a short-form merger, whereas other States do not. Compare Bryan v. Brock & Blevins Co., 490 F.2d 563 (CA5), cert. denied, 419 U.S. 844, 95 S.Ct. 77, 42 L.Ed.2d 72 (1974) (merger arranged by controlling stockholder for no business purpose except to eliminate 15% minority stockholder violated Georgia short-form merger statute) with Stauffer v. Standard Brands, Inc., 41 Del. Ch. 7, 187 A.2d 78 (Sup.Ct.1962) (Delaware short-form merger statute allows majority stockholder to eliminate the minority interest without any corporate purpose and subject only to an appraisal remedy). Thus to the extent that Rule 10b–5 is interpreted to require a valid corporate purpose for elimination of minority shareholders as well as a fair price for their shares, it would impose a stricter standard of fiduciary duty than that required by the law of some States.

funds to corporate directors on the understanding that, except where federal law *expressly* requires certain responsibilities of directors with respect to stockholders, state law will govern the internal affairs of the corporation." 422 U.S., at 84, 95 S.Ct., at 2091 (emphasis added).

We thus adhere to the position that "Congress by § 10(b) did not seek to regulate transactions which constitute no more than internal corporate mismanagement." Superintendent of Insurance v. Bankers Life & Cas. Co., 404 U.S., at 12, 92 S.Ct., at 169. There may well be a need for uniform federal fiduciary standards to govern mergers such as that challenged in this complaint. But those standards should not be supplied by judicial extension of § 10(b) and Rule 10b–5 to "cover the corporate universe." [28]

The judgment of the Court of Appeals is reversed, and the case is remanded for further proceedings consistent with this opinion.

So ordered.

MR. JUSTICE BRENNAN dissents and would affirm for substantially the reasons stated in the majority and concurring opinions in the Court of Appeals, 533 F.2d 1283 (CA2 1976).

MR. JUSTICE BLACKMUN, concurring in part. [This opinion is omitted.]

MR. JUSTICE STEVENS, concurring in part.

For the reasons stated by Mr. Justice Blackmun in his dissenting opinion in Blue Chip Stamps v. Manor Drug Stores, 421 U.S. 723, 761, 95 S.Ct. 1917, 1937, 44 L.Ed.2d 539, and those stated in my dissent in Piper v. Chris–Craft Industries, 430 U.S. 1, 53, 97 S.Ct. 926, 955, 51 L.Ed.2d 124 (1977), I believe both of those cases were incorrectly decided. I foresee some danger that Part IV of the Court's opinion in this case may incorrectly be read as extending the holdings of those cases. Moreover, the entire discussion in Part IV is unnecessary to the decision of this case. Accordingly, I join only Parts I, II, and III of the Court's opinion. I would also add further emphasis to the fact that the controlling stockholders in this case did not breach any duty owed to the minority shareholders because (a) there was complete disclosure of the relevant facts, and (b) the minority are entitled to receive the fair value of their shares.[29] The facts alleged in the complaint do not constitute "fraud" within the meaning of Rule 10b–5.

---

28. [By the Court] Cary, Federalism and Corporate Law: Reflections Upon Delaware, 83 Yale L.J. 663, 700 (1974) (footnote omitted). Professor Cary argues vigorously for comprehensive federal fiduciary standards, but urges a "frontal" attack by a new federal statute rather than an extension of Rule 10b–5. He writes, "It seems anomalous to jig-saw every kind of corporate dispute into the federal courts through the securities acts as they are presently written." Ibid. See also Note,

Going Private, 84 Yale L.J. 903 (1975) (proposing the application of traditional doctrines of substantive corporate law to problems of fairness raised by "going private" transactions such as short-form mergers).

29. [By the Justice] The motivation for the merger is a matter of indifference to the minority stockholders because they retain no interest in the corporation after the merger is consummated.

Notes

(1) Consider the implications of the discussion in Part IV of the majority opinion. Why should that discussion so divide the court? Why was it included at all?

(2) Despite the court's footnote (n. 27), at the time this case was decided, there was virtually no state law or precedent dealing with the propriety of "cash mergers," "going private" or similar transactions so long as the transactions followed the procedural requirements of the relevant merger provisions of the corporation act. The practical effect of the decision in the principal case was therefore to focus attention on state law as a possible regulator of transactions that literally followed state statute but were or might be unfair to defenseless interests. A number of state decisions after *Green* have imposed duties of "intrinsic fairness" or "fiduciary duties" to protect such interests. See Weinberger v. UOP, Inc., page 792 supra, and the cases cited in the notes following that case.

BASIC, INC. v. LEVINSON

Supreme Court of the United States, 1988.
485 U.S. 224, 108 S.Ct. 978, 99 L.Ed.2d 194.

JUSTICE BLACKMUN delivered the opinion of the Court.

This case requires us to apply the materiality requirement of § 10(b) of the Securities Exchange Act of 1934, and the Securities and Exchange Commission's Rule 10b–5, in the context of preliminary corporate merger discussions. We must also determine whether a person who traded a corporation's shares on a securities exchange after the issuance of a materially misleading statement by the corporation may invoke a rebuttable presumption that, in trading, he relied on the integrity of the price set by the market.

I

Prior to December 20, 1978, Basic Incorporated was a publicly traded company primarily engaged in the business of manufacturing chemical refractories for the steel industry. As early as 1965 or 1966, Combustion Engineering, Inc., a company producing mostly alumina-based refractories, expressed some interest in acquiring Basic, but was deterred from pursuing this inclination seriously because of antitrust concerns it then entertained. In 1976, however, regulatory action opened the way to a renewal of Combustion's interest. The "Strategic Plan," dated October 25, 1976, for Combustion's Industrial Products Group included the objective: "Acquire Basic Inc. $30 million."

Beginning in September 1976, Combustion representatives had meetings and telephone conversations with Basic officers and directors,[30] * * * concerning the possibility of a merger.[31] During 1977

---

30. [By the Court] In addition to Basic itself, petitioners are individuals who had been members of its board of directors prior to 1979: Anthony M. Caito, Samuel Eells, Jr., John A. Gelbach, Harley C. Lee, Max Muller, H. Chapman Rose, Edmund

31. See note 31 on page 978.

and 1978, Basic made three public statements denying that it was engaged in merger negotiations.[32] On December 18, 1978, Basic asked the New York Stock Exchange to suspend trading in its shares and issued a release stating that it had been "approached" by another company concerning a merger. On December 19, Basic's board endorsed Combustion's offer of $46 per share for its common stock, and on the following day publicly announced its approval of Combustion's tender offer for all outstanding shares.

Respondents are former Basic shareholders who sold their stock after Basic's first public statement of October 21, 1977, and before the suspension of trading in December 1978. Respondents brought a class action against Basic and its directors, asserting that the defendants issued three false or misleading public statements and thereby were in violation of § 10(b) of the 1934 Act and of Rule 10b–5. Respondents alleged that they were injured by selling Basic shares at artificially depressed prices in a market affected by petitioners' misleading statements and in reliance thereon.

The District Court adopted a presumption of reliance by members of the plaintiff class upon petitioners' public statements that enabled the court to conclude that common questions of fact or law predominated over particular questions pertaining to individual plaintiffs. See Fed.Rule Civ.Proc. 23(b)(3). The District Court therefore certified respondents' class. On the merits, however, the District Court granted summary judgment for the defendants. It held that, as a matter of law, any misstatements were immaterial: there were no negotiations ongoing at the time of the first statement, and although negotiations were taking place when the second and third statements were issued, those negotiations were not "destined, with reasonable certainty, to become a merger agreement in principle."

The United States Court of Appeals for the Sixth Circuit affirmed the class certification, but reversed the District Court's summary judg-

G. Sylvester, and John C. Wilson, Jr.
*   *   *

31. [By the Court] In light of our disposition of this case, any further characterization of these discussions must await application, on remand, of the materiality standard adopted today.

32. [By the Court] On October 21, 1977, after heavy trading and a new high in Basic stock, the following news item appeared in the Cleveland Plain Dealer:

"[Basic] President Max Muller said the company knew no reason for the stock's activity and that no negotiations were under way with any company for a merger. He said Flintkote recently denied Wall Street rumors that it would make a tender offer of $25 a share for control of the Cleveland-based maker of refractories for the steel industry."

On September 25, 1978, in reply to an inquiry from the New York Stock Exchange, Basic issued a release concerning increased activity in its stock and stated that

"management is unaware of any present or pending company development that would result in the abnormally heavy trading activity and price fluctuation in company shares that have been experienced in the past few days."

On November 6, 1978, Basic issued to its shareholders a "Nine Months Report 1978." This Report stated:

"With regard to the stock market activity in the Company's shares we remain unaware of any present or pending developments which would account for the high volume of trading and price fluctuations in recent months."

ment, and remanded the case. 786 F.2d 741 (1986). The court reasoned that while petitioners were under no general duty to disclose their discussions with Combustion, any statement the company voluntarily released could not be " 'so incomplete as to mislead.' " *Id.*, at 746, quoting *SEC v. Texas Gulf Sulphur Co.*, 401 F.2d 833, 862 (CA2 1968) (en banc), cert. denied *sub nom. Coates v. SEC*, 394 U.S. 976, 89 S.Ct. 1454, 22 L.Ed.2d 756 (1969). In the Court of Appeals' view, Basic's statements that no negotiations were taking place, and that it knew of no corporate developments to account for the heavy trading activity, were misleading. With respect to materiality, the court rejected the argument that preliminary merger discussions are immaterial as a matter of law, and held that "once a statement is made denying the existence of any discussions, even discussions that might not have been material in absence of the denial are material because they make the statement made untrue." 786 F.2d, at 749.

The Court of Appeals joined a number of other circuits in accepting the "fraud-on-the-market theory" to create a rebuttable presumption that respondents relied on petitioners' material misrepresentations, noting that without the presumption it would be impractical to certify a class under Fed.Rule Civ.Proc. 23(b)(3). See 786 F.2d, at 750–751.

We granted certiorari, 479 U.S. 1083, 107 S.Ct. 1284, 94 L.Ed.2d 142 (1987), to resolve the split, among the Courts of Appeals as to the standard of materiality applicable to preliminary merger discussions, and to determine whether the courts below properly applied a presumption of reliance in certifying the class, rather than requiring each class member to show direct reliance on Basic's statements.

II

The 1934 Act was designed to protect investors against manipulation of stock prices. Underlying the adoption of extensive disclosure requirements was a legislative philosophy: "There cannot be honest markets without honest publicity. Manipulation and dishonest practices of the market place thrive upon mystery and secrecy." H.R.Rep. No. 1383, 73d Cong., 2d Sess., 11 (1934). This Court "repeatedly has described the 'fundamental purpose' of the Act as implementing a 'philosophy of full disclosure.' " *Santa Fe Industries, Inc. v. Green*, 430 U.S. 462, 477–478, 97 S.Ct. 1292, 1303, 51 L.Ed.2d 480 (1977), quoting *SEC v. Capital Gains Research Bureau, Inc.*, 375 U.S. 180, 186, 84 S.Ct. 275, 280, 11 L.Ed.2d 237 (1963).

Pursuant to its authority under § 10(b) of the 1934 Act, the Securities and Exchange Commission promulgated Rule 10b–5. Judicial interpretation and application, legislative acquiescence, and the passage of time have removed any doubt that a private cause of action exists for a violation of § 10(b) and Rule 10b–5, and constitutes an essential tool for enforcement of the 1934 Act's requirements. See, *e.g.*, *Ernst & Ernst v. Hochfelder*, 425 U.S. 185, 196, 96 S.Ct. 1375, 1382, 47 L.Ed.2d 668 (1976); *Blue Chip Stamps v. Manor Drug Stores*, 421 U.S. 723, 730, 95 S.Ct. 1917, 1923, 44 L.Ed.2d 539 (1975).

The Court previously has addressed various positive and common-law requirements for a violation of § 10(b) or of Rule 10b–5. See, *e.g., Santa Fe Industries, Inc. v. Green, supra* ("manipulative or deceptive" requirement of the statute); *Blue Chip Stamps v. Manor Drug Stores, supra* ("in connection with the purchase or sale" requirement of the Rule); *Ernst & Ernst v. Hochfelder, supra* (scienter). The Court also explicitly has defined a standard of materiality under the securities law, see *TSC Industries, Inc. v. Northway, Inc.,* 426 U.S. 438, 96 S.Ct. 2126, 48 L.Ed.2d 757 (1976), concluding in the proxy-solicitation context that "[a]n omitted fact is material if there is a substantial likelihood that a reasonable shareholder would consider it important in deciding how to vote." *Id.,* at 449, 96 S.Ct., at 2132. Acknowledging that certain information concerning corporate developments could well be of "dubious significance," *id.,* at 448, 96 S.Ct., at 2132, the Court was careful not to set too low a standard of materiality; it was concerned that a minimal standard might bring an overabundance of information within its reach, and lead management "simply to bury the shareholders in an avalanche of trivial information—a result that is hardly conducive to informed decisionmaking." *Id.,* at 448–449, 96 S.Ct., at 2132. It further explained that to fulfill the materiality requirement "there must be a substantial likelihood that the disclosure of the omitted fact would have been viewed by the reasonable investor as having significantly altered the 'total mix' of information made available." We now expressly adopt the *TSC Industries* standard of materiality for the § 10(b) and Rule 10b–5 context.

III

The application of this materiality standard to preliminary merger discussions is not self-evident. Where the impact of the corporate development on the target's fortune is certain and clear, the *TSC Industries* materiality definition admits straightforward application. Where, on the other hand, the event is contingent or speculative in nature, it is difficult to ascertain whether the "reasonable investor" would have considered the omitted information significant at the time. Merger negotiations, because of the ever-present possibility that the contemplated transaction will not be effectuated, fall into the latter category.

A

Petitioners urge upon us a Third Circuit test for resolving this difficulty. Under this approach, preliminary merger discussions do not become material until "agreement-in-principle" as to the price and structure of the transaction has been reached between the would-be merger partners. See *Greenfield v. Heublein, Inc.,* 742 F.2d 751, 757 (CA3 1984), cert. denied, 469 U.S. 1215 (1985). By definition, then, information concerning any negotiations not yet at the agreement-in-principle stage could be withheld or even misrepresented without a violation of Rule 10b–5.

Three rationales have been offered in support of the "agreement-in-principle" test. The first derives from the concern expressed in *TSC Industries* that an investor not be overwhelmed by excessively detailed and trivial information, and focuses on the substantial risk that preliminary merger discussions may collapse: because such discussions are inherently tentative, disclosure of their existence itself could mislead investors and foster false optimism. The other two justifications for the agreement-in-principle standard are based on management concerns: because the requirement of "agreement-in-principle" limits the scope of disclosure obligations, it helps preserve the confidentiality of merger discussions where earlier disclosure might prejudice the negotiations; and the test also provides a usable, brightline rule for determining when disclosure must be made.

None of these policy-based rationales, however, purports to explain why drawing the line at agreement-in-principle reflects the significance of the information upon the investor's decision. The first rationale, and the only one connected to the concerns expressed in *TSC Industries,* stands soundly rejected, even by a Court of Appeals that otherwise has accepted the wisdom of the agreement-in-principle test. "It assumes that investors are nitwits, unable to appreciate—even when told—that mergers are risky propositions up until the closing." *Flamm v. Eberstadt,* 814 F.2d [1169], at 1175, [(7th Cir.) cert. denied 484 U.S. 853 (1987)]. Disclosure, and not paternalistic withholding of accurate information, is the policy chosen and expressed by Congress. We have recognized time and again, a "fundamental purpose" of the various securities acts, "was to substitute a philosophy of full disclosure for the philosophy of *caveat emptor* and thus to achieve a high standard of business ethics in the securities industry." *SEC v. Capital Gains Research Bureau, Inc.,* 375 U.S., at 186. The role of the materiality requirement is not to "attribute to investors a child-like simplicity, an inability to grasp the probabilistic significance of negotiations," *Flamm v. Eberstadt,* 814 F.2d, at 1175, but to filter out essentially useless information that a reasonable investor would not consider significant, even as part of a larger "mix" of factors to consider in making his investment decision. *TSC Industries, Inc. v. Northway, Inc.,* 426 U.S., at 448–449.

The second rationale, the importance of secrecy during the early stages of merger discussions, also seems irrelevant to an assessment whether their existence is significant to the trading decision of a reasonable investor. To avoid a "bidding war" over its target, an acquiring firm often will insist that negotiations remain confidential, and at least one Court of Appeals has stated that "silence pending settlement of the price and structure of a deal is beneficial to most investors, most of the time." *Flamm v. Eberstadt,* 814 F.2d, at 1177.[33]

---

33. [By the Court] Reasoning backwards from a goal of economic efficiency, that Court of Appeals stated: "Rule 10b–5 is about *fraud,* after all, and it is not fraudulent to conduct business in a way that makes investors better off. . . ." *Flamm v. Eberstadt,* 814 F.2d, at 1177.

We need not ascertain, however, whether secrecy necessarily maximizes shareholder wealth—although we note that the proposition is at least disputed as a matter of theory and empirical research [34]—for this case does not concern the *timing* of a disclosure; it concerns only its accuracy and completeness. We face here the narrow question whether information concerning the existence and status of preliminary merger discussions is significant to the reasonable investor's trading decision. Arguments based on the premise that some disclosure would be "premature" in a sense are more properly considered under the rubric of an issuer's duty to disclose. The "secrecy" rationale is simply inapposite to the definition of materiality.

The final justification offered in support of the agreement-in-principle test seems to be directed solely at the comfort of corporate managers. A bright-line rule indeed is easier to follow than a standard that requires the exercise of judgment in the light of all the circumstances. But ease of application alone is not an excuse for ignoring the purposes of the securities acts and Congress' policy decisions. Any approach that designates a single fact or occurrence as always determinative of an inherently fact-specific finding such as materiality, must necessarily be over- inclusive or underinclusive. In *TSC Industries* this Court explained: "The determination [of materiality] requires delicate assessments of the inferences a 'reasonable shareholder' would draw from a given set of facts and the significance of those inferences to him. . . ." 426 U.S., at 450. After much study, the Advisory Committee on Corporate Disclosure cautioned the SEC against administratively confining materiality to a rigid formula.[35] Courts also would do well to heed this advice.

We therefore find no valid justification for artificially excluding from the definition of materiality information concerning merger discussions, which would otherwise be considered significant to the trading decision of a reasonable investor, merely because agreement-in-princi-

34. [By the Court] See, *e.g.*, Brown, Corporate Secrecy, the Federal Securities Laws, and the Disclosure of Ongoing Negotiations, 36 Cath.U.L.Rev. 93, 145–155 (1986); Bebchuk, The Case for Facilitating Competing Tender Offers, 95 Harv.L.Rev. 1028 (1982); *Flamm v. Eberstadt,* 814 F.2d, at 1177, n. 2 (citing scholarly debate). See also *In re Carnation Co.,* Exchange Act Release No. 22214, 33 S.E.C. Docket 1025, 1030 (1985) ("The importance of accurate and complete issuer disclosure to the integrity of the securities markets cannot be overemphasized. To the extent that investors cannot rely upon the accuracy and completeness of issuer statements, they will be less likely to invest, thereby reducing the liquidity of the securities markets to the detriment of investors and issuers alike").

35. [By the Court] "Although the Committee believes that ideally it would be desirable to have absolute certainty in the application of the materiality concept, it is its view that such a goal is illusory and unrealistic. The materiality concept is judgmental in nature and it is not possible to translate this into a numerical formula. The Committee's advice to the [SEC] is to avoid this quest for certainty and to continue consideration of materiality on a case-by-case basis as problems are identified." Report of the Advisory Committee on Corporate Disclosure to the Securities and Exchange Commission 327 (House Committee on Interstate and Foreign Commerce, 95th Cong., 1st Sess.) (Comm. Print) (1977).

ple as to price and structure has not yet been reached by the parties or their representatives.

B

The Sixth Circuit [in the decision below] explicitly rejected the agreement-in-principle test, as we do today, but in its place adopted a rule that, if taken literally, would be equally insensitive, in our view, to the distinction between materiality and the other elements of an action under Rule 10b–5:

> "When a company whose stock is publicly traded makes a statement, as Basic did, that 'no negotiations' are underway, and that the corporation knows of 'no reason for the stock's activity,' and that 'management is unaware of any present or pending corporate development that would result in the abnormally heavy trading activity,' information concerning ongoing acquisition discussions becomes material *by virtue of the statement denying their existence.*

> "In analyzing whether information regarding merger discussions is material such that it must be affirmatively disclosed to avoid a violation of Rule 10b–5, the discussions and their progress are the primary considerations. However, once a statement is made denying the existence of any discussions, even discussions that might not have been material in absence of the denial are material because they make the statement made untrue." 786 F.2d, at 748–749 (emphasis in original).

This approach, however, fails to recognize that, in order to prevail on a Rule 10b–5 claim, a plaintiff must show that the statements were *misleading* as to a *material* fact. It is not enough that a statement is false or incomplete, if the misrepresented fact is otherwise insignificant.

C

Even before this Court's decision in *TSC Industries,* the Second Circuit had explained the role of the materiality requirement of Rule 10b–5, with respect to contingent or speculative information or events, in a manner that gave that term meaning that is independent of the other provisions of the Rule. Under such circumstances, materiality "will depend at any given time upon a balancing of both the indicated probability that the event will occur and the anticipated magnitude of the event in light of the totality of the company activity." *SEC v. Texas Gulf Sulphur Co.,* 401 F.2d, at 849. Interestingly, neither the Third Circuit decision adopting the agreement-in-principle test nor petitioners here take issue with this general standard. Rather, they suggest that with respect to preliminary merger discussions, there are good reasons to draw a line at agreement on price and structure.

In a subsequent decision, the late Judge Friendly, writing for a Second Circuit panel, applied the *Texas Gulf Sulphur* probability/magnitude approach in the specific context of preliminary merger negotiations. After acknowledging that materiality is something to be determined on the basis of the particular facts of each case, he stated:

"Since a merger in which it is bought out is the most important event that can occur in a small corporation's life, to wit, its death, we think that inside information, as regards a merger of this sort, can become material at an earlier stage than would be the case as regards lesser transactions—and this even though the mortality rate of mergers in such formative stages is doubtless high." *SEC v. Geon Industries, Inc.,* 531 F.2d 39, 47–48 (1976).

We agree with that analysis.[36]

Whether merger discussions in any particular case are material therefore depends on the facts. Generally, in order to assess the probability that the event will occur, a factfinder will need to look to indicia of interest in the transaction at the highest corporate levels. Without attempting to catalog all such possible factors, we note by way of example that board resolutions, instructions to investment bankers, and actual negotiations between principals or their intermediaries may serve as indicia of interest. To assess the magnitude of the transaction to the issuer of the securities allegedly manipulated, a factfinder will need to consider such facts as the size of the two corporate entities and of the potential premiums over market value. No particular event or factor short of closing the transaction need be either necessary or sufficient by itself to render merger discussions material.[37]

As we clarify today, materiality depends on the significance the reasonable investor would place on the withheld or misrepresented information.[38] The fact-specific inquiry we endorse here is consistent

---

36. [By the Court] The SEC in the present case endorses the highly fact-dependent probability/magnitude balancing approach of *Texas Gulf Sulphur.* It explains: "The *possibility* of a merger may have an immediate importance to investors in the company's securities even if no merger ultimately takes place." The SEC's insights are helpful, and we accord them due deference.

37. [By the Court] To be actionable, of course, a statement must also be misleading. Silence, absent a duty to disclose, is not misleading under Rule 10b–5. "No comment" statements are generally the functional equivalent of silence. See *In re Carnation Co.,* Exchange Act Release No. 22214, 33 S.E.C. Docket 1025 (1985). See also New York Stock Exchange Listed Company Manual § 202.01 [reprinted infra p. 1003] (premature public announcement may properly be delayed for valid business purpose and where adequate security can be maintained). It has been suggested that given current market practices, a "no comment" statement is tantamount to an admission that merger discussions are underway. See *Flamm v. Eberstadt,* 814 F.2d, at 1178. That may well hold true to the extent that issuers adopt a policy of truth-

fully denying merger rumors when no discussions are underway, and of issuing "no comment" statements when they are in the midst of negotiations. There are, of course, other statement policies firms could adopt; we need not now advise issuers as to what kind of practice to follow, within the range permitted by law. Perhaps more importantly, we think that creating an exception to a regulatory scheme founded on a prodisclosure legislative philosophy, because complying with the regulation might be "bad for business," is a role for Congress, not this Court.

38. [By the Court] We find no authority in the statute, the legislative history, or our previous decisions for varying the standard of materiality depending on who brings the action or whether insiders are alleged to have profited. See, *e.g., Pavlidis v. New England Patriots Football Club, Inc.,* 737 F.2d 1227, 1231 (CA1 1984) ("A fact does not become more material to the shareholder's decision because it is withheld by an insider, or because the insider might profit by withholding it").

We recognize that trading (and profit making) by insiders can serve as *an* indication of materiality, see *SEC v. Texas Gulf*

with the approach a number of courts have taken in assessing the materiality of merger negotiations.[39] Because the standard of materiality we have adopted differs from that used by both courts below, we remand the case for reconsideration of the question whether a grant of summary judgment is appropriate on this record.

IV

A

We turn to the question of reliance and the fraud-on-the-market theory. Succinctly put:

> "The fraud on the market theory is based on the hypothesis that, in an open and developed securities market, the price of a company's stock is determined by the available material information regarding the company and its business. . . . Misleading statements will therefore defraud purchasers of stock even if the purchasers do not directly rely on the misstatements. . . . The causal connection between the defendants' fraud and the plaintiffs' purchase of stock in such a case is no less significant than in a case of direct reliance on misrepresentations." *Peil v. Speiser*, 806 F.2d 1154, 1160–1161 (CA3 1986).

Our task, of course, is not to assess the general validity of the theory, but to consider whether it was proper for the courts below to apply a rebuttable presumption of reliance, supported in part by the fraud-on-the-market theory.

This case required resolution of several common questions of law and fact concerning the falsity or misleading nature of the three public statements made by Basic, the presence or absence of scienter, and the materiality of the misrepresentations, if any. In their amended complaint, the named plaintiffs alleged that in reliance on Basic's state-

---

Sulphur Co., 401 F.2d, at 851. We are not prepared to agree, however, that "[i]n cases of the disclosure of inside information to a favored few, determination of materiality has a different aspect than when the issue is, for example, an inaccuracy in a publicly disseminated press release." *SEC v. Geon Industries, Inc.*, 531 F.2d 39, 48 (CA2 1976). Devising two different standards of materiality, one for situations where insiders have traded in abrogation of their duty to disclose or abstain (or for that matter when any disclosure duty has been breached), and another covering affirmative misrepresentations by those under no duty to disclose (but under the ever-present duty not to mislead), would effectively collapse the materiality requirement into the analysis of defendant's disclosure duties.

39. [By the Court] See, *e.g.*, *SEC v. Shapiro*, 494 F.2d 1301, 1306–1307 (CA2 1974) (in light of projected very substantial increase in earnings per share, negotiations material, although merger still less than

probable); *Holmes v. Bateson*, 583 F.2d 542, 558 (CA1 1978) (merger negotiations material although they had not yet reached point of discussing terms); *SEC v. Gaspar*, CCH Fed.Sec.L.Rep. (1984–1985 Transfer Binder) ¶ 92,004, pp. 90,977–90,978 (SDNY 1985) (merger negotiations material although they did not proceed to actual tender offer); *Dungan v. Colt Industries, Inc.*, 532 F.Supp. 832, 837 (ND Ill. 1982) (fact that defendants were seriously exploring the sale of their company was material); *American General Ins. Co. v. Equitable General Corp.*, 493 F.Supp. 721, 744–745 (ED Va.1980) (merger negotiations material four months before agreement-in-principle reached). Cf. *Susquehanna Corp. v. Pan American Sulphur Co.*, 423 F.2d 1075, 1084–1085 (CA5 1970) (holding immaterial "unilateral offer to negotiate" never acknowledged by target and repudiated two days later); *Berman v. Gerber Products Co.*, 454 F.Supp. 1310, 1316, 1318 (WD Mich.1978) (mere "overtures" immaterial).

ments they sold their shares of Basic stock in the depressed market created by petitioners. Requiring proof of individualized reliance from each member of the proposed plaintiff class effectively would have prevented respondents from proceeding with a class action, since individual issues then would have overwhelmed the common ones. The District Court found that the presumption of reliance created by the fraud-on-the-market theory provided "a practical resolution to the problem of balancing the substantive requirement of proof of reliance in securities cases against the procedural requisites of [Federal Rule of Civil Procedure] 23." The District Court thus concluded that with reference to each public statement and its impact upon the open market for Basic shares, common questions predominated over individual questions, as required by Federal Rule of Civil Procedure 23(a)(2) and (b)(3).

Petitioners and their *amici* complain that the fraud-on-the-market theory effectively eliminates the requirement that a plaintiff asserting a claim under Rule 10b–5 prove reliance. They note that reliance is and long has been an element of common-law fraud, see *e.g.,* Restatement (Second) of Torts § 525 (1977), and argue that because the analogous express right of action includes a reliance requirement, see, *e.g.,* § 18(a) of the 1934 Act, as amended, so too must an action implied under § 10(b).

We agree that reliance is an element of a Rule 10b–5 cause of action. Reliance provides the requisite causal connection between a defendant's misrepresentation and a plaintiff's injury. There is, however, more than one way to demonstrate the causal connection. Indeed, we previously have dispensed with a requirement of positive proof of reliance, where a duty to disclose material information had been breached, concluding that the necessary nexus between the plaintiffs' injury and the defendant's wrongful conduct had been established. Similarly, we did not require proof that material omissions or misstatements in a proxy statement decisively affected voting, because the proxy solicitation itself, rather than the defect in the solicitation materials, served as an essential link in the transaction. See *Mills v. Electric Auto–Lite Co.,* 396 U.S. 375, 384–385 (1970).

The modern securities markets, literally involving millions of shares changing hands daily, differ from the face-to-face transactions contemplated by early fraud cases, and our understanding of Rule 10b–5's reliance requirement must encompass these differences.

> "In face-to-face transactions, the inquiry into an investor's reliance upon information is into the subjective pricing of that information by that investor. With the presence of a market, the market is interposed between seller and buyer and, ideally, transmits information to the investor in the processed form of a market price. Thus the market is performing a substantial part of the valuation process performed by the investor in a face-to-face transaction. The market is acting as the unpaid agent of the investor, informing him that given all the informa-

tion available to it, the value of the stock is worth the market price."
In re LTV Securities Litigation, 88 F.R.D. 134, 143 (ND Tex.1980).

Accord, *e.g., Peil v. Speiser,* 806 F.2d, at 1161 ("In an open and
developed market, the dissemination of material misrepresentations or
withholding of material information typically affects the price of the
stock, and purchasers generally rely on the price of the stock as a
reflection of its value"); *Blackie v. Barrack,* 524 F.2d 891, 908 (CA9
1975) ("[T]he same causal nexus can be adequately established indirectly, by proof of materiality coupled with the common sense that a stock
purchaser does not ordinarily seek to purchase a loss in the form of
artificially inflated stock"), cert. denied, 429 U.S. 816 (1976).

B

Presumptions typically serve to assist courts in managing circumstances in which direct proof, for one reason or another, is rendered
difficult. See, *e.g.,* 1 D. Louisell & C. Mueller, Federal Evidence 541–
542 (1977). The courts below accepted a presumption, created by the
fraud-on-the-market theory and subject to rebuttal by petitioners, that
persons who had traded Basic shares had done so in reliance on the
integrity of the price set by the market, but because of petitioners'
material misrepresentations that price had been fraudulently depressed. Requiring a plaintiff to show a speculative state of facts, *i.e.,*
how he would have acted if omitted material information had been
disclosed, or if the misrepresentation had not been made, would place
an unnecessarily unrealistic evidentiary burden on the Rule 10b–5
plaintiff who has traded on an impersonal market.

Arising out of considerations of fairness, public policy, and
probability, as well as judicial economy, presumptions are also useful
devices for allocating the burdens of proof between parties. The
presumption of reliance employed in this case is consistent with, and,
by facilitating Rule 10b–5 litigation, supports, the congressional policy
embodied in the 1934 Act. In drafting that Act, Congress expressly
relied on the premise that securities markets are affected by information, and enacted legislation to facilitate an investor's reliance on the
integrity of those markets:

> "No investor, no speculator, can safely buy and sell securities upon
> the exchanges without having an intelligent basis for forming his
> judgment as to the value of the securities he buys or sells. The idea of
> a free and open public market is built upon the theory that competing
> judgments of buyers and sellers as to the fair price of a security brings
> *[sic]* about a situation where the market price reflects as nearly as
> possible a just price. Just as artificial manipulation tends to upset the
> true function of an open market, so the hiding and secreting of
> important information obstructs the operation of the markets as indi-
> ces of real value." H.R.Rep. No. 1383, at 11.[40]

40. [By the Court] Contrary to the dissent's suggestion, the incentive for investors to "pay attention" to issuers' disclosures comes from their motivation to make
a profit, not their attempt to preserve a
cause of action under Rule 10b–5. Facili-

The presumption is also supported by common sense and probability. Recent empirical studies have tended to confirm Congress' premise that the market price of shares traded on well-developed markets reflects all publicly available information, and, hence, any material misrepresentations.[41] It has been noted that "it is hard to imagine that there ever is a buyer or seller who does not rely on market integrity. Who would knowingly roll the dice in a crooked crap game?" *Schlanger v. Four–Phase Systems Inc.,* 555 F.Supp. 535, 538 (SDNY 1982). Indeed, nearly every court that has considered the proposition has concluded that where materially misleading statements have been disseminated into an impersonal, well-developed market for securities, the reliance of individual plaintiffs on the integrity of the market price may be presumed.[42] Commentators generally have applauded the adoption of one variation or another of the fraud-on-the-market theory.[43] An investor who buys or sells stock at the price set by the market does so in reliance on the integrity of that price. Because most publicly available information is reflected in market price, an investor's reliance on any public material misrepresentations, therefore, may be presumed for purposes of a Rule 10b–5 action.

C

The Court of Appeals found that petitioners "made public, material misrepresentations and [respondents] sold Basic stock in an impersonal, efficient market. Thus the class, as defined by the district court, has established the threshold facts for proving their loss." 786 F.2d, at 751.[44] The court acknowledged that petitioners may rebut proof of the elements giving rise to the presumption, or show that the misrepresentation in fact did not lead to a distortion of price or that an individual

tating an investor's reliance on the market, consistently with Congress' expectations, hardly calls for "dismantling the federal scheme which mandates disclosure."

41. [By the Court] See *In re LTV Securities Litigation,* 88 F.R.D. 134, 144 (ND Tex.1980) (citing studies); Fischel, Use of Modern Finance Theory in Securities Fraud Cases Involving Actively Traded Securities, 38 Bus.Law. 1, 4, n. 9 (1982) (citing literature on efficient-capital-market theory). We need not determine by adjudication what economists and social scientists have debated through the use of sophisticated statistical analysis and the application of economic theory. For purposes of accepting the presumption of reliance in this case, we need only believe that market professionals generally consider most publicly announced material statements about companies, thereby affecting stock market prices.

42. [By the Editor] The Court cites seven appellate decisions, all after 1978.

43. [By the Court] See, *e.g.,* Black, Fraud on the Market: A Criticism of Dispensing with Reliance Requirements in Certain Open Market Transactions, 62 N.C.L.Rev. 435 (1984).

44. [By the Court] The Court of Appeals held that in order to invoke the presumption, a plaintiff must allege and prove: (1) that the defendant made public misrepresentations; (2) that the misrepresentations were material; (3) that the shares were traded on an efficient market; (4) that the misrepresentations would induce a reasonable, relying investor to misjudge the value of the shares; and (5) that the plaintiff traded the shares between the time the misrepresentations were made and the time the truth was revealed.

Given today's decision regarding the definition of materiality as to preliminary merger discussions, elements (2) and (4) may collapse into one.

plaintiff traded or would have traded despite his knowing the statement was false.

Any showing that severs the link between the alleged misrepresentation and either the price received (or paid) by the plaintiff, or his decision to trade at a fair market price, will be sufficient to rebut the presumption of reliance. For example, if petitioners could show that the "market makers" were privy to the truth about the merger discussions here with Combustion, and thus that the market price would not have been affected by their misrepresentations, the causal connection could be broken: the basis for finding that the fraud had been transmitted through market price would be gone.[45] Similarly, if, despite petitioners' allegedly fraudulent attempt to manipulate market price, news of the merger discussions credibly entered the market and dissipated the effects of the misstatements, those who traded Basic shares after the corrective statements would have no direct or indirect connection with the fraud.[46] Petitioners also could rebut the presumption of reliance as to plaintiffs who would have divested themselves of their Basic shares without relying on the integrity of the market. For example, a plaintiff who believed that Basic's statements were false and that Basic was indeed engaged in merger discussions, and who consequently believed that Basic stock was artificially underpriced, but sold his shares nevertheless because of other unrelated concerns, *e.g.,* potential antitrust problems, or political pressures to divest from shares of certain businesses, could not be said to have relied on the integrity of a price he knew had been manipulated. * * *

The judgment of the Court of Appeals is vacated, and the case is remanded to that court for further proceedings consistent with this opinion.

It is so ordered.

THE CHIEF JUSTICE, JUSTICE SCALIA, and JUSTICE KENNEDY took no part in the consideration or decision of this case.

JUSTICE WHITE, with whom JUSTICE O'CONNOR joins, concurring in part and dissenting in part.

I join Parts I–III of the Court's opinion, as I agree that the standard of materiality we set forth in *TSC Industries, Inc. v. Northway, Inc.,* 426 U.S. 438, 449 (1976), should be applied to actions under § 10(b) and

---

45. [By the Court] By accepting this rebuttable presumption, we do not intend conclusively to adopt any particular theory of how quickly and completely publicly available information is reflected in market price. Furthermore, our decision today is not to be interpreted as addressing the proper measure of damages in litigation of this kind.

46. [By the Court] We note there may be a certain incongruity between the assumption that Basic shares are traded on a well-developed, efficient, and information-hungry market, and the allegation that such a market could remain misinformed, and its valuation of Basic shares depressed, for 14 months, on the basis of the three public statements. Proof of that sort is a matter for trial, throughout which the District Court retains the authority to amend the certification order as may be appropriate. Thus, we see no need to engage in the kind of factual analysis the dissent suggests that manifests the "oddities" of applying a rebuttable presumption of reliance in this case.

Rule 10b–5. But I dissent from the remainder of the Court's holding because I do not agree that the "fraud-on-the-market" theory should be applied in this case.

I

Even when compared to the relatively youthful private cause-of-action under § 10(b), see *Kardon v. National Gypsum Co.,* 69 F.Supp. 512 (ED Pa.1946), the fraud-on-the-market theory is a mere babe.[47] Yet today, the Court embraces this theory with the sweeping confidence usually reserved for more mature legal doctrines. In so doing, I fear that the Court's decision may have many adverse, unintended effects as it is applied and interpreted in the years to come.

A

At the outset, I note that there are portions of the Court's fraud-on-the-market holding with which I am in agreement. Most importantly, the Court rejects the version of that theory, heretofore adopted by some courts, which equates "causation" with "reliance," and permits recovery by a plaintiff who claims merely to have been *harmed* by a material misrepresentation which altered a market price, notwithstanding proof that the plaintiff did not in any way *rely* on that price. I agree with the Court that if Rule 10b–5's reliance requirement is to be left with any content at all, the fraud-on-the-market presumption must be capable of being rebutted by a showing that a plaintiff did not "rely" on the market price. For example, a plaintiff who decides, months in advance of an alleged misrepresentation, to purchase a stock; one who buys or sells a stock for reasons unrelated to its price; one who actually sells a stock "short" days before the misrepresentation is made—surely none of these people can state a valid claim under Rule 10b–5. Yet, some federal courts have allowed such claims to stand under one variety or another of the fraud-on-the-market theory.[48]

47. [By the Justice] The earliest Court of Appeals case adopting this theory cited by the Court is *Blackie v. Barrack,* 524 F.2d 891 (CA9 1975), cert. denied, 429 U.S. 816 (1976). Moreover, widespread acceptance of the fraud-on-the-market theory in the Courts of Appeals cannot be placed any earlier than five or six years ago.

48. [By the Justice] *Abrams v. Johns-Manville Corp.,* [1981–1982] CCH Fed.Sec. L.Rep. ¶ 98,348, p. 92,157 (SDNY 1981) * * *.

The *Abrams* decision illustrates the particular pliability of the fraud-on-the-market presumption. In *Abrams,* the plaintiff represented a class of purchasers of defendant's stock who were allegedly misled by defendant's misrepresentations in annual reports. But in a deposition taken shortly after the plaintiff filed suit, she testified that she had bought defendant's stock primarily because she thought that favorable

changes in the federal tax code would boost sales of its product (insulation).

Two years later, after the defendant moved for summary judgment based on the plaintiff's failure to prove reliance on the alleged misrepresentations, the plaintiff resuscitated her case by executing an affidavit which stated that she "certainly [had] assumed that the market price of Johns-Manville stock was an accurate reflection of the worth of the company" and would not have paid the then-going price if she had known otherwise. Based on this affidavit, the District Court permitted the plaintiff to proceed on her fraud-on-the-market theory.

Thus, *Abrams* demonstrates how easily a *post hoc* statement will enable a plaintiff to bring a fraud-on-the-market action—even in the rare case where a plaintiff is frank or foolhardy enough to admit initially that

Happily, the majority puts to rest the prospect of recovery under such circumstances. A nonrebuttable presumption of reliance—or even worse, allowing recovery in the face of "affirmative evidence of nonreliance," *Zweig v. Hearst Corp.,* 594 F.2d 1261, 1272 (CA9 1979) (Ely, J., dissenting)—would effectively convert Rule 10b–5 into "a scheme of investor's insurance." *Shores v. Sklar,* 647 F.2d 462, 469, n. 5 (CA5 1981) (en banc), cert. denied, 459 U.S. 1102 (1983). There is no support in the Securities [Exchange] Act, the Rule, or our cases for such a result.

B

But even as the Court attempts to limit the fraud-on-the-market theory it endorses today, the pitfalls in its approach are revealed by previous uses by the lower courts of the broader versions of the theory. Confusion and contradiction in court rulings are inevitable when traditional legal analysis is replaced with economic theorization by the federal courts.

In general, the case law developed in this Court with respect to § 10(b) and Rule 10b–5 has been based on doctrines with which we, as judges, are familiar: common-law doctrines of fraud and deceit. Even when we have extended civil liability under Rule 10b–5 to a broader reach than the common law had previously permitted, we have retained familiar legal principles as our guideposts. The federal courts have proved adept at developing an evolving jurisprudence of Rule 10b–5 in such a manner. But with no staff economists, no experts schooled in the "efficient-capital-market hypothesis," no ability to test the validity of empirical market studies, we are not well equipped to embrace novel constructions of a statute based on contemporary microeconomic theory.[49]

The "wrong turns" in those Court of Appeals and district court fraud-on-the-market decisions which the Court implicitly rejects as going too far should be ample illustration of the dangers when economic theories replace legal rules as the basis for recovery. Yet the Court today ventures into this area beyond its expertise, beyond—by its own admission—the confines of our previous fraud cases. Even if I agreed with the Court that "modern securities markets . . . involving millions of shares changing hands daily" require that the "understanding

a factor other than price led her to the decision to purchase a particular stock.

49. [By the Justice] This view was put well by two commentators who wrote a few years ago:

"Of all recent developments in financial economics, the efficient capital market hypothesis ('ECMH') has achieved the widest acceptance by the legal culture. . . .

"Yet the legal culture's remarkably rapid and broad acceptance of an eco-

nomic concept that did not exist twenty years ago is not matched by an equivalent degree of *understanding.*" Gilson & Kraakman, The Mechanisms of Market Efficiency, 70 Va.L.Rev. 549, 549–550 (1984) (footnotes omitted; emphasis added).

While the fraud-on-the-market theory has gained even broader acceptance since 1984, I doubt that it has achieved any greater understanding.

of Rule 10b–5's reliance requirement" be changed, I prefer that such changes come from Congress in amending § 10(b). The Congress, with its superior resources and expertise, is far better equipped than the federal courts for the task of determining how modern economic theory and global financial markets require that established legal notions of fraud be modified. In choosing to make these decisions itself, the Court, I fear, embarks on a course that it does not genuinely understand, giving rise to consequences it cannot foresee.[50]

For while the economists' theories which underpin the fraud-on-the-market presumption may have the appeal of mathematical exactitude and scientific certainty, they are—in the end—nothing more than theories which may or may not prove accurate upon further consideration. Even the most earnest advocates of economic analysis of the law recognize this. Thus, while the majority states that, for purposes of reaching its result it need only make modest assumptions about the way in which "market professionals generally" do their jobs, and how the conduct of market professionals affects stock prices, I doubt that we are in much of a position to assess which theories aptly describe the functioning of the securities industry.

Consequently, I cannot join the Court in its effort to reconfigure the securities laws, based on recent economic theories, to better fit what it perceives to be the new realities of financial markets. I would leave this task to others more equipped for the job than we.

C

At the bottom of the Court's conclusion that the fraud-on-the-market theory sustains a presumption of reliance is the assumption that individuals rely "on the integrity of the market price" when buying or selling stock in "impersonal, well-developed market[s] for securities." Even if I was prepared to accept (as a matter of common sense or general understanding) the assumption that most persons buying or selling stock do so in response to the market price, the fraud-on-the-market theory goes further. For in adopting a "presumption of reliance," the Court *also* assumes that buyers and sellers rely—not just on the market price—but on the "*integrity*" of that price. It is this aspect of the fraud-on-the-market hypothesis which most mystifies me.

To define the term "integrity of the market price," the majority quotes approvingly from cases which suggest that investors are entitled to " 'rely on the price of a stock as a reflection of its value' " (quoting

---

50. [By the Justice] For example, Judge Posner in his Economic Analysis of Law § 15.8, pp. 423–424 (3d ed. 1986), submits that the fraud-on-the-market theory produces the "economically correct result" in Rule 10b–5 cases but observes that the question of damages under the theory is quite problematic. Notwithstanding the fact that "[a]t first blush it might seem obvious," the proper calculation of damages when the fraud-on-the-market theory is applied must rest on several "assumptions" about "social costs" which are "difficult to quantify." *Ibid.* Of course, answers to the question of the proper measure of damages in a fraud-on-the-market case are essential for proper implementation of the fraud-on-the-market presumption. Not surprisingly, the difficult damages question is one the Court expressly declines to address today.

Peil v. Speiser, 806 F.2d 1154, 1161 (CA3 1986)). But the meaning of this phrase eludes me, for it implicitly suggests that stocks have some "true value" that is measurable by a standard other than their market price. While the Scholastics of Medieval times professed a means to make such a valuation of a commodity's "worth," I doubt that the federal courts of our day are similarly equipped.

Even if securities had some "value"—knowable and distinct from the market price of a stock—investors do not always share the Court's presumption that a stock's price is a "reflection of [this] value." Indeed, "many investors purchase or sell stock because they believe the price *inaccurately* reflects the corporation's worth." See Black, Fraud on the Market: A Criticism of Dispensing with Reliance Requirements in Certain Open Market Transactions, 62 N.C.L.Rev. 435, 455 (1984) (emphasis added). If investors really believed that stock prices reflected a stock's "value," many sellers would never sell, and many buyers never buy (given the time and cost associated with executing a stock transaction). As we recognized just a few years ago: "[I]nvestors act on inevitably incomplete or inaccurate information, [consequently] there are always winners and losers; but those who have 'lost' have not necessarily been defrauded." *Dirks v. SEC,* 463 U.S. 646, 667, n. 27 (1983). Yet today, the Court allows investors to recover who can show little more than that they sold stock at a lower price than what might have been.[51]

I do not propose that the law retreat from the many protections that § 10(b) and Rule 10b–5, as interpreted in our prior cases, provide to investors. But any extension of these laws, to approach something closer to an investor insurance scheme, should come from Congress, and not from the courts.

II

Congress has not passed on the fraud-on-the-market theory the Court embraces today. That is reason enough for us to abstain from doing so. But it is even more troubling that, to the extent that any view of Congress on this question can be inferred indirectly, it is contrary to the result the majority reaches. * * *

[T]he majority's opinion ignores * * * the strong preference the securities laws display for widespread public disclosure and distribution to investors of material information concerning securities. This con-

---

51. [By the Court] This is what the Court's rule boils down to in practical terms. For while, in theory, the Court allows for rebuttal of its "presumption of reliance"—a proviso with which I agree—in practice the Court must realize, as other courts applying the fraud-on-the-market theory have, that such rebuttal is virtually impossible in all but the most extraordinary case.

Consequently, while the Court considers it significant that the fraud-on-the-market presumption it endorses is a rebuttable one, the majority's implicit rejection of the "pure causation" fraud-on-the-market theory rings hollow. In most cases, the Court's theory will operate just as the causation theory would, creating a nonrebuttable presumption of "reliance" in future Rule 10b–5 actions.

gressionally adopted policy is expressed in the numerous and varied disclosure requirements found in the federal securities law scheme.

Yet observers in this field have acknowledged that the fraud-on-the-market theory is at odds with the federal policy favoring disclosure. The conflict between Congress' preference for disclosure and the fraud-on-the-market theory was well expressed by a jurist who rejected the latter in order to give force to the former:

> "[D]isclosure . . . is crucial to the way in which the federal securities laws function. . . . [T]he federal securities laws are intended to put investors into a position from which they can help themselves by relying upon disclosures that others are obligated to make. This system is not furthered by allowing monetary recovery to those who refuse to look out for themselves. If we say that a plaintiff may recover in some circumstances even though he did not read and rely on the defendants' public disclosures, then no one need pay attention to those disclosures and the method employed by Congress to achieve the objective of the 1934 Act is defeated." *Shores v. Sklar,* 647 F.2d, at 483 (Randall, J., dissenting).

It is no surprise, then, that some of the same voices calling for acceptance of the fraud-on-the-market theory also favor dismantling the federal scheme which mandates disclosure. But to the extent that the federal courts must make a choice between preserving effective disclosure and trumpeting the new fraud-on-the-market hypothesis, I think Congress has spoken clearly—favoring the current pro-disclosure policy. We should limit our role in interpreting § 10(b) and Rule 10b–5 to one of giving effect to such policy decisions by Congress.

III

Finally, the particular facts of this case make it an exceedingly poor candidate for the Court's fraud-on-the-market theory, and illustrate the illogic achieved by that theory's application in many cases.

Respondents here are a class of sellers who sold Basic stock between October 1977 and December 1978, a 14–month period. At the time the class period began, Basic's stock was trading at $20 a share (at the time, an all-time high); the last members of the class to sell their Basic stock got a price of just over $30 a share. It is indisputable that virtually every member of the class made money from his or her sale of Basic stock.

The oddities of applying the fraud-on-the-market theory in this case are manifest. First, there are the facts that the plaintiffs are sellers and the class period is so lengthy—both are virtually without precedent in prior fraud-on-the-market cases. * * * [T]hese two facts render this case less apt to application of the fraud-on-the-market hypothesis.

Second, there is the fact that in this case, there is no evidence that petitioner's officials made the troublesome misstatements for the purpose of manipulating stock prices, or with any intent to engage in underhanded trading of Basic stock. Indeed, during the class period, petitioners do not appear to have purchased or sold *any* Basic stock whatsoever. I agree with *amicus* who argues that "[i]mposition of damages liability under Rule 10b–5 makes little sense . . . where a defendant is neither a purchaser nor a seller of securities." In fact, in previous cases, we had recognized that Rule 10b–5 is concerned primarily with cases where the fraud is committed by one trading the security at issue. And it is difficult to square liability in this case with § 10(b)'s express provision that it prohibits fraud "*in connection with* the purchase or sale of any security."

Third, there are the peculiarities of what kinds of investors will be able to recover in this case. As I read the District Court's class certification order, there are potentially many persons who did not purchase Basic stock until *after* the first false statement (October 1977), but who nonetheless *will* be able to recover under the Court's fraud-on-the-market theory. Thus, it is possible that a person who heard the first corporate misstatement and *disbelieved* it—*i.e.*, someone who purchased Basic stock thinking that petitioners' statement was false—may still be included in the plaintiff-class on remand. How a person who undertook such a speculative stock-investing strategy—and made $10 a share doing so (if he bought on October 22, 1977, and sold on December 15, 1978)—can say that he was "defrauded" by virtue of his reliance on the "integrity" of the market price is beyond me.[52] And such speculators may not be uncommon, at least in this case.

Indeed, the facts of this case lead a casual observer to the almost inescapable conclusion that many of those who bought or sold Basic stock during the period in question flatly disbelieved the statements which are alleged to have been "materially misleading." Despite three statements denying that merger negotiations were underway, Basic stock hit record-high after record-high during the 14–month class period. It seems quite possible that, like Casca's knowing disbelief of Caesar's "thrice refusal" of the Crown,[53] clever investors were skeptical of petitioners' three denials that merger talks were going on. Yet such investors, the saviest of the savvy, will be able to recover under the Court's opinion, as long as they now claim that they believed in the "integrity of the market price" when they sold their stock (between September and December 1978). Thus, persons who bought after hearing and relying on the *falsity* of petitioners' statements may be able to prevail and recover money damages on remand.

And who will pay the judgments won in such actions? I suspect that all too often the majority's rule will "lead to large judgments, payable in the last analysis by innocent investors, for the benefit of speculators and their lawyers." Cf. *SEC v. Texas Gulf Sulphur Co.*, 401

---

52. [By the Justice] The Court recognizes that a person who *sold* his Basic shares believing petitioners' statements to be false may not be entitled to recovery. Yet it seems just as clear to me that one who *bought* Basic stock under this same belief—hoping to profit from the uncertainty over Basic's merger plans—should not be permitted to recover either.

53. [By the Justice] See W. Shakespeare, Julius Caesar, Act I, Scene II.

F.2d 833, 867 (CA2 1968) (en banc) (Friendly, J., concurring), cert. denied, 394 U.S. 976 (1969). This Court and others have previously recognized that "inexorably broadening . . . the class of plaintiff[s] who may sue in this area of the law will ultimately result in more harm than good." *Blue Chip Stamps v. Manor Drug Stores, supra,* at 747–748. See also *Ultramares Corp. v. Touche,* 255 N.Y. 170, 179–180, 174 N.E. 441, 444–445 (1931) (Cardozo, C.J.). Yet such a bitter harvest is likely to be reaped from the seeds sewn by the Court's decision today [sic]. * * *

Notes

(1) Two preliminary aspects of this case should be noted: First, Justice Blackmun's opinion is a plurality opinion. Five of the nine sitting Justices did not sign this opinion, either by disqualification or dissent. Second, assuming that the various issues remanded by Justice Blackmun are resolved in favor of the plaintiffs (as seems likely), the defendants may be held liable for damages to all members of a class of plaintiffs who traded in Basic stock over a relatively long period. Depending on the number of members of the class and how damages are computed, the monetary liability of the defendants may be very substantial even though none of them apparently traded in Basic stock or benefitted from the violations. May the defendants who are directors take advantage of Del.Gen.Corp.Law section 102(a)(7), discussed at p. 730 supra?

(2) Carney, The Limits of the Fraud on the Market Doctrine, 44 Bus. Law. 1259, 1265–1266, 1271–1277 (1989): *

> The dissent in *Basic Inc. v. Levinson* expressed concerns over the pitfalls into which some lower courts have fallen "when traditional legal analysis is replaced with economic theorization by the federal courts" which, "with no staff economists, no experts schooled in the 'efficient-capital-market hypothesis,' no ability to test the validity of empirical market studies, . . . are not well equipped to embrace novel constructions of a statute based on contemporary microeconomic theory." The dissent expressed concern that while these theories had the appearance of mathematical exactitude, "they are—in the end—nothing more than theories which may or may not prove accurate upon further consideration."

> These remarks evidence an unwarranted suspicion of the knowledge on which the fraud on the market doctrine is based and of the use of this knowledge, which is only for the purpose of establishing a rebuttable presumption. All of our understanding of cause and effect is built upon observations of events and construction of theories, or hypotheses, to explain relationships between them. The "laws" of physics were not always laws. At one time the relationships now explained by these laws were mysteries to mankind. It took scientists such as Newton to hypothesize that a force called gravity explained certain phenomena in the physical world. Since we cannot observe the

forces themselves, but only the effects of these forces, our explanations, theories, and hypotheses can only be established by determining whether they have explanatory power. The power of the gravity hypothesis has been demonstrated by untold millions of observations that are consistent with the hypothesis. Yet these observations do not "prove" the truth of the gravity hypothesis, in a strict sense; they only corroborate it further. In non-scientific terms, such a thoroughly corroborated explanation of physical forces becomes a law of gravity. But a careful philosopher of science would avoid such usage. In any event, the presumptions about such well established relationships are generally conclusive, in the interest of judicial economy. Disputes about such hypotheses should first be raised in the laboratories and academic journals before the courts need concern themselves with the question of whether the presumption should only be rebuttable.

The Efficient Capital Markets Hypothesis ("ECMH") is a much younger hypothesis than Newton's. Questions remain about the extent to which markets operate efficiently.[54] Nevertheless, ECMH has been described as one of the best established hypotheses in all the social sciences.[55] * * * There is powerful evidence that "open and developed" capital markets operate quickly to reflect new information in security prices. It is also obvious that those prices influence prices paid and received by all traders. If all trading activity blindly relied on the fairness of market prices and nothing more, then an irrebuttable presumption of causation might be appropriate. But because human motives are complex and because traders operate on different information sets, the presumption established in *Basic* is only rebuttable. * * *

There are misunderstandings about what ECMH teaches about prices. The plurality opinion in *Basic* referred to legislative history suggesting that market processes lead to some kind of "fair" or "just" price. Justice White's dissent expressed doubts about expressions of reasonable reliance on the "integrity" of a market price and about statements that investors are entitled to "rely on the price of a stock as a reflection of its value." Justice White also expressed concern that questions of "true value" raise issues more suited to theologians than judges, noting that there are always individuals who decline to sell at

---

54. [By the Author] The market crash of October 1987 raised questions about how stocks could be fairly priced before and after October 19, 1987. One response is that virtually all stocks fell in proportion to their beta factors, thus retaining relative relationships to each other, but that response only avoids the larger issue of whether stocks were fairly priced with respect to other available investments. This is the fundamental criticism of Gordon & Kornhauser, Efficient Markets, Costly Information, and Securities Research, 60 N.Y.U.L.Rev. 761 (1985). * * * The difficulty in responding to arguments that stock prices do not fairly reflect value with respect to all other possible substitutes is that the hypothesis can be neither proved

nor disproved, since the only reliable way of measuring value ex ante is through prices, rather than ex post, through results. The absence of trading rules that allow investors systematically to earn above normal returns from "bargains" suggests the global efficiency of stock prices, even though there may be moments when, in hindsight, it appears that prices did not fairly reflect relative values.

55. [By the Author] Jensen, *The Takeover Controversy: Analysis and Evidence,* 4 Midland Corp.Fin.J., No. 2, at 6, 11 (1986). See also Gilson & Kraakman, The Mechanisms of Market Efficiency, 70 Va.L.Rev. 549, 549–50 (1984) (ECMH has wide acceptance).

the market price because they believe market prices are "inaccurate" reflections of value. The fact that sales occur at all in actively traded securities raises questions about the meaning of market prices. An understanding of what "value" means in this context is critical to understanding why it is reasonable for traders to rely on such prices. In this setting, it is fair to agree with the cynic who described an economist as one who knows the price of everything and the value of nothing, if by value something more than an individual's revealed reservation price is meant.

To say that prices reflect a security's "value" in the context of modern financial economics only means that the price is set in an unbiased manner and reflects a consensus view of its value. If a stock is perceived to be a bargain by a sufficient number of traders, they will proceed to buy it and sell others, until its price is driven up to the point where it is no longer a bargain, relative to other stocks.

Once this equilibrium is reached, a buyer ought to be able to sell any stock for exactly the price paid for it, if no changes take place. The number of traders who believe it is a bargain will be offset by those who think it is overpriced, so that for every willing buyer at that price there will always be a willing seller. Relative prices will change only upon the revelation of new information, which flows constantly and keeps stock prices in a state of flux. Thus a statement that price is "fair" is true at the moment of purchase but is no guarantee that a security will hold its value relative to the market as news about the issuer develops. * * *

The *Basic* plurality opinion not only quoted congressional language concerning market prices as "just" prices but also stated, "An investor who buys or sells stock at the price set by the market does so in reliance on the integrity of that price." Justice White expressed mystification at that remark. The mystification is probably a product of the confusion of the fairness of average stock prices with the fairness of particular stock prices.

Some lower courts have noted the distinction between reliance on the integrity of the market in a stock and reliance on the integrity of the market price of that stock. Relying on prices of particular stocks set by trading on publicly available information by itself provides no assurance that particular prices are honest with respect to real values. Market processes only assure that these prices are honest with respect to the news in the market. If all of the news is fraudulent, so are all of the prices based upon it. The problem of the emperor's new clothes could be universal if fraud were widespread. * * *

For a strong defense of the "fraud on the market" thesis, see Fischel, Use of Modern Finance Theory in Securities Fraud Cases Involving Actively Traded Securities, 38 Bus.Law. 1 (1982). Professors Carney and Fischel are both strongly identified with the "Chicago school" of law and economics. See also Black, Fraud on the Market: A Criticism of Dispensing with Reliance Requirements in Certain Open Market Transactions, 62 N.C.L. Rev. 435 (1984).

(3) The presumption of reliance created by Justice Blackmun greatly simplifies proof of the plaintiff's case, particularly in class actions. One

need only prove falsity, materiality, knowing participation by the defendants, and damages. Of course, the presumption of reliance is rebuttable, with the burden presumably being on the defendants. Assuming that the class of plaintiffs is relatively large—in the hundreds, say—how valuable is this right to rebut the presumption? Do the defendants have to interrogate the plaintiffs individually? Consider also the testimony accepted by the court in the *Abrams* decision (see n. 48 supra). Does that make the defendants' burden even more difficult?

(4) Liability may also be avoided if the defendants can establish that the misrepresented or undisclosed information was not material. The information in this case dealt with merger negotiations; is there any chance at all of the defendants establishing lack of materiality of such an important development? Consider the comments of Judge Easterbrook in Flamm v. Eberstadt, 814 F.2d 1169, 1174 (7th Cir.1987):

> From one perspective this conclusion [that merger negotiations were not material] is simply another cause for wonderment at the legal mind. Investors were looking at potential prices from $11.75 (if Microdot had defeated all bids) to $17 (if General Cable's bid had succeeded) to $21 (under Northwest's bid), and maybe more if a better bid were available. This is almost a 100% range. Only an addlepated investor would consider a 100% difference in price unimportant in deciding what to do.

Does this reasoning make all preliminary merger inquiries at attractive prices material? What about extremely preliminary or tentative inquiries? Might premature disclosure "chill" other possible bidders? If negotiations are disclosed before an agreement in principle is reached, might there be liability to a different class of plaintiffs—those who purchased on the basis of the announcement—if no agreement is ultimately reached? To handle these types of problems, Justice Blackmun substitutes a "fact-specific" inquiry into the significance the reasonable investor would place on the withheld or misrepresented information for the more mechanical "agreement in principle" test adopted by the lower court. Can you see any practical problems with the test applied by Justice Blackmun? Assume you are the general counsel of a corporation that receives a "feeler" from a third party; what do you have the corporation say and when should it say it? See Karjala, A Coherent Approach to Misleading Corporate Announcements, Fraud, and Rule 10b–5, 52 Albany L.Rev. 957, 977 (1989):

> A related potential problem with the materiality approach, especially likely to occur if an affirmative disclosure scheme is adopted, is determining the extent of disclosure necessary for completeness and the frequency of updates required to maintain it. Assuming, under the *Levinson* analysis, that someone inside the company has made a mistake by saying something more than "no comment" to an inquiry, the problem is not solved simply by saying that the company must now make "full disclosure." Even if the company announces, truthfully, that it is negotiating with corporation X concerning a possible merger and that X has been talking in terms of $50 per share while the company is seeking $70, what are the company's obligations when X raises its still tentative offer to $52, or $55 coupled with a more severe

condition on closing or some other new term? When an investment banker calls to say that he or she has a client who is considering offering $60? When a key high-tech engineer informs management that he or she does not want to work for X? There is virtually no end to the number of subsidiary events that can occur during this period that are arguably material. Do we really want to force litigation of these kinds of issues under a fact-specific test that, if properly applied, should almost invariably require a trial?

Given these problems, is not the only sensible approach to say "no comment" in response to all inquiries? And, thus, is not the practical consequence of Justice Blackmun's opinion to choke off rather than improve the flow of information into the market?

(5) What has happened to the scienter requirement of *Hochfelder?*

(6) Is the real problem with litigation of this type the point made by Justice White that one should not impose personal liability on defendants who neither traded nor profited in the securities during the period of the misrepresentation or failure to disclose?

(7) In S.E.C. v. Texas Gulf Sulphur Co., 401 F.2d 833 (2d Cir.1968), cert. denied sub nom. Coates v. S.E.C., 394 U.S. 976, 89 S.Ct. 1454, 22 L.Ed.2d 756 (1969), TGS had made one of the most important mineral discoveries of all time in North America. (The insider trading aspect of this famous case is set forth in the following section.) As rumors of the find spread in the trading markets, TGS, on April 12, 1964, attempted to quell these rumors by issuing the following press release:

New York, April 12—The following statement was made today by Dr. Charles F. Fogarty, executive vice president of Texas Gulf Sulphur Company, in regard to the company's drilling operations near Timmins, Ontario, Canada. Dr. Fogarty said:

"During the past few days, the exploration activities of Texas Gulf Sulphur in the area of Timmins, Ontario, have been widely reported in the press, coupled with rumors of a substantial copper discovery there. These reports exaggerate the scale of operations and mention plans and statistics of size and grade of ore that are without factual basis and have evidently originated by speculation of people not connected with TGS.

"The facts are as follows. TGS has been exploring in the Timmins area for six years as part of its overall search in Canada and elsewhere for various minerals—lead, copper, zinc, etc. During the course of this work, in Timmins as well as in Eastern Canada, TGS has conducted exploration entirely on its own, without the participation by others. Numerous prospects have been investigated by geophysical means and a large number of selected ones have been core-drilled. These cores are sent to the United States for assay and detailed examination as a matter of routine and on advice of expert Canadian legal counsel. No inferences as to grade can be drawn from this procedure.

"Most of the areas drilled in Eastern Canada have revealed either barren pyrite or graphite without value; a few have resulted in discoveries of small or marginal sulphide ore bodies.

"Recent drilling on one property near Timmins has led to preliminary indications that more drilling would be required for proper evaluation of this prospect. The drilling done to date has not been conclusive, but the statements made by many outside quarters are unreliable and include information and figures that are not available to TGS.

"The work done to date has not been sufficient to reach definite conclusions and any statement as to size and grade of ore would be premature and possibly misleading. When we have progressed to the point where reasonable and logical conclusions can be made, TGS will issue a definite statement to its stockholders and to the public in order to clarify the Timmins project."

401 F.2d at 845. A corrective release, describing accurately the magnitude of the find was released four days later. Two separate courts of appeal thereafter independently concluded that the April 12 press release was materially false and misleading, though it appeared that the decision to issue a press release was made with the best of motives and not to influence the market. S.E.C. v. Texas Gulf Sulphur Co., 446 F.2d 1301 (2d Cir.1971), cert. denied 404 U.S. 1004, 92 S.Ct. 561 (1971); Mitchell v. Texas Gulf Sulphur Co., 446 F.2d 90 (10th Cir.1971), cert. denied 404 U.S. 1005, 92 S.Ct. 564, 30 L.Ed.2d 558 (1971). As a result, two plaintiffs who claimed that they had sold on the basis of the misleading April 12 press release were permitted to recover damages from TGS. Damages for each plaintiff were measured as the difference between his selling price and "the amount it would have taken him to invest in the TGS market within a reasonable period of time after he became informed of the April 16 release." 446 F.2d at 105. Damages were based on the highest value of TGS stock during the period beginning Monday, April 20, and ending nine trading days later. Because class certification was denied and the plaintiffs were small investors, the amount of damages awarded in these two cases was modest.

(8) The genesis and background of Rule 10b–5 as described in the leading Supreme Court decisions of the 1970s is that it is an "antifraud" provision. See, for example, Ernst & Ernst v. Hochfelder, p. 961 supra. A rereading of Justice Blackmun's opinion in *Basic* from the beginning of part II of his opinion onward, however, reveals that he has a somewhat different perception of the function of Rule 10b–5. Justice Blackmun emphasizes the "fundamental purpose" of the securities acts as "full disclosure" of material facts. "Antifraud" and "full disclosure" are related but distinguishable concepts. See, for example, Roeder v. Alpha Industries, Inc., 814 F.2d 22 (1st Cir. 1987) [fact that corporation and its managers would probably be indicted for paying a bribe was "material" information for investors but failure to disclose that information was not actionable under Rule 10b–5 since that rule is an antifraud provision and there is no duty to disclose material information in absence of inaccurate, incomplete, or misleading prior disclosures]. Rule 10b–5(b), of course, does refer to an omission "to state a material fact necessary in order to make the statements made, in the light of the circumstances under which they were made, not misleading." That language has been construed to require affirmative disclosure in some limited situations:

(a) Disclosure is required if undisclosed information renders previous public statements by the corporation misleading.

(b) Disclosure is required if the corporation has reason to believe that individuals are engaged in trading in the securities markets on the basis of the information that has not been disclosed.

(c) Disclosure is required if there are rumors swirling through the brokerage community that are generally (though incorrectly) being attributed to the issuer.

On the other hand, one should not make too much of the distinction between "antifraud" and "full disclosure." Registration under section 12 of the 1934 Act carries with it substantial affirmative disclosure obligations. A failure to disclose merger negotiations or other major developments may render statements in these disclosure documents misleading or, equally likely, the affirmative disclosure requirements will themselves require prompt disclosure. For example, in the Roeder case, it is likely that the impending indictments would have to be disclosed in the next public filing in response to Item 103 of Regulation S–K requiring disclosure of material legal proceedings "known to be contemplated by government authorities" with respect to corporate officials. For discussion of the limited obligation to make affirmative disclosures under rule 10b–5 see Symposium, Affirmative Disclosure Obligations under the Securities Laws, 46 Md.L.Rev. 907 (1987), particularly Hazen, Rumor Control and Disclosure of Merger Negotiations or Other Control–Related Transactions: Full Disclosure or "No Comment"—The Only Safe Harbors, id., at 954; Goelzer, Disclosure of Preliminary Merger Negotiations—Truth or Consequences?, id., at 974; and Branson, SEC Nonacquiescence in Judicial Decisionmaking: Target Company Disclosure of Acquisition Negotiations, id., at 1001. All of these articles predate *Basic*.

(9) The only general SEC pronouncement on disclosure policies of publicly held corporations is SEC Rel. 8995, 35 Fed.Reg. 16733 (October 15, 1970), entitled "Timely Disclosure of Material Corporate Developments":

> The Securities and Exchange Commission today reiterated the need for publicly held companies to make prompt and accurate disclosure of information, both favorable and unfavorable, to security holders and the investing public. * * *

> Not only must material facts affecting the company's operations be reported; they must also be reported promptly. Corporate releases which disclose personnel changes, the receipt of new contracts, orders and other favorable developments but do not even suggest existing adverse corporate developments do not serve the public needs and may violate the antifraud provisions of the Securities Exchange Act of 1934, * * *.

> The policy of prompt corporate disclosure of material business events is embodied in the rules and directives of the major exchanges. It should be noted that unless adequate and accurate information is available, a company may not be able to purchase its own securities or make acquisitions using its securities, and its insiders may not be able to trade its securities without running a serious risk of [violating]

section 10(b) of the Securities Exchange Act of 1934 and Rule 10b–5 thereunder.

Corporate managements are urged to review their policies with respect to corporate disclosure and endeavor to set up procedures which will insure that prompt disclosure be made of material corporate developments, both favorable and unfavorable, so that investor confidence can be maintained in an orderly and effective securities market.

(10) New York Stock Exchange Listed Company Manual, §§ 202.03–202.06:

202.03   Dealing With Rumors or Unusual Market Activity

The market activity of a company's securities should be closely watched at a time when consideration is being given to significant corporate matters. If rumors or unusual market activity indicate that information on impending developments has leaked out, a frank and explicit announcement is clearly required. If rumors are in fact false or inaccurate, they should be promptly denied or clarified. A statement to the effect that the company knows of no corporate developments to account for the unusual market activity can have a salutary effect. It is obvious that if such a public statement is contemplated, management should be checked prior to any public comment so as to avoid any embarrassment or potential criticism. If rumors are correct or there are developments, an immediate candid statement to the public as to the state of negotiations or of development of corporate plans in the rumored area must be made directly and openly. Such statements are essential despite the business inconvenience which may be caused and even though the matter may not as yet have been presented to the company's Board of Directors for consideration.

*   *   *

202.04   Exchange Market Surveillance

The Exchange maintains a continuous market surveillance program through its Market Surveillance and Evaluation Division. An "on-line" computer system has been developed which monitors the price movement of every listed stock—on a trade-to-trade basis—throughout the trading session. *   *   * If the price movement of a stock exceeds a predetermined guideline, it is immediately "flagged" and review of the situation is immediately undertaken to seek the causes of the exceptional activity. Under these circumstances, the company may be called by its Exchange representative to inquire about any company developments which have not been publicly announced but which could be responsible for unusual market activity. Where the market appears to reflect undisclosed information, the company will normally be requested to make the information public immediately. Occasionally it may be necessary to carry out a review of the trading after the fact, and the Exchange may request such information from the company as may be necessary to complete the inquiry.

The Listing Agreement provides that a company must furnish the Exchange with such information concerning the company as the Exchange may reasonably require. * * *

202.05 Timely Disclosure of Material News Developments

A listed company is expected to release quickly to the public any news or information which might reasonably be expected to materially affect the market for its securities. This is one of the most important and fundamental purposes of the listing agreement which the company enters into with the Exchange.

A listed company should also act promptly to dispel unfounded rumors which result in unusual market activity or price variations.

202.06 Procedure for Public Release of Information

(A) Immediate Release Policy

The normal method of publication of important corporate data is by means of a press release. This may be either by telephone or in written form. Any release of information that could reasonably be expected to have an impact on the market for a company's securities should be given to the wire services and the press *"For Immediate Release."* * * *

(B) Telephone Alert to the Exchange

When the announcement of news of a material event or a statement dealing with a rumor which calls for immediate release is made shortly before the opening or during market hours (presently 9:30 A.M. to 4:00 P.M., New York time), it is recommended that the company's Exchange representative be notified by telephone at least ten minutes prior to release of the announcement to the news media. If the Exchange receives such notification in time, it will be in a position to consider whether, in the opinion of the Exchange, trading in the security should be temporarily halted. A delay in trading after the appearance of the news on the Dow Jones or Reuters news wires provides a period of calm for public evaluation of the announcement. * * * A longer delay in trading may be necessary if there is an unusual influx of orders. The Exchange attempts to keep such interruptions in the continuous auction market to a minimum. However, where events transpire during market hours, the overall importance of fairness to all those participating in the market demands that these procedures be followed.

(C) Release to Newspapers and News Wire Services

News which ought to be the subject of immediate publicity must be released by the fastest available means. The fastest available means may vary in individual cases and according to the time of day. Ordinarily, this requires a release to the public press by telephone, telegraph, or hand delivery, or some combination of such methods. Transmittal of such a release to the press solely by mail is not considered satisfactory. Similarly, release of such news exclusively to the local press outside of New York City would not be sufficient for adequate and prompt disclosure to the investing public.

To insure adequate coverage, releases requiring immediate publicity should be given to Dow Jones & Company, Inc., and to Reuters Economic Services.

Companies are also encouraged to promptly distribute their releases to Associated Press and United Press International as well as to newspapers in New York City and in cities where the company is headquartered or has plants or other major facilities. * * *

C. INSIDER TRADING

The first statement that trading on the basis of inside information in the anonymous securities markets might violate rule 10b–5 appeared in In the Matter of Cady, Roberts & Co., 40 S.E.C. 907 (1961). This was an administrative proceeding by the Securities and Exchange Commission to discipline a broker who learned from a director of Curtiss–Wright Corporation that Curtiss–Wright planned to reduce its dividend and who then sold Curtiss–Wright common stock (and entered into several short sales of that stock) before the announcement of the dividend cut was made. Chairman Cary's opinion for the Commission broadly stated that insider trading violated rule 10b–5:

> We have already noted that the anti-fraud provisions are phrased in terms of "any person" and that a special obligation has been traditionally required of corporate insiders, e.g., officers, directors and controlling stockholders. These three groups, however, do not exhaust the classes of persons upon whom there is such an obligation. Analytically, the obligation rests on two principal elements; first, the existence of a relationship giving access, directly or indirectly, to information intended to be available only for a corporate purpose and not for the personal benefit of anyone; and second, the inherent unfairness involved where a party takes advantage of such information knowing it is unavailable to those with whom he is dealing. In considering these elements under the broad language of the anti-fraud provisions we are not to be circumscribed by fine distinctions and rigid classifications. Thus our task here is to identify those persons who are in a special relationship with a company and privy to its internal affairs, and thereby suffer correlative duties in trading in its securities. Intimacy demands restraint lest the uninformed be exploited.

40 S.E.C. at 912. Chairman Cary also rejected arguments that an insider's responsibility was limited to existing shareholders and there was no prohibition against selling shares to members of the general public, and that rule 10b–5 was only applicable to face-to-face transactions or cases of misrepresentation or manipulation. "If purchasers on an exchange had available material information known by a selling insider, we may assume that their investment judgment would be affected and their decision whether to buy might accordingly be modi-

fied. Consequently, any sales by the insider must await disclosure of the information." 40 S.E.C. at 914.

CARLTON AND FISCHEL, THE REGULATION OF INSIDER TRADING

35 Stan.L.Rev. 857, 857–858, 866, 868 (1983).

Imagine two firms, A and B, which are identical in all respects except that, in its charter, firm A prohibits the trading of its shares based on inside (nonpublic) information. The firm requires insiders (employees) to report their trades, which a special committee or an independent accounting firm then checks to ensure compliance with the charter provision. Firm B, by contrast, neither prohibits insider trading nor requires reporting. Insiders openly trade shares of firm B and regularly earn positive abnormal returns. In competitive capital markets, which charter provision will survive?

Despite the deceptive simplicity of this question, it has no obvious answer. The consensus, to the extent that any exists, appears to be that firm A's charter will survive because it eliminates various perceived harmful effects of insider trading. Thus, investors would pay less for shares in B. The managers of B, in order to maximize the value of B shares, would have to adopt a similar charter provision.

As for these harmful effects, many believe that insider trading is "unfair" and undermines public confidence in capital markets. Other critics have argued that insider trading creates perverse incentives by allowing corporate managers to profit on bad news as well as good, encourages managers to invest in risky projects, impedes corporate decisionmaking, and tempts managers to delay public disclosure of valuable information. Some also have argued that insider trading is an inefficient compensation scheme because, in effect, it compensates risk-averse managers with a benefit akin to lottery tickets. Still others have claimed that insider trading allows insiders to divert part of the firm's earnings that would otherwise go to shareholders and therefore raises the firm's cost of capital. Under this "insider trading is harmful to investors" hypothesis, competitive capital markets would force firm B to prohibit insider trading.

The difficulty with this hypothesis is that it appears to be contradicted by the actions of firms. Although no one has conducted rigorous empirical research in this area, it is generally believed that firms have made little, if any, attempt to prohibit insider trading, at least until very recently and then perhaps only as a response to regulation. * * * Because unambiguous welfare statements can be very difficult to make even in simple economic models involving uncertainty, to expect any analysis to prove that insider trading is solely harmful or solely beneficial is unrealistic. The desirability of insider trading is ultimately an empirical question. Nevertheless, analyzing how insider trading affects information transmission and shapes incentives will enable us to understand better the consequences of different allocations of the property rights in valuable information.

A. INFORMATION EFFECTS

The social gains from efficient capital markets are well known. The more accurately prices reflect information, the better prices guide capital investment in the economy. * * *

Since the firm's shareholders value the ability to control information that flows to the stock market, they may also value insider trading because it gives the firm an additional method of communicating and controlling information. If insiders trade, the share price will move closer to what it would have been had the information been disclosed. How close will depend on the amount of "noise" surrounding the trade. The greater the ability of market participants to identify insider trading, the more information such trading will convey. * * *

Several reasons explain why communicating information through insider trading may be of value to the firm. Through insider trading, a firm can convey information it could not feasibly announce publicly because an announcement would destroy the value of the information, would be too expensive, not believable, or—owing to the uncertainty of the information—would subject the firm to massive damage liability if it turned out ex post to be incorrect. Conversely, firms also could use insider trading to limit the amount of information to be reflected in price. Controlling the number of traders who have access to information may be easier than controlling how much information gets announced over time. In other words, announcement of information need not be continuous, while trading on inside information can be. Thus, insider trading gives firms a tool either to increase or to decrease the amount of information that is contained in share prices.

Notes

(1) Following similar economic reasoning, the authors also suggest that corporations may prefer to permit insiders to trade on inside information because it "allows a manager to alter his compensation package in light of new knowledge, thereby avoiding continued renegotiation," and it "provides firms with valuable information concerning prospective managers." Id., at 870, 871.

(2) A somewhat earlier study of insider trading, primarily using economic analysis (but also examining the extent of the enforcement effort against such trading during the 1970s), concludes that "the harm caused by insider trading can be objectively measured and that so measured it does not cause any detectable injury to investors." Dooley, Enforcement of Insider Trading Restrictions, 66 Va.L.Rev. 1, 55 (1980). For an argument that some anonymous investor is inevitably harmed by such trading see Wang, Trading on Material Nonpublic Information on Impersonal Stock Markets: Who is Harmed, and Who Can Sue Whom Under SEC Rule 10b–5? 54 S.Cal.L.Rev. 1217 (1981).

(3) Is not all this simply beside the point because trading on inside information—a sure thing—is simply unfair and immoral? Carleton and Fischel respond to this argument as follows:

We have left for last the most common argument against insider trading—that it is unfair or immoral. The prevalence of this intuition is so powerful that many commentators have argued that insider trading should be prohibited even if it is efficient. What is commonly left unsaid is how and why insider trading is unfair.

Kenneth Scott has pointed out that if the existence of insider trading is known, as it surely is, outsiders will not be disadvantaged because the price they pay will reflect the risk of insider trading. This is a useful insight and in some sense is a complete response to the claim that investors are exploited by insider trading. * * *

A more powerful response to the argument that insiders profit at the expense of outsiders is that if insider trading is a desirable compensation scheme, it benefits insiders and outsiders alike. Nobody would argue seriously that salaries, options, bonuses, and other compensation devices allow insiders to profit at the expense of outsiders because these sums otherwise would have gone to shareholders. Compensating managers in this fashion increases the size of the pie, and thus outsiders as well as insiders profit from the incentives managers are given to increase the value of the firm. Insider trading does not come "at the expense of" outsiders for precisely the same reason.

Contrary to popular sentiment with respect to insider trading, therefore, there is no tension between considerations of fairness and of efficiency. To say that insider trading is a desirable method of compensating corporate managers is to say that shareholders would voluntarily enter into contractual arrangements with insiders giving them property rights in valuable information. If insider trading is efficient, no independent notions of fairness suggest that it should be prohibited.

Carlton and Fischel, The Regulation of Insider Trading, 35 Stan.L.Rev. 857, 880–882 (1983).

(4) The first real attack on the wisdom of a broad prohibition against insider trading appeared in a provocative little book by Professor Henry G. Manne entitled "Insider Trading and the Stock Market" (1966). [Professors Carlton and Fischel, incidentally, refer to this book as "brilliant" and state that it is the "starting point for anyone interested in the subject." Carlton and Fischel, The Regulation of Insider Trading, 35 Stan.L.Rev. 857, n. 1 (1983).] Manne also questioned the wisdom of a broad prohibition against insider trading on the basis of economic analysis by considering the theoretical market adjustment mechanisms where insiders were prohibited from trading on inside information and where they were permitted to do so. He concluded that "the odds against any long-term investor's being hurt by an insider trading on undisclosed information is almost infinitesimally small" but that a "rule *allowing* insiders to trade freely may be fundamental to the survival of our corporate system" (Page 110; emphasis added). His argument favoring such trading essentially was that such trading is a useful device to compensate true innovators within the corporation ("entrepreneurs") for their innovations, and that other, more traditional forms of compensation might not adequately do so.

This analysis was attacked (often caustically but not always successfully) in about fifteen book reviews in various law reviews. Professor Manne's riposte appears in Manne, Insider Trading and the Law Professors, 23 Vand. L.Rev. 547 (1970). The final word appears in Ferber, The Case Against Insider Trading: A Response to Professor Manne, 23 Vand.L.Rev. 621 (1970) and Manne, A Rejoinder to Mr. Ferber, 23 Vand.L.Rev. 627 (1970).

1. REGULATION UNDER RULE 10b–5

SECURITIES AND EXCHANGE COMM'N v. TEXAS GULF SULPHUR CO.

United States Court of Appeals, Second Circuit, 1968.
401 F.2d 833, certiorari denied, 394 U.S. 976, 89 S.Ct. 1454,
22 L.Ed.2d 756 (1969).

Before LUMBARD, CHIEF JUDGE, and WATERMAN, MOORE, FRIENDLY, SMITH, KAUFMAN, HAYS, ANDERSON and FEINBERG, CIRCUIT JUDGES.

WATERMAN, CIRCUIT JUDGE:

This action was commenced in the United States District Court for the Southern District of New York by the Securities and Exchange Commission (the SEC) pursuant to Sec. 21(e) of the Securities Exchange Act of 1934 (the Act), against Texas Gulf Sulphur Company (TGS) and several of its officers, directors and employees, to enjoin certain conduct by TGS and the individual defendants said to violate Section 10(b) of the Act, and Rule 10b–5 (the Rule) promulgated thereunder, and to compel the rescission by the individual defendants of securities transactions assertedly conducted contrary to law * * *

THE FACTUAL SETTING

This action derives from the exploratory activities of TGS begun in 1957 on the Canadian Shield in eastern Canada. In March of 1959, aerial geophysical surveys were conducted over more than 15,000 square miles of this area by a group led by defendant Mollison, a mining engineer and a Vice President of TGS. The group included defendant Holyk, TGS's chief geologist, defendant Clayton, an electrical engineer and geophysicist, and defendant Darke, a geologist. These operations resulted in the detection of numerous anomalies, i.e., extraordinary variations in the conductivity of rocks, one of which was on the Kidd 55 segment of land located near Timmins, Ontario.

On October 29 and 30, 1963, Clayton conducted a ground geophysical survey on the northeast portion of the Kidd 55 segment which confirmed the presence of an anomaly and indicated the necessity of diamond core drilling for further evaluation. Drilling of the initial hole, K–55–1, at the strongest part of the anomaly was commenced on November 8, and terminated on November 12 at a depth of 655 feet. Visual estimates by Holyk of the core of K–55–1 indicated an average copper content of 1.15% and an average zinc content of 8.64% over a length of 599 feet. This visual estimate convinced TGS that it was desirable to acquire the remainder of the Kidd 55 segment, and in order to facilitate this acquisition TGS President Stephens instructed the exploration group to keep the results of K–55–1 confidential and undisclosed even as to other officers,

Hamilton, Corps. 4th Ed. ACB—23

directors, and employees of TGS. The hole was concealed and a barren core was intentionally drilled off the anomaly. Meanwhile, the core of K–55–1 had been shipped to Utah for chemical assay which, when received in early December, revealed an average mineral content of 1.18% copper, 8.26% zinc, and 3.94% ounces of silver per ton over a length of 602 feet. These results were so remarkable that neither Clayton, an experienced geophysicist, nor four other TGS expert witnesses, had ever seen or heard of a comparable initial exploratory drill hole in a base metal deposit. So, the trial court concluded, "There is no doubt that the drill core of K–55–1 was unusually good and that it excited the interest and speculation of those who knew about it." [258 F.Supp.,] at 282. By March 27, 1964, TGS decided that the land acquisition program had advanced to such a point that the company might well resume drilling, and drilling was resumed on March 31.

During this period, from November 12, 1963 when K–55–1 was completed, to March 31, 1964 when drilling was resumed, certain of the individual defendants [56] and persons [57] said to have received "tips" from

---

56. [By the Court] The purchases by the parties during this period were:

Purchase		Shares		Calls	
Date	Purchaser	Number	Price	Number	Price

Hole K–55–1 Completed November 12, 1963

1963

Date	Purchaser	Number	Price	Number	Price
Nov. 12	Fogarty	300	$17^3/_4$–18		
15	Clayton	200	$17^3/_4$		
15	Fogarty	700	$17^5/_8$–$17^7/_8$		
15	Mollison	100	$17^7/_8$		
19	Fogarty	500	$18^1/_8$		
26	Fogarty	200	$17^3/_4$		
29	Holyk (Mrs.)	50	18		

Chemical Assays of Drill Core of K–55–1 Received December 9–13, 1963

1963

Date	Purchaser	Number	Price	Number	Price
Dec. 10	Holyk (Mrs.)	100	$20^3/_8$		
12	Holyk (or wife)			200	21
13	Mollison	100	$21^1/_8$		
30	Fogarty	200	22		
31	Fogarty	100	$23^1/_4$		

1964

Date	Purchaser	Number	Price	Number	Price
Jan. 6	Holyk (or wife)			100	$23^5/_8$
8	Murray			400	$23^1/_4$
24	Holyk (or wife)			200	$22^1/_4$–$22^3/_8$
Feb. 10	Fogarty	300	$22^1/_8$–$22^1/_4$		
20	Darke	300	$24^1/_8$		
24	Clayton	400	$23^7/_8$		
24	Holyk (or wife)			200	$24^1/_8$
26	Holyk (or wife)			200	$23^3/_8$
26	Huntington	50	$23^1/_4$		
27	Darke (Moran as nominee)			1000	$22^5/_8$–$22^3/_4$
Mar. 2	Holyk (Mrs.)	200	$22^3/_8$		
3	Clayton	100	$22^1/_4$		
16	Huntington			100	$22^3/_8$

---

57. See note 57 on page 1011.

Purchase		Shares		Calls	
Date	Purchaser	Number	Price	Number	Price
16	Holyk (or wife)			300	23¼
17	Holyk (Mrs.)	100	23⅞		
23	Darke			1000	24¾
26	Clayton	200	25		

Land Acquisition Completed March 27, 1964

Mar. 30	Darke			1000	25½
30	Holyk (Mrs.)	100	25⅞		

Core Drilling of Kidd Segment Resumed March 31, 1964

April 1	Clayton	60	26½		
1	Fogarty	400	26½		
2	Clayton	100	26⅞		
6	Fogarty	400	28⅛–28⅞		
8	Mollison (Mrs.)	100	28⅛		

First Press Release Issued April 12, 1964

April 15	Clayton	200	29⅜		
16	Crawford (and wife)	600	30⅛–30¼		

Second Press Release Issued 10:00–10:10 or 10:15 A.M., April 16, 1964

April 16 (app. 10:20 A.M.)

Coates (for family trusts)	2000	31–31⅝	

57. [By the Court]. The purchases made by "tippees" during this period were:

Purchase		Shares		Calls	
Date	Purchaser	Number	Price	Number	Price

Chemical Assays of K–55–1 Received Dec. 9–13, 1963

1963

Dec. 30	Caskey (Darke)			300	22¼

1964

Jan. 16	Westreich (Darke)	2000	21¼–21¾		
Feb. 17	Atkinson (Darke)	50	23¼	200	23⅛
17	Westreich (Darke)	50	23¼	1000	23¼ 23⅜
24	Miller (Darke)			200	23¾
25	Miller (Darke)			300	23⅜–23½
Mar. 3	E.W. Darke (Darke)			500	22½–22⅝
17	E.W. Darke (Darke)			200	23⅜
Mar. 30	Atkinson (Darke)			400	25¾–25⅞
	Caskey (Darke)	100	25⅞		
	E.W. Darke (Darke)			1000	25¾–25⅞
	Miller (Darke)			200	25½
	Westreich (Darke)	500	25¾		
30–31	Klotz (Darke)			2000	25½–26⅛

Second Press Release Issued April 16, 1964 (Reported over Dow Jones tape at 10:54 A.M.)

April 16 (from 10:31 A.M.)

Haemisegger (Coates)	1500	31¼–35	

In this connection, we point out that, though several of the Holyk purchases of shares and calls made between November 29, 1963 and March 30, 1964 were in the name of Mrs. Holyk or were in the names of both spouses, we have treated these purchases as if made in the name of defendant Holyk alone.

Defendant Mollison purchased 100 shares on November 15 in his name only and on April 8 100 shares were purchased in the name of Mrs. Mollison. We have made no distinction between those purchases.

Defendant Crawford ordered 300 shares about midnight on April 15 and 300 more shares the following morning, to be purchased for himself, and his wife, and these purchases are treated as having been made by the defendant Crawford.

them, purchased TGS stock or calls [58] thereon. Prior to these transactions these persons had owned 1135 shares of TGS stock and possessed no calls; thereafter they owned a total of 8235 shares and possessed 12,300 calls.

On February 20, 1964, also during this period, TGS issued stock options to 26 of its officers and employees whose salaries exceeded a specified amount, five of whom were the individual defendants Stephens, Fogarty, Mollison, Holyk, and Kline. Of these, only Kline was unaware of the detailed results of K–55–1, but he, too, knew that a hole containing favorable bodies of copper and zinc ore had been drilled in Timmins. At this time, neither the TGS Stock Option Committee nor its Board of Directors had been informed of the results of K–55–1, presumably because of the pending land acquisition program which required confidentiality. All of the foregoing defendants accepted the options granted them. * * *

[Editor: Texas Gulf had discovered one of the largest copper/zinc deposits in North America. As drilling explorations continued at the site to determine the size of the deposit, Texas Gulf also sought to acquire land or mineral rights in the area. Rumors leaked out that Texas Gulf had made a major mineral discovery. On April 12, Texas Gulf issued the press release quoted in the previous section, downplaying the importance of the exploration activity, but issued a corrective release four days later confirming the scope of the discovery.]

During the period of drilling in Timmins, the market price of TGS stock fluctuated but steadily gained overall. On Friday, November 8, when the drilling began, the stock closed at 17⅜; on Friday, November 15, after K–55–1 had been completed, it closed at 18. After a slight decline to 16⅜ by Friday, November 22, the price rose to 20⅞ by December 13, when the chemical assay results of K–55–1 were received, and closed at a high of 24⅛ on February 21, the day after the stock options had been issued. It had reached a price of 26 by March 31, after the land acquisition program had been completed and drilling had been resumed, and continued to ascend to 30⅛ by the close of trading on April 10, at which time the drilling progress up to then was evaluated for the April 12th press release. On April 13, the day on which the April 12 release was disseminated, TGS opened at 30⅛, rose immediately to a high of 32 and gradually tapered off to close at 30⅞. It closed at 30¼ the next day, and at 29⅜ on April 15. On April 16, the day of the official announcement of the Timmins discovery, the price climbed to a high of 37 and closed at 36⅜. By May 15, TGS stock was selling at 58¼.

In these particulars we have followed the lead of the court below. * * * It would be unrealistic to include any of these purchases as having been made by other than the defendants, and unrealistic to include them as having been made by members of the general public receiving "tips" from insiders.

58. [By the Court] A "call" is a negotiable option contract by which the bearer has the right to buy from the writer of the contract a certain number of shares of a particular stock at a fixed price on or before a certain agreed-upon date.

I. THE INDIVIDUAL DEFENDANTS

A. *Introductory*

Rule 10b–5, on which this action is predicated, * * * was promulgated * * * to prevent inequitable and unfair practices and to insure fairness in securities transactions generally, whether conducted face-to-face, over the counter, or on exchanges, see 3 Loss, Securities Regulation 1455–56 (2d ed. 1961). The Act and the Rule apply to the transactions here, all of which were consummated on exchanges. Whether predicated on traditional fiduciary concepts, see, e.g., Hotchkiss v. Fisher, 136 Kan. 530, 16 P.2d 531 (Kan.1932), or on the "special facts" doctrine, see, e.g., Strong v. Repide, 213 U.S. 419, 29 S.Ct. 521, 53 L.Ed. 853 (1909), the Rule is based in policy on the justifiable expectation of the securities marketplace that all investors trading on impersonal exchanges have relatively equal access to material information. The essence of the Rule is that anyone who, trading for his own account in the securities of a corporation has "access, directly or indirectly, to information intended to be available only for a corporate purpose and not for the personal benefit of anyone" may not take "advantage of such information knowing it is unavailable to those with whom he is dealing," i.e., the investing public. Matter of Cady, Roberts & Co., 40 SEC 907, 912 (1961). Insiders, as directors or management officers are, of course, by this Rule, precluded from so unfairly dealing, but the Rule is also applicable to one possessing the information who may not be strictly termed an "insider" within the meaning of Sec. 16(b) of the Act. Thus, anyone in possession of material inside information must either disclose it to the investing public, or if he is disabled from disclosing it in order to protect a corporate confidence, or he chooses not to do so, must abstain from trading in or recommending the securities concerned while such inside information remains undisclosed. So, it is here no justification for insider activity that disclosure was forbidden by the legitimate corporate objective of acquiring options to purchase the land surrounding the exploration site; if the information was, as the SEC contends, material,[59] its possessors should have kept out of the market until disclosure was accomplished. Cady, Roberts, supra at 911.

B. *Material Inside Information*

[Editor: The court concludes that K–55–1 constituted "material" information, an issue now controlled by the test of TSC Industries v. Northway, supra. In the course of this discussion the court included observations about insider trading that are relevant today:]

An insider is not, of course, always foreclosed from investing in his own company merely because he may be more familiar with company operations than are outside investors. An insider's duty to disclose information or his duty to abstain from dealing in his company's

---

59. [By the Court] Congress intended by the Exchange Act to eliminate the idea that the use of inside information for personal advantage was a normal emolument of corporate office. See Sections 2 and 16 of the Act.

securities arises only in "those situations which are essentially extraordinary in nature and which are reasonably certain to have a substantial effect on the market price of the security if [the extraordinary situation is] disclosed." Fleischer, Securities Trading and Corporate Information Practices: The Implications of the Texas Gulf Sulphur Proceeding, 51 Va.L.Rev. 1271, 1289.

Nor is an insider obligated to confer upon outside investors the benefit of his superior financial or other expert analysis by disclosing his educated guesses or predictions. 3 Loss, op. cit. supra at 1463. The only regulatory objective is that access to material information be enjoyed equally, but this objective requires nothing more than the disclosure of basic facts so that outsiders may draw upon their own evaluative expertise in reaching their own investment decisions with knowledge equal to that of the insiders. * * *

The speculators and chartists of Wall and Bay Streets are also "reasonable" investors entitled to the same legal protection afforded conservative traders. * * *

Our survey of the facts found below conclusively establishes that knowledge of the results of the discovery hole, K–55–1, would have been important to a reasonable investor and might have affected the price of the stock.[60] * * *

[A] major factor in determining whether the K–55–1 discovery was a material fact is the importance attached to the drilling results by those who knew about it. In view of other unrelated recent developments favorably affecting TGS, participation by an informed person in a regular stock-purchase program, or even sporadic trading by an informed person, might lend only nominal support to the inference of the materiality of the K–55–1 discovery; nevertheless, the timing by those who knew [of their stock purchases] and their purchases of *short-term calls* —purchases in some cases by individuals who had never before purchased calls or even TGS stock—virtually compels the inference that the insiders were influenced by the drilling results. This insider trading activity, * * * surely constitutes highly pertinent evidence and the only truly objective evidence of the materiality of the K–55–1 discovery. * * *

Our decision to expand the limited protection afforded outside investors * * * is not at all shaken by fears that the elimination of insider trading benefits will deplete the ranks of capable corporate

---

60. [By the Court] We do not suggest that material facts must be disclosed immediately; the timing of disclosure is a matter for the business judgment of the corporate officers entrusted with the management of the corporation within the affirmative disclosure requirements promulgated by the exchanges and by the SEC. Here, a valuable corporate purpose was served by delaying the publication of the K–55–1 discovery. We do intend to con-vey, however, that where a corporate purpose is thus served by withholding the news of a material fact, those persons who are thus quite properly true to their corporate trust must not during the period of non-disclosure deal personally in the corporation's securities or give to outsiders confidential information not generally available to all the corporations' stockholders and to the public at large.

managers by taking away an incentive to accept such employment. Such benefits, in essence, are forms of secret corporate compensation, see Cary, Corporate Standards and Legal Rules, 50 Calif.L.Rev. 408, 409–10 (1962), derived at the expense of the uninformed investing public and not at the expense of the corporation which receives the sole benefit from insider incentives. Moreover, adequate incentives for corporate officers may be provided by properly administered stock options and employee purchase plans of which there are many in existence. In any event, the normal motivation induced by stock ownership, i.e., the identification of an individual with corporate progress, is ill-promoted by condoning the sort of speculative insider activity which occurred here; for example, some of the corporation's stock was sold at market in order to purchase short-term calls upon that stock, calls which would never be exercised to increase a stockholder equity in TGS unless the market price of that stock rose sharply.

The core of Rule 10b–5 is the implementation of the Congressional purpose that all investors should have equal access to the rewards of participation in securities transactions. It was the intent of Congress that all members of the investing public should be subject to identical market risks,—which market risks include, of course, the risk that one's evaluative capacity or one's capital available to put at risk may exceed another's capacity or capital. The insiders here were not trading on an equal footing with the outside investors. They alone were in a position to evaluate the probability and magnitude of what seemed from the outset to be a major ore strike; they alone could invest safely, secure in the expectation that the price of TGS stock would rise substantially in the event such a major strike should materialize, but would decline little, if at all, in the event of failure, for the public, ignorant at the outset of the favorable probabilities would likewise be unaware of the unproductive exploration, and the additional exploration costs would not significantly affect TGS market prices. Such inequities based upon unequal access to knowledge should not be shrugged off as inevitable in our way of life, or in view of the congressional concern in the area, remain uncorrected.

We hold, therefore, that all transactions in TGS stock or calls by individuals apprised of the drilling results of K–55–1 were made in violation of Rule 10b–5. Inasmuch as the visual evaluation of that drill core (a generally reliable estimate though less accurate than a chemical assay) constituted material information, those advised of the results of the visual evaluation as well as those informed of the chemical assay traded in violation of law. The geologist Darke possessed undisclosed material information and traded in TGS securities. Therefore we reverse the dismissal of the action as to him and his personal transactions. The trial court also found that Darke, after the drilling of K–55–1 had been completed and with detailed knowledge of the results thereof, told certain outside individuals that TGS "was a good buy." These individuals thereafter acquired TGS stock and calls. The trial court also found that later, as of March 30, 1964, Darke not only used his material knowledge for his own purchases but that the substantial amounts of TGS stock and calls purchased by these outside individuals on that day, was "strong circumstantial evidence that Darke must have passed the word to one or more of his 'tippees' that drilling on the Kidd 55 segment was about to be resumed." 258 F.Supp. at 284. Obviously if such a resumption were to have any meaning to such "tippees," they must have previously been told of K–55–1.

Unfortunately, however, there was no definitive resolution below of Darke's liability in these premises for the trial court held as to him, as it held as to all the other individual defendants, that this "undisclosed information" never became material until April 9. As it is our holding that the information acquired after the drilling of K–55–1 was material, we, on the basis of the findings of direct and circumstantial evidence on the issue that the trial court has already expressed, hold that Darke violated Rule 10b–5(3) and Section 10(b) by "tipping" and we remand, pursuant to the agreement of the parties, for a determination of the appropriate remedy. As Darke's "tippees" are not defendants in this action, we need not decide whether, if they acted with actual or constructive knowledge that the material information was undisclosed, their conduct is as equally violative of the Rule as the conduct of their insider source, though we note that it certainly could be equally reprehensible. * * *

C. When May Insiders Act?

Appellant Crawford, who ordered [61] the purchase of TGS stock shortly before the TGS April 16 official announcement, and defendant Coates, who placed orders with and communicated the news to his broker immediately after the official announcement was read at the TGS-called press conference, concede that they were in possession of material information. They contend, however, that their purchases were not proscribed purchases for the news had already been effectively disclosed. We disagree.

Crawford telephoned his orders to his Chicago broker about midnight on April 15 and again at 8:30 in the morning of the 16th, with instructions to buy at the opening of the Midwest Stock Exchange that morning. The trial court's finding that "he sought to, and did, 'beat the news,'" 258 F.Supp. at 287, is well documented by the record. The rumors of a major ore strike which had been circulated in Canada and, to a lesser extent, in New York, had been disclaimed by the TGS press

---

61. [By the Court] The effective protection of the public from insider exploitation of advance notice of material information requires that the time that an insider places an order, rather than the time of its ultimate execution, be determinative for Rule 10b–5 purposes. Otherwise, insiders would be able to "beat the news," cf. Fleischer, supra, 51 Va.L.Rev. at 1291, by requesting in advance that their orders be executed immediately after the dissemina-

tion of a major news release but before outsiders could act on the release. Thus it is immaterial whether Crawford's orders were executed before or after the announcement was made in Canada (9:40 A.M., April 16) or in the United States (10:00 A.M.) or whether Coates's order was executed before or after the news appeared over the Merrill Lynch (10:29 A.M.) or Dow Jones (10:54 A.M.) wires.

release of April 12, which significantly promised the public an official detailed announcement when possibilities had ripened into actualities. The abbreviated announcement to the Canadian press at 9:40 A.M. on the 16th by the Ontario Minister of Mines and the report carried by The Northern Miner, parts of which had sporadically reached New York on the morning of the 16th through reports from Canadian affiliates to a few New York investment firms, are assuredly not the equivalent of the official 10–15 minute announcement which was not released to the American financial press until after 10:00 A.M. Crawford's orders had been placed before that. Before insiders may act upon material information, such information must have been effectively disclosed in a manner sufficient to insure its availability to the investing public. Particularly here, where a formal announcement to the entire financial news media had been promised in a prior official release known to the media, all insider activity must await dissemination of the promised official announcement.

Coates was absolved by the court below because his telephone order was placed shortly before 10:20 A.M. on April 16, which was after the announcement had been made even though the news could not be considered already a matter of public information. This result seems to have been predicated upon a misinterpretation of dicta in *Cady, Roberts,* where the SEC instructed insiders to "keep out of the market until the established procedures for public release of the information are *carried out* instead of hastening to execute transactions in advance of, and in frustration of, the objectives of the release," 40 SEC at 915 (emphasis supplied). This reading of a news release, which prompted Coates into action, is merely the first step in the process of dissemination required for compliance with the regulatory objective of providing all investors with an equal opportunity to make informed investment judgments. Assuming that the contents of the official release could instantaneously be acted upon,[62] at the minimum Coates should have waited until the news could reasonably have been expected to appear over the media of widest circulation, the Dow Jones broad tape, rather than hastening to insure an advantage to himself and his broker son-in-law.[63] * * *

62. [By the Court] Although the only insider who acted after the news appeared over the Dow Jones broad tape is not an appellant and therefore we need not discuss the necessity of considering the advisability of a "reasonable waiting period" during which outsiders may absorb and evaluate disclosures, we note in passing that, where the news is of a sort which is not readily translatable into investment action, insiders may not take advantage of their advance opportunity to evaluate the information by acting immediately upon dissemination. In any event, the permissible timing of insider transactions after disclosures of various sorts is one of the many

areas of expertise for appropriate exercise of the SEC's rulemaking power, which we hope will be utilized in the future to provide some predictability of certainty for the business community.

63. [By the Court] The record reveals that news usually appears on the Dow Jones broad tape 2–3 minutes after the reporter completes dictation.

Here, assuming that the Dow Jones reporter left the press conference as early as possible, 10:10 A.M., the 10–15 minute release (which took at least that long to dictate) could not have appeared on the wire before 10:22, and for other reasons

E.   May Insiders Accept Stock Options Without Disclosing Material Information To The Issuer?

On February 20, 1964, defendants Stephens, Fogarty, Mollison, Holyk and Kline accepted stock options issued to them and a number of other top officers of TGS, although not one of them had informed the Stock Option Committee of the Board of Directors or the Board of the results of K–55–1, which information we have held was then material. The SEC sought rescission of these options.   The trial court, in addition to finding the knowledge of the results of the K–55 discovery to be immaterial, held that Kline had no detailed knowledge of the drilling progress and that Holyk and Mollison could reasonably assume that their superiors, Stephens and Fogarty, who were directors of the corporation, would report the results if that was advisable; indeed all employees had been instructed not to divulge this information pending completion of the land acquisition program.   Therefore, the court below concluded that only directors Stephens and Fogarty, of the top management, would have violated the Rule by accepting stock options without disclosure, but it also found that they had not acted improperly as the information in their possession was not material.   In view of our conclusion as to materiality we hold that Stephens and Fogarty violated the Rule by accepting them.   However, as they have surrendered the options and the corporation has canceled them, we find it unnecessary to order that the injunctions prayed for be actually issued.   We point out, nevertheless, that the surrender of these options after the SEC commenced the case is not a satisfaction of the SEC claim, and a determination as to whether the issuance of injunctions against Stephens and Fogarty is advisable in order to prevent or deter future violations of regulatory provisions is remanded for the exercise of discretion by the trial court.

Contrary to the belief of the trial court that Kline had no duty to disclose his knowledge of the Kidd project before accepting the stock option offered him, we believe that he, a vice president, who had become the general counsel of TGS in January 1964, but who had been secretary of the corporation since January 1961, and was present in that capacity when the options were granted, and who was in charge of the mechanics of issuance and acceptance of the options, was a member of top management and under a duty before accepting his option to disclose any material information he may have possessed, and, as he did not disclose such information to the Option Committee we direct rescission of the option he received.[64]   As to Holyk and Mollison, the

unknown to us did not appear until 10:54. Indeed, even the abbreviated version of the release reported by Merrill Lynch over its private wire did not appear until 10:29. Coates, however, placed his call no later than 10:20.

64.   [By the Court] The options granted on February 20, 1964 to Mollison, Holyk, and Kline were ratified by the Texas Gulf directors on July 15, 1965 after there had been, of course, a full disclosure and after this action had been commenced. However, the ratification is irrelevant here, for we would hold with the district court that a member of top management, as was Kline, is required, before accepting a stock option, to disclose material inside information which, if disclosed, might affect the

SEC has not appealed the holding below that they, not being then members of top management (although Mollison was a vice president) had no duty to disclose their knowledge of the drilling before accepting their options. Therefore, the issue of whether, by accepting, they violated the Act, is not before us, and the holding below is undisturbed.

* * *

CONCLUSION

In summary, therefore, we affirm the finding of the court below that appellants Richard H. Clayton and David M. Crawford have violated 15 U.S.C.A. § 78j(b) and Rule 10b–5; we reverse the judgment order entered below dismissing the complaint against appellees Charles F. Fogarty, Richard H. Clayton, Richard D. Mollison, Walter Holyk, Kenneth H. Darke, Earl L. Huntington, and Francis G. Coates, as we find that they have violated 15 U.S.C.A. § 78j(b) and Rule 10b–5. As to these eight individuals we remand so that in accordance with the agreement between the parties the Commission may notice a hearing before the court below to determine the remedies to be applied against them. We reverse the judgment order dismissing the complaint against Claude O. Stephens, Charles F. Fogarty, and Harold B. Kline as recipients of stock options, direct the district court to consider in its discretion whether to issue injunction orders against Stephens and Fogarty, and direct that an order issue rescinding the option granted Kline and that such further remedy be applied against him as may be proper by way of an order of restitution. * * *

FRIENDLY, CIRCUIT JUDGE (concurring):

Agreeing with the result reached by the majority and with most of Judge Waterman's searching opinion, I take a rather different approach to two facets of the case.

I.

The first is a situation that will not often arise, involving as it does the acceptance of stock options during a period when inside information likely to produce a rapid and substantial increase in the price of the stock was known to some of the grantees but unknown to those in

price of the stock during the period when the accepted option could be exercised. Kline had known since November 1962 that K–55–1 had been drilled, that the drilling had intersected a sulphide body containing copper and zinc, and that TGS desired to acquire adjacent property.

Of course, if any of the five knowledgeable defendants had rejected his option there might well have been speculation as to the reason for the rejection. Therefore, in a case where disclosure to the grantors of an option would seriously jeopardize corporate security, it could well be desirable, in order to protect a corporation from selling securities to insiders who are in a posi-

tion to appreciate their true worth at a price which may not accurately reflect the true value of the securities and at the same time to preserve when necessary the secrecy of corporate activity, not to require that an insider possessed of undisclosed material information reject the offer of a stock option, but only to require that he abstain from exercising it until such time as there shall have been a full disclosure and, after the full disclosure, a ratification such as was voted here. However, as this suggestion was not presented to us, we do not consider it or make any determination with reference to it.

charge of the granting. I suppose it would be clear, under Ruckle v. Roto American Corp., 339 F.2d 24 (2 Cir.1964),[65] that if a corporate officer having such knowledge persuaded an unknowing board of directors to grant him an option at a price approximating the current market, the option would be rescindable in an action under Rule 10b–5. It would seem, by the same token, that if, to make the pill easier to swallow, he urged the directors to include others lacking the knowledge he possessed, he would be liable for all the resulting damage. The novel problem in the instant case is to define the responsibility of officers when a directors' committee administering a stock option plan proposes of its own initiative to make options available to them and others at a time when they know that the option price, geared to the market value of the stock, did not reflect a substantial increment likely to be realized in short order and was therefore unfair to the corporation.

A rule requiring a minor officer to reject an option so tendered would not comport with the realities either of human nature or of corporate life. If the SEC had appealed the ruling dismissing this portion of the complaint as to Holyk and Mollison, I would have upheld the dismissal quite apart from the special circumstance that a refusal on their part could well have broken the wall of secrecy it was important for TGS to preserve. Whatever they knew or didn't know about Timmins, they were entitled to believe their superiors had reported the facts to the Option Committee unless they had information to the contrary. Stephens, Fogarty and Kline stand on an altogether different basis; as senior officers they had an obligation to inform the Committee that this was not the right time to grant options at 95% of the current price. Silence, when there is a duty to speak, can itself be a fraud. I am unimpressed with the argument that Stephens, Fogarty and Kline could not perform this duty on the peculiar facts of this case, because of the corporate need for secrecy during the land acquisition program. Non-management directors would not normally challenge a recommendation for postponement of an option plan from the President, the Executive Vice President, and the Vice President and General Counsel. Moreover, it should be possible for officers to communicate with directors, of all people, without fearing a breach of confidence. Hence, as one of the foregoing hypotheticals suggests, I am not at all sure that a company in the position of TGS might not have a claim against top officers who breached their duty of disclosure for the entire damage suffered as a result of the untimely issuance of options, rather than merely one for rescission of the options issued to them.[66] Since

---

65. [By the Judge] * * * If we were writing on a clean slate, I would have some doubt whether the framers of the Securities Exchange Act intended § 10b to provide a remedy for an evil that had long been effectively handled by derivative actions for waste of corporate assets under state law simply because in a particular case the waste took the form of a sale of securities. * * *

66. [By the Judge] Though the Board of Directors of TGS ratified the issuance of the options after the Timmins discovery had been fully publicized, it obviously was of the belief that Kline had committed no serious wrong in remaining silent.

that issue is not before us, I merely make the reservation of my position clear. * * *

[The second issue discussed by Judge Friendly dealt with the April 12 press release.]

[Concurring opinions of JUDGES IRVING R. KAUFMAN, HAYS, and ANDERSON, and dissenting opinion of JUDGE MOORE (with whom CHIEF JUDGE LUMBARD concurs) are omitted.]

Notes

(1) On remand, the district court (1) enjoined defendants Clayton and Crawford from future violations of rule 10b–5, (2) denied injunctions against defendants Fogarty, Mollison, Stephens, Darke, Huntington, Holyk, and Kline although each was found to have violated 10b–5, (3) required Darke to pay to TGS the profits which he and his tippees made on TGS stock prior to April 17, 1964, (4) required Holyk, Huntington, and Clayton to pay to TGS the profits which each of them made on the TGS stock prior to April 17, 1964, and (5) required Kline's stock option to be canceled. The order stated that the payments were to be held in escrow in an interest-bearing account for a period of five years, subject to disposition in such manner as the court might direct upon application by the SEC or other interested person, or on the court's own motion. At the end of the five years any money remaining undisposed of would become the property of TGS. To protect the defendants against double liability, any private judgments against these defendants arising out of the events of this case were to be paid from this fund. This order was affirmed in its entirety by a panel consisting of Judges Friendly, Waterman and Hays. 446 F.2d 1301 (2d Cir.1971), cert. denied 404 U.S. 1005, 92 S.Ct. 561, 30 L.Ed.2d 558 (1971). The court specifically rejected the argument that the required restitution constituted a penalty:

> Restitution of the profits on these transactions merely deprives the appellants of the gains of their wrongful conduct. Nor does restitution impose a hardship in this case. The lowest purchase price of any of the transactions here was $17.75 per share paid by Clayton on November 15, 1963. The mean average price of the stock on April 17, 1964, has been stipulated by the parties to be $40.375 per share. By May 15, 1964, the stock was selling at $58.25 per share. The court's order requires only restitution of the profits made by the violators prior to general knowledge of the ore strike on April 17, 1964, and, in effect, leaves the appellants all the profits accrued after that date. It would severely defeat the purposes of the Act if a violator of Rule 10b–5 were allowed to retain the profits from his violation. The district court's

Throughout this litigation TGS has supported the legality of the actions of all the defendants—the company's counsel having represented, among others, Stephens, Fogarty and Kline. Consequently, I agree with the majority in giving the Board's action no weight here. If a fraud of this kind may ever be cured by ratification, compare Continental Securities Co. v. Belmont, 206 N.Y. 7, 99 N.E. 138, 51 L.R.A., N.S., 112 (1912), with Claman v. Robertson, 164 Ohio St. 61, 128 N.E.2d 429 (1955); that cannot be done without an appreciation of the illegality of the conduct proposed to be excused.

order corrects this by effectively moving the purchase dates of the violators' purchases up to April 17, 1964.

> As to the requirement that Darke make restitution for the profits derived by his tippees, admittedly more of a hardship is imposed. However, without such a remedy, insiders could easily evade their duty to refrain from trading on the basis of inside information. Either the transactions so traded could be concluded by a relative or an acquaintance of the insider, or implied understandings could arise under which reciprocal tips between insiders in different corporations could be given.

446 F.2d at 1308.

On what basis did the court conclude that Clayton and Crawford should be enjoined but that the other defendants should not even though all of them violated rule 10b–5? Are the defendants who violated rule 10b–5 but who were not enjoined in any different legal position as a result of this litigation than the persons who traded in TGS stock on the basis of inside information and who were referred to by name in the SEC's complaint but not made defendants?

Later cases recognize that full "disgorgement" or restitution may be sought from tippees as well as from insiders themselves. See e.g. S.E.C. v. Lund, 570 F.Supp. 1397 (C.D.Cal.1983). Presumably, Darke's tippees could have been required to restore the profits they made if they had been named as parties in the original suit by the Securities and Exchange Commission.

(2) Assume that you are the general counsel of a large corporation such as TGS. It seems desirable to issue a memorandum periodically reminding insiders of potential liability under rule 10b–5, and suggesting trading strategies that eliminate or minimize potential liability. Would you recommend a flat prohibition against all purchases or sales of stock by insiders? Isn't it desirable to encourage such persons to invest in the corporation? What kind of trading strategy might you recommend? The New York Stock Exchange Listed Company Manual § 309.00, discusses this problem and offers the following analysis:

> Shareholders have indicated however that they want directors and officers to have a meaningful investment in the companies they manage. So, in the interest of promoting better shareholder relationships, some general rules under which corporate officials may properly buy or sell stock in their company may be helpful. One appropriate method of purchase might be a periodic investment program where the directors or officers make regular purchases under an established program administered by a broker and where the timing of purchases is outside the control of the individual. It would also seem appropriate for officials to buy or sell stock in their companies for a 30–day period commencing one week after the annual report has been mailed to shareholders and otherwise broadly circulated (provided, of course, that the annual report has adequately covered important corporate developments and that no new major undisclosed developments occur within that period).

Transactions may also be appropriate under the following circumstances, provided that prior to making a purchase or sale a director or officer contacts the chief executive officer of the company to be sure there are no important developments pending which need to be made public before an insider could properly participate in the market:

- Following a release of quarterly results, which includes adequate comment on new developments during the period. This timing of transactions might be even more appropriate where the report has been mailed to shareholders.

- Following the wide dissemination of information on the status of the company and current results. For example, transactions may be appropriate after a proxy statement or prospectus which gives such information in connection with a merger or new financing.

- At those times when there is relative stability in the company's operations and the market for its securities. Under these circumstances, timing of transactions may be relatively less important. Of course such periods of relative stability will vary greatly from time to time and will also depend to a large extent on the nature of the industry or the company.

Where a development of major importance is expected to reach the appropriate time for announcement within the next few months, transactions by directors and officers should be avoided.

Corporate officials should wait until after the release of earnings, dividends, or other important developments have appeared in the press before making a purchase or sale. This permits the news to be widely disseminated and negates the inference that officials had an inside advantage. Similarly, transactions just prior to important press releases should be avoided.

In granting stock options to directors and key officers, the same philosophy that relates to purchases and sales may well apply. Where an established pattern or formula is part of a plan specifically approved by shareholders, the question of timing may not arise. In taking up an option, the timing of a purchase is not usually critical as the price is set at the time the option is granted. The reasoning relating to stock options might also apply to employee stock purchase plans in which directors and officers may be entitled to participate.

The considerations that affect director and officer transactions in stock of their own company may be pertinent to transactions in the shares of other companies with which discussions of merger, acquisition, important contracts, etc., are being considered or carried on. The same considerations apply to the families or close associates of directors and officers who are often presumed to have preferential access to information. As far as the public is concerned, they also are insiders. While this assumption may be unjustified in many cases, it is a fact of life which those in positions of leadership and responsibility cannot ignore.

Some companies have adopted policies for the guidance of their personnel relating to transactions in the company's stock, as well as other areas where conflicts of interest could arise. Such policies can be very helpful to employees who have access to important confidential information, as well as to the directors and officers.

In the final analysis, directors and officers must be guided by a sense of fairness to all segments of the investing public. * * *

CHIARELLA v. UNITED STATES

Supreme Court of the United States, 1980.
445 U.S. 222, 100 S.Ct. 1108, 63 L.Ed.2d 348.

MR. JUSTICE POWELL delivered the opinion of the Court.

The question in this case is whether a person who learns from the confidential documents of one corporation that it is planning an attempt to secure control of a second corporation violates § 10(b) of the Securities Exchange Act of 1934 if he fails to disclose the impending takeover before trading in the target company's securities.

I

Petitioner is a printer by trade. In 1975 and 1976, he worked as a "markup man" in the New York composing room of Pandick Press, a financial printer. Among documents that petitioner handled were five announcements of corporate takeover bids. When these documents were delivered to the printer, the identities of the acquiring and target corporations were concealed by blank spaces or false names. The true names were sent to the printer on the night of the final printing.

The petitioner, however, was able to deduce the names of the target companies before the final printing from other information contained in the documents. Without disclosing his knowledge, petitioner purchased stock in the target companies and sold the shares immediately after the takeover attempts were made public. By this method, petitioner realized a gain of slightly more than $30,000 in the course of 14 months. Subsequently, the Securities and Exchange Commission (Commission or SEC) began an investigation of his trading activities. In May 1977, petitioner entered into a consent decree with the Commission in which he agreed to return his profits to the sellers of the shares. On the same day, he was discharged by Pandick Press.

In January 1978, petitioner was indicted on 17 counts of violating § 10(b) of the Securities Exchange Act of 1934 (1934 Act) and SEC Rule 10b–5.[67] After petitioner unsuccessfully moved to dismiss the indictment, he was brought to trial and convicted on all counts.

The Court of Appeals for the Second Circuit affirmed petitioner's conviction. 588 F.2d 1358 (1978). We granted certiorari, 441 U.S. 942, 99 S.Ct. 2158, 60 L.Ed.2d 1043 (1979), and we now reverse.

---

67. [By the Court] Only Rules 10b–5(a) and (c) are at issue here. Rule 10b–5(b) provides that it shall be unlawful "[t]o make any untrue statement of a material fact or to omit to state a material fact necessary in order to make the statements made, in the light of the circumstances under which they were made, not misleading." The portion of the indictment based on this provision was dismissed because the petitioner made no statements at all in connection with the purchase of stock.

II

* * * This case concerns the legal effect of the petitioner's silence. The District Court's charge permitted the jury to convict the petitioner if it found that he willfully failed to inform sellers of target company securities that he knew of a forthcoming takeover bid that would make their shares more valuable. In order to decide whether silence in such circumstances violates § 10(b), it is necessary to review the language and legislative history of that statute as well as its interpretation by the Commission and the federal courts.

Although the starting point of our inquiry is the language of the statute, Ernst & Ernst v. Hochfelder, 425 U.S. 185, 197, 96 S.Ct. 1375, 1382, 47 L.Ed.2d 668 (1976), § 10(b) does not state whether silence may constitute a manipulative or deceptive device. Section 10(b) was designed as a catch-all clause to prevent fraudulent practices. But neither the legislative history nor the statute itself affords specific guidance for the resolution of this case. When Rule 10b–5 was promulgated in 1942, the SEC did not discuss the possibility that failure to provide information might run afoul of § 10(b).

The SEC took an important step in the development of § 10(b) when it held that a broker-dealer and his firm violated that section by selling securities on the basis of undisclosed information obtained from a director of the issuer corporation who was also a registered representative of the brokerage firm. In Cady, Roberts & Co., 40 S.E.C. 907 (1961), the Commission decided that a corporate insider must abstain from trading in the shares of his corporation unless he has first disclosed all material inside information known to him. The obligation to disclose or abstain derives from

> "[a]n affirmative duty to disclose material information[,] [which] has been traditionally imposed on corporate 'insiders,' particular officers, directors, or controlling stockholders. We, and the courts have consistently held that insiders must disclose material facts which are known to them by virtue of their position but which are not known to persons with whom they deal and which, if known, would affect their investment judgment." Id., at 911.

The Commission emphasized that the duty arose from (i) the existence of a relationship affording access to inside information intended to be available only for a corporate purpose, and (ii) the unfairness of allowing a corporate insider to take advantage of that information by trading without disclosure.

That the relationship between a corporate insider and the stockholders of his corporation gives rise to a disclosure obligation is not a novel twist of the law. At common law, misrepresentation made for the purpose of inducing reliance upon the false statement is fraudulent. But one who fails to disclose material information prior to the consummation of a transaction commits fraud only when he is under a duty to do so. And the duty to disclose arises when one party has information "that the other [party] is entitled to know because of a fiduciary or other similar relation of trust and confidence between them." In its *Cady, Roberts* decision, the Commission recognized a relationship of trust and confidence between the shareholders of a corporation and those insiders who have obtained confidential information by reason of their position with that corporation.[68] This relationship gives rise to a duty to disclose because of the "necessity of preventing a corporate insider from * * * [taking] unfair advantage of the uninformed minority stockholders." Speed v. Transamerica Corp., 99 F.Supp. 808, 829 (D.Del.1951).

The federal courts have found violations of § 10(b) where corporate insiders used undisclosed information for their own benefit. E.g., SEC v. Texas Gulf Sulphur Co., 401 F.2d 833 (CA2 1968), cert. denied, 404 U.S. 1005, 92 S.Ct. 561, 30 L.Ed.2d 558 (1971). The cases also have emphasized, in accordance with the common-law rule, that "[t]he party charged with failing to disclose market information must be under a duty to disclose it." Frigitemp Corp. v. Financial Dynamics Fund, Inc., 524 F.2d 275, 282 (CA2 1975). Accordingly, a purchaser of stock who has no duty to a prospective seller because he is neither an insider nor a fiduciary has been held to have no obligation to reveal material facts.

* * *

Thus, administrative and judicial interpretations have established that silence in connection with the purchase or sale of securities may operate as a fraud actionable under § 10(b) despite the absence of statutory language or legislative history specifically addressing the legality of nondisclosure. But such liability is premised upon a duty to disclose arising from a relationship of trust and confidence between parties to a transaction. Application of a duty to disclose prior to trading guarantees that corporate insiders, who have an obligation to place the shareholder's welfare before their own, will not benefit personally through fraudulent use of material nonpublic information.[69]

---

68. [By the Court] The dissent of Mr. Justice Blackmun suggests that the "special facts" doctrine may be applied to find that silence constitutes fraud where one party has superior information to another. This Court has never so held. In Strong v. Repide, 213 U.S. 419, 431–434, 29 S.Ct. 521, 525, 526, 53 L.Ed. 853 (1909), this Court applied the special facts doctrine to conclude that a corporate insider had a duty to disclose to a shareholder. In that case, the majority shareholder of a corporation secretly purchased the stock of another shareholder without revealing that the corporation, under the insider's direction, was about to sell corporate assets at a price that would greatly enhance the value of the stock. The decision in Strong v. Repide was premised upon the fiduciary duty between the corporate insider and the shareholder. See Pepper v. Litton, 308 U.S. 295, 307, n. 15, 60 S.Ct. 238, 245, n. 15, 84 L.Ed. 281 (1939).

69. [By the Court] "Tippees" of corporate insiders have been held liable under § 10(b) because they have a duty not to profit from the use of inside information that they know is confidential and know or should know came from a corporate insider, Shapiro v. Merrill Lynch, Pierce, Fenner & Smith, 495 F.2d 228, 237–238 (CA2 1974). The tippee's obligation has been viewed as arising from his role as a participant after the fact in the insider's breach of a fiduciary duty. Subcommittees of American Bar Association Section of Corporation, Banking, and Business Law, Comment Letter on Material, Non–Public Information (Oct. 15, 1973) reprinted in BNA, Securities Regulation & Law Report No. 233, at D–1, D–2 (Jan. 2, 1974).

III

In this case, the petitioner was convicted of violating § 10(b) although he was not a corporate insider and he received no confidential information from the target company. Moreover, the "market information" upon which he relied did not concern the earning power or operations of the target company, but only the plans of the acquiring company. Petitioner's use of that information was not a fraud under § 10(b) unless he was subject to an affirmative duty to disclose it before trading. In this case, the jury instructions failed to specify any such duty. In effect, the trial court instructed the jury that petitioner owed a duty to everyone; to all sellers, indeed, to the market as a whole. The jury simply was told to decide whether petitioner used material, nonpublic information at a time when "he knew other people trading in the securities market did not have access to the same information."

The Court of Appeals affirmed the conviction by holding that "[a]nyone—corporate insider or not—who regularly receives material nonpublic information may not use that information to trade in securities without incurring an affirmative duty to disclose." Although the court said that its test would include only persons who regularly receive material nonpublic information, its rationale for that limitation is unrelated to the existence of a duty to disclose.[70] The Court of Appeals, like the trial court, failed to identify a relationship between petitioner and the sellers that could give rise to a duty. Its decision thus rested solely upon its belief that the federal securities laws have "created a system providing equal access to information necessary for reasoned and intelligent investment decisions." The use by anyone of material information not generally available is fraudulent, this theory suggests, because such information gives certain buyers or sellers an unfair advantage over less informed buyers and sellers.

This reasoning suffers from two defects. First not every instance of financial unfairness constitutes fraudulent activity under § 10(b). See Santa Fe Industries Inc. v. Green, 430 U.S. 462, 474–477, 97 S.Ct. 1292, 1301–1303, 51 L.Ed.2d 480 (1977). Second, the element required

---

70. [By the Court] The Court of Appeals said that its "regular access to market information" test would create a workable rule embracing "those who occupy * * * strategic places in the market mechanism." 588 F.2d, at 1365. These considerations are insufficient to support a duty to disclose. A duty arises from the relationship between parties, and not merely from one's ability to acquire information because of his position in the market.

The Court of Appeals also suggested that the acquiring corporation itself would not be a "market insider" because a tender offeror creates, rather than receives, information and takes a substantial economic risk that its offer will be unsuccessful. Again, the Court of Appeals departed from the analysis appropriate to recognition of a duty. The Court of Appeals for the Second Circuit previously held, in a manner consistent with our analysis here, that a tender offeror does not violate § 10(b) when it makes preannouncement purchases precisely because there is no relationship between the offeror and the seller: "We know of no rule of law * * * that a purchaser of stock, who was not an 'insider' and had no fiduciary relation to a prospective seller, had any obligation to reveal circumstances that might raise a seller's demands and thus abort the sale." General Time Corp. v. Talley Industries, 403 F.2d 159, 164 (1968), cert. denied, 393 U.S. 1026, 89 S.Ct. 631, 21 L.Ed.2d 570 (1969).

to make silence fraudulent—a duty to disclose—is absent in this case. No duty could arise from petitioner's relationship with the sellers of the target company's securities, for petitioner had no prior dealings with them. He was not their agent, he was not a fiduciary, he was not a person in whom the sellers had placed their trust and confidence. He was, in fact, a complete stranger who dealt with the sellers only through impersonal market transactions.

We cannot affirm petitioner's conviction without recognizing a general duty between all participants in market transactions to forgo actions based on material, nonpublic information. Formulation of such a broad duty, which departs radically from the established doctrine that duty arises from a specific relationship between two parties, should not be undertaken absent some explicit evidence of congressional intent.

As we have seen, no such evidence emerges from the language or legislative history of § 10(b). Moreover, neither the Congress nor the Commission ever has adopted a parity-of-information rule. * * *

We see no basis for applying such a new and different theory of liability in this case. As we have emphasized before, the 1934 Act cannot be read " 'more broadly than its language and the statutory scheme reasonably permit.' " Touche Ross & Co. v. Redington, 442 U.S. 560, 578, 99 S.Ct. 2479, 2490, 61 L.Ed.2d 82 (1979). Section 10(b) is aptly described as a catch-all provision, but what it catches must be fraud. When an allegation of fraud is based upon nondisclosure, there can be no fraud absent a duty to speak. We hold that a duty to disclose under § 10(b) does not arise from the mere possession of nonpublic market information. The contrary result is without support in the legislative history of § 10(b) and would be inconsistent with the careful plan that Congress has enacted for regulation of the securities markets. Cf. Santa Fe Industries Inc. v. Green, 430 U.S., at 479, 97 S.Ct., at 1304.[71]

IV

In its brief to this Court, the United States offers an alternative theory to support petitioner's conviction. It argues that petitioner

---

71. [By the Court] Mr. Justice Blackmun's dissent would establish the following standard for imposing criminal and civil liability under § 10(b) and Rule 10b–5:

"[P]ersons having access to confidential material information that is not legally available to others generally are prohibited * * * from engaging in schemes to exploit their structural information advantage through trading in affected securities."

This view is not substantially different from the Court of Appeals theory that anyone "who regularly receives material nonpublic information may not use that information to trade in securities without incurring an affirmative duty to disclose," and must be rejected for the reasons stated in Part III. Additionally, a judicial holding that certain undefined activities "generally are prohibited" by § 10(b) would raise questions whether either criminal or civil defendants would be given fair notice that they have engaged in illegal activity.

It is worth noting that this is apparently the first case in which criminal liability has been imposed upon a purchaser for § 10(b) nondisclosure. Petitioner was sentenced to a year in prison, suspended except for one month, and a five-year term of probation.

breached a duty to the acquiring corporation when he acted upon information that he obtained by virtue of his position as an employee of a printer employed by the corporation. The breach of this duty is said to support a conviction under § 10(b) for fraud perpetrated upon both the acquiring corporation and the sellers.

We need not decide whether this theory has merit for it was not submitted to the jury. * * *

The jury instructions demonstrate that petitioner was convicted merely because of his failure to disclose material, nonpublic information to sellers from whom he bought the stock of target corporations. The jury was not instructed on the nature or elements of a duty owed by petitioner to anyone other than the sellers. Because we cannot affirm a criminal conviction on the basis of a theory not presented to the jury, we will not speculate upon whether such a duty exists, whether it has been breached, or whether such a breach constitutes a violation of § 10(b).

The judgment of the Court of Appeals is reversed.

[The separate opinions of MR. JUSTICE STEVENS, concurring in the majority opinion and judgment, and MR. JUSTICE BRENNAN, concurring in the judgment, are omitted.]

MR. CHIEF JUSTICE BURGER, dissenting.

I believe that the jury instructions in this case properly charged a violation of § 10(b) and Rule 10b–5, and I would affirm the conviction.

I

As a general rule, neither party to an arm's length business transaction has an obligation to disclose information to the other unless the parties stand in some confidential or fiduciary relation. See Prosser, Law of Torts § 106 (2d ed.1955). This rule permits a businessman to capitalize on his experience and skill in securing and evaluating relevant information; it provides incentive for hard work, careful analysis, and astute forecasting. But the policies that underlie the rule also should limit its scope. In particular, the rule should give way when an informational advantage is obtained, not by superior experience, foresight, or industry, but by some unlawful means. * * * I would read § 10(b) and Rule 10b–5 to encompass and build on this principle: to mean that a person who has misappropriated nonpublic information has an absolute duty to disclose that information or to refrain from trading.

The language of § 10(b) and of Rule 10b–5 plainly support such a reading. By their terms, these provisions reach *any* person engaged in *any* fraudulent scheme. This broad language negates the suggestion that congressional concern was limited to trading by "corporate insiders" or to deceptive practices related to "corporate information." [72]

72. [By the Chief Justice] Academic writing in recent years has distinguished between "corporate information"—infor- mation which comes from within the corporation and reflects on expected earnings or assets—and "market information." See,

Just as surely Congress cannot have intended one standard of fair dealing for "white collar" insiders and another for the "blue collar" level. The very language of § 10(b) and Rule 10b–5 "by repeated use of the word 'any' [was] obviously meant to be inclusive." Affiliated Ute Citizens v. United States, 406 U.S. 128, 151, 92 S.Ct. 1456, 1471, 31 L.Ed.2d 741 (1972).

The history of the statute and of the rule also supports this reading [73] * * *

II

The Court's opinion, as I read it, leaves open the question whether § 10(b) and Rule 10b–5 prohibit trading on misappropriated nonpublic information.[74] Instead, the Court apparently concludes that this theory of the case was not submitted to the jury. In the Court's view, the instructions given the jury were premised on the erroneous notion that the mere failure to disclose nonpublic information, however acquired, is a deceptive practice. And because of this premise, the jury was not instructed that the means by which Chiarella acquired his informational advantage—by violating a duty owed to the acquiring companies— was an element of the offense.

The Court's reading of the District Court's charge is unduly restrictive. * * * In sum, the evidence shows beyond all doubt that Chiarella, working literally in the shadows of the warning signs in the printshop, misappropriated—stole to put it bluntly—valuable nonpublic information entrusted to him in the utmost confidence. He then exploited his ill-gotten informational advantage by purchasing securities in the market. In my view, such conduct plainly violates § 10(b) and Rule 10b–5. Accordingly, I would affirm the judgment of the Court of Appeals.

Mr. Justice Blackmun, with whom Mr. Justice Marshall joins, dissenting.

e.g., Fleischer, Mundheim & Murphy, An Initial Inquiry into the Responsibility to Disclose Market Information, 121 U.Pa.L. Rev. 798, 799 (1973). It is clear that the § 10(b) and Rule 10b–5 by their terms and by their history make no such distinction. See Brudney, Insiders, Outsiders, and Informational Advantages Under the Federal Securities Laws, 93 Harv.L.Rev. 322, 329– 333 (1979).

73. [By the Chief Justice] This interpretation of the antifraud provisions also finds support in the recently proposed Federal Securities Code prepared by the American Law Institute under the direction of Professor Louis Loss. The ALI code would construe the antifraud provisions to cover a class of "quasi-insiders," including a judge's law clerk who trades on information in an unpublished opinion or a Government employee who trades on a secret

report. See ALI Federal Securities Code § 1603, comment 3(d), pp. 538–539. These quasi-insiders share the characteristic that their informational advantage is obtained by conversion and not by legitimate economic activity that society seeks to encourage.

74. [By the Chief Justice] There is some language in the Court's opinion to suggest that only "a relationship between petitioner and the sellers * * * could give rise to a duty [to disclose]." The Court's holding, however, is much more limited, namely that mere possession of material nonpublic information is insufficient to create a duty to disclose or to refrain from trading. Accordingly, it is my understanding that the Court has not rejected the view, advanced above, that an absolute duty to disclose or refrain arises from the very act of misappropriating nonpublic information.

Although I agree with much of what is said in Part I of the dissenting opinion of The Chief Justice, I write separately because, in my view, it is unnecessary to rest petitioner's conviction on a "misappropriation" theory. The fact that petitioner Chiarella purloined, or, to use The Chief Justice's word, "stole," information concerning pending tender offers certainly is the most dramatic evidence that petitioner was guilty of fraud. He has conceded that he knew it was wrong, and he and his co-workers in the print shop were specifically warned by their employer that actions of this kind were improper and forbidden. But I also would find petitioner's conduct fraudulent within the meaning of § 10(b) [and] Rule 10b–5, even if he had obtained the blessing of his employer's principals before embarking on his profiteering scheme. Indeed, I think petitioner's brand of manipulative trading, with or without such approval, lies close to the heart of what the securities laws are intended to prohibit.

The Court continues to pursue a course, charted in certain recent decisions, designed to transform § 10(b) from an intentionally elastic "catchall" provision to one that catches relatively little of the misbehavior that all too often makes investment in securities a needlessly risky business for the uninitiated investor. See, e.g., Ernst & Ernst v. Hochfelder, 425 U.S. 185, 96 S.Ct. 1375, 47 L.Ed.2d 668 (1976); Blue Chip Stamps v. Manor Drug Stores, 421 U.S. 723, 95 S.Ct. 1917, 44 L.Ed. 2d 539 (1975). Such confinement in this case is now achieved by imposition of a requirement of a "special relationship" akin to fiduciary duty before the statute gives rise to a duty to disclose or to abstain from trading upon material nonpublic information.[75] The Court admits that this conclusion finds no mandate in the language of the statute or its legislative history. Yet the Court fails even to attempt a justification of its ruling in terms of the purposes of the securities laws, or to square that ruling with the long-standing but now much abused principle that the federal securities laws are to be construed flexibly rather than with narrow technicality. * * *

Whatever the outer limits of the Rule, petitioner Chiarella's case fits neatly near the center of its analytical framework. He occupied a relationship to the takeover companies giving him intimate access to concededly material information that was sedulously guarded from public access. The information, in the words of Cady, Roberts & Co., 40 S.E.C., at 912, was "intended to be available only for a corporate purpose and not for the personal benefit of anyone." Petitioner, moreover, knew that the information was unavailable to those with whom he dealt. And he took full, virtually riskless advantage of this artificial information gap by selling the stocks shortly after each takeover bid was announced. By any reasonable definition, his trading was "inherent[ly] unfai[r]." This misuse of confidential information was clearly placed before the jury. Petition-

---

75. [By the Justice] The Court fails to specify whether the obligations of a special relationship must fall directly upon the person engaging in an allegedly fraudulent transaction, or whether the derivative obligations of "tippees" that lower courts long have recognized, are encompassed by its rule.

er's conviction, therefore, should be upheld and I dissent from the Court's upsetting that conviction.

Notes

(1) Would the Court's construction of rule 10b–5 reach the following persons:

(a) The secretary or messenger who overhears snippets of conversations from his superiors, infers that a favorable development is about to occur, and buys shares of his employer?

(b) The person sitting in a restaurant who overhears conversations at the next table from which she infers that a favorable development is about to occur with respect to XX Company, and buys shares in XX Company?

(c) The reporter who attends a press conference at which a favorable development is announced, and then, immediately after the conference and before the news appears on the ticker services, telephones his broker and places an order to purchase?

(d) A subtippee who believes his tippee has "connections" with employees of the corporation but is not himself employed by the corporation?

(2) Approximately four months after *Chiarella* was decided, the Securities and Exchange Commission adopted rule 14e–3 pursuant to sections 14(e) and 23 of the Securities Exchange Act. S.E.C. Rel. No. 34–17120, 45 Fed.Reg. 60410 (1980). The SEC release describes the purpose and scope of this Rule as follows:

> The rule pertains to trading by persons in securities which may be the subject of a tender offer as well as tipping of material, nonpublic information relating to a contemplated tender offer. It should be noted that the rule applies only in the context of tender offers.

* * *

II. Synopsis of Rule

* * * Rule 14e–3(a) imposes a duty of disclosure under Section 14(e) on any person who trades in securities which will be sought or are being sought in a tender offer while that person is in possession of material information which he knows or has reason to know is nonpublic and has been acquired directly or indirectly from the offering person, from the issuer or from an officer, director, partner or employee or any other person acting on behalf of the offering person or the issuer. Since no duty to disclose would arise if a person subject to the rule does not purchase or sell or cause the purchase or sale of such securities while in possession of such information, the rule establishes a specific duty to "disclose or abstain from trading" under Section 14(e). The "disclose or abstain from trading" framework of Rule 14e–3(a) is similar to the approach taken in *Texas Gulf* and *Cady, Roberts* which the *Chiarella* Court cited with approval. In the Commission's view this framework is the least restrictive method of regulating this abusive practice. * * *

The operation of Rule 14e–3(a) may be illustrated by examples. It should be emphasized that these examples are not exclusive and do not constitute the only situations in which the duty under Rule 14e–3(a) would arise:

(1) If an offering person tells another person that the offering person will make a tender offer which information is nonpublic, the other person has acquired material, nonpublic information directly from the offering person and has a duty under Rule 14e–3(a). * * *

(3) If the offering person sends a nonpublic letter to a subject company notifying the subject company of a proposed tender offer at a specified price and upon specified terms and the management of the subject company learns the contents of the letter, the management of the subject company has acquired material, nonpublic information directly from the offering person. An individual member of such management will violate Rule 14e–3(a) if he purchases or sells or causes the purchase or sale of the securities to be sought in the tender offer.

(4) If, under the facts in the preceding example, the management of the subject company also tells other persons not affiliated with management of the letter, then those other persons have acquired material, nonpublic information indirectly from the offering person and are under a duty to disclose or abstain from trading under Rule 14e–3(a). * * *

(6) If a person steals, converts or otherwise misappropriates material, nonpublic information relating to a tender offer from an offering person, such person will have acquired the information directly from the offering person and has a duty under Rule 14e–3(a).

(7) If an offering person tells another person of his intention to make a tender offer, and such other person subsequently tells a third person that a tender offer will be made and this third person knows or has reason to know that this non-public information came indirectly from the offering person, then this third person has a duty under Rule 14e–3(a).

45 Fed.Reg. 60410–60414. Given *Chiarella*, is this rule valid?

(3) Vincent Chiarella was apparently the first person against whom criminal charges were filed for violation of rule 10b–5. The press noted at the time that he was a "blue collar" worker and commented that it seemed unfair to apply the criminal process only against persons in lower economic classes. A number of criminal proceedings have since been brought for insider trading under rule 10b–5, including attorneys and other "white collar" workers as well as at least one other printer.

(4) After *Chiarella*, lower courts have generally enthusiastically endorsed the notion set forth principally in Chief Justice Burger's opinion that an insider trading violation may be based on a breach of fiduciary duty by the trader, regardless of whether that duty runs to the issuer of the securities involved or to other parties. See, for example, United States v. Newman, 664 F.2d 12 (2d Cir.1981), cert. denied sub nom. Newman v. United States, 464 U.S. 863, 104 S.Ct. 193, 78 L.Ed.2d 170 (1983); Securities and Exchange Commission v. Materia, 745 F.2d 197 (2d Cir.1984), cert. denied 471 U.S. 1053, 105 S.Ct. 2112, 85 L.Ed.2d 477 (1985); S.E.C. v. Musella, 578 F.Supp. 425 (S.D.N.Y.1984). This theory became generally

known as the "misappropriation theory" and its correctness and desirability has been widely debated in the academic literature. If Chiarella is guilty under rule 10b–5 under this theory, have we not simply criminalized violations by employees of employer work rules? Is there any public harm if Chiarella disobeys the signs posted by his employer?

CARPENTER v. UNITED STATES

Supreme Court of the United States, 1987.
484 U.S. 19, 108 S.Ct. 316, 98 L.Ed.2d 275.

JUSTICE WHITE delivered the opinion of the Court.

Petitioners Kenneth Felis and R. Foster Winans were convicted of violating § 10(b) of the Securities Exchange Act of 1934, and Rule 10b–5, *United States v. Winans,* 612 F.Supp. 827 (SDNY 1985). They were also found guilty of violating the federal mail and wire fraud statutes, 18 U.S.C. §§ 1341,[76] 1343 [77] and were convicted for conspiracy under 18 U.S.C. § 371.[78] Petitioner David Carpenter, Winans' roommate, was convicted for aiding and abetting. With a minor exception, the Court of Appeals for the Second Circuit affirmed, 791 F.2d 1024 (1986); we granted certiorari, 479 U.S. 1016, 107 S.Ct. 666, 93 L.Ed.2d 718 (1986).

I

In 1981, Winans became a reporter for the Wall Street Journal (the Journal) and in the summer of 1982 became one of the two writers of a daily column, "Heard on the Street." That column discussed selected stocks or groups of stocks, giving positive and negative information

---

76. [By the Court] Section 1341 provides:

"Whoever, having devised or intending to devise any scheme or artifice to defraud, or for obtaining money or property by means of false or fraudulent pretenses, representations, or promises, or to sell, dispose of, loan, exchange, alter, give away, distribute, supply, or furnish or procure for unlawful use any counterfeit or spurious coin, obligation, security, or other article, or anything represented to be or intimated or held out to be such counterfeit or spurious article, for the purpose of executing such scheme or artifice or attempting so to do, places in any post office or authorized depository for mail matter, any matter or thing whatever to be sent or delivered by the Postal Service, or takes or receives therefrom, any such matter or thing, or knowingly causes to be delivered by mail according to the direction thereon, or at the place at which it is directed to be delivered by the person to whom it is addressed, any such matter or thing, shall be fined not more than $1,000 or imprisoned not more than five years, or both."

77. [By the Court] Section 1343 provides:

"Whoever, having devised or intending to devise any scheme or artifice to defraud, or for obtaining money or property by means of false or fraudulent pretenses, representations, or promises, transmits or causes to be transmitted by means of wire, radio, or television communication in interstate or foreign commerce, any writings, signs, signals, pictures, or sounds for the purpose of executing such scheme or artifice, shall be fined not more than $1,000 or imprisoned not more than five years, or both."

78. [By the Court] Section 371 provides:

"If two or more persons conspire either to commit any offense against the United States, or to defraud the United States, or any agency thereof in any manner or for any purpose, and one or more of such persons do any act to effect the object of the conspiracy, each shall be fined not more than $10,000 or imprisoned not more than five years, or both."

about those stocks and taking "a point of view with respect to investment in the stocks that it reviews." Winans regularly interviewed corporate executives to put together interesting perspectives on the stocks that would be highlighted in upcoming columns, but, at least for the columns at issue here, none contained corporate inside information or any "hold for release" information. Because of the "Heard" column's perceived quality and integrity, it had the potential of affecting the price of the stocks which it examined. The District Court concluded on the basis of testimony presented at trial that the "Heard" column "does have an impact on the market, difficult though it may be to quantify in any particular case."

The official policy and practice at the Journal was that prior to publication, the contents of the column were the Journal's confidential information. Despite the rule, with which Winans was familiar, he entered into a scheme in October 1983 with Peter Brant and petitioner Felis, both connected with the Kidder Peabody brokerage firm in New York City, to give them advance information as to the timing and contents of the "Heard" column. This permitted Brant and Felis and another conspirator, David Clark, a client of Brant, to buy or sell based on the probable impact of the column on the market. Profits were to be shared. The conspirators agreed that the scheme would not affect the journalistic purity of the "Heard" column, and the District Court did not find that the contents of any of the articles were altered to further the profit potential of petitioners' stock-trading scheme. Over a four-month period, the brokers made prepublication trades on the basis of information given them by Winans about the contents of some 27 Heard columns. The net profits from these trades were about $690,000.

In November 1983, correlations between the "Heard" articles and trading in the Clark and Felis accounts were noted at Kidder Peabody and inquiries began. Brant and Felis denied knowing anyone at the Journal and took steps to conceal the trades. Later, the Securities and Exchange Commission began an investigation. Questions were met by denials both by the brokers at Kidder Peabody and by Winans at the Journal. As the investigation progressed, the conspirators quarreled, and on March 29, 1984, Winans and Carpenter went to the SEC and revealed the entire scheme. This indictment and a bench trial followed. Brant, who had pled guilty under a plea agreement, was a witness for the Government.

The District Court found, and the Court of Appeals agreed, that Winans had knowingly breached a duty of confidentiality by misappropriating prepublication information regarding the timing and contents of the "Heard" columns, information that had been gained in the course of his employment under the understanding that it would not be revealed in advance of publication and that if it were, he would report it to his employer. It was this appropriation of confidential information that underlay both the securities laws and mail and wire fraud counts. With respect to the § 10(b) charges, the courts below held that

the deliberate breach of Winans' duty of confidentiality and concealment of the scheme was a fraud and deceit on the Journal. Although
the victim of the fraud, the Journal, was not a buyer or seller of the
stocks traded in or otherwise a market participant, the fraud was
nevertheless considered to be "in connection with" a purchase or sale of
securities within the meaning of the statute and the rule. The courts
reasoned that the scheme's sole purpose was to buy and sell securities
at a profit based on advance information of the column's contents. The
courts below rejected petitioners' submission, which is one of the two
questions presented here, that criminal liability could not be imposed
on petitioners under Rule 10b–5 because "the newspaper is the only
alleged victim of fraud and has no interest in the securities traded."

In affirming the mail and wire fraud convictions, the Court of
Appeals ruled that Winans had fraudulently misappropriated "property" within the meaning of the mail and wire fraud statutes and that its
revelation had harmed the Journal. It was held as well that the use of
the mail and wire services had a sufficient nexus with the scheme to
satisfy §§ 1341 and 1343. The petition for certiorari challenged these
conclusions.

The Court is evenly divided with respect to the convictions under
the securities laws and for that reason affirms the judgment below on
those counts. For the reasons that follow, we also affirm the judgment
with respect to the mail and wire fraud convictions.

II

Petitioners assert that their activities were not a scheme to defraud
the Journal within the meaning of the mail and wire fraud statutes,[79]
and that in any event, they did not obtain any "money or property"
from the Journal, which is a necessary element of the crime under our
decision last Term in *McNally v. United States,* 483 U.S. ___, 107 S.Ct.
2875, 97 L.Ed.2d 292 (1987). We are unpersuaded by either submission
and address the latter first.

We held in *McNally* that the mail fraud statute does not reach
"schemes to defraud citizens of their intangible rights to honest and
impartial government," *id.,* at ___, 107 S.Ct., at 2879, and that the
statute is "limited in scope to the protection of property rights." *Id.,* at
___, 107 S.Ct., at 2879. Petitioners argue that the Journal's interest in
prepublication confidentiality for the "Heard" columns is no more than
an intangible consideration outside the reach of § 1341; nor does that
law, it is urged, protect against mere injury to reputation. This is not a
case like *McNally,* however. The Journal, as Winans' employer, was
defrauded of much more than its contractual right to his honest and
faithful service, an interest too ethereal in itself to fall within the
protection of the mail fraud statute, which "had its origin in the desire
to protect individual property rights." *McNally, supra,* at ___, n. 8, 107

---

79. [By the Court] The mail and wire
fraud statutes share the same language in
relevant part, and accordingly we apply
the same analysis to both sets of offenses
here.

S.Ct., at 2881, n. 8. Here, the object of the scheme was to take the Journal's confidential business information—the publication schedule and contents of the "Heard" column—and its intangible nature does not make it any less "property" protected by the mail and wire fraud statutes. *McNally* did not limit the scope of § 1341 to tangible as distinguished from intangible property rights.

Both courts below expressly referred to the Journal's interest in the confidentiality of the contents and timing of the "Heard" column as a property right, 791 F.2d, at 1034–1035; 612 F.Supp., at 846, and we agree with that conclusion. * * *

Petitioners' arguments that they did not interfere with the Journal's use of the information or did not publicize it and deprive the Journal of the first public use of it, miss the point. The confidential information was generated from the business and the business had a right to decide how to use it prior to disclosing it to the public. * * *

We cannot accept petitioners' further argument that Winans' conduct in revealing prepublication information was no more than a violation of workplace rules and did not amount to fraudulent activity that is proscribed by the mail fraud statute. Sections 1341 and 1343 reach any scheme to deprive another of money or property by means of false or fraudulent pretenses, representations, or promises. * * *

The concept of "fraud" includes the act of embezzlement, which is " 'the fraudulent appropriation to one's own use of the money or goods entrusted to one's care by another.' " *Grin v. Shine,* 187 U.S. 181, 189, 23 S.Ct. 98, 101, 47 L.Ed. 130 (1902).

The District Court found that Winans' undertaking at the Journal was not to reveal prepublication information about his column, a promise that became a sham when in violation of his duty he passed along to his co-conspirators confidential information belonging to the Journal, pursuant to an ongoing scheme to share profits from trading in anticipation of the "Heard" column's impact on the stock market. * * * As the New York courts have recognized, "It is well established, as a general proposition, that a person who acquires special knowledge or information by virtue of a confidential or fiduciary relationship with another is not free to exploit that knowledge or information for his own personal benefit but must account to his principal for any profits derived therefrom." *Diamond v. Oreamuno,* 24 N.Y.2d 494, 497, 301 N.Y.S.2d 78, 80, 248 N.E.2d 910, 912 (1969); see also Restatement (Second) of Agency §§ 388, Comment *c,* 396(c) (1958).

We have little trouble in holding that the conspiracy here to trade on the Journal's confidential information is not outside the reach of the mail and wire fraud statutes, provided the other elements of the offenses are satisfied. The Journal's business information that it intended to be kept confidential was its property; the declaration to that effect in the employee manual merely removed any doubts on that score and made the finding of specific intent to defraud that much easier. Winans continued in the employ of the Journal, appropriating its confidential business information for his own use, all the while pretending to perform his duty of safeguarding it. In fact, he told his editors twice about leaks of confidential information not related to the stock-trading scheme, demonstrating both his knowledge that the Journal viewed information concerning the "Heard" column as confidential and his deceit as he played the role of a loyal employee. Furthermore, the District Court's conclusion that each of the petitioners acted with the required specific intent to defraud is strongly supported by the evidence.

Lastly, we reject the submission that using the wires and the mail to print and send the Journal to its customers did not satisfy the requirement that those mediums be used to execute the scheme at issue. The courts below were quite right in observing that circulation of the "Heard" column was not only anticipated but an essential part of the scheme. Had the column not been made available to Journal customers, there would have been no effect on stock prices and no likelihood of profiting from the information leaked by Winans.

The judgment below is *Affirmed.*

Notes

(1) Prosecutorial concern about the reach and validity of the "misappropriation theory" under rule 10b–5 evaporated abruptly after announcement of this decision, since it opened up criminal prosecutions under the wire and mail fraud statutes for "insider trading" violations by outsiders— i.e. by persons unconnected with the issuer of the securities in question. In view of the rather opaque and uninformative nature of Justice White's opinion, there has been some speculation about the reasons for the four-four division on the securities act violations and the portent for the future. See Aldave, The Misappropriation Theory: Carpenter and Its Aftermath, 49 Ohio St.L.J. 373, 377–78, 380–82 (1988): *

> The most plausible explanation for the division of the Court in *Carpenter* is that four Justices rejected the proposition that "[a]lthough the victim of the fraud, the Journal, was not a buyer or seller," Winans' fraud nevertheless had occurred " 'in connection with' a purchase or sale of securities." The petitioners' brief hammered away at the point that "[t]he only victim of fraud alleged by the government . . . was the Journal, a financial newspaper which had absolutely no interest in the purchase, sale or value of any of the securities traded by petitioners." Even before the *Carpenter* case arose, some commentators had questioned whether any fraud perpetrated on a non-trading party could be said to have occurred "in connection with" a securities transaction.[80] *   *   *
>
> The Court's expansive reading of the mail and wire fraud statutes, in conjunction with its failure to endorse the misappropriation theory,

* Copyright © 1988 The Ohio State University.

80. [By the Author] *See, e.g.,* Langevoort, Insider Trading and the Fiduciary Principle: A Post–Chiarella Restate-ment, 70 Calif.L.Rev. 1, 47 (1982); Wang, Recent Developments in the Federal Law Regulating Stock Market Inside Trading, 6 Corp.L.Rev. 291, 302 (1983).

could accelerate the "criminalization" of insider-trading law.[81] Because the Securities and Exchange Commission cannot be certain that the Supreme Court will sustain any judgment dependent on the misappropriation theory, it may hesitate to bring civil actions in some cases in which it must rely on that theory. The Department of Justice, on the other hand, does not need to invoke the misappropriation theory, or to depend solely on that theory, to support criminal charges against defendants who have used the wires or mails in furtherance of an insider-trading scheme. A possible result is that proportionally more persons accused of insider trading will be pursued by a U.S. Attorney, and proportionally fewer by the SEC. * * *

(2) For a negative evaluation of *Carpenter* on the grounds that it "overcriminalizes" what should essentially be a matter for the civil law and that it tends to "trivialize" the mail and wire fraud case of *McNally,* see Coffee, Hush!: The Criminal Status of Confidential Information after *McNally* and *Carpenter* and the Enduring Problem of Overcriminalization, 26 Am.Crim.L.Rev. 121 (1988). For the perspective of an official of the Department of Justice on the *Carpenter* decision and background on the mail and wire fraud statute, see Dreeben, Insider Trading and Intangible Rights: The Redefinition of the Mail Fraud Statute, 26 Am.Crim.L.Rev. 181 (1988). See generally, Cox and Fogarty, Bases of Insider Trading Law, 49 Ohio St.L.Rev. 353 (1988); Mitchell, The Jurisprudence of the Misappropriation Theory and the New Insider Trading Legislation,: From Fairness to Efficiency and Back, 52 Albany L.Rev. 775 (1988).

DIRKS v. SEC

Supreme Court of the United States, 1983.
463 U.S. 646, 103 S.Ct. 3255, 77 L.Ed.2d 911.

JUSTICE POWELL delivered the opinion of the Court.

Petitioner Raymond Dirks received material nonpublic information from "insiders" of a corporation with which he had no connection. He disclosed this information to investors who relied on it in trading in the shares of the corporation. The question is whether Dirks violated the antifraud provisions of the federal securities laws by this disclosure.

I.

In 1973, Dirks was an officer of a New York broker-dealer firm who specialized in providing investment analysis of insurance company securities to institutional investors. On March 6, Dirks received information from Ronald Secrist, a former officer of Equity Funding of America. Secrist alleged that the assets of Equity Funding, a diversified corporation primarily engaged in selling life insurance and mutual funds, were vastly overstated as the result of fraudulent corporate practices. Secrist also stated that various regulatory agencies had

---

81. [By the Author] *See* Peloso, *Securities, Commodities Litigation: The Criminalization of Securities Laws,* N.Y. L.J., May 28, 1987, at 1, col. 1 (arguing that the SEC is abdicating part of its enforcement function by allowing the U.S. Attorney to decide for himself which defendants to prosecute, and for what offenses).

failed to act on similar charges made by Equity Funding employees. He urged Dirks to verify the fraud and disclose it publicly.

Dirks decided to investigate the allegations. He visited Equity Funding's headquarters in Los Angeles and interviewed several officers and employees of the corporation. The senior management denied any wrongdoing, but certain corporation employees corroborated the charges of fraud. Neither Dirks nor his firm owned or traded any Equity Funding stock, but throughout his investigation he openly discussed the information he had obtained with a number of clients and investors. Some of these persons sold their holdings of Equity Funding securities, including five investment advisers who liquidated holdings of more than $16 million.[82]

While Dirks was in Los Angeles, he was in touch regularly with William Blundell, The *Wall Street Journal*'s Los Angeles bureau chief. Dirks urged Blundell to write a story on the fraud allegations. Blundell did not believe, however, that such a massive fraud could go undetected and declined to write the story. He feared that publishing such damaging hearsay might be libelous.

During the two-week period in which Dirks pursued his investigation and spread word of Secrist's charges, the price of Equity Funding stock fell from $26 per share to less than $15 per share. This led the New York Stock Exchange to halt trading on March 27. Shortly thereafter California insurance authorities impounded Equity Funding's records and uncovered evidence of the fraud. Only then did the Securities and Exchange Commission (SEC) file a complaint against Equity Funding [83] and only then, on April 2, did the *Wall Street Journal* publish a front-page story based largely on information assembled by Dirks. Equity Funding immediately went into receivership.[84]

The SEC began an investigation into Dirks' role in the exposure of the fraud. After a hearing by an administrative law judge, the SEC found that Dirks had aided and abetted violations of § 17(a) of the Securities Act of 1933,[85] § 10(b) of the Securities Exchange Act of 1934, and SEC Rule 10b–5, by repeating the allegations of fraud to members

---

82. [By the Court] Dirks received from his firm a salary plus a commission for securities transactions above a certain amount that his clients directed through his firm. But "[i]t is not clear how many of those with whom Dirks spoke promised to direct some brokerage business through [Dirks' firm] to compensate Dirks, or how many actually did so." The Boston Company Institutional Investors, Inc., promised Dirks about $25,000 in commissions, but it is unclear whether Boston actually generated any brokerage business for his firm.

83. [By the Court] As early as 1971, the SEC had received allegations of fraudulent accounting practices at Equity Funding. Moreover, on March 9, 1973, an offi-

cial of the California Insurance Department informed the SEC's regional office in Los Angeles of Secrist's charges of fraud. Dirks himself voluntarily presented his information at the SEC's regional office beginning on March 27.

84. [By the Court] A federal grand jury in Los Angeles subsequently returned a 105–count indictment against 22 persons, including many of Equity Funding's officers and directors. All defendants were found guilty of one or more counts, either by a plea of guilty or a conviction after trial.

85. [By the Editor] Section 17 is set forth at p. 340, supra.

of the investment community who later sold their Equity Funding stock. The SEC concluded: "Where 'tippees'—regardless of their motivation or occupation—come into possession of material 'information that they know is confidential and know or should know came from a corporate insider,' they must either publicly disclose that information or refrain from trading." Recognizing, however, that Dirks "played an important role in bringing [Equity Funding's] massive fraud to light," the SEC only censured him.

Dirks sought review in the Court of Appeals for the District of Columbia Circuit. The court entered judgment against Dirks "for the reasons stated by the Commission in its opinion." * * *

In view of the importance to the SEC and to the securities industry of the question presented by this case, we granted a writ of certiorari. 459 U.S. 1014, 103 S.Ct. 371, 74 L.Ed.2d 506 (1982). We now reverse.

II.

In the seminal case of In re Cady, Roberts & Co., 40 S.E.C. 907 (1961), the SEC recognized that the common law in some jurisdictions imposes on "corporate 'insiders,' particularly officers, directors, or controlling stockholders" an "affirmative duty of disclosure * * * when dealing in securities." Id., at 911, and n. 13.[86] The SEC found that not only did breach of this common-law duty also establish the elements of a Rule 10b–5 violation,[87] but that individuals other than corporate insiders could be obligated either to disclose material nonpublic information [88] before trading or to abstain from trading altogether. In *Chiarella* we accepted the two elements set out in *Cady, Roberts* for establishing a Rule 10b–5 violation: "(i) the existence of a relationship affording access to inside information intended to be available only for a corporate purpose, and (ii) the unfairness of allowing a corporate insider to take advantage of that information by trading without disclosure." 445 U.S., at 227, 100 S.Ct., at 1114. In examining whether Chiarella had an obligation to disclose or abstain, the Court found that there is no general duty to disclose before trading on material nonpub-

---

86. [By the Court] The duty that insiders owe to the corporation's shareholders not to trade on inside information differs from the common-law duty that officers and directors also have to the corporation itself not to mismanage corporate assets, of which confidential information is one. In holding that breaches of this duty to shareholders violated the Securities Exchange Act, the *Cady, Roberts* Commission recognized, and we agree, that "[a] significant purpose of the Exchange Act was to eliminate the idea that use of inside information for personal advantage was a normal emolument of corporate office." See 40 S.E.C., at 912, n. 15.

87. [By the Court] Rule 10b–5 is generally the most inclusive of the three provi-

sions on which the SEC rested its decision in this case, and we will refer to it when we note the statutory basis for the SEC's inside-trading rules.

88. [By the Court] The SEC views the disclosure duty as requiring more than disclosure to purchasers or sellers: "Proper and adequate disclosure of significant corporate developments can only be effected by a public release through the appropriate public media, designed to achieve a broad dissemination to the investing public generally and without favoring any special person or group." In re Faberge, Inc., 45 S.E.C. 249, 256 (1973).

lic information, and held that "a duty to disclose under § 10(b) does not arise from the mere possession of nonpublic market information." *Id.,* at 235, 100 S.Ct., at 1118. Such a duty arises rather from the existence of a fiduciary relationship.

Not "all breaches of fiduciary duty in connection with a securities transaction," however, come within the ambit of Rule 10b–5. Santa Fe Industries, Inc. v. Green, 430 U.S. 462, 472, 97 S.Ct. 1292, 1300, (1977). There must also be "manipulation or deception." Id., at 473, 97 S.Ct., at 1300. In an inside-trading case this fraud derives from the "inherent unfairness involved where one takes advantage" of "information intended to be available only for a corporate purpose and not for the personal benefit of anyone." In re Merrill Lynch, Pierce, Fenner & Smith, Inc., 43 S.E.C. 933, 936 (1968). Thus, an insider will be liable under Rule 10b–5 for inside trading only where he fails to disclose material nonpublic information before trading on it and thus makes "secret profits." *Cady, Roberts,* 40 S.E.C., at 916, n. 31.

III.

We were explicit in *Chiarella* in saying that there can be no duty to disclose where the person who has traded on inside information "was not [the corporation's] agent, * * * was not a fiduciary, [or] was not a person in whom the sellers [of the securities] had placed their trust and confidence." 445 U.S., at 232, 100 S.Ct., at 1116. Not to require such a fiduciary relationship, we recognized, would "depar[t] radically from the established doctrine that duty arises from a specific relationship between two parties" and would amount to "recognizing a general duty between all participants in market transactions to forgo actions based on material, nonpublic information." Id., at 232, 233, 100 S.Ct., at 1116, 1117. This requirement of a specific relationship between the shareholders and the individual trading on inside information has created analytical difficulties for the SEC and courts in policing tippees who trade on inside information. Unlike insiders who have independent fiduciary duties to both the corporation and its shareholders, the typical tippee has no such relationships.[89] In view of this absence, it has been unclear how a tippee acquires the *Cady, Roberts* duty to refrain from trading on inside information.

---

89. [By the Court. This famous footnote is number 14 in the original opinion.] Under certain circumstances, such as where corporate information is revealed legitimately to an underwriter, accountant, lawyer, or consultant working for the corporation, these outsiders may become fiduciaries of the shareholders. The basis for recognizing this fiduciary duty is not simply that such persons acquire nonpublic corporate information, but rather that they have entered into a special confidential relationship in the conduct of the business of the enterprise and are given access to information solely for corporate purposes. When such a person breaches his fiduciary relationship, he may be treated more properly as a tipper than a tippee. See Shapiro v. Merrill Lynch, Pierce, Fenner & Smith, Inc., 495 F.2d 228, 237 (CA2 1974) (investment banker had access to material information when working on a proposed public offering for the corporation). For such a duty to be imposed, however, the corporation must expect the outsider to keep the disclosed nonpublic information confidential, and the relationship at least must imply such a duty.

A.

The SEC's position, as stated in its opinion in this case, is that a tippee "inherits" the *Cady, Roberts* obligation to shareholders whenever he receives inside information from an insider:

> "In tipping potential traders, Dirks breached a duty which he had assumed as a result of knowingly receiving confidential information from [Equity Funding] insiders. Tippees such as Dirks who receive non-public material information from insiders become 'subject to the same duty as [the] insiders.' Shapiro v. Merrill Lynch, Pierce, Fenner & Smith, Inc. [495 F.2d 228, 237 (CA2 1974) (quoting Ross v. Licht, 263 F.Supp. 395, 410 (SDNY 1967))]. Such a tippee breaches the fiduciary duty which he assumes from the insider when the tippee knowingly transmits the information to someone who will probably trade on the basis thereof. * * * Presumably, Dirks' informants were entitled to disclose the [Equity Funding] fraud in order to bring it to light and its perpetrators to justice. However, Dirks—standing in their shoes— committed a breach of the fiduciary duty which he had assumed in dealing with them, when he passed the information on to traders." 21 S.E.C. Docket, at 1410, n. 42.

This view differs little from the view that we rejected as inconsistent with congressional intent in *Chiarella*. In that case, the Court of Appeals agreed with the SEC and affirmed Chiarella's conviction, holding that " '[a]nyone—corporate insider or not—who regularly receives material nonpublic information may not use that information to trade in securities without incurring an affirmative duty to disclose.' " United States v. Chiarella, 588 F.2d 1358, 1365 (CA2 1978) (emphasis in original). Here, the SEC maintains that anyone who knowingly receives nonpublic material information from an insider has a fiduciary duty to disclose before trading.[90]

In effect, the SEC's theory of tippee liability in both cases appears rooted in the idea that the antifraud provisions require equal information among all traders. This conflicts with the principle set forth in *Chiarella* that only some persons, under some circumstances, will be barred from trading while in possession of material nonpublic informa-

---

90. [By the Court] Apparently, the SEC believes this case differs from *Chiarella* in that Dirks' receipt of inside information from Secrist, an insider, carried Secrist's duties with it, while Chiarella received the information without the direct involvement of an insider and thus inherited no duty to disclose or abstain. The SEC fails to explain, however, why the receipt of nonpublic information from an insider automatically carries with it the fiduciary duty of the insider. As we emphasized in *Chiarella*, mere possession of nonpublic information does not give rise to a duty to disclose or abstain; only a specific relationship does that. And we do not believe that the mere receipt of information from an insider creates such a special relationship between the tippee and the corporation's shareholders.

Apparently recognizing the weakness of its argument in light of *Chiarella*, the SEC attempts to distinguish that case factually as involving not "inside" information, but rather "market" information, i.e., "information generated within the company relating to its assets or earnings." This Court drew no such distinction in *Chiarella* and, as The Chief Justice noted, "[i]t is clear that § 10(b) and Rule 10b–5 by their terms and by their history make no such distinction." 445 U.S., at 241, n. 1, 100 S.Ct., at 1121, n. 1 (dissenting opinion).

tion. * * * We reaffirm today that "[a] duty [to disclose] arises from the relationship between parties * * * and not merely from one's ability to acquire information because of his position in the market." 445 U.S., at 232–233, n. 14, 100 S.Ct., at 1116–17, n. 14.

Imposing a duty to disclose or abstain solely because a person knowingly receives material nonpublic information from an insider and trades on it could have an inhibiting influence on the role of market analysts, which the SEC itself recognizes is necessary to the preservation of a healthy market.[91] It is commonplace for analysts to "ferret out and analyze information," 21 S.E.C., at 1406,[92] and this often is done by meeting with and questioning corporate officers and others who are insiders. And information that the analysts obtain normally may be the basis for judgments as to the market worth of a corporation's securities. The analyst's judgment in this respect is made available in market letters or otherwise to clients of the firm. It is the nature of this type of information, and indeed of the markets themselves, that such information cannot be made simultaneously available to all of the corporation's stockholders or the public generally.

B.

The conclusion that recipients of inside information do not invariably acquire a duty to disclose or abstain does not mean that such tippees always are free to trade on the information. The need for a ban on some tippee trading is clear. Not only are insiders forbidden by their fiduciary relationship from personally using undisclosed corporate information to their advantage, but they may not give such information to an outsider for the same improper purpose of exploiting the information for their personal gain. * * * Similarly, the transactions of those who knowingly participate with the fiduciary in such a breach are "as forbidden" as transactions "on behalf of the trustee himself."

91. [By the Court] The SEC expressly recognized that "[t]he value to the entire market of [analysts'] efforts cannot be gainsaid; market efficiency in pricing is significantly enhanced by [their] initiatives to ferret out and analyze information, and thus the analyst's work redounds to the benefit of all investors." 21 S.E.C., at 1406. The SEC asserts that analysts remain free to obtain from management corporate information for purposes of "filling in the 'interstices in analysis'. * * *" But this rule is inherently imprecise, and imprecision prevents parties from ordering their actions in accord with legal requirements. Unless the parties have some guidance as to where the line is between permissible and impermissible disclosures and uses, neither corporate insiders nor analysts can be sure when the line is crossed.

92. [By the Court] On its facts, this case is the unusual one. Dirks is an analyst in a broker-dealer firm, and he did interview management in the course of his investigation. He uncovered, however, startling information that required no analysis or exercise of judgment as to its market relevance. Nonetheless, the principle at issue here extends beyond these facts. The SEC's rule—applicable without regard to any breach by an insider—could have serious ramifications on reporting by analysts of investment views.

Despite the unusualness of Dirks' "find," the central role that he played in uncovering the fraud at Equity Funding, and that analysts in general can play in revealing information that corporations may have reason to withhold from the public, is an important one. Dirks' careful investigation brought to light a massive fraud at the corporation. And until the Equity Funding fraud was exposed, the information in the trading market was grossly inaccurate. But for Dirks' efforts, the fraud might well have gone undetected longer.

Mosser v. Darrow, 341 U.S. 267, 272, 71 S.Ct. 680, 682 (1951). As the Court explained in *Mosser,* a contrary rule "would open up opportunities for devious dealings in the name of the others that the trustee could not conduct in his own." 341 U.S., at 271, 71 S.Ct., at 682. See SEC v. Texas Gulf Sulphur Co., 446 F.2d 1301, 1308 (CA2), cert. denied, 404 U.S. 1005, 92 S.Ct. 561, (1971). Thus, the tippee's duty to disclose or abstain is derivative from that of the insider's duty. As we noted in *Chiarella,* "[t]he tippee's obligation has been viewed as arising from his role as a participant after the fact in the insider's breach of a fiduciary duty." 445 U.S., at 230, n. 12, 100 S.Ct., at 1115, n. 12.

Thus, some tippees must assume an insider's duty to the shareholders not because they receive inside information, but rather because it has been made available to them *improperly.* And for rule 10b–5 purposes, the insider's disclosure is improper only where it would violate his *Cady, Roberts* duty. Thus, a tippee assumes a fiduciary duty to the shareholders of a corporation not to trade on material nonpublic information only when the insider has breached his fiduciary duty to the shareholders by disclosing the information to the tippee and the tippee knows or should know that there has been a breach. As Commissioner Smith perceptively observed in *Investors Management Co.:* "[T]ippee responsibility must be related back to insider responsibility by a necessary finding that the tippee knew the information was given to him in breach of a duty by a person having a special relationship to the issuer not to disclose the information * * *." 44 S.E.C., at 651 (concurring in the result). Tipping thus properly is viewed only as a means of indirectly violating the *Cady, Roberts* disclose-or-abstain rule.[93]

C.

In determining whether a tippee is under an obligation to disclose or abstain, it thus is necessary to determine whether the insider's "tip" constituted a breach of the insider's fiduciary duty. All disclosures of

---

93. [By the Court] We do not suggest that knowingly trading on inside information is ever "socially desirable or even that it is devoid of moral considerations." Dooley, Enforcement of Insider Trading Restrictions, 66 Va.L.Rev. 1, 55 (1980). Nor do we imply an absence of responsibility to disclose promptly indications of illegal actions by a corporation to the proper authorities—typically the SEC and exchange authorities in cases involving securities. Depending on the circumstances, and even where permitted by law, one's trading on material nonpublic information is behavior that may fall below ethical standards of conduct. But in a statutory area of the law such as securities regulation, where legal principles of general application must be applied, there may be "significant distinctions between actual le-

gal obligations and ethical ideals." SEC, Report of the Special Study of Securities Markets, H.R.Doc. No. 95, 88th Cong., 1st Sess., pt. 1, pp. 237–238 (1963). The SEC recognizes this. At oral argument, the following exchange took place:

> "QUESTION: So, it would not have satisfied his obligation under the law to go to the SEC first?
>
> "[SEC's counsel]: That is correct. That an insider has to observe what has come to be known as the abstain or disclosure rule. Either the information has to be disclosed to the market if it is inside information * * * or the insider must abstain."

Thus, it is clear that Rule 10b–5 does not impose any obligations simply to tell the SEC about the fraud before trading.

confidential corporate information are not inconsistent with the duty insiders owe to shareholders. In contrast to the extraordinary facts of this case, the more typical situation in which there will be a question whether disclosure violates the insider's *Cady, Roberts* duty is when insiders disclose information to analysts. In some situations the insider will act consistently with his fiduciary duty to shareholders, and yet release of the information may affect the market. For example, it may not be clear—either to the corporate insider or to the recipient analyst—whether the information will be viewed as material nonpublic information. Corporate officials may mistakenly think the information already has been disclosed or that it is not material enough to affect the market. Whether disclosure is a breach of duty therefore depends in large part on the purpose of the disclosure. This standard was identified by the SEC itself in *Cady, Roberts:* a purpose of the securities laws was to eliminate "use of inside information for personal advantage." 40 S.E.C., at 912, n. 15. Thus, the test is whether the insider personally will benefit, directly or indirectly, from his disclosure. Absent some personal gain, there has been no breach of duty to stockholders. And absent a breach by the insider, there is no derivative breach. As Commissioner Smith stated in *Investors Management Co.:* "It is important in this type of case to focus on policing insiders and what they do * * * rather than on policing information *per se* and its possession. * * *" 44 S.E.C., at 648 (concurring in the result).

The SEC argues that, if inside-trading liability does not exist when the information is transmitted for a proper purpose but is used for trading, it would be a rare situation when the parties could not fabricate some ostensibly legitimate business justification for transmitting the information. We think the SEC is unduly concerned. In determining whether the insider's purpose in making a particular disclosure is fraudulent, the SEC and the courts are not required to read the parties' minds. Scienter in some cases is relevant in determining whether the tipper has violated his *Cady, Roberts* duty.[94] But to determine whether the disclosure itself "deceive[s], manipulate[s], or defraud[s]" shareholders, Aaron v. SEC, 446 U.S. 680, 686, 100 S.Ct. 1945, 1950 (1980), the initial inquiry is whether there has been a breach of duty by the insider. This requires courts to focus on objective criteria, i.e., whether the insider receives a direct or indirect personal

---

94. [By the Court] *Scienter*—"a mental state embracing intent to deceive, manipulate, or defraud," Ernst & Ernst v. Hochfelder, 425 U.S. 185, 193, n. 12, 96 S.Ct. 1375, 1381, n. 12 (1976)—is an independent element of a Rule 10b–5 violation. See Aaron v. SEC, 446 U.S. 680, 695, 100 S.Ct. 1945, 1955, (1980). * * * It is not enough that an insider's conduct results in harm to investors; rather, a violation may be found only where there is "intentional or willful conduct designed to deceive or defraud investors by controlling or artifi-

cially affecting the price of securities." Ernst & Ernst v. Hochfelder, supra, at 199, 96 S.Ct., at 1383. The issue in this case, however, is not whether Secrist or Dirks acted with *scienter,* but rather whether there was any deceptive or fraudulent conduct at all, i.e., whether Secrist's disclosure constituted a breach of his fiduciary duty and thereby caused injury to shareholders. Only if there was such a breach did Dirks, a tippee, acquire a fiduciary duty to disclose or abstain.

benefit from the disclosure, such as a pecuniary gain or a reputational benefit that will translate into future earnings. Cf. 40 S.E.C., at 912, n. 15; Brudney, Insiders, Outsiders, and Informational Advantages Under the Federal Securities Laws, 93 Harv.L.Rev. 324, 348 (1979) ("The theory ＊ ＊ ＊ is that the insider, by giving the information out selectively, is in effect selling the information to its recipient for cash, reciprocal information, or other things of value for himself. ＊ ＊ ＊"). There are objective facts and circumstances that often justify such an inference. For example, there may be a relationship between the insider and the recipient that suggests a *quid pro quo* from the latter, or an intention to benefit the particular recipient. The elements of fiduciary duty and exploitation of nonpublic information also exist when an insider makes a gift of confidential information to a trading relative or friend. The tip and trade resemble trading by the insider himself followed by a gift of the profits to the recipient.

Determining whether an insider personally benefits from a particular disclosure, a question of fact, will not always be easy for courts. But it is essential, we think, to have a guiding principle for those whose daily activities must be limited and instructed by the SEC's inside-trading rules, and we believe that there must be a breach of the insider's fiduciary duty before the tippee inherits the duty to disclose or abstain. In contrast, the rule adopted by the SEC in this case would have no limiting principle.[95]

IV.

Under the inside-trading and tipping rules set forth above, we find that there was no actionable violation by Dirks. It is undisputed that Dirks himself was a stranger to Equity Funding, with no pre-existing fiduciary duty to its shareholders. He took no action, directly or indirectly, that induced the shareholders or officers of Equity Funding to repose trust or confidence in him. There was no expectation by Dirks' sources that he would keep their information in confidence. Nor did Dirks misappropriate or illegally obtain the information about Equity Funding. Unless the insiders breached their *Cady, Roberts* duty to shareholders in disclosing the nonpublic information to Dirks, he breached no duty when he passed it on to investors as well as to the *Wall Street Journal*.

It is clear that neither Secrist nor the other Equity Funding employees violated their *Cady, Roberts* duty to the corporation's shareholders by providing information to Dirks.[96] The tippers received no

---

95. [By the Court] Without legal limitations, market participants are forced to rely on the reasonableness of the SEC's litigation strategy, but that can be hazardous, as the facts of this case make plain.

＊ ＊ ＊

96. [By the Court] In this Court, the SEC appears to contend that an insider invariably violates a fiduciary duty to the corporation's shareholders by transmitting nonpublic corporate information to an outsider when he has reason to believe that the outsider may use it to the disadvantage of the shareholders. "Thus, regardless of any ultimate motive to bring to public attention the derelictions at Equity Funding, Secrist breached his duty to Equity Funding shareholders." Brief for Respondent

monetary or personal benefit for revealing Equity Funding's secrets, nor was their purpose to make a gift of valuable information to Dirks. As the facts of this case clearly indicate, the tippers were motivated by a desire to expose the fraud. In the absence of a breach of duty to shareholders by the insiders, there was no derivative breach by Dirks. Dirks therefore could not have been "a participant after the fact in [an] insider's breach of a fiduciary duty." Chiarella, 445 U.S., at 230, n. 12, 100 S.Ct., at 1115, n. 12.

V.

We conclude that Dirks, in the circumstances of this case, had no duty to abstain from use of the inside information that he obtained. The judgment of the Court of Appeals therefore is

Reversed.

JUSTICE BLACKMUN, with whom JUSTICE BRENNAN and JUSTICE MARSHALL join, dissenting.

The Court today takes still another step to limit the protections provided investors by § 10(b) of the Securities Exchange Act of 1934. See Chiarella v. United States, 445 U.S. 222, 246, 100 S.Ct. 1108, 1123, 63 L.Ed.2d 348 (1980) (dissenting opinion). The device employed in this case engrafts a special motivational requirement on the fiduciary duty doctrine. This innovation excuses a knowing and intentional violation of an insider's duty to shareholders if the insider does not act from a motive of personal gain. Even on the extraordinary facts of this case, such an innovation is not justified. ＊ ＊ ＊

In my view, Secrist violated his duty to Equity Funding shareholders by transmitting material nonpublic information to Dirks with the intention that Dirks would cause his clients to trade on that information. Dirks, therefore, was under a duty to make the information publicly available or to refrain from actions that he knew would lead to trading. Because Dirks caused his clients to trade, he violated § 10(b)

---

31. This perceived "duty" differs markedly from the one that the SEC identified in *Cady, Roberts* and that has been the basis for federal tippee-trading rules to date. In fact, the SEC did not charge Secrist with any wrongdoing, and we do not understand the SEC to have relied on any theory of a breach of duty by Secrist in finding that Dirks breached his duty to Equity Funding's shareholders. ＊ ＊ ＊

Chiarella made it explicitly clear there is no general duty to forgo market transactions "based on material, nonpublic information." 455 U.S., at 233, 100 S.Ct., at 1117. Such a duty would "depar[t] radically from the established doctrine that duty arises from a specific relationship between two parties."

Moreover, to constitute a violation of Rule 10b–5, there must be fraud. See Ernst & Ernst v. Hochfelder, 425 U.S. 185, 199, 96 S.Ct. 1375, 1383, 47 L.Ed.2d 668 (1976) (statutory words "manipulative," "device," and "contrivance ＊ ＊ ＊ connot[e] intentional or willful conduct designed to *deceive or defraud* investors by controlling or artificially affecting the price of securities") (emphasis added). There is no evidence that Secrist's disclosure was intended to or did in fact "deceive or defraud" anyone. Secrist certainly intended to convey relevant information that management was unlawfully concealing, and—so far as the record shows—he believed that persuading Dirks to investigate was the best way to disclose the fraud. Other efforts had proved fruitless. Under any objective standard, Secrist received no direct or indirect personal benefit from the disclosure.

and Rule 10b–5. Any other result is a disservice to this country's attempt to provide fair and efficient capital markets. I dissent.

Notes

(1) Academic commentary on the "benefit" requirement imposed by Dirks has been generally negative: "This benefit requirement is a curious and largely unnecessary wrinkle; if there is one clear understanding in the common law of fiduciary responsibility, it is that an intent to benefit is not a necessary element." Langevoort, Commentary—The Insider Trading Sanctions Act of 1984 and its Effect on Existing Law, 37 Vand.L.Rev. 1273, 1292 (1984). On the other hand, the Securities and Exchange Commission appears to have little problem in finding a "benefit" in order to meet this requirement. When Paul Thayer, then Deputy Secretary of Defense and former CEO of LTV, Inc. was charged with passing information to a group of eight friends, including a young woman who was a former LTV employee, for example, the S.E.C. charged that Mr. Thayer received a personal benefit because of his "close personal relationship" with the woman. New York Times, Jan. 5, 1984, pt. A, p. 1, col. 3–4; Jan. 6, 1984, pt. A, p. 1, col. 2. In United States v. Reed, 601 F.Supp. 685 (S.D.N.Y.1985), the court refused to dismiss an indictment of a tippee who was the son of the tipper even though there was no evidence that the father intended to benefit his son by the disclosure; see also S.E.C. v. Gaspar (S.D.N.Y.1985) (1985 WL 521) [tipper received an "enhanced professional relationship" from tippee].

(2) In S.E.C. v. Switzer, 590 F.Supp. 756 (W.D.Okl.1984), Barry Switzer, the coach of the University of Oklahoma football team, was attending a high school track meet in which his son was competing. He decided to take a sun bath on a row of bleachers; while lying there inobtrusively he happened to overhear an acquaintance, Mr. Platt, talking with Mrs. Platt about problems facing his business. Switzer traded profitably on the information he thereby learned, but was absolved of liability under the Dirks standard since Switzer was basically an eavesdropper and the information was not disclosed by Mr. Platt for his own benefit.

(3) Courts have also readily accepted the idea, set forth in footnote 89 (footnote number 14 in Justice Powell's opinion) that a person may become a "temporary insider." See S.E.C. v. Lund, 570 F.Supp. 1397 (C.D.Cal.1983) [a confidant of a corporate officer]; S.E.C. v. Musella, 578 F.Supp. 425 (S.D. N.Y.1984) [the manager of office services of Sullivan and Cromwell]; S.E.C. v. Tome, 638 F.Supp. 596 (S.D.N.Y.1986) [social friend and adviser to CEO]. Following the original decision in *Musella* (relating to the manager of office services of Sullivan and Cromwell), the SEC proceeded against two New York City police officers who were "third tier tippees" utilizing the same information (but who did not know the original source of the information on which they were trading). S.E.C. v. Musella, 678 F.Supp. 1060 (S.D.N.Y. 1988). The police officers nevertheless were required to disgorge the rather modest profits they made since they had "made a conscious and deliberate choice not to ask [the second tier tippee] any questions about the confidential source whose existence they suspected." The court concluded that the police officers had reason to know that the "first tier tippee" [the office

manager at Sullivan and Cromwell and a "temporary insider"] had breached a fiduciary duty by misappropriating confidential information.

2. REGULATION UNDER THE INSIDER TRADING AND SECURITIES FRAUD ENFORCEMENT ACT OF 1988

During the 1980s Congress enacted two statutes dealing with insider trading. The first of these statutes, the Insider Trading Sanctions Act of 1984, Pub.Law 98–376 (98th Cong.2d Sess.) ("ITSA"), introduced statutory civil penalties into the law of insider trading. The second, the Insider Trading and Securities Fraud Enforcement Act of 1988, Pub.Law 100–704 (100th Cong.2d Sess.) amended and codified ITSA and added important new concepts. These two statutes obviously reflect the contemporaneous Congressional intent to enforce vigorously and militantly the current prohibition against insider trading.

Two important points about these statutes should be made at the outset. First, one will recall arguments made primarily by members of the "Chicago School" of law and economics that insider trading is a "victimless crime" and that such trading should be legalized since it serves important social and economic functions. This thesis has been emphatically rejected by Congress in these two statutes. "[T]he far greater number of commentators support efforts to curb insider trading, viewing such efforts as crucial to the capital formation process that depends on investor confidence in the fairness and integrity of our securities markets. Insider trading damages the legitimacy of the capital market and diminishes the public's faith." House Rep. No. 100–910 (House Energy and Commerce Committee) to accompany H.R. 5133 (100th Cong.2d Sess.), 8 (1988). Second, neither ITSA nor ITSFEA define what constitutes illegal "insider trading." We thus have the apparent anomaly of substantial civil penalties being prescribed for conduct whose legality is to be determined by a set of principles established in a series of judicial decisions that can hardly be described as setting clear boundaries of illegal conduct. The decision not to define the boundaries of unlawful conduct in this area was highly controversial in the consideration of ITSFEA (and indeed the SEC finally decided that a definition was undesirable only after its unexpected victory in *Carpenter*). See Symposium: Defining "Insider Trading," 39 Ala.L.Rev. 337 (1988), particularly the articles by Kripke, A Note on Insider Trading: An Example of How Not to Make Law, 39 Ala.L.Rev. 349 (1988); Cox, Choices: Paving the Road Toward a "Definition" of Insider Trading, 39 Ala.L.Rev. 381 (1988); and Pitt and Shapiro, The Insider Trading Proscriptions Act of 1987: A Legislative Initiative For a Sorely Needed Clarification of the Law Against Insider Trading, 39 Ala.L.Rev. 415 (1988).

Notes

Do you believe that a statutory definition of illegal insider trading is really necessary? Is it unconstitutional for Congress to impose substantial criminal and civil penalties for conduct that is defined only by judicial opinion? Can a lawyer advise a client as to what is legal and what is not when there is no statutory definition of illegal conduct? The Committee Report accompanying ITSFEA explains why the attempt to develop a statutory definition was abandoned:

> While cognizant of the importance of providing clear guidelines for behavior which may be subject to stiff criminal and civil penalties, the Committee nevertheless declined to include a statutory definition in this bill for several reasons. First, the Committee believed that the court-drawn parameters of insider trading have established clear guidelines for the vast majority of traditional insider trading cases, and that a statutory definition could potentially be narrowing, and in an unintended manner facilitate schemes to evade the law. Second, the Committee did not believe that the lack of consensus over the proper delineation of an insider trading definition should impede progress on the needed enforcement reforms encompassed within this legislation. Accordingly, the Committee does not intend to alter the substantive law with respect to insider trading with this legislation. The legal principles governing insider trading cases are well-established and widely-known.

House Rep. No. 100–910 (House Energy and Commerce Committee) to accompany H.R. 5133 (100th Cong.2d Sess.), 11.

SECURITIES EXCHANGE ACT OF 1934

15 U.S.C.A. § 78u–1 (1989).

SEC. 21A. CIVIL PENALTIES

(a) AUTHORITY TO IMPOSE CIVIL PENALTIES.—

(1) Judicial actions by commission authorized.—Whenever it shall appear to the Commission that any person has violated any provision of this title or the rules or regulations thereunder by purchasing or selling a security while in possession of material, nonpublic information in, or has violated any such provision by communicating such information in connection with, a transaction on or through the facilities of a national securities exchange or from or through a broker or dealer, and which is not part of a public offering by an issuer of securities other than standardized options, the Commission—

> (A) may bring an action in a United States district court to seek, and the court shall have jurisdiction to impose, a civil penalty to be paid by the person who committed such violation; and

> (B) may, subject to subsection (b)(1), bring an action in a United States district court to seek, and the court shall have jurisdiction to impose, a civil penalty to be paid by a person who, at the time of the violation, directly or indirectly controlled the person who committed such violation.

(2) Amount of penalty for person who committed violation.— The amount of the penalty which may be imposed on the person who committed such violation shall be determined by the court in light of the facts and circumstances, but shall not exceed three times the profit gained or loss avoided as a result of such unlawful purchase, sale, or communication.

(3) Amount of penalty for controlling person.—The amount of the penalty which may be imposed on any person who, at the time of the violation, directly or indirectly controlled the person who committed such violation, shall be determined by the court in light of the facts and circumstances, but shall not exceed the greater of $1,000,000, or three times the amount of the profit gained or loss avoided as a result of such controlled person's violation. If such controlled person's violation was a violation by communication, the profit gained or loss avoided as a result of the violation shall, for purposes of this paragraph only, be deemed to be limited to the profit gained or loss avoided by the person or persons to whom the controlled person directed such communication.

(b) LIMITATIONS ON LIABILITY.—

(1) Liability of controlling persons.—No controlling person shall be subject to a penalty under subsection (a)(1)(B) unless the Commission establishes that—

(A) such controlling person knew or recklessly disregarded the fact that such controlled person was likely to engage in the act or acts constituting the violation and failed to take appropriate steps to prevent such act or acts before they occurred; or

(B) such controlling person knowingly or recklessly failed to establish, maintain, or enforce any policy or procedure required under section 15(f) of this title [97] or section 204A of the Investment Advisers Act of 1940 and such failure substantially contributed to or permitted the occurrence of the act or acts constituting the violation.

(2) Additional restrictions on liability.—No person shall be subject to a penalty under subsection (a) solely by reason of employing another person who is subject to a penalty under such subsection, unless such employing person is liable as a controlling person

97. [By the Editor] The referenced section (also added by Pub.L. 100–174) reads as follows:

Sec. 15(f) Every registered broker or dealer shall establish, maintain and enforce written policies and procedures reasonably designed, taking into consideration the nature of such broker's or dealer's business, to prevent the misuse in violation of this title, or the rules or regulations thereunder, of material, non-public information by such broker or dealer or any person associated with such broker or dealer. The Commission, as it deems necessary or appropriate in the public interest or for the protection of investors, shall adopt rules or regulations to require specific policies or procedures reasonably designed to prevent misuse in violation of this title (or the rules or regulations thereunder) of material, nonpublic information.

under paragraph (1) of this subsection. Section 20(a) of this title [98] shall not apply to actions under subsection (a) of this section.

(c) AUTHORITY OF COMMISSION.—The Commission, by such rules, regulations, and orders as it considers necessary or appropriate in the public interest or for the protection of investors, may exempt, in whole or in part, either unconditionally or upon specific terms and conditions, any person or transaction or class of persons or transactions from this section.

(d) PROCEDURES FOR COLLECTION.—

(1) Payment of penalty to treasury.—A penalty imposed under this section shall (subject to subsection (e)) be payable into the Treasury of the United States.

(2) Collection of penalties.—If a person upon whom such a penalty is imposed shall fail to pay such penalty within the time prescribed in the court's order, the Commission may refer the matter to the Attorney General who shall recover such penalty by action in the appropriate United States district court.

(3) Remedy not exclusive.—The actions authorized by this section may be brought in addition to any other actions that the Commission or the Attorney General are entitled to bring.

(4) Jurisdiction and venue.—For purposes of section 27 of this title, actions under this section shall be actions to enforce a liability or a duty created by this title.

(5) Statute of limitations.—No action may be brought under this section more than 5 years after the date of the purchase or sale. This section shall not be construed to bar or limit in any manner any action by the Commission or the Attorney General under any other provision of this title, nor shall it bar or limit in any manner any action to recover penalties, or to seek any other order regarding penalties, imposed in an action commenced within 5 years of such transaction.

(e) AUTHORITY TO AWARD BOUNTIES TO INFORMANTS.—Notwithstanding the provisions of subsection (d)(1), there shall be paid from amounts imposed as a penalty under this section and recovered by the Commission or the Attorney General, such sums, not to exceed 10 percent of such amounts, as the Commission deems appropriate, to the person or persons who provide information leading to the imposition of such penalty. Any determinations under this subsection, including whether, to whom, or in what amount to make payments, shall be in the sole discretion of the Commission, except that no such payment shall be

---

98. [By the Editor] Section 20(a) provides:

Sec. 20(a) Every person who, directly or indirectly, controls any person liable under any provision of this title or of any rule or regulation thereunder shall also be liable jointly and severally with and to the same extent as such controlled person to any person to whom such controlled person is liable, unless the controlling person acted in good faith and did not directly or indirectly induce the act or acts constituting the violation or cause of action.

made to any member, officer, or employee of any appropriate regulatory agency, the Department of Justice, or a self-regulatory organization. Any such determination shall be final and not subject to judicial review.

(f) DEFINITION.—For purposes of this section, "profit gained" or "loss avoided" is the difference between the purchase or sale price of the security and the value of that security as measured by the trading price of the security a reasonable period after public dissemination of the nonpublic information. * * *

Notes

(1) ITSFEA increased the criminal penalties for willful violation of the Securities Acts or regulations issued thereunder from $100,000 and five years to $1,000,000 and ten years for individuals, and a fine of up to $2,500,000 when the defendant is a "person other than a natural person." ITSFEA, § 4.

(2) The power to impose civil penalties, first granted under ITSA and now codified in section 20A added by ITSFEA, greatly increases the risks of insider trading. Courts have consistently added substantial civil penalties to the disgorgement of insider trading profits. In S.E.C. v. Wang, 699 F.Supp. 44 (S.D.N.Y.1988), for example, the court stated that under the circumstances it planned to impose a penalty equal to the amount of disgorgement, thereby doubling the amount that must be repaid.

(3) While courts determine the amount of civil penalty imposed in litigated cases, most insider trading cases are settled. When discussing settlements, the amount of the penalty is, of course, negotiated by the defendant and the SEC or Department of Justice. Since 1984, widely publicized settlements in the hundreds of millions of dollars have been negotiated with Ivan Boesky, Drexel Burnham Lambert, Inc., and Michael Milken. These settlements involve criminal and civil proceedings and claims under RICO, mail fraud, and other criminal statutes as well as under the securities acts. These widely publicized cases do not give a true picture of the enforcement effort in the insider trading area.

(4) Many settlements of insider trading charges involve persons with modest means while others involve settlements running into the millions of dollars. The following anecdotal sampling of cases brought under ITSA and ITSFEA indicate that the SEC and Department of Justice appear to be quite willing to invest prosecutorial resources in order to pursue "small fry" as well as the Ivan Boeskys:

(a) Dennis Levine, an investment banker, agreed to repay $11.6 million in insider trading profits, plead guilty to four felony counts, and to testify against Ivan Boesky and other defendants, if necessary.

(b) First Boston Corporation settled charges of trading on nonpublic information concerning CIGNA Corporation, a client, by agreeing to disgorge $132,138 of profits and pay a civil penalty of $664,276.

(c) Martin Siegal, a senior manager of Kidder Peabody Inc., agreed to plead guilty to criminal violations and to settle SEC civil injunction and administrative proceedings by disgorging $13,676,101 of profits and pay a civil penalty of $11,618,674.

(d) A typesetting supervisor for Applied Graphics Technology, Inc., a printing company where Business Week is published, agreed to pay $46,000, (about the amount that he, his girlfriend, and his girlfriend's family made on 43 securities transactions over six months), based on advance knowledge of stories that later appeared in Business Week.

(e) In an unrelated case involving Business Week, a broker pleaded guilty to criminal charges of wire fraud, because he misappropriated and traded on information later appearing in Business Week; the broker purchased advance copies of Business Week from employees of the printer and then traded in advance of the distribution of the magazine. The trading profits from these transactions were about $74,000 for the broker's own account and $20,000 for the account of another person.

(f) A former partner in the law firm of Dorsey & Whitney of Minneapolis was charged with making illegal profits of $4.3 million on trading in stock and options in Pillsbury Corporation based on information learned from other lawyers in the firm about a tender offer to be made for that corporation. The attorney was also charged with diversion of clients' funds and did not contest an order of disbarment.

(g) A former employee of Household International Inc., her husband and a family friend settled charges that they traded on information about Household's plans to acquire a Texas company. The employee resigned from Household and agreed to disgorge $1,383 in profits plus a civil penalty of $2,320; the family friend, a broker at A.G. Edwards Co., agreed to disgorge $2,950, representing profits he and two of his clients made on the information, plus a civil penalty of $937 and a one-year suspension from the securities business.

(h) A "second tier tippee" settled SEC charges that he traded on nonpublic information involving a tender offer for two trucking companies; he agreed to disgorge profits of $29,250 and pay a penalty of $21,343.75. The tippee learned of the information from a business associate and his "live-in companion" while vacationing in the British West Indies.

(i) The CEO of Continental Can agreed to disgorge $154,086 in profits and a $128,412 penalty. The profits were earned by a "friend" of the CEO on the basis of information about a pending acquisition between unrelated companies unconnected with Continental Can that the CEO learned about from a relative. The identity of the friend was not disclosed.

(5) The SEC has also not hesitated to pursue law firm partners, associates, paralegals, and others who engage in insider trading on the basis of information obtained through law firms. One cannot assume that even modest profits will not be discovered and vigorously pursued. It is unlikely that a law firm would provide any assistance to, or retain, a partner, associate, or staff employee charged with insider trading. The prohibitions against insider trading are therefore of particular concern to partners and employees of law firms. The temptation to engage in even a discreet amount of trading on inside information obtained from one's work should be sternly resisted.

(6) Consider section 21A(a)(1)(B). The liability of controlling persons was added by ITSFEA in 1988. Under these provisions, would Texas Gulf Sulphur, Inc. have been liable for the insider trading transactions of Darke (the geologist)? Would Pandick Press have been liable for the transactions entered into by Chiarella? What about Sullivan and Cromwell being held liable for the inside trading of its office manager? Certainly a wide variety of employers whose employees may have access to valuable inside information will have to "establish, maintain, [and] enforce" policies or procedures designed to prevent the misuse of such information: issuers, law firms, accounting firms, financial printing companies, and the like. Furthermore, the policies or procedures will have to go much deeper down into the organization than merely the officers, directors, partners, and top level personnel. It is likely that many readers of this note will have first-hand experience with such procedures, either by being subject to them personally or by creating and applying such policies on behalf of clients, or both.

(7) Assume that you overhear a colleague talking about or appearing to execute a transaction that sounds suspiciously like insider trading. May you turn him or her in and claim a "bounty" for doing so? See section 21A(e). Senator D'Amato described the objective of this provision as follows on the floor of the United States Senate:

> To those who oppose bounty I ask that they put themselves in the place of an employee or coworker of an insider trader. What incentive is there to blow the whistle that can counteract the clear risk to profession and livelihood? They may answer that civic duty is enough, and one would hope they were right. But I disagree. Bounty is a positive incentive we can offer and I see no real cost in doing so.

134 Cong.Rec. S17219 (Oct. 21, 1988). The SEC has issued regulations describing the procedures for applying for, and obtaining, bounties under this section. SEC Rel. 34–26944, 54 Fed.Reg. 28,797 (1989).

SECURITIES EXCHANGE ACT OF 1934

15 U.S.C. § 78t–1.

§ 20A. Liability to contemporaneous traders for insider trading

(a) PRIVATE RIGHTS OF ACTION BASED ON CONTEMPORANEOUS TRADING.—Any person who violates any provision of this title or the rules or regulations thereunder by purchasing or selling a security while in possession of material, nonpublic information shall be liable in an action in any court of competent jurisdiction to any person who, contemporaneously with the purchase or sale of securities that is the subject of such violation, has purchased (where such violation is based on a sale of securities) or sold (where such violation is based on a purchase of securities) securities of the same class.

(b) LIMITATIONS ON LIABILITY.—

(1) Contemporaneous trading actions limited to profit gained or loss avoided.—The total amount of damages imposed under subsection (a) shall not exceed the profit gained or loss avoided in the transaction or transactions that are the subject of the violation.

(2) Offsetting disgorgements against liability.—The total amount of damages imposed against any person under subsection (a) shall be diminished by the amounts, if any, that such person may be required to disgorge, pursuant to a court order obtained at the instance of the Commission, in a proceeding brought * * * relating to the same transaction or transactions.

(3) Controlling person liability.—No person shall be liable under this section solely by reason of employing another person who is liable under this section, but the liability of a controlling person under this section shall be subject to section 20(a) of this title.

(4) Statute of limitations.—No action may be brought under this section more than 5 years after the date of the last transaction that is the subject of the violation.

(c) JOINT AND SEVERAL LIABILITY FOR COMMUNICATING.—Any person who violates any provision of this title or the rules or regulations thereunder by communicating material, nonpublic information shall be jointly and severally liable under subsection (a) with, and to the same extent as, any person or persons liable under subsection (a) to whom the communication was directed.

(d) AUTHORITY NOT TO RESTRICT OTHER EXPRESS OR IMPLIED RIGHTS OF ACTION.—Nothing in this section shall be construed to limit or condition the right of any person to bring an action to enforce a requirement of this title or the availability of any cause of action implied from a provision of this title.

(e) PROVISIONS NOT TO AFFECT PUBLIC PROSECUTIONS.—This section shall not be construed to bar or limit in any manner any action by the Commission or the Attorney General under any other provision of this title, nor shall it bar or limit in any manner any action to recover penalties, or to seek any other order regarding penalties.

Notes

(1) Section 20A was added by ITSFEA in 1988.

(2) Prior to the enactment of this section, the question whether private actions may be maintained against persons trading on inside information arose in a number of cases; the leading cases in which such suits were permitted are Elkind v. Liggett & Myers, Inc., 635 F.2d 156 (2d Cir.1980), and Shapiro v. Merrill Lynch, Pierce, Fenner & Smith, Inc., 495 F.2d 228 (2d Cir.1974). Some courts, however, did not permit such suits—presumably dismayed by the complex and erratic consequences of such litigation particularly in the computation of damages. Among the cases in which private actions were not permitted against defendants trading on the basis of inside information are Fridrich v. Bradford, 542 F.2d 307 (6th Cir.1976), cert. denied 429 U.S. 1053, 97 S.Ct. 767, 50 L.Ed.2d 769 (1977) [defendants did not purchase shares from plaintiffs and their trading in no way affected the plaintiffs' decision to sell; private civil liability does not need to be coextensive with the reach of the SEC]; Moss v. Morgan Stanley Inc., 719 F.2d 5 (2d Cir.1983), cert. denied sub nom. Moss v. Newman, 465 U.S. 1025,

104 S.Ct. 1280, 79 L.Ed.2d 684 (1984) [defendants were tippees of aggressor in proposed tender offer and traded in the target's stock; the court held that the tippees owed no duty to the plaintiffs on an impersonal market]. See also State Teachers Retirement Bd. v. Fluor Corp., 654 F.2d 843 (2d Cir. 1981) [defendants had actually purchased shares sold by plaintiff on the basis of insider information; dismissal of complaint reversed].

(3) Section 20A(b)(1) establishes the manner in which damages are to be measured in a narrow fashion. Since they are limited to "profit gained" or "loss avoided," and are subject to reduction for amounts disgorged in suits brought by the SEC, there may not be extensive litigation under this section. Does the definition of "profit gained" or "loss avoided" in section 21A also apply to the measurement of damages under section 20A(b)(1)?

(4) For attempts to determine whether investors or speculators are harmed by insider trading, see Karjala, Statutory Regulation of Insider Trading in Impersonal Markets, 1982 Duke L.J. 627; Wang, Trading on Material Nonpublic Information on Impersonal Stock Markets: Who is Harmed, and Who Can Sue Whom Under SEC Rule 10b–5?, 54 S.Cal.L.Rev. 1217 (1981).

(5) Is a person injured in some direct way by insider trading who is not a "contemporaneous trader" restricted by section 20A? The House Committee Report contains the following discussion:

> [T]he Committee recognized that there clearly are injuries caused by insider trading to others beyond contemporaneous traders. In the view of the Committee, Section 10(b), Rule 10b–5, and other relevant provisions of the Exchange Act have sufficient flexibility to recognize and protect any person defrauded, or harmed by a violation of any provision of this title or the rules or regulations thereunder by another person's purchasing or selling a security while in the possession of material, nonpublic information, or communicating such information to others.

> The most prominent example of the non-contemporaneous trader suit which came to the attention of the Committee involved a suit filed by Anheuser–Busch Companies, Inc. against Paul Thayer, a former director of the corporation. See Anheuser–Busch Companies, Inc., v. Thayer, et al., CA3–85–0794–R (N.D.Texas 1986). In that case, the plaintiff alleged that it was defrauded not as a result of trading with the defendant, but by having information secretly stolen and by having the subsequent trading on the information concealed. According to the complaint in this case, prior to public dissemination, the tipper disclosed to several parties the plans of Anheuser–Busch to acquire Campbell Taggart, Inc. The alleged misappropriation of Anheuser–Busch's confidential information proximately caused a significant increase in the market price of Campbell Taggart stock before Anheuser–Busch announced its offer. This forced Anheuser–Busch to raise its tender offer price, and the company eventually paid approximately $80 million more as a result of the illegal insider trading. Clearly, in such a case, the plaintiff corporation was a victim of the defendant's misap-

propriation. In the view of the Committee, where the plaintiff can prove that it suffered injury as a result of the defendant's insider trading, the plaintiff has standing to sue in this circumstance, and the remedial purposes of the securities laws require recognition of such an action.

In the view of the Committee, it was also important to note that in situations such as the Anheuser–Busch case and others, the potential harm to the plaintiff from the defendant's insider trading or tipping may be far greater than the profit gained or loss avoided by that defendant. The Committee recognizes that where the plaintiff demonstrates that he was defrauded by the defendant's insider trading and suffered actual damages proximately caused by the defendant's behavior, a cap of profit gained or loss avoided by the defendant, which is applicable for actions by contemporaneous traders, is not appropriate. Rather, in such an implied private cause of action, the plaintiff should be able to recover the full extent of those actual damages.

House Rep. (Energy and Commerce Committee) No. 100–910 (To accompany H.R. 5133) (10th Cong. 2nd Sess.) 27–28.

(6) Should a person receiving a false tip have a claim against his tipper? Of course, if the information had been accurate, the tippee would have himself violated rule 10b–5, and a plausible argument may be made that he has unclean hands and should not be permitted to maintain a suit against his tipper. Several lower courts split on the issue whether the *in pari delicto* defense should be applied in such a case, but the United States Supreme Court firmly resolved the disagreement in Eichler v. Berner, 472 U.S. 299, 105 S.Ct. 2622, 86 L.Ed.2d 215 (1985). The Court stated that a plaintiff should be barred in these circumstances only where "(1) as a direct result of his own actions, the plaintiff bears at least substantially equal responsibility for the violations he seeks to redress, and (2) preclusion of suit would not significantly interfere with the effective enforcement of the securities laws and protection of the investing public." Id. at 310, 105 S.Ct. at 2629.

SECURITIES EXCHANGE ACT OF 1934

15 U.S.C.A. § 78t (1989).

§ 20. Liability to contemporaneous traders for insider trading.

* * * (d) Wherever communicating, or purchasing or selling a security while in possession of, material nonpublic information would violate, or result in liability to any purchaser or seller of the security under any provision of this chapter, or any rule or regulation thereunder, such conduct in connection with a purchase or sale of a put, call, straddle, option, or privilege with respect to such security or with respect to a group or index of securities including such security, shall also violate and result in comparable liability to any purchaser or seller of that security under such provision, rule, or regulation.

Notes

(1) Section 20(d) was added by ITSA in 1984.

(2) In Laventhall v. General Dynamics Corp., 704 F.2d 407 (8th Cir. 1983), cert. denied 464 U.S. 846, 104 S.Ct. 150, the court held that a plaintiff who sold call options did not have standing to sue a defendant who had bought stock under rule 10b–5. The court relied primarily on language in *Chiarella* that rule 10b–5 required a "special relationship" between a buyer and a seller. Is not this decision now moot because of section 20(d)? See Wang, A Cause of Action for Option Traders Against Insider Option Traders, 101 Harv.L.Rev. 1056 (1988). Apparently no litigation has arisen under section 20(d) since its enactment.

D. SECTION 16(b) OF THE SECURITIES EXCHANGE ACT

SECURITIES EXCHANGE ACT OF 1934
48 Stat. 896 (1934), 15 U.S.C.A. § 78p (1989).

§ 16. Directors, officers, and principal stockholders

(a) Every person who is directly or indirectly the beneficial owner of more than 10 per centum of any class of any equity security (other than an exempted security) which is registered pursuant to section 12 of this title, or who is a director or an officer of the issuer of such security, shall file, at the time of the registration of such security on a national securities exchange or by the effective date of a registration statement filed pursuant to section 12(g) of this title, or within ten days after he becomes such beneficial owner, director, or officer, a statement with the Commission (and, if such security is registered on a national securities exchange, also with the exchange) of the amount of all equity securities of such issuer of which he is the beneficial owner, and within ten days after the close of each calendar month thereafter, if there has been a change in such ownership during such month, shall file with the Commission (and if such security is registered on a national securities exchange, shall also file with the exchange), a statement indicating his ownership at the close of the calendar month and such changes in his ownership as have occurred during such calendar month.

(b) For the purpose of preventing the unfair use of information which may have been obtained by such beneficial owner, director, or officer by reason of his relationship to the issuer, any profit realized by him from any purchase and sale, or any sale and purchase, of any equity security of such issuer (other than an exempted security) within any period of less than six months, unless such security was acquired in good faith in connection with a debt previously contracted, shall inure to and be recoverable by the issuer, irrespective of any intention on the part of such beneficial owner, director, or officer in entering into such transaction of holding the security purchased or of not repurchasing the security sold for a period exceeding six months. Suit to recover such profit may be instituted at law or in equity in any court of competent jurisdiction by the issuer, or by the owner of any security of the issuer in the name and in behalf of the issuer if the issuer shall fail or refuse to bring such suit within sixty days after request or shall fail diligently to prosecute the same thereafter; but no such suit shall be brought more than two years after the date such profit was realized. This subsection shall not be construed to cover any transaction where such beneficial owner was not such both at the time of the purchase and sale, or the sale and purchase, of the security involved, or any transaction or transactions which the Commission by rules and regulations may exempt as not comprehended within the purpose of this subsection.

Notes

(1) Read section 16(b) again, carefully. From the first, the courts have held that this section establishes a "crude rule of thumb" and that it is no defense to argue that the offsetting transactions were entered into for innocent reasons unconnected with inside information about the corporation's affairs. If a purchase and sale take place within a six month period, the "profit" is automatically recoverable by the corporation.

(2) How are violations discovered? Nothing could be easier, since the reports required by section 16(a) are made publicly available in a periodical published by the SEC. It is simply a matter of comparing transactions.

(3) Is there any incentive to find violations given the fact that the recovery inures to the corporation? Again from the first, the courts recognized that attorneys for plaintiff shareholders who locate section 16(b) violations, bring them to the attention of the corporation, and if necessary, bring suit on them [as contemplated by section 16(b)] are entitled to attorneys' fees. Further, "[s]ince in many cases such as this the possibility of recovering attorney's fees will provide the sole stimulus for the enforcement of § 16(b), the allowance must not be too niggardly." Smolowe v. Delendo Corp., 136 F.2d 231, 241 (2d Cir.1943), cert. denied 320 U.S. 751, 64 S.Ct. 56, 88 L.Ed. 446 (1943). Finally, it is not necessary to actually resort to litigation in order to earn the fee. Gilson v. Chock Full O'Nuts Corp., 326 F.2d 246 (2d Cir.1964).

(4) How difficult is it to find a plaintiff in whose name a suit may be brought to recover for a section 16(b) violation? Not difficult at all, since there is no requirement that the plaintiff be a shareholder at the time of either the purchase or sale, and apparently the ownership of a single share purchased specifically for bringing the suit is sufficient. See generally 2 Loss, Securities Regulation 1042, 1052. See also Hamilton, Convertible Securities and Section 16(b): The End of an Era, 44 Tex.L.Rev. 1447, 1450, n. 18 (1966):

> In Magida v. Continental Can Co., 231 F.2d 843 (2d Cir.), cert. denied, 351 U.S. 972, 76 S.Ct. 1031, 100 L.Ed. 1490 (1956), the court refused to allow the assertion of the defense of champerty even though the plaintiff's pro rata share of recovery could amount to only $1.10 and costs and expenses would reach many times that amount. Plaintiff's original counsel of record testified that plaintiff, "under the terms of an oral retainer, had agreed to pay such costs and expenses," but the

court commented that "the true facts of the arrangements between them were * * * heavily obscured by numerous invocations of the attorney-client privilege by the attorney of record." Id. at 847–48. Counsel of record in this case was Morris J. Levy, who has represented a large number, if not the majority, of § 16(b) stockholder-plaintiffs.

The stockholder-plaintiff in a number of the § 16(b) cases is one Isadore Blau. In Blau v. Lamb, 314 F.2d 618 (2d Cir.), cert. denied, 375 U.S. 813, 84 S.Ct. 44, 11 L.Ed.2d 49 (1963), the district court "sought to determine the beneficial ownership" of one hundred shares of stock in Blau's name which formed the basis of his entitlement to act as plaintiff. The district court had "held unbelievable Blau's own testimony that he had cash funds adequate to pay the account, noting the lack of any bank accounts or signs of wealth beyond Blau's own statement" and had concluded that he was holding the stock as nominee for some undisclosed person and was not the real party in interest so that he was not a proper party plaintiff. Id. at 619. The court of appeals reversed on the ground that the corporation was the real party in interest and the stockholder did not have to be a beneficial owner of the stock to be a § 16(b) plaintiff. The court of appeals commented that "Blau obviously had sufficient indicia of ownership to protect his right under the statute * * *." Id. at 620.

(5) How are profits computed if there is a series of transactions? In a word, punitively. "The only rule whereby all possible profits can surely be recovered is that of lowest price in, highest price out—within six months." Smolowe v. Delendo Corp., supra, at 239, Gratz v. Claughton, 187 F.2d 46 (2d Cir.1951), cert. denied 341 U.S. 920, 71 S.Ct. 741, 95 L.Ed. 1353 (1951). To illustrate:

Assume that an insider enters into the following transactions, which are grouped together for simplicity of analysis:

(1) 7/1/75   Buys 100 shares @   115
(2) 5/15/76   Sells 100 shares @   93
(3) 5/18/76   Buys 100 shares @   90
(4) 5/21/76   Buys 100 shares @   95
(5) 5/23/76   Sells 100 shares @   97
(6) 5/26/76   Buys 100 shares @   105
(7) 5/29/76   Sells 100 shares @   108
(8) 8/10/76   Sells 100 shares @   115

A businessman examining this sequence of transactions would probably conclude that the insider made a profit of $300 on transactions (2) and (3), $200 on (4) and (5), $300 on (6) and (7), and $0 on (1) and (8), closing the account, for a total trading profit of $800. However, by matching lowest price in with highest price out, the following tabulation is made:

Purchases	Sales	Profit
100 @ 90 (trans. (3))	100 @ 115 (trans. (8))	2500
100 @ 95 (trans. (4))	100 @ 108 (trans. (7))	1300
100 @ 105 (trans. (6))	100 @ 97 (trans. (5))	0

Thus appears a total § 16(b) profit of $3,800. In this computation all transactions which yield losses are to be ignored.

(6) An officer, director or ten per cent shareholder, subject to section 16(b), must accommodate his or her securities transactions to the requirements of that section. In order to avoid application of that section, a person who purchases or sells securities of the corporation must avoid entering into an offsetting transaction—a sale if the other transaction was a purchase, or a purchase if the other transaction was a sale—for a period that begins six months before the transaction in question and ends six months after the transaction. In effect, in-and-out trading is proscribed for a one year period surrounding every transaction. Of course, as the court in Diamond v. Oreamuno pointed out, section 16(b) is not violated if there are either a succession of purchase transactions or a succession of sale transactions without any offsetting transactions, no matter how much inside information is used. Further, there is no "profit" to return to the corporation if the highest sale price during every possible six month period is below the lowest purchase price during every possible six month period surrounding the transaction; however, as described in note (5) above transactions are matched in such a way that a single purchase at a lower price than any sale price will generate section 16(b) profits no matter what the net profit or loss in the account was over the same or a different period.

(7) Anyone dealing with the application of section 16(b) in real life quickly recognizes the complexity of the application of the section, particularly when unusual transactions not involving ordinary sales and purchases are involved. Officers and directors of an issuer are quite likely to violate the section inadvertently by transactions that in fact do not involve the use of nonpublic information, often after getting informal advice from accountants or financial people who themselves do not understand the legal intricacies of section 16(b). As a result, general counsel of issuers of registered securities regularly distribute cautionary memoranda to directors, officers, large shareholders, and employees who may have access to nonpublic material information. Since 1988 these memoranda have been virtually required by ITSFEA, but even before the enactment of that statute, such memoranda were widely used. They universally described the possible application of section 16(b), cautioning the reader of the dangers of inadvertent violations from innocent transactions and recommending that officers, directors, and ten per cent shareholders obtain legal advice before exercising employee stock options, making gifts of securities, exercising conversion privileges, or generally acquiring or disposing of equity securities when any possible offsetting transactions exist. Persons subject to section 16(b) are also in effect rewarned periodically of the pitfalls of this section when information relating to possible filings under section 16(a) is solicited.

(8) Presumably, officers and directors are sophisticated individuals well able to understand warnings. One can only assume that everyone subject to section 16(b) is aware of the existence of that statute, and one should therefore expect that violations of this section are relatively uncommon and that the principal effect of the section is to impose strong deterrents against short term in-and-out trading and speculation by officers, directors, and ten per cent shareholders. In fact, nothing could be further from the truth. This apparently simple and straightforward piece of legislation has given rise to hundreds of litigated cases, and such cases

continue to appear in substantial numbers. Furthermore, there are numerous, uncountable instances in which officers and directors voluntarily repay section 16(b) "profits" to the issuer because there is no conceivable defense, even though the transaction involved no misuse of confidential information. These voluntary repayments often involve large sums that in some instances must have devastating financial consequences for the long term or retirement planning of the unfortunate officer or director.

(9) It is difficult to give the flavor of section 16(b) litigation. Every important word in section 16(b)—e.g. "officer," "director," "six months," "more than 10 per centum of any class," "equity security," "realized by him" has been the subject of litigation. The cases below, decided during the late 1980s, are representative of the section 16(b) jurisprudence.

WINSTON v. FEDERAL EXPRESS CORPORATION

United States Court of Appeals, Sixth Circuit, 1988.
853 F.2d 455.

Before MARTIN, JONES, and NORRIS, CIRCUIT JUDGES.

BOYCE F. MARTIN, JR., CIRCUIT JUDGE.

Charles D. Winston appeals the district court's decision to grant summary judgment in favor of the Federal Express Corporation. 659 F.Supp. 647. Winston contends that the court erroneously concluded that he was an "officer" within the meaning of section 16(b) of the Securities Exchange Act of 1934, such that the profits realized from his short-swing purchase and sale of stock in Federal Express must be surrendered. We affirm.

In September 1981, Winston was hired by Federal Express to be Vice President of Network Systems. About two years later, he was promoted to Senior Vice President of Electronic Products. In that capacity, Winston was responsible for the development and implementation of the company's electronic products and systems, such as the company's overnight package delivery service and the company's same-day document delivery service. Winston reported directly to the chief operating officer, and he had substantial supervisory responsibilities.

On August 27, 1985, Winston resigned from Federal Express. Although his resignation was not to become effective until September 30, 1985, Winston ceased performing any duties for Federal Express as of August 27, and he was replaced almost immediately. Until September 30, however, Winston remained on the Federal Express payroll. Moreover, until the date of his resignation became effective, Winston was available to discuss transition matters with his successor, although he was never actually consulted by the company after August 27.

In fact, Winston's only contact with Federal Express after he resigned occurred on September 30 when he visited the company's offices in order to exercise options to purchase 8,298 shares of Federal Express stock. According to Winston, the sole reason that the effective date of his resignation was postponed was that the option to purchase 2,000 of those shares did not vest until September 26, 1985.

On March 26, 1986, Winston sold the shares he had purchased on September 30 for a profit in excess of $176,000. The stock was sold through a brokerage house which erroneously advised him that the "settlement date," as opposed to the "trade date," determined the date of the transaction for both tax and securities law purposes. Section 16 of the Exchange Act, which was designed to prevent insiders from taking advantage of their access to non-public information, provides that any profit realized by a beneficial owner, officer, or director of an issuer of stock from the purchase and sale of that issuer's stock within any six-month period shall be retained by the issuer. If the brokerage house's advice had been accurate, the transaction would have fallen outside the six-month short-swing profit period. When Winston informed Federal Express of the transaction, however, the company explained to him that the trade date was determinative. Therefore, Winston had technically engaged in a short-swing transaction under section 16(b), and Federal Express was entitled to recoup the profits from the sale.

Winston brought suit in federal court to recover those profits. In his complaint, Winston alleged that, because he did not actively participate in the duties of his office after August 27, he was not an officer of the company for the purposes of section 16(b) when he bought the stock at issue here on September 30. The district court, however, granted Federal Express' motion for summary judgment, finding that Winston was an officer within the meaning of section 16(b). We agree.

Section 16(b) was intended to protect the investing public from the "evils of insider trading" by enacting "a flat rule taking the profits out of a class of transactions in which the possibility of abuse was believed to be intolerably great." *Reliance Electric Co. v. Emerson Electric Co.*, 404 U.S. 418, 422, 92 S.Ct. 596, 599, 30 L.Ed.2d 575 (1972). "It does not matter whether the insider actually received the information, or utilized it; his mere status makes him liable." *National Medical Enterprises, Inc. v. Small*, 680 F.2d 83, 84 (9th Cir.1982). A strict-liability "approach maximize[s] the ability of the rule to eradicate speculative abuses by reducing difficulties in proof." *Bershad v. McDonough*, 428 F.2d 693, 696 (7th Cir.1970), *cert. denied*, 400 U.S. 992, 91 S.Ct. 458, 27 L.Ed.2d 440 (1971). Because Congress intended section 16(b) to be a "relatively arbitrary rule capable of easy administration," *id.*, courts generally interpret the statute so as to preserve its "mechanical quality." *Reliance Electric Co. v. Emerson Electric Co.*, 404 U.S. at 425, 92 S.Ct. at 600. In deciding whether an individual is an officer for purposes of section 16(b), therefore, courts tend to look solely at the title the individual holds.

An exception exists, however, "where the title is essentially honorary or ceremonial," *National Medical Enterprises, Inc. v. Small*, 680 F.2d at 84, or where the "title was purely 'titular' and not real." *Gold v. Sloan*, 486 F.2d 340, 351 (4th Cir.1973), *reh'g denied*, 491 F.2d 729, *cert. denied*, 419 U.S. 873, 95 S.Ct. 134, 42 L.Ed.2d 112 (1974). In such cases, the individual's transactions are not subject to section 16(b) restrictions because the person does not actually perform executive functions that put him or her in a position of being able to acquire the kind of confidential information about the company's affairs that provides an advantage in dealing in the company's securities. In effect, a title

> does no more than raise an inference that the person who holds the title has the executive duties and the opportunities for confidential information that the title implies. The inference can be overcome by proof that the title . . . did not carry with it any of the executive responsibilities that might otherwise be assumed.

Merrill Lynch, Pierce, Fenner & Smith v. Livingston, 566 F.2d 1119, 1122 (9th Cir.1978).

Here, however, we are presented with a rather unusual case. Winston concedes that, up until he tendered his resignation, he exercised substantial executive responsibilities and that he did have access to confidential information. He contends, though, that he ceased performing such duties after August 27 and that, therefore, the stock he purchased on September 30 is not subject to the short-swing profit rule. In such a circumstance, however, the presumption that the officer continues to have access to confidential information during the interim period is a strong one, and the officer must produce substantial evidence to overcome this presumption.

We believe the evidence adduced by Winston is clearly insufficient to rebut the presumption that he continued to have access to confidential information until September 30. Winston testified that, after he tendered his resignation on August 27, he only returned to the company's office once, on September 30, to exercise his stock options. He also testified that, although he was available to help his successor during the interim period, he was never actually consulted. This testimony is uncontroverted. It is also inconsequential, however, because Winston failed to produce any evidence that, had he requested access to the kind of confidential information which routinely crossed his desk prior to his resignation, such access would have been denied by the company. Winston also failed to offer any evidence that other officers and management personnel were expressly instructed that they were not to provide him confidential information. In short, although he was an officer in title only during the interim period, Winston offered no evidence that the company had constructed a kind of "Chinese wall" around him, shielding him from potential access to current confidential information. * * *

We recognize that the result in this case may appear harsh. There have been no allegations that Winston exploited confidential information, and he sold the stock only four days before the expiration of the six-month short-swing profit period on the basis of erroneous "expert" advice. Moreover, had he waited those few days, his profit would have been even greater because the price of Federal Express continued to rise after he sold his shares. Unfortunately for Mr. Winston, however, such seemingly unjust results are an inevitable consequence of a strict-liability rule which is necessarily arbitrary. The statutory scheme "place[s] responsibility for meticulous observance of the provision upon the shoulders of the insider. . . . [and he or she] must bear the risks of any inadvertent miscalculation." *Bershod v. McDonough,* 428 F.2d at 696. * * *

Accordingly, the judgment of the district court in favor of Federal Express is hereby affirmed.

C.R.A. REALTY CORP. v. CROTTY
United States Court of Appeals, Second Circuit, 1989.
878 F.2d 562.

Before OAKES, CHIEF JUDGE, and TIMBERS and MESKILL, CIRCUIT JUDGES.

TIMBERS, CIRCUIT JUDGE:

The essential question presented by this appeal is whether an employee's functions, rather than his title, determine whether he is an "officer" within the meaning of § 16(b) of the Securities Exchange Act of 1934. The district court held that the employee's functions were determinative. We agree. We affirm.

Appellant C.R.A. Realty Corp. appeals from a judgment entered December 27, 1988 in the Southern District of New York, Robert L. Carter, *District Judge,* dismissing after trial appellant's complaint which alleged that appellee Joseph R. Crotty (Crotty), an "officer" of appellee United Artists Communications, Inc. (United Artists or the company) engaged in short-swing trading in United Artists' securities in violation of § 16(b) of the Securities Exchange Act of 1934, * * * The district court held that Crotty was not an "officer" within the meaning of § 16(b)—despite his position as a corporate vice-president—because he was "a middle management employee of United Artists whose duties did not provide access to any confidential information about the company's financial plans or future operations".

Appellant asserts on appeal that the district court erred in holding that Crotty was not an officer because (1) Crotty's lack of access to confidential or inside information is irrelevant since § 16(b) imposes strict liability on *any* officer engaging in short-swing trading regardless of whether he has access to inside information, and (2) in the alternative, appellant demonstrated in the district court that Crotty had access to inside information.

For the reasons which follow, we affirm. * * *

I.

Appellant is an organization incorporated to act as a private attorney general to purchase stock and commence actions against corporate officials for violations of the federal securities laws. During the period in question, appellant owned 10 shares of United Artists, then a nationwide distributor and exhibitor of motion pictures. Crotty, a vice-president of United Artists, was the head film buyer of its western division, a territory encompassing six western states.

Crotty was first employed by United Artists in December 1969. He became head film buyer for the western division in 1980. He was elected a vice-president of United Artists in 1982 and continued to serve as head film buyer for the western division. As head film buyer, he obtained movies to be shown at the 351 movie screens in the western division theaters. He supervised their distribution. This included negotiating and signing agreements pursuant to which United Artists obtained movies for exhibition, supervising the distribution of the movies to the company's theaters, and settling contracts after the movies had been shown in the theaters. Crotty also had some supervisory responsibility for advertising in his division.

Crotty supervised a staff of 30 people. He had virtually complete and autonomous control of film buying in the western division. He was required to consult with higher authority only if he wanted to exceed a certain limit on the amount of the cash advance paid to a distributor for the exhibition of a particular movie. This occurred no more than two or three times a year. The gross revenue from Crotty's division routinely was about 35–36% of United Artists' gross revenue from movie exhibition, or around 15–18% of the company's total gross revenue.

The short-swing transactions here involved took place between December 19, 1984 and July 24, 1985. During this period Crotty purchased 7500 shares of United Artists and sold 3500 of its shares. He realized a large profit which appellant seeks to recover on behalf of United Artists. Following an unsuccessful demand on United Artists that it proceed against Crotty to recover this profit, appellant commenced the instant action against appellees pursuant to § 16(b). Following trial, the district court entered a judgment which dismissed the complaint. The court held that, although Crotty was a vice-president of United Artists, he was not an officer within the purview of § 16(b) because he had no access to inside information regarding the company's financial plans or future operations. This appeal followed. * * *

II.

* * * This provision of the statute "imposes a strict prophylactic rule with respect to insider, short-swing trading". *Foremost–McKesson, Inc. v. Provident Securities Co.,* 423 U.S. 232, 251 (1976). Any corporate official within the statutory meaning of an "officer" who engages in short-swing trading automatically will be required to surrender any profit from the trading, "without proof of actual abuse of insider information, and without proof of intent to profit on the basis of such information". *Kern County Land Co. v. Occidental Petroleum Corp.,* 411 U.S. 582, 595 (1973); *Smolowe v. Delendo Corp.,* 136 F.2d 231, 235–36 (2 Cir.), *cert. denied,* 320 U.S. 751 (1943). This objective test was

chosen by Congress because of the difficulty of proving whether a corporate insider actually abused confidential information to which he had access or purchased or sold an issuer's stock with the intention of profiting from such information. *Reliance Elec. Co. v. Emerson Elec. Co.,* 404 U.S. 418, 422 (1972) (quoting *Bershad v. McDonough,* 428 F.2d 693, 696 (7 Cir.1970), *cert. denied,* 400 U.S. 992 (1971)). Since the statute imposes strict liability, it is to be applied only when doing so "best serves the congressional purpose of curbing short-swing speculation by corporate insiders". *Reliance Elec., supra,* 404 U.S. at 424.

Appellant challenges the district court's holding by asserting that Crotty automatically was an officer within the meaning of § 16(b) by virtue of his title of vice-president of United Artists. The district court, however, held that it was Crotty's actual duties at the time of the short-swing trading—rather than his corporate title—that determined whether he was an officer within the meaning of § 16(b). We believe that the district court's holding was correct.

Appellant's starting point in challenging the district court's holding is the Securities and Exchange Commission rule which defined the term "officer" in the 1934 Act as including a vice-president of an issuer. 15 U.S.C. § 78c(b) (1982) (SEC has power to define 1934 Act terms in manner consistent with Act); Rule 3b–2, 17 C.F.R. 240.3b–2 (1988).[99] Appellant asserts that, since Crotty is a vice-president of United Artists, this rule places him within the purview of § 16(b). We believe it is significant, however, that the SEC itself does not believe that this rule should be rigidly applied in determining who is an officer within the meaning of § 16. For example, two SEC releases show that the Commission does not consider an employee's title as an officer to bring the employee automatically under § 16. Release on Ownership Reports and Trading by Officers, Directors and Principal Stockholders, Exchange Act Release No. 26333 (December 2, 1988)[100]; Release on Rules Applicable to Insider Reporting and Trading, Exchange Act Release No. 18114 (Sept. 23, 1981) (vice-president might not be an officer subject to reporting requirements of § 16(a) if officer's duties are "insignificant" and he or she has no access to inside information). We do not believe that Rule 3b–2 requires us to hold that Crotty is an

---

99. [By the Court] SEC Rule 3b–2 states:

"The term 'officer' means a president, *vice-president,* secretary, treasurer or principal financial officer, comptroller or principal accounting officer, and any person routinely performing corresponding functions with respect to any organization whether incorporated or unincorporated." (emphasis added).

100. [By the Court] In proposing new rules in this Release to clarify the term "officer" under § 16, the SEC stated:

"If applied literally, the Rule 3b–2 definition of 'officer' can be too broad in the context of Section 16; *of particular concern is the inclusion of all vice presidents in the definition.* Many businesses give the title of vice president to employees who do not have significant managerial or policymaking duties and are not privy to inside information.

The reporting and short-swing profit recovery provisions of Section 16 *were intended to apply to those officers who have routine access to material non-public information, not those with particular titles.*"

Release No. 26333 (emphasis added) (footnote omitted).

officer within the purview of § 16(b) merely by virtue of his title as a vice-president of the company.

Moreover the district court's holding is consistent with the law of this Circuit. It relied primarily on *Colby v. Klune,* 178 F.2d 872 (2 Cir. 1949). In *Colby* we held that a corporate employee who did not hold the title of a corporate officer nevertheless could be an officer within the meaning of § 16(b) if he "perform[ed] important executive duties of such character that he would be likely, in discharging these duties, to obtain confidential information about the company's affairs that would aid him if he engaged in personal market transactions". *Id.* at 873.

Colby is not factually on all fours with the instant case; indeed it is a correlative of the instant case. Here we must decide whether Crotty's title as a vice-president in and of itself brings him within the purview of § 16(b), whereas the issue in *Colby* was whether an employee's duties could bring him under § 16(b) even if he lacked a title as a corporate officer. We believe that the reasoning of *Colby* applies here. In *Colby* we held that "[i]t is immaterial how [an employee's] functions are labelled or how defined in the by-laws, or that he does or does not act under the supervision of some other corporate representative". In short, *Colby* established as the law of this Circuit that it is an employee's duties and responsibilities—rather than his actual title—that determine whether he is an officer within the purview of § 16(b). Three other circuits have followed a similar functional approach in determining the liability of officers under § 16(b). * * *

The general approach established by our Court in *Colby* is consistent with that of the Supreme Court in § 16(b) cases in which the Court has emphasized that potential access to inside information is the key to finding liability, rather than rigid application of statutory designations. In *Kern County,* the Court held that, even if a hostile bidder held 10% or more of the stock of a target company when it exchanged the issuer's stock for stock issued as part of a merger designed to fend off the bidder, the bidder did not come within the ambit of § 16(b), since its hostile status precluded it from having any inside information about the target issuer. These cases, as well as the approach followed by the district court in the instant case, reflect an interpretation of § 16(b) that "best serves the congressional purpose of curbing short-swing speculation by corporate insiders". *Reliance Elec. Co., supra,* 404 U.S. at 424.

It is significant that the approach set forth in *Colby* implements the objective standard established by § 16(b). *Colby*'s approach will require more proof that an employee is an officer under § 16(b) than merely showing that the employee holds a title as a corporate officer. We emphasize, however, that all that is required by *Colby* is that a plaintiff establish that it is more likely than not that the employee's duties gave him access to inside information. A plaintiff need not show that the employee actually obtained inside information or used it to his advantage.

We hold that it is the duties of an employee—especially his potential access to inside information—rather than his corporate title which determine whether he is an officer subject to the short-swing trading restrictions of § 16(b) of the 1934 Act.

III.

We turn next to the district court's finding that Crotty's duties did not give him access to inside information concerning United Artists. Since we hold that this finding was supported by substantial evidence and was not clearly erroneous, we discuss it only briefly.

The evidence indicated that Crotty's appointment as a vice-president—two years after he became a head film buyer—was essentially honorary. The appointment was accompanied by no raise in pay or change in responsibilities. Viewing his responsibilities both before and after the appointment, Crotty had no access to inside information such as the financial or operational plans of United Artists. He was not a director of the company, never attended a directors meeting, and never received any information from the Board of Directors that was not available to the general public. * * *

We hold that there was substantial evidence to support the district court's finding that Crotty did not have access to inside information. This finding was not clearly erroneous. * * *

Affirmed.

MESKILL, CIRCUIT JUDGE, dissenting: I respectfully dissent.

The plain language of both section 16(b) of the Securities Exchange Act of 1934, and the applicable Securities and Exchange Commission (SEC) regulation, contains no exception that exempts appellee Crotty from liability in this case. * * * The definition of "officer" for purposes of [section 16(b)], as determined by the SEC, is "a president, vice president, secretary, treasurer or principal financial officer, comptroller or principal accounting officer, and any person routinely performing corresponding functions with respect to any organization whether incorporated or unincorporated." 17 C.F.R. § 240.3b–2.

While * * * [section 16(b) and rule 3b–2] clearly leave room to construe as officers those who do not possess the titles of officers, *see Colby v. Klune*, 178 F.2d 872, 873 (2d Cir.1949), they do not permit the reverse inference.

Where the language of a statute is clear, as it is in this case, any extraneous considerations, such as the statute's legislative history, are irrelevant to an analysis of the statute's meaning. Crotty's title, vice president, is explicitly included within the list of titles that the SEC has determined constitute officers per se under section 16(b). He is, therefore, liable under that section. There is nothing within the terms of either section 16 or 17 C.F.R. § 240.3b–2 that makes either provision ambiguous. While a pragmatic approach may be proper when interpreting the outer reaches of section 16, which is a strict liability statute, it is not called for in this situation. There is no reason to ignore the unambiguous language of the statute. Therefore, under the plain terms of the statute and regulation, Crotty is liable to United Artists (UA) for the profits on his transactions. * * *

It makes no difference that since the time of his purchases and sales, the SEC has proposed amendments that, Crotty argues, would explicitly exempt him from the coverage of section 16(b). *See* 53 Fed. Reg. 49,997 (proposed Dec. 13, 1988). Not only were those provisions not in effect at the time in question, they are not in effect today. * * *

Because of the plain language of the statute alone, I believe that Crotty is bound by the provisions of section 16(b) as a matter of law, and I therefore would reverse the judgment of the district court.

There is, however, a second reason why I believe the district court's decision should be reversed. Even under the majority's reading of the statute and regulation, Crotty is an insider. The majority opinion itself reveals the great responsibility and control that Crotty had over the financial affairs of UA * * *.

For these reasons, I believe that Crotty was an officer subject to the restrictions of section 16(b) as a matter of law. Furthermore, even if he were not subject to section 16(b) as a matter of law, the district court's finding that Crotty had insufficient access to inside information for him to be deemed an insider was clearly erroneous. I would therefore reverse the judgment of the district court.

JAMMIES INTERN., INC. v. LAZARUS

United States District Court, S.D. New York, 1989.
713 F.Supp. 83.

CEDARBAUM, DISTRICT JUDGE.

This is an action brought under section 16(b) of the Securities Exchange Act of 1934, to recover "short-swing profits" allegedly realized by defendant Charles Lazarus from his wife's sales and his purchase of common stock of Toys "R" Us, Inc. A one-day bench trial was held on May 1, 1989. Two witnesses testified in court. Plaintiff called Dr. Helen S. Kaplan Lazarus as a witness. Defendant Charles Lazarus was a defense witness. After observing the demeanor of the witnesses and evaluating the plausibility and credibility of their testimony, and after examining the documentary evidence introduced at trial, I make the following findings of fact and conclusions of law pursuant to Fed.R. Civ.P. 52(a).

FINDINGS OF FACT

First, I adopt the facts to which the parties have expressly agreed:
* * *

3. Defendant Charles Lazarus ("Lazarus") is and has been since 1978 Chairman of the Board, a Director and Chief Executive Officer of Toys.

4. Lazarus and Dr. Helen S. Kaplan Lazarus ("Kaplan") are husband and wife. Lazarus and Kaplan were married on November 2, 1979.

5. During the month of June 1987 Kaplan sold from her own account shares of Toys' common stock, as follows:

Date	No. Shs. Sold	Price Per Share	Net Proceeds of Sale
6/5/87	5,000	$35½	$ 176,407.06
6/5/87	5,000	35	173,907.16
6/8/87	5,000	34⅞	173,284.14
6/8/87	4,000	34½	137,127.40

TOTAL—19,000 Shares   TOTAL NET PROCEEDS—$660,725.76

6. On October 5, 1987 Lazarus exercised his stock option for 1,442,706 shares of Toys' common stock at $.96 per share which had been granted to him pursuant to his 1978 Employment Agreement with Toys. Lazarus made full payment for such shares in accordance with the provisions of the Employment Agreement by delivering his check payable to Toys in the amount of $276,997.76 and by delivering his promissory note payable to Toys in the amount of $1,108,000.00. * * *

8. On November 12, 1987, the attorneys for plaintiff, Jammies International, Inc. ("Jammys"), sent a letter to Toys requesting Toys to institute suit to recover the profits purported to have been realized from the alleged short-swing transactions in its securities. Toys did not institute an action and 60 days have elapsed since Jammys made its request. * * *

20. On November 11, 1987, Jammys purchased one share of the common stock of Toys.

21. Jammys is and has been the beneficial owner of one share of common stock of Toys since November 11, 1987.

22. Kaplan is a psychiatrist who specializes in sexual problems. She has M.D., M.A., and Ph.D. degrees, and is board certified in psychiatry. Her writings in her field have been published.

23. Since 1970, she has had a private practice in psychiatry and has been a part-time faculty member at New York Hospital.

24. The marriage between Lazarus and Kaplan was a second marriage for both of them.

25. Kaplan has three children from her prior marriage, and Lazarus has two children from his prior marriage. Kaplan and Lazarus have not had any children during their marriage to each other.

26. Prior to her marriage to Lazarus, Kaplan owned the apartment in which she lived as well as a house at Red Cedar Point in the Hamptons.

27. Lazarus and Kaplan entered into a prenuptial agreement in which Lazarus gave up all rights to Kaplan's estate.

28. In the early period of their marriage, the couple lived in Kaplan's apartment and country house.

29. In the early period of their marriage, Kaplan paid a larger share of the household expenses than did her husband.

30. As Lazarus' income increased, he gradually paid more of their joint household expenses.

31. Lazarus always paid for their vacations.

32. Sometime during 1984 or 1985, Kaplan sold her apartment and country house in which they had lived since their marriage.

33. Kaplan deposited the proceeds of these sales in a bank money market account in her own name.

34. During the same period, Lazarus purchased an apartment into which the couple moved. He also bought two country houses, one in Quogue, the other at Nassau in the Bahamas.

35. Lazarus paid for the purchase and renovation of these three residences which are owned jointly by the couple.

36. Since that time, Lazarus has paid for all of the household expenses and all of Kaplan's clothing. Lazarus has also given Kaplan a Mercedes Benz convertible automobile. In Kaplan's words: "Since Charles has made a great deal of money, he has kept his money separate."

*   *   *

40. Kaplan, who loves gardening, has an ongoing program of purchasing trees and bushes for the Quogue house. To date, she has spent approximately $170,000 for such landscaping costs.

41. Kaplan also uses her earnings for the purchase of works of art.

42. During the period of the couple's courtship, Kaplan bought about 5,000 shares of Toys. After the marriage, she purchased additional shares.

43. Immediately prior to her sales of 19,000 shares in June of 1987, Kaplan owned 44,000 shares of Toys' stock.

44. Kaplan has used only her own funds—her professional earnings and the earnings from her personal investments—to buy all of the securities held in her name, including her shares of Toys' stock.

*   *   *

46. Kaplan does not have a financial advisor for the investment of her personal funds, *   *   * For her personal funds, Kaplan makes her own investment decisions, but she does solicit Lazarus' advice when she can get his attention because she considers him a brilliant business man.

48. When they do discuss her investments, they do not discuss them in depth because Lazarus is hesitant to give Kaplan financial advice.

49. Before each purchase of Toys' stock, Kaplan discussed the purchase with Lazarus.

50. Every year, Lazarus has discussed the matter with Kaplan before exercising his stock options in Toys.

51. Several days prior to her sales of the 19,000 shares, Kaplan discussed the planned transactions with Lazarus.

52. Lazarus always opposed the sale of Toys' stock.

53. Lazarus did not like anyone connected with Toys to buy or sell stock in the fourth quarter of the year when profit is taken, and Kaplan knew that it was "not O.K." to buy or sell Toys' stock between November 1 and January 31.

54. Lazarus said that "it was O.K. with him although he did not think it was a good idea from a financial point of view."

55. Kaplan understood Lazarus' comment to mean that there were no legal or technical impediments to her selling the 19,000 shares, but that he was not in favor of the sale from a financial point of view.

56. Kaplan wanted to sell her Toys' stock because the building in which she had rented her professional office for many years was converted into condominiums. She wanted to purchase a large condominium in that building for the price of $1.1 million. She used all of the proceeds of the sale of her Toys' stock toward the purchase of space for her professional practice. * * *

70. In five filings of Form 4 with the Securities and Exchange Commission, Lazarus reported Kaplan's holdings of Toys' stock and disclaimed ownership of her shares.

71. The lowest market price for Toys' stock within six months of June 5, 1987 and June 8, 1987 was $22 per share.

DISCUSSION AND CONCLUSIONS OF LAW

Jurisdiction of this action is based on sections 16(b) and 27 of the Securities Exchange Act of 1934 * * *.

Even though Jammys purchased its stock after the transaction complained of, courts have uniformly held that the plaintiff need not have been a shareholder at the time of the transaction which gave rise to the suit. *See Blau v. Oppenheim,* 250 F.Supp. 881, 883 (S.D.N.Y. 1966).

Although the intimacy and shared interest of the marital relationship provides both the temptation and the opportunity for the exchange of inside information, the courts have not adopted the *per se* rule that the SEC is currently proposing. *See* 53 Fed.Reg. 50,002 (proposed Dec. 13, 1988). Nevertheless, it is clear that a corporate officer and director may be held to have "realized profit" within the meaning of section 16(b) as a result of a matching of his wife's sales and his own purchase of his company's securities within the statutory six month period. *Whiting v. Dow Chemical Company,* 523 F.2d 680, 681–82 (2d Cir.1975). But the legal standard that does apply in determining when such a holding is appropriate is not clear. In the governing opinion in this Circuit, and indeed in the only appellate opinion on the matching of a spouse's sales with the other spouse's purchase of securities under section 16(b), the Second Circuit concluded that this is "a situation that cannot be resolved by legal interpretation but which requires a determination of questions of fact." *Whiting,* 523 F.2d at 687. In order to extract the teaching of *Whiting*, it is necessary to examine both the facts emphasized by the Second Circuit, and the Court's reason for attributing significance to those facts.

One of the premises on which the Second Circuit examined the facts in that case was that "shares to which legal title is held by one spouse may be said to be 'beneficially owned' by the other, the insider, if the ordinary rewards of ownership are used for their joint benefit." *Id.* at 688. The facts of *Whiting* establish that in order to attribute ownership to the insider, it is not necessary that the proceeds of the other spouse's particular sales be traceable to household or family support since money is fungible. But there must be some benefit, however indirect, to the insider from the ownership of the securities by the other spouse. In the *Whiting* case, that common benefit was shown by the fact that the larger part of the common maintenance of the couple's household came from the wife's personal inheritance which consisted primarily of shares of the insider's company. Mrs. Whiting also lent her husband the money needed for his purchase of shares.

In this case, it cannot fairly be said that after 1984 or 1985 Lazarus received any benefit from Kaplan's ownership of the 19,000 shares of Toys' stock that she sold in June of 1987. Kaplan contributed nothing to Lazarus' support, except that she purchased the landscaping for their Quogue house and some works of art. As a family unit, Kaplan and Lazarus share only Lazarus' property. Kaplan's independently-acquired property has been kept entirely separate, and Lazarus, pursuant to a prenuptial agreement, has given up all rights to Kaplan's separate property.

I turn then to the question of control. As I read *Whiting*, even in the absence of contributions of household funds by the other spouse, the exercise of control by the insider over the other spouse's investment decisions would justify treating the insider as the owner of the other spouse's securities for purposes of section 16(b). This is because one of the important attributes of ownership is the ability to control the disposition of the property owned. *Whiting* establishes that exclusive control is not necessary. Shared control is sufficient. In *Whiting*, the insider shared control of his wife's property through their joint financial planning. For financial planning purposes, their joint advisors treated their separate accounts as a common fund. Both spouses participated in joint planning sessions for the investment and disposition of each other's property as if the property of each was the property of both.

In this case, the credible evidence shows that Lazarus did not share control of Kaplan's investment decisions. Although Kaplan solicited Lazarus' advice in connection with her investment decisions, he was hesitant to give her financial advice. Several days prior to her sales, Kaplan discussed with Lazarus her plan to sell 19,000 shares of Toys' stock. But she did not follow his advice. Lazarus told Kaplan that "it was O.K. with him although he did not think it was a good idea from a financial point of view." Kaplan understood Lazarus' comment to mean that there were no legal or technical impediments to her selling the 19,000 shares, but that he was not in favor of the sale from a financial point of view. Even though Lazarus did not favor Kaplan's decision to sell the shares, Kaplan followed her own plan. Thus, the evidence negates that Lazarus shared control of the 19,000 shares of Toys' stock owned by Kaplan.

For the reasons discussed above, I conclude that Lazarus was not the beneficial owner of Kaplan's 19,000 shares of Toys' stock. Thus, Lazarus' purchase of Toys' stock should not be matched with Kaplan's sales, and Lazarus has not realized any profit within the meaning of section 16(b). Judgment is entered for defendants and against plaintiff on the claim in this action.

SO ORDERED.

Notes

(1) The lawyer for the plaintiffs in *C.R.A. Realty* and *Jammies International* was Morris J. Levy, of the law firm of Levy & Levy, New York City.

(2) The 10 per cent shareholder provision of section 16(b) obviously makes the section potentially applicable in takeover situations wherever the aggressor acquires more than 10 per cent of the target's shares but fails to acquire control of the target and thereafter disposes of the purchased shares within six months. That disposition may be to the target by private sale at a premium (greenmail), to a successful competitor for control, or on the open market by a series of sales usually to risk arbitragers, or conceivably to a long term investor who is not seeking control of the target. Since takeover disputes rarely extend for long periods, the probability is relatively high that the sale will occur within six months of some or all of the purchases. The United States Supreme Court addressed this issue in a series of opinions during the 1970s, and like the lower federal courts, became trapped by the irreconcilable tensions between section 16(b) as a crude rule of thumb and an objective standard, on the one hand, and the unjust or irrational results often reached when that objective standard is literally applied, on the other. The three principal cases are Reliance Electric Co. v. Emerson Electric Co., 404 U.S. 418, 92 S.Ct. 596, 30 L.Ed.2d 575 (1972); Kern County Land Co. v. Occidental Petroleum Corporation, 411 U.S. 582, 93 S.Ct. 1736, 36 L.Ed.2d 503 (1973); and Foremost–McKesson, Inc. v. Provident Securities Co., 423 U.S. 232, 96 S.Ct. 508, 46 L.Ed.2d 464 (1976). *Foremost–McKesson* solved many section 16(b) problems in the takeover context by holding that the transaction by which a person becomes a 10 per cent shareholder is not itself a purchase that may be matched with subsequent sales. On the perhaps debatable assumption that the aggressor who accepts cash tenders from tens or hundreds of thousands of shareholders does so in a single transaction, most of the problems of applying section 16(b) to takeover situations disappeared. Of course, all purchases after the one that increases the holding to above ten per cent are subject to section 16(b).

(3) Not all problems relating to takeover disputes and section 16(b) have disappeared, however, as a result of *Foremost–McKesson*. In Mayer v. Chesapeake Ins. Co. Ltd., 877 F.2d 1154 (2d Cir.1989), for example, various corporate entities controlled by Victor Posner purchased shares of Peabody International Corporation in an apparent takeover attempt. Posner subsequently agreed to enter into a five year "stand still" agreement for a cash consideration of $5.6 million and immediately sold all the Peabody shares on the open market. In determining the application of section 16(b), the court refused to aggregate all the holdings of the various Posner interests both for purposes of determining "profit" and for determining which transactions are subject to section 16(b). Judge Sweet dissented "respectfully" but vigorously.

(4) The last sentence of section 16(b) grants the SEC power to exempt transactions from that section if they are "not comprehended within the purpose of this subsection." The SEC has exercised the power of exemption sparingly. Perhaps the exemptions with the widest applicability are (a) section 240.16b–3, relating to certain transactions occurring under employee benefit plans and stock appreciation rights plans, (b) section 240.16b–6, relating to the manner of computation of profits incident to the sale of stock within six months after the exercise of a long term option, and (c) section 240.16b–9, relating to transactions involving the conversion of equity securities. In SEC Rel. 34–27148 (Aug. 19, 1989), the SEC withdrew the proposed regulations discussed in *Winston* and *Crotty,* and proposed a new set of regulations under both sections 16(a) and 16(b). These proposed regulations cover a number of topics not covered in the existing regulations, including transfers by gift and inheritance and hedging transactions in derivative securities.

(5) In *Foremost–McKesson* Justice Powell used the availability of rule 10b–5 as justification for the narrow reading of section 16(b) adopted in that case. Do you think that with the growth of rule 10b–5, and particularly with the enactment by Congress of ITSA and ITSFEA during the 1980s, that section 16(b) is now obsolete and should be repealed? Is any real purpose served by requiring Winston to return his employee benefits profits to Federal Express? May there be sufficient benefit in the prohibition against in-and-out trading by officers, directors, and large shareholders provided by section 16(b) that that section should be retained, despite the inequities and champertous litigation that it generates?

E. SALE OF CONTROL

ZETLIN v. HANSON HOLDINGS, INC.

Court of Appeals of New York, 1979.
48 N.Y.2d 684, 421 N.Y.S.2d 877, 397 N.E.2d 387.

MEMORANDUM

The order of the Appellate Division should be affirmed, with costs.

Plaintiff Zetlin owned approximately 2% of the outstanding shares of Gable Industries, Inc., with defendants Hanson Holdings, Inc., and

Sylvestri together with members of the Sylvestri family, owning 44.4% of Gable's shares. The defendants sold their interests to Flintkote Co. for a premium price of $15 per share, at a time when Gable was selling on the open market for $7.38 per share. It is undisputed that the 44.4% acquired by Flintkote represented effective control of Gable.

Recognizing that those who invest the capital necessary to acquire a dominant position in the ownership of a corporation have the right of controlling that corporation, it has long been settled law that, absent looting of corporate assets, conversion of a corporate opportunity, fraud or other acts of bad faith, a controlling stockholder is free to sell, and a purchaser is free to buy, that controlling interest at a premium price (see Barnes v. Brown, 80 N.Y. 527; Levy v. American Beverage Corp., 265 App.Div. 208, 38 N.Y.S.2d 517; Essex Universal Corp. v. Yates, 2nd Cir., 305 F.2d 572).

Certainly, minority shareholders are entitled to protection against such abuse by controlling shareholders. They are not entitled, however, to inhibit the legitimate interests of the other stockholders. It is for this reason that control shares usually command a premium price. The premium is the added amount an investor is willing to pay for the privilege of directly influencing the corporation's affairs.

In this action plaintiff Zetlin contends that minority stockholders are entitled to an opportunity to share equally in any premium paid for a controlling interest in the corporation. This rule would profoundly affect the manner in which controlling stock interests are now transferred. It would require, essentially, that a controlling interest be transferred only by means of an offer to all stockholders, i.e., a tender offer. This would be contrary to existing law and if so radical a change is to be effected it would best be done by the Legislature.

COOKE, C.J., and JASEN, GABRIELLI, JONES, WACHTLER, FUCHSBERG and MEYER, JJ., concur in memorandum.

DEBAUN v. FIRST WESTERN BANK AND TRUST CO.

Court of Appeals of California, 1975.
46 Cal.App.3d 686, 120 Cal.Rptr. 354.

THOMPSON, ASSOCIATE JUSTICE.

This appeal primarily concerns the duty of a majority shareholder to the corporation whose shares he holds in selling the shares when possessed of facts establishing a reasonable likelihood that the purchaser intends to exercise the control to be acquired by him to loot the corporation of its assets. We conclude that in those circumstances the majority shareholder owes a duty of reasonable investigation and due care to the corporation.

FACTS

Alfred S. Johnson Incorporated (Corporation) was incorporated by Alfred S. Johnson in 1955 to process color photographs to be reproduced in printed form. All of the 100 outstanding shares of Corporation were originally owned by Johnson. Subsequently, Johnson sold 20 of his shares to James DeBaun, Corporation's primary salesman, and 10 shares to Walter Stephens, its production manager. In November of 1964, Johnson was seriously ill so that managerial control of Corporation was assumed by DeBaun, Stephens, and Jack Hawkins, Corporation's estimator.

Johnson died testate on January 15, 1965. His will named appellant First Western Bank and Trust Company (Bank) as executor and trustee of a trust created by the will. The 70 shares of Corporation owned by Johnson at the time of his death passed to the testamentary trust. George Furman, an employee of Bank, was charged with the direct administration of the trust. While Bank took no hand in the management of Corporation leaving it to the existing management team, Furman attended virtually all directors' meetings. Bank, through its nominee, voted the 70 shares at stockholders' meetings.

Under the guidance of DeBaun and Stephens, the net after tax profit of Corporation increased dramatically as illustrated by the following table:

Fiscal year ending August 31	Net Profit
1964	$15,903
1965	$42,316
1966	$58,969
1967	$37,583
1968 (10 mos.)	$56,710

On October 27, 1966, Bank's trust department determined that the investment in Corporation was not appropriate for the trust and decided to sell the 70 shares. Bank also decided that no one connected with Corporation should be made aware of its decision to sell until a sale was firm. It caused an appraisal of Corporation to be made by General Appraisal Company which estimated the value of Corporation as a going concern at $326,000. Bank retained W.H. Daum Investment Company (Daum) to find a buyer and to assist it in the sale.

DeBaun and Stephens were not told of the Bank's plans. In March of 1968, a competitor of Corporation showed DeBaun a letter from Daum indicating that Corporation was for sale. Subsequently, both DeBaun and Stephens were contacted by two potential buyers who sought to purchase their shares. They refused to sell, agreeing to hold their shares because they had " * * * a good job * * * and percentage of the company * * * " At the request of Daum's representative, DeBaun submitted an offer for the 70 shares held by Bank. The offer was rejected as inadequate.

On May 15 and 20, 1968, Bank received successive offers for the 70 shares from Raymond J. Mattison, acting in the name of S.O.F. Fund, an inter vivos revocable trust of which he was both settlor and trustee. A sketchy balance sheet of S.O.F. Fund was submitted with the second offer. The offers were rejected. Anticipating a further offer from Mattison and his trust, Furman, acting for Bank, ordered a Dun & Bradstreet report on Mattison and the fund. The report was received on May 24, 1968. It noted pending litigation, bankruptcies, and tax liens against corporate entities in which Mattison had been a principal, and suggested that S.O.F. Fund no longer existed.

As of May 24, I. Earl Funk, a vice-president of Bank, had personal knowledge that: (1) on October 24, 1957, the Los Angeles Superior Court had entered a judgment against Mattison in favor of Bank's predecessor in interest for compensatory and punitive damages as the result of Mattison's fraudulent misrepresentations and a fraudulent financial statement to obtain a loan; and (2) the judgment remained unsatisfied in 1968 and was an asset of Bank acquired from its predecessor in an acquisition of 65 branch banks.

On May 27, 1968, Mattison submitted a third offer to purchase the 70 shares of Corporation held by Bank. The offer proposed that S.O.F. Fund would pay $250,000 for the shares, $50,000 in marketable securities as a down payment with the balance payable over a five-year period. Bank made a counter offer, generally accepting the terms of the Mattison proposal but providing that: (1) the $200,000 balance of the purchase price was to be secured by a pledge of marketable securities valued at a like amount; and (2) Corporation would pay no dividends out of "pre-sale" retained earnings. On June 4, 1968, representatives of Bank met with Oroville McCarrol, who had been a trust officer of Bank's predecessor in interest and was counsel for Mattison. McCarrol proposed that Corporation use its assets to secure the unpaid balance of the purchase price rather than Mattison supplying the security in the form of marketable securities. He proposed also the elimination of the restriction against dividends from pre-sale retained earnings. Despite reservations by Bank personnel on the legality of the use of corporate assets to secure an obligation of a major shareholder, Bank determined to pursue the McCarrol modification further. Troubled by the Dun & Bradstreet report, personnel of Bank met with Mattison and McCarrol on June 27. Mattison explained that it had been his practice to take over failing companies so that the existence of the litigation and tax liens noted in the Dun & Bradstreet report was not due to his fault. Not entirely satisfied, Furman wrote to McCarrol requesting a written report on the status of all pending litigation in which Mattison was involved. McCarrol telephoned his response, declining to represent the status of the litigation but noting that the information was publicly available. Partly because Ralph Whitsett, Furman's immediate superior at Bank, knew McCarrol as a former trust officer of Bank's predecessor in interest, and partly because during a luncheon with Mattison at the Jonathan Club Robert Q. Parsons, the officer at Daum in charge of the transaction, had noted that Mattison was warmly received by his fellow members and reported that fact to Furman, Bank did not pursue its investigation into the public records of Los Angeles County where a mass of derogatory information lay.

As of July 1, 1968, the public records of Los Angeles County revealed 38 unsatisfied judgments against Mattison or his entities totalling $330,886.27, and 54 pending actions claiming a total of $373,588.67 from them. The record also contained 22 recorded abstracts of judgments against Mattison or his entities totalling $285,704.11, and 18 tax liens aggregating $20,327.97. Bank did not investigate the public record and hence was unaware of Mattison's financial track record.

While failing to pursue the investigation of the known information adverse to Mattison, Bank's employees knew or should have known that if his proposal through McCarrol were accepted the payment of the $200,000 balance of the purchase price would necessarily come from Corporation. They assumed that the payments would be made by Mattison from distributions of the Corporation which he would cause it to make after assuming control. They were aware that Corporation would not generate a sufficient aftertax cash flow to pay dividends in a sufficient amount to permit the payments of interest and principal on the $200,000 balance as scheduled in the McCarrol proposal, and knew that Mattison could make those payments only by resorting to distribution of "pre-sale" retained earnings and assets of Corporation.

On July 11, 1968, Bank accepted the McCarrol modification by entering into an exchange agreement with S.O.F. Fund. The agreement obligated S.O.F. to retain a working capital of not less than $70,000, to refrain from intercompany transactions except in the ordinary course of business for adequate consideration, and to furnish monthly financial statements and a certified annual audit report to Bank. It provides that Bank is to transfer its 70 shares of Corporation to Mattison as trustee of S.O.F. Fund, and that the stock will be held by Bank in pledge to secure the fund's obligation. There is provision for acceleration of the unpaid balance of the purchase price if Mattison defaults in any provision of the agreement. The contract obligated Mattison to cause Corporation to execute a security agreement to secure Mattison's obligation to Bank covering all "furniture, fixtures and equipment of [Corporation]." Mattison agreed also to cause Corporation's principal banking business to be maintained with Bank.

The exchange agreement having been executed, Bank gave Mattison a proxy to vote the 70 shares of Corporation at a special meeting of shareholders of Corporation to be held on July 11 at 3 p.m. Furman attended that meeting and an ensuing directors' meeting, as did Mattison. At the shareholders' meeting, DeBaun and Stephens were told that the shares of Corporation owned by Bank had been sold by it on an installment basis to Mattison and that Bank intended to take a pledge of those shares. A new board of directors was elected of which Mattison had control although DeBaun and Stephens remained as directors. DeBaun and Stephens were informed by Furman that a security agreement had been signed to protect Corporation in the event of death or default of Mattison and that in such an event Bank would "foreclose on the stock." Furman did not supply DeBaun or Stephens with a copy of the security agreement or inform them that in fact [it] hypothecated corporate assets as security for Mattison's debt to Bank. Relying upon Furman's statement of the effect of the agreement and misled by his failure to disclose its material terms, and by the further representation that the document was simply a formal requirement of Mattison's purchase of the majority shares, DeBaun and Stephens participated in a unanimous vote approving the execution by Corporation of the security agreement. A directors' meeting was then convened at which Mattison was elected president of Corporation.

At the moment of Bank's sale of the controlling shares to Mattison, Corporation was an eminently successful going business with a bright future. It had cash of $76,126.15 and other liquid assets of over $122,000. Its remaining assets were worth $60,000. Its excess of current assets over current liabilities and reserve for bad debts was $233,391.94, and its net worth about $220,000. Corporation's earnings indicated a pattern of growth. Mattison immediately proceeded to change that situation. Beginning with the date that he acquired control, Mattison implemented a systematic scheme to loot Corporation of its assets. His first step was to divert $73,144 in corporate cash to himself and to MICO, a shell company owned by Mattison. The transfer was made in exchange for unsecured noninterest bearing notes but for no other consideration. On August 2, 1968, Mattison caused Corporation to assign to MICO all of Corporation's assets, including its receivables in exchange for a fictitious agreement for management services. He diverted all corporate mail to a post office box from which he took the mail, opened it, and extracted all incoming checks to the corporation before forwarding the mail on. He ceased paying trade creditors promptly, as had been Corporation's practice, delaying payment of trade creditors to the last possible moment and, to the extent he could, not paying some at all. He delayed shipments on new orders. To cover his activities, Mattison removed the corporate books and records.

In September 1968, DeBaun left Corporation's employ as a salesman because of Mattison's policy of not filling orders and because Mattison had drastically reduced DeBaun's compensation. * * * Mattison continued to loot the corporation, although at a reduced pace by reason of its depleted assets. He collected payments from employees to pay premiums on a voluntary health insurance plan although the policy covering the plan was terminated in September for failure to pay premiums. He issued payroll checks without sufficient funds and continued not to pay trade creditors. Mattison did not supply Bank with the financial reports required by the exchange agreement.

While Bank was not aware of the initial transfer of cash to MICO, it did learn of the other misconduct of Mattison as it occurred. Although the conduct was a breach of the exchange agreement, Bank took no action beyond seeking an oral explanation from Mattison. In December 1968, Stephens also left Corporation's employ.

Bank took no action in the matter until April 25, 1969. On that date, it filed an action in the superior court seeking the appointment of a receiver. On April 30, Bank called a special shareholders' meeting of Corporation at which it voted its shares with those of DeBaun and Stephens to elect a new board of directors replacing the Mattison group. Faced with resistance from Mattison, Bank pursued neither its receivership nor its ouster of the board until June 20, 1969, when it shut down the operations of Corporation. By that time, Corporation was hopelessly insolvent. Its debts exceeded its assets by over $200,000, excluding its contingent liability to Bank, as a result of the fraudulently obtained hypothecation of corporate assets to secure Mattison's debt. Both the federal Internal Revenue Service and California State Board of Equalization had filed liens upon corporate assets and notices to withhold funds. A trade creditor had placed a keeper on the corporate premises.

On July 10, 1969, Bank, pursuant to the security agreement, sold all of Corporation's then remaining assets for $60,000. $25,000 of the proceeds of sale was paid to release the federal tax lien while the remaining $35,000 was retained by Bank. After the sale, Corporation had no assets and owed $218,426 to creditors.

Respondents filed two related actions against Bank. One asserted their right to recover, as shareholders, for damage caused by Bank. The other was a stockholders' derivate [sic] action brought on behalf of Corporation pursuant to Corporations Code section 834. The two cases were consolidated. Bank demurred to both complaints. In the demurrer to the first action, it contended that respondents DeBaun and Stephens, as shareholders, lacked capacity to pursue their claim. In the demurrer to the second complaint, Bank took the opposite tack, contending that its liability did not run to Corporation. The demurrer to the first complaint was sustained without leave to amend, and the demurrer to the second complaint was overruled. The case at bench proceeded to trial before a judge as a derivate [sic] action. The trial court held for respondents, finding that Bank had breached duties it owed as a majority controlling shareholder to the corporation it controlled. It assessed monetary damages in the amount of $473,836, computed by adding to $220,000, the net asset value of the corporation as the date of transfer of the shares to Mattison, an amount equal to anticipated after-tax earnings of the corporation for the ensuing 10–year period, taking into account an 8 percent growth factor. The court additionally awarded Corporation an amount equal to the sum it would be required to pay and the cost of defending valid claims existing against it when it became defunct. Pursuant to Fletcher v. A.J. Industries, Inc., 266 Cal.App.2d 313, 320–321, 72 Cal.Rptr. 146, the trial court awarded counsel for respondents attorneys' fees payable from the fund recovered for Corporation's benefit. It denied respondents' claim for punitive damages. This appeal from the resulting judgment followed. ∗ ∗ ∗

BREACH OF DUTY

Early case law held that a controlling shareholder owed no duty to minority shareholders or to the controlled corporation in the sale of his stock. (See e.g., Ryder v. Bamberger, 172 Cal. 791, 158 P. 753.) Decisional law, however, has since recognized the fact of financial life that corporate control by ownership of a majority of shares may be misused. Thus the applicable proposition now is that "In any transaction where the control of the corporation is material," the controlling majority shareholder must exercise good faith and fairness "from the viewpoint of the corporation and those interested therein." (Remillard Brick Co. v. Remillard–Dandini, 109 Cal.App.2d 405, 420, 241 P.2d 66, 75 quoted in Jones v. H.F. Ahmanson & Co., 1 Cal.3d 93, 110, 81 Cal. Rptr. 592, 600, 460 P.2d 464, 472.) That duty of good faith and fairness encompasses an obligation of the controlling shareholder in possession of facts "[s]uch as to awaken suspicion and put a prudent man on his guard [that a potential buyer of his shares may loot the corporation of its assets to pay for the shares purchased] ∗ ∗ ∗ to conduct a reasonable adequate investigation [of the buyer]." (Insuranshares Corporation v. Northern Fiscal Corp. (E.D.Pa.1940) 35 F.Supp. 22, 25.)

Here Bank was the controlling majority shareholder of Corporation. As it was negotiating with Mattison, it became directly aware of facts that would have alerted a prudent person that Mattison was likely to loot the corporation. Bank knew from the Dun & Bradstreet report that Mattison's financial record was notable by the failure of entities controlled by him. Bank knew that the only source of funds available to Mattison to pay it for the shares he was purchasing lay in the assets of the corporation. The after-tax net income from the date of the sale would not be sufficient to permit the payment of dividends to him which would permit the making of payments. An officer of Bank possessed personal knowledge that Mattison, on at least one occasion, had been guilty of a fraud perpetrated on Bank's predecessor in interest and had not satisfied a judgment Bank held against him for damages flowing from that conduct.

Armed with knowledge of those facts, Bank owed a duty to Corporation and its minority shareholders to act reasonably with respect to its dealings in the controlling shares with Mattison. It breached that duty. Knowing of McCarrol's refusal to express an opinion on litigation against Mattison and his entities, and that the information could be obtained from the public records, Bank closed its eyes to that obvious source. Rather, it relied upon Mattison's friendly reception by fellow members of the Jonathan Club and the fact that he was represented by a lawyer who had been a trust officer of Bank's predecessor in interest to conclude that indicators that Mattison was a financial bandit should be ignored. Membership in a club, whether it be the Jonathan or the informal group of ex-trust officers of Bank, does not excuse investigation. Nor can Bank be justified in accepting Mattison's uncorroborated statement that the past financial disasters of his entities reported by Dun & Bradstreet were due to his practice of acquiring failing companies. Only one who loots a failed company at the expense of its creditors can profit from its acquisition. Mattison's constantly repeated entry into the transactions without ever pulling a company from the morass was a strong indication that he was milking the companies profitably. Had Bank investigated, as any prudent man would have done, it would have discovered from the public records the additional detail of Mattison's long, long trail of financial failure that would have precluded its dealings with him except under circumstances where his obligation was secured beyond question and his ability to loot Corporation precluded.

Bank, however, elected to deal with Mattison in a fashion that invited rather than tended to prevent his looting of Corporation's assets. It agreed to a payment schedule that virtually required Mattison to do so. By fraudulently concealing its nature from DeBaun and Stephens, Bank obtained corporate approval of a security agreement which hypothecated corporate assets to secure Mattison's obligation to it. Thus, to permit it to sell its majority shares to Mattison, Bank placed the assets and business of Corporation in peril. Not content with so doing, Bank used its control for still another purpose of its own by requiring Mattison to agree to cause Corporation to give its major banking business to Bank.

Thus the record establishes the duty of Bank and its breach. Appellant Bank seeks to avoid responsibility for its action by reversing the position taken by it in its demurrer to the complaint filed by DeBaun and Stephens individually for injury to their minority stock position by now claiming that its duty ran only to the minority shareholders and not to the controlled corporation. California precedent is to the contrary, holding that the duty runs to both. (Remillard Brick Co. v. Remillard–Dandini, supra, 109 Cal.App.2d 405, 420, 241 P.2d 66; see also Jones v. H.F. Ahmanson & Co., supra, 1 Cal.3d 93, 110, 81 Cal.Rptr. 592, 460 P.2d 464.)

Contributory Negligence

Contrary to appellant's contention, there is no substantial evidence that any conduct on the part of DeBaun and Stephens contributed to the injury caused Corporation. Appellant argues that by agreeing between themselves not to sell their combined 30 percent of the shares of Corporation unless they both consented, respondents limited the market for Corporation's shares because some buyers would insist upon 80 percent control so that Corporation might constitute part of an affiliated group permitting the filing of consolidated income tax returns. Assuming that Bank's argument correctly states the facts, its premise is misplaced. However DeBaun and Stephens had limited the market for the 70 percent of Corporation's shares held by Bank, they did nothing at all to induce or cause Bank to sell to a corporate pirate. That idea was strictly Bank's. ∗ ∗ ∗

MEASURE OF DAMAGES

Appellant contends finally that the trial court improperly multiplied the measure of damages by adding to net asset value on the date of Bank's tortious conduct an estimate for future net profit and an obligation that Bank discharge the valid existing obligations of Corporation. The record refutes the contention.

The trial judge arrived at a value of the corporation as a going concern at the time of appellant's breach by adding to the value of Corporation's tangible assets a goodwill factor computed on the basis of future net income reasonably to be anticipated from the Corporation's past record. This the trial court was authorized to do in determining "the amount which will compensate for all the detriment proximately caused ∗ ∗ ∗" by appellant's breach of duty. Appellant's breach damaged Corporation not only in the loss of its assets but also in the loss of its earning power. Since the trial court's determination of loss of earning power was based upon a past record of earnings and not speculation, it is supported by substantial evidence. The trial court's order requiring appellant to pay all valid claims of creditors against Corporation is also proper as necessary to restore Corporation to the condition in which it existed prior to the time that Bank contributed to its destruction. Prior to Bank's action, Corporation was a going concern with substantial net assets. As a proximate result of Bank's dereliction of duty, Corporation acquired a negative net worth of about $218,000. Total damage to Corporation is thus the sum necessary to restore the negative net worth, plus the value of its tangible assets, plus its going business value determined with reference to its future profits reasonably estimated. That is the measure which the trial court applied. Since the derivative action is equitable in nature, the court properly framed part of its judgment in terms of an obligation dependent upon future contingencies rather than at a fixed dollar amount.

DISPOSITION

The judgment is affirmed. The matter is, however, remanded to the trial court with directions to hold a hearing to determine the additional amount payable to respondents from the fund recovered by them for benefit of Corporation for counsel fees due for services on this appeal.

Notes

(1) What is the source of the duty owed by the bank to the plaintiffs in the principal case? As a practical matter, if you were advising an owner of a business who was planning to sell his controlling interest to unknown purchasers, how would you go about meeting this duty?

(2) Most of the looting cases involve investment companies, i.e. companies whose principal or sole assets constituted cash and readily marketable securities. Why should such companies be likely candidates for looters?

(3) Many cases involve a purchase price that seems unreasonably high given the business being purchased. Should the manifest willingness of an unknown purchaser to pay an unreasonably high price of itself be a suspicious circumstance? Some courts have refused to draw an adverse inference even though the premium seems extreme. In Clagett v. Hutchison, 583 F.2d 1259 (4th Cir.1978), for example, the majority shareholder was offered $43.75 per share at a time when the price in a "thinly traded * * * public market" varied between $7.50 and $10.00 per share; the court held that this price "cannot be said to be so unreasonable as to place [the seller] on notice of the likelihood of fraud on the corporation or the remaining stockholders." 583 F.2d at 1262. One Judge dissented.

(4) Consider the following analyses of the looting cases: (a) Easterbrook and Fischel, Corporate Control Transactions, 91 Yale L.J. 698, 718–719 (1982): *

> [L]ooting is a profitable transaction under some circumstances. Existing holders of control, no less than prospective purchasers, however, have an incentive to put their hands in the till, and a proposal to ban sales of control at a premium as an antidote to looting is like a proposal to ban investments in common stocks as an antidote to bankruptcy.

> If it were feasible to detect looters in advance, it might make sense to put the sellers of control blocs under a duty not to allow shares to pass to the knaves—certainly the sellers of control can detect knavery at a lower cost than the public shareholders who are not parties to the transaction. Indeed, some cases have held that a seller of a control bloc can be liable for failing to investigate adequately a prospective purchaser of control. The wisdom of such holdings is suspect, however, because it is difficult if not impossible to detect looters as they approach. A looter takes the money and runs, and looting is by nature a one-time transaction. Once looters have absconded with the assets of one firm, they acquire a reputation that prevents them from repeating this act. But when they first obtain control, they may appear quite innocuous. Any requirement that owners of control blocs investigate buyers and not sell to suspected looters is equivalent to a program of preventive detention for people who have never robbed banks but have acquisitive personalities.

> Although sellers could spend substantial sums investigating buyers and investors still more in litigating about the quality of investigation, and the result of some investigations would be a refusal to sell, almost all of these refusals would be false positives. That is, they would be refusals that reduced the gains available from transferring control. Sometimes the best way to manage a firm is to break it up—to sell off unprofitable operations and reorganize the rest. Some managers are especially skilled in reorganizing or liquidating seriously ailing firms.

* Reprinted by permission of The Yale Law Journal Company and Fred B. Rothman & Company from *The Yale Law Journal*, Vol. 91, pp. 718–719.

Yet it seems likely that the suspicion of looting would fall most heavily on such people, for it is hard to say in advance whether a radical restructuring of a firm would be good or bad for the shareholders. A legal rule that has its greatest bite when a firm is approached by a buyer with a proposal for radical (and potentially highly beneficial) surgery is unlikely to increase the value of investments.

We do not suggest that the legal system should disregard looting, but we think it likely that the best remedies are based on deterrence rather than prior scrutiny. Looters, when caught, could be heavily fined or imprisoned, taking into account the frequency with which looting escapes detection. Penalties for looting could be made high enough to be effective. The costs of deterrence are probably much lower than the costs of dealing with looting through a system of prior scrutiny that would scotch many valuable control shifts as a byproduct.

(b) Hamilton, Private Sale of Control Transactions: Where We Stand Today, 36 Case W.Res.L.Rev. 248, 267–8 (1985):

It is possible that Easterbrook and Fischel are correct when they infer that the costs of an *ex ante* requirement exceed its benefits, but I doubt it. In the first place, in my personal experience, it is not true that looters abscond and only first-time looters ply their trade. Rather, persons on the fringe of the law often quietly merge into the general economy and surface from time to time, hoping that their background is not discovered, and if it is, quietly disappear again. As a result, routine and inexpensive credit checks on persons offering to buy asset-rich companies often turn up substantially negative factors.

* * *

Second, while it is possible that the *ex ante* investigation would turn up some "false positives," I do not see why this should be so. What is supposed to be investigated is not whether the purchaser has dismantled companies in the past, but whether he has a reputation for honesty and the apparent wherewithal to finance a transaction of the magnitude under consideration without recourse to the corporation's assets in a way that defrauds creditors and minority shareholders.[101] If a person does not meet this standard, one wonders whether he is really a "false positive."

Finally, the *ex post* deterrence proposed by Easterbrook and Fischel in the form of criminal sanctions is not very attractive. Even if it is assumed that punishment for this type of conduct will be quick and sure—hardly characteristics of current criminal sanctions against white-collar crime—the result is that the innocent shareholders and others "left behind" will usually suffer the entire economic loss, while the majority shareholders who sold to the thieves may keep the entire

---

101. [By the Author] It is important to distinguish the use of corporate assets in "leveraged buy-outs" from their use in looting transactions. When the purchaser acquires all the shares of the corporation, as is the normal pattern in leveraged buy-outs, the purchaser may use the assets as he wishes, consistent with his obligations to creditors. As a result, he may use corporate assets to discharge his loans used to purchase the outstanding shares, * * * It is quite different to use corporate assets to discharge the purchasers' individual loans when there are minority shareholders; that is looting.

purchase price, premium and all. The thieves, of course, go to jail. This result seems so obviously unjust from the standpoint of the minority shareholders that it seems unreasonable to embrace it on the basis of entirely theoretical considerations of economic "efficiency."

(5) The word "looting," of course, has an emotional context, and often, as in *DeBaun*, the misuse of funds is blatant. However, what about paying out corporate assets in the form of dividends? What about salaries that are high but arguably not enough to constitute waste? Should such conduct be described as "looting"?

PERLMAN v. FELDMANN

United States Court of Appeals, Second Circuit, 1955.
219 F.2d 173.

Clark, Chief Judge.

This is a derivative action brought by minority stockholders of Newport Steel Corporation to compel accounting for, and restitution of, allegedly illegal gains which accrued to defendants as a result of the sale in August, 1950, of their controlling interest in the corporation. The principal defendant, C. Russell Feldmann, who represented and acted for the others, members of his family,[102] was at that time not only the dominant stockholder, but also the chairman of the board of directors and the president of the corporation. Newport, an Indiana corporation, operated mills for the production of steel sheets for sale to manufacturers of steel products, first at Newport, Kentucky, and later also at other places in Kentucky and Ohio. The buyers, a syndicate organized as Wilport Company, a Delaware corporation, consisted of end-users of steel who were interested in securing a source of supply in a market becoming ever tighter in the Korean War. Plaintiffs contend that the consideration paid for the stock included compensation for the sale of a corporate asset, a power held in trust for the corporation by Feldmann as its fiduciary. This power was the ability to control the allocation of the corporate product in a time of short supply, through control of the board of directors; and it was effectively transferred in this sale by having Feldmann procure the resignation of his own board and the election of Wilport's nominees immediately upon consummation of the sale.

The present action represents the consolidation of three pending stockholders' actions in which yet another stockholder has been permitted to intervene. Jurisdiction below was based upon the diverse citizenship of the parties. Plaintiffs argue here, as they did in the court below, that in the situation here disclosed the vendors must account to the nonparticipating minority stockholders for that share of their profit

---

102. [By the Court] The stock was not held personally by Feldmann in his own name, but was held by the members of his family and by personal corporations. The aggregate of stock thus had amounted to 33% of the outstanding Newport stock and gave working control to the holder. The actual sale included 55,552 additional shares held by friends and associates of Feldmann, so that a total of 37% of the Newport stock was transferred.

which is attributable to the sale of the corporate power. Judge Hincks denied the validity of the premise, holding that the rights involved in the sale were only those normally incident to the possession of a controlling block of shares, with which a dominant stockholder, in the absence of fraud or foreseeable looting, was entitled to deal according to his own best interests. Furthermore, he held that plaintiffs had failed to satisfy their burden of proving that the sales price was not a fair price for the stock per se. Plaintiffs appeal from these rulings of law which resulted in the dismissal of their complaint.

The essential facts found by the trial judge are not in dispute. Newport was a relative newcomer in the steel industry with predominantly old installations which were in the process of being supplemented by more modern facilities. Except in times of extreme shortage Newport was not in a position to complete profitably with other steel mills for customers not in its immediate geographical area. Wilport, the purchasing syndicate, consisted of geographically remote end-users of steel who were interested in buying more steel from Newport than they had been able to obtain during recent periods of tight supply. The price of $20 per share was found by Judge Hincks to be a fair one for a control block of stock, although the over-the-counter market price had not exceeded $12 and the book value per share was $17.03. But this finding was limited by Judge Hincks' statement that "[w]hat value the block would have had if shorn of its appurtenant power to control distribution of the corporate product, the evidence does not show." It was also conditioned by his earlier ruling that the burden was on plaintiffs to prove a lesser value for the stock.

Both as director and as dominant stockholder, Feldmann stood in a fiduciary relationship to the corporation and to the minority stockholders as beneficiaries thereof. Pepper v. Litton, 308 U.S. 295, 60 S.Ct. 238, 84 L.Ed. 281. His fiduciary obligation must in the first instance be measured by the law of Indiana, the state of incorporation of Newport. Although there is no Indiana case directly in point, the most closely analogous one emphasizes the close scrutiny to which Indiana subjects the conduct of fiduciaries when personal benefit may stand in the way of fulfillment of trust obligations. In Schemmel v. Hill, 91 Ind.App. 373, 169 N.E. 678, 682, 683, McMahan, J., said: "Directors of a business corporation act in a strictly fiduciary capacity. Their office is a trust. When a director deals with his corporation, his acts will be closely scrutinized. Directors of a corporation are its agents, and they are governed by the rules of law applicable to other agents, and, as between themselves and their principal, the rules relating to honesty and fair dealing in the management of the affairs of their principal are applicable. They must not, in any degree, allow their official conduct to be swayed by their private interest, which must yield to official duty. In a transaction between a director and his corporation, where he acts for himself and his principal at the same time in a matter connected with the relation between them, it is presumed, where he is thus potential on both sides of the contract, that self-interest will overcome his fidelity to his principal, to his own benefit and to his principal's hurt." And the judge added: "Absolute and most scrupulous good faith is the very essence of a director's obligation to his corporation. The first principal duty arising from his official relation is to act in all things of trust wholly for the benefit of his corporation."

In Indiana, then, as elsewhere, the responsibility of the fiduciary is not limited to a proper regard for the tangible balance sheet assets of the corporation, but includes the dedication of his uncorrupted business judgment for the sole benefit of the corporation, in any dealings which may adversely affect it. Irving Trust Co. v. Deutsch, 2 Cir., 73 F.2d 121, certiorari denied 294 U.S. 708, 55 S.Ct. 405, 79 L.Ed. 1243; Meinhard v. Salmon, 249 N.Y. 458, 164 N.E. 545, 62 A.L.R. 1. Although the Indiana case is particularly relevant to Feldmann as a director, the same rule should apply to his fiduciary duties as majority stockholder, for in that capacity he chooses and controls the directors, and thus is held to have assumed their liability. Pepper v. Litton, supra, 308 U.S. 295, 60 S.Ct. 238. This, therefore, is the standard to which Feldmann was by law required to conform in his activities here under scrutiny.

It is true, as defendants have been at pains to point out, that this is not the ordinary case of breach of fiduciary duty. We have here no fraud, no misuse of confidential information, no outright looting of a helpless corporation. But on the other hand, we do not find compliance with that high standard which we have just stated and which we and other courts have come to expect and demand of corporate fiduciaries. In the often-quoted words of Judge Cardozo: [The Court quotes from Meinhard v. Salmon, page 71 supra]. The actions of defendants in siphoning off for personal gain corporate advantages to be derived from a favorable market situation do not betoken the necessary undivided loyalty owed by the fiduciary to his principal.

The corporate opportunities of whose misappropriation the minority stockholders complain need not have been an absolute certainty in order to support this action against Feldmann. If there was possibility of corporate gain, they are entitled to recover. In Young v. Higbee Co., 324 U.S. 204, 65 S.Ct. 594, two stockholders appealing the confirmation of a plan of bankruptcy reorganization were held liable for profits received for the sale of their stock pending determination of the validity of the appeal. They were held accountable for the excess of the price of their stock over its normal price, even though there was no indication that the appeal could have succeeded on substantive grounds. And in Irving Trust Co. v. Deutsch, supra, an accounting was required of corporate directors who bought stock for themselves for corporate use, even though there was an affirmative showing that the corporation did not have the finances itself to acquire the stock. Judge Swan speaking for the court pointed out that "The defendants' argument, contrary to Wing v. Dillingham [5 Cir., 239 F. 54], that the equitable rule that fiduciaries should not be permitted to assume a position in which their individual interests might be in conflict with those of the corporation can have no application where the corporation is unable to undertake the venture, is not convincing. If directors are permitted to justify their conduct on such a theory, there will be a temptation to refrain from exerting their strongest efforts on behalf of the corporation since, if it does not meet the obligations, an opportunity of profit will be open to them personally." [73 F.2d 121, 124]

This rationale is equally appropriate to a consideration of the benefits which Newport might have derived from the steel shortage. In the past Newport had used and profited by its market leverage by operation of what the industry had come to call the "Feldmann Plan." This consisted of securing interest-free advances from prospective purchasers of steel in return for firm commitments to them from future production. The funds thus acquired were used to finance improvements in existing plants and to acquire new installations. In the summer of 1950 Newport had been negotiating for cold-rolling facilities which it needed for a more fully integrated operation and a more marketable product, and Feldmann plan funds might well have been used toward this end.

Further, as plaintiffs alternatively suggest, Newport might have used the period of short supply to build up patronage in the geographical area in which it could compete profitably even when steel was more abundant. Either of these opportunities was Newport's, to be used to its advantage only. Only if defendants had been able to negate completely any possibility of gain by Newport could they have prevailed. It is true that a trial court finding states: "Whether or not, in August, 1950, Newport's position was such that it could have entered into 'Feldmann Plan' type transactions to procure funds and financing for the further expansion and integration of its steel facilities and whether such expansion would have been desirable for Newport, the evidence does not show." This, however, cannot avail the defendants, who— contrary to the ruling below—had the burden of proof on this issue, since fiduciaries always have the burden of proof in establishing the fairness of their dealings with trust property. Pepper v. Litton, supra.

Defendants seek to categorize the corporate opportunities which might have accrued to Newport as too unethical to warrant further consideration. It is true that reputable steel producers were not participating in the gray market brought about by the Korean War and were refraining from advancing their prices, although to do so would not have been illegal. But Feldmann plan transactions were not considered within this self-imposed interdiction; the trial court found that around the time of the Feldmann sale Jones & Laughlin Steel Corporation, Republic Steel Company, and Pittsburgh Steel Corporation were all participating in such arrangements. In any event, it ill becomes the defendants to disparage as unethical the market advantages from which they themselves reaped rich benefits.

We do not mean to suggest that a majority stockholder cannot dispose of his controlling block of stock to outsiders without having to account to his corporation for profits or even never do this with impunity when the buyer is an interested customer, actual or potential, for the corporation's product. But when the sale necessarily results in a sacrifice of this element of corporate good will and consequent unusual profit to the fiduciary who has caused the sacrifice, he should account for his gains. So in a time of market shortage, where a call on a corporation's product commands an unusually large premium, in one form or another, we think it sound law that a fiduciary may not appropriate to himself the value of this premium. Such personal gain at the expense of his coventurers seems particularly reprehensible when made by the trusted president and director of his company. In this case the violation of duty seems to be all the clearer because of this triple role in which Feldmann appears, though we are unwilling to say, and are not to be understood as saying, that we should accept a lesser obligation for any one of his roles alone.

Hence to the extent that the price received by Feldmann and his codefendants included such a bonus, he is accountable to the minority stockholders who sue here. And plaintiffs, as they contend, are entitled to a recovery in their own right, instead of in right of the corporation (as in the usual derivative actions), since neither Wilport nor their successors in interest should share in any judgment which may be rendered. See Southern Pacific Co. v. Bogert, 250 U.S. 483, 39 S.Ct. 533, 63 L.Ed. 1099. Defendants cannot well object to this form of recovery, since the only alternative, recovery for the corporation as a whole, would subject them to a greater total liability.

The case will therefore be remanded to the district court for a determination of the question expressly left open below, namely, the value of defendants' stock without the appurtenant control over the corporation's output of steel. We reiterate that on this issue, as on all others relating to a breach of fiduciary duty, the burden of proof must rest on the defendants. Judgment should go to these plaintiffs and those whom they represent for any premium value so shown to the extent of their respective stock interests.

The judgment is therefore reversed and the action remanded for further proceedings pursuant to this opinion.

SWAN, CIRCUIT JUDGE (dissenting).

With the general principles enunciated in the majority opinion as to the duties of fiduciaries I am, of course, in thorough accord. But, as Mr. Justice Frankfurter stated in Securities and Exchange Comm. v. Chenery Corp., 318 U.S. 80, 85, 63 S.Ct. 454, 458, 87 L.Ed. 626, "to say that a man is a fiduciary only begins analysis; it gives direction to further inquiry. To whom is he a fiduciary? What obligations does he owe as a fiduciary? In what respect has he failed to discharge these obligations?" My brothers' opinion does not specify precisely what fiduciary duty Feldmann is held to have violated or whether it was a duty imposed upon him as the dominant stockholder or as a director of Newport. Without such specification I think that both the legal profession and the business world will find the decision confusing and will be unable to foretell the extent of its impact upon customary practices in the sale of stock.

The power to control the management of a corporation, that is, to elect directors to manage its affairs, is an inseparable incident to the ownership of a majority of its stock, or sometimes, as in the present instance, to the ownership of enough shares, less than a majority, to control an election. Concededly a majority or dominant shareholder is ordinarily privileged to sell his stock at the best price obtainable from the purchaser. In so doing he acts on his own behalf, not as an agent of the corporation. If he knows or has reason to believe that the purchaser intends to exercise to the detriment of the corporation the power of management acquired by the purchase, such knowledge or reasonable suspicion will terminate the dominant shareholder's privilege to sell and will create a duty not to transfer the power of management to such purchaser. The duty seems to me to resemble the obligation which everyone is under not to assist another to commit a tort rather than the obligation of a fiduciary. But whatever the nature of the duty, a violation of it will subject the violator to liability for damages sustained by the corporation. Judge Hincks found that Feldmann had no reason to think that Wilport would use the power of management it would acquire by the purchase to injure Newport, and that there was no proof that it ever was so used. Feldmann did know, it is true, that the reason Wilport wanted the stock was to put in a board of directors who would be likely to permit Wilport's members to purchase more of Newport's steel than they might otherwise be able to get. But there is nothing illegal in a dominant shareholder purchasing from his own corporation at the same prices it offers to other customers. That is what the members of Wilport did, and there is no proof that Newport suffered any detriment therefrom.

My brothers say that "the consideration paid for the stock included compensation for the sale of a corporate asset", which they describe as "the ability to control the allocation of the corporate product in a time of short supply, through control of the board of directors; and it was effectively transferred in this sale by having Feldmann procure the resignation of his own board and the election of Wilport's nominees immediately upon consummation of the sale." The implications of this are not clear to me. If it means that when market conditions are such as to induce users of a corporation's product to wish to buy a controlling block of stock in order to be able to purchase part of the corporation's output at the same mill list prices as are offered to other customers, the dominant stockholder is under a fiduciary duty not to sell his stock, I cannot agree. For reasons already stated, in my opinion Feldmann was not proved to be under any fiduciary duty as a stockholder not to sell the stock he controlled.

Feldmann was also a director of Newport. Perhaps the quoted statement means that as a director he violated his fiduciary duty in voting to elect Wilport's nominees to fill the vacancies created by the resignations of the former directors of Newport. As a director Feldmann was under a fiduciary duty to use an honest judgment in acting on the corporation's behalf. A director is privileged to resign, but so long as he remains a director he must be faithful to his fiduciary duties and must not make a personal gain from performing them. Consequently, if the price paid for Feldmann's stock included a payment for voting to elect the new directors, he must account to the corporation for such payment, even though he honestly believed that the men he voted to elect were well qualified to serve as directors. He can not take pay for performing his fiduciary duty. There is no suggestion that he did do so, unless the price paid for his stock was more than its value. So it seems to me that decision must turn on whether finding 120 and conclusion 5 of the district judge are supportable on the evidence. They are set out in the margin.[103]

Judge Hincks went into the matter of valuation of the stock with his customary care and thoroughness. He made no error of law in applying the principles relating to valuation of stock. Concededly a controlling block of stock has greater sale value than a small lot. While the spread between $10 per share for small lots and $20 per share for the controlling block seems rather extraordinarily wide, the $20 valuation was supported by the expert testimony of Dr. Badger, whom the district judge said he could not find to be wrong. I see no justification for upsetting the valuation as clearly erroneous. Nor can I agree with my brothers that the $20 valuation "was limited" by the last sentence in finding 120. The controlling block could not by any possibility be shorn of its appurtenant power to elect directors and through them to control distribution of the corporate product. It is this "appurtenant power" which gives a controlling block its value as such block. What evidence could be adduced to show the value of the block "if shorn" of such appurtenant power, I cannot conceive, for it cannot be shorn of it. * * *

The final conclusion of my brothers is that the plaintiffs are entitled to recover in their own right instead of in the right of the corporation. This appears to be completely inconsistent with the theory advanced at the outset of the opinion, namely, that the price of the stock "included compensation for the sale of a corporate asset." If a corporate asset was sold, surely the corporation should recover the compensation received for it by the defendants. Moreover, if the plaintiffs were suing in their own right, Newport was not a proper party. The case of Southern Pacific Co. v. Bogert, 250 U.S. 483, 39 S.Ct.

---

103. [By the Judge] "120. The 398,927 shares of Newport stock sold to Wilport as of August 31, 1950, had a fair value as a control block of $20 per share. What value the block would have had if shorn of its appurtenant power to control distribution of the corporate product, the evidence does not show."

"5. Even if Feldmann's conduct in cooperating to accomplish a transfer of control to Wilport immediately upon the sale constituted a breach of a fiduciary duty to Newport, no part of the moneys received by the defendants in connection with the sale constituted profits for which they were accountable to Newport."

533, 63 L.Ed. 1099, relied upon as authority for the conclusion that the plaintiffs are entitled to recover in their own right, relates to a situation so different that the decision appears to me to be inapposite.

I would affirm the judgment on appeal.

Notes

(1) On remand, Judge Hincks took a deep breath and concluded that the "enterprise value" of a share of Newport stock was $14.67, so that Feldmann had received a premium of $5.33 per share, or a total premium of $2,126,280. The plaintiffs, representing sixty-three per cent of the stock, were therefore entitled to a judgment of $1,339,769, plus interest. Perlman v. Feldmann, 154 F.Supp. 436 (D.Conn.1957).

(2) Consider the following analysis of *Perlman* by Easterbrook and Fischel, Corporate Control Transactions, 91 Yale L.J. 698, 716, 717–718 (1982): *

There are several problems with * * * [the court's analysis in Perlman v. Feldmann]. Foremost is its assumption that the gain resulting from the "Plan" was not reflected in the price of Newport's stock. Newport stock was widely traded, and the existence of the Feldmann Plan was known to investors. The going price of Newport shares prior to the transaction therefore reflected the full value of Newport, including the value of advances under the Feldmann Plan. The Wilport syndicate paid some two-thirds more than the going price and thus could not profit from the deal unless (a) the sale of control resulted in an increase in the value of Newport, or (b) Wilport's control of Newport was the equivalent of looting. To see the implications of the latter possibility, consider the following simplified representation of the transaction. Newport has only 100 shares, and Wilport pays $20 for each of 37 shares. The market price of shares is $12, and hence the premium over the market price is $8 \times 37 = $296. Wilport must extract more than $296 from Newport in order to gain from the deal; the extraction comes at the expense of the other 63 shares, which must drop approximately $4.75 each, to $7.25.

Hence, the court's proposition that Wilport extracted a corporate opportunity from Newport—the functional equivalent of looting—has testable implications. Unless the price of Newport's outstanding shares plummeted, the Wilport syndicate could not be extracting enough to profit. In fact, however, the value of Newport's shares rose substantially after the transaction. Part of this increase may have been attributable to the rising market for steel companies at the time, but even holding this factor constant, Newport's shares appreciated in price.[104] The data refute the court's proposition that Wilport appropriated a corporate opportunity of Newport.

* Reprinted by permission of The Yale Law Journal Company and Fred B. Rothman & Company from *The Yale Law Journal*, Vol. 91, pp. 716–718.

104. [By the Author] Charles Cope has computed changes in the price of Newport shares using the market model, well developed in the finance literature, under which the rate of return on a firm's shares is a function of the market rate of return, the volatility of the firm's price in the past, a constant, and a residual component that represents the consequences of unanticipated events. Increases in this residual

It seems, then, that the source of the premium in Perlman is the same as the source of the gains for the shares Wilport did not buy: Wilport installed a better group of managers and, in addition, furnished Newport with a more stable market for its products. The gains from these changes must have exceeded any loss from abolition of the Feldmann Plan.

See also Booth, A Note on Individual Recovery in Derivative Suits, 16 Pepperdine L.Rev. 1025 (1989).

(3) In Birnbaum v. Newport Steel Corp., 193 F.2d 461 (2d Cir.1952), cert. denied 343 U.S. 956, 72 S.Ct. 1051, 96 L.Ed. 1356, Judge A. Hand offered the following description of the facts of this case as alleged in a complaint under rule 10b–5:

"* * * [During the period June to August 1950] Follansbee Steel Corporation and Newport were negotiating for a merger of the two corporations, which merger, on the terms offered by Follansbee, would have been highly profitable to all the stockholders of Newport. However, in August of 1950, Feldmann, acting in his official capacity as president of Newport, rejected the Follansbee offer, and on August 31, 1950, sold his stock to the defendant Wilport Company * * *. Immediately following the sale, Feldmann and the other directors of Newport resigned and * * * [persons who] were officers of and directors of Wilport took their place. * * *"

Does this brief description suggest an alternative basis for grounding recovery against Feldmann? Incidentally, the rule 10b–5 complaint was ultimately dismissed because the plaintiff was neither a purchaser nor a seller of securities.

(4) Just what theory did Judge Clark adopt? One commentator offers this comparison with the looting cases:

The looting cases have most often involved investment companies. A purchaser buys a controlling block of stock at a premium over value, whether that be taken as market value of the investment company's shares or the net asset value of its portfolio securities. As a condition of closing, the seller is to cause the purchaser and his nominees to be elected directors and officers. Then the purchaser utilizes his new place of power to steal from the corporation, selling portfolio securities and converting the proceeds to his personal use. The sellers have been held liable to the corporation for the amount of the premium and for the amount of the loss to the corporation, on a finding that circumstances were such as to put the seller on notice of the possibility of the looting that in fact occurred. *Feldmann* is said to fall in the same mold, except that the harm to the corporation, instead of the loss of cash and negotiable securities, is the loss of opportunities for Feldmann Plan financing and generation of local patronage.

But there is a vast difference between the corporate losses in *Feldmann* and in the looting cases. The loss in the looting cases is one

reflect good news for the firm. Cope found a significant positive residual for Newport in the month of the sale to Wilport. See Cope, Is the Control Premium Really a Corporate Asset? (April 1981) (unpublished paper on file with *Yale Law Journal*).

for which the purchaser, that is, the thief, would be held primarily liable if he were amenable to process and solvent enough to pay. The selling stockholder's liability for the loss is secondary, for facilitating, with notice, the purchaser's wrongdoing. There is nothing in *Feldmann* to suggest, however, that anything Wilport did or was likely to do after acquiring Feldmann's stock was actionable. It is a nice question whether Wilport incurred any liability on account of the purchase itself, for paying the control premium to Feldmann instead of to the corporation or to all its stockholders pro rata; but if it did, that liability was secondary, for participating in Feldmann's wrong, not the primary liability of a looter for misconduct after the transfer of control is consummated. There is no reason why suit could not have been brought against Wilport if its acts of mismanagement were the gravamen of the plaintiffs' complaint.

Andrews, The Stockholder's Right to Equal Opportunity in the Sale of Shares, 78 Harv.L.Rev. 505, 509–510 (1965).*

(5) Is it desirable for courts to evolve a single, consistent position with respect to premiums paid for controlling shares? (To date they have not done so.) At least the following arguments seem defensible:

(a) In the absence of fraud or foreseeable looting, a person may sell his or her property for what he can get or refuse to sell it at all. That is what economic freedom is all about. [A number of cases, like *Zetlin*, have adopted this position which is the dominant position today.

(b) A purchaser is really seeking control of the corporate assets when he buys the controlling shares. If he wants the assets he should buy them from the corporation, in which case all the shareholders would receive the same amount per share. In effect, this translates all sale of control cases into corporate opportunity cases [Some courts have adopted this position, particularly where the purchasers first approached the corporation seeking to buy its assets, and the controlling shareholder proposes a stock deal. See e.g. Commonwealth Title Ins. & Trust Co. v. Seltzer, 227 Pa. 410, 76 A. 77 (1910).]

(c) If it is part of the deal for the selling shareholder to resign his position with the corporation (as it almost always is), that is what the premium *really* is for. This approach in effect translates virtually all sale of control cases into sale of corporate office cases. [Some courts have tried this approach, particularly where the premium is set aside and its payment is made contingent on the resignations. E.g. Porter v. Healy, 244 Pa. 427, 91 A. 428 (1914).]

(d) It is simply immoral for a shareholder knowingly to take a greater price for his shares than other shareholders, since each share is actually identical with every other share. The additional amount must be for the control and that should belong to the corporation. See, e.g. Bayne, The Noninvestment Value of Control Stock, 45 Ind.L.J. 317 (1970).

(6) Of course, if the controlling shareholder hides or misrepresents the price she is getting, other shareholders who sell may have a right of recission under Rule 10b–5.

* Copyright © 1965 by the Harvard Law Review Association.

(7) Professor Andrews suggests the following "rule":

> The rule to be considered can be stated thus: whenever a controlling stockholder sells his shares, every other holder of shares (of the same class) is entitled to have an equal opportunity to sell his shares, or a prorata part of them, on substantially the same terms. Or in terms of the correlative duty: before a controlling stockholder may sell his shares to an outsider he must assure his fellow stockholders an equal opportunity to sell their shares, or as high a proportion of theirs as he ultimately sells of his own. * * *
>
> Now let us look briefly at what the rule means. First, it neither compels nor prohibits a sale of stock at any particular price; it leaves a controlling stockholder wholly free to decide for himself the price above which he will sell and below which he will hold his shares. The rule only says that in executing his decision to sell, a controlling stockholder cannot sell pursuant to a purchase offer more favorable than any available to other stockholders. Second, the rule does not compel a prospective purchaser to make an open offer for all shares on the same terms. He can offer to purchase shares on the condition that he gets a certain proportion of the total. Or he can even make an offer to purchase 51 per cent of the shares, no more and no less. The only requirement is that his offer, whatever it may be, be made equally or proportionately available to all stockholders. * * *

78 Harv.L.Rev., at 515–517.* Do you think this is a sensible solution to the control premium problem? For a critical analysis see Javaras, Equal Opportunity in the Sale of Controlling Shares: A Reply to Professor Andrews, 32 U.Chi.L.Rev. 420 (1965). Several courts have rejected the rule, one describing it as, "while nice theoretically, * * * simply not the law;" Clagett v. Hutchison, 583 F.2d 1259 (4th Cir.1978).

(8) Easterbrook and Fischel, Corporate Control Transactions, 91 Yale L.J. 698, 709–710 (1982):

> A sharing requirement also may make an otherwise profitable transaction unattractive to the prospective seller of control. To illustrate, suppose that the owner of a control bloc of shares finds that his perquisites or the other amenities of his position are worth $10. A prospective acquiror of control concludes that, by eliminating these perquisites and other amenities, he could produce a gain of $15. The shareholders in the company benefit if the acquiror pays a premium of $11 to the owner of the controlling bloc, ousts the current managers, and makes the contemplated improvements. The net gains of $4 inure to each investor according to his holdings, and although the acquiror obtains the largest portion because he holds the largest bloc, no one is left out. If the owner of the control bloc must share the $11 premium with all of the existing shareholders, however, the deal collapses. The owner will not part with his bloc for less than a $10 premium. A sharing requirement would make the deal unprofitable to him, and the other investors would lose the prospective gain from the installation of better managers.[105]

---

105. [By the Author] The common law recognizes that unequal distribution of

Compare Hamilton, Private Sale of Control Transactions: Where We Stand Today, 36 Case W.L.Rev. 248, 256–7 (1985):

There are several problems with this kind of analysis, however. The hypothetical the authors create assumes the correctness of their thesis. The assumption [is] that the purchasers of control will reduce the "perquisites or the other amenities" enjoyed as a result of the seller's position by $10, thereby producing a corporate gain of $15, * * *. One can equally plausibly assume that the buyer feels that he can enjoy the same "perquisites or the other amenities" as the seller enjoyed, and even increase them to, for instance, $14. On this assumption, the minority shareholders are clearly worse off as a result of the sale, and both the purchaser and seller of the control shares are benefiting at the minority shareholders' expense. * * *

There is another problem with the Easterbrook–Fischel hypothetical. Assume that the control stock sold in the hypothetical consists of 55% of the outstanding shares; if the buyers are content to allow the $15 increase in value to remain in the corporation, they will obtain 55% of the $15 increase in value by reason of their 55% stock ownership, or $8.25. In other words, if they abandon the "perquisites and other amenities," they will pay $11 in order to obtain an increase in investment value of only $8.25. They would obviously be better off if they retain the sellers' "percs" worth $10 and seek to squeeze out another couple of dollars here and there from additional "percs," rather than eliminating the "percs." * * *

The basic question is: If the new purchasers are rational profit maximizers, why should they share the $15 increase in value with the minority? It is not true that minority shareholders always share ratably in all increases in value with the majority shareholders. It would appear to be rational (and certainly practical) to place the minority shareholders on "starvation returns" from the corporation while increasing salaries or other "percs" to the new controlling shareholders in order to obtain all the additional $15 in gains. Why should the minority be given any of it? Starvation returns may also persuade the minority to sell their shares at low prices to the majority so that at some time thereafter the purchasers may own all of the outstanding shares and obtain all of the benefits of their skills. In short, I do not view hypothetical examples, such as those put forth by Easterbrook and Fischel, to prove anything more than that there *may be* idealized situations where everyone is better off as a result of the transfer of control; they do not prove that there are such situations, or their frequency.

gains facilitates the transfer of assets to higher-valued uses. Someone who discovers a lode of ore need not share the knowledge (and the profits) with the farmer under whose land the ore lies but may, instead, send an agent to buy the farm for the going price of farmland. A sharing requirement would lead to less searching for ore and lower wealth for society. *See* Leitch Gold Mines v. Texas Gulf Sulfur, 1 Ont.2d 469 (1969). See also Laidlaw v. Organ, 15 U.S. (2 Wheat.) 178 (1817). * * *

JONES v. H.F. AHMANSON & CO.

Supreme Court of California, 1969.
1 Cal.3d 93, 81 Cal.Rptr. 592, 460 P.2d 464.

TRAYNOR, CHIEF JUSTICE.

June K. Jones, the owner of 25 shares of the capital stock of United Savings and Loan Association of California brings this action on behalf of herself individually and of all similarly situated minority stockholders of the Association. The defendants are United Financial Corporation of California, fifteen individuals, and four corporations, all of whom are present or former stockholders or officers of the Association. Plaintiff seeks damages and other relief for losses allegedly suffered by the minority stockholders of the Association because of claimed breaches of fiduciary responsibility by defendants in the creation and operation of United Financial, a Delaware holding company that owns 87 percent of the outstanding Association stock.

Plaintiff appeals from the judgment entered for defendants after an order sustaining defendants' general and special demurrers to her third amended complaint without leave to amend. Defendants have filed a protective cross-appeal. We have concluded that the allegations of the complaint and certain stipulated facts sufficiently state a cause of action and that the judgment must therefore be reversed.

[Editor: United States Savings and Loan Association of California was a savings and loan association. The defendants owned about 85 per cent of the stock of the Association; the plaintiffs the remaining 15 per cent. Over the years the Association prospered. The Association retained the major part of its earnings in tax-free reserves with the result that the book value of each share increased from $1,131 in 1959 to $4,143.70 in 1966. However, because of the high price, the shares were only infrequently traded. In order to take advantage of increased public interest in savings and loan association shares, the defendants formed a new corporation, United Financial Corporation, to which they transferred all their shares of United States Savings and Loan Association in exchange for United Financial shares. The plaintiffs were not given an opportunity to exchange their shares. The savings and loan company shares represented the major asset of United Financial. United Financial then made a successful public offering of its shares and thereafter several of the defendants sold publicly some of their shares of United Financial. An active market developed in United Financial shares.

United Financial later offered to buy the remaining 15 percent of the shares of United States Savings and Loan Association or to exchange United Financial shares for United States Savings and Loan Association shares. However, the shares offered by United Financial to the shareholders of the savings and loan association had a market value of only $2,400 for each share of the savings and loan association, while the shares previously received by the defendants when United

Financial was created were worth about $8,800 per share. Previously, this value had been as high as $13,127.41 per share.] * * *

Plaintiff contends that in following this course of conduct defendants breached the fiduciary duty owed by majority or controlling shareholders to minority shareholders. She alleges that they used their control of the Association for their own advantage to the detriment of the minority when they created United Financial, made a public market for its shares that rendered Association stock unmarketable except to United Financial, and then refused either to purchase plaintiff's Association stock at a fair price or exchange the stock on the same basis afforded to the majority. She further alleges that they also created a conflict of interest that might have been avoided had they offered all Association stockholders the opportunity to participate in the initial exchange of shares. Finally, plaintiff contends that the defendants' acts constituted a restraint of trade in violation of common law and statutory antitrust laws. * * *

II

MAJORITY SHAREHOLDERS' FIDUCIARY RESPONSIBILITY

Defendants take the position that as shareholders they owe no fiduciary obligation to other shareholders, absent reliance on inside information, use of corporate assets, or fraud. This view has long been repudiated in California. The Courts of Appeal have often recognized that majority shareholders, either singly or acting in concert to accomplish a joint purpose, have a fiduciary responsibility to the minority and to the corporation to use their ability to control the corporation in a fair, just, and equitable manner. Majority shareholders may not use their power to control corporate activities to benefit themselves alone or in a manner detrimental to the minority. Any use to which they put the corporation or their power to control the corporation must benefit all shareholders proportionately and must not conflict with the proper conduct of the corporation's business.

The extensive reach of the duty of controlling shareholders and directors to the corporation and its other shareholders was described by the Court of Appeal in Remillard Brick Co. v. Remillard–Dandini, 109 Cal.App.2d 405, 241 P.2d 66, where, quoting from the opinion of the United States Supreme Court in Pepper v. Litton, 308 U.S. 295, 60 S.Ct. 238, 84 L.Ed. 281, the court held: * * * In *Remillard* the Court of Appeal clearly indicated that the fiduciary obligations of directors and shareholders are neither limited to specific statutory duties and avoidance of fraudulent practices nor are they owed solely to the corporation to the exclusion of other shareholders.

Defendants assert, however, that in the use of their own shares they owed no fiduciary duty to the minority stockholders of the Association. They maintain that they made full disclosure of the circumstances surrounding the formation of United Financial, that the creation of United Financial and its share offers in no way affected the control of the Association, that plaintiff's proportionate interest in the Association was not affected, that the Association was not harmed, and that the market for Association stock was not affected. Therefore, they conclude, they have breached no fiduciary duty to plaintiff and the other minority stockholders.

Defendants would have us retreat from a position demanding equitable treatment of all shareholders by those exercising control over a corporation to a philosophy much criticized by commentators and modified by courts in other jurisdictions as well as our own. In essence defendants suggest that we reaffirm the so-called "majority" rule reflected in our early decisions. This rule, exemplified by the decision in Ryder v. Bamberger, 172 Cal. 791, 158 P. 753, but since severely limited recognized the "perfect right [of majority shareholders] to dispose of their stock * * * without the slightest regard to the wishes and desires or knowledge of the minority stockholders; * * *" (p. 806, 158 P. p. 759) and held that such fiduciary duty as did exist in officers and directors was to the corporation only. The duty of shareholders as such was not recognized unless they, like officers and directors, by virtue of their position were possessed of information relative to the value of the corporation's shares that was not available to outside shareholders. In such case the existence of special facts permitted a finding that a fiduciary relationship to the corporation and other shareholders existed.

We had occasion to review these theories as well as the "minority rule" that directors and officers have an obligation to shareholders individually not to profit from their official position at the shareholders' expense in American Trust Co. v. California etc. Ins. Co., 15 Cal.2d 42, 98 P.2d 497. Each of the traditional rules has been applied under proper circumstances to enforce the fiduciary obligations of corporate officers and directors to their *cestuis*. (Lawrence v. I.N. Parlier Estate Co., 15 Cal.2d 220, 100 P.2d 765 [directors may not engage in any transaction that will conflict with their duty to the shareholders or make use of their power or of the corporate property for their own advantage]; Hobart v. Hobart Estate Co., 26 Cal.2d 412, 159 P.2d 958 [officer must disclose knowledge of corporate business to shareholder in transaction involving transfer of stock]; In re Security Finance Co., 49 Cal.2d 370, 317 P.2d 1 [majority shareholders' statutory powers subject to equitable limitation of good faith and inherent fairness to minority].) The rule that has developed in California is a comprehensive rule of "inherent fairness from the viewpoint of the corporation and those interested therein." (Remillard Brick Co. v. Remillard–Dandini, supra, 109 Cal.App.2d 405, 420, 241 P.2d 66, 75.) The rule applies alike to officers, directors, and controlling shareholders in the exercise of powers that are theirs by virtue of their position and to transactions wherein controlling shareholders seek to gain an advantage in the sale or transfer or use of their controlling block of shares. Thus we held in In re Security Finance, supra, 49 Cal.2d 370, 317 P.2d 1, that majority shareholders do not have an absolute right to dissolve a corporation, although ostensibly permitted to do so by Corporations Code, section 4600, because their statutory power is subject to equitable limitations in favor of the minority. We recognized that the majority had the right to dissolve the corporation to protect their investment *if* no alternative means were available *and* no advantage was secured over other shareholders, and noted that "there is nothing sacred in the life of a corporation that transcends the interests of its shareholders, but because dissolution falls with such finality on those interests, above all corporate powers it is subject to equitable limitations." (49 Cal.2d 370, 377, 317 P.2d 1, 5.)

The extension of fiduciary obligations to controlling shareholders in their exercise of corporate powers and dealings with their shares is not a recent development. * * *

The increasingly complex transactions of the business and financial communities demonstrate the inadequacy of the traditional theories of fiduciary obligation as tests of majority shareholder responsibility to the minority. These theories have failed to afford adequate protection to minority shareholders and particularly to those in closely held corporations whose disadvantageous and often precarious position renders them particularly vulnerable to the vagaries of the majority. Although courts have recognized the potential for abuse or unfair advantage when a controlling shareholder sells his shares at a premium over investment value (Perlman v. Feldmann, 219 F.2d 173, 50 A.L.R.2d 1134 [premium paid for control over allocation of production in time of shortage]; Gerdes v. Reynolds, Sup., 28 N.Y.S.2d 622 [sale of control to looters or incompetents]; Brown v. Halbert, supra, 271 A.C.A. 307, 76 Cal.Rptr. 781 [sale of only controlling shareholder's shares to purchaser offering to buy assets of corporation or all shares]) or in a controlling shareholder's use of control to avoid equitable distribution of corporate assets (Zahn v. Transamerica Corporation (3rd Cir.1946) 162 F.2d 36, 172 A.L.R. 495 [use of control to cause subsidiary to redeem stock prior to liquidation and distribution of assets]), no comprehensive rule has emerged in other jurisdictions. Nor have most commentators approached the problem from a perspective other than that of the advantage gained in the sale of control. Some have suggested that the price paid for control shares over their investment value be treated as an asset belonging to the corporation itself (Berle and Means, The Modern Corporation and Private Property (1932) p. 243), or as an asset that should be shared proportionately with all shareholders through a general offer (Jennings, Trading in Corporate Control (1956) 44 Cal.L. Rev. 1, 39), and another contends that the sale of control at a premium is always evil (Bayne, The Sale-of-Control Premium: the Intrinsic Illegitimacy (1969) 47 Tex.L.Rev. 215).

The additional potential for injury to minority shareholders from majority dealings in its control power apart from sale has not gone unrecognized, however. * * * The case before us, in which no sale or transfer of actual control is directly involved, demonstrates that

* * * injury * * * can be inflicted with impunity under the traditional rules and supports our conclusion that the comprehensive rule of good faith and inherent fairness to the minority in any transaction where control of the corporation is material properly governs controlling shareholders in this state.

We turn now to defendants' conduct to ascertain whether this test is met.

III

FORMATION OF UNITED FINANCIAL AND MARKETING ITS SHARES

Defendants created United Financial during a period of unusual investor interest in the stock of savings and loan associations. They then owned a majority of the outstanding stock of the Association. This stock was not readily marketable owing to a high book value, lack of investor information and facilities, and the closely held nature of the Association. The management of the Association had made no effort to create a market for the stock or to split the shares and reduce their market price to a more attractive level. Two courses were available to defendants in their effort to exploit the bull market in savings and loan stock. Both were made possible by defendants' status as controlling stockholders. The first was either to cause the Association to effect a stock split (Corp.Code, § 1507) and create a market for the Association stock or to create a holding company for Association shares and permit all stockholders to exchange their shares before offering holding company shares to the public. All stockholders would have benefited alike had this been done, but in realizing their gain on the sale of their stock the majority stockholders would of necessity have had to relinquish some of their control shares. Because a public market would have been created, however, the minority stockholders would have been able to extricate themselves without sacrificing their investment had they elected not to remain with the new management.

The second course was that taken by defendants. A new corporation was formed whose major asset was to be the control block of Association stock owned by defendants, but from which minority shareholders were to be excluded. The unmarketable Association stock held by the majority was transferred to the newly formed corporation at an exchange rate equivalent to a 250 for 1 stock split. The new corporation thereupon set out to create a market for its own shares. Association stock constituted 85 percent of the holding company's assets and produced an equivalent proportion of its income. The same individuals controlled both corporations. It appears therefrom that the market created by defendants for United Financial shares was a market that would have been available for Association stock had defendants taken the first course of action.[106]

106. [By the Court] The situation of minority stockholders and the difficulties they faced in attempting to market their savings and loan stock were described in The Savings and Loan Industry in California, a report prepared by the Stanford Research Institute for the California Savings and Loan Commissioner, and published by

After United Financial shares became available to the public it became a virtual certainty that no equivalent market could or would be created for Association stock. United Financial had become the controlling stockholder and neither it nor the other defendants would benefit from public trading in Association stock in competition with United Financial shares. Investors afforded an opportunity to acquire United Financial shares would not be likely to choose the less marketable and expensive Association stock in preference. Thus defendants chose a course of action in which they used their control of the Association to obtain an advantage not made available to all stockholders. They did so without regard to the resulting detriment to the minority stockholders and in the absence of any compelling business purpose. Such conduct is not consistent with their duty of good faith and inherent fairness to the minority stockholders. Had defendants afforded the minority an opportunity to exchange their stock on the same basis or offered to purchase them at a price arrived at by independent appraisal, their burden of establishing good faith and inherent fairness would have been much less. At the trial they may present evidence tending to show such good faith or compelling business purpose that would render their action fair under the circumstances. On appeal from the judgment of dismissal after the defendants' demurrer was sustained we decide only that the complaint states a cause of action entitling plaintiff to relief.

Defendants gained an additional advantage for themselves through their use of control of the Association when they pledged that control over the Association's assets and earnings to secure the holding compa-

the Commissioner in 1960. The attractiveness of the holding company as a device to enhance liquidity was recognized:

"The majority and minority stockholders in the original associations often found that they had difficulties in selling their shares at a price approximating their book value. Their main difficulties arose from the fact that book values and prices of shares often ran into many thousands of dollars, a price not generally suitable for wide public sale. These shares were usually owned by a relatively small number of stockholders. When one of them, or his heirs, wished to sell his shares, he had to negotiate with a buyer in this small group or attempt to find an outside purchaser. Minority stockholders had a special problem, because they could not sell control with their stock.

"The holding company was regarded by many stockholders as an attractive device to solve the problem of the marketability of their shares. Through this method, the control of one, two, or several associations could be consolidated and offered to the investing public in a single large stock issue at relatively low prices, either over the counter or through a stock exchange. The wide public ownership of holding company shares would thus provide a more active market and more protection against large capital losses in the event the original owners or their heirs wished to sell their holding company stock. * * *

"Large capital gains on the sale of holding company stock to the public have been an important incentive and consequence of this form of organization. The issuance of holding company stock to the general public usually found an enthusiastic demand which made it possible to sell the stock for as much as two to three times book value. In many but not all cases, the majority stockholders in the original associations have offered less than 50 percent of the holding company's stock to the public, thus retaining control of the association and the holding companies." (The Savings and Loan Industry in California (1960) pp. VI–6– VI–7.) * * *

ny's debt, a debt that had been incurred for their own benefit.[107] In so doing the defendants breached their fiduciary obligation to the minority once again and caused United Financial and its controlling shareholders to become inextricably wedded to a conflict of interest between the minority stockholders of each corporation. Alternatives were available to them that would have benefited all stockholders proportionately. The course they chose affected the minority stockholders with no less finality than does dissolution and demands no less concern for minority interests.

In so holding we do not suggest that the duties of corporate fiduciaries include in all cases an obligation to make a market for and to facilitate public trading in the stock of the corporation. But when, as here, no market exists, the controlling shareholders may not use their power to control the corporation for the purpose of promoting a marketing scheme that benefits themselves alone to the detriment of the minority. Nor do we suggest that a control block of shares may not be sold or transferred to a holding company. We decide only that the circumstances of any transfer of controlling shares will be subject to judicial scrutiny when it appears that the controlling shareholders may have breached their fiduciary obligation to the corporation or the remaining shareholders.

IV

DAMAGES

Plaintiff contends that she should have been afforded the opportunity to exchange her stock for United Financial shares at the time of and on the same basis as the majority exchange. She therefore proposes that upon tender of her Association stock to the defendants she be awarded the fair market value of a derived block of United Financial shares during 1960–1962 plus interest from the date of her action as well as a return of capital of $927.50 plus interest from the date the same was made to the former majority shareholders. In addition she seeks exemplary damages and other relief.

Defendants, on the other hand, claim that plaintiff seeks a "free ride" after they have taken all of the risks in creating United Financial and marketing its stock. They maintain that plaintiff has not been damaged by their conduct and that they have breached no duty owed to plaintiff and the other minority stockholders. We are thus without guidance from defendants as to the remedy that a court of equity might appropriately fashion in these circumstances.

---

107. [By the Court] Should it become necessary to encumber or liquidate Association assets to service this debt or to depart from a dividend policy consistent with the business needs of the Association, damage to the Association itself may occur. We need not resolve here, but note with some concern, the problem facing United Financial, which owes the same fiduciary duty to its own shareholders as to those of the Association. Any decision regarding use of Association assets and earnings to service the holding company debt must be made in the context of these potentially conflicting interests.

From the perspective of the minority stockholders of the Association, the transfer of control under these circumstances to another corporation and the resulting impact on their position as minority stockholders accomplished a fundamental corporate change as to them. Control of a closely held savings and loan association, the major portion of whose earnings had been retained over a long period while its stockholders remained stable, became an asset of a publicly held holding company. The position of the minority shareholder was drastically changed thereby. His practical ability to influence corporate decision-making was diminished substantially when control was transferred to a publicly held corporation that was in turn controlled by the owners of more than 750,000 shares. The future business goals of the Association could reasonably be expected to reflect the needs and interest of the holding company rather than the aims of the Association stockholders thereafter. In short, the enterprise into which the minority stockholders were now locked was not that in which they had invested.

The more familiar fundamental corporate changes, merger, consolidation, and dissolution, are accompanied by statutory and judicial safeguards established to protect minority shareholders. Shareholders dissenting from a merger of their corporation into another may demand that the corporation purchase their shares at the fair market value. If the shareholders and the corporation fail to agree on that value, the shareholders may call upon the court, which may in turn appoint independent appraisers to assist in evaluating the shares. This procedure makes possible determination of value unaffected by any market distortion caused by the merger (Gallois v. West End Chemical Co., 185 Cal.App.2d 765, 8 Cal.Rptr. 596) and enables stockholders in a closely held corporation whose shares are not publicly marketed to obtain an independent judgment as to the value of their shares. Protection of shareholder interests is achieved in voluntary corporate dissolution by judicial supervision to assure equitable settlement of the corporation's affairs. * * *

Although a controlling shareholder who sells or exchanges his shares is not under an obligation to obtain for the minority the consideration that he receives in all cases, when he does sell or exchange his shares the transaction is subject to close scrutiny. When the majority receives a premium over market value for its shares, the consideration for which that premium is paid will be examined. If it reflects payment for that which is properly a corporate asset all shareholders may demand to share proportionately. (Perlman v. Feldmann, supra, 219 F.2d 173.) Here the exchange was an integral part of a scheme that the defendants could reasonably foresee would have as an incidental effect the destruction of the potential public market for Association stock. The remaining stockholders would thus be deprived of the opportunity to realize a profit from those intangible characteristics that attach to publicly marketed stock and enhance its value above book value. Receipt of an appraised value reflecting book value and earnings alone could not compensate the minority shareholders for the loss of this potential. Since the damage is real, although the amount is speculative, equity demands that the minority stockholders be placed in a position at least as favorable as that the majority created for themselves.

If, after trial of the cause, plaintiff has established facts in conformity with the allegations of the complaint and stipulation, then upon tender of her Association stock to defendants she will be entitled to receive at her election either the appraised value of her shares on the date of the exchange, May 14, 1959, with interest at 7 percent a year from the date of this action or a sum equivalent to the fair market value of a "derived block" of United Financial stock on the date of this action with interest thereon from that date, and the sum of $927.50 (the return of capital paid to the original United Financial shareholders) with interest thereon from the date United Financial first made such payments to its original shareholders, for each share tendered. The appraised or fair market value shall be reduced, however, by the amount by which dividends paid on Association shares during the period from May 14, 1959 to the present exceeds the dividends paid on a corresponding block of United Financial shares during the same period.

* * *

PETERS, TOBRINER, BURKE, and SULLIVAN, JJ., and COUGHLIN, J. pro tem., concur.

McCOMB, JUSTICE (dissenting).

I dissent. I would affirm the judgment in favor of defendants for the reasons expressed by Mr. Justice Shinn and Mr. Justice Moss in the opinions prepared by them for the Court of Appeal in Jones v. H.F. Ahmanson & Company (Cal.App.) 76 Cal.Rptr. 293.

Notes

(1) Judge Traynor, of course, sometimes painted with a broad brush. Is the problem dealt with in this case the same as the control premium problem? Or is it more like Zahn v. Transamerica Corp., p. 827 supra?

(2) The measure of damages authorized in this case is essentially the "recissory damage" recovery discussed in Weinberger v. UOP, Inc., p. 792, supra.

PETITION OF CAPLAN

Supreme Court of New York, Appellate Division, First Department, 1964.
20 A.D.2d 301, 246 N.Y.S.2d 913.

STEUER, JUSTICE.

On March 8, 1963, Defiance Industries, Inc. entered into a transaction with Roy Cohn which, though unusual in form, amounted to a deferred sale of 55,000 shares of Lionel Corporation then owned by Cohn. * * * The 55,000 shares constituted 3% of the outstanding stock of Lionel Corporation.

The board of directors of Lionel consisted of ten directors, of whom Cohn was one. Six of the other directors were his nominees. Just how his holdings, amounting to 3%, enabled him to have this representation does not appear. Immediately after making the contract, these six directors resigned and their places were filled by nominees of Defiance.

On October 9, 1963, Defiance sold its interest in the above-described contract to A.M. Sonnabend, the transaction to close October 23, 1963. It was a condition of that agreement that prior to closing the six Defiance directors should be replaced by nominees of Sonnabend. On October 16 this was done. On November 14, 1963, Cohn resigned as a director and was replaced by a Sonnabend nominee. All of these changes in the board were effected by the directors filling the vacancy as each was created by resignation.

This proceeding is brought by a stockholder of Lionel to set aside and vacate the elections of the seven directors so elected. Special Term found the elections to be illegal and vacated them. With this finding and disposition we are in accord. The underlying principle is that the management of a corporation is not the subject of trade and cannot be bought apart from actual stock control (McClure v. Law, 161 N.Y. 78, 55 N.E. 388). Where there has been a transfer of the majority of the stock, or even such a percentage as gives working control, a change of directors by resignation and filling of vacancies is proper (Barnes v. Brown, 80 N.Y. 527). Here no claim was made that the stock interest which changed hands even approximated the percentage necessary to validate the substitution. * * *

All concur.

Notes

(1) Carter v. Muscat, 21 A.D.2d 543, 251 N.Y.S.2d 378 (1964) involved seriatim resignations of directors in connection with transfer of 9.7 per cent of the outstanding shares. Full disclosure of the change in control was made to the shareholders and some of the new directors were thereafter reelected at annual shareholders meetings. After quoting from *Petition of Caplan*, the Court said: "When a situation involving less than 50% of the ownership of stock exists, the question of what percentage of ownership of stock is sufficient to constitute working control is likely to be a matter of fact, at least in most circumstances." * * * 251 N.Y.S.2d at 381. The change in control was upheld, the Court relying on the disclosure, the absence of objection, and the subsequent election of directors as "endorsements" of the substituted directors.

(2) In the modern publicly held corporation, incumbent management usually owns an insignificant fraction of the outstanding shares. Because of their control of the "proxy machinery," the managers usually have the power to determine who will be nominated, and therefore elected, to the board of directors. Hence the basic explanation of how Roy Cohn could control so much while owning so little is really not very difficult. Independence of directors, however, has doubtless increased since the early 1960s.

What would happen today if a modern board of directors predominantly composed of outside directors (many of whom are CEOs or former CEOs of other corporations) were presented by management with the request that they resign seriatim and vote to replace sitting directors with a new slate of individuals who are strangers to the board members?

(3) The validity of contract provisions requiring seriatim resignations of directors in connection with sales of small percentages of voting shares also may arise in the context of breach of contract suits between the buyer and seller, rather than suits brought by shareholders not party to the contract. In the leading case of Essex Universal Corp. v. Yates, 305 F.2d 572 (2d Cir.1962), suit was brought on a contract to sell about 28% of the stock of the corporation. The sellers were committed to deliver the resignations of a majority of the board of directors and to cause the election of successors nominated by the purchaser at the closing of the transaction. The defendants argued that the contract was against public policy because of the provisions relating to the transfer of directorships. The case was complicated by reason of the *Erie* doctrine: The panel of the Second Circuit was forced to divine New York law in the absence of any really controlling precedent. Chief Judge Lumbard argued as follows: (1) if the block being transferred were a majority of the shares, the clause would not be against public policy since a majority of the shares inherently carries with it the power to name at least a majority of the board of directors; (2) it is unlawful to transfer control as such (accompanied by no stock or insufficient stock to carry voting control); (3) a 28% interest "is *usually* tantamount to majority control" in a publicly held corporation; and (4) the case should therefore be remanded to determine whether, assuming neutrality on the part of the selling shareholders, a holder of 28% of the outstanding shares might fail to obtain the election of its candidates at a regular election. Judge Clark concurred in the result, suggesting that the inquiry proposed by Judge Lumbard required "hypothetical findings" and should not be determinative of the outcome. Judge Clark also stated that the agreement did not involve a "naked transfer of corporate office," and there was "no ground for declaring the present agreement void on its face." Judge Friendly, starting from a somewhat different perspective than Judge Clark, suggested tentatively that "if I were sitting on the New York Court of Appeals, I would hold a provision like Paragraph 6 violative of public policy save when it was entirely plain that a new election would be a mere formality, such as where the seller owned more than 50% of the stock." See also Goode v. Powers, 97 Ariz. 75, 397 P.2d 56 (1964), where the purchasers of a 25% interest in the voting shares of an insurance company were sued for the balance of the agreed purchase price. The defendants argued that the stock was only inherently worth $200 per share, but was sold for $500 per share because of the transfer of control provisions. Not surprisingly, this argument was rejected by the court, though some evidence as to valuation was considered by the trial court. The issue in these cases of the validity of the contract for the sale of shares that contains provisions relating to transfer of control is quite different from the issue presented by a nonselling shareholder complaining of the transfer of control. There seems to be no reason to permit a party to a contract to

avoid its commitment on the theory that the agreement may injure other parties unless those parties complain of the injury.

(4) When the Federal cash tender offer legislation was adopted in 1969, a section was added to the Securities Exchange Act of 1934 dealing with the transfer of control by seriatim resignations of directors. Section 14(f), 82 Stat. 454 (1970), 15 U.S.C.A. § 78n(f) (1989), applies if there is an "arrangement or understanding" with persons acquiring more than five per cent of the stock of an issuer by tender offer or purchase, by which "any persons are to be elected or designated as directors of the issuer, otherwise than at a meeting of security holders, and the persons so elected or designated will constitute a majority of the directors." However, the section only requires the issuer to disseminate certain information to all holders of record entitled to vote at a meeting (and to the SEC). The information must identify the persons to whom control was transferred, describe the transaction by which control was transferred, the source of any consideration paid, the identity of the new directors, transactions with the issuer, the remuneration to be paid to directors and management, and the amount of securities held by principal shareholders. Rule 14f–1, 17 C.F.R. § 240.14f–1 (1989).

Do you believe that such disclosure provides ample protection? What other kind of approach might be adopted by courts or by the Congress? What about *Petition of Caplan,* where control was based on 3 percent of the outstanding shares?

Chapter Fourteen

INDEMNIFICATION AND INSURANCE

MERRITT–CHAPMAN & SCOTT CORP. v. WOLFSON

Superior Court of Delaware, 1974.
321 A.2d 138.

BALICK, JUDGE.

These actions arise over claims of Louis Wolfson, Elkin Gerbert, Joseph Kosow and Marshal Staub (claimants) for indemnification by Merritt–Chapman & Scott Corporation (MCS) against expenses incurred in a criminal action. All parties seek summary judgment.

Claimants were charged by indictment with participation in a plan to cause MCS to secretly purchase hundreds of thousands of shares of its own common stock. Count one charged all claimants with conspiracy to violate federal securities laws. Count two charged Wolfson and count three charged Gerbert with perjury before the Securities and Exchange Commission (SEC). Counts four and five charged Wolfson, Gerbert, and Staub with filing false annual reports for 1962 and 1963 respectively with the SEC and New York Stock Exchange.

At the first trial the court dismissed part of the conspiracy count but the jury returned guilty verdicts on all charges against all claimants. At that stage this court held that Wolfson, Gerbert, and Kosow were not entitled to partial indemnification. Merritt–Chapman & Scott v. Wolfson, 264 A.2d 358 (Del.Super.1970). Thereafter the convictions were reversed. United States v. Wolfson, 437 F.2d 862 (2nd Cir.1970).

There were two retrials of the perjury and filing false annual report charges against Wolfson and Gerbert. At the first retrial the court entered a judgment of acquittal on count four at the end of the State's case, and the jury could not agree on the other counts. At the second retrial the jury returned a guilty verdict on count three, but could not agree further.

The charges were then settled as follows: Wolfson entered a plea of *nolo contendere* to count five and the other charges against him were dropped.   He was fined $10,000 and given a suspended sentence of eighteen months.   Gerbert agreed not to appeal his conviction of count three, on which he was fined $2,000 and given a suspended sentence of eighteen months, and the other charges against him were dropped. The prosecution also dropped the charges against Kosow and Staub.

Indemnification of corporate agents involved in litigation is the subject of legislation in Delaware.   Title 8 Delaware Code § 145. Subsection (a), which permits indemnification, and subsection (c), which requires indemnification, provide as follows:

> (a) A corporation may indemnify any person who was or is a party or is threatened to be made a party to any threatened, pending or completed action, suit or proceeding, whether civil, criminal, administrative or investigative (other than an action by or in the right of the corporation) by reason of the fact that he is or was a director, officer, employee or agent of the corporation, or is or was serving at the request of the corporation as a director, officer, employee or agent of another corporation, partnership, joint venture, trust or other enterprise, against expenses (including attorneys' fees), judgments, fines and amounts paid in settlement actually and reasonably incurred by him in connection with such action, suit or proceeding if he acted in good faith and in a manner he reasonably believed to be in or not opposed to the best interests of the corporation, and, with respect to any criminal action or proceeding, had no reasonable cause to believe his conduct was unlawful.   The termination of any action, suit or proceeding by judgment, order, settlement, conviction, or upon a plea of *nolo contendere* or its equivalent, shall not, of itself, create a presumption that the person did not act in good faith and in a manner which he reasonably believed to be in or not opposed to the best interests of the corporation, and, with respect to any criminal action or proceeding, had reasonable cause to believe that his conduct was unlawful.
>
> *   *   *
>
> (c) To the extent that a director, officer, employee or agent of a corporation has been successful on the merits or otherwise in defense of any action, suit or proceeding referred to in [subsection (a)], or in defense of any claim, issue or matter therein, he shall be indemnified against expenses (including attorneys' fees) actually and reasonably incurred by him in connection therewith.

The policy of the statute and its predecessor has been described as follows, Folk, The Delaware General Corporation Law, 98 (1972):

> The invariant policy of Delaware legislation on indemnification is to "promote the desirable end that corporate officials will resist what they consider" unjustified suits and claims, "secure in the knowledge that their reasonable expenses will be borne by the corporation they have served if they are vindicated."   Beyond that, its larger purpose is "to encourage capable men to serve as corporate directors, secure in the knowledge that expenses incurred by them in upholding their

honesty and integrity as directors will be borne by the corporation they serve."

MCS argues that the statute and sound public policy require indemnification only where there has been vindication by a finding or concession of innocence. It contends that the charges against claimants were dropped for practical reasons, not because of their innocence, and that in light of the conspiracy charged in the indictment, the judgment of acquittal on count four alone is not vindication.

The statute requires indemnification to the extent that the claimant "has been successful on the merits or otherwise." Success is vindication. In a criminal action, any result other than conviction must be considered success. Going behind the result, as MCS attempts, is neither authorized by subsection (c) nor consistent with the presumption of innocence.

The statute does not require complete success. It provides for indemnification to the extent of success "in defense of any claim, issue or matter" in an action. Claimants are therefore entitled to partial indemnification if successful on a count of an indictment, which is an independent criminal charge, even if unsuccessful on another, related count. * * *

Notes

(1) In its opinion in the earlier proceeding, 264 A.2d 358, 360 (Del. Super.1970), the Court described the purpose of § 145 as follows:

"Indemnification statutes were enacted in Delaware, and elsewhere, to induce capable and responsible businessmen to accept positions in corporate management. [§ 145] is a new statute, enacted to clarify its predecessor, and to give vindicated directors and others involved in corporate affairs a judicially enforcible right to indemnification.

"It would be anomalous, indeed, and diametrically opposed to the spirit and purpose of the statute and sound public policy to extend the benefits of indemnification to these defendants under the circumstances of this case." * * *

If the corporation had wished, could it have indemnified Wolfson and Gerbert for the expenses incurred in connection with the claims on which they pleaded nolo contendere? See RMBCA § 8.51(c).

(2) As a practical matter, the grant of broad indemnification rights to directors is important—nay, virtually essential—if a publicly held corporation is to persuade desirable individuals to serve as directors. Such individuals are usually experienced, relatively affluent, and able to command significant salaries in their chosen professions. They are also apt to be relatively risk adverse and quite aware of the growth in litigation against directors, particularly in situations involving defensive tactics in takeovers, and in other types of derivative litigation involving judicial review of difficult business decisions generally. While fees paid to directors may seem relatively generous, they do not begin to cover the out-of-pocket

costs, particularly attorneys fees, incurred by a director who is named as a defendant in any major litigation. The decision by the Delaware Supreme Court in *Van Gorkom* (p. 704 supra) doubtless contributed to the concern of directors about personal liability generally and the need for iron clad indemnification rights against the corporation in particular. The elimination of most due care liability by statutory provisions such as Del.Gen.Corp. Law, § 102(b)(7) obviously helps to reduce the over-all risk but does not really eliminate the need for indemnification from the standpoint of a person considering an invitation to become a director of a publicly held corporation. Why not?

(3) The need for indemnification to attract directors seems clearest in the case of litigation that ultimately vindicates the actions of the director on the merits. However, reflection should also indicate that a test limited to complete vindication on the merits is too narrow. For example, should directors be entitled to indemnification for costs if a settlement is available that involves a relatively nominal payment to the plaintiffs and their attorneys? Should not the corporation and the defendant directors be able to settle nuisance suits by nominal payments to or on behalf of the plaintiffs without shifting litigation costs from the corporation back to the defendant directors? Can one distinguish such settlements from genuine settlements which directors settle because the probability that they will lose is high? Should there be indemnification in such cases? Questions such as these raise the fundamental issue of what should be the outside limits of the power of indemnification.

(4) Subchapter E of Chapter 8 of the Revised Model Business Corporation Act (sections 8.50 through 8.58) attempts to define the scope of permissible indemnification. This subchapter is a complex series of sections that cannot be adequately digested in a single reading, or even in two readings. These sections are based on the principles appearing in section 5 of the 1969 Model Act, as amended in 1980; the division of a single section into nine separate sections was designed to improve the readability and comprehensibility of a section that was similar in appearance to section 146 of the Delaware statute, quoted in part in *Wolfson*. The goal of the RMBCA provisions relating to indemnification are laudatory:

> Indemnification provides financial protection by the corporation for its directors, officers, and employees against expenses and liabilities incurred by them in connection with proceedings based on an alleged breach of some duty in their service to or on behalf of the corporation. Today, when both the amount and the cost of litigation have skyrocketed, it would be difficult or impossible to persuade responsible persons to serve as directors if they were compelled to bear personally the cost of vindicating the propriety of their conduct in every instance in which it might be challenged. While reasonable people may differ as to what constitutes a meritorious case, almost all would agree that corporate directors should have some protection against personal risk and that the rule of New York Dock Co. v. McCollom, 173 Misc. 106, 16 N.Y.S.2d 844 (Sup.Ct.1939), which denied reimbursement to the directors who successfully defended their case on the merits, should as a matter of policy be overruled by statute.

Indemnification, if permitted too broadly, may violate equally basic tenets of public policy. It is inappropriate to permit management to use corporate funds to avoid the consequences of wrongful conduct or conduct involving bad faith. A director, officer, or employee who acted wrongfully or in bad faith should not expect to receive assistance from the corporation for legal or other expenses and should be required to satisfy not only any judgment entered against him but also expenses incurred in connection with the proceeding from his personal assets. Any other rule would tend to encourage socially undesirable conduct.

A further policy issue is raised in connection with indemnification against liabilities or sanctions imposed under express provisions of state or federal civil or criminal statutes. A shift of these liabilities from the individual director or officer to the corporation by way of indemnification may in some instances be viewed as frustrating the public policy of those statutes which expressly impose the sanctions on the director or officer.

The fundamental issue that must be addressed by an indemnification statute is the establishment of policies consistent with these broad principles: to ensure that indemnification is permitted only where it will further accepted corporate goals and to prohibit indemnification where it might protect or encourage wrongful or improper conduct. As phrased by one commentator, the goal of indemnification is to "seek the middle ground between encouraging fiduciaries to violate their trust, and discouraging them from serving at all." Johnston, "Corporate Indemnification and Liability Insurance for Directors and Officers," 33 Bus.Law 1993, 1994 (1978). The increasing number of suits against directors, the increasing cost of defense, and the increasing emphasis on broadening membership of boards of directors of public companies all militate in favor of establishing workable arrangements to protect directors and officers against liability for action taken in good faith to the extent consistent with broad public policy.

Introductory Comment to Subchapter E.

(5) When read carefully, Subchapter E contains some surprises and some value judgments that may seem questionable about the circumstances in which indemnification may be permitted, the persons who can decide whether to grant indemnification, and the time when indemnification payments may be made.

(a) Compare RMBCA §§ 8.51, 8.52, and 8.53. What are the relationships among these three sections?

(b) RMBCA § 8.52 requires that a corporation indemnify a director "who was wholly successful, on the merits or otherwise." The word "wholly" was added to reverse the result in the principal case. Does it? More basically, consider the phrase "on the merits *or otherwise.*" Does this really mean what it says? For example, assume that a director is charged with egregious criminal conduct that seriously harms the corporation. She concedes that she engaged in the conduct but defends successfully on the ground that the statute of limitations has run. Should she be entitled to indemnification as a matter of right? She clearly is under RMBCA § 8.52, the theory being that a person with a valid procedural defense should not be required to proceed to a trial on the merits, which may be prolonged and expensive, in order to establish eligibility for indemnification. See also n. 20, p. 178 supra.

(c) Consider a director who has probably violated section 16(b). A demand is made, and the director consults an attorney who advises the director to repay the profits to the corporation, and sends a bill for legal services rendered. The director repays the profits and then requests the corporation to pay the attorney. May the corporation do so without court approval under RMBCA § 8.51 on the theory the director acted in "good faith" and in a manner he reasonably believed to be "*not opposed to* [the] best interests [of the corporation]?" RMBCA § 8.51(d)(2) was obviously designed to prevent indemnification in section 16(b), rule 10b–5, and other cases where the defendant is found liable after a trial but the corporation is arguably not injured. It seems clear on the literal language of the statute, however, that the director who makes voluntary repayment is not precluded from indemnification in this situation since he or she has not been "adjudged" liable for anything.

(d) Who is to make decisions about optional indemnification? See RMBCA § 8.55. Is there any requirement that a court or the shareholders be advised that the corporation has decided to indemnify someone? See RMBCA § 16.21(a).

(e) Under what circumstances can a director be indemnified for a criminal fine (as contrasted with expenses incurred in connection with a criminal proceeding)? See RMBCA §§ 8.51(a)(3), 8.51(d), 8.54.

(f) If a director defends a proceeding to the bitter end and a judgment is entered against him, he is entitled to indemnification for either expenses only, or the judgment plus expenses, only with court approval. See RMBCA §§ 8.51(d), 8.54. What if he fears he may lose and offers to settle? Who determines whether he is entitled to indemnification in connection with the settlement? Do you think these persons may be more favorably disposed toward the director or officer than a judge?

(g) Consider the position of a director who has been named as a defendant and is incurring expenses to prepare her defense. Does she have to advance funds out of her own pocket until she is ultimately vindicated or is determined to be eligible for optional indemnification, or can the corporation pay for her defense from the outset? See RMBCA § 8.53. If the corporation makes advances to cover her expenses the director must file an undertaking to repay the advances if it is ultimately determined that she is not entitled to indemnification. However, why should such an undertaking to repay be unsecured and why "may [it] be accepted without reference to financial ability to make repayment?" RMBCA § 8.53(b). The theory of this clause is that it is not fair to favor wealthy directors who may be in less need of financial assistance in mounting their defense over directors whose financial resources are modest or meagre.

(h) Assume that a director is called as a witness before a grand jury in connection with corporate matters. He hires counsel; appears as a witness but is never notified that he is a target of the investigation or indicted. Must his expenses be paid by the corporation? Cf. RMBCA § 8.58(b).

(i) In most boards of directors, there are some directors who are employees of the corporation and some who are not. Is there any difference in the power or duty of a corporation to indemnify outside directors as contrasted with director/employees? See RMBCA § 8.56(1) and (2). The Official Comment states that it was the intent of this section that "all directors should be treated alike; complications may be created if directors who are not officers have potentially less protection under the statute than directors who are officers. It would also be difficult in many instances to distinguish in what capacity an officer-director is acting."

(j) Assume that a director is also an executive of a trade association or the trustee of an employee pension trust. Presumably these positions were assumed either at the request of the corporation or with its implicit approval were assumed. May that director seek indemnification *from the corporation* for expenses or liabilities incurred while serving the trade association or pension trust? See RMBCA §§ 8.50(2), 8.50(5), 8.51(b).

(k) What is the difference between a "determination" of indemnification under RMBCA § 8.55(b) and an "authorization" of indemnification under RMBCA § 8.55(c)?

(6) The indemnification provisions of the MBCA and RMBCA have gone through several substantial revisions over the years. Collectively, these provisions have been extremely influential, having been followed in some 42 states.

(7) For evaluations of the statutory approach toward indemnification, see Bishop, Sitting Ducks and Decoy Ducks: New Trends in the Indemnification of Corporate Directors and Officers, 77 Yale L.J. 1078 (1968); Symposium, Officers' and Directors' Responsibilities and Liabilities, 27 Bus. Law. 1, 109–164 (Spec. Issue, 1972); Knepper, Officers and Directors: Indemnification and Liability Insurance—An Update, 30 Bus.Law. 951 (1975).

(8) Hanks, Evaluating Recent State Legislation on Director and Officer Liability Limitation and Indemnification, 43 Bus.Law. 1207, 1221, 1240 (1988):

> At least ten states * * * have enacted statutes expanding the right of corporations to indemnify their directors for expenses, settlements, and adverse judgments in derivative suits. * * * The most far-reaching statutory developments affecting derivative suits are provisions eliminating or substantially eliminating the distinction between third-party and derivative suits and permitting indemnification against judgments, settlements, and expenses for any director or officer who meets the general statutory standards for indemnification without a requirement of court approval.[1] * * *

---

1. [By the Author] These standards typically require good faith conduct, reasonable belief that the individual's conduct was in or not opposed to the corporation's best interests, and in a criminal proceeding, no reason to believe the individual's conduct was unlawful. E.g., Revised Model Business Corp. Act § 8.51(a) (1984); Md. Corps. & Ass'ns Code Ann. § 2–418(b)(1) (1985 & Supp.1987). These statutory standards for indemnification differ from the typical statutory standards of conduct for directors by omitting the requirement for the care of an ordinarily prudent person in similar circumstances and by modifying the reasonable belief requirement in the indemnification standards to require only a reasonable belief that the director's con-

In the absence of any applicable liability limitation, the disadvantage of permitting indemnification against settlements and adverse judgments and derivative suits is its circularity. Any money recovered from the director or officer is paid, less the stockholders' attorneys' fees, by the individual to the corporation, which then returns the money, together with reimbursement for the individual's legal expenses, to the individual as indemnification. Although the individual is made whole, the corporation winds up paying not only the amount of the loss but also the stockholders' and individual's attorneys' fees and costs. Thus, the corporation is actually in a worse economic position than if it had simply sustained the loss without the cost of recovery and consequent reimbursement. The real beneficiaries of circular indemnification are the stockholders' lawyers. Since the corporation's loss really belongs to the stockholders, no rational stockholder would initiate a derivative suit unless the corporation were able to pass the risk along to an insurance company. Of course, it was the unavailability of affordable insurance that gave rise to the search for legislative solutions in the first place.

Moreover, while statutes may permit a corporation to indemnify a director or officer held liable for negligence in a derivative suit, they do not * * * require indemnification. Thus, unless the charter or by-laws require indemnification in such circumstances, the individual is left in a state of uncertainty as to whether indemnification will actually be authorized in his particular case. This type of uncertainty has caused many directors to leave corporate boards. While expanded indemnifiability helps directors and officers by giving them at least one source of reimbursement (assuming the corporation can afford to pay at the time of the loss), it will not provide any relief for the insurance carriers.

Mr. Hanks was discussing developments in indemnification that occurred essentially between 1984, the enactment of the RMBCA, and 1988. These four years were tumultuous years for directors with widely publicized cases imposing liability on directors, the "drying up" of liability insurance, and the enactment of state statutes limiting the monetary liability of directors.

(9) Mr. Hanks also summarizes briefly two other recent developments in the area of indemnification:

(a) At least twenty-nine states have recently expanded the provisions of their indemnification statutes permitting corporations to provide rights [broader] than [statutory] indemnification by charter, by-law, board resolution, contract, or otherwise. * * * The broad form of nonexclusivity provision has been typified by section 145(f) of the Delaware General Corporation Law, which provides that statutory indemnification "shall not be deemed exclusive of any other rights to which those seeking indemnification or advancement of expenses may be entitled under any by-law, agreement . . . or otherwise." Even the Delaware statute, however, could be read to limit any indemnifica-

---

duct "was at least not opposed to [the corporation's] best interests" in the case of conduct not in the director's official capaci-

ty. E.g., Revised Model Business Corp. Act § 8.30(a) (1984).

tion right to section 145, although "other rights" would not be deemed to be excluded by section 145.

The narrow form of nonexclusivity provision was formerly typified by Maryland, which until earlier this year * * * was based upon section 8.58(a) of the Revised Model Business Corporation Act. The official comment to section 8.58(a) notes that the nonexclusive statutory provisions, such as Delaware's, make "no attempt to limit the non-statutory creation of rights of indemnification. This kind of language is subject to misconstruction . . . since non-statutory conceptions of public policy limit the power of the corporation to indemnify or to contract to indemnify directors." Significantly, however, the official comment also notes that

> the phrase "to the extent that it is consistent with" is not synonymous with "exclusive." Situations may well develop from time to time in which indemnification is permissible under Section 8.58 but would be precluded if all portions of [the indemnification section] were viewed as exclusive.

The Maryland statute has been changed to state specifically that indemnification "shall not be deemed exclusive of any other rights, by indemnification or otherwise, to which a director [or officer] may be entitled." * * *

In states like Delaware and Maryland, which have no express limits in their nonexclusivity provisions, there is always the possibility—probably the likelihood—that a court will add its own public policy limits. Thus, the outer parameters of these provisions will always be unclear. * * *

Finally, in the past two years, Delaware, Maryland, New York, Pennsylvania, and several other states have amended their statutes to add advancement of expenses to indemnification in their nonexclusivity provisions. * * *

43 Bus.Law. at 1224–1226.

(b) The typical indemnification statute permits the corporation to purchase insurance for directors and officers "whether or not the corporation would have the power to indemnify [the individual] against such liability" under the other provisions of the indemnification statute. However, as conventional insurance has become more expensive or even not available at any price, alternative sources of reimbursement have emerged. Examples include captive insurance subsidiaries, association captives formed by industry groups, trust funds, letters of credit, guaranties, and sureties. Virtually all of these devices amount to self-insurance, since the corporation remains the ultimate source of payment. * * *

Louisiana has authorized corporations to "create a trust fund or other form of self-insurance arrangement for the benefit of persons indemnified by the corporation" and has authorized the formation of a captive insurance subsidiary. Louisiana has also provided that in the absence of actual fraud, insurance or self-insurance arrangements shall not be subject to voidability and the board of directors shall not be subject to liability on any ground in approving such an arrangement, "regardless of whether directors participating in approving such insurance arrangement shall be beneficiaries thereof." Texas incorporates substantively identical alternative reimbursement provisions in its indemnification statute. * * *

Legislation authorizing reimbursement from sources other than conventional third-party insurance generally results in the stockholders retaining the economic risk of the director's misconduct (except as limited) since the funds for reimbursement are derived, either initially or ultimately, from the corporation.

43 Bus.Law. at 1230–1231. The justification for these alternative sources of reimbursement may be traced in Louisiana and Texas (though similar provisions were enacted in a number of other states as well) to the impact of the decline of oil prices on publicly held but marginally financed energy companies. By the middle 1980s, insolvency and bankruptcy reorganization of many of these companies was a strong possibility. What is the status of indemnification rights in bankruptcy? In the absence of alternative reimbursement sources, the answer just about has to be that the director entitled to indemnification is merely one more unsecured creditor. To a potential director in a marginal or shaky corporation, an unsecured right to indemnification is just about worthless since there can be no assurance that either advance or ultimate indemnification is going to be in fact available. D & O insurance avoids the problem if the corporation can afford the premiums, and if that insurance is in fact available to a marginally financed company mired in the oil patch. In part because of the risk of insolvency and subsequent litigation against directors, insurance became unavailable or extraordinarily expensive just when it was needed the most. This justification for authorizing alternative sources of reimbursement was persuasive in about ten states.

(10) Consider RMBCA § 8.57. Most states have adopted a provision relating to liability insurance for directors and officers, usually referred to as "D & O insurance." Even in states without express authorization, the provision of such insurance may be implicit in other corporate powers relating to the compensation of officers and directors. Is such insurance erosive of the public policy underlying the securities acts and other rules providing for liability? Of course, § 8.57 is only enabling, and the following excerpt reveals there are significant exceptions, exclusions, and public policy limitations applicable to such insurance.

JOHNSTON, CORPORATE INDEMNIFICATION AND LIABILITY INSURANCE FOR DIRECTORS AND OFFICERS *

33 Bus.Law. 1993, 2012–2014, 2017–2021, 2024–2027, 2029–2031, 2033 (1978).

The D & O policies currently available provide a substantial measure of protection against certain of the gaps in corporate indemnification (e.g., judgments or settlements in a derivative action alleging negligence, and liabilities for negligent violations of the federal securities laws), but, as will be indicated below, they do not provide protection for liabilities involving self-dealing, bad faith, knowing violations of the securities laws, or other willful misconduct. * * *

D & O insurance is a relatively new form of liability insurance. Although the policies have been marketed since the 1950s, the coverage had little attention until the mid–1960s. * * *

When D & O insurance first appeared, it was somewhat controversial and its validity was sometimes questioned, particularly where the corporation paid all of the premium. There were even some commentators who could argue, on the one hand, that the policy was so badly drafted and contained so many exclusions that it was doubtful whether a lawyer could recommend that his clients purchase it, and, on the other hand, simultaneously assert that the contract was contrary to public policy because it provided more coverage than the state indemnification statutes permitted.[2] The public policy arguments against the purchase by the corporation of D & O insurance are now largely moot in view of the statutes in most jurisdictions specifically permitting the purchase of such insurance at the expense of the corporation. In any event, the argument that D & O insurance was contrary to the indemnification statutes had little merit since the indemnification payment was to be made by the insurance company and not by the corporation. Although the corporation may have paid the premiums, this was nothing more than another form of compensation for the executives and a way of attracting capable managers.

* * * [M]ost D & O policies are issued in the form of two separate policies, or one policy with two parts. The first policy, commonly called the "Corporate Reimbursement" form, insures the corporation against "loss" (as defined) arising from claims against directors and officers for "wrongful acts" (as defined), but only when the corporation is required or permitted to indemnify the directors or officers under applicable statutory or by-law provisions. The second policy, called the "Directors and Officers" form, covers the directors and officers against loss arising from claims against them for wrongful acts in cases where they are *not* indemnified by the corporation. * * *

It is important to understand that the Corporate Reimbursement form covers *only* the corporation's obligation to indemnify its directors and officers. It does *not* cover any liability which the corporation itself may have to the plaintiff in any given action. For example, in an action under the federal securities laws charging the corporation and its directors and officers with disseminating false information, whatever liability the corporation may have to the plaintiff-shareholder will not be covered by the D & O policy. The Corporate Reimbursement

---

2. [By the Author] See Bishop, New Cure for an Old Ailment: Insurance Against Directors' and Officers' Liability, 22 Bus.Law. 92 (1966).

form will cover only the corporation's obligation (if any) to indemnify the directors and officers.

The Directors and Officers form—the second part of the dual form—is much more important from the standpoint of the directors and officers, since what they are most interested in is protecting themselves in situations where the corporation cannot indemnify them. * * *

1. Self-insured Amounts

(a) Retentions

All D & O policies are subject to self-insured "retentions" or deductibles. There are normally two deductibles in the Directors and Officers form: * * * For example, in a typical policy, there might be a $5,000 deductible for each individual director and officer, subject to a maximum of $25,000 in the aggregate for all directors and officers, with respect to each loss.

It is now customary to include a still higher deductible for the corporation itself in the Corporate Reimbursement form. For example, the deductible applicable to the corporation might be $50,000 or $100,000 for each loss, or even higher. * * *

(b) 5 Percent Co-insurance Feature

Most standard D & O policies also require the insureds to bear 5 percent of each loss at their own risk and uninsured. It is often possible, however, to negotiate the elimination of the 5 percent co-insurance feature with respect to losses in excess of $1,000,000. * * *

7. Exclusions

There are only three exclusions under the Corporate Reimbursement form—these include claims insured by another existing policy, or a prior policy, and pollution claims. No other exclusions are deemed necessary under this form because it covers only matters as to which the corporation is required or permitted to indemnify its directors and officers under the applicable indemnification statute.

In the Directors and Officers form, however, there are a number of very important exclusions and a number of "non-standard" exclusions that may be added to the policy by the insurers and which limit the coverage even further.

(a) *Libel and Slander.* * * *

(b) *Personal Profit or Advantage.* The policy excludes any claim against the insureds "based upon or attributable to their gaining in fact of any personal profit or advantage to which they were not legally entitled." This clause is written so broadly that it excludes virtually any kind of case where the directors or officers are held liable for conflicts of interest or self-dealing. * * *

It should be noted that this clause excludes claims based on the gaining in fact of an unlawful "advantage" as well as a personal profit.

Thus, if a director or officer were held to have misspent corporate funds to preserve himself in office, this would be a personal "advantage" within the meaning of the exclusion even though he was no richer as a result.

(c) *Illegal Remuneration.* This clause excludes any claim for the return by directors and officers of any remuneration paid to them "without the previous approval of the stockholders of the Company which payment shall be held by a court to have been illegal." The purpose of this provision is to exclude all claims against the directors and officers for excessive compensation, except where such compensation is approved by stockholders. * * *

(d) *Section 16(b) Exclusion.* * * * The insurers apparently have deemed it necessary to include a special exclusion for section 16(b) liability, in addition to the "personal profit" exclusion, because of the unusual rules applied by the courts in section 16(b) cases to "squeeze out" paper profits even though the insider might not have netted any actual profit from his transactions.

It is noteworthy that the policy does not purport to exclude claims under rule 10b–5. This means that claims for violation of rule 10b–5 would, in theory, be covered by the policy unless they fell within some specific exclusion or are excluded by reason of public policy. Any liability of a director or officer for trading for his own account in the corporation's stock would certainly be excluded by the "personal profit" exclusion, and perhaps also by considerations of federal public policy. Even if he were vindicated, as indicated earlier, the insurance company might deny coverage on the ground that he was not acting in his capacity as a director or officer and the suit was not brought against him solely by reason of his being a director or officer. A claim against the director or officer for making misstatements or omissions in public documents, releases or other corporate publicity in his capacity as a director or officer would presumably be covered to the extent that it involved conduct no graver than ordinary negligence. After Ernst & Ernst v. Hochfelder, however, it would appear that claims for damages cannot be brought under rule 10b–5 in the absence of "scienter". Such claims, if successful, would probably be uninsurable as a matter of federal public policy, although there might be a "gray area" of gross negligence or recklessness that could conceivably fall within the standard of *Hochfelder* and still be insurable. It thus appears that the D & O policy may not provide much meaningful coverage for liability for money damages under rule 10b–5. On the other hand, the policy would cover defense costs, at least in cases where the directors and officers are vindicated and where they are sued for action in their official capacity or solely by reason of being directors or officers.

(e) *Dishonesty Exclusion.* This clause excludes liability with respect to claims brought about or contributed to by the dishonesty of the insureds, but they are nevertheless protected "unless a judgment or other final adjudication * * * adverse to the Assureds shall establish that acts of active and deliberate dishonesty committed by the Assureds with actual dishonest purpose and intent were material to the cause of action so adjudicated."

(f) *Failure to Maintain Insurance.* A derivative action might be brought against directors and officers alleging that they had failed to maintain adequate insurance coverage—e.g., on a major plant that was destroyed by fire. Such a claim would be excluded by this clause. The intention of this exclusion is to avoid making the D & O policy a substitute for the corporation's normal liability and property insurance coverage. * * *

(j) *Pollution Exclusion.* This exclusion is now standard in most D & O forms. Its intent is to exclude all types of claims based on pollution or other "environmental" damage. The exclusion is expressed somewhat differently in the various policies. * * *

(k) *ERISA Exclusion.*[3] Although the ERISA exclusion is not included in the Lloyd's policy form itself, it is nearly always included as a rider, both by Lloyd's and other D & O insurers, and therefore should be classified as a "standard" exclusion. This exclusion eliminates from coverage all liability based upon violations of ERISA. * * *

8. *"Non-standard" Exclusions*

In addition to the exclusions discussed in the previous section, which are now standard in most D & O policies, there are a number of non-standard exclusions that will be added by insurers depending upon their assessment of the risk. These may include exclusions for antitrust claims, discrimination claims, claims resulting from political contributions or "improper payments" and claims arising out of pending or prior litigation. Most corporations can expect to find one or more of these "non-standard" exclusions in their D & O policies. * * *

C. MATTERS WHICH ARE UNINSURABLE ON GROUNDS OF PUBLIC POLICY

As noted earlier, the D & O policies contain a clause excluding coverage for "fines or penalties imposed by law or other matters which are uninsurable under the law pursuant to which this policy shall be construed." The exclusion of "other matters which are uninsurable" requires a consideration of the concept of uninsurability on grounds of public policy.

It is a well-established principle of the law of liability insurance that an insurance policy indemnifying an insured against liability due to his willful wrong is void as against public policy. It has been said that the basis for the rule that willful conduct is uninsurable is "the

3. [By the Editor] The Employee Retirement Income Security Act of 1974 imposes broad fiduciary duties by statute on administrators of employee retirement income plans. 29 U.S.C.A. § 1104.

fundamental principle that no one shall be permitted to take advantage of his own wrong. *   *   *" [4]

The case of Globus v. Law Research Service, Inc.,[5] held that a securities underwriter could not recover from the issuer under a contract of indemnity where the underwriters had actual knowledge of the omission of material facts from the prospectus. The principle stated by the court—that "one cannot insure himself against his own reckless, wilful or criminal misconduct"—is broad enough to preclude insurance for directors and officers against damages resulting from knowing violations of the federal securities laws. *   *   *

There is a split of authority as to whether punitive damages are insurable. To the extent that the object of punitive damages is penal and deterrent rather than compensatory, it would appear that such damages should not be insurable. It makes little sense to award punitive damages against a defendant to punish him for his outrageous conduct, and then to permit him to shift the "punishment" to an insurance company. Nevertheless, a number of cases have held that liability insurance may properly cover punitive damages. *   *   *

Applying the above principles to D & O insurance, it would appear likely that willful or intentional misconduct by directors and officers will be held to be uninsurable. The reason is that "an insurance contract relieving executives of their responsibility to reimburse those whom they injure through deliberate misconduct would appear to reduce measurably the deterrence of unlawful conduct." It should be emphasized that the court need not resort to "public policy" considerations to exclude coverage for intentional misconduct. In most cases, such misconduct would fall either within the "dishonesty" exclusion or within the "personal profit" exclusion and would accordingly be excluded as a contractual matter.

It has been argued that conduct which is reckless, in addition to intentional or deliberate misconduct, should be uninsurable as a matter of public policy. An example would be a case involving a transaction entered into by the directors when they knew or should have known that the transaction could result in a loss for the corporation, but could never result in a gain.[6] The basis for this conclusion is the belief that deterring reckless managerial behavior is more important than having a fund from which to compensate the corporation and its shareholders for the result of the directors' recklessness.

But this result does not necessarily follow where the insured's conduct is not so reckless as to amount to willful abdication of duty but amounts only to gross negligence. In contrast to deliberate misconduct,

---

4. [By the Author] Messersmith v. American Fidelity Co., 232 N.Y. 161, 165, 133 N.E. 432, 433 (1921) (Cardozo, J.).

5. [By the Editor] 418 F.2d 1276 (2d Cir. 1969), certiorari denied 397 U.S. 913, 90 S.Ct. 913, 25 L.Ed. 93 (1970).

6. [By the Author] For an example of such a case, see Litwin v. Allen, 25 N.Y.S.2d 667 (Sup.Ct.N.Y.Co.1940).

the consequences of negligent conduct are not considered in advance and, as a practical matter, such conduct is unlikely to be deterred by the prospect of uninsurability. In the experience of those who work with corporate boards on a daily basis, there is no evidence that directors have been made either more or less careful as a result of the availability of D & O insurance. * * *

D. INSURER'S RIGHT TO RESCIND POLICY BASED ON MISREPRESENTATION: BIRD V. PENN CENTRAL COMPANY

In order to obtain D & O insurance, the insureds or their representative must submit an application to the insurance company providing certain information that the insurance company requires in order to evaluate the risk.

It is elementary contract law that when the manifestation of assent by a party to a contract is induced by a fraudulent or a material misrepresentation by the other party upon which the recipient of the misrepresentation is justified in relying, the contract is voidable by the recipient. * * *

The only reported case involving the right to rescind a D & O policy is Bird v. Penn Central Company.[7] Plaintiffs in this case were members of a syndicate of Lloyd's of London, which had issued a D & O policy covering Penn Central Co. and its directors and officers. The application (or "proposal form") for the policy had been executed by David C. Bevan, chairman of the finance committee of the company. The policy was the standard Lloyd's dual policy. Item 10 of the application reads as follows:

> No person proposed for this insurance is cognizant of any act, error, or omission which he has reason to suppose might afford valid grounds for any future claim such as would fall within the scope of the proposed insurance except as follows:

Mr. Bevan's reply on the application to Item 10 was "None Known". Plaintiffs contended that this response was false, and that it was known to be so at the time of the application by Mr. Bevan, as well as by unspecified directors and officers proposed for coverage under the policy. It was claimed that they were aware of at least three conflict-of-interest situations at the time of application which should have been indicated in response to Item 10. Plaintiffs further alleged that the answer given to Item 10 was made in bad faith, was material to the risk, and was justifiably relied on so as to entitle them to rescind the policy because of fraud. Certain of the outside directors, who contended that they had no knowledge of any possible claims, moved for summary judgment. The court, however, held in favor of Lloyd's and denied the directors' motion for summary judgment. * * *

7. [By the Author] 334 F.Supp. 255 (E.D.Pa.1971), motions denied on rehearing 341 F.Supp. 291 (1972).

The outside directors ＊ ＊ ＊ argued that the policy should not be rescinded as to them, since they were altogether innocent and had no knowledge of any probable claims. Thus, if these directors had filled out the application, their answers would have been something similar to "none known" and such answers would have been truthful. They further asserted that they never authorized Mr. Bevan to make representations on their behalf in the application.

The court rejected this argument ＊ ＊ ＊.

E. SEVERABILITY IN THE LIGHT OF BIRD V. PENN CENTRAL COMPANY

In ＊ ＊ ＊ *Bird,* the court intimated that the result might have been different if each insured director and officer had submitted a separate application. Subsequent to the *Bird* decision, this practice has in fact been adopted by some applicants. However, it is not certain that such an approach would be effective to preclude rescission, at least in the absence of clear severability language in the policy, because the insurance company could still take the position that the contract was a unitary risk which it would not have accepted if it had known that one of the applicants had misrepresented the facts—particularly if that applicant happened to be the officer who signed for the corporation.

Notes

Until the mid–1980s, D & O insurance was relatively inexpensive and easy to obtain. This pattern has changed abruptly, a phenomenon that has also occurred with respect to other types of liability or malpractice insurance. See Businesses Struggling to Adapt as Insurance Crisis Spreads, Wall St.J., January 21, 1986 at 31, col. 1. According to this story, at least six outside directors of publicly held companies resigned in 1985 because of the inability of the company to obtain D & O insurance. Because insurers on the average paid out three or four times as much in D & O claims as they received in premiums, the story continued, such insurance has become much more expensive and difficult to obtain. An example involved a Massachusetts shoe company which saw its premium increase from $7,000 per year to $122,000 per year while its coverage was reduced from $10 million per lawsuit to $5 million per lawsuit. The following excerpt indicates that the experience of the shoe company during this period was not uncommon.

ROMANO, WHAT WENT WRONG WITH DIRECTORS' AND OFFICERS' LIABILITY INSURANCE *

14 Del.J.Corp.L. 1, 2, 9–13 (1989).

Management's perception of an insurance problem is further evident in the shift in reasons firms provide for not carrying D & O insurance. In 1984, the most frequently stated reason for not purchas-

* Reprinted in 14 Del.J.Corp.L. 1 (1989).

ing such insurance was that there was no need for it, whereas in 1987 the main reason was affordability.[8]

The turbulent conditions in the D & O insurance market persisted until mid–1986, when the rate of cost escalation and capacity reduction declined. While many corporations reported having difficulty in securing D & O insurance coverage in 1986, only a small number failed to resolve the problem. The increased capacity in D & O insurance appears to be due, in part, to the emergence of new institutions, policyholder-formed insurers. In 1986, new policyholder-formed insurers accounted for approximately half of all premiums in the excess D & O insurance market and over one-quarter of the premiums in the primary market. * * *

* * * Because most claims come under the corporate reimbursement portion [of D & O policies], as claims have increased, corporate reimbursement deductibles have risen over time while personal coverage deductibles have not. Corporate deductibles surged upwards recently, for an average increase of 1,326% from 1984 to 1987. Personal coverage deductibles, after declining steadily for a decade, have also begun to drift upward, increasing an average of 44% from 1984 to 1987, although the deductible amount is still lower than it was in the 1970s.

* * *

Concurrent with the rise in policy deductibles, premiums have gone up, reversing a downward trend of several years. Over 80% of firms renewing policies from mid–1985 through 1986 experienced a premium increase, and over half reported an increase in excess of 200%. Of course, the effective rate of premium increase is far greater than this, because new policies have higher deductibles and provide less coverage. Taking 1974 as a premium index base year equaling 100%, the Wyatt Survey computes an index that incorporates deductible levels as well as other factors, such as policy limit and corporate asset size, in determining the premium. Based on this calculation, the average premium index for 1987 was 682.4%, in contrast to a 1984 average of 54.3%.

Coverage has also been restricted by adding exclusions and revising coverage extension provisions. While there have always been exclusions in D & O policies, such as exclusions for losses caused by dishonesty or personal profit, which mitigate obvious moral hazard concerns, the proportion of policies with exclusions, as well as the number of exclusions per policy, have sharply increased. In particular, traditional exclusions, such as exclusions for losses due to pollution, pending and prior litigation, and failure to maintain insurance, were reported as included in D & O policies in 1987 at a rate approximately double their reported inclusion in policies in effect in 1984. In addition, the newer exclusions for losses due to litigation by an insured

8. [By the Author] The Wyatt Co., 1987 Wyatt Directors and Officers Liability Insurance Survey 55 (1987); The Wyatt Co., 1984 Wyatt Directors and Officers and Fiduciary Liability Survey, Comprehensive Report (1984). [Ed.: Virtually all of the data in the balance of this excerpt is taken from the 1987 Wyatt Co. survey.]

against another insured, mergers and acquisitions, tender offer resistance, actions by regulatory agencies, and securities transactions appeared in more than 10% of D & O policies in 1986. While some of the exclusions, such as the pollution exclusion, are relatively innocuous as they prevent D & O policies from being used as umbrella or substitute general liability policies, others, such as the acquisitions and takeover resistance exclusions, undercut the very rationale for acquiring D & O insurance as they eliminate from coverage shareholder claims that have been a traditional impetus for purchasing insurance.

A further method of restricting coverage, besides the addition of specific exclusions, is reducing the policy's duration. * * *

Extended discovery provisions extend the period of coverage during which the insured can report claims to the insurer concerning wrongful acts committed during the original policy period, for payment of an additional premium. These provisions can be crucial for the insured because D & O policies are written on a claims-made basis, in contrast to the occurrence basis of general liability policies.[9] As these provisions often come into play when the insurer has exercised its cancellation right, they protect the insured against a potential gap in coverage that could not arise under an occurrence policy—a wrongful act occurring during the policy period with no claim having been filed before the policy is terminated.

During the recent crisis, the number of policies with shorter extended discovery periods has been increasing. For instance, 41.2% of new policies had a one-year extended discovery period compared to 56.5% of old policies, while 41.1% of new policies had a 90–day period compared to 29.9% of old policies. This particular revision is a significant loss of protection for insureds because insurers frequently cancel policies when a claim appears likely. For instance, one-third of directors who submitted D & O insurance claims reported that the insurer tried to cancel the policy or narrow its coverage.[10] Cancellation under these circumstances creates severe problems for an insured, as a new policy application asks whether the insured knows of any past acts that could produce a claim and then will typically exclude losses from any acts so disclosed.

The final important change in D & O policies during the current crisis is a sharp reduction in policy limits. From early 1985 to mid–1986, an increasing number of companies found their D & O policies renewable only at substantially lower levels of coverage, despite premium and deductible increases. The Wyatt Survey reported an average decrease in policy limits of 50% in the first quarter of 1986. Virtually

9. [By the Author] A claims-made policy covers losses for claims that are filed against the insured during the policy period, whereas occurrence insurance covers losses arising out of acts occurring during the policy period even if the policy has expired when the claim is brought. Extended discovery period provisions, thus, move a claims-made policy in the direction of an occurrence policy.

10. [By the Author] Scheibla, *A Plague of Lawyers,* Barron's, Nov. 17, 1986, at 38. * * *

all insurers remaining in the market cut back their capacity from 1984 to 1986. By the end of 1986, however, the situation improved somewhat, as newly organized policyholder-formed insurance groups offered increased limits for their members. As a result, there was a net reduction in policy limits of only 10% in the last quarter of 1986 and, on average, the limits were higher than pre–1984 levels.

Notes

Professor Romano considers whether the insurance crisis of the mid–1980s could have been caused by a variety of non-legal or legal factors: e.g. (1) changes in the structure of the insurance industry; (2) changes in economic conditions that caused more transactions that were claim-generating during this period than in earlier periods; (3) changes in liability standards; (4) increases in uncertainty as to the application of liability standards; and (5) unexpected judicial constructions of insurance contract provisions that increase the allocation of risk to insurers. While her conclusions "are, at times tentative, and there are a number of important loose ends," 14 Del.J.Corp.Law, at 2 (1989), Professor Romano concludes that the explanation was multi-causal. The developments discussed earlier in this casebook—e.g. the Delaware Supreme Court decision in *Van Gorkom,* page 704, supra—may have contributed to increases in rates primarily because of increases in uncertainty. Her strongest comments, however, are reserved for judicial decisions that construe (or misconstrue) provisions in D & O insurance contracts unexpectedly in favor of the insureds:

> The problem confronting D&O insurers in assessing the risks of unanticipated, novel lawsuits is exacerbated by court rulings on insurance contracts which are all too often, to be blunt, lawless. In their reading of D&O insurance contracts, courts frequently rewrite the allocation of risk against the insurer. Insurers have had, for example, to pay defense costs as incurred, even though the action may not be covered by the policy, the insured refuses to respect the insurer's reservation of rights, and the policy explicitly gives the insurer the option to make defense advances.[11] Insurers have not been permitted to litigate the applicability of the dishonesty exclusion when the underlying action has been settled without an adjudication of guilt.[12] They have also not been permitted to exercise their cancellation rights when the insured is bankrupt.[13] Related transactions have been found to constitute "separate loss occurrences," increasing the liability of the insurer,[14] and knowing misrepresentations in financial statements have been held not to void policies because the documents were not explicitly incorporated by reference in the policy application's cogni-

---

11. [By the Author] Okada v. MGIC Indemnity Corp., 795 F.2d 1450 (9th Cir. 1986); Pepsico, Inc. v. Continental Casualty Co., 640 F.Supp. 656 (S.D.N.Y.1986).

12. [By the Author] Pepsico, Inc. v. Continental Casualty Co., 640 F.Supp. 656 (S.D.N.Y.1986).

13. [By the Author] Minoco Group v. First State Underwriters Agency, 799 F.2d 517 (9th Cir.1986).

14. [By the Author] Okada v. MGIC Indemnity Corp., 795 F.2d 1450 (9th Cir. 1986); North River Ins. Co. v. Huff, 628 F.Supp. 1129 (D.Kan.1985).

zance warranty.[15] In addition, insurers have been held liable for losses arising from suits involving an outside directorship—an insured individual serving on the board of a company different from the insured corporation—when the policy was silent on the issue.[16] The two notable decisions favorable to insurers have permitted the voiding of a policy as to all insureds when there has been a material misrepresentation in the application process.[17]

Courts have also construed D&O policies as placing the risk of all new perils on insurers. The recent spate of cases in which banks have directly sued officers and directors for negligently approving what with hindsight were bad loans, in order to recover upon the D&O insurance policy, illustrates this tendency. Such claims could not have been anticipated by insurers because a corporation suing its employees for negligence was theretofore unthinkable. Yet in National Union Fire Insurance Co. v. Seafirst Corp.,[18] the court cavalierly rejected the insurer's contention that its D&O policy was not intended to cover such a claim by citing the policy language that the insurer would pay losses suffered as a result of "any" claims against directors.

The corporate strategy followed in the bank cases, when successful, converts what is priced as third-party insurance into first-party insurance, because the corporation can trigger a payment to itself by suing its employees. * * * Moreover, the liability on such claims has been substantial: Chase Manhattan settled a $175 million claim for $32.5 million covered by insurance; Bank of America settled a $95 million claim for an $8.2 million payment from insurers; and Seafirst Corporation entered into a $110 million settlement with its directors and officers limiting recovery to its $70 million remaining policy limits.[19] The inevitable consequence of such litigation is higher insurance premiums. * * *

[This] insurance contract litigation may be contributing to the crisis. When courts rewrite an insurance contract, the price insurers received will not have been commensurate with the risk they actually bore. Higher premiums are necessary on new policies, with terms identical to older, cheaper policies, to compensate the insurer for the court-added risk. * * *

14 Del.J.Corp.Law at 25–27, 29.

15. [By the Author] National Union Fire Ins. Co. v. Continental Ill. Corp., 673 F.Supp. 267 (N.D.Ill.1986).

16. [By the Author] Continental Copper & Steel Indus. v. Johnson, 491 F.Supp. 360 (S.D.N.Y.1980), aff'd, 641 F.2d 59 (2d Cir.1981).

17. [By the Author] Shapiro v. American Home Assurance Co., 584 F.Supp. 1245 (D.Mass.1984); Bird v. Penn Central Co., 341 F.Supp. 291 (E.D.Pa.1972).

18. [By the Author] No. C85–396R (W.D.Wash. Mar. 19, 1986), *reprinted* in Directors' and Officers' Liability Insurance 1987, at 307 (1987).

19. [By the Author] *BankAmerica's Settlements*, N.Y. Times, Jan. 5, 1988, at D4, col. 5. See also National Union Fire Ins. v. Seafirst Corp., 662 F.Supp. 36 (W.D. Wash.1986) (the primary insurer paid $15 million in addition to paying $5 million in defense costs, while the excess insurer is contesting paying its $55 million share). Bank of America settled related shareholder litigation with payments from its D & O insurers totaling $60.4 million. Waldman, *BankAmerica Settles Suits Tied to Losses, Posts Gain on Sale of Bank–Firm Stake*, Wall St. J., Jan. 5, 1988, at 12, col. 2.

Chapter Fifteen

SHAREHOLDER LITIGATION

A. ATTITUDES TOWARD SHAREHOLDER LITIGATION

COHEN v. BENEFICIAL INDUS. LOAN CORP.

Supreme Court of the United States, 1949.
337 U.S. 541, 69 S.Ct. 1221, 93 L.Ed. 1528.

MR. JUSTICE JACKSON delivered the opinion of the Court.

The ultimate question here is whether a federal court, having jurisdiction of a stockholder's derivative action only because the parties are of diverse citizenship, must apply a statute of the forum state which makes the plaintiff, if unsuccessful, liable for all expenses, including attorney's fees, of the defense and requires security for their payment as a condition of prosecuting the action.

Petitioners' decedent as plaintiff, brought in the United States District Court for New Jersey an action in the right of the Beneficial Industrial Loan Corporation, a Delaware corporation doing business in New Jersey. The defendants were the corporation and certain of its managers and directors. The complaint alleged generally that since 1929 the individual defendants engaged in a continuing and successful conspiracy to enrich themselves at the expense of the corporation. Specific charges of mismanagement and fraud extended over a period of eighteen years and the assets allegedly wasted or diverted thereby were said to exceed $100,000,000. The stockholder had demanded that the corporation institute proceedings for its recovery but, by their control of the corporation, the individual defendants prevented it from doing so. This stockholder, therefore, sought to assert the right of the corporation. One of 16,000 stockholders, he owned 100 of its more than two million shares, so that his holdings, together with 150 shares held by the intervenor, approximated 0.0125% of the outstanding stock and had a market value that had never exceeded $9,000.

The action was brought in 1943, and various proceedings had been taken therein when, in 1945, New Jersey enacted the statute which is here involved. Its general effect is to make a plaintiff having so small an interest liable for all expenses and attorney's fees of the defense if he fails to make good his complaint and to entitle the corporation to indemnity before the case can be prosecuted. These conditions are made applicable to pending actions. The corporate defendant therefore moved to require security, pointed to its by-laws by which it might be required to indemnify the individual defendants, and averred that a bond of $125,000 would be appropriate.

The District Court was of the opinion that the state enactment is not applicable to such an action when pending in a federal court, 7 F.R.D. 352. The Court of Appeals was of a contrary opinion and reversed, 3 Cir., 170 F.2d 44, and we granted certiorari. 336 U.S. 917, 69 S.Ct. 639. * * *

CONSTITUTIONALITY

Petitioners deny the validity of the statute under both Federal and New Jersey Constitutions. The latter question is ultimately for the state courts, and since they have made no contrary determination, we shall presume in the circumstances of this case that the statute conforms with the State constitution.

Federal Constitutional questions we must consider, because a federal court would not give effect, in either a diversity or nondiversity case, to a state statute that violates the Constitution of the United States.

The background of stockholder litigation with which this statute deals requires no more than general notice. As business enterprise increasingly sought the advantages of incorporation, management became vested with almost uncontrolled discretion in handling other people's money. The vast aggregate of funds committed to corporate control came to be drawn to a considerable extent from numerous and scattered holders of small interests. The director was not subject to an effective accountability. That created strong temptation for managers to profit personally at expense of their trust. The business code became all too tolerant of such practices. Corporate laws were lax and were not self-enforcing, and stockholders, in face of gravest abuses, were singularly impotent in obtaining redress of abuses of trust.

Equity came to the relief of the stockholder, who had no standing to bring civil action at law against faithless directors and managers. Equity, however, allowed him to step into the corporation's shoes and to seek in its right the restitution he could not demand in his own. It required him first to demand that the corporation vindicate its own rights but when, as was usual, those who perpetrated the wrongs also were able to obstruct any remedy, equity would hear and adjudge the corporation's cause through its stockholder with the corporation as a defendant, albeit a rather nominal one. This remedy born of stockholder helplessness was long the chief regulator of corporate management and has afforded no small incentive to avoid at least grosser forms of betrayal of stockholders' interests. It is argued, and not without reason, that without it there would be little practical check on such abuses.

Unfortunately, the remedy itself provided opportunity for abuse which was not neglected. Suits sometimes were brought not to redress real wrongs, but to realize upon their nuisance value. They were bought off by secret settlements in which any wrongs to the general body of share owners were compounded by the suing stockholder, who was mollified by payments from corporate assets. These litigations were aptly characterized in professional slang as "strike suits." And it was said that these suits were more commonly brought by small and irresponsible than by large stockholders, because the former put less to risk and a small interest was more often within the capacity and readiness of management to compromise than a large one.

We need not determine the measure of these abuses or the evils they produced on the one hand or prevented and redressed on the other. The Legislature of New Jersey, like that of other states, considered them sufficient to warrant some remedial measures.

The very nature of the stockholder's derivative action makes it one in the regulation of which the legislature of a state has wide powers. Whatever theory one may hold as to the nature of the corporate entity, it remains a wholly artificial creation whose internal relations between management and stockholders are dependent upon state law and may be subject to most complete and penetrating regulation, either by public authority or by some form of stockholder action. Directors and managers, if not technically trustees, occupy positions of a fiduciary nature, and nothing in the Federal Constitution prohibits a state from imposing on them the strictest measure of responsibility, liability and accountability, either as a condition of assuming office or as a consequence of holding it.

Likewise, a stockholder who brings suit on a cause of action derived from the corporation assumes a position, not technically as a trustee perhaps, but one of a fiduciary character. He sues, not for himself alone, but as representative of a class comprising all who are similarly situated. The interests of all in the redress of the wrongs are taken into his hands, dependent upon his diligence, wisdom and integrity. And while the stockholders have chosen the corporate director or manager, they have no such election as to a plaintiff who steps forward to represent them. He is a self-chosen representative and a volunteer champion. The Federal Constitution does not oblige the State to place its litigating and adjudicating processes at the disposal of such a representative, at least without imposing standards of responsibility, liability and accountability which it considers will protect the interests he elects himself to represent. It is not without significance that this Court has found it necessary long ago in the Equity Rules and now in the Federal Rules of Civil Procedure [1] to impose procedural regulations of the class action not applicable to any other. We conclude that the state has plenary power over this type of litigation.

In considering specific objections to the way in which the State has exercised its power in this particular statute, it should be unnecessary to say that we are concerned only with objections which go to constitutionality. The wisdom and the policy of this and similar statutes are involved in controversies amply debated in legal literature [2] but not for us to judge, and, hence not for us to remark upon. The Federal Constitution does not invalidate state legislation because it fails to embody the highest wisdom or provide the best conceivable remedies. Nor can legislation be set aside by courts because of the fact, if it be such, that it has been sponsored and promoted by those who advantage from it. In dealing with such difficult and controversial subjects, only experience will verify or disclose weaknesses and defects of any policy and teach lessons which may be applied by amendment. Within the area of constitutionality, the states should not be restrained from devising experiments, even those we might think dubious, in the effort to preserve the maximum good which equity sought in creating the derivative stockholder's action and at the same time to eliminate as much as possible its defects and evils.

It is said that this statute transgresses the Due Process Clause, Amend. 14, by being "arbitrary, capricious and unreasonable;" [and] the Equal Protection Clause by singling out small stockholders to burden most heavily; * * *.

In considering whether the statute offends the Due Process Clause we can judge it only by its own terms, for it has had no interpretation or application as yet. It imposes liability and requires security for "the *reasonable* expenses, including counsel fees which may be incurred" (emphasis supplied) by the corporation and by other parties defendant. The amount of security is subject to increase if the progress of the litigation reveals that it is inadequate or to decrease if it is proved to be excessive. A state may set the terms on which it will permit litigations in its courts. No type of litigation is more susceptible of regulation than that of a fiduciary nature. And it cannot seriously be said that a state makes such *unreasonable* use of its power as to violate the Constitution when it provides liability and security for payment of *reasonable* expenses if a litigation of this character is adjudged to be unsustainable. It is urged that such a requirement will foreclose resort by most stockholders to the only available judicial remedy for the

1. [By the Editor] The Rule referred to by the Court is now Fed.Civ.Proc. Rule 23.1, 28 U.S.C.A.

2. [By the Court] See [e.g.] Hornstein, Problems of Procedure in Stockholders' Derivative Suits, 42 Col.L.R. 574; Hornstein, Directors' Expenses and Stockholders' Suits, 43 id. 301; Hornstein, The Death

Knell of Stockholders' Derivative Suits in New York, 32 California L.R. 123; Zlinkoff, The American Investor And The Constitutionality of Section 61–b of the New York General Corporation Law, 54 Yale L.J. 352. See Douglas, Directors Who Do Not Direct, 47 Harv.L.R. 1305.

protection of their rights. Of course, to require security for the payment of any kind of costs or the necessity for bearing any kind of expense of litigation has a deterring effect. But we deal with power, not wisdom; and we think, notwithstanding this tendency, it is within the power of a state to close its courts to this type of litigation if the condition of reasonable security is not met.

The contention that the statute denies equal protection of the laws is based upon the fact that it enables a stockholder who owns 5% of a corporation's outstanding shares, or $50,000 in market value, to proceed without either security or liability and imposes both upon those who elect to proceed with a smaller interest. We do not think the state is forbidden to use the amount of one's financial interest, which measures his individual injury from the misconduct to be redressed, as some measure of the good faith and responsibility of one who seeks at his own election to act as custodian of the interests of all stockholders, and as an indication that he volunteers for the large burdens of the litigation from a real sense of grievance and is not putting forward a claim to capitalize personally on its harassment value. These may not be the best ways of precluding "strike lawsuits," but we are unable to say that a classification for these purposes, based upon the percentage or market value of the stock alleged to be injured by the wrongs, is an unconstitutional one. Where any classification is based on a percentage or an amount, it is necessarily somewhat arbitrary. It is difficult to say of many lines drawn by legislation that they give those just above and those just below the line a perfectly equal protection. A taxpayer with $10,000.01 of income does not think it is equality to tax him at a different rate than one who has $9,999.99, or to require returns from one just above and not from one just below a certain figure. It is difficult to say that a stockholder who has 49.99% of a company's stock should be unable to elect any representative to its Board of Directors while one who owns 50.01% may name the entire Board. If there is power, as we think there is, to draw a line based on considerations of proportion or amount, it is a rare case, of which this is not one, that a constitutional objection may be made to the particular point which the legislature has chosen. * * *

APPLICABILITY IN FEDERAL COURT

* * * [T]his statute is not merely a regulation of procedure. With it or without it the main action takes the same course. However, it creates a new liability where none existed before, for it makes a stockholder who institutes a derivative action liable for the expense to which he puts the corporation and other defendants, if he does not make good his claims. Such liability is not usual and it goes beyond payment of what we know as "costs." If all the Act did was to create this liability, it would clearly be substantive. But this new liability would be without meaning and value in many cases if it resulted in nothing but a judgment for expenses at or after the end of the case. Therefore, a procedure is prescribed by which the liability is insured by

entitling the corporate defendant to a bond of indemnity before the outlay is incurred. We do not think a statute which so conditions the stockholder's action can be disregarded by the federal court as a mere procedural device.

It is urged, however, that Federal Rule of Civil Procedure No. [23.1] deals with plaintiff's right to maintain such an action in federal court and that therefore the subject is recognized as procedural and the federal rule alone prevails. Rule [23.1] requires the stockholder's complaint to be verified by oath and to show that the plaintiff was a stockholder at the time of the transaction of which he complains or that his share thereafter devolved upon him by operation of law. In other words, the federal court will not permit itself to be used to litigate a purchased grievance or become a party to speculation in wrongs done to corporations. It also requires a showing that an action is not a collusive one to confer jurisdiction and to set forth the facts showing that the plaintiff has endeavored to obtain his remedy through the corporation itself. It further provides that the class action shall not be dismissed or compromised without approval of the court, with notice to the members of the class. These provisions neither create nor exempt from liabilities, but require complete disclosure to the court and notice to the parties in interest. None conflict with the statute in question and all may be observed by a federal court, even if not applicable in state court.

We see no reason why the policy stated in Guaranty Trust Co. of New York v. York, 326 U.S. 99, 65 S.Ct. 1464, 89 L.Ed. 2079, 160 A.L.R. 1231, should not apply.

We hold that the New Jersey statute applies in federal courts and that the District Court erred in declining to fix the amount of indemnity reasonably to be exacted as a condition of further prosecution of the suit.

The judgment of the Court of Appeals is affirmed.

MR. JUSTICE DOUGLAS, with whom MR. JUSTICE FRANKFURTER concurs, dissenting in part.

The cause of action on which this suit is brought is a derivative one. Though it belongs to the corporation, the stockholders are entitled under state law to enforce it. The measure of the cause of action is the claim which the corporation has against the alleged wrongdoers. This New Jersey statute does not add one iota to nor subtract one iota from that cause of action. It merely prescribes the method by which stockholders may enforce it. Each state has numerous regulations governing the institution of suits in its courts. They may favor the litigation or they may affect it adversely. But they do not fall under the principle of Erie R. Co. v. Tompkins, 304 U.S. 64, 58 S.Ct. 817, 82 L.Ed. 1188, 114 A.L.R. 1487, unless they define, qualify or delimit the cause of action or otherwise relate to it.

This New Jersey statute, like statutes governing security for costs, regulates only the procedure for instituting a particular cause of action and hence need not be applied in this diversity suit in the federal court. Rule [23.1] of the Federal Rules of Civil Procedure defines that procedure for the federal courts.

MR. JUSTICE RUTLEDGE, dissenting.

I am in accord with the dissenting opinion of MR. JUSTICE DOUGLAS in this case. * * *

SUROWITZ v. HILTON HOTELS CORP.

Supreme Court of the United States, 1966.
383 U.S. 363, 86 S.Ct. 845, 15 L.Ed.2d 807.

MR. JUSTICE BLACK delivered the opinion of the Court.

Petitioner, Dora Surowitz, a stockholder in Hilton Hotels Corporation, brought this action in a United States District Court on behalf of herself and other stockholders charging that the officers and directors of the corporation had defrauded it of several million dollars by illegal devices and schemes designed to cheat the corporation and enrich the individual defendants. The acts charged, if true, would constitute frauds of the grossest kind against the corporation, and would be in violation of the Securities Act of 1933, the Securities Exchange Act of 1934, and the Delaware General Corporation Law. Summarily stated, the detailed complaint, which takes up over 60 printed pages, charges first that defendants conceived and carried out a deceptive plan under which the Hilton Hotels Corporation through a formal "offer" mailed to all the stockholders, purchased from them some 300,000 shares of its outstanding common stock, that these defendants manipulated the stock's market price to an artificially high level and then at this inflated price sold some 100,000 shares of their own stock to the corporation, and that the effect of this offer and purchase was to reduce the corporation's working capital more than $8,000,000 at a time when its financial condition was weak, and the funds were badly needed to run the corporation's business. The second deceptive scheme charged in the complaint was that the same defendants, all of whom were stockholders of the Hilton Credit Corporation, caused the Hilton Hotels Corporation to purchase, also at an artificially high price, more than a million shares of Hilton Credit Corporation stock, paying about $3,441,000 for it, of which over $2,000,000 was personally received by the defendants. The complaint was signed by counsel for Mrs. Surowitz in compliance with Rule 11 of the Federal Rules of Civil Procedure which provides that "The signature of an attorney constitutes a certificate by him that he has read the pleading; that to the best of his knowledge, information, and belief there is good ground to support it; and that it is not interposed for delay." Also pursuant to Rule [23.1] of the Federal Rules, the complaint was verified by Mrs. Surowitz, the petitioner, who stated that some of the allegations in the complaint were true and that she "on information and belief" thought that all the other allegations were true.

So far as the language of the complaint and of Mrs. Surowitz's verification was concerned, both were in strict compliance with the provisions of Rule [23.1] which states that a shareholder's complaint in a secondary action must contain certain averments and be verified by the plaintiff. Notwithstanding the sufficiency of the complaint and verification under Rule [23.1], however, the court, without requiring defendants to file an answer and over petitioner's protest, granted defendants' motion to require Mrs. Surowitz to submit herself to an oral examination by the defendants' counsel. In this examination Mrs. Surowitz showed in her answers to questions that she did not understand the complaint at all, that she could not explain the statements made in the complaint, that she had a very small degree of knowledge as to what the lawsuit was about, that she did not know any of the defendants by name, that she did not know the nature of their alleged misconduct, and in fact that in signing the verification she had merely relied on what her son-in-law had explained to her about the facts in the case. On the basis of this examination, defendants moved to dismiss the complaint, alleging that "1. It is a sham pleading, and 2. Plaintiff, Dora Surowitz, is not a proper party plaintiff * * *" In response, Mrs. Surowitz's lawyer, in an effort to cure whatever infirmity the court might possibly find in Mrs. Surowitz's verification in light of her deposition, filed two affidavits which shed much additional light on an extensive investigation which had preceded the filing of the complaint. Despite these affidavits the District Judge dismissed the case holding that Mrs. Surowitz's affidavit was "false," that being wholly false it was a nullity, that being a nullity it was as though no affidavit had been made in compliance with Rule [23.1], that being false the affidavit was a "sham" and Rule [23.1] required that he dismiss her case, and he did so, "with prejudice."

The Court of Appeals affirmed the District Court's dismissal, saying in part:

> "We can only conclude, as did the court below, that plaintiff's verification of the complaint was false because she swore to the verity of alleged facts of which she was wholly ignorant." 342 F.2d, at 606.

The Court of Appeals reached its conclusion that the case must be dismissed under Rule [23.1] and Rule 41(b) despite the fact that the charges made against the defendants were viewed as very serious and grave charges of fraud and that "many of the material allegations of the complaint are obviously true and cannot be refuted." 342 F.2d, at 607. We cannot agree with either of the courts below and reverse their judgments. We do not find it necessary in reversing, however, to consider all the numerous arguments made by respondents based on the origin, history and utility of Rule [23.1], and of derivative causes of action and class suits. No matter how much weight we give to the function of the Rule and of class action proceedings in protecting corporate management against so-called "nuisance" or "strike suits," we hold that the Rule cannot justify dismissal of this case on the record shown here. * * *

Mrs. Surowitz, the plaintiff and petitioner here, is a Polish immigrant with a very limited English vocabulary and practically no formal education. For many years she has worked as a seamstress in New York where by reason of frugality she saved enough money to buy some thousands of dollars worth of stocks. She was of course not able to select stocks for herself with any degree of assurance of their value. Under these circumstances she had to receive advice and counsel and quite naturally she went to her son-in-law, Irving Brilliant. Mr. Brilliant had graduated from the Harvard Law School, possessed a master's degree in economics from Columbia University, was a professional investment advisor, and in addition to his degrees and his financial acumen, he wore a Phi Beta Kappa key. In 1957, six years before this litigation began, he bought some stock for his mother-in-law in the Hilton Hotels Corporation, paying a little more than $2,000 of her own money for it. He evidently had confidence in that corporation because by 1960 he had purchased for his wife, his deceased mother's estate, a trust fund created for his children, and Mrs. Surowitz some 2,350 shares of the corporation's common stock, at a cost of about $45,000 in addition to one of the corporation's $10,000 debentures.

About December 1962, Mrs. Surowitz received through the mails a notice from the Hilton Hotels Corporation announcing its plan to purchase a large amount of its own stock. Because she wanted it explained to her, she took the notice to Mr. Brilliant. Apparently disturbed by it, he straightway set out to make an investigation. Shortly thereafter he went to Chicago, Illinois, where Hilton Hotels has its home office and talked the matter over with Mr. Rockler. Mr. Brilliant and Mr. Rockler had been friends for many years, apparently ever since both of them served as a part of the legal staff representing the United States in the Nuremberg trials. The two decided to investigate further, and for a number of months both pursued whatever avenues of information that were open to them. By August of 1963 on the basis of their investigation, both of them had reached the conclusion that the time had come to do something about the matter. In the meantime the value of the corporation's stock had declined steadily, and in August the corporation failed to pay its usual dividend. In October, while a complaint was being prepared charging defendants with fraud and multiple violations of the federal securities acts and state law, Mr. Rockler met with defendants' lawyers. This conference, instead of producing an understanding merely provided Mr. Brilliant and Mr. Rockler with information, not previously available to them, which increased their grave suspicions about the corporation's stock purchase and its management. For instance it was learned at this meeting that at the time of the stock purchase the president and chairman of the board of Hilton Hotels Corporation had purchased for an unusually high price over 100,000 shares of the corporation's stock from several trusts established by a vice president and director of the corporation. Finally, in December, or almost exactly one year after the corporation had submitted its questionable offer to purchase stock from its shareholders, this complaint was filed charging the defendants with creating and participating in a fraudulent scheme which had taken millions of dollars out of the corporation's treasury and transferred the money to the defendants' pockets.

Soon after these investigations began Rockler prepared a letter for Mrs. Surowitz to send to the corporation protesting the alleged fraudulent scheme. Mr. Brilliant, her son-in-law, took the communication to Mrs. Surowitz, explained it to her, and she signed it. Later, in August 1963, when the corporation declined to pay its dividend, Mrs. Surowitz, who had purchased the stock for the specific purpose of gaining a source of income, was sufficiently disturbed to seek Mr. Brilliant's counsel. He explained to her that he and Mr. Rockler were of the opinion that the corporation's management had wrongfully damaged the corporation, and together at that time Mrs. Surowitz and her son-in-law discussed the matter of her bringing this suit. When, on the basis of this conversation, Mrs. Surowitz stated that she agreed that suit be filed in her name, Mr. Rockler prepared a formal complaint which he mailed to Mr. Brilliant. Mr. Brilliant then, according to both his affidavit and Mrs. Surowitz's testimony, read and explained the complaint to his mother-in-law before she verified it. Her limited education and her small knowledge about any of the English language, except the most ordinarily used words, probably is sufficient guarantee that the courts below were right in finding that she did not understand any of the legal relationships or comprehend any of the business transactions described in the complaint. She did know, however, that she had put over $2,000 of her hard-earned money into Hilton Hotels stock, that she was not getting her dividends, and that her son-in-law who had looked into the matter thought that something was wrong. She also knew that her son-in-law was qualified to help her and she trusted him. It is difficult to believe that anyone could be shocked or harmed in any way when, in the light of all these circumstances, Mrs. Surowitz verified the complaint, not on the basis of her own knowledge and understanding, but in the faith that her son-in-law had correctly advised her either that the statements in the complaint were true or to the best of his knowledge he believed them to be true.

We assume it may be possible that there can be circumstances under which a district court could stop all proceedings in a derivative cause of action, relieve the defendants from filing an answer to charges of fraud, and conduct a pre-trial investigation to determine whether the plaintiff had falsely sworn either that the facts alleged in the complaint were true or that he had information which led him to believe they were true. And conceivably such a pre-trial investigation might possibly reveal facts surrounding the verification of the complaint which could justify dismissal of the complaint with prejudice. However, here we need not consider the question of whether, if ever, Federal Rule

[23.1] might call for such summary action. Certainly it cannot justify the court's summary dismissal in this case. Rule [23.1] was not written in order to bar derivative suits. Unquestionably it was originally adopted and has served since in part as a means to discourage "strike suits" by people who might be interested in getting quick dollars by making charges without regard to their truth so as to coerce corporate managers to settle worthless claims in order to get rid of them. On the other hand, however, derivative suits have played a rather important role in protecting shareholders of corporations from the designing schemes and wiles of insiders who are willing to betray their company's interests in order to enrich themselves. And it is not easy to conceive of anyone more in need of protection against such schemes than little investors like Mrs. Surowitz.

When the record of this case is reviewed in the light of the purpose of Rule [23.1]'s verification requirement, there emerges the plain, inescapable fact that this is not a strike suit or anything akin to it. Mrs. Surowitz was not interested in anything but her own investment made with her own money. Moreover, there is not one iota of evidence that Mr. Brilliant, her son-in-law and counselor, sought to do the corporation any injury in this litigation. In fact his purchases for the benefit of his family of more than $50,000 of securities in the corporation, including a $10,000 debenture, all made years before this suit was brought, manifest confidence in the corporation, not a desire to harm it in any way. The Court of Appeals in affirming the District Court's dismissal, however, indicated that whether Mrs. Surowitz and her counselors acted in good faith and whether the charges they made were truthful were irrelevant once Mrs. Surowitz demonstrated in her oral testimony that she knew nothing about the content of the suit. That court said:

> "Those affidavits reveal that substantial and diligent investigation by Brilliant, Rockler and others preceded the filing of this complaint. * * * Neither affidavit, however, does anything, if anything could be done, to offset plaintiff's positive disavowal of any relevant knowledge or information other than the fact of her stock ownership." 342 F.2d, at 607.

In fact the opinion of the Court of Appeals indicates in several places that a woman like Mrs. Surowitz, who is uneducated generally and illiterate in economic matters, could never under any circumstances be a plaintiff in a derivative suit brought in the federal courts to protect her stock interests.

We cannot construe Rule [23.1] or any other one of the Federal Rules as compelling courts to summarily dismiss, without any answer or argument at all, cases like this where grave charges of fraud are shown by the record to be based on reasonable beliefs growing out of careful investigation. The basic purpose of the Federal Rules is to administer justice through fair trials, not through summary dismissals as necessary as they may be on occasion. These rules were designed in large part to get away from some of the old procedural booby traps which common-law pleaders could set to prevent unsophisticated litigants from ever having their day in court. If rules of procedure work as they should in an honest and fair judicial system, they not only permit, but should as nearly as possible guarantee that bona fide complaints be carried to an adjudication on the merits. Rule [23.1], like the other civil rules, was written to further, not defeat the ends of justice. The serious fraud charged here, which of course has not been proven, is clearly in that class of deceitful conduct which the federal securities laws were largely passed to prohibit and protect against. There is, moreover, not one word or one line of actual evidence in this record indicating that there has been any collusive conduct or trickery by those who filed this suit except through intimations and insinuations without any support from anything any witness has said. The dismissal of this case was error. It has now been practically three years since the complaint was filed and as yet none of the defendants have even been compelled to admit or deny the wrongdoings charged. They should be. The cause is reversed and remanded to the District Court for trial on the merits.

Reversed and remanded.

Mr. Justice Fortas took no part in the decision of this case.

The Chief Justice took no part in the consideration or decision of this case.

[A concurring opinion by Mr. Justice Harlan is omitted.]

Notes

(1) Derivative litigation by shareholders has been influenced by two fundamentally inconsistent attitudes exemplified in these two cases: (1) the need to have some procedure by which persons in control of a corporation can be called to account for their misdeeds that enrich themselves at the expense of the corporation, and (2) the fear of encouraging questionable or groundless lawsuits brought solely for their settlement value by plaintiff-shareholders with little financial interest in recovery by the corporation, the so-called strike suit. Historically, the fear of strike suits was not academic:

> The characteristics of strike suits may be illustrated by the activities of Clarence H. Venner, referred to as "an artificer of litigation and a menace to corporate society." Continental Securities Co. v. Belmont, 183 Misc. 340, 343, 144 N.Y.Supp. 801, 804 (Sup.Ct.1913). During his career he conducted at least 23 campaigns against such defendants as the United States Steel Corp., the Great Northern Railway Co., the Interborough Rapid Transit Co., the American Telephone and Telegraph Co. These campaigns involved at least 40 separate actions and have left over 100 cases in the reports. The campaign against the New York Central extended over 14 years, involved 12 suits in 4 jurisdictions, employed 4 nominal plaintiffs, left 29 cases in the reports, and reached the United States Supreme Court 5 times. Of the total

number of actions brought he lost 34 and won 5, one having been discontinued. This, however, is no measure of his success. He received $300,000 for $70,000 worth of Union Pacific Railroad stock (see N.Y. Herald Tribune, June 26, 1933, at 13); between one and two million dollars was his price for dismissing the suit against the Great Northern Railway Co. [A History of the Libel Suit of Clarence H. Venner against August Belmont, (published by the Interborough Rapid Transit Co., 1913) 136]; and he received "a large sum" to discontinue against the Chicago, R.I. and P. Ry. Co. (id. at 123–128). Moreover, it is known that he brought many other actions which do not appear in the reports, an indication of success (id. at 141).

Note, Extortionate Corporate Litigation: The Strike Suit, 34 Colum.L.Rev. 1308, n. 1 (1934). Assuming that such activity may be a problem, how should it be attacked? Is the New Jersey statute upheld in *Cohen* a reasonable solution?

(2) In recent years, concern has also been expressed about the development of plaintiffs' firms that specialize in entrepreneurial corporate litigation. See the Coffee excerpt quoted at page 655, supra. The concern often comes down to charges of champerty, and is similar to the problem under section 16(b) of the Securities Exchange Act of 1934, discussed earlier. Attorneys familiar with derivative litigation from the standpoint of management generally believe that most such litigation is groundless and of no benefit to shareholders. This perspective is well illustrated by Duesenberg, The Business Judgment Rule and Shareholder Derivative Suits: A View From the Inside, 60 Wash.U.L.Q. 311, 331–333 (1982):

> [I]t is often stated that the shareowners' derivative suit has "long played a crucial role in assuring a modicum of integrity and competence in the management of corporations,"[3] or that it is the "chief regulator of corporate management."[4] In a competent and scholarly discourse of this subject, two academics have opined that "the organizing principle around which the derivative action should be reconstructed is a deterrent one: the derivative action should serve as the principal means by which to enforce the fiduciary duties of corporate officials and to penalize the violation thereof."[5] In this observer's view, nothing is further off base or potentially more inimical to the interests of corporate governance and therefore to the welfare of shareowners than this view of the derivative action.

> Lawyers and the legal profession often assign excessive credit to the value of lawsuits or the threat of lawsuit in shaping the conduct of society. No empirical evidence suggests that lawsuits or their threat have any major impact in keeping others in line. Would lawyers, for example, concede that their conduct is determined in any meaningful measure by the threat of malpractice actions, as distinguished from a

3. [By the Author] Dent, The Power of Directors to Terminate Shareholder Litigation: The Death of the Derivative Suit?, 75 Nw.U.L.Rev. 96 (1980).

4. [By the Author] Cohen v. Beneficial Indus. Loan Corp., 337 U.S. 541, 548, 69 S.Ct. 1221, 1226, 93 L.Ed. 1528 (1949).

5. [By the Author] Coffee & Schwartz, The Survival of the Derivative Suit: An Evaluation and a Proposal for Legislative Reform, 81 Colum.L.Rev. 261, 302 (1981).

culturally derived attitude to perform in a respectable and professional manner? Do lawyers put the interests of clients foremost simply to avoid war with the law or the particular client? The view that shareowner derivative actions should be used as the "principal means" for enforcing managerial fiduciary responsibilities reflects either a cynical view of human action or an uninformed perspective of how management works.

Those who manage or guide the management of corporate enterprises are, except in the aberrant case, dominantly driven by the desire to perform effective and superior wealth-producing roles, and to perform these in a culturally acceptable manner. They are not motivated toward proper and effective leadership by the kind of adversarial relationship or climate that shareowner challenges, especially lawsuits, precipitate. This is not to say that the threat of potential liability has not swayed management or board room actions; it doubtless has. The norm of board and management conduct, however, is to take action without transgressions of morality and ethics because the ethos and culture of the participants so demand. To believe that boards and managers consciously skirt close to the margin of illegality or moral turpitude to achieve private aggrandizement or gain competitive advantage is to indulge in fantasy. The real world seldom orders itself in that manner. Directors and managers of American enterprises are products of the same culture as are other professionals, including lawyers, judges, and law professors, and their integrity and sense of justice and injustice are no less finely tuned, nor more flawed in execution.

To the business manager, litigation is a nonproductive, highly expensive adversity to be suffered. Its cost is measured not only in dollars, but also in the injury it brings to organizational morale and the diversion it requires of management time and talent. In view of the discipline forfeited by American courts over the discovery process, it is an easy matter for opposing lawyers, through depositions, interrogatories, and subpoenas of documents, literally to tie in knots a target organization. What can be and is done through these tactics belies any rational justification. Filing lawsuits with little or no merit has become, it seems, a way of life with many lawyers, nurtured by a number of practices that managers see as pernicious in consequence. These include contingency fees, treble damage statutes, and discovery abuses. Another contributing factor, and perhaps the more significant, is the failure of our system to impose a penalty on claimants who are inspired by counsel to seek draconian relief when an appropriate remedy actually may be only a fraction of that prayed for, or nothing at all. The over-deposed, over-interrogated and over-discovered defendant, pursued by teams of lawyers, becomes victimized by the process, not by the effects of the allegedly wrongful conduct. Pragmatists as they are, managers reluctantly turn their attention to settlement, not to avoid adjudication of their alleged guilt, but to end the process and return their labors to the ongoing affairs of the entities they are charged to manage. Because the shareowner-plaintiff is not the recipient of what may be left in any such settlement after lawyers' fees, the real winner in these forays are not the shareowners, but the lawyers.

Mr. Deusenberg is General Counsel of Monsanto Company. There is relatively little empirical evidence one way or the other as to the value of modern derivative litigation. One study of some 531 derivative suits brought against 205 corporations between 1970 and 1978 produced these conclusions:

> From these aggregate figures, some revealing statistics emerge. Plaintiffs as a class obtained some relief—settlement, compliance, or favorable judgment—in 75.3% (262 of 348) of these suits. The vast majority of them, 74.7% (260 of 348), were resolved out of court through settlement or compliance. Of the 88 suits which were decided by the court in some manner, plaintiffs as a class prevailed in only two, a paltry 2.3%. Of the 15 judgments rendered, plaintiffs again prevailed in only two, a success rate of 13.3%.

Jones, An Empirical Examination of the Resolution of Shareholder Derivative and Class Action Lawsuits, 60 Bos.U.L.Rev. 542, 545. Further refinement of this data, however, reveals that in many of the "favorable" outcomes, no cash recovery was obtained but only a change in corporate procedures accompanied by the award of attorney's fees to the "successful" attorney. See generally Conard, Winnowing Derivative Suits Through Attorneys Fees, 47 Law & Contemp.Prob. 269 (Winter, 1984); Garth, Nagel and Plager, Empirical Research and the Shareholder Derivative Suit: Toward a Better–Informed Debate, 48 Law & Contemp.Prob. 137, 146–7 (Summer, 1985); Coffee, The Unfaithful Champion: The Plaintiff as Monitor in Shareholder Litigation, 48 Law & Contemp.Prob. 5, 26–33 (Summer, 1985). For an inconclusive attempt to assess empirically the value of derivative litigation based on movements of stock prices, see Fischel and Bradley, The Role of Liability Rules and the Derivative Suit in Corporate Law: A Theoretical and Empirical Analysis, 71 Corn.L.Rev. 261 (1986) and the comments on that study beginning on page 299.

(3) In a broad sense, the controversy over the role and value of derivative litigation in modern corporate governance has been the driving force behind important developments in corporation law during the 1980s: the development of litigation committees (see page 734, supra), the continued controversy over the American Law Institute's Corporate Governance Project, and the gradual decline of securities-for-expenses statutes discussed below.

(4) The security-for-expenses statute upheld in *Cohen* is really extraordinary legislation. Where else does a plaintiff with a small financial stake become responsible for a defendant's litigation expenses while a person with a larger financial interest does not? The amount of the required bond has often been set at a high amount—often in six figures—and its cost is prohibitive as a practical matter. The result of the statute has been to skew corporate derivative litigation. For example, since the statute is not applicable to federal claims e.g. under rule 10b–5, McClure v. Borne Chemical Co., 292 F.2d 824 (3d Cir.1961), cert. denied 368 U.S. 939, 82 S.Ct. 382, 7 L.Ed.2d 339, it has undoubtedly encouraged the growth of rule 10b–5 and the other areas of federal law that may relate to corporate management. It should

perhaps be added that under *Cohen*, security for expenses in federal courts may be applied to suits based on diversity of citizenship and to claims based on state law that are in federal court based on the principle of pendent jurisdiction. A second area of impact of these security-for-expenses statutes is on the distinction between direct claims [i.e. those based on a direct injury to the shareholder as such] and derivative ones [i.e. those based on an injury to the corporation which constitutes only an indirect injury to the shareholder]. Claims may sometimes be phrased so as to state a direct injury rather than a derivative one, and to the extent the security-for-expense statutes apply only to derivative claims, there is a strong incentive to frame the complaint so as to avoid the requirement. Finally, the statutes lead to considerable pre-hearing skirmishing. For example, a plaintiff subject to the statute may seek to obtain a shareholders' list in order to persuade other shareholders to intervene. See Stern v. South Chester Tube Co., 390 U.S. 606, 88 S.Ct. 1332, 20 L.Ed.2d 177 (1968). It appears to be established that if the other shareholders qualify as plaintiffs, their holdings may be tacked together and if the aggregate exceeds the statutory amount, the plaintiff need not comply with the statute. Kaufman v. Wolfson, 136 F.Supp. 939 (S.D.N.Y.1955).

(5) Consider RMBCA §§ 7.40–7.47. These sections, approved in 1989, replace an interim statute adopted in 1984. The most significant changes made in 1989 relate to the universal demand requirement of § 7.42 and the grounds for dismissal of a derivative proceeding in § 7.44. These sections are discussed in connection with the litigation committee issue. See page 767, supra.

(a) The 1984 interim statute did not include a security-for-expenses statute. This is noteworthy because it replaced a 1969 Model Act provision that did contain such a provision. The Official Comment to the 1984 interim statute explained this omission as follows:

> Earlier versions of the Model Act and the statutes of many states required a plaintiff to give security for reasonable expenses, including attorneys' fees, if his holdings of shares did not reach a specified size or value—five percent of the outstanding shares or a value of $25,000 in the earlier version of the Model Act. This requirement has been deleted. The security-for-expenses requirement, to the extent it was based on the size or value of the plaintiff's holdings rather than on the apparent good faith of his claim, was subject to criticism that it unreasonably discriminated against small shareholders.

> The basic policy question with respect to the requirement of a bond for small shareholders is how far to go in protecting the corporation and its officers and directors from suits. The choice is between making the right to sue widely available, without obstacles except in obviously baseless cases, or imposing obstacles in the way of the small shareholder without imposing a similar obstacle in the way of the large shareholder. Moreover, no bond requirement exists for class actions, antitrust cases, or individual actions for personal injury, all of which involve the corporation in substantial expense of defending against suit.

> Several states have concluded on the basis of these considerations that the bond requirement for small plaintiffs should be repealed or not adopted.

(b) Earlier versions of the Model Act (and the statutes of many states) required a plaintiff to be a "shareholder of record." Compare RMBCA § 7.40(2). Is this mild relaxation of the prerequisites for suit desirable? The Official Comment to § 7.40 states that "in the context of subchapter D, beneficial owner means a person having a direct economic interest in the shares.

(c) RMBCA § 7.41 also requires the plaintiff to be a shareholder "at the time of the act or omission complained of or become a shareholder through transfer by operation of law from one who was a shareholder at that time." This is usually referred to as the "contemporary ownership" requirement. Why should there be such a requirement at all? The Committee rejected a proposal, based generally on the California statute, that this requirement be relaxed to permit suit by a shareholder who acquired his security "before the earlier of the time when the material facts relating to the alleged wrong were publicly disclosed or were known by the holder." [This quoted language is not precisely in the form presented to the Committee on Corporate Laws.] Would that language be an improvement?

The Federal Rules of Civil Procedure, rule 23.1, also contain a contemporaneous ownership requirement. Is there any additional reason for such a requirement in federal diversity actions? See 7C C. Wright, A. Miller, and M. Kane, Federal Practice and Procedure: Civil 2d § 1828 (1986).

(d) Section 7.41(2) is similar to the language of Rule 23.1 of the Federal Rules of Civil Procedure except that Rule 23.1 refers to the interests of "shareholders similarly situated" rather than the "interests of the corporation." Is this difference in formulation significant from either a practical or theoretical standpoint?

(e) The 1984 interim statute required that a derivative complaint be verified but this requirement was omitted in the 1989 revision. In light of *Surowitz* would you recommend that such a requirement be retained?

(f) Consider RMBCA § 7.46. The Official Comment to this section states:

> Section 7.46(1) is intended to be a codification of existing case law. See, e.g., Mills v. Electric Auto-Lite Co., 396 U.S. 375 (1970). It provides that the court may order the corporation to pay the plaintiff's reasonable expenses (including counsel fees) if it finds that the proceeding has resulted in a substantial benefit to the corporation. The subsection requires that there be a "substantial" benefit to the corporation to prevent the plaintiff from proposing inconsequential changes in order to justify the payment of counsel fees. While the subsection does not specify the method for calculating attorneys' fees since there is a substantial body of court decisions delineating this issue, it does require that the expenses be reasonable which would include taking into account the amount or character of the benefit to the corporation.

> Section 7.46(2) provides that on termination of a proceeding the court may require the plaintiff to pay the defendants' reasonable expenses, including attorneys' fees, if it finds that the proceeding "was commenced or maintained without reasonable cause or for an improper purpose." The phrase "for an improper purpose" has been added to parallel Federal Rule of Civil Procedure 11 as recently amended in order to prevent proceedings which may be brought to harass the

corporation or its officers. The test in this section is similar to but not identical with the test utilized in section 13.31, relating to dissenters' rights, where the standard for award of expenses and attorneys' fees is that dissenters "acted arbitrarily, vexatiously or not in good faith" in demanding a judicial appraisal of their shares. The derivative action situation is sufficiently different from the dissenters' rights situation to justify a different and less onerous test for imposing costs on the plaintiff. The test of section 7.46 that the action was brought without reasonable cause or for an improper purpose is appropriate to deter strike suits, on the one hand, and on the other hand to protect plaintiffs whose suits have a reasonable foundation.

Section 7.46(3) has been added to deal with other abuses in the conduct of derivative litigation which may occur on the part of the defendants and their counsel as well as by the plaintiffs and their counsel. The section follows generally the provisions of Rule 11 of the Federal Rules of Civil Procedure. Section 7.46(3) will not be necessary in states which already have a counterpart to Rule 11.

(g) Consider RMBCA § 7.47. The Official Comment explains:

* * * [T]he distinction between what is procedural and what is substantive is not clear. See, e.g., Cohen v. Beneficial Indus. Loan Corp., 337 U.S. 541, 555–57 (1949). For example, in Susman v. Lincoln American Corp., 550 F.Supp. 442, 446 n.6 (N.D.Ill.1982), the court suggested that the standing requirement might be considered a federal procedural question under Federal Rule of Civil Procedure 23.1 and a matter of substantive law under the Delaware statute.

In view of the uncertainties created by these decisions, section 7.47 sets forth a choice of law provision for foreign corporations. It provides, subject to three exceptions, that the matters covered by the subchapter shall be governed by the laws of the jurisdiction of incorporation of the foreign corporation. In this respect, the section is similar to section 901 of the Revised Uniform Limited Partnership Act which provides that the laws of the state under which a foreign limited partnership is organized govern its organization and internal affairs.

The three exceptions to the general rule are areas which are traditionally part of the forum's oversight of the litigation process: section 7.43 dealing with the ability of the court to stay proceedings; section 7.45 setting forth the procedure for settling a proceeding; and section 7.46 providing for the assessment of reasonable expenses (including counsel fees) in certain situations.

(h) A few states require that a demand be made on shareholders as well as directors. See e.g. Wolgin v. Simon, 722 F.2d 389 (8th Cir.1983) [Missouri law]; Zimmerman v. Bell, 585 F.Supp. 512 (D.Md.1984) [Maryland law]. Most states, like RMBCA § 7.40 do not contain this requirement, which, if carried to its logical conclusion, might require a full-scale proxy solicitation before suit is filed. See generally D. DeMott, Shareholder—Derivative Actions: Law and Practice, § 5.02 (1987).

(6) How did Mrs. Surowitz fare after her preliminary trip to the United States Supreme Court to establish her right to serve as a champion for others and herself? The New York Times, Nov. 17, 1966, at 69, col. 6 reports

that the directors of Hilton settled, agreeing to pay $825,000 to the corporation over six and one half years. The directors did not admit wrongdoing, and the corporation stated to its shareholders that the suit was "without merit" but was settled to avoid the expenses and burden of litigation.

B. PROCEDURAL PROBLEMS

SCHIFF v. METZNER

United States Court of Appeals, Second Circuit, 1964.
331 F.2d 963.

SWAN, CIRCUIT JUDGE.

Almost immediately after the decision in United States v. E.I. du Pont de Nemours & Co., 353 U.S. 586, 77 S.Ct. 872, 1 L.Ed.2d 1057 (June 3, 1957) holding that du Pont's ownership of stock in General Motors Corporation was a violation of Section 7 of the Clayton Act, four derivative actions were brought by shareholders of General Motors to recover on its behalf damages caused it by du Pont's violation of the anti-trust laws. In February 1958, on motion of the defendants, three of the derivative actions (the fourth having been dismissed) were consolidated under the title Rita Gottesman et al. v. General Motors Corporation and E.I. du Pont de Nemours & Co. In the Gottesman case Judge Weinfeld entered an order on July 3, 1958 restraining all stockholders of General Motors from prosecuting any derivative action except Gottesman. On October 6, 1959 the consolidated Gottesman action was assigned to Judge Metzner for all purposes.

On February 25, 1963 Margot B. Schiff, Individually and as Executrix of the Estate of Herbert Schiff, deceased, filed a derivative action as owner of General Motors stock. This action was assigned to Judge Metzner on March 6, 1963, the plaintiff consenting thereto. The Schiff action raises substantially the same issues of law and of fact that are presented in the consolidated Gottesman action. In that action Judge Metzner has ruled that the earliest date for which damages are recoverable is May 4, 1950. In Schiff plaintiff claims that her holding of General Motors stock can be traced back to prior to November 25, 1936.

The order of July 15, 1963 which the petition for mandamus seeks to have vacated provides that the time of the defendants General Motors and du Pont to move or answer with respect to the Schiff complaint "is extended to and including a day thirty (30) days following termination of the stay provided for in paragraph 9 of the order of" Judge Weinfeld dated July 3, 1958 in the Gottesman case, and that "the application for modification of the provisions of said paragraph 9" is denied. It is obvious that denial of Schiff's application for modification of the stay ordered by Judge Weinfeld involved the exercise of discretion by Judge Metzner.

While the motion for modification was pending, and before its decision, Schiff also moved to consolidate her derivative action with the

Gottesman action. This motion was also denied. This, too, involved the exercise of discretion by Judge Metzner.

The Supreme Court definitely recognized in Landis v. North American Co., 299 U.S. 248, 254, 57 S.Ct. 163, 166, 81 L.Ed. 153 that "[t]he power to stay proceedings is incidental to the power inherent in every court to control the disposition of the causes on its docket with economy of time and effort for itself, for counsel, and for litigants." See also Mottolese v. Kaufman, 2 Cir., 176 F.2d 301. No type of case is more appropriate for "economy" than derivative suits by stockholders. Schiff's action is the seventh proceeding in the court below to raise the issues being litigated in the Gottesman case. Her suit was started nearly six years after Gottesman and was stayed for five years by Judge Weinfeld's order without protest by her. Trial preparation of the Gottesman case was well under way long before her action was filed. Both actions have been assigned to Judge Metzner for all purposes.

The orders Schiff seeks to have vacated will not deprive her of her day in court. Decision of the common issues in Gottesman will simplify the issues to be tried in the Schiff case and will promote "economy" of effort for all concerned. Under the circumstances there was no abuse of discretion in denying her motions. Consequently we hold that her application for a writ of mandamus is unjustified and deny it.

Notes

(1) In most derivative litigation there are large numbers of potential plaintiff-shareholders, and often suit is instituted by several of them in different courts, state or federal. If, as in the principal case, all the suits are filed in federal courts, consolidation may be practical. Where litigation is pending in both federal and state courts, one or more courts may be persuaded to grant a stay so as to permit the other suit to proceed. In making a decision whether to consolidate or grant a stay, courts have to have some kind of criteria. Who should be permitted to proceed? The one who filed first? All of them? The one with the most competent attorney? The one which has been filed in the Court with the broadest discovery rights? The one that is in a court that does not have a securities-for-expenses statute? See generally, 7C C. Wright, A. Miller, and M. Kane, Federal Practice and Procedure: Civil 2d § 1838 (1986).

(2) Is there any problem with the res judicata effect of a final decision? If the corporation is bound, does not that mean that no other shareholder can attack the decision, at least on a derivative basis? See generally 7C C. Wright, A. Miller, and M. Kane, supra, § 1840.

ROSS v. BERNHARD

Supreme Court of the United States, 1970.
396 U.S. 531, 90 S.Ct. 733, 24 L.Ed.2d 729.

MR. JUSTICE WHITE delivered the opinion of the Court.

The Seventh Amendment to the Constitution provides that in "[s]uits at common law, where the value in controversy shall exceed twenty dollars, the right of trial by jury shall be preserved." Whether the Amendment guarantees the right to a jury trial in stockholders' derivative actions is the issue now before us.

Petitioners brought this derivative suit in federal court against the directors of their closed-end investment company, the Lehman Corporation and the corporation's brokers, Lehman Brothers. They contended that Lehman Brothers controlled the corporation through an illegally large representation on the corporation's board of directors, in violation of the Investment Company Act of 1940, and used this control to extract excessive brokerage fees from the corporation. The directors of the corporation were accused of converting corporate assets and of "gross abuse of trust, gross misconduct, willful misfeasance, bad faith, [and] gross negligence." Both the individual defendants and Lehman Brothers were accused of breaches of fiduciary duty. It was alleged that the payments to Lehman Brothers constituted waste and spoliation, and that the contract between the corporation and Lehman Brothers had been violated. Petitioners requested that the defendants "account for and pay to the Corporation for their profits and gains and its losses." Petitioners also demanded a jury trial on the corporation's claims.

On motion to strike petitioners' jury trial demand, the District Court held that a shareholder's right to a jury on his corporation's cause of action was to be judged as if the corporation were itself the plaintiff. Only the shareholder's initial claim to speak for the corporation had to be tried to the judge. 275 F.Supp. 569. * * * The Court of Appeals reversed, holding that a derivative action was entirely equitable in nature, and no jury was available to try any part of it. 403 F.2d 909. * * *

We reverse the holding of the Court of Appeals that in no event does the right to a jury trial preserved by the Seventh Amendment extend to derivative actions brought by the stockholders of a corporation. We hold that the right to jury trial attaches to those issues in derivative actions as to which the corporation, if it had been suing in its own right, would have been entitled to a jury. * * *

The common law refused * * * to permit stockholders to call corporate managers to account in actions at law. The possibilities for abuse, thus presented, were not ignored by corporate officers and directors. Early in the 19th century, equity provided relief both in this country and in England. Without detailing these developments, it suffices to say that the remedy in this country, first dealt with by this Court in Dodge v. Woolsey, 18 How. 331, 15 L.Ed. 401 (1856), provided redress not only against faithless officers and directors but also against third parties who had damaged or threatened the corporate properties and whom the corporation through its managers refused to pursue. The remedy made available in equity was the derivative suit, viewed in this country as a suit to enforce a *corporate* cause of action against officers, directors, and third parties. As elaborated in the cases, one precondition for the suit was a valid claim on which the corporation could have sued; another was that the corporation itself had refused to proceed after suitable demand, unless excused by extraordinary conditions. Thus the dual nature of the stockholder's action: first, the plaintiff's right to sue on behalf of the corporation and, second, the merits of the corporation claim itself.

Derivative suits posed no Seventh Amendment problems where the action against the directors and third parties would have been by a bill in equity had the corporation brought the suit. Our concern is with cases based upon a legal claim of the corporation against directors or third parties. Does the trial of such claims at the suit of a stockholder and without a jury violate the Seventh Amendment?

* * * [L]egal claims are not magically converted into equitable issues by their presentation to a court of equity in a derivative suit. The claim pressed by the stockholder against directors or third parties "is not his own but the corporation's." Koster v. Lumbermens Mut. Cas. Co., 330 U.S. 518, 522, 67 S.Ct. 828, 831 (1947). The corporation is a necessary party to the action; without it the case cannot proceed. Although named a defendant, it is the real party in interest, the stockholder being at best the nominal plaintiff. The proceeds of the action belong to the corporation and it is bound by the result of the suit. The heart of the action is the corporate claim. If it presents a legal issue, one entitling the corporation to a jury trial under the Seventh Amendment, the right to a jury is not forfeited merely because the stockholder's right to sue must first be adjudicated as an equitable issue triable to the court. * * *

Derivative suits have been described as one kind of "true" class action. We are inclined to agree with the description, at least to the extent it recognizes that the derivative suit and the class action were both ways of allowing parties to be heard in equity who could not speak at law. 3B J. Moore, Federal Practice ¶¶ 23.02[1], 23.1.16[1] (2d ed. 1969). After adoption of the rules there is no longer any procedural obstacle to the assertion of legal rights before juries, however the party may have acquired standing to assert those rights. Given the availability in a derivative action of both legal and equitable remedies, we think the Seventh Amendment preserves to the parties in a stockholder's suit the same right to a jury trial that historically belonged to the corporation and to those against whom the corporation pressed its legal claims.

In the instant case we have no doubt that the corporation's claim is, at least in part, a legal one. The relief sought is money damages. There are allegations in the complaint of a breach of fiduciary duty, but there are also allegations of ordinary breach of contract and gross negligence. The corporation, had it sued on its own behalf, would have been entitled to a jury's determination, at a minimum, of its damages against its broker under the brokerage contract and of its rights against its own directors because of their negligence. Under these circumstances it is unnecessary to decide whether the corporation's other claims are also properly triable to a jury. The decision of the Court of Appeals is reversed.

It is so ordered.

MR. JUSTICE STEWART, with whom THE CHIEF JUSTICE and MR. JUSTICE HARLAN join, dissenting.

In holding as it does that the plaintiff in a shareholder's derivative suit is constitutionally entitled to a jury trial, the Court today seems to rely upon some sort of ill-defined combination of the Seventh Amendment and the Federal Rules of Civil Procedure. Somehow the Amendment and the Rules magically interact to do what each separately was expressly intended not to do, namely, to enlarge the right to a jury trial in civil actions brought in the courts of the United States. * * *

The Court begins by assuming the "dual nature" of the shareholder's action. While the plaintiff's right to get into court at all is conceded to be equitable, once he is there the Court says his claim is to be viewed as though it were the claim of the corporation itself. If the corporation would have been entitled to a jury trial on such a claim, then, it is said, so would the shareholder. This conceptualization is without any historical basis. For the fact is that a shareholder's suit was not originally viewed in this country, or in England, as a suit to enforce a *corporate* cause of action. Rather, the shareholder's suit was initially permitted only against the managers of the corporation—not third parties—and it was conceived of as an equitable action to enforce the right of a beneficiary against his trustee. The shareholder was not, therefore, in court to enforce indirectly the corporate right of action, but to enforce directly his own equitable right of action against an unfaithful fiduciary. Later the rights of the shareholder were enlarged to encompass suits against third parties harming the corporation, but "the postulated 'corporate cause of action' has never been thought to describe an actual historical class of suit which was recognized by courts of law." Indeed the commentators, including those cited by the Court as postulating the analytic duality of the shareholder's derivative suit, recognize that historically the suit has in practice always been treated as a single cause tried exclusively in equity. They agree that there is therefore no constitutional right to a jury trial even where there might have been one had the corporation itself brought the suit. * * *

If history is to be so cavalierly dismissed, the derivative suit can, of course, be artificially broken down into separable elements. But so then can any traditionally equitable cause of action, and the logic of the Court's position would lead to the virtual elimination of all equity jurisdiction. An equitable suit for an injunction for instance, often involves issues of fact which, if damages had been sought, would have been triable to a jury. Does this mean that in a suit asking only for injunctive relief these factual issues *must* be tried to the jury, with the judge left to decide only whether, given the jury's findings, an injunction is the appropriate remedy? Certainly the Federal Rules make it *possible* to try a suit for an injunction in that way, but even more certainly they were not intended to have any such effect. Yet the Court's approach, it seems, would require that if any "legal issue" procedurally *could* be tried to a jury, it constitutionally *must* be tried to a jury.

The fact is, of course, that there are, for the most part, no such things as inherently "legal issues" or inherently "equitable issues." There are only factual issues, and, "like chameleons [they] take their color from surrounding circumstances." Thus the Court's "nature of the issue" approach is hardly meaningful.

As a final ground for its conclusion, the Court points to a supposed analogy to suits involving class actions. It says that before the Federal Rules such suits were considered equitable and not triable to a jury, but that since promulgation of the Rules the federal courts have found that "plaintiffs may obtain a jury trial on any legal issues they present." Of course the plaintiff *may* obtain such a trial even in a derivative suit. Nothing in the Constitution or the Rules precludes the judge from granting a jury trial as a matter of discretion. But even if the Court means that some federal courts have ruled that the class action plaintiff in some situations has a constitutional right to a jury trial, the analogy to derivative suits is wholly unpersuasive. For it is clear that the draftsmen of the Federal Rules intended that Rule [23.1] as it pertained to class actions should be applicable, like other rules governing joinder of claims and parties, "to all actions, whether formerly denominated legal or equitable." This does not mean that a formerly equitable action is triable to a jury simply *because* it is brought on behalf of a class, but only that a historically legal cause of action can be tried to a jury *even if* it is brought as a class action. Since a derivative suit is historically wholly a creation of equity, the class action "analogy" is in truth no analogy at all.

The Court's decision today can perhaps be explained as a reflection of an unarticulated but apparently overpowering bias in favor of jury trials in civil actions. It certainly cannot be explained in terms of either the Federal Rules or the Constitution.

Note

Based on your consideration of a rather large number of cases involving actual or possible derivative litigation, do you think the conclusion is correct as a matter of efficient judicial administration? In other words, are the issues in such cases of the general type on which the use of a jury seems desirable? See generally, 7C C. Wright, A. Miller, and M. Kane, Federal Practice and Procedure: Civil 2d § 1837 (1986).

CANNON v. U.S. ACOUSTICS CORP.

United States District Court of Illinois, 1975.
398 F.Supp. 209.

MARSHALL, DISTRICT JUDGE.

Charles B. Cannon, Richard L. Davis, John G. Marsh, and Jeffrey Ross brought this derivative shareholder's action, as well as personal claims, against the defendants, U.S. Acoustics Corporation (hereinafter "Acoustics"), a Florida corporation, and National Perlite Products, S.A., (hereinafter "Perlite"), a Panamanian corporation. The six-count complaint alleges violations of the Securities Exchange Act of 1934, and the common and statutory laws of Florida and Illinois. * * *

There are pending for decision cross-motions to disqualify counsel and a motion to disqualify Cannon as a party plaintiff. Shortly after Robert J. Gareis, Peter J. Mone and the firm of Baker & McKenzie filed their appearances on behalf of the corporate and individual defendants, plaintiffs moved to disqualify them from representing the corporate defendants and requested that the court appoint independent counsel. Plaintiffs base their motion on the theory that dual representation in a shareholder derivative suit creates a conflict of interest that the court can order terminated.

Concomitant with filing their answer to the plaintiffs' motion, defendants moved to strike Cannon as a party plaintiff. * * *

Defendants argue that by virtue of Canon 4 of the American Bar Association's Code of Professional Responsibility (hereinafter "CPR"), Cannon (who is a lawyer), and the lawyers and law firm which represent him, cannot maintain the pending suit because each previously represented the corporate defendants in legal matters that are substantially related to the present litigation.

I. PLAINTIFFS' MOTION TO STRIKE THE APPEARANCE OF THE ATTORNEYS ON BEHALF OF THE CORPORATE DEFENDANTS

Plaintiffs' motion to disqualify the lawyers from the firm of Baker & McKenzie from representing the corporate defendants raises fundamental questions of legal ethics and the extent to which a court should interfere with the right of any litigant to be represented by counsel of his own choosing. Furthermore, a motion to disqualify calls to question not only the probity of the individual lawyer, but the legal profession as a whole. Mindful of these problems and considerations we have reached the conclusion that independent counsel must be selected for the defendant corporations. * * *

[T]he anomalous position of the corporation in a derivative suit is that it is both a defendant and a plaintiff. An examination of plaintiffs' complaint amply reveals this position. Count 1 alleges that beginning in 1968 and continuing to the present, the individual defendants committed numerous violations of Rule 10b–5: illegal stock options were allegedly granted, stock was issued and purchased upon false representations that the stock was for services, rent, and other expenses, stock was issued for little or no consideration, corporate opportunities were usurped, illegal profits were retained by certain officers and directors, and illegal and excessive compensation was paid to Stedman.

The remaining derivative counts allege the same misconduct but seek recovery under Section 16(b) of the Securities Exchange Act of 1934, and the common law of Florida and Illinois.

Even a cursory examination of the foregoing allegations demonstrates that should they be established at trial, Acoustics and Perlite will benefit substantially. For this reason plaintiffs argue that Mone, Gareis, and the firm of Baker & McKenzie cannot represent the alleged wrongdoers and the ultimate beneficiaries of any judgment that might be obtained.

Defendants' position is that although there is a theoretical conflict of interest, no real conflict exists. They argue that the corporations are really inactive participants in the lawsuit, and that should any conflict arise they will withdraw their representation of the individual defendants and continue their representation of the corporations. Defendants further argue that their present position is that all the transactions complained of are legal and should be upheld. * * *

When a single lawyer or law firm undertakes to represent both the individual and corporate defendants in a derivative action, at least two potential ethical problems arise. First, there exists, as previously discussed, a potential conflict of interest between the individual and corporate defendants, and second, there is the threat that confidences and secrets obtained from each client may be jeopardized because of the dual nature of the representation. The CPR addresses each of these problems in varying degrees of particularity. No code of ethics could establish unalterable rules governing all possible eventualities. Ultimately, therefore, the resolution of these problems rests in the reasoned discretion of the court. * * *

In the instant case Gareis, Mone and their firm represent two clients with, at a minimum, potentially conflicting interests. The pleadings charge the individual defendants with serious corporate misconduct, and although counsel has in good faith represented there is no present conflict between the two sets of defendants, the subtle influences emanating from the representation of the individual defendants that might lead counsel to reach this position on behalf of the corporations are troubling.

Fortunately there are several other ethical considerations that deal more specifically with multiple clients. * * * [T]hese two ethical considerations convincingly establish that in a derivative suit the better course is for the corporation to be represented by independent counsel from the outset, even though counsel believes in good faith that no conflict of interest exists. * * *

The Canons and Ethical Considerations are aspirational; consequently, they provide only guidance. Thus, while the CPR supports plaintiffs' position, a study of the relevant case law is necessary.

Although there is not a wealth of cases dealing with the problem of dual representation in derivative shareholder's suits, the position of the federal courts has developed along two lines. The older cases have refused to disqualify counsel, while the more recent trend is to require the corporation to obtain independent counsel. This trend has also manifested itself in a number of cases under the Labor–Management Reporting and Disclosure Act, 29 U.S.C.A. § 501 et seq. (1970).

* * * [T]he appropriate course * * * is for the corporation to retain independent counsel. Under this procedure, once counsel has examined the evidence, a decision can be made regarding the role the corporation will play in the litigation. This decision will be made without the possibility of any influence emanating from the representation of the individual defendants, and will also eliminate the potential problem of confidences and secrets reposed by the individual defendants being used adverse to their interests by former counsel should new counsel have had to have been selected under the approach suggested by defense counsel. This solution, concededly, is not without its disabilities. The corporations' rights to counsel of their choice are infringed and in a closely held corporation, as here, the financial burden is increased. Nevertheless, on balance, the corporations must obtain independent counsel.

Two questions remain. The first is how new counsel should be selected. Plaintiffs urge the court to make the selection because the individual defendants still serve as the board of directors and thus will make the selection unless prevented from doing so. There is no precedent in the reported decisions to support plaintiffs' suggestion. * * *

The defendant corporations may select their own counsel. Certainly new counsel will recognize their duty to represent solely the interests of the corporate entities. And should difficulties arise, the parties or counsel may apply to the court for additional relief.

The final question is whether the corporations' answer should be stricken and new pleadings filed. * * *

In accord with the foregoing, plaintiffs' motion to strike the appearance of Gareis, Mone and the firm of Baker & McKenzie as counsel for defendants Acoustics and Perlite, is granted, and the answer of these defendants is stricken with leave to new counsel to answer anew within 20 days.

II. Defendant's Motion to Strike the Appearance of Plaintiffs' Attorneys and to Disqualify Charles B. Cannon as a Plaintiff

* * * Although the record does not justify the disqualification of plaintiffs' counsel either for impropriety or the appearance thereof, Cannon, who is a lawyer, must be disqualified as a party plaintiff.

In support of their motion to disqualify Cannon, defendants have submitted documentary evidence which is so voluminous that it compels the conclusion that Cannon must have acquired information in the past representation of the corporations and their officers that he now seeks to use to his advantage and to their detriment. Stedman's affidavit reveals that Cannon performed a multitude of legal matters for the two corporations and the individual defendants acting on their behalf, during the years 1961–1973. * * *

Although the previously discussed case law related to disqualifying attorneys, the same rules and canons apply to counsel turned litigant. In the leading case of Richardson v. Hamilton International Corp., 469 F.2d 1382 (3d Cir.1972), cert. denied 411 U.S. 986, 93 S.Ct. 2271, 36 L.Ed.2d 964 (1973), the court affirmed a district court order (333 F.Supp. 1049 (E.D.Pa.1971)) disqualifying a plaintiff from maintaining a derivative shareholder's suit and class action against Alexander Hamilton Life Insurance Company of America, its directors, officers and parent corporation. The complaint alleged various securities violations in connection with a merger of the parent and subsidiary. Reviewing the record, the court found that the plaintiff, while an associate with the firm retained to represent Hamilton, spent a considerable time interviewing defendants and examining their personal files, as well as the files of Hamilton.

> Although the exact nature of the information received is unknown, it is known that he had access to confidential information about Hamilton Life's finances, corporate structure and operations, which he would not have received had he not been its attorney. 469 F.2d at 1385.

In affirming the district court order, the court also observed that direct evidence that the previous representation is related to the present suit is not needed. * * * [T]he court held that defendants need only show Richardson might have acquired substantially related information. 469 F.2d at 1385.

In the instant case the record requires that Cannon be disqualified as a plaintiff. He represented defendants for 12 years, five of which he was their sole counsel. There is no question that in the course of that former representation he might have acquired information which is substantially related to the pending suit. * * *

Notes

(1) The Seventh Circuit affirmed the portions of the District Court's opinion set forth above. Cannon v. U.S. Acoustics Corp., 532 F.2d 1118 (7th Cir.1976).

(2) Rule 1.7 of the Model Rules of Professional Conduct, dealing with multiple representation of clients is quoted at page 135 supra.

RULE 1.9 CONFLICT OF INTEREST: FORMER CLIENT

MODEL RULES OF PROFESSIONAL CONDUCT *
(1989)

(a) A lawyer who has formerly represented a client in a matter shall not thereafter represent another person in the same or a substantially related matter in which that person's interests are materially adverse to the interests of the former client unless the former client consents after consultation.

(b) A lawyer shall not knowingly represent a person in the same or a substantially related matter in which a firm with which the lawyer formerly was associated had previously represented a client,

(1) whose interests are materially adverse to that person; and

(2) about whom the lawyer had acquired information protected by Rules 1.6 and 1.9(c) that is material to the matter;

unless the former client consents after consultation.

(c) A lawyer who has formerly represented a client in a matter or whose present or former firm has formerly represented a client in a matter shall not thereafter:

(1) use information relating to the representation to the disadvantage of the former client except as Rule 1.6 or Rule 3.3 would permit or require with respect to a client, or when the information has become generally known; or

(2) reveal information relating to the representation except as Rule 1.6 or Rule 3.3 would permit or require with respect to a client.

C. INDIVIDUAL RECOVERY OF DAMAGES

GLENN v. HOTELTRON SYSTEMS

Court of Appeals of New York, 1989.
74 N.Y.2d 386, 547 N.Y.S.2d 816, 547 N.E.2d 71.

WACHTLER, CHIEF JUDGE.

* * * The dispute here is between Jacob Schachter and Herbert Kulik, the founders of Ketek Electric Corporation. Schachter and Kulik each own 50% of the corporation's shares and serve as the corporation's only officers. The circumstances underlying the dispute are set forth in detail in the Appellate Division memorandum in an earlier appeal in this matter (Schachter v. Kulik, 96 A.D.2d 1038, 466 N.Y.S.2d 444, appeal dismissed 61 N.Y.2d 758, 472 N.Y.S.2d 1030, 460 N.E.2d 1363) and need not be repeated here. It is sufficient to note that, although Supreme Court initially determined after trial that neither Schachter nor Kulik had proved a breach of duty by the other,

the Appellate Division, on the prior appeal, found Schachter liable for diverting Ketek assets and opportunities to Hoteltron Systems, Inc., a corporation wholly owned by Schachter.

Following the trial on damages, Supreme Court concluded that Hoteltron had earned profits of $362,242.84 from Schachter's usurpation of Ketek assets and opportunities. Of this total, $5,000 was used by Schachter to pay legal expenses in connection with this litigation and the balance was withdrawn from the corporation for his personal use. * * * Supreme Court ordered that these principal sums, together with nearly $54,000 in legal expenses and attorneys' fees incurred by Kulik, be paid by Schachter and that the entire award, after payment of attorneys' fees, should be paid to Kulik.

On Schachter's appeal, the Appellate Division modified the judgment in several respects. * * * In addition, the court concluded that the Hoteltron profits should be awarded to the injured corporation, Ketek, rather than the innocent shareholder Kulik, and that legal expenses and attorneys' fees should be paid by Ketek Corp. out of this award, rather than by Schachter (Glenn v. Hoteltron Sys., 138 A.D.2d 568, 526 N.Y.S.2d 149).

The parties cross-appeal, pursuant to leave granted by this court. We affirm. * * *

It is the general rule that, because a shareholders' derivative suit seeks to vindicate a wrong done to the corporation through enforcement of a corporate cause of action, any recovery obtained is for the benefit of the injured corporation (see, Business Corporation Law § 626[e]; Wolff v. Wolff, 67 N.Y.2d 638, 499 N.Y.S.2d 665, 490 N.E.2d 532; Clarke v. Greenberg, 296 N.Y. 146, 149, 71 N.E.2d 443). Where, however, the plaintiff sues in an individual capacity to recover damages resulting in harm, not to the corporation, but to individual shareholders, the suit is personal, not derivative, and it is appropriate for damages to be awarded directly to those shareholders (see, Sautter v. Fulmer, 258 N.Y. 107, 179 N.E. 310; Norte & Co. v. Huffines, 416 F.2d 1189 (2d Cir.) [explaining Perlman v. Feldmann, 219 F.2d 173 (2d Cir.)].

In this case, the diversion of Ketek's corporate assets by Schachter for his own profit resulted in a corporate injury because it deprived Ketek of those profits (see, Abrams v. Donati, 66 N.Y.2d 951, 498 N.Y.S.2d 782, 489 N.E.2d 751). Kulik, the innocent shareholder, was injured only to the extent that he was entitled to share in those profits. His injury was real, but it was derivative, not direct. Thus, the Appellate Division properly ruled that those profits should be returned to Ketek Corp.

Kulik argues that this result is inequitable because Schachter, as a shareholder of Ketek, will ultimately share in the proceeds of the damage award. But that prospect exists in any successful derivative action in which the wrongdoer is a shareholder of the injured corporation. An exception based on that fact alone would effectively nullify the general rule that damages for a corporate injury should be awarded to the corporation.

It is true that this anomaly is magnified in cases involving closely held corporations, because the errant fiduciary is likely to own a large share of the corporation—as Schachter owns 50% of Ketek—and will share proportionately in the restitution to the corporation generated by a successful suit against him. Thus, it may be argued that in such circumstances an award of damages to the corporation does not provide a sufficient deterrent to the potential wrongdoer. We conclude, however, that this consideration does not require a different damage rule for close corporations.

While awarding damages directly to the innocent shareholder may seem equitable with respect to the parties before the court, other interests, particularly those of the corporation's creditors, should not be overlooked. The fruits of a diverted corporate opportunity are properly a corporate asset. Awarding that asset directly to a shareholder could impair the rights of creditors whose claims may be superior to that of the innocent shareholder (see, Note, Individual Pro Rata Recovery in Stockholders' Derivative Suits, 69 Harv.L.Rev. 1314, 1318).

Thus, while we do not rule out the possibility that an award to innocent shareholders rather than to the corporation would be appropriate in some circumstances, we find no need to invoke such an exception here.

ATTORNEYS' FEES

The rule in New York remains that "attorneys' fees and disbursements are incidents of litigation and the prevailing party may not collect them from the loser unless an award is authorized by agreement between the parties or by statute or court rule." Although Business Corporation Law § 626(e) provides that a successful plaintiff in a shareholders' derivative action may recoup legal expenses and attorneys' fees from the proceeds of a judgment, compromise or settlement in favor of the corporation, it does not authorize the imposition of such expenses on the losing party.

The basis for an award of attorneys' fees in a shareholders' derivative suit is to reimburse the plaintiff for expenses incurred on the corporation's behalf. Those costs should be paid by the corporation, which has benefited from the plaintiff's efforts and which would have borne the costs had it sued in its own right. Thus, the Appellate Division was correct in modifying Supreme Court's judgment to provide for the payment of Kulik's legal expenses out of the award to Ketek Corp. rather than by Schachter. * * *

Accordingly, the order of the Appellate Division should be affirmed, without costs.

Notes

(1) Despite the "general rule" set forth in this case, several cases permit pro-rata recovery in derivative suits. The leading case is Perlman v. Feldman, page 1090, supra. The ALI's Corporate Governance Project lists nine such cases, and summarizes their holdings as follows:

In general, when a substantial portion of the shares are held either by persons who had aided or abetted the defendants to commit the fiduciary breach or by non-contemporaneous holders who had suffered no injury because they had bought their shares at a price reflecting the injury done to the corporation, the case for a pro-rata recovery in favor of the other eligible shareholders will be strongest. However, it should not be assumed that pro-rata recovery should be granted merely because persons who committed or aided the breach remain as shareholders. A corporate recovery in such an instance does not mean that the defendants will receive unjust enrichment. To the contrary, proration of a partial recovery among other shareholders reduces the damages defendants must pay and thereby minimizes both the sanction against them and the amount of compensation that will benefit creditors and others affected by an injury to the corporation. That defendants continue as shareholders is, however, highly relevant if the court determines that there is a possibility that defendants will divert the recovery. This possibility will be greatest when the defendants remain in control of the corporation.

Another instance in which a pro-rata recovery is justified arises when shareholders who were earlier injured by a wrong for which they have not been adequately compensated have been eliminated as the result of a fundamental corporate change. In these circumstances, a derivative action is a more practical means by which to address such a wrong than is the appraisal remedy, because the appraisal remedy grants relief only against the corporation (and thus indirectly against its current shareholders) rather than against the alleged wrongdoer.

* * *

ALI Corporate Governance Project, Tent. Draft No. 8, 236–7 (1988).*

(2) The American Law Institute's Corporate Governance Project generalizes these cases as follows:

(d) If a corporation is closely held, the court may in its discretion treat an action raising derivative claims as a direct action, exempt it from those restrictions and defenses applicable only to derivative actions, and direct an individual recovery, if it finds that to do so will not (i) unfairly expose the corporation or the defendants to a multiplicity of actions, (ii) materially prejudice the interests of creditors in the corporation, or (iii) interfere with a fair distribution of the recovery among all interested persons.

American Law Institute, Corporate Governance Project, § 7.01(d) (Tent. Draft No. 6, 1986). See also Crosby v. Bream, 47 Ohio St.3d 105, 548 N.E.2d 217 (1989).

D. SETTLEMENT AND DISMISSAL

See RMBCA § 7.45. Rule 23.1 of the Federal Rules of Civil Procedure similarly provides that an action may not be "dismissed or compromised" without the approval of the court and notice of the proposed dismissal or compromise must be given the shareholders "in such manner as the court directs."

WOLF v. BARKES

United States Court of Appeals, Second Circuit, 1965.
348 F.2d 994, certiorari denied, 382 U.S. 941, 86 S.Ct. 395, 15 L.Ed.2d 351.

FRIENDLY, CIRCUIT JUDGE:

Appellant's contention is that the pendency in a federal court of a stockholder's derivative action challenging arrangements between a corporation and its officers deprives the corporation and officers of power to make any out-of-court settlement—that is, one not requiring action by the court in the derivative suit—and that once the suit has been brought, there must be notice to stockholders and court approval as provided in F.R.Civ.P. [23.1], even though the settlement itself calls for no judicial action. Although the contention is interesting and by no means without force, we think the rule does not go that far.

In May, 1964, plaintiff Miriam J. Wolf, a stockholder of Curtis Publishing Company, brought an action in the District Court for the Southern District of New York against the Company and various individuals, who were said to have been directors, officers, or both, at relevant dates. In support of federal jurisdiction the complaint alleged violation of § 14(a) of the Securities Exchange Act, see § 27; and the doctrine of pendent jurisdiction was relied upon to bring further alleged wrongdoing before the district court. The complaint alleged, *inter alia,* that in 1962 Curtis had employed defendants Culligan and Clifford, Culligan being elected President and Clifford Executive Vice President; that their employment agreements contained common stock options which (save for 15,500 shares in Culligan's case) were contingent upon approval of an increase in Curtis' authorized common stock; that the proxy statement for the 1963 annual meeting of stockholders, at which the management sought approval for such an increase primarily to meet the requirements of these contracts and of a general Restricted Stock Option Incentive Plan, was false and misleading in various respects; that the proposal to increase the authorized common stock did not receive a two-thirds vote of the prior preferred stock although this was required; that ratification of the Restricted Stock Option Incentive Plan was unlawfully obtained because of the lack of separate approval of the additional common stock by the prior preferred; that the grant of stock options to Culligan and Clifford and to the defendant Kantor was wrongful in other respects; that an increase in Culligan's salary agreed to in 1963 constituted a waste of corporate assets; and that the proxy statement had concealed facts the defendants knew or should have known as to the value of mineral rights in Canadian timberlands owned by a subsidiary of Curtis which would result in an increase in the value of Curtis' stock unrelated to any efforts of Culligan, Clifford or other recipients of stock options. Demand upon the directors to sue was alleged to be futile because of their participation in the transactions complained of and their consequent liability; demand upon the stockholders was claimed to be unnecessary and futile. The complaint prayed that the actions taken at the 1963 annual meeting be annulled; that Culligan's, Clifford's and Kantor's stock options be cancelled; that the Restricted Stock Option Incentive Plan and all options thereunder be rescinded; that holders of options surrender any stock obtained by the exercise of options and account for any profits; and that the directors be held liable for any damage suffered by Curtis as a result of the acts alleged.

Various extensions of the time to answer were obtained. The stipulation covering the period from November 3 to November 16, 1964, was given after Curtis promised plaintiff's attorneys not to enter into any agreements with executives or employees settling claims under any of the employment agreements referred to in the complaint. When Curtis and other defendants refused to renew this undertaking and a newspaper article indicated that Curtis was about to make settlements with four defendant-employees who had resigned, plaintiff moved for an order enjoining any compromise or settlement of claims in favor of Curtis asserted in the complaint save with the approval of the district court on notice to all stockholders, as provided in F.R.Civ.P. [23.1]. Judge Palmieri denied the motion without opinion, and plaintiff appeals. * * * There can be little doubt that if we look only at the letter of the rule, it does not apply. No one has sought to dismiss or compromise the class suit. If we go behind the letter to the prime "mischief and defect" the rule was intended to prevent, to wit, "private settlements under which the plaintiff stockholder and his attorney got the sum paid in settlement, and the corporation got nothing," Craftsman Finance & Mortgage Co. v. Brown, 64 F.Supp. 168, 178 (S.D.N.Y. 1945), the instant case likewise is not within it. But plaintiff insists it to be anomalous that although she could not compromise the suit without complying with rule [23.1], the corporation should have what she considers to be a greater liberty, and contends that various decisions point in her favor.

The plaintiff argues that a settlement by the corporation with the officers will give them a presumptively valid defense to the claims now being pressed in the derivative suit; and that if the settlement includes a general release this may extinguish the corporation's claims against the defendants, not only as recipients of corporate property but also as directors, as neatly as if a derivative plaintiff had dismissed his own suit secretly or after the statute of limitations had run, or if an unfavorable consent judgment had been rendered—schemes against which rule [23.1] was clearly directed. But the situations differ in many important respects.

In the hypothesized cases, the court's own process is being used to obtain a determination which, in one way or another, will bind or prejudice the class on whose behalf the suit was brought. * * *

From a practical standpoint also there are important differences between the hypothesized cases and that here before us. While a board of directors dominated by the defendants with whom settlements are made would find it hard to provide a release that would survive charges of self-dealing, dismissal or compromise by an independent stockholder, with the corporation simply standing idle, would not be subject to such easy attack. A new derivative suit against management for fraud or waste in releasing corporate claims for inadequate payment can redress improper settlements even without setting them aside; finding a management target when the derivative shareholder has terminated the corporate claim may be a harder assignment. When the acquiescence of a derivative plaintiff to a dismissal or a consent judgment has in effect been purchased by the defendants, the supposed vigorous champion of the shareholders at large has been retired; far from policing the disposition of the corporate claim, he may well assist in seeing that the news does not leak out to stir other shareholders to inquiry. No such silencing of the derivative plaintiff occurs when the corporation settles out of court with some of the defendants. Indeed, he is the very person most likely to challenge the settlement, either by pursuing the original action and attempting to overthrow the settlement or by bringing a new action against the directors in which the settlement itself is the gravamen of the complaint.

No one would contend that a corporation could not negotiate a release of corporate claims, even against insiders, before a derivative suit was started. The corporation's interest in achieving a favorable settlement does not cease because derivative litigation has begun; especially is this so when some of the defendants in the derivative suit have taken the initiative—as in the present case—in bringing their own actions against the corporation and settlement with them may be impossible unless it can be promptly consummated.

It is true that the commencement of a derivative suit provides a handle for judicial supervision not present when the corporation negotiates at an earlier stage, and that permitting out-of-court settlements may be discouraging to attorneys for derivative plaintiffs. It is also true that some suspicion may attach to a settlement made by a board of directors that has shown no inclination to collect corporate claims until its hand is forced by the start of a derivative suit. But though the plaintiff's argument is not one to be lightly overruled, we conclude that the corporation's power to make its own out-of-court settlements, subject to normal shareholder redress, is not abolished by a procedural rule that does not embrace these either in its language or in its primary rationale. Whether it would not be well to expand the principle of rule [23.1] to cover a case like that here presented, and how that can be lawfully done, are not here before us. * * *

What we have written should not be taken as saying that there can never be circumstances under which a federal court, seized of a stockholder's suit, could properly enjoin the corporation, temporarily or finally, from entering into a settlement of a claim for improper dealings with it. We cite, simply by way of illustrating what we have in mind, a case where the beneficiaries of the alleged improper dealing still dominated the board of directors and plaintiffs were able to make some proof that wrongdoing was afoot. But any such action would be taken under the general equity powers of the court * * * and on the facts of the particular case, not in response to a supposed universal command of rule [23.1]. The papers here presented to the district judge not merely did not compel but would hardly have justified the taking of such action.

Affirmed.

[The concurring opinion of Waterman, Circuit Judge, is omitted].

Notes

(1) The requirement of court approval of settlements and dismissals obviously has greatly reduced the possibility of successful strike suits. Would it not be sensible to repeal all security-for-expenses statutes and rely exclusively on court approval?

(2) Does Judge Friendly state too narrowly the purposes underlying the last sentence of Rule 23.1? Consider 7C C. Wright, A. Miller and M. Kane, Federal Practice and Procedure: Civil 2d § 1839 (1986):

> In bona fide actions, the last sentence of Rule 23.1 serves to protect the corporation and its shareholders in the event that plaintiff becomes faint hearted prior to the litigation's completion and would be willing to settle the action even though it might not be in the best interests of all concerned. Furthermore, the rule prevents any prejudice to the corporate claim that might result from a discontinuance of the suit. This might occur, for example, when an advantage that already has been obtained is surrendered by the dismissal or settlement or when the statute of limitations precludes the institution of a new action. Special caution is warranted in the context of derivative suits inasmuch as plaintiff is affecting a right that belongs to the corporation.

(3) D. DeMott, Shareholder Derivative Actions: Law and Practice, § 7.05 (1987): *

> Conflicts may arise in derivative litigation between the interests of the corporation (and its shareholders) and those of the attorney repre-

---

* Reprinted with permission from De-Mott, Shareholder Derivative Actions: Law & Practice (§ 7.05, 1987), published by Callaghan & Co., 155 Pfingsten Rd., Deerfield, IL 60015.

senting the stockholder-plaintiff in the action; conflicts may also develop between the plaintiff's attorney and the plaintiff. * * *

The potential divergence in interests between the plaintiff and the plaintiff's attorney is most likely to materialize in the settlement context for the reasons explained by the Second Circuit in Saylor v. Lindsley,[6] in which the plaintiff himself opposed a settlement proposal to which his attorney assented. The plaintiff's economic interest is limited to his proportionate interest (typically a small shareholding) in the corporation's recovery minus any award of fees to his attorney, which represent the costs to the corporation of attaining its recovery. Counsel's economic interest is more complex: it consists of the amount of fees recovered, less the time and effort invested in the action, or, stated differently, the ratio between the fee recovered versus the investment of counsel's time and effort required to achieve it. Counsel may thus disfavor larger corporate recoveries that are achieved only after an extensive investment of additional time and work.

It is * * * conventional practice for the defendants and the corporation to agree in the settlement proposal not to oppose an application for fees up to a ceiling amount. One question this raises is the defendants' possible exposure for liability to the corporation for the difference if the court ultimately approves fees in an amount *less* than the ceiling. That is, it may be argued that by agreeing to a settlement proposal containing a ceiling on fees, the defendants effectively agreed to pay the ceiling amount (in addition to the agreed-to damage amount) in exchange for the termination of the claims against them. This argument was decisively rejected by the Second Circuit in Blatt v. Dean Witter Reynolds Intercapital, Inc., in which the court held that such a settlement agreement commits the defendant only to paying the amount of attorney fees awarded by the court.[7]

6. [By the Author] 456 F.2d 896 (2d Cir. 1972).

7. [By the Author] 732 F.2d at 306–307.

Chapter Sixteen

FUNDAMENTAL CHANGES: CORPORATION LAW ASPECTS

BOVE v. COMMUNITY HOTEL CORP. OF NEWPORT, RHODE ISLAND

Supreme Court of Rhode Island, 1969.
105 R.I. 36, 249 A.2d 89.

JOSLIN, JUSTICE.

This civil action was brought in the superior court to enjoin a proposed merger of The Community Hotel Corporation of Newport, Rhode Island, a defendant herein, into Newport Hotel Corp. Both corporations were organized under the general corporation law of this state and are hereinafter referred to respectively as "Community Hotel" and "Newport." No oral testimony was presented and a trial justice sitting without a jury decided the case on the facts appearing in the exhibits and as assented to by the parties in the pretrial order. The case is here on the plaintiffs' appeal from a judgment denying injunctive relief and dismissing the action.

Community Hotel was incorporated on October 21, 1924, for the stated purpose of erecting, maintaining, operating, managing and leasing hotels; and it commenced operations in 1927 with the opening of the Viking Hotel in Newport. Its authorized capital stock consists of 6,000 shares of $100 par value six per cent prior preference cumulative preferred stock, and 6,000 shares of no par common stock of which 2,106 shares are issued and outstanding. The plaintiffs as well as the individual defendants are holders and owners of preferred stock, plaintiffs having acquired their holdings of approximately 900 shares not later than 1930. At the time this suit was commenced, dividends on the 4,335 then-issued and outstanding preferred shares had accrued, but had not been declared, for approximately 24 years, and totalled about $645,000 or $148.75 per share.

Newport was organized at the instance and request of the board of directors of Community Hotel solely for the purpose of effectuating the

1172

merger which is the subject matter of this action. Its authorized capital stock consists of 80,000 shares of common stock, par value $1.00, of which only one share has been issued, and that to Community Hotel for the consideration of $10.

The essentials of the merger plan call for Community Hotel to merge into Newport, which will then become the surviving corporation. Although previously without assets, Newport will, if the contemplated merger is effectuated, acquire the sole ownership of all the property and assets now owned by Community Hotel. The plan also calls for the outstanding shares of Community Hotel's capital stock to be converted into shares of the capital stock of Newport upon the following basis: Each outstanding share of the constituent corporation's preferred stock, together with all accrued dividends thereon, will be changed and converted into five shares of the $1.00 par value common stock of the surviving corporation; and each share of the constituent corporation's no par common stock will be changed and converted into one share of the common stock, $1.00 par value, of the surviving corporation.

Consistent with the requirements of G.L.1956, § 7–5–3,[1] the merger will become effective only if the plan receives the affirmative votes of the stockholders of each of the corporations representing at least two-thirds of the shares of each class of its capital stock. For the purpose of obtaining the required approval, notice was given to both common and preferred stockholders of Community Hotel that a special meeting would be held for the purpose of considering and voting upon the proposed merger. Before the scheduled meeting date arrived, this action was commenced and the meeting was postponed to a future time and place. So far as the record before us indicates, it has not yet been held.

The plaintiffs argue that the primary, and indeed, the only purpose of the proposed merger is to eliminate the priorities of the preferred stock with less than the unanimous consent of its holders. Assuming that premise, a preliminary matter for our consideration concerns the merger of a parent corporation into a wholly-owned subsidiary created for the sole purpose of achieving a recapitalization which will eliminate the parent's preferred stock and the dividends accumulated thereon, and whether such a merger qualifies within the contemplation of the

---

1. [By the Court] Section 7–5–3 in pertinent part provides:

"Said agreement shall be submitted to the stockholders of each constituent corporation at a meeting thereof called separately for the purpose of taking the same into consideration. * * * At said meeting said agreement shall be considered and the stockholders of said corporation shall vote by ballot, in person or by proxy, for the adoption or rejection of the said agreement, each share entitling the holder thereof to one (1) vote, and if the votes of the stockholders of each such corporation representing at least two-thirds of the shares of each class of its capital stock shall be for the adoption of said agreement * * * the agreement so adopted and certified * * * shall thence be taken and deemed to be the agreement and act of consolidation or merger of said corporations * * *."

statute permitting any two or more corporations to merge into a single corporation.

It is true, of course, that to accomplish the proposed recapitalization by amending Community Hotel's articles of association under relevant provisions of the general corporation law [2] would require the unanimous vote of the preferred shareholders, whereas under the merger statute, only a two-third vote of those stockholders will be needed. Concededly, unanimity of the preferred stockholders is unobtainable in this case, and plaintiffs argue, therefore, that to permit the less restrictive provisions of the merger statute to be used to accomplish indirectly what otherwise would be incapable of being accomplished directly by the more stringent amendment procedures of the general corporation law is tantamount to sanctioning a circumvention or perversion of that law.

The question, however, is not whether recapitalization by the merger route is a subterfuge, but whether a merger which is designed for the sole purpose of cancelling the rights of preferred stockholders with the consent of less than all has been authorized by the legislature. The controlling statute is § 7–5–2. Its language is clear, all-embracing and unqualified. It authorizes any two or more business corporations *which were or might have been organized* under the general corporation law to merge into a single corporation; and it provides that the merger agreement shall prescribe " * * * the terms and conditions of consolidation or merger, the mode of carrying the same into effect * * * *as well as the manner of converting the shares of each of the constituent corporations into shares or other securities of the corporation resulting from or surviving such consolidation or merger,* with such other details and provisions as are deemed necessary." [3] (italics ours) Nothing in that language even suggests that the legislature intended to make *underlying purpose* a standard for determining permissibility. Indeed, the contrary is apparent since the very breadth of the language selected presupposes a complete lack of concern with whether the merger is designed to further the mutual interests of two existing and nonaffiliated corporations or whether alternatively it is proposed solely upon effecting a substantial change in an existing corporation's capital structure.

2. [By the Court] Section 7–2–18, as amended, provides that a corporation may " * * * from time to time when and as desired amend its articles of association * * * " and § 7–2–19, as amended, provides that "Unless otherwise provided in the articles of association, every such amendment shall require the affirmative vote of the following proportion of the stockholders, passed at a meeting duly called for the purpose:

"(a) * * *

"(b) Where the amendment diminishes the stipulated rate of dividends on any class of stock or the stipulated amount to be paid thereon in case of call or liquidation, the unanimous vote of the stockholders of such class and the vote of a majority in interest of all other stockholders entitled to vote."

3. [By the Court] The quoted provision is substantially identical to the Delaware merger statute (Del.Rev.Code (1935) C. 65, § 2091) construed in Federal United Corp. v. Havender, 24 Del.Ch. 318, 11 A.2d 331.

Moreover, that a possible effect of corporate action under the merger statute is not possible, or is even forbidden, under another section of the general corporation law is of no import, it being settled that the several sections of that law may have independent legal significance, and that the validity of corporate action taken pursuant to one section is not necessarily dependent upon its being valid under another. Hariton v. Arco Electronics, Inc., 40 Del.Ch. 326, 182 A.2d 22, aff'd, 41 Del.Ch. 74, 188 A.2d 123.

We hold, therefore, that nothing within the purview of our statute forbids a merger between a parent and a subsidiary corporation even under circumstances where the merger device has been resorted to solely for the purpose of obviating the necessity for the unanimous vote which would otherwise be required in order to cancel the priorities of preferred shareholders. Federal United Corp. v. Havender, supra; Hottenstein v. York Ice Machinery Corp., 3 Cir., 136 F.2d 944.

A more basic problem, narrowed so as to bring it within the factual context of this case, is whether the right of a holder of cumulative preferred stock to dividend arrearages and other preferences may be cancelled by a statutory merger. That precise problem has not heretofore been before this court, but elsewhere there is a considerable body of law on the subject. There is no need to discuss all of the authorities. For illustrative purposes it is sufficient that we refer principally to cases involving Delaware corporations. That state is important as a state of incorporation, and the decisions of its courts on the precise problem are not only referred to and relied on by the parties, but are generally considered to be the leading ones in the field.

The earliest case in point of time is Keller v. Wilson & Co., 21 Del. Ch. 391, 190 A. 115 (1936). Wilson & Company was formed and its stock was issued in 1925 and the law then in effect protected against charter amendments which might destroy a preferred shareholder's right to accumulated dividends. In 1927 that law was amended so as to permit such destruction, and thereafter the stockholders of Wilson & Company, by the required majorities, voted to cancel the dividends which had by then accrued on its preferred stock. In invalidating that action the rationale of the Delaware court was that the right of a holder of a corporation's cumulative preferred stock to eventual payment of dividend arrearages was a fixed contractual right, that it was a property right in the nature of a debt, that it was vested, and that it could not be destroyed by corporate action taken under legislative authority subsequently conferred, without the consent of all of the shareholders.

Consolidated Film Industries, Inc. v. Johnson, 22 Del.Ch. 407, 197 A. 489 (1937), decided a year later, was an almost precisely similar case. The only difference was that Consolidated Film Industries, Inc. was not created until after the adoption of the 1927 amendment, whereas in the earlier case the statutory amendment upon which Wilson & Company purported to act postdated both its creation and the issuance of its stock. Notwithstanding the *Keller* rationale that an investor should be entitled to rely upon the law in existence at the time the preferred stock was issued, the court in this case was " * * * unable to discover a difference in principle between the two cases." In refusing to allow the proposed reclassification, it reasoned that a shareholder's fixed contractual right to unpaid dividends is of such dignity that it cannot be diminished or eliminated retrospectively even if the authorizing legislation precedes the issuance of its stock.

Two years elapsed before Federal United Corp. v. Havender, supra, was decided. The issue was substantially the same as that in the two cases which preceded. The dissenting stockholders had argued, as might have been expected, that the proposed corporate action, even though styled a "merger," was in effect a *Keller* type recapitalization and was entitled to no different treatment. Notwithstanding that argument, the court did not refer to the preferred stockholder's right as "vested" or as "a property right in the nature of a debt." Neither did it reject the use of *Keller*-type nomenclature as creating "confusion" or as "substitutes for reason and analysis" which are the characterizations used respectively in Davison v. Parke, Austin & Lipscomb, Inc., 285 N.Y. 500, 509, 35 N.E.2d 618, 622; Meck, Accrued Dividends on Cumulative Preferred Stocks; The Legal Doctrine, 55 Harv.L.Rev. 7, 76. Instead, it talked about the extent of the corporate power under the merger statute; and it held that the statute in existence when Federal United Corp. was organized had in effect been written into its charter, and that its preferred shareholders had thereby been advised and informed that their rights to accrued dividends might be extinguished by corporate action taken pursuant thereto.

Faced with a question of corporate action adjusting preferred stock dividends, and required to apply Delaware law under Erie R.R. v. Tompkins, 304 U.S. 64, 58 Sup.Ct. 817, 82 L.Ed. 1188, it is understandable that a federal court in Hottenstein v. York Ice Machinery Corp., 3 Cir., 136 F.2d 944, 950, found *Keller, Johnson* and *Havender* irreconcilable and said,

> "If it is fair to say that the decision of the Supreme Court of Delaware in the Keller case astonished the corporate world, it is just to state that the decision of the Supreme Court in Havender astounded it, for shorn of rationalization the decision constitutes a repudiation of principles enunciated in the Keller case and in Consolidated Film Industries v. Johnson, supra." at 950.[4]

4. [By the Court] To the same effect the court in Western Foundry Co. v. Wicker, 403 Ill. 260, said at 277, 85 N.E.2d 722 at 730:

"Thus, what was formerly regarded as an almost inviolable vested property right was now considered a mere defeasible right, subject to cancellation by merger by reason of the consent of the preferred shareholders granted at the time the stock was originally issued. There being little or no difference between a recapitalization by corporate amendment and recapitalization by merger of a parent corporation with a wholly-owned subsidiary, the present status of the *Keller* case is obscure. While not expressly overruled, the theory of the *Keller* case was entirely repudiated. Consequently, as an authority for the

With Keller's back thus broken, *Hottenstein* went on to say that under Delaware law a parent corporation may merge with a wholly-owned inactive subsidiary pursuant to a plan cancelling preferred stock and the rights of holders thereof to unpaid accumulated dividends and substituting in lieu thereof stock of the surviving corporation.

Only four years intervened between *Keller* and *Havender,* but that was long enough for Delaware to have discarded "vested rights" as the test for determining the power of a corporation to eliminate a shareholder's right to preferred stock dividend accumulation, and to have adopted in its stead a standard calling for judicial inquiry into whether the proposed interference with a preferred stockholder's contract has been authorized by the legislature. The *Havender* approach is the one to which we subscribe as being the sounder, and it has support in the authorities.

The plaintiffs do not suggest, other than as they may have argued that this particular merger is a subterfuge, that our merger statute will not permit in any circumstances a merger for the sole reason that it affects accrued, but undeclared, preferred stock dividends. Rather do they argue that what should control is the date of the enactment of the enabling legislation, and they point out that in *Havender,* Federal United Corp. was organized and its stock was issued subsequent to the adoption of the statute authorizing mergers, whereas in this case the corporate creation and the stock issue preceded adoption of such a statute. That distinguishing feature brings into question what limitations, if any, exist to a state's authority under the reserved power to permit by subsequent legislation corporate acts which affect the preferential rights of a stockholder. More specifically, it raises the problem of whether subsequent legislation is repugnant to the federal and state constitutional prohibitions against the passage of laws impairing the obligations of contracts, because it permits elimination of accumulated preferred dividends by a lesser vote than was required under the law in existence at the time of the incorporation and when the stock was issued.

The mere mention of the constitutional prohibitions against such laws calls to mind Trustees of Dartmouth College v. Woodward, 17 U.S. 518, 4 Wheaton 518, 4 L.Ed. 629, where the decision was that a private corporation charter granted by the state is a contract protected under the constitution against repeal, amendment or alteration by subsequent legislation. Of equal significance in the field of corporation law is Mr. Justice Story's concurring opinion wherein he suggested that application of the impairment clause upon acts of incorporation might be avoided if a state legislature, coincident with granting a corporate charter, reserved as a part of that contract the right of amendment or repeal. With such a reservation, he said, any subsequent amendment

---

proposition that the power to change the 'rights' of preferred stock does not include the right to cancel unpaid cumula- tive dividends, Keller v. Wilson & Co. is highly questionable."

or repeal would be pursuant, rather than repugnant, to the terms of the contract and would not therefore impair its obligation.

Our own legislature was quick to heed Story's advice, and in the early part of the 19th century, when corporations were customarily created by special act, the power to alter, amend, or revoke was written directly into each charter. Later, when the practice changed and corporations, instead of being created by special enactment, were incorporated under the general corporation law, the power to amend and repeal was reserved in an act of general application, and since at least as far back as 1844 the corporation law has read in substance as it does today viz., " * * * The charter or articles of association of every corporation hereafter created may be amended or repealed at the will of the general assembly." Section 7-1-13.

The language in which the reserved power is customarily stated is not, however, self-explaining, and the extent of the legislative authority under it has frequently been a source of difficulty. Recognizing that problem, but not answering it, the United States Supreme Court said in a frequently quoted passage:

> "The authority of a state under the so-called reserve power is wide; but it is not unlimited. The corporate charter may be repealed or amended, and, within limits not now necessary to define, the interrelations of state, corporation and stockholders may be changed; but neither vested property rights nor the obligation of contracts of third persons may be destroyed or impaired." Coombes v. Getz, 285 U.S. 434, 441–442, 52 S.Ct. 435, 436, 76 L.Ed. 866, 871. * * *

On the one side, there is a body of law which speaks of the threefold nature of the stockholder's contract and, while agreeable to an exercise of the reserved power affecting only the contractual relationship between the state and the corporation, rejects as unconstitutional any exercise which affects the relationship between the stockholder and the corporation or between the stockholders inter sese. Under this view, subsequent legislation purporting to permit a corporate act to cancel accrued preferred dividends would obviously be an improper exercise of the power inasmuch as the essence of a preferred stockholder's contract is its definition of his relationship with the corporation and with the other stockholders vis-à-vis such matters as the distribution of the profits of the enterprise or the division of its capital and surplus account in the event of liquidation.

The other side of the argument considers that the question is primarily one of statutory construction and that so long as the statute authorizes the corporate action, it should make no difference whether its enactment preceded or postdated the birth of the corporation or the issuance of its stock.[5] The basis for this viewpoint is that the terms of

---

5. [By the Court] This, in substance was the basis for the decision in Consolidated Firm Industries, Inc. v. Johnson. The corporation there, as distinguished from the one in Keller v. Wilson & Co., was created subsequent to the amendment which permitted recapitalization. Nonetheless, the court was " * * * unable to discover a difference in principle between the two cases."

the preferred stockholder's contractual relationship are not restricted to the specifics inscribed on the stock certificate, but include also the stipulations contained in the charter or articles of association as well as the pertinent provisions of the general corporation law. One of those provisions is, of course, the reserved power; and so long as it is a part of the preferred shareholder's contract, any subsequent legislation enacted pursuant to it, even though it may amend the contract's original terms, will not impair its obligation in the constitutional sense. It is as if the stock certificate were inscribed with the legend "All of the terms and conditions hereof may be changed by the legislature acting pursuant to the power it has reserved in G.L.1956, § 7–1–13." * * *

On the basis of our own precedents we conclude that the merger legislation, notwithstanding its effect on the rights of its stockholders, did not necessarily constitute an improper exercise of the right of amendment reserved merely because it was subsequent.

In addition to arguing that the proposed plan suffers from a constitutional infirmity, plaintiffs also contend that it is unfair and inequitable to them, and that its consummation should, therefore, be enjoined. By that assertion they raise the problem of whether equity should heed the request of a dissenting stockholder and intervene to prevent a merger notwithstanding that it has received the vote [6] of the designated proportions of the various classes of stock of the constituent corporations.

In looking to the authorities for assistance on this question, we avoided those involving recapitalization by charter amendment where a dissident's only remedy against allegedly unfair treatment was in equity. In those situations the authorities generally permit equitable intervention to protect against unfair or inequitable treatment. They are founded on the concept that otherwise there might be confiscation without recompense. The same rationale, however, is not available in the case of a merger, because there the dissenting stockholders usually can find a measure of protection in the statutory procedures giving them the option to compel the corporation to purchase their shares at an appraised value. This is a significant difference and is ample reason for considering the two situations as raising separate and distinct issues.

This case involves a merger, not a recapitalization by charter amendment, and in this state the legislature, looking to the possibility that there might be those who would not be agreeable to the proposed merger, provided a means whereby a dissatisfied stockholder might demand and the corporation be compelled to pay the fair value of his securities. G.L.1956, §§ 7–5–8 through 7–5–16 inclusive. Our inquiry then is to the effect of that remedy upon plaintiff's right to challenge

---

6. [By the Court] For purposes of this proceeding we have accepted the implied assumption of all of the parties that the proposed merger will receive the required vote and we have not sua sponte suggested that the suit might more properly have awaited that eventuality.

the proposed merger on the ground that it is unfair and inequitable because it dictates what shall be their proportionate interests in the corporate assets. Once again there is no agreement among the authorities. Vorenberg, "Exclusiveness of the Dissenting Stockholder's Appraisal Right," 77 Harv.L.Rev. 1189. Some authorities appear to say that the statutory remedy of appraisal is exclusive. Beloff v. Consolidated Edison Co., 300 N.Y. 11, 87 N.E.2d 561. Others say that it may be disregarded and that equity may intervene if the minority is treated oppressively or unfairly, Barnett v. Philadelphia Market Co., 218 Pa. 649, 67 A. 912; or if the merger is tainted with fraud or illegality, Adams v. United States Distributing Corp., 184 Va. 134, 147, 34 S.E.2d 244, 250, 162 A.L.R. 1227. To these differing views must also be added the divergence of opinion on whether those in control or those dissenting must bear the burden of establishing that the plan meets whatever the required standard may be. Vorenberg, supra; 77 Harv.L.Rev. 1189, 1210–1215.

In this case we do not choose as between the varying views, nor is there any need for us to do so. Even were we to accept that view which is most favorable to plaintiffs we still would not be able to find that they have been either unfairly or inequitably treated. The record insofar as it relates to the unfairness issue is at best sparse. In substance it consists of the corporation's balance sheet as of September 1967, together with supporting schedules. That statement uses book, rather than the appraised, values, and neither it nor any other evidentiary matter in any way indicates, except as the same may be reflected in the surplus account, the corporation's earning history or its prospects for profitable operations in the future.

Going to the figures we find a capital and surplus account of $669,948 of which $453,000 is allocable to the 4,530 issued and outstanding shares of $100 par value preferred stock and the balance of $316,948 to surplus. Obviously, a realization of the book value of the assets in the event of liquidation, forced or otherwise, would not only leave nothing for the common stockholders, but would not even suffice to pay the preferred shareholders the par value of their stock plus the accrued dividends of $645,000.

If we were to follow a rule of absolute priority, any proposal which would give anything to common stockholders without first providing for full payment of stated value plus dividend accruals would be unfair to the preferred shareholders. It could be argued that the proposal in this case violates that rule because an exchange of one share of Community Hotel's preferred stock for five shares of Newport's common stock would give the preferred shareholders securities worth less than the amount of their liquidation preference rights while at the same time the one to one exchange ratio on the common would enrich Community Hotel's common stockholders by allowing them to participate in its surplus.

An inherent fallacy in applying the rule of absolute priority to the circumstances of this case, however, is its assumption that assets would be liquidated and that nothing more than their book value will be realized. But Community Hotel is not in liquidation. Instead it is a going concern which, because of its present capitalization, cannot obtain the modern debt-financing needed to meet threatened competition. Moreover, management, in the call of the meeting at which it was intended to consider and vote on the plan, said that the proposed recapitalization plan was conceived only " * * * after careful consideration by your Board of Directors and a review of the relative values of the preferred and common stocks by the independent public accountants of the Corporation. The exchange ratio of five new common shares for each share of the existing preferred stock was determined on the basis of the book and market values of the preferred and the inherent value of the unpaid preferred dividends." Those assertions are contained in a document admitted as an exhibit and they have testimonial value.

When the varying considerations—both balance sheet figures and management's assertions—are taken into account, we are unable to conclude, at least at this stage of the proceedings, that the proposed plan is unfair and inequitable, particularly because plaintiffs as dissidents may avail themselves of the opportunity to receive the fair market value of their securities under the appraisal methods prescribed in § 7-5-8 through § 7-5-16 inclusive.

The plaintiffs argue that due consideration will not be given to their dividend accruals under the appraisal. We do not agree. Jeffrey v. American Screw Co., 98 R.I. 286, 201 A.2d 146, requires that the securities of a dissident invoking the statute must be appraised by a person "versed in the intricacies of corporate finance." Such a person will find when he looks to *Jeffrey* for guidance that the evaluation process requires him to consider " * * * all relevant value factors including market value, book value, asset value, and other intrinsic factors probative of value." Certainly, unpaid dividend arrearages fall within that directive and are a relevant factor to be considered in arriving at the full and fair cash value of the plaintiffs' preferred stock. While we make no decision one way or the other on the exclusiveness of appraisal as a remedy for a dissident, we do decide that its availability is an element or a circumstance which equity should weigh before intervening. When that is done in this case, we find no ground for intervention.

For the reasons stated, the judgment appealed from is affirmed.

Notes

(1) The notion that certain rights of securities holders are "vested property rights" is superficially appealing, and, as indicated in the principal case, has been judicially adopted in a few instances. The effect of it, however, is to require unanimous consent for transactions, and that is

usually impractical. Most modern corporation law commentators accept the idea that rights of securities holders may be modified by appropriate corporate action, subject to the statutory protections afforded: the right to vote as a class in certain situations, the right to dissent and receive in cash a judicially determined "fair market value" in certain instances, and the requirement in many state statutes that more than a majority vote is needed to approve certain proposals. The provision in the Rhode Island statute referred to in note 2 requiring unanimous consent for a certain type of amendment is atypical. See RMBCA §§ 10.03, 10.04, 13.02. In addition to these statutory protections, minority shareholders may rely on the fiduciary duties of controlling shareholders and directors in connection with the treatment of minority interests.

(2) In considering fundamental or organic changes, it is important to recognize that there is usually more than one way to skin a cat. Essentially the same final result may often be obtained through several different routes. These routes may involve the exercise of statutory powers (e.g. amendments to articles of incorporation, mergers, share exchanges) or nonstatutory transactions (e.g. the purchase of shares or assets in exchange for stock) or a combination of statutory and nonstatutory transactions. The route that is followed is important because some of the fundamental protections of minority interests described in the preceding paragraph— particularly class voting by senior securities and appraisal rights—are literally available only in connection with certain types of statutory transactions. Fiduciary duties of controlling shareholders and directors, of course, are more generally applicable to all transactions.

(3) It is also important to recognize that equality of treatment is often not guaranteed in statutory transactions. See Weinberger v. UOP, Inc., p. 792 supra. Under most merger statutes, for example, some shareholders in a corporation may be compelled to accept cash while other shareholders receive stock in the continuing venture. See, e.g. RMBCA §§ 11.01(b)(3), 11.04(b)(2).

FARRIS v. GLEN ALDEN CORP.

Supreme Court of Pennsylvania, 1958.
393 Pa. 427, 143 A.2d 25.

COHEN, JUSTICE.

We are required to determine on this appeal whether, as a result of a "Reorganization Agreement" executed by the officers of Glen Alden Corporation and List Industries Corporation, and approved by the shareholders of the former company, the rights and remedies of a dissenting shareholder accrue to the plaintiff.

Glen Alden is a Pennsylvania corporation engaged principally in the mining of anthracite coal and lately in the manufacture of air conditioning units and fire-fighting equipment. In recent years the company's operating revenue has declined substantially, and in fact, its coal operations have resulted in tax loss carryovers of approximately $14,000,000. In October 1957, List, a Delaware holding company owning interests in motion picture theaters, textile companies and real estate, and to a lesser extent, in oil and gas operations, warehouses and aluminum piston manufacturing, purchased through a wholly owned subsidiary 38.5% of Glen Alden's outstanding stock.[7] This acquisition enabled List to place three of its directors on the Glen Alden board.

On March 20, 1958, the two corporations entered into a "reorganization agreement," subject to stockholder approval, which contemplated the following actions:

1. Glen Alden is to acquire all of the assets of List, excepting a small amount of cash reserved for the payment of List's expenses in connection with the transaction. These assets include over $8,000,000 in cash held chiefly in the treasuries of List's wholly owned subsidiaries.

2. In consideration of the transfer, Glen Alden is to issue 3,621,703 shares of stock to List. List in turn is to distribute the stock to its shareholders at a ratio of five shares of Glen Alden stock for each six shares of List stock. In order to accomplish the necessary distribution, Glen Alden is to increase the authorized number of its shares of capital stock from 2,500,000 shares to 7,500,000 shares without according preemptive rights to the present shareholders upon the issuance of any such shares.

3. Further, Glen Alden is to assume all of List's liabilities including a $5,000,000 note incurred by List in order to purchase Glen Alden stock in 1957, outstanding stock options, incentive stock options plans, and pension obligations.

4. Glen Alden is to change its corporate name from Glen Alden Corporation to List Alden Corporation.

5. The present directors of both corporations are to become directors of List Alden.

6. List is to be dissolved and List Alden is to then carry on the operations of both former corporations.

Two days after the agreement was executed notice of the annual meeting of Glen Alden to be held on April 11, 1958, was mailed to the shareholders together with a proxy statement analyzing the reorganization agreement and recommending its approval as well as approval of certain amendments to Glen Alden's articles of incorporation and bylaws necessary to implement the agreement. At this meeting the holders of a majority of the outstanding shares, (not including those owned by List), voted in favor of a resolution approving the reorganization agreement.

On the day of the shareholders' meeting, plaintiff, a shareholder of Glen Alden, filed a complaint in equity against the corporation and its officers seeking to enjoin them temporarily until final hearing, and perpetually thereafter, from executing and carrying out the agreement.

---

7. [By the Court] Of the purchase price of $8,719,109, $5,000,000 was borrowed.

The gravamen of the complaint was that the notice of the annual shareholders' meeting did not conform to the requirements of the Business Corporation Law, in three respects: (1) It did not give notice to the shareholders that the true intent and purpose of the meeting was to effect a merger or consolidation of Glen Alden and List; (2) It failed to give notice to the shareholders of their right to dissent to the plan of merger or consolidation and claim fair value for their shares, and (3) it did not contain copies of the text of certain sections of the Business Corporation Law as required.[8]

By reason of these omissions, plaintiff contended that the approval of the reorganization agreement by the shareholders at the annual meeting was invalid and unless the carrying out of the plan were enjoined, he would suffer irreparable loss by being deprived of substantial property rights.[9]

The defendants answered admitting the material allegations of fact in the complaint but denying that they gave rise to a cause of action because the transaction complained of was a purchase of corporate assets as to which shareholders had no rights of dissent or appraisal. For these reasons the defendants then moved for judgment on the pleadings.[10]

The court below concluded that the reorganization agreement entered into between the two corporations was a plan for a *de facto* merger, and that therefore the failure of the notice of the annual meeting to conform to the pertinent requirements of the merger provisions of the Business Corporation Law rendered the notice defective and all proceedings in furtherance of the agreement void. Wherefore, the court entered a final decree denying defendants' motion for judgment on the pleadings, entering judgment upon plaintiff's complaint and granting the injunctive relief therein sought. This appeal followed.

When use of the corporate form of business organization first became widespread, it was relatively easy for courts to define a "merger" or a "sale of assets" and to label a particular transaction as one or the other. But prompted by the desire to avoid the impact of adverse, and to obtain the benefits of favorable, government regulations, partic-

---

8. [By the Court] The proxy statement included the following declaration:

"Appraisal Rights.

"In the opinion of counsel, the shareholders of neither Glen Alden nor List Industries will have any rights of appraisal or similar rights of dissenters with respect to any matter to be acted upon at their respective meetings."

9. [By the Court] The complaint also set forth that the exchange of shares of Glen Alden's stock for those of List would constitute a violation of the pre-emptive rights of Glen Alden shareholders as established by the law of Pennsylvania at the time of Glen Alden's incorporation in 1917. The defendants answered that under both statute and prior common law no preemptive rights existed with respect to stock issued in exchange for property.

10. [By the Court] Counsel for the defendants concedes that if the corporation is required to pay the dissenting shareholders the appraised fair value of their shares, the resultant drain of cash would prevent Glen Alden from carrying out the agreement. On the other hand, plaintiff contends that if the shareholders had been told of their rights as dissenters, rather than specifically advised that they had no such rights, the resolution approving the reorganization agreement would have been defeated.

ularly federal tax laws, new accounting and legal techniques were developed by lawyers and accountants which interwove the elements characteristic of each, thereby creating hybrid forms of corporate amalgamation. Thus, it is no longer helpful to consider an individual transaction in the abstract and solely by reference to the various elements therein determine whether it is a "merger" or a "sale". Instead, to determine properly the nature of a corporate transaction, we must refer not only to all the provisions of the agreement, but also to the consequences of the transaction and to the purposes of the provisions of the corporation law said to be applicable. We shall apply this principle to the instant case.

Section 908 subd. A of the Pennsylvania Business Corporation Law provides: "If any shareholder of a domestic corporation which becomes a party to a plan of merger or consolidation shall object to such plan of merger or consolidation * * * such shareholder shall be entitled to * * * [the fair value of his shares upon surrender of the share certificate or certificates representing his shares]." 15 P.S. § 2852–908, subd. A.[11]

This provision had its origin in the early decision of this Court in Lauman v. Lebanon Valley R.R. Co., 1858, 30 Pa. 42. There a shareholder who objected to the consolidation of his company with another was held to have a right in the absence of statute to treat the consolidation as a dissolution of his company and to receive the value of his shares upon their surrender.

The rationale of the Lauman case, and of the present section of the Business Corporation Law based thereon, is that when a corporation combines with another so as to lose its essential nature and alter the original fundamental relationships of the shareholders among themselves and to the corporation, a shareholder who does not wish to continue his membership therein may treat his membership in the original corporation as terminated and have the value of his shares paid to him.

Does the combination outlined in the present "reorganization" agreement so fundamentally change the corporate character of Glen Alden and the interest of the plaintiff as a shareholder therein, that to refuse him the rights and remedies of a dissenting shareholder would in reality force him to give up his stock in one corporation and against his will accept shares in another? If so, the combination is a merger within the meaning of section 908, subd. A of the corporation law.

If the reorganization agreement were consummated plaintiff would find that the "List Alden" resulting from the amalgamation would be quite a different corporation than the "Glen Alden" in which he is now

---

11. [By the Court] Furthermore, section 902, subd. B provides that notice of the proposed merger and of the right to dissent thereto must be given the shareholders. "There shall be included in, or enclosed with * * * notice [of meeting of share-holders to vote on plan of merger] a copy or a summary of the plan of merger or plan of consolidation, as the case may be, and * * * a copy of subsection A of section 908 and of subsections B, C and D of section 515 of this act."

a shareholder. Instead of continuing primarily as a coal mining company, Glen Alden would be transformed, after amendment of its articles of incorporation, into a diversified holding company whose interests would range from motion picture theaters to textile companies. Plaintiff would find himself a member of a company with assets of $169,000,000 and a long-term debt of $38,000,000 in lieu of a company one-half that size and with but one-seventh the long-term debt.

While the administration of the operations and properties of Glen Alden as well as List would be in the hands of management common to both companies, since all executives of List would be retained in List Alden, the control of Glen Alden would pass to the directors of List; for List would hold eleven of the seventeen directorships on the new board of directors.

As an aftermath of the transaction plaintiff's proportionate interest in Glen Alden would have been reduced to only two-fifths of what it presently is because of the issuance of an additional 3,621,703 shares to List which would not be subject to pre-emptive rights. In fact, ownership of Glen Alden would pass to the stockholders of List who would hold 76.5% of the outstanding shares as compared with but 23.5% retained by the present Glen Alden shareholders.

Perhaps the most important consequence to the plaintiff, if he were denied the right to have his shares redeemed at their fair value, would be the serious financial loss suffered upon consummation of the agreement. While the present book value of his stock is $38 a share after combination it would be worth only $21 a share. In contrast, the shareholders of List who presently hold stock with a total book value of $33,000,000 or $7.50 a share, would receive stock with a book value of $76,000,000 or $21 a share.

Under these circumstances it may well be said that if the proposed combination is allowed to take place without right of dissent, plaintiff would have his stock in Glen Alden taken away from him and the stock of a new company thrust upon him in its place. He would be projected against his will into a new enterprise under terms not of his own choosing. It was to protect dissident shareholders against just such a result that this Court one hundred years ago in the Lauman case, and the legislature thereafter in section 908, subd. A, granted the right of dissent. And it is to accord that protection to the plaintiff that we conclude that the combination proposed in the case at hand is a merger within the intendment of section 908, subd. A.

Nevertheless, defendants contend that the 1957 amendments to sections 311 and 908 of the corporation law preclude us from reaching this result and require the entry of judgment in their favor. Subsection F of section 311 dealing with the voluntary transfer of corporate assets provides: "The shareholders of a business corporation which acquires by sale, lease or exchange all or substantially all of the property of another corporation by the issuance of stock, securities or otherwise shall not be entitled to the rights and remedies of dissenting shareholders * * *."

And the amendment to section 908 reads as follows: "The right of dissenting shareholders * * * shall not apply to the purchase by a corporation of assets whether or not the consideration therefor be money or property, real or personal, including shares or bonds or other evidences of indebtedness of such corporation. The shareholders of such corporation shall have no right to dissent from any such purchase."

Defendants view these amendments as abridging the right of shareholders to dissent to a transaction between two corporations which involves a transfer of assets for a consideration even though the transfer has all the legal incidents of a merger. They claim that only if the merger is accomplished in accordance with the prescribed statutory procedure does the right of dissent accrue. In support of this position they cite to us the comment on the amendments by the Committee on Corporation Law of the Pennsylvania Bar Association, the committee which originally drafted these provisions. The comment states that the provisions were intended to overrule cases which granted shareholders the right to dissent to a sale of assets when accompanied by the legal incidents of a merger.[12] Whatever may have been the intent of the *committee,* there is no evidence to indicate that the *legislature* intended the 1957 amendments to have the effect contended for. But furthermore, the language of these two provisions does not support the opinion of the committee and is inapt to achieve any such purpose. The amendments of 1957 do not provide that a transaction between two corporations which has the effect of a merger but which includes a transfer of assets for consideration is to be exempt from the protective provisions of section 908, subd. A and 515. They provide only that the shareholders of a corporation which acquires the property or purchases the assets of another corporation, *without more,* are not entitled to the right to dissent from the transaction. So, as in the present case, when as part of a transaction between two corporations, one corporation dissolves, its liabilities are assumed by the survivor, its executives and

12. [By the Court] "The amendment to Section 311 expressly provides that a sale, lease or exchange of substantially all corporate assets in connection with its liquidation or dissolution is subject to the provisions of Article XI of the Act, and that no consent or authorization of shareholders other than what is required by Article XI is necessary. The recent decision in Marks v. Autocar Co., D.C.E.D.Pa., [153 F.Supp. 768] is to the contrary. This amendment, together with the proposed amendment to Section 1104 expressly permitting the directors in liquidating the corporation to sell only such assets as may be required to pay its debts and distribute any assets remaining among shareholders (Section 1108, [subd.] B now so provides in the case of receivers) have the effect of overruling Marks v. Autocar Co., * * * which permits a shareholder dissenting from such a sale to obtain the fair value of his shares. The Marks case relies substantially on Bloch v. Baldwin Locomotive Works, 75 [Pa.] Dist. & Co. R. 24, also believed to be an undesirable decision. That case permitted a holder of stock in a corporation which *purchased* for stock all the assets of another corporation to obtain the fair value of his shares. That case is also in effect overruled by the new Sections 311 [subd.] F and 908 [subd.] C." 61 Ann.Rep. Pa.Bar Ass'n, 277, 284 (1957).

directors take over the management and control of the survivor, and, as consideration for the transfer, its stockholders acquire a majority of the shares of stock of the survivor, then the transaction is no longer simply a purchase of assets or acquisition of property to which sections 311, subd. F and 908, subd. C apply, but a merger governed by section 908, subd. A of the corporation law. To divest shareholders of their right of dissent under such circumstances would require express language which is absent from the 1957 amendments.

Even were we to assume that the combination provided for in the reorganization agreement is a "sale of assets" to which section 908, subd. A does not apply, it would avail the defendants nothing; we will not blind our eyes to the realities of the transaction. Despite the designation of the parties and the form employed, Glen Alden does not in fact acquire List, rather, List acquires Glen Alden, and under section 311, subd. D [13] the right of dissent would remain with the shareholders of Glen Alden.

We hold that the combination contemplated by the reorganization agreement, although consummated by contract rather than in accordance with the statutory procedure, is a merger within the protective purview of sections 908, subd. A and 515 of the corporation law. The shareholders of Glen Alden should have been notified accordingly and advised of their statutory rights of dissent and appraisal. The failure of the corporate officers to take these steps renders the stockholder approval of the agreement at the 1958 shareholders' meeting invalid. The lower court did not err in enjoining the officers and directors of Glen Alden from carrying out this agreement. [14]

Decree affirmed at appellants' cost.

Notes

(1) Is the holding of the principal case that shareholder appraisal rights must be recognized whenever it is possible to structure a transaction as a statutory merger?

(2) Compare Hariton v. Arco Electronics, Inc., 41 Del.Ch. 74, 188 A.2d 123 (1963), where the Court upheld a plan of reorganization involving a two-step transaction:

13. [By the Court] "If any shareholder of a business corporation which sells, leases or exchanges all or substantially all of its property and assets otherwise than (1) in the usual and regular course of its business, (2) for the purpose of relocating its business, or (3) in connection with its dissolution and liquidation, shall object to such sale, lease or exchange and comply with the provisions of section 515 of this act, such shareholder shall be entitled to the rights and remedies of dissenting shareholders as therein provided."

14. [By the Court] Because of our disposition of this appeal, it is unnecessary for us to consider whether the plaintiff had any pre-emptive rights in the proposed issuance of newly authorized shares as payment for the transfer of assets from List, or whether amended sections 908 subd. C and 311 subd. F of the corporation law may constitutionally be applied to the present transaction to divest the plaintiff of his dissenter's rights.

(a) First, Corporation A sells its assets to Corporation B (a larger corporation) in exchange for common stock of Corporation B; and

(b) Second, Corporation A dissolves, distributing the common stock of Corporation B to its shareholders.

The Court refused to apply the *de facto* merger doctrine because it would "create uncertainty in the law and invite litigation." The Court also stated that "the framers of a reorganization plan may resort to either type of corporate mechanics to achieve the desired end." In commenting approvingly on this decision Professor Folk has stated that the decision "displays, consciously or unconsciously, a profound distrust of appraisal rights." He continues:

> The basic premise implicitly adopted in *Hariton* may perhaps be stated more affirmatively. One does not invest in a unique corporate entity or even a particular business operation, but rather in a continuous course of business which changes over a long period of time. Certainly the best investments are growth investments—investments in enterprises which change with time, technology, business opportunities, and altered demand; and the worst investments are those which diminish in value because the type of business has lost importance and the corporation has been unable to adapt to the changed conditions. Although a shareholder's enthusiasm dwindles when an enterprise changes internally for the worst, no one suggests that he should have an option to compel the return of his investment. Viewed this way, the fact that the change—for better or for worse—comes through marriage, whether by merger or assets sale, seems purely incidental. The fact that the corporate entity in which one invested disappears as a result of a merger or of a sale of assets coupled with dissolution is also beside the point. One's investment may gain immortality when it takes a new form, i.e., a share in a successor enterprise. The fact is that, closely held corporations aside, an investment in a corporation is really an investment in the judgment, business acumen, integrity, and vigor of management, whose personnel and policy change over time. Management ability may have its finest hour in negotiating and implementing arrangements which conceptually change the shareholder's investment and his original relationship to the corporation and its shareholders, but which actually improve his investment.

> This is not meant to be a paean in praise of management. It does not mean that management (with or without a majority or more of the shareholders) should be omnipotent or that every distinctive Delaware doctrine, e.g., the narrow scope of fraud, the light treatment of preferred stock rights, is sound. It does seem, however, that an unrealistic importance has been attached to the investor's interest in changes in corporate form. Certainly, "fundamental corporate change" is too undiscriminating a basis on which to adopt a *de facto* merger concept, and in so far as *Hariton* rejects such a basis, the decision seems entirely sound.

Folk, De Facto Mergers in Delaware: Hariton v. Arco Electronics, Inc., 49 Va.L.Rev. 1261, 1278, 1280–1281 (1963). Do you agree with this point of view?

(3) There are relatively few recent cases in which the de facto merger doctrine was invoked in an effort to obtain the procedural protections that would be available if the transaction were cast as a merger. One recent attempt is Irving Bank Corp. v. Bank of New York Co., Inc., 140 Misc.2d 363, 530 N.Y.S.2d 757 (Sup.1988), where the Irving Bank unsuccessfully argued that Bank of New York's takeover attempt (involving open market purchases, a cash tender offer, and a cash-out merger) constituted a de facto merger that required the affirmative vote of two-thirds of Bank of New York's shareholders.

(4) Presumably the decline in the de facto merger doctrine is attributable in part to the systemization of the procedures relating to the approval of mergers and economically equivalent transactions. Under the RMBCA, for example, there is no immediate procedural advantage in structuring an acquisition in the form of a sale of assets for stock followed by the distribution of the stock to shareholders of the selling corporation and dissolution of that corporation. The shareholders of the selling corporation have the right to vote on the sale of assets and shareholders opposing that transaction have the right of dissent and appraisal. However, not all states follow this pattern. Delaware and a handful of other states require a shareholder vote on sales of substantially all the assets of a corporation but do not grant dissenters' rights to shareholders voting against a sale of assets. In addition, other procedural rights in some states may be involved in the characterization of the procedure as a "merger" or as something else. It is therefore likely that cases involving the de facto merger doctrine will arise from time to time even though such attempts to restructure transactions should lose if the reasoning of *Hariton* is accepted.

(5) A few states have statutes that attempt to negate the de facto merger doctrine. See, for example, Tex.Bus.Corp.Act Ann. art. 5.01B (Vernon 1980).

> B. A disposition of all, or substantially all, of the property and assets of a corporation requiring the special authorization of the shareholders of the corporation under Section A of this article:
>
> > (1) is not considered to be a merger or consolidation pursuant to this Act or otherwise; and
>
> > (2) except as otherwise expressly provided by another statute, does not make the acquiring corporation responsible or liable for any liability or obligation of the selling corporation that the acquiring corporation did not expressly assume.

The Bar Committee Comment to this section states that its purpose "is to preclude the application of the doctrine of *de facto* merger in any sale, lease, exchange or other disposition of all or substantially all the property and assets of a corporation requiring authorization [of shareholders] * * *."

(6) One class of cases in which the de facto merger doctrine has been applied with regularity is the product liability case. A plaintiff is injured by the use of some product; investigation reveals that the manufacturer disappeared years earlier in an asset transaction, with the purchaser usually being a large publicly held corporation that is continuing the

business of the manufacturer under the same name and often, with some of the same manufacturing assets and personnel. The acquisition agreement contained clauses specifically disclaiming the assumption of contingent or unknown liabilities. Cases holding the successor liable in such circumstances are so common that in most jurisdictions attorneys refuse to express an opinion as to whether the asset purchaser will be free of product liability claims. These cases often stress the degree of continuity between the old business and the new and the test is not always phrased in terms of "de facto merger." See e.g., Marks v. Minnesota Min. & Mfg. Co., 187 Cal. App.3d 1429, 232 Cal.Rptr. 594 (1986); Dayton v. Peck, Stow and Wilcox Co. (Pexto), 739 F.2d 690 (1st Cir.1984); Grant–Howard Associates v. General Housewares, 115 Misc.2d 704, 454 N.Y.S.2d 521 (Sup.Ct.1982); Ray v. Alad Corp., 19 Cal.3d 22, 136 Cal.Rptr. 574, 560 P.2d 3 (1977); Turner v. Bituminous Cas. Co., 397 Mich. 406, 244 N.W.2d 873 (1976); Haney v. Bendix Corp., 88 Mich.App. 747, 279 N.W.2d 544 (1979); Gee v. Tenneco, Inc., 615 F.2d 857 (9th Cir.1980) (California law). Not all courts, however, have broadly accepted the de facto merger doctrine in this type of case. See e.g. Weaver v. Nash International, Inc., 730 F.2d 547 (8th Cir.1984); Armour–Dial, Inc. v. Alkar Engineering Corp., 469 F.Supp. 1193 (E.D.Wis. 1979) (Wisconsin law). See RMBCA § 14.07 which attempts to address this general problem by broadening the right to proceed against the shareholders of the disappearing corporation receiving liquidating distributions rather than addressing the issue of successor liability directly.

Appendix One

RESTATEMENT OF AGENCY, SECOND *

Definitions

§ 4. Disclosed Principal; Partially Disclosed Principal; Undisclosed Principal

(1) If, at the time of a transaction conducted by an agent, the other party thereto has notice that the agent is acting for a principal and of the principal's identity, the principal is a disclosed principal.

(2) If the other party has notice that the agent is or may be acting for a principal but has no notice of the principal's identity, the principal for whom the agent is acting is a partially disclosed principal.

(3) If the other party has no notice that the agent is acting for a principal, the one for whom he acts is an undisclosed principal.

§ 7. Authority

Authority is the power of the agent to affect the legal relations of the principal by acts done in accordance with the principal's manifestations of consent to him.

§ 8. Apparent Authority [1]

Apparent authority is the power to affect the legal relations of another person by transactions with third persons, professedly as agent

---

1. [By the Editor] The distinction between "authority" and "apparent authority" is a basic one that reappears throughout the Restatement of Agency. A principal may grant "authority" to an agent to act on his behalf (§ 7); this grant directly to the agent is often called "actual authority." The principal may also create "apparent authority" in the agent by his actions or manifestations of consent to third persons which gives the agent the power to bind the principal (§ 8) even though actual authority is lacking. See Comment a to section 8:

a. Apparent authority results from a manifestation by a person that another is his agent, the manifestation being made to a third person and not, as when authority is created, to the agent. It is entirely distinct from authority, either express or implied. The power to deal for the other, arising from and in accordance with the other's manifestations to such third persons.

Creation of Relation

§ 15. Manifestations of Consent

An agency relation exists only if there has been a manifestation by the principal to the agent that the agent may act on his account, and consent by the agent so to act.

Creation and Interpretation of Authority and Apparent Authority

§ 26. Creation of Authority: General Rule

* * * [A]uthority to do an act can be created by written or spoken words or other conduct of the principal which, reasonably interpreted, causes the agent to believe that the principal desires him so to act on the principal's account.

§ 27. Creation of Apparent Authority: General Rule

* * * [A]pparent authority to do an act is created as to a third person by written or spoken words or any other conduct of the principal which, reasonably interpreted, causes the third person to believe that the principal consents to have the act done on his behalf by the person purporting to act for him.

§ 33. General Principle of Interpretation

An agent is authorized to do, and to do only, what it is reasonable for him to infer that the principal desires him to do in the light of the principal's manifestations and the facts as he knows or should know them at the time he acts.

§ 34. Circumstances Considered in Interpreting Authority

An authorization is interpreted in light of all accompanying circumstances, including among other matters:

    (a) the situation of the parties, their relations to one another, and the business in which they are engaged;

with third persons which results from it may, however, be identical with the power created by authority as it is where the principal's statements to the third person are the same as to the agent and are similarly interpreted. On the other hand the power may be greater or smaller than that resulting from authority. If it exists, the third person has the same rights with reference to the principal as where the agent is authorized. * * * Further, one who is authorized to act for the principal makes the latter a party to the transaction whether or not the third person believes the agent to be authorized or is even aware of the existence of the principal. * * * On the other hand, apparent authority exists only with regard to those who believe and have reason to believe that there is authority; there can be no apparent authority created by an undisclosed principal. The rules of interpretation of apparent authority are, however, the same as those for authority, substituting the manifestation to the third person in place of that to the agent. * * *

(b) the general usages of business, the usages of trades or employments of the kind to which the authorization relates, and the business methods of the principal;

(c) facts of which the agent has notice respecting the objects which the principal desires to accomplish;

(d) the nature of the subject matter, the circumstances under which the act is to be performed and the legality or illegality of the act; and

(e) the formality or informality, and the care, or lack of it, with which an instrument evidencing the authority is drawn.

§ 43. Acquiescence by Principal in Agent's Conduct

(1) Acquiescence by the principal in conduct of an agent whose previously conferred authorization reasonably might include it, indicates that the conduct was authorized; if clearly not included in the authorization, acquiescence in it indicates affirmance.

(2) Acquiescence by the principal in a series of acts by the agent indicates authorization to perform similar acts in the future.

§ 49. Interpretation of Apparent Authority Compared with Interpretation of Authority

The rules applicable to the interpretation of authority are applicable to the interpretation of apparent authority except that:

(a) manifestations of the principal to the other party to the transaction are interpreted in light of what the other party knows or should know instead of what the agent knows or should know, and

(b) if there is a latent ambiguity in the manifestations of the principal for which he is not at fault, the interpretation of apparent authority is based on the facts known to the principal.

§ 82. Ratification

Ratification is the affirmance by a person of a prior act which did not bind him but which was done or professedly done on his account, whereby the act, as to some or all persons, is given effect as if originally authorized by him.

Termination

§ 105. [By] Lapse of Time

Authority conferred for a specified time terminates at the expiration of that period; if no time is specified, authority terminates at the end of a reasonable period.

§ 106. [By] Accomplishment of Authorized Act

The authority of an agent to perform a specified act or to accomplish a specified result terminates when the act is done or the result is accomplished by the agent or by another, except that if the act is done or the result is accomplished by a person other than the agent, the manifestations of the principal to the agent determine whether the authority terminates at once or when the agent has notice of it.

§ 117. [By] Mutual Consent

The authority of an agent terminates in accordance with the terms of an agreement between the principal and agent so to terminate it.

§ 118. [By] Revocation or Renunciation

Authority terminates if the principal or the agent manifests to the other dissent to its continuance.

§ 119. Manner of Revocation or Renunciation

Authority created in any manner terminates when either party in any manner manifests to the other dissent to its continuance or, unless otherwise agreed, when the other has notice of dissent.

§ 124A. Effect of Termination of Authority upon Apparent Authority and Other Powers

The termination of authority does not thereby terminate apparent authority. All other powers of the agent resulting from the relation terminate except powers necessary for the protection of his interests or of those of the principal.

§ 125. [Termination of Apparent Authority]

Apparent authority, not otherwise terminated, terminates when the third person has notice of:

(a) the termination of the agent's authority;

(b) a manifestation by the principal that he no longer consents; or

(c) facts, the failure to reveal which, were the transaction with the principal in person, would be ground for rescission by the principal.

Liability of Principal to Third Persons in General

§ 140. Liability Based upon Agency Principles

The liability of the principal to a third person upon a transaction conducted by an agent, or the transfer of his interests by an agent, may be based upon the fact that:

(a) the agent was authorized;

(b) the agent was apparently authorized; or

(c) the agent had a power arising from the agency relation and not dependent upon authority or apparent authority.

§ 141. Liability Based on Other Than Agency Principles

A principal, although not subject to liability because of principles of agency, may be liable to a third person on account of a transaction with an agent, because of the principles of estoppel, restitution or negotiability.

§ 143. Effect of Ratification

Upon ratification with knowledge of the material facts, the principal becomes responsible for contracts and conveyances made for him by one purporting to act on his account as if the transaction had been authorized, if there has been no supervening loss of capacity by the principal or change in the law which would render illegal the authorization or performance of such a transaction.

(a) Liability of Disclosed or Partially Disclosed Principals

§ 144. General Rule

A disclosed or partially disclosed principal is subject to liability upon contracts made by an agent acting within his authority if made in proper form and with the understanding that the principal is a party.

§ 159. Apparent Authority

A disclosed or partially disclosed principal is subject to liability upon contracts made by an agent acting within his apparent authority if made in proper form and with the understanding that the apparent principal is a party. The rules as to the liability of a principal for authorized acts, are applicable to unauthorized acts which are apparently authorized.

§ 160. Violation of Secret Instructions

A disclosed or partially disclosed principal authorizing an agent to make a contract, but imposing upon him limitations as to incidental terms intended not to be revealed, is subject to liability upon a contract made in violation of such limitations with a third person who has no notice of them.

§ 161. Unauthorized Acts of General Agent

A general agent for a disclosed or partially disclosed principal subjects his principal to liability for acts done on his account which usually accompany or are incidental to transactions which the agent is authorized to conduct if, although they are forbidden by the principal, the other party reasonably believes that the agent is authorized to do them and has no notice that he is not so authorized.

§ 165. Agent Acts for Improper Purpose

A disclosed or partially disclosed principal is subject to liability upon a contract purported to be made on his account by an agent authorized to make it for the principal's benefit, although the agent acts for his own or other improper purposes, unless the other party has notice that the agent is not acting for the principal's benefit.

§ 166. Persons Having Notice of Limitations of Agent's Authority

A person with notice of a limitation of an agent's authority cannot subject the principal to liability upon a transaction with the agent if he should know that the agent is acting improperly.

§ 168. Power of Agent as to Statements of His Authority

A disclosed or partially disclosed principal is not thereby subject to liability because of untrue representations by an agent as to the existence or extent of his authority or the facts upon which it depends.

(b) Liability of Undisclosed Principals

§ 186. General Rule

An undisclosed principal is bound by contracts and conveyances made on his account by an agent acting within his authority * * *.

§ 194. Acts of General Agents

A general agent for an undisclosed principal authorized to conduct transactions subjects his principal to liability for acts done on his account, if usual or necessary in such transactions, although forbidden by the principal to do them.

§ 195. Acts of Manager Appearing to be Owner

An undisclosed principal who entrusts an agent with the management of his business is subject to liability to third persons with whom the agent enters into transactions usual in such businesses and on the principal's account, although contrary to the directions of the principal.

Liability of Principal to Third Persons for Torts

§ 212. Principal Intends Conduct or Consequences

A person is subject to liability for the consequences of another's conduct which results from his directions as he would be for his own personal conduct if, with knowledge of the conditions, he intends the conduct, or if he intends its consequences, unless the one directing or the one acting has a privilege or immunity not available to the other.

§ 213. Principal Negligent or Reckless

A person conducting an activity through servants or other agents is subject to liability for harm resulting from his conduct if he is negligent or reckless:

> (a) in giving improper or ambiguous orders or in failing to make proper regulations; or

> (b) in the employment of improper persons or instrumentalities in work involving risk of harm to others;

(c) in the supervision of the activity; or

(d) in permitting, or failing to prevent, negligent or other tortious conduct by persons, whether or not his servants or agents, upon premises or with instrumentalities under his control.

§ 215. Conduct Authorized But Unintended by Principal

A master or other principal who unintentionally authorizes conduct of a servant or other agent which constitutes a tort to a third person is subject to liability to such person.

§ 216. Unauthorized Tortious Conduct

A master or other principal may be liable to another whose interests have been invaded by the tortious conduct of a servant or other agent, although the principal does not personally violate a duty to such other or authorize the conduct of the agent causing the invasion.

§ 219. When Master Is Liable for Torts of His Servants

(1) A master is subject to liability for the torts of his servants committed while acting in the scope of their employment.

(2) A master is not subject to liability for the torts of his servants acting outside the scope of their employment, unless:

(a) the master intended the conduct or the consequences, or

(b) the master was negligent or reckless, or

(c) the conduct violated a non-delegable duty of the master, or

(d) the servant purported to act or to speak on behalf of the principal and there was reliance upon apparent authority, or he was aided in accomplishing the tort by the existence of the agency relation.

§ 222. Servants of Agent of Undisclosed Principal

An undisclosed principal is subject to liability to third persons for conduct within the scope of employment of servants and of subservants employed for him by a servant or other agent empowered to employ them.

§ 228. General Statement [as to Scope of Employment]

(1) Conduct of a servant is within the scope of employment if, but only if:

(a) it is of the kind he is employed to perform;

(b) it occurs substantially within the authorized time and space limits;

(c) it is actuated, at least in part, by a purpose to serve the master; and

(d) if force is intentionally used by the servant against another, the use of force is not unexpectable by the master.

(2) Conduct of a servant is not within the scope of employment if it is different in kind from that authorized, far beyond the authorized time or space limits, or too little actuated by a purpose to serve the master.

§ 230. Forbidden Acts

An act, although forbidden, or done in a forbidden manner, may be within the scope of employment.

§ 231. Criminal or Tortious Acts

An act may be within the scope of employment although consciously criminal or tortious.

§ 232. Failure to Act

The failure of a servant to act may be conduct within the scope of employment.

§ 250. Non-liability for Physical Harm by Non–Servant Agents

A principal is not liable for physical harm caused by the negligent physical conduct of a non-servant agent during the performance of the principal's business, if he neither intended nor authorized the result nor the manner of performance, unless he was under a duty to have the act performed with due care.

Liability of Third Party to Principal

§ 292. General Rule [with respect to a Disclosed or Partially Disclosed Principal]

The other party to a contract made by an agent for a disclosed or partially disclosed principal, acting within his authority, apparent authority or other agency power, is liable to the principal as if he had contracted directly with the principal, unless the principal is excluded as a party by the form or terms of the contract.

§ 302. General Rule [With Respect to an Undisclosed Principal]

A person who makes a contract with an agent of an undisclosed principal, intended by the agent to be on account of his principal and within the power of such agent to bind his principal, is liable to the principal as if the principal himself had made the contract with him, unless he is excluded by the form or terms of the contract, unless his existence is fraudulently concealed or unless there is set-off or a similar defense against the agent.

§ 304. Agent Misrepresents Existence of Principal

A person with whom an agent contracts on account of an undisclosed principal can rescind the contract if he was induced to enter into it by a representation that the agent was not acting for a principal and if, as the agent or principal had notice, he would not have dealt with the principal.

Liability of Agent to Third Person

§ 320. Principal Disclosed

Unless otherwise agreed, a person making or purporting to make a contract with another as agent for a disclosed principal does not become a party to the contract.

§ 321. Principal Partially Disclosed

Unless otherwise agreed, a person purporting to make a contract with another for a partially disclosed principal is a party to the contract.

§ 322. Principal Undisclosed

An agent purporting to act upon his own account, but in fact making a contract on account of an undisclosed principal, is a party to the contract.

§ 326. Principal Known to Be Nonexistent or Incompetent

Unless otherwise agreed, a person who, in dealing with another, purports to act as agent for a principal whom both know to be nonexistent or wholly incompetent, becomes a party to such a contract.

§ 329. Agent Who Warrants Authority

A person who purports to make a contract, conveyance or representation on behalf of another who has full capacity but whom he has no power to bind, thereby becomes subject to liability to the other party thereto upon an implied warranty of authority, unless he has manifested that he does not make such warranty or the other party knows that the agent is not so authorized.

§ 330. Liability for Misrepresentation of Authority

A person who tortiously misrepresents to another that he has authority to make a contract, conveyance, or representation on behalf of a principal whom he has no power to bind, is subject to liability to the other in an action of tort for loss caused by reliance upon such misrepresentation.

§ 331. Agent Making No Warranty or Representation of Authority

A person who purports to make a contract, conveyance or representation on behalf of a principal whom he has no power to bind thereby is not subject to liability to the other party thereto if he sufficiently manifests that he does not warrant his authority and makes no tortious misrepresentation.

§ 343. General Rule [With Respect to Torts]

An agent who does an act otherwise a tort is not relieved from liability by the fact that he acted at the command of the principal or on account of the principal, except where he is exercising a privilege of the principal, or a privilege held by him for the protection of the principal's interests, or where the principal owes no duty or less than the normal duty of care to the person harmed.

———

Sections 376 through 528 of the Restatement of Agency, Second, define in great detail the duties agent and principal owe to each other. The duties of an agent include care, skill, obedience, good conduct, loyalty, and the preservation of confidentiality; a principal's duties include performance of contract obligations, good conduct, non-interference, and cooperation.

Appendix Two

PARTNERSHIP AGREEMENT *

Typhoon Marine Sales

The Parties agree to form a Partnership on the terms and conditions set forth in this Agreement.

ART. 1—GENERAL

1.1 Parties. The Parties (sometimes called the Partners) to this Agreement are Al Anchor (sometimes called "Anchor"), Bill Boat (sometimes called "Boat") and Charlie Cash (sometimes called "Cash").

1.2 Effective Date. The effective date of this Agreement shall be January 1, 19__.

1.3 Name. The Partnership name is TYPHOON MARINE SALES.

COMMENT. If the name differs from the Partners' names, the fictitious name statutes should be consulted. * * * If it is intended that the same name may be used after the death or retirement of a Partner, specific provision should be made; see par. 6.6. Such use is permitted by U.P.A. § 41(10) without liability for the estate of a deceased Partner.

1.4 Purpose. The purpose of the Partnership is to engage in the sale, service, and repair of all types of outboard and inboard motor boats, outboard and inboard motors, and all character of marine equipment and accessories.

COMMENT. This paragraph serves to define the scope of the Partnership business, within which each Partner has authority (actual or apparent) to act for the Partnership, U.P.A. § 9(1).

1.5 Place. The Partnership business shall be conducted at 12345 Tidal Avenue, Sunbay, Texas, and/or such other places as the Partners may determine.

* This form of partnership agreement appears as Appendix V in J. Crane and A. Bromberg: Law of Partnership (1968).

1.6 Term. The Partnership shall continue until dissolved pursuant to par. 6.1.

1.6 Term (Alternate). The Partnership shall continue for two years unless dissolved by the occurrence of one of the events listed in par. 6.1(b) or 6.1(c). After the expiration of two years, the Partnership shall continue until dissolved pursuant to par. 6.1.

COMMENT. The first alternative gives an indefinite term; the second superimposes a minimum. A third alternative would be a fixed term without provision for continuation thereafter. In such a case, expiration of the term automatically dissolves the partnership, U.P.A. § 31(1)(a), * * * but any continuation of the business would be presumptively pursuant to the original agreement, U.P.A. § 23. The principal effect of a fixed term (alone or followed by an indefinite extension) is to subject a Partner to damages for breach of contract if he deliberately dissolves the partnership before the fixed term is over, and to let the other Partners continue the business if they choose. U.P.A. §§ 38(2), 31(2) * * *. With an indefinite term, any Partner may dissolve at will, U.P.A. § 31(1)(b).

ART. 2—CAPITAL, INCOME, DRAWINGS

2.1 Initial Capital Contributions. The initial capital contributions of each Partner shall be as follows:

(a) Anchor: That certain tract of land locally known as 12345 Tidal Avenue, Sunbay, Texas, and all improvements thereon, consisting of a portable metal canopy covering an area 25′ × 50′, which property has a fair market value of $10,000 as of the effective date of this Agreement. This tract is more specifically described in Schedule A attached hereto.

(b) Boat: Those certain boats, motors and marine accessories described in Schedule B attached hereto, which have a fair market value of $10,000 as of the effective date of this Agreement.

(c) Cash: $10,000 in cash.

2.2 Subsequent Capital Contributions. The Partners, in proportion to their distributive shares (as defined in par. 3.3), shall make such subsequent capital contributions as are needed by the Partnership. If any Partner fails to make such contribution, the other Partners (at their option) may consider the sums thus advanced by them to be loans to the Partnership.

COMMENT. This provision could easily be omitted in favor of letting the Partners make this decision as circumstances develop. A distinction is suggested between a loan and a capital contribution in the event one partner defaults because loans have priority over capital contributions in distributions after dissolution, par. 6.9, U.P.A. §§ 40(b), 18(a), U.P.A. § 18(c), authorizes interest on advances. Cf. par. 3.4(a).

2.3 Capital Accounts. An individual Capital Account shall be maintained for each Partner. It shall be credited with his contributions and debited and credited in accordance with pars. 2.6 and 2.8.

COMMENT. The elaborate scheme of accounting prescribed by pars. 2.3–2.8 is convenient but not essential. It is designed so that the books of account will show, at a glance, all the different financial relations between Partners and Partnership. It could be replaced by a bare statement that books shall be kept in accordance with generally accepted accounting principles, but this leaves many questions unanswered.

Several alternative procedures might be specified:

(A) Capital account only. Capital contributions, income and withdrawals are all entered in it. This has the virtue of simplicity.

(B) Capital account and income account. Income and withdrawals are entered in the income account which is ultimately closed to the capital account.

(C) Capital account, accumulated income account and drawing account. This would be the same as in the Agreement, except that the capital account would be credited only with capital contributions and debited only with withdrawals of capital. Income would be entered in the accumulated income account which would be a balance sheet account (like earned surplus) to which drawings are closed. Such an arrangement would facilitate liquidation, in which capital contributions are repaid before profits, par. 6.9, U.P.A. §§ 40(b), 18(a).

Wherever feasible, the Partnership accountant should be consulted before drafting provisions on accounting matters. This is particularly important where the Agreement concerns an existing partnership with established records.

2.4 Income Accounts. An individual Income Account shall be maintained for each Partner. It shall be credited with his Distributive Share of profits and debited with his Distributive Share of losses (subject to par. 2.6) as soon as practicable after the close of each fiscal year and at such times during the fiscal year as the Partners may determine.

2.5 Drawing Accounts. An individual Drawing Account shall be maintained for each Partner. It shall be debited with his withdrawals.

2.6 Relation of Income Accounts to Capital Accounts. Any losses exceeding the credit balances in the Income Accounts shall be debited to the individual Capital Accounts. If the Capital Account of a Partner is depleted by thus debiting losses, future profits of that Partner shall be credited to his Capital Account until such depletion has been made good.

2.7 Limitation on Withdrawals. Except by unanimous agreement of the Partners, no Partner shall make a withdrawal which would:

(a) Reduce Partnership cash below $_____, or

(b) Make the balance in his Drawing Account exceed the combined net credit balance of (i) his Capital Account,

(ii) his Income Account and (iii) his Distributive Share of estimated profits or losses since the last entries in his Income Account.

Any excessive withdrawal shall be promptly restored.

COMMENT. This provision is designed to discourage excessive withdrawals and can be made more stringent if desired. The last sentence creates a duty to repay any excessive withdrawals; this provision can presumably be enforced without dissolving the Partnership. Par. (a) is designed to keep a minimum working capital in the Partnership. Par. (b) is intended to assure that no Partner is ever a net debtor to the Partnership.

2.8 Closing of Accounts. As soon as practicable after the closing of each fiscal year, the Income and Drawing Accounts shall be closed to the Capital Accounts.

ART. 3—OTHER FINANCIAL AND ACCOUNTING MATTERS

3.1 Method of Accounting. The Partnership shall keep accounts on the accrual basis. The accounts shall readily disclose items which the Partners take into account separately for income tax purposes. As to matters of accounting not provided for in this agreement, generally accepted accounting principles shall govern.

COMMENT. The simpler cash method of accounting will be preferred in many instances. However, the accrual method is required in virtually all instances where inventories are maintained; Income Tax Regulations Sec. 1.446–1(b)(2)(i). Separately treated items are identified in IRC Sec. 702(a) (26 U.S.C.A.) and Regulations thereunder. Except in very unusual cases, the Partnership books should be kept in accordance with income tax requirements.

3.2 Fiscal Year. The fiscal year of the Partnership shall be the calendar year.

COMMENT. In most instances this is the only fiscal year a Partnership can have for tax purposes; see IRC 706(b) (26 U.S.C.A.).

3.3 Distributive Shares. The profits or losses of the Partnership shall be distributable or chargeable, as the case may be, in the following proportions (sometimes called Distributive Shares):

Al Anchor ⅓

Bill Boat ⅓

Charlie Cash ⅓

COMMENT. Sharing of profits equally and sharing losses in proportion to profits is provided by U.P.A. § 18(a) * * *. Any variation shall be specified in the Partnership Agreement. The phrase "distributive share" is from IRC Sec. 704 (26 U.S.C.A.). The distributive share need not be the same for all items (e.g. gain v. loss, ordinary income v. capital gain) but variations must comply with IRC 704 (26 U.S.C.A.) and Income Tax Regulations Sec. 1.704–1(b)(2) to be effective for tax purposes. Non-partners may be compensated by a share of the profits; see U.P.A. § 7(4).

3.4 Other Compensation to Partners.

(a) No interest shall be paid on Capital Accounts.

(b) Anchor and Boat shall receive salaries of $75 per week. No increase in salaries shall be made without unanimous agreement. The payment of salaries to Partners shall be an obligation of the Partnership only to the extent that Partnership assets are available therefor, and shall not be an obligation of the Partners individually. Salaries shall, to this extent, be treated as an expense of the Partnership in determining profits or losses.

COMMENT. Unless the Agreement provides otherwise, interest is allowed on Capital Accounts from the date when repayment should be made (U.P.A. § 18(d)) and salaries are not allowed (U.P.A. § 18(f)). See par. 4.2 on rent.

3.5 Indemnification of Partners. The Partnership shall promptly indemnify each Partner in respect of payments reasonably made and personal liabilities reasonably incurred by him in the ordinary conduct of its business, or for the preservation of its business or property.

COMMENT. Since U.P.A. § 18(b) so provides, this need not be repeated in the Agreement, although it is important that the Partners understand it.

ART. 4—PROPERTY

4.1 Partnership Property. The property described in par. 2.1 (Initial Capital Contributions) shall become Partnership property. Other property may be contributed to the Partnership upon the same terms by unanimous agreement of the Partners. All Partnership property shall be so recorded in the Partnership accounts.

COMMENT. An enormous volume of litigation has resulted from failure to distinguish partnership property from property owned by the Partners individually but made available for Partnership use. Typical of the problems have been: (1) creditors' priorities, (2) partners' rights in property, (3) who shares gain or loss on disposition, and (4) who is entitled to the property on dissolution. The intent of the Partners has generally been held to govern. Pars. 4.1 and 4.2 are designed to make intent explicit and to require Partnership records to be kept accordingly. Capital contributions are credited to a Partner's capital account pursuant to par. 2.3.

A number of consequences flow from the characterization of property as partnership or individual. For example, partnership creditors have prior rights in partnership property and individual creditors in individual property. U.P.A. § 40(h), (i). * * * The designation of partnership property is of vital significance because of the limited rights of an individual partner therein. These rights are itemized in U.P.A. § 25(2) * * *. They might well be paraphrased in the Agreement to avoid misunderstandings among the Partners. A Partner's interest in the partnership is legally distinct from his rights in specific partnership property.

4.2 Property Made Available for Partnership Use. Schedule C to this Agreement identifies certain property being made available for Partnership use. This property shall remain the property of the Partner presently owning it, but it shall not be withdrawn from Partnership use prior to dissolution without unanimous consent of the Partners. (However, the tractor and trailer described in Item _____ of the Schedule is being made available to the Partnership by Cash for one year after the effective date of this Agreement; then Cash shall be free to withdraw the same.) No rental shall be paid by the Partnership for the use of such equipment, but all usual and customary operating expenses shall be treated as an expense of the Partnership in determining profits or losses. Such property shall not be recorded as Partnership assets in the Partnership accounts. Other property may be made available for Partnership use on such terms as the Partners may unanimously agree.

COMMENT. See Comment to Par. 4.1.

4.3 Method of Holding Partnership Property. Partnership property (including real estate) may, by unanimous consent of the Partners, be acquired and conveyed in the name of any Partner or other person as nominee for the Partnership. Such property shall be recorded as Partnership property in the Partnership accounts.

COMMENT. Although all property, including real estate, can be held and conveyed in the partnership name (U.P.A. §§ 8(3), 10), it may be simpler to use a partner or someone else as nominee or trustee. It is important that the partnership accounts reflect the ownership; see Comment to Par. 4.1.

ART. 5—OPERATIONS

5.1 Management. All Partners shall have equal rights in the management of the Partnership business. Decisions shall be by majority vote (each Partner having one vote) except as provided in par. 5.2.

COMMENT. This restates U.P.A. § 18(e), (h).

5.2 Matters Requiring Unanimity. No Partner shall, without the consent of the other Partners (which consent shall not be unreasonably withheld), do any of the following:

(a) Assign the partnership property in trust for creditors or on the assignee's promise to pay the debts of the Partnership.

(b) Dispose of the good will of the business.

(c) Do any other act which would make it impossible to carry on the ordinary business of the Partnership.

(d) Confess a judgment.

(e) Submit a partnership claim or liability to arbitration or reference.

(f) Make, execute or deliver for the Partnership any bond, mortgage, deed of trust, guarantee, indemnity bond, surety bond or accommodation paper or accommodation endorsement.

(g) Borrow money in the partnership name or use Partnership property as collateral.

(h) Assign, transfer, pledge, compromise or release any claim of or debt owing to the Partnership except upon payment in full.

(i) Convey any Partnership real property.

(j) Pledge or transfer in any manner his interest in the Partnership except to another Partner.

(k) Any of the acts for which unanimity is required by other paragraphs of this Agreement, e.g. 2.7, 3.4, 4.1, 4.2, 4.3 and 6.1.

COMMENT. Limitations on a Partner's authority are generally not binding on third persons without knowledge. U.P.A. § 9(4), * * *. However, they are binding on the Partners; any breach might give rise to damages and might dissolve the partnership. Subpars. (a)–(e) of the Agreement restate U.P.A. § 9(3), * * * and are therefore presumably binding on third persons (by force of the Act) as well as upon Partners.

5.3 Time. Anchor and Boat shall each devote his entire time and attention to the business of the Partnership, except that each may devote reasonable time to civic, family, and personal affairs. Cash shall be free to devote his time and attention to other business matters.

COMMENT. This settles the legally uncertain extent of a Partner's duty to perform services. * * * It also contains an implied non-competition agreement for Anchor and Boat, but not for Cash, which may be made explicit. Unless otherwise agreed, Partners are not free to compete with their firm.

5.4 Books. The Partnership books shall be kept at the principal place of business of the Partnership, and every Partner shall at all times have access to and may inspect and copy any of them.

COMMENT. Since U.P.A. § 19 so provides, this need not be repeated in the Agreement.

5.5 Bank Accounts. The Partnership shall maintain such bank accounts as the Partners shall determine. Checks shall be drawn for Partnership purposes only, and may be signed by any person or persons designated by the Partners. All moneys received by the Partnership shall be deposited in such account or accounts.

COMMENT. In establishing bank accounts, the bank's form of deposit agreement should be carefully scrutinized. It may modify the Partnership Agreement, e.g. as to borrowing authority.

ART. 6—DISSOLUTION

6.1 Causes of Dissolution. The Partnership shall be dissolved by the first of the following which happens:

(a) Retirement of a Partner,

(b) Death, disability or bankruptcy of a Partner,

(c) Unanimous agreement of the Partners to dissolve.

COMMENT. These are not the only causes of dissolution recognized by U.P.A. §§ 31, 32 * * *. In particular, they do not deprive a Partner of the power to dissolve in violation of the Agreement, U.P.A. § 31(2) * * *. They should, however, convert such a dissolution into a retirement, with consequent advantages to the remaining Partners, e.g., Par. 6.6 and perhaps rights to damages if during a fixed term, U.P.A. § 38(2) * * *. U.P.A. § 38(2)(b) * * * allows a similar continuation of the business without express provision in the Agreement, but subject to rather more restrictive requirements. See also Comment to Par. 1.6.

6.2 Manner of Retirement. Any Partner may retire upon 60 days prior written notice to the other Partners.

6.3 Definition of "Disability." Disability shall mean permanent physical or mental disability.

6.4 Notice of Dissolution. Actual notice of dissolution shall be given to all persons who have had dealings with the Partnership during the two years prior to dissolution.

COMMENT. U.P.A. §§ 35(1)(b) and 35(3)(c) encourage such notice by relieving the Partners from unauthorized post-dissolution liabilities if it is given. The agreement may well go further and call for notice of dissolution by newspaper advertisement which gives further protection under the sections cited.

6.5 Accounting on Dissolution. The Capital, Income and Drawing Accounts shall be posted as of the date of dissolution. Assets and liabilities shall be taken at book value but no value shall be assigned to good will or firm name.

COMMENT. In some circumstances it will be desirable to have the assets appraised or to include value for good will or firm name.

6.6 Right to Continue. If dissolution occurs under Par. 6.1(a) or (b), the remaining Partners shall have the right to continue the Partnership business under the same name, by themselves or with any other person or persons they may select. If the remaining Partners desire to continue the business, but not together, the Partnership shall be liquidated in accordance with Par. 6.9.

COMMENT. * * * For continued use of the name, see Comment to Par. 1.3.

6.7 Payment if Partnership Continued. If the remaining Partners continue the Partnership business under Par. 6.6, they shall pay to the other Partner or his legal representatives the value of his interest as of the date of dissolution, as determined under Par. 6.8 and no more. Payment shall be made at least one-half within six months of dissolution and the remainder within twelve months of dissolution.

COMMENT. See U.P.A. § 42, * * * for an alternative (foreclosed by this paragraph) allowing the retiring Partner or a deceased Partner's estate to leave property in the firm and receive a share of the profits.

6.8 Value of Interest. The value of a Partner's interest shall be:

(a) The sum of:

(1) His Capital Account,

(2) His Income Account,

(3) Any other amounts due and owing to him by the Partnership;

(b) Less the sum of:

(1) His Drawing Account,

(2) Any other amounts due and owing by him to the Partnership.

COMMENT. See Comment to Par. 6.5 concerning revaluation of the assets. In certain instances (e.g. professional or construction firms) it will be desirable to include the value of unrealized profits on uncompleted employments or projects. This method of valuation takes partnership liabilities into account; the continuing partnership remains responsible for them. U.P.A. § 41(1).

6.9 Winding Up and Liquidation. Upon dissolution, if the Partnership business is not continued under Par. 6.6, it shall be wound up and liquidated as rapidly as business circumstances will permit. The assets shall be applied to the following purposes in the following order:

(a) To pay or provide for all amounts owing by the Partnership to creditors other than Partners, and for expenses of winding up.

(b) To pay or provide for all amounts owing by the Partnership to Partners other than for capital and profits.

(c) To pay or provide for all amounts owing by the Partnership to Partners in respect of capita.

(d) To pay or provide for all amounts owing to the Partners in respect of profits.

COMMENT. Since U.P.A. § 40(b) generally so provides, this need not be repeated in the Agreement. A frequent alternative is to provide for the division among the partners in proportion to their capital accounts after payment or provision for loans to partners and other creditors. Depending on the method of computation of the capital accounts, this may well provide a different distribution from U.P.A. § 40(b). In particular, it impliedly relieves the partners from the obligations of U.P.A. §§ 40(d), 18(a) * * * to make contributions sufficient to satisfy all the liabilities of the partnership, even those in respect of profits.

6.10 Authority to Wind Up. If dissolution occurs under Par. 6.1(a) or (b), the remaining Partners shall have the authority to wind up. If dissolution occurs under Par. 6.1(c), all Partners jointly shall have the authority to wind up.

COMMENT. U.P.A. § 37, * * * generally so provides. Implied authority and duty to convert assets into cash is supplied by Sec. 38(1).

6.11 Method of Distribution of Assets. To the extent feasible, all distributions in liquidation shall be made pro rata to the partners in kind.

COMMENT. This is a warning not to become entangled in IRC Sec. 751 (collapsible partnerships). Pro rata distributions are usually preferable for income tax purposes. See Comment to Par. 6.10. If property contributed by a particular partner is to be returned to him, the Agreement should so state.

ART. 7—MISCELLANEOUS

7.1 Notice. Any notice to a partner required or permitted by this Agreement shall be in writing and shall be sufficient if sent by registered or certified mail to the last known address of the person to whom such notice is to be given. Any notice may be waived in writing by the person entitled to receive it.

7.2 Construction of Agreement. The captions used in this Agreement are for convenience only and shall not be construed in interpreting this Agreement. Whenever the context so requires, the masculine shall include the feminine and neuter, and the singular shall include the plural and conversely. If any portion of this Agreement shall be held invalid or inoperative, then, so far as is reasonable and possible:

(a) The remainder of this Agreement shall be considered valid and operative, and

(b) Effect shall be given to the intent manifested by the portion held invalid or inoperative.

7.3 Binding Effect. This Agreement shall bind the partners, their heirs, personal representatives and assigns.

COMMENT. Consideration should be given to reciting that the wives of Partners are also bound, and having them sign the Agreement. This may be particularly important in a community property state. * * * In any state it blunts a possible attack by a wife on continuation and payment provisions after a Partner's death. But making them signatories may require their consent to any amendment of the Agreement, unless provision is included for amendment by the Partners alone.

    EXECUTED at Sunbay, Texas, in multiple copies December _____, 19__.

AL ANCHOR

BILL BOAT

CHARLIE CASH

COMMENT. See Comment to Par. 7.3.

Appendix Three

FORM OF BYLAWS FOR USE UNDER MODEL ACT *

BY-LAWS OF * * *

ARTICLE I. OFFICES

The principal office of the corporation in the State of _____ shall be located in the City of _____, County of _____. The corporation may have such other offices, either within or without the State of _____, as the board of directors may designate or as the business of the corporation may require from time to time.

The registered office of the corporation, required by the _____ Business Corporation Act to be maintained in the State of _____ may be, but need not be, identical with the principal office in the State of _____, and the address of the registered office may be changed from time to time by the board of directors. [§ 5.01] [§ 1.40(17)]

ARTICLE II. SHAREHOLDERS

Section 1. **Annual Meeting.** The annual meeting of the shareholders shall be held on the _____ in the month of _____ in each

* [By the Editor] This is Form No. 51, Model By-Laws—A Long Form, 3 Mod.Bus. Corp.Act Ann. (2d Ed.) 194 (1971), prepared for use with the 1969 Model Act. While there has been discussion about preparing model documents for use with the Revised Model Business Corporation Act (1984), as of 1989 no concrete steps had been taken to prepare such documents. The numbers in [brackets] in this Appendix are references to the RMBCA. In a number of instances, the cited section does not fully support the provision based on the 1969 Act because of the elimination of obsolescent provisions in the RMBCA or because of simplification of statutory provisions in that statute. Of more importance, several new sections of the RMBCA that contemplate bylaw provisions for their implementation have no

counterpart in the 1969 Model Act, and are therefore not treated at all in these bylaws. Sections of this type include, e.g. RMBCA §§ 2.07 (emergency bylaws), 6.27 (restrictions on share transfer), 7.28 (election of directors by plurality vote of shareholders at meeting at which quorum is present), 7.20 (shareholders' list available before meeting), 7.25 (reduction of quorum of shareholders to one-third upon election of corporation), 8.03 (size of board of directors), 10.21 (bylaws increasing quorum and voting requirements of shareholders), 10.22 (bylaw provisions increasing quorum and voting requirements of directors), subpart E of Chapter 8 (indemnification), subpart F of Chapter 8 (conflict of interest) and Chapter 16 (inspection rights of shareholders and disclosure obligations of corporations).

year, beginning with the year 19___, at the hour of _____ o'clock ___. M., or at such other time on such other day within such month as shall be fixed by the board of directors, for the purpose of electing directors and for the transaction of such other business as may come before the meeting. If the day fixed for the annual meeting shall be a legal holiday in the State of _____, such meeting shall be held on the next succeeding business day. If the election of directors shall not be held on the day designated herein for any annual meeting of the shareholders, or at any adjournment thereof, the board of directors shall cause the election to be held at a special meeting of the shareholders as soon thereafter as conveniently may be. [§ 7.01]

Section 2. **Special Meetings.** Special meetings of the shareholders, for any purpose or purposes, unless otherwise prescribed by statute, may be called by the president or by the board of directors, and shall be called by the president at the request of the holders of not less than one-tenth of all outstanding shares of the corporation entitled to vote at the meeting. [§ 7.02]

Section 3. **Place of Meeting.** The board of directors may designate any place, either within or without the State of _____, as the place of meeting for any annual meeting or for any special meeting called by the board of directors. A waiver of notice signed by all shareholders entitled to vote at a meeting may designate any place, either within or without the State of _____, as the place for the holding of such meeting. If no designation is made, or if a special meeting be otherwise called, the place of meeting shall be the principal office of the corporation in the State of _____. [§§ 7.01; 7.02]

Section 4. **Notice of Meeting.** Written notice stating the place, day and hour of the meeting and, in case of a special meeting, the purpose or purposes for which the meeting is called, shall, unless otherwise prescribed by statute, be delivered not less than ten nor more than sixty days before the date of the meeting, either personally or by mail, by or at the direction of the president, or the secretary, or the officer or other persons calling the meeting, to each shareholder of record entitled to vote at such meeting. If mailed, such notice shall be deemed to be delivered when deposited in the United States mail, addressed to the shareholder at his address as it appears on the stock transfer books of the corporation, with postage thereon prepaid. [§§ 7.05; 1.41]

Section 5. **Fixing of Record Date.** For the purpose of determining shareholders entitled to notice of or to vote at any meeting of shareholders or any adjournment thereof, or shareholders entitled to receive payment of any dividend, or in order to make a determination of shareholders for any other proper purpose, the board of directors of the corporation may fix in advance a date as the record date for any such determination of shareholders, such date in any case to be not more than seventy days and, in case of a meeting of shareholders, not less than ten days prior to the date on which the particular action, requiring such determination of shareholders, is to be taken. If no record date is fixed for the determination of shareholders entitled to notice of or to vote at a meeting of shareholders, or shareholders entitled to receive payment of a dividend, the date on which notice of the meeting is mailed or the date on which the resolution of the board of directors declaring such dividend is adopted, as the case may be, shall be the record date for such determination of shareholders. When a determination of shareholders entitled to vote at any meeting of shareholders has been made as provided in this section, such determination shall apply to any adjournment thereof. [§ 7.07]

Section 6. **Voting Record.** The officer or agent having charge of the stock transfer books for shares of the corporation shall make a complete record of the shareholders entitled to vote at each meeting of shareholders or any adjournment thereof, arranged in alphabetical order, with the address of and the number of shares held by each. Such record shall be produced and kept open at the time and place of the meeting and shall be subject to the inspection of any shareholder during the whole time of the meeting for the purposes thereof. [§ 7.20]

Section 7. **Quorum.** A majority of the outstanding shares of the corporation entitled to vote, represented in person or by proxy, shall constitute a quorum at a meeting of shareholders. If less than a majority of the outstanding shares are represented at a meeting, a majority of the shares so represented may adjourn the meeting from time to time without further notice. At such adjourned meeting at which a quorum shall be present or represented, any business may be transacted which might have been transacted at the meeting as originally noticed. The shareholders present at a duly organized meeting may continue to transact business until adjournment, notwithstanding the withdrawal of enough shareholders to leave less than a quorum. [§ 7.25]

Section 8. **Proxies.** At all meetings of shareholders, a shareholder may vote in person or by proxy executed in writing by the shareholder or by his duly authorized attorney-in-fact. Such proxy shall be filed with the secretary of the corporation before or at the time of the meeting. No proxy shall be valid after eleven months from the date of its execution, unless otherwise provided in the proxy. [§ 7.22(a)]

Section 9. **Voting of Shares.** Subject to the provisions of Section 12 of this Article II, each outstanding share entitled to vote shall be entitled to one vote upon each matter submitted to a vote at a meeting of shareholders. [§ 7.21]

Section 10. **Voting of Shares by Certain Holders.** Shares standing in the name of another corporation may be voted by such officer, agent or proxy as the by-laws of such corporation may prescribe, or, in the absence of such provision, as the board of directors of such other corporation may determine. [§ 7.24]

Shares held by an administrator, executor, guardian or conservator may be voted by him, either in person or by proxy, without a transfer of such shares into his name. Shares standing in the name of a trustee may be voted by him, either in person or by proxy, but no trustee shall be entitled to vote shares held by him without a transfer of such shares into his name. [§ 7.24]

Shares standing in the name of a receiver may be voted by such receiver, and shares held by or under the control of a receiver may be voted by such receiver without the transfer thereof into his name if authority so to do be contained in an appropriate order of the court by which such receiver was appointed. [§ 7.24]

A shareholder whose shares are pledged shall be entitled to vote such shares until the shares have been transferred into the name of the pledgee, and thereafter the pledgee shall be entitled to vote the shares so transferred. [None]

Neither treasury shares of its own stock held by the corporation, nor shares held by another corporation if a majority of the shares entitled to vote for the election of directors of such other corporation are held by the corporation, shall be voted at any meeting or counted in determining the total number of outstanding shares at any given time for purposes of any meeting. [§ 7.21(b)]

Section 11. **Informal Action by Shareholders.** Any action required or permitted to be taken at a meeting of the shareholders may be taken without a meeting if a consent in writing, setting forth the action so taken, shall be signed by all of the shareholders entitled to vote with respect to the subject matter thereof. [§ 7.04]

[Optional Section.] Section 12. **Cumulative Voting.** At each election for directors every shareholder entitled to vote at such election shall have the right to vote, in person or by proxy, the number of shares owned by him for as many persons as there are directors to be elected and for whose election he has a right to vote, or to cumulate his votes by giving one candidate as many votes as the number of such directors multiplied by the number of his shares shall equal, or by distributing such votes on the same principle among any number of such candidates. [§ 7.28]

ARTICLE III. BOARD OF DIRECTORS

Section 1. **General Powers.** The business and affairs of the corporation shall be managed by its board of directors. [§ 8.01(b)]

Section 2. **Number, Tenure and Qualifications.** The number of directors of the corporation shall be _____. Each director shall hold office until the next annual meeting of shareholders and until his successor shall have been elected and qualified. Directors need not be residents of the State of _____ or shareholders of the corporation. [§§ 8.02, 8.03, 8.05]

Section 3. **Regular Meetings.** A regular meeting of the board of directors shall be held without other notice than this by-law immediately after, and at the same place as, the annual meeting of shareholders. The board of directors may provide, by resolution, the time and place, either within or without the State of _____, for the holding of additional regular meetings without other notice than such resolution. [§ 8.22]

Section 4. **Special Meetings.** Special meetings of the board of directors may be called by or at the request of the president or any two directors. The person or persons authorized to call special meetings of the board of directors may fix any place, either within or without the State of _____, as the place for holding any special meeting of the board of directors called by them. [§§ 8.20, 8.22]

Section 5. **Notice.** Notice of any special meeting shall be given at least two days previously thereto by written notice delivered personally or mailed to each director at his business address, or by telegram. If mailed, such notice shall be deemed to be delivered when deposited in the United States mail, so addressed, with postage thereon prepaid. If notice be given by telegram, such notice shall be deemed to be delivered when the telegram is delivered to the telegraph company. Any director may waive notice of any meeting. The attendance of a director at a meeting shall constitute a waiver of notice of such meeting, except where a director attends a meeting for the express purpose of objecting to the transaction of any business because the meeting is not lawfully called or convened. Neither the business to be transacted at, nor the purpose of, any regular or special meeting of the board of directors need be specified in the notice or waiver of notice of such meeting. [§§ 8.22, 8.23]

Section 6. **Quorum.** A majority of the number of directors fixed by Section 2 of this Article III shall constitute a quorum for the transaction of business at any meeting of the board of directors, but if less than such majority is present at a meeting, a majority of the directors present may adjourn the meeting from time to time without further notice. [§ 8.24]

Section 7. **Manner of Acting.** The act of the majority of the directors present at a meeting at which a quorum is present shall be the act of the board of directors. [§ 8.24(c)]

Section 8. **Action Without a Meeting.** Any action required or permitted to be taken by the board of directors at a meeting may be taken without a meeting if a consent in writing, setting forth the action so taken, shall be signed by all of the directors. [§ 8.21]

Section 9. **Vacancies.** Any vacancy occurring in the board of directors may be filled by the affirmative vote of a majority of the remaining directors though less than a quorum of the board of directors. A director elected to fill a vacancy shall be elected for the unexpired term of his predecessor in office. Any directorship to be filled by reason of an increase in the number of directors may be filled by election by the board of directors for a term of office continuing only until the next election of directors by the shareholders. [§§ 8.10, 8.05(d)]

Section 10. **Compensation.** By resolution of the board of directors, each director may be paid his expenses, if any, of attendance at each meeting of the board of directors, and may be paid a stated salary as director or a fixed sum for attendance at each meeting of the board of directors or both. No such payment shall preclude any director from serving the corporation in any other capacity and receiving compensation therefor. [§ 8.11]

Section 11. **Presumption of Assent.** A director of the corporation who is present at a meeting of the board of directors at which action on any corporate matter is taken shall be presumed to have assented to the action taken unless his dissent shall be entered in the minutes of the meeting or unless he shall file his written dissent to such action with the person acting as the secretary of the meeting before the adjournment thereof or shall forward such dissent by registered mail to the secretary of the corporation immediately after the adjournment of the meeting. Such right to dissent shall not apply to a director who voted in favor of such action. [§ 8.24(d)]

ARTICLE IV. OFFICERS

Section 1. **Number.** The officers of the corporation shall be a president, one or more vice-presidents (the number thereof to be determined by the board of directors), a secretary, and a treasurer, each of whom shall be elected by the board of directors. Such other officers and assistant officers as may be deemed necessary may be elected or appointed by the board of directors. Any two or more offices may be held by the same person, except the offices of president and secretary. [§ 8.40]

Section 2. **Election and Term of Office.** The officers of the corporation to be elected by the board of directors shall be elected annually by the board of directors at the first meeting of the board of directors held after each annual meeting of the shareholders. If the election of officers shall not be held at such meeting, such election shall be held as soon thereafter as conveniently may be. Each officer shall hold office until his successor shall have been duly elected and shall have qualified or until his death or until he shall resign or shall have been removed in the manner hereinafter provided. [None]

Section 3. **Removal.** Any officer or agent may be removed by the board of directors whenever in its judgment the best interests of the corporation will be served thereby, but such removal shall be without prejudice to the contract rights, if any, of the person so removed. Election or appointment of an officer or agent shall not of itself create contract rights. [§§ 8.43, 8.44]

Section 4. **Vacancies.** A vacancy in any office because of death, resignation, removal, disqualification or otherwise, may be filled by the board of directors for the unexpired portion of the term. [None]

Section 5. **President.** The president shall be the principal executive officer of the corporation and, subject to the control of the board of directors, shall in general supervise and control all of the business and affairs of the corporation. He shall, when present, provide at all meetings of the shareholders and of the board of directors. He may sign, with the secretary or any other proper officer of the corporation thereunto authorized by the board of directors, certificates for shares of the corporation and deeds, mortgages, bonds, contracts, or other instruments which the board of directors has authorized to be executed, except in cases where the signing and execution thereof shall be expressly delegated by the board of directors or by these By–Laws to some other officer or agent of the corporation, or shall be required by law to be otherwise signed or executed; and in general shall perform all duties incident to the office of president and such other duties as may be prescribed by the board of directors from time to time. [§§ 8.40, 8.41]

Section 6. **The Vice–Presidents.** In the absence of the president or in the event of his death, inability or refusal to act, the vice-president (or in the event there be more than one vice-president, the vice-presidents in the order designated at the time of their election, or in the absence of any designation, then in the order of their election) shall perform the duties of the president, and when so acting, shall have all the powers of and be subject to all the restrictions upon the president. Any vice-president may sign, with the secretary or an assistant secretary, certificates for shares of the corporation; and shall perform such other duties as from time to time may be assigned to him by the president or by the board of directors. [§§ 8.40, 8.41]

Section 7. **The Secretary.** The secretary shall: (a) keep the minutes of the proceedings of the shareholders and of the board of directors in one or more books provided for that purpose; (b) see that all notices are duly given in accordance with the provisions of these By–Laws or as required by law; (c) be custodian of the corporate records and of the seal of the corporation and see that the seal of the corporation is affixed to all documents the execution of which on behalf of the corporation under its seal is duly authorized; (d) keep a register of the postoffice address of each shareholder which shall be furnished to the secretary by such shareholder; (e) sign with the president, or a vice-president, certificates for shares of the corporation, the issuance of which shall have been authorized by resolution of the board of directors; (f) have general charge of the stock transfer books of the corporation; and (g) in general perform all duties incident to the office of secretary and such other duties as from time to time may be assigned to him by the president or by the board of directors. [§§ 8.40(c), 8.41, 1.40(20)]

Section 8. **The Treasurer.** The treasurer shall: (a) have charge and custody of and be responsible for all funds and securities of the corporation; (b) receive and give receipts for moneys due and payable to the corporation from any source whatsoever, and deposit all such moneys in the name of the corporation in such banks, trust companies or other depositaries as shall be selected in accordance with the provisions of Article V of these By–Laws; and (c) in general perform all of the duties incident to the office of treasurer and such other duties as from time to time may be assigned to him by the president or by the board of directors. If required by the board of directors, the treasurer shall give a bond for the faithful discharge of his duties in such sum and with such surety or sureties as the board of directors shall determine. [§§ 8.40, 8.41]

Section 9. **Assistant Secretaries and Assistant Treasurers.** The assistant secretaries, when authorized by the board of directors, may sign with the president or a vice-president certificates for shares of the corporation the issuance of which shall have been authorized by a resolution of the board of directors. The assistant treasurers shall respectively, if required by the board of directors, give bonds for the faithful discharge of their duties in such sums and with such sureties as the board of directors shall determine. The assistant secretaries and assistant treasurers, in general, shall perform such duties as shall be assigned to them by the secretary or the treasurer, respectively, or by the president or the board of directors. [§§ 8.40, 8.41]

Section 10. **Salaries.** The salaries of the officers shall be fixed from time to time by the board of directors and no officer shall be prevented from receiving such salary by reason of the fact that he is also a director of the corporation. [None]

ARTICLE V. CONTRACTS, LOANS, CHECKS AND DEPOSITS

Section 1. **Contracts.** The board of directors may authorize any officer or officers, agent or agents, to enter into any contract or execute and deliver any instrument in the name of and on behalf of the corporation, and such authority may be general or confined to specific instances. [None]

Section 2. **Loans.** No loans shall be contracted on behalf of the corporation and no evidences of indebtedness shall be issued in its name unless authorized by a resolution of the board of directors. Such authority may be general or confined to specific instances. [None]

Section 3. **Checks, Drafts, etc.** All checks, drafts or other orders for the payment of money, notes or other evidences of indebtedness issued in the name of the corporation shall be signed by such officer or officers, agent or agents of the corporation and in such manner as shall from time to time be determined by resolution of the board of directors. [None]

Section 4. **Deposits.** All funds of the corporation not otherwise employed shall be deposited from time to time to the credit of the corporation in such banks, trust companies or other depositaries as the board of directors may select. [None]

ARTICLE VI. CERTIFICATES FOR SHARES AND THEIR TRANSFER

Section 1. **Certificates for Shares.** Certificates representing shares of the corporation shall be in such form as shall be determined by the board of directors. Such certificates shall be signed by the president or a vice-president and by the secretary or an assistant secretary and sealed with the corporate seal or a facsimile thereof. The signatures of such officers upon a certificate may be facsimiles if the certificate is manually signed on behalf of a transfer agent or a registrar, other than the corporation itself or one of its employees. Each certificate for shares shall be consecutively numbered or otherwise identified. The name and address of the person to whom the shares represented thereby are issued, with the number of shares and date of issue, shall be entered on the stock transfer books of the corporation. All certificates surrendered to the corporation for transfer shall be cancelled and no new certificate shall be issued until the former certificate for a like number of shares shall have been surrendered and cancelled, except that in case of a lost, destroyed or mutilated certificate a new one may be issued therefor upon such terms and indemnity to the corporation as the board of directors may prescribe. [§ 6.25]

Section 2. **Transfer of Shares.** Transfer of shares of the corporation shall be made only on the stock transfer books of the corporation by the holder of record thereof or by his legal representative, who shall furnish proper evidence of authority to transfer, or by his attorney thereunto authorized by power of attorney duly executed and filed with the secretary of the corporation, and on surrender for cancellation of the certificate for such shares. The person in whose name shares stand on the books of the corporation shall be deemed by the corporation to be the owner thereof for all purposes. [None]

ARTICLE VII. FISCAL YEAR

The fiscal year of the corporation shall begin on the first day of January and end on the thirty-first day of December in each year. [None]

ARTICLE VIII. DIVIDENDS

The board of directors may, from time to time, declare and the corporation may pay dividends on its outstanding shares in the manner and upon the terms and conditions provided by law and its Articles of Incorporation. [§ 6.40]

ARTICLE IX. CORPORATE SEAL

The board of directors shall provide a corporate seal which shall be circular in form and shall have inscribed thereon the name of the corporation and the state of incorporation and the words "Corporate Seal." [§ 3.02(2)]

ARTICLE X. WAIVER OF NOTICE

Whenever any notice is required to be given to any shareholder or director of the corporation under the provisions of these By–Laws or under the provisions of the Articles of Incorporation or under the provisions of the _____ Business Corporation Act, a waiver thereof in writing signed by the person or persons entitled to such notice, whether before or after the time stated therein, shall be deemed equivalent to the giving of such notice. [§§ 7.06, 8.23]

ARTICLE XI. AMENDMENTS

These By–Laws may be altered, amended or repealed and new By–Laws may be adopted by the board of directors or by the shareholders at any regular or special meeting. [§§ 10.20, 10.21, 10.22]

Appendix Four

PROXY STATEMENT FOR AMERICAN EXPLORATION COMPANY

American Exploration Company

April 28, 1989

Dear Fellow Stockholder:

You are cordially invited to attend the Annual Meeting of Stockholders on Thursday, June 8, 1989, at 9:30 a.m., at The Drake Hotel, 440 Park Avenue at 56th Street, New York, New York.

Walter Curley, who will be resigning from our Board to accept a position as the United States Ambassador to France, is not a nominee for director. We are grateful to him for his many contributions to the growth and success of our company and wish him well in Paris.

We are very pleased that O. Donaldson Chapoton, Senior Partner of Baker & Botts, Irvin K. Culpepper, Jr., Vice President of Kelso & Company, Richard M. Kernan, Jr., Senior Vice President of New York Life Insurance Company, and John H. Moore, formerly Chairman and Chief Executive Officer of Ladd Petroleum Corporation, have agreed to join our Board and are nominees for election as directors at this meeting.

Please sign and return the enclosed proxy form in the envelope provided as soon as possible so your shares can be voted at the meeting in accordance with your instructions.

A copy of American's 1988 Annual Report to Stockholders is also enclosed.

Sincerely,

Mark Andrews
Chairman of the Board and
Chief Executive Officer

AMERICAN EXPLORATION COMPANY
NOTICE OF ANNUAL MEETING OF STOCKHOLDERS
To Be Held June 8, 1989

To THE STOCKHOLDERS OF
AMERICAN EXPLORATION COMPANY:

NOTICE IS HEREBY GIVEN that the Annual Meeting of Stockholders of American Exploration Company ("American") will be held at The Drake Hotel, 440 Park Avenue at 56th Street, New York, New York, on Thursday, June 8, 1989, at 9:30 a.m., New York time, for the following purposes:

(1) to elect 14 members to the Board of Directors for the ensuing year;

(2) to approve the amendment and restatement of American's 1983 Stock Option Plan;

(3) to approve the appointment of Arthur Andersen & Co. as independent public accountants of American for 1989; and

(4) to transact such other business as may properly come before the meeting.

American has fixed the close of business on April 10, 1989, as the record date for determining stockholders entitled to notice of, and to vote at, such meeting or any adjournment thereof.

You are cordially invited to attend the meeting in person. Even if you plan to attend the meeting, you are requested to mark, sign, date and return the accompanying proxy as soon as possible.

By Order of the Board of
Directors

Russell P. Pennoyer
Secretary

April 28, 1989
700 Louisiana
Houston, Texas 77002

AMERICAN EXPLORATION COMPANY

700 Louisiana
Houston, Texas 77002
(713) 237–0800

PROXY STATEMENT

The accompanying proxy is solicited by the Board of Directors of American Exploration Company, a Delaware corporation ("American"), to be voted at the Annual Meeting of Stockholders of American to be held on June 8, 1989 ("Annual Meeting"), at the time and place and for the purposes set forth in the accompanying Notice of Annual Meeting of Stockholders and at any adjournments thereof.

This proxy statement and the accompanying proxy card are being mailed to stockholders on or about April 28, 1989. In addition to the solicitation of proxies by mail, regular officers and employees of American may solicit the return of proxies by mail, telephone, telegram or personal contact. American will pay the cost of soliciting proxies in the accompanying form. American will reimburse brokers or other persons holding stock in their names or in the names of their nominees for their reasonable expenses in forwarding proxy materials to beneficial owners of stock.

VOTING

Holders of the Common Stock, par value $.05 per share ("Common Stock"), of American as of April 10, 1989, the record date for determining persons entitled to notice of, and to vote at, the Annual Meeting, are entitled to vote on all matters at the Annual Meeting. Each share of Common Stock entitles the holder to one vote on each matter submitted to a vote of the stockholders. As of April 10, 1989, American had outstanding and entitled to vote 21,058,948 shares of Common Stock.

All duly executed proxies received prior to the Annual Meeting will be voted in accordance with the choices specified thereon and, in connection with any other business that may properly come before the meeting, in the discretion of the persons named in the proxy. As to any matter for which no choice has been specified in a proxy, the shares represented thereby will be voted by the persons named in the proxy, to the extent applicable, (1) for the election as a director of each nominee listed herein; (2) for the proposal to approve the amendment and restatement of American's 1983 Stock Option Plan; (3) for the proposal to approve the appointment of Arthur Andersen & Co. as independent public accountants of American for 1989; and (4) in the discretion of such persons in connection with any other business that may properly come before the meeting. A stockholder giving a proxy may revoke it at any time before it is voted at the Annual Meeting. A stockholder who attends the Annual Meeting may, if he or she wishes, vote by ballot at the Annual Meeting and such vote will cancel any proxy previously given.

PRINCIPAL SECURITY HOLDERS

The following table sets forth certain information with respect to the only persons known by American to own beneficially in excess of 5% of the Common Stock of American as of March 31, 1989.

Name and Address of Beneficial Owner	Number of Shares	Percent of Class [1]
New York Life Insurance Company ..... 51 Madison Avenue New York, NY 10010	6,073,000 [2]	26.3%
Mark Andrews .... 885 Third Avenue New York, NY 10022	1,826,229 [3]	6.7

ELECTION OF DIRECTORS (Proposal No. 1)

It is intended that the persons named below will be placed in nomination for election as directors at the Annual Meeting and that the persons named in the proxy will vote in favor of such nominees unless authority to vote in the election of directors is withheld. The terms of office of the directors will be until the next annual meeting of stockholders and until their successors are elected and qualified. The persons named in the proxy may act with discretionary authority in the event any nominee should become unavailable for election, although management is not aware of any circumstances likely to render any nominee unavailable or unable to continue to serve. Except for Messrs. Chapoton, Culpepper, Kernan and Moore, each of the nominees is a current director of American.

NAMES AND BUSINESS EXPERIENCE OF THE NOMINEES

Name	Principal Occupation During Past Five Years	Age	Director Since
Mark Andrews	Chairman of the Board and Chief Executive Officer of American [4]	38	1980

1. See explanation of computation of percent of class under "Election of Directors—Security Ownership of Directors and Nominees."

2. Includes 300,000 shares issuable upon exercise of American's Common Stock Warrants ("Warrants").

3. See Note (15) * * * Mr. Andrews is a director of American and has been nominated for reelection.

4. Mr. Andrews has been Chairman of the Board and Chief Executive Officer since 1980 and was President from 1980 to October, 1988. Mr. Andrews is also a director of IVAX Corporation.

Name	Principal Occupation During Past Five Years	Age	Director Since
O. Donaldson Chapoton	Senior Partner of the law firm of Baker & Botts [5]	51	_____
Irvin K. Culpepper, Jr.	Vice President, Kelso & Company, a merchant banking firm engaged in the leveraged buyout business [6]	40	_____
Peter C. Forbes	President of American [7]	44	1988
Phillip Frost, M.D.	Chairman of the Board and Chief Executive Officer of IVAX Corporation, a pharmaceutical, medical diagnostic and specialty chemical company [8]	52	1983
Peter G. Gerry	President of Citicorp Venture Capital Ltd.[9]	43	1983
H. Phipps Hoffstot, III	Private investor [10]	32	1983
John E. Justice, III	Private investor [11]	60	1980

5. Mr. Chapoton has been partner-in-charge of the Washington office of Baker & Botts since February 1989. From May, 1986 to January, 1989 he served in the U.S. Treasury, most recently (from October 1987 to January 1989) as Assistant Secretary of the Treasury for Tax Policy. He joined the Treasury from Baker & Botts, where he had been a Senior Partner in its Houston office. Mr. Chapoton was a director of American from 1980 to 1986.

6. Mr. Culpepper joined Kelso & Company in 1988. From 1986 to 1988, he was Vice President and head of Private Finance for New York Life Insurance Company. He was an Investment Vice President of New York Life Insurance Company from 1982 to 1986. Mr. Culpepper is also a director of The New York City Industrial Development Agency.

7. Mr. Forbes was elected President and a director of American in October, 1988. From 1975 to 1985 he worked in the treasury division of Texas Eastern Transmission Corporation, including four years as Treasurer. From 1985 to January 1988, he served as Chief Financial Officer of Zapata Corporation, an offshore drilling company. He joined American from

Browning Ferris Industries, Inc., a waste management company, where he was Vice President—Finance from February to October, 1988.

8. Dr. Frost has been Chairman of the Board and Chief Executive Officer of IVAX Corporation since March, 1987. He was Chairman of the Board of Key Pharmaceuticals Company until June 1986, when it was acquired by Schering–Plough Corp. He is also Chairman of the Department of Dermatology of Mount Sinai Medical Center of Greater Miami and a director of American Vaccine Corp. and Atico Financial Corp.

9. Mr. Gerry is also a director of Pond Hill Homes, Ltd. and Tigera Group, Inc.

10. Mr. Hoffstot is also a Vice President and director of Commonwealth National Company, a real estate consulting and development company.

11. Mr. Justice was Vice President of the investment banking firm of Lovett Mitchell Webb & Garrison, Inc. from 1984 to 1989 and Vice Chairman of the Board of Rotan Mosle Inc., an investment banking firm, from 1979 to 1984.

Name	Principal Occupation During Past Five Years	Age	Director Since
Mark Kavanagh.......	Chairman of Kavanagh Securities Ltd., an Irish investment company [12]	44	1982
Richard M. Kernan, Jr.	Senior Vice President in charge of the Investment Department, New York Life Insurance Company	48	_____
John H. Moore	Petroleum Consultant [13]	63	_____
Peter P. Nitze	Chairman of Nitze–Stagen & Company Inc., a real estate and financial consulting firm	53	1983
John B. Quay	President and Director of Plymouth Steel Corporation [14]	35	1982
Peter G. Schiff........	General Partner of Northwood Ventures, a venture capital limited partnership	37	1983

COMPENSATION OF DIRECTORS

Walter J.P. Curley, who is not standing for re-election as a director because he has been appointed United States Ambassador to France, received compensation of $10,000 per quarter for his services as Chairman of the Executive Committee. Otherwise, directors of American have not received compensation for services rendered in their capacities as directors, but have been reimbursed for certain expenses incurred by them in attending meetings of the Board of Directors and committees thereof.

BOARD ORGANIZATION AND MEETINGS

The Board of Directors of American has three standing committees—the Executive Committee, the Audit Committee and the Compensation Committee. The Executive Committee is composed of Messrs. Andrews, Curley, Frost, Gerry and Nitze. The function of this Committee is to exercise all the powers and authority of the Board of Directors during the intervals between the meetings of the Board, except to the extent that such authority is limited by law. In 1988, the Executive Committee held three meetings.

12. Mr. Kavanagh is also a director of Imry International Plc.

13. Mr. Moore was President and Chief Executive Officer from 1979 to 1986 and Chairman of the Board and Chief Executive Officer from 1986 to 1988 of Ladd Petroleum Corporation. Mr. Moore is also a director of First Interstate Bank of Denver, Hersey Oil Company and New Jersey Natural Resources Company.

14. Mr. Quay was Vice President of Plymouth Steel Corporation from 1978 until September, 1985. Since September, 1985, he has also been President of Cuyahoga Steel and Wire Corp. Mr. Quay is the brother of Mr. Andrews' wife.

The Audit Committee is composed of Messrs. Curley, Gerry and Nitze. Its function is to recommend to the Board of Directors the independent public accountants to be employed by American, to confer with the independent public accountants concerning the scope of their audit and, on completion of their audit, to review the accountants' findings and recommendations and to review the adequacy of American's system of internal accounting controls. In 1988, the Audit Committee held two meetings.

The Compensation Committee is composed of Messrs. Frost, Justice, Curley and Quay. Its functions are to approve, or in some cases to recommend to the Board of Directors, remuneration arrangements and compensation plans involving American's executive officers and certain other employees whose compensation exceeds certain levels and to administer, and grant stock options under, American's stock option plan. It will continue to administer the plan as amended and restated, if such amendment and restatement is approved by stockholders. (See "Proposal to Approve the Amendment and Restatement of American's 1983 Stock Option Plan," below.) In 1988, the Compensation Committee held three meetings.

During 1988 the Board of Directors held four regular meetings and one special meeting. No incumbent director, except Mr. Curley, Dr. Frost and Mr. Kavanagh, attended less than seventy-five percent of the meetings of the Board of Directors and of any Committee of which he was a member.

SECURITY OWNERSHIP OF DIRECTORS AND NOMINEES

The following table sets forth information concerning the shares of Common Stock beneficially owned by each director and nominee, and by all directors and officers as a group, as of March 31, 1989. The table includes shares of Common Stock that can be acquired through the exercise of options or Warrants or the conversion of convertible securities within 60 days. Pursuant to Rule 13d–3(d)(1) under the Securities Exchange Act of 1934, the percent of the class owned by each such person has been computed assuming the exercise of all such options and Warrants and conversion of all such securities where the number of shares beneficially owned includes shares issuable upon exercise of any such options or Warrants or upon conversion of such securities. Except as indicated, each individual has sole voting power and sole investment power over all shares listed opposite his name.

Name	Number of Shares of Common Stock	Percent of Class
Mark Andrews..................	1,826,229 [15]	6.7%

15. Includes 492,980 shares (including 40,000 shares issuable upon conversion of Series A Cumulative Convertible Preferred Stock ("Preferred Stock") of American) held directly or indirectly by Plymouth Steel Corporation, of which Mr. Andrews' wife is a principal shareholder and a director, and as to which shares he disclaims any beneficial ownership. Also includes 100,000 shares issuable upon conversion of

Name	Number of Shares of Common Stock	Percent of Class
O. Donaldson Chapoton	53,351	*
Irvin K. Culpepper, Jr.............	0	*
Walter J.P. Curley	115,000 [16]	*
Peter C. Forbes	7,976 [17]	*
Phillip Frost, M.D.	1,044,302 [18]	3.9
Peter G. Gerry....................	756,002 [19]	3.6
H. Phipps Hoffstot, III	671,746 [20]	2.5
John E. Justice, III	48,771	*
Mark Kavanagh	213,333 [21]	1.0
Richard M. Kernan, Jr.	6,073,000 [22]	26.3
John H. Moore	0	*
Peter P. Nitze	340,550 [23]	1.3
John B. Quay....................	492,980 [24]	2.0
Peter G. Schiff....................	296,690 [25]	1.3
All current directors and officers as a group (19 persons)	5,752,177 [26]	21.2

* Less than one percent.

Preferred Stock owned by Mr. Andrews, 40,000 shares issuable upon conversion of Preferred Stock owned by a partnership in which Mr. Andrews is a general partner, 11,000 shares issuable upon exercise of Warrants, 131,250 shares issuable upon exercise of stock options and 11,394 shares allocated to Mr. Andrews under American's Employee Stock Ownership Plan.

16. Includes 5,000 shares issuable upon exercise of Warrants. Ambassador Curley is not standing for re-election as a director (see "Compensation of Directors").

17. Includes 4,000 shares issuable upon exercise of Warrants owned by Mr. Forbes' wife, 400 shares owned by Mr. Forbes' son as to which shares Mr. Forbes disclaims beneficial interest and 2,576 shares allocated to Mr. Forbes under American's Employee Stock Ownership Plan.

18. Includes 36,106 shares owned by a pension plan of which Dr. Frost is a trustee and as to which shares he disclaims beneficial interest, 100,000 shares issuable upon conversion of Preferred Stock and 25,000 shares issuable upon exercise of Warrants.

19. Includes 619,752 shares held directly by Citicorp Venture Capital Ltd., of which Mr. Gerry is President. Mr. Gerry shares investment and voting power over such shares and disclaims beneficial interest in such shares. Also includes 125,000 shares owned by a limited partnership of which Mr. Gerry is a limited partner.

20. Includes 6,000 shares issuable upon exercise of Warrants and 500,746 shares, including 132,000 shares issuable upon conversion of Preferred Stock, over which Mr. Hoffstot shares investment and voting power.

21. These shares are owned by Kavex Limited, of which Mr. Kavanagh is Managing Director.

22. These shares are owned by New York Life Insurance Company of which Mr. Kernan is a Senior Vice President. See "Principal Security Holders." Mr. Kernan shares investment and voting power over such shares and disclaims beneficial interest in such shares.

23. Includes 40,000 shares issuable upon conversion of Preferred Stock and 27,150 shares issuable upon exercise of Warrants.

24. These shares, which include 40,000 shares issuable upon conversion of Preferred Stock, are held directly or indirectly by Plymouth Steel Corporation, of which Mr. Quay is President and a director. See also Note (1).

25. Includes 47,000 shares issuable upon exercise of Warrants.

26. Includes 164,000 shares issuable upon exercise of options held by officers other than Messrs. Andrews and Forbes that were exercisable at March 31, 1989 or within 60 days of such date. Also includes 138,817 shares (including 60,000 shares issuable upon conversion of Preferred Stock) owned by partnerships in which an officer is a limited partner, 8,100 shares issuable

EXECUTIVE COMPENSATION

The following table sets forth certain information regarding the cash compensation of the five executive officers of American who were most highly compensated during 1988 and of all executive officers of American as a group during that period.

CASH COMPENSATION TABLE

Name of Individual or Number in Group	Capacities in Which Served During 1988	Cash Compensation
Mark Andrews	Chairman of the Board and Chief Executive Officer	$ 303,484
J. Curtis Grindal [27]	Executive Vice President and Chief Operating Officer	$ 243,625
Russell P. Pennoyer	Senior Vice President, Secretary and General Counsel	$ 201,606
Stephen W. Haines	Senior Vice President—Production	$ 133,938
William G. Pattillo	Senior Vice President—Land	$ 127,514
All executive officers as a group (11 persons, including those named above)		$1,553,028

BENEFIT PLANS

1983 Stock Option Plan. The 1983 Stock Option Plan of American was originally approved by American's stockholders in 1984 and was amended and restated in 1987 (the "1983 Option Plan"). It is proposed that the stockholders approve a further amendment and restatement of the 1983 Option Plan at the Annual Meeting. See "Proposal to Approve the Amendment and Restatement of American's 1983 Stock Option Plan," below.

All employees of American are eligible to participate in the 1983 Option Plan. The Compensation Committee of the Board of Directors administers the 1983 Option Plan and determines the amount of any grants thereunder. At March 31, 1989, 2,018,500 shares of Common Stock were subject to outstanding options at an average per share

upon exercise of Warrants owned by officers other than Messrs. Andrews and Forbes and 27,970 shares allocated under American's Employee Stock Ownership Plan to officers other than Mr. Andrews and Mr. Forbes. See also Notes (1) through (11).

27. Mr. Grindal resigned as an executive officer of American in October 1988. In connection with his resignation, the Company agreed to pay Mr. Grindal $50,000 in cash, transfer to him an automobile and certain computer equipment valued at $21,000, pay him $13,750 a month through October 31, 1989 and extend the exercise period for certain options to purchase Common Stock. Such payments are in addition to the amounts set forth in the table above.

exercise price of $2.63. The outstanding options include options to purchase an aggregate of 865,000 shares which were granted to various employees, subject to, and contingent upon, amendment and restatement of the 1983 Option Plan, among other things, to increase the number of shares issuable pursuant to such plan from 1,500,000 to 2,900,000. If American's stockholders do not approve the amendment and restatement of the 1983 Option Plan to be presented at the Annual Meeting, such options will be cancelled. On the basis of the closing price of the Common Stock on the American Stock Exchange on April 19, 1989, $3.25 per share, the market value of the shares of Common Stock subject to stock options as of March 31, 1989 was $6,560,125, and the market value of all shares of Common Stock issuable, if American's stockholders approve the amendment and restatement of the 1983 Option Plan, would be $9,354,000.

Generally, stock options under the 1983 Option Plan become exercisable twenty-five percent (25%) for each full year of employment with American, or a parent or subsidiary thereof, after grant. The maximum duration of such outstanding options is ten years and one day from the date of grant. All options are granted at not less than 100% of the fair market value of the shares on the date of grant. As of March 31, 1989, 72 persons held options under the 1983 Option Plan, out of approximately 300 employees who were eligible to participate therein.

The table below shows for the individuals named in the Cash Compensation Table, for all executive officers as a group and for all employees of American, the aggregate number of shares of Common Stock subject to stock options under the 1983 Option Plan granted from January 1, 1986 through December 31, 1988, and the average per share exercise price thereof. No options were exercised during the period.

	Options Granted January 1, 1986 through December 31, 1988	
	Number of Shares [28]	Average Per Share Exercise Price
Mark Andrews	350,000	$2.37
J. Curtis Grindal	125,000	2.05
Russell P. Pennoyer	220,000	2.25
Stephen W. Haines	140,000	2.50

28. Options to purchase an aggregate of 865,000 shares of Common Stock have been granted contingent upon stockholder approval of the amendment and restatement of the 1983 Option Plan to be presented at the Annual Meeting; these options will automatically be cancelled if such approval is not received. Included in this column are shares subject to such cancellable options with an exercise price of $2.50 per share which were granted on December 9, 1988 to Messrs. Andrews (125,000 shares), Pennoyer (100,000 shares), Haines (100,000 shares) and Pattillo (100,000 shares), to other executive officers (50,000 shares) and to employees who were not executive officers (275,000 shares). Not included in this column are shares subject to such cancellable options with an exercise price of $2.75 per share which were granted on March 1, 1989 to employees who were not executive officers (115,000 shares).

	Number of Shares	Average Per Share Exercise Price
William G. Pattillo..............	108,000	2.52
All executive officers as a group (11 persons, including those named above)	1,360,500	2.33
All employees (72 persons, including all executive officers)......	1,707,000	2.38

Employee Stock Ownership Plan. In 1988, the Board of Directors of American adopted an Employee Stock Ownership Plan ("ESOP"). All current employees of American, including officers, participate in the ESOP. Pursuant to the terms of the ESOP, a trust (the "ESOP Trust") was created and authorized to purchase and hold shares of Common Stock for the benefit of participants in the ESOP.

Shares of Common Stock purchased by the ESOP Trust are allocated at the end of each calendar year to the account of each participant in the ESOP according to a formula based upon the participant's compensation. Allocated shares of Common Stock become vested over a period of four years beginning with the year after the participant joined the employ of American. Upon a participant's retirement or other termination of employment, vested ESOP benefits will generally be payable over not more than a five-year period.

Participants have the right to vote shares of Common Stock allocated to their accounts under the ESOP. Unallocated shares of Common Stock will be voted by the Trustees of the ESOP Trust. The Trustees have dispositive power with respect to Common Stock held for the ESOP; provided, however, that in the event of a tender or exchange offer, the Trustees will tender or exchange only those allocated shares for which they receive such instructions.

Although the ESOP also has the ability to borrow to acquire shares of Common Stock, it is the present intention of American that acquisitions of Common Stock by the ESOP will be funded through contributions made by American. Such contributions will be made at such times, and in such amounts, as the Board of Directors of American determines in its sole discretion.

As of March 31, 1989, the ESOP held 253,500 shares of Common Stock, of which 213,500 shares had been allocated to participant accounts. This amount represents approximately 1% of the outstanding shares of Common Stock. Contributions to the ESOP during 1988, the first year of operation of the ESOP, for the accounts of Messrs. Andrews, Pennoyer, Haines and Pattillo were $30,000, $18,700, $9,100 and $9,300, respectively. No contribution was payable with respect to Mr. Grindal's account. Contributions to the ESOP for the accounts of all executive officers as a group were $110,500 and for all employees as a group were $562,000.

Royalty Compensation Plan. Pursuant to American's Royalty Compensation Plan, certain key employees of American involved in exploration were awarded an overriding royalty interest of up to 3% in each exploratory prospect. Royalties with respect to three exploratory prospects were granted in 1986. No amount has ever been paid with respect to awards granted under this plan and none is expected to be paid in the future.

Other. American has agreed to pay Peter C. Forbes, who joined American in October 1988 to serve as its President, a base salary of $180,000, subject to review in July, 1989, and a performance bonus for 1989. The amount of the performance bonus will be determined by the Compensation Committee of the Board of Directors, but will be no less than 25% of his base salary. American has also agreed that should Mr. Forbes' employment with the Company be terminated on or before October 21, 1991, otherwise than for cause, he will be entitled to continued payment of his base salary as in effect on the date of termination until the earlier of the date when he begins other employment or 12 months after the date of such termination, together with normal employment benefits throughout such period and a bonus based upon his annual salary rate as of the date of termination.

PROPOSAL TO APPROVE THE AMENDMENT AND RESTATEMENT OF AMERICAN'S 1983 STOCK OPTION PLAN (Proposal No. 2)

The Board of Directors recommends that stockholders approve the amendment and restatement of the 1983 Stock Option Plan of American Exploration Company (the "1983 Option Plan"), which has been adopted by the Board of Directors, effective as of December 9, 1988, subject to the approval of the stockholders. As so amended and restated, the 1983 Option Plan will be called the American Exploration Company Stock Compensation Plan (the "Plan"). A copy of the Plan is set forth in Appendix A. The summary of Plan provisions contained below is qualified in its entirety by reference to the actual provisions of the Plan * * *.

The Plan has been designed to incorporate provisions of the 1983 Option Plan previously approved by the stockholders and to amend certain of such provisions. The major changes that would be effected by the amendment and restatement of the 1983 Option Plan are (i) the increase in the number of shares of Common Stock issuable thereunder from 1,500,000 shares to 2,900,000 shares, (ii) the authorization of the issuance of stock appreciation rights in conjunction with stock options, (iii) the authorization of the granting of Restricted Common Stock and Performance Shares and (iv) the acceleration of payment of certain awards in the event of a change in control of American. The Compensation Committee of the Board of Directors of American (the "Committee") will be responsible for the granting of awards under, and the administration of, the Plan. No member of the Committee will be eligible to receive awards or grants under the Plan. ∗ ∗ ∗

[The detailed description of the proposed amendment and restatement of American's 1983 stock option plan is omitted.]

Unless stockholders specify otherwise in the proxy, proxies solicited by the Board of Directors will be voted for approval of the American Exploration Company Stock Compensation Plan. The affirmative vote of a majority of the outstanding shares of Common Stock will be required for approval of this proposal.

The Board of Directors recommends that stockholders vote FOR approval of the American Exploration Company Stock Compensation Plan.

APPOINTMENT OF INDEPENDENT PUBLIC ACCOUNTANTS (Proposal No. 3)

The Board of Directors has appointed and recommends the approval of the appointment of Arthur Andersen & Co. as independent public accountants of American for 1989. This firm has acted as independent public accountants for American since its incorporation in 1980.

Representatives of Arthur Andersen & Co. are expected to attend the Annual Meeting and will have an opportunity to make a statement if they desire to do so and to respond to appropriate questions raised by stockholders.

The Board of Directors recommends that stockholders vote FOR appointment of Arthur Andersen & Co.

OTHER BUSINESS

Management does not intend to bring any business before the Annual Meeting other than the matters referred to in the accompanying notice and at this date has not been informed of any matters that may be presented at the Annual Meeting by others. If, however, any other matters properly come before the Annual Meeting, it is intended that the persons named in the accompanying proxy will vote pursuant to the proxy in accordance with their best judgment on such matters.

ANNUAL REPORT

American's 1988 Annual Report to Stockholders, including financial statements for the year ended December 31, 1988, is being mailed to all stockholders concurrently herewith. The 1988 Annual Report to Stockholders is not part of the proxy solicitation material.

STOCKHOLDER PROPOSALS

Proposals intended to be presented by stockholders at American's 1990 Annual Meeting must be received by American, at the address set forth on the first page of this proxy statement, no later than December 29, 1989 in order to be included in American's proxy materials and form of proxy relating to that meeting. Stockholder proposals must also be otherwise eligible for inclusion.

CERTAIN RELATIONSHIPS AND RELATED TRANSACTIONS

New York Life Insurance Company ("New York Life"), holder of 26.3% of the outstanding Common Stock, and one of its wholly owned subsidiaries are investors in certain of American's institutional property acquisition programs. In addition, wholly owned subsidiaries of New York Life and of American act as general partners of the NYLOG programs, a series of producing property acquisition partnerships being offered to the public through agents of New York Life and several independent broker dealers.

New York Life provides a revolving credit facility to American to finance acquisitions of producing oil and gas properties and companies on a bridge basis. This facility was set at $100 million in 1987 and increased to $175 million in 1988. In early 1989, it was increased again to $200 million and extended through April, 1990. During 1988, American used the facility to finance four acquisitions and paid New York Life commitment fees of $875,000, usage fees of $2,530,000 and interest of $8,640,000. The facility currently provides for a commitment fee of $\frac{1}{2}$% per annum, a usage fee of 1.25% of funds advanced and interest on amounts outstanding at rates ranging from 3% to 6% over the 30–day A1/P1 commercial paper rate depending on the time that amounts are outstanding.

During 1988, Mark Andrews was a special general partner in five institutional partnerships in which American acts as managing general partner. As special general partner, Mr. Andrews paid .1% of all costs and received .1% of all revenues of such partnerships. Subject to certain limitations, Mr. Andrews was indemnified by each partnership for any costs, expenses, losses or damages incurred by reason of his being a special general partner. Mr. Andrews purchased his interest from each partnership at its book value; such purchases were financed through a $130,000 demand loan from American which was extended on December 8, 1987. The loan bore interest at the federal short-term rate, as announced by the Commissioner of the Internal Revenue Service. During 1988, the rate was fixed at 7.42% on January 1 and at 7.74% on July 1. Early in 1989, Mr. Andrews completed the conveyance of all of his special general partnership interests in the five institutional partnerships in which American acts as managing general partner to American; in consideration for its acquisition of such interests, American cancelled the $130,000 demand loan described above, together with all interest accrued thereon.

The law firm of Baker & Botts provides legal services to American. O. Donaldson Chapoton, a nominee for election as a director, is a partner of this firm. During 1988, Nitze–Stagen & Company, Inc., of which Peter P. Nitze is chairman, performed financial consulting services for American. During 1988, the law firm of Patterson, Belknap, Webb & Tyler provided legal services to American. American paid this firm $971,000 for these services during the year. The father of Russell P. Pennoyer is a partner in this firm.

[The 1988 Annual Report to Shareholders referred to in Mr. Andrews' covering letter and the text of the Stock Compensation Plan set forth as "Appendix A" to the proxy statement are not reproduced.]

*

Index

References are to Pages

---

†